Lecture Notes in Computer Science 6470

Commenced Publication in 1973
Founding and Former Series Editors:
Gerhard Goos, Juris Hartmanis, and Ja

Services Science

Subline of Lectures Notes in Computer Science

Paul P. Maglio   Mathias Weske   Jian Yang
Marcelo Fantinato (Eds.)

Service-Oriented Computing

8th International Conference, ICSOC 2010
San Francisco, CA, USA, December 7-10, 2010
Proceedings

 Springer

Volume Editors

Paul P. Maglio
IBM Almaden Research Center
San Jose, CA, USA
E-mail: pmaglio@almaden.ibm.com

Mathias Weske
University of Potsdam
Potsdam, Germany
E-mail: mathias.weske@hpi.uni-potsdam.de

Jian Yang
Macquarie University
Sydney, Australia
E-mail: jian@ics.mq.edu.au

Marcelo Fantinato
University of São Paulo
São Paulo, Brazil
E-mail: m.fantinato@usp.br

Library of Congress Control Number: Applied for

CR Subject Classification (1998): D.2, C.2, H.4, H.3, H.5, J.1

LNCS Sublibrary: SL 2 – Programming and Software Engineering

ISSN	0302-9743
ISBN-10	3-642-17357-8 Springer Berlin Heidelberg New York
ISBN-13	978-3-642-17357-8 Springer Berlin Heidelberg New York

springer.com

© Springer-Verlag Berlin Heidelberg 2010
Printed in Germany

Typesetting: Camera-ready by author, data conversion by Scientific Publishing Services, Chennai, India
Printed on acid-free paper   06/3180

Preface

Welcome to the 8th International Conference on Service Oriented Computing (ICSOC 2010), held in San Francisco, December 2010. These proceedings represent high-quality research and industry papers, tutorials, demos, and posters that showcase new developments in service oriented computing and related fields.

Since the first meeting in beautiful Trento in 2003, ICSOC has become the premier conference in the rapidly evolving areas of service research. While keeping its roots in scientific excellence and technical depth of service technology, ICSOC 2010 aimed to combine technical aspects of service computing with application and business-oriented aspects of service design, following the recent emergence of service science as an interdisciplinary foundation for understanding and integrating service systems. Located in the center of technology innovation, the San Francisco Bay Area, this year's ICSOC, through its Local Advisory Board, reached out to local industry and academia for keynotes and panels on current topics and to connect technical invention with commercial innovation.

The Program Committee faced some tough decisions this year. We received 238 submissions, signalling a growing community of researchers and practitioners working in this multidisciplinary field. All papers were considered carefully by the Program Committee in originality, novelty, rigor, and relevance. In the end, 33 full research papers and three full industry papers were selected, resulting in an acceptance rate of 15%. An additional 18 submissions were accepted as short papers. There were also three PhD symposium posters and four regular posters accepted. Paper and poster presentations were complemented by tutorial and demo programs. All represented the state of the art in service oriented computing.

We were fortunate to work with some 100 Program Committee members on paper selection. Without their expertise and dedication, these proceedings—and this conference—would not have been possible. The high-quality papers resulted from the joint effort of these researchers, who each carefully read, commented on, and corresponded over many submissions. We thank them for their hard work.

We were privileged to work with many talented and dedicated colleagues on the Organizing Committee and the Local Advisory Board, particularly Bernd Kraemer, Registration Co-chair, Marcelo Fantinato, Publications Chair, Matthias Weidlich, Publicity Chair, and Maja Vukovic, Web Chair. We apologize that we cannot list all who helped. Please find the complete list in the proceedings.

A special thanks goes to the authors, keynote speakers, panelists, and tutorial speakers, who together made the conference happen. And of course, our biggest thanks goes to the participants, who make the conference worthwhile. It is our great pleasure and privilege to present these proceedings. We hope you find the volume inspiring for years to come.

December 2010

Heiko Ludwig
Fu-ren Lin
Paul P. Maglio
Mathias Weske
Jian Yang

Organization

Honorary General Chair

Jim Spohrer   IBM, USA

General Chairs

Heiko Ludwig   IBM Research, USA
Fu-Ren Lin   National Tsing Hua University, Taiwan

Program Committee Chairs

Mathias Weske   Univ. Potsdam, Germany
Jian Yang   Mcquarry University, Australia
Paul Maglio   IBM Research, USA

Advisory Board

Avi Borthakur   Oracle, USA
Claudio Bartolini   HP Labs, USA
Christoph Bussler   Saba Software, USA
Axel Hochstein   Stanford University, USA
Ramesh Jakka   360 Fresh and Carnegie Mellon Silicon Valley, USA
Yuecel Karabulut   SAP, USA
Michael Maximilien   IBM Research, USA

Workshop Chairs

Gustavo Rossi   UNLP, Argentina
Soe-Tsyr Yuan   National Chengchi University, Taiwan
Michel Maximilien   IBM Research, USA

Tutorial Chairs

Thomas Sandholm   HP Labs, USA
Jyoti Bhat   Infosys, India
Haluk Demirkan   Arizona State University, USA

Demonstration Chairs

Florian Daniel   University of Trento, Italy
Christian Zirpins   Karlsruhe Institute of Technology, Germany

Poster Chairs

Andreas Wombacher   University of Twente, The Netherlands

Finance/Registration Chairs

Bernd J. Kraemer   Fernuni Hagen, Germany
Christian Zirpins   Karlsruhe Institute of Technology, Germany

PhD Symposium Chairs

Eleni Stroulia   University of Alberta, Canada
Boualem Benatallah   University of New South Wales, Australia
Jianwen Su   University of California at Santa Barbara, USA

Web Chair

Maja Vukovic   IBM Research, USA

Publications Chair

Marcelo Fantinato   University of São Paulo, Brazil

Publicity Chair

Matthias Weidlich   University of Potsdam, Germany

Conference Operations Management

Beatriz Raggio   Xparency, USA

Program Committee

Marco Aiello	University of Groningen, The Netherlands
Rama Akkiraju	IBM Research, USA
Alvaro Arenas	STFC Rutherford Appleton Laboratory, USA
Karim Baina	Mohammed V-Souissi University, Morocco
Luciano Baresi	Politecnico di Milano, Italy
Claudio Bartolini	HP Labs, USA
Samik Basu	Iowa State University, USA
Boualem Benatallah	University of New South Wales, Australia
Salima Benbernou	University of Paris, France
Antonia Bertolino	ISTI-CNR, Italy
Walter Binder	University of Lugano, Switzerland
Athman Bouguettaya	CSIRO, Australia
Christoph Bussler	BEA, USA
Manuel Carro	Universidad Politécnica de Madrid, Spain
Shiping Chen	CSIRO ICT, Australia
Lawrence Chung	University of Texas at Dallas, USA
Emmanuel Coquery	Université Claude Bernard Lyon 1, France
Francisco Curbera	IBM Research, USA
Vincenzo D'Andrea	University of Trento, Italy
Florian Daniel	University of Trento, Italy
Joseph Davis	University of Sydney, Australia
Mark Davis	Bentley University, USA
Flavio De Paoli	Universita di Milano, Italy
Haluk Demirkan	Arizona State University, USA
Frederic Desprez	INRIA, France
Khalil Drira	LAAS Toulouse, France
Marlon Dumas	University of Tartu, Estonia
Schahram Dustdar	University of Technology Vienna, Austria
Markus Endler	PUC-Rio de Janeiro, Brazil
Gregor Engels	University of Paderborn, Germany
Rik Eshuis	Eindhoven University of Technology, The Netherlands
Ioannis Fikouras	Ericsson, Sweden
Howard Foster	City University London, UK
Andreas Friesen	SAP, USA
Hiroaki Fukuda	Keio University, Japan
Dragan Gasevic	Athabasca University, Canada
Paolo Giorgini	University of Trento, Italy
Carlo Ghezzi	Politecnico di Milano, Italy
Sven Graupner	HP Labs, Palo Alto, USA
Jeff Gray	University of Alabama at Birmingham, USA
Paul Grefen	Eindhoven University of Technology, The Netherlands

Colette Roland	University of Paris, France
Florian Rosenberg	ICT CSIRO, Australia
Gustavo Rossi	UNLP, Argentina
Masoud Sadjadi	Florida International University, USA
Mohand-Said Hacid	University of Lyon, France
Jorge Sanz	IBM Almaden Research Center, USA
Regis Saint-Paul	CREATE-NET International Research Center, Italy
Ramesh Jakka	360 Fresh and Carnegie Mellon Silicon Valley, USA
Daniel Schwabe	PUC-Rio de Janeiro, Brazil
Michael J. Shaw	University of Illinois, Urbana Champaign, USA
Jane Siegel	Carnegie Mellon Silicon Valley, USA
Munindar P. Singh	North Carolina State University, USA
Ignacio Silva-Lepe	IBM T.J. Watson Research Center, USA
George Spanoudakis	City University London, UK
Bruce Spencer	NRC, Canada
Jianwen Su	UC Santa Barbara, USA
York Sure	GESIS Inst. and University of Koblenz-Landau, Germany
Jun Suzuki	University of Massachusetts, Boston, USA
Stefan Tai	University of Karlsruhe, Germany
Wang-Chiew Tan	IBM Research, USA
Zahir Tari	RMIT University, Australia
M. Beatriz F. Toledo	Unicamp, Brazil
Farouk Toumani	Blaise Pascal University, France
Peter Troeger	HI, University of Potsdam, Germany
Jos van Hillegersberg	University of Twente, The Netherlands
Changzhou Wang	The Boeing Company, USA
Yan Wang	Macquarie University, Australia
Bruno Wassermann	University College London, UK
Michael Weiss	Carleton University, Canada
Karsten Wolf	University of Rostock, Germany
Andreas Wombacher	University of Twente, The Netherlands
Lai Xu	Bournemouth University, UK
Ramin Yahyapour	TU Dortmund University, Germany
Yelena Yesha	University of Maryland, USA
Hossein Zadeh	RMIT, Australia
Konstantinos Zachos	City University London, UK
Weiliang Zhao	Macquarie University, Australia
Andrea Zisman	City University London, UK
Yan Zheng	Nokia Research Center Helsinki, Finland

Table of Contents

Service Management (2)

Quality of Service

Service Science and Design

Service Development and Run-Time Management

High-Level Description Languages

Service Level Agreements

Service Engineering Methodologies

Service Security, Privacy, and Trust

Industry Papers

Short Papers

Business Service Modeling

Run-Time Service Management

Formal Methods

Quality of Service

Service Applications

Posters

PhD Symposium Posters

Demonstration Papers

Tutorial Abstracts

Business Process Model Abstraction Based on Behavioral Profiles

Sergey Smirnov[1], Matthias Weidlich[1], and Jan Mendling[2]

[1] Hasso Plattner Institute, Potsdam, Germany
{sergey.smirnov,matthias.weidlich}@hpi.uni-potsdam.de
[2] Humboldt-Universität zu Berlin, Germany
jan.mendling@wiwi.hu-berlin.de

Abstract. A variety of drivers for process modeling efforts, from low-level service orchestration to high-level decision support, results in many process models describing one business process. Depending on the modeling purpose, these models differ with respect to the model granularity. Business process model abstraction (BPMA) emerged as a technique that given a process model delivers a high-level process representation containing more coarse-grained activities and overall ordering constraints between them. Thereby, BPMA reduces the number of models capturing the same business process on different abstraction levels. In this paper, we present an abstraction approach that derives control flow dependencies for activities of an abstract model, once the groups of related activities are selected for aggregation. In contrast to the existing work, we allow for arbitrary activity groupings. To this end, we employ the behavioral profile notion that captures behavioral characteristics of a process model. Based on the original model and the activity grouping, we compute a new behavioral profile used for synthesis of the abstract process model.

1 Introduction

Business process management is a methodology that allows companies to stay competitive and shorten the time to market periods of their products and services [14]. Typically, each product or service is supported by a series of operational business processes. Companies that adopt business process management use models to explicitly capture the knowledge about their processes. In large companies such initiatives often yield several thousand models. Not only the number is a challenge to maintenance of these models, but also the fact that often several models relate to the same process. This is, for instance, the case when there exists a BPEL model capturing the service orchestration, a detailed conceptual model describing the work steps, and an overview model for senior management. In this context, business process model abstraction (BPMA) emerged as a technique that works on the most detailed model. It preserves essential process properties leaving out insignificant details. In this way, maintenance can be centered around the most fine-grained model from which the more abstract models are generated.

P.P. Maglio et al. (Eds.): ICSOC 2010, LNCS 6470, pp. 1–16, 2010.

BPMA is related to different use cases. These include, for instance, discovering the perspective of a particular collaboration partner or filtering out activities of minor interest. A user study with industry has revealed that getting a quick overview of a detailed process is urgently required in practice [26]. Technically, a more high-level process model has to be derived with more coarse-grained activities and their control flow relations. A corresponding BPMA technique has to tackle two questions. First, which activities should be grouped into more coarse-grained ones? Second, what are the control flow relations between them? Most of the existing work has made structural assumptions regarding the first question, such that the second question becomes trivial, cf. [6,12,16,21]. Meanwhile, these restrictions are often not realistic given the requirements in practice [22,29].

In this paper, we address the abstraction problem, assuming that arbitrary activity groupings are specified. Our contribution is a technique for discovering control flow relations of an abstract model given an unrestricted grouping of activities in the initial model. Our novel approach builds on behavioral profiles, a mechanism that captures control relations between each pair of activities in terms of strict order, exclusiveness, or interleaving. Furthermore, we develop an approach for the synthesis of a process model from a behavioral profile. The synthesis builds on the newly defined notion of consistency for behavioral profiles.

The rest of the paper is structured accordingly. Section 2 motivates the problem and introduces the basic notations. Section 3 presents the developed BPMA technique including the derivation of an abstract profile and the synthesis of the model. Section 4 discusses the related work. Finally, Section 5 concludes the paper and provides an outline on the future work.

2   Background

This section discusses BPMA and explains the limitations of the existing approaches supporting the argumentation with an example. Once the motivation is provided, we introduce the formalism further used in the paper.

2.1   Business Process Model Abstraction

In essence, business process model abstraction is an operation on a model which preserves essential properties by leaving out insignificant details in order to retain information relevant for a particular purpose. BPMA is realized by means of two basic abstraction operations: elimination and aggregation (respectively, inverse of the extension and refinement operations for behavior inheritance [24]). While elimination omits insignificant activities, aggregation groups several semantically related activities into one high-level activity. As the question of which activities shall be aggregated has been partially answered by prior research, e.g., cf. [25], we focus on how the ordering relations between high-level activities are derived.

Existing approaches restrict the choice of activities to be aggregated and derive the ordering relations between high-level activities analyzing the initial model control flow, cf. [6,16,21]. In these works each coarse-grained activity is

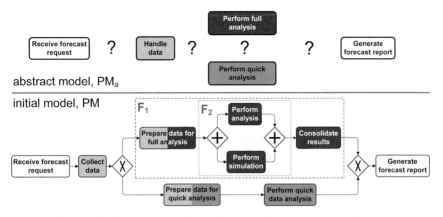

Fig. 1. Motivating example: initial model and activity grouping

mapped to a process model fragment. The fragments are either explicitly given by patterns or specified through properties. The latter enables aggregation of fragments with an arbitrary inner structure and rests upon model decomposition techniques [21]. However, the direct analysis of the control flow has limitations. In practice, semantically related activities can be allocated in the original model independently of the control flow structure, while one activity may belong to several semantically related activity sets [22,29]. Consider the example model PM in Fig. 1. The model describes a business process, where a forecast request is processed. Once a forecast request is received, the required data is collected. Then, there are two options: either to perform a full data analysis, or its short version. The process concludes with a forecast report creation. Model PM contains several semantically related activities that can be aggregated together into more coarse-grained ones. In model PM related activities are marked by the same background color, for instance, {*Prepare data for quick analysis, Perform quick data analysis*}. Each activity set corresponds to a respective high-level activity in the abstract model PM_a, e.g., *Perform quick analysis*. Activities *Receive forecast request* and *Generate forecast report* are not aggregated and, hence, appear in the abstract model as is. The abstraction techniques proposed in prior research allow to aggregate activities that belong, for instance, to fragment F_1 or F_2. However, none of the existing approaches is capable of suggesting the ordering constraints between activities *Handle data, Perform full analysis*, and *Perform quick analysis* in the abstract model. In this paper, we define a more flexible approach to determine the control structure. We utilize *behavioral profiles* [30] as the underlying formalism. Behavioral profiles capture the essential behavior of a process model in terms of strict order, exclusiveness, and interleaving order relations for each activity pair.

Further, addressing the user demand revealed in [26], our BPMA technique comprises a slider control that manages the ordering constraints loss. The slider allows the user to select an appropriate model from a spectrum of models: from the model with an arbitrary execution of high-level activities to the model where the ordering constraints of PM are best-effort preserved.

2.2   Preliminaries

For our discussion, we use a formal notion of a process model. It captures the commonalities of process modeling languages, such as BPMN or EPCs.

Definition 1 (Process Model). A tuple $PM = (A, G, F, s, e, t)$ is a *process model* , where:

- A is a finite nonempty set of activities;
- G is a finite set of gateways;
- $N = A \cup G$ is a finite set of nodes with $A \cap G = \emptyset$;
- $F \subseteq N \times N$ is the flow relation, such that (N, F) is a connected graph;
- $\bullet n = \{n' \in N | (n', n) \in F\}$ and $n \bullet = \{n' \in N | (n, n') \in F\}$ denote, respectively, the direct predecessors and successors of a node $n \in N$;
- $\forall\, a \in A : | \bullet a| \leq 1 \wedge |a \bullet | \leq 1$
- $s \in A$ is the only start activity, such that $\bullet s = \emptyset$;
- $e \in A$ is the only end activity, such that $e \bullet = \emptyset$;
- $t : G \rightarrow \{and, xor\}$ is a mapping that associates each gateway with a type.

The execution semantics of such a process model is given by a translation into a Petri net following on common formalizations, cf., [1,10]. As our notion of a process model comprises a dedicated start activity and a dedicated end activity, the resulting Petri net is a workflow net (WF-net) [1]. All gateways are of type *and* or *xor*, such that the WF-net is free-choice [1]. In order to arrive at a behavioral profile, we consider the set of all complete traces (or execution sequences) from start s to end e. The set of *complete process traces* $\mathcal{T}_{PM}$ for a process model PM contains lists of the form $s \cdot A^* \cdot e$ such that a list comprises the execution order of activities. We use $a \in \sigma$ with $\sigma \in \mathcal{T}_{PM}$ to denote that an activity a is a part of a complete process trace. The behavioral profile is grounded on the notion of *weak order* between activities within this set of traces. Two activities of a process model are in weak order, if there exists a trace in which one activity occurs after the other. This relation requires the *existence* of such a trace and does not have to hold for all traces of the model.

Definition 2 (Weak Order Relation). Let $PM = (A, G, F, s, e, t)$ be a process model, and $\mathcal{T}_{PM}$—its set of traces. The *weak order relation* $\succ_{PM} \subseteq (A \times A)$ contains all pairs (x, y), such that there is a trace $\sigma = n_1, \ldots, n_m$ in $\mathcal{T}_{PM}$ with $j \in \{1, \ldots, m-1\}$ and $j < k \leq m$ for which holds $n_j = x$ and $n_k = y$.

Depending on how two activities of a process model are related by weak order, we define three relations forming the behavioral profile.

Definition 3 (Behavioral Profile). Let $PM = (A, G, F, s, e, t)$ be a process model. A pair $(x, y) \in (A \times A)$ is in one of the following relations:

- *strict order relation* $\rightsquigarrow_{PM}$, if $x \succ_{PM} y$ and $y \nsucc_{PM} x$;
- *exclusiveness relation* $+_{PM}$, if $x \nsucc_{PM} y$ and $y \nsucc_{PM} x$;
- *interleaving order relation* $||_{PM}$, if $x \succ_{PM} y$ and $y \succ_{PM} x$.

The set of all three relations is the *behavioral profile* of PM.

The relations of the behavioral profile, along with the inverse strict order $\rightsquigarrow^{-1} = \{(x, y) \in (A \times A) \mid (y, x) \in \rightsquigarrow\}$, partition the Cartesian product of activities.

The behavioral profile relations allow different levels of freedom for activities. While interleaving order relation allows the activities to appear in an arbitrary order, (inverse) strict order specifies a particular execution order, and exclusiveness prohibits appearance of two activities in one trace. Thus, we organize the relations into a hierarchy presented in Fig. 2. At the top of the hierarchy the "strictest" relation appears, while at the bottom—the least restrictive.

Fig. 2. Behavioral relation hierarchy

3 Abstract Model Synthesis

In this section, we describe the developed abstraction technique. We realize the technique in the following steps.

Step 1 derive the behavioral profile BP_{PM} for model PM

Step 2 construct the behavioral profile BP_{PM_a} for model PM_a

Step 3 if a model consistent with profile BP_{PM_a} exists

Step 4 then create PM_a, **else** report an inconsistency.

The remainder of this section is structured according to the above mentioned steps: each subsection discusses one step.

3.1 Deriving Behavioral Relations from a Process Model

Derivation of the behavioral profile of a process model can be done efficiently under the assumption of soundness. Soundness is a correctness criteria often used for process models that guarantees the absence of behavioral anomalies, such as deadlocks or livelocks [2]. It has been defined for WF-nets. As discussed in Section 2.2, semantics for our notion of a process model is given by a translation into free-choice WF-nets. Hence, the soundness criterion can be directly applied to a process model. Moreover, we are able to reuse techniques for the derivation of behavioral profiles that have been introduced for sound free-choice WF-nets in [30]. Based thereon, behavioral profiles can be derived in $O(n^3)$ time with n as the number of nodes of the respective WF-net. In essence, this approach establishes a relation between the structure of a net and the relations of its behavioral profile.

3.2 Abstract Model Behavioral Profile Construction

We assume that each high-level activity in $PM_a = (A_a, G_a, F_a, s_a, e_a, t_a)$ is the result of aggregation of several activities in $PM = (A, G, F, s, e, t)$. Then, the construction of coarse-grained activities is formalized by a function *aggregate*:

Definition 4 (Function Aggregate). Let $PM = (A, G, F, s, e, t)$ be a process model and $PM_a = (A_a, G_a, F_a, s_a, e_a, t_a)$—its abstract counterpart. Function $aggregate : A_a \rightarrow \mathcal{P}(A)$ specifies a correspondence between one activity in PM_a and the set of activities in PM.

Algorithm 1. Derivation of a behavioral relation for an activity pair

1: **deriveBehavioralRelation(Activity** x, **Activity** y, **Double** w_t)
2: $w(x \succ_{PM_a} y) = |\{\forall(a,b) \in aggregate(x) \times aggregate(y) : a \rightsquigarrow_{PM} b \vee a||_{PM} b\}|$
3: $w(y \succ_{PM_a} x) = |\{\forall(a,b) \in aggregate(x) \times aggregate(y) : a \rightsquigarrow_{PM}^{-1} b \vee a||_{PM} b\}|$
4: $w(x \not\succ_{PM_a} y) = |\{\forall(a,b) \in aggregate(x) \times aggregate(y) : a \rightsquigarrow_{PM}^{-1} b \vee a +_{PM} b\}|$
5: $w(y \not\succ_{PM_a} x) = |\{\forall(a,b) \in aggregate(x) \times aggregate(y) : a \rightsquigarrow_{PM} b \vee a +_{PM} b\}|$
6: $w_{prod} = |aggregate(x)| \cdot |aggregate(y)|$
7: $w(x +_{PM_a} y) = \dfrac{min(w(x \not\succ_{PM_a} y), w(y \not\succ_{PM_a} x))}{w_{prod}}$
8: $w(x \rightsquigarrow_{PM_a} y) = \dfrac{min(w(x \succ_{PM_a} y), w(y \not\succ_{PM_a} x))}{w_{prod}}$
9: $w(x \rightsquigarrow_{PM_a}^{-1} y) = \dfrac{min(w(y \succ_{PM_a} x), w(x \not\succ_{PM_a} y))}{w_{prod}}$
10: $w(x||_{PM_a} y) = \dfrac{min(w(x \succ_{PM_a} y), w(y \succ_{PM_a} x))}{w_{prod}}$
11: **if** $w(x +_{PM_a} y) > w_t$ **then**
12:     **return** $x +_{PM_a} y$
13: **if** $w(x \rightsquigarrow_{PM_a} y) > w_t$ **then**
14:     **if** $w(x \rightsquigarrow_{PM_a}^{-1} y) > w(x \rightsquigarrow_{PM_a} y)$ **then**
15:         **return** $x \rightsquigarrow_{PM_a}^{-1} y$
16:     **else**
17:         **return** $x \rightsquigarrow_{PM_a} y$
18: **if** $w(x \rightsquigarrow_{PM_a}^{-1} y) > w_t$ **then**
19:     **return** $x \rightsquigarrow_{PM_a}^{-1} y$
20: **return** $x||_{PM_a} y$

Considering the example in Fig. 1, for instance, it holds *aggregate(Perform quick analysis)* = {*Prepare data for quick analysis, Perform quick data analysis*} and *aggregate(Handle data)*={*Collect data, Prepare data for full analysis, Prepare data for quick analysis*}. The behavioral profile of model PM_a defines the relations between each pair of activities in PM_a. To discover the behavioral profile for PM_a we analyze the relations among activities in PM and consider the function *aggregate*. For each pair of coarse-grained activities x, y, where $x, y \in A_a$, we study the relations between a and b, where $a \in aggregate(x), b \in aggregate(y)$. This study reveals a dominating behavioral relation between elements of $aggregate(x)$ and $aggregate(y)$. We assume that the behavioral relations between activity pairs of PM_a can be discovered independently from each other, i.e., the relation between x and y, where $x, y \in A_a$ depends on the relations between activities in $aggregate(x)$ and $aggregate(y)$, but does not depend on the relations between $aggregate(x)$ and $aggregate(z), \forall z \in A_a$.

Algorithm 1 formalizes the derivation of behavioral relations. The input of the algorithm is a pair of activities, x and y, and w_t—the user-specified threshold telling significant relation weights from the rest and, hence, managing the ordering constraints loss. The output of the algorithm is the relation between x and y. Algorithm 1 derives behavioral profile relations between x and y from the observable frequencies of relations between activities (a, b), where $(a, b) \in aggregate(x) \times aggregate(y)$. According to Definition 3 each of the behavioral profile relations is specified by the corresponding weak order relations. Thereby, to conclude about the behavioral profile relation between x and y we first evaluate the frequencies of weak order relations for x and y. The latter are found in the assumption that each weak order relation holding for $(a, b) \in$ $aggregate(x) \times aggregate(y)$, contributes to the weak order relation between x and y. This rationale allows to find the weight for each weak order relation between x and y (lines 2–5). The overall number of relations is stored in variable w_{prod} (line 6). Algorithm 1 continues finding the relative weight for each behavioral profile relation (lines 7–10). The relative weights of behavioral relations together with the relation hierarchy are used to choose the dominating relation (lines 11–20). The behavioral relations are ranked according to their relative weights. Threshold w_t selects significant relations, omitting those which relative weights are less than w_t. Finally, the relation hierarchy allows to choose the strictest relation among the significant ones. Notice that the input parameter w_t implements the slider concept: by means of w_t the user expresses the preferred ordering constraint loss level and obtains the corresponding behavioral relations for model PM_a.

To illustrate Algorithm 1 we refer to the motivating example and derive the behavioral relation between activities *Handle data* (*HD*) and *Perform quick analysis* (*PQA*) given the threshold $w_t = 0.5$. Following Algorithm 1, $w(HD \succ_{PM_a} PQA) = 4$, $w(PQA \succ_{PM_a} HD) = 1$, $w(HD \not\succ_{PM_a} PQA) = 2$,

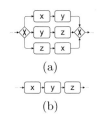

Fig. 3. Slider example

$w(PQA \not\succ_{PM_a} HD) = 5$, and $w_{prod} = 6$. Then, $w(HD +_{PM_a} PQA) = 2/6$, $w(HD \leadsto_{PM_a} PQA) = 4/6$, $w(HD \leadsto^{-1}_{PM_a} PQA) = 1/6$, and $w(HD \leadsto^{-1}_{PM_a} PQA) = 1/6$. The constellation of behavioral relation weights is shown in Fig. 3. Each relation weight w_r defines a segment $[0, w_r]$, where the respective behavioral relation r is valid. If the maximum weight of the relations w_{max} is less than 1, we claim that the interleaving order relation is valid in segment $[w_{max}, 1]$ (it provides most freedom in execution of two activities). While the resulting segments overlap, the relation hierarchy defines the dominating relation in a particular point of $[0, 1]$. For only $w(HD \leadsto_{PM_a} PQA) > 0.5$, we state *Handle data* $\leadsto_{PM_a}$ *Perform quick analysis*.

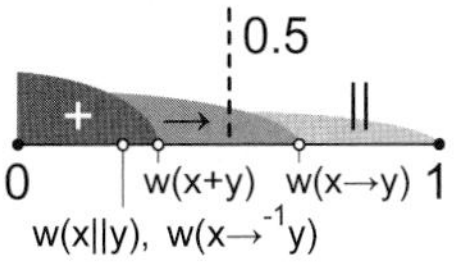

3.3 Behavioral Profile Consistency Validation

The creation of the behavioral profile for the abstract model as introduced above might yield an *inconsistent* profile. Hence, this section first introduces a notion of consistency for behavioral profiles and then elaborates on how it can be decided.

Consistent Behavioral Profiles. A behavioral profile is inconsistent, if there exists no process model that satisfies all the constraints of the behavioral profile. Whether such a process model exists depends on the applied notion of a process model and the intended structural and behavioral characteristics of the synthesized model. For instance, the strict order relation might define a cyclic dependency between three activities x, y, and z: $x \leadsto y$, $y \leadsto z$, and $z \leadsto x$.

(a)

(b)

Fig. 4. Exemplary model fragments

The process model fragment in Fig. 4(a) satisfies these behavioral constraints at the expense of duplicating activities. However, the result is clearly inappropriate against the background of our use case: an abstract model should provide a concise and compact view on the process. Hence, extensive activity duplication should be avoided. For our notion of a process model, the aforementioned behavioral constraints cannot be satisfied as exemplified by the model in Fig. 4(b), where constraint $z \rightsquigarrow x$ is violated. Moreover, structural and behavioral properties of a process model, e.g., the absence of deadlocks, impact on the existence of a process model for a given behavioral profile.

Our notion of behavioral profile consistency is motivated by the goal of deriving a sound process model. That is, the resulting model should be free of behavioral anomalies, cf., Section 2.2.

Definition 5 (Consistent Behavioral Profile). Let $PM = (A, G, F, s, e, t)$ be a process model with the behavioral profile $\mathcal{BP} = \{\rightsquigarrow_{PM}, +_{PM}, \|_{PM}\}$. $\mathcal{R} \subseteq (A \times A)$ is a *dependency relation* derived from the behavioral profile with:
  - $(x, y) \notin \mathcal{R}$ and $(y, x) \notin \mathcal{R}$, if $x +_{PM} y$.
  - $(x, y) \in \mathcal{R}$ and $(y, x) \notin \mathcal{R}$, if $x \rightsquigarrow_{PM} y$.
  - either $(x, y), (y, x) \in \mathcal{R}$ or $(x, y), (y, x) \notin \mathcal{R}$, if $x \|_{PM} y$.
Then, $\mathcal{BP}$ is *consistent*, iff $\mathcal{R}$ is a transitive relation.

For the aforementioned example of three activities x, y, and z with $x \rightsquigarrow y$, $y \rightsquigarrow z$, and $z \rightsquigarrow x$ the profile is inconsistent: $x \rightsquigarrow y$ and $y \rightsquigarrow z$ induce $x \mathcal{R} y$ and $y \mathcal{R} z$, whereas $x \not\mathcal{R} z$ is derived from $z \rightsquigarrow x$.

In order to prove that consistency of a behavioral profile coincides with the existence of a sound process model that shows this profile, we need auxiliary results on the relation between behavioral and structural dependencies.

Proposition 1. Let $PM = (A, G, F, s, e, t)$ be a sound process model and $\mathcal{BP} = \{\rightsquigarrow_{PM}, +_{PM}, \|_{PM}\}$—its behavioral profile. Then, for $x, y \in A$ it holds:
S1 there is no path between them, $x \not F^+ y$ and $y \not F^+ x$, if $x +_{PM} y$.
S2 there is a path between them, $x F^+ y$ and $y \not F^+ x$, if $x \rightsquigarrow_{PM} y$.
S3 there is either no path between them or they are a part of a control flow cycle, $(x \not F^+ y) \wedge (y \not F^+ x)$ or $(x F^+ y) \wedge (y F^+ x)$, if $x \|_{PM} y$.
S4 they are exclusive or in interleaving order, $x +_{PM} y$ or $x \|_{PM} y$, if $x \not F^+ y$ and $y \not F^+ x$.
S5 they are in strict order, $x \rightsquigarrow_{PM} y$, if $x F^+ y$ and $y \not F^+ x$.
S6 they are in interleaving order, $x \|_{PM} y$, if $x F^+ y$ and $y F^+ x$.

Proof. We have already mentioned that any sound process model can be transformed into a corresponding sound free-choice WF-net. Hence, we reuse the results that have been proven for this class of nets in [30].

S1 Follows from Lemma 3 in [30], stating that activities that cannot be enabled concurrently are exclusive if and only if there is no path between them.

S2 Follows from the proof of Theorem 1 in [30], which includes the statement that for activities that cannot be enabled concurrently, the path relations $x F^+ y$ and $y \not F^+ x$ coincide with strict order $x \rightsquigarrow y$.

S3 According to Lemma 2 in [30], activities that cannot be enabled concurrently are in interleaving order, if and only if they are a part of a common control flow cycle. It remains to show that potential concurrent enabling of activities x and y implies that there is either no path between them, $x \not\!F^+ y$ and $y \not\!F^+ x$, or they belong to a common control flow cycle, $x F^+ y$ and $y F^+ x$. Assume that x and y can be enabled concurrently and that $x F^+ y$ and $y \not\!F^+ x$ hold. The path $x F^+ y$ induces a sequence of activities that can be executed starting with x and leading to a state in which y is enabled (this property has been shown for sound free-choice WF-nets in [15]). Due to $y \not\!F^+ x$, any token enabling y in the first state cannot impact on the execution of this activity sequence. Thereby, a state in which y is enabled concurrently to itself is reached. This contradicts the process model soundness property. Again, that follows from transferring the results shown for free-choice sound WF-nets to our setting. In [2] such nets are shown to be safe, so that no activity can be enabled concurrently to itself.

S4 Follows directly from Lemma 1 in [30] and Lemma 3 in [30], cf. also S1.

S5 Follows from the proof of Theorem 1 in [30], cf. also S2.

S6 Follows directly from Lemma 2 in [30].   □

The requirements imposed by Definition 5 for relation $\mathcal{R}$ coincide with the properties of the flow relation in sound process models, cf., Proposition 1. In other words, Definition 5 ensures that the structural requirements induced by the behavioral profile are satisfiable. We see that every sound process model shows a consistent behavioral profile.

Lemma 1. *The behavioral profile of a sound process model is consistent.*

Proof. Let $PM = (A, G, F, s, e, t)$ be a sound process model with the behavioral profile $\mathcal{BP} = \{\leadsto_{PM}, +_{PM}, \|_{PM}\}$ and assume that $\mathcal{BP}$ is not consistent. According to Proposition 1 S1, S2, and S3, the transitive closure of the flow relation F of PM qualifies for being a dependency relation as defined in Definition 5. However, the flow relation F is transitive by definition, which yields a contradiction with our assumption of $\mathcal{BP}$ being inconsistent.   □

Deciding Behavioral Profile Consistency. According to Lemma 1, consistency of the behavioral profile is a necessary condition for the existence of a sound process model. Hence, we have to clarify how to decide consistency for a given behavioral profile.

In the general case the consistency check for a behavioral profile cannot be done efficiently: interleaving order between two activities stems either from the potential concurrent enabling, or from the existence of a control flow cycle spanning both activities. Hence, to decide whether there exists a transitive relation $\mathcal{R}$ according to Definition 5, both possibilities have to be explored for each pair of activities in interleaving order. Analysis of alternatives yields an exponential time complexity of any algorithm for checking consistency.

Still, consistency can be decided efficiently under certain assumptions. Consistency of a behavioral profile comprising solely strict order and exclusiveness relations can be decided in polynomial time. In addition, two stricter notions of consistency can be applied. First, all pairs of activities x and y with $x\|y$ may be required to be in the dependency relation, i.e., $(x, y), (y, x) \in \mathcal{R}$. In this case, the existence of a transitive relation $\mathcal{R}$ indicates the existence of a sound process model for the profile that does not show any concurrency of activities. That is due to the fact that interleaving order between activities stems solely from control flow cycles. We refer to this consistency as *non-concurrent consistency*. Second, all pairs of activities x and y with $x\|y$ may be required not to be in the dependency relation, i.e., $(x, y), (y, x) \notin \mathcal{R}$. Then, interleaving order is expected to stem solely from concurrent enabling of activities. This consistency, referred to as *acyclic consistency*, hints at the existence of a sound process model for the profile that is acyclic. As both notions avoid to check two possibilities for interleaving pairs of activities, they can be decided in polynomial time.

Corollary 1. The following problems can be decided in $O(n^3)$ time with n as the number of activities of a behavioral profile.
1. Given a behavioral profile, to decide consistency in the absence of activities in interleaving order.
2. Given a behavioral profile, to decide non-concurrent consistency.
3. Given a behavioral profile, to decide acyclic consistency.

Proof. According to Definition 5, a dependency relation is built from the behavioral profile. In all three cases, the derivation is straight-forward as for every pair of activities it is defined whether or not it is part of the dependency relation. Hence, building the dependency relations takes $O(n^2)$ time with n as the number of activities. Then, the dependency relations is checked for transitivity, which takes $O(n^3)$ time with n as the number of activities of the process model.   □

3.4   Abstract Model Synthesis from a Consistent Behavioral Profile

Once consistency of a behavioral profile is validated, we derive the abstract model structure from the behavioral profile. Due to consistency and according to Definition 5 there is a transitive dependency relation between the activities. This dependency relation induces the abstract process model flow relation. Still, to arrive at a well-structured process model in which every activity has at most one predecessor and successor, several additional steps have to be done. We outline these steps in Algorithm 2 and explain them in detail in the following paragraphs.

First, the dependency relation $\mathcal{R}$ between activities is determined. Then, a transitive reduction is performed on $\mathcal{R}$ yielding the relation $\mathcal{R}'$. Intuitively, the dependency relation corresponds to the transitive closure of the flow relation. Thereby, it is reduced by all activity pairs that can be derived through transitivity of two other activity pairs. In the case of cyclic dependencies, there are different options to remove activity pairs during transitive reduction. We can choose one pair arbitrarily, since the activity order inside a control flow cycle does not impact on the relations of the behavioral profile between these activities.

Algorithm 2. Deriving a process model from a consistent behavioral profile

1: **deriveProcessModelFromBehavioralProfile**($\mathcal{BP}$)
2: $\mathcal{R} :=$ determineDependencyRelation($\mathcal{BP}$)
3: $\mathcal{R}' :=$ doTransitiveReduction($\mathcal{R}$)
4: $A :=$ extractOneDomainOfRelation($\mathcal{BR}$)
5: $G := \emptyset$
6: $s :=$ determineOrCreateStartActivity($\mathcal{R}'$)
7: $e :=$ determineOrCreateEndActivity($\mathcal{R}'$)
8: $A := A \cup \{s, e\}$
9: $\mathcal{R}' :=$ updateRelationBasedOnStartAndEndActivities($s, e, \mathcal{R}'$)
10: $F := \mathcal{R}'$
11: $t := \emptyset$
12: **for all** $a \in A$ with more than one successor in $\mathcal{R}'$ **do**
13:     $G_a :=$ createSplitGatewaysBetweenActivityAndSuccessors($a, \mathcal{R}'$)
14:     $t := t \cup$ determineGatewayTypes($a, G_a, \mathcal{R}'$)
15:     $F :=$ updateRelationForGatewaysAfterActivity(G, a, F)
16:     $G := G \cup G_a$
17: **for all** $a \in A$ with more than one predecessor in $\mathcal{R}'$ **do**
18:     $G_a :=$ createJoinGatewaysBetweenActivityAndSuccessors($a, \mathcal{R}'$)
19:     $t := t \cup$ determineGatewayTypes($a, G_a, \mathcal{R}'$)
20:     $F :=$ updateRelationForGatewaysAfterActivity(G, a, F)
21:     $G := G \cup G_a$
22: **return** $PM = (A, G, F, s, e, t)$

Second, we extract the set of activities of the process model, which corresponds to one of the domains of the behavioral profile relations. Further, we determine a start and an end activity as follows. If there is exactly one activity that has no predecessor in the reduced dependency relation $\mathcal{R}'$, this activity is selected as the start activity s. When there are multiple start activity candidates, an auxiliary activity is created and added to the set of activities. Relation $\mathcal{R}'$ is updated, so that there is an entry between the auxiliary activity and all start activity candidates. In the same vein, an end activity is selected or created, respectively.

Third, the abstract model flow relation is defined as the reduced dependency relation $\mathcal{R}'$. Then, the result is a process model consisting of activities and flow arcs with dedicated start and end activities. However, activities might show multiple incoming or outgoing flow arcs. In a post-processing step, we introduce gateways to realize the splitting and joining of control flow. For an activity with multiple outgoing arcs split gateways are applied. Notice that more than one gateway might be introduced to implement the behavioral relations between succeeding activities correctly. Thus, there might be a sequence of gateways, inserted between the activity and its successors, such that the flow relation and the relation that types gateways have to be updated accordingly. For an activity a the sequence of succeeding split gateways is created as follows.

1. All successors of a, for which there is a path to a, are connected to a new *xor* split gateway. Note that these successors are part of one control flow cycle.

2. All successors of a are grouped iteratively, so that each group has the same behavioral relations to the other successors of a (or groups of successors). All these groups are either exclusive to each other, or in interleaving order.

3. All successors of a in a dedicated group are connected to a new split gateway. The gateway type is defined by the behavioral relation between the group members: exclusiveness yields a *xor* gateway, interleaving order—an *and* gateway.

4. The gateways created for all groups are chained according to the order of activity grouping. Any *xor* gateway for the activities in a control flow cycle is added as the last gateway.

We illustrate these steps by the model fragment depicted in the left part of Fig. 5. Assume there is a path from b to a and from c to a, whereas there is no path from activities d, e, and f to a. Thus, activities b and c are grouped and connected to an *xor* split. Assume that activities d and e are exclusive, while both of them are in interleaving order with activity f. Then, d and e are grouped first and connected

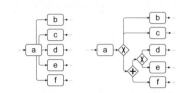

Fig. 5. Post-processing of activities with multiple outgoing flow arcs

to an *xor* split. Taking both activities as a single fragment, the second group consists of this fragment and activity f. Due to interleaving order, both are connected to an *and* split. Finally, the group containing the activities in a control flow cycle, i.e., b and c, is connected. The right part of Fig. 5 depicts the post-processing result for activity a. The approach described for activities with more than one outgoing flow arc is mirrored for activities with more than one incoming flow arc in order to introduce the respective join gateways.

After the activities with multiple incoming or outgoing flow arcs have been post-processed, the complete abstract model derived from the consistent behavioral profile is returned by the algorithm.

Lemma 2. *Given a consistent behavioral profile, the process model derived by Algorithm 2 shows the same behavioral profile.*

Proof. Let $\mathcal{BP} = \{\leadsto, +, ||\}$ be a consistent behavioral profile and $PM = (A, G, F, s, e, t)$ the derived process model with the behavioral profile $\mathcal{BP}' = \{\leadsto_{PM}, +_{PM}, ||_{PM}\}$. The algorithm translates the transitive dependency relation into the transitive closure of the flow relation F. Therefore, $x \leadsto y$ implies xF^+y and $y\not{F^+}x$. According to Proposition 1 S5, $x \leadsto_{PM} y$ holds. The same argument holds for interleaving activities $x||y$ that translate to xF^+y and yF^+x, yielding $x||_{PM}y$ by Proposition 1 S6. For activities x and y with $x\not{F^+}y$ and $y\not{F^+}x$, it holds either $x||y$ or $x+y$. It remains to show that in both cases the same relation can be observed in the derived process model. As the process model is a connected graph, there must be a node n for which we have a path to x and a path to y, while for two successors of n, $n_1, n_2 \in n\bullet$, it holds n_1F^+x, $n_1\not{F^+}y$, $n_2\not{F^+}x$, and n_2F^+y. As n has more than one successor, it is a gateway. The type of gateway n, *and* or *xor*, determines whether it holds $n_1 +_{PM} n_2$ or $n_1||_{PM}n_2$ and, therefore, $x +_{PM} y$ or $x||_{PM}y$. As this gateway type is selected by our algorithm based on the behavioral relation between x and y in the original profile $\mathcal{BP} = \{\leadsto, +, ||\}$, the relations of both profiles $\mathcal{BP}$ and $\mathcal{BP}'$ coincide for activities x and y. □

After we studied the relation between consistency of a behavioral profile and the existence of a sound process models in both directions, we conclude the following.

Theorem 1. *There is a sound process model, if and only if, the behavioral profile is consistent.*

Proof. The $\Rightarrow$ direction follows from Lemma 1, the $\Leftarrow$ direction from Lemma 2.

$\square$

We conclude this section returning to the motivating example presented in Section 2. Fig. 6 illustrates the complete abstract model derived from the initial model according to the developed abstraction technique. We see that the activities aggregated into *Handle data* are in strict order with most of the other activities to aggre-

Fig. 6. Abstract model for the initial example in Fig. 1

gate. Hence, the strict order relation holds also between the aggregated activities in the abstract model. For the other two aggregated activities, exclusiveness turns out to be the dominating behavioral relation.

4   Related Work

The work presented in this paper complements two research areas: business process model abstraction and process model synthesis. The former studies methods of process model transformation and criteria of model element abstraction.

The related process model transformation techniques constitute two groups. The first group builds on an explicit definition of a fragment to be transformed. Here, Petri net reduction rules preserving certain behavioral properties play an important role [19]. Such rules have also been defined for workflow graphs [23], EPCs [11,18], and YAWL [31]. The second group of transformation techniques hierarchically decomposes a model into fragments, e.g., cf. [28]. The reduced process model can be regarded as a view in terms of [20] and typically preserves properties of behavior inheritance [3]. Unfortunately, such hierarchical decomposition is not sufficient in many scenarios, cf. [29]. The technique developed in this paper shows how the abstract model control flow can be discovered even for non-hierarchical abstractions. Model element abstraction criteria, for instance, execution cost, duration, and path frequency, have been studied in a number of works [12,13,26]. These works have in common that their major focus is on identifying abstraction candidates. The current paper complements this stream of research demonstrating how abstracted process models can be constructed even if aggregated activities are not structurally close to each other. There is a series of works that address the requirements of business process model abstraction. The approaches of [6,7,16] build on an explicit definition of a fragment that can be abstracted to provide a process overview. In [5,21,27] such fragments are discovered without user specification according to the model structure.

The developed method for the construction of an abstract process model from the behavioral profile extends the family of process model synthesis techniques.

In process mining the alpha algorithm is used for the construction of a process model from event logs [4]. The mining relations used by the alpha algorithm differ to ours as they are only partially transitive. In this paper, we use the behavioral profile relations, which permit the reconstruction of the process model if the profile is consistent. There are further approaches to synthesis that take the state space as an input to generate process models including [8,9,17], which all build on Petri net formalism.

5   Conclusion and Future Work

In this paper, we have presented a novel approach to process model abstraction that addresses existing industry demand. Given a process model and sets of related activities in it, we are capable to deliver a high-level process model preserving the overall properties of the initial model or tell the user that such a model cannot be created. The suggested abstraction approach bases on an aggregation of the initial model elements and, in contrast to the available techniques, is capable of non-hierarchical aggregation. To synthesize a high-level process model we leverage behavioral profiles. Once a profile for the initial model is created, we propose how to abstract it and synthesize a high-level model out of it. Notice that in the synthesis step we assume the resulting model to be a sound process model—a reasonable assumption in practice.

This paper motivates several directions of the future work. In the context of BPMA, it is imperative to investigate criteria and methods allowing to learn which activities in the initial model are related. A corresponding solution would complement the approach developed in this paper and their combination may support the user with an automated BPMA solution. Another direction of the future work is the further research on model synthesis out of behavioral profiles. In particular, it is interesting to broaden the class of synthesized models.

References

1. van der Aalst, W.M.P.: The Application of Petri Nets to Workflow Management. JCSC 8(1), 21–66 (1998)
2. van der Aalst, W.M.P.: Workflow Verification: Finding Control-Flow Errors Using Petri-Net-Based Techniques. In: van der Aalst, W.M.P., Desel, J., Oberweis, A. (eds.) Business Process Management. LNCS, vol. 1806, pp. 161–183. Springer, Heidelberg (2000)
3. van der Aalst, W.M.P., Basten, T.: Life-Cycle Inheritance: A Petri-Net-Based Approach. In: Azéma, P., Balbo, G. (eds.) ICATPN 1997. LNCS, vol. 1248, pp. 62–81. Springer, Heidelberg (1997)
4. van der Aalst, W.M.P., Weijters, A.J.M.M., Maruster, L.: Workflow Mining: Discovering Process Models from Event Logs. IEEE TKDE 16(9), 1128–1142 (2004)
5. Basu, A., Blanning, R.W.: Synthesis and Decomposition of Processes in Organizations. ISR 14(4), 337–355 (2003)
6. Bobrik, R., Reichert, M., Bauer, T.: View-Based Process Visualization. In: Alonso, G., Dadam, P., Rosemann, M. (eds.) BPM 2007. LNCS, vol. 4714, pp. 88–95. Springer, Heidelberg (2007)

7. Cardoso, J., Miller, J., Sheth, A., Arnold, J.: Modeling Quality of Service for Workflows and Web Service Processes. Technical report, University of Georgia, Web Services (2002)
8. Cortadella, J., Kishinevsky, M., Lavagno, L., Yakovlev, A.: Deriving Petri Nets from Finite Transition Systems. IEEE TC 47(8), 859–882 (1998)
9. Dehnert, J., van der Aalst, W.M.P.: Bridging The Gap Between Business Models And Workflow Specifications. IJCIS 13(3), 289–332 (2004)
10. Dijkman, R.M., Dumas, M., Ouyang, C.: Semantics and Analysis of Business Process Models in BPMN. IST 50(12), 1281–1294 (2008)
11. van Dongen, B., Jansen-Vullers, M., Verbeek, H., van der Aalst, W.M.P.: Verification of the SAP Reference Models Using EPC Reduction, State-space Analysis, and Invariants. CAIE 58(6), 578–601 (2007)
12. Eshuis, R., Grefen, P.: Constructing Customized Process Views. DKE 64(2), 419–438 (2008)
13. Günther, C.W., van der Aalst, W.M.P.: Fuzzy Mining Adaptive Process Simplification Based on Multiperspective Metrics. In: Alonso, G., Dadam, P., Rosemann, M. (eds.) BPM 2007. LNCS, vol. 4714, pp. 328–343. Springer, Heidelberg (2007)
14. Hammer, M., Champy, J.: Reengineering the Corporation: A Manifesto for Business Revolution. HarperBusiness (April 1994)
15. Kiepuszewski, B., ter Hofstede, A.H.M., van der Aalst, W.M.P.: Fundamentals of Control Flow in Workflows. Acta Informatica 39(3), 143–209 (2003)
16. Liu, D., Shen, M.: Workflow Modeling for Virtual Processes: an Order-preserving Process-view Approach. ISJ 28(6), 505–532 (2003)
17. Massuthe, P., Serebrenik, A., Sidorova, N., Wolf, K.: Can I Find a Partner? Undecidability of Partner Existence for Open Nets. IPL 108(6), 374–378 (2008)
18. Mendling, J., van der Aalst, W.M.P.: Formalization and Verification of EPCs with OR-Joins Based on State and Context. In: Krogstie, J., Opdahl, A.L., Sindre, G. (eds.) CAiSE 2007 and WES 2007. LNCS, vol. 4495, pp. 439–453. Springer, Heidelberg (2007)
19. Murata, T.: Petri Nets: Properties, Analysis and Applications. Proceedings of the IEEE 77(4), 541–580 (1989)
20. Pankratius, V., Stucky, W.: A Formal Foundation for Workflow Composition, Workflow View Definition, and Workflow Normalization based on Petri Nets. In: APCCM 2005, pp. 79–88. ACS, Inc, Darlinghurst (2005)
21. Polyvyanyy, A., Smirnov, S., Weske, M.: The Triconnected Abstraction of Process Models. In: Dayal, U., Eder, J., Koehler, J., Reijers, H.A. (eds.) Business Process Management. LNCS, vol. 5701, pp. 229–244. Springer, Heidelberg (2009)
22. Reijers, H.A., Mendling, J., Dijkman, R.M.: On the Usefulness of Subprocesses in Business Process Models. BPM Center Report BPM-10-03, BPMcenter.org (2010)
23. Sadiq, W., Orlowska, M.E.: Analyzing Process Models Using Graph Reduction Techniques. ISJ 25(2), 117–134 (2000)
24. Schrefl, M., Stumptner, M.: Behavior-Consistent Specialization of Object Life Cycles. ACM TOSEM 11(1), 92–148 (2002)
25. Smirnov, S., Dijkman, R., Mendling, J., Weske, M.: Meronymy-based Aggregation of Activities in Business Process Models. In: ER 2010. LNCS, Springer, Heidelberg (2010)
26. Smirnov, S., Reijers, H., Nugteren, T., Weske, M.: Business Process Model Abstraction: Theory and Practice. Technical report, Hasso Plattner Institute (2010), http://bpt.hpi.uni-potsdam.de/pub/Public/SergeySmirnov/abstractionUseCases.pdf

27. Streit, A., Pham, B., Brown, R.: Visualization Support for Managing Large Business Process Specifications. In: van der Aalst, W.M.P., Benatallah, B., Casati, F., Curbera, F. (eds.) BPM 2005. LNCS, vol. 3649, pp. 205–219. Springer, Heidelberg (2005)
28. Vanhatalo, J., Völzer, H., Koehler, J.: The Refined Process Structure Tree. In: Dumas, M., Reichert, M., Shan, M.-C. (eds.) BPM 2008. LNCS, vol. 5240, pp. 100–115. Springer, Heidelberg (2008)
29. Weidlich, M., Barros, A., Mendling, J., Weske, M.: Vertical Alignment of Process Models - How Can We Get There? In:BPMDS 2009 LNBIP, vol. 29, pp. 71–84. Springer, Heidelberg (1975)
30. Weidlich, M., Mendling, J., Weske, M.: Efficient Consistency Measurement based on Behavioural Profiles of Process Models. In: IEEE TSE (to appear 2010)
31. Wynn, M.T., Verbeek, H.M.W., van der Aalst, W.M.P., ter Hofstede, A.H.M., Edmond, D.: Reduction Rules for YAWL Workflows with Cancellation Regions and OR joins. IST 51(6), 1010–1020 (2009)

Root-Cause Analysis of Design-Time Compliance Violations on the Basis of Property Patterns

Amal Elgammal[*], Oktay Turetken, Willem-Jan van den Heuvel,
and Mike Papazoglou

European Research Institute in Service Science (ERISS), Tilburg University,
Tilburg, The Netherlands
{a.f.s.a.elgammal,o.turetken,w.j.a.m.vdnheuvel,
m.p.papazoglou}@uvt.nl

Abstract. Today's business environment demands a high degree of compliance of business processes with business rules, policies, regulations and laws. Compliance regulations, such Sarbanes-Oxley force enterprises to continuously review their business processes and service-enabled applications and ensure that they satisfy the set of relevant compliance constraints. Compliance management should be considered from the very early stages of the business process design. In this paper, a taxonomy of compliance constraints for business processes is introduced based on property specification patterns, where patterns can be used to facilitate the formal specification of compliance constraints. This taxonomy serves as the backbone of the root-cause analysis, which is conducted to reason about and eventually resolve design-time compliance violations. Based on the root-cause analysis, appropriate guidelines and instructions can be provided as remedies to alleviate design-time compliance deviations in service-enabled business processes.

Keywords: Regulatory compliance, Compliance constraint detection and prevention, Design-time compliance management, Formal compliance model, Compliance patterns, root-cause analysis.

1 Introduction

SOA is an integration framework for connecting loosely coupled software modules into on-demand business processes. Business processes form the foundation for SOAs and require that multiple steps occur between physically independent yet logically dependent software services [1]. Where business processes stretch across many cooperating and coordinated systems, possibly crossing organizational boundaries, technologies like XML and Web services are making system-to-system interactions commonplace.

Business processes form the foundation for all organizations, and as such, are impacted by industry regulations. Without explicit business process definitions,

---

[*] This work is a part of the research project "COMPAS: Compliance-driven Models, Languages and Architectures for Services", which is funded by the European commission, funding reference FP7-215175.

P.P. Maglio et al. (Eds.): ICSOC 2010, LNCS 6470, pp. 17–31, 2010.

flexible rule frameworks, and audit trails that provide for non-repudiation, organizations face litigation risks and even criminal penalties. Compliance regulations, such as HIPAA, Basel II, Sarbanes-Oxley (SOX) and others require all organizations to review their business processes and ensure that they meet the compliance standards set forth in the legislation. In all cases, these new control and disclosure requirements create auditing demands for SOAs.

SOAs should play a crucial role in compliance, allowing management to ascertain that internal control measures that govern their key business processes can be checked, tested, and potentially certified with their underlying web-services.

Compliance is about ensuring that business processes, operations and practices are in accordance with a prescribed and/or agreed on set of norms [2] . A *compliance constraint* (*requirement*) refers to any explicitly stated rule or regulation that prescribes any aspect of an internal or cross-organizational business process. Compliance constraints may emerge from different sources and can take various forms. They may originate from legislation and regulatory bodies (such as Sarbanes-Oxley and Basel II), standards and code of practices (such as: ISO 9001) and/or business partner contracts.

Not only the large and ever-increasing number of compliance constraints but also the diversity and complexity of these constraints, complicate the compliance management process [3]. Consequently, a comprehensive compliance management solution is of utmost importance to support compliance throughout all the stages of the complete business process lifecycle. A major requirement of a generic compliance management approach is that it should be sustainable [2]. A preventive focus is fundamentally required in order to achieve the sustainability requirement. Compliance should be considered at the very early stages of business process design, thus enforcing compliance by design.

Compliance constraints should be based on a formal foundation of a logical language to facilitate the application of future automatic reasoning techniques for verifying and ensuring business process compliance. However, formal specifications in general are difficult to write and understand by users. The notion of *property specification patterns* (Dwyer's property patterns) was introduced in [4] as high-level abstractions of frequently used logical formulas. Property patterns assist users in understanding and defining formal specifications, which significantly facilitates the work of the user, as she doesn't need to go into the lower-level and complex details of the adapted formal language.

By applying the automated verification tools that are associated with the utilized logical language (e.g. NuSMV2 model-checker [5]), compliance between specifications and the applicable set of compliance constraints can be automatically checked. However, the verification results are usually a list of which compliance rules have been violated and which have been satisfied. Clearly, existing practices and approaches are by far insufficient to effectively assist business process/service designers in resolving potential conflicts or violations between service-enabled processes and associated rules, laws and regulations. A structured approach is critical to allow designers –many of which are non-experts in formal languages- to formally capture compliance rules and policies, and then semi-automatically detect the root-cause of compliance anomalies and provide heuristics to create corrective actions to resolve them. The main focus of this paper is on *design-time* compliance management and analysis.

In this paper, we use Dwyer's property specification patterns [4] and Linear Temporal Logic (LTL) [6] to formally represent compliance constraints. Furthermore, we present pattern extensions and we introduce new patterns that are frequently used to specify compliance constraints. Then, a compliance constraint taxonomy is built up on top of these patterns, which represents the backbone of the root-cause analysis conducted in this paper. Finally, the root-cause analysis approach is presented to reason about design-time compliance violations. The *Current Reality Tree (CRT)* of Goldratt's Theory of Constraints (TOC) [7], [8] is adapted as the root-cause analysis technique. By traversing the CRTs, appropriate remedies are provided as guidelines/suggestions that help the user/expert to resolve the compliance deviations.

The rest of this paper is organized as follows: a design-time compliance management approach is briefly discussed in Section 2. Section 3 presents a scenario used as the running example throughout this paper. Section 4 presents the proposed root-cause analysis approach to reason about design-time compliance violations. Related work is summarized in Section 5. Finally, conclusions and outlook are highlighted in Section 6.

2   Design-Time Compliance Management

To provide a brief overview of the compliance management approach maintained in this paper, this section briefly discusses important aspects of a comprehensive compliance management framework, underlining the features that deal with managing compliance during the *design-time*. Fig. 1 depicts an overview of the key practices and components of this approach, and highlights the parts that outline the *scope* of this paper. There are two primary roles involved in this approach: (i) a *business expert,* who is responsible for defining and managing service-enabled business processes in an organization while taking compliance constraints into account, and (ii) a *compliance expert,* who is responsible for the internalization, specification and management of compliance requirements stemming from external and internal sources in close collaboration with the business expert.

The approach encompasses two logical repositories; the *business process repository* and the *compliance requirements repository*, which are semantically aligned and may reside in a shared environment. Process models including service descriptions are defined and maintained in the business process repository, while the compliance requirements and all relevant concepts are defined, maintained and organized in the compliance requirements repository. These repositories foster the reusability of business and compliance specifications. We assume that these two specifications (business processes and compliance requirements) use the same constructs through the usage of a shared domain-specific ontology.

The approach assumes the overall process to start either from the business process side (the right-hand side of Fig. 1) or from the compliance requirements side (left part of Fig. 1). Process models can be specified in Business Process Execution Language

(BPEL [1]) de facto standard; However, as BPEL is not grounded on a formal model, any BPEL specification should be transformed into a formal representation (e.g. a finite state automaton, such as Buchi automata [9]) to enable the verification of these formal definitions against formally specified compliance rules.

On the other hand, the *internalization* of compliance constraints originating from regulations, policies, standards and other compliance sources into a set of organization-specific compliance requirements involves not only compliance but also business process domain knowledge. It may require compliance expert to work in collaboration with the business expert to define and iterate an effective set of requirements to address these constraints.

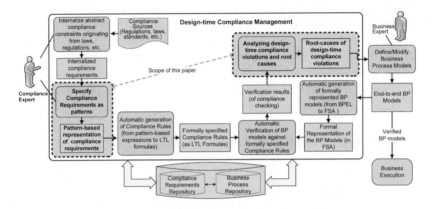

Fig. 1. Design-time compliance management approach

A compliance expert may apply patterns to render compliance constraints, which represents an intermediate step between internalized compliance requirements and formal statements (as LTL formulas for our case). These pattern-based expressions are then automatically transformed into LTL formulas, based on the mapping rules between patterns and LTL. As shown in Fig. 1, the inputs to the 'automatic verification' component of the approach are; the formally specified end-to-end business process models; and the LTL rules capturing compliance requirements. Then, automatic verification is supported by 'model-checkers' [10].

Analysis of the verification results and their root-causes should be assisted by a component of the approach, which also directs the business expert in modifying the business process model so she may resolve any compliance violation. The counter-example tracing facility, typically provided by the model-checkers, can also aid user by highlighting the fragments in the business process model that are the sources of non-compliance. The business process models are updated based on the compliance verification and analysis results and re-mapped to their formal forms and re-verified against the set of applicable compliance requirements. This process iterates until no violations are detected.

---

[1] BPEL: Business Process Execution Language, http://en.wikipedia.org/wiki/BPEL

This paper focuses on the parts in Fig. 1 that are enclosed (with dotted lines), which are: the pattern-based specification of compliance requirements and analyses of design-time violations and root-causes. Our work on the other components of the approach are kept outside the scope of this paper.

3 Running Scenario

The Internet reseller scenario, which is used as the running example throughout this paper, is one of the industry scenarios explored within the EU funded COMPAS research project [12]. The scenario is set in an e-business application domain, and more particularly, online product selling systems.

The scenario starts with the customer checking product information on a website. Next, if the customer chooses a specific item, she submits an order along with her customer data. Next, the sales department validates the order by contacting the credit bureau to check the credit worthiness of the customer. Afterwards, the financial department creates the invoice and checks for payments. Finally, a delivery request is sent to the supplier.

Table 1 shows excerpts of the compliance requirements relevant to this scenario. Each compliance requirement is described in terms of: (i) an ID (ii) internalized compliance requirement (iii) its representation as patterns (as discussed in Section 2), and (iv) an explanation of its pattern representation.

Table 1. An excerpt of the relevant compliance requirements

ID	Compliance Requirement	Pattern Representation	Description
R1	Computer-generated sales order confirmations or cancelations are sent to customers after validating the order.	*ValidateOrder(x,y)* **LeadsTo** *(SendConfirm(x)* **MutexChoice** *SendCancel(x))*	*ValidateOrder* for sales order y and customer x is followed by either sending a confirmation or cancelation to customer x.
R2	Sales orders over a set threshold require approval by management before acceptance by the system.	*(SalesOrder(y,threshold)* **exists**) **Imply** *(Approve(y, manager)* **Precedes** *Accept(y))*	If there is a *salesOrder* y that exceeds a threshold *threshold* then *Approve* action performed by *manager* should precedes *Accept* of order y.
R3	Appropriate segregation of duties is maintained between credit checking and cashing functions.	*CreditChecking(x)* **SegregatedFrom** *Cashing(x)*	*CreditChecking* function for customer x should be segregated from the *Cashing* function for the same customer

4 Compliance Patterns and Compliance Constraints Taxonomy

This section presents a taxonomy of pattern-based compliance constraints for business processes. As shown in Fig. 2, the compliance pattern is the core element of the taxonomy, and each pattern is a sub-type of it. The compliance pattern is sub-divided in two main classes of patterns; namely *atomic* and *composite*. The lower part of Fig. 2 presents the atomic patterns, which are adapted from Dwyer's property specification pattern system [4].

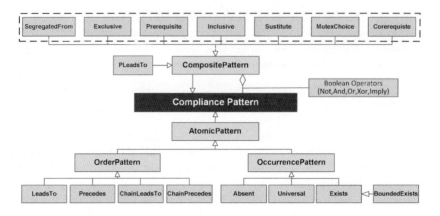

Fig. 2. Compliance constraints taxonomy based on patterns

Atomic patterns introduce two main sub-classes: *Occurrence* and *Order* pattern classes. Their properties can be described as follows:
Occurrence patterns are:

- *Absent*: Indicates that a given state[2] *P* does not occur within the system.
- *Universal*: Indicates that *P* occurs throughout the system.
- *Exists*: Indicates that *P* must occur within the system.
- *Bounded exists*: Indicates that *P* must occur at least/exactly/at most *k* times within the system.

Order patterns are:

- *Precedes*: A given state *P* must always be preceded by a given state *Q*.
- *LeadsTo*: *P* must always be followed by *Q*.
- *Chain precedes*: A sequence of states $P_1, \ldots P_n$ must always be preceded by a sequence of states $Q_1, \ldots Q_m$.
- *ChainLeadsTo*: A sequence of states $P_1, \ldots P_n$ must always be followed by a sequence of states $Q_1, \ldots Q_m$.

As shown in the upper part of Fig. 2, compliance patterns can be nested using Boolean logic operators including *Not, And, Or, Xor* and *Imply* to help the definition of complex requirements in terms of other compliance patterns (composite patterns). For instance, the *PLeadsTo* pattern introduced in [11] is an 'And' composition of the two atomic patterns (*P Precedes Q*) *And* (*P LeadsTo Q*).

In addition to the patterns described above, this paper introduces seven new compliance patterns, namely: *Exclusive, Substitute, Corequiste, Inclusive, Prerequiste, MutexChoice,* and *SegregatedFrom*. Although these patterns commonly

---

[2] *State* represents a node in finite state automata (used for formal representation of a BP model as discussed in Section 2). In our context, it indicates a certain BP activity or a condition on any related artifact. '*ValidateOrder*' activity and '*OrderAmount > 500*' branching condition are examples of states.

occur within the domain of business process compliance, they are also applicable for the specification of properties in different domains and context.

The *SegregatedFrom* pattern captures the typical separation-of-duties security principle, which mandates that two specific activities should be performed by two different roles. Table 2 presents the mapping from the newly introduced compliance patterns to atomic patterns together with their meaning and their formal representation as LTL formulae

Table 2. Mapping of new compliance patterns

Composite Compliance Pattern	Description	Atomic Pattern Equivalence	LTL Representation
P *Segregated-From* Q	(Activities) P and Q should be assigned to different roles	(P*PLeads* Q) $\wedge$ (P.Role1) $\neq$ (Q.Role2)	$G(\neg Q\ W\ P)) \wedge G(P \rightarrow F(Q)) \wedge G((P.Role(\text{Role1}) \rightarrow G(\neg(Q.Role(\text{Role1})))$
P *Inclusive* Q	The presence of P mandates that Q is also present	(P *exists*) $\rightarrow$ (Q *exists*) = $\neg$ (P *exists*) $\vee$ (Q *exists*)	$\neg F(P) \vee F(Q)$
P *Prerequisite* Q	The absence of P mandates that Q is also absent	(P *isabsent*) $\rightarrow$ (Q *isabsent*) = $\neg$ (P*isabsent*) $\vee$ (Q *isabsent*)	$\neg G(\neg P) \vee G(\neg(Q))$
P *Exclusive* Q	The presence of P mandates the absence of Q. And presence of Q mandates the absence of P	($\neg$P *exists*) $\vee$ (Q *isabsent*) $\wedge$ ($\neg$Q *exists*) $\vee$ (P *isabsent*)	$(\neg (F(P)) \vee G(\neg Q)) \wedge (\neg (F(Q)) \vee G(\neg P))$
Q *Substitute* P	Q substitutes the absence of P	(P *isabsent*) $\rightarrow$ (Q *exists*) = $\neg$(P *isabsent*) $\vee$ (Q *exists*)	$\neg G(\neg(P)) \vee F(Q)$
P *Corequisite* Q	Either activities P and Q should exist together or to be absent together	(P *exists*) iff (Q *exists*) = ((P *exists*) $\wedge$ (Q *exists*)) $\vee$ ((P *isabsent*) $\wedge$ (Q *isabsent*))	$(F(P) \wedge F(Q)) \vee (G(\neg P) \wedge G(\neg Q))$
P *MutexChoice* Q	Either P or Q exists but not any of them or both of them	(P *exists*) Xor (Q *exists*) = ((P *exists*) $\wedge$ (Q *isabsent*)) $\vee$ ((Q *exists*) $\wedge$ (P *isabsent*))	$(F(P) \wedge G(\neg(Q))) \vee (F(Q) \wedge G(\neg(P)))$

In LTL [6], [10]; G, F and U correspond to the temporal operators 'always', 'eventually' and 'until' respectively. 'G' denotes that formula f must be true in all the states of the business process model. 'F' indicates that formula f will be true at some state in the future. 'U' means that if at some state in the future the second formula g will be true, then, the first formula f must be true in all the subsequent states.

5   Root-Cause Analysis of Design-Time Compliance Violations

A compliance violation in a business process definition may occur due to a variety of reasons and it is of upmost importance to provide the compliance expert intelligent feedback that reveals the root-causes of these violations and aids their resolution. This feedback should contain a set of rationale explaining the underlying reasons why the violation occurred and what strategies can be used as remedies. Based on the compliance constraint taxonomy proposed in Section 2, we have further analyzed and formalized root-causes for each pattern in the taxonomy. Particularly, we investigated and reported all possible causes of a violation of a compliance constraint represented by a specific pattern. However, based on the root-cause analysis, only the exact deduced cause(s) of the violation(s) is communicated to the user (as explained in Section 5.5).

For this purpose, we have adapted the *Current Reality Tree (CRT)* technique from Goldratt's Theory of Constraints (TOC) [7]. A *current reality tree* is a statement of a core problem and the symptoms that arise from it. It maps a sequence of causes and effects from the core problem to the symptoms arising from one core problem or a core conflict. If the core problem is removed, each of the symptoms may be removed. Operationally the process works backwards from the apparent undesirable effects or symptoms to uncover or discover the underlying core causes [7]. The CRT has been chosen due to its simplicity and the visual representation of the causes and effects.

A CRT usually starts with a list of problems called *Undesirable Effects* (*UDEs*), which represent negative or bad conditions. They are also 'effects' because for most part they are caused by something else [8]. The key question begins with 'why a violation occurs?' (the root of the tree). The answer to this question will generate child-(eren) of the UDE under consideration. For each child, which might be a UDE, the same "why" question is applied, and the answer is depicted as a deeper level in the tree. This process continues iteratively until the UDE under consideration is the root-cause(s) of the problem (in the leaf level of the tree). Incoming connections to an UDE from its children are connected via logical '*or*' operator; unless otherwise specified. Due to space limitation, we do not present all the current reality trees corresponding to each pattern given in the taxonomy (in Fig. 2).

5.1   Current Reality Trees for Atomic Patterns

One of the main advantages of using the Current Reality Tree technique (CRT) is that it is self-explanatory. Fig. 3 presents the CRTs for *Exists, Precedes, LeadsTo, PleadsTo, Absence and Universal* patterns. The root of each CRT represents an undesirable effect (UDEs). For our purpose, an UDE is a violation of a specific pattern. Hence, the root of each tree represents a violation to a specific pattern. For example, as shown in Fig. 3, the violation to '(P *Precedes* Q) pattern' is considered as the UDE of the *Precedes* CRT.

Deeper levels in the tree are guided by answering the same 'why' question. For example, the question that should be addressed here is: why (P *Precedes* Q) is violated. The answer to this question is: because (Q *Exists* is satisfied) and (P *exists* is violated) before it. This is depicted as the second level of the tree. The same 'why' question is applied to the UDE under consideration and analysis continues until the root-causes of the problem, i.e. the leaves of the tree are reached. For each leaf, the user is provided with guidelines as remedies to compliance violations. These guidelines are depicted in the CRTs as squared brackets linked to the leaves, e.g. 'Swap the occurrence of P and Q', where P and Q are business process activities that will be parameterized with the actual activity names. In case the leaf is a composite pattern, it will be replaced by its corresponding CRT. This process iterates continuously until all the leaves of the tree are atomic patterns.

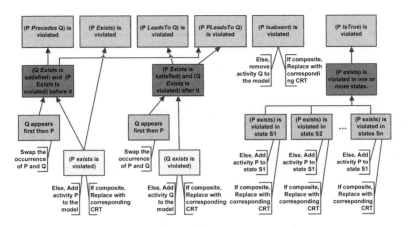

Fig. 3. CRT for Exists, Precedes, LeadsTo and PLeadsTo patterns

5.2 Current Reality Trees for Composite Patterns

Fig. 4 presents the CRTs for the composite patterns that comprise one or more compliance patterns connected with a Boolean operator. An example output from the analysis process could be the UDE '(PropertyPattern1 *and* PropertyPattern2) is violated'. Let this UDE be *UDE1*. According to the truth table of the '*and*' operator, the '*and*' statement is only true if its two operands are evaluated to true, otherwise the statement is evaluated to false. By applying the same 'Why' question to *UDE1*, the answer is either:

    i.   *UDE1.2:* PropertyPattern1 is violated, or
    ii.   *UDE1.2*: PropertyPattern2 is violated, or
    iii.   *UDE1.3:* PropertyPattern1 is violated and PropertyPattern2 is violated.

UDE1.1, *UDE1.2* and *UDE1.3* correspond to the violation of other compliance patterns. Hence, each UDE corresponds to a compliance pattern will be replaced with its corresponding CRT.

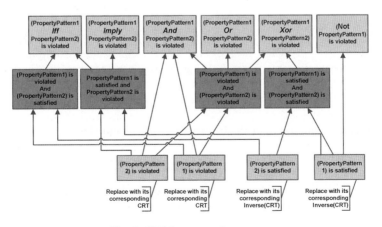

Fig. 4. CRT for composite patterns

Notably, for the negation operator, '(*Not* PropertyPattern1) is violated', the undesirable effect in this case is '(PropertyPattern1) is satisfied', which semantically represents the opposite of the CRTs analyzed above. For this purpose, each compliance pattern is re-analyzed the same way, with the undesirable effect (UDE) being 'property pattern is satisfied' (e.g. the lower levels of MutexChoice CRT in Fig. 5).

5.3   Current Reality Trees for the New Compliance Patterns

The CRTs of the newly introduced compliance patterns (e.g. SegregatedFrom, Inclusive, etc.) are instances from the CRTs of composite patterns given in Fig. 4. Two examples of the CRTs of these compliance patterns are presented in Fig. 5; namely: *Exclusive* and *Mutexchoice*.

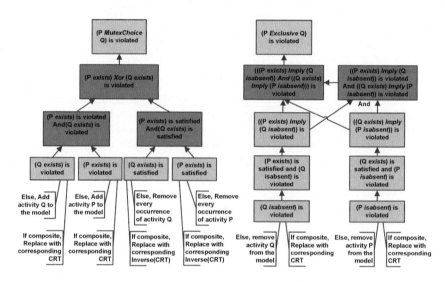

Fig. 5. CRTs for Exclusive and MutexChoice Composite Patterns

As shown in Fig. 5, the *MutexChoice* composite pattern is an '*Xor*' composition between two atomic patterns: (P *Exists*) and (Q *Exists*). Hence, for the *MutexChoice* composite pattern, the CRT of the '*Xor*' composite pattern is instantiated. The instantiation process starts from the outermost pattern to the innermost pattern. Similarly, the CRT of the *Exclusive* pattern is built based on the CRTs of '*And*', '*Imply*' composite patterns and *isabsent* atomic pattern.

5.4   Current Reality Trees of the Internet Reseller Scenario

This section presents briefly due to space limitations the application of the pattern based representation approach and relevant CRTs of the second and third compliance constraints (R2 & R3) given in Table 1 from the Internet reseller scenario.

In case violations are detected to R2 and R3 (e.g. the model-checker detects the violations), the CRTs to reason about violations are automatically constructed and traversed. Fig. 6 presents the CRTs of the violations to R2 and R3. The CRT of the violation to R2 is an *'Imply'* composition between two atomic patterns; *exists* and *precedes*. The CRT of the violation to the segregation-of-duty compliance constraints (R3) is shown in the right-hand side of Fig. 6.

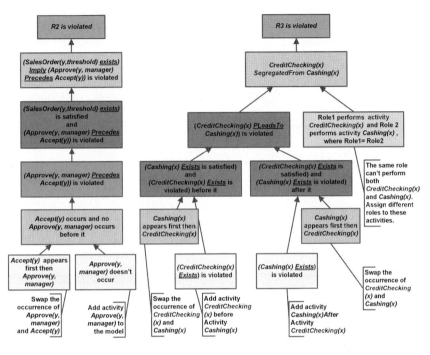

Fig. 6. CRTs for the violation to R2 and R3

5.5   Implementation of the Root Cause Analysis Approach

An effective and scalable implementation of the concepts discussed above is a challenging yet necessary step to help to ascertain the soundness of the approach proposed in this paper. We are currently implementing an environment as a part of a comprehensive tool-suite for business process compliance management, based on the concepts described in above sections. The prototype is a web-based environment[3], which also incorporates standalone tools for building graphical representation of requirements using patterns. The web-based environment is implemented using 'PHP'[4] as the main scripting language and Oracle database (ver.8i)[5] as the repository for compliance data and meta-data. The integration with Reo toolkit [13], which is used for process verification, is ongoing. The integration is achieved through a group of asynchronous web services, which mainly forwards BPEL representation and

---

[3] http://eriss.uvt.nl/compas
[4] http://en.wikipedia.org/wiki/PHP
[5] http://en.wikipedia.org/wiki/Oracle_Database

relevant formal compliance rules specified in LTL as input to Reo toolkit and retrieve back the verification result listing the rules that have been checked and whether they are satisfied or not.

Fig. 7 presents one of the user interfaces from the implementation reflecting how the results of the root cause analysis are communicated to experts. Only relevant remedies extracted from traversing the appropriate CRTs are displayed in the last column of the table in the user interface ('Result Description/Remedy' column). The user interface exemplifies the case of Internet reseller scenario, where R1 is satisfied, while, R2 and R3 are violated.

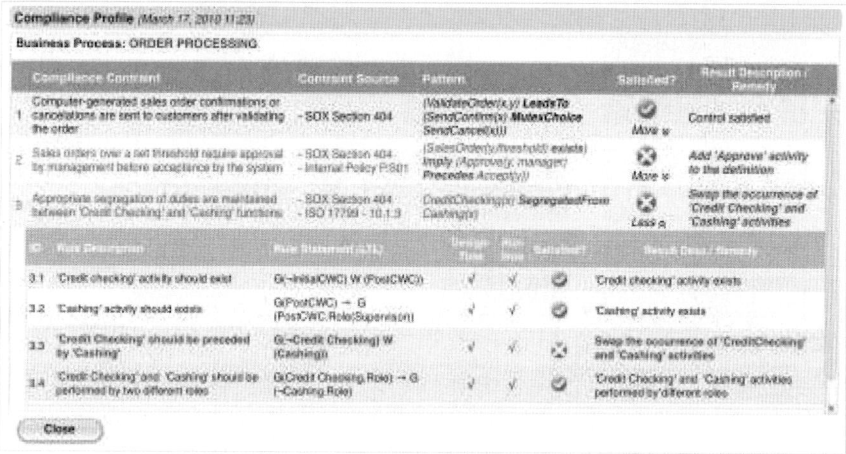

Fig. 7. A user interface implementation for the running scenario

6 Related Work

Deontic logic and temporal logic families have been successfully utilized in the literature as the formal foundation of compliance constraints. Key work examples utilizing languages based on Deontic logic are: [2], [14], [15], [16], [17], [18], [19] and [20]. On the other hand, major works built on top of temporal logic are: [5], [11], [21], [22], [23], [24], and [25]. Due to space limitation, we are listing here key works grounded on temporal logic.

Authors in [5] proposed a static-compliance checking framework that includes various model transformations. Compliance constraints are modeled using the graphical Business Property Specification Language (BPSL) tool. Next, NuSMV2 model checker is used to check the compliance. The study in [21] utilized π-Logic to formally represent compliance constraints. On the other hand, business process models are abstractly represented using BP-Calculus. Using HAL toolkit, a BPEL program equivalent to the abstract representation can be automatically generated if the two specifications are compliant. The study in [23] utilized past LTL (PLTL), where properties about the past can be represented. However sequential compliance constraints are just considered. On the other hand, the study in [24] utilizes the original pattern-based system, however, it considers aspects relevant to monitoring compliance during runtime. Furthermore, authors in [25] have extended Dwyer's property pattern to capture time-related property specifications. E.g. activity A must always be followed by activity B within k time units. Integrating real-time dimension to the proposed approach entails an ongoing research direction. The study in [11] has utilized Dwyer's patterns for the verification of service compositions. In [22], real-time temporal object logic was proposed for the formal specification of compliance requirements based on a pre-defined domain ontology. Real-time temporal object logic is an expressive logic, however it is excessively difficult to be used.

Assisting the user to resolve non-compliance during design-time has been addressed in [26], [27] and [23]. The notion of *proximity relation* has been introduced in [26] that quantitatively compare how much a modified business process model deviated from the original one. The goal is to resolve non-compliance violations by identifying minimally different process models. They also introduced heuristic guidance for detecting and resolving compliance violations. A major distinction to our work is that we provide concrete guidelines and our work is based on a compliance constraint taxonomy based on extended patterns. The notion of *compliance distance* has been introduced in [20, 27], as a quantification of the effort required to transform a non-compliant business process model to a compliant one, which can take the values between 0 and 1. A visualization of compliance violations has been introduced in [23] by utilizing Temporal Logic Querying (TLQ). To the best of our knowledge, this is the first study that considers an exhaustive analysis of root-causes of compliance violations, and providing the user with only relevant guidelines/ suggestions as remedies to resolve the compliance deviations based on high-level patterns.

7   Conclusions and Outlook

Business processes –many of which are implemented as a SOA these days - form the foundation for all organizations, and as such, are impacted by laws, policies and industry regulations. Without an explicit auditing SOA framework to ensure compliance of service-enabled processes, organizations face litigation risks and even criminal penalties. One of the significant provisions towards business process compliance is a framework that would enable service engineers to define compliance constraints and weave them into service-enabled processes. Compliance management should be considered from the very early stages of the business process design, such that compliance constraints are designed into service-enabled processes. To enable automatic reasoning techniques for verifying and ensuring compliance, these compliance constraints should be grounded on a formal language. Using property specification patterns to specify compliance constraints and automatically generate formal specifications significantly facilitate the work of the compliance expert.

Moreover, recovering from compliance violations in service-enabled processes is an important issue that has not paid much attention by the research community. The compliance expert should be provided with intelligent feedback that reveals the root-causes of these violations and aids their resolution; not merely an indication whether the constraint is violated. To address this problem, we have proposed a taxonomy of compliance constraints based on Dwyer's property patterns and extended this taxonomy with patterns that are frequently used to specify compliance constraints. Next, we have introduced a root-cause analysis approach to automatically reason about design-time compliance violations rooted on the proposed taxonomy. Based on the root-cause analysis, the compliance expert is provided with only relevant guidelines/suggestions.

The root-cause analysis approach including its compliance constraint taxonomy is validated in three ways. Firstly, the internal and construct validity are verified by formalizing the taxonomy, and particularly, the atomic and composite patterns in LTL. Secondly, the implementability of our approach is ascertained with an experimental prototype. Lastly, we have explored and tested our approach with several case studies drawn from industrial partners in the COMPAS EU project in which we participate. Furthermore, the validation of the proposed approach will further be intensified by its application on various empirical experiments and/or case studies on prospective users of the developed prototype toolset.

Design-time and runtime compliance management are complementary and indispensable phases for ensuring and enforcing the compliance. The main focus of this work is on design-time verification and analysis. Addressing compliance verification and analysis during runtime, based on the proposed compliance pattern taxonomy, and integrating it to the proposed design-time verification and analysis approach entails another important ongoing research direction. This course of research will pave the way for a comprehensive compliance management solution that verifies, analyses and ensures the compliance of business processes on both design-time and runtime dimensions. Future work will concentrate on extending the compliance constraints taxonomy with additional domain-specific compliance patterns. This requires intensive involvement in the specification of various industrial large-scale use case scenarios.

References

1. Papazoglou, M., Traverso, P., Dustdar, S., Leymann, F.: Service-Oriented Computing: State of the Art and Research Challenges. Computer 40, 38–45 (2007)
2. Sadiq, S., Governatori, G., Naimiri, K.: Modeling Control Objectives for Business Process Compliance. In: 10th International Conference on BPM, Australia, pp. 149–164 (2007)
3. ITIL: Information Technology Infrastructure Library (2010)
4. Dwyer, M., Avrunin, G., Corbett, J.: Property Specification Patterns for Finite-State Verification. In: Workshop on Formal Methods on Software Practice, USA, pp. 7–15 (1998)
5. Liu, Y., Muller, S., Xu, K.: A Static Compliance-Checking Framework for Business Process Models. IBM Systems Journal 46 (2007)
6. Pnueli, A.: The Temporal Logic of Programs. In: 18th IEEE Symposium on Foundations of Computer Science, pp. 46–57 (1977)
7. Dettmer, H.: Goldratt's Theory of Constraints: a systems approach to continuous improvement, pp. 62–119. ASQC Quality Press (1997)
8. Mosely, H.: Current Reality Trees: An Action Learning Tool for Root Cause Analysis (2006),
   http://www.jhuccp.org/training/scope/starguide/toc/rootcause
   analysis.ppt

9. Buchi, K.: On a Decision Method in Restricted Second Order Arithmetic. In: International Congress on Logic, Method, Philosophy of Science, Stanford, pp. 1–11 (1960)
10. Clarke, E., Grumberg, J., Peled, D.: Model Checking. MIT Press, Cambridge (2000)
11. Yu, J., Manh, T., Han, J., Jin, Y.: Pattern-Based Property Specification and Verification for Service Composition. In: Aberer, K., Peng, Z., Rundensteiner, E.A., Zhang, Y., Li, X. (eds.) WISE 2006. LNCS, vol. 4255, pp. 156–168. Springer, Heidelberg (2006)
12. COMPAS official web site – Project description, http://www.compas-ict.eu/project.php
13. Arbab, F., Kokash, N., Meng, S.: Towards Using Reo for Compliance-Aware Business Process Modeling. In: ISOLA 2008, Greece, pp. 108–123 (2008)
14. Governatori, G., Milosevic, Z., Sadiq, S.: Compliance Checking Between Business Processes and Business Contracts. In: EDOC 2006, Hong Kong, pp. 221–232 (2006)
15. Governatori, G., Milosevic, Z.: Dealing with Contract Violations: Formalism and Domain-Specific Language. In: EDOC 2005, pp. 46–57 (2005)
16. Goedertier, S., Vanthienen, J.: Designing Compliant Business Processes with Obligations and Permissions. In: The International BPM Workshops, Austria, pp. 5–14 (2006)
17. Governatori, G., Rotolo, A.: Logic of Violations: A Gentzen System for Reasoning with Contrary-to-duty Obligations. Australasian Journal of Logic (2006)
18. Governatori, G.: Representing Business Contracts in RuleML. International Journal of Cooperative Information Systems (2005)
19. Milosevic, Z., Sadiq, S., Orlowska, M.: Translating business contract into compliant business processes. In: EDOC 2006, pp. 211–220 (2006)
20. Lu, R., Sadiq, S., Governatori, G.: Compliance Aware Business Process Design. In: ter Hofstede, A.H.M., Benatallah, B., Paik, H.-Y. (eds.) BPM Workshops 2007. LNCS, vol. 4928, pp. 120–131. Springer, Heidelberg (2008)
21. Abouzaid, F., Mullins, J.: A Calculus for Generation, Verification, and Refinement of BPEL Specifications. In: WWV 2007, pp. 43–68 (2007)
22. Giblin, C., Liu, A., Muller, S.: Regulations Expressed As Logical Models. In: 18th Conference of Legal Knowledge and Information Systems, Belgium, pp. 37–48 (2005)
23. Awad, A., Weidlich, M., Weske, M.: Specification, Verification and Explanation of Violation for Data Aware Compliance Rules. In: Baresi, L., Chi, C.-H., Suzuki, J. (eds.) ICSOC-ServiceWave 2009. LNCS, vol. 5900, pp. 500–515. Springer, Heidelberg (2009)
24. Namiri, K., Stojanovic, N.: Pattern-based Design and Validation of Business Process Compliance. LNCS, pp. 59–76 (2007)
25. Gruhn, V., Laue, R.: Specification Patterns for Time-Related Properties. In: 12th Int'l Symposium on Temporal Representation and Reasoning, pp. 191–198 (2005)
26. Ghose, A., Koliadis, G.: Auditing Business Process Compliance. In: Krämer, B.J., Lin, K.-J., Narasimhan, P. (eds.) ICSOC 2007. LNCS, vol. 4749, pp. 169–180. Springer, Heidelberg (2007)
27. Lu, R., Sadiq, S., Governatori, G.: Measurement of Compliance Distance in Business Processes. Information Systems Management 25, 344–355 (2008)

Artifact-Centric Choreographies

Niels Lohmann and Karsten Wolf

Universität Rostock, Institut für Informatik, 18051 Rostock, Germany
{niels.lohmann,karsten.wolf}@uni-rostock.de

Abstract. Classical notations for service collaborations focus either on the control flow of participating services (interacting models) or the order in which messages are exchanged (interaction models). None of these approaches emphasizes the evolution of data involved in the collaboration. In contrast, artifact-centric models pursue the converse strategy and begin with a specification of data objects.

This paper extends existing concepts for artifact-centric business process models with the concepts of *agents* and *locations*. By making explicit *who* is accessing an artifact and *where* the artifact is located, we are able to automatically generate an interaction model that can serve as a contract between the agents and by construction makes sure that specified global goal states on the involved artifacts are reached.

1 Introduction

During the last few years, *artifact-centric* modeling of business processes received more and more attention [21,14,8,10,13,15]. In essence, this paradigm is about modeling the main data objects and then to derive a process which manipulates these data objects for achieving a given business goal. Some authors propose to mirror this paradigm in the implementation of business process engines by proposing an artifact hub which drives the actual business process [15]. Artifact-centric approaches have also been proposed in a service-oriented setting [10,13]. Here, services are discovered and employed for performing actions which manipulate artifacts. Although different in many details, this approach has a bit of an orchestration flavor.

In this paper, we study the use of artifacts in a more choreography-like setting. That is, we abandon the concept of having a single artifact hub. Instead, we introduce the idea of having several *agents* each of which operates only on some of the artifacts in the overall system. We believe that this setting is more appropriate for interorganizational business collaborations than the idea of central artifact hubs.

We observe that some artifacts can move between agents and that their actual location may matter for the executability of actions performed on them. That is, we extend the idea of "moving data throughout a process" [8] by the idea of "moving artifacts between agents". In consequence, we contribute

- a systematic approach for modeling artifact location and its impact on the accessibility of actions, and
- an approach to automatically derive an interaction model between the agents which may serve as a contract between them.

P.P. Maglio et al. (Eds.): ICSOC 2010, LNCS 6470, pp. 32–46, 2010.

The derivation of the interaction model is solely based on existing methods and tools [18,24,20,19]. Local policies of the involved agents can easily be incorporated.

Models using a single artifact hub appear as a special case in our approach where there is only a single agent. In a setting with more than one agent, however, our approach reaches beyond the single agent setting: We derive not only the actions that need to be performed on the artifacts for reaching a goal but also the messages that need to be exchanged between agents for this purpose.

The paper is organized as follows. The next section briefly describes how artifacts can be modeled with Petri nets. Section 3 introduces location-aware extensions and their impact to artifact models. Section 4 provides a categorization of location information which may serve as suggestion for a high-level language for location-aware artifacts. The construction of an interaction model out of location-aware artifacts is described in Sect. 5. Section 6 shows our approach in the context of related work before Sect. 7 concludes and discusses several possible extensions to the work of this paper.

2   Modeling Artifacts

Being concerned with an interorganizational setting, we assume that there is a set $\mathcal{A}$ of *agents* (or roles, organizations, locations, etc.). In our approach, agents are principals in the role-based access control for artifacts. Additionally, agents may (permanently or temporarily) *posses* artifacts, so they play the role of locations that messages containing artifacts may be sent to.

Informally, an artifact consists of data fields that can be manipulated (changed) by agents. Thereby, the change of data is constrained by the role-based access control. Hence, we model an artifact as a state machine. States represent the possible valuations of the data fields whereas transitions are the potential atomic changes that can happen to the data fields. In this paper, we use Petri nets for implicitly representing state machines. When data fields in an artifact evolve independently of each other, the size of a Petri net grows much slower than the number of represented states.

Definition 1 (Petri net). *A Petri net $N = [P, T, F, m_0]$ consists of two finite and disjoint sets P (places) and T (transitions), a flow relation $F \subseteq (P \times T) \cup (T \times P)$, and an initial marking m_0. A marking $m : P \to \mathbb{N}$ represents a state of the Petri net and is visualized as a distribution of tokens on the places. Transition t is enabled in marking m iff, for all $[p, t] \in F$, $m(p) > 0$. An enabled transition t can fire, transforming m into the new state m' with $m'(p) = m(p) - W(p, t) + W(t, p)$ where $W([x, y]) = 1$ if $[x, y] \in F$, and $W([x, y]) = 0$, otherwise.*

Transitions are triggered by *actions*. The available actions form the *interface* to the artifact. For modeling role based access control, each action is associated to an agent, meaning that this agent is permitted to perform that action.

In Fig. 1(a), we show an example of an artifact model for a direct debit authorization (automated clearing house). Data fields of such an artifact include an amount authorized, account information, and Booleans showing whether it has been signed, respectively whether it has been validated. In the state machine model, we abstract away the amount and account information fields. These fields do not influence the control flow in our

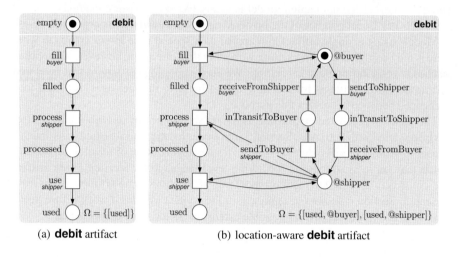

(a) **debit** artifact

(b) location-aware **debit** artifact

Fig. 1. Direct debit authorization artifact (a) with location information (b)

example. We silently assume that each artifact has finitely many states which typically can be achieved by a suitable abstraction.

Throughout this paper fix a set $\mathcal{L}$ of *action labels* and a mapping $c : \mathcal{L} \to \mathcal{A}$ representing the *access control*. In figures, the access control is written as additional transition labels, for instance *buyer* and *shipper* in Fig. 1(a).

Definition 2 (Artifact). *An artifact $A = [N, \ell, \Omega]$ consists of*

- *A Petri net $N = [P, T, F, m_0]$;*
- *a transition labeling $\ell : T \to \mathcal{L}$ associating actions with Petri net transitions;*
- *a set Ω of markings of N representing endpoints in the life cycle of the artifact.*

Action $x \in \mathcal{L}$ is enabled in marking m iff some transition $t \in T$ with $l(t) = x$ is enabled in m. Executing the enabled action x amounts to firing any (nondeterministically chosen) such transition.

Nondeterminism in an artifact may sound unusual at first glance but may occur due to prior abstraction. The final marking of the **debit** artifact (cf. Fig. 1(a)) consists of the marking [used] modeling successful debit authorization.

3   Location-Aware Artifacts

If we want to derive a protocol from a set of given artifacts, we have to understand the reasons for which messages are sent around in an artifact context. It turns out that there exist different shapes of artifacts which cause message transfer for different reasons. We give a few examples.

Consider first an artifact that is materialized as, say, a physical form. Actions in this artifact correspond to filling in fields in this form. Still, some actions may be bound

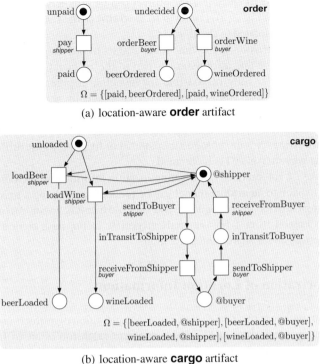

(a) location-aware **order** artifact

(b) location-aware **cargo** artifact

Fig. 2. Online order artifact (a) and cargo artifact (b)

to particular agents (e.g., signatures), so the artifact itself must be passed to that agent. Passing the artifact corresponds to sending a message. The act of sending would, at the same time, disable any actions by the sending agent. In another scenario, an artifact manifests itself as a database record. In this case, the artifact is not passed, but a message may be required to announce the existence of the artifact and to transmit some kind of access link which then enables the other agent to perform actions on the artifact by remote access to the data base.

Taking the artifact-centric approach seriously, we propose to include the acts of sending a message, receiving a message, and synchronous communication steps as specific actions of the artifact. Likewise, the actual location of the artifact (at an agent or "in transit") becomes an additional data field. The additional data field can be used for modeling the actual effect of the messaging activity such as enabling or disabling other actions. In the example, remote access to the artifact is ruled out. Figure 1(b) shows the augmented model for the direct debit authorization from Fig. 1(a). It expresses the fact that transition "fill" can only be executed when the artifact resides at the buyer, whereas the other actions can only be performed when the artifact is at the shipper. Note that the augmented model is required to leave "in transit" states to reach a final marking.

As a second example, consider an online **order** artifact. Figure 2(a) shows the functional part of such an artifact which happens to be identical to its location-aware extension. This reflects the idea that the artifact can be remotely accessed at any time. The artifact **cargo** (cf. Fig. 2(b)) is similar to the **debit** artifact and models the fact that the cargo can only be loaded to the shipper.

We see that the extension to the functional artifact model may vary a lot. Hence, it is reasonable to provide this information as part of the artifact. One possible approach is to make the modeler fully responsible for modeling location-specific information about the artifact. Another option would be to automatically generate an extension of the model from a more high level specification. The latter approach has the advantage that the added information is consistent (e.g., a message can only be received after it has been sent). However, our subsequent treatment of location-aware artifacts does not depend on the way they have been obtained.

For the sake of automatically generating location information, we observe that the necessary extension to an artifact model can be reduced to applying a reasonably sized set of recurring patterns. In consequence, we suppose that it is possible to automatically derive the extension from a few general categories. In the next section, we make a preliminary proposal for such a categorization.

4   Categorization of Location Information

In this section, we propose a two-dimensional categorization of artifacts and discuss the consequences on the derivation of a location-aware extension of an artifact. The first dimension is concerned with the possible changes of ownership and remote visibility of the artifact. The second dimension deals with remote accessibility to actions.

In the first dimension, we distinguish *mobile*, *persistent*, and *transient* artifacts.

A mobile artifact may change its location over time. A typical example is a physical form that is exchanged between agents, for instance for collecting information or just signatures from different agents. The direct debit authorization discussed in previous sections is a particular instance of a mobile artifact. Messages caused by a mobile artifact typically correspond to a change of location of the artifact. This can be modeled using an additional data element that records the location which may be at a particular agent or "in transit" between two agents. Actions correspond to sending an artifact (move the location field from "at X" to "in transit from X to Y" and receiving an artifact (move the location field from "in transit from X to Y" to "at Y"). The location field may then be used for constraining remote access as discussed later in this section.

Persistent and transient artifacts are both immobile; that is, their location does not change over time. The difference between these two categories concerns the visibility of the artifact to other agents. An example for a persistent artifact could be a commonly known Web front-end such as a popular book-ordering platform. Access to actions on the artifact, including creation of an order (an actual instance of the artifact) can happen at any time from any agent. In contrast, consider a journal reviewing record as an example for a transient artifact. This artifact resides in the editorial office at all time — like the ordering artifact resides with the seller. However, the reviewer cannot access the artifact from the beginning as he or she simply does not know of its existence. Only after having been invited to review the paper, the reviewer can start to act on the artifact (including downloading the paper and filling in the fields in the recommendation form).

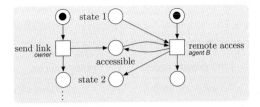

Fig. 3. Excerpt of a transient artifact whose *owner* needs to send a link prior to remote access of *agent B*

In essence, the reviewer invitation contains a *link* to the artifact, possibly in the form of login information thus announcing the existence to the artifact. This link message makes the artifact remotely accessible. For a persistent artifact, no such information is required. At least, passing the link to the artifact to the remote (customer) agent, is typically not part of the interorganizational business process model for book selling.

Persistent artifacts basically do not require any location-specific extension (such as the **order** example). It is just necessary to be aware of the particular location for the purpose of distinguishing remote from local access to the artifact. For a transient model, we propose to add a place for each agent that is marked as soon as the artifact is visible to that agent. An action "send link" marks that place thus modeling the fact that the artifact can be accessed after having received the link (or login) information. Once a place is marked, the artifact can be accessed indefinitely by the respective agent. See Fig. 3 for an example.

The second dimension determines, whether and how an artifact can be accessed by remote agents. For a mobile artifact, an agent is remote if it is not currently owning the artifact. For a persistent or transient artifact, all agents are remote, except the one that currently possesses it. Remote accessibility may differ between actions, so we suggest to specify this information for each action separately.

We distinguish three options for remote accessibility of an action: *none, synchronous,* and *asynchronous.* For a real paper form, the standard option would be none. The form is not remote accessible. Performing an action requires physical presence of the artifact. An exception may be a situation where two agents are actually present in a single location such as in the case of a contract that is signed by a customer directly at a desk which does not require passing the contract from the clerk to the customer. Synchronous transfer is an obvious option for artifacts with interactive Web forms as front-end. An example for an asynchronously accessible artifact can be found in the once popular tool *Majordomo*[1] for managing electronic mailing lists. Participants could manipulate their recorded data (like subscription and unsubscription) by writing e-mails containing specific commands to a particular e-mail address.

Although there is a certain correlation between the dimensions, we can think of examples for all possible combinations of values for the two discussed dimensions. Even for a mobile artifact, asynchronous remote access may be reasonable. Think of a product that is about to be assembled where the delivery and mounting of a part from a

---

[1] http://www.greatcircle.com/majordomo/

Table 1. Dimensions of location information with examples

	no remote access	synchronous remote access	asynchronous remote access
mobile artifact	physical form	insurance claim with delegation	
persistent artifact	—	database	majordomo
transient artifact	—	online survey	review form

supplier may be modeled as an asynchronous access to the artifact. Thus, there is a need to explicitly state the remote accessibility scheme for each action.

We do not claim that the above categorization (see Table 1 for an overview) is complete. However, we argue that this categorization provides enough evidence to support the claim that location-based information about artifacts can be systematically specified and then transformed into an extended artifact model. Potential refinements include, for example, restrictions concerning the set of agents to which the artifact may be passed or made visible. However, it is safe to assume for the remainder of this paper that a location-aware artifact model be given.

5   Choreography Construction

With location-aware artifacts, we can model the evolution (life cycle) of distributed data objects. As these life cycles evolve independently, several problems may arise:

1. Each artifact may reach a local final state, but the respective global state might model an unreasonable combination of final states. For instance, a beer order together with a wine-loaded cargo is reachable in the running example.
2. Even worse, undesired situations such as deadlocks (nonfinal markings without successors) or livelocks (infinite runs without reachable final marking) might be reachable.
3. Furthermore, not every reachable behavior is actually permitted: Policies may additionally restrict the order of actions that reaches a final state. For instance, a shipper must not load the cargo before the ordered goods have been paid.

In the course of this section, we address these three problems as follows. With *goal states*, we restrict the set of all possible final states to a subset of desired global final states. This addresses the first problem. To avoid deadlocks and livelocks, the artifacts' actions need to be *controlled* by the environment, resulting in an interaction model (i.e., a choreography) which may serve as a contract between the agents. This interaction model provides the necessary coordination to deal with the second problem. Finally, we introduce *policies* to further refine the interdependencies between artifacts. This tackles the third problem. Figure 4 provides an overview.

5.1   Goal States and Controller Synthesis

To simplify subsequent definitions, we first unite the artifacts. The union of a set of artifacts is again an artifact.

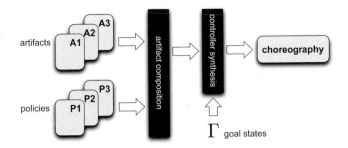

Fig. 4. Overview: Artifact composition and controller synthesis (Sect. 5.1) and policies (Sect. 5.2) yield a choreography

Definition 3 (Artifact union). *Let $A_1, \ldots, A_n$ be artifacts with pairwise disjoint Petri nets $N_1, \ldots, N_n$. Define the artifact union $\bigcup_{i=1}^{n} A_i = [N, \ell, \Omega]$ to be the artifact consisting of*

- $N = [\bigcup_{i=1}^{n} P_i, \bigcup_{i=1}^{n} T_i, \bigcup_{i=1}^{n} F_i, m_{0_1} \oplus \cdots \oplus m_{0_n}]$,
- $\ell(t) = \ell_i(t)$ *iff* $t \in T_i$ $(i \in \{1, \ldots, n\})$, *and*
- $\Omega = \{m_1 \oplus \cdots \oplus m_n \mid m_i \in \Omega_i \wedge 1 \leq i \leq n\}$

Thereby, $\oplus$ denotes the composition of markings: $(m_1 \oplus \cdots \oplus m_n)(p) = m_i(p)$ iff $p \in P_i$.

The previous definition is of rather technical nature. The only noteworthy property is that the set of final markings of the union consists of all combinations of final markings of the respective artifacts. We shall later restrict this set of final markings to a subset of *goal states*.

The next definition captures the interplay between two artifacts A_1 and A_2 and uses their interfaces (i.e., the labels associated to artifact transitions) to synchronize artifacts. In the resulting *composition*, each pair of transitions t_1 and t_2 of artifact A_1 and A_2, respectively, with the same label (i.e., $\ell_1(t_1) = \ell_2(t_2)$) is replaced by a new transition $[t_1, t_2]$ which models synchronous firing of t_1 and t_2. Consequently, the composition of two artifacts restricts their behavior by synchronization.

Definition 4 (Artifact composition). *Let A_1 and A_2 be artifacts. Define their shared labels as $S = \{l \mid \exists t_1 \in T_1, \exists t_2 \in T_2 : \ell(t_1) = \ell(t_2) = l\}$. The composition of A_1 and A_2 is the artifact $A_1 \oplus A_2 = [N, \ell, \Omega]$ consisting of:*

- $N = [P, T, F, m_{0_1} \oplus m_{0_2}]$ *with*
  - $P = P_1 \cup P_2$;
  - $T = (T_1 \cup T_2 \cup \{[t_1, t_2] \in T_1 \times T_2 \mid \ell(t_1) = \ell(t_2)\}) \setminus (\{t \in T_1 \mid \ell_1(t) \in S\} \cup \{t \in T_2 \mid \ell_2(t) \in S\})$,
  - $F = ((F_1 \cup F_2) \cap ((P \times T) \cup (T \times P))) \cup \{[[t_1, t_2], p] \mid [t_1, p] \in F_1 \vee [t_2, p] \in F_2\} \cup \{[p, [t_1, t_2]] \mid [p, t_1] \in F_1 \vee [p, t_2] \in F_2\}$,
- *for all $t \in T \cap T_1$: $\ell(t) = \ell_1(t)$, for all $t \in T \cap T_2$: $\ell(t) = \ell_2(t)$, and for all $[t_1, t_2] \in T \cap (T_1 \times T_2)$: $\ell([t_1, t_2]) = \ell_1(t_1)$, and*

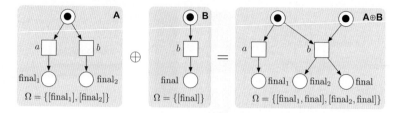

Fig. 5. Example for the composition of two artifacts

- $\Omega = \{m_1 \oplus m_2 \mid m_1 \in \Omega_1 \land m_2 \in \Omega_2\}$.

The composition $A_1 \oplus A_2$ is complete if for all $t_1 \in T_1$ and $t_2 \in T_2$ holds: $\ell_1(t_1) \in S$ and $\ell_2(t_2) \in S$.

Figure 5 depicts an example for the composition of two artifacts. Final markings of the composition are built just like in the union. We call a composition *complete* if for each transition in one artifact exists a transition in the other artifact that carries the same label. Intuitively, a complete composition does not contain "unsynchronized" transitions. To avoid undesired behavior, a complete composition plays an important role.

Given an artifact A and a set $\Gamma \subseteq \Omega$ of *goal states* of A, we call another artifact A' a *controller* for A iff (1) their composition $A \oplus A'$ is complete and (2) for each reachable markings of the composition, a marking $m \oplus m'$ is reachable such that $m \in \Gamma$ and m' is a final marking of A'. Intuitively, this controller synchronizes with A such that a goal state $m \in \Gamma$ of A always remains reachable.

The existence of controllers (also called *controllability* [24]) is a fundamental correctness criterion for communicating systems such as services. It can be decided constructively [24]: If a controller for an artifact exists, it can be constructed automatically.

With the concept of controller synthesis, we are now able to reason about artifacts. Given a set of artifacts and a set of goal states, we can synthesize a controller which rules out any behavior that makes the goal states unreachable. At the same time, the controller provides a global model which specifies the order in which the agents may perform actions on the artifacts. Furthermore, we can derive communication actions from the labels that were introduced in the location-aware versions.

For the three artifacts of the running example and the set of goal states

$$\Gamma = \{[\text{used}, \textbf{debit}@\text{shipper}, \text{paid}, \text{beerOrdered}, \text{beerLoaded}, \textbf{cargo}@\text{buyer}],$$
$$[\text{used}, \textbf{debit}@\text{shipper}, \text{paid}, \text{wineOrdered}, \text{wineLoaded}, \textbf{cargo}@\text{buyer}]\}$$

expressing successful purchase of beer or wine, respectively, the synthesized controller has 1120 states and is too large to be shown here. Although free of deadlocks and livelocks, it still contains undesired behavior which we rule out with policies in the next subsection.

5.2 Policies

Artifact-centric approaches follow a declarative modeling style. The same holds for artifact-centric choreographies: instead of explicitly modeling global state changes, we

Table 2. Required policies to rule out unintended behavior

policy	description	artifacts
P1	only load cargo after buyer has paid	**order**, **cargo**
P2	only pay when filled debit form is at shipper	**order**, **debit**
P3	do not send unloaded cargo to buyer	**cargo**
P4	only send debit form if it is filled and at the buyer	**debit**

only modeled the local object life cycle of every artifact. Consequently, the order of actions in the generated choreography is only constrained to avoid deadlocks and live-locks with respect to goal states. As a downside of this approach, a lot of unreasonable behavior is exposed. For instance, sending of unloaded cargo or even sending without prior payment is possible.

To rule out this undesired behavior, we employ *policies* (also called *behavioral constraints* [18]). In the setting of this paper, we also model policies with artifacts; that is, labeled Petri nets with a set of final markings. These artifacts have no counterpart in reality and are only used to model dependencies between actions of different artifacts. The application of policies then boils down to the composition of the artifacts with these policies. In principal, goal states can be expressed by policies as well. We still decided to split these concepts, because the former express liveness properties whereas the latter express safety properties.

For the running example, we used four policies, listed in Table 2. To avoid, for instance, loading the cargo without payment (P1), the **order** and **cargo** artifacts need to be constrained. Specifically, the **cargo**'s transitions with label "loadBeer" and "load-Wine" must not fire before **order**'s transition "pay" has fired. Such a dependency can be straightforwardly expressed by Petri nets, for instance by the constraint net in Fig. 6(a). Figure 6(b) depicts the similar constraint net for policy P3. Their composition with the **order** and **cargo** artifacts is shown in Fig. 6(c).

By applying more and more policies to the artifacts, we exclude more and more unintended behavior. This effect can be observed in the number of states of the choreography. Without any constraints, the choreography has 1120 states. After the application of policy P1, this number is reduced to 736. With more policies, this number is quickly reduced to 216 (P1, P2), 60 (P1, P2, P3), and finally 30 states with all four policies.

Figure 7 depicts the Petri net representing this final choreography. Each transition is labeled with an action (what is done), an artifact (which data are accessed), and an agent (who performs the action). This Petri net model exposes the concurrency between the handling of the direct debit authorization and the buyer's order choice. This choreography has been calculated by Wendy [19] as an automaton model which then was transformed into a Petri net model using the tool Genet [11]. With a preprocessing tool to compose artifacts and policies, Wendy as controller synthesis tool, and Genet as Petri net transformation, we have a continuous tool chain for location-aware artifact-centric choreographies available. Although the running example is rather trivial, case studies with Wendy [19] show that it is able to cope with input models with millions of states.

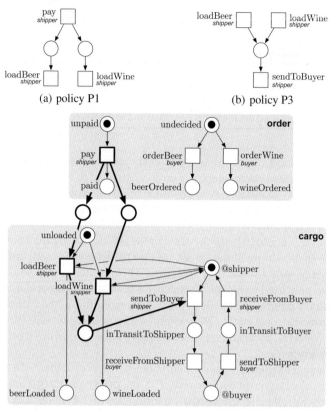

(a) policy P1   (b) policy P3

(c) policy P1 and P3 applied to artifacts **order** and **cargo**.

Fig. 6. Application of policies to artifacts

6   Related Work

There exists a variety of approaches dealing with artifact-centric modeling of business processes.

Workflow construction. Küster et al. [17] study the interplay between control flow models and object life cycles. Beside an extended soundness notion which also respects object life cycles, the authors present an algorithm to automatically derive a sound process model from given object life cycles. Compared to our approach, this workflow model is not aware of artifact locations and hence plays an orchestrating role.

Object life cycle inheritance. Aalst and Basten [2,3] model object life cycles as labeled Petri nets and investigate the relationships between different versions of object life cycles. These *inheritance* notions may complement our work and can, for instance, be used in our context to compare artifacts and choreographies. Such an application to contracts is described by Aalst et al. [4].

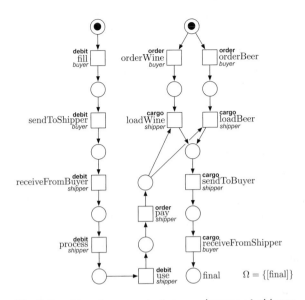

Fig. 7. Resulting choreography between *buyer* and *shipper*

Artifacts and service orientation. The idea of encapsulating functionality as services also influenced artifact-centric approaches. Several authors investigated how services can be used to manipulate the state of artifacts. Keeping a declarative modeling style, services are described by preconditions and postconditions formulated in different logics.

Bhattacharya et al. [8] study several questions related to artifacts and services, including reachability of goal states, absence of deadlocks, and redundancy of data. Their employed logics is similar to OWL-S. Similar settings are investigated by Calvanese et al. [10] and Fritz et al. [13] for first order logics. Gerede and Su [14] language based on CTL to specify artifact behaviors in artifact-centric process models. Each paper provides complexity and decidability results for the respective problems.

These approaches share the idea of using service calls to manipulate artifacts. The artifact itself, however, is assumed to be immobile, resulting in orchestrating workflows rather than our choreography-like setting.

Artifact hosting. Hull et al. [15] introduce *artifact-centric hubs* as central infrastructure hosting data that can be read and written by participants. The authors motivate that, compared to autonomous settings such as choreographies, the centralized storage of data has the advantage of providing a conceptual rendezvous point to exchange status information. This centralized approach can be mimicked by our location-aware approach by remotely accessible immobile artifacts.

Proclets. Aalst et al. [1,5] introduce *proclets* to specify business processes in which object life cycles can be modeled in different levels of granularity and cardinality. Consequently, proclets are well-suited to deal with settings in which several instances of data objects are involved. Being introduced as workflow models, proclets have no concept of locations.

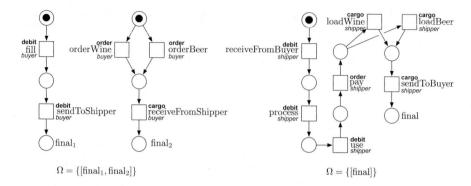

Fig. 8. Local models for the *buyer* (left) and the *shipper* (right)

To the best of our knowledge, this is the first approach to explicitly add information on agents and locations to artifact models. As a result, we can naturally reason about sending and receiving of artifacts resulting in a choreography of agents. Consequently, our approach is a first step toward artifact-based *interorganizational* business processes.

7 Conclusion

We extended the idea of artifact-centric process design to a choreography setting where artifacts are not necessarily gathered in artifact hubs. We observed that in such a setting the actual location of the artifact has a significant impact on executability of actions and on the message flow that is required to transform artifacts into desired goal states. We propose to enhance artifacts with explicit information on location and its impact on remote access to actions. This information can be modeled manually or derived systematically from a high level description. We suggest a principal two-dimensional categorization into mobile, persistent, and transient artifacts on one hand, and no, synchronous, or asynchronous remote access to actions on the other as an initial proposal for a high level description. From location-aware artifacts and goal states for the artifacts, we can derive a global interaction model that may serve as a contract between the involved agents. The interaction model can be derived in such a way that it respects specified policies of the involved agents. The whole approach relies on only one simple formalism. Petri nets express the functional part of an artifacts, location information, as well as policies. This way, it is possible to employ existing tools for the automated construction of a choreography and the invocation of policies. These tools have already proven their capability to cope with nontrivial problem instances.

In our modeling approach to artifacts, we did not include mechanisms for creating new artifact instances. If the overall number of artifacts in the system is bounded, this is not a serious problem since the creation of a new artifact instance can be modeled by a transition from a state "not existing" to the actual initial state of the artifact. This approach does not work in the case of an unbounded number of artifacts. Similar problems are known in the area of verification of parameterized programs where parts of the program may spawn a finite but not a priori bounded number of threads which run identical programs. There exist ways to finitely model such systems and several verification problems turn out to be decidable [12,6]. Future research is required to find out whether the methodology used there extends to the problems and solutions proposed in this paper.

Another interesting issue is the further transformation of the choreography derived in this paper into local processes for the agents. We see two potential directions which need to be further explored. First, we could exploit existing research on *accordance* (e.g., [7,9,23]). In [4], we showed that it is possible for each agent to replace its part of a contract by an accordant private process. Relying on the accordance criterion, soundness of the original interaction model is inherited by the collaboration of private processes. The approach requires a suitable decision procedure for checking accordance [23,22] or powerful transformation rules which preserve accordance [16]. Both appear to be more advanced for establishing deadlock freedom than for livelock freedom, so more progress needs to be made there.

A second opportunity for deriving local processes is to use the *realizability* approach proposed in [20]. There, local processes are constructed from a choreography for the sake of proving that the choreography can be implemented (realized). To this end, the choreography is transformed into a service where the local processes are computed as correctly interacting partners, cf. Fig. 8. Adding results from [24] to this approach, we can even compute a finite representation of a *set* of processes for each agent such that each combination of one process per agent yields a correct set of realizing partners for the choreography. The concept was called *autonomous controllability* in [24]. In the artifact setting, such a finite representation of a set of processes could be used to derive, at least to some degree, a local process that not only respects the artifacts and policies known to all involved agents, but also artifacts and policies that are hidden from the other agents. Again, past research focused on deadlock freedom, so further work is required to make that technology available in the context of this paper. Nevertheless, the discussion suggests that the chosen approach connects artifact centric choreographies to promising methods for further tool support.

We believe that we can further exploit ideas for bridging the gap between the global interaction model and the local processes of the agents. It is also worth to explore ideas known from program verification for the purpose of supporting unbounded creation of artifact instances.

References

1. van der Aalst, W.M.P., Barthelmess, P., Ellis, C.A., Wainer, J.: Proclets: A framework for lightweight interacting workflow processes. Int. J. Cooperative Inf. Syst. 10(4), 443–481 (2001)
2. van der Aalst, W.M.P., Basten, T.: Life-cycle inheritance: A Petri-net-based approach. In: Azéma, P., Balbo, G. (eds.) ICATPN 1997. LNCS, vol. 1248, pp. 62–81. Springer, Heidelberg (1997)
3. van der Aalst, W.M.P., Basten, T.: Identifying commonalities and differences in object life cycles using behavioral inheritance. In: Colom, J.-M., Koutny, M. (eds.) ICATPN 2001. LNCS, vol. 2075, pp. 32–52. Springer, Heidelberg (2001)
4. van der Aalst, W.M.P., Lohmann, N., Massuthe, P., Stahl, C., Wolf, K.: Multiparty contracts: Agreeing and implementing interorganizational processes. Comput. J. 53(1), 90–106 (2010)

5. van der Aalst, W.M.P., Mans, R.S., Russell, N.C.: Workflow support using proclets: Divide, interact, and conquer. IEEE Data Eng. Bull. 32(3), 16–22 (2009)
6. Ball, T., Chaki, S., Rajamani, S.K.: Parameterized verification of multithreaded software libraries. In: Margaria, T., Yi, W. (eds.) TACAS 2001. LNCS, vol. 2031, pp. 158–173. Springer, Heidelberg (2001)
7. Benatallah, B., Casati, F., Toumani, F.: Representing, analysing and managing Web service protocols. Data Knowl. Eng. 58(3), 327–357 (2006)
8. Bhattacharya, K., Gerede, C.E., Hull, R., Liu, R., Su, J.: Towards formal analysis of artifact-centric business process models. In: Alonso, G., Dadam, P., Rosemann, M. (eds.) BPM 2007. LNCS, vol. 4714, pp. 288–304. Springer, Heidelberg (2007)
9. Bravetti, M., Zavattaro, G.: Contract based multi-party service composition. In: Arbab, F., Sirjani, M. (eds.) FSEN 2007. LNCS, vol. 4767, pp. 207–222. Springer, Heidelberg (2007)
10. Calvanese, D., Giacomo, G.D., Hull, R., Su, J.: Artifact-centric workflow dominance. In: Baresi, L., Chi, C.-H., Suzuki, J. (eds.) ICSOC-ServiceWave 2009. LNCS, vol. 5900, pp. 130–143. Springer, Heidelberg (2009)
11. Carmona, J., Cortadella, J., Kishinevsky, M.: Genet: A tool for the synthesis and mining of petri nets. In: ACSD 2009, pp. 181–185. IEEE Computer Society Press, Los Alamitos (2009)
12. Emerson, E.A., Kahlon, V.: Reducing model checking of the many to the few. In: McAllester, D. (ed.) CADE 2000. LNCS, vol. 1831, pp. 236–254. Springer, Heidelberg (2000)
13. Fritz, C., Hull, R., Su, J.: Automatic construction of simple artifact-based business processes. In: ICDT 2009. International Conference Proceeding Series, vol. 361, pp. 225–238. ACM Press, New York (2009)
14. Gerede, C.E., Su, J.: Specification and verfication of artifact behaviors in business process models. In: Krämer, B.J., Lin, K.-J., Narasimhan, P. (eds.) ICSOC 2007. LNCS, vol. 4749, pp. 181–192. Springer, Heidelberg (2007)
15. Hull, R., Narendra, N.C., Nigam, A.: Facilitating workflow interoperation using artifact-centric hubs. In: Baresi, L., Chi, C.-H., Suzuki, J. (eds.) ICSOC-ServiceWave 2009. LNCS, vol. 5900, pp. 1–18. Springer, Heidelberg (2009)
16. König, D., Lohmann, N., Moser, S., Stahl, C., Wolf, K.: Extending the compatibility notion for abstract WS-BPEL processes. In: WWW 2008, pp. 785–794. ACM, New York (April 2008)
17. Küster, J.M., Ryndina, K., Gall, H.: Generation of business process models for object life cycle compliance. In: Alonso, G., Dadam, P., Rosemann, M. (eds.) BPM 2007. LNCS, vol. 4714, pp. 165–181. Springer, Heidelberg (2007)
18. Lohmann, N., Massuthe, P., Wolf, K.: Behavioral constraints for services. In: Alonso, G., Dadam, P., Rosemann, M. (eds.) BPM 2007. LNCS, vol. 4714, pp. 271–287. Springer, Heidelberg (2007)
19. Lohmann, N., Weinberg, D.: Wendy: A tool to synthesize partners for services. In: Lilius, J., Penczek, W. (eds.) Applications and Theory of Petri Nets. LNCS, vol. 6128, pp. 297–307. Springer, Heidelberg (2010)
20. Lohmann, N., Wolf, K.: Realizability is controllability. In: Laneve, C., Su, J. (eds.) Web Services and Formal Methods. LNCS, vol. 6194, pp. 110–127. Springer, Heidelberg (2010)
21. Nigam, A., Caswell, N.S.: Business artifacts: An approach to operational specification. IBM Systems Journal 42(3) (2003)
22. Stahl, C.: Service Substitution - A Behavioral Approach Based on Petri Nets. Ph.D. thesis, Humboldt-Universität zu Berlin, Mathematisch-Naturwissenschaftliche Fakultät II; Eindhoven University of Technology (2009)
23. Stahl, C., Massuthe, P., Bretschneider, J.: Deciding substitutability of services with operating guidelines. In: Jensen, K., van der Aalst, W.M.P. (eds.) Transactions on Petri Nets. LNCS, vol. 5460, pp. 172–191. Springer, Heidelberg (2009)
24. Wolf, K.: Does my service have partners? In: Jensen, K., van der Aalst, W.M.P. (eds.) Transactions on Petri Nets. LNCS, vol. 5460, pp. 152–171. Springer, Heidelberg (2009)

Resolving Business Process Interference via Dynamic Reconfiguration*

Nick R.T.P. van Beest[1], Pavel Bulanov[2], Hans Wortmann[1], and Alexander Lazovik[2]

[1] Department of Business & ICT, Faculty of Economics and Business,
University of Groningen, Nettelbosje 2, 9747 AE Groningen, The Netherlands
[2] Johann Bernoulli Institute for Mathematics and Computer Science, Faculty of Mathematics
and Natural Sciences, University of Groningen, Nijenborgh 9,
9747 AG Groningen, The Netherlands
{n.r.t.p.van.beest,p.bulanov,j.c.wortmann,a.lazovik}@rug.nl

Abstract. For business processes supported by service-oriented information systems, concurrent execution of business processes still may yield undesired business outcomes as a result of process interference. For instance, concurrent processes may partially depend on a semantically identical process variable, causing inconsistencies during process execution. Current design-time verification of service-based processes is not always sufficient to identify these issues. To identify and resolve potentially erroneous situations, run-time handling of interference is required. In this paper, dependency scopes are defined to represent the dependencies between processes and data sources. In addition, intervention patterns are developed to repair inconsistencies using dynamic reconfiguration during execution of the pro-cess. These concepts are implemented on top of a BPMS platform and tested on a real case study, based on the implementation of a Dutch Law in e-Government.

Keywords: business process, configuration, variability, concurrency.

1 Introduction

Concurrent execution of business processes, supported by distributed or service-oriented information systems, may result in an unexpected behavior due to process interference. Different concurrent processes may partially depend on the same resource. Data, modified by an external process, may cause inconsistencies during process execution, resulting in the aforementioned undesired business outcomes. Such business processes are designed with an inherent assumption of independence of processes. Consequently, if business processes are executed concurrently, it is implicitly assumed that they cannot affect each other. For many business processes it is not always feasible to foresee all interdepen-dencies. Assuming independent execution of the processes, current design-time verifica-tion of process models is insufficient to identify all conflicts and, more importantly, resolve these issues during run-time [8].

---

* The research is supported by the NWO SaS-LeG project, http://www.sas-leg.net, contract No. 638.000.000.07N07.

P.P. Maglio et al. (Eds.): ICSOC 2010, LNCS 6470, pp. 47–60, 2010.

Traditionally, locking mechanisms are used to resolve the issues with concurrent access to shared data. Unfortunately, in practice it is not possible to lock data for a long period of time, which is quite typical for long-term business processes. Consider, for example, a business process for issuing a wheelchair for disabled people in the Netherlands. It takes up to 6 weeks from sending the initial request to receiving an actual wheel chair. What if in the meantime the person, which requested the wheel chair, has moved to a different place, e.g., to a care home with a nursing support? The original process has to be adjusted, either by forwarding the wheel chair to a new place, or by cancelling the request (whatever is more suitable in a concrete situation). To resolve this issue by locking, one would "force" the person not to change his address until the first process is finished, which is unfeasible in real life.

In this paper, process interference is prevented by awareness of process dependencies and automatic execution of compensation activities. Dependency scopes are introduced to represent the dependencies between processes and data sources. In addition, intervention patterns are developed to repair inconsistencies during execution of the process. These modeling concepts can be seamlessly integrated in existing Business Process Modeling platforms. The Cordys Business Operations Platform is used as a basis for the implemen-tation of the proposed concepts. The implemented solution is demonstrated and tested on a real case study from e-Government that concerns the Dutch WMO law business process.

The remainder of the paper is organized as follows. Section 2 provides a background showing the current methods for dealing with the problem of concurrent process execution. A detailed description of the problem and the research methodology are both presented in Section 3. The developed modeling concepts are presented in Section 4. The introduced approach is applied to the WMO law case study in Section 5. In Section 6, an overview of the implementation of the dependency scopes and intervention patterns is presented. Finally, the paper is concluded in Section 7.

2   Related Work

Much work has been done on verification of workflow and data specifications, e.g. [14]. However, workflow verification as presented in [14] assumes that the analysis is performed in the context of a single party, who has full access to the processes and data involved. However, many business processes are designed in a distributed manner, and their execution is spread among several parties. Often, such business processes are supported by, for instance, various autonomous Web services environments [9]. Work-flow and data verification, as described by e.g. [14], cannot be applied to interference resolution due to absence of a single ownership over the business processes involved in the execution. The parts of the business process owned by other partners are not specified in detail, as the implementation details are typically only known to the external party.

[18] propose an approach that deals with failing processes as the point of failure for the analysis of data dependencies and process interference. Similarly, compensation activities have been introduced to restore consistency in e.g. aborted long-lived transactions

[7]. In practice, however, interfering processes do not necessarily fail. More often, they execute without any noticeable problems from inside the organization, as no error message is signaled. In contrast, the problem is primarily noticed by the external stakeholders (mostly customers) as the final result is undesirable to them [16].

The handling of the process interference at run-time is desirable by identifying and resolving erroneous situations. This may, for example, be realized by a run-time re-confi-guration of the business process to repair it and bring it back to a consistent state. Such a concept has been proposed in [15], but the solution emphasizes on re-solving *design-time* modeling contradictions in business process specifications rather than run-time ones. Unfortunately the interference issues at *run-time* cannot be identi-fied as a contradicting specification, as each business process runs without any inter-ference in isolation. As a result, abnormal run-time interference situations are not covered by this technique.

In general, the idea to deal with run-time business process reconfiguration is not new. The most notable examples of handling run-time reconfiguration are the ADEPT project [6], the DECLARE framework [10], and more general techniques like ad-hoc sub-processes [5] and run-time case handling [2]. A more detailed overview of vari-ous dynamic business process reconfiguration techniques can be found in [11], while detailed requirements for such systems are overviewed in [4].

The ADEPT project is designed to support the synchronization between several run-ning instances of the same process. The idea is to catch any changes made by the user and incorporate those changes into all of the running instances without interrupting their execution. The DECLARE framework utilizes the idea of a declarative process speci-fica-tion [13] in order to attain flexible process execution. As a result, the process de-fined inside this framework is not a strictly written sequence of actions, but rather a set of rules, which guide the user through the process execution in an interactive manner.

The primary aim of both case handling and ad-hoc sub-processes is to enhance the specification of a business process with conditions, which are left undecided until run-time. At run-time, users can choose whether a part of the process should be included or not, based on their own experience. In the same way, parts of business processes may be left undefined in order to be specified at run-time, using the so-called late binding technique. This technique is supported by the YAWL workflow language [3] and also adopted in a form of reconfigurable sub-processes by [12].

The frameworks and techniques listed above focus on supporting run-time process specification, which provides a design-time defined execution flexibility to the user. However, ad-hoc compensation to prevent inconsistent process execution requires an automated mechanism to determine which activities need to be executed. In this paper, design-time modeling concepts are developed to manage run-time discovered interfer-ence and provide automatic execution of compensation activities to restore consistency.

3 A Case Study: Business Process for the Dutch WMO Law

To demonstrate the proposed solution, and also to evaluate and to show feasibility of the approach, a business process supporting the Dutch Law for Societal Support (known as the WMO[1] law) is examined. The purpose of this law is to enable people with a chronic disease, a disability or physical decline due to aging to live in their own homes and take part in society for as long as possible. Facilities are provided to offer support to such citizens by means of, for example, domestic care, transportation, a wheelchair or a home modification. Both the responsibility and the execution of the business process are located at the municipalities. The business process under investigation concerns the handling of the requests from citizens at one of the 430 municipalities in the Netherlands.

Fig. 1 shows a business process representing the request for a facility taken from one of the municipalities in the Netherlands. The business process consists of activities, which are provided by various services. First, the citizen contacts the municipality and submits an application for a provision. Such a provision may concern, for example, a wheelchair, domestic help, or a home modification. Based on that application, it is decided whether a home visit is necessary, to have a better understanding of the situation. Then, it might be necessary to ask for additional information, by means of a medical advice. This information will finally result in an indication and decision made by the municipality. If the decision is unsatisfactory for the citizen, there is a possibility for appeal.

Depending on the requested service, the citizen can choose between a Personal Budget and Care in Kind. Very often, this choice is already made in the initial application. In case of a Personal Budget, the citizen periodically receives a certain amount of money for the granted provision(s). If Care in Kind is chosen, suppliers are contacted, which will eventually supply the citizen with the granted provisions. The process ends with the payment of the invoices received from the suppliers.

Concurrently executed processes may constitute a potential risk of erroneous workflow execution. That is, although the process does finish regularly without any system errors, the final result may be undesirable from a business perspective. Activity branches with a rather long execution time that strongly depend on the consistency of certain process variables are the most vulnerable to inconsistencies caused by concurrent processes.

In Fig. 1, the four distinct activity branches following "Designation and report" (Domestic help, Transportation, Wheelchair and Major home modification) may potentially suffer from process interference. The throughput time for both the wheelchair provisioning and major home modification may take up to 6 weeks, whereas they strongly depend on the address of the citizen and the content of the designation. This implies that a change in either of these process variables (e.g. address) may have strong consequences for the consistency of the business process.

For instance, assume that the tender for major home modification will be approved and the order will be sent to the supplier. If the citizen moves from a regular house to a nursing home during or right after "Check tender with designation", the home modification will not be necessary anymore. However, in the process above, the supplier or the municipality are not notified of the address change and the request for home modification is not cancelled.

---

[1] http://nl.wikipedia.org/wiki/Wet_maatschappelijke_ondersteuning

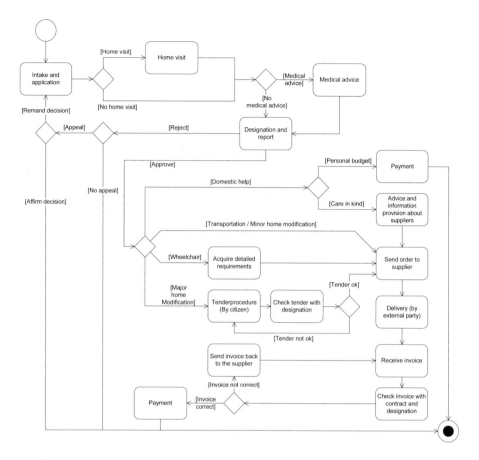

Fig. 1. Process model of the request for a provision at a municipality in the Netherlands

A similar situation occurs in case of a request for a wheelchair. The requirements (and constraints) of a wheelchair may depend on certain architectural characteristics of the citizen's home. Therefore, an address change between "acquire detailed requirements" and delivery might result in a wheelchair that does not fit the actual requirements.

4 Dependency Scopes and Intervention Patterns

The situations described in Section 3 may occur when several concurrent processes, that are wrongly assumed to be independent, use the same data at a particular point in time or within a certain timeframe. As a result, this may affect the data used in subsequent activities or even the sub-processes that follow an evaluation of a condition.

In order to analyze this situation, let us formalize the concept of a business process.

Definition 1. A *business process* is a set of linked activities, constructors and process variables that collectively realize a business objective or a policy goal, where:

- Each activity is an atomic piece of work representing an interaction with some service.
- Constructors represent the flow of execution, e.g. sequence, choice, parallelism, join synchronization. These constructors have well-defined semantics, e.g. defined in [1].
- A process variable is a variable over arbitrary domain, and is typically mapped into input/output parameters of activities (services).

In this paper, we do not distinguish between the business process and the business process model, assuming that the business process engine is able to execute the provided business process model. Consequently, the difference between a business process and its modeling representation is irrelevant in the context of this paper.

Definition 2. A *sub-process* is a business process that is enacted or called from another (initiating) business process (or sub-process), and which forms part of the overall (initiating) business process [17].

The process definitions presented above are not new. They have been implemented in different workflow and business process management systems, e.g. using BPMN, or BPEL notation.

In Fig. 2, two processes are presented. The decision made in Process 1 is based on the value of process variable D. That specific decision determines whether activities A1 and A2 are executed or rather A3 and A4. If D is changed by another process (e.g. Process 2) during execution of A2, this may have consequences for the decision made. That is, as a result of the data change, currently the wrong branch of activities is being executed. In such a situation, the execution of A2 needs to be cancelled and followed by compensating activities to compensate A2 and A1. Subsequently, the process should continue at A3. Therefore, it is desirable to know what activities are implicitly relying on that process variable (D). Furthermore, these activities should be notified if that data has changed, even if those changes happened externally to the process being currently executed.

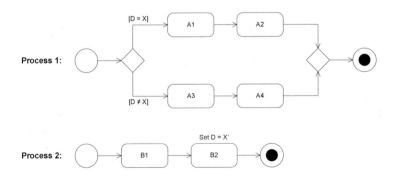

Fig. 2. Two business processes with concurrent data modification

To identify the specific part of the process that depends on certain process variable, we introduce a notion of dependency-scope. A *dependency-scope* (DS) is defined as a structurally correct subset of the business process, in which the activities are implicitly or explicitly relying on the accuracy of a volatile process variable accessed in the first activity of that set. This implies that the process variable is assumed to remain unchanged (or within a certain range of values) by an external process during the execution of the entire DS. Note that this definition implies that an update of this process variable by the process *will* end the DS of that particular process variable, whereas it *may* start a new DS. In Fig. 3, Process 1 is represented with a corresponding dependency scope.

At an instance level, a DS can be active or inactive. It is activated when the first activity is started, which is part of the set that defines the DS. It is active as long as an activity is executed that belongs to the DS. If the last activity of the set of consecutive activities is finished, the DS switches to be inactive.

Definition 3. A *volatile process variable* is a process variable that can be changed externally during execution of the process.

A change of a volatile process variable can have various origins. That is, it can be changed by another process in the same organization or it can be changed externally to the organization that is executing the business process.

Definition 4. A *dependency-scope* (DS) is a part of the business process with a set of volatile process variables D, where:

- The activities of the dependency scope are relying on the correct value of D.
- There exists only one start activity (first activity in the dependency scope).
- The dependency scope is activated when its first activity starts.

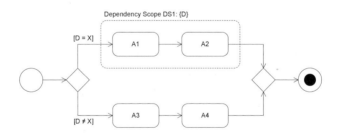

Fig. 3. Business process with a dependency scope definition

Consider an example shown in Fig. 2: even if dependencies are identified, as shown in Fig. 3, an intervention may happen in any part of the dependency scope, both after A1 and A2. More specifically, if A2 is notified that B2 of Process 2 has just changed the variable D, A1 has already executed. In order to resolve the conflict, the process should restart again from the decision point prior to activity A1, which requires both A1 and A2 to be rolled back to the initial state.

This rollback may in some cases be prevented by a number of alternative activities to be executed before starting A3, in order to regain consistency. For example, the state of process 1 is undesirable from a business perspective, due to the incorrect decisions made as a result of the data mutation. A repairing activity should be interposed between A2 and A3, to recover process 1 to a consistent state that corresponds to reality again.

Definition 5. An *intervention pattern* is a sub-process that is linked to a DS, comprising a set of compensation activities, which together restore the consistent state of a business process. An intervention pattern has the following properties:

- A condition over the set D of the DS determines when the set of compensation activities needs to be executed.
- If the condition is true then the currently executed activity in the DS is stopped and the compensation process is executed.
- The last activity provides a re-entry point in the business process.

Note that intervention patterns are not expected to contain dependency scopes by themselves. They are considered to be relatively simple repairing activities. Fig. 4 shows a sequence of compensation activities, which is defined as an intervention pattern.

Fig. 4. Specification of intervention activities

The activities required to restore consistency may vary, even concerning the same volatile process variable. A DS can comprise several intervention patterns. Depending on the condition, the corresponding intervention pattern is executed. However, if more intervention patterns are connected to one DS, then the conditions should be mutually exclusive. In addition, the activities required to restore consistency may vary between processes. In most cases, it may be sufficient to update the process variables in the currently executed activity and proceed, whereas in a more severe case the activity needs to be cancelled and the process should be resumed with another activity.

An example of the process including both a DS and an inserted intervention pattern is shown in Fig. 5. This solution allows for execution without manual process reconfiguration. As a result of the firing of the trigger on DS1, the activity currently being executed (A2) is halted. Next, the process is continued at the 'Continue' mark, where the execution of the intervention activities starts. After the intervention activities have been finished, the process proceeds with the correct activity in the regular process flow (A3).

The concepts described above prevent the process designer from being forced to check the value of the condition after every activity within the DS. That is, in order to predefine the error-handling in case of process interference without the presented concepts, for every activity the values of volatile process variables have to be tested. A (simplified) example of such an undesirable situation is represented in Fig. 6.

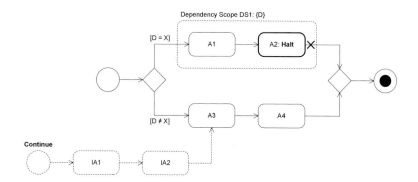

Fig. 5. Business process with dependency scope and connected intervention activities

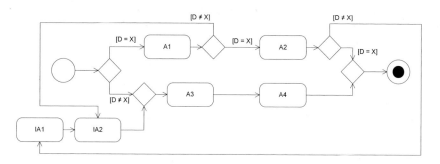

Fig. 6. Alternate solution to resolve dependencies

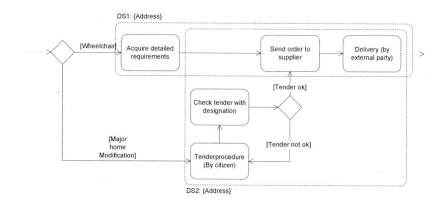

Fig. 7. Dependency scope for the case study

In more complex business processes, this would require a high amount of checks pre-defined in the business process. It is to be expected that this way of overcoming inter-dependency issues will strongly increase the complexity of each process model and, accordingly, result in a cascading change after the model is to be updated.

5   Case Study: Repairing the WMO Process

In Fig. 1, the four distinct activity branches following "Designation and report" (Domestic help, Transportation, Wheelchair and Major home modification) may potentially suffer from the process interference. In this section, we enrich two of them ([Wheelchair] and [Major home modification]) with dependency scopes that are referring to the variable {Address}. Each dependency scope has a trigger on the corresponding process variable {Address}. As shown in Fig. 7, both DS1 and DS2 start at the first activity in the branch and end after the final delivery, when the process variable {Address} is no longer required to remain unchanged.

If the trigger of one of the dependency scopes fires, the main process is halted, and corresponding compensation activities are executed. These activities are defined within the intervention patterns. In Fig. 8, the intervention pattern on [Wheelchair] (DS1) is shown. The intervention pattern on [Major home modification] (DS2) is shown in Fig. 9.

The decision concerning which intervention activity is to be executed first for each intervention pattern depends on the cancelled activity in the main process. For instance, if the order for home modification is already sent to the supplier, it must be cancelled first. If the order is not sent yet, it will suffice to start with a home visit.

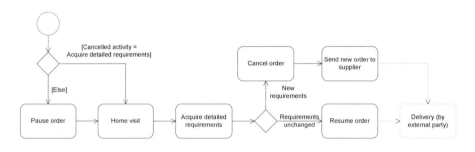

Fig. 8. Intervention pattern on [Wheelchair]

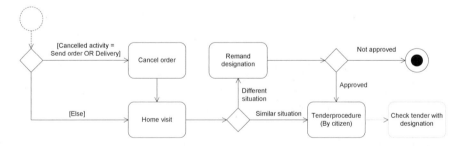

Fig. 9. Intervention pattern on [Major home modification]

6 Implementation

To show the feasibility of the approach, a prototype has been implemented on top of the Cordys Business Operations Platform[2]. Cordys is a business process management platform, which also adheres to modern variability management techniques, such as case handling and process inheritance, thus providing run-time reconfiguration abilities. This prototype adds dependency scopes over existing business process models, and maps each of the defined dependency scopes to an appropriate trigger.

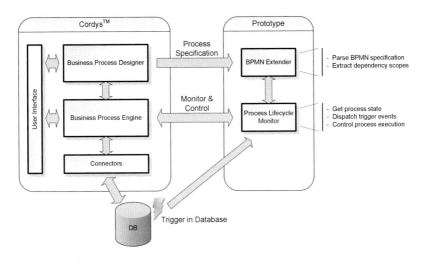

Fig. 10. Architectural overview of the prototype

Fig. 10 depicts the architectural overview, where the left box represents the simplified Cordys architecture, while the right box represents the structure of the prototype itself. In the Cordys box, the major parts are Business Process Designer and Business Process Engine. The former provides visual process design facilities, whereas the latter provides the business process lifecycle support (i.e. process execution and monitoring). Connectors at the bottom of the Cordys box provide communication with external data, e.g. databases, or data provided by external services. Finally, the user interface provides means for interacting with users, and is usually represented by a web-based application.

In the prototype box, the BPMN Extender parses the BPMN process specification in order to extract dependency scopes. Such dependency scopes can be designed using standard Cordys process design facilities, and the information about dependency scopes is saved along with a process's BPMN specification in the internal process repository. After that, the process specification can be retrieved via the Cordys public API.

---

[2] http://www.cordys.com

When the data modification occurs, a trigger is fired, which passes the corresponding information to the Process Lifecycle Monitor (PLM). This monitor has access to the information about existing business processes and their dependency scopes, which is provided by BPMN Extender. Based on the information about the processes being currently executed by the Cordys platform, PLM makes the decision whether or not to stop process(es) and fire appropriate intervention pattern(s). In order to support decision making, additional information must be associated with every dependency scope, such as a table in the database, the criteria to find a row in the table, and the criteria to identify which changes in the data are significant.

In Fig. 11, the business process from Fig. 7 is modeled using Cordys process designer with BPMN Extender on top of it. Two overlapping dependency scopes ([Wheelchair] and [Major home modification]) are designed. Both dependency scopes are assigned to one variable {Address}. Both dependency scopes are associated with the table "Citizens" in the underlying database and, whenever the {Address} is changed, the corresponding intervention pattern is executed.

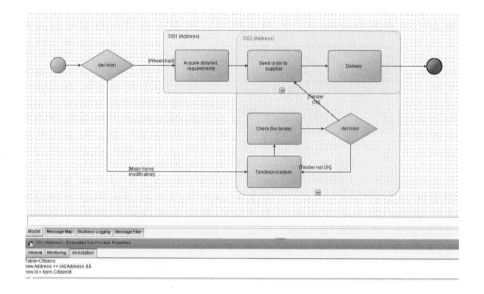

Fig. 11. Screenshot of dependency scope implementation within Cordys platform

For example, imagine the situation in which some process instance went on the "Wheelchair" path, i.e., after the decision steps "Acquire detailed requirements" and "Send order to supplier" were executed, and the step "Delivery" is about to be executed. Now, suppose that the customer's address is changed due to the moving to another city. Since the process is now within DS1, the intervention actions must be undertaken.

The sequence of actions in this case is the following:

- The Process Lifecycle Monitor is called with the information that a row is modified in the "Citizens" table.

- The dependency scopes associated with the "Citizens" table (which are DS1 and DS2) are identified.
- The currently running process instances that are now inside one of those scopes (there is one running process instance, and activated dependency scope is DS1) are fetched.
- Check if data modification is significant for those process instances (since the address has been changed, then the modification is significant.

When all conditions are met, the intervention pattern is automatically executed as follows:

- The original process is stopped.
- The compensation process assigned to DS1 is executed, as shown in Fig. 8.

7   Conclusion

In this paper, intervention patterns are used for repairing inconsistencies in process execution as a result of process and data interference. The main advantage of intervention patterns is that continuity of the process can be ensured in a predefined way. We have shown that both dependency scopes and intervention patterns can easily be integrated within an existing BPMS platform. Furthermore, the problem of business process interference can be resolved using the concepts introduced in the paper, namely, dependency scopes and intervention patterns. A real case scenario (Dutch WMO law) is implemented and is planned to be integrated into the implementation of the law in one of the Dutch municipalities.

A situation might occur that does require intervention, but the predefined intervention patterns attached to the dependency scope do not apply for this particular situation. In these cases, two possible solutions can be suggested. First, the process can be paused and require a human decision on how to proceed. Second, a rollback can be executed. This is, however, the least desirable solution, especially in processes with a long lead time. Furthermore, it is important that intervention patterns are defined as generic as possible, in order to make sure they cover potential inconsistency cases that might occur within a dependency scope.

Currently, intervention patterns are built manually by a domain expert and specific to a certain dependency scope. More complex interacting processes require the number of intervention patterns as well. For future work, we plan to generalize the intervention concept, to allow for automatic DS and intervention pattern generation. This way, it can be ensured that all cases of interference are covered, potentially without the need for human intervention.

References

1. van der Aalst, W.M.P., Hofstede, A.H.M., Kiepuszewski, B., Barros, A.P.: Workflow Patterns. Distributed and Parallel Databases 14(1), 5–51 (2003)
2. van der Aalst, W.M.P., Weske, M., Grünbauer, D.: Case handling: a new paradigm for business process support. Data and Knowledge Engineering 53(2), 129–162 (2005)

3. van der Aalst, W.M.P., Hofstede, ter, A.H.M.: Yet Another Workflow Language. Information Systems 30(4), 245–275 (2005)
4. Aiello, M., Bulanov, P., Groefsema, H.: Requirements and Tools for Variability Management. In: IEEE workshop on Requirements Engineering for Services at IEEE COMPSAC (2010) (to appear)
5. OMG: Business Process Model and Notation (BPMN) 2.0, Request For Proposal. OMG Document: BMI/2007-06-05 (2007)
6. Dadam, P., Reichert, M.: The ADEPT project: a decade of research and development for robust and flexible process support. Computer Science - R&D 23(2), 81–97 (2009)
7. Garcia-Molina, H., Salem, K.: Sagas. In: Proc. of the ACM SIGMOD Int. Conf. on Management of Data, pp. 249–259 (1987)
8. Klai, K., Tata, S., Desel, J.: Symbolic Abstraction and Deadlock-Freeness Verification of Inter-enterprise Processes. In: Dayal, U., Eder, J., Koehler, J., Reijers, H.A. (eds.) Business Process Management. LNCS, vol. 5701, pp. 294–309. Springer, Heidelberg (2009)
9. Li, Q., Zhou, J., Peng, Q.R., Li, C.Q., Wang, C., Wu, J., Shao, B.E.: Business processes oriented heterogeneous systems integration platform for networked enterprises. Computers In Industry 61(2), 127–144 (2010)
10. Pesic, M., Schonenberg, M.H., Sidorova, N., van der Aalst, W.M.P.: Constraint-Based Workflow Models: Change Made Easy. In: OTM Conferences, vol. (1), pp. 77–94 (2007)
11. Rinderle, S., Reichert, M., Dadam, P.: Correctness Criteria for Dynamic Changes in Workflow Systems – A Survey. Data and Knowledge Engineering 50(1), 9–34 (2004)
12. Sadiq, S., Sadiq, W., Orlowska, M.: Pockets of Flexibility in Workflow Specifications. In: Kunii, H.S., Jajodia, S., Sølvberg, A. (eds.) ER 2001. LNCS, vol. 2224, pp. 513–526. Springer, Heidelberg (2001)
13. Schonenberg, M.H., Mans, R., Russell, N., Mulyar, N., van der Aalst, W.M.P.: Process Flexibility: A Survey of Contemporary Approaches. In: CIAO! / EOMAS, LNBIP, vol. 10, pp. 13–16. Springer, Heidelberg (2008)
14. Trčka, N., van der Aalst, W.M.P., Sidorova, N.: Data-Flow Anti-Patterns: Discovering Data-Flow Errors in Workflows. In: van Eck, P., Gordijn, J., Wieringa, R. (eds.) CAiSE 2009. LNCS, vol. 5565, pp. 425–439. Springer, Heidelberg (2009)
15. Van Beest, N.R.T.P., Szirbik, N.B., Wortmann, J.C.: A Vision for Agile Model-driven Enterprise Information Systems. In: Proc. of the 11th Int. Conf. on EIS, Inf. Syst. Analysis and Specification, pp. 94–188 (2009)
16. Van Beest, N.R.T.P., Szirbik, N.B., Wortmann, J.C.: Assessing The Interference In Concurrent Business Processes. In: Proc. of the 12th Int. Conf. on EIS, Inf. Syst. Analysis and Specification (2010)
17. WfMC: The Workflow Management Coalition Specification, Terminology & Glossary. Document Number WFMC-TC-1011 (1999)
18. Xiao, Y., Urban, S.D.: Using Data Dependencies to Support the Recovery of Concurrent Processes in a Service Composition Environment. In: Proc. of Coop. Inf. Syst. Monterrey, Mexico (2008)

Linked Data and Service Orientation

Erik Wilde

School of Information
UC Berkeley

Abstract. *Linked Data* has become a popular term and method of how to expose structured data on the Web. There currently are two school of thought when it comes to defining what *Linked Data* actually is, with one school of thought defining it more narrowly as a set of principles describing of how to publish data based on *Semantic Web* technologies, whereas the other school more generally defines it as any form of properly linked data that follows the *Representational State Transfer (REST)* architectural style of the Web. In this paper, we describe and compare these two schools of thoughts with a particular emphasis on how well they support principles of service orientation.

1   Introduction

In the recent past, the term of *Linked Data* has become a popular meme for referring to approaches which are publishing structured data on the Web. However, the exact meaning of that term has been contentious, which is not an unusual thing to happen to terms which attract a certain attention and are not rigidly defined by any specific standard or product. This paper is an attempt to explore, explain, and clarify the major world views in this area, and more importantly, to investigate how well they work under the perspective of service orientation.

Unfortunately, the term *service orientation* itself is not all that well-defined, which means that it takes a little bit of explanation in itself. For the purpose of this paper, we refer to service orientation as an approach which allows the providers or information-intensive services to expose services which can be easily used, reused, and recombined using Web technologies. One of the main goals of service orientation should be to achieve *loose coupling* [24] between services, and between service providers and service consumers, so that the service landscape exposed by service providers, and the service landscape used by service consumers, are as agile and as easy to repurpose as possible.

For the purpose of this paper, the main property of service orientation is that it is on a higher level of abstraction and functionality than structured data. In order to implement service-oriented architectures, it is necessary to have some representation for the data that is exchanged between service providers and consumers, but the exact nature of that data, in particular the specific structured data standard used to represent that data, is secondary. Of course, in order to make services easily usable and easily mashable it is advantageous to use standardized and well-established structured data standards, but this is

P.P. Maglio et al. (Eds.): ICSOC 2010, LNCS 6470, pp. 61–76, 2010.

only one of the facets of service orientation. Another important facet is that the exact patterns in which data is exchanged is essential to service design as well, and there are several popular design patterns such as downloads, incremental data transfers, pull-based data feeds, and push-based architectures with various subscription and notification mechanisms using light or fat ping approaches.

The goal of this paper is to provide an overview and a qualitative comparison between the two dominant "world views" of linked data that are currently in use. One of the world views is a more constrained one which is based on Semantic Web technologies and architecture, and this approach is described in Section 2. The other world view is less constrained in terms of technologies and is based on Web technologies and architecture, this approach is described in Section 3. Recently, a third world view has been proposed, seeking the middle ground by not rigidly prescribing the RDF metamodel[1] of the Semantic Web world view, but still mandating that the metamodel used for structured data should be based on triples. This third world view so far has not gained a lot of momentum, though, probably caused by a lack of available candidates for a metamodel which is not RDF, but still based on triples.

The main reason for comparing the different approaches for linked data is that in the end, they are just implementation variants to achieve non-technical goals, which in many cases revolve around ideas of accessibility and usability (of data, and not of user interfaces), openness (non-proprietary ways of accessing and representing data), extensibility (the ability of the environment to adapt to unforeseen needs and use cases), and transparency (giving users the ability to understand where data originates, and easier ways to interact with a larger set of back-end data and service providers). Looking at service orientation is one way of comparing different approaches, so that from the business perspective it becomes easier to decide which technical approach best fits the requirements of the business goals.

2   Narrow Linked Data World View

The *Narrow Linked Data World View* is based on the approach of the *Semantic Web* [6], most importantly mandating the used of Semantic Web standards for structured data models and access. The most important standards in this space are the *Resource Description Framework (RDF)* [19] as the metamodel for any data being published on the Semantic Web, and *SPARQL* [27] as the query language for extracting subgraphs from large RDF graphs. While the original Semantic Web approach focused mainly on the core technologies, the term "linked data" emerged in conjunction with usage patterns around those technologies,

---

[1] In this paper, the term *metamodel* refers to the model of a model language, i.e. it is the foundation that is provided by a modeling language for building application-specific models. For example, the RDF metamodel is defined by *RDF Concepts and Abstract Syntax* [19], whereas the (most popular) XML metamodel is defined by the *XQuery 1.0 and XPath 2.0 Data Model (XDM)* [4].

and one of the important sources being cited frequently in this context is the *Linked Data* design note,[2] which defines the following rules:

1. Use URIs as names for things.
2. Use HTTP URIs so that people can look up those names.
3. When someone looks up a URI, provide useful information, using the standards (RDF, SPARQL).
4. Include links to other URIs, so that they can discover more things.

This set of rules can be regarded as repeating the pattern that has made the HTML Web successful: Use URIs for Web pages, use HTTP URIs so that people can point their browser at Web pages, make information available in HTML so that a standard browser can render the Web page, and include links to more pages so that people can click on links and follow them to retrieve even more Web pages. Because this approach focuses on the utility of a single metamodel that is consistently used by all information providers, and the utility of a standardized query language for providers of large datasets, for the remainder of this paper we refer to this approach as *Homogeneous Linked Data (HoLD)*.

The most important implications of the HoLD approach are that it fixes two design options that are left open by the Web itself: It mandates the use of HTTP URIs so that the identities of anything identified can also be used as a way to access it, and it mandates the use of RDF as the metamodel so any structured information made available at those HTTP URIs can be expected to be in a format that is prescribed in advance, instead of being discovered at runtime.

One of the important value propositions of HoLD is that data harvesting and/or aggregation becomes relatively easy because the two most important tasks (how to get access to data about an identified entity, and what to expect when accessing that data) are backed by the constraints defined by this approach. Since RDF is a metamodel with a small unit of atomicity (everything is based on triples, and there is no bigger unit of granularity, such as a concept of a "document," in RDF's metamodel), there is little built-in "bias" in RDF when it comes to mapping existing non-RDF data models to RDF. As discussed in more detail in Section 4, this can be a boon or a bane, depending on the data models in question and the requirements of data publishers and users, but regardless of these individual "data model usability" issues, the overall integrative qualities of the HoLD approach are largely undisputed.

3   Wide Linked Data World View

The *Wide Linked Data World View* is based on general principles of the *Architecture of the World Wilde Web* [18], and more specifically, on the *Representational State Transfer (REST)* [13] architectural style underlying the Web. Whereas HoLD is promoting a specific set of technology choices, this second view is more agnostic in terms of technologies and is operating on the layer of

---

[2] http://www.w3.org/DesignIssues/LinkedData.html

architectural styles, which are design patterns for architectures. In this wider view, the main constraints are derived from the REST architectural style, which underlies the Web and more specifically, the core Web technologies. The REST constraints can be summarized as follows:

1. *Resource Identification:* Anything that should be available for interactions should have an identifier.
2. *Uniform Interface:* Interactions with identified things should be based on a uniform interface, so that anything that is identified is readily available for interactions. Different identification schemes can have different interfaces, and not all identified things have to respond to all interactions defined by their uniform interface.
3. *Self-Describing Messages:* Interactions should be based on exchanges of messages (or documents) which are labeled with their type.[3]
4. *Hypermedia Driving Application State:* Messages should be based on data formats that may contain links (in most cases these are typed links), and interactions with RESTful services essentially means following those links according to the goals of the service consumer, and the semantics of the link types.
5. *Stateless Interactions:* The uniform interface should be usable in a way that interactions are independent of each other and only rely on either client state or resource state. This decouples interactions and allows clients and servers to be more independent of each other (servers do not need to remember clients, and clients can take advantage of scalability optimizations such as caching and replication).

Whereas HoLD to a large part reflects the specific technologies of the human-oriented Web, the wide view reflects the architectural style of the Web and its openness to new technologies, where identification is done by *Uniform Resource Identifier (URI)* [5] but allows a multitude of identification schemes to co-exist and new ones to be invented, where most of the interactions are based on the uniform interface of *Hypertext Transfer Protocol (HTTP)* [12], but other protocols can be used as well, and where structured data standards such as HTML [28], XML [7] or JSON [11] can be used, but new ones can be invented, as long as they are registered and subsequently identified according to the constraint of self-describing messages. Since this wider view thus allows a more open and evolving universe of concrete technologies, it will be referred to as *Heterogeneous Linked Data (HeLD)* for the rest of this paper.

In the same sense as HoLD is established as a set of constraints and patterns for publishing linked data using the Semantic Web's set of technologies, it is

---

[3] For clarification: REST uses the term "self-describing" in a considerably weaker form than this term is being used in more semantics-oriented research communities. "Self-describing" simply means that the type of the message can be inferred by looking at the message; it does not mean that any higher-level semantics are necessarily made available through advanced semantic descriptions.

possible to come up with some patterns and established best practices for publishing linked data according to HeLD approach. Since this approach is based in Web architecture itself, it can been dubbed the *Plain Web* [31], which is a general attempt to use established Web technologies instead of building entirely new stacks of technology on top of the Web, essentially treating the Web as a transport infrastructure instead of the information system it is.

Plain Web principles and HeLD results in approaches which can also be called *Lightweight Linked Data* [32], using established core Web technologies such as *Atom* [22] and the *Atom Publishing Protocol (AtomPub)* [15]. One of the main motivations of this approach is that HeLD data can be processed using basic Web technology toolsets (instead of the new toolset required for handling HoLD).

While the basic approach of using Atom and XML for exposing services and representing data might seem limiting, it is important to notice that because of the reliance of established and widely-used Web technologies, HoLD can benefit from developments in that rapidly developing space. One example is *PubSub-Hubbub (PuSH)*, a protocol that is based on Atom's model of exposing services via feeds, but that extends Atom's pull mechanics with a *Publish/Subscribe (Pub/Sub)* mechanism that can be used to implement push mechanics (this is described in more detail in Section 5).

4   Data Model Issues

One of the most striking differences between the two approaches is the fact that HoLD has a fixed metamodel, whereas in HeLD there is no fixed metamodel, and as long as the representation is properly labeled with its type (*self-describing*) and contains links (*hypermedia*), it can be used in a HeLD scenario. From the service point of view, this can be both good and bad. It can be good because it allows services to expose linked data in metamodels that fit their needs, and may be a good fit for the data model they are using (Section 4.1 contains a more in-depth discussion). It can be bad, because it means that service consumers may have to deal with a variety of metamodels, and this requires a variety of toolsets and may make it hard to combine data from different sources.

One of the interesting observations in this area is that the degree of freedom allowed by HeLD allows an "evolution" of metamodels used by services. As a popular example, for a while many Web-based services published structured data in XML, which was the first established Web-wide metamodel for structured data, and was reasonably easy to process in many client-side environments. However, because the majority of service consumers were using JavaScript (and processing XML in JavaScript involved some extra steps and created somehow awkward data structures), many services started providing the data in JSON, an alternative representation. JSON is a bit more limited than XML in its metamodel, but most XML models can be mapped to JSON in a fairly straightforward way. Because many developers preferred JSON's more straightforward mapping of data structures into programming language abstractions, JSON has now replaced XML in popularity for many Web-based services. This evolution has not changed anything about the data being exchanged and the way how it is linked and used, but it has allowed developers to move to a metamodel that better fits their needs.

4.1 Metamodel Bias

The example of XML and JSON highlights the fact that in many cases (at least in reasonably simple cases), data models can be mapped between metamodels. However, there are also many examples where data models, and especially more sophisticated data models, gain a lot of their expressiveness and convenience from the underlying metamodel. A good example for this are markup languages such as SGML or XML, which are metamodels specifically designed for representing human-readable documents. Many document types can be expressed rather conveniently in these metamodels, because of the specific design bias of the metamodel.

Metamodel bias is important in many scenarios where the data is non-trivial in its internal structure, and where there's a certain "natural order" to data, such as in documents which often are quite naturally a sequence of a variety of content objects. Metamodel bias has two main impacts: If there is a good match between a metamodel and a data model, then defining the model and representing and managing data with it are made easier by the metamodel's properties, and maybe the technologies and toolsets that have evolved around that metamodel. If there is a bad match between a metamodel and a data model, then defining the model becomes awkward, and representing and managing data with it become tasks where technologies and tools often feel like they work against the developer.

Metamodels can be roughly classified into three classes (without making any attempt to create a precise classification scheme), which at least for the purpose of a rough classification are sufficient:

- *Hierarchical:* In this case, models are always a *Directed Acyclic Graph (DAG)*, and sometimes they may be trees (having only one root node), sometimes they are allowed to have multiple root nodes. Another possible distinction is whether models can use a built-in ordering, or wether there is no ordering of nodes in the graph. Examples for hierarchical models are IBM's *Information Management System (IMS)* for a rather old model, and more recently the *Extensible Markup Language (XML)*.
- *Linked Tables:* Instead of having the inherently hierarchical structure of trees or other kinds of DAGs, the model of linked tables (as formalized by relational algebra) is less concerned with one predefined structure for a model instance, and instead is based on relations and operators on those relations. The most prominent example of this metamodel is the relational model introduced by Codd [10], which nowadays has its most popular representation in the *Structured Query Language (SQL)*.
- *Generalized Graphs:* The two previously discussed metamodels have a structural bias, for the hierarchical model this is some variation of DAG, and for the linked table model the bias are relations (i.e., connected n-tuples).

The third approach to metamodel structure is to try to avoid as much bias as possible, and just use generalized graphs. RDF can be seen as such a metamodel, where each triple represents an edge (the predicate) connecting two nodes (the subject and the object).

This categorization of metamodel structures is rough and only an approximation, but it does illustrate that various modeling languages may be based on different classes of metamodel structures, and based on this bias (and on the underlying use cases and derived technologies and tools), they provide differently specialized environments for certain classes of applications. The most important thing to realize is that this specialization is both a constraint in terms of these environment working better for some classes of problems than for others, and an opportunity for optimization, because it is possible to develop more effective and more efficient solutions for those problems that do fit the environments' bias.

As an example, while an ordered tree model (a DAG-based model with additional constraints) such as XML can feel like a good fit and almost natural for scenarios involving structured text, its built-in bias can become inconvenient and hard to adjust to when the scenarios become more advanced and include concepts such as overlapping or concurrent markup, which cannot be easily represented in XML-based data models. However, for the majority of document processing environments, tree-based models have proven to be the most convenient foundations, and metamodels such as SGML and XML and associated processing technologies and tools have produced an environment with a good mix of built-in bias, and freedom for customization and specialization.

In terms of comparing the two linked data approaches, HeLD allows data to use any media type as long as it is properly declared, and thus services are free to use models that fit their needs. HoLD, on the other hand, prescribes RDF's generalized graph as the only acceptable metamodel and thus does not introduce any particular structural bias (DAGs and relations have considerably more of a structural bias to them), but on the other hand also does not allow services to use the more biased metamodels if they would fit their needs. Many popular services prefer exposing XML or JSON over exposing RDF, because the installed base of both tools and developers is much bigger.

As a side note, it is interesting to see that recently, the W3C has started work on a standardized mapping of relational models to RDF models [26], recognizing the fact that a lot of data today is managed in relational systems. However, since this mapping is intended to be generic (i.e., it maps any relational model to an RDF model), it is likely that working with the RDF "view" of the relational data will be rather awkward, and figuring out the SPARQL queries to retrieve model-level data, and making sure that they can run with similar efficiency than in a fine-tuned RDBMS will likely be a challenge.

4.2   Data Granularity

One of the issues not discussed in the previous discussion of metamodel bias is that of *data granularity*. From the service perspective, in many cases data has a certain natural granularity in the sense that some data only makes sense as a unit, whereas other data is more loosely linked and can exist even if some of the linked resources cease to exist. This idea of data granularity is addressed in *document engineering* [14], and many frameworks have constructs to deal with it.

One example is the *Unified Modeling Language (UML)* [17], which supports various level of how tightly coupled data is. *Association, aggregation,* and *composition* are the different levels which are supported, and while the exact difference between these constructs is out of the scope of this paper, it is important to realize that these concepts were deemed important enough to be hardcoded into the metamodel.

The *Extensible Markup Language (XML)* and the *JavaScript Object Notation (JSON)* are two other examples where there is a level of granularity between a model's "atoms" (elements/attributes in XML and fields in JSON) and the global view of all data available. Data granularity is important for issues such as *provenance, versioning,* and *security,* where the "natural unit" of the data model (for example an XML document or a JSON object) makes it easier to express document-level semantics such as the origin, a version number, or a digital signature.

RDF does not have the concept of documents in the metamodel, there is no granularity concept beyond the triple. This has been noticed by the HoLD community as a problem, because *reification* as one way to solve this problem has the unfortunate side-effect of increasing data size several-fold, and *named graphs* [8] as the other way to solve this problem are not a part of RDF itself, but have been introduced by SPARQL. This means that as long as all data in a HoLD scenario is treated as merging seamlessly into one graph (an approach which for a while was dubbed the *giant global graph*), RDF works well and provides a good fit for processing this accumulation of all data into one big graph. However, when document boundaries become important because of the provenance, versioning, and security issues mentioned above, there is no support in the metamodel for modeling this, and applications have to come up with their own ways of introducing such an intermediate level of granularity between the "atom" and the "universe" as a whole.

4.3   Data Processing

Maybe the biggest difference between the two linked data approaches are in how data processing is supposed to work. Data processing can be considered on at least two different levels: One is the level of metamodels, where the question is which metamodel processed data is based on, and thus which technologies and tools are required to be able to process this data. The other level is that of understanding the meaning of the data, and being able to relate it to other models or other data. Unsurprisingly, the HoLD approach makes processing and understanding/combining data simpler, because it is based on a single metamodel, whereas the HeLD approach allows data to be more diverse, which has both positive and negative implications.

Processing Mechanics. Because HoLD is based on a single metamodel, processing can be reliably based on technologies and tools supporting this metamodel, and then by definition all structured data can be reliably processed.[4] HeLD mandates that structured data must be labeled with its format (*self-describing*), but if a client encounters data using a metamodel that it does not support, then it cannot process this data. This allows for new metamodels to be introduced and gain in popularity (such as the XML/JSON example mentioned earlier), but it does introduce an element of uncertainty in terms of what clients can encounter when following links.

Semantics and Mashups. The main difference between the basic *Semantic Web* and *Linked Data* (the HoLD variety) is that the latter establishes a set of patterns and best practices that are intended to actually link data, either because entities have well-known URIs, or because data and data models are created using existing data models, allowing data and data models from various sources to be joined. Again, the mandated use of a single metamodel not only make processing of individual resource representations easier as discussed above, they also provide a unified framework within which clients can infer the "meaning" of data (because concepts in RDF are identified by URI), and a simple way to "mash up" all data, because all data uses the same metamodel. This ability to combine data from any source is the biggest strength of HoLD, and is much harder to accomplish in HeLD. HeLD allows different metamodels to co-exist, and has no unified way of representing structured data, or identifying concepts. HeLD clients thus have to deal with heterogeneity on two different levels: models may be hard to relate because there is no standardized way of identifying concepts, and data can hard to combine because it may be based on different metamodels.

5   Service Orientation

When looking at data processing as discussed in the previous section, it becomes apparent that HoLD's approach allows users to deal with a more unified environment, whereas HeLD may require users to deal with various metamodels, and even for environments where all data is using the same metamodel (for example, XML), each model has its "private" semantics and there is no established way in which different models can be related or mapped [30]. This makes it easier to use data in HoLD, but HeLD does have the advantage of allowing services to use the metamodel that has the bias that makes most sense for their scenario. However, this is still looking at the data model level alone, and the next interesting area to look at is *service orientation*. How well can services be represented and exposed in these two approaches, and how do they compare?

---

[4] This is not entirely true because RDF supports various representations and the only standardized one, RDF/XML [3], has been on a steady decline in popularity, whereas alternative but not yet standardized syntaxes have become more popular.

On a very abstract level, a service can be defined as a well-defined unit of functionality that is accessible through some well-defined interface.[5] While this definition is probably general enough to not conflict with any other definition of services, it is also too wide to serve as a starting point for deciding on how good or bad specific services are exposed, or even more importantly, for deciding how well a certain architecture is suited for exposing services, and for allowing service innovation.

HeLD allows for service innovation in a variety of places, and most importantly, in the architecture itself. It is possible to introduce new identification methods, new interfaces, and new metamodels, and while this flexibility makes it necessary for clients to cope with the potential of new things being invented, it allows the service ecosystem to evolve over time and to adjust to the varied and unforeseeable needs and evolution of service providers and consumers. One good example on the human Web is Flash: Regardless of its merits as a well-designed or not-so-well-designed container for multimedia content, the open architecture of the Web allowed this new media type to flourish and succeed. All it needed was the `application/x-shockwave-flash` media type to be supported by a substantial share of clients, and to be provided by an increasing share of services. With the recent advances in HTML5 and the problematic support for Flash on mobile devices, combined with the rise of the mobile Web, it may happen that multimedia content will increasingly use HTML again, and move away from Flash. For many content producers, this is not even a major issue, because they produce their content with tools which increasingly will be able to export Flash or HTML5 representations of multimedia content. The important observation is that in this scenario, the service is to provide a multimedia representation of some content at some URI, and whether this is done in Flash or HTML5 is an implementation question that has no "correct" answer, but only a "best" answer given the constraints of content production tools and support for specific media types on the client side.

From this point of view, the "service" in HeLD is on a more abstract level than it is in HoLD, and spelling out the specific "service" definition implicitly asserted by these two approaches is crucial for understanding the differences between them:

– *Service as defined by HoLD:* Homogeneity is a top concern in HoLD, because it allows the seamless joining of both data and models across services. For this reason, a service in HoLD in required to only use RDF's metamodel. HoLD also encourages service providers to reuse existing identifiers, so that data retrieved from a variety of sources is more likely to be joinable on the data and/or the model level. From the interaction perspective, the services currently supported by HoLD are simple resource retrieval (HTTP GET of a URI), or SPARQL queries at an endpoint that exposes the SPARQL protocol via HTTP [9].

---

[5] For comparison, this is the definition of a service as given by the OASIS SOA reference model [20]: "A service is a mechanism to enable access to one or more capabilities, where the access is provided using a prescribed interface and is exercised consistent with constraints and policies as specified by the service description."

- *Service as defined by HeLD:* Heterogeneity is the biggest differentiating factor of HeLD, and it starts with identification, which can use a variety of schemes. Most schemes have well-defined interactions, and the uniform interface constraint of REST should allow clients to interact with a service if it supports the scheme linking to that service. REST's self-description constraint allows the service to consume and/or provide whatever metamodel it wants to, as long as the media type is exposed in the interactions.[6] The semantics of interactions often may be described or at least constrained by the interaction protocol associated with the URI scheme (for example, HTTP's methods describe basic safe/unsafe and idempotent/non-idempotent semantics for the HTTP methods), but this is not required by HeLD itself.

When contrasting these two approaches on how to define services, the differences between the approaches become strikingly apparent: HoLD's homogeneous approach defines an architecture where everything is predictable: data is always based on the same metamodel, and services always expose the same functionality. Because of this homogeneity, HoLD makes it possible basically ignore the underlying machinery of HTTP for resource retrieval and SPARQL for remote query execution: the virtual world view provided by HoLD is that of a seamlessly interconnected graph of data across all HoLD providers.

HeLD's world view is less homogeneous and thus supports a less virtualized world view. In HeLD, clients have to be prepared for heterogeneity on a variety of levels, which means that by definition they can never have a complete and definitive view across all HeLD providers, because that would require global knowledge across an unrealistic set of variables:

- *Identification:* Identification can use a variety of schemes and new schemes can be introduced at runtime.
- *Interaction:* Schemes in most cases imply interaction through a uniform interface, and this uniform interface must be implemented when interaction with a resource using that scheme is required.
- *Representation:* There is no fixed metamodel and services are free to consume and provide their preferred metamodel. Discovery of metamodels is done through registration and runtime labeling of representations with the metamodel they are based on, but new metamodels can be introduced at runtime.
- *Interpretation:* Even if a metamodel is supported, most metamodels do not have an overarching concept of how models encode and reuse semantics. Thus, often it is necessary to specifically support the interpretation of models, which thus must be detectable in representations.[7]

---

[6] HTTP's content negotiation adds a dynamic and negotiable pattern to this basic setup, but we will not discuss the specifics of HTTP here.

[7] In XML, for example, this is traditionally done with DTD declarations, XML namespaces, or XSD-specific attributes, but a recent W3C specification [16] proposes to use a unified syntax (based on processing instructions) for all these association mechanisms.

Thus, when comparing HoLD and HeLD, the trade-offs between the approaches become probably best visible on the service level: HoLD standardizes all services into RDF producers (static RDF or SPARQL endpoints), whereas HeLD provides an environment which is open and extensible on a variety of levels. Since HoLD standardizes a lot of this (thus making things more interoperable), extensions to this picture have to published as additional standards. One example is *SPARQL Update* [29], which extends the currently read-only nature of SPARQL to support create, update, and delete operations as well.

Since HeLD is more open, evolution and development can happen in a more informal way. One good example for this is in the area of feeds. Feeds have become the de-facto standard for lightweight data distribution on the Web, either using one of the various RSS formats, or the more recent Atom [22]. Feeds are a good example for HeLD because they provide an evidently working framework for implementing large scale data distribution and aggregation, but they also allow publishers to decide on the actual contents of the feed. Podcasts, for example, are just feeds which happen to carry audio or video content instead of more static media types. The big disadvantage of feeds has always been their *pull* model, which has been a great advantage for achieving loose coupling and scalability, but also produces a lot of polling in time-critical scenarios. Recently, *PubSubHubbub (PuSH)* has achieved some success by layering a push-oriented overlay on top of the pull model of feeds. PuSH allows clients to register callbacks with "hubs" (layered designs of multiple hubs are supported), and whenever a feed is updated, the clients will be notified via their callbacks. The basic information flow remains unaltered (services produce entries which are exposed via feeds), but the reversed control flow allows to eliminate polling. From the HeLD perspective, this was a straightforward innovation, with the only difference being that the media types involved in the scenario now are reversed in the HTTP interactions (the service provider or the hub acting on behalf of it acts as an HTTP client pushing the entry, and the service consumer accepts the entry by running a server at the callback URI).

Interestingly, recent work on combining SPARQL and PuSH in *sparqlPuSH* [23] has replicated this behavior in HoLD, adding a new service to the HoLD picture. How this new capability (which introduces something that could be described as "SPARQL triggers" and uses PuSH feeds carrying RDF as the notification mechanism) fits into the existing picture of HoLD services remains to be seen, but it fits well into the general direction of the HoLD and Semantic Web research community, where there is an increasingly strong push to move past the currently established model of "all RDF data accessible via one SPARQL endpoint," and is moving towards a more distributed scenario, including issues such as provenance and versioning.

The first draft of SPARQL 1.1 Federation Extensions [25] is looking at the fact that the current view of a service in HoLD is limited, because it is either retrieval of a fixed resource from a URI, or submitting a SPARQL query to an endpoint which then returns a subset of the RDF data managed behind that endpoint. SPARQL federation is supposed to work across a variety of RDF-oriented data sources, and introduces the SERVICE keyword. Because of the more constrained view of what a service is, this keyword allows a query to contain a query to another SPARQL endpoint, and the results of this query will then become available in the context of the "outer" query. While SPARQL federation will allow interesting new patterns of how to combine multiple RDF stores, it does not move outside of the basic assumption that services always consume and produce RDF, and that the only interactions possible with a service are retrieval and SPARQL-based querying.

6   Which One Is Better?

To a certain extent, research communities both from the HoLD and the HeLD side picture these two approaches as competing. This does not necessarily have to be the case. It also is misleading to picture the HoLD approach (or the Semantic Web in general) as the "next step in Web evolution." It is much more helpful to think of both approaches as being complementary, and of having different strengths and weaknesses.

HoLD shines when it comes to providing an abstraction layer that essentially makes the Web go away, and allows information to be viewed as the proverbial giant global graph. This capability can be very valuable when it comes to making sense of a large dataset, but it also comes at the price of having to do the homogenization of all data and services. Often, many of the most expensive tasks for producing good linked data in HoLD are non-technical, such as when data is aggregated from a wide variety of sources and entity resolution becomes a cumbersome process made expensive by data quality and a lack of transparency [33].

HeLD allows a more heterogeneous perspective on linked data and thus allows a greater variety of data sources and services to be used and possibly combined [2]. One possible use for this available data and the combination of available data sources is to map it to a HoLD view of these sources [1], available in some RDF mapping of the underlying sources and a SPARQL endpoint for using this mapped data.

It is probably unrealistic to assume that all data and service providers will subscribe to the HoLD set of technologies. Thus, it is likely that both approaches will co-exist for the foreseeable future, and both will have application areas where they are good fits, or not so good fits. In the HoLD world, the most exiting development for the near future is probably the inclusion of write features into the general architecture, and a more decentralized view of how HoLD data can be used. In the HeLD world, it is necessary to continuously improve the ways in which fundamental pieces of the infrastructure can use agreed-upon semantics, such as will be made possible for link relations [21] with a new registry of link types on the Web.

One way of benefiting from the differences in approach and strengths in both HoLD and HeLD can be to encourage the use of the less harmonized but still useful and accessible HeLD style in scenarios where the added expense of harmonizing models and metamodels is not justified, and to layer the more harmonized HoLD style on top of those HeLD services, if a more harmonized view is required, and the expenses for it are justified. Converting a set of HeLD services into a HoLD service (or, more accurately speaking, providing a HoLD perspective of a set of HeLD services) can be a value-added service in itself, but it also can be a costly service to implement. In many cases, most of the costs of this service will be caused by the expensive and often manual or semi-automatic tasks of data cleansing and entity resolution.

7   Conclusions

The goal of this paper is to compare the two approaches to *Linked Data* that are currently under discussion in the research and developer communities. For the purpose of this paper, we refer to the approach based on Semantic Web technologies as *Homogeneous Linked Data (HoLD)*, and to the approach based on Web architecture and REST as *Heterogeneous Linked Data (HeLD)*. The main goal of the comparison is to understand how well these approaches work in the context of service-orientation, and how open they are to service innovation on a variety of levels. The goal of this paper is a qualitative comparison, pointing out the strengths and weaknesses of both approaches. The service level turns out to be a very good comparison between those two approaches, because HoLD's more homogenous approach allows clients to work in a very predictable landscape of data and services, whereas HeLD's heterogeneous approach requires clients to deal with heterogeneity on at least four different levels (identification, interaction, representation, and interpretation).

In summary, HoLD can be described as defining more constraints, thus providing a more predictable environment, but also providing less potential for innovation, whereas HeLD with its more open approach has less constraints, thus provides a less predictable environment, but on the other hand has more potential for innovation. We don't think that these two approaches have to be mutually exclusive. In tightly coupled and cooperating environments, the HoLD approach has obvious benefits by providing a more integrated view of the available data and services, and allowing developers to better abstract from the underlying fabric of the Web. In loosely coupled and decentralized environments, the HeLD approach provides a more flexible and open solution that still establishes patterns and practices for data and services to be linked, but allows a more open ecosystem that can change over time, introducing new tools and technologies as service providers and consumers as well as their needs evolve.

References

1. Alarcòn, R., Wilde, E.: From RESTful Services to RDF: Connecting the Web and the Semantic Web. Tech. Rep. 2010-041, School of Information, UC Berkeley, Berkeley, California (June 2010)

2. Alarcón, R., Wilde, E.: Linking Data from RESTful Services. In: Third Workshop on Linked Data on the Web, Raleigh, North Carolina (April 2010)
3. Beckett, D.: RDF/XML Syntax Specification (Revised). World Wide Web Consortium, Recommendation REC-rdf-syntax-grammar-20040210 (February 2004)
4. Berglund, A., Fernández, M.F., Malhotra, A., Marsh, J., Nagy, M., Walsh, N.: XQuery 1.0 and XPath 2.0 Data Model (X DM) (2 eds.) World Wide Web Consortium, Proposed Edited Recommendation PER-xpath-datamodel-20090421 April 2009)
5. Berners-Lee, T., Fielding, R.T., Masinter, L.: Uniform Resource Identifier (URI): Generic Syntax. Internet RFC 3986 (January 2005)
6. Berners-Lee, T., Hendler, J.A., Lassila, O.: The SemanticWeb. Scientific American 284(5), 34–43 (2001)
7. Bray, T., Paoli, J., Sperberg-McQueen, C.M., Maler, E., Yergeau, F.: Extensible Markup Language (XML) 1.0 (Fifth Edition). World Wide Web Consortium, Recommendation REC-xml- 20081126 (November 2008)
8. Carroll, J.J., Bizer, C., Hayes, P., Stickler, P.: Named Graphs, Provenance and Trust. In: Ellis, A., Hagino, T. (eds.) 14th International World Wide Web Conference, pp. 613–622. ACM Press, Chiba (May2005)
9. Clark, K.G., Feigenbaum, L., Torres, E.: SPARQL Protocol for RDF. World Wide Web Consortium, Recommendation REC-rdf-sparql-protocol-20080115 (January 2008)
10. Codd, E.F.: A Relational Model of Data for Large Shared Data Banks. Communications of the ACM 13(6), 377–387 (1970)
11. Crockford, D.: The application/json Media Type for JavaScript Object Notation (JSON). Internet RFC 4627 (July 2006)
12. Fielding, R.T., Gettys, J., Mogul, J.C., Frystyk Nielsen, H., Masinter, L., Leach, P.J., Berners- Lee, T.: Hypertext Transfer Protocol | HTTP/1.1. Internet RFC 2616 (June 1999)
13. Fielding, R.T., Taylor, R.N.: Principled Design of the Modern Web Architecture. ACM Transactions on Internet Technology 2(2), 115–150 (2002)
14. Glushko, R.J., McGrath, T.: Document Engineering, The MIT Press, Cambridge (August 2005)
15. Gregorio, J., de Hóra, B.: The Atom Publishing Protocol. Internet RFC 5023 (October 2007)
16. Grosso, P., Kosek, J.: Associating Schemas with XML documents 1.0 (1eds.) World Wide Web Consortium, Note NOTE-xml-model-20100415 (April 2010)
17. International Organization for Standardization: Information Technology– Open Distributed Processing – Unified Modeling Language (UML) Version 1.4.2. ISO/IEC 19501 (April 2005)
18. Jacobs, I., Walsh, N.: Architecture of the World Wide Web, Volume One. World Wide Web Consortium, Recommendation REC-webarch-20041215 (December 2004)
19. Klyne, G., Carroll, J.J.: Resource Description Framework (RDF): Concepts and Abstract Syntax. World Wide Web Consortium, Recommendation REC-rdf-concepts-20040210 (February 2004)
20. MacKenzie, C.M., Laskey, K., McCabe, F., Brown, P.F., Metz, R.: Reference Model for Service Oriented Architecture 1.0. Organization for the Advancement of Structured Information Standards, OASIS Standard (October 2006)
21. Nottingham, M.: Web Linking. Internet Draft draft-nottingham-http-link-header-10 (May 2010)

22. Nottingham, M., Sayre, R.: The Atom Syndication Format. Internet RFC 4287 (December 2005)

23. Passant, A., Mendes, P.N.: sparqlPuSH: Proactive notification of data updates in RDF stores using PubSubHubbub. In: 6th Workshop on Scripting and Development for the Semantic Web, Crete, Greece (May 2010)

24. Pautasso, C., Wilde, E.: Why is the Web Loosely Coupled? A Multi-Faceted Metric for Service Design. In: Quemada, J., León, G., Maarek, Y.S., Nejdl, W. (eds.) 18th International World Wide Web Conference, pp. 911–920. ACM Press, Madrid (April 2009)

25. Prud'hommeaux, E.: SPARQL 1.1 Federation Extensions. World Wide Web Consortium, Working Draft WD-sparql11-federated-query-20100601 (June 2010)

26. Prud'hommeaux, E., Hausenblas, M.: Use Cases and Requirements for Mapping Relational Databases to RDF. World Wide Web Consortium, Working Draft WD-rdb2rdf-ucr-20100608 (June 2010)

27. Prud'Hommeaux, E., Seaborne, A.: SPARQL Query Language for RDF. World Wide Web Consortium, Recommendation REC-rdf-sparql-query-20080115 (January 2008)

28. Raggett, D., Le Hors, A., Jacobs, I.: HTML 4.01 Speci_cation. World Wide Web Consortium, Recommendation REC-html401-19991224 (December 1999)

29. Schenk, S., Gearon, P., Passant, A.: SPARQL 1.1 Update. World Wide Web Consortium, Working Draft WD-sparql11-update-20100601 (June 2010)

30. Wilde, E.: Model Mapping in XML-Oriented Environments. Tech. Rep. TIK Report 257, Co mputer Engineering and Networks Laboratory, ETH Zürich, Zürich, Switzerland (July 2006)

31. Schenk, S., Gearon, P., Passant, A.: SPARQL 1.1 Update. World Wide Web Consortium, Working Draft WD-sparql11-update-20100601 (June 2010)

32. Wilde, E., Liu, Y.: Lightweight Linked Data. In: 2008 IEEE International Conference on Information Reuse and Integration, Las Vegas, Nevada (July 2008)

33. Yee, R., Kansa, E.C., Wilde, E.: Improving Federal Spending Transparency: Lessons Drawn from Recovery.gov. Tech. Rep. 2010-040, School of Information, UC Berkeley, Berkeley, California (May 2010)

Risk Sensitive Value of Changed Information for Selective Querying of Web Services

John Harney and Prashant Doshi

THINC Lab, Dept. of Computer Science,
University of Georgia, Athens, GA 30602
{jfh,pdoshi}@cs.uga.edu

Abstract. A key challenge associated with compositions is that they must often function in volatile environments, where the parameters of the component Web services may change during execution. Failure to adapt to such changes may result in sub-optimal compositions. Value of changed information (VOC) offers a principled and recognized approach for selectively querying component services for their revised information. It does so in a rational (risk neutral) way. However, risk preferences often constitute an important part of the organization's decision analysis cycle and determine its desired business goals. We show how VOC may be generalized to consider preferences such as risk seeking and aversion using a utility based approach. Importantly, considerations of risk preferences lead to different services being used in the compositions and selected for querying for revised information. This is intuitive and provides evidence toward the validity of our approach for modeling risk preferences in VOC.

1 Introduction

A key benefit of Web services (WS) is the potential for automatically and flexibly formulating compositions of services resulting in integrated software processes. Many of the proposed approaches for optimally composing WSs utilize fixed information about the component WSs available at design time [1,18,21,24]. A notable exception is [14] where parameters of WSs are obtained again just before execution. However, the approaches predominantly result in compositions that may soon become suboptimal if the environment is volatile. For example, a product may go out of stock affecting the usefulness of the corresponding WS, the network bandwidth may fluctuate affecting the WS response time, or costs of using a service may increase. Such changes may negatively impact the performance of the composition, making it critical that the compositions identify and adapt to changes appropriately to maintain optimality.

This is not a new problem and several adaptation techniques have been proposed [4,7,9,17] to improve composition performance in the presence of volatile information. They seek to maintain an updated model of the composition environment, some of them by querying for revised information [9,17]. One such approach uses the *value of changed information (VOC)* to decide which WS to query for its revised parameters [8,9]. VOC is a principled and recognized way for selectively querying WSs participating in a composition. Recently, He et al. [10] expanded the applicability of VOC to multiple different workflow patterns. Experimental results reveal that VOC based

P.P. Maglio et al. (Eds.): ICSOC 2010, LNCS 6470, pp. 77–91, 2010.

querying leads to adaptive compositions that perform better than those that do not adapt, in simulations.

Approaches such as VOC aim to adapt compositions in a rational – risk neutral – manner. However, risk preferences often strongly influence a modern organization's decision analysis cycle and play a pivotal role in determining the goals of its many different business processes. This was demonstrated in a recent survey conducted by Corner and Corner [6], which found that more than a quarter of all business processes show some sensitivity to risk. For example, an organization may be conservative by nature, willing to sacrifice some cost in exchange for more stability and reduced risk of incurring greater costs in the future. In contrast to such *risk aversion*, *risk-seeking* behavior involves making decisions that could yield large gains at the risk of incurring heavier losses.

Clearly, a comprehensive approach to composition and adaptation should allow for considerations of risk preferences. This is because distinct preferences toward risk could significantly affect which WSs are selected in the composition and how the composition is adapted. In this paper, we generalize VOC toward modeling risk preferences in deciding which WS to query for revised information. Although we focus on VOC, our general approach toward considering risk is applicable to other adaptation techniques as well. We model risk preferences using *utility functions* [22] – a well-known way of modeling different attitudes toward risk. However, its principled integration within the traditional VOC is not trivial.

We show that considerations of risk preferences affect which WSs are included for participation in compositions, and which WSs are selected for querying of revised information. This in turn affects how compositions are adapted. We experimentally demonstrate that while the rational costs of the adapted compositions may be high, its utility to the risk-sensitive designer is optimal. This conforms to the intuition generally held about risk and its role in automation. It also provides evidence about the validity of our risk-sensitive model. The outcome is a novel approach for guiding the querying of WSs in volatile environments that models and acts on risk preferences as well.

The remainder of this paper is organized as follows. Section 2 presents a composition problem that is simple to understand yet demonstrative of the impact of considering risk preferences. Section 3 gives a brief overview of a specific composition technique and VOC. Section 4 shows how we may extend these models to include risk preferences. In Section 5, we present our experimental results that demonstrate the validity of our approach. Section 6 gives a concise summary of research related to this paper. We conclude with Section 7 which gives a brief summary and ideas for future work.

2   Scenario: Risk Sensitive Supply Chain

In order to demonstrate our approach, we present a *manufacturer's* supply chain process designed according to the supply-chain operations reference (SCOR) [25] model. We assume that the component activities are all available as WSs. As the SCOR model is highly complex, we focus on the subtask of parts procurement and assembly, where the manufacturer must obtain a specific part to finish assembling a larger product for delivery.

We illustrate the activities involved in parts procurement in Fig. 1. The manufacturer must optimally decide between three different service providers from whom to obtain specific parts. The first option is to obtain the parts from its own inventory (shown as Inventory in Fig. 1), an inexpensive option that would allow the manufacturer to acquire the part quickly and cheaply. The manufacturer has limited storage available, however, making this method of obtaining the part unreliable. The manufacturer may also choose to obtain the parts directly from its preferred supplier. The part is more expensive to obtain from the supplier, but its availability is significantly better than from the inventory. Finally, the manufacturer may rely on the spot market, which almost certainly guarantees that the part will be obtained, but is more expensive than the previous two options. For the sake of simplicity, we assume that the manufacturer may invoke a single WS only. If the manufacturer is unable to complete the parts procurement task (i.e., a service is used that is not able to satisfy the order for the parts), a penalty is incurred in addition to the cost of invoking the WS. This penalty is representative of the recovery costs needed to heal the process (manufacturing halts, process rollbacks, compensations, etc.). In Fig. 1, we also indicate example QoS properties of each of the available services.

A rational (risk neutral) manufacturer would optimize the composition by selecting the WS that maximizes the mathematical expectation of total cost given the probability of obtaining the parts using the WS. For the quality of service (QoS) parameters given in Fig. 1, a rational manufacturer would elect to use the preferred supplier. However, pragmatic manufacturers are not always rational. A manufacturer that is *averse* to risk

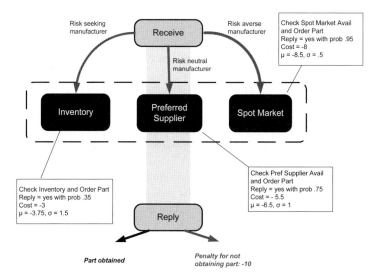

Fig. 1. Parts procurement in a manufacturer's supply chain. The manufacturer may choose between obtaining parts from its own inventory WS, a preferred supplier service or the spot market service. The inventory supplies parts cheaply but is less available in general, while the spot market provides parts reliably but expensively. The preferred supplier has intermediate cost and availability of parts. A penalty is incurred if the process does not complete.

would opt for a more sure bet – a reliable service whose probability of meeting the order is thought to be high – despite the potentially higher cost. For our scenario, it seems intuitive that a risk-averse manufacturer would likely select the spot market due to almost guaranteed availability of the parts. On the other hand, a *risk seeker* would likely bet on a WS that is least expensive despite its lower reliability, such as the inventory. Subsequently, although our scenario is simple, it is appropriate for demonstrating the impact that distinct risk preferences may have.

An adaptive manufacturer would seek to modify its choice based on the updated information about the component WSs. In this regard, we indicate the mean (μ) and standard deviation (σ) that guides the Gaussian distribution of the volatile cost of each participating service, in Fig. 1. While we restrict our analysis to Gaussian distributions, it applies to other distributions as well. Per domain knowledge, we expect inventory to be most volatile (high standard deviation) while the spot market to be least volatile.

3   Background: Web Service Composition and VOC

We briefly describe a framework for WS composition that provides a guarantee of expected cost based optimality. Consequently, we model both the cost and availability of the services that may participate in the composition. We then describe the *value of changed information* and how it may be used to pick a WS to query for revised information. While we show its usage in the context of the previous WS composition framework, Chafle et al. [5] demonstrate that VOC may be coupled with other WS composition frameworks as well. We refer the reader to [7] and [9] for more details about the WS composition framework and VOC, respectively.

3.1   WS Composition Using Markov Decision Processes

We model the problem of WS composition as a Markov decision process (MDP) [19] using the sextuplet:

$$WP = (S, A, T, R, H, s_0)$$

where $S = \Pi_{i=1}^n X^i$, S is the set of all possible states of the composition factored into a set, X, of n variables, $X = \{X^1, X^2, \ldots, X^n\}$; A is the set of all possible actions ie. WS invocations; T is the transition function, $T : S \times A \rightarrow \Delta(S)$, which specifies the probability distribution over the next states of the composition given the current state and action. T models the uncertain availability of the WS itself and the service it provides; R is a reward function, $R : S \times A \times S \rightarrow \mathbb{R}$, which specifies the reward obtained (or cost) for performing each transition that has a non-zero probability. R models the summation of the cost of invoking a WS and the cost of consuming the service it provides, and is thus often independent of the source and resulting states. For our example, the reward depends only on the action; H is the period of consideration over which the composition must be optimal, also known as the horizon. While $1 \leq H \leq \infty$, for the sake of understanding we use a horizon of 1 (greedy actions) in this paper. Our approach is applicable to longer horizons in a straightforward manner; and s_0 is the starting state of the composition.

In order to gain insight into the use of the above framework for WS composition, let us model the parts procurement problem of Section 2. The state of the corresponding WS composition is captured by the random variables – **Inventory available, Preferred-Supplier available, SpotMarket available** – and is a conjunction of assignments of either *Yes, No,* or *Unknown* to each variable. As we mentioned, actions are WS invocations: A={Inventory, PreferredSupplier, SpotMarket}. The transition function, T, models the nondeterministic effect of a WS invocation. For example, invoking the PreferredSupplier WS causes **PreferredSupplier available** to be assigned *Yes* with a probability of T(**PreferredSupplier available**=*Yes*|PreferredSupplier, **Preferred-Supplier available**=*Unknown*) = 0.75. The reward function, R, models the cost of using a service. We model this cost as a combination (e.g., a sum) of the cost of invoking the WS and the cost of the parts the service offers. For example, the cost of using the inventory is R(Inventory).

Given that the manufacturer has modeled its WS composition problem in the above framework, it may apply standard MDP solution techniques to arrive at an optimal composition. Here, optimality is with respect to the expected cost summed over the horizon. These solution techniques use stochastic dynamic programming [19] for calculation of the optimal policy using *value iteration*:

$$V^n(s) = \begin{cases} 0 & s \in \mathbb{G} \\ \max_{a \in A} \sum_{s' \in S} T(s'|a, s)[R(s, a, s') + V^{n-1}(s')] & s \notin \mathbb{G} \end{cases} \qquad (1)$$

where $V^n(s)$ quantifies the maximum long-term expected reward of reaching each state s with n actions remaining to be performed, and could be written concisely as $V^n(s) = \max_{a \in A} E_{s'}^{s,a}[r_0 + V^{n-1}(s')]$; $\mathbb{G}$ represents the set of goal states, indicating that the composition has completed successfully. As we employ a one step approach, $n = 1$ for our analysis. Here, $V^0(s') = 0, \forall s \in \mathbb{G}$, and $V^0(s') \leq 0, \forall s \notin \mathbb{G}$.

Because the reward is negative (cost), Eq. 1 implies that the expected value of a non-goal state is less than or equal to the expected value of a goal state. In our example, $V^0(s') \leq 0$ for non-goal states represents the penalty of not procuring the desired parts from the selected supplier.

Once we know the expected reward (or cost) associated with each state, the optimal action for each state is the one which results in the maximum expected reward.

$$\pi^*(s) = \underset{a \in A}{argmax} \sum_{s' \in S} T(s'|a, s)[R(s, a, s') + V^0(s')] \qquad (2)$$

In Eq. 2, π^* is the optimal policy which is a mapping from states to action(s), $\pi^* : S \rightarrow \Delta(A)$. The WS composition is obtained by performing the WS invocation prescribed by the policy given the state of the composition and observing the result of the invocation in order to obtain the next state. Doshi et al. [7] details this procedure and provides an algorithm for translating the policy to a WS composition.

3.2   VOC for Selective Querying

The parameters of the participating services may change during the lifetime of a WS composition. For example, the cost of the parts from the preferred supplier service may increase (requiring an update of R) or the probability with which the **preferred supplier** satisfies an order for parts may reduce (requiring an update of T). In order to remain optimal in such volatile environments, one approach we may adopt is to query the component WSs for their revised parameters [17]. However, queries may be costly or tedious to perform. We must therefore manage them carefully.

Harney and Doshi [9] introduced the *value of changed information (VOC)* that intelligently selects which service to query for its revised information. VOC employs a myopic approach to information revision, in which we query a single provider at a time for new information. For example, the manufacturer may query for revised information about the cost of using the **inventory** thereby updating the reward function to R'(Inventory).

Let $V_{\pi^*}(s|R')$ denote the expected reward of following the optimal policy, π^*, from the state s given updated costs, R'. Let $V_{\pi}(s|R')$ be the expected reward of following the original policy, π, from state s in the context of the revised costs. The policy, π, is optimal in the absence of revised information. Since the updated costs are not known unless we query the service provider, we average over all possible values of the revised costs, using our subjective belief distribution over the values. We formulate the VOC pertaining to the revised costs at some state, s, as:

$$VOC_{R'}(s) = \int_r Pr(R'(s,a,s') = r)[V_{\pi^*}(s|R') - V_{\pi}(s|R')]dr \qquad (3)$$

where $R'(s,a,s')$ denotes the cost that may be queried and subsequently may get revised, $Pr(\cdot)$ is our *belief* over the possible costs of WS a. As we mentioned previously, the cost may be independent of s and s'.

The subscript to VOC, R', denotes the revised information inducing the change. Intuitively, Eq. 3 represents how badly, on average, the original policy, π, performs in the changed environment as formalized by the MDP model with the revised R'. We may model our beliefs over the possible cost of a WS, $Pr(R'(s,a,s') = r)$ in Eq. 3, using density functions, which could be obtained from the service provider initially in the service-level agreement or may be learnt from previous interactions. We let the densities for the WSs take the form of *Gaussian* density functions[1].

Of all the participating WSs in the composition, we select the one whose possible new cost is expected to bring about the most change in the WS composition, and this change exceeds the cost of querying that provider. We first select the service provider associated with the WS for whom the VOC is maximum:

$$a = \underset{a \in A}{argmax} \ [VOC_{R'}(s)] \qquad (4)$$

Let $VOC^*(s)$ represent the corresponding maximum VOC at state s. We query for new information only if the VOC due to the revised information in that state is greater than the query cost: $VOC^*(s) > QueryCost(R'(a))$. This revised parameter information is integrated into the MDP model, and the optimal policy, π^*, is regenerated. The WS composition resumes execution using an updated policy. Harney and Doshi [9] provide further details about the algorithm that integrates VOC within WS composition.

---

[1] Note that that these densities are marginalizations of the more complex ones that would account for all the factors that may influence the cost of the WS.

4 Risk Sensitive VOC

The traditional business analysis cycle views risk preferences as an important criteria for designing business processes [11]. Although rational process design stipulates risk indifference (often called risk neutrality), pragmatic composition design often involves either implicit or explicit considerations of risk preferences. For example, surveys [6] have found that 27% of all business processes are designed with some sensitivity to risk. Typically, risk considerations are predominant in processes involving high-stakes decisions, or those involving large sums of money or resources, in order to either avoid disastrous consequences or obtain huge financial gains [15]. A process designer may be *risk averse* – it is willing to incur some cost in exchange for more reliability and reduced risk of incurring greater costs in future. Some designers may have opposite preferences and are *risk seeking* – they make decisions that could yield large possible gains, at the risk of sustaining heavy losses.

A known way of modeling risk preferences is by adjusting the *utility function* that maps the actual expected reward to the subject's utility [20,22]. Risk aversion is associated with a large drop in utility for low reward (high cost) while risk-seeking behavior is thought to associate a large increase in utility for positive expected reward. On the other hand, risk neutrality involves considering the expected reward as is. We show example utility functions for the three distinct risk preferences in Fig. 2.

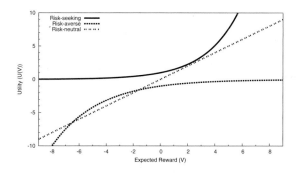

Fig. 2. Utility functions for different risk preferences. Risk aversion is modeled using a concave function while risk seeking is represented by a convex utility function. The utility function for risk neutrality is linear.

Typically, utility functions that model risk assume an exponential form. Consequently, we model risk-averse utility as, $U^n(s) = max_{a \in A} E_{s'}^{s,a}[-\gamma^{r_0+V^{n-1}(s')}]$, where γ is between 0 and 1 not inclusive, and $n \geq 1$. Parameter γ is often called the risk factor and decides the degree of risk. Smaller values of γ signify greater aversion. Risk-seeking utility is modeled as, $U^n(s) = max_{a \in A} E_{s'}^{s,a}[\gamma^{r_0+V^{n-1}(s')}]$, where γ is greater than 1. Analogously, larger values of γ signify greater risk. If $\gamma = 1$ we get the risk-neutral utility and $U^n(s) = max_{a \in A} E_{s'}^{s,a}[r_0 + V^{n-1}(s')]$. In Fig. 2, $\gamma = 1.5$ for the risk-seeking function while it is 0.75 for the risk-averse utility function.

As previously shown by Avila-Godoy [2], we may incorporate the utility functions in the solution of an MDP. Because the utility is an expectation of the exponential function of the value, we may rewrite Eq. 1 with $n = 1$ as:

$$U^1(s) = \begin{cases} \iota & s \in \mathbb{G} \\ \max_{a \in A} \; [\sum_{s' \in S} \gamma^{R(s,a,s')} T(s'|a,s) U^0(s')] & s \notin \mathbb{G} \end{cases} \qquad (5)$$

Here, $\iota = sgn(ln\,\gamma)$; in other words, ι is 1 is $\gamma > 1$ and -1 if $0 < \gamma < 1$. Notice that ι is obtained by applying the appropriate utility function to the corresponding $V^0(s)$ for goal states, $\mathbb{G}$, in Eq. 1. In case of risk aversion, $U^0(s) = -\gamma^{V^0(s)} = -\gamma^0 = -1$. For risk-seeking, $U^0(s) = \gamma^{V^0(s)} = \gamma^0 = 1$. $U^0(s')$ is the appropriate utility function applied to $V^0(s')$ for any state, s'. Thus, $U^0(s') = \iota$ for all goal states and $U^0(s') \leq \iota$ for all non-goal states. Note that the utility of non-goal states continues to be less than that of goal states.

We note that considerations of risk could impact the utility of the different states of the WS composition to the designer, and potentially which WS invocations are optimal at different states. This implies that the optimal policy, π^*, may be different as well leading to possibly distinct WS compositions for different utility functions.

Given the risk-sensitive composition using utility functions, we may generalize VOC to include considerations of risk preferences. In order to do this, Eq. 3 may be rewritten as:

$$\mathcal{VOC}_{R'}(s) = \int_r Pr(R'(s,a,s') = r)[U_{\pi^*}(s|R') - U_\pi(s|R')]dr \qquad (6)$$

where $\mathcal{VOC}$ denotes the generalized version of the traditional VOC, $U_{\pi^*}(s|R')$ denotes the risk-sensitive utility of the state s given the optimal policy in the context of revised information and $U_\pi(s|R')$ denotes the risk-sensitive utility of s given the original policy in the context of revised information. The utility function, U, is as defined in Eq. 5.

Subsequently, we select the WS to query which has the maximum $\mathcal{VOC}$, analogously to Section 3.2. However, the query is issued only if the $\mathcal{VOC}^*$ is greater than the utility of the query cost to the designer. Formally, if $\mathcal{VOC}^*(s) > U(QueryCost)$, then the query is issued to the provider whose service led to the maximum expected change.

Observe that considerations of risk preferences may alter which WS is selected for querying in comparison to risk neutrality. In our example, the composition of a risk-averse manufacturer may be more sensitive to changes in the parameters of the spot market. This is because the risk-averse manufacturer could be relying on the spot market to satisfy its parts order. This is in contrast to a risk-neutral manufacturer whose composition is expected to be most affected by changes in the parameters of the pre-ferred supplier.

5 Experiments

We evaluate the performance of our risk-sensitive VOC and subsequent adaptation of the compositions in the context of our example problem domain of Section 2. Our service-oriented architecture involving VOC is identical to the one used previously by Harney and Doshi [9]. In particular, VOC computations are performed within internal

WSDL WSs. The benefit of using VOC for selectively querying services for revised information and adapting compositions using the updated information has been demonstrated previously [8,9,10]. Specifically, compositions adapted using VOC lead to significantly better performance in volatile environments compared to compositions that are not adapted and to those that are adapted using adhoc techniques. Hence, we will not demonstrate the benefits of VOC here; rather we will focus on illustrating the influence of risk preferences on composition and adaptation, and thereby demonstrate the intuitive validity of our general approach.

5.1   Impact of Risk Preferences on Composition

Columns 1-3 of Table 1 summarize the cost and availability parameters of the participating supplier WSs that the manufacturer could use for procuring parts. Although the inventory is least costly, its likelihood of satisfying the order is the lowest. On the other hand, the spot market is most expensive but almost guaranteed to satisfy the manufacturer's order.

Table 1. Parameters of the participating WSs in our parts procurement problem domain. Existing rewards are slightly away from the means to facilitate potential querying.

WS	Reward	Availability	Volatility	
			Mean	Std. dev.
Inventory	-3	0.35	-3.75	1.5
Preferred Supplier	-5.5	0.75	-6.5	1
Spot Market	-8	0.95	-8.5	0.5

A rational, risk-neutral manufacturer should choose the preferred supplier for placing its order. This is because the expected reward of using it (see Eq. 5 with $\gamma = 1$ which becomes identical to Eq. 1) is the largest (lowest expected cost) among all three suppliers. However, let us consider the case where the manufacturer is *risk seeking* with $\gamma = 1.5$. The utility of the inventory for a risk-seeking manufacturer is the highest $(U^1(s_0) = 0.11)$ compared to that of the inventory and the spot market. This is intuitive because the inventory is a risky bet with the potential for a large reward (low cost of using it successfully) but also low chances of winning it (low availability). In contrast, both preferred supplier and spot market represent less attractive bets (action utility of 0.08 and 0.04, respectively) for the risk seeker. On the other hand, a risk-averse manufacturer with $\gamma = 0.75$ opts for the spot market because it represents a safe bet – its order would almost certainly be met although the cost is high $(U^1(s_0) = -18.36)$.

These outcomes demonstrate the impact of risk preferences while formulating compositions. Differing compositions also influence how they get adapted using VOC; we investigate this next.

5.2   Impact of Risk Preferences on Adaptation

As we mentioned previously, in the absence of risk preferences a rational manufacturer would choose the preferred supplier's WS to order parts. Given the volatility in the environment (see columns 4 and 5 of Table 1), let the manufacturer use a VOC-driven approach toward querying service providers for revised information. If the updated information leads to a change in the optimal policy, the composition is adapted. In this context, we show the performance of the risk-neutral manufacturer's compositions in Fig. 3. We show the average reward obtained by three distinct *adaptive* compositions that invoke the **inventory, preferred supplier** and **spot market** WSs, respectively. Here, each data point is the average of 500 executions of the composition in 1,000 simulations of our problem domain. The simulations are constructed by sampling the Gaussian distributions of parameters of the participating volatile WSs. Each of the three different compositions experienced identical simulations in order to facilitate a valid comparison. A possible VOC-driven query is issued at the starting state of the composition.

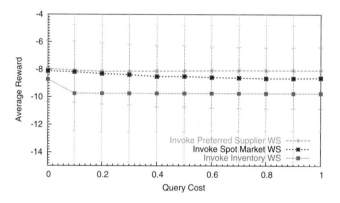

Fig. 3. Performance of the VOC-driven adaptive compositions for a risk-neutral manufacturer. We compare between policies prescribing the three different WSs. Higher average reward indicates better performance. The vertical bars represent the standard deviations. Large deviations are mainly due to the high penalty when the composition does not procure the parts.

We first observe that all three compositions show a drop in expected reward as the query cost increases. This is typical of VOC-driven adaptations. While adaptations are frequent when the query cost is low, they occur less as querying becomes more expensive. Notice that the composition prescribing the invocation of the **preferred supplier** continues to do the best. This implies that for low query costs, possible adaptations continue to outperform those in compositions that prescribed invoking other WSs. Furthermore, the risk-neutral manufacturer queried the **preferred supplier** the most because the associated VOC was often the largest. For large query costs, there is no adaptation and it is rational to choose the **preferred supplier**.

In Fig. 4, we demonstrate how the adaptive compositions of a *risk-seeking* manufacturer would perform when using VOC-driven selective querying. Our methodology for generating the data is same as before except for γ which is 1.5 and we show the utility of the reward obtained by the compositions. Risk-sensitive VOC was computed according to Eq. 6. As we mentioned previously, a risk-seeking manufacturer opts to

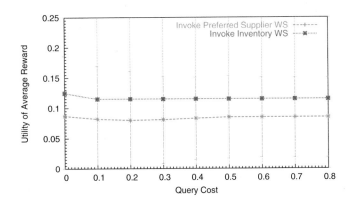

Fig. 4. Utility of VOC-driven adaptive compositions for a risk-seeking manufacturer ($\gamma = 1.5$). We compare between policies that recommend **preferred supplier** and **inventory** WSs. Higher utility indicates better performance.

invoke the **inventory** in comparison to a rational manufacturer who chooses the **preferred supplier**. Fig. 4 demonstrates that possible adaptations of this composition have a larger utility to the risk-seeking manufacturer than the adaptive **preferred supplier** based WS composition, which is the choice of a rational manufacturer. Thus, although the composition that prescribes the **inventory** performs worst in the absence of risk preferences, it becomes the optimal choice for a risk seeker.

We observed that for low query costs, the risk-seeking manufacturer queried the **inventory** the largest number of times indicating that its $\mathcal{VOC}$ was the largest. This is because of the high standard deviation of its cost coupled with its importance in the composition of the manufacturer. About a fraction of one-tenth of these queries led to adaptations where the **preferred supplier** was selected.

Finally, in Fig. 5 we demonstrate the utility to a risk-averse manufacturer of the performance of adaptive compositions. We use $\gamma = 0.75$ (recall that risk aversion is modeled using $\gamma < 1$) and each data point is generated as before. In comparison to a risk seeker, our risk-averse manufacturer continues to find the adaptive composition that recommends invoking the **spot market** most preferable. Its utility remains consistently high compared to that of the adaptive composition that involves the **preferred supplier** which is the choice of a rational manufacturer. Furthermore, the risk-averse manufacturer queried the **preferred supplier** most number of times. This is intuitive because while the **spot market** is important its deviation is very low. Significant changes in **preferred supplier's** costs could make it the WS of choice for the risk-averse manufacturer. Despite the querying the number of times that adaptations do occur is low because of the significant value of the **spot market** to the risk-averse manufacturer. About one-fifth of these queries led to adaptations.

In summary, risk-sensitive VOC leads to different services being selected for querying based on the risk preferences, in comparison to queries in the absence of risk. This is in part due to the varying compositions induced by different risk preferences.

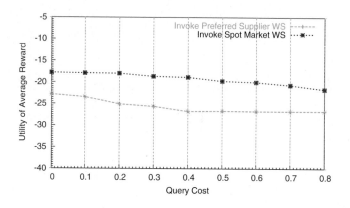

Fig. 5. Utility of VOC-driven adaptive compositions for a risk-averse manufacturer ($\gamma = 0.75$). We compare between policies that select **preferred supplier** and **spot market** WSs. Higher average utility indicates better performance.

6 Related Work

Our paper borrows, in large part, from recent work in quantitative risk analysis. This line of research uses modern decision-theoretic planning and von-Neuman-Morgenstern utility theory concepts [22] that exist in the artificial intelligence [20] and decision analysis [12] literature. Avila-Godoy [2] derived straightforward methods to compute value functions for process designers that utilize exponential utility functions to model their risk attitudes. Liu [15] extended this line of work so that value functions may be computed using more general (i.e. non-exponential) risk-sensitive utility functions. While their focus was strictly on MDPs, these methods provide a means to include risk preferences in process creation.

Other lines of work have attempted to represent risk attitude in different ways. Kokash and D'Andrea [13] use traditional risk management strategies to derive contingency plans (such as quality of service re-negotiation or adopting other component services) when the risk of using a composition is found to be high. They operate with the notions of threats (danger sources), probabilities of threats, and their quantifiable impact on the provider of the composition (monetary losses, time losses and breach of reputation). These threats are juxtaposed against the possible gains of the composition. Decisions are made whether to utilize a contingency plan of composition based on these comparisons. Wiesemann et al. [23] incorporate the average value at risk (AVaR) measure, widely used in economic studies, into the decision making of a WS composition. They introduce risk-preferences using the β-AVaR metric, which is defined as the mean value of the $(1-\beta)$ worst losses sustained by making a particular decision. Parameter $\beta \in [0, 1]$ represents the degree to which a decision maker considers the worst case loss of a particular decision. When β is 0, the decision maker is risk-neutral. As β increases it becomes more pessimistic, and thus, risk-averse. The β-AVaR metric is introduced in their value maximization equations and decisions are based on the modified equations. Although both approaches apply quantitative methods, they quantify the risks in different ways, and neither handle run-time adaptation of WS compositions in the presence of risk preferences as we do in this paper.

Finally, risk management in processes has long received attention in economic and business enterprise research communities. Traditionally, this line of research has adopted an orthogonal and external perspective to risk by seeking to identify the risks posed to business processes and outlining options that process managers may undertake to deal with the risks [16]. Unlike the formal concepts discussed in this paper, their strategies implement qualitative approaches to risk management. Human specialists oversee the processes and identify potential hazards that could upset its functionality. After the risks are identified, they are addressed in a systematic manner.

7   Discussion and Future Work

Real world environments in which WS compositions must function are seldom static. Parameters of WSs and the of service it provides such as the cost and availability are volatile. In this context, compositions must adapt to remain optimal. A crucial step in adaptation is finding out the updated information about the component WSs. VOC offers a principled and recognized approach for deciding which WS to query for revised information.

Although designers are often advised to be rational and objective while designing processes, risk preferences invariably play a role in the composition. Therefore, we presented an approach for considering risk preferences while composing and querying, leading to the *risk sensitive VOC*. We used utility functions to model risk preferences and showed how these may be integrated with the traditional VOC. Our experimental results on a simulated parts procurement domain confirmed our intuition about the impact of risk – its consideration leads to changes in how we compose and issue queries compared to rational behavior.

While we experimented with a simple scenario in order to promote clarity, we think that our results are indicative of more complex scenarios as well. In particular, the risk-sensitive utility as defined in Eq. 5 may be generalized straightforwardly to multiple steps and the corresponding computation of the risk-sensitive VOC continues to proceed as shown in Eq. 6.

Although we used particular exponential utility functions, other forms of exponential utility functions could be used as well such as those often utilized in economics and those which allow a switch in risk preference depending on the accumulated reward [15]. We speculate that our analysis would hold for these forms of utility functions as well. Finally, it would be interesting to demonstrate the beneficial role of risk in real-world compositions. In this regard, we are seeking a case study.

Acknowledgment

We would like to thank Bob Bostrom, professor in the business school of the University of Georgia for useful discussions related to this work.

References

1. Agarwal, V., Chafle, G., Dasgupta, K., Karnik, N., Kumar, A., Mittal, S., Srivastava, B.: Synthy: A system for end to end composition of web services. Journal of Web Semantics 3, 311–339 (2005)
2. Avila-Godoy, M.: Controlled Markov Chains with Exponential Risk-Sensitive Criteria: Modularity, Structured Policies and Applications. Ph.D. thesis, Department of Mathematics, University of Arizona (1999)
3. Andrieux, A., Czajkowski, K., Dan, A., Keahey, K., Ludwig, H., Nakata, T., Pruyne, J., Rofrano, J., Tuecke, S., Xu, M.: WS-Agreement Specification (2005)
4. Chafle, G., Dasgupta, K., Kumar, A., Mittal, S., Srivastava, B.: Adaptation in web service composition and execution. In: International Conference on Web Services (ICWS), Industry Track, pp. 549–557 (2006)
5. Chafle, G., Doshi, P., Harney, J., Mittal, S., Srivastava, B.: Improved Adaptation of Web Service Compositions Using Value of Changed Information. In: International Conference on Web Services (ICWS), Industry Track, pp. 784–791 (2007)
6. Corner, J., Corner, P.: Characteristics of decisions in decision analysis practice. The Journal of Operational Research Society 46, 304–314 (2006)
7. Doshi, P., Goodwin, R., Akkiraju, R., Verma, K.: Dynamic workflow composition using markov decision processes. Journal of Web Services Research 2(1), 1–17 (2005)
8. Harney, J., Doshi, P.: Adaptive Web Processes Using the Value of Changed Information. In: Dan, A., Lamersdorf, W. (eds.) ICSOC 2006. LNCS, vol. 4294, pp. 179–190. Springer, Heidelberg (2006)
9. Harney, J., Doshi, P.: Selective querying for adapting web service compositions using the value of changed information. In: IEEE Transactions on Services Computing (2008) (in press)
10. He, Q., Yan, J., Jin, H., Yang, Y.: Adaptation of Web Service Composition Based on Workflow Patterns. In: Bouguettaya, A., Krueger, I., Margaria, T. (eds.) ICSOC 2008. LNCS, vol. 5364, pp. 22–37. Springer, Heidelberg (2008)
11. Holtzman, S.: Intelligent Decision Systems. Addison-Wesley, Reading (1989)
12. Kirkwood, C.: Approximating Risk Aversion in Decision Analysis Applications. Decision Analysis, 55–72 (2004)
13. Kokash, N., D'Andrea, V.: Evaluating Quality of Web Services: A Risk-Driven Approach. Business Information Systems, 180–194 (2007)
14. Kuter, U., Sirin, E., Nau, D.S., Parsia, B., Hendler, J.A.: Information gathering during planning for web serivce composition. Journal of Web Semantics 3(2-3), 183–205 (2005)
15. Liu, Y.: Decision-Theoretic Planning Under Risk-Sensitive Planning Objectives. Ph.D. thesis, College of Computing, Georgia Institute of Technology (2005)
16. zur Muehlen, M., Ho, D.: Risk Management in the BPM Lifecycle. In: Bussler, C.J., Haller, A. (eds.) BPM 2005. LNCS, vol. 3812, pp. 454–466. Springer, Heidelberg (2006)
17. Au, T.C., Kuter, U., Nau, D.: Web service composition with volatile information. In: Gil, Y., Motta, E., Benjamins, V.R., Musen, M.A. (eds.) ISWC 2005. LNCS, vol. 3729, pp. 52–66. Springer, Heidelberg (2005)
18. Pathak, J., Basu, S., Honavar, V.: Moscoe: A specification-driven framework for modeling web services using abstraction, composition and reformulation. In: Ph.D. Symposium, International Conference on Services-Oriented Computing (ICSOC), pp. 1–6 (2007)
19. Puterman, M.L.: Markov Decision Processes:Discrete Stochastic Dynamic Programming. Wiley series in probability and mathematical statistics. Wiley-Interscience, Hoboken (1994)
20. Russell, S., Norvig, P.: Artificial Intelligence: A Modern Approach, 2nd edn. Prentice-Hall, Englewood Cliffs (2003)

21. Sirin, E., Parsia, B., Wu, D., Hendler, J.A., Nau, D.S.: Htn planning for web service composition using shop2. Journal of Web Semantics 1(4), 377–396 (2004)
22. von Neumann, J., Morgenstern, O.: Theory of Games and Economic Behavior. Princeton University Press, Princeton (1944)
23. Wiesemann, W., Hochreiter, R., Kuhn, D.: A Stochastic Programming Approach for QoS-Aware Service Composition In. IEEE International Symposium on Cluster Computing and the Grid (CCGrid 2008), pp. 226–233 (2008)
24. Zhao, H., Doshi, P.: Haley: An end-to-end scalable web service composition tool. In: Developers Track, World Wide Web, (WWW 2008)
25. The Supply-Chain Council, `http://archive.supply-chain.org/cs/root/scor_tools_resources/scor_model/scor_model` (last accessed June 14, 2010)

Adaptive Service Composition Based on Reinforcement Learning*

Hongbing Wang[1], Xuan Zhou[2], Xiang Zhou[1], Weihong Liu[1],
Wenya Li[1], and Athman Bouguettaya[2]

[1] School of Computer Science and Engineering,
Southeast University, China
{hbw,szs,chw}@seu.edu.cn
[2] CSIRO ICT Centre, Australia
{xuan.zhou,athman.bouguettaya}@csiro.au

Abstract. The services on the Internet are evolving. The various properties of the services, such as their prices and performance, keep changing. To ensure user satisfaction in the long run, it is desirable that a service composition can automatically adapt to these changes. To this end, we propose a mechanism for adaptive service composition. The mechanism requires no prior knowledge about services' quality, while being able to achieve the optimal composition solution by leveraging the technology of reinforcement learning. In addition, it allows a composite service to dynamically adjust itself to fit a varying environment, where the properties of the component services continue changing. We present the design of our mechanism, and demonstrate its effectiveness through an extensive experimental evaluation.

1 Introduction

In the emerging paradigm of Service Oriented Computing (SOC), data, software and hardware can all be encapsulated as services shared on the Internet. Applications would no longer be built from scratch, but as compositions of the available services. In this way, application builders can focus on business logics, without overly spending time and efforts on infrastructures. To realize SOC, a variety of technologies have been proposed. They include the stack of Web Service technologies, e.g. SOAP and BPEL, and a variety of mashup tools, e.g. Yahoo Pipe and Google Mashup Editor. Most of these technologies aim to help engineers / users create service compositions efficiently.

The services on the Internet keep evolving. Some services may stop functioning, once their providers go out of business. Some may keep upgrading themselves, to achieve improved Quality of Service (QoS). For instance, Amazon EC2 has decreased its prices for several times (the latest one was a 15% cut in Nov 2009), but continually improve its architecture to achieve better performance.

---

* This work is partially supported by the NSFC project No. 60673175 and the Jiangsu NSF project titled "Cloud-Service Oriented Autonomic Software Development".

P.P. Maglio et al. (Eds.): ICSOC 2010, LNCS 6470, pp. 92–107, 2010.

For those services that do not evolve, their quality may change with the varying environment. For instance, the growth of customers will usually increase the response time of a service. Due to the evolvement of services and the dynamicity of the environment, a service composition has to be continually adjusted, to keep functioning in a cost-effective manner. This imposes intensive workload to engineers in monitoring, tuning and re-engineering service compositions. It is desirable that a service composition can be self-adaptive in a dynamic environment, so that it will incur less maintenance cost.

In recent years, extensive research efforts have been spent on the development and the optimization of service compositions [13,19]. However, most of the existing approaches assume a static environment. As a common practice [19,1,18], an abstract service composition is firstly created to meet users' requirements on functionality. Then, concrete services are selected based on their non-functional properties to create a concrete service composition of the best possible quality. A service composition created out of this approach runs in a static workflow and is not self-adaptive. When its environment or its component services change, the composition has to be manually adjusted to adapt to the changes.

In this paper, we present a novel mechanism to enable a service composition to adapt to its environment autonomously. Our mechanism achieves self-adaptivity by utilizing Reinforcement Learning, a typical technology used for planning and optimization in dynamic environments. We model a service composition as a Markov Decision Process (MDP), so that multiple alternative services and workflows can be incorporated into a single service composition. The optimization of the composition is conducted at runtime (when users consume the services), through reinforcement learning. The learning aims to obtain the optimal policy of the Markov decision process that delivers the best quality of service. In contrast to the existing approaches of service composition and optimization, our mechanism requires no prior knowledge of services' non-functional properties, which are anyway uncertain in most real world circumstances. Instead, it learns these properties by actually executing the services. As the learning process continues throughout the life-cycle of a service composition, the composition can automatically adapt to the change of the environment and the evolvement of its component services. We have conducted extensive experiments to evaluate our approach and observed a number of its merits.

The remainder of this paper is organized as follows. Section 2 defines our model of service composition. Section 3 shows how reinforcement learning can be conducted to run the service compositions. Section 4 presents the results of our experimental evaluation. Section 5 compares our approach against some related work. Finally, Section 6 provides a conclusion.

2   A MDP Model for Service Composition

Some recent approaches [5,6] to automatic service composition have used Markov Decision Process (MDP) to model service compositions. We use this model too, as it allows us to apply reinforcement learning to dynamically optimize the quality of a service composition.

We first define the key concepts of the model.

Definition 1 (Web Service). A Web service is modeled as a tuple $WS =< ID, QoS >$, where
- ID is the identifier of the Web service.
- QoS is a n-tuple $< att_1; att_2; ...; att_n >$, where each att_i denotes a QoS attribute of WS.   ∎

Example 1: Some example Web services are defined as follows:

ID: StorkID
QoS: <price:free, response_time:1ms, availability:99%>

ID: StorkPrice
QoS: <price:free, response_time:1ms, availability:99%>

ID: StrokInfo1
QoS: <price:$1, response_time:200ms, availability:80%>

ID: StockInfo2
QoS: <price:$2, response_time:1ms, availability:99%>

ID: Transaction
QoS: <price:$1, response_time:200ms, availability:99%>

We use these services as walk-through examples to illustrate our approach. Among these services, StockID allows a user to know the identification code of a stock. StockPrice allows a user to check the current price of a stock. Stock-Info1 and StockInfo2 are two alternative services for providing user with more information about stocks. They charge different fees and offer different QoS. Finally, Transaction allows a user to buy or sell stock. In our example, we use only three typical QoS attributes.   ∎

As we use Markov Decision Process (MDP) to model service composition, we first define MDP. In [8], a MDP is defined as:

Definition 2 (Markov Decision Process (MDP)). A MDP is a 4-tuple $M =< S, A(.), P, R >$, where
- S: a finite set of states of the world. When an agent arrives at a state, the agent can observe the complete state of the world.
- $A(s)$: a finite set of actions. The set of available actions depends on the current state $s \in S$.
- P: when an action $a \in A$ is performed, the world makes a probabilistic transition from its current state s to a resulting state s' according to a probability distribution $P(s'|s, a)$.
- R: Similarly, when action a is performed and the world makes its transition from s to s', the agent receives a real-valued (possibly stochastic) reward r, whose expected value is $r = R(s'|s, a)$.   ∎

A MDP involves multiple actions and paths for a agent to choose. By using it to model service compositions, we are able to integrated multiple alternative work-flows and services into a single composition. We call our model of service composition WSC-MDP, which simply replaces the actions in a MDP with Web services.

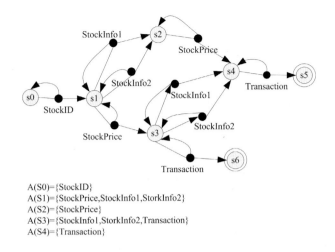

A(S0)={StockID}
A(S1)={StockPrice,StockInfo1,StorkInfo2}
A(S2)={StockPrice}
A(S3)={StockInfo1,StorkInfo2,Transaction}
A(S4)={Transaction}

Fig. 1. The WSC-MDP of a Composite Service for Stock Transaction

Definition 3 (Web Service Composition MDP (WSC-MDP)). A Web service composition MDP is 6-tuple WSC-MDP=$< S, s_0, S_r, A(.), P, R >$, where

- S: a finite set of states of the world.
- $s_0 \in S$ is the initial state. An execution of the service composition starts from this state.
- $S_r \subset S$ is the set of terminal states. Upon arriving at one of the states, an execution of the service composition terminates.
- $A(s)$ represents the set of Web services that can be executed in state $s \in S$. A service ws belongs to $A(s)$, only if the precondition ws^P is satisfied by s.
- P: When a Web service $ws \in A(s)$ is invoked , the world makes a transition from its current state s to a resulting state s', where the effect of ws is satisfied. For each s, the transition occurs with a probability $P(s'|s, ws)$.
- R: When a Web service $ws \in A(s)$ is invoked, the environment makes a transition from s to s', and the service consumer receives an immediate reward r, whose expected value is $R(s'|s, ws)$. ∎

A WSC-MDP can be visualized as a transition graph [15]. As illustrated by Fig. 1, the graph contains two kinds of nodes, i.e., state nodes and service nodes, which are represented by open circles and solid circles respectively. $s0$ represents the initial state node. The terminal states nodes are those with double circles. A state node can be followed by a number of service nodes, representing the possible services that can be invoked in the state. There is at least one arrow pointing from a service node to the next state node. Each arrow is labeled with a transition probability $P(s'|s, ws)$, and the expected reward for that transition $R(s'|s, ws)$, which are determined by the P and R in the WSC-MDP. (For simplicity, we omit the labels in Fig. 1.) The transition probabilities on the arrows rooted at a single action node always sum to one.

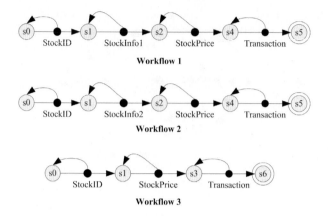

Fig. 2. Three Workflows contained by the WSC-MDP in Fig. 1

Example 2: The services introduced in Example 1 can be composed into a integrated service for stock transaction. We model it as a WSC-MDP transition graph in Fig. 1. (For simplicity, we assume only two resulting states for each service. If the service is invoked successfully, the world changes to the next state predicated by the service's post-condition. Otherwise, the world remains in the current state.) This service composition provides multiple workflows for users to purchase or sell stocks. When executing the composition, the system can choose the workflow that offers the best results. ∎

As shown in the related work [5,6], WSC-MDP is expressive enough to describe the control flows of a general business process. In addition, WSC-MDP can express a super service composition composed of multiple alternative workflows. Each of the workflows corresponds to a service composition constructed by traditional approaches, such as BPEL.

Definition 4 (Service Workflow). Let wf be a subgraph of a WSC-MDP. wf is a service workflow if and only if there is at most one service that can be invoked at each state wf. In other words, $\forall s \in wf, |A(s) \cap wf| \leq 1$. ∎

A service workflow is actually analogous to a deterministic state machine. A tradition service composition usually corresponds a single workflow. In contrast, a WSC-MDP based composition can consist of multiple workflows.

Example 3: The WSC-MDP in Example 2 consists of multiple service workflows. Fig. 2 shows three of them. Which workflow will be executed by the service composition is determined the policy of the Markov decision process. ∎

We define a policy (or execution policy) of a WSC-MDP as follows.

Definition 5 (Policy). A policy π is a mapping from state $s \in S$ to a service $ws \in A$, which tells which service $ws = \pi(s)$ to execute when the world is in state s. ∎

Example 4: A policy for the WSC-MDP in Example 2 can be expressed as π = $\{s0 : StockID, s1 : StockInfo1, s2 : StockPrice, s4 : Transaction\}$. It tells our system to execute the service composition using Workflow 1 in Fig. 2(a). ■

Each policy can uniquely determine a workflow of a WSC-MDP. By executing a workflow, the service customer is supposed to receive a certain amount of reward, which is equivalent to the cumulative reward of all the executed services. Given a WSC-MDP, the task of our service composition system is to identify the optimal policy or workflow that offers the best cumulative reward. As the environment of a service composition keep changing, the transition function P and the reward function R of a WSC-MDP changes too. As a result, the optimal policy changes with time. If our system is able to identify the optimal policy at any given time, the service composition will be highly adaptive to the environment.

It worth noting that this paper only deals with how to model a service composition using WSC-MDP. Regarding the design and construction of WSC-MDP, we schedule it in our future work. In practice, a WSC-MDP can either be created manually by engineers or using some automatic composition approaches, such as an AI planner [11,14].

3   Reinforcement Learning for Service Composition

The MDP model introduced previously allows service engineers to integrate multiple alternative workflows and services into a single service composition. During the execution of a service composition, the system can dynamically choose the optimal policy / workflow that would give the best possible reward to the users. When the complete WSC-MDP is known, the theoretically optimal policy can always be calculated. However, this is not true in practice. Firstly, we may not have complete knowledge about the state transition functions of the WSC-MDP, as the results of a service are not always predicable. Secondly, we may not have sufficient knowledge about the reward functions of the WSC-MDP. Especially for human oriented services, the user experience of a service composition is rarely predicable, until it has been tried out. Moreover, as the environment of a service composition keep changing, both the state transition functions and the reward functions change with time.

Due to the above issues, we choose to learn the optimal policy of a WSC-MDP at runtime. In this section, we introduce a reinforcement learning scheme to orchestrate WSC-MDP based service compositions. We first give a brief overview of a reinforcement learning algorithm called Q-Learning. Following that, we show how to apply reinforcement learning to WSC-MDP.

3.1   Q-Learning

In reinforcement learning, the task of the learner or decision-maker is to learn a policy of the MDP that maximizes the expected sum of reward. As there is no initial and terminal states in a generic MDP (Definition 2), an agent is supposed to live in the MDP forever. Therefore, the cumulative reward of starting from an arbitrary state s_t and following a policy π is defined as:

$$V^\pi(s_t) = r_t + \gamma r_{t+1} + \gamma^2 r_{t+2} + \ldots = \sum_{i=0}^{\infty} \gamma^i r_{t+i} \tag{1}$$

where r_{t+i} is the *expected* reward received in each step, and γ is a discount factor.

Based on Equation 1, the optimal policy is the policy that maximizes $V^\pi(s_t)$ for all s_t. Let π^* denote the optimal policy. Therefore,

$$\pi^* = argmax_\pi V^\pi(s_t), (\forall s_t \in S) \tag{2}$$

We use $V^*(.)$ to represent the cumulative reward of the optimal policy π^*.

As mentioned earlier, the state transition function and reward function of a MDP may not be known. Thus, π^* cannot be calculated directly. It has to be learned through a trial-and-error process.

To facilitate the learning process, Q-Learning [17] uses a Q function to simulate the cumulative reward. Let s be the current state of the agent. Let a be the action taken by the agent. Let s' be the resulting state of action a. Then, the Q function of taking action a at state s is

$$Q(s,a) = \sum_{s'} P(s'|s,a)[R(s'|s,a) + \gamma V^*(s')] \tag{3}$$

The Q function represents the best possible cumulative reward of taking action a at state s.

Based on Equation 3, we obtain the optimal policy for each single state s.

$$\pi^*(s) = argmax_a Q(s,a), (\forall a \in A(s)) \tag{4}$$

Applying Equation 4 to resolve the $V^*(s')$ in Equation 3, we obtain a recursive definition of $Q(s,a)$.

$$Q(s,a) = \sum_{s'} P(s'|s,a)[R(s'|s,a) + \gamma max_{a'} Q(s',a')] \tag{5}$$

This recursive definition of Q forms the basis of the Q-Learning algorithm [17]. Q-learning starts with some initial values of $Q(s,a)$, and updates $Q(s,a)$ recursively using the actual reward received by the agent in a trial-and-error process. The complete learning process is depicted in the algorithm in Fig. 3.

In this algorithm, we assume that there is a single initial state, i.e. s_0, and a set of terminal states, i.e. S_r, in a given MDP. In the beginning, $Q(s,a)$ is initialized. For instance, $Q(s,a)$ can be set to 0 for all s and a. Then, the learning process is performed recursively. In each episode (round), the learner starts from the initial state s_0, and takes a sequence of actions by following the ϵ-greedy policy (which is introduced subsequently). The episode ends when the agent reaches a

Initialize $Q(s,a)$;
for each episode **do**
    $s \leftarrow s_0$;
    for $s \notin S_r$ **do**
        Choose $a \in A(s)$ based on ϵ-greedy policy;
        Execute a, observe reward r and new state s';
        $Q(s,a) \leftarrow Q(s,a) + \alpha[r + \gamma max_{a'}Q(s',a') - Q(s,a)]$;
        $s \leftarrow s'$;
    end for
end for

Fig. 3. The Q-Learning Algorithm

terminal state $s \in S_r$. After executing each action, the learner updates $Q(s,a)$ using the following equation.

$$Q(s,a) \leftarrow Q(s,a) + \alpha[r + \gamma max_{a'}Q(s',a') - Q(s,a)] \tag{6}$$

On the right side of Equation 6, $r+\gamma max_{a'}Q(s',a')$ represents the newly observed reward (see Equation 5), and $Q(s,a)$ represents the previously observed reward. We can see that the function does not intend to use the newly observed value to completely replace the old $Q(s,a)$ value. Instead, it only updates a certain portion of the $Q(s,a)$ value, which is quantified by $\alpha(0 \leq \alpha \leq 1)$. α is called learning ratio, which is an important tuning factor in Q-Learning. Intuitively, the higher the learning ratio, the faster the learner will find the optimal policy. However, the higher the learning ratio, it is more likely that the learner be locked in a local optimal region.

The ϵ-greedy policy is used by the learner for executing the MDP during the learning. $\epsilon(\epsilon < 1)$ is the deterministic parameter of this policy. Given a state s, based on the current $Q(s,a)$ function, the ϵ-greedy policy chooses to execute the optimal action (i.e. $argmax_a Q(s,a)$) with a probability of $1 - \epsilon$. With a probability ϵ, the policy chooses a random action to execute. On the one hand, the ϵ-greedy policy ensures that $Q(s,a)$ is being optimized continuously. On the other hand, it guarantees that all the available actions are given chances to be tried out by the learner.

3.2   Applying Q-Learning to WSC-MDP

Our mechanism applies the Q-Learning algorithm to a WSC-MDP based service composition to determine the optimal or near-optimal policy at runtime. Rather than treating the Q-Learner as a learning system, our framework uses it directly as the execution engine of service compositions. Upon receiving a user request's, the system starts an execution of the service composition. It applies the ϵ-greedy policy of the Q-Learner to pick a service workflow to execute. This execution is in turn treated as an episode of the learning process. The ϵ-greedy policy and the Q-functions are updated afterwards, based on the newly observed reward.

By combining execution and learning, our framework achieves self-adaptivity automatically. When the environment changes, a service composition will change its policy accordingly, based on its new observation of reward. It does not require prior knowledge about the QoS attributes of the component services, but is able to achieve the optimal execution policy through learning.

Reward Assessment

To apply Q-Learning to a WSC-MDP, an important issue is to define the reward of the learning process. As the ultimate objective of our mechanism is to maximize user satisfaction. The reward should be a certain measure of user satisfaction. Information about user satisfaction can be obtained through two channels in a service composition system. This first channel is the QoS attributes that can be measured after the execution of each service. These QoS attributes include service fee, response time, availability, etc.. Our framework uses the following function to aggregate the various QoS attributes into a single reward value:

$$R(s) = \sum w_i \times \frac{Att_i^s - Att_i^{min}}{Att_i^{max} - Att_i^{min}} \tag{7}$$

where Att_i^s represent the observed value of the ith attribute of service s, and Att_i^{max} and Att_i^{min} represent the maximum and minimum values of Att_i for all services. w_i is the weighting factor of Att_i. w_i is positive if users prefer Att_i to be high (e.g. availability). w_i is negative if users prefer Att_i to be low (e.g. service fee and response time).

The second channel to assess user satisfaction is user feedback. A service composition system can allow a user to rate the composite service after each transaction. The rating is a kind of direct measure of the final reward received by the user. User feedback allow the learner to capture some properties that cannot be directly quantified. A typical property of such kind is user experience. Different from the QoS based reward, which can be measured at each learning step, users' feedback can only be measured at the final step of a episode. Fortunately, the Q-Learning approach is able to propagate the influence of the final reward to the intermediate services of the composition. Even when QoS attributes are not used, user feedbacks can still allow the learner to obtain a near-optimal policy.

Q-Function Initialization

Using Q-Learning, our framework does not need to know the QoS attributes of services to obtain the optimal execution policy. However, knowledge about QoS is still beneficial, as it allows the learner to obtain the optimal policy quickly. To incorporate the known QoS information into the learning process, we use this information to initialize the Q-Functions, i.e., $Q(s,a)$. In other words, for a service s whose QoS attributes are known, we calculate its initial $Q(s,a)$ by applying Equation 7 to its QoS attributes directly. For a service s whose QoS attributes are unknown, we approximate its initial QoS attributes by averaging the QoS values of other services, and apply Equation 7 to the approximated values to calculate $Q(s,a)$. As shown in our experiments, this initialization method is able to remarkably accelerate the learning process.

4   Experimental Evaluation

We conducted simulation to evaluate the properties of our service composition mechanism. This section presents some of the results.

4.1   Simulation Setup

We randomly generated WSC-MDP transition graphs to simulate service compositions. Each simulated WSC-MDP had a single initial state and two terminal states. The number of state nodes and the number of service nodes in a WSC-MDP graph ranged between $1,000 - 10,000$ and $1,000 - 40,000$ respectively. Each service node in a simulated WSC-MDP graph had at least one out-edge. The average number of out-edges per service node was set to 2.

We considered two QoS attributes of services. They were service fee and execution time. We assigned each service node in a simulated WSC-MDP graph with random QoS values. The values followed normal distribution. To simulate the dynamic environment, we periodically varied the QoS values of existing services based on a certain frequency.

We applied the Q-Learner introduced in Section 4 to execute the simulated service compositions. The reward function used by the learner were solely based on the two QoS attributes. We did not consider the reward information obtained from user feedback, as a simulation of user feedback may not reflect the reality. However, we believe that reward based on QoS can provide an adequate view of how a service composition can adapt to the environment through reinforcement learning. In the experiment results, without special announcement, the discount factor γ of the Q-Learner is set to 0.9, the learning rate α is set to 0.2 and the ϵ is set to 0.6.

Our experiments were performed on a 2.13GHz Intel Core2 PC with 2GB of RAM.

4.2   Efficiency of Learning

In the first stage of the evaluation, we studied how efficiently reinforcement learning would enable our service compositions to achieve the optimal execution policy. We assumed that the service composition system has zero knowledge about the QoS of the component services, and let the Q-Learner guide the service compositions to gradually reach the optimal policy. We conducted three sets of experiments to evaluate the efficiency.

In the first set of experiments, we fixed the number of states of the simulated WSC-MDP to 1,000 and the number of services for each state to 4. We varied the learning rate α from 0.1 to 0.6. For each α, we executed the service composition for 400 times. In other words, the learning was performed for 400 episodes for each α. We plot the cumulative reward of each episode in Fig. 4. As the figure shows, for all α, the cumulative rewards started converging before the 400th episodes. We can see that a higher learning rate can accelerate the learning process, whereas a smaller learning rate is helpful to avoid local optimality. As shown

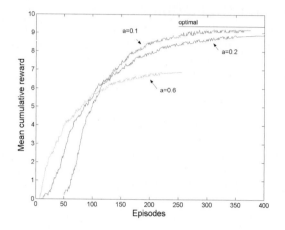

Fig. 4. Efficiency of Learning with Different Learning Rates

in Fig. 4, when α=0.6, although the cumulative reward increases very fast, the service composition failed to find the optimal policy. When α=0.1, the cumulative reward increases slowly, while it guarantee to achieve the optimal policy. When α=0.2, the learner seemed to achieve a good tradeoff between speed and effectiveness. Hence, we set α to 0.2 in the rest of our experiments. Fig. 4 also shows that the improvement made by the learning in the early stage is usually much higher than that in the late stage. This implies that a near-optimal policy can usually be identified much more quickly than the final optimal policy.

In the second set of experiments, we fixed the learning rate α to 0.2, but varied the parameter of the ϵ-greedy policy from 0.2 to 0.8. We studied how fast the cumulative reward converged to the optimal value during the learning. The cumulative reward is regarded to converge if the difference between its values in previous 10 consecutive episodes is below 1%. As shown in Fig. 5, the convergence time varies with ϵ. When $\epsilon = 0.6$, the convergence speed is the fastest. Hence, we set ϵ to 0.6 in the rest of our experiments.

Our third set of experiments aimed to analyze the relationship between the learning speed and the size of service composition.

Firstly, we fixed the number of services of each state to 4 and varied the number of states in a WSC-MDP graph from 1,000 to 10,000. We observed

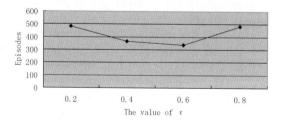

Fig. 5. Learning Speed vs ϵ

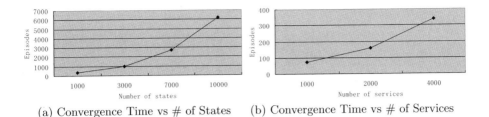

(a) Convergence Time vs # of States   (b) Convergence Time vs # of Services

Fig. 6. Influence of Service Composition Size on Learning Speed

how fast the cumulative reward converged to optimal value during the learning. The results are shown in Fig. 6(a). As expected, the convergence time increases polynomially with the number of states. This is because the number of alternative workflows in a service composition usually increase exponentially with the number of states. Because of the efficiency of Q-Learning, the convergence time actually increases much slower than the number of workflows.

Secondly, we fixed the number of states to 1,000, and varied the number of alternative services in each state from 1 to 4. The results are shown in Fig. 6(b). The convergence time increases almost linearly with the number of services. This also shows the efficiency of Q-Learning, as the number of alternative workflows in a composition increases polynomially with the number of services.

A WSC-MDP graph with 10,000 states and 40,000 services seems to represent a fairly complex service composition. By using Q-Learning, our framework is able to identify the optimal execution policy with 6,000 episodes. In other words, once the composition has been executed for 6,000 times, it will reach the optimal status. As indicated by Fig. 4, a composition can reach a near-optimal status with a even faster speed.

4.3   Adaptivity to Changes

In the second stage of our evaluation, we studied how well our service compositions adapt to the changes of the environment.

In the first set of experiments, we simulated the changes of the environment by changing the QoS attributes of the services periodically. We assumed that the system have no knowledge about the services' QoS attributes, and let it rely on Q-Learning to learn the optimal execution policy. During the learning process, we changed the QoS attributes of the service in three kinds of frequencies. Namely, for every 100 episodes of learning, we varied 1%, 5% and 10% of the service's QoS attributes respectively. We observed how these changes would influence the effectiveness of learning.

Fig. 7 shows the growth of the cumulative reward during the learning process. We can see that by increasing the change rate we can delay a service composition to reach its optimal execution policy. However, the changes do not stop the optimization process. The execution policy is still being continually optimized when the learning goes on. When the turnover is as high as 10% per 100 episodes,

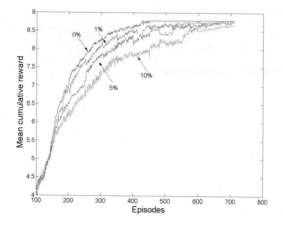

Fig. 7. Influence of Changes on Learning

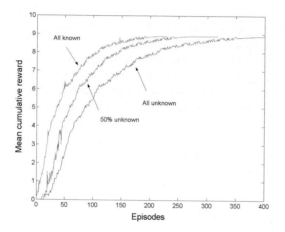

Fig. 8. Influence of Initial Knowledge

the service composition can still eventually reach a near optimal policy and stick to it afterwards.

In the final set of experiments, we studied how initial knowledge of services' QoS attributes can accelerate the learning process. We investigated in three cases. In the first case, all services' QoS attributes were known. In the second case, 50% of services' QoS attributes were known. In the last case, no QoS information is known. We applied the approach introduced in Section 4.2 to initialize the Q-function of the Q-Learner. The resulting learning processes are plotted in Fig. 8. The results show that the learning speed can be significantly improved by exploring the prior knowledge about services.

5   Related Work

The existing technologies for service composition mainly aim to achieve two objectives [19,1,18]. On the one hand, a service composition should provide the functionalities required by customers. On the other hand, the quality of a service composition should be optimized. Most of the previous approaches address the two issues in two separate phases.

In the first phase, a set of tools are used to create an abstract workflow of a service composition, which aims to satisfy users' requirements on functionality [13]. The applied techniques include AI planning [11,14], π-Calculus [16], Petri Nets [7], Model Checking [12], Finite State Machines [3], as well as Markov Decision Process (MDP) [5,6,4].

In the second phase, an optimal set of concrete services are selected to instantiate the abstract workflow. It generates a concrete service composition with the optimal Quality of Service (QoS). This phase is also known as service optimization. In [19], Zeng et al proposed a service quality model based on non-functional attributes, which has been widely used by the others [2,20,18] to perform service optimization. While the non-functional attributes of component services can reflect the quality of a service composition. However, they do not capture all the features of a composition. For example, user experience usually cannot be directly assessed using these attributes. In contrast, our learning based approach is able to take some implicit features into account. For instance, user feedbacks can be used by the learner to optimize the composition.

Recently, there have been a number of proposals for performing service optimization at runtime. An example is the work of Mei et al [9]. They applied social network analysis to rank services. Based on the ranking, their approach automatically selects the best service to run a workflow. Similarly, in [10], a tree-based algorithm was used to conduct runtime service selection. In theory, these two approaches are able to cope with evolving service quality. However, as they assume that information about QoS is known and up to date, they cannot deal with the real world cases where such information is unknown. Furthermore, they all assume a static workflow.

A fundamental difference between our approach and the previous approaches is that our service composition does not rely on an static workflow. By contrast, a service composition in our framework is able to integrate multiple alternative workflows and services. When executing the composition, our system decides which workflow and services to execute using its real-time knowledge. In addition, our system do not need to know the non-functional properties of services a-priori. Instead, it applies reinforcement learning to obtain the optimal solution by directly studying the results of execution. Therefore, our mechanism of service composition can be highly adaptive to a dynamic environment.

6   Conclusion

This paper introduces a novel framework for service composition. In contrast to most of the previous approaches, which develop service compositions upon static workflow, our framework integrates multiple workflows and alternative services into a single composition. The concrete workflows and services used for execution are determined at runtime, based on the environment and the status of component services. By applying reinforcement learning, our framework is able to obtain the optimal execution policies of service compositions at runtime. Our experimental results show that our service compositions can obtain (near-)optimal execution policies efficiently, and they are highly adaptive to the changes of the component services.

References

1. Agarwal, V., Dasgupta, K., Karnik, N.M., Kumar, A., Kundu, A., Mittal, S., Srivastava, B.: A service creation environment based on end to end composition of web services. In: WWW, pp. 128–137 (2005)
2. Ardagna, D., Pernici, B.: Global and local qos guarantee in web service selection. In: Bussler, C.J., Haller, A. (eds.) BPM 2005. LNCS, vol. 3812, pp. 32–46. Springer, Heidelberg (2006)
3. Berardi, D., Calvanese, D., Giacomo, G.D., Lenzerini, M., Mecella, M.: Automatic service composition based on behavioral descriptions. Int. J. Cooperative Inf. Syst. 14(4), 333–376 (2005)
4. Chen, K., Xu, J., Reiff-Marganiec, S.: Markov-htn planning approach to enhance flexibility of automatic web service composition. In: ICWS, pp. 9–16 (2009)
5. Doshi, P., Goodwin, R., Akkiraju, R., Verma, K.: Dynamic workflow composition: Using markov decision processes. Int. J. Web Service Res. 2(1), 1–17 (2005)
6. Gao, A., Yang, D., Tang, S., Zhang, M.: Web service composition using markov decision processes. In: Fan, W., Wu, Z., Yang, J. (eds.) WAIM 2005. LNCS, vol. 3739, pp. 308–319. Springer, Heidelberg (2005)
7. Hamadi, R., Benatallah, B.: A petri net-based model for web service composition. In: ADC, pp. 191–200 (2003)
8. Kaelbling, L.P., Littman, M.L., Moore, A.P.: Reinforcement learning: A survey. J. Artif. Intell. Res (JAIR) 4, 237–285 (1996)
9. Mei, L., Chan, W.K., Tse, T.H.: An adaptive service selection approach to service composition. In: ICWS, pp. 70–77 (2008)
10. Oh, M., Baik, J., Kang, S., Choi, H.-J.: An efficient approach for qos aware service selection based on a tree-based algorithm. In: ACIS-ICIS, pp. 605–610 (2008)
11. Oh, S.-C., Lee, D., Kumara, S.R.T.: Effective web service composition in diverse and large-scale service networks. IEEE TSC 1(1), 15–32 (2008)
12. Rao, J., Küngas, P., Matskin, M.: Composition of semantic web services using linear logic theorem proving. Inf. Syst. 31(4-5), 340–360 (2006)
13. Rao, J., Su, X.: A survey of automated web service composition methods. In: Cardoso, J., Sheth, A.P. (eds.) SWSWPC 2004. LNCS, vol. 3387, pp. 43–54. Springer, Heidelberg (2005)
14. Shin, D.-H., Lee, K.-H., Suda, T.: Automated generation of composite web services based on functional semantics. J. Web Sem. 7(4), 332–343 (2009)
15. Sutton, R.S., Barto, A.G.: Reinforcement Learning: An Introduction. The MIT Press, Cambridge (1998)
16. Wang, Y.-L., Yu, X.-L.: Formalization and verification of automatic composition based on pi-calculus for semantic web service, December 1-30, vol. 1, pp. 103–106 (2009)

17. Watkins, C.J.C.H.: Learning from Delayed Rewards. PhD thesis, Kings College, Oxford (1989)
18. Yu, Q., Bouguettaya, A.: Framework for web service query algebra and optimization. TWEB 2(1) (2008)
19. Zeng, L., Benatallah, B., Ngu, A.H.H., Dumas, M., Kalagnanam, J., Chang, H.: Qos-aware middleware for web services composition. IEEE Trans. Softw. Eng. 30(5), 311–327 (2004)
20. Zeng, L., Ngu, A., Benatallah, B., Podorozhny, R., Lei, H.: Dynamic composition and optimization of web services. Distributed and Parallel Databases 24(1), 45–72 (2008)

A Service Execution Control Framework for Policy Enforcement

Masahiro Tanaka, Yohei Murakami, and Donghui Lin

Language Grid Project, National Institute of Information and Communications
Technology (NICT),
3-5 Hikaridai, Seika-cho, Kyoto, Japan
{mtnk,yohei,lindh}@nict.go.jp

Abstract. Service-oriented collective intelligence, which creates new value by combining various programs and data as services, requires many participants. Therefore it is crucial for an infrastructure for service-oriented collective intelligence to satisfy various policies of service providers. Some previous works have proposed methods for service selection and adaptation which are required to satisfy service providers' policies. However, they do not show how to check if the selected services and adaptation processes certainly satisfy service providers' policies. In this paper, we propose an execution control framework which realizes service selection and adaptation in order to satisfy service providers' policies. On the framework, the behaviors of composite services are verified against service providers' policies based on model checking. We also formally defined the effect of the proposed execution control APIs. This enabled us to update models for verification at runtime and reduce the search space for verification.

1 Introduction

Services computing technologies had initially aimed to realize flexible development and management of information system of enterprises. However, services computing are now applied to service-oriented collective intelligence, which creates new values by combining a wide variety of programs and contents provided by various providers.

For example, the Language Grid[1] is one of the infrastructures for service-oriented collective intelligence and has achieved interoperability of language resources such as machine translators and dictionaries by wrapping them as Web services with standardized interfaces. More than 120 organizations have joined the Language Grid and 90 language services are available on the infrastructure.

It is crucial to have many service providers join in order to realize for service-oriented collective intelligence. Service providers usually have their own policies about use of their service including limitation of transferred data, constraints on combinations of services and so on. Therefore an infrastructure for service-oriented collective intelligence must be capable of satisfying their policies. From this aspect, service-oriented collective intelligence is quite different with traditional collective knowledge which relies on single license e.g. Wikipedia. As for

P.P. Maglio et al. (Eds.): ICSOC 2010, LNCS 6470, pp. 108–121, 2010.

the Language Grid, it allows service providers to set permission to use their service for each user and limit amount of transferred data.

One of the major advantages of services computing is a flexibility of development and management. This is the reason why a composite service is usually defined as a workflow. Users can select services which are assigned to tasks in the workflow at runtime according to his/her requirements. On the other hand, in the context of service-oriented collective intelligence, the combination of selected services must satisfy service providers' policy. Otherwise, some adaptation process should be applied in order to change the behavior of the services and make them follow the given policy.

Many previous works have proposed methods for service selection for composite services[2,3]. Moreover, to adapt behaviors of services without changing models of the composite services, various methods using Aspect-oriented Programming (AOP)[4] or proxy for message exchange[5] have been proposed. In [6], a comprehensive process for service selection and adaptation is also proposed.

However, service selection and adaptation during execution make it difficult to verify that service providers' policies are satisfied. Applying an adaptation process to satisfy a policy may lead to violation of another policy which was satisfied before the adaptation. Although model checking for composite services[7] can verify behaviors, such method has the following problems.

Dynamic change of model. Runtime adaptation changes the behavior of the target composite service during execution. It is unrealistic to manually change the model for verification.

Verification cost. Verification is performed by exhaustively searching execution states. Runtime verification may decline the performance of the composite service.

To solve the problems, we propose an execution control framework whose behaviors can be verified by extending the methods proposed in [8] and [6]. We also show a reduction of search space for runtime verification according to service selection and adaptation during execution.

The rest of the paper is organized as follows. In Section 2, we show a scenario which represents the problems to be solved. In Section 3, we overview the system architecture which solves the problems. Then we detail the solution, which consists of an execution control framework for composite service and application of model checking in Section 4 and Section 5 respectively. After introducing related works in Section 6, we conclude this paper in Section 7.

2   Scenario

In this section, we show a typical scenario and the problems to be solved by taking a composite service for translation on the Language Grid[1] as an example. Suppose a composite service combines a morphological analyzer, a machine translator, and technical term dictionaries. This service improves translation quality of technical documents by translating technical terms in the given sentences using the technical term dictionaries, not the machine translator.

Figure 1 shows the overview of the composite service. A square which contains a circle represents a service invocation. First the given sentences are divided into morphemes by the morphological analyzer. Next dictionaries find technical terms which consist of the morphemes and return the translation of the technical terms. Finally the translator translates the whole sentences.

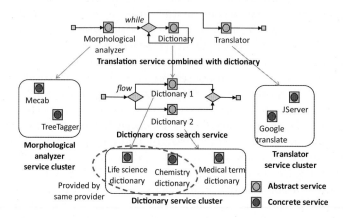

Fig. 1. A composite service for translation

As shown in Fig. 1, we assume that a composite service is defined in a workflow description language such as WS-BPEL[9]. In a composite service, the constituent services define only the interface and are not bound to any endpoint. We refer to such a service as an *abstract service*. For example, on the Language Grid, an abstract service is defined for each service type such as translators and dictionaries. Endpoints for the services are determined when the composite service is invoked or during execution. A service to which an endpoint is bound is called a *concrete service*.

A set of concrete services which can be bound to an abstract service is called a service cluster. In Fig. 1, there are more than one concrete services in each service cluster. In our example, we bind one concrete service to the morphological analyzer and the machine translator. For the dictionary, we first bind a composite service for cross search and then bind two concrete services to abstract services in the cross search composite service.

When we use the composite service, we need to select concrete services which satisfy service providers' policies. Assume that both the life science dictionary and the chemistry dictionary are provided by the same provider and that the provider prohibits concurrent access to the two services to prevent a user from giving too much load. On the other hand, the composite service allows two dictionary services to be concurrently executed because the designer of the composite service does not know which services are bound. In the case that the two dictionaries are bound, the execution of the composite service violates the provider's policy. Since the providers' policies must be certainly satisfied, some verification method such as model checking should be applied.

However, the uncertainty of service execution often causes the following problems. Assume the dictionary service replaces the technical terms found in the input sentences with words in the target languages and that the translator does not translate words in the target language. In this way, we can obtain a translation result whose technical terms are translated by the dictionary, not by the translator. But this may cause a failure of execution of the translator because the length of input sentences changes by the word replacement and may exceeds the limit of input length of the translator.

One of the solutions to this failure is adding an adaptation process, which divides the input string into sentences, translates each of them and merge the translation results. But applying adaptation processes may cause other violation of service providers' policies because the business logic is changed. For example, the service provider for a dictionary service and translator service may give discount for a plan of the same count of invocation of the services. Therefore we need to modify the model for verification according to the changes of business logic and perform verification again.

The first problem of the above approach is that it is unrealistic for the user or the human operator to modify models for verification during execution. Another problem is that verification during execution may decline the performance of the composite service.

3   System Architecture

In this section, we describe the system architecture which contains an execution control framework for runtime service selection and adaptation and a verification framework for dynamic changes of the business change.

Figure 2 shows the overview of the system proposed in this paper. The system consists of the composite service execution engine, service selector and behavior verifier.

The composite service execution engine interprets and executes the deployed composite services. It is extended to provide APIs for adaptation which allows changing business logics of composite services and get/set execution state of running instance of a composite service. Using the APIs, we can define an adaptation service, which is a composite service and implements adaptation process for other composite services. The interaction between the adaptation service and the target composite service is configured by a supervision service, which is also a composite service and uses the APIs.

The service selector finds a combination of services which satisfy service providers' policies and binds them to abstract services. If there is no combination which satisfies the given policies, it searches for adaptation processes which can change properties of the services and satisfy given policies referring to profiles of available services and adaptation processes.

The verifier checks that a composite services satisfies given policy based on the model of the composite service, the model of the adaptation service and changes of business logic defined in the supervision service. It uses SPIN model checker.

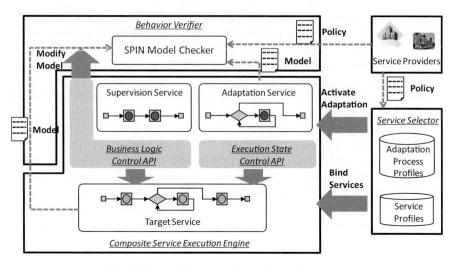

Fig. 2. An architecture for policy enforcement

We describe the steps of service execution on the architecture below. First the composite service execution engine is invoked by a request from a user. Since abstract composite services are deployed on the engine, user can specify bindings for constituent services of the composite services. For abstract services to which the user does not bind a concrete service, the service selector selects concrete services to be bound. Adaptation processes to be applied are also activated if needed.

Through execution of the composite service, the following two types of check are performed.

Execution state check. Check if the combination of services and variables defined in a composite service satisfy the given policies. This check is performed before each service invocation.

Behavioral check. Check if the execution state and protocols of service invocation. This check is performed before an adaptation process is executed.

Both checks are also performed when execution of a composite service starts. If the service selector cannot find a combination which passes execution state check, it applies adaptation processes to services. For example, when the system finds that the input string exceeds the limit of length, the adaptation process which divides an input string into sentences can be applied to pass the check. The selected adaptation process must pass behavioral check using SPIN model checker[10]. When it cannot finally find an appropriate combination of services or adaptation processes, the execution of the composite service fails. The method for finding a combination of services and adaptation processes is proposed in [6].

4   Adaptation Using Execution Control

The architecture shown in the previous section contains adaptation mechanism. The adaptation requires flexible changes of behaviors of composite services, e.g.

adding a parallel process and skipping defined a service invocation. We defined two types of execution control APIs to realize the adaptation. In this section, we describe the details of the APIs and a framework for adaptation using the APIs.

4.1   Execution State Control

The composite service defined in WS-BPEL, the standard language for describing composite services, consists of *activities*. An activity corresponds to an atomic process in a composite service such as service invocation and assignment of variables. Most of WS-BPEL execution engines define state for activities. We assume that an activity is in one of the following states: Ready, Running, Finished, Suspended.

A composite service defined in WS-BPEL also has variables and partner links which are information about service to be invoked. A partner link has an endpoint address of the invoked service. Therefore we can change invoked services at runtime by changing the endpoint address set to the partner link, without changing the model of the composite service.

In this paper, we assume the state of a running instance of a composite service is defined by the combination of states of activities, values of variables and endpoint addresses set to partner links. Most of constraints which come from service providers' policies are defined by the information. For example, the violation of the limit of input length can be found by checking the value of the variable input to the translator before invocation.

Table 1. Execution control APIs

API	Effect
getVariable(pid, varname)	Get the value of the specified variable. This API takes a process ID and a variable name as parameters.
setVariable(pid, varname, value)	Set a value to the specified variable. This API takes a process ID, variable name and values to be set as parameters.
getPartnerLink(pid, plname)	Get the specified partner link. This API takes a process ID and a partner link name as parameters.
setPartnerLink(pid, plname, address)	Set a partner link. This API takes a process ID, a partner link and an endpoint address to be set to the partner link as parameters.
getActivityState(pid)	Get states of all activities in the specified process. This takes a process ID as parameters.
suspend(pid, activity)	Suspend the specified running activity. This API takes a process ID and activity as parameters.
resume(pid, activity)	Resume the specified suspended activity. This API takes a process ID and activity as parameters.
getProcessIds(sid)	Get process IDs of running instances of the specified composite service. This API takes a service ID as a parameter.

On the basis of the above assumption, we realized the APIs for execution control shown in Table 1. These APIs get/set variables, partner links and states of activities. We also provide an API for getting information of a target process.

WS-BPEL provides functionalities for getting/setting variables and partner links in the same running instance. On the other hand, we provide APIs for access information in other instances of composite services. This is because we need to consider all processes which use a service in order to satisfy policies of the provider of the service.

Moreover, even in the same instance, WS-BPEL does not provide functionalities for getting/setting states of activities. Therefore we usually need to modify the model of the composite services and add an interface which allows access to the execution state of the composite services. However, the designer of the composite service does not know what interface is required because a combination of services are decided at runtime.

Generally speaking, human operator monitors and manages execution state of composite services. They usually have a process or a workflow for the monitoring and management. Therefore we allow them to implement a composite service which realizes the same process as they perform by providing the APIs as Web service. The composite service can be defined also in WS-BPEL. Therefore we apply existing methods or tools for business process modeling.

4.2   Business Logic Control

After defining an adaptaion process, we need to integrate it into the target composite service. For example, using the APIs shown in Table 1, we can implement a composite service which gets an input string to translator, divides it into sentences, and merges after translating each of them. We need to define the protocol between the target composite service and the composite service for adaptation.

Most of previous works on adaptation for composite services have proposed methods for adding processes to existing composite services based on AOP[4,5]. But more flexible adaptations such as adding a parallel process or skipping activity are often required for adaptation in order to satisfy service providers' policies. Moreover, we need to apply adaptation at runtime because some violations of policies are found during execution.

According to these requirements, we provide the APIs shown in Table 2 for changing business logic. We also make these APIs accessible as Web service. Therefore we can define a composite services for changing business logic in order to integrate a certain adaptation process.

4.3   Adaptation Example

We can realize various adaptation processes by implementing composite services which use the APIs shown in this Section. We refer to a composite service which uses APIs for getting/setting execution state as an adaptation service, and a composite service which uses APIs for changing business logic as a supervision service.

Table 2. Business logic control APIs

API	Effect
`skip(pid, start, end)`	Skip activities in the specified range. This API takes a process ID and activity locations which specify the range to be skipped.
`fork_join(pid, start, end, invocation)`	Add a parallel process to the specified instance. This takes a process ID, activity locations where the parallel process starts/finishes and invocation information (endpoint address, operation and input data) as parameters.
`fork(pid, start, invocation)`	Add a parallel process to the specified instance. This takes a process ID, an activity location where the parallel process starts and invocation information as parameters.
`insert(pid, start, pname, param)`	Invoke a service at the specified location. This takes a process ID, an activity location where the invoked process starts and invocation information as parameters.

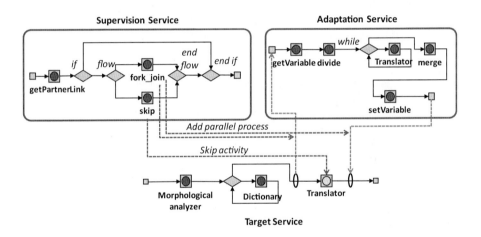

Fig. 3. Adaptation for division and merging

Figure 3 shows an example of adaptation for the composite service shown in Fig. 1. The adaptation divides input string to translator and merges them after translating each of them.

The Supervision Service shown in Fig. 3 is invoked after Service Selector decides to use the Adaptation Service. First it checks the endpoint for translator `getPartnerLink`, and then integrates the Adaptation Service into the target composite service (`fork_join`) and skip invocation of translator defined in the target service (`skip`).

The adaptation service first reads the variable which is set as the input to the translator (`getVariable`). Then it divides the input to sentences and translates each of them in loop. The traslation results are merged and set to the variable which is set to the output of the translator (`setVariable`).

5 Verification during Execution

When a supervision process is executed, the business logic of the target service is changed as shown in Fig. 3. Therefore execution of the target service may violate policies which were once satisfied. This is the reason we should perform behavioral check whenever adaptation is applied. In this section, we first show how models for verification are changed based on business logic APIs described in the previous section. Then we propose an idea for reducing computational cost for verification in order to prevent decline of performance.

5.1 Updating Model

Behavioral check described in Section 3 uses SPIN model checker and requires model of composite services described in Promela. We assume the models for SPIN can be generated from WS-BPEL processes. Although it is impossible to generate models which represents complete behaviors of a composite service, in [7], the author shows the method generating a model described in Promela from composite services described in WS-BPEL by introducing some abstraction.

Using SPIN and model described in Promela, we can verify that policies represented as LTL (Liner Temporal Logic) formula are satisfied. For example, the following formula f represents that the life science dictionary service ($S_{life\_science}$) and the chemistry dictionary service ($S_{chemistry}$) are not concurrently executed. $state()$ returns the state of the given service.

$$f = \Box\neg((state(S_{life\_science}) = Running) \wedge (state(S_{chemistry}) = Running))$$

SPIN transforms models described in Promela into an automaton which represents behaviors of the system. The automaton of the whole system including the target composite services and adaptation services can be obtained as an asynchronous product of automatons of target composite services $S_1...S_m$ and those of adaptation services $a_1...a_n$ as shown below.

$$M_A = M_{S_1} \times ...M_{S_m} \times M_{a_1} \times ... \times M_{a_n}$$

The LTL formula f is satisfied if a synchronous product of M_A and $\overline{M_f}$, which is an automaton corresponding to the negation of f, is empty.

M_A needs to be changed when business logic control APIs are executed. Since it is unrealistic to manually modify the model during execution, we defined modification of an automaton for each API in Table 2.

Figure 4 shows the process for fork_join. The idea of the modification is to add states for sending requests/receiving response. In Fig. 4, we omit the process ID from the parameter list for simplicity. Channels which represent sending a request to/receiving a response from the adaptation service are defined. States which correspond to activity location specified as start or end are also defined. The automaton can have more than one state which corresponds to start or end because the states can have the values of variables and partner links.

```
fork_join(start, end, invocation)

ch!op <- send action on channel which represents invocation
Sstart <- set of states which corresponds to start
ch?op <- receive action on channel which represents invocation
Send <- set of states which corresponds to end

for each Sstart in Sstart
  Sto_start <- set of states which have transition to Sstart
  for each Sto_start in Sto_start
    create node Snew
    replace transition(Sto_start, Sstart, act) with transition(Sto_start, Snew, act)
    create transition(Snew, Sstart, ch!op)
  end for
end for
for each Send in Send
  Sto_end <- set of states which have transition to Send
  for each Sto_end in Sto_end
    create node Snew
    replace transition(Sto_end, Send, act) with transition(Sto_end, Snew, act)
    create transition(Snew, Send, ch?op)
  end for
end for
```

Fig. 4. Updating automaton of verification model (fork_join)

In the first loop, the algorithm inserts a new state before the activity location specified as start. The transition from/to the new state are also created. The transition from the new state to the state which corresponds to the activity location specified as start is performed when the send action on the channel is executed. In the latter part of the algorithm, the same goes for states which correspond to the activity location specified as end.

The modification process for other APIs are shown in Fig. 5.

5.2 Reducing Execution State Space

Behavioral check requires exhaustive search on state space and may decline the performance of composite services. Therefore reducing search space contributes to improving the performance.

Business logic control APIs does not affect states between the initial state and states which corresponds to the activity location specified as start. This is the reason the states do not have to be checked once verification is performed before starting execution of the composite service.

On the other hand, we need to check reachability from the current state to the states which are added by the processes shown in Fig. 4 and Fig. 5.

Based on the above idea, we search only transition to states which are newly added by the processes in Fig. 4 and Fig. 5 if the search reaches the state which has a transition to the newly added states.

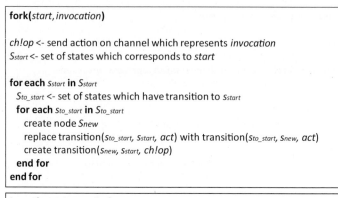

fork(*start, invocation*)

ch!op <- send action on channel which represents *invocation*
S_{start} <- set of states which corresponds to *start*

for each S_{start} **in** S_{start}
  S_{to_start} <- set of states which have transition to S_{start}
  for each S_{to_start} **in** S_{to_start}
    create node S_{new}
    replace transition(S_{to_start}, S_{start}, *act*) with transition(S_{to_start}, S_{new}, *act*)
    create transition(S_{new}, S_{start}, *ch!op*)
  end for
end for

---

insert(*start, invocation*)

ch!op <- send action on channel which represents *invocation*
ch?op <- receive action on channel which represents *invocation*
S_{start} <- set of states which corresponds to *start*

for each S_{start} **in** S_{start}
  S_{to_start} <- set of states which have transition to S_{start}
  for each S_{to_start} **in** S_{to_start}
    create node S_{new1}, S_{new2}
    replace transition(S_{to_start}, S_{start}, *act*) with transition(S_{to_start}, S_{new1}, *act*)
    create transition(S_{new1}, S_{new2}, *ch!op*)
    create transition(S_{new2}, S_{start}, *ch?op*)
  end for
end for

---

skip(*start, end*)

S_{start} <- set of states which corresponds to *start*
S_{end} <- set of states which corresponds to *end*

for each S_{start} **in** S_{start}
  S_{to_start} <- set of states which have transition to S_{start}
  for each S_{to_start} **in** S_{to_start}
    for each S_{end} **in** S_{end}
      act <- *action* for transition from S_{to_start} to S_{start}
      replace path(S_{to_start}, S_{end}) with transition(S_{to_start}, S_{new}, *act*)
    end for
  end for
end for

Fig. 5. Updating automaton of verification model (`fork`, `insert`, `skip`)

Figure 6 shows the algorithm. First $Initialize()$ is executed, then search is recursively executed. This is based on depth-first search, which is used by SPIN as default, and `satisfy` checks if the condition are satisfied or not. The condition is given according to f which represents service providers' policies. If any of states does not satisfy the condition, the algorithm immediately exits and returns error.

```
Initialize()
  Add the initial state to State Space
  Push the initial state to stack

search()
  Stop <- top of stack

  if Stop does not satisfy the condition
    exit(error)
  end if

  Snext <- set of states to which can be directly moved from Stop
  for each Snew in Snext
    if Snew is a state added by business logic control APIs
      if Snew is not in State Space
        add Snew to State Space
        push Snew to stack
        search()
      end if
    end if
  end for
  pop from stack
```

Fig. 6. An execution state search algorithm

6   Related Works

This work shows architecture based on runtime service selection and adaptation with verification for an infrastructure where many service providers join. In this section, we introduce some related works on verification of composite services, service selection and adaptation.

For verification, various approaches including process algebra, Petri net, finite state machine or logic have been proposed. Nakajima proposed a method for generating description in Promela, which is used for SPIN model checker, from a WS-BPEL process[7]. In the paper, the author shows an abstraction for verification and refers to features which are characteristic of WS-BPEL such as dead path elimination. Our paper assumes that the initial model of composite services are generated by such a method.

Narayanan et al. modeled composite Web services in OWL-S using Petri nets in order to verify the composite Web services [11]. Their work verifies the reachability to certain states and detects deadlocks.

Ankolekar et al. proposed a method transforming a composite Web service in OWL-S into descriptions in a language for model checking[12]. This makes it possible to verify not only control flow but also dataflow. Fu et al. focused on interactions between services in a composite Web service[13]. They transformed interaction protocols described in BPEL into Guarded Automata(GA), which reacts to certain messages. Then the GA is transformed into descriptions in a language for model checking. Their method can flexibly adopt various combinations of languages for composite Web service and languages for model checking.

Many previous works have proposed methods for service selection. For example, the method proposed in [2] focuses on finding a combination of services which gives the best QoS. The method proposed in [3] selects services considering interfaces of services in addition to QoS. These works assume that vast amount of services are stored in a service cluster. In reality, however, the number of services which have equivalent functions is limited. That is the reason the previous works often cannot find a combination of services. Moreover, to handle the policies of service providers, we need not only finding a static combination of services but also dynamic adaptation and meta-level control of composite services.

Also in the area of dynamic adaptation, there have been some previous works. Most of the works can be classified into three types: weaving a new process based on AOP (Aspect-oriented Programming), using a proxy to monitor/change messages exchanged between a composite service and invoked services, and transforming the model of a composite service based on definition of additional processes.

AO4BPEL[4] is one of the framework for realizing AOP of composite services. It allows a user to define a pointcut in a WS-BPEL process and weave a process described in WS-BPEL as an advice. This can add processes for adaptation without changing the model of a composite service.

For service-oriented collective intelligence, however, it is required to satisfy various policies of service providers. AOP is suitable for adaptation as described in the previous section, but it is not flexible enough to coordination such as controlling order of service execution.

The work proposed in [5] adopts a framework using a proxy. It checks if messages exchanged among a composite services and the constituent services satisfy the given conditions when the composite service execution engine invokes the constituent services. If any of conditions is not satisfied, it performs some recovering processes, retries invocation, or changes the service to an alternative[14]. But this focuses on adaptation of single service and does not deal with policies of all service provider concerned.

7   Conclusion

In this paper, we proposed a framework of execution control for composite services. The framework realizes service selection and adaptation in order to satisfy service providers' policies. Moreover, adaptation applied at runtime can be verified using model checking.

The contributions of this paper are as follows.

- We defined procedures which update description of model checking for each business logic control operation used for adaptation.
- We showed an algorithm which reduces the search space for verification by focusing on search states updated by business logic control operations.

Although there have been many previous works on adaptation and verification, they have not focused on verifying composite services which are adapted at runtime. This paper is the first work that tries to verify service providers' policies are satisfied even when adaptation is applied by formally defining effects of execution control for adaptation.

For future works, we are going to propose generation of adaptation process which satisfies service providers' policies based on formal definition of execution control APIs and business logic control APIs.

Acknowledgments

This works was partially supported by Strategic Information and Communications R&D Promotion Programme from Ministry of Internal Affairs and Communications.

References

1. Ishida, T.: Language Grid: An infrastructure for intercultural collaboration. In: IEEE/IPSJ Symposium on Applications and the Internet (SAINT 2006), pp. 96–100 (2006)
2. Zeng, L., Benatallah, B., Ngu, A.H., Dumas, M., Kalagnanam, J., Chang, H.: Qos-aware middleware for web services composition. IEEE Transactions on Software Engineering 30, 311–327 (2004)
3. Hassine, A.B., Matsubara, S., Ishida, T.: A constraint-based approach to horizontal web service composition. In: Cruz, I., Decker, S., Allemang, D., Preist, C., Schwabe, D., Mika, P., Uschold, M., Aroyo, L.M. (eds.) ISWC 2006. LNCS, vol. 4273, pp. 130–143. Springer, Heidelberg (2006)
4. Charfi, A., Mezini, M.: AO4BPEL: An aspect-oriented extension to bpel. World Wide Web 10(3), 309–344 (2007)
5. Baresi, L., Guinea, S., Plebani, P.: Policies and aspects for the supervision of BPEL processes. In: Krogstie, J., Opdahl, A.L., Sindre, G. (eds.) CAiSE 2007 and WES 2007. LNCS, vol. 4495, pp. 340–354. Springer, Heidelberg (2007)
6. Tanaka, M., Murakami, Y., Lin, D., Ishida, T.: Service supervision for service-oriented collective intelligence. In: IEEE 7th International Conference on Services Computing (SCC 2010) (to appear 2010)
7. Nakajima, S.: Model-checking behavioral specification of bpel applications. Electronic Notes in Theoretical Computer Science 151, 89–105 (2006)
8. Tanaka, M., Ishida, T., Murakami, Y., Morimoto, S.: Service supervision: Coordinating web services in open environment. In: IEEE International Conference on Web Services (ICWS 2009), pp. 238–245 (2009)
9. Business process execution language for web services (BPEL), version 1.1 (2003), http://www.ibm.com/developerworks/library/ws-bpel/
10. Holzmann, G.: The SPIN Model Checker. Addison-Wesley, Reading (2004)
11. Narayanan, S., McIlraith, S.A.: Simulation, verification and automated composition of web services. In: The 11th International Conference on World Wide Web (WWW 2002), pp. 77–88 (2002)
12. Ankolekar, A., Paolucci, M., Sycara, K.: Towards a formal verification of owl-s process models. In: Gil, Y., Motta, E., Benjamins, V.R., Musen, M.A. (eds.) ISWC 2005. LNCS, vol. 3729, pp. 37–51. Springer, Heidelberg (2005)
13. Fu, X., Bultan, T., Su, J.: Analysis of interacting bpel web services. In: The 13th conference on World Wide Web (WWW2004), pp. 621–630 (2004)
14. Mosincat, A., Binder, W.: Transparent runtime adaptability for bpel processes. In: Bouguettaya, A., Krueger, I., Margaria, T. (eds.) ICSOC 2008. LNCS, vol. 5364, pp. 241–255. Springer, Heidelberg (2008)

An Integrated Solution for Runtime Compliance Governance in SOA

Aliaksandr Birukou[1], Vincenzo D'Andrea[1], Frank Leymann[3],
Jacek Serafinski[2], Patricia Silveira[1], Steve Strauch[3], and Marek Tluczek[2,*]

[1] DISI, University of Trento, TN 38123, Italy
[2] Telcordia Poland, Poznan
[3] IAAS, University of Stuttgart, 70569, Germany

Abstract. In response to recent financial scandals (e.g. those involving Enron, Fortis, Parmalat), new regulations for protecting the society from financial and operational risks of the companies have been introduced. Therefore, companies are required to assure compliance of their operations with those new regulations as well as those already in place. Regulations are only one example of compliance sources modern organizations deal with every day. Other sources of compliance include licenses of business partners and other contracts, internal policies, and international standards. The diversity of compliance sources introduces the problem of compliance governance in an organization. In this paper, we propose an integrated solution for runtime compliance governance in Service-Oriented Architectures (SOAs). We show how the proposed solution supports the whole cycle of compliance management: from modeling compliance requirements in domain-specific languages through monitoring them during process execution to displaying information about the current state of compliance in dashboards. We focus on the runtime part of the proposed solution and describe it in detail. We apply the developed framework in a real case study coming from EU FP7 project COMPAS, and this case study is used through the paper to illustrate our solution.

Keywords: compliance governance, business process, monitoring, SOA, complex event processing.

1 Introduction

During the last decade several companies, such as Enron in US, Fortis and Parmalat in Europe, unexpectedly collapsed. In response to those events, new regulations for protecting society from financial and operational risks of companies have been introduced. The goal of those regulations is to avoid similar bancruptcies in the future, and companies must comply with them. Compliance become more and more important in modern organizations [12]. In this paper, we use the term "compliance" in the sense of the conformance of a company in

---

* This work was supported by funds from the European Commission (contract no. 215175 for the FP7-ICT-2007-1 project COMPAS).

P.P. Maglio et al. (Eds.): ICSOC 2010, LNCS 6470, pp. 122–136, 2010.

fulfilling compliance requirements, i.e. constraints or assertions that are the results of the interpretation of the compliance sources. Modern organizations deal with three main types of compliance sources: legislature and regulatory bodies (e.g., Sarbanes-Oxley Act, Basel II, Solvency II), standards and codes of practice (e.g., ISO9000, ISO/IEC 27002, internal regulations), and business partner contracts (e.g., licenses of service providers).

The diversity of compliance sources introduces the problem of compliance governance in an organization. Compliance governance refers to the overall management approach for controlling the state of compliance in the entire organization and, in general, consists of: (1) selecting the sources to be compliant with and designing corresponding compliance requirements; (2) (re-)designing business processes compliant with the selected requirements; (3) monitoring compliance of processes during their execution; (4) informing interested parties (managers, auditors) on the current state of compliance; (5) taking specific actions or changing the processes in cases of (predicted or happened) non-compliance.

There are solutions for automating one or several steps of the compliance governance, i.e. deriving requirements from sources (Global Information Rules Database[1]), modeling and automating design time compliance checks [10], monitoring [17] and informing interested parties [20]. However, the existing approaches rarely deal with different types of compliance sources and cover only a few steps of the compliance governance.

There are several research challenges arising when speaking about an integrated solution for compliance governance: (i) Is it possible to create a system dealing with the whole process of compliance management, from selecting compliance sources to dealing with cases of non-compliance? (ii) Is the service-oriented technology mature enough to be used as the basis for such a solution? (iii) Can we reuse the knowledge about achieving compliance within the company, or, even, across companies?

With the research challenges above in mind, we propose an integrated solution for runtime compliance governance in SOA. The framework is based on the service-oriented technology and includes tools for: modeling compliance requirements for different compliance sources; linking the requirements to the business processes; monitoring process execution using Complex Event Processing (CEP); displaying the current state of compliance in a Compliance Governance Dashboard (CGD) and analyzing cases of non-compliance in order to find what causes such situations. In the description of framework we focus on the runtime aspects, such as process execution and monitoring, but the design-time aspects (modeling processes and requirements) are also briefly described. For a number of issues (besides technical issues there are also organizational issues, legal responsibility, acceptance of an active role of the technology in the work practices), in this paper, we do not address the issue of taking specific actions for achieving compliance (also known as *enforcement*) and process re-design. This topic deserves dedicated research. Therefore, our framework covers selection and modeling compliance requirements and business processes, monitoring the compliance

---

[1] http://www.grcroundtable.org/grc-grid.htm

at runtime and informing interesting parties on the state of compliance. The framework and the prototypes of the licensing Domain-Specific Language (DSL) for expressing compliance requirements, the business process engine, CEP-based monitoring tool, the warehouse, the dashboard, etc. have been applied in a real case study in the context of the EU FP7 project COMPAS[2] (Compliance-driven Models, Languages, and Architectures for Services). The case study focuses on checking compliance of telecom service provider to licenses of its business partners.

This paper is continuation of our work on the compliance governance. Previously, we introduced: compliance governance lifecycle and conceptual model [9], which we adapt in the presented framework; a model-aware repository and service environment (MORSE) [25], a licensing DSL [3], an approach for developing compliance governance dashboards [20], and algorithms for root-cause analysis [7], which are used withing the proposed framework. This paper connects the proposed pieces within an integral runtime compliance governance framework and shows how the whole framework is applied in the case study scenario.

The paper has the following structure: in Section 2 we review existing approaches for compliance governance in SOA. Section 3 introduces the scenario we use through the paper to illustrate our solution. Section 4 presents the compliance governance lifecycle in an organization, while Section 5 presents our solution for runtime compliance governance, according to the considered lifecycle. We conclude the paper in Section 6.

2   Related Work

Our approach is different from related work as it enables the adaption to various domains of compliance by extending the conceptual model for compliance governance introduced in [9] and customizing the related components in the compliance governance architecture accordingly. We deal with the domains of Quality of Service (QoS), security, and licensing, while most of the existing approaches in the field of compliance governance in SOAs are focusing on one single specific compliance domain. For example, the approach presented by Kuster et al. [13] is limited to the compliance of business processes with respect to data object lifecycles. A data object lifecycle is specified as a model, which captures allowed states and state transitions for a particular data object. The generated process model complies to the object lifecycle based on automata theory.

Most of the scientific publications regarding compliance involves annotation of business processes. For instance, Wolter and Schaad [27] investigated an extension for the Business Process Model And Notation (BPMN) [19], enabling the modeling of task-based authorization constraints and supporting resource allocation patterns such as separation of duties and role-task assignments. In contrast to our approach, this later focuses on task-based access control, which is a subtopic of the compliance domain regarding business process security. Sadiq [23] presents an approach based on a formal contract language to specify and describe

---

[2] http://www.compas-ict.eu/

compliance constraints, and to define compliance rules to annotate business processes. Namiri et al. [18] propose a semantic-based approach for modeling and implementation of internal controls in business processes, focusing on the separation of business and internal control processes. An approach focusing on the integration of semantic constraints in process management systems and its usage for the verification of the integrated semantic constraints is introduced in [14]. Those approaches only consider the modeling phase of compliance constrains or controls, lacking support for runtime compliance checking and monitoring.

The current studies involving policy-based frameworks are also restrict to the modeling phase and far from having a full and well defined framework to manage compliance. They have been extending and integrating semantic of business process and compliance policies in the form of ontologies in order to provide compliant business process [15], [16]. In fact, the same lack of completeness is also present when policy frameworks (e.g., IETF, Ponder, KAoS, Rei and WS-Policy) are adopted to manage compliance in SOA as describe in this survey [26]. Hence, a lot of open issues are still around in the compliance field.

The work of Governatori et al. [10] checks compliance of business process to regulations. They propose a framework for assessing if a given business process complies with a set of regulatory control objectives. The compliance governance framework proposed in this paper aims at an integral management of compliance of all business processes in an organization. Differently from Governatori et al., whose framework provides diagnostic support for business process design, our framework focuses on the aspect of compliance of process instances, with the current status of compliance being updated on dedicated CGDs.

Business Activity Monitoring (BAM) aims at providing aggregated information suitable for performing various types of analysis on data obtained from the execution of business activities. For example, tools such as Oracle BAM, Nimbus and IBM Tivoli aim at providing their users with real-time visual information and alerts based on business events in a SOA environment. The information provided to users comes in the form of dashboards for reporting on key performance indicators (KPIs) and violations of service level agreements (SLAs). The compliance management part of these tools, if any, comes in the form of monitoring of SLA violations, which need the SLA formal specifications as one of its inputs.

In the context of our research it is worth to mention event-based related work, since our framework checks compliance taking in consideration the content of the events produced during the execution of business processes or as a result of CEP. The following works present solutions to monitor and evaluate process events, but not taking into account their compliance. Michelson et al. [17] presented a complete report overview about event-driven architecture (EDA) in SOA environments. Their content is composed of many definitions and concepts involving events, as well as strategies to process them in a SOA. Additionally, they also describe event flows and the main components expected in an EDA. Many of those components are presented in our solution (e.g., repositories, events, process engine). However, even if with some similarities, the approaches are different, in the sense that Michelsons work does not focus on and mention compliance.

Sriraman et al. [24] also claim the business utility and agility provided by the union of SOA, EDA and model driven architecture (MDA). They present different perspectives containing SOA, EAD, and MDA together with different domains (e.g., user, development, business) and views (e.g., user centric view). They also show how to implement the proposed architectures in Java. However, also this work does not explicitly comment or focus on event-based compliance monitoring. Still, both paper are important to understand the role of events and how they can be useful in a business process environment.

Giblin et al. [6] propose a compliance meta-model for uniform description and management of compliance policies and show how subsets of compliance sources, expressed in terms of the meta-model, can be (semi-)automatically transformed into event monitoring rules. While the experience of authors in generation of rules from requirement is definitely useful for this step in our framework, we go beyond this, providing runtime monitoring and informing interested parties on the state of compliance.

Robinson [22] proposes a generic framework for defining, monitoring, and modifying (based on feedback) requirements in information systems. This work lies in the area of system verification, while our framework rather deals with compliance to requirements coming from different sources.

3   Motivating Scenario: Advanced Telecom Services

In this section, we describe the Advanced Telecom Services scenario we use through the paper to illustrate our solution. This scenario is one of the case studies of the EU FP7 project COMPAS. The scenario deals with a service "WatchMe" that provides customers with on-demand aggregated audio and video streaming content. Service clients can use the service to see videos with soundtracks in different languages. This service is provided by a fictitious company called Mobile Virtual Network Operator (MVNO).

The case study focuses on particularly challenging environment: a provision of advanced telecom services by a mobile operator that does not have its own network, but uses existing networks of other operators to provide services. Therefore, network infrastructure and many applications that provide the MVNO service components are owned and managed by different enterprises, which include third party application providers, network carriers, and the MVNO company. We place the proposed architecture inside the MNVO company for managing and monitoring the compliance with the licenses of content providers.

In this scenario, the WatchMe service serves as a content aggregator placed between customers (cellphone owners) and the audio and video streaming third party providers. For example, customers access the WatchMe service to see sport events with audio comments in the language they prefer. The service processes customer requests and provides streaming of the selected audio and video content. In the scenario, we assume the MVNO company is providing synchronization between video and audio. The process describing the services offered by the company (presented in Figure 1) includes the following operations:

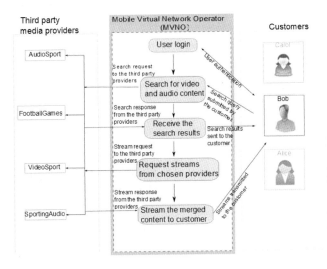

Fig. 1. The business process of the WatchMe service

- authorization of a customer,
- processing search queries for audio and video streams received from customers and forwarding them to third party providers,
- collecting the results of the queries from the providers,
- merging all the results into a single list,
- sending the merged list of results to the customer,
- receiving requests for specific audio and video streaming content from the customer,
- acquiring requested video and audio endpoints from the selected providers,
- receiving streams from the acquired endpoints, merging them online and streaming the resulting content to the customer.

The terms and conditions of using the WatchMe service are regulated by appropriate licenses between MVNO (the WatchMe service provider) and its customers, and between the third party providers and MVNO. In this scenario, we focus on the latter, which is the compliance of MVNO to the licenses of third party providers. Licenses of audio and video providers specify conditions related to various payment plans, as well as to types of allowed compositions of audio and video streams. We consider two payment plans in this scenario. The Time-based plan allows MVNO to acquire and resell any stream for an unlimited number of times in a certain period, based on the amount paid to the media supplier. The Pay-per-view plan allows the company to acquire and resell a certain number of streams based on the amount paid to the supplier, without time constraints. In both plans, the composition permission specifies predefined combinations of video and audio providers, i.e., video streams from VideoSport can only be combined with audio streams from AudioSport, a company from the same media group.

Table 1. Licensing compliance requirements of the Advanced Telecom Services scenario

Compliance Requirement	Description of Compliance Requirement	Control
Pay-per-view plan	When the WatchMe company subscribes for the Pay-per-view plan it acquires a *limited* number of streams based on *the amount paid* to the media supplier.	When WatchMe company subscribes for the Pay-per-view plan it has to pay *29.90 euro first* and *then receive 300* streams from the media supplier.
Time-based plan	When the WatchMe company subscribes for the Time-based plan it acquires *any* number of times *any* possible streams in a certain period, based on *the amount paid* to the media supplier.	When WatchMe company subscribes for the time-based plan it has to pay *89.90 euro first* and then receive an *unlimited* number of times *any* available stream from the media supplier *in a 30 days* period starting from the contract start date.
Composition permission	*Only pre-defined combinations of* video and audio streams from providers are allowed due to the licenses specified by the video provider.	Video streams from *Football Games* can be *assembled* with audios streams from *AudioSport or SportingAudio*. Videos from *VideoSport* can *only be assembled* with audio streams from *AudioSport*.

All licensing compliance requirements for the business process of the WatchMe service are listed and described in Table 1. For each requirement we list the control, which describes what has to be done to realize the corresponding compliance requirement. The compliance sources from where requirements have been derived are licenses of the content providers. In order to model the requirements, we use Licensing DSL, developed in COMPAS [3]. For the sake of simplicity we focus on the composition permission compliance requirement throughout this paper and use it to show the application of our framework to the Advanced Telecom Services scenario.

4   Compliance Governance Lifecycle

Figure 2 shows the overall compliance governance lifecycle considered in the COMPAS project. The compliance governance lifecycle starts with the step of internalization of the external compliance sources, such as regulations, business contracts, standards. This step is performed by a compliance officer.

The next step is the design or modeling of business processes and compliance requirements that must be met by the processes. At this step, requirements are derived from internalized external sources and also from internal policies defined by the organization. This step involves a process analyst, a compliance officer and a technical specialist.

In COMPAS the compliance requirements are modeled in DSLs [1] using the corresponding DSL Editors. For instance, in the Advanced Telecom Services scenario we use the Licensing DSL [3] , which is an extension of the Open Digital

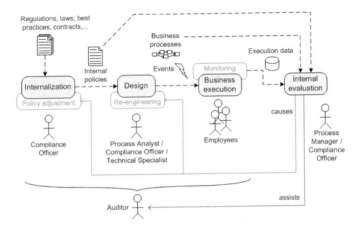

Fig. 2. The compliance governance lifecycle

Rights Language (ODRL) [21], for modeling the composition permission compliance requirement. Other DSLs include QoS [1] and Security [4] DSLs. The processes are specified using the View-based Modeling Framework (VbMF) [11], which is a Model-driven Software Development (MDSD) software framework based on the Eclipse Modeling Framework (EMF). The EMF Models specifying the business process as well as the compliance requirements specified in the corresponding DSLs are the input for the Code Generator, a component integrated in VbMF to generate (semi-automatically) business processes defined in BPEL. In addition to the BPEL process the configuration artifacts, e.g., CEP rules for monitoring components are generated depending on the concrete compliance requirements the execution of the business process has to conform to. The framework currently does not deal with the problem of conflicts and redundancy among the selected requirements, introduced in [5], but, rather, aims at fulfilling all specified compliance requirements. Conflicts and redundancy can be detected at later stages, for instance, applying root-cause analysis.

All artifacts used for the generation of the compliant business process and the configuration artifacts such as compliance requirements, the EMF models, and process models are stored in the Model Repository, which is part of the Model-Aware Service Environment (MORSE) [25]. For the unique identification of each artifact stored in the Model Repository we use Universal Unique Identifier (UUID). Thus this important information might be requested for finding the cause in case a compliance violation is detected during compliance monitoring, by querying the Web service interface of the Model Repository. Finally, the compliant BPEL process containing the UUIDs is deployed in the process engine and the configuration artifacts containing UUIDs are deployed to the corresponding compliance monitoring and checking components.

The third step of the lifecycle is business execution, where employees participate in execution of a business process. During such execution, the process emits events that are used for the monitoring, and also produces data about process execution. Such data, together with models of the business processes and compliance requirements is used by a process manager or a compliance officer at the fourth step: internal evaluation. During this step the compliance of the process is assessed and the data is analyzed in order to find what causes non-compliance. The results of the analysis assist an auditor and can be also used for process re-engineering and re-thinking of initial requirements. These two latter steps are out of the scope of this paper.

The reader can find the detailed definitions of terms and concepts of the compliance governance in COMPAS, stemming from an effort of the whole team of the COMPAS project at http://www.compas-ict.eu/terminology.php. An initial version of the compliance management lifecycle and of the terminology has been presented in [9].

5 Runtime Compliance Governance Framework

In this section we describe the compliance governance framework for monitoring the compliance of business processes at runtime and show how to apply it in the Advanced Telecom Services scenario.

5.1 Runtime Compliance Governance Architecture

Figure 3 shows the components of the runtime compliance governance architecture, described in the following. Runtime governance starts with deploying a BPEL business process that contains the UUIDs of the process model and

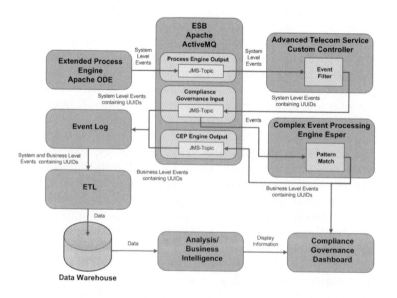

Fig. 3. Runtime compliance governance architecture

those of the activities relevant for monitoring and checking of the compliance requirements to the *Extended Process Engine Apache ODE*. After the deployment a `Process Deployed` system-level event containing the BPEL file of the process including UUIDs is emitted and published to the Java Message Service Topic named Process Engine Output within the *Enterprise Service Bus Apache ActiveMQ*, used as messaging infrastructure. The *Advanced Telecom Service Custom Controller (ATSCC)* is subscribed to this JMS-Topic and therefore receives all events emitted by the Apache ODE. The purpose of the ATSCC is to select pre-defined events, e.g., `Activity Completed` system-level events, emitted by the engine that are related to the deployed process.

The system-level events augmented with the corresponding UUIDs passing the ATSCC internal event filter are published to the JMS-Topic named Compliance Governance Input. Both the *Event Log* and the *CEP Engine Esper* are subscribed to this topic to receive all system-level events relevant to runtime compliance monitoring and checking. The goal of CEP is to provide the possibility for finding complex event patterns within the low-level streams of events generated by the Business Process Engine or/and other Business Activity Monitoring tools. The CEP Engine Esper processes system-level events to create higher-level business-level events, for instance, subtracting timestamp of `ActivityStarted` event from the timestamp of `ActivityFinished` event for the calculation of the duration of an activity. The resulting business-level events also contain UUIDs, which are UUIDs of the CEP rules and generated semi-automatically during design phase using VbMF. Due to the fact that one business process may have to be compliant to several different compliance requirements affecting not necessarily a disjoint set of activities the UUIDs of the monitoring artifacts, e.g., CEP rules are additionally required for the sufficient querying of the Model Repository for drill-down. This enables a unique identification, because the relationship between a concrete compliance requirement and the corresponding CEP rule is always one-to-one as specified in the conceptual model [9]. The results of CEP are shown on the online tab of the *Compliance Governance Dashboard*, allowing for near real-time detection of violation patterns of events, which could lead to violation of any of the licenses signed with their contractors. Therefore, the runtime overhead of using CEP is required for the fast detection of patterns of events leading to violations. Such detection might prevent major financial losses for the company.

The Business Level Events augmented with UUIDs are published to the JMS-Topic named CEP Engine Output. The *Event Log* storing the system-level events augmented with UUIDs and Business Level Events containing UUIDs is subscribed to both JMS-Topics Compliance Governance Input and CEP Engine Output. The *ETL* extracts, transforms and loads the data including UUIDs from the Event Log and stores it in the *Data Warehouse*. After this the *Analysis/Business Intelligence* component retrieves the data from the Data Warehouse and executes the analysis on the data. In case a compliance violation is detected the Model Repository might be queried for drill-down to retrieve the corresponding compliance requirements, EMF models, and CEP rules uniquely identified by the corresponding UUIDs. Finally, the results of the offline compliance monitoring and checking are displayed in the *Compliance Governance Dashboard*.

5.2   Compliance Governance in the Advanced Telecom Services

In the following, we use the four steps of compliance governance to explain how our framework is applied in the Advanced Telecom Services scenario.

```
21    <!-- the Scope of rights clause of the license -->
22    <o-ex:permission>
23        <!-- allows composition under conditions listed below-->
24        <sl:composition />
25    </o-ex:permission>
26    <!-- Financial terms license clause -->
27    <o-ex:permission>
28        <!-- Allowed combinations of audio providers -->
29        <o-dd:play>
30            <o-ex:requirement>
31                <wm:combinations>
32                    <wm:type>ApprovedAudioProviderOnly</wm:type>
33                </wm:combinations>
34            </o-ex:requirement>
35            <o-ex:constraint>
36                <o-ex:context>
37                    <o-dd:name>ApprovedAudioProviders</o-dd:name>
38                    <o-ex:constraint>
39                        <o-ex:context>
40                            <o-dd:name>AudioSport</o-dd:name>
41                            <o-dd:uid>ASport</o-dd:uid>
42                        </o-ex:context>
43                    </o-ex:constraint>
44                </o-ex:context>
45            </o-ex:constraint>
46        </o-dd:play>
47    </o-ex:permission>
```

Fig. 4. The composition permission expressed in the Licensing DSL for the VideoSport provider

Step 1. Selecting compliance sources and compliance requirements. Figure 4 shows how the composition permission requirement (selected for the running example, as we discussed in Section 3), is modeled in the Licensing DSL.

Step 2. Designing business processes compliant with the selected requirements. The business process is modeled in EMF using the VbMF [1,2]. This EMF model as well as the composition permission compliance requirement modeled in Licensing DSL, as shown in Figure 4, serves as input for the Code Generator component, which is integrated in VbMF.

This step is still under development in COMPAS, the goal is to have a process model annotated with events that will be emitted during the execution. Such events will be used during the execution to check compliance. Currently, attaching events and generating rules requiring to monitor the compliance requirements is done manually. The result of the semi-automatic generation is the business process in BPEL containing the UUIDs of the process model itself as well as of the activities relevant for compliance checking. Moreover the CEP rules will be generated for processing the corresponding system-level events for creation of business-level events. Additionally the configuration file for the ATSCC specifying the type of events not to be filtered out and the configuration artifacts for the Analysis/Business Intelligence component are generated.

Step 3. Monitoring compliance of processes during their execution. In order to be able to quickly react to any compliance violation, it is essential to monitor business processes online. For this purpose we chose CEP as a perfect solution for efficient and fast detection of events that match violation patterns. Business process engine generates the events at every step of process execution, according to the annotations. A specialized CEP engine catches and uses them for the evaluation of predefined rules. The rules can be used to specify any complex patterns (including temporal logic), various operators (mathematical, logical) and operations for filtering and aggregation. Finally the configuration artifacts are deployed on the corresponding component involved in compliance monitoring and checking and the BPEL process is deployed on the extended Apache ODE.

The following rule for monitoring violations of composition permission is used to detect patterns of video and audio request events that are not compliant with a license.

```
select * from pattern [ every ( VidProvVideoSport = Event
(name = 'WatchMeGetVideoStreamEvent' AND VideoProviderID= 'VideoSport' )
AND ( AudProvAudioSport = Event ( name = 'WatchMeGetAudioStreamEvent'
AND NOT (AudioProviderID = 'AudioSport') )))]
where AudProvAudioSport.sessionID =VidProvVideoSport.sessionID
```

In this case, the pattern includes combinations of `WatchMeGetAudioStream` events from the audio stream of AudioSport and from the video stream of VideoSport for a given session. The query has to match only the events related to the same session (matching is done by "sessionID" property of the events). The system-level events emitted by the ATSCC as well as the Business Level Events generated and emitted by the CEP Engine are afterwards stored in the Event Log as described in Section 5.1. The ETL component extracts the data from the Event Log and loads it into the Data Warehouse. Then the Analysis/Business Intelligence component checks compliance based on the data. In case a compliance violation is detected the Model Repository may be queried in order to perform a drill-down.

Step 4. Informing interested parties on the current state of compliance. The current state of compliance of the processes of the organization is shown in offline and online dashboards. Using the monitoring table in the online view, it is possible to verify event violations detected on the fly and take actions to avoid violations in the future. Such view is mainly used by technical project resources that could change the business process implementation to correct wrong behaviors. Using the offline view, composed of Key Compliance

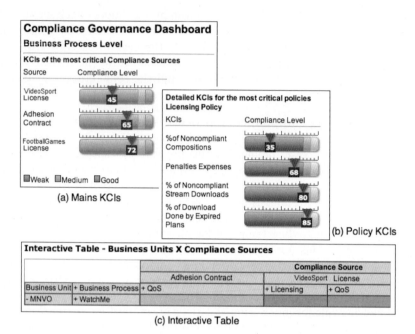

Fig. 5. The current state of compliance of the WatchMe Business Process displayed at the dashboard

Indicators (KCIs) widgets and an interactive table, it is possible to quickly check violations in different perspectives (e.g., business or compliance) and summarization levels (e.g., compliance source, requirement, or policies, which group related requirements, such as licensing requirements). In our example of monitoring the composition permission, ad-hoc KCIs can be defined and their values will be displayed in the dashboard. Having both business and compliance perspective and different summarization levels, it is possible to show high-level information (e.g., KCIs of compliance sources) useful for CEOs and CFOs and low-level information (e.g., list of events violations per compliance requirement) to technical experts. Figure 5 (a) illustrates the KCIs of the different compliance sources from the Advanced Telecom Services scenario in descendant order, where the first widget always contains the compliance source with the highest compliance performance (the worst case). CGD also provides indicators for the compliance requirements concerning licensing (Figure 5 (b)) and an interactive table (Figure 5 (c)). The later also allows users to drill-down KCIs from the highest level information until the lowest level. The values showed by the KCIs are calculated based on the data stored into the Data Warehouse (DW), which were previously temporally stored into the Event log. More details about the CGD design and implementation are available in [20] or at the CGD website[3].

---

[3] http://compas.disi.unitn.it/CGD/home.html

6   Conclusion and Future Work

We have presented an integral framework for runtime compliance governance supporting all the steps of the compliance governance lifecycle: from selecting compliance sources to runtime monitoring and reporting on violations. This addresses the first research question posed in the introduction: *(i) Is it possible to create a system dealing with the whole process of compliance management, from selecting compliance sources to dealing with cases of non-compliance?* In this paper we presented runtime aspects of such a system, while design aspects have been presented in [1], [2].

Since the solution is service-oriented, we also address the second question: *(ii) Is the service-oriented technology is mature enough to be used as the basis for such a solution?* The service-oriented technology seems to be capable of dealing with the matter, since the solution has been tested in a real case study and we are currently working on testing it in another real case study dealing with the loan approval scenario.

Future work includes support of other compliance domains, such as compliance to security or QoS requirements and addressing the third research question: *(iii) Can we reuse the knowledge about achieving compliance within the company, or, even, across companies?* In this regard, we are studying the application of business process fragments [8]. We are also planning applying the presented solution in different settings in order to evaluate its performance and feasibility for real-time business processes.

References

1. COMPAS Deliv. D1.2: Core Meta-models, Templates, and Languages (2009)
2. COMPAS Deliv. D1.3: MDSD Software Framework for Business Compliance (2009)
3. COMPAS Deliverable D5.3: Final Goal-oriented Data Model (2009)
4. COMPAS Deliverable D5.4: Reasoning Mechanisms to Support the Identification and the Analysis of Problems Associated with User Requests (2009)
5. Awad, A., Weidlich, M., Weske, M.: Consistency checking of compliance rules. In: Business Information Systems. ch.10, vol. 47, Springer, Heidelberg (2010)
6. Giblin, C., et al.: From regulatory policies to event monitoring rules: Towards model-driven compliance automation. Technical report, IBM Zurich (2006)
7. Rodríguez, C., et al.: Analyzing compliance of service-based business processes for root-cause analysis and prediction. In: Proceedings of ESW 2010, Springer, Heidelberg (2010)
8. Schumm, D., et al.: Integrating Compliance into Business Processes: Process Fragments as Reusable Compliance Controls. In: Proc. of the Multikonferenz Wirtschaftsinformatik (MKWI 2010), Universitätsverlag, Göttingen (2010)
9. Daniel, F., et al.: Business compliance governance in service-oriented architectures. In: Proceedings of the IEEE Twenty-Third International Conference on Advanced Information Networking and Applications (AINA 2009), Bradford, UK (May 2009)
10. Governatori, G., et al.: Detecting regulatory compliance for business process models through semantic annotations. In: Ardagna, D., Mecella, M., Yang, J. (eds.) Business Process Management Workshops. ch. 2, vol. 17, Springer, Heidelberg (2009)

11. Tran, H., et al.: Modeling Process-Driven SOAs - a View-Based Approach. In: Cardoso, J., van der Aalst, W. (eds.) Information Science Reference (2009)
12. Henry, T.: Product for managing governance, risk, and compliance: Market fluff or relevant stuff? Report of Burton Group (March 2008)
13. Kuester, J., Ryndina, K., Gall, H.: Generation of business process models for object life cycle compliance. In: Alonso, G., Dadam, P., Rosemann, M. (eds.) BPM 2007. LNCS, vol. 4714, pp. 165–181. Springer, Heidelberg (2007)
14. Ly, L.T., et al.: Integration and verification of semantic constraints in adaptive process management systems. Data Knowl. Eng. 64(1), 3–23 (2008)
15. El Kharbili, M., et al.: Policy-based semantic compliance checking for business process management. In: Proceedings of the Workshops co-located with the MobIS2008 Conference,CEUR Workshop Proceedings, aarbrücken, Germany. CEUR Workshop Proceedings, vol. 420, pp. 178–192 (November 2008) CEUR-WS.org
16. El Kharbili, M., et al.: Towards a framework for semantic business process compliance management (2008)
17. Michelson, B.M.: Event-driven architecture overview. Report of Patricia Seybold Group (2006)
18. Namiri, K., Stojanovic, N.: Pattern-based design and validation of business process compliance. In: Meersman, R., Tari, Z. (eds.) OTM 2007, Part I. LNCS, vol. 4803, pp. 59–76. Springer, Heidelberg (2007)
19. Object Management Group (OMG). Business Process Model And Notation (BPMN). Version 1.2, OMG Specification (January 2009)
20. Silveira, P., et al.: On the design of compliance governance dashboards for effective compliance and audit management. In: Proc. of the 3rd Workshop on Non-Functional Properties and SLA Management in SOC, NFPSLAM-SOC 2009 (2009)
21. Iannella, R.: Open Digital Rights Language (ODRL). Version 1.1, (Septmeber 2002)
22. Robinson, W.: A requirements monitoring framework for enterprise systems. Requirements Engineering 11(1), 17–41 (2006)
23. Sadiq, S.W., Governatori, G., Namiri, K.: Modeling control objectives for business process compliance. In: Alonso, G., Dadam, P., Rosemann, M. (eds.) BPM 2007. LNCS, vol. 4714, pp. 149–164. Springer, Heidelberg (2007)
24. Sriraman, B., Radhakrishnan, R.: Event driven architecture augmenting service oriented architectures. Report of Unisys and Sun Microsystems (2005)
25. Holmes, T., et al.: Monitoring and analyzing service-based internet systems through a model-aware service environment. In: Pernici, B. (ed.) Advanced Information Systems Engineering. LNCS, vol. 6051, pp. 98–112. Springer, Heidelberg (2010)
26. Phan, T., et al.: A survey of policy-based management approaches for service oriented systems. In: Proceedings of the 19th Australian Conference on Software Engineering (ASWEC 2008), Washington, DC, USA, pp. 392–401 (2008)
27. Wolter, C., Schaad, A.: Modeling of task-based authorization constraints in BPMN. In: Alonso, G., Dadam, P., Rosemann, M. (eds.) BPM 2007. LNCS, vol. 4714, pp. 64–79. Springer, Heidelberg (2007)

A Differentiation-Aware Fault-Tolerant Framework for Web Services

Gerald Kotonya[1] and Stephen Hall[2]

[1] Computing Department, Lancaster University, InfoLab21, Lancaster LA1 4WA UK
[2] ESRC Centre for Economic and Social Aspects of Genomics (Cesagen),
Institute of Advanced Studies, Lancaster University, Lancaster LA1 4YD, UK
{gerald,s.hall}@comp.lancs.ac.uk

Abstract. Late binding to services in business-to-business operations pose a serious problem for dependable system operation and trust. If third party services are to be trusted they need to be dependable. One way to address the problem is by adding fault tolerance (FT) support to service-oriented systems. However, FT techniques are yet to be adopted in a systematic way within service oriented computing. Current FT frameworks for service-oriented computing are largely protocol-specific, have poor service quality differentiation and poor support for the FT process model. This paper describes a service differentiation-aware, FT framework based on the FT process model that can be used to support service-oriented computing.

Keywords: Service-oriented systems, fault-tolerance, differentiation-aware.

1 Introduction

Service-oriented architectures (SOA) such as web services, pose a serious problem for dependable system operation because they promise late binding. Late binding delegates the decision to trust a service to an external software agent. However, if third party services are to be trusted they need to be dependable. One way to address the problem is by adding fault tolerance support to service-oriented systems. Fault tolerance (FT) build reliable systems using mediated replication techniques. However, the adoption of FT techniques within service-oriented computing is still patchy and variable. Current FT frameworks used in service oriented computing suffer from a number of limitations:

- *Limited coverage of fault tolerance techniques.* There is a tendency for approaches to be problem or protocol specific [1]. Some frameworks provide extensibility mechanisms, but these are limited to simple active and passive replication techniques. A direct consequence of this limited coverage is a lack of evaluation of known FT protocols with regards to reliability and performance in service-oriented computing.
- *Poor support for the FT process model.* The FT process model [2] is based on a pure asynchronous messaging environment to remove all implicit timing assumptions about interactions. Current FT frameworks struggle in to work with

P.P. Maglio et al. (Eds.): ICSOC 2010, LNCS 6470, pp. 137–151, 2010.
© Springer-Verlag Berlin Heidelberg 2010

standard SOAs to provide asynchronism. Some are based on SOAs that only support synchronous request-response exchanges by being tied the underlying transport protocol such as HTTP [3], [4], [5]. Others bypass the SOA in favour of a hard-wired approach [6], [7], severely limiting extensibility.

- *Lack of discoverable FT services.* Existing service- oriented frameworks do not support discoverable fault tolerance services. FT protocols are embedded at a transport level using indirection. This makes them transparent to processes that may have specific FT requirements.

- *Poor support for service differentiation.* Existing FT frameworks do not provide a means for the system to select different protocols at runtime. In addition, current frameworks do not provide a means to differentiate between services that fulfil the same well-known role.

Our solution has been to provide FT support through an asynchronous messaging framework that provides a pluggable means to represent fault tolerance protocols as process models and to expose them as discoverable services. The framework provides runtime service differentiation mechanism based on quality of service and is supported by a decentralised platform. The rest of this paper is structured as follows. Section 2 reviews related work. Section 3 introduces our FT framework. Section 4 describes how a real *Trading Floor* application was used to evaluate the framework. Finally, we provide some closing thoughts in section 5.

2   Related Work

There are a number of initiatives for fault tolerance (FT) in service-oriented computing (SOC). Table 1 provides a summary of some notable FT frameworks in SOC. Because of space considerations, these are representative rather than exhaustive.

The Generic FT Container for SOA [8] is a mediated FT approach for synchronous SOAP invocations. Its limitations lie in its centralised approached to FT. Failure of the mediator would result in overall failure of the system. Its failure detection is also weak because it relies primarily on faults being raised by the services it mediates or the underlying connection time outs. Web Service-Fault Tolerance Mechanism (WS-FTM) [3] is a simple framework that is based on NVP [9]. WS-FTM is very limited in its scope and can only operate with stateless web services. It is preconfigured and cannot be reconfigured. It only allows active replication where most frameworks provide support for passive replication. Lastly, it can only use synchronous RPC type messaging.

FAult tolerance for Web Services (FAWS) [4] adopts a similar approach to the Generic FT Container and has similar limitations. It uses a mediator to route messages to variant implementations of the same service interface. It communicates with a management component, the FT-Admin, using Java based RMI calls. The FT-Admin component is responsible for informing the FT-Front of policy based on input from a failure detection component.

CORBA provides transference to service-oriented computing with the FT-CORBA standard. FT-CORBA has two implementations, FT-SOAP and FT-Web. FT-SOAP provides many useful properties including pseudo group membership, but suffers from a singleton topology where management component themselves can fail. FTWeb [5] provides a similar approach, but decentralises the management components. However, it is limited to synchronous RPC interactions.

Thema [6] is a FT framework for web services that provides an implementation of the Castro and Liskov Byzantine Fault Tolerance protocol (CLBFT) [10] by extending the BASE library [11]. Thema requires three libraries that extend the BASE libraries to provide integration to SOAP. A major problem with Thema is its requirement of UDP based IP multicast for its fault-tolerant framework for Web Services. CLBFT is very complex and using reliable TCP connections diminishes the efficiency of the process significantly. The Byzantine Fault-Tolerance framework for Web Services (BFT-WS) [7] addresses the topology problems of Thema by implementing the CLBFT algorithm directly on top of Web Services Reliable Messaging (WS-RM) [12]. However, there are major concerns over the performance of BFT-WS. Multicasting is replaced by a series of unicasts that degrades the performance. In addition, both Thema and BFT-WS are fixed implementations in two ways. Firstly, they are tied to the CLBFT protocol. Secondly, replicas are not free to join or leave at any time.

WS-Reliable Messaging (WS-RM) is a standard developed by the OASIS consortium [12]. The standard works by the sender indexing outgoing messages whilst requiring the receiver to send acknowledgements for all messages received. WS-RM suffers from several limitations. It does not support the broadcast of primitives required for state machine replication. While several reference implementations of WS-RM exist, the standard provides poor performance because of the overhead of starting/terminating sequences and acknowledgements.

Table 1. FT-SOC frameworks

Framework / Feature	Generic Container	WS-FTM	FAWS	FT-Web	THEMA	BFT-WS
Approach	Intermediary	Intermediary (Client)	Intermediary	CORBA	CLBFT	CLBFT
Passive replication	√	×	√	√	×	×
Active replication	√	√	×	√	×	×
State machine replication	×	×	×	×	√	√
Crash model	√	√	√	√	√	√
Byzantine model	≈	≈	×	≈	√	√
Requires synchrony	√	√	√	√	×	×
Decentralization	×	×	×	×	√	√
Messaging complexity	$\varphi=2(f+1)$	$\varphi=2n$	$\varphi=2(f+1)$	$\varphi=2(f+1)$	$\varphi=2n$	$\varphi=2n(n-1)^{\#}$
Scalable	√	√	√	√	×	×
Diversity	√	√	×	√	√	√
Late binding	×	×	×	√	×	×

Key

√ - Feature supported

≈ - Feature partially supported

× - Feature not supported

- Includes $2n^2$ digital signature validations.

3   A Differentiation-Aware Fault-Tolerant Framework

This section describes our proposed FT framework. The framework comprises two main components; Late Asynchronous Message Brokering system (LAMB) and Sandbox (shown in Figure 1). LAMB is an asynchronous message brokering system that routes SOAP messages to services based on their header and content. LAMB brokers messages to services based on name matching. We assume all semantic decisions including deep interface matching are made at design-time [13]. Sandbox is a container for web services that provides logging, authentication, failure detection, synchronization and election. LAMB and Sandbox are supported by a JXTA-based platform for peer connectivity, organization and distribution of WSDL-based services.

Every host that forms part of our architecture possesses one instance of LAMB and Sandbox. Communications between hosts take place over protocols provided by the JXTA P2P protocols [14]. We adopt JXTA to provide a distributed information model based on adapted WSDL (with bindings to LAMB and QoS metrics). This is achieved by wrapping WSDL in a new type of JXTA advertisement, the WS-Advertisement forming the basis for service discovery. We also make use of JXTA's ability to share peer information and self-organize. Finally, we use the JXTA pipe that abstracts unreliable asynchronous unicast and broadcast primitives. JXTA supports implementation bindings, but these are passive. To link the LAMB and Sandbox infrastructure to JXTA we provide the FT platform.

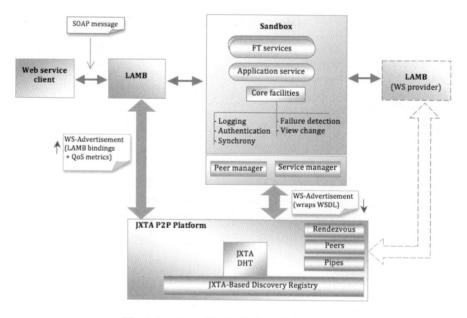

Fig. 1. Peer-based fault tolerance for web services

3.1 LAMB

LAMB is a message-oriented middleware (MOM) that asynchronously routes messages to web services, based on content. LAMB differs from other MOMs [18], [16], [17] by adhering to the following propositions:

1. *Any message* $m_x \longmapsto \{i_1...i_n\}$, *where* i_x *is a service interface. In turn the interface* $i_x \longmapsto \{s_1...s_n\}$, *where* s_x *is a service definition. Finally, the service* $s_x \longmapsto \{e_1...e_n\}$, *where* e_x *is a service endpoint.*

   A message has a name that identifies its content. LAMB uses the message name to identify candidate services that are able to consume the message. A WSDL defined service provides a set of endpoints to which the message can be routed. The assumptive part of this proposition is that a message will always uniquely identify services. Finally, if a message is consumed by two different interfaces then they intersect to form another interface $m_i \longmapsto i_x \wedge m_i \longmapsto i_y \Rightarrow m_i \longmapsto i_z : i_z \equiv i_x \cap i_y$

   All LAMB entities $\{m_x, i_x, s_x, e_x\}$ are uniquely identified by URIs.

2. *Everything is exposed as asynchronous web services.* LAMB treats the world as asynchronous web services that consume messages. This means that any orthogonal policies (in our case, FT) are also treated as services. Every service, FT or not, that is discovered by a LAMB broker must have a WSDL description.

3. *Policy Agnosticism.* Stemming from proposition point 2, a LAMB broker is not tied to any specific policy. Unlike other MOMs, such as WS-BUS [2], JMS [4] or Narada Brokering [19], it does not assume publish-subscribe interactions.

4. *Transport Agnosticism.* A LAMB broker should be able to use any well-known protocol to deliver messages to their endpoint; this includes HTTP, TCP/IP, SMTP or JXTA protocols.

5. *Optimistic brokering.* LAMB implements no specific infrastructure to ensure FT. It optimistically assumes all messages get delivered. If a failure occurs, LAMB neither notes it nor takes remedial action.

6. *Interoperability with SOAP and WSDL.* LAMB has bindings to SOAP and WSDL to ensure web service interoperability. In common with standards such as WS-Addressing [20], LAMB annotates SOAP message headers with its brokering information.

7. *Support for stateful services.* Web services can be stateful between different interactions. LAMB assumes that services are partitioned according to state and maintains a causal service history for each message.

8. *All brokers are equal.* LAMB brokers can reside on any host and see the same set of services within a domain. Service discovery does not depend on the topological or geographical location of a LAMB broker.

9. *LAMB Enabled Web-Services.* Web services must be altered to work with LAMB. Firstly, all outbound messages relative to a service must be passed directly to a LAMB broker service. Secondly, web services must correlate causally related messages by copying any LAMB headers between them.

10. *Zero recursion.* LAMB prevents a broker from selecting the service that a message has just come from to avoid *recursion*.

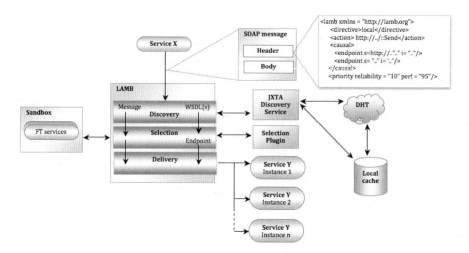

Fig. 2. Architecture of LAMB

As shown in Figure 2 LAMB consists of three services:

- *Discovery*. Take a message and search for matching WSDL descriptions based on qualified and URI names.
- *Selection*. Given a set of discovered services for m_x, the selection service chooses the most appropriate. We have implemented a simple priority scheme where a message can define its requirements in terms of QoS, performance and reliability. A service publishes similar QoS and the selection service chooses a service based on these criteria. The benefits of this priority scheme are discussed in section 4.
- *Delivery*. A service may consist of 1 or more endpoints. LAMB sends the message to all endpoints of a selected service using the most appropriate transport protocol. This may be over JXTA or using transport such as HTTP.

By setting a special field within the LAMB header of a SOAP message, discovery and selection modes can be changed. A *direct* mode means that a service endpoint is embedded in the header and the message gets routed without discovery or selection. *New* mode ensures that no service in the causal header is used. A *local* mode ensures discovery only looks for services on the same host. A *broadcast* mode bypasses the selection service. A *default* mode uses all three services with a bias towards services in the causal history. We have integrated LAMB with the JXTA Peer-to-Peer framework to provide decentralised discovery. It uses a *WSAdvertisment* an extended *JXTA Advertisement*, to index web service descriptions against message URIs to provide fast lookup times. Service publication and discovery is simply the distribution of *WSAdvertisements* over the JXTA SRDI a distribute hash table. This provides a consistent view across all LAMB brokers. Service descriptions are cached within all JXTA peers to further improve discovery times.

3.2 Sandbox

Sandbox is a container that houses FT protocol implementations and exposes them as services. It stems from the *Engine* API in [21] and container described in [8]. Sandbox uses introspection to expose FT protocols as process models enabled with WSDL service descriptions. Sandbox provides a core set of APIs or facilities that provide many common FT abstractions including failure detection and bounded synchronisation. These facilities include:

- *Message Routing.* Sandbox provides a conduit for incoming SOAP messages to reach FT services. Sandbox inspects an incoming message for a service URI and context identifier. The service URI is used to lookup a deployed service class. The context is used to lookup a service instance.

- *Service Lifecycle.* It manages the creation, destruction and state of embedded service instances.

- *Logging.* Many FT protocols require that messages and events get logged either in memory or to stable-storage. Our mechanism, called Domesday, stores arbitrary objects or messages, allowing querying in a variety of chronological ways.

- *Authentication.* Gatekeeper is a facility available to embedded services that provides message authentication and encryption using either RSA digital signatures or Message Authentication Codes (MACs). This allows FT services to check if a message has been tampered with and to verify that it is truly from the sender.

- *Crash Failure Detection.* We have developed a distributed crash failure detector, called *Eternity*, using heartbeats over a ring-topology to inform embedded services of the liveliness of other processes.

- *Synchronisation.* We have developed *Clockwork,* an API that records message-received times for incoming messages. Clockwork generates events when two correlated messages do not synchronise within an upper-bound.

- *Deterministic view changes.* We have developed *Viewpoint*, an API that supports the view-change protocol [22]. Viewpoint allows processes to be chosen deterministically as leaders across the network. It works by taking a view number and selecting the leader from a set of identifiers.

3.3 Fault Tolerance Protocols

To demonstrate the agnosticism and coverage of our framework we have implemented six different protocols that are exposed as FT services:

- *Patmos.* This is a distributed version of ubiquitous recovery block protocol for passive replication, as also found in [4], [5], [8]. However, in our version the intermediary is rotated between, and monitored by, multiple protocol instances so that there are not single points of failure.

- *Elegant.* This protocol provides N-Version Programming like [3], [5], [8] without voting. The protocol has no service implementation, hence it is elegant, and it relies on the distribution of endpoints for one functional service.

- *Atakos*. Enhances *Elegant* to provide voting on multiple service responses, this enables the leverage of diversity.
- *Ionian*. As far as we are aware this is the first web service implementation of the Paxos protocol for state-machine replication (SMR) [1]. Ionian is a clone of multi-Paxos instances that includes an extra messaging step to regulation of total-order proposals.
- *IonianNB*. Ionian non-blocking is an extension to Ionian that removes the proposal regulation step and instead internally consensus decisions.
- *Andros*. Andros is a clone of the CLBFT protocol [10] as supported by [6], [7]. It uses three-step consensus and authentication (through Gatekeeper) to provide Byzantine FT. Andros has both RSA digital-signatures and MAC based variants.

4   Case Study – Trading Floor System

Our case study is based on the Trading Floor system used by one of London's large financial institutions. The system provides real-time information on stocks, bonds, commodities, derivatives and currency to many traders simultaneously. The system consists of three core services as shown in Figure 3. A coordinator service initiates the cycle by sending a fetch indicator message to one or more source services, which fetch the data from online systems. Once the source has fetched an indicator it sends a show indicator message to all available screen services. Each screen service displays the indicator value on the chart shown in the actual trading floor screen. The screen service keeps a record of all indicators. To complete the cycle a screen service sends a log indicator message back to the coordinator. The coordinator can determine what screen services are currently operating or if a source service has failed.

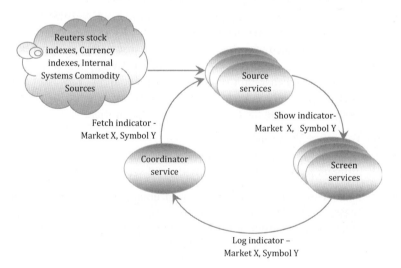

Fig. 3. Trading floor services

This type of application is suitable for evaluating our FT framework as it depends on the plurality of both the sources and the screens. The test case also allows us to contrast the effect of different FT protocols. To evaluate the effect of errors, we doped the source services to generate deterministic pseudo-random values based on the indicator name and a clock value set by the coordinator. Hence unless instructed otherwise, the sources service instances generated the same "random" value.

We scripted doping profiles to generate a wide range of failure conditions including conditional, stochastic and periodic. The doping mechanism was used to drive the injection of requests. The client dope used send methods in the trading floor coordinator service to perform each request. We used two forms of injection; soak injection to create client requests at a fixed rate for a given time and load injection to increase the rate of requests over time.

4.1 Performance Monitoring

The framework incorporates an interface to assess the performance and reliability of the FT protocols. The interface takes snapshots of messages at predefined points in time, during the system operation and sends the results to a monitoring peer that stores all snapshots. Relevant FT metrics are computed by sampling the snapshots over a given period of time. Snapshots are grouped using a correlation identifier to provide start and end points. The in-rate can be computed from the start points, and the out-rate from the end points. Based on this, the throughput, cumulative loss and average latency can be determined. It is also possible to determine when messages are received out of order.

4.2 FT Configuration

A configuration in this context is the deployment of test-case and FT services across a set of nodes. Table 2 shows all configurations used in our case study. A selection of the FT scenarios applied to the case study are describe next.

Table 2. Configuration used in case study

Configuration	Coordinator Nodes		Sources Nodes			Screen Nodes	
	Services	Instances	Services	n	f	Services	Instances
No-FT	TF Coordinator	1	TF Source	1	0	TF Screen	1
Elegant	TF Coordinator	1	TF Source	3,5,7	2,4,6	TF Screen	1
Atakos	TF Coordinator	1	TF Source	3,5,7	1,2,3	TF Screen Atakos	1
Patmos	TF Coordinator	1	TF Source Patmos	3,5,7	2,4,6	TF Screen	1
Ionian	TF Coordinator	1	TF Source Ionian	3,5,7	1,2,3	TF Screen Atakos	1
IonianNB	TF Coordinator	1	TF Source IonianNB	3,5,7	1,2,3	TF Screen Atakos	1
Andros MAC	TF Coordinator	1	TF Source Andros MAC	4,5,10	1,2,3	TF Screen Atakos	1
Andros RSA	TF Coordinator	1	TF Source Andros RSA	4,5,10	1,2,3	TF Screen Atakos	1

4.3 Normal Operation Scenario

This scenario evaluated the framework's general performance and scalability. It was divided into two parts. First, the soak variant injected requests at a fixed rate for a given time allowing the user to contrast all configurations directly. By testing different values of n for each protocol (for example *Andros* with n = 4,7,10) we observed the properties of n-scalability directly. Secondly, a load variant was used to linearly increase load to test the maximum throughput that each configuration could tolerate, therefore assessing the load-scalability.

For the soak case our expectation was that latency would increase with the complexity of the underlying protocol, results. The results, shown in Table 3, are in-line with the expectation. At a fixed, one client request per second, there is a near zero percent loss (given a 1.5% margin for error in the metric API). *No-FT* has the lowest latency and *Andros* the highest.

Table 3. Normal operation with soak results

Name	n	Inject 1 Request/sec			Inject 3 Requests/sec		
		Loss %	Latency (ms)	MD Msg/sec	Loss %	Latency (ms)	MD Msg/sec
No-FT	1	0	177	2.2	0	177	3.2
Elegant	3	0	220	3.5	0.25	150	11.5
Elegant	5	0	270	3.65	0	260	12.75
Elegant	7	0	340	4.25	0.25	310	14.1
Atakos	3	0	625	3.6	0.25	322	13.6
Atakos	5	0	375	3.1	0.5	380	14.5
Atakos	7	0	405	3.25	0.25	430	15.0
Patmos	3	0.5	375	2.8	0.3	350	4.3
Patmos	5	0.5	302	3.3	0	390	6.2
Patmos	7	0	375	4.15	0.31	432	7.5
Ionian	3	0	500	3.5	0	700	9.0
Ionian	5	0	600	5.9	0	750	15.0
Ionian	7	0	1250	8.8	0	15000	27.0
IonianNB	3	0	625	3.0	0	500	5.0
IonianNB	5	0	760	8.0	0	620	12.5
IonianNB	7	0	740	12.0	9.0	4300	37.0
Andros MAC	4	0	1130	5.0	0	1200	5.0
Andros MAC	7	1.2	1170	15.0	85.0	28000	35.0
Andros MAC	10	0	1220	53.0	98.0	20000	10.0
Andros RSA	4	0.8	775	5.0	0	1000	6.0
Andros RSA	7	0.8	1050	22.5	75.0	17000	34.0
Andros RSA	10	1.0	1030	22.0	90.0	30000	19

As Figure 4 shows, all FT protocols had a maximum throughput, however we did not manage to overload the *No-FT* configuration. *Elegant, Patmos* and *Atakos* reached a throughput of 4-5 trans/s whereas *Ionian* was limited to a throughput of 2 trans/s. Andros demonstrated the poorest maximum throughput. All the consensus-based protocols are erratic one their maximum throughput is exceeded.

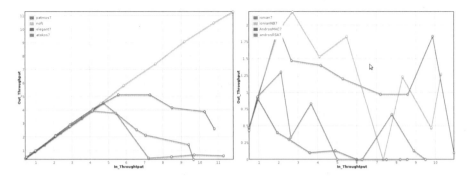

Fig. 4. Behaviour with increasing load ($n=7$)

4.4   Runtime Reconfiguration Scenario (Differentiation-Awareness)

The aim of this scenario was to test the property of dynamism that is enabled by the priority service selection scheme. We wanted to show that when a more resilient FT protocol (indicated by a higher reliability metric) is deployed, incoming requests are delegated to it rather than lesser protocols. So, for example, *Andros* would be chosen over *Ionian*, *Ionian* over *IonianNB* and so forth. To do this we constructed a series of configuration deployments over time whilst soak injecting requests. The result, shown in Figure 5, indicates that the transitions were smooth without the expected problems, clearly demonstrating the effectiveness of the FT priority selection scheme.

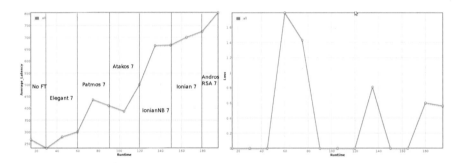

Fig. 5. Runtime reconfiguration results

4.5   Concurrent Fail-Stop Scenario

The aim of this scenario was to establish whether the protocols could support concurrent crash failures within a fail-stop distributed system model. We created two boundary cases when $n-1$ and n nodes crash concurrently. To tolerate concurrent fail-stop the configurations needed to survive $n-1$ crashes but not, trivially, n. For No-FT $n-1 = 0$ so we did not run that case.

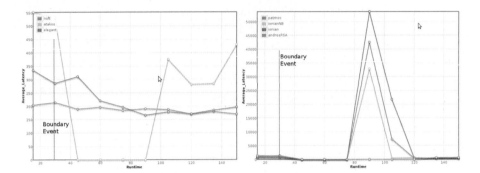

Fig. 6. Concurrent fail-stop (*n-1*)

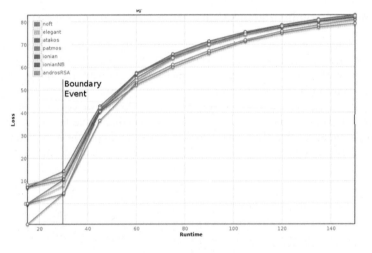

Fig. 7. Concurrent fail-stop (*n*)

Figure 6 shows that all the configurations tolerated *n−1* concurrent fail stops successfully (the latency is measured in milliseconds). Both Andros RSA and *Atakos* showed a much slower recovery than the other protocols. Though in both cases there was slightly recovery towards the end of the run. Figure 7 clearly shows that all the protocols failed totally completing the boundary case.

4.6   Byzantine Scenario

The aim of the Byzantine scenario was to demonstrate that our framework is able to tolerate arbitrary failures in common with [6], [7]. We divided the scenario into four cases: *f* and *f+1* concurrent failures; stochastic failures with an increasing probability; post recovery state. A Byzantine failure is an alternation between the following: fail-silent, omission, timing, denial-of-service or commission.

We expected that only *Andros* would be able to tolerate *f* Byzantine failures. This result is demonstrated in Figure 8 where *Andros* has less loss than either *Ionian* or

IonianNB. However, the result was not perfect. Through observational evidence we noted that a fail-silent, omission, timing or Byzantine attack caused some less power-ful nodes to fail-stop. This triggered constant reconfigurations inside the SMR proto-cols leading to a temporary increase in loss, this result is reflected in Figure 8. In the Byzantine *f+1* scenario as expected all configurations showed an upward trend in loss and latency times.

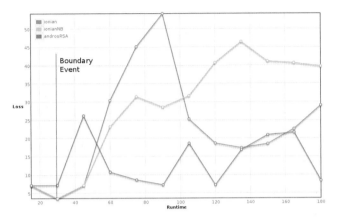

Fig. 8. Byzantine failures (f) for SMR protocols

Figure 9 shows part of the test-bed running the Trading Floor application

Fig. 9. Test-bed

5 Conclusions

In existing service-oriented frameworks FT is treated as an orthogonal issue to services. Service-oriented frameworks do not support discoverable fault tolerance services. In-stead FT protocols are embedded at the transport level making them transparent to the application. Current FT frameworks provide poor support for the FT process model and protocol differentiation restricting the applications ability to select appropriate FT protocols at runtime. Our solution is a differentiation-aware FT framework that provides a pluggable means to represent fault tolerance protocols and to expose them as discoverable web services. We have demonstrated using a real case study how our framework addresses the problems outlined in section 1 (introduction). We have evaluated the framework over many different fault scenarios covering common failure models and showed it to be effective.

Our framework provides a messaging environment for fault tolerance protocols to operate using LAMB, an asynchronous message brokering system. LAMB improves on existing message-oriented middleware by providing a full service-oriented architecture. We have addressed the issue of representing FT protocols as process models and exposing them as services by using Sandbox. Sandbox is container for FT services that allows protocols to be represented as process models. Sandbox extends the approach described in [5] by adding structure and introspection. We have provided a decentralised platform for FT by implementing our framework over a P2P overlay. Ensuring the framework has no singleton components.

We have provided a means for discovering FT services by providing LAMB with the ability to publish and discover WSDL descriptions. To ensure that the descriptions are disseminated to all LAMB brokers we use the JXTA SRDI as the information model. Lastly, our framework supports runtime protocol differentiation by incorporating a simple QoS matching scheme within LAMB. All services have a priority based on reliability and performance metrics.

While our FT framework is a significant improvement on existing frameworks for service-oriented computing, further improvements are needed if it is to address complex service-oriented systems. We are currently exploring ways to improve its performance and to make it more scalable.

Acknowledgements. The support of the Economic and Social Research Council (ESRC) is gratefully acknowledged. This work is part of the Research Programme of the ESRC Genomics Network at Cesagen (ESRC Centre for Economic and Social Aspects of Genomics).

References

1. Lamport, L.: Paxos Made Simple. ACM SIGACT News (Distributed Computing Column) 32(4), 51–58 (2001)
2. Guerraoui, R., Rodrigues, L.: An Introduction to Reliable Distributed Programming. Springer, Heidelberg (2006)
3. Looker, N., Munro, M., Xu, J.: Increasing web service dependability through consensus voting. In: Proc. of the 29th Annual International Computer Software and Applications Conference, vol. 2, pp. 66–69. IEEE Computer Society, Los Alamitos (2005)
4. Jayasinghe, D.: FAWS for Soap-based Web Services. IBM Developerworks. (2005), http://www.ibm.com/developerworks/webservices/library/ws-faws/

5. Santos, G.T., Lung, L.C., Montez, C.: FTWeb: A Fault Tolerant Infrastructure for Web Services. In: Proc. of the 9th IEEE International EDOC Enterprise Computing Conference (EDOC 2005), pp. 95–105. IEEE Computer Society, Los Alamitos (2005)
6. Merideth, M.G., Iyengar, A., Mikalsen, T., Tai, S., Rouvellou, I., Narasimhan, P.: Thema: Byzantine-Fault-Tolerant Middleware for Web-Service Applications. In: Proc. of the 24th IEEE Symposium on Reliable Distributed Systems, pp. 131–142. IEEE Computer Society, Los Alamitos (2005)
7. Zhao, W.: BFT-WS: A Byzantine Fault Tolerance Framework for Web Services. In: Proc. of.Enterprise Computing Conference (EDOC 2007). Eleventh International IEEE, pp. 89–96 (2007)
8. Sommerville, I., Hall, S., Dobson, G.: A Generic Mechanism for Implementing Fault Tolerance in Service-Oriented Architectures. Tech. Report, Computing Dept., University of Lancaster (2005)
9. Avizienis, A.: The N-Version Approach to Fault-tolerant Software. IEEE Trans. Software Engineering 11(12), 1491–1501 (1985)
10. Castro, M., Liskov, B.: Practical Byzantine Fault Tolerance and Proactive Recovery. ACM Trans. Comput. Syst. 20(4), 398–461 (2002)
11. Rodrigues, R., Castro, M., Liskov, B.: Base: Using Abstraction to Improve Fault Tolerance. In: Proc. of the 18th ACM Symposium on Operating Systems Principles (SOSP 2001), pp. 15–28. ACM Press, New York (2001)
12. Davis, D., Karmarkar, A., Pilz, G., Winkler, S., Yalinalp, U.: Web Services Reliable Messaging (WS-ReliableMessaging) Version 1.1. Web, (2007), http://DOCS.OASIS-OPEN.ORG/WS-RX/WSRM/200702/WSRM-1.1-Spec-OS-01.html
13. Alonso, G.: Myths of Web Services. IEEE Data Engineering Bulletin 23(4), 3–9 (2002)
14. Verstrynge, J.: Practical JXTA, Lulu.com (2008)
15. Erradi, A., Maheshwari, P.: WSBUS: A Framework for Reliable Web Services Interactions. In: Proc. of the 2005 ACM Symposium on Applied Computing (SAC 2005), pp. 1739–1740. ACM, New York (2005)
16. Hapner, M., Burridge, R., Sharma, R., Fialli, J., Stout, K.: Java Messaging Service. Web, (2002), http://java.sun.com/products/jms/docs.html
17. Pallickara, S., Fox, G.: NaradaBrokering: A Distributed Middleware Framework and Architecture for Enabling Durable Peer-to-Peer Grids. In: Proc. of Middleware 2003, pp. 41–61. Springer, Heidelberg (2003)
18. Chinnici, R., Haas, H., Lewis, A., Moreau, J.-J., Orchard, D., Weerawarana, S.: Web Services Description Language (WSDL) Version 2.0 part 2: Adjuncts. Web, (2005), http://www.w3.org/TR/wsdl20-adjuncts
19. Reiter, M.K.: The Rampart Toolkit for Building High-Integrity Services. In: Birman, K.P., Mattern, F., Schiper, A. (eds.) Dagstuhl Seminar 1994. LNCS, vol. 938, pp. 99–110. Springer, Heidelberg (1995)
20. Gudgin, M., Hadley, M., Rogers, T.: Web services addressing 1.0 - core. Web,(2006), http://www.w3.org/TR/ws-addr-core
21. Hall, S., Kotonya, G.: An adaptable fault-tolerance for SOA Using a Peer-to-Peer Framework. In: Proc. of the IEEE International Conference on E-Business Engineering (ICEBE 2007), pp. 520–527. IEEE Computer Society, Los Alamitos (2007)
22. Liskov, B.: From Viewstamped Replication to BFT, (2007), http://www.inf.unisi.ch/30YearsOfReplication/pps/Liskov.pdf, 30 Years of Replication Lecture Series

Repair vs. Recomposition
for Broken Service Compositions

Yuhong Yan[1], Pascal Poizat[2,3], and Ludeng Zhao[1]

[1] Concordia University, Montreal, Canada
yuhong@encs.concordia.ca
[2] University of Evry Val d'Essonne, Evry, France
[3] LRI UMR 8623 CNRS, Orsay, France
pascal.poizat@lri.fr

Abstract. Service composition supports the automatic construction of value-added distributed applications. However, this is nowadays mainly a static affair, with compositions being built once and for all. Moving from a static to a dynamic world, where both available services and needs may change, requires automated techniques to correct broken compositions. Recomposition is a working solution but it requires to rebuild composition models from scratch. With graph planning as the service composition framework, we propose repair as an alternative to recomposition. Rather than discarding broken compositions, repair reuses and corrects them for fast generating new service compositions. Our approach is completely tool-supported. This enables us to compare repair and recomposition using both a case study and a data set from a service composition benchmark framework.

1 Introduction and Motivating Example

Software architects benefit from automatic service composition (ASC) techniques and tools [27,8,16] to foster the rapid design, implementation and deployment of distributed applications. Still, ASC enables a more dynamic and on-demand way to develop software, where end-users directly expose their needs to composition engines. The conjunction of technical developments (ubiquitous computing and service pervasiveness), social usages (smart devices equipment rate and user nomadism), together with an adequate business model (cloud computing) makes this vision a close reality. Still, ASC has to support the automatic evolution of compositions, taking into account changes both in the needs of the (possibly mobile) end-users and in the services availability.

A motivating example: the eMeet scenario. Let us imagine the following scenario. Alice is on her way to meet a friend, Bob, who works at a University. To reach him, Alice needs an itinerary map. Since she could get out of her way inadvertently, Alice wants that itinerary can be updated. To achieve her goals, Alice can use services in her vicinity (Fig. 1): M:map (localized map), M:way (itinerary map from location p_1 to location p_2), F:gps (friend position),

P.P. Maglio et al. (Eds.): ICSOC 2010, LNCS 6470, pp. 152–166, 2010.
© Springer-Verlag Berlin Heidelberg 2010

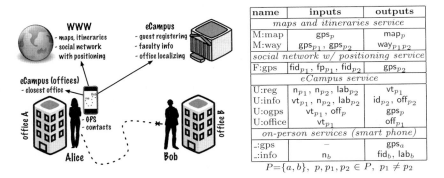

name	inputs	outputs
maps and itineraries service		
M:map	gps_p	map_p
M:way	gps_{p_1}, gps_{p_2}	$way_{p_1 p_2}$
social network w/ positioning service		
F:gps	fid_{p_1}, fp_{p_1}, fid_{p_2}	gps_{p_2}
eCampus service		
U:reg	n_{p_1}, n_{p_2}, lab_{p_2}	vt_{p_1}
U:info	vt_{p_1}, n_{p_2}, lab_{p_2}	id_{p_2}, off_{p_2}
U:ogps	vt_{p_1}, off_p	gps_p
U:office	vt_{p_1}	off_{p_1}
on-person services (smart phone)		
_:gps	–	gps_a
_:info	n_b	fid_b, lab_b

$P=\{a,b\}$, $p, p_1, p_2 \in P$, $p_1 \neq p_2$

Fig. 1. eMeet scenario – architecture (left) and services (right)

U:reg (guest registration), U:info (faculty member information), U:ogps (office location), U:office (closest office), _:gps (own position), _:info (friend id and lab). Services are equipped with semantic descriptions to support their automatic discovery and composition. These refer to GPS positions (gps), social network ids and passwords (fid, fp), names and labs (n, lab), faculty ids, office ids, and visitor authorization tokens (id, off, vt), maps and itineraries (map, way).

Alice wants a way to Bob (way_{ab}) and agrees to give her name (n_a), her social network information (fid_a, fp_a) and Bob's name (n_b). Using a service composition algorithm, *e.g.*, based on chaining between service inputs/output one would obtain that one must first call _:gps to get Alice's position, _:info and then F:gps to get Bob's one, and finally M:way to get an itinerary from Alice to Bob.

Solving out broken compositions. Let us now suppose that Alice moves and looses the GPS signal. The found composition gets broken (no _:gps service).

A first solution is **replacement**, *i.e.*, replacing a broken (disappeared, faulty, or with a bad QoS) service by another one. There are different solutions for this, a typical one is that service s' can replace service s if it produces more outputs using less inputs. Replacement is an efficient technique as far as computation time is concerned (one comparison with each available service). It also yields compositions resembling to the original ones, which is desirable both for technical (commitment to used services) and social (transparency of the process) reasons. A limit of replacement is that a broken service often cannot be replaced by a unique one. It is the case in our example. The only other way to get a gps position for Alice is by calling three services, namely U:reg, U:office, and U:ogps. Further, while replacement can deal with broken services, it cannot deal with added composition needs since in such a case no service is there to be replaced.

A second solution, that deals both with broken services and new needs is **recomposition**, *i.e.*, computing a new composition. However, this means rebuilding models used in the underlying composition technique, while parts of them may still be valid. *Substitution* is often used as a generic term for the way to react to some service that has to be replaced. Technically, in case of 1-1 substitution we will refer to it as replacement, while in case of 1-n substitution we will refer to it as recomposition (causal input/output relation between the n services have to be computed). It should be noted that recomposition goes further, since computing a brand new composition may result in using a completely different set of services and hence would correspond to a kind of n-m substitution.

Contributions. To correct broken service compositions, we propose **repair** as an alternative solution that goes beyond the limits of service replacement while avoiding recomposition. This technique aims not only at keeping most of the above mentioned models as-is (*i.e.*, not recompute them), but also take benefit from them while computing a corrected composition. As such, repair is a form of *heuristic and guided partial recomposition.* In case of 1-1 substitution, repair performs as replacement and is as efficient. In other cases and for added needs, repair yields better computation time than recomposition while retrieving solutions of the same quality. Setting up composition in the AI planning domain, we propose to apply plan repair principles [22] to ASC. We evaluate and compare our repair algorithm with reference to planning-based recomposition, *i.e.*, replanning, using both a case study and a data set generated with a standard ASC benchmark framework. Our approach is completely tool-equipped, including going beyond models, *i.e.*, reading ontologies and service descriptions files and generating WS-BPEL orchestrations.

Organization. Preliminaries on AI planning are given in Sect. 2. Thereafter, our formal models and the application of AI planning to ASC are given in Sect. 2. Our repair algorithm and its principles are presented in Sect. 4. Details on our prototype implementation and experimental comparative evaluation of repair *vs.* recomposition are given in Sect. 5. Related work is presented in Sect. 6 and we end up with conclusions and our perspectives in Sect. 7.

2   Preliminaries

In this section we introduce AI planning [12]. It been applied with success to service composition [25,7], among others due to its support for under-specified composition requirements which are well-suited to end-user composition.

Definition 1. *Given a finite set* $L = \{p_1, \ldots, p_n\}$ *of proposition symbols, a planning problem [12] is a triple* $P = ((S, A, \gamma), s_0, g)$, *where:*

- $S \subseteq 2^L$ *is a set of states.*
- A *is a set of actions, an action* a *being a couple* $(pre, effects^+)$ *where* $pre(a) \subseteq L$ *and* $effects^+(a) \subseteq L$ *denote respectively the preconditions and the (positive) effects of* a.
- γ *is a state transition function such that, for any state* s *where* $pre(a) \subseteq s$, $\gamma(s, a) = s \cup effects^+(a)$.
- $s_0 \in S$ *and* $g \subseteq L$ *are respectively the initial state and the goal.*

The definition in [12] takes into account predicates and constant symbols which are then used to define states (ground atoms made with predicates and constants). We directly use propositions here. It also includes negative effects of actions. Since we do not use them in our approach we remove them for clarity.

A *plan* is a sequence of actions $\pi = a_1; \ldots; a_k$ such that $\exists s_1 \in S, \ldots, s_k \in S$, $s_1 = s_0$, $\forall i \in [1, k]$, $precond(a_i) \in s_{i-1} \wedge \gamma(s_{i-1}, a_i) = s_i$. Different algorithms have been proposed to solve planning problems and get plans from them, *e.g.,* depending on whether they are building the underlying graph structure in a forward (from initial state) or backward (from goal) way. We propose to use an algorithm based on planning graphs [4] since they yield a compact representation of relations between actions and represent the whole problem world. Even after some changes, whole parts of planning graphs would then still be valid. Moreover, recent works have demonstrated the suitability of this model for ASC [3,32].

A planning graph G is a directed acyclic leveled graph (see, Fig. 2). The levels alternate proposition levels P_i and action levels A_i. The initial proposition level P_0 contains the initial propositions (s_0). The planning graph is constructed from P_0 using a polynomial algorithm. An action a is put in layer A_i iff $pre(a) \subseteq P_{i-1}$ and then $effects^+(a) \subseteq P_i$. The planning graph actually explores multiple search paths at the same time when expanding the graph, which stops at a layer A_k iff the goal is reached ($g \subseteq A_k$) or in case of a fixpoint ($A_k = A_{k-1}$). In the former case there exists at least a solution, while in the later there is not. Solution(s) can be obtained using backward search from the goal. Planning graphs whose computation has stopped at level k enable to retrieve all solutions up to this level (while other planning techniques are only able to retrieve a single one). Additionally, planning graphs enable to retrieve solutions in a concise form, taking benefit of actions that can be done in parallel (denoted with $\parallel$).

3   Models

A service signature is made up of a set of operations which can be described in terms of their inputs and outputs. Still, service being developed by different third-parties, one can hardly imagine, and further, achieve service interoperability at the service signature level. Semantic annotations help in solving this issue [27]. Therefore, we associate semantic information to inputs and outputs.

Definition 2. *Given a set D of concepts, a service w is a set Op of operations where for each o in Op, $in(o) \subseteq D$ (resp. $out(o) \subseteq D$) denote the inputs (resp. the outputs) of o.*

Our service model can be related to WSDL, with semantic annotations for inputs and outputs described using SAWSDL and ontologies supporting annotations described using OWL. Most Web services currently posted online are stateless black boxes (no conversations). For example, numerous services listed by webservicelist.com and xmethods.net are this kind of Web services, with capabilities that range from checking stock prices, weather, or driving directions to calculating currency exchanges, mortgages, etc. Therefore, for each service w with n operations $o_1, \ldots, o_n$ we may do as if we had n services $w : o_1, \ldots, w : o_n$.

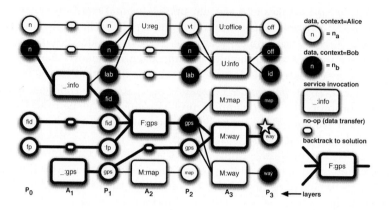

Fig. 2. Planing graph for $WSC_1 = (\{\text{services in Fig. 1, right}\}, \{n_a, n_b, \text{fid}_a, \text{fp}_a\}, \{\text{wayd}_{ab}\})$

Definition 3. *A service composition problem is a triple* $(W, D_{\text{in}}, D_{\text{out}})$, *where* W *is a set of services,* D_{in} *are provided inputs, and* D_{out} *are expected outputs.*

Following [32], it is possible to map a service composition problem $(W, D_{\text{in}}, D_{\text{out}})$ to a planning problem $P = ((S, W, \gamma), D_{\text{in}}, D_{\text{out}})$ with service inputs being mapped to action preconditions $(in(w) \mapsto pre(w))$ and outputs to positive effects $(out(w) \mapsto effects^+(w))$. Plans can be encoded in any orchestration language with assignment and sequence operators, *e.g.*, WS-BPEL. Additionally, planning graphs enable to retrieve plans with parallel invocations. These can be encoded using parallel operations (WS-BPEL flow).

Application. The planning graph for our example is given in Fig. 2. To keep figures legible, in a layer P_i we draw only data that is used in some layer $A_{j,j>i}$. We do not draw a service in a layer A_i if it is already in some layer $A_{j,j<i}$, unless if its input data can be re-generated meanwhile. Finally, in the sequel we will not take into consideration the fact that M:way can be used in layer A_3 to produce way$_{ba}$ (it is dual to it producing way$_{ab}$). Backtracking from the goal, we get a plan, (_:info || _:gps) ; F:gps ; M:way, which can be flattened into two sequential plans: _:info ; _:gps ; F:gps ; M:way and _:gps ; _:info ; F:gps ; M:way.

4   Repairing Service Compositions

4.1   Change Modelling

Service composition should be considered in a world that is subject to change. Accordingly, a service composition problem model, $(W, D_{\text{in}}, D_{\text{out}})$, should be updated to accommodate inputs (D_{in}), goals (D_{out}) and service (W) changes.

Goals may change, some getting out of interest while new ones may appear. We denote them respectively with D_{out}^- and D_{out}^+. Services become unavailable due to many reasons, *e.g.*, network failure or user mobility, and accordingly new

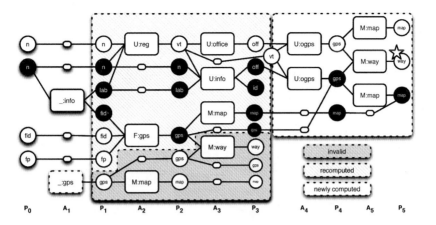

Fig. 3. Planing graph for WSC$_1$ after removal of _:gps (recomposition)

services may appear. We denote them respectively with W^- and W^+. We may then set $D'_{\text{out}} = D_{\text{out}} \backslash D^-_{\text{out}} \cup D^+_{\text{out}}$ and $W' = W \backslash W^- \cup W^+$.

When change has to be considered during execution, we update D_{in} to the state of the partially executed composition. We also update D_{in} if the inputs of the service composition problem change. In other cases, we have $D'_{\text{in}} = D_{\text{in}}$. Finding a solution for an updated problem may require to rollback an executed service, w, and accordingly its effects. We do not constraint how the effects are canceled (operation in the same service or not), but we set $D'_{\text{in}} = D_{\text{in}} \backslash effects^+(w)$.

With this modelling, change yields a new service composition problem, $(W', D'_{\text{in}}, D'_{\text{out}})$, and, in turn, a new planning problem, $P' = ((S', W', \gamma'), D'_{\text{in}}, D'_{\text{out}})$.

Application. In our example we have $D'_{\text{in}} = D_{\text{in}}$, $D^-_{\text{out}} = D^+_{\text{out}} = W^+ = \emptyset$, and $W^- = \{\_:\text{gps}\}$. Using recomposition on the planning graph we get Fig. 3. One can see that an important part of the graph is rebuilt, before a new part is grown and yields a composition solution, either _:info ; (U:reg || F:gps) ; U:office ; U:ogps ; M:way (way between the building next to Alice and Bob's position), or _:info ; U:reg ; (U:office || U:info) ; (U:ogps || U:ogps) ; M:way (itinerary between the building next to Alice and Bob's office).

4.2 Repair Algorithm

Broken preconditions and broken plans. After impacting change, we get a partial planning graph G with a set of *Broken Preconditions* $BP^G_{m \in [1,n]}$, $BP^G_m \subseteq P_i$. BP^G_n are unsatisfied goals, while $BP^G_{m \in [1,n-1]}$ are inputs of actions in A_{m+1} that are no longer available. Let A be a set of actions, we denote $out(A)$ (resp. $in(A)$) the set $\bigcup_{a \in A} out(a)$ (resp. the set $\bigcup_{a \in A} in(a)$). We have $BP^G_{m \in [1,n-1]} = \{p \in in(A_{m+1}) | p \notin D_{\text{in}} \bigcup_{k \in [1,m]} out(A_k)\}$ and $BP^G_n = \{p \in D_{\text{out}} | p \notin D_{\text{in}} \bigcup_{k \in [1,n]} out(A_k)\}$. We may also focus on a given plan, say π. Let π_i be the set of actions in π at step m. Due to π computation with the planning graph we have

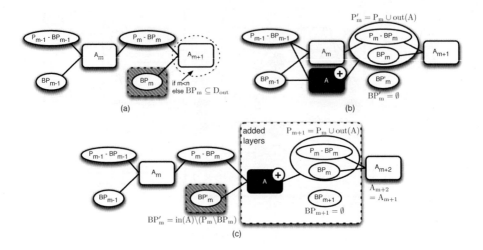

Fig. 4. Broken preconditions at level m, $m \leq n$ (basic repair)

$\pi_m \subseteq A_m$. We have then broken preconditions related to π, $BP^\pi_{m \in [1,n-1]} = \{p \in in(\pi_{m+1}) | p \not\subseteq D_{\text{in}} \bigcup_{k \in [1,m]} out(\pi_k)\}$ and $BP^\pi_n = \{p \in D_{\text{out}} | p \notin D_{\text{in}} \bigcup_{k \in [1,n]} out(\pi_k)\}$. Note that BP^G_m and BP^π_m are incomparable.

We then proceed as follows. If π is not broken ($\forall m \in [1,n]$, $BP^\pi_m = \emptyset$) we have nothing to do. π is still a valid solution. Else, we run our algorithm for BP^π (hence, in the sequel, we will use BP_m for BP^π_m for simplicity). Note that if π is broken but G is not ($\forall m \in [1,n]$, $BP^G_m = \emptyset$) then there is still at least a solution in G, which we may retrieve using backtracking. However, this may yield a solution which is very different from π. Running our algorithm we try first to get a resembling solution. If this fails, any other solution will be found too by the algorithm.

Repair principles. For a proposition level where BP_m is not empty (Fig. 4 (a)), we search for candidate services A which can produce BP_m and insert them into action level m (Fig. 4 (b)). This promotes shorter repair solutions. Sometimes, the lower proposition level P_{m-1} does not contain all the inputs needed by A. We then insert A into a new action level $m+1$ (Fig. 4 (c)). By doing this, we can use more propositions since $P_{m-1} \subseteq P_m$ but increase the plan length by one.

This technique can fail if we cannot find a set of services A that produce all the broken preconditions in BP_m. As a solution we may degrade our basic repair principle. If it is not the goal layer ($m < n$), we remove the unrepairable part (Fig. 5). New broken preconditions may appear at level $m + 1$ and will be treated in a next iteration. If it is the goal layer ($m = n$), then there is no solution, neither with repair nor with recomposition. Degraded repair increases computation time wrt. basic repair since it gets closer to recomposition. Still, it enables to find a solution whenever it exists.

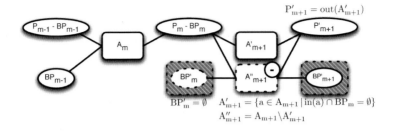

Fig. 5. Broken preconditions at level m, $m < n$ (degraded repair)

Repair algorithms. The main algorithm is the graph repair algorithm, Algorithm 1. It corresponds to the repair principles that are applied for each layer with broken preconditions, starting with the upper layer first. Once we get a repaired graph, a solution is computed with backward search, as with replanning.

Algorithm 1. $G' = \text{Repair}(G,W)$

---

inputs: partial planning graph G with size n, available services W
outputs: repaired planning graph or `fail`

1: **while** $\exists BP_i, i \in [1, n]$, $BP_i \neq \emptyset$ **do**
2:    $m = \max \{i \in [1, n] | BP_i \neq \emptyset\}$;
3:    $candidates = \{w \in W | out(w) \cap BP_m \neq \emptyset\}$;
4:    **if** $BP_m \subseteq out(candidates)$ **then** {//fixable}
5:       $\{A, C\} = \text{SelectServices}(candidates, G, BP_m, m)$;
6:       **if** $C = \emptyset$ **then** {//insert A into action level m}
7:          $A_m = A_m \cup A$; $P_m = P_m \cup out(A)$; $BP_m = \emptyset$;
8:       **else** {//add A into action level $m + 1$}
9:          $\{A, C\} = \text{SelectServices}(candidates, G, BP_m, m + 1)$;
10:         insert a new proposition level P_{m+1} and a new action level A_{m+1};
11:         $A_{m+1} = A$; $P_{m+1} = P_m \cup out(A)$; $BP_{m+1} = \emptyset$;
12:         $BP_m = in(A) \backslash (P_m \backslash BP_m)$;
13:   **else** {// not directly fixable}
14:      **if** $degradeOption = no \vee m = n$ **then** {// no degradation or last layer}
15:         **return** `fail`
16:      **else** {//degradation is possible}
17:         $A_{m+1} = \{a \in A_{m+1} | in(a) \cap BP_m = \emptyset\}$; $P_{m+1} = out(A_{m+1})$
18:         $BP_m = \emptyset$; recompute BP_{m+1}

In this algorithm, SelectServices (Alg. 2) is in charge of selecting the best services from candidate services to obtain some broken preconditions.

It is a greedy search algorithm. We use (1) and (2) to select the best services. The evaluation depends on the layer where w is to be added. At the highest level n, we define:

$$f1(w, G, m) = \frac{|BP_n \cap out(w)|}{\max_{\Omega}} \times 2 + \frac{|in(w) \cap P_{m-1}|}{\max_{Pi}} - \frac{|in(w) - P_{m-1}|}{\max_{Pe}}, \text{if } m = n; \tag{1}$$

Algorithm 2. $\{W_{\text{selected}}, BP_{\text{new}}\} = \text{SelectServices}(candidates, G, BP_{\text{old}}, m)$

---

inputs: candidate services $candidates$, planning graph G whose highest level is n, broken preconditions BP_{old}, level m where services to be added
outputs: selected services W_{selected}, new broken precondition BP_{new}
1: $W_{\text{selected}} = \emptyset; BP_{\text{new}} = \emptyset$;
2: **while** $BP_{\text{old}} \neq \emptyset$ **do**
3:     $w \in candidates$ is the best services by (1) or (2), depending on m;
4:     $candidates = candidates \backslash w; W_{\text{selected}} = W_{\text{selected}} \cup \{w\}$;
5:     $BP_{\text{old}} = BP_{\text{old}} \backslash out(w); BP_{\text{new}} = BP_{\text{new}} \cup in(w) \backslash P_{m-1}$;
6: **return** $\{W_{\text{selected}}, BP_{\text{new}}\}$;

---

where $|BP_n \cap out(w)|$ is the number of unimplemented goals that can be implemented by w; $|in(w) \cap P_{m-1}|$ is the number of w inputs that can be provided by propositions in P_{m-1}; $|in(w) - P_{m-1}|$ is the number of w inputs that cannot be provided by propositions in P_{m-1}. This set needs to be added into BP if w is added. $\max_\Omega$, $\max_{Pi}$, and $\max_{Pe}$ are the maximum value of the nominators in the neighborhood respectively normalize each term. The first term is given a weight of 2 to increase its significance.

If w is to be added in another layer $(m < n)$ then the evaluation function is:

$$f2(w, G, m) = f1(w, G, m) + \frac{\sum_{i \in [m,n]} |BP_i \cap out(w)|}{\max_{BP}}, \text{if } m < n; \qquad (2)$$

Compared to (1), the added term $(\sum_{i \in [m,n]} |BP_i \cap out(w)|)$ is the number of the broken propositions in the level P_m and above that can be satisfied by w outputs. $\max_{BP}$ is the maximum value in the neighborhood to normalize each term. For clarity, we have not put selection exception cases. To ensure repair termination, we do not select services that would reproduce the same set of broken preconditions $(B = C)$, nor do we select a service that has been removed in degraded mode.

According to [4], the size of the full planning graph is polynomial to the size of services and the size of propositions. In the worst case, Algorithm 1 explores all the possible paths in the graph, therefore it terminates in polynomial time.

Application. The application of repair to our example is given in Fig. 6. We begin (a) with $BP_2 = \{gps_a\}$. We select $A = \{U : ogps\}$ but since $in(A) = \{off_a\} \not\subseteq P_1$ we add a new level and add A in the new action layer (b). Still, BP_2 (now $\{off_a\}$) is not empty. We then select $A = \{U : office\}$ and since $in(A) = \{vt_a\} \not\subseteq P_1$ we add again a new level (c). We then observe that $BP_2 = \emptyset$ since $in(A) \subseteq P_2$. There is no more any $BP_i \neq \emptyset$ so repair has succeeded. We find the solution which is the closest to the original one, namely _:info ; (U:reg || F:gps) ; U:office ; U:ogps ; M:way. As one can see, the new graph is grown *on top* of the existing one and computed parts are smaller than with recomposition (Fig. 3).

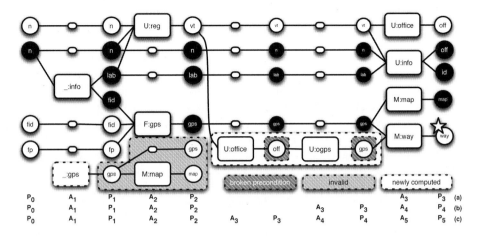

Fig. 6. Planing graph for WSC_1 after removal of _:gps (repair)

5   Implementation and Experimental Evaluation

5.1   Evaluation Criteria

In order to evaluate efficiency and quality of repair *vs.* recomposition (replanning), we use four criteria. *Composition Time* is the time to get the first feasible solution or report nonexistence of it. *Time Steps* and *Number of Services* are respectively the number of layers and the number of services used in the solution. Smaller values lead to more parallelism and less invocations, hence more efficiency at execution time. We assume here that all services have the same execution cost. A perspective is to take into account QoS both in the service model and our heuristic service selection. Finally, *Plan Stability* [9] given two plans π and π' is defined as the number of actions in π not in π' plus the number of actions in π' not in π. Stability is beneficial for transparency and for keeping commitment to services.

5.2   Implementation and Benchmark

The PGA tool. Our approach is fully automated thanks to a tool we have implemented in Java, PGA (Planning Graph with Adaptation). PGA includes three main algorithms. The first one is a Java implementation of the standard graph planning algorithm [4]. It is used to build the original planning graph for a service composition problem and to find a solution for it (or detect there is none). The second algorithm is used to apply change on a planning graph. One may then either call the first algorithm to perform replanning, or use the third one, which implements our repair technique. As far as input files are concerned, PGA can read an OWL file describing ontology concepts and a set of Web service interfaces described in WSDL. Note that the later are annotated with a simple extension mechanism instead of using full-fledged SAWSDL. PGA is also connected to the

WSC platform[1] which is used to generate WS-BPEL orchestrations from XML descriptions of compositions.

Experimental benchmark. PGA has been used to generate solutions for our example (represented in Fig. 3 and Fig. 6). However, this example contains only 20 ground concepts (gps_a, gps_b, n_a, n_b, etc.) and 18 operations (corresponding to the operations in Fig. 1, with duplicates due to genericity, *e.g.*, we have two M:map operations, one for gps_a and one for gps_b). To perform comparison of recomposition and repair, we needed a larger benchmark.

The WSC testset generator is a tool that enables to compare service composition algorithms by generating sets of semantically annotated service interfaces. We use a data set with 351 services. The services can use in their input and output messages parameters in a list of 2891 parameters which are from 6209 instances of 3081 semantic concepts. Given a solution depth, the data generator generates several groups of solutions, each of which has the given solution depth. The solution groups do not share services. Within a group, some services can directly substitute others as they use the same input set and produce the same outputs. The generator randomly generates a lot of "padding" Web services around the services used in solutions. These "padding" services do not have the outputs that can be used by the services within a solution. The data set has four solution groups (1–4) with respectively 9, 18, 19, and 27 levels.

5.3   Experiment Results

We present here the comparative evaluation made for repair and replanning in case of service removal and with group 1 (initial solution: 9 layers and 10 services) Each point is obtained from the average of 100 independent runs. We remove different percentage of services from the service set. We stop at 30% since after it the success rate both for repair and replanning falls down below 50%.

Figure 7(left) shows that our repair algorithm is faster than replanning. Figure 7(right) compares the quality of the solutions. We can see that repair retrieve solutions with the same quality than replanning (plots at superposed).

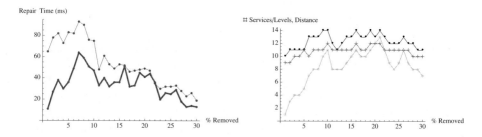

Fig. 7. Repair *vs.* replanning – composition time (thick: repair, thin:replanning) and quality (same for repair/replanning, ●/blue: services, +/red: levels, */green: distance)

---

[1] http://ws-challenge.georgetown.edu/wsc09/software.html

6   Related Work

Service composition has been studied under various assumptions and models [27,8,16]. Among these, planning has successfully been used to support under-specified composition requirements [25,7]. Still, to quote [24], service composition is today largely a static affair. In this paper we address the evolution and adaptation of composition under changes.

When the issue is to react to a disappeared or faulty service, or to a service with a bad QoS, strict *replacement* can be used, *e.g.*, [10,13,6] for some recent works. Some works support a less strict notion of replacement, *e.g.*, with transformers to solve out message mismatching [20]. Replacement is limited to 1-1 substitution. Further, it focuses on finding replacement for broken services, while solving a broken composition may require removing other ones. Supporting the substitution of one service by several ones, and using repair degradation, our algorithm has therefore higher success rate than replacement.

Going further than 1-1 substitution, supporting both 1-n substitution and added needs, can be done with *recomposition, i.e.*, running a composition algorithm on an updated composition problem. Any algorithm defined for service composition [27,8,16] would apply there, including many ones based on some form of planning, *e.g.*, using heuristic search [19,23], linear programming [31], automated reasoning [14,29]. In our previous works we have proposed to build on planning graphs [32,3]. In this paper we have thoroughly compared our repair algorithm wrt. graph planning recomposition. We get solutions of the same quality in less computation time.

A complementary domain of research is *software adaptation*, devoted to the generation of *mediators* (also called *software adaptors*, or simply adaptors) to solve mismatch between components or services [28]. Software adaptation can be used as a composition technique (when adapting between the composition need and available services). It can also be used as a repair technique that keeps the original (broken) composition unmodified and builds a mediator in between this and available services. This technique has been employed for 1-1 replacement (adaptation between one client and one server), *e.g.*, in [5,21]. Some other works have applied software adaptation in the large between n services, *e.g.*, [17,1]. Computing a mediator is as expensive as computing a composition. Our repair technique then share the same benefits wrt. software adaptation than wrt. recomposition. Moreover, n-ary adaptation applies to services with conversations, hence it requires that the services to adapt are previously discovered (which is complex in case of conversations). Our repair technique does not require this since it takes the assumption that services have no conversation.

Composition repair and reuse has been proposed for fault recovery. Substitution and compensation actions are predefined in [10]. Whenever an erroneous condition is encountered, the execution of the process is stopped and a repair plan generated by automated reasoning is inserted and executed. [18] proposes to substitute the faulty services and rebind to new services, or completely recompose a solution. Still, [18] does not present specific solutions to these strategies. [2] proposes a language to define the substitution actions and uses them in a self-healing mechanism implemented in the JBOSS rule engine. In work-flow management, people also study how to dynamically handle failures. For example, [11] proposes mechanisms like termination of failed activity instances and replanning. Considering possible new opportunities is another motivation for composition evolution. [15] alternates planning and execution of the composition in order to adapt to new opportunities. Compared the above work, our method can be used for both fault recovery and plan evolution.

Plan Repair has been introduced in AI planning. [22] claims that repair is not better than planning in the worst case, still in many cases the new planning problem resembles the original one, hence repair is a technique that works in practice. We have proposed a preliminary service composition repair technique in [30]. But for its objective (repair *vs.* recompose), it is not a direct ancestor of the approach we have presented here. The [30] algorithm degraded into backward search whenever a service without a possible (1-1 or 1-n) substitution at the same layer was removed. Also, the service selection process could lead to dead-ends, *i.e.*, repair failure while there was indeed a solution to the broken composition. Using layer insertion and repair degradation we are able to avoid these draw-backs. Performing comparison, using WSC generated testsets, between the [30] algorithm and the one presented here, we achieve a stable quality of the solutions but a better success rate and shorter composition time.

7   Conclusions and Future Work

Automatically generated service compositions may get broken upon change in their envisioned environment, *e.g.,* upon service disappearance, service failure, or added needs. We have addressed this issue with a repair approach based on planning graphs, an alternative to replacement and to recomposition. Our approach is completely automatic and tool-equipped. Repair does as good as replacement when 1-1 substitution is possible, but goes beyond this limit, supporting 1-n/n-m substitution and added needs. Empirical evaluation has shown that repair gets solutions of the same quality than recomposition in better computation time. Repair may sometimes fail to find a solution while one is found with recomposition. To overcome this issue, we have proposed degradation techniques in our repair algorithm. Experiments have shown that in practice we still get better computation time with repair than with recomposition.

So far, we have compared our repair algorithm with the standard planning graph algorithm. It would be interesting to further compare our repair technique with more recomposition algorithms, especially those in AI replanning studies. In this paper we took into account that many services do not expose a conversation. A promising direction is to support more expressive models [16] with both service conversations and a rich conversation-based requirement language. We made a first step in this direction with a technique based on planning graphs for the composition of services with conversations in [26]. QoS models could also enrich our heuristic service selection process. By now, our PGA tool is only used to repair broken compositions at the model and process level, not for running instances. The next step is then to study its integration in an existing runtime monitoring and adaptation framework for services composition such as [20].

Acknowledgement. This work is supported by project "Building Self-Manageable Web Service Process" (RGPIN/298362-2007) of Canada NSERC Discovery Grant, and by project "PERvasive Service cOmposition" (ANR-07-JCJC-0155-01, PERSO) of the French National Agency for Research.

References

1. van der Aalst, W.M.P., Mooij, A.J., Stahl, C., Wolf, K.: Service Interaction: Patterns, Formalization, and Analysis. In: Bernardo, M., Padovani, L., Zavattaro, G. (eds.) SFM 2009. LNCS, vol. 5569, pp. 42–88. Springer, Heidelberg (2009)
2. Baresi, L., Guinea, S., Pasquale, L.: Self-healing bpel processes with dynamo and the jboss rule engine. In: Proc. of ESSPE, pp. 11–20 (2007)
3. Beauche, S., Poizat, P.: Automated Service Composition with Adaptive Planning. In: Bouguettaya, A., Krueger, I., Margaria, T. (eds.) ICSOC 2008. LNCS, vol. 5364, pp. 530–537. Springer, Heidelberg (2008)
4. Blum, A.L., Furst, M.L.: Fast Planning through Planning Graph Analysis. Artificial Intelligence Journal 90(1–2), 281–300 (1997)
5. Brogi, A., Popescu, R.: Automated generation of bpel adapters. In: Dan, A., Lamersdorf, W. (eds.) ICSOC 2006. LNCS, vol. 4294, pp. 27–39. Springer, Heidelberg (2006)
6. Cavallaro, L., Nitto, E.D., Pradella, M.: An automatic approach to enable replacement of conversational services. In: Baresi, L., Chi, C.-H., Suzuki, J. (eds.) ICSOC-ServiceWave 2009. LNCS, vol. 5900, pp. 159–174. Springer, Heidelberg (2009)
7. Chan, K.S.M., Bishop, J., Baresi, L.: Survey and comparison of planning techniques for web service composition. Tech. rep, Dept Computer Science, University of Pretoria (2007)
8. Dustdar, S., Schreiner, W.: A survey on web services composition. Int. J. Web and Grid Services 1(1), 1–30 (2005)
9. Fox, M., Gerevini, A., Long, D., Serina, I.: Plan Stability: Replanning versus Plan Repair. In: Proc. of ICAPS, pp. 212–221 (2006)
10. Friedrich, G., Ivanchenko, V.: Model-based repair of web service processes. Tech. Rep. 2008/001, ISBI research group, Alpen-Adria-Universität Klagenfurt (2008)
11. Gajewski, M., Momotko, M., Meyer, H., Schuschel, H., Weske, M.: Dynamic failure recovery of generated workflows. In: Proc. of DEXA Workshops, pp. 982–986 (2005)
12. Ghallab, M., Nau, D., Traverso, P.: Automated Planning: Theory and Practice. Morgan Kaufmann Publishers, San Francisco (2004)
13. Grigori, D., Corrales, J.C., Bouzeghoub, M.: Behavioral matchmaking for service retrieval: Application to conversation protocols. Inf. Syst. 33(7-8), 681–698 (2008)
14. Hashemian, S.V., Mavaddat, F.: A logical reasoning approach to automatic composition of stateless components. Fundam. Inform. 89(4), 539–577 (2008)
15. Lazovik, A., Aiello, M., Papazoglou, M.P.: Planning and monitoring the execution of web service requests. Int. J. on Digital Libraries 6(3), 235–246 (2006)
16. Marconi, A., Pistore, M.: Synthesis and Composition of Web Services. In: Bernardo, M., Padovani, L., Zavattaro, G. (eds.) SFM 2009. LNCS, vol. 5569, pp. 89–157. Springer, Heidelberg (2009)

17. Mateescu, R., Poizat, P., Salaün, G.: Adaptation of service protocols using process algebra and on-the-fly reduction techniques. In: Bouguettaya, A., Krueger, I., Margaria, T. (eds.) ICSOC 2008. LNCS, vol. 5364, pp. 84–99. Springer, Heidelberg (2008)
18. Meyer, H., Kuropka, D., Tröger, P.: Asg - techniques of adaptivity. In: Proc. of AAWS (2007)
19. Meyer, H., Weske, M.: Automated service composition using heuristic search. In: Dustdar, S., Fiadeiro, J.L., Sheth, A.P. (eds.) BPM 2006. LNCS, vol. 4102, pp. 81–96. Springer, Heidelberg (2006)
20. Moser, O., Rosenberg, F., Dustdar, S.: Non-intrusive monitoring and service adaptation for ws-bpel. In: Proc. of WWW, pp. 815–824 (2008)
21. Motahari Nezhad, H.R., Xu, G.Y., Benatallah, B.: Protocol-aware matching of web service interfaces for adapter development. In: Proc. of WWW, pp. 731–740 (2010)
22. Nebal, B., Koehler, J.: Plan Reuse versus Plan Generation: A Theoretical and Empirical Analysis. Artificial Intelligence Journal 76(1-2), 427–454 (1995)
23. Oh, S.C., Lee, D., Kumara, S.: Web Service Planner (WSPR): An Effective and Scalable Web Service Composition Algorithm. International Journal of Web Service Research 4(1), 1–22 (2007)
24. Papazoglou, M., Traverso, P., Dustdar, S., Leymann, F.: Service-oriented computing research roadmap (2006), technical report, http://infolab.uvt.nl/staff/mikep/publications/
25. Peer, J.: Web Service Composition as AI Planning – a Survey. Tech. rep., University of St.Gallen (2005)
26. Poizat, P., Yan, Y.: Adaptive Composition of Conversational Services through Graph Planning Encoding. In: Proc. of ISoLA (to appear 2010)
27. Rao, J., Su, X.: A survey of automated web service composition methods. In: Cardoso, J., Sheth, A.P. (eds.) SWSWPC 2004. LNCS, vol. 3387, pp. 43–54. Springer, Heidelberg (2005)
28. Seguel, R., Eshuis, R., Grefen, P.: An overview on protocol adaptors for service component integration (2008), working Paper from, http://is.tm.tue.nl/staff/heshuis/publications.html
29. Sohrabi, S., Prokoshyna, N., McIlraith, S.A.: Web service composition via the customization of golog programs with user preferences. In: Borgida, A.T., Chaudhri, V.K., Giorgini, P., Yu, E.S. (eds.) Conceptual Modeling: Foundations and Applications. LNCS, vol. 5600, pp. 319–334. Springer, Heidelberg (2009)
30. Yan, Y., Poizat, P., Zhao, L.: Repairing service compositions in a changing world. In: Proc. of SERA (2010)
31. Yoo, J.W., Kumara, S., Lee, D., Oh, S.C.: A Web Service Composition Framework Using Integer Programming with Non-functional Objectives and Constraints. In: Proc. of CEC/EEE. pp. 347–350 (2008)
32. Zheng, X., Yan, Y.: An Efficient Web Service Composition Algorithm Based on Planning Graph. In: Proc. of ICW 2008, pp. 691–699 (2008)

Interoperation, Composition and Simulation of Services at Home

Eirini Kaldeli, Ehsan Ullah Warriach, Jaap Bresser,
Alexander Lazovik, and Marco Aiello*

Distributed Systems Group
Johann Bernoulli Institute
University of Groningen
Nijenborgh 9, 9747 AG, The Netherlands
{e.kaldeli,e.u.warriach,j.bresser,a.lazovik,m.aiello}@rug.nl

Abstract. Pervasive computing environments such as our future homes are the prototypical example of a dynamic, complex system where Service-Oriented Computing techniques will play an important role. A home equipped with heterogeneous devices, whose services and location constantly change, needs to behave as a coherent system supporting its inhabitants. In this paper, we present a fully implemented architecture for domotic applications which uses the concept of a service as its fundamental abstraction. The architecture distinguishes between a pervasive layer where devices and their basic internetworking live, and a composition layer where services can be dynamically composed as a reaction to user desires or home events. Next to the architecture, we also illustrate a visualization and simulation environment to test home coordination scenarios. From the technical point of view, the implementation uses UPnP as the basic device connection protocol and techniques from Artificial Intelligence planning for composing services at runtime.

Keywords: Pervasive Services, Internet of Things, Composition.

1 Introduction

The vision of the Internet of Things brings a number of fresh challenges, that the field of Service-Oriented Computing can help to address. Having a large number of autonomous and heterogeneous objects whose location, connectivity, and set of functionalities may change during a home's life cycle, requires a rich and flexible infrastructure. Support for interoperation, dynamic discovery, sensing of the current execution context, and run-time service compositions are among the most notable elements of such an infrastructure.

In this paper, we focus our attention on the smart home. Following the vision of the Smart Homes for All project [19], we design and implement a software architecture based on the concept of service, that supports the integration of

---

* The research is supported by the EU project Smart Homes for All (http://www.sm4all-project.eu), contract FP7-224332.

P.P. Maglio et al. (Eds.): ICSOC 2010, LNCS 6470, pp. 167–181, 2010.

heterogeneous home devices, the inference of the home context, and the possibility to compose services inside the home as a response to a user need or a home event. Technologies based on Service Orientation are not new for pervasive systems. UPnP and Jini [6] have been proposed as protocols and architectures for dynamic device and functionality discovery, based on describing services in terms of WSDL and Java interfaces respectively. These are excellent starting points for our study, as they provide support for basic interoperation, but to realize genuinely smart homes, more aspects need to be designed in terms of home sensing and composition.

Our approach is driven by the proposition that domestic events, may these be generated by a user's desire or by a home situation that needs to be handled, can be best addressed by designing a complex behavior specific to the event and the current home context. When a fire breaks for example, one does not simply want to turn on a fire alarm, but rather, based on what services are available in the home in terms of alarms, sprinklers, automatic doors, and so on, infer the status of the home and the location of the user, and then compose the available services to ensure maximum safety for the home inhabitants, as well as protection for the home itself. Such a philosophy of design for pervasive systems also brings an extra added value: the system is portable to several homes with minimal reconfiguration. In fact, the same event will be dealt with differently in different homes, simply because the available services will be diverse, as well as the state of the environment.

The paper makes concrete the vision and philosophy above by resorting to Artificial Intelligence (AI) planning techniques for service composition, and UPnP as the basic protocol for interoperation. Building on our previous work on service composition [12,9] and creating a framework for integrating devices, we implement an instance of a SM4All architecture which is able to deal with physical and simulated devices, and also visualize home behaviors. The implementation is then evaluated to show that, despite the fact that we use elaborate AI techniques, the system performs rapidly, and a road to actual home deployment is definitely feasible.

The paper is organized as follows. A description of a possible scenario in a smart home, working as our running example, is presented in Section 2. Then we introduce the SM4All architecture, and we focus on the composition and pervasive layers in Section 3. Section 4 provides details of the RuG ViSi visualization tool. The results of performance evaluation for the framework at both its composition and pervasive layer are presented in Section 5. A discussion of related work and conclusions are presented in Sections 6 and 7 respectively.

2   Getting a Beer

The soccer World Cup is well under way and the user of our smart home, as many others, likes to watch TV with a cold beer in his hands. Without too much planning, he simply has to make sure that there is beer available in the house, and that he has paid the electricity bills so that the TV can work. This simple scenario can help illustrate the behavior of our smart home.

Let's assume that the inhabitant of the house has just taken his bath, and wants to move to the sitting room to watch the forthcoming soccer match. Such a request may include instructions about how the sitting room atmosphere should be prepared—by adjusting the lights, probably opening the window if the temperature is too high, and turning on the TV. During the halftime break, the user decides to go to the kitchen to prepare something to eat. While being there, the smoke detector in the kitchen identifies a potentially dangerous smoke leak—but fortunately not due to fire. As a result, a predefined home goal for dealing with this situation is automatically triggered: after having ensured that the user has safely moved out of the kitchen (let's say to the adjacent sitting room), the door leading to the kitchen is closed to isolate the smoke in a single room. The ventilator, if present, is turned on and the kitchen window is also opened, so that the foul air is expelled, while an alarm notification appears on the TV screen. While waiting in the sitting room, the user wants to move back to the kitchen, but only after having assured that the environment there is safe, and the smoke has been eliminated. This wish implies resorting to sensing to identify the current situation in the kitchen. Let's assume that after some time the smoke is indeed eliminated, causing the alarm on the TV and the ventilator to automatically turn off, and the user can finally move to the kitchen. After verifying that no serious damage has been caused, he decides to move back to the sitting room in order not to miss the second half of the match, that has just started.

While sitting on the sofa, and trying to overcome the stress from the unfortunate smoke leak incident, the user wishes to have a cold beer in his hand. Assuming that the household is equipped with a robot device, which is able to move around the house, get and put items at particular places and sense their temperature, the task for getting a cold beer can be assigned to the robot. Let's say that the user has neglected to put any beers in the fridge, however the system finds out that there are some beers left on the store shelf. Having this information in hand, the robot will move to the storage room and get a beer from there. In order to satisfy the requirement that the beer should be cold, it will proceed in placing the beer it has taken in the fridge, and leave it there for two minutes to cool. Then it will take it out again and bring it to the sofa. It should be noted that if the same goal was issued in another home instance, in which the robot device has only the capability of getting items from the fridge, the user would be unfortunate enough to be left without his highly desired cold beer, if there is no one such available in the fridge.

3   Architecture

The middleware is the software layer that abstracts from distribution, providing a coherent application interface. In the case of the Smart Home the middleware is a *thick* layer that has to offer a number of services to the participating components. It has to accommodate for dynamic group membership, asynchronous communication, provide a common message ontology, support heterogeneous and mobile devices, mobility of the user. Most notably, it has to coordinate atomic

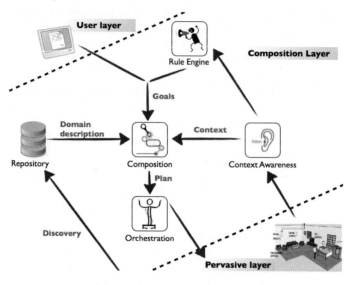

Fig. 1. Architectural overview

device functionalities to satisfy elaborate application needs, that is, not simply expose a de-localized remote function, but rather aggregate and temporize existing functions in order to provide an added-value complex functionality.

In the context of the Smart Homes for All project, we propose a middleware architecture split into three macro layers. At the bottom is the *pervasive layer*, where the heterogeneous sensors, actuators and mobile devices of the house live. In the middle sits the *composition layer*, which is responsible for registering and inferring the state of the home, as well as coordinating it on behalf of the user. On top is the *user layer* which provides the interface to the home. This schematization is illustrated in Figure 1 with the main control and information flows represented by arrows. In this paper, we focus on the composition and pervasive layer, and provide an instance of the architecture. The user layer using touch screen and brain computer interface [8] is beyond the scope of the present treatment.

The central composition layer is further abstracted into five major components. The *context awareness* module is responsible for the collection of the sensed information from the home, and the maintenance of a representation of the execution and user context in the home, by reading information directly from the pervasive layer [5]. The *repository* keeps a number of key data bases which include a registry of description of abstract devices, a registry of currently active devices, semantic descriptions of service invocations, and the layout of the house (e.g., the rooms that comprise it, and how they are arranged). A *rule engine* is constantly informed about any changes in the context, and identifies whether certain conditions hold. If the conditions entail that some action has to be taken, the rule engine directly invokes the composition module. The *composition* module is the central one of the composition layer. It is responsible for finding the right combination of service operations that can satisfy the high level complex goals, issued either by the rule engine (e.g., an emergency goal for combating some dangerous gas that has been identified) or by the user layer (e.g., a request for a beer). The composition module has to be aware of the home description stored in the repository, as well as of the current state of the environment, as seamlessly provided by the context awareness component. The working of the module is based on AI planning [7], therefore we shall interchangeably refer to it as the composition module or *planner*. Once a composition of services is computed, it needs to be executed. The execution is controlled by the *orchestration* module, which retrieves and invokes the physical services. Since the current state of the environment constantly changes, and these changes may interfere with the process in execution, the orchestrator should be able to use the feedback from each invocation to drive the rest of the execution.

In the context of the SM4All project, we have instantiated the general architecture described above using state-of-the-art and novel approaches we have developed. In particular, we use a constraint-based approach to planning in order to compose services [9], and UPnP [1] and OSGi [2] to provide a uniform infrastructure at the pervasive layer. In the followings, we describe in more details the characteristics of each component and how it functions.

Pervasive Layer. The pervasive layer is a dynamic and open environment where devices join and leave while offering and consuming services. A number of requirements have to be satisfied. Firstly, new services should be automatically detected, and the interested parties should be notified accordingly. Secondly, the services should be described in a standardized programmatic manner, and it should be possible to control them in accordance with this description. Thirdly, interested parties should be notified about changes of services' states in a event-driven manner, and communication between services should be enabled regardless of the platform each service runs on. Moreover, the pervasive layer should be able to perform well with varying loads and number of participating devices.

To realize the layer and satisfy the above requirements, we use *Universal Plug and Play (UPnP)* [1] as the protocol for the direct access to hardware services, WSDL and SOAP protocols to expose high-level services, and the *OSGi framework* [2] as the intermediate between the physical UPnP and the WSDL-level service invocations. Figure 2 provides an overview of the architecture of the pervasive layer. At the bottom sits the *network layer* where physical devices can dock. UPnP devices use TCP/IP and UDP as basic networking protocols, but alternatives to UPnP, such as Bluetooth or ZigBee (www.zigbee.org), are also possible. According to the UPnP specification, a device includes a set of services, each of which maintains some *actions*, i.e., operations that can be invoked, and involves some *state variables*, which model the current state of the service.

OSGi provides the framework for the wrapping of devices (UPnP or non-UPnP through the use of a proxy), providing a standard interface for interacting with them. All components participating in the OSGi framework are deployed as so-called bundles. The *Controller* is a special OSGi bundle that is responsible for

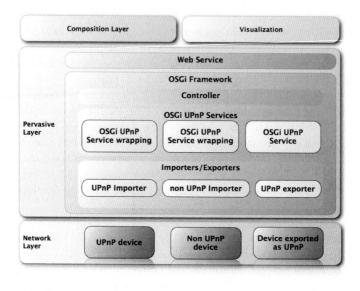

Fig. 2. Pervasive layer architecture

handling events and controlling the services available in the framework, functioning as a bridge between the OSGi layer and the *Web Service (WS) layer*, which provides a standardized API to the upper layers. On top are the clients, which can invoke the services exposed by the available devices. Thanks to an event propagation mechanism, registered clients are notified when UPnP services become available or unavailable, and can subscribe to change events concerning the state variables they are interested in. The clients may be a visualization and simulation tool (see Section 4), a BPEL orchestration engine [13], or a composition layer.

The composition layer. The planner is the module standing at the core of the composition layer. Its task is to compute a *plan*, that is, a sequence of actions that need to be applied in order to satisfy a given goal. Starting from an initial state, which in our case is reflected by the current values of all variables that describe the home domain, the application of each action in the plan leads to a new state, as prescribed by its effects. Referring to Figure 1, we go through the interactions that take place between the planner and the other components of the composition layer. The planner first retrieves the description of the home stored in the repository, and forms the planning domain, by mapping each UPnP action to a planning-level action, specified in terms of preconditions and effects (see Figure 3). This process has to take place once for each house instance, and be repeated only when a new service is discovered or removed.

The planner is being constantly informed about the current values of the variables describing the house by the context module, which receives the notifications about any changes in the environment in accordance with the event

turn_on_ventilator
Preconditions:
  $ventilator := OFF$
Effects:
  $ventilator := ON$

move_robot(destination)
Preconditions:
  $robotLocation \neq destination \wedge$
  $(adjacent\_same\_room(robotLocation, destination) \vee$
  $adjacent\_same\_room(robotLocation, destination) \wedge$
  $door\_open(room(robotLocation), room(destination)))$
Effects:
  $robotLocation := destination$

Fig. 3. Examples of two planning-level actions

propagation mechanism mentioned in Section 3. Upon getting this information, the planner updates its initial state accordingly. Whenever a goal is issued, the planner performs a search to satisfy the goal under the conditions entailed by the specific home and the current initial state. Then the actual plan is generated, and passed further to the orchestrator, which maps each planning-level abstract action to the equivalent concrete UPnP action to be executed in the pervasive layer. In Figure 3 we provide two examples of actions, as described at the planner level. The first action *turn_on_ventilator* states that the action can be applied if the ventilator is OFF in the current state, and has as a result that it will be ON in the next state. The action *move_robot(destination)* instructs how the robot can move to a *destination*, provided as a parameter. The action can be applied if the *destination* does not coincide with the robot's current location *robotLocation*, and if either the current and the destination locations are adjacent to each other and belong to the same room, or, in the case they are neighbor locations but in different rooms, the door between these two rooms is open. Other actions, such as opening doors, can be applied to satisfy the preconditions of the *move_robot* action. This way, the moving will take place in steps, with the robot maneuvering between neighbor locations, based on how these are arranged in the specific house instance. Abiding by such a generic and loosely-coupled encoding, the actions that are common in all houses have to be specified once, without being tied to the details of each specific house.

The planner is a domain-independent CSP-based planner [9], which provides a number of features that are of particular relevance to the requirements associated with smart domotic environments. Firstly, it supports efficient handling of variables with large domains, which are frequently present in intelligent component interactions—e.g., temperature measurements, or the number of beers in our example. Moreover, current advances in the CSP field allow the employment of powerful inference and search techniques to speed-up the search. An important characteristic of the planner, that makes it especially well-suited for adaptable and user-centric environments, is that it allows the expression and satisfaction of extended goals. The supported goal language accommodates for temporal constructs and maintainability properties, and adopts a clear distinction between sensing and achievement goals. The goal is expressed in a declarative way, i.e., it prescribes what properties should be satisfied and under which conditions, but not how the operations should be combined. A set of predefined-defined goals

Table 1. The goals corresponding to the test-case scenario

Goal 1:
watch TV
	achieve-maint($TvState = ON \ \wedge \ sitrLight1 = ON \ \wedge$
	      $sitrLight2 = OFF \ \wedge \ userLocation = AT\_SOFA) \ \wedge$
	(achieve-maint($sitrWindow = OPEN$)
	  under_condition_or_not(
	    find_out-maint($sitrTemperature > 30$)))

Goal 2:
address smoke leak
(by Rule engine)
	achieve-maint($kitchVentilator = ON \ \wedge$
	      $TvState = ALARM \ \wedge kitchWindow = OPEN) \ \wedge$
	(achieve-final($doorsLeadTo(KITCHEN) = CLOSED$)
	  under_condition(
	    achieve-maint($personRoom \neq KITCHEN$)))

Goal 3: smoke eliminated (by Rule engine)	achieve-maint($kitchVentilator = OFF \ \wedge \ TV = OFF$)

Goal 4:
go to kitchen if safe
	achieve-maint($userLocation = AT\_OVEN$))
	  under_condition(
	    find_out-maint($kitchSmoke = OFF$))

Goal 5: bring cold beer	achieve-final($robotLocation = userLocation \ \wedge$ $robotHolds = BEER \ \wedge \ beerTaken = COLD$)

can be made available to the user, hidden behind the buttons that appear in the user interface panel. If the goal issued can be satisfied, the generated plan is executed and the UPnP devices change state accordingly. If the goal is not satisfiable under the current context, a message is shown on the user interface. Table 1 summarizes the goals that correspond to the scenario informally described in Section 2. The syntax and semantics of most constructs can be found in [9] (the language has been enriched with a couple of constructs thereafter). In the case of Goal 1, the under_condition_or_not structure ensures that the subgoal $sitrWindow = OPEN$ will be satisfied if the temperature is higher than 30 degrees, while if the temperature is lower than that, then only the rest of the subgoals will be looked after. This is to be contrasted with the semantics of the under_condition construct, which in Goal 4 for example dictates that $kitchSmoke = OFF$ should necessarily hold, otherwise the goal will fail. The find_out type of subgoals take care of sensing. In the case of achieve-final subgoals, the respective proposition has to be satisfied at the final state, but is allowed to hold or not throughout the plan execution, like for example in Goal 5 where $robotLocation$ will change many times while the robot is moving around to find and get the beers. On the other hand, the maint annotation implies that once the proposition is satisfied, it should remain true in all subsequent states, preventing the variables involved to change many times in the plan states traversal.

It is worth noting that the user does not have to know about the operational details of the service instances available in each specific house. It is up to the planner to find a "creative" solution based on the capabilities of the particular house and the current context, without depending on any ad-hoc business processes. Another useful feature is that, thanks to a mechanism of dynamic addition and removal of constraints, continual planning for newly-issued goals can be performed in an effectual way, as well as the incorporation of recent changes reported by the context-awareness component, after removing the obsolete information.

4   Simulation and Visualization

Testing and verifying the behavior of service orchestration in large pervasive systems is a costly and error prone enterprise, which demands a vast amount of time and effort. Therefore, an environment that mimics as closely as possible the real setting, and is able to simulate a number of interactions and behaviors can greatly help the development and testing of service-based pervasive computing applications. Following our initial implementation of a visualization tool for home environments—the RuG ViSi tool—based on Google SketchUp [13], we have upgraded it to a module compliant with the SM4All architecture, which is capable of full bidirectional interactions with UPnP services or devices deployed with a UPnP proxy. The visualization module is registered as a client of the server on top of the OSGi framework. This way, one can control the devices at the pervasive layer through their virtual equivalents, while the invocations of the actual devices are in turn reflected at the visualization layer, by changing its state. Figure 4 depicts a screenshot from the RuG ViSi tool, with a virtual house

Fig. 4. Simulated UPnP devices in the home

(in the center) surrounded by a number of UPnP devices: a door controller, a wall-fan, a light, two window controllers, a fire alarm and a television set. A UPnP module which represents the position of a user in the house, and can be coupled with a location detector that provides information about the position of the user, is also there (at the bottom). Real physical devices, that may follow different standards and communication protocols, such as Bluetooth or ZigBee, can also be linked to the RuG ViSi tool. For instance, we have coupled a light service with a Sentilla mote (www.sentilla.com) equipped with an accelerometer and a radio connection. The hardware is plugged in the OSGi layer and, when shaken, turns on and off a specific light in the virtual home.[1]

5 Evaluation

We have implemented the architecture described in Section 3 and the simulation and visualization tool described in Section 4. Next, we provide an evaluation of our implementation to show the viability of a home solution based on such an architecture. We start by evaluating the pervasive layer, and then look into the composition layer and consider its interactions with the other modules in the system.

Evaluating the pervasive layer. First, we test the latency in the pervasive layer. The setup is based on using a 2.66 Ghz computer running Windows 7, 64 bit and Java 1.6.0_18. The devices used for the test are implemented as OSGi bundles, i.e., the devices are simulated and wrapped in OSGi. Every device has one service which has a single state variable and action. The clients are implemented in Java using Apache CXF 2.2.5. For the purposes of the evaluation, we define the following quantities and measures: $t\_stimulus$ is the time at the beginning of a UPnP action invocation at one of the test devices, and $t\_response$ the time a client receives a notification that a state variable changed as the result of an action invocation. *Latency* is the absolute temporal difference between stimulus and response of an action. This way, latency includes both service control latency (latency related to the invocation of the action) and eventing latency (latency related to the event notification mechanism).

In the context of this test, a device is a simulated OSGi UPnP device, with one service, one state variable *count* of type integer, and one action called *setCount*, which acts as a setter for *count*. Since each device has one service, the terms (UPnP) device and (UPnP) service are used interchangeably. A client is an instance of a WS client whose only function is to record the time, when it is informed about state variable changes. Real clients, such as the visualization client or the composition layer, would of course include more functionalities.

The testing protocol is as follows. After bootstrapping, each client subscribes to *device_count* state variables (of *device_count* different devices). Then, the following step is repeated *iteration_count* times, with increasing values of *current_iteration*: for each device $t\_stimulus$ is stored, its action is invoked with

---

[1] A demo is available at www.youtube.com/watch?v=2w_UIwRqtBY..

current_iteration as a value, and then a sleeping time of *sleep_time* ms is issued. Upon receiving a notification that a state variable has changed, each client stores the current time in the *t_response* which corresponds to the specific state variable and iteration (as reflected by the received value *current_iteration*).

Finally, the time measurements are aggregated to compute latency. Figure 5 shows how the performance of the system behaves when the number of clients increases, by plotting the average latency. We also tried to increase the number of devices up to 2.000 and have experienced latency times in the order of 6 ms. It should be noted that domotic systems involve more complex devices, and therefore the results of these tests should not be used to make exact predictions on how a real system will perform. The evaluation however indicates that the tool can support many clients and a high number of devices, still providing very low response times. Next, we consider a very special type of client: the composition module based on planning.

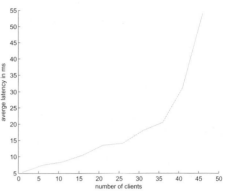

Fig. 5. Average latency with iteration_count = 10, device_count = 100, sleep_time = 100ms

Evaluating the composition Layer. Considering the scenario of Section 2, we implement all devices and services according to our architecture, and provide an initial evaluation of the performance of the composition layer. The tests have been run on a 1.83 Ghz computer running Debian GNU/Linuz 5.0, 32 bit and Java 1.6.0_12. The components are described with respect to the OSGI UPnP Device Specification and are exposed as OSGi bundles, with each device supporting one or more services, each of which involves a number of actions and state variables. The constraint solver standing at the core of the planner is the Choco v2.1.1 constraint solving library (www.emn.fr/x-info/choco-solver). The composition layer is registered as a client to the WS server of the middleware, and subscribes to all services comprising the domain. In the specific evaluation, we model a home with 5 rooms, and 10 devices providing 21 UPnP actions (plus the sensing operations that are defined for each state variable in the domain), which affect 22 different state variables. The user himself is represented as one of the services at the pervasive layer. It should be noted that a state variable can be accessed or affected by more than one services, possibly belonging to different devices, like the *FridgeDoor* variable, which, besides the *Fridge* device, can also be directly set by the *Robot*, when for instance it wants to cool a beer. Each of the exposed UPnP actions is mapped to an equivalent planner-level action, as the ones shown in Figure 3.

We have tested the planner on each of the goals in Table 1, for different initial states in accordance with our testing scenario. Table 2 shows two examples of such plans. Each plan is represented as a partially ordered set of actions, with comma-separated actions $a1, a2$ indicating that a_1 has to be performed before a_2, while the actions included in the same set $\{a_1, \ldots, a_n\}$ can be executed in parallel. As one can see, the same goal for getting a cold beer results in different plans, depending on the current context: if there are no beers in the fridge ([5a]) the robot has first to move to the storage to get a beer from there, and then cool it by moving back to the fridge, while in the second case ([5b]) it can save some effort by getting the requested beer directly from the fridge. It should be noted that because of the use of random search strategies, the plans returned may slightly vary between different runs.

Table 2. The plans generated for Goal 5 (getting a cold beer), for two different initial states (only the initial values that are of interest to the goal are mentioned)

Goal/Initial state	Plan
[5a] Goal 5 (get cold beer) with initial state : *robotLocation=AT_START,* *userLocation=AT_SOFA,* *kitchStorDoor=CLOSED,* *sitrKitchDoor = CLOSED,* *numOfBeersInFridge=0,* *numOfBeersInStorage=8,* *robotHolds=EMPTY,* *fridgeDoor=CLOSED*	*open_fridgeDoor,* { *open_sitrKitchDoor,* *open_kitchStorDoor*}, *move_robot_to(AT_OVEN),* *move_robot_to(AT_STOR_SHELF),* *robotGetsBeerFromStorage,* *move_robot_to(AT_FRIDGE),* *robotCoolsBeer,* { *open_fridgeDoor,* *close_kitchStorDoor*}, *robotGetsBeerFromFridge,* { *move_robot_to(AT_SOFA),* *close_fridgeDoor*}
[5b] Same as above but with *numOfBeersInFridge = 1*	*open_fridgeDoor, open_sitrKitchDoor,* *move_robot_to(AT_FRIDGE),* { *robotGetsBeerFromFridge,* *open_kitchStorDoor, open_bedrBathrDoor,* *open_sitrBedrDoor*}, { *move_robot_to(AT_SOFA),* *close_fridgeDoor*}

The time required by the planner to subscribe to the available UPnP services, build the planning-level domain description, and sense the first initial state, by invoking the UPnP sensing actions for all state variables, is 9.7 sec. This is the 'home bootstrap' time and needs to be executed only once per house and per set of devices. We have measured the time the planner takes to generate a plan for each of the goals, for a given initial state (the time taken by the other components of the composition layer is negligible for the tests we run), as well as the time needed for each plan to be actually executed by invoking the respective simulated UPnP actions. These results are summarized in Table 3, along with the number of actions included in the respective plan. We have used a random branching strategy during constraint solving, by restarting the search after a maximum number of backtracks. The reported times both for composition and execution

Table 3. The time required for composition and execution. In [5a], which includes the *CoolBeer* action, we have subtracted the time the robot waits for the beer to cool.

Test	Number of actions in plan	Plan Composition (time in sec.)	Plan execution (time in sec.)
[1] (watch TV)	10	1.5	1.1
[2] (address smoke leak)	9	1.1	0.8
[3] (smoke eliminated)	2	0.7	0.3
[4a] (go to kitchen, smoke on)	0	0.1	–
[4b] (go to kitchen, smoke off)	4–5	0.7	0.4
[5a] (get beer, fridge empty)	12–15	2.4	0.6
[5b] (get beer, fridge full)	6–9	2.1	0.5

are averaged over 5 separate runs. As already mentioned, the plans may differ in some of the test situations, in which cases we mention both the minimum and the maximum number of actions in the produced plans. It turns out that the most demanding goal is 5 (getting a cold beer), especially in the case where there are no beers already stored in the fridge, mainly due to the substantial backtracking required to find a solution (up to 478 backtracks, compared to 47 backtracks in the worst case concerning the other goals). In general, the more indirect the inter-relations between the different actions required to satisfy the goal are, the more search and backtracks are needed to compute the desired plan.

The changes entailed by the generated plan can also be visualized in the simulated home environment. The visualization client has been tested on a more restricted modelling of a house consisting of two rooms (see footnote 1 in Section 4).

6   Related Work

In [4,3] we survey domotic standards and propose to use the Web service stack as a means to solve the interoperability problem at home. We show how WS-Notification can be used as an event-based mechanism for addressing emergency situations in the home, most notably, the fall of an elder. The basic architecture is an eventing one with no notion of context and coordination of service beyond basic action/reaction interactions. The issue of composing domotic components has been addressed in [18], where composite services are deployed as BPEL processes, which are made available in a semantically enriched OSGi platform. These BPEL processes are predefined and not created at run-time, based on sensed information. A more dynamic approach inspired from AI techniques is adopted in [17], where the problem of service integration is cast to Distributed Constraint Optimization. This is a highly distributed framework, however it suffers from an inflexible and cumbersome domain modelling process, while the requests the user can make are restricted to a set of rather simple commands that involve only a limited number of devices. AI planning techniques for Web Service composition have been proposed by a number of authors, e.g., [12,11,14]. A common denominator of most of the approaches in this area is that they can support a restricted variety of composite functionalities, either because they rely on—to a lesser or greater extent—fixed templates of pre-anticipated user behaviors, or because they support simple goals, with limited expressive power.

From the pervasive layer perspective, Service Oriented Architectures have been widely proposed, e.g., UPnP or Jini [6]. A richer form of "pervasive SOA" is proposed in [15], where the importance for home networks with platform independence and loose coupling is advocated. In [15] the challenges that currently exist in interconnecting home devices are described, and it is recognized that OSGi can be useful for developing smart homes. In [16], a semantic annotation of the OSGi description is proposed to improve the discovery process. Looking at UPnP [1], its use as low level home middleware has been often proposed, e.g., [10].

7   Concluding Remarks

Service-Oriented computing provides an advanced approach to building dynamic systems. If its initial thrust came from the need of integration of business information systems, the future may add a new important area: pervasive computing with our homes being an important instance. We have designed, implemented and evaluated a generic SOA for homes which supports highly dynamic computing context. Our initial evaluation indicates that the approach using AI planning, context awareness, and OSGi/UPnP device wrapping is a viable one.

To achieve a robust, scalable and user-friendly solution, many research challenges remain open. Dealing with *concurrency* and possible contradictions that may arise when events interfere with the execution of a plan, is an important extension of our framework. Improving the *efficiency* of the planner used for composition, and moving towards generating optimal plans, is also high in our agenda, as are *context* updates and efficiency in sensing. Another direction of future work involves further automating the process of transforming the pervasive-level services to planning-level actions by using an ontology that provides the necessary semantic annotations. Security, privacy, and user interfacing are also important topics currently investigated by other partners of the SM4All project.

References

1. Upnp[TM] device architecture version 1.1 (2008), http://www.upnp.org
2. OSGi service platform core specification release 4 (2009), http://www.osgi.org
3. Aiello, M.: The Role of Web Services at Home. In: IEEE Web Service-based Systems and Applications, WEBSA (2006)
4. Aiello, M., Dustdar, S.: A domotic infrastructure based on the web service stack. Pervasive and Mobile Computing 4(4), 506–525 (2008)

5. Baldoni, R., Cerocchi, A., Lodi, G., Montanari, L., Querzoni, L.: Designing highly available repositories for heterogeneous sensor data in open home automation systems. In: Lee, S., Narasimhan, P. (eds.) SEUS 2009. LNCS, vol. 5860, pp. 144–155. Springer, Heidelberg (2009)
6. Dobrev, P., Famolari, D., Kurzke, C., Miller, B.A.: Device and service discovery in home networks with osgi. Communications Magazine, IEEE 40(8), 86–92 (2002)
7. Ghallab, M., Nau, D., Traverso, P.: Automated Planning: Theory and Practice. Morgan Kaufmann, Amsterdam (2004)
8. Guger, C., Daban, S., Sellers, E., Holzner, C., Krausz, G., Carabalona, R., Gramatica, F., Edlinger, G.: How many people are able to control a P300-based brain-computer interface (BCI)? Neuroscience Letters 462, 94–98 (2009)
9. Kaldeli, E., Lazovik, A., Aiello, M.: Extended goals for composing services. In: Proceedings of the 19th International Conference on Automated Planning and Scheduling, ICAPS 2009, Thessaloniki, Greece, September 19-23, AAAI, Menlo Park (2009)
10. Kim, D.S., Lee, J.M., Kwon, W.H., Yuh, I.K.: Design and implementation of home network systems using upnp middleware for networked appliances. IEEE Transactions on Consumer Electronics, 963–972 (2002)
11. Kuter, U., Sirin, E., Nau, D., Parsia, B., Hendler, J.: Information Gathering During Planning for Web Service Composition. Journal of Web Semantics (2004)
12. Lazovik, A., Aiello, M., Papazoglou, M.: Planning and monitoring the execution of web service requests. In: Orlowska, M.E., Weerawarana, S., Papazoglou, M.P., Yang, J. (eds.) ICSOC 2003. LNCS, vol. 2910, pp. 335–350. Springer, Heidelberg (2003)
13. Lazovik, E., den Dulk, P., de Groote, M., Lazovik, A., Aiello, M.: Services inside the smart home: A simulation and visualization tool. In: Baresi, L., Chi, C.-H., Suzuki, J. (eds.) ICSOC-ServiceWave 2009. LNCS, vol. 5900, pp. 651–652. Springer, Heidelberg (2009)
14. Martínez, E., Lespérance, Y.: Web Service Composition as a Planning Task: Experiments using Knowledge-Based Planning. In: Proc. of the Workshop on Planning and Scheduling for Web and Grid Services, ICAPS 2004 (2004)
15. Ngo, L.: Service-oriented architecture for home networks. In: Seminar on Internet-working, pp. 1–6 (2007)
16. Panagiotis Gouvas, T.B., Mentzas, G.: An OSGi-Based Semantic Service-Oriented Device Architecture. In: OTM 2007, pp. 773–782 (2007)
17. Pecora, F., Cesta, A.: DCOP for Smart Homes: a Case Study. Computational Intelligence 23(4), 395–419 (2007)
18. Redondo, R.P.D., Vilas, A.F., Cabrer, M.R., Arias, J.J.P., Duque, J.G., Solla, A.G.: Enhancing residential gateways: A semantic OSGi platform. IEEE Intelligent Systems 23(1), 32–40 (2008)
19. SM4All: Smart hoMes for All (2008-2011), http://www.sm4art-project.eu

Efficient QoS-Aware Service Composition with a Probabilistic Service Selection Policy

Adrian Klein[1], Fuyuki Ishikawa[2], and Shinichi Honiden[1,2]

[1] The University of Tokyo, Japan
[2] National Institute of Informatics, Tokyo, Japan
{adrian,f-ishikawa,honiden}@nii.ac.jp

Abstract. Service-Oriented Architecture enables the composition of loosely coupled services provided with varying Quality of Service (QoS) levels. Given a composition, finding the set of services that optimizes some QoS attributes under given QoS constraints has been shown to be NP-hard. Until now the problem has been considered only for a single execution, choosing a single service for each workflow element. This contrasts with reality where services often are executed hundreds and thousands of times. Therefore, we modify the problem to consider repeated executions of services in the long-term. We also allow to choose multiple services for the same workflow element according to a probabilistic selection policy. We model this modified problem with Linear Programming, allowing us to solve it optimally in polynomial time. We discuss and evaluate the different applications of our approach, show in which cases it yields the biggest utility gains, and compare it to the original problem.

1 Introduction

1.1 SOA

Service-Oriented Architecture (SOA) consists of a set of design principles which enable defining and composing interoperable services in a loosely coupled way. The value of SOA lies in assuring such compositions are easily and rapidly possible with low costs. Thus, service composition is a key to SOA. Especially, achieving an automatic service composition remains a major challenge [1].

When selecting a service not only functional requirements, but also the non-functional requirements [2], expressed by Quality of Service (QoS) attributes, are very important. Especially, when there are many functionally equivalent services, the QoS becomes the deciding factor. Thus, QoS-awareness is of crucial importance in service composition.

QoS-aware automatic service composition is employed in two different problem settings: In the planning problem the composition itself is computed by taking into consideration available input data and desired output data. While the heuristics used for the planning can be geared towards optimizing QoS [3], finding a functionally sufficient composition is the main focus.

P.P. Maglio et al. (Eds.): ICSOC 2010, LNCS 6470, pp. 182–196, 2010.

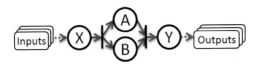

Fig. 1. Sample Composition

This contrasts the traditional composition problem[1] where the functional part, the composition itself, is already given, e.g. as a business process specified with BPEL [4], requiring some inputs, invoking some tasks, and producing some desired outputs (Fig. 1).

The main focus lies in selecting the set of services, with one service per task, to execute the composition optimally with regards to QoS. This means to maximize the overall QoS of the composition according to given preferences while adhering to given QoS constraints [5]. Of course, the output of the planning problem could be used as an input for the composition problem.

1.2 Composition Problem

In this paper we will focus on the latter, the composition problem. For example, if we take a simple workflow consisting of a sequence of two tasks X and Y, and corresponding services S_1, S_2 and S_3, S_4 that can fulfill X and Y, respectively, there are four possibilities to execute this workflow (Fig. 2). Out of those possibilities, the most common approach is to select the optimal set of services regarding QoS preferences and constraints given [5,6].

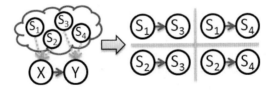

Fig. 2. Sample Composition Problem

Trying all combinations obviously takes exponential time. Modeling it as a Multi-Choice Multidimensional Knapsack problem (MMKP) gives the same result, as MMKP is known to be NP-hard [7]. In order to make use of existing solvers, the problem is usually modeled by Integer (Linear) Programming (IP), which is also NP-hard to solve in the general case. Thus, as of today, the problem cannot be solved efficiently in polynomial time. This is an obstacle to the vision of SOA encompassing a future "Enabling a Web of billions of services"[2] where

---

[1] We will refer to this problem as the composition problem from now on.
[2] Credo & goal of the SOA4ALL project (part of the European FP7): www.soa4all.eu

efficient algorithms are crucial in order to enable fast composition queries and adaptation at runtime.

1.3   Contribution

In the present state of the art, approaches for the composition problem implicitly assume that a service is executed only a single time. As a result, one service is statically assigned to each task. We believe that in many situations a service composition will be executed repeatedly. Thus, we propose to optimize the QoS for the long-term, which implies the following:

1. There is no need to choose always the same set of services for each execution.
2. QoS constraints should also be applied for the long-term, e.g. keeping to a monthly budget or assuring an hourly throughput.

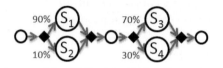

Fig. 3. Sample Probabilistic Composition

For instance, the combinations $\{S_1, S_3\}$ and $\{S_2, S_4\}$ could represent different trade-offs to execute the given workflow: One being fast/expensive and the other cheap/slow. In such a case, for the long-term an optimal solution will most likely contain a probabilistic mix of those two combinations in a certain ratio (Fig. 3) in order to satisfy constraints on budget and throughput while adhering to the QoS preferences given. We propose that such a solution is represented by a set of probabilistic service selection policies. For each task a policy defines the probability that a service is chosen for it at runtime.

As for the computational approach, we propose to use linear programming (LP). We do not restrict our problem to integer solutions, as we represent the decision to choose a certain service with a continuous probability value, not a (binary) integer value. Thus, besides this difference, we can use identical modeling as in IP, and, at the same time, profit from efficient polynomial algorithms to solve the problem. The only caveat is that such probabilistic modeling also changes the nature of the specified QoS constraints, forcing them to apply to the long-term. Later we will discuss the detailed implications of this fact, and show some alternative ways to still guarantee QoS constraints for each execution, if needed.

To summarize, we propose an approach for the service composition problem that is both efficient and QoS-aware, maximizes QoS over the long-term, and results in a set of probabilistic service selection policies. According to this policies the services will be chosen probabilistically at runtime.

The structure of this paper is as follows: Section 2 surveys related work. Section 3 defines our approach. Section 4 explains the possible applications of our approach. Section 5 evaluates the performance and effectiveness of our approach. Finally, Section 6 concludes the paper.

2   Related Work

In this section we survey related work which can be roughly classified into four different categories: work laying the foundation for our approach, work presenting an alternative to our approach, complementary work, and work sharing similar ideas.

The foundation for the QoS-aware composition problem is given in [5]. Many common notions we use are introduced there, and the problem is formalized and solved using IP.

As performance is such an important issue there are many alternative approaches tackling it. One popular theme is to to reduce the search space with heuristics [6,8,9]. Another alternative is to use a genetic algorithm to solve the problem [10]. Only optimizing locally is also an option [11], though its conception is slightly opposite to our idea that multiple services can be mixed and (globally) compensate each others QoS. In comparison to our approach, all this approaches are also efficient, but find only approximate solutions to the given optimization problem.

A complementary approach is to compute the skyline of the services involved in the composition beforehand in order to prune services that can never be part of an optimal solution [12]. Obviously, this can be easily integrated with our approach.

There is also work that shares ideas on a conceptual level. In [13] multiple services for the same task are provisioned for adaptation at runtime in the case that one of them fails. For instance, if the first service for a task fails, the second one will be called, and so on. The goal is to improve the failure resilience of a service execution, but not to combine those multiple services by calling them probabilistically at runtime. Regarding considering several executions over the long-term, there is not much related work, but in [14] we already showed an approach that optimizes the service selection for a specific user given his expected usage over the long-term. To the best of our knowledge no related work exists that considers repeated executions of services in the long-term for QoS-aware optimization though.

In conclusion our contribution lies in optimizing the QoS in the long-term efficiently in polynomial time and in selecting between multiple services probabilistically at runtime.

3   Approach

In this section we define our approach formally. The notions, which we will briefly introduce in this section, follow the IP versions of the problem given in [5,6]. Afterwards, we explain what the consequences of modeling the problem as LP are with regards to the properties that hold for the solutions found.

3.1   Formal Definition

As in [6], the following composition patterns are supported: Seq (sequential execution), AND (parallel execution), XOR (alternative execution with certain probabilities p_i) and Loop (with maximum loop count x).

Fig. 4. Composition patterns: Seq, AND, XOR, Loop

For any given workflow, we have to aggregate the QoS according to the composition patterns. As usual, we unroll any loop to a sequence according to the maximum loop count. Then, the QoS gets aggregated according to the aggregation functions presented in [15]. (Also attributes and their corresponding constraints aggregated by non-linear functions are linearized for the LP formalization, e.g. by taking their logarithm.) Given n aggregated QoS attributes $q_1, \ldots, q_n$, we normalize them like in [5] in order to limit their values to $[0, 1]$ and to be able to simply maximize the weighted sum of their normalized values $\tilde{q}_1, \ldots, \tilde{q}_n$:

$$\sum_{i=1}^{n} w_i \tilde{q}_i \qquad (1)$$

Regarding the constraints, we first consider a sample workflow that consists of the four tasks $\{X, Y, A, B\}$ (Fig. 5). A and B are executed in parallel, while the rest is executed sequentially. Thus, each execution of this workflow will execute all four tasks. In addition, there are two paths through the workflow, namely $\{X, A, Y\}$ and $\{X, B, Y\}$. Therefore, we maximize the sum of (1) over all paths, as this has been proven to produce the best results in [6].

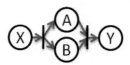

Fig. 5. Sample Workflow

The constraints Q_i^{min}/Q_i^{max} are applied on the aggregated non-normalized QoS of the workflow:

$$q_i \geq Q_i^{min} \land q_i \leq Q_i^{max} \qquad (2)$$

We follow [6] in that a constraint needs to be applied to the whole workflow, and/or to each path, depending on the particular kind of QoS and the workflow. For example, for response time in conjunction with parallel executions paths, we have to apply the constraint for each path (e.g. $\{X, A, Y\}$ and $\{X, B, Y\}$), while for price we have to apply its constraint to the whole execution (e.g. $\{X, Y, A, B\}$).

Regarding the selection variables, for each task t_i, we introduce as many variables s_{ij} as there are services capable of performing that task. This variables represent the possible choices in our LP problem. In our approach, they represent probabilities and, thus, are not constrained to be integers which is a difference to the notions in [5,6]. Only their sum must be equal to one for each task, as usual.

3.2   Relaxation

In general, removing the integer restriction on the variables of an IP problem is called relaxing the IP problem. Thus, from now on, we will refer to the former IP problem as the original problem and to our LP problem as the relaxed problem.

One important consequence is that we can solve our relaxed problem with regular linear programming for which efficient algorithms like Simplex or Interior Point exist that solve the problem in polynomial time. This is opposed to the algorithms needed for IP that are exponential in the worst-case as IP is NP-hard. The corresponding caveat is that this changes the nature of our constraints. For instance a solution to the relaxed problem does not necessarily solve the original problem, as seen from a small example workflow consisting of a single task with two services A and B chosen for it according to Table 1. Such a probabilistic combination of A and B will perfectly satisfy a constraint of 100ms on the response time, as the QoS of A and B are multiplied by their probabilities before being compared to the constraint. Thus, individual executions will violate the constraint, even if in the long-term the expected value of the response time fulfills the constraint. We will show some approaches that deal with this issue in the next section where we describe how our approach can be applied. Those enable us to get closer to guaranteeing QoS constraints for each execution, if needed.

Regarding the utility obtained, the solution to our relaxed problem is guaranteed to be at least as good, or better than the solution to the original problem. That is because the feasible solutions of the original problem are only a subset of the feasible solutions of the relaxed problem. The absolute difference in utility depends on the formalization of the problem (e.g. scaling of QoS), but the relative difference can become arbitrary large. Intuitively, a constraint could forbid to choose a good solution in the original problem, even if the constraint is only violated slightly. On the contrary, in the relaxed problem we can choose this solution, if we can compensate this small violation in the long-term.

Table 1. Example Service Combination

Service	Probability	Response time
A	50%	150ms
B	50%	50ms

3.3   Result

As for the result of our approach, we get a set of probabilistic service selection policies, as illustrated in Fig. 6. At runtime the services are chosen according to those policies. An approach that also tries to limit the deviation from the policies at any given time should be preferred to a purely random strategy.

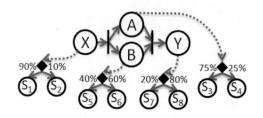

Fig. 6. Probabilistic Service Selection Policy

4   Application

In this section we show four different ways of applying our approach in practice: We apply it to solve the original and the relaxed problem. Also it can be applied to solve a refinement of our relaxed problem, and, as part of a computer-aided decision process, it can be applied, too.

4.1   Original Problem

One interesting application is to use the solution of the relaxed problem to find a solution for the original problem. The advantage of doing this is the performance gain compared to using IP. This raises the questions, if this is possible, and, if such solutions are optimal. To answer these questions, it is important to examine how the solution to the relaxed problem differs from the one for the original problem. As we get a set of probabilistic service selection policies instead of a set of concrete services, a single solution to the relaxed problem contains many potential solutions to the original problem. But, as we know, those solutions only satisfy the QoS constraints in the long-term.

For example, the probabilistic composition in Fig. 7 satisfies a constraint of 3.2 seconds on its response time[3], and to assure this constraint for each execution, we can choose the subset of possible executions colored in grey. Apparently, if we have just a single constraint, a solution that satisfies the QoS constraint for each execution must exist. Given multiple QoS constraints this is no longer true, as no single solution might satisfy all constraints. For example with constraints Q and R, we might have two solutions, one over-satisfying Q, but not satisfying R, and the other one vice versa. Thus, in the long-term their combination may satisfy Q and R, but none of them satisfies both. This means that we may not find such a solution in all cases, especially, if there are many constraints. In

---

[3] The services are annotated with their response times in s(econds) in the figure.

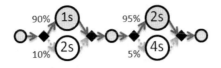

Fig. 7. Choosing a Subset of a Probabilistic Composition

general, it is quite difficult to answer how good the quality of such a solution will be compared to the optimal solution. Therefore, we will rely on giving some empirical results later in the evaluation part. One note regarding the scalability: In order to find such a solution, we have to look at all possible solutions induced by the probabilistic policies. If the number of possible solutions becomes too large, it might be necessary to use a Monte-Carlo approach, just probabilistically checking some solutions instead of an exhaustive search in order not to loose the original performance benefit.

4.2   Relaxed Problem

The most obvious application is, of course, to apply the obtained solution to the relaxed problem. We already discussed that this gives us a better utility than solving the original problem. Also the constraints on the QoS are only guaranteed for the long-term. We already mentioned some cases for which this works really well, e.g. for a budget or throughput applied monthly, daily, et cetera. The question is in which cases this is not acceptable. The most general answer is: when a QoS constraint is important for each and every single execution. While it is difficult to imagine a budget, throughput, or availability to be required for every execution, QoS that directly correspond to the experience of the service user might be a concern. One prime example is response time: a user might only tolerate a certain maximum response time when he calls a service. Also, even if a certain deviation is still acceptable, it might affect the impression of how good a service is. In such cases, not only guaranteeing the QoS constraint in the long-term, but additionally assuring only a limited deviation from it seems better than directly taking the solution to the relaxed problem. This takes us to next application of our approach.

4.3   Refined Relaxed Problem

Applying our approach to solve a refinement of the relaxed problem is the next logical step. The idea is to solve the problem iteratively over and over again, refining it slightly in each iteration to get closer to the desired result, e.g. guaranteeing some QoS constraints for every execution, or at least for a sufficient percentage (e.g. 99.9%) of the executions. If a refinement with a sufficiently good solution can be obtained in a limited (e.g. constant) number of iterations, then we do not even lose the performance benefit either. In general, there are two basic refinements: changing an existing constraint, and adding an additional constraint. Both share the common refinement process shown in Fig. 8.

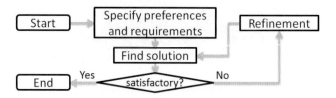

Fig. 8. Refinement Process

For example, to guarantee a better response time for each execution we can make the constraint on response time tighter. This will improve QoS in the long-term and also for each execution on average. Doing this many times might finally produce a solution that satisfies our original constraint for every execution. As we are constraining an average value to guarantee a certain maximum value, this might not always succeed though. Depending on the problem, no matter how good the average is, some outliers might still get included; till the point where a even better average is not possible anymore. Therefore, this kind of refinement might fail and also produce suboptimal solutions, because constraining the average is not our real goal.

An alternative is to add additional constraints with each iteration. The idea is that the found solution contains many combinations of which some over-satisfy our QoS constraints and some under-satisfy them. If we can limit the amount of those under-satisfying them, we can increase the probability that the QoS constraints hold for every execution. In order to do so, we can analyze all found combinations, and restrict a weighted sum of the probabilities of services contributing to under-satisfying such a constraint. Lowering the upper bound on this sum and heuristically determining those weights by how often and how much a service contributes to the under-satisfaction should restrict the maximum value of the QoS in question, and give a good utility. Apparently, this assumes two things:

1. Services not selected in prior iterations cannot be selected in later iterations.
2. At least some of the solution's combinations satisfy the QoS constraints.

Regarding the first point, we only want to analyze a hopefully small number of combinations found in the LP problem instead of an exponential number of all combinations possible. As we saw, the latter is not guaranteed, but guaranteeing only a small number of QoS for each execution might still work out quite often and provide better results than the first refinement given a good heuristic for the weights mentioned. Also combining both types of refinements is possible: tighten the corresponding QoS constraint till a satisfying combination is found, and then constrain all under-satisfying combinations as far as needed.

4.4   Computer-Aided Decision Process

The previous applications all had in common that the problem is solved in an automated way. Of course, this is useful in many cases, but it may not be possible

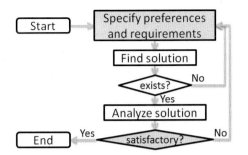

Fig. 9. Decision Process

or desirable in all cases. For such cases we suggest applying our approach as part of a computer-aided decision process. It has some similarities with the previous application in that the problem gets refined in the process. Only the decision of refining itself and of the kind of refinement is left up to a human. The motivation behind that is the difficulty of defining the optimization problem in terms of the objective function and the constraints. Thus, the idea is to let a human actively control and evaluate the refinement of an initial solution till it fits his needs, instead of forcing him to perfectly specify the objective and constraints in the beginning that would automatically lead to a solution. The decision process could then look similar to Fig. 9 which shows the human activities in grey. In the analysis part e.g. each QoS constraint could be analyzed in depth:

- How often is the constraint kept for each execution?
- How big is the possible deviation from the target value?
- How does the probability distribution of the possible values look like?

A small deviation might for example be acceptable. Interpreting the problem as a multi-objective optimization would also be possible, so instead of computing just one optimal solution, several Pareto-optimal solutions could be computed, each representing different trade-offs. Our approach is particularly suited for such kind of applications, because of its performance: being able to run our computations with different problem settings over and over again in a reasonable time, and, thus, being able to explore different scenarios makes it possible to realize such a computer-aided design process.

5   Evaluation

In this section we evaluate our approach taking into account the applications mentioned in the previous section. We evaluate its performance and scalability. Also we analyze the obtained utility gains, and show the results of applying our approach to the original problem.

5.1   Settings

The evaluation was run on a machine with an Intel Core 2 Quad CPU with 3 GHz. As a solver we used CPLEX, a state of the art IP solver from IBM, called from within our Java program which was given 1.5 GB of memory. We generated our workflows as follows: given the workflow size we randomly inserted some control structures, like AND, XOR, et cetera. Unless stated otherwise, the QoS attributes were independently generated with random uniform distributions and typical aggregation patterns. We varied the weights and constraints systematically. The execution time for the optimization was limited to 40 seconds for each individual problem.

5.2   Performance and Scalability

For comparing the performance of LP and IP, we chose 4 attributes with 4 corresponding constraints. For each possible workflow size, 4 different workflows were generated and solved with different weights and constraints for the QoS, resulting in about 250 solved problems per datapoint for both Fig. 10(a) and 10(b). First we compare the performance our LP approach with IP: as shown in Fig. 10(a), the performance is much better for our approach, compared using workflow size 5. We increased the number of services that are available for each task in the workflow from 10 to 40. We can see that already at this small scale using IP at runtime for adaptation or queries is not possible anymore. This is not surprising, because efficient polynomial algorithms are only available for LP. Secondly, we look at the scalability of our LP approach. In Fig. 10(b) we can see the performance of the approach for different workflow sizes (#10–40) and different number of services per task again. The times are below 100ms even for workflows with 40 tasks and 80 services available for each of the tasks. Such performance allows the use even at runtime or under strict performance requirements, e.g. if we want to apply our approach as discussed in the previous section, solving the problem not only once, but several times with different settings.

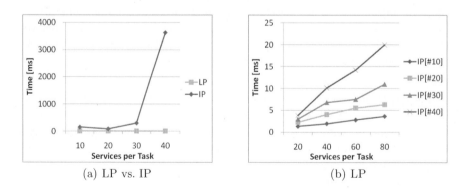

(a) LP vs. IP   (b) LP

Fig. 10. Solution Time

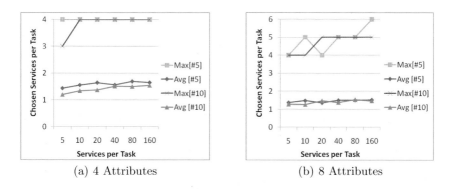

(a) 4 Attributes   (b) 8 Attributes

Fig. 11. Chosen Services per Task

In addition to this, we also analyze how the number of combinations contained by the solutions found scales with the size of the problem. By comparing Fig. 11(a) and Fig. 11(b) we can observe that the maximum number of chosen services per task for each solution seems to be limited only by the number of attributes. Additionally, there is no significant increase in the the average number of services chosen per task. The observed limit is plausible, because each combination represents a specific trade-off that contributes to an optimal solution, and the number of trade-offs is obviously limited by the number of attributes. Still, the number of combinations per workflow increases exponentially in the worst-case. Hence Monte-Carlo methods will indeed be required to explore the combinations efficiently.

5.3 Utility

For evaluating the utility obtained by our approach, we chose 6 attributes of which 3 were bounded with constraints. We generated 4 different workflows of size 5 with 5 services available for each task. Then, we solved the problem with some different weights and many different constraints for the QoS, resulting in

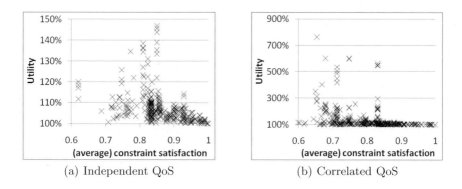

(a) Independent QoS   (b) Correlated QoS

Fig. 12. Utility vs. Constraint Satisfaction

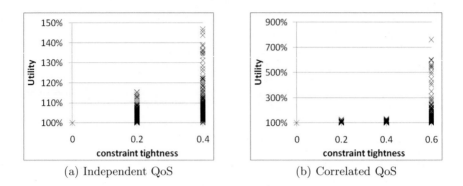

(a) Independent QoS   (b) Correlated QoS

Fig. 13. Utility vs. Tightness of Constraints

over 1200 solved problems for each of the following figures. The most important factor that we varied was how to generate the QoS attributes. First, we generated them independently, and, secondly, we generated them assuming a correlation: all QoS attributes x_i were generated independently, except for one attribute x_p which we calculated from the formula[4] $e^{\sum_{i \neq p} x_i}$. Thus, x_p represents a common price attribute, reflecting that services with better QoS are more expensive. As we can see in Fig. 12(a), the utility obtained does not exceed the utility of the IP approach (which corresponds to 100%) by much in most cases given independent QoS, but at the same time the constraint satisfaction is still quite high on average: each constraint is satisfied in at least over 60% of all executions induced by the probabilistic policies. Still there are some cases, where the utility of the composition is improved to 150% of the IP solution. In the second setting with correlated QoS, we see much higher utility gains shown in Fig. 12(b). One reason is obvious: if we want to achieve good QoS, because of the high cost of selecting a single service that is exceptionally good for all QoS attributes, it is cheaper to achieve the same QoS by combining several services that may only be average on most QoS and good for some QoS. Another observation that we can make from Fig. 13(a) and 13(b) is that the tightness of the constraints chosen influences the (potential) utility gains. We define the tightness as a percentage value regarding the location of the constraint between the minimum and maximum QoS possible for a workflow. For loose constraints the solutions of the IP and LP problem converge, and for tighter constraints they diverge greatly.

5.4   Original Problem

We again chose 6 attributes of which 3 were bounded by constraints, and generated 4 different workflows for each size (#5 and #10) with 5 or 10 services available for each task. Then, we solved the problem with different weights and constraints for the QoS which were either independent (ind) or correlated (corr),

---

[4] Other linear formulas also produced the same tendencies.

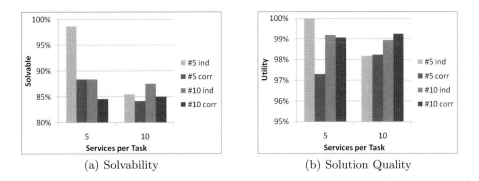

(a) Solvability   (b) Solution Quality

Fig. 14. Solving the Original Problem

resulting in over 600 solved problems for each data point in the following figures. From Fig. 14(a) we can see that for each data point a solution of the original problem can be derived in over 80% of the problems. The solution quality in terms of utility achieved is not as good as when solving the IP directly, but, with less than 3% deviation from the optimal IP solution, the approximation quality is very high, as we can see in Fig. 14(b).

6 Conclusion

In this paper we introduced an efficient approach for the composition problem that optimizes QoS for repeated executions of services in the long-term. Our approach produces a set of probabilistic service selection policies that must be evaluated at runtime to choose a particular service accordingly. We demonstrated several potential applications of our approach beyond the mentioned scenario, including a computer-aided decision process. We evaluated our approach and showed that it is indeed efficient and scalable for the needs envisioned in SOA. We also showed in which cases our approach yields the most utility gains over common approaches. Additionally, we showed that our approach can be used to solve the traditional composition problem in many cases and produces near-optimal solutions.

Exploring the various applications of our approach in depth, and developing corresponding methodologies and tools are possible extensions of our work. Using our approach in conjunction with a genetic algorithm to compute a multi-objective optimization yielding multiple Pareto-optimal solutions for different trade-offs would also be a possible extension of our work.

Acknowledgments

We thank Nobuaki Hiratsuka for his work using multiple services that challenged our assumption to just select a single service for each workflow element. We also like to thank Florian Wagner and Benjamin Klöpper for the fruitful discussions that helped form our approach.

References

1. Papazoglou, M.P., Traverso, P., Dustdar, S., Leymann, F., Kramer, B.J.: Service-oriented computing: A research roadmap. In: Service Oriented Computing (SOC). Dagstuhl Seminar Proceedings (2006)
2. O'Sullivan, J., Edmond, D., Ter Hofstede, A.: What's in a Service? Distributed and Parallel Databases 12(2–3), 117–133 (2002)
3. Chen, K., Xu, J., Reiff-Marganiec, S.: Markov-HTN Planning Approach to Enhance Flexibility of Automatic Web Service Composition. In: ICWS 2009: IEEE International Conference on Web Services, pp. 9–16 (2009)
4. OASIS Committee Draft: Web Service - Business Process Execution Language (WS BPEL), Version 2.0 (2006)
5. Zeng, L., Benatallah, B., Dumas, M., Kalagnanam, J., Sheng, Q.Z.: Quality Driven Web Services Composition. In: WWW 2003: Proceedings of the 12th International Conference on World Wide Web, pp. 411–421 (2003)
6. Yu, T., Zhang, Y., Lin, K.-J.: Efficient algorithms for Web services selection with end-to-end QoS constraints. ACM Transactions on the Web 1(1), 6 (2007)
7. Pisinger, D.: Algorithms for Knapsack Problems. PhD thesis, University of Copenhagen, Dept. of Computer Science (1995)
8. Menascé, D.A., Casalicchio, E., Dubey, V.: On optimal service selection in Service Oriented Architectures. Performance Evaluation 67(8), 659–675 (2009)
9. Lecue, F., Mehandjiev, N.: Towards Scalability of Quality Driven SemanticWeb Service Composition. In: ICWS 2009: IEEE International Conference on Web Services, pp. 469–476 (2009)
10. Canfora, G., Di Penta, M., Esposito, R., Villani, M.L.: An approach for QoS-aware service composition based on genetic algorithms. In: GECCO 2005: Proceedings of the 2005 onference on Genetic and volutionary Computation, pp. 1069–1075 (2005)
11. Alrifai, M., Risse, T.: Combining global optimization with local selection for efficient QoS-aware service composition. In: WWW 2009: Proceedings of the 18th International Conference on World Wide Web, pp. 881–890 (2009)
12. Alrifai, M., Skoutas, D., Risse, T.: Selecting Skyline Services for QoS-based Web Service Composition. In: WWW 2010: Proceedings of the 19th International Conference on World Wide Web, pp. 11–20 (2010)
13. Stein, S., Payne, T.R., Jennings, N.R.: Flexible provisioning of web service workflows. ACM Transactions on Internet Technology 9(1), 1–45 (2009)
14. Klein, A., Ishikawa, F., Bauer, B.: A Probabilistic Approach to Service Selection with Conditional Contracts and Usage Patterns. In: Baresi, L., Chi, C.-H., Suzuki, J. (eds.) ICSOC-ServiceWave 2009. LNCS, vol. 5900, pp. 253–268. Springer, Heidelberg (2009)
15. Jaeger, M.C., Rojec-Goldmann, G., Muhl, G.: QoS Aggregation for Web Service Composition using Workflow Patterns. In: EDOC 2004: Proceedings of the Eighth IEEE International Enterprise Distributed Object Computing Conference, pp. 149–159 (2004)

Using Real-Time Scheduling Principles in Web Service Clusters to Achieve Predictability of Service Execution

Vidura Gamini Abhaya, Zahir Tari, and Peter Bertok

School of Computer Science and Information Technology
RMIT University, Melbourne, Australia
{vidura.abhaya,zahir.tari,peter.bertok}@rmit.edu.au

Abstract. Real-time scheduling algorithms enable applications to achieve predictability in request execution. This paper proposes several request dispatching algorithms based on real-time scheduling principles that enable clusters hosting web services to achieve predictability in service execution. Dispatching decisions are based on request properties (such as deadline, task size and laxity) and they are scheduled to achieve designated deadlines. All algorithms follow three important steps to achieve a high level of predictability. Firstly, requests are scheduled based on their hard deadlines. Secondly, requests are selected for execution based on their laxity. Thirdly, the underlying software infrastructure provides means of achieving predictability with high precision operations. The algorithms use various techniques to increase the number of deadlines met. One decreases the variance of task sizes at each executor while another increases the variance of laxity at an executor. The algorithms are implemented in a real-life cluster using real-time enabled Apache Synapse as the dispatcher and services hosted in real-time aware Apache Axis2 instances. The algorithms are compared with common algorithms used in clusters such as Round-Robin and Class-based dispatching. The empirical results show the proposed algorithms outperform the others by meeting at least 95% of the deadlines compared to less than 10% by the others.

1 Introduction

With the advent of cloud computing and the trend of exposing 'things' as services on the internet, web services have firmly established itself as the de-facto standard for distributed computing [8,9]. As platforms and infrastructure are being exposed as services, the Quality of Service (QoS) aspects of web service execution mandates an increased importance than before. With applications and systems joining the cloud bandwagon, the performance of web services becomes pivotal to its overlaid applications, thereby requiring stringent QoS levels in their operations. A common practice in alleviating performance bottlenecks, is the use of clusters in hosting web services. The simple idea is to balance the load among service replicas to gain performance. Although a cluster results in a performance gain having multiple hosts and improves the availability of services [18], it does not improve the predictability of web service execution.

Web service middleware are seldom designed to achieve predictability in service execution. Over the years, this has prevented web services being used for applications with critical time requirements and precision in execution. SOAP engines and application

P.P. Maglio et al. (Eds.): ICSOC 2010, LNCS 6470, pp. 197–212, 2010.

servers contain many optimisations for throughput [2,14,16]. For instance, they employ thread pools to service requests in parallel using processor sharing [11]. Although this increases the number of requests being executed within a unit of time, it results in the proportionate increase of the average execution time of a service.

Real-time applications consider predictability of execution with utmost importance. In such systems, missing an execution deadline usually renders even a correctly obtained result useless. As a result, they mandate the use of special scheduling techniques that repeatedly guarantee completion of tasks within requested deadlines. Such stringent requirements in service execution has hindered the use of web services as middleware in real-time systems. In [5,6] we identified three important requirements to achieve predictability of execution. Firstly, the main attribute considered for scheduling a request must be its *deadline* for completion. Secondly, there must be support from the underlying infrastructure (development platform and OS) and thirdly, requests must be selected for execution based on their laxity, which is the indicator of slacktime in a request.

When predictability of execution is considered, previous work on execution time QoS of web services and request dispatching in clusters fail due to many reasons. A common approach for web services is to consider multiple classes of requests [7,15] and provide them with differentiated service. The classes are scheduled to share the processor in a ratio defined by a Service Level Agreement (SLA). They fail due to deadline not being considered as a scheduling parameter. Moreover the infrastructure and software used, do not support predictability. Others [10] use heuristic techniques such as fuzzy logic which cannot guarantee a specific outcome every time. Some [4] support other QoS aspects such as reliability, fault tolerance and does not give prominence to execution. Some of the well known work in request dispatching in distributed systems [3,13,12] cannot be considered as they do scheduling with the goal of reducing the mean waiting time and slowdown of requests, therefore are unable guarantee execution times without specifically scheduling based on deadlines. Neither are they supported by a suitable infrastructure.

In our previous work [5,6] we introduced a solution based on real-time scheduling principles, to achieve predictability in execution on a single server. We selected requests for execution based on their laxity with a guarantee of meeting their deadlines through a schedulability check. The selected requests were pre-emptively executed using earliest deadline first scheduling policy. Furthermore, we presented a real-implementation of the techniques supported by a development platform and an operating system with real-time features. In this paper, we extend our solution to support a cluster.

To address the lack of real-time execution support in web service clusters, our primary contribution through this paper is a set of dispatching algorithms that select and execute requests to meet hard execution deadlines on multiple executors in a cluster. As a secondary contribution, implementation details of these algorithms in a real system, is presented. The uniqueness of our solution lies in the use of real-time scheduling principles and how each of the algorithms function. With RT-RoundRobin we show how a simple algorithm can be made real-time ready by extending it to select requests for execution, based on laxity. The round-robin (RR) nature increases the inter-arrival times at executors which helps them to achieve deadlines. The schedulability check introduced guarantees that a request will not compromise the deadlines of others. RT-ClassBased is an extension to the popular method of service differentiation through traffic classes. Candidate executors are selected based on the traffic class of a request and the schedulability check tries to place the request among the already accepted, based on its laxity. As traffic classes are based on the execution times, this reduces the variance of task sizes at an executor. RT-LaxityBased makes use of laxities the best possible way. It keeps track of the laxities of requests assigned to each executor and ensures a high variance of laxities at each cluster. As large laxities enable more requests to be scheduled together, spreading them evenly increases the schedulability of requests on the cluster. These three algorithms conduct only a single schedulability check per request on the selected executor. RT-Sequential attempts to achieve a higher schedulability by conducting multiple checks for a single request on different executors. This method makes the best possible use of processing resources, although with a slightly lower deadline achievement rate than the others. All four algorithms make use of our schedulability check from [6] and executors schedule the selected requests using earliest deadline first scheduling principle.

The algorithms are evaluated using a real-life implementation with Apache Synapse [1] used for the dispatcher and Apache Axis2 [2] for cluster servers. We augment the functionality of both these products to be real-time aware in execution. While there are many aspects of QoS in web services, we only consider execution time as as the most important, in this research. Moreover, network communication aspects are considered to be reliable and we make the assumption of communication cost not being significant, in service invocation.

Rest of this paper is organised as follows. In Sect. 2 we provide a background about important task properties for predictable execution. Next we present our solution in Sect. 3 followed by details of the implementation. We present the empirical evaluation in Sect. 5 and discuss some related work in Sect. 6. Finally we conclude in Sect. 7 with a summary and brief look at the way forward.

2 Background

In this section we discuss some important properties of tasks with deadlines to achieve predictability of execution. For a task in execution with a start time S, a deadline D and remaining execution time C, its slack time can be defined as L, where $L = (D - S) - C$. Laxity of a task gives an indication of the same prior to the start of execution, as a ratio between deadline and execution time.

$$Laxity = \frac{Deadline}{ExecutionTime}$$

In the context of deadline based scheduling, laxity and slack time indicates how long a request (or its remaining execution) could be delayed without compromising its deadline. A higher laxity gives ability to delay a task more and schedule other tasks that need to finish earlier. Similarly, a lower laxity means less tasks could be scheduled together.

Figure 2 gives an example on the effect of laxity on scheduling tasks. Tasks T1 and T2 have executed pre-emptively enabling T3, T4 and T5 to be scheduled within their lifespan. It has been possible as a result of T1 and T2 having large laxities. Even with smaller laxities T3 and T4 enable T5, which starts within their lifespan to achieve

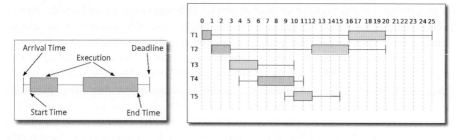

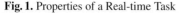

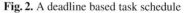

Fig. 1. Properties of a Real-time Task   **Fig. 2.** A deadline based task schedule

its deadline due to its larger laxity. If T5 had a smaller laxity it may not have been schedulable with T3 and T4 as its execution could not have been delayed.

The schedulability check in our previous work [6], selects tasks for execution based on the same principles. Depending on the laxities of tasks it tries to schedule tasks together and ensures that deadline of the target task can be met while not compromising the deadlines of the others. Furthermore, it also prevents a server being overloaded with requests. This check is used by all algorithms presented in this paper for the same purpose and can be identified by the method call *IsSchedulable(newTask, Executor)* where the schedulability of *newTask* is considered with all accepted requests on *Executor*.

3   Real-Time Dispatching Algorithms for Web Service Clusters

The envisioned solution enables a web service cluster to function in a real-time aware manner. Herein, the cluster will honour a hard deadline specified with each request. The deadline for a request is communicated to the cluster using SOAP headers. The solution consists of two components. First, we introduce several real-time aware algorithms to be used at the dispatcher. These would match a request to an executor and ensure the its deadline requirement could be met. The second part of the solution pre-emptively schedules the requests at executors using *Earliest Deadline First* scheduling principle.

3.1   Dispatching Algorithms

The algorithms in our solution perform the task of assigning requests to executors, however with the additional guarantee of meeting the requested deadline. Each of the following algorithms perform in a different way and impacts the variance of laxity at an executor. The goal of the algorithms is to increase the variance of laxities at each executor, thereby increase the number of requests schedulable to meet their deadlines. All algorithms, use our schedulability check presented in [6]. The following algorithms are introduced for request dispatching.

RT-RoundRobin

Round-robin scheduling distributes requests evenly among the executors in a cluster. Adapting this simple yet widely used scheduling technique, RT-RoundRobin (RT-RR) takes it a step further with an additional schedulability check prior to dispatching a request. Even though RT-RR scheme has little effect on the distribution of request sizes or laxities at an executor, it effectively reduces the arrival rate of tasks. As a result, requests arrive further apart and reduces the number of requests vying to be scheduled within the same window of time. This increases the number of requests schedulable to meet their deadlines.

Algorithm 1 details the steps in RT-RR. The RR nature of it is maintained by keeping track of the last executor a request was assigned to and assigning the new request to the next executor in the list. A check ensures the previous executor assigned is not the last of the list, in which case the list is reset to the beginning (Lines 2-4). Using the index the executor is fetched and schedulability of the request is checked (Lines 7-8). If the request is schedulable, it is assigned to the executor (Lines 9,11) and a reference to the executor is kept as the last one to be assigned (Line 10). A negative result from the check results in the request being rejected (Line 13). Executor information is kept in a data structure with constant time access when the index is used. The schedulability check has a worst case time complexity of $O(n)$ as with the rest of RT-RR. Therefore it results in an overall worst case time complexity of $O(n)$. Moreover, RT-RR is the simplest of the checks with the possible processing overhead kept to a minimum.

RT-ClassBased

Most of the related work on execution level QoS, follow the class based approach where requests are divided into classes based on a priority scheme. These classes get processing time allocations depending on the associated priority in a pre-determined ratio. For instance, consider a system with 3 traffic classes A,B and C. The dispatcher may schedule them based on a 3:2:1 ratio among the executors, where for every 3 requests of class A it schedules 2 requests of class B and 1 of C.

The RT-ClassBased (RT-CB) algorithm follows the same principle with the additional step of ensuring the deadlines of the requests could be met. The class of a request is based on the size of the task identified by the execution time. Executors are mapped with request size ranges, offline and based on it the executor for a given request is selected. With requests assigned to executors based on task size, RT-CB scheduling results in similar sized requests arriving at the same executor. This prevents small and large requests competing for the same executor, thereby increasing the number of small and medium sized requests accepted.

Algorithm 3 contains the steps of RT-CB. The size of the request is used to obtain the executor, through a function that looks-up the mapping information (Lines 1-2). The request is directly checked for schedulability with the executor (Line 3) and assigned to it on being successful (Lines 4-5). On a negative result, the request is rejected (Line 7). Line 1 shows the class of the request being retrieved from itself for brevity. As there is no knowledge of a request prior to its arrival, the size of the request has to be inferred from information at hand. Profiled execution times or execution time history can be used for this purpose. For this, we decided use a combination where profiled times were used when a service was invoked first for a given set of inputs and execution time history was used thereafter. The executor to task size mapping was stored in a data structure with constant access time. As a result the worst case time complexity of the algorithm is $O(n)$ due to the schedulability check.

RT-LaxityBased

The goal of RT-LaxityBased (RT-Lax) is to ensure the even distribution of tasks with higher and lower laxities among the executors. While the schedulability check selects a request for execution based on its laxity and that of already accepted requests, RT-Lax takes it a step further with distributing requests based on laxity prior to using the check. RT-Lax keeps track of the last two laxities assigned to an executor and ensures the same laxities are not assigned to it consecutively. Moreover, it remembers the last executor a request was assigned to and prevents it being considered first for the next request assignment. This increases the variance of laxities at an executor and enables more requests to be scheduled together.

Algorithm 4, describes the steps in the algorithm. Upon receiving a request, the laxity is calculated (Line 1). It is checked to ensure not to be one of the last two laxities assigned to the executor (Line 3-4). In the case of the calculated laxity being in the last two laxities assigned to the last executor, next executor in the list is considered (Lines 13-14). The schedulability check is done on the selected executor (Line 18-19) and the request is either assigned to it or rejected based on the result (Lines 19-24). The first time a request is scheduled through the algorithm, there is no last executor information available. In such a scenario the request is checked for schedulability with the first executor in the list (Lines 30-40). Executor information and details of last laxities assigned to executors are kept in data structures with linear and constant access time complexities respectively. Although a request maybe matched with more than one executor, the schedulability check is conducted only with a single executor. The algorithm bar the schedulability check exhibits a worst case execution time complexity of $O(n)$. Together with the schedulability check, the complete algorithm therefore still results in a time complexity of $O(n)$.

RT-Sequential

RT-Sequential (RT-Seq) algorithm tries to make the best possible match for a request by trying for schedulability more than once. In turn it tries to make best possible use of the server resources by checking the schedulability of a request with more than one executor. If the schedulability check for a request fails with one executor, RT-Seq continues to check its schedulability with the rest of the executors in the cluster until it is schedulable on one of them or the list exhausted. Like RT-Lax this achieves a larger variance of laxity at an executor due to fitting a request ultimately to the best executor. However,it does this with the additional cost of multiple schedulability checks per request. The other algorithms keeps it to a minimum to ensure its cost being too significant, as the lifetime of a request starts from the moment it enters the system.

Algorithm 2 details the steps in RT-Seq. To prevent RT-Seq always starting with the same executor, the successful executor from the last run is kept track of and is considered first (Lines 1,11,22). Requests are repeatedly assigned to it until the check fails (Lines 1-4), in which case another executor is considered (Lines 6-16). Executor information is kept in a data structure with linear access time complexity when accessed sequentially.

The worst case time complexity of the algorithm without the schedulability check is $O(n)$. As multiple schedulability checks may happen for a given request, the overall complexity becomes $O(mn)$ where m has an upper bound on the number of executors in the cluster.

Algorithm 1. RT-RoundRobin

Require: New request R, List of Executors E, Last Executor L

Ensure: R assigned to an executor or rejected
1. lastExecIndx ← L.getIndex
2. **if** lastExecIndx = E.size-1 **then**
3.   lastExecIndx = 0
4. **else**
5.   lastExecIndx ← lastExecIndx + 1
6. **end if**
7. nextExec ← E.getExec(lastExecIndx)
8. S ← IsSchedulable(R,nextExec)
9. **if** S = true **then**
10.   L ← nextExec
11.   Assign R to nextExec
12. **else**
13.   Reject R
14. **end if**

Algorithm 2. RT-Sequential

Require: New request R, List of Executors E, Last executor
Ensure: R assigned to an executor or rejected
1. **if** lastExec is not $\emptyset$ **then**
2.   S ← IsSchedulable(R,lastExec)
3.   **if** S = true **then**
4.   Assign R to lastExec
5.   **else**
6.   **while** E.hasMore() AND R not assigned **do**
7.   nextExec ← E.getNextExec
8.   **if** nextExec is not lastExec **then**
9.   S ← IsSchedulable(R,nextExec)
10.   **if** S = true **then**
11.   lastExec ← nextExec
12.   Assign R to nextExec
13.   **end if**
14.   **end if**
15.   **end while**
16.   **end if**
17. **else**
18.   **while** E.hasMore() AND R not assigned **do**
19.   nextExec ← E.getNextExec
20.   S ← IsSchedulable(R,nextExec)
21.   **if** S = true **then**
22.   lastExec ← nextExec
23.   Assign R to nextExec
24.   **end if**
25.   **end while**
26. **end if**
27. **if** R is not assigned **then**
28.   Reject R
29. **end if**

Algorithm 3. RT-ClassBased

Require: New request R, List of Executors E
Ensure: R assigned to an executor rejected
1. C ← R.getRequestClass
2. nextExec ← E.GetExecforReqClass(C)
3. S ← IsSchedulable(nextExec)
4. **if** S = true **then**
5.   Assign R to nextExecutor
6. **else**
7.   Reject R
8. **end if**

Algorithm 4. RT-LaxityBased

Require: New request R, List of Executors E, Laxity Map LM, Last Executor L
Ensure: R assigned to an endpoint or rejected
1. Laxity ← $\left(\frac{R.getDeadline}{R.getExecutionTime} \right)$
2. **if** lastExec is not $\emptyset$ **then**
3.   LL ← lastExec.LastLaxities
4.   **if** Laxity is not in LL **then**
5.   S ← IsSchedulable(R,lastExec)
6.   **if** S = true **then**
7.   lastExec.setLastLaxities(Laxity)
8.   Assign R to nextExecutor
9.   **else**
10.   Reject R
11.   **end if**
12.   **else**
13.   **while** E.hasMore() and R is not assigned **do**
14.   nextExec ← E.getNextExec
15.   **if** nextExec is not lastExec **then**
16.   LL ← nextExec.LastLaxities
17.   **if** Laxity not in LL **then**
18.   S ← IsSchedulbl(R,nextExec)
19.   **if** S = true **then**
20.   nextEx.setLstLaxities(Lax)
21.   lastExec ← nextExec
22.   Assign R to nextExec
23.   **else**
24.   Reject R
25.   **end if**
26.   **end if**
27.   **end if**
28.   **end while**
29.   **end if**
30. **else**
31.   nextExec ← E.getfirstExec
32.   S ← IsSchedulable(R,nextExec)
33.   **if** S = true **then**
34.   nextExec.setLastLaxities(Laxity)
35.   lastExec ← nextExec
36.   Assign R to nextExec
37.   **else**
38.   Reject R
39.   **end if**
40. **end if**

4   Implementation

Dispatcher Component

The algorithms presented were implemented in Synapse using its mediation framework. To support the real-time aspects of the algorithm, all thread-pools in Synapse were replaced with real-time implementations. A real-time scheduler component introduced into Synapse manages the scheduling of the worker threads. Moreover, these additional features were facilitated by running Synapse on Java Real-time System version 2.1 [17] supported by Sun Solaris 10 08/05 real-time operating system (SunOS). The development platform and the operating system provides Synapse with better control, runtime accuracy and precision at the system level which is unavailable for the default implementation.

Executor Component

The executor portion of our solution conducts the important task of scheduling the requests for execution to achieve the deadlines requested. The requests received are scheduled using Earliest Deadline First (EDF) policy in a pre-emptive manner. The real-time enabled Axis2 (RT-Axis2) from our previous work is used at the executors with a few modifications. Unlike in [6], it is relieved of conducting schedulability checks as this is done at the dispatcher. Its functionality is supported by RTSJ and SunOS at the system level.

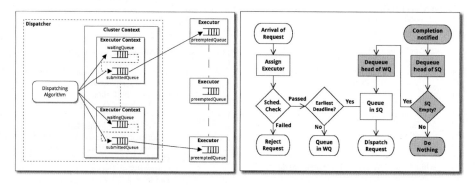

Fig. 3. RT-Synapse Internals   **Fig. 4.** RT-Synapse Functionality

Cluster Functionality

Figure 3, shows the design of the cluster. Request processing in Synapse is handled by worker-threads and the internal representation of a request is an instance of *RTTask* class. The dispatcher stores the state of the cluster in *Cluster Context* and the state of each executor in instances of *Executor Context* (EC). It keeps track of all tasks assigned to an executor in two ordered queues based on deadlines.

Figure 4 summaries the functionality of the dispatcher. On dispatching a request its RTTask instance is queued on *submittedQueue* (SQ). Requests waiting to be dispatched are queued in *waitingQueue* (WQ). Once a request is accepted for execution, its deadline is compared with already accepted requests. If the new request has the earliest deadline, its RTTask instance is queued in SQ and it is dispatched to the executor. If the new request should not be the earliest to finish, it is queued in WQ. The dispatcher receives a notification from the executor at the completion of a request and its RTTask is removed from the head of SQ. If SQ becomes empty the head of WQ is removed, queued in SQ and the request dispatched to the executor. Conversely if SQ is not empty, requests from the waiting queue are not dispatched to the executor as the executor would be busy processing requests. When the executor is busy, the dispatcher only dispatches a request having an earlier deadline than the one being processed at the executor.

Upon receiving a request, one of two things may happen at the executor. If the executor was idle, the request is taken for processing straight-away. If the executor was busy, deadlines of all requests present is evaluated and the one with the earliest gets the processor to run. The rest are queued on *preemptedQueue* (PQ) which is also ordered on deadlines. At the completion of a request, once the result is returned back to the dispatcher, the head of PQ is removed and its execution resumed. The worker threads that requests are assigned to at arrival, are suspended when a request is pre-empted and woken back up when its execution resumed.

Multi Core/Processor Support

The schedulability check evaluates requests on a single time line of execution. This does not benefit from multi-core and multi-processors hardware. In order to take advantage of such deployments, our solution makes the executors configurable for a number of execution lanes. An execution lane represents a processor core. If an executor is configured for N execution lanes, the same number of requests in the order of their deadlines, would be executed in parallel. On the dispatcher, each lane has its own EC and is considered as a separate executor. As each lane gets its own processor core for execution, no processor sharing takes place among the requests executing in parallel at each executor.

5   Empirical Evaluation

Our implementation is empirically evaluated with traffic generated to resemble various conditions. Our previous work [6] indicated that it is best to test such an implementation with a good mixture of request sizes making the composition of the stream totally random. Hence, for all experiments conducted we use a uniform distribution for task sizes. The deadline for each request is calculated by picking a value between 1.5 and 10 from a uniform distribution and multiplying the profiled execution time for the request. For each run we pick inter-arrival times of requests from a uniform distribution bounded by a low and a high value. We use a web service that allows us to create task sizes with fine-grain precision, using input parameters.

The proposed algorithms select requests for execution based on the schedulability check and those selected are scheduled at the executors using EDF policy.

Table 1. Performance Comparison of Round Robin vs. RT-RoundRobin

	Round Robin (Non real-time)						RT-RoundRobin					
	2 Executors		3 Executors		4 Executors		2 Executors		3 Executors		4 Executors	
Inter-arrival time(sec)	% Acc.	% D. Met off % Acc.	% Acc.	% D. Met off % Acc	% Acc.	% D. Met off % Acc	% Acc.	% D. Met off % Acc	% Acc.	% D. Met off % Acc	% Acc.	% D. Met off % Acc
0.25 - 1	99.5	28.8	99.8	37.2	99.9	51.5	88.0	99.0	99.0	100	99.9	100
0.1 - 0.5	62.3	20.3	89.0	28.4	98.0	39.7	52.0	96.4	74.0	99.0	99.4	99.9
0.1 - 0.25	49.0	15.0	67.3	20.0	74.1	33.2	28.0	96.0	47.0	97.6	78.0	99.0
0.05 - 0.1	38.8	6.3	52.6	9.1	68.0	13.6	20.5	90.0	37.5	95.0	46.3	99.0

Table 2. Performance Comparisons of Class based vs. RT-ClassBased

	Class based (Non real-time)						RT-ClassBased					
	2 Executors		3 Executors		4 Executors		2 Executors		3 Executors		4 Executors	
Inter-arrival time(sec)	% Acc.	% D. Met off % Acc.	% Acc.	% D. Met off % Acc	% Acc.	% D. Met off % Acc	% Acc.	% D. Met off % Acc	% Acc.	% D. Met off % Acc	% Acc.	% D. Met off % Acc
0.25 - 1	100	27.8	99.2	40.8	99.9	58.2	99.2	99.0	100.0	99.0	100	100
0.1 - 0.5	82.0	26.0	98.6	36.6	99.4	42.4	62.2	95.4	76.7	94.8	90.9	100
0.1 - 0.25	74.8	18.0	83.3	30.0	86.9	30.2	45.4	94.6	66.0	99.0	74.4	97.7
0.05 - 0.1	52.7	7.8	75.6	13.5	78.0	20.5	28.6	98.9	44.7	91.4	55.1	99.0

Table 3. Performance of RT-Sequential and RT-LaxityBased

	RT-Sequential						RT-LaxityBased					
	2 Executors		3 Executors		4 Executors		2 Executors		3 Executors		4 Executors	
Inter-arrival time(sec)	% Acc.	% D. Met off % Acc.	% Acc.	% D. Met off % Acc	% Acc.	% D. Met off % Acc	% Acc.	% D. Met off % Acc	% Acc.	% D. Met off % Acc	% Acc.	% D. Met off % Acc
0.25 - 1	99.0	96.8	100	97.0	100	97.2	99.2	99.9	100.0	99.9	100	100
0.1 - 0.5	86.0	91.0	96.1	96.3	100	95.0	89.0	99.8	80.5	99.8	99.8	100
0.1 - 0.25	38.6	87.4	76.5	95.0	84.6	96.2	47.4	99.2	66.0	99.6	75.2	100
0.05 - 0.1	29.1	90.0	57.2	95.3	66.7	95.8	38.5	99.0	50.7	99.2	54.3	100

The non-real-time algorithms we compare ours against do not conduct any check for task acceptance. They are implemented directly on non-real-time Synapse and non-real-time Axis2 deployments with best-effort request execution. The three tables listed below summarise the results from different experimental runs. Herein, the success of an algorithm is measured using the percentage of requests accepted (% Acc.) for execution (from the schedulability check) and out of that, the percentage of deadlines met (% D.Met off % Acc.). We conduct all runs with 2 to 4 executors being used in the cluster. % Acc. under non-real-time algorithms used for comparison, signify the percentage accepted due to server overloads resulted by those algorithms.

Round-robin vs. RT-RoundRobin

To illustrate the effect of scheduling based on deadlines, we compare the simple RR algorithm with RT-RR. In RT-RR executors are selected in a RR fashion and the request is checked for schedulability once with the selected executor. Requests that pass the check are accepted for execution on that executor. Table 1 details the results of all runs

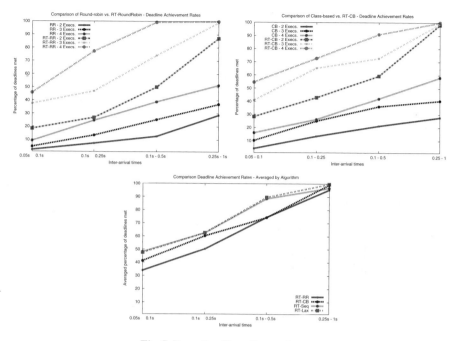

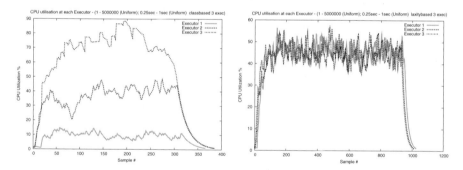

Fig. 5. Execution Time Comparisons

Fig. 6. CPU Utilisation at Executors

conducted. The graph on the left side of the first row in Fig. 5 summarises the deadline acceptance rates. It can be seen that, RT-RR performs better than simple-RR. Simple RR results in better task acceptance rates due to not having an explicit check that rejects request. However, it performs badly with the number of deadlines met. Although RT-RR accepts less requests, it still outperforms simple-RR in meeting more than 90% of the deadlines even in very high request arrivals. With best-effort request execution, the resultant execution times easily miss the deadlines.

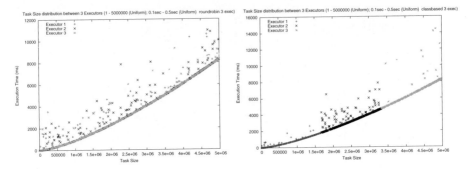

Fig. 7. Task Size distribution at Executors

Class based vs. RT-ClassBased

Next we compare the performance (Table 2) of the class based service differentiation technique with RT-CB, which matches an executor to a request in the same manner, however only accepting the request through a schedulability check. Moreover RT-CB schedules requests for execution based on their deadlines. The graph on the right side of the first row in Fig. 5 summarises the deadline acceptance rates. In both algorithms, requests were sorted into classes based on the size of the request (resultant execution time) and executors were assigned based on the request class. This results in requests of similar sizes being assigned to the same executor and avoids scenarios where a large request and small requests competing for the same server (Fig. 7). As a result, class-based algorithms performs better than simple-RR. However, the percentage of deadlines met are still quite low compared to RT-CB and RT-RR. The first graph on Fig. 6 shows the processor utilisation levels of each executor for an RT-CB runs. The executors exhibit different levels of utilisation due to the classes being based on task sizes.

Performance of RT-Sequential and RT-LaxityBased

RT-Seq checks the schedulability of a request with all executors in the cluster prior to rejecting a request. As a result it returns the highest acceptance rates of all algorithms. However, the total time taken for carrying out multiple checks can become significant for certain requests. Therefore, RT-Seq results in the lowest values for percentage of deadlines met out of all algorithms. These values are still better than the non-real-time algorithms we compare them with. RT-Lax ensures the equal distribution of laxities among cluster members. This creates a higher variance of laxities at each executor thereby enables more requests to be scheduled together. As a result, RT-Lax performs the best in meeting request deadlines. This property of RT-Lax, enables it to make use of the processing resources the best possible way. Compared to a policy such as RT-CB, Fig. 6 shows RT-Lax resulting in equal utilisation levels for all executors in the cluster.

Factors Affecting Request Acceptance and Deadlines Met

From the results presented, it is visible that other factors affect the amount of requests accepted for execution and the deadlines met. As the inter-arrival times of requests decreases, the number of requests accepted and deadlines met also decreases with it. A reduction in inter-arrival times transforms to an increase of requests arriving at the cluster in a given time period. As a result more requests compete for the processor within a single window of time. However, only a portion of them could be accepted for execution. Another factor affecting the acceptance rates and deadlines met is the number of executors in the cluster. Having more executors in the cluster would mean more processing power is available for requests to be executed. Moreover, spreading requests across more executors also results in a reduction of request arrivals at an executor, in a time unit. This enables the executors to successfully achieve the deadlines of requests. Having more executors would mean an increase of workload at the dispatcher. However, when the worst case time complexities of the algorithms are considered, introducing additional executors would not have a big impact on the performance of the dispatcher.

Discussion

The experimental results clearly demonstrate that predictability of execution can be achieved in a web services cluster. In these experiments, we tested the proposed algorithms for the worst possible scenario where there is an equal mixture of task sizes with all requests having hard-deadlines. Moreover, the implementation was exposed to very high request arrival rates. With RT-RR, we demonstrate how a simple scheduling policy could be transformed into being real-time aware. This combines the simplicity of the RR dispatching with the objective scheduling of real-time algorithms. Supported by the underlying software infrastructure RT-RR results in more than 90 % of deadlines being met in all runs. Although simple RR results in higher rates of requests being executed due to its best-effort nature, it fails to guarantee the deadlines of most of them, at times being less than 10%.

With RT-CB we demonstrated how a request-aware dispatching policy could be transformed in being real-time aware. With the additional steps of selecting requests based on their laxity through a schedulability check and deadline based scheduling, it achieves 95% of the deadlines under any traffic condition with more than 50% acceptance rates, at most times. The proposed approach of defining traffic classes based on request sizes and assigning requests for traffic classes, replicate a common tactic used in many other dispatching algorithms. Through this, a request stream consisting of any mixture of requests gets transformed into a request stream with similar sizes at each executor (Fig. 7). This prevents small and large tasks competing for the same executor. This phenomenon, together with decreased arrival rates at executors due to requests being disseminated across many executors enable many requests to be scheduled to meet their requested deadlines. Although the simple class based policy receives the same benefits, the best effort nature of request execution results in deadlines being lost. RT-CB would be suitable for request streams with comparatively more smaller sized requests.

Experimental results confirm that RT-Seq makes the best use of processing resources. It achieved the highest acceptance rates out of all algorithms. Trying to schedule a request repeatedly on different executors ensures that, a request will be scheduled on the cluster if required processing time is available on any one of the executors. This effectively fills the gaps on processor time lines making the maximum use of their processing resources. However, conducting multiple checks may incur a significant overhead depending on the size of the request. The life of a request, starts on its arrival at the cluster. Therefore, the time spent on being dispatched and being checked for schedulability, has to be subsumed within the execution time requirement of a request. For small sized requests, the overhead incurred by multiple checks may result in them missing their deadlines. As a result, RT-Seq is not suitable for request streams predominantly containing smaller sized requests.

The distribution of requests based on laxity, ensures that requests with large and small laxities are evenly distributed. If an executor gets too many requests with small laxities, eventually some of them will end up being rejected, as they compete for the same window of time. Requests with large laxities are able to shift or stagger their execution within a larger time window enabling more requests to be scheduled within their lifespan. This principle results in RT-Lax meeting the highest number of deadlines, with more than 50% acceptance rate in most cases (second row of Fig. 5). All algorithms show that they could achieve higher performance with the cluster scaling up with more executors. With cost of hardware becoming cheaper by the day, the acceptance rates could be increased with more executors being added to the cluster. In such a setup RT-Lax will be the best algorithm to use with a good mixture of task sizes and laxities in the request stream.

6   Related Work

Much work on dispatching in clusters can be found in the literature. Many of them are for clusters hosting static web content and follow the premise of static web traffic taking a heavy tailed distribution. In [12], no prior knowledge of task sizes are assumed and requests are sent through several executors assigned with increasing quanta until the request is completed in a non-work conserving manner. Requests are mapped to executors based on task sizes in [3,13] and as a result the dispatching transforms the heavy tailed work load into that of type exponential. These work with the goal of reducing the mean waiting time, mean slowdown of tasks and not the predictability of execution. Moreover, with the assumptions they make on static web content such as the heavy-tailed nature of traffic, they seem unsuitable to be used with the highly dynamic nature of web services.

Similarly, evidence of work specific to web service clusters can be found in the literature. In [7] requests are dispatched to achieve probabilistic limits of maximum response time defined in SLAs. A QoS controller monitors the response times resulted in each executor for different types of requests and accepts or rejects requests to maintain the agreed upon limits in the SLAs. While this allows the cluster to achieve a method of controlling response times, the scheduling algorithms used do not consider any deadlines or give a guarantee of achieving them. Requests are divided into traffic classes in [15] and they are scheduled to achieve average response times defined in SLAs. The solution uses a utility function to compute the actual performance of executors and compare them with the rate promised. A discrepancy identified would change the ratio of the number of requests executed from each class by the executors. Similarly, [10] uses a class based approach where a controller based on fuzzy logic is used to optimise the ratio of requests executed by the cluster.

Commonly, all the work discussed use some aspect related to execution time as a QoS parameter. However, they all fail to guarantee predictable execution times mainly for two reasons. None of them purposely schedule tasks to achieve a deadline in a definite manner. Furthermore, their implementations and infrastructure does not support predictability of execution, by design. Additionally, none of them contain means of validating the schedulability of a request with requests already executing in the cluster.

7 Conclusion

In this paper, we presented four algorithms to achieve predictability of execution in web service clusters. Execution time predictability becomes more important with web services being used to integrate distributed platforms and infrastructure. Moreover, it will enable the use of web services in applications with real-time requirements and enable the real-time development space to enjoy the benefits and advantages web services bring. The proposed algorithms were compared with commonly used request dispatching techniques and experimental results confirm the inability for those techniques to achieve the level of predictability the proposed algorithms demonstrate. We discussed the use of specific algorithms in different types of request streams and their suitability. We also provided brief details about how these algorithms can be implemented in real-life using real-time enabled versions of Apache Synapse and Axis2 for a cluster setup. The software infrastructure used for the implementation also plays a large part in enabling the proposed algorithms to achieve the levels of predictability they demonstrate.

To completely achieve predictability of execution, the network communication aspects of web services would also need to be considered. As future work, we hope to extend our solution to the network level by ensuring the delays are minimised along the path of the web service invocation. We continue to research on more cluster based scheduling algorithms that are more application specific, which would enable them to achieve better acceptance rates.

Acknowledgements. This work is supported by the ARC (Australian Research Council) under the Linkage scheme (No. LP0667600, Titled "An Integrated Infrastructure for Dynamic and Large Scale Supply Chain").

References

1. Apache Software Foundation: Apache Synapse (June 9, 2008),
   http://synapse.apache.org/
2. Apache Software Foundation: Apache Axis2 (June 8, 2009),
   http://ws.apache.org/axis2/
3. Ciardo, G., Riska, A., Smirni, E.: EquiLoad: a load balancing policy for clustered web servers. Performance Evaluation 46(2-3), 101–124 (2001)

4. Erradi, A., Maheshwari, P.: wsbus: Qos-aware middleware for reliable web services interactions. e-Technology, e-Commerce and e-Service, 2005. In: Proceedings of The 2005 IEEE International Conference on EEE 2005, pp. 634–639 (March April 1, 2005)
5. Gamini Abhaya, V.: Achieving Predictabiliy and Service Differentiation in Web Service Execution. Tech. rep., School of CS and IT, RMIT University, Melbourne, Australia (April 17, 2009), http://goanna.cs.rmit.edu.au/~vabhaya/publications/TechReport1.pdf
6. Gamini Abhaya, V., Tari, Z., Bertok, P.: Achieving Predictability and Service Differentiation in Web Services. In: Baresi, L., Chi, C.-H., Suzuki, J. (eds.) ICSOC-ServiceWave 2009. LNCS, vol. 5900, pp. 364–372. Springer, Heidelberg (2009)
7. García, D.F., García, J., Entrialgo, J., García, M., Valledor, P., García, R., Campos, A.M.: A qos control mechanism to provide service differentiation and overload protection to internet scalable servers. IEEE Transactions on Services Computing 2(1), 3–16 (2009)
8. Gartner : SOA Is Evolving Beyond Its Traditional Roots (April 2, 2009), http://www.gartner.com/it/page.jsp?id=927612
9. Gartner and Forrester: Use of Web services skyrocketing (Septmeber 30, 2003), http://utilitycomputing.com/news/404.asp
10. Gmach, D., Krompass, S., Scholz, A., Wimmer, M., Kemper, A.: Adaptive quality of service management for enterprise services. ACM Transactions on the Web (TWEB) 2(1), 1–46 (2008)
11. Graham, S., Davis, D., Simeonov, S., Daniels, G., Brittenham, P., Nakamura, Y., Fremantle, P., Konig, D., Zentner, C.: Building Web Services with Java: Making Sense of XML, SOAP, WSDL and UDDI, 2nd edn. Sams Publishing, Indianapolis (2004)
12. Harchol-Balter, M.: Task Assignment with Unknown Duration. Journal of the ACM 49(2), 260–288 (2002)
13. Harchol-Balter, M., Crovella, M., Murta, C.: On Choosing a Task Assignment Policy for a Distributed Server System. Journal of Parallel and Distributed Computing 59(2), 204–228 (1999)
14. Microsoft: Windows Communications Foundation, http://msdn.microsoft.com/library/ee958158.aspx
15. Pacifici, G., Spreitzer, M., Tantawi, A., Youssef, A.: Performance management for cluster-based web services. EEE Journal on Selected Areas in Communications, I 23(12), 2333–2343 (2005)
16. Sun Microsystems: Glassfish Application Server - Features (2009), http://www.oracle.com/us/products/middleware/applicationserver/oracleglassfishserver/index.html
17. Sun Microsystems: Sun Java Real-time System (2009), http://java.sun.com/javase/technologies/realtime/
18. Vilas, J., Arias, J., Vilas, A.: High availability with clusters of web services. Advanced Web Technologies and Applications pp, 644–653

Aggregate Quality of Service Computation for Composite Services

Marlon Dumas[2], Luciano García-Bañuelos[2], Artem Polyvyanyy[3],
Yong Yang[1], and Liang Zhang[1]

[1] School of Computer Science, Fudan University, China
{081024011,lzhang}@fudan.edu.cn
[2] Institute of Computer Science, University of Tartu, Estonia
{marlon.dumas,luciano.garcia}@ut.ee
[3] Hasso Plattner Institute at the University of Potsdam, Germany
Artem.Polyvyanyy@hpi.uni-potsdam.de

Abstract. This paper addresses the problem of computing the aggregate QoS of a composite service given the QoS of the services participating in the composition. Previous solutions to this problem are restricted to composite services with well-structured orchestration models. Yet, in existing languages such as WS-BPEL and BPMN, orchestration models may be unstructured. This paper lifts this limitation by providing equations to compute the aggregate QoS for general types of irreducible unstructured regions in orchestration models. In conjunction with existing algorithms for decomposing business process models into single-entry-single-exit regions, these functions allow us to cover a larger set of orchestration models than existing QoS aggregation techniques.

1 Introduction

The ability to rapidly and effectively build new services by composing existing services – a practice known as *service composition* – is one of the key pillars of Service-Oriented Computing (SOC). Service orchestration is a popular approach for service composition [14]. The idea of service orchestration is to assign the responsibility for coordinating the execution of a composite service to a single entity (the *orchestrator*). The orchestrator is responsible for handling incoming requests for the composite service and to interact with the services participating in the composition (the *component services*) in order to fulfill these requests. The interactions between the orchestrator and the component services are governed by a *orchestration model* that usually takes the form of a process model in which each task represents either an internal action (e.g. a data transformation) or an interaction with a component service. In practice, these process models are specified using a specialized language such as the Business Process Execution Language (WS-BPEL) or the Business Process Modeling Notation (BPMN).

One of the key issues in service composition is that of predicting and managing the Quality-of-Service (QoS) of composite services. If we assume that each component service advertises its QoS, or that this QoS information can be derived

P.P. Maglio et al. (Eds.): ICSOC 2010, LNCS 6470, pp. 213–227, 2010.

based on past observations (as detailed in [18] for example), we can estimate the QoS of the composite service by aggregating the available information about the component services' QoS. This estimation can then be used to detect undesirable QoS variance as early as possible [19,2] and to trigger corrective actions when such variance is detected [4].

In this setting, this paper addresses the following problem: How to compute the expected QoS of a composite service given its orchestration model specified in a language such as WS-BPEL or BPMN, and a binding that assigns each task in the orchestration to a concrete service? Following previous work, we assume that QoS is captured in terms of numerical attributes (e.g. time, cost and reputation) and that the QoS attribute values for each component service are given. Gathering QoS attribute values for non-composite services is a separate problem addressed in previous work [18].

Previous solutions to this problem [5,8,18,9,12] only work for composite services with well-structured orchestration models, that is, models described as graphs made up of split and join points, such that for every split there is a corresponding join such that the region of the graph between the split and the join is a single-entry-single-exit region. Yet, both WS-BPEL and BPMN allow orchestration models to be unstructured. In the case of WS-BPEL, one can obtain unstructured models by using so-called *control links*. These links allow tasks to be connected in arbitrary topologies, with the restriction that links cannot cross the boundaries of loop activities. Therefore, WS-BPEL orchestration models may contain unstructured acyclic fragments that cannot be handled by existing QoS aggregation methods. BPMN orchestration models are even less restricted, and they may contain both acyclic and cyclic unstructured fragments. The contribution of this paper is a generalized method for computing the QoS of composite services that can handle unstructured acyclic fragments, and a larger set of unstructured cyclic fragments than existing methods.

The rest of the paper is organized as follows. Section 2 introduces the orchestration model and the QoS model. Next, Section 3 describes the data structures used to represent service orchestrations, while Section 4 outlines the QoS aggregation method. Section 5 then discusses the implementation of the method and its evaluation using models of various sizes and topologies. Finally, Section 6 discusses related work and Section 7 draws conclusions.

2   Background

In this section, we introduce an orchestration model covering the core features of languages used in practice for specifying orchestration models, particularly WS-BPEL and BPMN. We also introduce the basic model for capturing Quality of Service that is used in the rest of the paper.

2.1   Orchestration Model

We consider service compositions whose internal logic is specified in terms of orchestration models. An orchestration model is essentially a process graph in

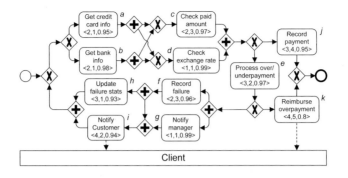

Fig. 1. Example of Composite Service

which the tasks are mapped to interactions with the client of the composite service and with services drawn from a service repository (the component services).

Definition 1 (Composite Service, Orchestration Model)

A *composite service* is a tuple *(Orc, Binding)*, where *Orc* is a service orchestration model and *Binding* is a function that maps tasks in the orchestration model to component services or to a predefined *Client* role. An *orchestration model* is a directed graph consisting of edges (n_1, p, n_2) such that n_1 and n_2 are process nodes (the source and the target of the edge) and p is the probability of taking the edge assuming that the execution of the orchestration has reached node n_1.

Process nodes are of two types: *tasks* and *gateways*. Tasks represent units of work that are delegated to component services, while gateways represent control-flow routing points. There are two types of gateways: XOR gateways represent conditional branching (XOR-split) or merging of exclusive branches (XOR-join), wheres AND gateways represent parallel forking (AND-split) or synchronization points (AND-join). Split gateways are gateways with multiple outgoing edges, while join gateways are gateways with multiple incoming edges.

The binding of a composite service is not necessarily a total function – some tasks might not be bound to any service. A task in a composite service that is not bound to a service is called an *empty task*.

We impose the following *well-formedness* conditions: (i) an orchestration model has a single source node (i.e., a node with no incoming edges), and a single sink node (i.e., a node with no outgoing edges), and every node is on a path from the source to the sink; (ii) every task node has a single incoming and a single outgoing edge, and every gateway is either a split or a join. If these latter conditions are not satisfied, the orchestration model can be trivially restructured into one that satisfies these conditions; (iii) the sum of the probabilities attached to the outgoing edges of an XOR-split gateway is 1; (iv) an edge whose source is not an XOR-split gateway has a probability of 1, meaning that such edges are always traversed when their source node is reached.

As an illustrative example, we consider a simplified *Payment* composite service depicted in Fig.1. The figure shows the orchestration model of the composite service in BPMN. Tasks are represented as rounded rectangles while gateways are represented as diamonds labelled with 'X' (XOR) or '+' (AND). Not shown in the figure is the binding of the composite service which maps each task to a service (except tasks "Notify Customer" and "Reimburse Overpayment" which consist of interactions with the customer).

2.2   Quality of Service Model

QoS computations on composite services are performed with respect to a fixed set of QoS attributes $\{Attr_i \mid i \in 1..n\}$ such as execution time, cost and reliability. The assumption of a fixed set of attributes is made for presentation purposes and does not constitute a limitation since we can make this set as large as required.

We further postulate the existence of a function that given a service, returns its QoS. This function is initially given for pre-existing (non-composite) services. Our goal is to lift this function so that it can also be applied to composite services.

Definition 2 (QoS Function). The QoS of a service s, denoted by $QoS(s)$, is a vector $\langle v_1, \cdots, v_n \rangle$, where v_i is the value of QoS attribute $Attr_i$ for service s. By extension, QoS is also defined over tasks as follows: $QoS(T) = QoS(binding(T))$.

Numerous QoS attributes have been proposed in previous studies (e.g., [5,6,7,8,9,18]). With respect to the method for computing QoS attribute values for composite services, we classify existing QoS attributes into three categories:

1. **Critical path.** The value of the QoS attribute for the composite service is determined by the *critical path* of the orchestration. Examples include *execution time* (longest critical path) and fault-tolerance (weakest path) [5].
2. **Additive.** The value of the QoS attribute for the composite service is a sum of the QoS values of the component services taking into account how often each service is invoked. Examples include *cost* and *carbon footprint*.
3. **Multiplication.** The QoS attribute value for the composite service is a product of the QoS values of the component services taking into account how often each service is invoked. Examples include *reliability* and *availability* [18].

Below, we only consider three representative attributes. For each service s, $QoS(s) = \langle T, C, R \rangle$, where T, C and R stand for time, cost and reliability. In Fig.1, for example, the numbers in each service denote its QoS attributes.

3   Anatomizing Service Orchestration

This section presents an approach for parsing service compositions. Given a service orchestration, it gets decomposed into a collection of orchestration components, each with clear structural characteristics. The approach is founded on two techniques: a technique for structuring orchestration models [15] and a technique for discovery of SESE components in orchestration models [16,17]. Sect.3.1 presents the overall approach. Sect.3.2 and Sect.3.3 discuss two special types of orchestration components: SEMELoop and DAG components.

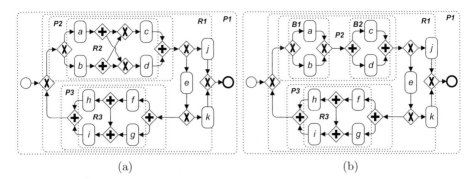

(a)   (b)

Fig. 2. (a) Service orchestration, (b) maximally-structured representation of (a)

3.1 Orchestration Component

In order to analyze service orchestrations, we decompose them into *orchestration components*. An orchestration component is a subgraph of the orchestration model with a single-entry and single-exit point (including individual tasks in the orchestration, but also larger subgraphs). QoS is then computed independently for each orchestration component. This section discusses the approach we employ for identifying orchestration components in orchestrations.

The Refined Process Structure Tree (RPST) [16,17] is a technique to parse orchestration models into a tree of SESE components. A component in the RPST contains all components at the lower level, whereas all components at a given level are disjoint. Each component in the RPST belongs to one out of four classes: A *trivial* (T) component consists of a single flow arc. A *polygon* (P) represents a sequence of components. A *bond* (B) stands for a set of components that share two common nodes. Any other component is a *rigid* (R) component.

Fig.2(a) exemplifies the RPST of the running example given in Fig.1. Note that Fig.2(a) uses short-names for tasks $(a, b, c, \ldots)$, which appear next to each task in Fig.1. In the figure, each dotted box represents a component in the RPST that is formed by flow arcs that are inside or intersect the box. Names of components hint at their class, e.g., $P1$ is a polygon component and $R1$ is a rigid component. Each flow arc forms a trivial component. Trivial components, as well as polygons that are composed of two flow arcs, are not visualized for simplicity reasons.

Rigid components determine what makes a service orchestration unstructured. The service orchestration in Fig.2(a) contains three rigid components. To maximize the amount of structural information derived at the parsing step, we employ the technique from [15]. The technique allows to derive maximally-structured representation of a service orchestration under the fully concurrent bisimulation equivalence notion [3]. By employing the technique from [15] to the model in Fig.2(a), one obtains a service orchestration that is given in Fig.2(b); rigid component $R2$ gets an equivalent representation that consists of bond components $B1$ and $B2$. Importantly, at the stage of maximally-structured representation we are able to define syntax of an orchestration component as follows.

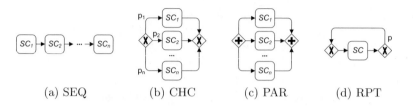

Fig. 3. Structured orchestration components

Definition 3 (Syntax of an Orchestration Component)

Let P be the range of real numbers from 0.0 to 1.0.

$$ServiceComponent(SC) \;::=\; \tau \mid Service \mid C^+ \mid C^-$$

$$OrchestrationElement(OE) \;::=\; SC \mid AND \mid XOR$$

$$StructuredComponent(C^+) \;::=\; SEQ([SC]) \mid CHC(\{P \times SC\}) \mid$$
$$\mid PAR(\{SC\}) \mid RPT(SC \times P)$$

$$UnstructuredComponent(C^-) \;::=\; SEMELoop([SC \times P \times SC]) \mid$$
$$\mid DAG(\{OE \times P \times OE\})$$

We distinguish the following types of orchestration components: empty (τ) tasks, regular tasks (tasks bound to services), structured orchestration components, and unstructured orchestration components. Fig.3 exemplifies four types of structured orchestration components: sequence (SEQ), choice (CHC), parallel (PAR), and repeat (RPT). A sequence component is a list of orchestration components. A choice component is a set of orchestration components along with probabilities for executing each orchestration component. A parallel component is a set of orchestration components. Finally, a repeat component is an orchestration component along with the probability of repeating it. In Fig.2(b), bond $B1$ is a choice component, bond $B2$ is a parallel component, and polygon $P2 = [B1, B2]$ is a sequence component.

3.2   Single-Entry-Multi-Exit Loop Component

In the context of flowcharts, it has been shown that loops with multiple entry points can be restructured into loops with single entry point by means of node duplication [13]. However, subsequent transformation of loops with multiple exit points into loops with single exit point requires introduction of variables and branching conditions on these variables. In these cases, it is not straightforward to abstract branching conditions as a branching probability. Therefore, we explicitly deal with single-entry-multi-exit loop components (SEMELoop components) that capture single entry point loop topologies. Fig.4(a) shows a 1-Entry-2-Exit loop component, whereas Fig.4(b) gives a general topology of a SEMELoop component of size $n \in \mathbb{N}, n \geq 2$.

We treat a SEMELoop component as a list of tuples (SC_i, p_i, eSC_i), where p_i is the probability of proceeding with loop execution after an accomplishment

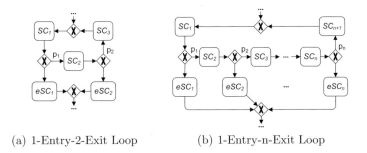

(a) 1-Entry-2-Exit Loop   (b) 1-Entry-n-Exit Loop

Fig. 4. SEMELoop components

of an orchestration component SC_i and eSC_i is an orchestration component that is executed if the loop is left after an accomplishment of SC_i. For instance, a SEMELoop component that is given in Fig.4(a) is represented by the list $[(SC_1, p_1, eSC_1), (SC_2, p_2, eSC_2), (SC_3, 1.0, \tau)]$. Note that the last element in the list shows that the loop component cannot be left after SC_3 (the probability of staying in the loop is equal to 1.0) and, hence, no orchestration component can be executed after leaving the loop after SC_3 (denoted by a silent service τ). Observe that $R1$, both in Fig.2(a) and in Fig.2(b), is a 1-Entry-2-Exit loop component. Loop topologies that cannot be classified as SEMELoop components within service orchestrations are left for future work.

3.3 DAG Component

Acyclic rigids that are present in maximally-structured representations of service orchestrations are classified as irreducible acyclic components, or DAG components. Fig.5 exemplifies DAG components: Fig.5(a) shows the simplest DAG component—a well-known N-structure [10], whereas Fig.5(b) visualizes a DAG component that is a composition of N-structures. Observe that rigid $R3$, both in Fig.2(a) and in Fig.2(b), is a DAG component.

We treat a DAG component as a set of tuples (OE_1, p, OE_2), where OE_1 and OE_2 are orchestration elements, i.e., either an orchestration component or a gateway, and p is the probability that OE_2 will be executed after accomplishment of OE_1. For instance, the N-structure in Fig.5(a) is described by the set

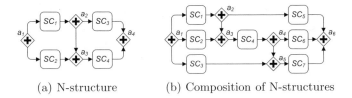

(a) N-structure   (b) Composition of N-structures

Fig. 5. DAG components

$\{(a_1, 1.0, SC_1), (a_1, 1.0, SC_2), (SC_1, 1.0, a_2), (SC_2, 1.0, a_3), (a_2, 1.0, a_3), (a_2, 1.0, SC_3), (a_3, 1.0, SC_4), (SC_3, 1.0, a_4), (SC_4, 1.0, a_4)\}$.

DAG components are analyzed by employing the notion of a *run*. A *run* is a subgraph of a DAG component that can be interpreted as its concurrent execution along with the probability to observe this run. The notion which is relevant to runs is that of *configuration*. A configuration is a set of tuples (OE_1, p, OE_2), where OE_1 is a XOR-split gateway, OE_2 is an orchestration element, and p is the probability that OE_2 will be executed after visiting OE_1. Moreover, a configuration must define a run. For instance, $\{(x_1, p_{11}, x_2), (x_2, p_{21}, SC_2)\}$ and $\{(x_1, p_{11}, x_2), (x_2, p_{22}, SC_3)\}$ are configurations of the DAG in Fig.6(a).

Individual runs allow us to treat each DAG component as a choice component. A choice component that corresponds to a DAG component is a set of runs of the DAG, each together with the probability to observe the run. We use Alg.1 to compute all configurations of a process graph.

Algorithm 1. Compute Configurations of a DAG Component

Input: G—a DAG component
Output: Θ—the set of configurations of G
$X = \{x_1, x_2, \ldots, x_n\}$ // XOR-split gateways of G
$\Theta = \prod_{i=1}^{|X|} out(x_i)$ // Cartesian product of outgoing flow arcs
foreach $\theta = (e_1, e_2, \ldots, e_n) \in \Theta$ **do**
    foreach $e_i, e_j \in set(\theta)$ **do**
        if $\exists\, path : src(e_i), e_j \in path \wedge tgt(e_i) \notin path$ **then** $\theta = \theta - e_j$
Remove duplicates from Θ
return Θ

Example 1. We exemplify the steps of Alg.1 for the DAG component in Fig.6(a):
1. $X = \{x_1, x_2, x_3\}$ is the set of XOR-split gateways, with outgoing flow arcs given as: $out(x_1) = \{e_1, e_4\}$, $out(x_2) = \{e_2, e_3\}$, $out(x_3) = \{e_5, e_6\}$.
2. $\Theta = \prod_{i=1}^{3} out(x_i) = \{(e_1, e_2, \underline{e_5}), (e_1, e_2, \underline{e_6}), (e_1, e_3, \underline{e_5}), (e_1, e_3, \underline{e_6}), (e_4, e_5, \underline{e_2}), (e_4, e_5, \underline{e_3}), (e_4, e_6, \underline{e_2}), (e_4, e_6, \underline{e_3})\}$, where the underlining elements will be removed in the next step.
3. $\Theta = \{(e_1, e_2), (e_1, e_2), (e_1, e_3), (e_1, e_3), (e_4, e_5), (e_4, e_5), (e_4, e_6), (e_4, e_6)\}$.
4. $\Theta = \{(e_1, e_2), (e_1, e_3), (e_4, e_5), (e_4, e_6)\}$, after removing duplicate entries.

Given a DAG component and the set of its configurations, Alg.2 computes the set of its runs. Consequently, one can construct a choice component that corresponds to the original DAG component. A choice component is obtained by introducing a single XOR-split gateway which leads to entry of each run with the probability that reflects the chance to observe the run. Accordingly, exits of all runs must be merged by a single XOR-join gateway. A choice component that corresponds to the DAG component in Fig.6(a) is given in Fig.6(b).

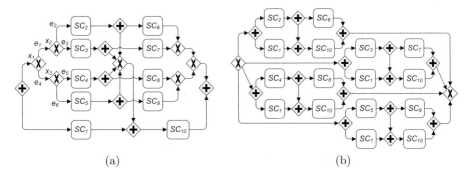

$$(a) \qquad\qquad\qquad\qquad (b)$$

Fig. 6. (a) a DAG component, (b) a choice component that corresponds to (a)

Algorithm 2. Compute Runs of a DAG Component

Input: G—a DAG component, Θ— the set of configurations of G
Output: Γ—the set of runs of G
$\Gamma = \{\}$ // Initialize Γ as empty set
foreach $\theta \in \Theta$ **do** Compute corresponding run for θ
    $\gamma = G$ // Initialize the run
    $q = 1.0$ // Initialize the probability of observing the run
    foreach $(x, p, m) \in \theta$ **do**
        foreach $(x, h, n) \in \gamma \wedge n \neq m$ **do** $\gamma = \gamma - (x, h, n)$
    while $\exists (y, k, z) \in \gamma : \nexists (y', k', y) \in \gamma$ **do** $\gamma = \gamma - (y, k, z)$
    foreach XOR-split gateway $x \in \gamma$ **do** $\gamma = \gamma - (x, p, y) + (x.precede, 1.0, y)$
    $q = q \times p$ // Update the probability of observing the run
    $\Gamma = \Gamma \cup (q, \gamma)$
return Γ

---

4 Quality of Service Aggregation

In this section, we discuss the aggregation of QoS of orchestration components. Sect.4.1 proposes functions for computing QoS of service orchestration components, and Sect.4.2 proposes an algorithm that combines these component-specific functions into comprehensive approach for computing QoS.

4.1 Aggregation of Orchestration Component

Structured Component. The QoS of structured orchestration components is computed based on the following equations, which are taken from [5].

$$QoS(SEQ[SC_i]) = \langle \sum T_{SC_i}, \sum C_{SC_i}, \prod R_{SC_i} \rangle$$

$$QoS(CHC\{(p_i, SC_i)\}) = \langle \sum p_i T_{SC_i}, \sum p_i C_{SC_i}, \sum p_i R_{SC_i} \rangle$$

$$QoS(RPT(SC, p)) = \langle (1-p)^{-1} T_{SC}, \; (1-p)^{-1} C_{SC}, \; R_{SC}^{(1-p)^{-1}} \rangle$$

$$QoS(PAR\{SC_i\}) = \langle max\{T_{SC_i}\}, \sum C_{SC_i}, \prod R_{SC_i} \rangle \qquad (1)$$

Note that, for repeat composition $RPT(SC, p)$, the computation considers that SC may be executed one or more times. Following the well-known power series relation, SC is expected to be executed $(1 - p)^{-1}$ times[1], where p is the probability of staying in the loop.

Single-Entry-Multi-Exit Loop Component. As for repeat components, in SEMELoop components a collection of orchestration components is executed one or more times. However, for a given component the expected number depends on its position in the loop.

Let $L = SEMELoop[(SC_i, p_i, eSC_i)], i \in [1..n + 1]$, be a SEMELoop and $\{\alpha_i\} = \{SC_i\} \cup \{eSC_i\}$ be an orchestration component of L. Then, QoS of L can be computed as follows:

$$\langle \sum_{i=1}^{n+1} avg(\alpha_i) \bullet T_{\alpha_i}, \sum_{i=1}^{n+1} avg(\alpha_i) \bullet C_{\alpha_i}, \prod_{i=1}^{n+1} R_{SC_i}^{avg(SC_i)} \times \sum_{i=1}^{n} p(eSC_i) \bullet R_{eSC_i} \rangle \ (2)$$

Here, $avg(\alpha_i)$ stands for the average number of times that α_i gets executed in the loop, $p(eSC_i)$ stands for the probability of exiting the loop along orchestration component eSC_i, and $avg(eSC_i) = p(eSC_i)$ for each service eSC_i.

For each service α_i, $avg(\alpha_i)$ can be computed as follows:

$$avg(SC_1) = 1 + \rho_n + \rho_n^2 + \cdots = \sum_{i=0}^{\infty} \rho_n^i = (1 - \rho_n)^{-1}$$

$$avg(SC_k) = \rho_{k-1} + \rho_{k-1}\rho_n + \rho_{k-1}\rho_n^2 + \cdots = \rho_{k-1} \sum_{i=0}^{\infty} \rho_n^i = \rho_{k-1}(1 - \rho_n)^{-1}$$

$$avg(eSC_k) = p(eSC_k) = \rho_{k-1}(1 - p_k) + \rho_{k-1}(1 - p_k)\rho_n + \rho_{k-1}(1 - p_k)\rho_n^2 + \cdots$$

$$= (1 - p_k)\rho_{k-1} \sum_{i=0}^{\infty} \rho_n^i = (1 - p_k)\rho_{k-1}(1 - \rho_n)^{-1}$$

Wherein, $\rho_k = \prod_{i=1}^{k} p_i$, $k \in [1..n]$ and $\rho_0 = 1$.

Example 2. The average number of times of each orchestration component in Fig.4(a) is computed as follows:
$$avg(SC_1) = \sum_{i=0}^{\infty}(p_1 p_2)^i = (1 - p_1 p_2)^{-1}$$
$$avg(SC_2) = p_1 \sum_{i=0}^{\infty}(p_1 p_2)^i = p_1(1 - p_1 p_2)^{-1}$$
$$avg(SC_3) = p_1 p_2 \sum_{i=0}^{\infty}(p_1 p_2)^i = p_1 p_2(1 - p_1 p_2)^{-1}$$
$$p(eSC_1) = (1 - p_1) \sum_{i=0}^{\infty}(p_1 p_2)^i = (1 - p_1)(1 - p_1 p_2)^{-1}$$
$$p(eSC_2) = p_1(1 - p_2) \sum_{i=0}^{\infty}(p_1 p_2)^i = p_1(1 - p_2)(1 - p_1 p_2)^{-1}$$

DAG Component. A DAG orchestration component can be transformed into an equivalent choice component as explained in Sect.3.3. Each of the branches in this choice component corresponds to a run of the DAG component. The QoS

---

[1] Power series: $p^0 + p^1 + \ldots + p^n = \sum_{i=0}^{\infty} p^i = (1 - p)^{-1}$.

values calculated for individual runs are then aggregated taking into account the probability of each run as follows:

$$\langle \sum p_{\gamma_k} T_{\gamma_k}, \sum p_{\gamma_k} C_{\gamma_k}, \sum p_{\gamma_k} R_{\gamma_k} \rangle \tag{3}$$

For a given run γ_k, the execution time can be computed with the well-known *critical path method*, i.e. compute the longest duration path in the run. Meanwhile, the cost of a run is the sum of the costs of the orchestration components in the run, and the reliability of a run is the product of the reliabilities of the orchestration components in the run.

For each run γ, therefore, QoS can be computed as follows:

$$\langle CriticalPath(T_{path_i}), \sum C_{SC_i}, \prod R_{SC_i} \rangle \tag{4}$$

Example 3. The QoS of the DAG component shown in Fig.5(a) is the following: $\langle max\{T_{SC_1} + max\{T_{SC_3}, T_{SC_4}\}, T_{SC_2} + T_{SC_4}\}, \sum C_{SC_i}, \prod R_{SC_i} \rangle$.

4.2   QoS of Composite Services

The overall QoS for a composite service is computed by aggregating the QoS of its orchestration components according to their structure and relation, i.e., maximally-structured representation in Fig.2(b). To this end, the RPST of the composite service is traversed in pre-order, i.e., computing the aggregate QoS from leaf nodes up to the root node.

Alg. 3 details the procedure of computing QoS for a service orchestration.

Algorithm 3. Compute QoS for Service Orchestration: ComputeQoS(SC)

Input: SC — node of the RPST
Output: QoS — QoS of SC
if SC is an atomic service **then return** $\langle T_{SC}, C_{SC}, R_{SC} \rangle$
foreach $SC_i \in$ ChildrenOf(SC) **do** ComputeQoS(SC_i)
if SC is a structured orchestration component **then**
    Compute $QoS(SC)$ as according to Formula 1
if SC is a SEMELoop component **then**
    Compute $QoS(SC)$ according to Formula 2
if SC is a DAG component **then**
    Compute configurations Θ of SC
    foreach $\theta \in \Theta$ **do**
        Compute runs γ for θ according to Alg. 2
        Compute $QoS(\gamma)$ according to Formula 4
    Compute $QoS(SC)$ according to Formula 3
return QoS

Example 4. To exemplify the Alg.3, we compute QoS for the composite service that is proposed in Fig.1.

$QoS(B1) = \langle 2 \cdot 0.6 + 1 \cdot 0.4, 1 \cdot 0.6 + 2 \cdot 0.4, 0.95 \cdot 0.6 + 0.98 \cdot 0.4 \rangle = \langle 1.6, 1.4, 0.962 \rangle;$
$QoS(B2) = \langle max\{2, 1\}, 3 + 1, 0.97 \cdot 0.99 \rangle = \langle 2, 4, 0.9603 \rangle;$
$QoS(P2) = \langle 1.6 + 2, 1.4 + 4, 0.962 \cdot 0.9238 \rangle = \langle 3.6, 5.4, 0.8887 \rangle;$
$QoS(P3) = QoS(B2) = \langle max\{2 + 3, 2 + 4, 1 + 4\}, 3 + 1 + 1 + 2, 0.96 \cdot 0.99 \cdot 0.93 \cdot$
$0.94 \rangle = \langle 6, 7, 0.8308 \rangle;$

$avg(P2) = 1/(1 - 0.8 \cdot 0.6) = 1.9231;$
$avg(j) = p(j) = (1 - 0.8)/(1 - 0.8 \cdot 0.6) = 0.3846;$
$avg(e) = 0.8/(1 - 0.8 \cdot 0.6) = 1.5385;$
$avg(k) = p(k) = 0.8 \cdot (1 - 0.6)/(1 - 0.8 \cdot 0.6) = 0.6154;$
$avg(P3) = 0.6 \cdot 0.8/(1 - 0.8 \cdot 0.6) = 0.9231;$

$QoS(P1) = QoS(R1) = \langle 3.6 \cdot 1.9231 + 3 \cdot 0.3846 + 3 \cdot 1.5385 + 4 \cdot 0.6154 + 6 \cdot$
$0.9231, 5.4 \cdot 1.9231 + 4 \cdot 0.3846 + 2 \cdot 1.5385 + 5 \cdot 0.6154 + 7 \cdot 0.9231, 0.8887^{1.9231} \cdot$
$0.97^{1.5385} \cdot 0.80^{0.6154} \cdot (0.95 \cdot 0.3846 + 0.8308 \cdot 0.9231) \rangle = \langle 20.6927, 24.5388, 0.7506 \rangle.$

5   Implementation and Evaluation

We have implemented the proposed QoS aggregation method in a tool that takes as inputs service orchestrations described in BPMN[2] and computes the aggregate value for each QoS attribute. The QoS values for each service and the branching probabilities of gateways in the BPMN model are defined in separate (text) files. The tool is distributed as an extension of the BPStruct tool and is available at: `http://sep.cs.ut.ee/Main/Bpstruct`. Below we present an evaluation of the scalability of the QoS aggregation method using the implemented tool.

5.1   Dataset

We collected a dataset consisting of 28 BPMN models from the following sources: 8 models from the public Oryx repository[3], 8 models from BPMN-to-BPEL case study of the Grabats'2009 graph transformation challenge[4], and 12 models from a repository of process models for local government authorities in China collected by Fudan University. We discarded incomplete/incorrect models, and models containing OR gateways, complex gateways, error events and boundary events, which are out of the scope of this paper. The size of models in the dataset (number of process nodes) range from 5 to 32, with an average of 17.5 nodes. Some of these models were larger, but they were structured into a top-level process with subprocess invocations. In this case, the process and its subprocesses are handled separately. The models cover all types of components: 72 SEQ components, 19 CHC components, 24 PAR components, 20 SESE Loop components, 2 DAG components, and 4 SEME Loop components. Links to all the models in the dataset are included in the tool distribution Web page. We assigned random probability to each XOR-split branch of each model (using a uniform distribution), and random QoS to each service (i.e., time, cost and reliability).

---

[2] Specifically, the tool accepts BPMN models exported from Oryx
   (`http://oryx-project.org/`)
[3] `http://oryx-editor.org/`
[4] `http://fots.ua.ac.be/events/grabats2008/cases.html`

5.2   Results

We used the tool to compute the aggregate QoS for each models in the dataset and measured execution times (in milliseconds). All tests were performed on a laptop with a dual core Intel processor, 2.53 GHz, 3 GB memory, running Microsoft Vista and SUN Java Virtual Machine version 1.6 (with 512MB of allocated memory). To eliminate load time from the measures, each test was executed five times, and we recorded the average execution time of the second to fifth run. The measured execution time included the time required to compute the RPST and to calculate the QoS.

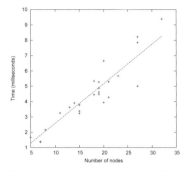

Fig. 7. Execution times for QoS aggregation

The resulting histogram of execution times is plotted in Fig. 7. The figure shows that the QoS aggregation technique can deal with models of realistic size and complexity and that it scales quasi-linearly.

6   Related Work

Several previous studies have addressed the problem of aggregating QoS in terms of different structures in the orchestration model. Jaeger *et al* [8,9] discuss the QoS aggregation problem for process models consisting of sequence, conditional and parallel. The approach does not deal with loops. In order to cope with the problem of binding and re-binding for composite services, Canfora *et al* [4] propose QoS aggregation functions for four constructs: sequence, switch, flow and loop, while Mukherjee *et al* [12] propose a model to estimate QoS of an executable BPEL process definition, but without considering unstructured BPEL activities (i.e. BPEL "flow" activities with control links). Cardoso *et al* [5] proposed a Stochastic Workflow Reduction (SWR) algorithm which takes as input a process graph and computes the expected QoS by repeatedly applying a set of reduction rules for sequential, parallel, conditional and simple loop. Hwang *et al* [6,7] represent composite services using a tree structure and compute the aggregate QoS of composite services recursively by traversing the tree. This tree is similar with the RPST structure, but the trees in the work of Hwang *et al* do not contain any unstructured blocks. In summary, all of the above approaches are related to ours, but all of them deal with well-structured orchestration models only.

The problem of computing QoS for composite services is related to that of QoS-aware service composition [1,11,18], where the input is an orchestration model and a set of service candidates for each task in the orchestration model. The goal is to find a binding that optimizes a given objective function while satisfying a given set of constraints. Zeng *et al* [18] study a local and a global optimization approach to this problem using Simple Additive Weighting (SAW) and Integer Programming (IP), respectively. Meanwhile, Liu *et al* [11] propose a dynamic QoS computation model for web services selection in order to deal with runtime QoS selection. Like [18], the authors construct a QoS matrix and compute QoS of a composite service via normalization and then multiplication with weights given by a user. A combination of the local optimization and the global optimization approaches is studied in Alrifai *et al* [1]. This latter work considers three types of QoS aggregation functions: summation, multiplication and minimum relation. The classification of QoS attributes that we use is inspired by this latter work.

The above studies address a more complex problem, in the sense that the binding is not given, but instead needs to be computed based on the set of candidate services for each task. On the other hand, the above work also suffer from an inability to deal with unstructured components. In addition, the global optimization approach proposed by Zeng *et al* [18] cannot deal with loops (not even structured loops). Instead, it is assumed that loops are expanded by putting an upper-bound to the number of times a loop is executed and unfolding the loop into a sequential structure.

7   Conclusion

In this paper, we proposed a method for computing the QoS of composite services. Unlike previous work, the proposed method can deal with orchestration models containing unstructured components, specifically models containing single-entry-multi-exit loop (SEMELoop) and DAG components. The proposed method has been implemented as a tool and tested with a collection of models taken from multiple sources.

Our future work includes computing QoS for composite services with more complex types of loops (e.g., overlapping loops) and extending the proposed method to address the problem of QoS-aware service composition.

Acknowledgments. Work supported by the NSF of China grant 60873115, the Chinese National Basic Research Program (973) grant 2005CB321905 and the Fudan Short-Term Visits Program for Doctoral Students. Work also supported by the ERDF via the Estonian Centre of Excellence in Computer Science.

References

1. Alrifai, M., Risse, T.: Combining Global Optimization with Local Selection for Efficient QoS-aware Service Composition. In: Proc. 18th Int. Conf. on World Wide Web, pp. 881–890. ACM Press, New York (2009)
2. Becker, C., Kulovits, H., Kraxner, M., Gottardi, R., Rauber, A.: An Extensible Monitoring Framework for Measuring and Evaluating Tool Performance in a Service-Oriented Architecture. In: Gaedke, M., Grossniklaus, M., Díaz, O. (eds.) Web Engineering. LNCS, vol. 5648, pp. 221–235. Springer, Heidelberg (2009)
3. Best, E., Devillers, R.R., Kiehn, A., Pomello, L.: Concurrent Bisimulations in Petri Nets. Acta Informatica 28(3), 231–264 (1991)

4. Canfora, G., Di Penta, M., Esposito, R., Villani, M.L.: A framework for QoS-aware binding and re-binding of composite web services. Systems and Software 81(10) (2008)
5. Cardoso, J., Sheth, A., Miller, J., Arnold, J., Kochut, K.: Quality of Service for Workflows and Web Service Processes. Web Semantics 1(3), 281–308 (2004)
6. Hwang, S.Y., Wang, H., Srivastava, J., Paul, R.A.: A Probabilistic QoS Model and Computation Framework for Web Services-Based Workflows. In: Atzeni, P., Chu, W., Lu, H., Zhou, S., Ling, T.-W. (eds.) ER 2004. LNCS, vol. 3288, pp. 596–609. Springer, Heidelberg (2004)
7. Hwang, S.Y., Wang, H., Tang, J., Srivastava, J.: A probabilistic approach to modeling and estimating the QoS of web-services-based workflows. Information Sciences 177(23), 5484–5503 (2007)
8. Jaeger, M.C., Rojec-Goldmann, G., Muhl, G.: QoS Aggregation for Web Service Composition using Workflow Patterns. In: Proc. of Enterprise Distributed Object Computing Conf., pp. 149–159. IEEE, Los Alamitos (2004)
9. Jaeger, M.C., Rojec-Goldmann, G., Muhl, G.: QoS Aggregation in Web Service Compositions. In: Proc. IEEE Int. Conf. EEE, pp. 181–185 (2005)
10. Kiepuszewski, B., ter Hofstede, A.H.M., Bussler, C.: On Structured Workflow Modelling. In: Wangler, B., Bergman, L.D. (eds.) CAiSE 2000. LNCS, vol. 1789, pp. 431–445. Springer, Heidelberg (2000)
11. Liu, Y., Ngu, A.H., Zeng, L.Z.: QoS Computation and Policing in Dynamic Web Service Selection. In: WWW Alt, pp. 66–73 (2004)
12. Mukherjee, D., Jalote, P., Gowri Nanda, M.: Determining QoS of WS-BPEL compositions. In: Bouguettaya, A., Krueger, I., Margaria, T. (eds.) ICSOC 2008. LNCS, vol. 5364, pp. 378–393. Springer, Heidelberg (2008)
13. Oulsnam, G.: Unravelling Unstructured Programs. Computer Journal 25(3) (1982)
14. Peltz, C.: Web services orchestration and choreography. IEEE Computer 36(10), 46–52 (2003)
15. Polyvyanyy, A., García-Bañuelos, L., Dumas, M.: Structuring Acyclic Process Models. In: Hull, R., Mendling, J., Tai, S. (eds.) BPM 2010. LNCS, vol. 6336, pp. 276–293. Springer, Heidelberg (2010)
16. Polyvyanyy, A., Vanhatalo, J., Völzer, H.: Simplified Computation and Generalization of the Refined Process Structure Tree. In: Proc. of the 7th Int. Workshop on Web Services and Formal Methods, WS-FM (2010) (in press)
17. Vanhatalo, J., Völzer, H., Koehler, J.: The Refined Process Structure Tree. Data and Knowledge Engineering 68(9), 793–818 (2009)
18. Zeng, L., Benatallah, B., H.H. Ngu, A., Dumas, M., Kalagnanam, J., Chang, H.: QoS-Aware Middleware for Web Services Composition. IEEE Transactions on Software Engineering 30(5), 311–327 (2004)
19. Zeng, L., Lei, H., Chang, H.: Monitoring the QoS for Web Services. In: Krämer, B.J., Lin, K.-J., Narasimhan, P. (eds.) ICSOC 2007. LNCS, vol. 4749, pp. 132–144. Springer, Heidelberg (2007)

Creating Context-Adaptive Business Processes

Gabriel Hermosillo, Lionel Seinturier, and Laurence Duchien

INRIA Lille - Nord Europe, ADAM Project-Team
Univ. Lille 1 - LIFL CNRS UMR 8022
Lille, France
firstname.lastname@inria.fr

Abstract. As the dynamicity of today's business environments keeps increasing, there is a need to continuously adapt business processes to respond to the changes in those environments and keep a competitive level. By using complex event processing, we can discover information that is relevant to our organization, which is usually hidden among the data generated in the environment, and use it to adapt the processes accordingly to respond to the changing conditions in an optimal way. Unfortunately, the static nature of business process definitions makes it impossible to adapt them at runtime and the redeployment of a modified process is required. By using a component-based approach, we can transform the existing business processes into dynamically bound components, adding the flexibility needed to adapt the processes at runtime. In this paper we present CEVICHE, a framework that combines the strengths of complex event processing and dynamic business process adaptation, which allows to respond to the needs of the rapidly changing environment, and its adaptation language called SBPL, an extension to BPEL which adds flexibility to business processes.

1 Introduction

In order to maintain a competitive level, organizations are increasingly using services to facilitate the integration of their business processes. These services are loosely-coupled instances, which enable the separation of concerns. To orchestrate them, organizations rely mainly in well known standards such as BPEL (*Business Process Execution Language*). As business processes evolve and get more complex, the data around them increases exponentially, to the point where it becomes almost impossible to find valuable information among it.

Complex Event Processing (CEP) is an emerging technology that can help the organizations to benefit from this data, since it allows them to find real-time relationships between different events, using elements such as timing, causality, and membership in a stream of data to extract relevant information [1]. CEP can be used in a wide variety of applications, like preventing theft of merchandise [2], monitoring the stock market [3], and interacting with RFID systems [4].

However, there are some occasions in which it is not enough just to be able to obtain this information from simple raw data. A better approach would be that, once the information is found, the system could automatically adapt itself

P.P. Maglio et al. (Eds.): ICSOC 2010, LNCS 6470, pp. 228–242, 2010.

accordingly to respond to the presented scenario. In this case, we want to apply this approach to business processes, allowing them to be dynamically and automatically adapted, according to the information discovered using CEP to continue in an optimal way, and this is why we developed CEVICHE (*Complex EVent processIng for Context-adaptive processes in pervasive and Heterogeneous Environments*).

The purpose of CEVICHE is to create context-aware business processes that are able to adapt dynamically to respond to different unpredictable scenarios. CEVICHE relies on BPEL, since it is the most common orchestration language, it is an OASIS standard [5], and it is an execution language and not a modeling language (like BPMN). With CEVICHE the adaptation of the business process happens at runtime during the execution. The decisions of how to respond to a specific scenario are done by collecting data from different sources and transforming it into useful information, using CEP. Separating the decision making process from the core business process can help to keep a better understanding of the process, by avoiding to have cross-cutting code in the main process definition. In this paper we present the *Standard Business Process Language* (SBPL), an extension of BPEL which allows the user define the adaptation points in a business process. By using a component-oriented approach, we can define alternative processes that can be integrated into the existing business process at runtime, allowing the business process to adapt in a dynamic way.

We have already presented CEVICHE in previous work, where we used an aspect-oriented approach to monitor and maintain the Quality of Service (QoS) of a business process, by monitoring the performance and availability of the different tasks of the process, adapting the process to maintain a good QoS whenever a decrease of those parameters was detected [6]. In this paper we are using a component-oriented approach to show the flexibility of CEVICHE to deal with different adaptation approaches, however we mainly want to focus on the way in which this adaptation is defined by the user using CEVICHE's adaptation language, called SBPL, and the event definitions.

The rest of this paper is organized as follows. In Section 2, we use a scenario to illustrate the motivation and challenges of our proposal. Section 3 presents a background of the different domains used in this paper. In Section 4, we present the SBPL and show how events are defined in CEVICHE. Section 5 explains the CEVICHE framework and its architecture. In Section 6, we discuss our proposal and how it solves the presented challenges. Section 7 presents some of the related work. Finally, Section 8 concludes and discusses some future work.

2   Motivation and Challenges

In order to show how CEVICHE can help to improve the business process by adding dynamic adaptation, we will use a small health-care scenario. The goal of the process is to diagnose a patient, given her vital signs (*i.e.* temperature, blood pressure and heart-beat rate), as can be seen in Fig. 1. If the vital signs are normal, the results are logged and the process finishes, otherwise, the process diagnoses the problem and logs the results.

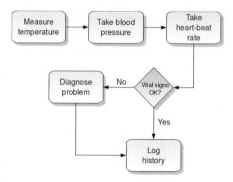

Fig. 1. The health-care sample process

Even though this is a very simple scenario, we can identify several limitations. For example, if the information provided by the previous steps of the process were not enough to diagnose a problem, and we needed other information to accurately diagnose it (*e.g.* saliva PH, blood oxygen), there is no way to add it to the process. We would need the user to start a new process that requests the missing information in order to complete the diagnostic.

We could add additional steps to the process, like a validation in which, if the first steps of the process do not provide enough information to diagnose the problem, then the process will continue gathering other information until the diagnostic can be completed. However, these additional steps are different for each scenario, since the information needed to diagnose each problem is not the same. Moreover, we do not want to have all the code for every case in the main process definition, since this will generate code scattering and create a very complex code that will be very hard to maintain. Finally, given the static nature of business process definitions, whenever we want to add a new problem detection to the process, or change the way in which an existing problem is being diagnosed, we would need to modify and redeploy the whole process, stopping the service while doing so and losing all the unfinished transactions.

Given these limitations, we can extract three challenges for the scenario:

1. *Situation identification.* In certain cases, the process needs to collect additional information about the patient, but we cannot anticipate what information is needed in each case.
2. *Code scattering.* Even when we can anticipate the additional information, the request for such information would have to be included in the main process definition, generating code scattering and a complex logic in the process.
3. *Process redeployment.* If we need to add a new problem to diagnose, or change the way an existing problem is being diagnosed, the whole process would need to be redeployed.

3   Background

In this section, we present a brief introduction to the main domains addressed in this paper: complex event processing, business process execution language, and component-oriented programming.

3.1   Complex Event Processing

CEP is an emerging technology for finding relationships between series of simple and independent events from different sources, using previously defined rules [1]. The CEP technology can be used, among a lot of other things, to enrich the enterprise's existing processes, by introducing rules that will allow the capture of relevant information from the different steps of their business process [7].

For example, let us consider the scenario of a retail store that keeps a record of its inventory in an existing *Enterprise Resource Planning* (ERP) system and wants to keep a live monitoring of its stocks to prevent shortage. To achieve this, the store installs a CEP engine that will monitor the products' movements through their life cycle in the store process by receiving and analyzing all the events generated by every change in the state. Since the objective is to monitor inventory, the CEP engine will only keep the events related to changes in the inventory and forget about the rest. By creating the necessary CEP rules, the configuration is set to specify the lowest acceptable stock of product that the store can have to avoid a shortage, *e.g.*, a 10% for normal products and a 5% for some low-demand products. Whenever a product reaches a minimum, the CEP engine alerts the managers so they can make a supply order.

In addition to that, CEP can also be used to predict unexpected situations. To complement the previous example, we can say that because of a global pandemic alert, hand sanitizers are very popular and are selling a lot more than usual. Given this demand, the store will run out of hand sanitizer before they can resupply it, even with the minimum stock alert. By adding some specialized CEP rules to analyze the frequency of sells of each product during the last 4 or 5 hours, the engine can polarize these values to know in advance (if the sells rates are kept) that it will need to resupply before the expected time, which will allow them to react in time even before it reaches the minimum level.

3.2   Business Process Execution Language

The *Business Process Execution Language* (BPEL) is an XML-based language for composing services, created by IBM, BEA Systems and Microsoft in 2002, and later approved as an OASIS Standard as WS-BPEL 2.0 [5]. There are two types of service composition: orchestration (execution) and choreography (control). BPEL is an orchestration language, which means that it focuses on the flow of control and data among the different services of the business process, rather than on the specification of peer-to-peer collaboration.

BPEL uses web services as a way to communicate with the different parties involved in the business process. It has two types of activities: primitive and structured. The former refers to atomic or single activities while the latter refers to composite activities (a combination of several activities). Some instructions like `invoke`, `receive` or `assign` refer to the primitive activities, while `sequence` and `flow` are part of the structured activities and refer to the order in which the activities will execute.

In order to interact with the different parties of the business process (called `partners`), we need to define a `partner` link, which specifies the roles of the partner and the caller. We also need to define the different input and output variables that we will use to send information to and receive information from the service. Finally, BPEL also provides some facilities for transaction and exception handling.

3.3 Component-Oriented Programming

Taylor *et al.* define a software component as an architectural entity that encapsulates a subset of the system's functionality and/or data, restricts access to that subset via an explicitly defined interface, and has explicitly defined dependencies on its required execution context [8].

Component-oriented programming enables programs to be constructed from prebuilt software components, which are reusable, self-contained blocks of computer code. These components have to follow certain predefined standards including interface, connections, versioning, and deployment [9]. Component-oriented programming enables the development of software by assembling independent components into a software architecture.

4 Events Definitions and the SBPL

The CEVICHE framework uses events to identify the situations where a process adaptation is required. In this section we present how these events are defined and how they are used by CEVICHE's extension to BPEL, the *Standard Business Process Language* (SBPL), to trigger the business process adaptation.

4.1 Event Definitions

Event definitions are one of the main parts of the CEVICHE framework. Since the goal of CEVICHE is to work with any CEP engine, we need to provide the user with a powerful enough event descriptor, in order to be able to use the engine's capabilities in the best possible way, after the event definitions are translated. We are also concerned about standards, since it will be easier to develop a translation plug-in for a specific CEP engine if the source were in a well documented format, and this is why we use XPath[1] expressions for our event definitions, a query language for XML defined by the World Wide Web Consortium. With XPath, the event conditions can be explicitly described and therefore easily translated to other query languages. Besides, some CEP engines,

---

[1] http://www.w3.org/TR/xpath20

like Esper[2], already support XPath event definitions, the translation plug-in can be very simple or even non-existent.

An example of an event definition is shown in Fig. 2. Here we define an event called Hypertension, which is triggered whenever the systolic blood pressure is above 140 *mmHg* and the diastolic blood pressure is above 90 *mmHg*. For more information about the use of XPath expressions, please refer to the specification.

```
1  <event name='Hypertension'>
2    <condition>
3      /event[@name='BloodPressure']
4      and /event/pressure[@type='Systolic'] > 140
5      and /event/pressure[@type='Diastolic'] > 90
6    </condition>
7  </event>
```

Fig. 2. Event definition example

4.2   Standard Business Process Language

In order to respond to the lack of adaptation specifications in the current standards, we created the *Standard Business Process Language* (SBPL), an extension of BPEL which allows the user to include, in the business process definitions, the adaptation points, conditions and alternative processes to create dynamically adaptable business processes. The syntaxis of the SBPL can be seen in Fig. 3. As an adaptation language, in SBPL we need to answer four basic questions: *Where* to adapt?, *When* to adapt it?, *How* to adapt it?, and *What* to adapt?

To answer the first adaptation question, we need to identify the exact place where we want to adapt the process, for which we use the adaptatioPoint tag (line 11). We can use several adaptation points throughout the business process definition. To define when adaptation that will take place, we need to specify the conditions under which such adaptation is expected, and we do so by using the situation tag (line 13). The first element is the event (line 14), which refers to the name or alias of either a simple event generated by the process or a complex event, generated by the CEP engine.

The conditions to identify these events will be defined as CEP rules and deployed in the CEP engine using the translation plug-in. By separating the event definitions from the business process definitions, we can increase the flexibility of the process adaptation, since the conditions of the event definitions can be easily managed, inserting, updating and deleting events without affecting the business process. This also helps to the separation of concerns, avoiding to mix the decision making process with the business process definition.

After declaring the expected event, we specify how the process should be adapted, using the adaptationType tag (line 15). Inspired by the aspect-oriented approach, the adaptation can be done either *before, after* or *around* the adaptation point [10,11]. The first two types can be understood by their name, and the

---

[2] http://esper.codehaus.org

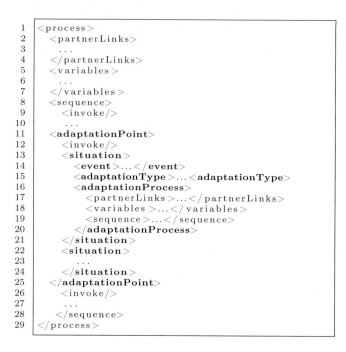

```
1   <process>
2     <partnerLinks>
3       ...
4     </partnerLinks>
5     <variables>
6       ...
7     </variables>
8     <sequence>
9       <invoke/>
10      ...
11    <adaptationPoint>
12      <invoke/>
13      <situation>
14        <event>...</event>
15        <adaptationType>...<adaptationType>
16        <adaptationProcess>
17          <partnerLinks>...</partnerLinks>
18          <variables>...</variables>
19          <sequence>...</sequence>
20        </adaptationProcess>
21      </situation>
22      <situation>
23        ...
24      </situation>
25    </adaptationPoint>
26      <invoke/>
27      ...
28    </sequence>
29  </process>
```

Fig. 3. The SBPL definition

third is a combination of both, meaning that additional tasks will be executed before and after the adaptation point. Also, when the *around* adaptation is used, the task marked on the adaptation point can even be excluded from the process and not executed at all.

Finally, we need to define what is to be adapted in the process, and for this we use the `alternativeProcess` tag (line 16). This tag allows the user to introduce the alternative business process that will be used to adapt the current process. When using the *around* adaptation type, a tag called *proceed* should be added in the alternative process to indicate the place where the adaptation point should be inserted. Several situations can be defined for a single adaptation point, allowing the process to be adapted in a different way according to the context information.

5   The CEVICHE Framework

In this section we present the CEVICHE framework. We start by giving an overview of the system, then we present the framework's architecture and finally we show how the process adaptation is executed.

5.1   Overview and Architecture

CEVICHE is a framework that intends to facilitate the integration of CEP into existing business processes and to allow these processes to be dynamically adapted to different circumstances. With this framework we want to address mainly four issues: adaptation, dynamicity, integration of CEP into business process, and non-dependency to a specific CEP engine.

To address the first issue, adaptation, we use a component-oriented approach. We specifically use Easy BPEL[3], a library that provides a BPEL 2.0 engine to orchestrate services based on a WSDL description. With this library, each task of the business process is transformed into a component that exposes its interfaces, which are bound according to the process definition, and the whole process is exposed as a service using an *Enterprise Service Bus* (ESB). These bindings can be changed at runtime, adding or removing components to the architecture, which allows the process to be adapted dynamically, giving also a solution to our second issue.

By analyzing the current events with CEP and using context information, CEVICHE can automatically decide when and how to adapt the process, integrating CEP into business processes (third issue). To achieve this, we need to provide CEVICHE with the definition of the adaptation points for the business process and the events that will trigger that adaptation. This information is defined using the SBPL, which contains also the complete business process. In Section 4.2 we discussed the SBPL in more detail.

Finally, CEVICHE aims to be able to work with any CEP engine available. For that, as part of this framework, we use a plug-in approach, which will allow us to translate our events and conditions into the desired CEP engine. This approach allows the users to define their business processes only once and deploy them using their preferred CEP engine.

The architecture of CEVICHE is composed of four main parts: 1) a user interface to create the SBPL definitions, 2) a translation framework that separates the main business process from the adaptation conditions, 3) a translation plug-in in charge of adapting the event definitions for each CEP engine, and 4) an adaptation manager to deal with the process adaptation. CEVICHE also relies on different technologies to achieve the process adaptation, like the CEP and BPEL engines, as shown in Fig. 4.

To configure the system, the user needs to be able to specify where the process has to be adapted and the conditions that will trigger such an adaptation. In order to fulfill this need, CEVICHE requires a language that can describe the business process along with all the adaptation points and conditions, and that is just what the SBPL provides.

CEVICHE needs to kinds of information: first, the event definitions that identify the special situations that require process adaptation, and second, the business process definition and adaptation points using the SBPL. Separating the decision making process from the core business process, helps to reduce the cross-cutting code and improves the maintainability of the process. The information in the process definition is sent to the translation framework, which separates the adaptation data from the core business process. The business process information is sent to the BPEL engine, while the adaptation information is sent to CEVICHE's adaptation manager.

---

[3] http://easybpel.petalslink.com

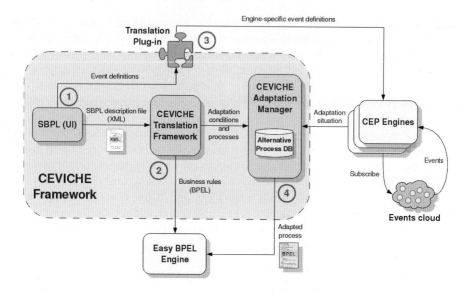

Fig. 4. The CEVICHE framework

Since there is no standard yet to define the events and CEP rules, CEVICHE uses a specialized plug-in approach to send the information in the second file in the specific CEP engine's format. This plug-in will need to be developed for each specific CEP language, unless until a standard is defined by the *Event Processing Technical Society*[4]. This way, whenever the user wants to use another CEP engine, the only thing that needs to be done is to change the plug-in, without rewriting all the specifications of the business processes. The event definitions are explained in more detail in Section 4.1.

5.2 Process Adaptation

Once the initial setup is ready and all the components have been properly configured, the process starts and the information begins to flow from one component to the other. First, the BPEL engine transforms the business process into components and exposes the process as a service in the ESB. When a request message is received, a new instantiation of the BPEL process is triggered. Then, the CEP engine subscribes to the different sources of events, here called the `events cloud`, which will provide the engine with the information it needs to take decisions and create complex events.

The CEP engine will gather all the events, filter the interesting ones according to the business rules and find relations that can generate complex events. When an adaptation situation is detected, the CEP engine notifies the adaptation manager, which in turn searches for the corresponding condition in the *alternative process DB* and adapts the process accordingly at runtime.

---

[4] http://www.ep-ts.com

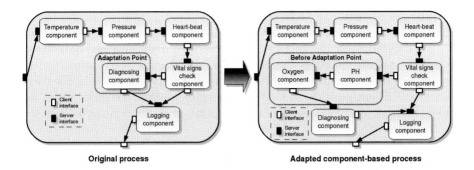

Fig. 5. A process adaptation example

The adaptation is achieved by taking advantage of the reconfiguration capabilities of the component-oriented approach in our model. The components from the adaptation points are unbound from the process and the alternative process is bound instead. Depending on the type of adaptation (before, after or around), the adaptation point is bound again into the process in the proper place.

We can see an example of a component-based process adaptation in Fig. 5. Here, the process presented in Fig. 1 is transformed into components on the left-hand side of the figure. Then, on the right-hand side we add an alternative process using a *before* adaptation type. As can be noticed, the input bindings of the adaptation point are changed and bound to the alternative process. The output of the last component of the alternative process is then bound to the service of the adaptation point. Since the bindings in the component model can be modified at run-time, the process is dynamically adapted.

6   Discussion and Validation

In this section we will show how CEVICHE can be used to deal with the challenges presented in Section 2, and discuss the advantages of our approach. In our motivation scenario, we had mainly three challenges: 1) *Situation identification*, 2) *Code scattering*, and 3) *Process redeployment*.

Situation identification. In certain cases, the process needed to collect additional information about the patient, but we cannot anticipate what information was needed in each case. In CEVICHE, we use CEP rules to identify special situations. These situations allow us to provide the scenarios and special circumstances that we are interested in and to define how we want to respond to them. Using the information from the process and even other sources, the CEP engine matches the corresponding rules and alert the system when such a situation is found.

Code scattering. If we could anticipate the additional information, the request for such information would have to be included in the main process definition, generating code scattering and a complex logic in the process. To deal with code scattering, we separated the event definitions from the business process definition. By doing this, we can focus all the decision making code in a separate file which can be easily maintained without modifying or even interrupting the business process execution. The adaptation rules only need to be written once, even when the CEP engine is changed. This also helps to share the event definitions among different partners, or even a community, without limiting its use to a specific software.

Process redeployment. If we needed to add a new problem to diagnose, or change the way an existing problem is being diagnosed, the whole process would need to be redeployed. Given the dynamic reconfiguration of the components provided by the component-oriented model, once our business processes is transformed to bound components, these bindings can be modified at runtime, allowing the process to be adapted without redeploying it and without losing any current transactions in the process.

Evaluation and Performance. CEVICHE can be used to dynamically adapt business processes according to a wide number of situations. In previous work, we have shown how CEVICHE can be used to monitor and maintain the Quality of Service (QoS) of a business process by monitoring the performance and availability of the different tasks of the process, adapting the process to maintain a good QoS whenever a decrease of those parameters was detected [6].

As it can be expected, adding an external engine to deal with event processing, to discover the adaptation situations, require some additional time and resources. This overhead may vary depending on the number and the complexity of rules that need to be processed by the CEP engine. However, the overhead induced to the original process is negligible compared to the cost of the whole process, specially when dealing with Internet interactions with partners, increasing only around 1% or 2% the execution time. For the CEP engine, the overhead is insignificant, taking it less than 1 *ms* to process each event through the whole set of rules. In this case we used the Esper engine, which is an open source stream event processing engine. The efficiency of the CEP engine to process the events is such that it exceeds over 500,000 events per second.

7   Related Work

In this section we describe some of the works related to CEVICHE. Since our project covers several topics, we divided the related work in three sections: CEP and BPEL, business process adaptation, and BPEL context adaptation.

7.1   CEP and BPEL

As mentioned earlier in this paper, CEP is an emerging technology and the use of it in the business processes is a recent topic of interest and research [12,13]. An analysis of scenarios of composite event patterns comparing BPEL and BPMN is done in [12]. The authors analyze patterns of events that go from conjunction and cardinality to time relations and event consumption possibilities. The conclusion of their study is that neither BPEL nor BPMN are capable of supporting complex event scenarios in their specifications, so there is a need to integrate event pattern descriptions into the process definitions language, but they do not mention the need to adapt the process according to those complex events.

In [13], we present a service to add traceability to the RFID tagged products by using Complex Event Processing. When the RFID events are captured, they are transformed into business events that correspond to the business rules defined in the process which allows the users to have a better understanding of the status of their products, *i.e.*, the product's location and the environment it has been exposed to.

7.2   Business Process Adaptation

The need to adapt a process has been a topic of interest in the recent years and there have been different approaches that offer solutions to it [14,15,16,17]. In [14], the authors propose to deal with process adaptation by adding a web service repository that handles the web services to invoke in each case. Whenever an invocation of a web service is done, the call is intercepted and the repository is checked for changes in the process definition, before the invocation of a web service. If there have been some changes, then it examines the available web services in the repository and chooses the one that best suits the criteria, otherwise the invocation is executed as usual.

The authors in [15] use an aspect-oriented approach introducing `executable models`, which are used to represent the cross-cutting concerns. They use `open objects`, which are representations of the state of the elements in the model, to monitor the invocation of services and adapt the process by weaving the interaction with other models before (activation) and after (deactivation) the call to the service.

Another aspect oriented implementation, using the Spring .NET framework, is presented in [16]. They use a contract-based approach to assign a web service to each instance of an execution call. To achieve adaptation of the process they can change the contract at runtime to assign a new web service for the call. They can also adapt an existing implementation of a web service by using aspects to weave the new behavior.

An adaptation of the BPEL language called VxBPEL is presented in [17]. The authors insist on the need of flexibility and variability in the service-based systems and the lack of them when deploying BPEL processes. They extend the BPEL language to add new elements like `Variation Points`, which are the places where the process can be adapted and `Variants`, which define the alternative steps of the process that can be used. VxBPEL also accepts new `Variants` to be added at runtime, allowing the systems to be adapted without redeploying the process.

7.3   BPEL Context Adaptation

The work that is closer to our proposal is the one presented in [18]. The authors present a plug-in based architecture for self-adaptive processes that uses AO4BPEL. Their proposal is to have different plug-ins with a well-defined objective. Each plug-in has two types of aspects: the `monitoring aspects` that check the system to observe when an adaptation is needed and the `adaptation aspects` that handle the situations detected by the monitoring aspects. Whenever the conditions of a `monitoring aspect` are met, it uses AO4BPEL to weave the `adaptation aspects` into the process at runtime. In our approach we deal with the monitoring part using the rules deployed in the CEP engine, which detect special situations (by relating simple events) and select the aspects to be used to adapt the process.

An advantage of their work is that the monitoring aspects can be hot-deployed to their BPEL engine while with our approach the changes in the rules might not be considered at runtime, depending on the CEP engine. However, even if we needed to restart the CEP engine in order to consider the new rules, this would not affect any active running processes, as it would if we restarted the BPEL engine. On the other hand, this difference also shows an advantage for our proposal, since we are not tied to a single CEP engine and we can use any CEP rules already defined for the monitoring process, while in their case we would need to create a new plug-in for each new situation we want to monitor.

8   Conclusions and Future Work

Process adaptation and Complex Event Processing are two topics that are creating a lot of interest in the research community, however there is still no integration of both domains. In this paper we presented CEVICHE, a framework that intends to facilitate the integration of CEP into existing business processes and to allow these processes to be dynamically adapted to different circumstances.

With CEVICHE we addressed four issues: adaptation, dynamicity, integration to business process, and non-dependency to a specific CEP engine. As part of the CEVICHE framework, we proposed the SBPL, an extension of BPEL that allows the user to include the adaptation points and conditions to create dynamically adaptable business processes. We also presented how users can define their own events to trigger the process adaptations. These event definitions are sent to a special plug-ins to deal with the different languages of the CEP engines, allowing the users to write their process specifications only once and deploy it in the engine they want.

With a simple scenario we showed how CEVICHE can be used to monitor the context information of a business process and adapt it dynamically to respond to it, without the need to redeploy the process and without loosing any current transactions. Using CEVICHE, we managed to respond to the three challenges on the scenario: 1) *Situation identification*, 2) *Code scattering*, and 3) *Process redeployment*.

Thanks to the modular architecture of CEVICHE, it is not strongly linked to any third party technology. In previous work, we have shown how CEVICHE can also work in an aspect-oriented approach to monitor and maintain the quality of service of a business process, showing that be used with different technologies and approaches to deal with dynamic process adaptation. This architecture also allows our work to be completely componentized in the future, facilitating the integration with other technologies and the interaction with the different parts of the architecture.

We plan to work on the definition of a RESTful architecture to leverage on the deployment of CEVICHE components and facilitate the evolution of the architecture by adding or changing components. Finally, we are creating a couple of plug-ins for some open-source CEP engines, to demonstrate the feasibility of our approach for standardizing event definitions.

Acknowledgements

This work was supported by the French Ministry of Higher Education and Research, Nord-Pas de Calais Regional Council and FEDER through the *Contrat de Projets Etat Region* (CPER) 2007-2013.

References

1. Luckham, D.C.: The Power of Events: An Introduction to Complex Event Processing in Distributed Enterprise Systems. Addison-Wesley Longman Publishing Co., Inc., Amsterdam (2001)
2. Huber, N., Michael, K.: Minimizing Product Shrinkage across the Supply Chain using Radio Frequency Identification: a Case Study on a Major Australian Retailer. In: ICMB 2007: Proceedings of the International Conference on the Management of Mobile Business, p. 45. IEEE Computer Society, Los Alamitos (2007)
3. Mangkorntong, P.: A Domain-Driven Approach for Detecting Event Patterns in E-Markets: A Case Study in Financial Market Surveillance. VDM Verlag, Saarbrücken (2009)
4. Zang, C., Fan, Y., Liu, R.: Architecture, implementation and application of complex event processing in enterprise information systems based on RFID. Information Systems Frontiers 10(5), 543–553 (2008)
5. OASIS: OASIS Standard. Web Services Business Process Execution Language Version 2.0. (April 2007),
http://docs.oasis-open.org/wsbpel/2.0/wsbpel-v2.0.html
6. Hermosillo, G., Seinturier, L., Duchien, L.: Using complex event processing for dynamic business process adaptation. In: SCC 2010: Proceedings of the 2010 IEEE International Conference on Services Computing, IEEE Computer Society, Los Alamitos (2010)
7. Ku, T., Zhu, Y., Hu, K.: A Novel Complex Event Mining Network for Monitoring RFID-Enable Application. In: PACIIA 2008: Proceedings of the 2008 IEEE Pacific-Asia Workshop on Computational Intelligence and Industrial Application, pp. 925–929. IEEE Computer Society, Los Alamitos (2008)

8. Taylor, R.N., Medvidovic, N., Dashofy, E.M.: Software Architecture: Foundations, Theory and Practice. Addison-Wesley, Reading (2007)

9. Wang, A.J.A., Qian, K.: Component-Oriented Programming. Wiley Interscience, Hoboken (2005)

10. Kiczales, G., Lamping, J., Mendheka, A., Maeda, C., Lopes, C.V., Loingtier, J.M., Irwin, J.: Aspect-Oriented Programming. In: Gjessing, S., Nygaard, K. (eds.) ECOOP 1997. LNCS, vol. 1241, pp. 220–242. Springer, Heidelberg (1997)

11. Kiczales, G., Hilsdale, E., Hugunin, J., Kersten, M., Palm, J., Griswold, W.G.: An overview of aspectj. In: Knudsen, J.L. (ed.) ECOOP 2001. LNCS, vol. 2072, pp. 327–353. Springer, Heidelberg (2001)

12. Barros, A.P., Decker, G., Großkopf, A.: Complex events in business processes. In: Abramowicz, W. (ed.) BIS 2007. LNCS, vol. 4439, pp. 29–40. Springer, Heidelberg (2007)

13. Hermosillo, G., Ellart, J., Seinturier, L., Duchien, L.: A Traceability Service to Facilitate RFID Adoption in the Retail Supply Chain. In: Proceedings of the 3rd International Workshop on RFID Technology - Concepts, Applications, Challenges IWRT 2009, pp. 49–58. INSTICC Press, Portugal (May 2009)

14. Lins, F.A.A., dos Santos Júnior, J.C., Rosa, N.S.: Adaptive web service composition. SIGSOFT Softw. Eng. Notes 32(4), 6 (2007)

15. Sánchez, M., Villalobos, J.: A flexible architecture to build workflows using aspect-oriented concepts. In: AOM 2008: Proceedings of the 2008 AOSD workshop on Aspect-oriented modeling, pp. 25–30. ACM, New York (2008)

16. Rahman, S.S.u., Aoumeur, N., Saake, G.: An adaptive eca-centric architecture for agile service-based business processes with compliant aspectual.net environment. In: iiWAS 2008: Proceedings of the 10th International Conference on Information Integration and Web-based Applications & Services, pp. 240–247. ACM, New York (2008)

17. Koning, M., Sun, C.a., Sinnema, M., Avgeriou, P.: Vxbpel: Supporting variability for web services in bpel. Inf. Softw. Technol. 51(2), 258–269 (2009)

18. Charfi, A., Dinkelaker, T., Mezini, M.: A plug-in architecture for self-adaptive web service compositions. In: ICWS 2009: Proceedings of the 2009 IEEE International Conference on Web Services, pp. 35–42. IEEE Computer Society, Los Alamitos (2009)

Statistical Quality Control for Human-Based Electronic Services

Robert Kern, Hans Thies, and Gerhard Satzger

Karlsruhe Institute of Technology (KIT), Karlsruhe Service Research Institute,
Englerstraße 11, 76131 Karlsruhe, Germany
{robert.kern,gerhard.satzger}@kit.edu,
hans.thies@gmx.de

Abstract. Crowdsourcing in form of human-based electronic services (people services) provides a powerful way of outsourcing tasks to a large crowd of remote workers over the Internet. Research has shown that multiple redundant results delivered by different workers can be aggregated in order to achieve a reliable result. However, existing implementations of this approach are rather inefficient as they multiply the effort for task execution and are not able to guarantee a certain quality level. As a starting point towards an integrated approach for quality management of people services we have developed a quality management model that combines elements of statistical quality control (SQC) with group decision theory. The contributions of the workers are tracked and weighted individually in order to minimize the quality management effort while guaranteeing a well-defined level of overall result quality. A quantitative analysis of the approach based on an optical character recognition (OCR) scenario confirms the efficiency and reach of the approach.

1 Introduction

The idea of human-based electronic services is that they look like Web services but they are not performed by a computer, instead they use human workforce out of a crowd of Internet users. The success of Amazon's Mechanical Turk[1] (MTurk) platform and the growing number of companies that build their business model entirely on that platform demonstrate the potential of this approach. The MTurk platform acts as a broker between requesters who publish human intelligence tasks (HITs) and workers who work on those tasks in return for a typically small monetary compensation. Kern et al. proposed the term people services (pServices) for this type of human-based electronic services [10]. As there is limited control over the individual contributors, particular attention has to be paid to the quality of the work results.

One quality assurance approach that is heavily used in practise and that can be applied to a broad set of pServices scenarios is the majority vote (MV) approach which *introduces redundancy by passing the same task to multiple workers*

---

[1] www.mturk.com

P.P. Maglio et al. (Eds.): ICSOC 2010, LNCS 6470, pp. 243–257, 2010.

and aggregating the results in order to compute the result with the highest probability for correctness [9]. Existing applications of this approach typically apply a fixed level of redundancy to each individual task, i.e. each task is performed by multiple workers. From the perspective of quality management that means that the quality of each individual task is validated. However, the concepts of statistical quality control (SQC) teach us, that the quality management effort can usually be drastically reduced by taking only samples rather than by performing a full inspection of all individual items. [16]. Moreover, a fixed degree of redundancy is both inefficient and incapable of assuring a certain level of result quality because the level of agreement (and so the expected result quality) varies depending on the error rates of the involved workers.

For some tasks, the agreement might be extremely high (e.g. all workers agree on exactly the same result), for others the worker results might be at odds (e.g. half of the workers return result A, while the other half returns B).

In this paper, a quality management (QM) approach for pServices is proposed which improves the traditional MV approach in three ways: (1) It reduces the QM effort in *horizontal* direction by validating only a sample of tasks rather than all tasks. (2) It reduces the QM effort in *vertical* direction by dynamically adjusting the level of redundancy rather than working with a fixed level of redundancy. (3) It allows to guarantee a certain quality level by taking individual worker error rates into account.

Within the multifaceted dimensions of quality, this paper concentrates on the correctness dimension as the ability to return a minimum percentage of results that are free of error [10]. According to Jurans definition of quality as *fitness for use* [8], the paper assumes that the service requester can clearly categorize a task result as correct or incorrect. The level of correctness is determined by a comparison with the ideal result (gold standard) provided by the service requester. After providing some fundamentals of SQC in section 2, the QM approach for pServices is presented in section 3. It has been implemented as a QM component on top of the MTurk platform and it has been evaluated using an optical character recognition (OCR) scenario. The results are provided in section 4. The paper closes with related work and a summary and outlook in sections 5 and 6.

2   Fundamentals

This chapter describes some fundamentals about SQC which are required for the considerations in section 3. Specifically, the paper leverages the concept of *sampling plans*.

Acceptance Sampling is the process to decide based on a sample whether a set of units meets certain quality requirements or not. Acceptance sampling determines the probability of a lot of units being within the specified quality levels, and accepts or rejects lots based on its quality characteristics. A sampling plan is a procedure where a sample of n units is drawn from a lot of size N. If the number of defects in the sample is higher than the *acceptance number* c, the lot is rejected. Otherwise it is accepted. If the units do not occur in batches, but in a continuous production, such as in line assembly or in a service scenario, the process has to be decomposed into artificial batches. However, before a whole batch has been handled, quality levels for this batch cannot be guaranteed and the results of this batch cannot be further processed. In order to overcome this restriction, *continuous sampling plans* have been developed.

Continuous Sampling Plans (CSPs) control the inspection frequency and replacement of defects in such a way that a certain *average outgoing quality limit* (AOQL) is not exceeded. Dodge developed the first continuous sampling plan, the CSP-1. This plan has been further developed and adapted by Dodge et. al and Lieberman et al. amongst others [4,12]. The most celebrated and most used continuous sampling plan still is the CSP-1. The reason is not only its relative simplicity, but also its efficiency, which in few cases is exceeded by other continuous sampling plans like the CSP-2 [5]. Dodge made the following assumptions developing the CSP-1: (1) The process of incoming units is under statistical control and follows a Bernoulli distribution. (2) Sample inspection is perfect. (3) Defective units are replaced by good ones.

The sampling plan is designed for attributes, thus quality parameters are categorized as either good or defective. This means that if the incoming process is under statistical control i.e. the incoming fraction defective p does not change over time, the process can be described by a Bernoulli process with defect probability p. As illustrated by figure 4, the sampling plan starts with 100% inspection. If i consecutive units are found free of defects, only a fraction f of the units are inspected. If a unit is found to be defective, the model returns to 100% inspection and the process starts from the beginning. Defective units are either reworked or replaced with good ones [16]. Important characteristics of the CSP-1 are the *average fraction inspected* (AFI), the *average outgoing quality* (AOQ) and the *average outgoing quality limit* (AOQL) [16].

The average fraction inspected (AFI) depends on the parameters i and f and on the incoming fraction defective p:

$$AFI(p|i;f) = \frac{1}{1 + (\frac{1}{f} - 1)(1 - p)^i} \tag{1}$$

The average outgoing quality is equal to the average amount of defective units passing through without being inspected.

$$AOQ(p|i;f) = \frac{(\frac{1}{f} - 1)p(1 - p)^i}{1 + (\frac{1}{f} - 1)(1 - p)^i} \tag{2}$$

The AOQ depends on the incoming fraction defective p. It is monotonically increasing with p until reaching its maximum AOQL at p_M. For values higher than p_M, AOQ is monotonically decreasing because CSP-1 is moving more and more to full inspection and is thus detecting and replacing more of the defective items. AOQL is called the *average outgoing quality limit*, it is the worst (highest) value of AQL that can be reached depending on the incoming fraction defective p. AOQL can be determined as:

$$AOQL = \frac{(i+1)p_M - 1}{i} \tag{3}$$

There are multiple combinations of i and f which result in the same value of AOQL. In order to guarantee the average outgoing quality limit AOQL with minimum inspection effort, i and f must be determined in such a way that AFI is minimized. The optimal selection of i and f depends on the scenario, e.g. on the overall number of units (run length). Several increments of the CSP-1 have been provided in order to adapt it to different scenarios. Two of them are outlined in the following:

In case of **imperfect inspection**, two major inspection errors can be made:

- E_1: a good item can be classified as defective, also referred to as a *type 1 inspection error*.
- E_2: a defective item can be classified as good, also referred to as a *type 2 inspection error*.

In the following, A refers to the event that an item is defective. The probability of the event that an item is classified as defective (B) can be calculated as:

$$P(B) = P(A) * P(\neg E_2) + P(\neg A) * P(E_1) \tag{4}$$

Wang and Chen have presented a model to calculate a minimal AFI under the assumption of imperfect inspection [24]. According to them, under the assumption that the optimal value for $i = i^*$ is already known, an optimal value for f^* can be calculated by

$$f^* = \frac{(1 - P(B))^{i^*}(1 - \frac{AOQL}{\hat{p}})}{((1 - P(B))^{i*} - 1)(1 - \frac{AOQL}{\hat{p}}) + (1 - P(E_2))} \tag{5}$$

where AOQL is the specified value for the average outgoing quality limit and $\hat{p}$ is the incoming fraction defective.

Blackwell developed a Markov-chain model for the CSP-1 under **short production runs** [1]. McShane and Turnbull extended his model to compute probability limits on outgoing quality [15]. Although computationally expensive, their model can be used to determine a CSP-1 with minimal inspection by iteratively increasing i, determining the smallest value of f that meets the AOQL, and finally calculating the AFI. The details model go beyond the scope of this paper and can be found in [15].

3   Statistical Quality Control for People Services

3.1   Assumptions

Because of the nature of pServices as *Web based software services that deliver human intelligence, perception, or action to customers as massively scalable resources* [10], it is obvious that pServices require some kind of Web platform.

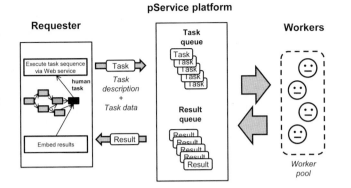

Fig. 1. Scenario of basic pService platform

Figure 1 gives an overview of the basic pService scenario which comprises three roles: the pService *requester*, the *pService platform* and the *workers* who belong to a worker pool. The pService platform acts as a mediator between the pService requester who publishes pService tasks and pService workers who select tasks and work on it in return for a typically small compensation. The paper makes some additional assumptions about the underlying pService platform: (1) It allows for tracking individual workers based on an individual *worker ID* which is returned to the requester for each result delivered by the worker. (2) It provides means for making specific tasks only available to a well-defined group of workers, e.g. by performing qualification tests.

It is further assumed that there is a large number of equivalent tasks which consist of the same *task description* but different *task data*. The task description primarily contains the instructions for the workers how to perform the task as well as information about the expected result quality. The task data is the variable part which might represent different pictures to be annotated, different addresses to be validated or different products to be classified. A *task instance* represents a task for an individual item of the task data, e.g. for an individual picture to be annotated.

3.2   Acceptance Sampling for pServices

The objective of the model described in this paper is to leverage acceptance sampling in order to ensure that pService results are delivered within a certain average outgoing quality limit AOQL, while the inspection costs in terms of labor work are minimized. The model can be seen as a quality management (QM) component on top of the basic pService platform described in the previous section. The overall scenario is given by figure 2. The model assumes that for a given task type there is an individual error rate p_x for each worker x (A). This error rate is the same for all tasks of the same type, but it may change over time, since workers may learn and therefore improve their skills.

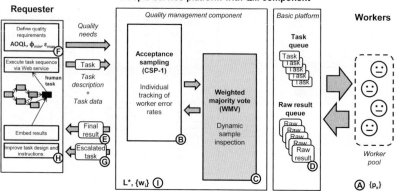

Fig. 2. Schematic overview of pService platform with QM component

Because the error rates of individual workers are independent from each other, the sampling has to be done at worker-level. The results are aggregated, and the same AOQL is applied to all workers that work on this task type i.e. the same quality of work results is requested from all participating workers. The QM component uses continuous acceptance sampling in order to guarantee a certain long-run average outgoing quality limit AOQL defined by the service requester.

The QM component consists of two functional parts: an acceptance sampling component (B) and a sample inspection component (C). The acceptance sampling component leverages the basic continuous sampling plan (CSP-1) with the increment of imperfect inspection and replacement and the increment of limited runtimes as presented in section 2. The CSP-1 leverages continuous sampling of *raw results* (D) delivered by the workers and turns them into *final results* (E) in order to guarantee an average outgoing quality limit AOQL that is defined by the requester along with other quality requirements (F). The CSP-1 requires a mechanism for sample inspection. For this purpose, a *weighted majority vote approach* (WMV) was designed which will be described in detail in section 3.3. The WMV dynamically increases the redundancy by including additional workers in the MV decision until a predefined significance φ_{min} is reached. Because the inspection process performed by the WMV is not perfect but only meets a quality level of φ_{min}, Case et al.'s model for CSP-1 with imperfect inspection is utilized in combination with Wang and Chen's increment. As some tasks may not conform to the specifications of that task type, e.g. they are harder to solve than the others or the task description does not apply to all individual tasks, they are escalated back to the requester (G) if a predefined *escalation limit* ε_{max} (F) is reached. That way, he can use this information to improve task design and provide the correct results himself (H). As we assume a fixed payment per task, the QM costs can be minimized by minimizing the total number of tasks. Because the WMV (as well as the traditional MV) appraoch assumes that the raw results delivered by multiple workers can be compared to each other or aggregated into a consolidated result, the mechanism works only for *deterministic tasks* i.e. for tasks that have a certain well-defined optimal result [9].

Additional parameters are administrated by the platform itself (I): The Markov chain CSP-1 model developed by McShane and Turnbull (see section 2) is used to take into account that some workers may contribute only few results. It determines a starting value of i, considering the expected run length L^*. L^* specifies the expected *run length* of a process per worker, that is the average amount of tasks of the same task type each worker will work on. The CSP-1 is implemented using an inspection status w_x for each worker. The initial value will be $w_x = i$ which will be reduced by 1 for each consecutive result that the worker has been submitted and that has been classified as correct. If $w_x = 0$, only fractional inspection will take place. Once, a result submitted by the worker is classified as incorrect, his inspection status will be reset to $w_x = i$. The worker error rate p_x describes the expected error rate of worker x, anticipated from historical values. Due to the nature of human work, p_x should never completely reach 0.

Worker Pool Management. A worker who constantly stays in full inspection mode leads to high costs, so depending on the availability of workers and the costs for inspection, a decision has to be made as to which workers are not profitable and should be removed from the worker pool. Therefore, the maximum error rate e has been introduced. If a worker's error rate exceeds the maximum error rate $p_x > e$, he may not participate.

3.3 Sample Inspection Process - The Weighted Majority Vote (WMV) Approach

The weighted majority vote (WMV) is used for sample inspection. All raw results that have to be inspected according to the CSP-1 for the respective worker, are validated by passing redundant task assignments to other workers in order to be able to come to a group decision which meets a minimum inspection quality

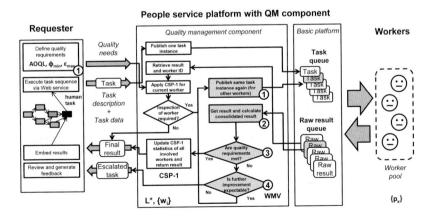

Fig. 3. Detailed overview of pService platform with QM component

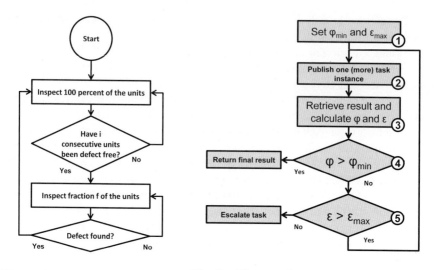

Fig. 4. Procedure of the continuous sampling plan CSP-1

Fig. 5. The weighted majority vote (WMV) approach

level φ_{min}. The process of the WMV is explained based on figure 3. The basic idea is to publish one additional (redundant) task assignment (2), retrieve the result (3) and calculate based on his individual error rate whether the required minimum inspection quality φ_{min} has already been met (4). If this is the case, the final result is returned (4). If the required quality has not yet been met, it is checked in step (5), whether a quality improvement can be expected by adding more workers. If that is not the case, the task is escalated back to the requester. Otherwise, the process continues with step (2) where another redundant task assignment is published. The process is continued until either the raw results delivered by several workers can be aggregated into a reliable result (4) which is returned as the final result to the requester or until the escalation limit is reached in step (5). Figure 5 provides an overview of the WMV. Assuming each worker x has an individual failure rate p_x when working on task y and returns raw result r_{xy}, the process is the following:

1. Specify desired level of inspection quality φ_{min} and escalation limit ε_{max}.
2. Make one (more) redundant assignment for task y available to the workers.
3. Retrieve the worker result r_{xy} and identify the result with the highest probability of correctness ε as well as the actual escalation limit ε.
4. If the φ exceeds the desired level inspection quality φ_{min}, return the result r_c with the highest probability of correctness and update the qualification values q_x of all participating workers, where $q_x = 1 - p_x$.
5. Escalate the task back to the requester if the overall probability ε for getting a result set R_y is lower or equal than the escalation limit ε_{max}, with $R_y = \{r(x_1), r(x_2), ..r(x_k)\}$, $x_1, x_2..x_k$ being the IDs of the workers who have worked on the task and k being the number of assignments for the task.

Steps 2 to 5 are repeated until the final result is returned in step 4 or the task is escalated in step 5. In step 3, the values φ and ε are calculated using equations 6, 7 and 8. Equation 6 determines the Bayes-conditional likelihood for result r_c being correct under the condition that the result set R_y was received.

$$\varphi_c = P(r_c \; is \; correct | R = R_y) = \frac{P(r_c \; is \; correct \cap R = R_y)}{P(R = R_y)} \tag{6}$$

$$= \frac{\prod_{\forall r_i = r_c} r_c q_i \prod_{\forall r_i \neq r_c} p_i}{\sum_{j=1}^{k} \prod_{\forall r_i = r_j} q_i \prod_{\forall r_i \neq r_j} p_i + \prod_{j=1}^{N} p_j} \tag{7}$$

$$\varepsilon_y = P(R = R_y) = (\sum_{j=1}^{k} \prod_{\forall r_i = r_j} q_i \prod_{\forall r_i \neq r_j} p_i) + \prod_{j=1}^{N} p_j \tag{8}$$

4   Evaluation

4.1   Experimental Design

The QM approach has been implemented as a QM component on top of MTurk, accessing the platform through the SOAP interface available to service requesters. An *optical character recognition* (OCR) scenario was used for evaluation, which consists of a dataset of 1176 handwritten words. In each of the tasks, a worker was asked to type in a single handwritten word which was displayed as an image file (JPEG). The expected optimal result (gold standard) was specified by the author of the handwriting himself. On February 1st, 10 instances (assignments) of each task were uploaded to the MTurk platform. It was prohibited that a worker handles the exact same task more than once. The task payment was $0.01 per task, with Amazon receiving a service charge of $0.005 for each task. Consequently a total amount of $1,176 \times 10 = 11,760$ data sets has been collected during the evaluation leading to total expenses of $11,760(\$0.01 + \$0.005) = \$176.40$. The QM mechanism was simulated on the raw results in order to be able to run multiple simulations at different parameters and in order to have a baseline for comparing with the performance of the traditional MV mechanism.

4.2   Qualification Testing

The MTurk platform provides means for limiting the access to tasks to those workers who have successfully completed a so called *qualification test*. Such a test can be designed individually for each type of task. The QM approach described in this paper implicitly determines the error rates of the workers, therefore there is typically no need to restrict the participation to those who have passed a qualification test. However, as the actual test was only simulated on a fixed number of instances (assignments) of each task, a qualification test was used to reduce the overall cost of the experiment as it excludes spammers and workers who submit bad quality right from the start. The test consisted of a series of 10 simple OCR tasks (10 words). All of them had to be typed in correctly in order to pass the test.

4.3 Execution Performance

Probably the most astonishing result of the experiment was the speed with which the results were submitted. In the first pre-tests, a batch of 3,528 tasks was completed by 112 workers in less than 15 minutes at an execution rate of 14,088 tasks per hour. During other experiments we even observed total execution speeds up to 3 times as fast, because of more workers participating. We assume that the execution speed besides the payment also depends on the time of day, since most workers are U.S.- or Indian citizens [19]. Figure 6 illustrates the execution of the actual experiment in which 11,760 tasks have been processed by 36 workers in about 2:40 hours. One can observe how workers successively join the process. A similar chart is used by the crowdsourcing provider crowdflower.com.

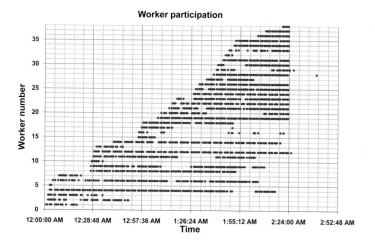

Fig. 6. worker participation

4.4 Full Inspection

The first simulation was a full inspection by running the WMV for all tasks. The CSP-1 was not used in this experiment. Running only the WMV leads to remarkably good quality. The inspection quality goal of 0.99 was almost perfectly met. Figure 7 shows the results of WMV compared to the traditional MV approach. The traditional MV was simulated based on the same data as the WMV by averaging all possible combinations of 2 to 9 answers within each set of 10 available answers per task for the two-fold up to the 9-fold MV. For each combination, the most occurring answer was chosen. If several answers occur the same amount of times (tie), a random choice between the answers occurring most was made, as suggested by Snow et al. [21].

We see that our WMV (98.36%) even outperforms the accuracy of a ninefold traditional MV (97.76%). That is a remarkable result given that the WMV is 4 times more efficient as it requires only 2.25 workers per task compared to

Approach	MV 2	WMV	MV 3	MV 4	MV 5	MV 6	MV 7	MV 8	MV 9	MV 10
Average redundancy	2	2.25	3	4	5	6	7	8	9	10
Accuracy	0.927	0.984	0.954	0.958	0.962	0.974	0.975	0.977	0.978	0.977

Fig. 7. Comparison of the accuracy of different majority vote approaches

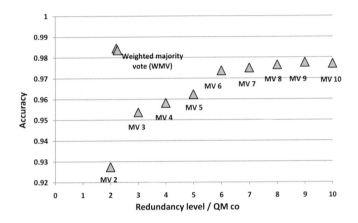

Fig. 8. Comparison of the accuracy of different majority vote approaches

9 workers per task for the basic ninefold MV approach. In other words: the WMV approach has reduced the quality management effort by some 75 percent compared to the traditional MV approach. Figure 8 illustrates this relation.

4.5 Acceptance Sampling

In a series of tests, the QM approach was used with CSP-1 for 3 different quality goals i.e. three different values of AOQL. Figure 9 shows the results of 10 simulation runs with an AOQL of 0.05:

$AOQL = 0.05;\ i = 6;\ f = 0.249;\ \varphi_{min} = 0.99;\ \varepsilon_{max} = 0.01$

Simulation #	1	2	3	4	5	6	7	8	9	10	Average	Average per HIT
Run length	1176	1176	1176	1176	1176	1176	1176	1176	1176	1176	1176.0	1.0000
Assignments	1783	1744	1830	1823	1741	1797	1793	1836	1782	1762	1789.1	1.5213
Escalated	20	25	23	25	21	24	16	26	22	23	22.5	0.0191
Inspected	439	427	469	475	433	471	489	482	453	458	459.6	0.3908
Incoming failures	84	88	90	92	85	91	87	95	88	76	87.6	0.0745
Outgoing failures	59	62	48	55	67	58	64	58	56	50	57.7	0.0491

Fig. 9. Results of the acceptance sampling test for 10 simulations with AOQL=0.05

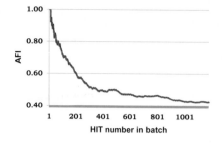

Average per HIT	AOQL=0.025	AOQL=0.05	AOQL=0.075
Run length	1.0000	1.0000	1.0000
Assignments	1.7954	1.5213	1.0930
Escalated	0.0404	0.0191	0.0032
Inspected	0.6331	0.3908	0.0601
Incoming failures	0.0723	0.0745	0.0745
Outgoing failures	0.0287	0.0491	0.0710

Fig. 10. Decrease of the average fraction inspected (AFI) over time with AOQL=0.05

Fig. 11. Results of the acceptance sampling tests for different values of AOQL

A total of 1.52 assignments per HIT was observed on average, which is a significant improvement even compared to the 100%-inspection with 2.25 assignments per HIT. A number of 1.91 percent of the HITs are escalated. Some 39 percent of all tasks are inspected. Figure 10 illustrates the decrease of the inspection rate over time, therefore a smaller inspection rate can be expected in the long run. The AOQL value was achieved in 6 out of the 10 cases. It is not surprising that in some runs the quality is slightly worse than the specified AOQL because of the short run time of only 1176 tasks. When averaging over several runs, we obtain a reliable outgoing fraction of 0.0491, which can be considered optimal as the goal is to minimize the QM effort rather than to overachieve the quality objective.

We further tested the quality model with different AOQL levels (Figure 9):

$AOQL = 0.025; i = 5; f = 0.582; \varphi_{min} = 0.99; \varepsilon_{max} = 0.01$
$AOQL = 0.075; i = 1; f = 0.039; \varphi_{min} = 0.99; \varepsilon_{max} = 0.01$

For AOQL=0.075 the quality is again precisely met. However, when increasing the quality demands to AOQL=0.025, the model does not manage to achieve the desired level anymore. The reason for that lies in the gap between the gold standard and the majority decision of the workers: In several cases, the majority of the workers identified a certain word (e.g. "five") even if the writer (who represented the gold standard) had written a different word (e.g. "fine").

5   Related Work

The concept of majority vote is widely used in the context of pServices. Redundant task execution is a basic feature for quality improvement provided by platforms like MTurk. Sorokin and Forsyth as well as Snow et al. have analyzed the effect of the approach based on annotation scenarios [22,21]. Snow et al. have investigated how many non-experts out of the crowd are needed in order to achieve better results than one expert. Depending on the scenario, they report a required number of non-experts between two and more than ten. Whitehill et al. consider how to integrate labeler's expertise into a majority vote mechanism for image labeling [25]. They propose a probabilistic model and use it to simultaneously infer the label of each image, the expertise of each labeler, and the difficulty of each image. Complementary approaches for quality management of pServices include iterative work processes [13], review processes [9] and the injection of gold standard tasks [22]. A maximum likelihood estimation can be used to estimate worker error rates as well as the correct categories of the task results [7,9]. The approach leverages the EM algorithm dating back to Dawid and Skene [3]. Raykar et al. propose a specific form of an EM algorithm which is capable of generating a gold standard [17].

The validity of the majority vote model has been first mathematically proven by Condorcet's Jury Theorem [2]. Under the assumption that one of two outcomes is correct and each decision maker has the independent probability $p > 0.5$ to make the right decision, the probability for a correct group decision is greater than the individual one. Latif-Shabgahi et al. have examined and classified a large number of software voting algorithms used in safety-critical systems [11]. Surowiecki illustrated that the aggregation of group responses may lead to better results than the information of any single group member - if the opinions are diverse, independent, decentralized, and an appropriate aggregation mechanism exists [23]. This phenomenon has been described as the wisdom of the crowds. Typical applications that leverage crowd intelligence are prediction markets [6], Delphi methods [20] and extensions of the traditional opinion poll. In the field of machine learning, Littlestone and Warmuth developed a weighted majority algorithm, that acts as a "master algorithm" and aggregates the answers of several prediction algorithms in order to determine the best prediction possible [14]. The aggregation mechanism is a vital part of each majority vote model. Revow et al. compare five combination strategies (majority vote, Bayesian, logistic regression, fuzzy integral, and neural network) and arrive at the conclusion that majority vote is as effective as the other, more complicated schemes to improve the recognition rate for the data set used [18].

6   Conclusion and Future Work

We have presented a statistical model for managing the correctness of human-based electronic services (people services) which leverages continuous acceptance sampling and group decision theory. The mechanism consists of two parts: The continuous acceptance sampling plan CSP-1 is used to track the contributions of each worker individually based on samples taken from their work results. A *weighted majority vote* (WMV) approach was introduced for the inspection of the samples which leverages a group decision of multiple workers. The number of workers participating in that group decision is adjusted dynamically depending on their individual error rates. By validating only a fraction of the tasks and keeping the validation effort per task at a minimum, the model is capable of guaranteeing a certain predefined level of result quality at minimum costs. An evaluation on Amazon's Mechanical Turk platform has shown a reduction of the quality management effort of up to 75 percent compared to existing approaches.

In our ongoing research we are expanding the scope of our QM mechanism to other aspects of quality like performance and availability. Furthermore, we are investigating the effect of worker feedback on the result quality.

References

1. Blackwell, M.: The effect of short production runs on CSP-1. Technometrics 19(3), 259–263 (1977)
2. le marquis de Condorcet, M., Caritat, A.N.: Essai sur l'application de l'analyse la probabilit des dcisions rendues la pluralit des voix (1785)
3. Dawid, A., Skene, A.: Maximum likelihood estimation of observer Error-Rates using the EM algorithm. Journal of the Royal Statistical Society 28(1), 20–28 (1979)
4. Dodge, H., Torrey, M.: Additional continuous sampling inspection plans. Industrial Quality Control (7), 7–12 (1951)
5. Gosh, D.T.: An optimum continuous sampling plan CSP-2 with k i to minimise the amount of inspection when incoming quality p follows a distribution. The Indian Journal of Statistics 58(1), 105–117 (1996)
6. Gruca, T.S., Berg, J.E., Cipriano, M.: Consensus and differences of opinion in electronic prediction markets. Electronic Markets 15(1), 13–22 (2005)
7. Ipeirotis, P.G., Provost, F., Wang, J.: Quality management on amazon mechanical turk (2010)
8. Juran, J., Godfrey, A.: Juran's Quality Handbook, 5th edn. McGraw-Hill, New York (2000)
9. Kern, R., Bauer, C., Thies, H., Satzger, G.: Validating results of human-based electronic services leveraging multiple reviewers. In: Proceedings of the 16th Americas Conference on Information Systems (AMCIS), Lima, Peru (2010) (forthcoming)
10. Kern, R., Zirpins, C., Agarwal, S.: Managing quality of Human-Based eServices. In: Feuerlicht, G., Lamersdorf, W. (eds.) ICSOC 2008.December 1st, 2008, Revised Selected Papers, LNCS, vol. 5472, pp. 304–309. Springer, Heidelberg (2009)
11. Latif-Shabgahi, G., Bass, J.M., Bennett, S.: A taxonomy for software voting algorithms used in safety-critical systems. IEEE Transactions on Reliability 53(3), 319 (2004)
12. Lieberman, G.J., Solomon, H.: Multi-Level continuous sampling plans. The Annals of Mathematical Statistics 26(4), 686–704 (1955)
13. Little, G., Chilton, L.B., Goldman, M., Miller, R.C.: Turkit: Tools for iterative tasks on mechanical turk. In: Proceedings of the ACM SIGKDD Workshop on Human Computation, pp. 29–30 (2009)
14. Littlestone, N., Warmuth, M.K.: The weighted majority algorithm. Information and Comutation 108, 212–261 (1994)
15. McShane, L.M., Turnbull, B.W.: Probability limits on outgoing quality for continuous sampling plans. Technometrics 33(4), 393–404 (1991)
16. Montgomery, D.: Introduction to statistical quality control, 6th edn. Wiley & Sons, New York (2008)
17. Raykar, V.C., Yu, S., Zhao, L.H., Valadez, G.H., Florin, C., Bogoni, L., Moy, L.: Learning from crowds. Journal of Machine Learning Research 11, 1297–1322 (2010)
18. Revow, M., Williams, C.K.I., Hinton, G.E.: Using generative models for handwritten digit recognition. IEEE Trans. Pattern Anal. Mach. Intell. 18(6), 592–606 (1996)

19. Ross, J., Irani, L., Silberman, M., Zaldivar, A., Tomlinson, B.: Who are the crowd-workers?: shifting demographics in mechanical turk. In: Proceedings of the 28th of the International Conference Extended Abstracts on Human Factors in Computing Systems, pp. 2863–2872 (2010)
20. Rowe, G., Wright, G.: The delphi technique as a forecasting tool: issues and analysis. International Journal of Forecasting 15(4), 353–375 (1999)
21. Snow, R., OConnor, B., Jurafsky, D., Ng, A.Y.: Cheap and fast but is it good? evaluating non-expert annotations for natural language tasks. In: EMNLP 2008: Proceedings of the Conference on Empirical Methods in Natural Language Processing, pp. 254–263. ACL, Stroudsburg (2008)
22. Sorokin, A., Forsyth, D.: Utility data annotation with amazon mechanical turk. In: CVPRW 2008: Proceedings of the Conference on Computer Vision and Pattern Recognition Workshops, pp. 1–8. IEEE Computer Society, Washington (June 2008)
23. Surowiecki, J.: The Wisdom of Crowds, 1st edn. Doubleday, New York (2004)
24. Wang, R., Chen, C.: Minimum average fraction inspected for continuous sampling plan CSP-1 under inspection error. Journal of Applied Statistics 24(5), 539–548 (1997)
25. Whitehill, J., Ruvolo, P., Wu, T., Bergsma, J., Movellan, J.: Whose vote should count more: Optimal integration of labels from labelers of unknown expertise. In: Advances in Neural Information Processing Systems, vol. 22, pp. 2035–2043 (2009)

A Requirement-Centric Approach to Web Service Modeling, Discovery, and Selection

Maha Driss[1,2], Naouel Moha[1], Yassine Jamoussi[2],
Jean-Marc Jézéquel[1], and Henda Hajjami Ben Ghézala[2]

[1] IRISA/INRIA,University of Rennes 1, France
{mdriss,moha,jezequel}@irisa.fr
[2] ENSI, RIADI-GDL Laboratory, University of Manouba, Tunisia
{yassine.jamoussi,henda.benghezala}@ensi.rnu.tn

Abstract. Service-Oriented Computing (SOC) has gained considerable
popularity for implementing Service-Based Applications (SBAs) in a flexible and effective manner. The basic idea of SOC is to understand users'
requirements for SBAs first, and then discover and select relevant services
(i.e., that fit closely functional requirements) and offer a high Quality of
Service (QoS). Understanding users' requirements is already achieved
by existing requirement engineering approaches (e.g., TROPOS, KAOS,
and MAP) which model SBAs in a requirement-driven manner. However,
discovering and selecting relevant and high QoS services are still challenging tasks that require time and effort due to the increasing number of
available Web services. In this paper, we propose a requirement-centric
approach which allows: (i) modeling users' requirements for SBAs with
the MAP formalism and specifying required services using an Intentional
Service Model (ISM); (ii) discovering services by querying the Web service search engine Service-Finder and using keywords extracted from the
specifications provided by the ISM; and(iii) selecting automatically relevant and high QoS services by applying Formal Concept Analysis (FCA).
We validate our approach by performing experiments on an e-books application. The experimental results show that our approach allows the
selection of relevant and high QoS services with a high accuracy (the
average precision is 89.41%) and efficiency (the average recall is 95.43%).

Keywords: Service-Based Applications, Users' Requirements Modeling,
Service Discovery, Service Selection, QoS, Formal Concept Analysis.

1 Introduction

Service-Oriented Computing (SOC) is an emerging paradigm for developing
low-cost, flexible, and scalable distributed applications based on Web services
(WSs) [1]. SOC is becoming broadly adopted as it offers the ability to build
efficiently and effectively added-value Service-Based Applications (SBAs) by
composing ready-made services. The basic idea of SOC is to understand users'
requirements for SBAs first, and then discover and select WSs that fit closely expected functional and non-functional requirements. Functional requirements define functionalities provided by WSs. We refer to services which fit closely users'

P.P. Maglio et al. (Eds.): ICSOC 2010, LNCS 6470, pp. 258–272, 2010.

functional requirements as 'relevant' services. Non-functional requirements are expressed by the term Quality of Service (QoS) that refers to various properties such as availability, response time, security, and throughput [2]. If multiple WSs offer the same functionality, then a QoS requirement can be used as a secondary criterion for service selection.

Understanding users' requirements includes requirements elicitation, analysis, and modeling which provide a full support for SBAs engineering. Discovering services is achieved by querying a WS search engine to browse WSs using several criteria (e.g., functionalities and QoS). Among the set of services obtained by discovery, only services that best match users' functional and non-functional requirements are selected. Understanding users' requirements is already achieved by traditional requirement engineering approaches that are extended and refined to meet the SBAs characteristics. To this end, goal modeling techniques such as TROPOS [3], KAOS [4], and MAP [5] are used to model SBAs. However discovering and selecting relevant and high QoS WSs is still a challenging task because of two main issues. First, the growing number and diversity of WSs in addition to their publication over multiple public and private registries make service discovery difficult to accomplish. Second, the frequent large number of WSs returned by discovery requires costly and time-consuming selection of relevant and high QoS services.

In this paper, we propose a new requirements-centric approach for: (i) modeling SBAs in terms of functional and non-functional users requirements; (ii) discovering potential services that match expected requirements; and (ii) selecting relevant and high QoS services. This approach consists of three successive steps 1-3 as it is shown by Figure 1.

In the first step, our approach allows an intentional-driven modeling of SBAs using the MAP formalism [5]. The MAP elicits and analyzes users' requirements in a set of graphs composed of intentions and strategies, called *maps*. In previous work [6], an Intentional Service Model (ISM) is proposed to specify intentional services presented by maps. In this paper, the same model will be enhanced to include QoS aspects and will be used to specify intentional services. In the second step, our approach permits discovery of operational services by querying the WS search engine Service-Finder using keywords extracted from ISM models. To efficiently

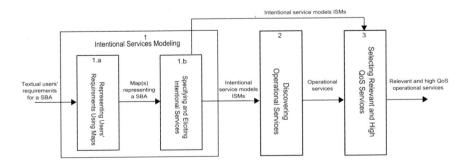

Fig. 1. A requirement-centric approach to WS modeling, discovery, and selection

discover relevant and high QoS services, we propose two-level filtration. In the first level, some QoS properties are considered namely validity (i.e., we verify if the service URI is valid) and availability (i.e., we verify if the service is operational). Services which pass the first level are filtered according to a semantic matchmaking between the intentional specification provided by ISM and the operational specification provided by WSDL. In the third step, the remaining set of services is classified into an ordered structure called concept lattice by applying Formal Concept Analysis (FCA) [7]. FCA is a formal framework that allows grouping individuals that share common properties and organizes them into concept lattices. The FCA will automate the selection task by providing a clear and organized view of potential services to enable users to easily check out relevant and high QoS services. We validate our approach by performing experiments on an e-books WS-based application. The experimental results show that our approach allows the selection of relevant and high QoS services with a high accuracy (the average precision is 89.41%) and efficiency (the average recall is 95.43%).

The remainder of the paper is structured as follows. In Section 2, we present the intentional-driven modeling of SBAs. In Section 3, we describe the WS discovery conducted using Service-Finder. In Section 4, we explain how to apply FCA to select relevant and high QoS WSs. Experimental results are documented in Section 6. Section 5 surveys related work. This paper ends with concluding remarks and future work.

2 Intentional Services Modeling

A considerable number of research efforts on SBAs modeling are conducted both in industry and academia. Indeed, these initiatives aimed to propose languages (e.g., BPEL4WS [8] and OWL-S [9]) and formalisms (e.g., Petri nets [10]) for modeling SBAs. All these initiatives adopt a 'function-driven' service modeling focusing on 'low level' technical statements (e.g., coordination messages, input/output parameters, and bindings) that are understandable by software programmers but far to be comprehensible by users. However, users need to interact with programmers to obtain SBAs satisfying their requirements. Thus, SBAs must be modeled in terms of users' requirements and not in terms of technical statements.

In this paper, we adopt a 'requirement-driven' approach that allows a 'high level' modeling of SBAs. This approach uses the MAP formalism to represent users' requirements. We refer to services presented by maps as intentional services. These services are specified by an Intentional Service Model (ISM).

In the following, we present an overview of the MAP formalism, we introduce the ISM model, and we provide guidelines to elicit intentional services and their composition from maps.

2.1 Representing Users' Requirements with Maps

A MAP is a meta-process formalism which allows designing several processes, i.e., maps, under a single representation. A map is a labelled directed graph

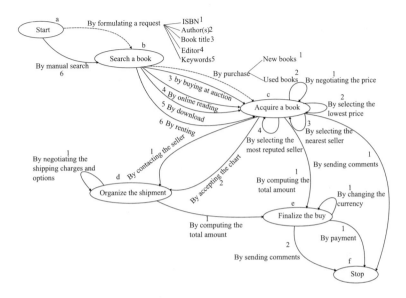

Fig. 2. The e-books application map

with intentions as nodes and strategies as edges between intentions. A strategy is a manner to achieve an intention. An intention is a requirement that can be achieved by following different strategies. Each map has two distinct intentions *Start* and *Stop* to respectively begin and end the navigation in the map. There are two main reasons for using the MAP formalism: first, the MAP was already applied to service modeling domain [11], so we can use previous knowledge and experiences. Second, the MAP permits to capture variability by focusing on the strategy to achieve an intention and the potential alternatives to accomplish the same intention. This explicit representation of variability offered by maps is missing in other requirement engineering formalisms such as TROPOS or KAOS.

Figure 2 represent users' requirements for an e-books application with the MAP formalism. The e-books application map has four key intentions to be achieved, namely *Search a book*, *Acquire a book*, *Organize the shipment*, and *Finalize the buy*. To achieve the *Search a book* intention, users can follow the *By manual search* strategy or the *By formulating a request* strategy.

A map is composed of one or more sections. A section is a triplet <Source Intention I_i, Target Intention I_j, Strategy S_{ij}> that captures a specific manner to achieve the target intention I_j starting from the source intention I_i with the strategy S_{ij}. For instance, <*Start, Search a book, By formulating a request*> represents a way to achieve the target intention *Search a book* from the source intention *Start* following the *By formulating a request* strategy.

There exist four relationships between sections: *bundle*, *multi-thread*, *path*, and *multi-path* relationships.

Bundle relationship: sections in a bundle are mutually exclusive; exactly one strategy can be used to realize the target intention. In Figure 2, *By formulating a request* is a bundle consisting of five different strategies: *By ISBN*, *By author(s)*, *By book title*, *By editor*, and finally *By Keywords*.

Multi-thread relationship: a target intention can be achieved from a source intention in many different ways. Each of these ways is expressed as a section in the map. One or more of these sections can be used to realize the target intention. For example, *By formulating a request* and *By manual search* are two different strategies to *Search a book*. These two strategies are in a *multi-thread* relationship.

Path relationship: this establishes a precedence/succession relationship between sections. For example, the sections <*Start*, *Search a book*, *By formulating a request*> and <*Search a book*, *Acquire a book*, *By purchase*> constitute a *path*.

Multi-path relationship: given the three previous strategies, a target intention can be achieved by combining several sections. For instance, there are two distinct paths to achieve the intention *Finalize the buy* from *Start*. The first is the path via *Search a book*, *Acquire a book*, and *Organize the shipping* intentions. The second is the path via only the *Search a book* and the *Acquire a book* intentions.

In general, a map from its *Start* to its *Stop* intention is a *multi-path* and may contain *multi-threads*. Finally, it is possible to refine a section of a map into another map. Refinement is an abstraction mechanism by which a complex assembly of sections at level i+1 is viewed as a unique section at level i. Figure 3 shows the refinement of the section <*Finalize the buy*, *Stop*, *By payment*> as a map. This map is composed of two key intentions *Sign in* and *Finish the payment* and it provides several strategies to achieve each of them.

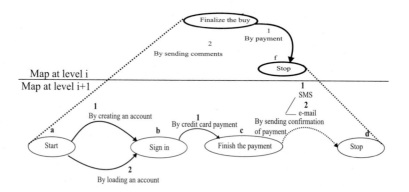

Fig. 3. The refinement of the section <*Finalize the buy*, *Stop*, *By payment*>

2.2   Specifying Intentional Services

Intentional services are services presented by maps. Intentional services allow the achievement of users' requirements represented as intentions using the MAP formalism. Intentional services are specified by the Intentional Service Model

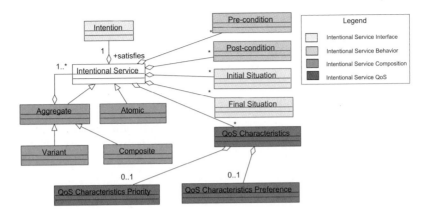

Fig. 4. The intentional service model (ISM)

(ISM). Figure 4 presents the ISM meta-model using UML notations. As shown by colors used in Figure 4, the ISM describes intentional services through four main aspects: the intentional service interface, behavior, composition, and QoS. We describe each of these aspects in the following paragraphs.

The Intentional Service Interface. There are three elements *that constitute* interface, namely *Intention*, *Initial Situation*, and *Final Situation*. The key idea of the ISM is that an *intentional* service allows the achievement of an intention given an initial situation and terminating with a final situation. The intention replaces the functionalities that can be achieved by the service. The achievement of an intention will ultimately lead to a state that is expected to be reached or to be maintained. The *Initial Situation* and the *Final Situation* represent respectively the input and output parameters of the intentional service.

The Intentional Service Behavior. *Pre-condition* and *Post-condition* describe the service behavior aspect. *Pre-condition* and *Post-condition* are respectively the initial and final state, i.e., the state requiring the achievement of the intention and the state resulting from its achievement.

The Intentional Service Composition. *Atomic* and *Aggregate* services are involved in the service composition aspect. An *Atomic* service has an operationalized intention that can be achieved directly by an atomic operational service. An *Aggregate* service has a high level intention that should be decomposed till atomic operational services are identified. Aggregation of services can result either by *Composite* or *Variant* services. *Composite* services express the precedence/succession relationship between intentional services. We distinguish three types of composition: *Sequential*, *Parallel*, and *Iterative*. *Variant* services describe variability needed for SBAs. There are three variants in the ISM, namely *Alternative*, *Choice*, and *Multi-path*.

The Intentional Service QoS. There are three elements specifying QoS of intentional services, namely *QoS Characteristic*, *QoS Characteristic Priority*, and

QoS Characteristic Preference. *QoS Characteristic* is the quality to be attained or preserved. *QoS Characteristic Priority* allows the expression of a priority over a *QoS Characteristic*. *QoS Characteristic Preference* allows the expression of a preference over a *QoS Characteristics*.

2.3 Eliciting Intentional Services from Maps

The MAP is used to represent intentional services satisfying users' requirements. To elicit intentional services and their composition from maps, we follow three key guidelines [6]:

1. The first guidline consists of associating every non-refined section of a map to an atomic service. In the case of the e-books application map, this correspondence leads to a set of 29 atomic services including for instance: $ab1_i$ → $S_{Search\ a\ book\ by\ ISBN}$ and $bc1_{i+1}$ → $S_{Pay\ with\ credit\ card}$[1].
2. The second guideline consists of identifying paths of a map by applying an algorithm that calculates paths in a graph. This algorithm is an adaptation of the MacNaughton and Yamada's algorithm [12]. This algorithm is based on formula that calculate the set of all possible paths between an initial node and a final node of a graph which, in our case, are respectively the intentions *Start* and *Stop*.
3. The third guideline consists of determining aggregate services by establishing the following correspondences between section relationships in the map and aggregate service types in the ISM model: *<Path-Composite>*, *<Bundle-Alternative>*, *<Multi-thread-Choice>*, and *<Multi-path-Multi-path>*.

3   Discovering Operational Services

Discovering operational services is proceeded by querying Service-Finder [13]. Service-Finder is a Web 2.0 platform for WS discovery. It is managed to search and access existing WSs on the Web. It searches among almost 25.000 WSs from more than 200.000 related Web pages [13]. In order to understand the problem of WS discovery and selection, we are going to demonstrate an example of a WS from the e-books application. Naturally, discovery and selection should be processed for all intentional services in order to build the e-books application. We consider the service $S_{Pay\ with\ credit\ card}$ presented by the section bc1 of the e-books application map at level i+1. This service performs payment with a credit card. Figure 5 shows the intentional model of the service $S_{Pay\ with\ credit\ card}$ according to the ISM.

$S_{Pay\ with\ credit\ card}$ is an atomic service that ensures the achievement of the intention *Pay with credit card*. $S_{Pay\ with\ credit\ card}$ takes 2 input parameters that are *Book* and *Card* and provides *Payment* as output. $S_{Pay\ with\ credit\ card}$

---

[1] For sake of conciseness, we use an abbreviated notation to refer to a section of a map. We refer to each intention by a letter starting from a and to each strategy by a digit starting from 1. Levels of maps start from i.

```
<?xml version="1.0" encoding="ASCII"?>
<ism:Map xmi:version="2.0"
xmlns:xmi="http://www.omg.org/XMI"
xmlns:xsi="http://www.w3.org/2001/XMLSchema-instance"
xmlns:ism="http://ism/1.0"
xsi:schemaLocation="http://ism/1.0 ISM.ecore">
  <service xsi:type="ism:Atomic"
  intention="//@Intention.0"
  pre_condition="//@Pre-Condition.0"
  post_condition="//@Post-Condition.0"
  initial_situation="//@Initial Situation.0"
  final_situation="//@Final Situation.0"
qos_characteristic="//@QoS Characteristic.0"
qos_characteristic="//@QoS Characteristic.1"
  id="Pay with credit card"/>
  <Intention description="Pay with credit card"/>
  <Pre-Condition value="Book.Cart=true"/>
  <Post-Condition value="Payment.State=true"/>
  <resource name="Book"/>
  <resource name="Payment"/>
  <resource name="Card"/>
  <Initial Situation input="//@resource.0 //@resource.2"/>
  <Final Situation output="//@resource.1"/>
  <QoS Characteristic id="Respons time">
    <QoS Priority value="3"/>
    <Qos Preference value="Very low"/>
  </QoS Characteristic>
  <QoS Characteristic id="Availability">
    <QoS Priority value="1"/>
    <Qos Preference value="Very high"/>
  </QoS Characteristic>
</ism:Map>
```

Fig. 5. The intentional model of the service $S_{Pay\ with\ credit\ card}$

has as pre-condition *Book.Cart=true* and as post-condition *Payment.State=true*. $S_{Pay\ with\ credit\ card}$ is characterized by a very high availability and a very low response time. Response time is three time more important for the users than the availability. The QoS preferences and priorities are given by users.

We query Service-Finder using the keywords 'payment + credit + card'. We extract these keywords from the intentional model $S_{Pay\ with\ credit\ card}$ using a well known Information Retrieval (IR) metric called TF/IDF [14]. All words of a service specification are weighted with TF/IDF metric. TF/IDF metric allows us to filter out both stop words and low frequency words. Only meaningful words (i.e., keywords) having a high TF/IDF weight are maintained. Service-Finder returns a result set of 77 WSs[2]. To reduce this set, we process two-level filtration. In the first level, we consider some QoS properties namely validity and availability. These two properties are checked as follows: (1) validity is verified by checking whether the endpoint URI exists or not; (2) Availability is verified by checking if the service is operational or not. This first filtration level generates a new reduced set that contains 37 WSs. These services are passed to a second level filtration which is based on a semantic matchmaking between the intentional model of the service $S_{Pay\ with\ credit\ card}$ and WSDLs of the returned operational services. This is done by parsing every service WSDL in order to check if required operation with specified signature exists or not. An operation signature is the combination of the operation name, its input parameters, and its output. In our example, the required operation is *Pay with credit card*, its inputs are *Book* and

---

[2] The discovery result set is obtained on June 13th, 2010.

Card, and its output is *Payment*. A final set of 16 WSs is obtained after the second level filtration. These remaining services will be organized into concept lattices using FCA in order to facilitate the selection task.

4 Selecting Relevant and High QoS Operational Services

To automate the selection of relevant and high QoS services, Formal Concept Analysis (FCA) [7] is used.

4.1 Introducing FCA

FCA offers a formal framework for clustering individuals along the properties they share. It describes clusters, called formal concepts, both extensionally and intentionally, i.e., as sets of individuals and sets of shared properties, and organises them hierarchically, according to a binary incidence relation, into a complete lattice, called the concept lattice [7]. FCA considers a dataset as being organised into a formal context, i.e., a triple $\mathcal{K} = (\mathcal{O}, \mathcal{A}, \mathcal{I})$, where $\mathcal{O}$ is a set of individuals, $\mathcal{A}$ is a set of properties, and $\mathcal{I}$ is the binary incidence relation between $\mathcal{O}$ and $\mathcal{A}$, $\mathcal{I} \subseteq \mathcal{O} \times \mathcal{A}$.

For our problem, we define a context $\mathcal{K}$ where individuals represent services and properties represent QoS properties. We consider 2 QoS properties: availability and response time. Real time monitoring information of service availability and response time are provided by Service-Finder. The binary incidence relation is the *service-has-QoS property* relationship. To spread out availability and response time values, we use the boxplot statistical technique [15]. A boxplot splits a set of numerical values into four quarters called quartiles. We map these quartiles into a five-point Likert scale with the following ordinal values: very high, high, medium, low, and very low. Then, we associate QoS values with these ordinal values. As specified in the intentional model of the service $S_{Pay\ with\ credit\ card}$, users give three time more importance to the service response time than to the availability (see Figure 5). So, we define for each response time ordinal value three sub-values in order to express the priority. For instance, we consider the sub-values: very low 1, very low 2, and very low 3 for the ordinal value very low. Service having a very low response time should has an incidence relationship with the three sub-values of the ordinal value very low. Also, we consider that if a service has an incidence relationship with a response time ordinal value (availability ordinal value, respectively), it should has incidence relationship with all ordinal values that comes after (that comes before, respectively). For instance, if a service has a very low response time (very high availability, respectively) it has also low, medium, high and very high response time (high, medium, low , and very low availability, respectively). Relevant and high QoS of services are services which have more incidence relationships with context properties.

Table 1 illustrates the context drawn from the final obtained set of services. It shows the 16 services (individuals in rows), and their has-relationship links with availability and response time (properties in columns).

Table 1. Context $\mathcal{K}$ linking services to QoS characteristics

	(A1) Very Low Availability	(A2) Low Availability	(A3) Medium Availability	(A4) High Availability	(A5) Very High Availability	(RT11) Very Low Response Time 1	(RT12) Very Low Response Time 2	(RT13) Very Low Response Time 3	(RT21) Low Response Time 1	(RT22) Low Response Time 2	(RT23) Low Response Time 3	(RT31) Medium Response Time 1	(RT32) Medium Response Time 2	(RT33) Medium Response Time 3	(RT41) High Response Time 1	(RT42) High Response Time 2	(RT43) High Response Time 3	(RT51) Very High Response Time 1	(RT52) Very High Response Time 2	(RT53) Very High Response Time 3
(s0) XWebCheckOut	×	×	×	×								×	×	×	×	×	×	×	×	×
(s1) PaymentWS	×	×							×	×	×	×	×	×	×	×	×	×	×	×
(s2) Pay-Service	×	×	×	×					×	×	×	×	×	×	×	×	×	×	×	×
(s3) Checkout	×	×	×	×								×	×	×	×	×	×	×	×	×
(s4) Book247XMLWebServices	×	×										×	×	×	×	×	×	×	×	×
(s5) ExigoAPI	×	×										×	×	×	×	×	×	×	×	×
(s6) FSI	×	×	×	×					×	×	×	×	×	×	×	×	×	×	×	×
(s7) CEPayProcessor	×	×	×												×	×	×	×	×	×
(s8) SmartPayment2	×	×	×															×	×	×
(s9) BasicOperations	×	×	×	×					×	×	×	×	×	×	×	×	×	×	×	×
(s10) Order	×								×	×	×	×	×	×	×	×	×	×	×	×
(s11) MemberServices	×	×	×	×					×	×	×	×	×	×	×	×	×	×	×	×
(s12) SmartPayments	×	×	×															×	×	×
(s13) SBWebServices	×	×	×	×								×	×	×	×	×	×	×	×	×
(s14) MWService	×														×	×	×	×	×	×
(s15) OMService	×																	×	×	×

4.2 Using Concept Lattices to Select Relevant and High Quality Operational Services

FCA organizes formal concepts into complete lattices, called concept lattices. The lattice structure allows easy navigation and search as well as optimal representation of information. Figure 6 depicts a simplified (reduced) labeling of the concept lattice derived from our context $\mathcal{K}$. This lattice is built using the Galicia (Galois Lattice Interactive Constructor) [16] tool. Galicia is a multi-tool open-source platform for creating, visualizing, and storing concept lattices. Our lattice contains information that can be interpreted using the following set of rules:

- The concepts are represented using the intent (I) and the extent (E) sets.
  - A service that appears in the extent set E of a concept is inherited by all the concepts that are above it.
  - A QoS value that appears in the intent set I of a concept is inherited by all the concepts that are below.

- When the extent set E is not empty, the concept represents exactly the service(s) that is/are in the extent set E with its/their QoS value(s) in the I set.

- When the extent set E is empty, this signifies that the concept represents a service specification that does not exist in the services set.

From these rules, we can conclude that relevant and high QoS services are services presented by the concept which is in the bottom of our lattice (node 4). The extent set of this concept includes 4 services: *Basicoperations*, *FSI*, *MemberServices*, and *Pay-Service*. These services have a high availability (A4) and a low response time (RT21, RT22, and RT23).

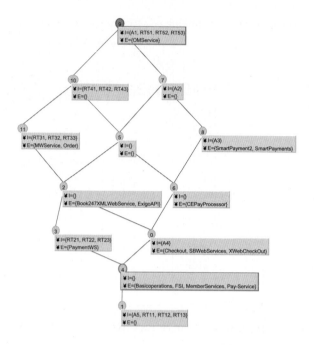

Fig. 6. The lattice of the context $\mathcal{K}$

5   Experiments

We validate our approach on the 29 intentional services of the e-books application. We verify manually that the services returned by our approach correspond to real relavant and high QoS services. We recast our work in the domain of information retrieval and we use the precision and recall measures [17]. Precision assesses the number of true relevant and high QoS operational services identified among the returned set of operational services, while recall assesses the number of returned operational services among the existing relevant and high QoS services, according to the following equations:

$$
\mathrm{precision} = \frac{\left|\left\{\text{true relevant and high QoS operational services}\right\} \cap \left\{\text{returned operational services}\right\}\right|}{\left|\left\{\text{returned operational services}\right\}\right|}
$$

$$
\mathrm{recall} = \frac{\left|\left\{\text{true relevant and high QoS operational services}\right\} \cap \left\{\text{returned operational services}\right\}\right|}{\left|\left\{\text{true relevant and high QoS operational services}\right\}\right|}
$$

Due to the limitation of paper space, we show only, in Table 2, experimental results related to 10 intentional services. However, we provide the precision and recall average of the 29 intentional services of the e-books application. In Table 2, the first column corresponds to intentional services. In the second column, we list, first, the keywords used to query Service-Finder; then, the number of

Table 2. Precision and recall of services of the e-books application

Intentional services	Service-Finder			Our Approach			Precision	Recall
	Keywords	Returned operational services	True relevant and high QoS operational services	Discovery	Selection	True relevant and high QoS operational services		
$ab1_i \rightarrow$ $S_{Search\ a\ book\ by\ ISBN}$	'search + book + isbn'	7	2/7	4/7	2/4	2/2	2/2 (100%)	2/2 (100%)
$ab2_i \rightarrow$ $S_{Search\ a\ book\ by\ author(s)}$	'search + book + author'	16	3/16	10/16	4/10	3/4	3/4 (75%)	3/3 (100%)
$ab3_i \rightarrow$ $S_{Search\ a\ book\ by\ title}$	'search + book + title'	31	5/31	22/31	6/22	5/6	5/6 (83.33%)	5/5 (100%)
...	...	...	...	...	...	...	...	...
$cc2_i \rightarrow$ $S_{Sort\ books\ by\ price}$	'sort + price'	64	11/64	52/64	9/52	8/9	8/9 (88.89%)	8/11 (72.73%)
$cc3_i \rightarrow$ $S_{Sort\ books\ by\ seller\ location}$	'sort + location'	58	12/58	40/58	11/40	11/11	11/11 (100%)	11/12 (91.67%)
...	...	...	...	...	...	...	...	...
$ee1_i \rightarrow$ $S_{Change\ the\ currency}$	'change + currency'	55	8/55	30/55	7/30	6/7	6/7 (85.71%)	6/8 (75%)
$ab1_{i+1} \rightarrow$ $S_{Create\ an\ account}$	'create + account'	330	26/330	203/330	25/203	22/25	22/25 (88%)	22/26 (84.62%)
$ab2_{i+1} \rightarrow$ $S_{Load\ an\ account}$	'load + account'	29	4/29	20/29	5/20	4/5	4/5 (80%)	4/4 (100%)
$bc1_{i+1} \rightarrow$ $S_{Pay\ with\ credit\ card}$	'payment + credit + card'	77	4/77	16/77	4/16	4/4	4/4 (100%)	4/4 (100%)
$cd1_{i+1} \rightarrow$ $S_{Send\ sms}$	'send + sms'	162	17/162	105/162	18/105	15/18	15/18 (83.33%)	15/17 (88.24%)
						Average	89.41%	95.43%

services returned by Service-Finder; and finally, the number of services identified manually as true relevant and high QoS services. In the third column, we enumerate the number of services obtained, first, after the discovery step of our approach, and then, after the selection step, and finally the number of true services among those returned after selection step. The two last columns correspond to the precision and the recall. For example, the two keywords of the intentional service $S_{Send\ sms}$ are: 'send + sms'. The query returns an initial set of 162 operational services. Among this set, only 17 services are verified manually as true relevant and high QoS services. The discovery step reduces the initial set to a second set of 105 services. The selection step using FCA reduces the second set to 18 services. Among these services, only 15 services are verified manually as true relevant and high QoS services. The precision of $S_{Send\ sms}$ is 83.33% and he recall is 88.24%.

Table 2 shows that the precision and recall of our approach are both very high. The average precision is 89.41% and the average recall is 95.43%.

To increase the robustness of our approach, we need to use more advanced semantic techniques for the filtration of the discovered operational services. Moreover our selection is based only on two QoS properties. Thus, we need to enhance our selection method with multiple QoS properties to identify more efficiently high QoS services.

6   Related Work

Recently, several requirements-driven approaches for service composition have been proposed. The work presented by Pistore *et al.* [18] is the first work that takes in the challenge of deriving service compositions by refining TROPOS requirements models. The key idea of this work is to enrich formal TROPOS models with BPEL4WS code and exploit model checking techniques to ensure verification and validation. More recently, the MAP formalism has been used in [6] to describe services compositions. Main contribution of this work takes on the proposition of an Intentional Service Model (ISM) to model, retrieve, and compose services in an intentional manner. Unfortunately, this model omits QoS aspects. All the works mentioned above focus only on modeling service composition in a requirement driven manner. They do not provide solutions for service discovery and selection to ensure the satisfaction of the users' requirements. A similar work to ours is provided by Zachos *et al.* [19]. The goal of this work is to align and refine requirements to the available services. The key idea of the proposed approach is to create an initial requirements specification, transform it into a registry query and use the query results to refine the specification. This work suffers from several problems: (i) the textual and incomplete requirements description; (ii) the lack of the non-functional requirements description; and finally (iii) the difficulty to refine the initial requirements based on service query result.

The solution that we present in this paper is complementary to [18], [6], and [19] since our approach permits not only SBAs modeling in terms of functional and non-functional requirements but also the discovery and the selection of services that fit closely expected functional requirements and offer a high QoS. To handle the problem of service selection we apply the FCA. Several approaches using FCA in the context of WSs have been proposed. We detail these approches in the following paragraphs.

Peng *et al.* [20] present an approach to classify and select services. They build lattices starting from contexts where individuals are WSs and properties represent the operations of these services. The approach allows similar services clustering by applying similarity search techniques that compare operation descriptions and input/output messages' data type. The contributions of this work are complementary to ours, insofar as they do not deal with QoS properties in the selection task. Azmeh *et al.* [21] present a similar approach to classify and select services using the FCA. They propose WSPAB (Web Service Personal Address Book) tool that permits the discovery, the automatic classification, and the selection of WSs. This tool processes by multiple successive steps. It first queries the service registry to find a first set of candidate services. Secondly, it filters this service set according to functional and non-functional criteria. Finally, the set of remaining services is classified into a service lattice using FCA. Classification is accomplished by defining a binary relation between services and operation signatures. The obtained lattice can be used to identify relevant services and their substitutes. In contrast to our approach, this work does not consider QoS properties to process WS selection. Also, this work is purely syntactic (signature-based) while our work proposes a semantic filtration of discovered services based on the intentional models.

7   Conclusion

In this paper, we presented a requirement-centric approach to WS modeling, discovery, and selection. This approach consists of three successive steps. First, our approach allows an intentional-driven modeling of SBAs using the MAP formalism. Intentional services, that are presented by maps, are specified with the ISM model. Secondly, our approach permits discovery of operational services by querying the WS search engine Service-Finder using keywords extracted from specifications provided by ISM. To efficiently discover relevant services, we propose two-level filtration. In the first level, some QoS properties are considered namely validity and availability. Services which pass the first level are filtered according to a semantic matchmaking between the intentional specification provided by ISM and the operational specification provided by WSDL. Finally, the remaining set of services is classified into concept lattices using FCA. We consider contexts with services as individuals and QoS characteristics as properties. The obtained concept lattices are used to check out relevant and high QoS services. We validate our approach by performing experiments on an e-books application. The experimental results show that our approach allows the selection of relevant and high QoS services with a high accuracy (the average precision is 89.41%) and efficiency (the average recall is 95.43%). Future work includes: (i) studying semantic similarity techniques to enhance the filtration of the discovered operational services; (ii) considering multiple QoS properties, during the selection step, to identify more efficiently high QoS services; and (iii) applying Relational Concept Analysis (RCA) to identify high QoS composite services since the presented approach is applicable to atomic services.

Acknowledgments. This work has been supported by the European Communitys Seventh Framework Programme FP7/2007-2013 under grant agreement 215483 (S-Cube). (http://www.s-cube-network.eu/).

References

1. Huhns, M.N., Singh, M.P.: Service-oriented computing: Key concepts and principles. IEEE Internet Computing 9(1), 75–81 (2005)
2. Menascé, D.A.: Qos issues in web services. IEEE Internet Computing 6(6), 72–75 (2002)
3. Bresciani, P., Perini, A., Giorgini, P., Giunchiglia, F., Mylopoulos, J.: Tropos: An agent-oriented software development methodology. Autonomous Agents and Multi-Agent Systems 8(3), 203–236 (2004)
4. Lamsweerde, A.V., Letier, E.: Handling obstacles in goal oriented requirements engineering. IEEE Transactions on Software Engineering 26(10), 978–1005 (2000)
5. Rolland, C., Prakash, N.: Bridging the gap between organizational needs and erp functionality. Requirements Engineering 5(3), 180–193 (2000)
6. Rolland, C., Kaabi, R.S., Kraiem, N.: On isoa: Intentional services oriented architecture. In: Krogstie, J., Opdahl, A.L., Sindre, G. (eds.) CAiSE 2007 and WES 2007. LNCS, vol. 4495, pp. 158–172. Springer, Heidelberg (2007)

7. Ganter, B., Wille, R.: Formal Concept Analysis: Mathematical Foundations. Springer, New York (1999)
8. BPEL4WS,
   http://www.oasis-open.org/committees/tc_home.php?wg_abbrev=wsbpel
9. OWLS, http://www.w3.org/Submission/OWLS/
10. Mecella, M., Presicce, F.P., Pernici, B.: Modeling e-service orchestration through petri nets. In: Buchmann, A., Casati, F., Fiege, L., Hsu, M.-C., Shan, M.-C. (eds.) TES 2002. LNCS, vol. 2444, pp. 38–47. Springer, Heidelberg (2002)
11. Kaabi, R.K., Souveyet, C., Rolland, C.: Eliciting service composition in a goal driven manner. In: ICSOC 2004, New York, USA, pp. 308–315 (2004)
12. MacNaughton, R., Yamada, H.: Regular expressions and state graphs for automata. IEEE Transactions on Electronic Computers 9(1), 39–47 (1960)
13. Service-Finder, http://www.service-finder.eu/
14. Salton, G., Buckley, C.: Term-weighting approaches in automatic text retrieval. Information Processing and Management 24(5), 513–523 (1988)
15. Chambers, J.M., Clevelmd, W.S., Kleiner, B., Tukey, P.A.: Graphical methods for data analysis. Wadsworth & Brooks / Cole, Belmont (1983)
16. Galicia, http://galicia.sourceforge.net/
17. Frakes, W.B., Baeza-Yates, R.: Information Retrieval: Data Structures and Algorithms. Prentice-Hall, Englewood Cliffs (1992)
18. Pistore, M., Roveri, M., Busetta, P.: Requirements-driven verification of web service. In: WSFM 2004, Pisa, Italy, pp. 95–108 (2004)
19. Zachos, K., Maiden, N., Zhu, X., Jones, S.: Discovering web services to specify more complete system requirements. In: Krogstie, J., Opdahl, A.L., Sindre, G. (eds.) CAiSE 2007 and WES 2007. LNCS, vol. 4495, pp. 142–157. Springer, Heidelberg (2007)
20. Peng, D., Huang, S., Wang, X., Zhou, A.: Management and retrieval of web services based on formal concept analysis. In: CIT 2005, Shanghai, China, pp. 269–275 (2005)
21. Azmeh, Z., Huchard, M., Tibermacine, C., Urtado, C., Vauttier, S.: Wspab: A tool for automatic classification & selection of web services using formal concept analysis. In: ECOWS 2008, Dublin, Ireland, pp. 31–40 (2008)

Spreadsheet as a Generic Purpose Mashup Development Environment

Dat Dac Hoang[1], Hye-Young Paik[1], and Anne H.H. Ngu[2]

[1] School of Computer Science & Engineering, University of New South Wales, Sydney
[2] Department of Computer Science, Texas State University, San Marcos
{ddhoang,hpaik}@cse.unsw.edu.au, angu@txstate.edu

Abstract. Mashup development is done using purposely created tools. Because each tool offers a different paradigm and syntax for wiring mashup components, users need to learn different tools for different tasks. We believe that there is a need for a generic purpose mashup environment catering for a wider range of mashup applications. In this paper we introduce MashSheet - a spreadsheet-based, generic purpose mashup tool. Using MashSheet, mashups can be built using spreadsheet paradigms that many users are already familiar with. We use a generic data model (XML-based) to represent mashup components and data produced by them, which enables the reuse of intermediate mashup results. We support three classes of mashup operations: data, process and visualization.

1 Introduction

Mashup is a new application development method enabling users to create applications by reusing existing contents and functionalities. Recently, we have witnessed rapidly growing interests in mashup tools and applications in the web community. In programmableweb.com, for example, there are over 4815 mashup applications and 1995 Web APIs registered[1]. However, many mashup programmings today are done in "special-purpose" and "hand-crafted" manners using a purposely created development environment [8]. For example, MapCruncher [1] is designed for users to create mashups involving maps. Swivel.com makes it easy for users to create graph mashups from multiple data tables. Yahoo Pipes [5] is best suited to generate feeds. Due to the ad-hoc nature of the popular mashups tools, users are required to learn different tools, paradigms and syntaxes to write mashup applications. We believe that there is a need for a generic purpose mashup environment that can cater for a wider range of mashup applications with a uniform mashup paradigm.

In this paper, we propose a spreadsheet-based mashup programming framework called MashSheet. Spreadsheets are frequently used to analyze data imported from different sources (e.g, database, file, data service), particularly in the context of decision support. They also have been tagged as the most successful end-user development environment with millions of users [11,16].

We believe that spreadsheets can provide a programming paradigm that many users are already familiar with, hence would be a good environment for designing a generic

---

[1] The figures are as of 18 May 2010, from [2].

P.P. Maglio et al. (Eds.): ICSOC 2010, LNCS 6470, pp. 273–287, 2010.

purpose mashup tool. In fact, there have been some efforts in spreadsheet-based mashup tools (e.g., [4,18,14,12]) with varying degree of success [10]. There is still much work left to do in order to create a spreadsheet-based mashup framework which can be generically applied to multiple situations. We use these existing systems to benchmark our prototype to show that our tool is more widely applicable for mashup programming.

1.1 Reference Scenario

Let us consider the following scenario as our running example. Tom wants to create a mashup application that will help him to find Points of Interest (POI) (e.g., restaurant, cinema) when he travels to a city. Tom considers the following five services:

- RL: with read() operation, it returns a list of restaurants with addresses,
- CL: with read() operation, it returns a list of cinemas with addresses,
- DG: with getDR() operation, it returns car driving direction,
- WF: with getWeather() operation, it returns weather forecast information,
- BU: with getBU() operation, it returns bus itinerary.

Some services require SOAP-based interactions and some are RSS feeds (Figure 1(b)). Figure 1(a) shows the scenario of the application. Tom inputs the address of a hotel, calls RL and CL, merges and sorts the results. He would use DG only when the WF service reports rain, otherwise he prefers to use public transport, so information from BU will suffice. Finally, Tom visualizes the direction results in a grid of cells.

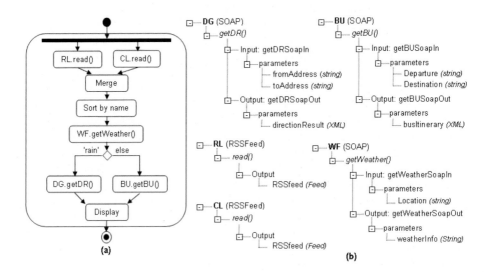

Fig. 1. Tom's scenario

1.2   Contributions

To make the tool generic, we start with a generic data model that will support a wide-range of data types we need to deal with in the framework. We name the data type 'MashSheet Object Type' (MOT) and it is an XML-based data model. MOT is based on [12], where the conventional spreadsheet data model is extended to include complex data types to represent RSS feeds. Using MOT, we introduce two components to represent a web service (`service`) and web service output (`service-output`). At present, MashSheet can work with SOAP-based services and RSS data feeds. However, it is not difficult to extend the range in the future, e.g., REST-based services.

MashSheet offers the following advantages over existing approaches:

- MashSheet defines all operations as spreadsheet formula: data, process and visualization. This means that the mashup operations would be like another spreadsheet formula to the users - the concept many users are already familiar with.
- MashSheet provides different classes of mashup operations to make the framework applicable to many mashup scenarios.
  - *Data operators:* In spreadsheet, the data is represented as simple data types (e.g., string, number). Web service invocation, on the other hand, often returns complex data type such as XML document. In other spreadsheet-based mashup tools, users have to "flatten" the complex data into two-dimensional grid of spreadsheet before data operations (e.g., sort, filter, join) can be applied. This creates unnecessary step in mashup creation process. In MashSheet, users can manipulate the complex data "as-is" by applying data mashup operation directly on MOT. In addition, any intermediary result created by data operations can be reused by other data and visualization mashup operators at any stage. This increases the reusability of intermediate data in the application.
  - *Process operators:* Evaluation of spreadsheet's formula is driven by data dependencies between cells. This data-flow model allows users to define some process mashup operations using natural spreadsheet programming metaphor (e.g., sequence by using cell referencing mechanism).

    However, the semantics of some control flow patterns are not inherently supported in spreadsheets and none of the existing spreadsheet-based mashup tools address this issue (e.g., exclusive choice, synchronization). Supporting a basic set of control flow patterns are important for mashup component composing scenarios. We introduce an extension to the spreadsheet formula language so that the basic control flow patterns [17] are supported.
  - *Visualization operators.* Data visualization needs in mashup cover a wide range of options (e.g., grid, map, chart, timeline). In current spreadsheet-based mashup tools we investigated, data can only represented in a grid of cells by using either simple grid (i.e., column, row) [14,4] or nested grid (i.e., hierarchical, index, repeater) [12,18]. Also, the data view needs to reflect any change in the data source and make it immediately visible to users.

    We define visualization operators as components to present service output data using different visualization types (e.g., grid, map). The benefits of having these operators are: (i) *flexibility*: the layout of data is automatically updated when there is a change in the data source); (ii) *generic applicability*: we can apply different visualization operators to produce different layouts of data; (iii) *easiness to use*: can be called like spreadsheet functions.

The remainder of this paper is organized as follows. The related work is discussed in section 2. We introduce the architecture of MashSheet in section 3. Sections 4 and 5 explain the application model and operators of MashSheet. Implementation, mashup formula evaluation mechanism and a brief evaluation are discussed in sections 6 and 7. Section 8 presents conclusion and future work.

2   Overview of Spreadsheet-Based Mashup Tools

According to Fischer et al. [7], spreadsheet is one of the six programming paradigms for mashup development, along with integrated development environment, scripting languages, wiring paradigm, programming by demonstration and automatic creation of mashup. In this section, we present mashup tools that use spreadsheet paradigm[2].

StrikeIron [4] is a Microsoft Excel plugin allowing users to pull data from SOAP web services into Excel worksheet. Using StrikeIron, users can create mashup applications by 'wiring' output data of one service with the input parameter of another service (via cell referencing). However the main limitation of this approach is that it does not support all of the basic control flow patterns. In addition, data visualization in StrikeIron is limited to conventional spreadsheet data visualization (i.e., data is visualized by a grid of cells and a cell can only accommodate simple types such as number, string).

AMICO:CALC [14] is an OpenOffice Calc extension that lets users to create mashups within Calc spreadsheet by using AMICO-Read and Amico-Write functions. The execution of mashup application is based on a middleware named Adaptable Multi-Interface COmmunicator. By using a combination of Read and Write functions, users can model basic control flow patterns in their mashup application. However, AMICO:CALC does not provide data manipulation and visualization operators.

Mashroom [18] is a mashup tool that relies on nested table algebra and spreadsheet programming metaphor to simplify the mashup creation process. However, Mashroom is not a generic mashup framework since it focuses only on data mashup and its data visualization is limited to nested table.

In SpreadMash [12], web data is modeled using entity relations, then browsed and visualized using widgets. SpreadMash, however, is limited to data importation and visualization. It does not mention control flow and is not a generic mashup tool. Spreadator [15], as SpreadMash's earlier prototype, mainly provides means for accessing/manipulating web data from spreadsheet. MashSheet builds further on the early ideas presented in SpreadMash and Spreadator, focusing on generic applicability and mashup component composition. We will discuss these tools further in section 7.

3   MashSheet Overview

This section sketches the overall design of MashSheet and explains how it draws inspiration from spreadsheet. As depicted in Figure 2, the architecture of MashSheet comprises of four elements:

---

[2] Please refer to [10] for more detailed analysis.

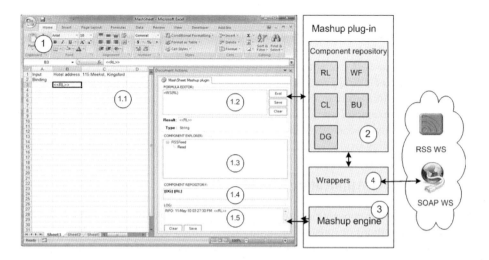

Fig. 2. The architecture of MashSheet

- **MashSheet's graphical user interface (GUI) (1).** This element is a conventional
  spreadsheet interface which includes a grid of cells (1.1) and a mashup plugin implemented as a Task Pane. Cells are capable of storing values and formulas, while
  mashup plugin allows users to build mashup applications by specifying composition logic and layout information. The GUI plays a role as a development environment and users mainly interact with this element. The mashup plugin includes:
    - *Formula editor (1.2).* This element allows users to enter mashup formulas. Note
      that our formula input area is different with the conventional formula input in
      spreadsheets. The reason for this design is that most of the spreadsheets do not
      allow developer to modify their evaluation engine with conventional input.
    - *Component explorer (1.3).* This element lets users to visualize structure of web
      service (e.g., WSDL) and service output (e.g., XML) in a tree view.
    - *Component repository (1.4).* This element shows to the users a list of com-
      ponents (i.e., representations of web services in the tool). It is a front-end of
      "Component repository" element which will be defined below.
    - *Log (1.5).* This element displays the output message of each operation.
- **Component Repository (2).** This element is a repository of all mashup components available in the tool. Users can choose an external web service and create a
  component that allows them to interact with the service within the tool. This service component can be assigned a friendly name (i.e., alias) and can be called in the
  MashSheet formula editor. For example, in the Tom's scenario, DG is a component
  representing a SOAP-based service that provides driving direction information.
- **Mashup Engine (3).** This key element is responsible for evaluating the mashup
  formula (i.e., composition logic) and "wiring" components together. Since most
  of spreadsheet tools do not allow users to modify their formula evaluation mechanisms, mashup engine could be developed as an extension to spreadsheet evaluation
  engine. Mashup engine is also responsible for maintaining the formula evaluation

context and facilitate the reaction to cell modification by triggering the re-evaluation of dependent formula (i.e., upon a service invocation returns, the corresponding references need to be updated with the returning value). We will explain the working of the engine with examples in the later sections.

- **Wrappers (4).** Wrappers facilitate interoperability among services which have different data formats (e.g., XML, RSS) or use different access protocols (e.g., SOAP, RSS). For example, we need different wrappers to create components to correctly serve the Tom's scenario, such as SOAP wrapper for DG, RSS wrapper for RL. We rely on existing works (e.g., RSS.NET library [3]) to provide wrappers for services.

4   MashSheet Application Model

MashSheet extends conventional spreadsheet to provide its application model. We use the formal definitions of spreadsheet application in [6] to describe our model as follow:

A MashSheet application (S) is a spreadsheet contains a collection of cells organized in a tabular grid. Each cell is identified by its address (a), value (v) and formula (f). An address uses absolute coordinates of the cell in the grid (e.g., A1). A formula can contain a value (v) (e.g., a number), a reference to another cell address (a) (e.g., A1) or mashup operators (ω) (e.g., invoke()). A cell's value is obtained by evaluating the cell's formula. In MashSheet, a value (v) can be either a simple data type (α) (e.g., number, string) or complex data type. We model the complex type as XML-based data type and name it MashSheet Object Type (MOT). Using MOT, we build two components: service (SC) and service $-$ output (OC) to represent web service and its output data, respectively. Figure 3 illustrates the MashSheet's model. We use the notion $\|(\mathtt{a}, \mathtt{f})\|_\mathtt{S}$ to denote the evaluation of a MashSheet cell with address a and formula f. Cell reference can use single cell address (e.g., A1) or a range of cells (e.g., A1 : C3).

We use regular tree languages and tree automata from [13] to define MOT:

MashSheet Object Type (MOT) is a quadruples $(\mathtt{N}, \mathtt{T}, \mathtt{B}, \mathtt{P})$, where:

- N is a finite set of nonterminals which are regular expressions represented by capitalized *Italic* characters (ϵ is a null sequence of nonterminals),
- T is a set of terminals which are symbols represented by lowercase characters (*pcdata* is a special terminal character matched with any node in the tree),

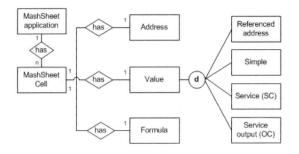

Fig. 3. MashSheet application model

- B is a set of start symbols, where $B \in N$,
- P is a set of rules in the form of $X \rightarrow \mathbf{a}r$, where $X \in N$, $\mathbf{a} \in T$, and r is a regular expression over N.

Figure 4 shows an example of data produced by RL's read() operation and its MOT representation (for visibility issue, we remove some fields such as Link, PubDate).

```
<rss version="2.0">
<channel>
    <title>Restaurant Listing service</title>
    <descriptionRestaurants in Kensington</description>
        <item>
            <title>Grotta Carpi</title>
            <description>97-101 Anzac Pde</description>
        </item>
        <item>
            <title>Golden Kingdom</title>
            <description>147-151 Anzac Pde</description>
        </item>
        <item>
            <title>Kensington Peking</title>
            <description>172 Anzac Pde</description>
        </item>
</channel>
</rss>
```

$N = \{Rss, Channel, Item, Title, Description, PCdata\}$,
$T = \{rss, channel, item, title, description, pcdata\}$,
$S = \{Rss\}$,
$P = \{Rss \rightarrow rss\ (Channel)$,
$\quad Channel \rightarrow channel\ (Title, Description, Item)$,
$\quad Item \rightarrow item\ (Title, Description, PCData)$,
$\quad Title \rightarrow title\ (PCData)$,
$\quad Description \rightarrow description\ (PCData)$,
$\quad PCData \rightarrow pcdata\ (\epsilon)\}$

Fig. 4. Example of RL data and its MOT representation

Service component (SC) is a triplet (Name, Type, URL),where:

- Name is an unique identifier of a web service (WS) to be used in MashSheet,
- Type is the type of the WS,
- URL is unified resource locater of the WS,

When a SC is bound to a MashSheet cell, MashSheet creates an instance of the SC in the application. We call the instance of the SC as 'bound SC' and denote as SC^*. SC^* inherits all the attributes of the SC and has a new attribute: Location which is the address (a) of the SC in MashSheet.

Service-output component (OC) is a triplet (Name, OprCell, OutputCell), where:

- Name is an unique identifier of a service − output component,
- OprCell is the address (a) of the SC ,
- OutputCell is the address (a) of the OC.

For example, consider a simple MashSheet application as follow:

```
create('http : //www.ecubicle.net/driving.asmx?WSDL', 'DG')
(A1, = bind('DG'));
(B2, = invoke(A1.getDR(C1, C2)))
```

The first formula creates SC_{DG} = {DG, SOAP, http : //www.ecubicle.net/driving.asmx?WSDL} in the component repository. Evaluation of the formula in cell A1 creates: SC^*_{DG} = {DG, SOAP, http : //www.ecubicle.net/driving.asmx?WSDL, A1} and evaluation of the formula in cell B2 creates: OC_{DG} = {DG, A1, B2}.

5   MashSheet's Mashup Operators

MashSheet offers operators that support data, process (orchestration of services) and visualization operations in a mashup application. They are used in MashSheet formula and can be classified into four main categories: *life cycle, process, data* and *visualization*. In this section, we briefly introduce these operators.

5.1   Life Cycle Operators

MashSheet has three life cycle operators for the purpose of managing SC and SC* in the application: component creation, component deletion, service binding.

Component creation: create() registers a new SC to the component repository by importing the service interface referenced. This operator does not produce any data value in the MashSheet grid. For example, the following formula creates SC_{DG}:

$$= \texttt{create('http://www.ecubicle.net/driving.asmx?WSDL', 'DG')}$$

Component deletion: delete() removes the referenced SC from the component repository. Similar to create(), delete() does not affect the MashSheet's cell values since it is repository management operator. For example, the following formula removes SC_{DG} from the repository:

$$= \texttt{delete('DG')}$$

Component binding: bind() binds a SC to a specific cell and creates SC*. When the SC* is created, cell address (a) is used to identify the component and its operations are accessible by using dot notation. The incentive of using binding operator is that users can interact with a specific web service invocation within cells. For example, evaluation of the following cell binds SC_{DG} to cell B3 and creates (SC^*_{DG}):

$$(B3, = \texttt{bind('DG')})$$

Thereafter, Tom can refer to the operation of DG as B3.getDR(String, String). bind() has one input parameter which is SC and returns SC*. That is, it can be expressed as $\|(a, \texttt{bind(SC)})\|_s \rightarrow SC^*$.

5.2   Process Operators

MashSheet has three process operators for the purpose of supporting orchestration of web services: simple invocation, extended IF and synchronization. They are used to support modeling basic control flow patterns [17] in the application.

Simple invocation: invoke() is defined much of the same way as other spreadsheet-based mashup tools, however, in MashSheet, the output is held in a *OC* for further access and manipulation. For example, evaluation of the following cell invokes getDR() operation provided by SC^*_{DG} in cell B3 and holds the output data (OC_{DG}) in cell B5:

$$(B5, = \texttt{invoke(B3.getDR(B1, B13))})$$

invoke() has one parameter which is SC* and returns OC. That is, it would be expressed as $\|(a, \texttt{invoke(SC}^*))\|_s \rightarrow OC$.

Extended if: iff() is provided to model an exclusive choice pattern in conventional spreadsheet. Consider the exclusive choice case in our reference scenario. The pseudo code is represented as: If WF ='rain' Then DG Else BU. The semantically correct interpretation of this situation is that there is only one execution between DG and BU. But in conventional spreadsheets (and any other spreadsheet mashup tools we investigated), both DG and BU will run in order for the code/formula can be evaluated.

iff() has a condition and two SC* parameters and returns OC. It would be expressed as $\|(a, iff(condition, SC^*, SC^*))\|_s \rightarrow OC$. The semantic of iff() is defined as follow:

$$\|(a, iff(condition, opr_1, opr_2)\|_S = \begin{cases} \|(a, opr_1)\|_S & \text{if } condition = True \\ \|(a, opr_2)\|_S & \text{if } condition = False \end{cases}$$

For example, Figure 5 illustrates an exclusive choice scenario.

	A	B
1	Hotel address	115 Meeks st, Kingsford
2	=bind('RL')	=bind('DG')
3	=bind('BU')	=bind('WF')
4	=invoke(A2.read())	=invoke(B3.getForecast(B1))
5	=iff(B4.weatherInfo='Rain', invoke(B2.getDR(B1, A4.Channels[0].Items[0].Description)), invoke(A3.getBU(B1, A4.Channels[0].Items[0].Description)))	

Fig. 5. iff() example: User input is in cell B1; Service bindings are in cells A2:B3; Simple invocations are in cells A4:B4; Exclusive choice is in cell A5

Synchronization: sync() is provided to correctly support the semantic of AND-join (synchronization) and XOR-join (simple merge) in spreadsheet [17]. It has parameters which are SC* and a condition indicating the semantic of sync() (i.e., AND/XOR) and returns a Boolean value (α) indicating the joining status of participating service invocations: $\|(a, sync(SC^*, .., SC^*, condition))\|_s \rightarrow \alpha$. The semantic of AND-join is defined as follow:

$$\|(a, sync(opr_1, .., opr_n, AND)\|_S = \begin{cases} False & \text{if any } \|(a, opr_k)\|_S \,|k \in (1, n) \text{ has not evaluated} \\ True & \text{if all } \|(a, opr_k)\|_S \,|k \in (1, n) \text{ has evaluated} \end{cases}$$

The semantic of XOR-join is defined as follow:

$$\|(a, sync(opr_1, .., opr_n, XOR)\|_S = \begin{cases} False & \text{if no } \|(a, opr_k)\|_S \,|k \in (1, n) \text{ has evaluated} \\ True & \text{if any } \|(a, opr_k)\|_S \,|k \in (1, n) \text{ has evaluated} \end{cases}$$

For example, Figure 6 illustrates a synchronization scenario.

5.3 Data Operators

MashSheet provides eight data operators: union(), join(), merge(), merge_field(), rename_field(), filter(), filter_field() and sort() for manipulating with OC data. The main differences of these operators in comparison with data mashup operators in other spreadsheet-based mashup tools are:

	A	B
1	Hotel address	115 Meeks st, Kingsford
2	=bind('RL')	=bind('CL')
3	=sync(invoke(A2.read()), invoke(B2.read()), AND)	

Fig. 6. sync() example: User input is in cell B1; Service bindings are in cells A2:B2; sync() is in cell A3. Users check the value of A3 to see whether two invocations are synchronized or not.

- Input parameters of MashSheet data operators are XML data. Therefore, instead of mapping data into the grid before can run the operator (like in other tools), MashSheet data operators can run directly on the XML data. The operators can perform operations either on the structure of data (e.g., merge(), filter_field()) or on the data itself (e.g., filter(), sort()).
- Instead of immediately visualized in cells, the output of a data mashup operator are held in a cell for further processing by other data or visualization operators. These operators are motivated by the fact that intermediate data in a mashup application should be reused by others operators and visualized only when needed.

In this section, due to the space limitation, we only introduce the merge() operator. Full description of all operators is given in [9].

Merge: merge() combines two OCs in a uniform structure to an OC containing all the data from participating OCs. Evaluation of the cell containing merge() is defined as: $\|(a, \text{merge}(\text{OC}, \text{OC})\|_s \to \text{OC}$. We denote the first OC as $OS_1(N_1, T_1, B_1, P_1)$ and the second OC as $OC_2(N_2, T_2, B_2, P_2)$. The merge() operator runs on OC_1, OC_2 will produce a new $OC(N, T, B, P)$ with MOT representation as follow:

$$N = N_1 = N_2, T = T_1 = T_2, B = B_1 = B_2, P = P_1 = P_2$$

For example, consider the following cells. The formula in cell C3 merges the output data produced by RL's read() and CL's read() operations in cell A2 and B2.

$(A1, = \text{bind}(`RL'))$; $(B1, = \text{bind}(`CL'))$;
$(A2, = \text{invoke}(A1.\text{read}()))$; $(B2, = \text{invoke}(B1.\text{read}()))$;
$(C3, = \text{merge}(A2, B2))$

5.4   Visualization Operators

The goal of these operators is to separate the presentation layer from data layer so that users can visualize OC data using different layouts (e.g., grid, map). The separation is an important issue, especially when users want flexibility and reusability in creating their own display of OC data. Basically, visualization operators map a data space into a visual space. In our context, data space is OC and visual space is a set of cell addresses (A).

MashSheet visualization operator is a triplet $O = (D, V, R)$, where:

- D is an OC, OC = (N, T, B, P)
- V is a visual space including a set of cells addresses A
- R is a set of visualization rules, a rule $r \in R$ is a mapping $r : N \rightarrow V$

MashSheet contains two visualization operators: grid() and map():

Grid: grid() allows users to visualize OC data in a grid of cells. Evaluation of the cell containing grid() is defined as: $\|(a, grid(OC, \alpha, a)\|_s \rightarrow (a, .., a)$. There are two types of grid(): column and row identified by parameter α. Column (row) grid visualizes data as a horizontal (vertical) sequence of columns (rows) where a column (row) is constructed as a vertical (horizontal) sequence of attribute in N^* (N^* is a subset of N constructed by selecting all "leaf" nodes in the OC's tree). For example, Figure 7(a) and 7(b) present two scenarios when Tom visualizes the data produced by RL's read() operator in cell B1 by a range of cells which the top-left cell is cell A3.

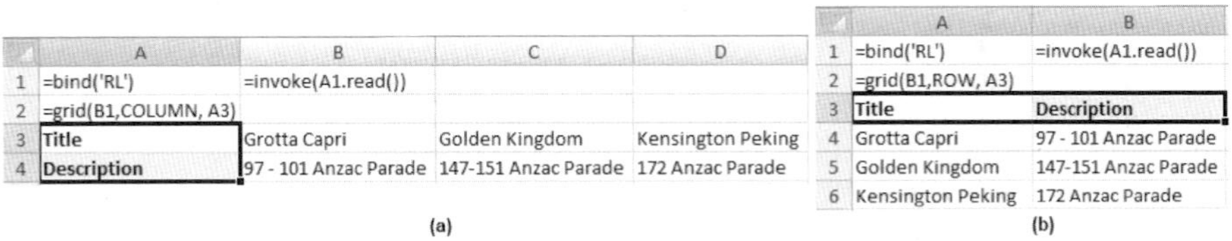

	A	B	C	D
1	=bind('RL')	=invoke(A1.read())		
2	=grid(B1,COLUMN, A3)			
3	Title	Grotta Capri	Golden Kingdom	Kensington Peking
4	Description	97 - 101 Anzac Parade	147-151 Anzac Parade	172 Anzac Parade

(a)

	A	B
1	=bind('RL')	=invoke(A1.read())
2	=grid(B1,ROW, A3)	
3	Title	Description
4	Grotta Capri	97 - 101 Anzac Parade
5	Golden Kingdom	147-151 Anzac Parade
6	Kensington Peking	172 Anzac Parade

(b)

Fig. 7. Visualize RL data by (a)column, (b)row

Map: map() lets users to visualize static data in an OC using a map interface. This operator creates a map object with points indicating the addresses and detail information about each point. For implementation purpose, we choose Google API as foundation of map provider. map() does not produce any data value in the MashSheet grid. Instead, it shows a map object as a gadget in the grid interface. We define a_0 is a special address representing a floating gadget. Evaluation of the cell containing map() is defined as: $\|(a, map(OC)\|_s \rightarrow (a_0)$. map() has two parameters which are addresses of the POIs and information adding to each POI. Users have to manually extract the data for these two parameters from an OC. Consider the following cells, evaluation of formula in cell B2 will get data produced by RL's read() operation in cell B1 and display it in a map object.

```
(A1, = bind('RL')); (B1, = invoke(A1.read()));
(B2, = map(B1.Channels.Items.Description, B1.Channels.Items.Title));
```

6   Building and Executing MashSheet Application

Figure 8 shows how Tom's scenario can be implemented using MashSheet. First, Tom defines cell B1 as the input area for entering hotel's address. He uses create() to register five components to the repository (not shown in the figure). He, then, binds five components to cells A3:B4, C3. Tom is now ready to invoke services and build the scenario:

	A	B	C
1	Hotel address	115 Meeks st, Kingsford	
2			
3	=bind('RL')	=bind('DG')	=bind('CL')
4	=bind('BU')	=bind('WF')	
5			
6	=invoke(A3.read())	=invoke(C3.read())	
7			=invoke(B4.getWeather(B1))
8	=sync(invoke(A3.read()), invoke(C3.read()), AND)		
9	=if(A8='True', merge(A6, B6))		
10			
11	=sort(A9, A9.Channels[0].Items, ASC)		
12			
13	=grid(A11, ROW, A14)		
14	Grotta Capri	97 - 101 Anzac Parade, Kensington	
15	Golden Kingdom	147-151 Anzac Parade, Kensington	
16	Kensington Peking	172 Anzac Parade, Kensington	
17			
18	=iff(C7.weatherInfo='Rain', invoke(B3.getDR(B1, B14), invoke(A4.getBU(B1, B14)))	=sync(invoke(B3.getDR(B1, B14), invoke(A4.getBU(B1, B14)), XOR)	
19			
20	=if (B18='True', grid(A18, COLUMN, A20))		
21	Head west on Meeks St toward Botany Ln	At the roundabout, take the 1st exit onto Harbourne Rd	Turn left at Barker St

Fig. 8. A running example implementing Tom's scenario. Note that in this figure we combine formula view and evaluation view in one worksheet due to the space limitation. In fact, the formulas will be evaluated to concrete data in the corresponding cells.

- He invokes the read() operations provided by RL and CL in cells A6 and B6 respectively, He also invokes getWeather() by WF in C7,
- Tom uses a sync() formula in cell A8 to check the synchronization status of two read() operations provided by RL and CL,
- After both RL and CL are completed, he merges the data in cell A6 and B6 and puts the result in cell A9[3],
- He then, sorts the content of A9 and put the result into A11. The sorting is done by the name column (i.e., A9.Channels[0].Items) in ascending order.
- In cell A13, Tom visualizes the data in cell A11 by a grid of cells which the top-left cell of the grid is cell A14.
- Tom enters the formula in cell A18 to get the direction from his hotel to the first POI in the list (in case WF reports rain, he uses DG otherwise he uses BU).
- Finally, he visualizes the direction produced in cell A18 in a grid of cells which the top-left cell is cell A21 by entering a formula in cell A20.

To build the MashSheet application, Tom needs to consider two aspects: (i) control flow: defines the order in which the cells' formulas are evaluated and the condition

---

[3] It is not shown in the figure for space reason, but the evaluation result of each operation is displayed on the component explorer (Figure 2 part 1.3) when associated cells are clicked.

under which a certain formula may or may not be evaluated; (ii) data flow: defines how data is passed between the evaluations of the formulas. We observe that spreadsheet evaluation engine only depends on data flow through cell referencing mechanism. In this framework, we extend the MashSheet language to support both control and data flows in a MashSheet application but still using spreadsheet-like language. We consider the basic control flow patterns as defined by [17], and explain how to model each pattern in the following:

Sequence can be modeled in MashSheet either by spatial arrangement of cells' formulas in a MashSheet application or by using cell referencing (the spatial arrangement of cells is considered first).

- Spatial arrangement: We define the spatial arrangement of the cell formulas as the evaluation order. Two formulas are sequentially evaluated if their cells are located in two *adjacent cells*. The evaluation order progresses from left to right and from top to bottom of the cell locations. For example, the group of cells A3: B4, C3 in Figure 8 are sequentially executed in the order:
  A3 → B3 → C3 → A4 → B4.
- Cell referencing: Two formulas are also considered sequentially evaluated if they have *input-output dependency* to each other. For example, the formula in cell A6 is evaluated after the evaluation of formula in cell A3 in Figure 8.

Parallel split can also be modeled either by spatial arrangement of cell's formulas or using cell referencing.

- Spatial arrangement: Two formulas are evaluated in parallel if their cells are located in two *non-adjacent cells without data dependency*. For example, cells A6 and C7 in Figure 8 are evaluated in parallel.
- Cell referencing: Two formulas are considered executed in parallel if they have *data dependency with the same data and have no data dependency to each other*. For example, cells A5 and B6 in Figure 9 are evaluated in parallel.

Exclusive choice can be modeled using iff() operator. For example, in Figure 8 the formula in cell A18 models an exclusive choice pattern.

Synchronization and Simple Merge can be modeled using sync() operator with AND and XOR parameters, respectively. For example, the sync() formula in A8 performs *synchronization* for the formulas in A6 and B6 are executed in parallel, whereas the sync() in B18 performs *simple merge* because the service invocations in iff() is done as *exclusive choice*.

	A	B	C
1	Original address	115 Meeks st, Kingsford	
2	Destination address	2 Addison st, Kensington	
3	=bind('DG')	=bind('BU')	
4			
5	=invoke(A3.getDR(B1, B2))		
6		=invoke(B3.getBU(B1, B2))	

Fig. 9. Parallel example with input-output dependency

Implementation. MashSheet is implemented as a plug-in of Microsoft Excel application. It extends the work presented in [15], which is mainly designed for presenting data services in spreadsheet. The language of choice for implementation is C# using Visual Studio for Office (VSTO) toolkit and the language for implementing evaluation engine is JScript. MashSheet GUI is implemented as a Task Pane in the Excel. RSS service is accessible by using open source library RSS.NET. We use applications provided in Microsoft .NET SDK to access SOAP services (e.g., wsdl.exe, csc.exe).

7   MashSheet Benchmark

In this section we evaluate the generic property of MashSheet against other spreadsheet-based mashup tools. The first group of dimensions examines the support for basic control flow patterns. The second group of dimensions looks at data mashup operation aspects and the last group includes visualization operators. Figure 10 shows the result. StrikeIron, SpreadMash and Mashroom do not support the dimensions in the first group since they are data mashup frameworks. SpreadMash supports "update to data" dimension since it allows users to update the change in spreadsheet to the data source. Mashroom supports all data dimensions. AMICO:CALC supports the basic control flow patterns, but it does not provide data mashup operators.

Dimensions		(1)	(2)	(3)	(4)	(5)	Dimensions		(1)	(2)	(3)	(4)	(5)
Basic control flow patterns	Sequence	-	+	-	-	+	**Data mashup operations**	Union	+	-	+	+	+
	Parallel split	-	+	-	-	+		Join	+	-	+	+	+
	Exclusive choice	-	+	-	-	+		Merge	+	-	-	+	+
	Sync	-	+	-	-	+		Merge field	-	-	+	+	+
	Simple merge	-	+	-	-	+		Rename field	-	-	-	+	+
Visualization operations	Create view	+	+	+	+	+		Filter	-	-	-	+	+
	Delete view	-	-	+	+	+		Filter field	+	-	+	+	+
	Update view	+	+	+	+	+		Sort	+	-	+	+	+
	Update to data	-	-	+	-	-							

Fig. 10. Benchmarking MashSheet and reviewed spreadsheet-based mashup tools: (1)StrikeIron, (2)AMICO:CALC, (3)SpreadMash, (4)Mashroom, (5)MashSheet

8   Conclusions and Future Works

In this paper, we introduced MashSheet - a generic purpose mashup framework that allows users to write mashup applications using spreadsheet formulas. In MashSheet, mashup applications can be built incrementally, producing intermediary results during the process. MashSheet has the following benefits: (i) the mashup language is based on a programming paradigm that many users are already familiar with, (ii) it considers not only data flow but also control flow in mashup development, and (iii) it allows flexible data visualization using visualization operators.

One might argue that the user interface for mashup development should be as simple as drag and drop, so that users do not have to write the formulas. However, drag-and-drop manipulations are only suitable for simple scenarios. We believe supporting formula-based scripting is more generic approach, making it applicable to more complex scenarios.

Currently, we are working on several areas to improve out framework. First, we are conducting an evaluation study to attain both qualitative and quantitative feedback on the feasibility of MashSheet as a generic mashup tool. We target the scientific workflow communities for obtaining concrete mashup scenarios for evaluating the tool. This will also lead to extending our range of supported service interface types. An important feature we would like to integrate into MashSheet is reusability. By supporting reuse, a mashup application in MashSheet will be considered as a service component which can be invoked from other applications.

References

1. Mapcruncher,
   http://research.microsoft.com/en-us/um/redmond/projects/mapcruncher
2. Programmableweb.com,
   http://www.programmableweb.com/mashups/directory
3. Rss.net library, http://www.rssdotnet.com
4. Strikeiron web services for excel, http://www.strikeiron.com
5. Yahoo pipes, http://pipes.yahoo.com
6. Abraham, R., Erwig, M.: Type inference for spreadsheets. In: Proceedings of the 8th ACM SIGPLAN, (PPDP 2006) (2006)
7. Fischer, T., Bakalov, F., Nauerz, A.: An overview of current approaches to mashup generation. In: Wissensmanagement, pp. 254–259 (2009)
8. D. Hinchcliffe. The 10 top challenges facing enterprise mashups,
   http://www.zdnet.com/blog/hinchcliffe/the-10-top-challenges-facing-enterpris
9. Hoang, D.D., Paik, H.Y.: Spreadsheet as a generic purpose mashup development environment. Technical report, The University of New South Wales, Sydney, Australia (2010)
10. Hoang, D.D., Paik, H.Y., Benatallah, B.: An analysis of spreadsheet-based services mashup. In: Proceeding of the ADC 2010, Brisbane, Australia (2010)
11. Jones, S.P., Blackwell, A., Burnett, M.: A user-centred approach to functions in excel. In: Proceedings of the ICFP 2003, Uppsala, Sweden (2003)
12. Kongdenfha, W., Benatallah, B., Saint-Paul, R., Casati, F.: Spreadmash: A spreadsheet-based interactive browsing and analysis tool for data services. In: Bellahsène, Z., Léonard, M. (eds.) CAiSE 2008. LNCS, vol. 5074, pp. 343–358. Springer, Heidelberg (2008)
13. Murata, M., Lee, D., Mani, M., Kawaguchi, K.: Taxonomy of xml schema languages using formal language theory. ACM T. Internet Tech. 5(4), 660–704 (2005)
14. Obrenovic, Z., Gasevicc, D.: End-user service computing: Spreadsheets as a service composition tool. IEEE Transactions on Services Computing (2008)
15. Saint Paul, R., Benatallah, B., Vayssière, J.: Data services in your spreadsheet! In: Proceedings of EDBT 2008 (Demo), Nantes, France, pp. 690–694 (2008)
16. Scaffidi, C., Shaw, M., Myers, B.: Estimating the numbers of end users and end user programmers. In: Proceedings of the VLHCC 2005, Dallas, USA (2005)
17. Van Der Aalst, W.M.P., Ter Hofstede, A.H.M., Kiepuszewski, B., Barros, A.P.: Workflow patterns. Distrib. Parallel Databases 14(1), 5–51 (2003)
18. Wang, G., Yang, S., Han, Y.: Mashroom: end-user mashup programming using nested tables. In: Proceedings of the WWW 2009, Madrid, Spain (2009)

Combining Enforcement Strategies
in Service Oriented Architectures

Gabriela Gheorghe[1], Bruno Crispo[1],
Daniel Schleicher[2], Tobias Anstett[2], Frank Leymann[2],
Ralph Mietzner[2], and Ganna Monakova[2]

[1] University of Trento, Italy
First.Last@disi.unitn.it
[2] University of Stuttgart, Germany
Last@iaas.uni-stuttgart.de

Abstract. Business regulations on enterprise applications cover both infrastructure and orchestration levels of the Service-Oriented Architecture(SOA) environment. Thus, for a correct and efficient enforcement of such requirements, full integration among different enforcement middleware is necessary. Based on previous work [1], we make a comparison between enforcement capabilities at business and infrastructure levels. Our contribution is to make a first step towards a policy enforcement model that combines the strengths of the orchestration level enforcement mechanisms with those of the message bus. The advantage of such a model is (1) that infrastructure and orchestration requirements are enforced by the most appropriate mechanisms, and (2) the ability to enforce regulations that would be otherwise impossible to enforce by a single mechanism. We present the architecture and a first prototype of such a model to show its feasibility.

Keywords: policy enforcement, SOA, BPEL, ESB.

1 Introduction

There is an increasing number of regulations that all enterprise applications have to comply with. These regulations usually concretise in policies on data protection, system behaviour and resource or organisational management (e.g., EU Directives[1], Basel3 and Sarbanes-Oxley[14]). Such constraints crosscut enterprise applications.

Achieving compliance with such regulations can be done through policy enforcement. From our point of view, this enforcement comes in two flavours: message or infrastructure level enforcement mechanisms and orchestration level enforcement mechanisms. Mechanisms at the message level focus on technical details like communication protocols (e.g., SOAP, REST), message transformation (e.g., XSLT) or choice of message routes. They are typically embedded within an Enterprise Service Bus (ESB). Regulatory enforcement at the ESB level cannot normally go higher than controlling message flows between physical endpoints or binding virtual endpoints to actual endpoints. Concepts

---

[1] European Commision EC-95/46 http://ec.europa.eu/justice_home/fsj/
privacy/docs/95-46-ce/dir1995-46_part1_en.pdf

P.P. Maglio et al. (Eds.): ICSOC 2010, LNCS 6470, pp. 288–302, 2010.

at higher levels address issues related to orchestration or choreography of activities. At this level business processes and business process engines are used. Examples on this level are based on the Business Process Execution Language (BPEL).

The gap between these two enforcement capabilities at the two levels is illustrated by a real use case: the Hong Kong Red Cross[2] implements its blood donation process in a SOA. In order to stay compliant with existing laws and regulations, the Red Cross needs to enforce the following policy: mutual exclusiveness of doctors approving blood donation and distribution. The first policy is a policy most easily enforced at the message level because location information is only managed at this level. The second is a Separation of Duty (SoD) requirement saying that the same actor in an application is not allowed to perform two conflicting operations. This can be enacted on a BPEL engine by inhibiting one operation if the other operation has been previously performed by the same actor. While the BPEL engine can disallow a process to handle the request to perform an action, the problem is that the process has *already* received the request. If this request contains sensitive information, the BPEL engine cannot prevent it from arriving on the machine where it will be inhibited, and this may cause a data privacy breach over which the BPEL process has no control.

It follows that enforcing policies of message level at the orchestration level or vice versa is awkward for a number of reasons. First, it requires pulling data and associations that are not available to one layer or the other. Second, the policy specification is more complicated and hence prone to errors. Third, there is a tight dependency between the policy languages at each level, and the limits of their enforcement. Also, for management reasons it is advisable to have all policies in one language, and in one place, since this makes deployment and review much easier. We follow this idea and suggest a centralised enforcement model that discovers enforcement capabilities advertised at both process engine and message level. The model decides where to enforce which policy constraints, and how to map these constraints to the existing capabilities at the right level. In our Red Cross example, presented in the next section, we envision the same SoD constraint enforced correctly by combining the BPEL-level check with ESB's capability to resolve the second operation to an endpoint that is surely operated by a different actor. Hence, our approach extends typical ESB and BPEL engine features, and combines rather than separates the resulting enforcement strengths.

The remainder of the paper is structured as follows. Giving a motivating example, the gaps between BPEL engine and ESB enforcement as non-integrated components are described in Section 2. Section 3 presents extensions of the ESB and BPEL engine to address the enforcement limitations and also a general enforcement model. Section 4 shows how to join the two different sets of capabilities. Implementation considerations are presented in Section 5. Problems with current approaches are given in Section 6, and Section 7 concludes.

2   Motivating Example

In this section we use a real example to show the drawbacks of performing enforcement by focusing on either BPEL engines or ESBs. In many countries the name *Red*

---

[2] http://www.redcross.org.hk/en/home.html

Cross encompasses those organisations dedicated to emergency situations and health care. The Hong Kong Red Cross (HKRC) organisation manages, among other things, blood donations for a number of public hospitals [12]. The organisation acts as an intermediary between blood donors, hospitals, and patients (blood receivers). Both the HKRC and the hospitals have to comply with regulations defined by government health agencies. These regulations relate to the blood treatment and donor data:

- The same doctor cannot approve both a blood donation and the distribution of that blood sample to a public hospital. (**Regulation 1**)
- The temperature of the blood samples must always be below zero degrees Celsius. (**Regulation 2**)
- The Red Cross must distribute the donated blood within 2 days after the blood is collected in an HKRC branch. (**Regulation 3**)

Complying with these regulations means understanding how to detect and react to violations. For example *Regulation 1* requires a differentiation between users of the Hong Kong Red Cross so that a doctor approving a blood donation cannot approve the blood distribution afterwards. *Regulation 2* requires sensors detecting temperature changes to a component responsible for monitoring temperatures and triggering reactions. *Regulation 3* requires that blood can only be collected from an HKRC branch and forbids blood distribution after more than 2 days after the collection.

Regulations 1-3 above also concern internal business processes of the HKRC, such as the *blood donation management process*. Figure 1 illustrates the interface between the donors and the blood donation management process. We use this process in a slightly changed form in the remainder of this work. The process is modeled as a WS-BPEL process that orchestrates the Web services connected by an ESB.

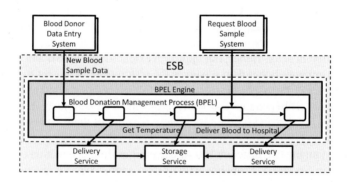

Fig. 1. The Red Cross blood sample management process

The blood donation management process is modeled with respect to regulation 2. For every blood donation a process instance is created; this instance continuously polls the temperature of the corresponding blood storage system until the blood sample is requested or regulation 2 was violated. The violation is detected by the evaluation of a condition (similar to if-else structures) defined on the returned temperature. Despite being the only implemented solution of enforcing SoD constraints, this BPEL-only implementation falls short in several respects: (1) tagging and sending the blood for cooling are logical invocations whose execution the BPEL engine cannot control down to the message level; (2) the BPEL process does not distinguish between service invocations emitted or served by the same host; (3) the BPEL process does not manipulate service location information. These three aspects are covered by ESB capabilities, and to our knowledge there is no approach that tries to link ESB with BPEL engine features for the purpose of fine-grained policy enforcement.

In the following section we discuss in more detail the limitations of performing policy enforcement only at the level of business processes, or only at the ESB level. We show how Regulations 1-3 can be realised with our combined approach.

3   SOA Enforcement: Current Approaches versus Our Approach

In this section we show architectural approaches to do enforcement and present the enforcement capabilities of current BPEL engines and ESBs. We also show a policy model describing how to use these enforcement capabilities in a distributed and automated environment. In what follows, we use the term *SOA enforcement* to refer to the operation of the service-oriented mechanisms whose job is to ensure that requirements of an enterprise policy (on security or performance) are satisfied. We also use the concept of an *enforcement life cycle* as a three-step mechanism. Given a policy to be enacted, the first step is *to detect* the events relevant to the policy; the second step is *to decide* whether the detected events constitute a violation of the policy. The last step is *to react* as specified by the policy. Drawing this line between the enforcement steps helps to localise the shortcomings of current approaches.

3.1   Different Architectural Approaches

Let us consider the separation of duty regulation (Regulation 1) from above: *The same doctor cannot approve both a blood donation and the distribution of that blood sample to a public hospital.* Enforcing this constraint requires to detect (1) on which doctor's behalf the donation approval service operates, (2) on which doctor's behalf the blood distribution service operates, and (3) the identifier of the blood sample. Figure 2 shows different approaches to enforce such a policy. An initial approach is to weave enforcement features into the donation approval service and the blood distribution service (Figure 2.A). The enforcement mechanism here couples all three stages of the enforcement life cycle (detect, decide, react). Changing the reaction or detection criteria implies that the donation approval service or blood distribution service code must be changed. An improved approach is wrapping: bundling the donation approval service and the blood distribution service with enforcement stubs to make any policy change independent from the service logic (Figure 2.B). This approach does not scale with the policy growth and burdens the two service nodes with heavy processing because the wrapper is on the same node as the business logic. Figure 2.C shows a further improvement: *enforcement as a service.* External enforcement services make enforcement reusable for

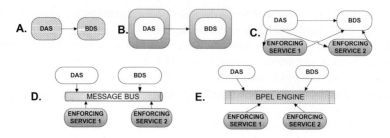

Fig. 2. Different architectures for SOA enforcement. BDS stands for Blood Distribution Service. DAS stands for Donation Approval Service.

other services, but are bypassable and not very scalable. If the blood distribution service or the donation approval service is contacted on a channel that cannot be reached by the enforcement service it cannot be detected that the same doctor performs the same operation for both services. Worse, for every new constraint on the communication between the two services there will have to be a new enforcement service to enforce it.

A further logical step is to employ the message bus (ESB) as a communication channel to and from all services in an enterprise system (Figure 2.D). The ESB solves the bypassability and overloading issues mentioned before. Since it mediates all communication between the donation approval service and the blood distribution service, all relevant messages will be unnoticed before they are dispatched to their destination. All enforcement mechanisms for any policy will have to be deployed to the bus, and the ESB will ensure that messages are dispatched to the right destinations. The ESB falls short in handling correlated enforcement actions that need access to the semantics of the messages: the ESB by itself cannot easily detect that the same doctor performs the same operation on the same blood sample. This correlation problem is solved by the BPEL engine (Figure 2.E). In case there are several constraints on the communication related to the donation approval service and the blood distribution service, an enhanced BPEL engine can be used to orchestrate the way in which the different policies are enforced by their respective services. Conversely, message routing and endpoint resolution is where BPEL falls short. The BPEL engine can enforce the separation of logical users running the approval and distribution of the blood sample. But it cannot impose that this happens in every case. The mapping between the users and their machines is done by the ESB and not BPEL. Hence for a given blood sample, the ESB can ultimately resolve the blood distribution service endpoint to a machine that is different from the one on which the donation approval service has happened. Since it is realistic to assume each doctor has its own machine, then the separation of duty constraint is satisfied because different machines mean different doctors.

Having shown some important limitations of current ESB and BPEL approaches, in what follows we present a more detailed study of the enforcement capabilities of these two SOA components. Based on this we show how the enforcement capabilities of the ESB and the ones of the BPEL engine can be combined to do policy enforcement.

3.2 BPEL Engine Enforcement Capabilities

There are three main categories of *standard capabilities* that a common BPEL engine can employ for the detection of policy violations: observation, event triggering, and event aggregation.

- Observation of events: BPEL engines can observe events occurring during the execution of a process. The execution history of all process instances is saved in the audit trail, and the data can be later used for an analysis if a certain condition has become true.
- Triggering of events: BPEL engines are capable of triggering events at state changes during the execution of a BPEL process. Events that occur during the execution of a BPEL process are saved in the audit trail. The audit trail can be used to monitor the execution of all running instances of all deployed process models on a BPEL engine. A process instance can also be started when a message or event has arrived at the BPEL engine.
- Aggregation of events. In a BPEL engine, event aggregation is implicitly done by an internal component called the process navigator. The navigator is responsible for the execution of the activities defined in a BPEL process. One feature of the navigator is the initialisation of a new activity if the required previous activities have completed or faulted. The navigator of a BPEL engine is notified by an event that the preceding activity has ended. Such events can also be made visible to the outside for complex event aggregation, e.g. by emitting an event containing the aggregated information of several events.

Functionalities covering the reaction step of the enforcement life cycle include the suspension and termination of process instances. These enforcement abilities are part of the standard abilities of the BPEL engine we use in our prototype. To further support enforcement we enriched the BPEL engine with *additional* reaction abilities: functionality to block and unblock processes, to insert, delete, and modify activities, and to modify variables [3].

- Termination and suspension of process instances: A BPEL engine is capable of terminating and suspending running process instances. This means it is possible to stop a process instance that behaves in a way that violates policies. Terminated process instances cannot be reactivated; suspended process instances can be resumed.
- Block or un-block process instances: The execution of running BPEL processes can be blocked when a certain event occurs. This is the difference to the suspension of a process instance described before. To unblock a process instance another event needs to occur. This can be, for example, an unblock message coming from a policy decision component.
- Insertion, deletion, and modification of activities of a running process instance: It is possible to insert new activities into running process instances. For long running process instances this is a means to implement new policies that were not present when the process instance was initiated. The changes performed onto process instances can be mapped to the underlying process model. This procedure has been previously called *instance migration* [10].

– Modification of variables and activities: Variables and activities of running process instances can be modified to lead the process execution to a direction that avoids the violation of policies.

The BPEL engine inherently keeps track of the state of the process instances running on it. In case of an emergency shut down most BPEL engines persist the states of all running processes on disk so that they can be resumed after a restart. BPEL internal fault and compensation handling is not always visible to the outside, thus it must be signalled and enforced within the BPEL engine. State keeping helps to make BPEL-level enforcement decisions, but an enforcement decision maker on the BPEL engine cannot come off-the-shelf.

3.3   ESB Enforcement Capabilities

In this section we show enforcement aspects that are typical for an ESB and cannot happen on a BPEL engine. Following the enforcement life cycle model, detection in the ESB happens specifically on message flows. It encompasses endpoint resolution, observation, triggering of events, blocking of a message flow and transformation of messages. This functionality is provided by default in standard ESB platforms.

– Endpoint resolution: Endpoint resolution is one of the two main functions of the ESB. Resolving endpoints means matching a virtual endpoint to a physical endpoint in a service registry. The ESB uses its own protocols for this matching.
– Observation: The ESB mediates all messages flowing through. These message flows can be logged for later analysis.
– Triggering of messages: ESBs are capable of emitting events, usually when a certain message arrives. Hence when a certain message is received, the system is injected with a generated event. At message-level, both the message and the event can be either a service invocation, a service response, or a fault raised in the application.
– Blocking message flows: ESBs offer the possibility to react synchronously to incoming or outgoing messages. This means that when a certain message has been received or is about to be dispatched, the ESB can perform an action before routing the message to its destination.
– Transformation of messages: ESBs are capable of aggregating, splitting, filtering, and processing the messages that they route from one endpoint to another. Processing of messages on certain criteria is covered generically by enterprise integration patterns. Standard patterns like the message splitter, message aggregator, and message filter are already implemented in a number of ESB platforms.

The added enforcement functionalities that were suggested and implemented in our previous work [1] cover the reaction step of the ESB enforcement life cycle. They include:

– Modification of a message: The ESB has control over the messages between the source endpoint and destination endpoint. This implies that it can modify parts of the message, be it the message metadata (source, destination, security headers, etc.) or the message payload. Usually the ESB can discern between payload and routing information. Still, the payload is not always accessible to the ESB, for instance when it is encrypted.

– Rerouting messages: Rerouting messages can be done on the fly by sending a message not to its intended destination, but to another endpoint. Rerouting can serve multiple enforcement functions, e.g., block the initial destination endpoint from receiving a message or to retain the message for a limited amount of time.
– Inserting messages: ESB traffic can be duplicated among endpoints, as the ESB can insert messages into existing flows.

While the BPEL engine handles logical flows between logical endpoints, the ESB handles correspondence with the real endpoints. The ESB features native endpoint name resolution, message processing, message reliability and delivery mechanisms. For instance, the ESB has access to service metadata such as: position information, interface information, intra-service protocols, user tags, and ranking or price of a service. Endpoint resolution means the ability to choose another endpoint for a message depending on various parameters. Non-functional runtime aspects like traffic load and trust can influence the flow of messages between endpoints. The message flow can be controlled by the ESB at the infrastructure level. Similar to the case of the BPEL engine, the ESB does not come with decision making support with respect to any kind of constraints.

Table 1 shows a comparison of the new enforcement capabilities we added to the ESB [1] and the BPEL engine. It summarises our efforts to provide two middleware components with extended support for enforcement in an SOA. The fact that the BPEL engine and the ESB have two distinct feature sets in terms of enforcement emphasises that there is a need to combine these enforcement capabilities.

Table 1. Comparison of new Enforcement Capabilities of ESB and BPEL engine

New Enforcement Capability	BPEL engine	ESB
Modification of Messages	-	×
Rerouting Messages	-	×
Insertion of Messages	-	×
Block / Unblock Process	×	-
Termination / Suspension of Process Instances	×	-
Insertion, Deletion, and Modification of Activities	×	-
Modification of Process Variables	×	-

3.4   Enforcement Policy Model

To automatically react to critical states of a system, there have to be machine readable policies describing what should happen when the system reaches a certain state or tries a transition from one state to another. In this section we present a model of the information needed in an enterprise policy for regulatory compliance. With this model it is possible to describe enforcement actions on single SOA components like a BPEL engine or an ESB or on a combination of these components. We use this policy model in the Sections 4 and 5 to show the interaction between an ESB and a BPEL engine during the execution of an enforcement action.

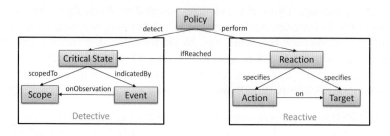

Fig. 3. Policy Content

Figure 3 shows the model specifying the content of the enforcement policy. It consists of two parts. The detective part specifies the critical state of the system to observe and how this state can be detected. The components that need to be observed in order to detect the critical state constitute the scope of the detective part. For example, in order to ensure encrypted communication between services S_1 and S_2, all messages sent between these services must be observed. A critical state in this case would be indicated by the detection of an unencrypted message. The reactive part specifies what actions should be taken if the critical state is reached and what are the targets of the actions. In the previous example, a reaction can be the encryption of the message. In this case *message* is the target of the action *encrypt*.

To enforce a policy, the decisions have to be made as to where the detective measures for the policy have to take place and where the reactions have to be executed. The decision is made based on the policy content, particularly on the observational scope and on the targets the reactive actions need to be performed on, and on the capabilities of the enforcement components, in particular ESB and BPEL engine, which are described in a service catalogue. Thereby detective and reactive parts can be performed by different enforcement components. Currently, the decision regarding whether the policy is enforced on a BPEL engine or on an ESB is made at the design time and must satisfy the following two criteria:

1. Detective part: The enforcement component must be able to observe the components specified in the scope
2. Reactive part: The enforcement component must be able to perform specified actions on the specified target

These criteria restrict the number of options to the components which are capable to enforce the given policy. For example, a BPEL engine would not be able to observe communications between services if this communication is not part of a business process running on this engine. Similarly, an ESB would not be able to control internal control and data flow of a business process. The ESB actions primarily target a *message* and are scoped to the observation of the messages that flow between the services that use this ESB. The BPEL engine actions, on the other hand, target *process, process instance, process activity, process activity instance*. Thus, if a policy specifies *Ensure that every instance of a business process performs activity Approve on Blood Sample*, then the target is clearly a business process and at least the detection of the critical state should go to the BPEL engine. If the policy on the other hand says *Ensure that all messages between $S_1, ..., S_n$ are encrypted*, then the observation scope and the action target is a *message* and clearly belongs to the ESB. However, service invocations can be controlled on both ESB and BPEL level: on the BPEL level by controlling *invoke* activities that invoke a service, and on the ESB level by controlling the invocation message.

To demonstrate the differences and similarities between ESB and BPEL level enforcements in our case, consider the first example regulation specified in Section 2: *The same doctor cannot approve both a blood donation and the distribution of that blood sample to a public hospital.* The critical state of a policy guarding this regulation can be specified as *The doctor to have approved a blood donation wants to distribute the blood sample* with the corresponding reactive part of *Block blood sample distribution by the doctor.* To detect the critical state, two services S_1 performing *blood donation* and S_2 performing *blood distribution* need to be observed. If these services are invoked from the same business process BP_1, then the observation can be mapped to the observation of the corresponding *invoke* activities of BP_1 and thus can be done on the BPEL engine level. The reactive part in this example is specified by action *block* on target S_2, which can also be mapped to the blocking of the corresponding *invoke* activity on BPEL level. However, if usage of S_1 and S_2 is not coordinated by a single business process, for example when blood donation and blood distribution are parts of different business processes, then additional correlation of the service invocations is required. In this case the ESB can carry out the necessary message correlation to detect a critical state and block messages to the service S_2. In general, when the policy controls the usage of services $S_1, ..., S_n$, both ESB and BPEL can be used for its enforcement. In this case, the decision of which to use must be made by the designer based on the current system implementation and with the goal to minimize distribution of the policy enforcement. For example, when these services are invoked from multiple points but all invocations flow through one ESB, this ESB can intercept requests from different processes and services at one centralized point. A BPEL engine in this case would need an extra policy for each BPEL engine that runs processes that invoke these services, and thus would have multiple enforcement points. Similarly, if a set of services that need to be observed are invoked from a single business process, then their usage can be controlled at one centralized point on the BPEL engine level.

4 Combination of Enforcement Capabilities

The ESB complements the process engine enforcement because it performs complete mediation, endpoint resolution and leverages communication disparities. These disparities are often unavoidable because providers do not reveal the implementation of their services. To the usually stateless controls offered by the ESB, the BPEL engine provides a central point of coordination and global state management. ESB capabilities fit better with a cross-domain stateless enforcement, while the process engine better serves enforcing complex actions to achieve adherence to a common policy.

As described in sections 3.2 and 3.3, we have extended an ESB and a BPEL engine with added functionality for enforcement. Both components have been extended independently to meet enforcement requirements in their respective domain. In order to

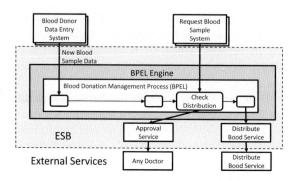

Fig. 4. Original implementation of the blood donation management process

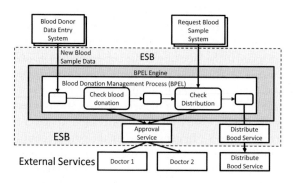

Fig. 5. Modified implementation of the blood donation management process. Also shows ESB responsible for choosing the doctor to approve the requests.

make best use of enforcement functionalities of both ESBs and BPEL engines we need to combine them. In the following we show how the combination of both enforcement capabilities works in a use case scenario.

Let us assume the Hong Kong Red Cross has a BPEL process for managing blood donations shown in Figure 4. This process is out-dated: it does not implement Regulation 1 as stated in Section 2 because it only has one check activity instead of the required two. There also is no policy deployed in the ESB ensuring the adherence to Regulation 1. The activity labelled *Check Distribution* is responsible to check if a blood sample can be distributed. The ESB forwards any approval request to any doctor being currently in charge for approvals in the hospital.

Figure 5 shows the new blood donation management process with Regulation 1 implemented. To implement Regulation 1, a new activity labelled *Check blood donation* has been inserted into the process model. Already running instances have been changed on the fly by using the activity insertion enforcement mechanism of the BPEL engine. The Approval service in the ESB has not been changed. No new endpoint has been introduced for the new check activity. Instead a new enforcement policy has been added to the ESB stating that two approval requests from the same process instance are routed

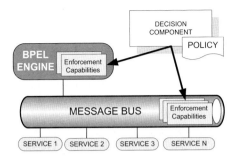

Fig. 6. The architecture implementing the enforcement life cycle. The arrows to the right indicate that the decision component uses the interfaces provided by the ESB and BPEL engine for detection and reaction to violations.

to distinct doctors. Of course, an underlying assumption is that every doctor is using the system from a physically different endpoint, so that the ESB can differentiate between doctors. When the same endpoint is operated by two different doctors for two different actions, the ESB cannot go beyond ESB endpoint information, which is normally not associated with user data. With extra information from the outside, the ESB can be helped to route to distinct doctor endpoints on the same machine.

Enforcement actions affecting the control flow of a business process are meant to be executed on a BPEL engine. It is possible to influence the control flow of a workflow from the outside by modifying input messages. To do this, deep knowledge of the workflow is needed in order to be capable of doing the right modifications to the input data. Therefore we propose to execute enforcement actions that affect the control flow of a workflow directly on the BPEL engine. On the other hand enforcement actions that have to do with message routing or endpoint resolution of Web services are better to be executed on the ESB.

We envision an architecture that joins the capabilities of the message bus with those of the BPEL engine, as shown in Figure 6. There can be one or more BPEL engines deployed to the bus to orchestrate the execution of a business process. The enforcement capabilities of these engines, as well as that of the ESB, are made available to a higher-level enforcement component that we call the *decision component*. As mentioned earlier, neither the message bus nor the BPEL engine offer any explicit support for enforcement decision making. Our suggested decision component will discover the ESB and BPEL detection capabilities (as described in Section 3.4), and will make a decision of how to react to a possible violation of a policy. This reaction can be either at the BPEL, at the ESB level, or at both levels. For the moment, the way to decide between these two cases is by checking an explicit flag in the policy, stating that its target it located at one level or the other. Thus, we rely on the policy writer to specify what part of the policy is linked to the ESB and what part to the BPEL instance. Keeping the decision component away from either the ESB or the BPEL engine makes the decision component independent of the limitations of either layer. In this way, the enforcement assurance of the composite will incorporate both types of message-level and BPEL engine capabilities.

5   Implementation Considerations

In this section we show how the prototypes of an ESB and a BPEL engine implement the enforcement life cycle. We use Regulation 1 from Section 2 to show an example of how the ESB and BPEL engine work together to perform an enforcement action.

First, we instrumented Apache ServiceMix 3.0[3] to offer hooks to message interception, default endpoint resolution and message modification. ServiceMix offers an interface for intercepting all messages at the level of the Normalised Message Router. We employ this interface for *detection*: we direct all intercepted messages to a Decision Component shown in Figure 6. Before being directed to this component, messages can be filtered based on message metadata like message destination, message source, and user data. As *reaction*, we added a set of Web services to the message bus that can perform the following enforcement actions: block a message, modify a message, delay a message for a defined period of time and insert a message into the message flow. These Web services act within the message router, before or after a message is dispatched.

Second, we extended the Apache ODE BPEL[4] engine with enforcement capabilities to block and unblock a running BPEL process. The concepts of the prototype are based on two previous approaches [3,4]. The first approach proposes an architecture to extend ODE to emit all events occurring when a process is executed. The BPEL engine is enhanced with a component to extract the internal events (*detection*). The other approach shows a management framework for BPEL based on Web service Resource Framework (WS-RF). Here, we use WS-RF to expose every BPEL process deployed on the Apache ODE BPEL engine as a resource (*detection*). This resource can be queried and changed. The changes are mapped back to the referred BPEL process (*reaction*).

Web service interfaces link enforcement on the Apache ODE BPEL engine with enforcement on the modified message bus. All SOAP messages produced by the ODE BPEL engine and possible application services are routed through the ESB. The ESB can access the BPEL engine capabilities, and hence ask for orchestration of enforcement actions or events occurring at the BPEL level. Conversely, the BPEL engine will access ESB messages and ask to perform message modification actions at the message level.

How is Regulation 1 enforced with this implementation? The ESB detects all incoming requests to the check blood donation and the check distribution services. All incoming requests to the former are let to pass unaltered. All incoming requests to the check distribution service are blocked waiting for an enforcement decision. A copy of the request to the check distribution services is sent to the decision component. The decision component will record in a forbidden address parameter the physical location of the doctor to which this request was directed, as well as the blood sample id. For each request, the decision component will check if the blood sample id is the same as in a previous check blood donation request.

If so, the decision component will invoke an enforcement operation at the BPEL engine in order to send the check distribution request again with a new addressee. The new request is again blocked by the ESB. After a check by the decision component, the block is released and the message is forwarded to the right doctor performing the check.

---

[3] http://servicemix.apache.org/home.html
[4] http://ode.apache.org

The Decision Component shown in Figure 6 is for now manual. It is performed by a human administrator declaring a list of doctors who cannot invoke the same Web service operations.

6   Related Work

In SOA enforcement, there has been no approach, yet that covers the enforcement life cycle in its entirety: (1) observation of events, (2) decision of right countermeasures, and (3) execution of a reaction. Moser et al. introduce the VieDAME4BPEL framework for monitoring BPEL processes and enforcing the replacement of partner services [8]. An interception and adaption layer allows to intercept outbound messages, monitor messages, apply message transformations, and replace services. Monitoring inbound messages and state changes is not discussed. This is a basic requirement to react to possible faulty behaviour of a BPEL process. Another approach supporting the dynamic change of workflows is $ADEPT_{flex}$ [9]. $ADEPT_{flex}$ defines a set of change operations which can be used to adapt the structure of a running workflow. Conducting automatic changes to the running workflow is not intended by the solution.

In [13] Tsai et al. propose an event driven framework to enforce policies in an SOA environment. In this work a BPEL engine is instrumented to emit events for certain state changes of a running BPEL process. These events are then aggregated by a so called global policy engine and forwarded to a local policy engine. This policy engine is responsible for executing the necessary enforcement action. There is no explanation on what enforcement actions are possible and how these actions are executed.

Research in SOA enforcement that considers message-level enforcement has a lot of generic models [11,5,2]. Neither of these solutions discusses how the enforcement at the message bus layer actually happens, so that it can be linked with the orchestration level. More relevant to our viewpoint are the message-level enforcement frameworks that are scoped to SOA governance [6,7]. These approaches hint to the centralization of policy management, when policies pertain to different abstraction layers. None of the solutions above separate between message-level and BPEL engine-level enforcement capabilities. To our knowledge, our work is the first to suggest to combine important SOA components on the stages of the enforcement life cycle.

7   Conclusion and Future Work

This paper introduces a new approach and model for ensuring policy enactment in enterprise applications. Our approach extends and combines BPEL and ESB capabilities on the framework of a SOA policy model. It is an architecture by which BPEL enforcement can use ESB abilities for policy enforcement, and vice versa. This is done by exposing these capabilities via enforcement interfaces and already implemented in the prototype. For future work, we will add mechanisms to automatically react to policy violations. For now, the decision making component decides whether to delegate the enforcement actions to the ESB or the BPEL levels based on flags contained in the policies. We aim to investigate the extent to wich this process can be automated, along with its granularity. Also, the ongoing work on our prototype will be extended with several case studies to show what is the impact of our model on the business process execution.

Acknowledgement

The work published in this article has partially received funding from the European Community's 7th Framework Programme Information Society Technologies Objective under the MASTER project[5] contract no. FP7-216917.

References

1. Gheorghe, G., Neuhaus, S., Crispo, B.: xESB: An enterprise service bus for access and usage control policy enforcement. In: Uehara, T. (ed.) IFIPTM 2010. LNCS, vol. 321, pp. 63–78. Springer, Heidelberg (2010)
2. Goovaerts, T., De Win, B., Joosen, W.: Infrastructural support for enforcing and managing distributed application-level policies. Electron. Notes Theor. Comput. Sci. 197(1), 31–43 (2008)
3. Khalaf, R., Karastoyanova, D., Leymann, F.: Pluggable framework for enabling the execution of extended bpel behavior. In: Di Nitto, E., Ripeanu, M. (eds.) ICSOC 2007. LNCS, vol. 4907, pp. 376–387. Springer, Heidelberg (2009)
4. van Lessen, T., Leymann, F., Mietzner, R., Nitzsche, J., Schleicher, D.: A Management Framework for WS-BPEL. In: Proceedings of the 6th IEEE European Conference on Web Services 2008, pp. 187–196. IEEE Computer Society, Los Alamitos (November 2008)
5. Leune, K., van den Heuvel, W.J., Papazoglou, M.: Exploring a multi-faceted framework for soc: how to develop secure web-service interactions? In: Proc. 14th Intl. Workshop on Research Issues on Data Engineering, pp. 56–61 (March 2004)
6. Maierhofer, A., Dimitrakos, T., Titkov, L., Brossard, D.: Extendable and adaptive message-level security enforcement framework. In: International conference on Networking and Services, ICNS 2006, pp. 72–72 (2006)
7. Hafner, M., Mukhtiar Memon, R.B.: SeAAS - a reference architecture for security services in SOA. Journal of Universal Computer Science 15(15), 2916–2936 (2009)
8. Moser, O., Rosenberg, F., Dustdar, S.: Non-intrusive monitoring and service adaptation for ws-bpel. In: WWW, pp. 815–824 (2008)
9. Reichert, M., Dadam, P.: Adeptflex: Supporting dynamic changes of workflow without loosing control. Journal of Intelligent Information Systems 10, 93–129 (1998)
10. Reichert, M., Rinderle-Ma, S., Dadam, P.: Flexibility in process-aware information systems. T. Petri Nets and Other Models of Concurrency 2, 115–135 (2009)
11. Svirskas, A., Isachenkova, J., Molva, R.: Towards secure and trusted collaboration environment for european public sector. In: Collaborative Computing: Networking, Applications and Worksharing. CollaborateCom 2007. International Conference on, pp. 49–56 (2007)
12. Trojer, T., Kwong Lee, C., Fung, B.C.M., Narupiyakul, L., Hung, P.C.K.: Privacy-aware health information sharing. In: Privacy Aware Knowledge Discovery: Novel Applications and New Techniques, Chapman and Hall/CRC Press, Boca Raton (2010)
13. Tsai, W.T., Zhou, X., Chen, Y.: Soa simulation and verification by event-driven policy enforcement. In: ANSS-41 2008: Proceedings of the 41st Annual Simulation Symposium (anss-41 2008), pp. 165–172. IEEE Computer Society, Washington (2008)
14. United States Code: Sarbanes-Oxley Act of 2002, pl 107-204, 116 stat 745. Codified in Sections 11, 15, 18, 28, and 29 USC (July 2002)

---

[5] http://www.master-fp7.eu

Fault Handling in the Web Service Stack

Oliver Kopp, Frank Leymann, and Daniel Wutke

Institute of Architecture of Application Systems, University of Stuttgart, Germany
Universitätsstraße 38, 70569 Stuttgart, Germany
lastname@iaas.uni-stuttgart.de

Abstract. The Web services platform architecture consists of different layers for exchanging messages. There may be faults happening at each layer during the message exchange. First, the paper presents current standards employed in the different layers and shows their interrelation. Thereby, the focus is on the fault handling strategies. Second, current service middleware is reviewed whether and how it follows the fault handling strategies.

1 Introduction

The service-oriented architecture (SOA) is an architectural style for building (enterprise) applications whose building blocks are services. One incarnation of the technology stack required to build SOA applications are Web services [1]. Web services are defined by a modular and composeable stack of standards ranging from low-level communication protocols, over standardized formats for description of services and the messages exchanged during a Web service interaction to high-level standards for defining potentially complex composite applications built from Web services. An important aspect of said enterprise applications is robustness, i. e. applications must be able to cope with faults occurring during run-time.

Although the issue of building robust applications has been addressed in numerous publications (see Sect. 2 for an overview), these typically focus on one specific aspect of fault handling. None of the work has regarded the different layers of the Web service stack altogether. To understand the cause of a fault in the application, it is necessary to understand how the lower levels work and when and how a fault in the lower levels is propagated to the upper levels. Thus, this paper aims at providing an overview of fault handling across all layers of the Web service stack used by an application with special focus on the interplay of the different functions involved in the fault handling process.

To achieve this goal, the contribution of this paper is two-fold: First, we provide an overview of the functionality required to build a service-oriented application and how it maps to different layers in the application's architecture. With this description, we then identify the different fault types that may occur during run-time of such an application and classify them according to the layer they occur on. As part of this description, we discuss different approaches to reacting to a fault both on the level of the employed middleware (i. e. the Web service run-time implementation or the workflow management system) and on the level of the composite application's logic. Second, we provide an overview of how fault handling has been implemented in one open-source technology stack comprising the BPEL [2] orchestration engine *Apache ODE*, the Web

P.P. Maglio et al. (Eds.): ICSOC 2010, LNCS 6470, pp. 303–317, 2010.
© Springer-Verlag Berlin Heidelberg 2010

service runtime *Apache Axis 2* and the WS-Reliable Messaging implementation *Apache Sandesha 2* and investigate how their implementation relates to identifies fault types.

The structure of the paper is as follows: First, we present an overview of existing work on fault handling in Web service-based applications Sect. 2. An identification and classification of different fault types according to the Web service platform layer they occur on is provided in Sect. 3. The properties of each fault class are discussed in detail on a conceptual level, relating them to existing Web service specifications where appropriate. During this discussion, special focus is placed on pointing out inter-dependencies among faults on different layers. Section 4 complements the conceptual fault classification presented in Sect. 3 by providing an analysis of the fault handling behavior of a workflow management system and corresponding Web service runtime implementation across all layers of the Web service technology stack. Finally, Sect. 5 concludes and provides and outlook on future work.

2   Related Work

Current work on investigating the parts of or the entire Web services platform architecture such as [1,3,4] regards the layers in isolation and does not provide an overview on the interplay between these layers.

The Web Service Business Process Execution Language (BPEL [2]) is the de-facto orchestration language for services. It provides concepts for fault and compensation handling. The specification does not state how faults from lower levels of the stack are propagated into the process.

There are several approaches enhancing BPEL engines by adding capabilities of the fault handling. For instance, Jijia et al. [5] present an extension to the invocation handler of the BPEL engine. It can be configured what action is taken in case a Web service fails. Current actions are retry, substitute, ignore and terminate. The authors rely on the infrastructure to propagate network faults to the extension. Modafferi et al. [6] propose enhancements to the architecture of BPEL engines with a similar functionality. Guidi et al. [7] regard synchronous invoke activities: they propose to wait for the reply message regardless of faults in parallel branches in the process before executing the termination handler. Ardissono et al. [8] shows how hypothesis about the cause of a fault can be constructed and how this information can be used in business processes. Friedrich at al. [9] follow a similar approach based on the WS-DIAMOND infrastructure [10]. A summary of all related work in the context of fault handling in the case of Web services is also presented in [9]. All these approaches do not regard the different layers of the WS stack, whereas our work focuses on the interplay between these layers.

The work by Russell et al. [11] presents workflow exception patterns. These patterns investigate the expressiveness of the workflow language and does not deal with the interplay between the workflow layer and the layers below.

To verify the conformance of a BPEL process, the process is represented as a formal system and then verified for properties given by a specification. Current formalizations of BPEL do not take the Web services stack into account [12]. State of the art formalizations such as the Petri net formalization [13] assume asynchronous communication, but do not regard faults in the layers below the interface layer. Lohmann [12] considers lost messages and buffer overflows, but disregards the interplay of the layers in the Web service stack.

A classification of faults with respect to workflows is given in [14, 15]. Here, workflow engine failures, activity failures (expected exceptions), communication failures and unexpected exceptions are distinguished. Workflow engine failures denote failures of the workflow engine itself. Activity failures are also called expected exceptions. They denote that an activity did not complete successfully and hence a special handling is needed. Communication failures are failures in the communication with the activity implementation. This is the focus of this paper. Unexpected exceptions are exceptions on the process definition level, where the structure of the modeled process cannot handle a special case. Mourao et al. [16] show how unexpected exceptions can be supported by special workflows involving humans.

A general taxonomy in the context of dependability is given by Avižienis et al. [17]. Faults in system components cause error states in the system, which manifest in failures. To be in line with the Web service specifications, we use the word "fault" whenever the specification also uses it, even if the word "failure" is more appropriate.

Looker et al. [18] analyze dependability of Web services by injecting faults in messages. They differentiate in physical faults, software faults, resource-management faults, communication faults and life-cycle faults. Gorbenko et al. [19] distinguish between errors in the "Network and service platform", in the "Web service software" and in the "Client software". Both works, however, do not consider all layers of the Web service stack as we do.

3   Fault Classification

The Web service platform architecture [1] categorizes the required middleware functions for facilitating interactions among the services of an SOA-based application in several layers. These layers are depicted Fig. 1 along with the Web service standards that specify the layer's functionality.

The *component layer* (Sect. 3.5) addresses the realization of an application's business logic which invokes the business functions the application is composed of, technologically rendered as Web services. One possible incarnation of a technology that is widely used for service orchestration in an SOA environment is the Web Service Business Process Execution Language (BPEL [2]), which hence is the focus of the discussion in the remainder of this paper. Composite applications often require nontrivial quality of service from the orchestrated services; typical examples of such nonfunctional component or service characteristics is reliability of interactions, transactional behavior of a set of services or security-related aspects, such as ensuring message integrity or message confidentiality. These functions are provided by the *quality of service* (Sect. 3.4) layer. Apart from nonfunctional properties, a (Web service) component is characterized by a *description* (Sect. 3.5) of its functional interface in form of a WSDL document [20], specifying the business functions supported by the service along with the message types they consume and produce. Concrete ordering of consumed and sent messages may be defined using BPEL. Requesting applications interact with service components by exchanging messages. Messages have a well-defined format that follows the SOAP specification; multiple messages may be interrelated to form potentially complex message

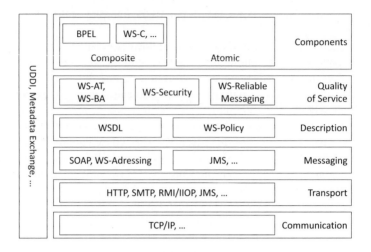

Fig. 1. Layers in the Web Service Platform Architecture, adapted from [1]

exchange patterns using the mechanisms provided by WS-Addressing [21] on the *messaging layer* (Sect. 3.3) such as means for identification of communicating entities and messages as well as message correlation. SOAP messages can be transmitted between components using different network transport protocols, depending on the requester's requirements, these are reflected by the *transport layer* (Sect. 3.2). The functions provided by the *communication layer* (Sect. 3.1) focus on the transmission of "raw data" among communication partners, potentially crossing the boundaries of one physical machine. Typically this functionality is provided by network transport protocols such as the Transmission Control Procotol (TCP) or the User Datagram Protocol (UDP), with themselves rely on lower level protocols such as the Internet Protocol (IP) for data transmission. In case the partners participating in the interaction reside on the same physical machine, machine-local data transmission mechanisms, such as shared memory, can be used on the communication layer (e. g. invoking a Web service implemented as an Enterprise Java Bean on the same machine). As Web services are defined as software systems that interact "over a network" [22] we focus on networked interactions in the remainder of this paper.

In the subsequent sections we discuss the fault handling behavior employed on each of the aforementioned layers in detail by describing a message flow between a service requester and service provider along with the faults that can occur on each layer and their respective fault handling strategies. For the following discussion we chose one concrete technology for the implementation of each layer: The application on the component layer is implemented using BPEL. Messages are exchanged reliably using WS-Reliable Messaging [23], encoded using SOAP and transported using HTTP over TCP/IP. Variants of these setting are briefly discussed in the respective sections. Figure 2 illustrates this setting. Each arc in the figure identifies a certain step in the overall message flow. During execution of the depicted interaction, messages are passed between the components implementing the individual layers of the application; message flow is thereby restricted

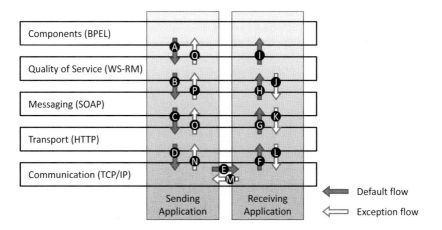

Fig. 2. Message Passing Through the Layers

to adjacent layers. In case a fault occurs it can be (i) either *handled* within the layer it occurred on or (ii) it can be *propagated* to a higher layer, which can then again decide to either handle the fault or propagate it to the next higher level. As the functionality provided by the description layer is not invoked during runtime of the depicted message exchange but during application build-time, this layer has been omitted from Fig. 2.

Note that faults occurring in the *runtime environment*, such as a component running out of memory during execution, errors due to bad memory and hard disk or system crashes are out of scope and hence not explicitly addressed in the discussion in the remainder of this paper. The same holds for faults resulting from *erroneous implementation*, i. e. implementations not conforming to their specification. Note that an implementation error may manifest in a fault in an arbitrary layer. Hence, such faults are out of scope of this paper and we focus on the specified behavior.

In the following sections we classify the faults according to the layers in the Web service stack. The individual layers are explained bottom-up from the communication layer to the component layer along with their respective fault types.

3.1 Communication Layer Faults

Generally, we subsume all protocols and mechanisms of the OSI Layered Network Model [24] below layer 7, i. e. the OSI application layer, as providing a platform for communicating data among the participants of an interaction and hence refer to them collectively as the communication layer of an SOA-based application.

The faults that may occur on this layer (triggered by a message flowing along arc D in Fig. 2) on the side of the sending application include *connectivity faults* where a sender cannot establish a connection with a receiver (arc E) or *data integrity faults* where the data exchanged between them is corrupted (arc E or arc M).

Examples for connectivity faults in applications are (i) problems in name resolution, i. e. a host name cannot be resolved to an IP address through DNS [25], (ii) problems during message routing from sender to receiver, i. e. host or network unreachable or

(iii) unavailability of a network endpoint, i. e. connection refused, due to the service provider not being ready to process incoming data. An example for a data integrity fault is loss of packets exchanged as part of an interaction.

Connectivity faults are typically not handled directly on the communication layer (e. g. by retrying a failed connection attempt at a later point in time) but are instead propagated up in the layered application architecture on the side of the sending application (arc N). If it is desired that these faults should be handled before reaching the requesting application's component layer, fault handling must be carried out on the quality of service layer as described in Sect. 3.4.

As data integrity faults may occur quite frequently—especially when using unreliable transports—some communication layer protocols, such as TCP, employ corresponding fault handling mechanisms directly on the communication layer, such as a retransmit of lost packets.

3.2 Transport Layer Faults

When a message is passed from the messaging layer down to the transport layer (arc C in Fig. 2) as part of the execution of the Web service runtime's binding implementation, the sending application encodes the message to be sent in a representation that can be conveyed using the chosen transport mechanism. In terms of the OSI layered model, this transport mechanism resides on layer seven, i. e. the application layer. Once the message has been encoded, the sending application uses the communication primitives provided by the chosen transport protocol to transmit the message to the receiving application— i. e. the component to be invoked—and potentially consumes response messages that may be sent by the service.

Each network transport protocol used on the transport layer may employ its own mechanisms for identifying and creating transport layer faults. In case of the Hypertext Transfer Protocol (HTTP) [26], transport layer faults are identified by an HTTP error code (e. g. "403 Forbidden" in case a requester is not allowed to access a certain resource exposed using HTTP). Note that—in contrast to communication layer faults— these faults do not occur on the side of the sending application, but at the receiving application and are then propagated back to the sender along the arcs L, M and N in Fig. 2. This is even the case for client-side error codes (4xx) indicating that the client made a wrong request (from the view of the server). Note that the communication along these arcs is a normal communication taking place in the established http connection. For the communication layer, the HTTP error is not an error. Communication layer faults propagated to the transport layer and transport layer faults are propagated to the next higher level (arc O in Fig. 2), i. e. the messaging layer.

3.3 Messaging Layer Faults

The messaging layer comprises the functionality of encoding messages coming through the quality of service layer from an application (along arc B in Fig. 2), processing the message according to the SOAP processing model [27], adding addressing information about the message's destination in form of corresponding WS-Addressing headers [21] and passing it on to the transport layer through the Web service runtime's binding implementation (arc C).

According to the SOAP specification, the following messaging layer fault types are distinguished: (i) a *VersionMismatch* fault identifies a fault due to an incompatible message format version; (ii) a *MustUnderstand* fault is generated when a receiver cannot process a mandatory SOAP header block; (iii) a *DataEncodingUnknown* is generated when a SOAP message uses an encoding that is not supported by a receiving SOAP node; (iv) a generic *Sender* fault represents invalid or missing message content as generated by the sending application and (v) a *Receiver* fault represents a fault that occurred due to (potentially transient) problems on the side of the receiving applications. In case of the latter fault type, resending the same SOAP envelope at a later point in time may result in successful server-side message processing. Similar to transport layer faults, these faults occur on the side of the receiving application and are propagated to the sender along the arcs K, L, M, N, O and P.

The mapping between messaging layer SOAP faults and transport layer fault status codes is defined as part of the specification of a Web service binding. In case of the SOAP/HTTP binding [28] all SOAP faults except *Sender* faults map to HTTP status code 500, which indicates a server-side processing error [26]. *Sender* faults map to a HTTP status code 400, which indicates a client-side error resulting in an invalid request message.

The SOAP processing model includes the definition of a routing concept from an initial sender over intermediary nodes to an ultimate receiver. This concept is one possible implementation of the enterprise integration patterns by Hohpe and Wolf [29]. Concrete examples are services for message encryption and message logging [30]. Messages may also be transmitted over different transports before reaching the ultimate receiver. For instance, SOAP/JMS may be used from the initial sender to the encryption service, the encryption service sends the encrypted message using SOAP/JMS to a messaging gateway. Finally, the messaging gateway uses SOAP/HTTP as the ultimate receiver only supports the SOAP/HTTP binding. As a consequence, a fault raised by an intermediary or the ultimate receiver may not just be propagated to the proceeding node which established a connection using a specific transport, but has to be routed to the initial sender. For that purpose, the WS-Addressing headers `ReplyTo` and `FaultTo` are defined. `ReplyTo` defines the endpoint reference, where the reply message should be directed. `FaultTo` is used to specify a different SOAP node to direct the fault to. In other words, the latter header is especially useful in multi-hop interactions, where a SOAP message is routed through several intermediaries, when only the original sender of the message should be notified about processing errors on any of the SOAP processing nodes along the message path.

Faults that may occur during message creation and processing on the side of the sending application are not rendered as SOAP faults but instead propagated to the component layer using the error handling mechanisms of the Web service runtime's implementation, e. g. Java exceptions when the runtime is implemented in the Java programming language. Note that this is not required by the SOAP specification, but typically implemented.

3.4   Quality of Service Layer Faults

The quality of service layer adds nonfunctional capabilities to Web services. These include support for transactions, security and reliable transfer of messages.

Transactions are implemented using the WS-Coordination framework, which in turn offers WS-AtomicTransactions (WS-AT) for interoperable two-phase commits and WS-BusinessActivity (WS-BA) for long-running compensation-based transactions [31]. WS-Security ensures message integrity and confidentiality [32]. In this paper, we focus on WS-ReliableMessaging (WS-RM) which enables reliable end-to-end messaging. That means even if SOAP intermediaries with different transports inbetween are used (see Sect. 3.3 for an example), the communication from the initial sender to the ultimate receiver is reliable. In case no component of the quality of service layer is used, messages from the component are directly passed to the messaging layer and messages from the messaging layer are directly passed to the component.

By using WS-RM, faults propagated from the messaging layer (arc P) are handled by the WS-RM component. WS-RM offers the configuration options AtLeastOnce, AtMostOnce, ExcactlyOnce and InOrder. WS-RM places messages in sequences. Each message takes a running number enabling in order delivery. Ranges of received messages are acknowledged by the receiver, which enables at least once and exactly once delivery. At most once delivery does not require acknowledgments as no delivery conforms to at most once. WS-RM defines faults which are propagated to the component layer. These faults indicate faults at the WS-RM processing itself, such as notifying that an endpoint is not WS-RM aware, an invalid acknowledgment is received or that the maximum value for numbering messages has been reached. They may be generated by the sending and the receiving quality of service layer. A sequence takes an expiry time. In case a sequence is not completed until the expiry, the sequence is terminated and a `SequenceTerminated` fault is raised through arc Q. The receiver may either discard the entire sequence, discard all messages following the first gap or discard nothing. A permanent fault at the client side (e. g. "403 Forbidden") is also propagated as SequenceTerminated fault to the sender application. A WS-RM implementation is not required to wait until the expiry is met and may propagate this fault earlier.

3.5   Component Layer Faults

Faults that may occur on the component layer, i. e. the layer on which an application's business logic resides, differ substantially from the fault types of the lower layers described so far.

As the latter are—under the given assumption of *absence* of erroneous implementations presented in Sect. 3—often transient errors that may be handled by retrying a message exchange after its failure, component layer faults are typically permanent in nature and an indication of an error in the application logic of a component that has technically been invoked successfully (by transmitting a request message along the arcs A to I and propagating the application fault by sending a new message). Component layer faults can be made more tangible by classifying them into two groups: faults reflected in the *component's interface description* or in the *component's implementation*.

Component Interface Description: WSDL. *Component interface faults* refer to faults which are specified as part of the functional component contract, i. e. the component's WSDL description (Fig. 1). These faults reflect an error situation in the application logic of a component and are hence—in contrast to the layers below the component layer—expected during application design time.

An example for a component interface fault is a calculator component, whose *divide* method signature defines a separate fault in addition to a request and a result message for notifying a requester when e. g. a division by zero or a range overflow occurs. Using this method, the requesting application gets notified about the component layer fault "out of band" of the regular response and can hence clearly identify the error situation and handle it accordingly.

In WSDL, component layer faults are specified through the `fault`-element of a `WSDL-operation` in WSDL 1.1 [20] or an `interface` in WSDL 2.0 [33] and typed using WSDL 2.0's typing mechanism. Whether a fault can be specified as part of the interface description of a component's operation is dependent on its *operation type* in WSDL 1.1 or its *message exchange pattern* in WSDL 2.0, respectively. In case an operation follows a *one-way/in-only* message exchange pattern, no faults may be propagated back to the sending application due to the "fire and forget" nature of the interaction. In the WSDL 2.0 specification this is referred to as *no faults propagation rule*. If this behavior is undesired, other message exchange patterns (e. g. *request-response/in-out*) should be chosen for the respective operation. In addition to these patterns, where a component is required to send a response even in case no fault occurs, WSDL 2.0 defines the *robust-in-only* message exchange pattern in which a fault may be propagated to the requesting application. The WSDL specification, however, lacks a clear description how requesting applications are supposed to handle these optional faults on a technical level, e. g. how long to wait for a fault for a particular component invocation until it is assumed that the invocation was successful. Thus, this pattern is underspecified [34].

Component Implementation: BPEL. A component interface fault is created during the execution of the implementation of a component's application logic. As not all faults that may occur during execution of a component should become visible outside the component itself, component implementation faults can be—similar to the other fault types—be either handled or propagated. Propagation of component layer faults typically result in involving a human in the fault handling process.

For component layer-internal fault handling, BPEL defines the concept of fault handlers which can be attached to either `scope` or `invoke` activities in which process modelers may specify application logic to be executed when a fault occurs. A fault can be created either explicitly as part of the process model through the `throw` activity, or can be raised implicitly during execution of e. g. an `invoke` interaction which results in a fault declared as part of a component's interface (cf. Sect. 3.5).

Although the BPEL specification defines how to react to interface layer faults, no explicit provisions are made how to treat faults that occur on layers below the component layer during the process of sending an invocation request to a component (i. e. when executing arcs A to E). Hence, implementations differ in their behavior with regard to handling such faults. A common way to treat transient transport layer faults, which is e. g. used in *Apache ODE*[1], is distinguishing business *faults* and technical *failures*. Whereas business faults are propagated into the process for "regular" fault handling through the processes fault handlers, failures result in suspending process instance execution and notification of an administrator who—after resolving the problem—may

---

[1] http://ode.apache.org

resume process instance execution. Another approach to handling lower layer faults is to propagate such faults to the process in form of custom typed BPEL faults which may then be handled using BPEL's fault handling mechanisms. The approach is applied in *ActiveBPEL*[2]. Apache ODE may be configured to this behavior by using the faultOnFailure attribute.

4   Implemented Fault Propagation

This section presents a concrete way to implement the presented exception handling strategies. We use Apache ODE 1.3.8, Apache Sandesha2[3] and Apache Axis2 1.3.1[4] to illustrate the implementation concepts. These implementations are put to relation to the layers of the Web service stack (Fig. 1) in Fig. 4: Being a BPEL engine, Apache ODE implements a component. Apache ODE calls Axis which implements the messaging and the transport layer. Sandesha is a plugin for Axis implementing WS-RM, which we focus on. Axis uses HTTP components to imple-

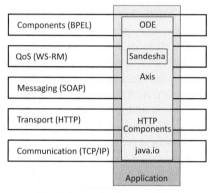

Fig. 3. Layer Implementations

ment the transport layer which in turn uses java.io from the Java runtime as implementation for the runtime layer.

4.1   Apache ODE

Apache ODE (ODE for short) is a BPEL engine developed by the Apache Software foundation. After a process is instantiated, a BpelRuntimeContext is available. In case of an invoke activity, its invoke method is called to invoke a service. This call reaches the SoapExternalService class. Depending on the type of the invoke, a OutOnlyAxisOperationClient or an OutInAxisOperationClient (cf. Sect. 4.2) is created. In the case of a one-way invoke, an exception raised by the OutOnlyAxis-OperationClient is logged without propagating into the process. In case of a two-way invoke, an exception raised by the OutInAxisOperationClient the exception is put as failure in a PartnerRoleMessageExchange object odeMex. If a SOAP fault is received as reply, this fault is put as fault in odeMex. Otherwise, the reply message is put there. An exception on the handling of the reply message is rendered as fault. Received faults and locally generated faults and failures are propagated to the parent activity by calling the completed or failure method. The ACTIVITYGUARD class implements the failure method. Here, the faultOnFailure property is checked and the failure either converted to a fault or an administrator involved. Faults are propagated up the activity hierarchy (using the completed method) until a scope is reached. Here, a failure

---

[2] http://www.activebpel.org

[3] http://ws.apache.org/sandesha/sandesha2/

[4] http://ws.apache.org/axis2

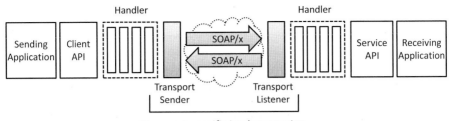

Fig. 4. Axis 2 Architecture

is converted to a fault and the `completed` method is called. Subsequently, the usual BPEL fault handling runs as described in the BPEL specification [2, 35, 36]. In short, all activities in the scope the activity belongs to are terminated and a fault handler of the scope is called. Here, completed activities of the scope may be compensated by calling compensation activities. A fault may be re-thrown to the parent scope, where the same handling starts.

4.2 Apache Axis2

Apache Axis 2 (Axis for short) is a Web service runtime that supports different Web service specifications and transport protocols. In Fig. 4, a high-level overview of Axis' architecture[5] is depicted.

Axis supports two different service invocation styles: client may (i) either use build-time tools to generate a client-side proxy object based on the service's WSDL description which wraps the interaction with the service provider or (ii) use Axis' `ServiceClient` API to dynamically construct the service invocation request at runtime. For this purpose, the API exposes several methods for SOAP message generation (e. g. `addHeader`, `setTargetEPR`) and sending (e. g. `fireAndForget`, `sendReceive`, `sendReceiveNonBlocking`, `sendRobust`). These methods can be used to implement different message exchange patterns such as *in-only* in case of `fireAndForget` or synchronous or asynchronous *in-out* in case of `sendReceive` and `sendReceiveNon-Blocking`, respectively.

The following description of the internal actions carried out by the Axis runtime during execution of a Web service interaction assumes that a client uses the `ServiceClient` API directly. As generated proxy objects rely on the `ServiceClient` API internally as well, there is no difference in fault handling behavior on the layers below the component layer when using either service invocation style. The invocation styles, however, differ with regard to their component layer fault handling behavior. Whereas the proxy objects generated during build-time render interface faults as typed faults in the client's programming language (e. g. an exception in Java), the `ServiceClient` API propagates them to the component layer in form of a generic `AxisFault`.

---

[5] Adapted from `http://ws.apache.org/axis2/1_4_1/userguide.html`

Once a client application has called an operation of the `ServiceClient` object, a `OperationClient` object is created that corresponds to the message exchange pattern implemented by the invoked `ServiceClient` method. In case the `fireAndForget` method of the `ServiceClient` is invoked, which implements an *in-only* WSDL message exchange pattern, a `OutOnlyAxisOperationClient` object is created, which furthermore contains the client-defined SOAP envelope and determines the transport protocol to be used to invoke the service based on the client-defined service endpoint address in form of a `TransportOutDescriptionObject`.

After creation of the request message, it is passed into the `AxisEngine` in form of a `MessageContext` object. The engine subsequently passes the message context object to several configurable handler objects (cf. Fig. 4) which may perform additional processing steps before the message is passed to the implementation of the `TransportSender` interface corresponding to the transport protocol that should be used for the respective interaction. The `TransportSender` implementation for using a HTTP transport is the `CommonsHTTPTransportSender`. Additional processing steps include WS-Security and WS-RM steps. In the case of WS-RM, the `SandeshaOutHandler` is used. Here, the WS-RM data are created or fetched from an internal storage (e. g. sequence number) and added to the message[6]. The message is put to a `SenderBeanManager`, where messages to send are persistently stored to have them available for a retransmit. The transport sender serializes the message payload in the `MessageContext` and sends it to the receiver using the `CommonsHTTPClient sendViaPost` method. The message transmission is carried out using the *Apache HttpComponents Client*[7].

Any exceptions occurring during message creation and processing within Axis (including the WS-RM phase) at the side of the message sender as described before result in the creation of an `AxisFault` which is propagated back to the calling client application. The reason of the fault (e. g. a `MailformedURLException` in case of an invalid URL in the defined endpoint address or an `IOException` in case of an unavailable receiver) is embedded in the generated `AxisFault` which allows clients to individually handle different fault types.

On the server-side Axis implementation, the request is received either through the `AxisServlet` or a stand-alone `HTTPTransportReceiver`. The SOAP request message is extracted from the incoming HTTP request and stored into a `MessageContext` object which is then passed through the handlers of the server-side Axis runtime (see Fig. 4) to the service's application logic. Any fault occurring on the way up to the component layer is rendered as a SOAP fault with its fault code chosen according to the description in Sect. 3.3. The WS-RM part checks if the message is a WS-RM message or if there are WS-RM headers present and executes the respective logic. For instance, in the case of the `SequenceAcknowledgement` header, acknowledged message numbers are compared with the numbers of the sent messages. In case a message is acknowledged, it is removed from the `SenderBeanManager`. The unacknowledged messages are sent using the `SandeshaThread`, which in turn periodically queries the sender bean manager.

---

[6] Details on the internal processing by Sandesha2 is provided by
http://ws.apache.org/sandesha/sandesha2/architectureGuide.html
[7] http://hc.apache.org/

After message transmission, the client-side transport sender interprets the status of the message submission based on the received HTTP status code (cf. mapping between SOAP faults and HTTP status codes in Sect. 3.2). In case the receiving side signals an HTTP code of 2xx, the message transmission is considered successful and the payload of the response message (which e.g. in case of an *in-out* message exchange pattern contains the result of the service invocation) is extracted and stored into a `MessageContext` object. In case an HTTP status code of 4xx (client error) or 5xx (server error) is received, the response message is checked for the presence of a SOAP fault which is extracted and stored into a `MessageContext` object similar to the response case.

Whether the response or fault is propagated back to the calling application through Axis' handlers is dependent on the concrete message exchange pattern of the executed operation. If the call is an *in-only* operation, the response and error messages are discarded and not processed further by Axis. If the call on the other hand is a *in-out* operation (realized by an `OutInAxisOperationClient`), either the created message context object is passed back to the sending client application through Axis' handlers or an exception corresponding to the occurred fault is thrown and propagated back, either directly in case of a blocking invocation of `sendReceive` or by invoking a client-provided callback in case of `sendReceiveNonBlocking`. Processing the response status codes even in case of a `fireAndForget` invocation allows for developing implementations of the `TransportSender` interface, which are independent of any concrete message exchange patterns.

Alternative binding implementations, such as the `MailTransport`, which are realized as further implementations of the `TransportSender` interface, generally follow the same approach to identifying, wrapping and propagating faults back to the calling client application.

5   Conclusions and Future Work

This paper provided an overview on the fault handling on all layers in the Web service stack. Special emphasis was put on the analysis of the interplay between the different layers. We showed that current related work in the field does not holistically regard the communication between different services. This paper helps to foster the awareness of the different layers of the Web service stack and enables a more detailed analysis of impacts of new solutions to the Web service stack.

Not all specifications cover fault handling completely. The fault-handling-mechanisms defined e.g. as part of the BPEL specification alone are not sufficient to enable a robust behavior of a business process in all cases: BPEL engine implementations differ e.g. in the way how they handle a fault occurring on the communication layer. Vendors include custom extensions; e.g. ODE suspends a process and allows an administrator to decide how to handle the situation. Thus, guidelines are needed to enable developing applications which are reaching a consistent state even in the case of a failure during the execution.

Currently, faults are handled by a component in each layer. In our future work, we plan to use BPEL to coordinate fault handling in the quality of service layer and below by extending the work presented in [30].

In this work, we discussed the implementations of Apache ODE and Apache Axis only. Future work has to investigate the behavior of other WS runtimes such as the Active BPEL engine and Apache CXF.

Current formalizations of BPEL and other process calculi currently do not capture the behavior of the Web service stack. Thus, our future work is to use our findings to include the behavior of the middleware in verification of processes.

References

1. Curbera, F., Leymann, F., Storey, T., Ferguson, D., Weerawarana, S.: Web Services Platform Architecture: SOAP, WSDL, WS Policy, WS Addressing, WS BPEL, WS-Reliable Messaging and More. Prentice Hall PTR, Englewood Cliffs (2005)
2. OASIS: Web Services Business Process Execution Language Version 2.0 – OASIS Standard (2007)
3. Papazoglou, M.P.: Web Services: Principles and Technology. Prentice-Hall, Englewood Cliffs (2007)
4. Coulouris, G., Dollimore, J., Kindberg, T.: Distributed Systems: Concepts and Design. In: Distributed Systems: Concepts and Design, 4th edn. (2005)
5. Jiajia, W., Junliang, C., Yong, P., Meng, X.: A Multi-Policy Exception Handling System for BPEL Processes. In: First International Conference on Communications and Networking in, China (2006)
6. Modafferi, S., Mussi, E., Pernici, B.: SH-BPEL: a Self-Healing Plug-In for WS-BPEL Engines. In: 1st Workshop on Middleware for Service Oriented Computing, ACM, New York (2006)
7. Guidi, C., Lanese, I., Montesi, F., Zavattaro, G.: On the Interplay Between Fault Handling and Request-Response Service Invocations. In: 8th International Conference on Application of Concurrency to System Design ACSD (2008)
8. Ardissono, L., Furnari, R., Goy, A., Petrone, G., Segnan, M.: Fault tolerant web service orchestration by means of diagnosis. In: Gruhn, V., Oquendo, F. (eds.) EWSA 2006. LNCS, vol. 4344, pp. 2–16. Springer, Heidelberg (2006)
9. Friedrich, G., Fugini, M., Mussi, E., Pernici, B., Tagni, G.: Exception Handling for Repair in Service-Based Processes. IEEE Transactions on Software Engineering 99(2), 198–215 (2010)
10. Console, L., et al.: WS-DIAMOND: Web Services-DIAgnosability, MONitoring, and Diagnosis. In: At Your Service: Service-Oriented Computing from an EU Perspective, pp. 213–239. MIT Press, Cambridge (June 2009)
11. Russell, N., van der Aalst, W., ter Hofstede, A.: Workflow Exception Patterns. In: Advanced Information Systems Engineering. In: Dubois, E., Pohl, K. (eds.) CAiSE 2006. LNCS, vol. 4001, pp. 288–302. Springer, Heidelberg (2006)
12. Lohmann, N.: Communication models for services. In: 2nd Central-European Workshop on Services and their Composition (ZEUS 2010), vol. 563, CEUR (2010)
13. Lohmann, N.: A Feature-Complete Petri Net Semantics for WS-BPEL 2.0. In: Dumas, M., Heckel, R. (eds.) WS-FM 2007. LNCS, vol. 4937, pp. 77–91. Springer, Heidelberg (2008)
14. Eder, J., Liebhart, W.: The Workflow Activity Model WAMO. In: Conference on Cooperative Information Systems (CoopIs), pp. 87–98 (1995)
15. Eder, J., Liebhart, W.: Workflow Recovery. In: COOPIS 1996: First International Conference on Cooperative Information Systems, IEEE Computer Society, Los Alamitos (1996)
16. Mourao, H., Antunes, P.: Supporting Effective Unexpected Exceptions Handling in Workflow Management Systems. In: SAC 2007, pp. 1242–1249. ACM, New York (2007)

17. Avižienis, A., Randell, B., Landwehr, C.: Basic Concepts and Taxonomy of Dependable and Secure Computing. IEEE Transactions on Dependable and Secure Computing 1(1), 11–33 (2004)
18. Looker, N., Munro, M., Xu, J.: Simulating errors in web services. International Journal of Simulation Systems 5(5), 29–37 (2004)
19. Gorbenko, A., Romanovsky, A., Kharchenko, V., Mikhaylichenko, A.: Experimenting with Exception Propagation Mechanisms in Service-Oriented Architecture. In: WEH 2008: 4th International Workshop on Exception Handling, ACM, New York (2008)
20. Christensen, E., Crubera, F., Meredith, G., Weerawarana, S.: Web Services Description Language (WSDL) 1.1. W3C Note (2001), http://www.w3.org/TR/wsdl
21. Gudgin, M., Hadley, M., Rogers, T.: Web Services Addressing 1.0 – Core. W3C Recommendation (2006), http://www.w3.org/TR/ws-addr-core/
22. Haas, H., Booth, D., Newcomer, E., Champion, M., Orchard, D., Ferris, C., McCabe, F.: Web Services Architecture. W3C Working Group Note (2004), http://www.w3.org/TR/ws-arch/
23. OASIS: Web Services Reliable Messaging (WS-ReliableMessaging) Version 1.2. (2009)
24. ISO 7498-1:1994: Information technology – Open Systems Interconnection – Basic Reference Model: The Basic Model. ISO, Geneva, Switzerland
25. Mockapetris, P.V.: Domain Names - Implementation and Specification. RFC 1035 (1987)
26. Fielding, R., Gettys, J., Mogul, J., Frystyk, H., Masinter, L., Leach, P., Berners-Lee, T.: Hypertext Transfer Protocol – HTTP/1.1. RFC 2616 (1999)
27. Gudgin, M., Hadley, M., Mendelsohn, N., Moreau, J.J., Nielsen, H.F., Karmarkar, A., Lafon, Y.: SOAP Version 1.2 Part 1: Messaging Framework. W3C Recommendation (2007), http://www.w3.org/TR/soap12-part1/
28. Gudgin, M., Hadley, M., Mendelsohn, N., Moreau, J.J., Nielsen, H.F., Karmarkar, A., Lafon, Y.: SOAP Version 1.2 Part 2: Adjuncts. W3C Recommendation (2007), http://www.w3.org/TR/soap12-part2/
29. Hohpe, G., Woolf, B.: Enterprise Integration Patterns: Designing, Building, and Deploying Messaging Solutions. Addison-Wesley Professional, Reading (2003)
30. Scheibler, T., Karastoyanova, D., Leymann, F.: Dynamic Message Routing Using Processes. In: KiVS 2009, Springer, Heidelberg (March 2009)
31. OASIS: OASIS Web Services Transaction (WS-TX) TC (2009), http://www.oasis-open.org/committees/ws-tx/
32. OASIS: Web Services Security: SOAP Message Security 1.1 (2006), http://docs.oasis-open.org/wss/v1.1/
33. Chinnici, R., Gudgin, M., Moreau, J.J., Schlimmer, J., Weerawarana, S.: Web Services Description Language (WSDL) Version 2.0 Part 1: Core Language. W3C Recommendation (2004), http://www.w3.org/TR/wsdl20/
34. Nitzsche, J., van Lessen, T., Leymann, F.: WSDL 2.0 Message Exchange Patterns: Limitations and Opportunities. In: 3rd International Conference on Internet and Web Applications and Services (ICIW), IEEE Computer Society, Los Alamitos (June 2008)
35. Curbera, F., Khalaf, R., Leymann, F., Weerawarana, S.: Exception Handling in the BPEL4WS Language. In: van der Aalst, W.M.P., ter Hofstede, A.H.M., Weske, M. (eds.) BPM 2003. LNCS, vol. 2678, pp. 276–290. Springer, Heidelberg (2003)
36. Khalaf, R., Roller, D., Leymann, F.: Revisiting the Behavior of Fault and Compensation Handlers in WS-BPEL. In: Meersman, R., Dillon, T., Herrero, P. (eds.) OTM 2009. LNCS, vol. 5870, pp. 286–303. Springer, Heidelberg (2009)

Conjunctive Artifact-Centric Services

Piero Cangialosi, Giuseppe De Giacomo, Riccardo De Masellis, and Riccardo Rosati

Dipartimento di Informatica e Sistemistica "Antonio Ruberti"
SAPIENZA – Università di Roma
Via Ariosto, 25, 00185 Rome, Italy
lastname@dis.uniroma1.it

Abstract. Artifact-centric services are stateful service descriptions centered around "business artifacts", which contain both a *data schema* holding all the data of interest for the service, and a *lifecycle schema*, which specifies the process that the service enacts. In this paper, the data schemas are full-fledged relational databases, and the lifecycle schemas are specified as sets of condition-action rules, where conditions are evaluated against the current snapshot of the artifact, and where actions are suitable updates to database. The main characteristic of this work is that conditions and actions are based on conjunctive queries. In particular, we exploit recent results in data exchange to specify through tuple-generating-dependencies (tgds) the effects of actions. Using such basis we develop sound and complete verification procedures, which, in spite of the fact that the number of states of an artifact-centric service can be infinite, reduce to the finite case through a suitable use of homomorphism induced by the conjunctive queries.

1 Introduction

In the past years, what can be called the artifact-centric approach to modeling workflows and services has emerged, with the fundamental characteristic of considering both data and processes as first-class citizens in service design and analysis [21,17,11], see also [27,1]. In this approach the key elements of services are *(i)* data manipulated, which correspond to key business-relevant entities, *(ii)* the service lifecycle (i.e., the process that the service follows), and *(iii)* the tasks invoked and executed. Executing a task has effects on the data managed by the service, on the service state, as well as on the information exchanged with the external world. This "artifact-centric" approach provides a simple and robust structure for workflow and services, and has been demonstrated in practice to permit efficiency in business transformation [5,6]. From the formal point of view, artifact-centric services deeply challenge the research community by requiring simultaneous attention to both data and processes. Indeed, on the one hand they deal with full-fledged processes and require analysis in terms of verification of sophisticated temporal properties [10]. On the other hand, the presence of data [2] makes the usual analysis based on model checking of finite-state systems impossible in general, since when data evolution is taken into account the whole system becomes infinite state. In this paper, we provide a formal model for a family of artifact-centric services, based on the notion of conjunctive queries, used both to define preconditions and effects of tasks. In this setting we take advantage of the recent literature on data exchange and data integration

P.P. Maglio et al. (Eds.): ICSOC 2010, LNCS 6470, pp. 318–333, 2010.

[15,18], which has deeply investigated mapping between databases based on correspondences between conjunctive queries, the so call tuple-generating dependencies (tgds) in the database jargon [2]. In a nutshell, the core idea of our work is to consider the current state of the data and their state after the performance of a task as two databases related through a set of tgds. More precisely, our model follows the spirit of [5,16], but with important generalizations. The artifact "data schema" is a full-fledged relational database, which is used to hold relevant information about the artifact as it passes through the workflow. The "lifecycle schema", which is used to specify the possible ways that the artifact can pass through the workflow, is specified as a set of condition-action rules, where the condition is evaluated against the current snapshot of the artifact (i.e., the current state of the database), and where the actions are "tasks" invocations, which query the current snapshot and generate the next snapshot possibly introducing existential values representing inputs from the outside world. Similar to the context of semantic web services [24], the behaviors of the tasks used here are characterized using pre- and postconditions. The key point, however, is that both pre-conditions and post-conditions are expressed as conjunctive queries. On top of such a system we introduce a powerful verification logic based on a variant of μ-calculus [19,22,13,7] to express temporal properties. Our verification logic is also based on conjunctive queries, in that it requires the atomic formulas to be conjunctive queries and disallows forms of negation of such queries. No limitations whatsoever are instead put on the fixpoint formulas that are the key element of the μ-calculus. The main result of the paper is showing that the resulting formalism, while quite expressive, and inherently infinite state, is decidable under a reasonable restriction, called *weak-acyclicity* [15], on the form of the tgds expressing the effects of actions. In particular we develop a sound, complete and terminating reasoning procedure for the verification formalism. The crux of the result is that conjunctive queries are unable to distinguish homomorphic equivalent databases, and under suitable but quite general circumstances, the number of homomorphically different states can be bounded to be finite. Thus we can reduce verification to model checking of a finite state abstraction (based on homomorphic equivalence) of the system.

2   Framework

The framework that we propose, called *conjunctive artifact-centric services*, merges data and processes following the artifact-centric approach. Namely an artifact is composed by the following three components:

- **Artifact Data Schema**, which captures the data schema of the information manipulated in the artifact. States of the processes correspond to instances to such a schema. Technically, the artifact data schema is a relational schema, and an instance is a relational database.
- **Artifact Tasks**, which is the set of atomic actions that can be used to manipulate data in the artifacts, i.e., to compute new states given the current one. We assume that the user can freely query (through certain answers, see later) the current data instance, and for simplicity we disregard a specific treatment of the output to the user. Technically, such tasks are specified in terms of dependencies between conjunctive queries.

– **Artifact lifecycle**, which specifies the actual process of the artifacts in terms of tasks that can be executed at each state of the process. Technically, the artifact lifecycle is specified in terms of condition-action rules, where the conditions are again based on conjunctive queries.

It should result immediately clear that such a setting produces in general infinite state processes, and that verification of such processes is in general undecidable. We will leverage on the notion of conjunctive query and the associated notion of homomorphism between instances to gain decidability of verification in spite of the infinite states.

2.1   Artifact Data Schema

Let us enter the formalism by showing how data are represented. As customary in relational databases, we consider an **artifact data schema** as a tuple $S = \langle R, c \rangle$ where:

– $R = R_1, \dots, R_n$ is a finite set of *relational (predicate) symbols* each one with an associated arity;
– $c = c_1, c_2, \dots$ is a finite or countably infinite set of *constants*.

Given an artifact data schema S, an **artifact data instance** over a schema S is a standard first-order interpretation with a *fixed interpretation doman*. More precisely a data instance is a couple $I = \langle \Delta, \cdot^I \rangle$ where:

– Δ is a countably infinite *domain* fixed a-priori for every data instance. For convenience we partition Δ into two countable infinite disjoint sets $const(\Delta)$ and $ln(\Delta)$, and we use the first set to interpret *constants*, while the second is needed to correctly interpret existentials, we call the latter *labeled nulls* (see later);
– $\cdot^I$ is an interpretation function that associates:
  • to each constant symbol c a constant $c^I \in const(\Delta)$ such that for each $c_1, c_2 \in const(\Delta)$ if $c_1 \neq c_2$ then $c_1^I \neq c_2^I$, namely we make the *Unique Name Assumption*, furthermore we require that every interpretation interprets contants in the same way, that i, given any two interpretation I and I', we have that $c_n^I = c_n^{I'}$ for each constant c_n;
  • to each m-ary relation symbol R_i a (finite) m-ary relation $R_i^I \subseteq \Delta^m$.

Intuitively, an artifact data instance is alike a relational database instance, since the $\cdot^I$ function lists all tuples belonging to each relation.

We call a **fact** an expression $R_i(d_1, \dots, d_m)$. We say that a fact belongs to and interpretation I iff $d = \langle d_1, \dots, d_m \rangle \in R_i^I$. We can characterize the interpretation function $\cdot^I$ simply by listing of its facts (notice that such a set is finite). Following the database literature [2], we call to the **active domain** $\bar{\Delta}_I$ of an instance I the set of domain elements appearing in facts of I.

To query data instances we use a special class of first-order formulas, widely used in database theory, which corresponds to relational algebra select-project-join queries: *conjunctive queries*. A **conjunctive query** is a formula cq of the form:

$$\exists \boldsymbol{y}.body(\boldsymbol{y}, \boldsymbol{x})$$

where *body* is a conjunction of atomic formulas involving constants (but no labeled nulls), existentially quantified variables y and free variables x.

Intuitively a conjunctive queries returns as answer the domain elements (both constants and nulls) that substitute to the free variables make the formula true in the data instance. More formally, let $I = \langle \Delta, \cdot^I \rangle$ an artifact instance, the *answer to a conjunctive query cq(x)* with free variables x, denoted by $cq(x)^I$ is defined as:

$$cq(x)^I = \{\eta \mid \langle I, \eta \rangle \models cq(x)\}$$

with $\eta : x \rightarrow \Delta$ an assignment for the free variables. In fact, as usual in the database literature [2], we see assignments η simply as tuples of domain elements to be substituted to the free variables.

The characterizing property of conjunctive queries from the semantical point of view is that they are invariant under homomorphic equivalence [2]. That is if two data instances I and I' are homomorphic, then each boolean (without free variables) conjunctive query cq produces exactly the same (boolean) answer: $cq(x)^I = cq(x)^{I'}$.

Homomorphism [8] indeed plays a key role in our setting, so we remind its definition here. Given two instances $I_1 = \langle \Delta, \cdot^{I_1} \rangle$ and $I_2 = \langle \Delta, \cdot^{I_2} \rangle$ over the same schema $\mathcal{S}$, a **homomorphism** from I_1 to I_2, denoted by $h : I_1 \rightarrow I_2$, is a function from Δ to Δ such that:

1. for every constant c, we have that $h(c) = c$ and
2. for every $\langle d_1, \ldots, d_m \rangle \in R_i^{I_1}$, we have that $\langle h(d_1), \ldots, h(d_m) \rangle \in R_i^{I_2}$.

Two instances I_1 and I_2 are **homomorphically equivalent**, written $I_1 \overset{h}{=} I_2$, if there exist two homomorphisms $h_1 : I_1 \rightarrow I_2$ and $h_2 : I_2 \rightarrow I_1$.

A homomorphism $h : I_1 \rightarrow I_2$ preserves the interpretation of constants but not of labeled nulls of I_1, which are mapped either to constants or nulls in I_2, that is the homomorphism can "determine" some nulls values assigning them to constants. In other words, homomorphism interprets nulls of I_1 as existential values.

The existential interpretation of labeled nulls given by homomorphisms suggest a different way of answering to a conjunctive query, that essentially sees an interpretation as a *theory* where all nulls are treated as existential values. To make this notion precise, given an interpretation I we define the (*infinite*) set W_I of all interpretations $I' = \langle \Delta, \cdot^{I'} \rangle$ over $\mathcal{S}$ such that there exists an homomorphism $h : I \rightarrow I'$. Then we define the **Certain Answers** of a conjunctive query cq as:

$$cert^I(cq) = \bigcap_{w \in W_I} cq^{I_w}$$

That is the certain answers to a query are all those tuples of (active domain) elements (in fact constants) in I that are produced by the query in every interpretation I' such that there exists an homomorphism $h : I \rightarrow I'$. Formally, it can be shown that, the certain answers correspond to the tuples of constants such that, substituted to the free variables of the query, would make the resulting query logically implied by the theory constituted by a single conjunctive query formed by the logical AND of all facts in I, considering all labeled nulls as existentially quantified. From a more pragmatical point of view, when using certain answers we consider the current instance as representative of several possible instances, and while we assume to have incomplete information on which is exactly the current instance, we still produce all answers that would be produced in all possible instances.

In our framework, we assume that the user can pose arbitrary conjunctive queries to the current instance, but require them to be evaluated returning the certain answers. In this way we become independent of the particular null values occurring in the data instance, since they are not returned as answers, though they can still be used as witness of existential quantified variables.

2.2   Artifact Tasks

A task is specified as a set of *effects* that it can produce, and when it is performed over the current (artifact) data instance, the result is a completely new data instance made up of a subset of the action's *effects*. The formalization of an effect is borrowed from the database and data exchange literature and in particular from the notion of *tuple generating dependencies* (tgds) [2,15]. A **(conjunctive) effect specification** ξ over a schema S is a formula of the form:

$$\exists y.\phi(x, y, c) \rightarrow \exists w.\psi(x, w, d)$$

where ϕ and ψ are conjunctions of atoms over S; x, y, w denote the variables and c, d the constants occurring in ϕ and ψ. We call the left-hand side of ξ the *premise*, and the right-hand side the *conclusion*. Notice that both the premise and the conclusion are *conjunctive queries*. Formally, let $I = \langle \Delta, \cdot^I \rangle$ be an artifact instance over the schema S, and $\xi = \exists y\ \phi(x, y, c) \rightarrow \exists w\ \psi(x, w, d)$ an effect specification. The result of **enacting effect specification** ξ on I, is a set of facts $\xi(I)$ defined as follows:

> Let $\eta = (\exists y\ \phi(x, y, c))^I$, be the answer to the query $\exists y\ \phi(x, y, c)$ in I, then for each $\eta_i \in \eta$ we proceed as follows. For each atomic formula $R_i(x, w, d)$ occurring in ψ, we include in $\xi(I)$ a new fact $R_i^{I'}(x, w, d)|_{\eta_i}^{\psi}$, obtained by substituting every variable in x with the corresponding element given by the assignment η_i, and every variable in w with a fresh (not appearing elsewhere) labeled null ln.

Intuitively, the premise, acting like a query, selects values form the current instance, while the conclusion builds the resulting instance by inserting them in possibly different positions of the schema, and by potentially introducing fresh elements, namely, the labeled nulls and fixed constants.

A **task** T for a schema S is specified as a set $\xi = \{\xi_1, \dots, \xi_n\}$ of conjunctive effect specifications. The result of **executing task** T on I, denoted by $I \xrightarrow{T} I^T$, is a new instance $I^T = \langle \Delta, \cdot^{I^T} \rangle$ on the same schema S, obtained as the union of the enactments of each effect specification. Namely $I^T = \langle \Delta, \cdot^{I^T} \rangle$ where is the interpretation function $\cdot^{I^T}$ characterized by the facts $\bigcup_{\xi \in \xi} \xi(I)$.

Let's make some key observations on such tasks. First, we observe that the role of the existential qualification on the two sides of an effect specification is very different.

The existential qualification on the left-hand side is the usual one used in conjunctive queries, which projects out variables used only to make joins. The existential qualification on the right-hand side, instead, is used as a witness of values that should be chosen by the user when executing the effect. In other words, the choice function used for assign witness to the existential on the right should be in the hand of the user. Here since we do not have such a choice at hand, we introduce a fresh null, to which we assign an existential meaning through homomorphism. Essentially we imply that there exists a choice made by the user of the value assigned to those variables.

The second observation is that we do not make any persistence (or frame [23]) assumption in our formalization. In principle at every move we substitute the whole old data instance with a new one. On the other hand, it should be clear that we can easily write effect specifications that *copy* big chunks of the old instance into the new one. For example, $R_i(x) \rightarrow R_i(x)$ copies the entire extension of a relation R_i.

2.3 Artifact Lifecycle

The artifact lifecyle is defined in terms of condition/action rules, that specify, for every instance, which tasks can be executed. A **(condition/action) rule** for a schema S is a couple $\varrho = \langle \pi, T \rangle$ where π is a precondition, and T is a task. The precondition is a *closed* formula over S of the following form:

$$\pi ::= cq \mid \neg \pi \mid \pi_1 \wedge \pi_2$$

where cq is a boolean conjunctive query. Preconditions are arbitrary boolean combinations of boolean conjunctive queries interpreted under the certain answer semantics, namely:

$$
\begin{aligned}
I &\triangleright cq & &\text{iff } cert^I(cq) = true \\
I &\triangleright \neg \pi & &\text{iff } I \not\triangleright \pi \\
I &\triangleright \pi_1 \wedge \pi_2 & &\text{iff } I \triangleright \pi_1 \text{ and } I \triangleright \pi_2
\end{aligned}
$$

In order to execute a task T, on an instance I, precondition π must certainly hold in I, written as $I \triangleright \pi$, and, if this is the case, a new instance I^T is generated, according to T's effects.

Observe that, while we disallow negation in task effects so as to exploit the theory of conjunctive queries, which do not include negation, in the condition/action rules we allow for it, but to do so we actually require conditions to be based on certain answers of conjunctive queries, in this way we force a sort of "negation-as-failure" for negation [9].

Example 1. We illustrate here an example of specification. The scenario concerns an institution, e.g. a bank, that provides services to its customers, such as loans or money transfers. Every service has a distinct cost, that has to be paid in advance by customers that asked for it. A customer may inquire for the provision of a service, that first has to be approved by a supervisor, then paid, and finally provisioned by the bank. Moreover there are special "premier customers" that do not need the service's approval.

The **artifact schema** S consists of the following relation symbols: $Customer(\underline{cust\_ssn}, name)$ is the relation containing customers information; $Service(\underline{serv\_code}, cost)$ contains information about the different types of services that the bank offers to its customers; $Service\_Claimed(\underline{serv\_code}, cust\_ssn)$ keeps track of information of services requested by clients; $Request\_Exam(\underline{serv\_code}, spv\_name, outcome)$ is the relation containing the names of supervisors in charge of evaluating customers' claims; $Payment(\underline{serv\_code}, cust\_ssn, amount)$ contains information about service payments; $Service\_Provided(\underline{serv\_code}, cust\_ssn)$ holds the services which have been provided; $Premier\_Member(\underline{cust\_ssn})$ contains the customers that reach the "premier" status; $Account(\underline{acc\_id}, cust\_ssn, maximum\_withdrawal, credit\_card)$ is the relation that holds information about bank accounts.

Tasks model the possible modifications that can be performed over the artifact schema. As syntactic sugar, we include some input parameters (the symbols between brackets after the task name). In order to execute them such parameters must be instantiated with constants.

- **Claim_service(cust_ssn, serv_code):**
  - $\xi_1 = \exists x, y. \, Customer(cust\_ssn, x) \wedge Service(serv\_code, y) \rightarrow Service\_Claimed(serv\_code, cust\_ssn)$
  - $\xi_2, \ldots, \xi_9 = copy\_frame$

  models the choice of the customer $cust\_ssn$ to apply for the provision of a new service of type $serv\_code$. Since the resulting instance is a completely new one consisting in tuples added by the task only, we need to explicitly "copy" all facts that we do not require to be dropped after the task execution. That is exactly the role of effects $\xi_2, \ldots, \xi_9$ that, for all relations $R_1, \ldots, R_m$, are defined as $\xi_i = R_i(x_1, \ldots, x_n) \rightarrow R_i(x_1, \ldots, x_n)$ with $i \in \{1, \ldots m\}$. Intuitively, the result of firing task $Claim\_service(cust\_ssn, \, serv\_code)$ on an instance I results in a new instance I' that either contains I but also include the new tuple $Service\_Claimed(cust\_ssn, serv\_code)$ provided that the premise are satisfied by I, or $I' = I$ if not.

- **Make_payment(cust_ssn, serv_code, amount):**
  - $\xi_1 = Service\_Claimed(cust\_ssn, serv\_code) \rightarrow Payment(serv\_code, cust\_ssn, amount)$
  - $\xi_2, \ldots, \xi_9 = copy\_frame$

  models the payment operation performed by a customer for a service that has been previously requested, i.e., the resulting instance may include the tuple $Payment(cust\_ssn, serv\_code, amount)$.

- **Grant_approval(serv_code):**
  - $\xi_1 = Service\_Claimed(serv\_code, x) \rightarrow \exists z. \, Request\_Exam(serv\_code, z, \text{``approved''})$
  - $\xi_2, \ldots, \xi_9 = copy\_frame$

  represents the approval of a service that has been requested, by including the fact $Request\_Exam(serv\_code, ln, \text{``approved''})$ where ln is a fresh labeled null that models a possible supervisor.

- **Provide_services():**
  - $\xi_1 = Service\_Claimed(x, y) \wedge Request\_Exam(x, v, \text{``approved''}) \rightarrow Service\_Provided(x, y)$
  - $\xi_2, \ldots, \xi_9 = copy\_frame$

models the delivery of all services that have had explicitly approved by a supervisor and that was already paid. The task

- **Quick_provide_service():**
  - $\xi_1 = Service\_Claimed(x, y) \rightarrow Service\_Provided(x, y)$
  - $\xi_2, \ldots, \xi_9 = copy\_frame$

delivers all the services for which it was paid the correct amount and that have been requested from a premier customer. Lastly

- **Award_premier_status():**
  - $\xi_1 = \exists y, u, w, t.\, Customer(x, y) \wedge Service\_Provided(y, x) \wedge Account(u, x, w, t) \rightarrow Premier\_Member(x)$
  - $\xi_2, \ldots, \xi_9 = copy\_frame$

awards the premier status to all customers holding a bank account that applied for the provision of a service that had already been accepted.

Finally, we assume that condition-action rules that specify the **artifact lifecycle** allow for executing every task in every state, except for the following rules:

$$\varrho_1 = \langle \exists x, y, u, v, w.\, Payment(x, y, w) \wedge Service(x, u) \wedge Request\_Exam(x, v, \text{``approved''}),$$
$$\textbf{Provide\_services()}\rangle$$
$$\varrho_2 = \langle \exists x, y, w.\, Payment(x, y, w) \wedge Service(x, w) \wedge Premier\_Member(y),$$
$$\textbf{Quick\_provide\_service()}\rangle$$
$$\varrho_3 = \langle \exists x, y, u, w, t.\, Service\_Provided(x, y) \wedge Account(u, y, w, t),$$
$$\textbf{Award\_premier\_status()}\rangle \qquad \qquad \Box$$

2.4 Artifact Executions

Let us consider an **artifact** as a tuple $A = \langle \mathcal{S}, \mathcal{T}, \mathcal{C} \rangle$, where: *(i)* $\mathcal{S}$ is an *artifact data schema*; *(ii)* $\mathcal{T}$ is a set of *tasks*; and *(iii)* $\mathcal{C}$ is a set of *condition/action rules*.

An **artifact transition system** for A starting from a initial data instance I_0 is a tuple $\mathfrak{A}_A = \langle \Sigma, \sigma_0, L, Tr \rangle$ where *(i)* Σ is the (possibly infinite) set of states; *(ii)* σ_0 is the initial state; *(iii)* $L : \Sigma \rightarrow \mathcal{I}$ is a labeling function that associates to each state in Σ a data instance of S, with the constraint that $L(\sigma_0) = I_0$; *(iv)* $Tr \subseteq \mathcal{I} \times \mathcal{T} \times \mathcal{I}$ is the transition relation such that $\langle \sigma, T, \sigma' \rangle \in Tr$, denoted $\sigma \xrightarrow{T} \sigma'$ if there exists a rule $\varrho = \langle \pi, T \rangle$ such that $L(\sigma) \rhd \pi$, and $L(\sigma') = I'$ where I' is the result of applying task T to data instance $I = L(\sigma)$, i.e we must have that $I \xrightarrow{T} I'$.

Notice that if an artifact A may generate an infinite number of data instances in its evolution, then every transition system associated to it must have and infinite number of states in order for the labeling function L to be correctly defined. Though transition systems may have more states than data instances, which implies that more states may be labelled with the same data instance. Among the various artifact transition systems for A starting from a initial data instance I_0 there is one of particular significance, the so called **execution tree** of an artifact A starting from I_0, in which each state of the transition system correspond to the full history that has generated it. Such an execution tree is a transition system $\mathfrak{T}_A = \langle \Sigma, \sigma_0, L, Tr \rangle$ whose set of states is defined as follows: *(i)* the root is σ_0; *(iii)* given a state σ for each task $T \in \mathcal{T}$ such that there exists a rule $\varrho = \langle \pi, T \rangle$ such that $L(\sigma) \rhd \pi$, add a state σ'_T, and define $L(\sigma'_T) = I'$ where I' is data instance resulting by applying T to $L(\sigma)$. We can interpret σ'_T as the T-successor of the node σ.

We observe that the number of states of the execution tree is indeed *infinite*, and also that given any state σ, by looking at the path from the root σ_0 to σ, we can reconstruct the full history that has lead to σ, including the sequence of tasks invoked and the resulting data instance at each step.

All transition systems for and artifact A starting from a given data instance I_0, even if different, denote the same behavior, namely the behavior of the artifact A starting from I_0 and executing the various tasks. To formally capture such and equivalence between transition system, we make use of the notion of *bisimulation* [20]. In fact in formally detailing such a notion, we consider right from the start that the user can only query data instances through conjunctive queries, evaluated to return certain answers.

Given two artifact transition systems $\mathfrak{A}_1 = \langle \Sigma_1, \sigma_{0,1}, L_1, Tr_1 \rangle$ and $\mathfrak{A}_2 = \langle \Sigma_2, \sigma_{0,2}, L_2, Tr_2 \rangle$ a **bisimulation** is a relation $B \subseteq \Sigma_1 \times \Sigma_2$ such that:

$\langle \sigma_1, \sigma_2 \rangle \in B$ implies that:

1. for every conjunctive query cq we have that $cert^{L_1(\sigma_1)}(cq) = cert^{L_2(\sigma_2)}(cq)$;
2. if $\sigma_1 \overset{a}{\Longrightarrow} \sigma'_1$ then there exists σ'_2 such that $\sigma_2 \overset{a}{\Longrightarrow} \sigma'_2$ and $\langle \sigma'_1, \sigma'_2 \rangle \in B$;
3. if $\sigma_2 \overset{a}{\Longrightarrow} \sigma'_2$ then there exists σ'_1 such that $\sigma_1 \overset{a}{\Longrightarrow} \sigma'_1$ and $\langle \sigma'_1, \sigma'_2 \rangle \in B$.

We say that two states σ_1 and σ_2 are *bisimilar*, denoted as $\sigma_1 \sim \sigma_2$ if there exists a bisimulation B such that $\langle \sigma_1, \sigma_2 \rangle \in B$. Two transition systems $\mathfrak{A}_1 = \langle \Sigma_1, \sigma_{0,1}, L_1, Tr_1 \rangle$ and $\mathfrak{A}_2 = \langle \Sigma_2, \sigma_{0,2}, L_2, Tr_2 \rangle$ are **bisimilar** if $\sigma_{0,1} \sim \sigma_{0,2}$. We are now able to introduce the verification formalism.

3   Verification Formalism

We turn to verification of conjunctive artifact-centric services. To specify dynamic properties we will use μ-calculus [14] which is one of the most powerful temporal logics for which model checking has been investigated, and indeed is able to express both linear time logics, as LTL, and branching time logics such as CTL or CTL* [10]. In particular, we need to introduce a variant of μ-calculus, called $\mu\mathcal{L}$ that conforms with the basic assumption of our formalism: the use of conjunctive queries and certain answers to talk about data instances. This intuitive requirement can be made formal as follows: our μ-calculus variant must by invariant with respect to the notion of bisimulation introduced above.

Given an artifact $A = \langle \mathcal{S}, \mathcal{T}, \mathcal{C} \rangle$, the **verification formulas** of $\mu\mathcal{L}$ for A have the following form:

$$\Phi ::= cq \mid \neg\Phi \mid \Phi_1 \wedge \Phi_2 \mid [T]\Phi \mid \langle T \rangle \Phi \mid \mu Z.\Phi \mid \nu Z.\Phi \mid Z$$

where cq is a boolean conjunctive query (interpreted through certain answers) over the artifact schema, Z is a predicate variable symbol.

The symbols μ and ν can be considered as quantifiers, and we make use of notions of scope, bound and free occurrences of variables, closed formulas, etc. The definitions of these notions are the same as in first-order logic, treating μ and ν as quantifiers. In fact, we are interested only in closed formulas as specification of temporal properties to verify. For formulas of the form $\mu Z.\Phi$ and $\nu Z.\Phi$, we require the *syntactic monotonicity* of Φ wrt Z: Every occurrence of the variable Z in Φ must be within the scope of an even number of negation signs. In μ-calculus, given the requirement of syntactic monotonicity, the least fixpoint $\mu Z.\Phi$ and the greatest fixpoint $\nu Z.\Phi$ always exist. In order to define the meaning of such formulas we resort to transition systems. Let $\mathfrak{A}_A = \langle \Sigma, \sigma_0, L, Tr \rangle$ be a transition system for A with initial data instance I_0, and let $\mathcal{V}$ be predicate valuation on $\mathfrak{A}$, i.e., a mapping from the predicate variables to subsets of the states in $\mathfrak{A}$. Then, we assign meaning to μ-calculus formulas by associating to $\mathfrak{A}$ and $\mathcal{V}$ an *extension function* $(\cdot)^{\mathfrak{A}}_{\mathcal{V}}$, which maps μ-calculus formulas to subsets of $\mathcal{I}$. The extension function $(\cdot)^{\mathfrak{A}}_{\mathcal{V}}$ is defined inductively as follows:

$$
\begin{aligned}
(cq)^{\mathfrak{A}}_{\mathcal{V}} &= \{\sigma \in \Sigma \mid cert^{L(\sigma)}(cq)\} \\
(Z)^{\mathfrak{A}}_{\mathcal{V}} &= \mathcal{V}(Z) \subseteq \Sigma \\
(\neg\Phi)^{\mathfrak{A}}_{\mathcal{V}} &= \Sigma - (\Phi)^{\mathfrak{A}}_{\mathcal{V}} \\
(\Phi_1 \wedge \Phi_2)^{\mathfrak{A}}_{\mathcal{V}} &= (\Phi_1)^{\mathfrak{A}}_{\mathcal{V}} \cap (\Phi_2)^{\mathfrak{A}}_{\mathcal{V}} \\
(\langle T \rangle \Phi)^{\mathfrak{A}}_{\mathcal{V}} &= \{\sigma \in \Sigma \mid \exists \sigma'. \sigma \overset{T}{\Longrightarrow} \sigma' \text{ and } \sigma' \in (\Phi)^{\mathfrak{A}}_{\mathcal{V}}\} \\
([T]\Phi)^{\mathfrak{A}}_{\mathcal{V}} &= \{\sigma \in \Sigma \mid \forall \sigma'. \sigma \overset{T}{\Longrightarrow} \sigma' \text{ implies } \sigma' \in (\Phi)^{\mathfrak{A}}_{\mathcal{V}}\} \\
(\mu Z.\Phi)^{\mathfrak{A}}_{\mathcal{V}} &= \bigcap\{\mathcal{E} \subseteq \Sigma \mid (\Phi)^{\mathfrak{A}}_{\mathcal{V}[Z \leftarrow \mathcal{E}]} \subseteq \mathcal{E}\} \\
(\nu Z.\Phi)^{\mathfrak{A}}_{\mathcal{V}} &= \bigcup\{\mathcal{E} \subseteq \Sigma \mid \mathcal{E} \subseteq (\Phi)^{\mathfrak{A}}_{\mathcal{V}[Z \leftarrow \mathcal{E}]}\}
\end{aligned}
$$

Intuitively, the extension function $(\cdot)^{\mathfrak{A}}_{\mathcal{V}}$ assigns to the various constructs of μ-calculus the following meanings:

- The boolean connectives have the expected meaning.
- The extension of $\langle T \rangle \Phi$ includes the states σ such that starting from σ, there is an execution of task T that leads to a successive state σ' included in the extension of Φ.
- The extension of $[T]\Phi$ includes the states σ such that starting from σ, each execution of task T leads to some successive state σ' included in the extension of Φ.
- The extension of $\mu Z.\Phi$ is the *smallest subset* $\mathcal{E}_{\mu}$ of Σ such that, assigning to Z the extension $\mathcal{E}_{\mu}$, the resulting extension of Φ is contained in $\mathcal{E}_{\mu}$. That is, the extension of $\mu X.\Phi$ is the *least fixpoint* of the operator $\lambda \mathcal{E}.(\Phi)^{\mathfrak{A}}_{\mathcal{V}[Z \leftarrow \mathcal{E}]}$ (here $\mathcal{V}[Z \leftarrow \mathcal{E}]$ denotes the predicate valuation obtained from $\mathcal{V}$ by forcing the valuation of Z to be $\mathcal{E}$).
- Similarly, the extension of $\nu X.\Phi$ is the *greatest subset* $\mathcal{E}_{\nu}$ of Σ such that, assigning to X the extension $\mathcal{E}_{\nu}$, the resulting extension of Φ contains $\mathcal{E}_{\nu}$. That is, the extension of $\nu X.\Phi$ is the *greatest fixpoint* of the operator $\lambda \mathcal{E}.(\Phi)^{\mathfrak{A}}_{\mathcal{V}[X \leftarrow \mathcal{E}]}$.

The reasoning problem we are interested in is **model checking**: verify whether a $\mu\mathcal{L}$ **closed formula Φ holds in an artifact A with initial data instance I_0**. Formally such problem is defined as checking whether $\sigma_0 \in I \in (\Phi)^{\mathfrak{T}^{I_0}_A}_{\mathcal{V}}$ (where $\mathcal{V}$ is any valuation, since Φ is closed), that is, whether Φ is true in the root of the A execution tree.

On the other hand we know that there are severals transition system that are bisimilar to the execution tree $\mathfrak{T}^{I_0}_A$. The following theorem state that the formula evaluation in $\mu\mathcal{L}$ is indeed invariant wrt bisimilarity, so we can equivalently check any such transition systems.

Theorem 1. *Let $\mathfrak{A}_1$ and $\mathfrak{A}_2$ be two bisimilar artifact transition systems. Then, for every pair of states σ_1 and σ_2 such that $\sigma_1 \sim \sigma_2$ (including the initial ones), for all formulas Φ of $\mu\mathcal{L}$, we have that $\sigma_{0,1} \in (\Phi)^{\mathfrak{A}_1}_{\mathcal{V}}$ iff $\sigma_{0,2} \in (\Phi)^{\mathfrak{A}_1}_{\mathcal{V}}$.*

Proof. The proof is analogous to the standard proof of bisimulation invariance of mu-calculus, see e.g., [7], though taking into account our specific definition of bisimulation, which makes use of conjunctive queries and certain answers as their evaluation.

In particular if, for some reason we can get a transition system that is bisimilar to the execution tree, and is *finite*, then we can apply the following theorem.

Theorem 2. *Checking a $\mu\mathcal{L}$ formula Φ over a finite transition system $\mathfrak{A}_A = \langle \Sigma, \sigma_0, L, Tr \rangle$ can be done in time*

$$O((|\mathfrak{A}| \cdot |\Phi|)^k)$$

where $|\mathfrak{A}| = |\Sigma| + |Tr|$, i.e., the number of states plus the number of transitions of $\mathfrak{A}$, $|\Phi|$ is the size of formula Φ (in fact, considering conjunctive queries as atomic), and k is the number of nested fixpoints, i.e., fixpoints whose variables are one within the scope of the other.

Proof. We can use the standard μ-calculus model checking algorithms [13], with the proviso that for atomic formulas we use the computation of certain answers of conjunctive queries.

Example 2. Continuing the example introduced above, suppose now we have an initial artifact data instance where: $Customer^{I_0} = \{\langle 337505, "JohnSmith" \rangle, \langle 125232, "MaryStewart" \rangle\}$, and $Service^{I_0} = \{\langle L057, 100 \rangle, \langle L113, 150 \rangle, \langle C002, 50 \rangle\}$, and all the other relations are empty. Consider the following liveness property, which aks if it is actually possible to obtain the provision of a service:

$$\mu Z. ((\exists\, x_1, x_2, x_3. Service(x_1, x_2) \wedge Service\_Provided(x_1, x_3)) \vee \bigvee_{T \in \mathcal{T}} \langle T \rangle Z$$

The formula is actually true: for example, a state in which $Service\_Provided(L057, 337505)$ holds can be reached after the following sequence of tasks: $Claim\_Service(337505, L057)$, $Make\_Payment(337505, L057, 100)$, $Grant\_Approval(L057)$ and finally $Provide\_Services()$. Next consider the safety property asking whether every possible reachable instance will always contain the information that the service $L113$ has been paid and provided:

$$\nu Z. (\exists\, x_1, x_2, x_3. Payment(L113, x_1, x_2) \wedge Service\_Provided(L113, x_3) \wedge \bigwedge_{T \in \mathcal{T}} [T](Z))$$

that is trivially false, since in the initial state I there is no payment for any service. More sophisticated properties such as strong form of fairness for example are also easily expressible in $\mu\mathcal{L}$, though for space limitation we don't report them here   □

4 Results

Notice that we still do not have a concrete technique for the verification problem, since model checking results in Theorem 2 only apply to finite structures. In fact, as a consequence of the undecidability of the implication problem for tgds (see e.g. [2]), it is obvious that, without any restrictions on effect specifications, the model checking in our setting is undecidable. Addressing condition of decidability is the purpose of this section. We start by introducing the notion of Skolem transition system and showing its relationship with the concept of execution tree of an artifact.

4.1 Skolem Transition System

For every effect specification $\xi = \exists y \ \phi(x, y, c) \rightarrow \exists w \ \psi(x, w, d)$ and for every $w \in w$ we define a Skolem term $f_w^\xi(x)$. Such Skolem term is interpreted as a fixed injective function $f_w^\xi : \Delta \rightarrow ln(\Delta)$. In this way, enacting an effect ξ on a the data instance I results in the set of facts $R_i^{I'}(x, f_{w_1}^\xi(x), \ldots, f_{w_n}^\xi(x), d)|_{\eta_i}^\psi$, for every for every atom $R_i^{I'}(x, w_1, \ldots, w_n), d)$ that occurs in ψ and every answer to the left-hand-side query $\eta_i \in (\exists y. \phi(x, y, c)^{I'})$. The **Skolem execution of a task** T in I is the data instance J formed by the union of all Skolem enactment of the effects in T. Notice that being the interpretation of Skolem terms an fixed function, the Skolem execution of a task is fully determined and functional.

Given an artifact $A = (\mathcal{S}, \mathcal{T}, \mathcal{C})$ and an initial artifact data instance I_0, we define the **Skolem transition system** $\mathfrak{S}_A = \langle \Sigma_s, \sigma_{0,s}, L_s, Tr_s \rangle$ inductively as follows:

- $\sigma_{0,s} \in \Sigma$ and such that $L_s(\sigma_{0,s}) = I_0$;
- for all instances $\sigma \in \Sigma_s$ and for each task $T \in \mathcal{T}$ such that there exists a rule $\varrho = \langle \pi, T \rangle$ such that $L_s(\sigma) \rhd \pi$, let J be data instance resulting from the Skolem execution of task T in $L_s(\sigma)$ then:
  - if there exists an instance $\sigma' \in \Sigma_s$ such that $L_s(\sigma') \stackrel{h}{=} J$ then add the transition $\sigma \stackrel{T}{\Longrightarrow} \sigma'$ to Tr_s;
  - if such a state does not exists, then add the new state σ_J to Σ with $L_s(\sigma_J) = J$ to $\mathcal{I}$ and add the transition edge $\sigma \stackrel{T}{\Longrightarrow} \sigma_J$ to Tr_s.

Theorem 3. *Let $A = (\mathcal{S}, \mathcal{T}, \mathcal{C})$ be an artifact and I_0 be a data instance over schema $\mathcal{S}$. Then, the execution tree $\mathfrak{T}_{A, I_o} = \langle \Sigma_t, \sigma_{0,t}, L_t, Tr_t \rangle$ is bisimilar to the Skolem transition system $\mathfrak{S}_{A, I_o} = \langle \Sigma_s, \sigma_{0,s}, L_s, Tr_s \rangle$.*

Proof. Let us consider the bisimulation relation $B_{ts} = \{ \langle \sigma_t, \sigma_s \rangle \mid \sigma_t \in \Sigma_t \wedge \sigma_s \in \Sigma_s \wedge L_t(\sigma_s) \stackrel{h}{=} L_t(\sigma_t) \}$. This is the relation formed by the pris of states of the two transition system such that their labeling data instances are homomorphically equivalent. We show that B_{ts} is bisimulation (according to our definition). Indeed consider $\langle \sigma_s, \sigma_t \rangle \in B_{ts}$. Then:

1. For each cq, since $L_t(\sigma_s) \stackrel{h}{=} L_t(\sigma_t)$ we have that $cert^{L_t(\sigma_s)}(cq) = cert^{L_t(\sigma_s)}(cq)$ from the definition of certain answers and homomorphical equivalence.
2. If $\sigma_t \stackrel{a}{\Longrightarrow} \sigma'_t$ then there is a rule $\varrho = \langle \pi, T \rangle$ and $L_t(\sigma_t) \rhd \pi$. Since $L_t(\sigma_s) \stackrel{h}{=} L_t(\sigma_t)$ then (i) $L_s(\sigma_s) \rhd \pi$ as well, so $\sigma_s \stackrel{a}{\Longrightarrow} \sigma'_s$ moreover it is easy to see that $L_t(\sigma'_t) \stackrel{h}{=} L_s(\sigma'_s)$ by considering definition of executing a task and a Skolem executing task.

3. Symmetric to the previous case.

Finally observe that since $L_t(\sigma_{0,t}) = L_s(\sigma_{0,s}) = I_0$ we trivially get that $\langle \sigma_{0,s}, \sigma_{O,t} \rangle \in B_{ts}$.

This theorem basically allow us to make use of a Skolem transition system rather than an execution tree for our verification tasks, taking advantage of Theorem 1. using *equivalence classes* of homomorphically equivalent instances for the purpose of verification. Notice, however, that this theorem it is not sufficient to achieve a decidability result, since the number of state in the Skolem transition system is bounded only by the number of homomorphically non-equivalent data instances, which is infinite in general. Next we concentrate on conditions that guarantee its finiteness.

4.2   Decidability

Given an artifact $A = \langle S, T, C \rangle$ and the set $\mathcal{I}$ of possible interpretations over S, we consider two different functions: the first one, $f : T \times \mathcal{I} \to \mathcal{I}$, is the usual result of Skolem executing a task on I; while the second one, $g : T \times \mathcal{I} \to \mathcal{I}$, is the *inflationary* variant of the first one: $g(T, I) = f(T, I) \cup I$, that is g generates the result of Skolem executing the task T on I and then copies all "old" facts of I. Notice that no contradiction can arise since effects of tasks, being based on conjunctive queries, are only positive. For f and g we have the following results:

Lemma 1. *Functions g and f are* monotonic *wrt set containment. Namely, for every task T and instance I, if $I \subseteq J$, we have both $f(T, I) \subseteq f(T, J)$ and $g(T, I) \subseteq g(T, J)$.*

Lemma 2. *Function g is* monotonically increasing, *namely for every task T and instance I, $I \subseteq g(T, I)$ holds.*

The same result does not hold for function f, because some facts may not be propagated.

Lemma 3. *For every task T and instance I, we have that $f(T, I) \subseteq g(T, I)$.*

Let us inductively define the set of instances $\mathcal{L}_{I_0}$ obtained, starting from I_0, by repeatedly applying $g(\cdot, \cdot)$ in all possible ways. This is the least set such that

- $I_0 \subseteq \mathcal{L}_{I_0}$;
- if $I' \subseteq \mathcal{L}_{I_0}$ then, for every $T \in \mathcal{T}$, $g(T, I') \subseteq \mathcal{L}_{I_0}$.

Notice also that, as an immediate consequence of its inductive definition, we get $g(T, \mathcal{L}_{I_0}) = \mathcal{L}_{I_0}$, since $\mathcal{L}_{I_0}$ is a *fixpoint*, indeed, the *least fixpoint* [26].

Lemma 4. *Let I_0 be an instance and $\mathcal{L}_{I_0}$ as above, then for every sequence of instances $I_0, \ldots, I_n$ such that $I_{i+1} = g(T_i, I_i)$, we have that $I_i \subseteq \mathcal{L}_{I_0}$, for $i = 0, \ldots, n$.*

Proof. By induction of length n of a task sequence.

Lemma 5. *Let $A = \langle S, T, C \rangle$ be an artifact, I_0 and initial data instance, and $\mathcal{L}_{I_0}$ as above. Then for every sequence of instances $I_0, \ldots, I_n$, such that $I_{i+1} = f(T_i, I_i)$, we have that $I_i \subseteq \mathcal{L}_{I_0}$, for $i = 0, \ldots, n$.*

Proof. By Lemma 3 and 4.

Roughly speaking, the above lemmas, guarantee that every possible instance that can be produced from I_0 by applying in every possible way both f and g functions is bounded by the least fixpoint $\mathcal{L}_{I_0}$. Notice however that $\mathcal{L}_{I_0}$ is infinite in general, in order to get decidability we will still need a finite bound on $\mathcal{L}_{I_0}$.

To get such condition we exploit results from [15] on *weakly-acyclic* tgds. Weak-acyclicity is a syntactic notion that involves the so-called *dependency graph* of the set of tgds TG. Informally, a set TG of tgds is weakly-acyclic if there are no cycles in the dependency graph of TG involving "existential" relation positions. The key property of *weakly-acyclic* tgds is that chasing a data instance with them (i.e., applying them in all possible way) generates a stet of facts (a database) that is finite. We refer to [15] for more details. We show that, under the assumption that the tgds of the artifact are weakly-acyclic, the set $\mathcal{L}_{I_0}$ introduced above is *finite*.

Lemma 6. *Let $A = \langle \mathcal{S}, \mathcal{T}, \mathcal{C} \rangle$ be an artifact. If all effect specifications in every task $T \in \mathcal{T}$ are weakly-acyclic, then the fixpoint $\mathcal{L}_{I_0}$ has finite cardinality.*

Proof. If the set of all effect specification is weakly-acyclic, from [15] we know that the *dependency graph* has no cycle going through a special edge [15]. Since every special edge represents the application of a Skolem function, it follows that for every Skolem execution task sequence, it is not possible to nest the same Skolem function. Indeed, suppose that at a certain point, an effect specification $\xi = \exists \boldsymbol{y}.\phi(\boldsymbol{x}, \boldsymbol{y}, \boldsymbol{c}) \rightarrow \exists \boldsymbol{w}.\psi(\boldsymbol{x}, \boldsymbol{w}, \boldsymbol{d})$ adds a fact $R_i^I(\boldsymbol{x}, f_{w_1}^\xi(\boldsymbol{x}), \dots, f_{w_i}^\xi(f_{w_j}^{\xi'}(\dots(f_{w_i}^\xi(\boldsymbol{x})), \dots, f_{w_n}^\xi(\boldsymbol{x}), \boldsymbol{d})|_{\eta_i}^\psi$, this means that: *(i)* there is at least a special edge from a position p_1 in a relation R_j that occurs in ϕ, to a position p_2 in R_i that occurs in ψ, due to the presence of the outermost Skolem function $f_{w_i}^\xi$, *(ii)* there is a sequence (eventually empty) of special edges that propagate values in position p_2 to position p_m, due to the presence of Skolem function between the outermost and the innermost one, and *(iii)* there is a sequence (of length at least one) of non-special edges that propagate values from p_m back to p_1, because the innermost Skolem function $f_{w_i}^\xi$ is nested in itself (the outermost). But this contradicts the hypothesis of weakly-acyclic set of effect specification. Since the domain and the image of a Skolem function is finite, and no nesting of the same Skolem function is possible, there is a bound on the number of different values that can exist in every position of the schema. As a consequence, the number of possible instances that can be obtained from a (finite) initial instance I_0 by applying g in every possible way is finite. Given that g is monotonic, the theorem is proved.

Based on the above theorem, we are able to derive our main result.

Theorem 4. *Let $A = \langle \mathcal{S}, \mathcal{T}, \mathcal{C} \rangle$ be an artifact such that all effect specifications in $\mathcal{T}$ are weakly-acyclic, and let I_0 be a data instance for A. Then, for every formula Φ of $\mu\mathcal{L}$, verifying that Φ holds in A with initial data instance I_0 is decidable.*

Proof. By Theorem 3 and Theorem 1, we can perform model checking of Φ on the Skolem transition system for A and I_0. Now, by Lemma 5, we have that all data instances that can be assigned to the states of the Skolem transition system for A and I_0

must be subsets of $\mathcal{L}_{I_0}$. And by Lemma 6, we get that $\mathcal{L}_{I_0}$ has a finite cardinality. This implies that Skolem transition system is finite and Theorem 2 can be applied.

5   Conclusions

In this paper we have introduced conjunctive artifact-based services, a class of services which pose balanced attention to both data (here a full-fledged relational database) and processes (acting on the database), and, through a suitable use of conjunctive queries in specifying tasks pre- and post-conditions, guarantees decidability.

It is worth noting that decidability results for formalisms that fully take into account both data and processes are rare. Here we mention three of them that are quite relevant for artifact-centric approaches. The most closely related one is [12]), which shares the general setting with our approach but differs in the conditions required to obtain decidability. These are not based on conjunctive queries, but on some decidability results of certain formulas of a first-order variant of linear time temporal logic [25]. Another relevant decidability result is that of SPOCUS relational transducers [3], where decidability is obtained through results on inflationary Datalog. Finally, the work on service composition according to the COLOMBO model [4] is also related. There, decidability is obtained through symbolic abstraction on data and the requirement that process are input bounded (i.e., take only a bounded number of new values (similar to our nulls) taken from input). The result presented here is not subsumed by (nor subsumes) any of the above results. But actually opens a new lode for research in the area, based on the connection with the theory of dependencies in databases that has been so fruitful in data exchange and data integration in recent years [15,18].

Acknowledgments. The authors would like to thank Diego Calvanese and Yves Lesperance for interesting discussions on the paper. This work has been supported by the EU Project FP7-ICT ACSI (257593).

References

1. Abiteboul, S., Bourhis, P., Galland, A., Marinoiu, B.: The axml artifact model. In: TIME, pp. 11–17 (2009)
2. Abiteboul, S., Hull, R., Vianu, V.: Foundations of Databases. Addison-Wesley, Reading (1995)
3. Abiteboul, S., Vianu, V., Fordham, B.S., Yesha, Y.: Relational transducers for electronic commerce. J. Comput. Syst. Sci. 61(2), 236–269 (2000)
4. Berardi, D., Calvanese, D., De Giacomo, G., Hull, R., Mecella, M.: Automatic Composition of Transition-based Semantic Web Services with Messaging. In: Proc. of VLDB 2005 (2005)
5. Bhattacharya, K., Gerede, C.E., Hull, R., Liu, R., Su, J.: Towards Formal Analysis of Artifact-Centric Business Process Models. In: Alonso, G., Dadam, P., Rosemann, M. (eds.) BPM 2007. LNCS, vol. 4714, pp. 288–304. Springer, Heidelberg (2007)
6. Bhattacharya, K., Guttman, R., Lyman, K., Heath III, F.F., Kumaran, S., Nandi, P., Wu, F.Y., Athma, P., Freiberg, C., Johannsen, L., Staudt, A.: A model-driven approach to industrializing discovery processes in pharmaceutical research. IBM Systems Journal 44(1), 145–162 (2005)

7. Bradfield, J., Stirling, C.: Modal mu-calculi. In: Handbook of Modal Logic, vol. 3, pp. 721–756. Elsevier, Amsterdam (2007)

8. Chandra, A.K., Merlin, P.M.: Optimal implementation of conjunctive queries in relational data bases. In: STOC, pp. 77–90 (1977)

9. Clark, K.L.: Negation as failure. In: Logic and Data Bases, pp. 293–322 (1977)

10. Clarke, E.M., Grumberg, O., Peled, D.A.: Model checking. The MIT Press, Cambridge (1999)

11. Cohn, D., Hull, R.: Business artifacts: A data-centric approach to modeling business operations and processes. IEEE Data Eng. Bull. 32(3), 3–9 (2009)

12. Deutsch, A., Hull, R., Patrizi, F., Vianu, V.: Automatic Verification of Data-Centric Business Processes. In: Proc. of ICDT (2009)

13. Emerson, E.A.: Model checking and the mu-calculus. In: Descriptive Complexity and Finite Models, pp. 185–214 (1996)

14. Emerson, E.A.: Model checking and the mu-calculus. In: Descriptive Complexity and Finite Models, pp. 185–214 (1996)

15. Fagin, R., Kolaitis, P.G., Miller, R.J., Popa, L.: Data exchange: semantics and query answering. Theor. Comput. Sci. 336(1), 89–124 (2005)

16. Fritz, C., Hull, R., Su, J.: Automatic construction of simple artifact-based business processes. In: ICDT, pp. 225–238 (2009)

17. Hull, R.: Artifact-centric business process models: Brief survey of research results and challenges. In: Meersman, R., Tari, Z. (eds.) OTM 2008. LNCS, vol. 5331, pp. 1152–1163. Springer, Heidelberg (2008)

18. Lenzerini, M.: Data Integration: A Theoretical Perspective. In: Proc. of PODS 2002, pp. 233–246 (2002)

19. Luckham, D.C., Park, D.M.R., Paterson, M.: On formalised computer programs. J. Comput. Syst. Sci. 4(3), 220–249 (1970)

20. Milner, R.: An algebraic definition of simulation between programs. In: Proc. of IJCAI, pp. 481–489 (1971)

21. Nigam, A., Caswell, N.S.: Business artifacts: An approach to operational specification. IBM Syst. J. 42(3), 428–445 (2003)

22. Park, D.: Finiteness is mu-ineffable. Theor. Comput. Sci. 3(2), 173–181 (1976)

23. Reiter, R.: Knowledge in Action: Logical Foundations for Specifying and Implementing Dynamical Systems. MIT Press, Cambridge (September 2001)

24. Sohrabi, S., Prokoshyna, N., McIlraith, S.A.: Web service composition via generic procedures and customizing user preferences. In: Cruz, I., Decker, S., Allemang, D., Preist, C., Schwabe, D., Mika, P., Uschold, M., Aroyo, L.M. (eds.) ISWC 2006. LNCS, vol. 4273, pp. 597–611. Springer, Heidelberg (2006)

25. Spielmann, M.: Verification of relational transducers for electronic commerce. J. Comput. Syst. Sci. 66(1), 40–65 (2003)

26. Tarski, A.: A lattice-theoretical fixpoint theorem and its applications. Pacific J. of Mathematics 5(2), 285–309 (1955)

27. van der Aalst, W.M.P., Barthelmess, P., Ellis, C.A., Wainer, J.: Proclets: A framework for lightweight interacting workflow processes. Int. J. Cooperative Inf. Syst. 10(4), 443–481 (2001)

Diagnosis of Service Failures by Trace Analysis with Partial Knowledge

Wolfgang Mayer[1], Gerhard Friedrich[2], and Markus Stumptner[1]

[1] Advanced Computing Research Centre, University of South Australia
{mayer.mst}@cs.unisa.edu.au
[2] Alpen-Adria Universität, Austria
gerhard.friedrich@uni-klu.ac.at

Abstract. The identification of the source of a fault ("diagnosis") of orchestrated Web service process executions is a task of growing importance, in particular in automated service composition scenarios. If executions fail because activities of the process do not behave as intended, repair mechanisms are envisioned that will try re-executing some activities to recover from the failure. We present a diagnosis method for identifying incorrect activities in service process executions. Our method is novel both in that it does not require exact behavioral models for the activities and that its accuracy improves upon dependency-based methods. Observations obtained from partial executions and re-executions of a process are exploited. We formally characterize the diagnosis problem and develop a symbolic encoding that can be solved using constraint solvers. Our evaluation demonstrates that the framework yields superior accuracy to classic dependency-based debugging methods on realistically-sized examples.

1 Introduction

The proliferation of orchestrated Web Services has increased the importance of diagnosing errors in process executions. Diagnosing the execution of concurrent applications is a challenging task even in local environments, but is exacerbated in large scale distributed business interactions, as acknowledged in a recent IEEE TSC special issue on Transactional behavior. Orchestrated Web Services define a process where individual activities are implemented by Web Services. If individual activities fail during execution, raising exceptions, repairs must be carried out [8], but as the authors explain, while languages such as WS-BPEL provide exception handling facilities, the construction of the logic to conduct fault handling is time consuming and itself error prone. (The other option at this point would be to fall back on compensation approach.) To provide complete and correct methods for repair, a complete and correct diagnosis method is of central importance. The goal of this paper is to infer minimal (irreducible) *diagnoses*, or problematic service behaviors that need to be avoided (e.g,. through re-execution) in terms of activity executions from observed execution traces.

While powerful techniques for runtime verification [5] or specification of fault handling logic [2,8] have been proposed, essentially they presuppose the existence of a detailed specification of intended service behavior in one case, and detailed fault models in the other. Unfortunately, these assumptions are not necessarily generally satisfied

P.P. Maglio et al. (Eds.): ICSOC 2010, LNCS 6470, pp. 334–349, 2010.

in practice. The correct control flow may be specified but precise models of individual services and activity behaviors are usually unavailable. Fortunately, the sequence of activity executions can be obtained from the execution engine. However, in case of failures (i.e., if exceptions are triggered), a repair-enabled execution engine needs the ability to execute and re-execute activities in order to achieve a successful process execution despite the fault. This increases the difficulty of the task, since repair executions (re-executions) do not necessarily follow the defined control flow. Our only assumption is that raising a fault will raise an exception.

To solve the problem of partial knowledge, earlier work has used dependency tracing [14,1]. As we will show in our example, such methods cannot always correctly compute the set of minimal diagnoses because they do not fully capture the semantics of the employed control elements. Also, to the best of our knowledge no current generic diagnostic approach can deal with (re-)executions of activities, nor deal with partially known behaviors.

We present an approach to isolate minimal sets of faulty activity executions based on the structure of a given process while assuming that the behavioral descriptions of individual activities may not be given fully. Our approach relies on partial models of individual activities that are gathered from observed input and output values that occur in execution traces. No complete formal specification of an activity is required.

The paradigm of *consistency-based diagnosis* [13] is based on the assumption that faults are expressed via inconsistencies between *observations* (observed results of the actual system behavior) and the expected system behavior. In our case, such inconsistencies are the result of raising an exception. A *diagnosis* specifies the set of observed activity executions that are assumed to be correct. These assumed-correct activity behaviors must be part of "guaranteed safe" behavioral models for the activities of a process definition s.t. (i) no exceptions will be triggered for all possible process executions and (ii) specified activity behavior constraints are fulfilled. Such behavior constraints express *partial* knowledge about activity behaviors. If such a process behavior cannot exist, then some activity behaviors must be incorrect. The lack of precise knowledge about activity behaviors creates the necessity to reason about all possibly correct behaviors of activities. We tackle this problem by introducing sets of possible behavior descriptions and the propagation of symbolic constants representing specific but unknown values that may be created during execution of the process. Our approach is highly flexible; particular workflow patterns such as XOR splits (our example in this paper) are merely special cases of activities with particular observed behaviors.

We develop a correct and complete diagnosis method for a sequence of activity (re-)executions. We introduce basic concepts and an example in Sec. 2 and present the process model in Sec. 3. In Sec. 4 we provide the diagnosis concepts for process (re-)executions. Sec. 5 introduces the diagnosis method based on symbolic values. Its implementation and evaluation are discussed in Sec. 6.

2   Example

We use the example depicted in Figure 1 to introduce core concepts of our approach. The upper part of this figure shows the process definition, the lower part depicts the executions of activities.

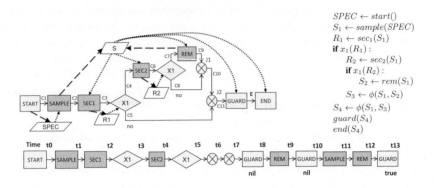

Fig. 1. Example process (top left), its Static Single Assignment form (right) and a sequence of activity executions (bottom)

The process definition includes processing activities (e.g. SAMPLE) connected by a control-flow using XOR-splits (i.e. X1) and XOR-joins (i.e. J1 and J2) as control activities. Activities read input variables and store their results in output variables. Process executions are started by the execution of activity START which provides the process inputs. A process execution is finished by the execution of END. The outputs of a process are the inputs of activity END. In our example the input to the process is a specification of a test sample (variable $SPEC$) which is used by activity SAMPLE to generate a sample placed at S. S is inspected by SEC1 and SEC2. Depending on the outcomes of SEC1 and SEC2, activity REM is eventually executed to remove some parts of the sample. Before ending the process a guard examines the sample for a final quality control. This guard can decide that the process failed by assigning nil to the control variable E thus stopping the execution. In keeping with other work in the area, e.g., [5], we assume for simplicity and without loss of generality, that a service has one operation and the invocation of that operation equates execution of the service.

Assume that the process was executed as shown in Fig. 1. Time points mark the end of an executed activity. The completion of activity executions are observed. GUARD raises an exception by assigning nil to E at time t8. We assume that only the processing activities SAMPLE, SEC1, SEC2, REM could be faulty. Given the flow of execution, activity executions $SAMPLE_{t1}$ and $SEC2_{t4}$ are the only ones that could have failed. $\langle SAMPLE_{t1}, SEC2_{t4} \rangle$ is the only minimal conflict so far; a correctness assumption of $SEC1_{t2}$ is not needed to predict that the guard will fail. Both branches of the first occurrence of X1 in the process will lead to an execution of GUARD that fails if $SAMPLE_{t1}$ and $SEC2_{t4}$ are assumed to be correct. Diagnosis methods based on tracing dependencies [14] would *not* exonerate $SEC1_{t2}$ since the computation of E depends on the output of $SEC1_{t2}$. (Recall that dependency based models implicate all activities that contribute to the derivation of an inconsistency in an execution trace. Our model is stronger in that we also consider inferences that involve hypothetical, unknown output values of activities. Hypothetical values allow us to prove that some explanations derived from a dependency based approach are in fact incorrect and result in an exception.)

Let us assume that a failure of $SAMPLE_{t1}$ is unlikely, so $[SEC2_{t4}]$ is the only leading diagnosis. It follows, that SEC2 must output to R_2 a value such that the second occurrence of X1 takes the upper branch. REM has to be executed to avoid the exception.

Let us assume a repair reasoner decides to execute REM and GUARD after the execution of GUARD at t8, but the execution of $GUARD_{t10}$ generates another exception. It follows that $\langle SAMPLE_{t1}, REM_{t9} \rangle$ is a further minimal conflict. Whatever branch is taken in the process, assuming executions $SAMPLE_{t1}$, REM_{t9} as correct leads to an exception raised by GUARD. Consequently, $[SAMPLE_{t1}]$ is the only single fault diagnosis. So the repair reasoner decides to execute SAMPLE again at t11. If we assume that the second execution of SAMPLE (at t11) outputs the same value as the execution of SAMPLE at t1, then the diagnosis $[SAMPLE_{t1}]$ has to be extended to $[SAMPLE_{t1}, SAMPLE_{t11}]$.

Consequently, there are two minimal diagnoses $[SAMPLE_{t1}, SAMPLE_{t11}]$ and $[SEC2_{t4}, REM_{t9}]$. If the first diagnosis is very unlikely (since we know that the probability for SAMPLE to fail twice is an order of magnitude lower than the second diagnosis) then the repair reasoner decides to execute REM again which now provides a different value than REM_{t9}. Next GUARD is executed which returns t (true). At this point we can conclude that the value provided by REM_{t12} corresponds to a value where the process is executed for the input provided by $START_{t0}$ and all activities worked correctly. Consequently, the faulty execution of the process is repaired.

In such a diagnosis/repair scenario two challenges must be addressed. (1) The execution follows the control path of the process definition until an exception is raised. At this point a repair reasoner takes over control and (re-)executes activities in an order that may differ from the one specified in the process definition. Note, if an activity can be re-executed is decided by the repair reasoner.

(2) It *cannot* be assumed that a complete definition of the behavior of the activities is available. In many cases only the structural description of the process and the execution trace is provided.

To deal with partially known behavior we present a process model that allows to define sets of possible activity behaviors. (For brevity, we will not address the mapping to and from BPEL and remain within the formal notation.)

3   Process Model

In our model, a process consists of activities that are connected by shared variables. To obtain a model that is suitable for simulation and diagnosis, the semantics of each activity and the control and data flow between activities must be captured. We follow the proposal of [11] and represent the semantics of the process as constraints over the process variables. Different from previous models, our approach explicitly captures alternative possible process behaviors in a single model. Our notation is based on Reiter's logic formalism [13], but the underlying ideas apply to other formalisms, such as transition systems. We first describe the flow-related modeling aspects:

Definition 1 (Process). *A process* $P = \langle A, V, I, O \rangle$ *consists of a set of literals* $A = \{A_1, \ldots, A_n\}$ *representing activities. Occurrences of each activity are defined over a* *set of process variables V. $I \subset V$ and $O \subseteq V$ represent the input and output variables of P, respectively.*

Each occurrence of activity A_i in P receives a vector of input values through some process variables (the vector of variables is denoted by $\widetilde{I}_i$) and outputs a vector of values to process variables (denoted by $\widetilde{O}_j$). Activities A_i may occur several times in the process exploiting different process variables. A process has a distinguished START activity with no predecessors and an END activity with no successors. Processes conform to the Static Single Assignment (SSA) form [3], values through some process variables and outputs values to some process variables. The vector of process variables serving as input (output) for A_{i_j} is denoted by $\widetilde{I}_{i_j}$ ($\widetilde{O}_{i_j}$). A process has a distinguished START activity with no predecessors and an END activity with no successors. Processes conform to the Static Single Assignment (SSA) form [3], where each variable is defined by exactly one activity. This is accomplished by creating new indexed "versions" of variables and by introducing so called ϕ-activities that are placed at control flow join points. The SSA form of our example process is shown (in pseudo-code syntax) in Figure 1.

The input variables taken by a process are defined by the START activity, and the output variables are inputs to the END activity. The structure of P is expressed as the conjunction of all its activity occurrences

$$P(V) = \bigwedge A_i(\widetilde{I}_j, \widetilde{O}_j), \qquad A_i \in A; \widetilde{I}_j, \widetilde{O}_j \subseteq V; i \in [1, n]$$

that defines the control and data flow admitted by the process. As noted, an activity A_i may occur several times in $P(V)$. We use upper case letters to denote variables in first-order logical sentences. We write $P(\widetilde{I}, \widetilde{X}, \widetilde{O})$ to denote the conjunction $P(V)$ where the process input variables are bound to input values $\widetilde{I}$, the output variables are bound to $\widetilde{O}$, and the remaining process-internal variables are bound to $\widetilde{X}$. Predicates A_i govern the *allowed* value combinations admitted by the correct behavior of all occurrences of activity A_i. Hence, value assignments to all process variables $\widetilde{I}, \widetilde{X}, \widetilde{O}$ which satisfy the predicates of the activities A_i in the conjunction $P(\widetilde{I}, \widetilde{X}, \widetilde{O})$ correspond to the allowed execution(s) where P receives input values $\widetilde{I}$ and produces output values $\widetilde{O}$. A value assignment that satisfies all predicates A_i in $P(\widetilde{I}, \widetilde{X}, \widetilde{O})$ is an *execution* of the process. For simplicity of presentation, we assume that END has only a single control input variable E that indicates success or failure of a process execution. The SSA from of the example process is represented as the conjunction

$$\begin{aligned}
P(SPEC, R_1, R_2, S_1, &\ldots, S_4, C_1, C_2, \ldots, E) = \\
&start(C_1, SPEC) \wedge sample(C_1, SPEC, C_2, S_1) \wedge \\
&sec1(C_2, S_1, C_3, R_1) \wedge x1(C_3, R_1, C_4, C_5) \wedge \\
&sec2(C_4, S_1, C_6, R_2) \wedge x1(C_6, R_2, C_7, C_8) \wedge \\
&rem(C_7, S_1, C_9, S_2) \wedge \phi(C_8, C_9, C_{10}) \wedge \phi(S_1, S_2, S_3) \wedge \\
&\phi(C_5, C_{10}, C_{11}) \wedge \phi(S_1, S_3, S_4) \wedge guard(C_{11}, S_4, E) \wedge end(E, S_4)
\end{aligned}$$

where the variables C_i and E model the control flow and the remaining variables model the data flow. Control- and data flow joins are uniformly represented as ϕ-activities.

From here on we define the relation describing the behavior of an activity over a set of *activity variables*. We focus on the possible relationships between input and output values of an activity and do not rely on detailed knowledge about the internal structure or implementation of an activity. Since an activity may occur several times in P, the activity variables (˙) may be bound to different process variables (˙) as shown in the example for X1. That is, the activity variables in the definition of the behavior relation serve as a placeholder for process variables.

Definition 2 (Behavior Relation). *Let A be an activity with activity variables $U_1, \ldots, U_t$ where the input variables are $\overline{I} = \langle U_1, \ldots, U_s \rangle$ and the output variables are $\overline{O} = \langle U_{s+1}, \ldots, U_t \rangle$, and let D_{U_k} denote the value domain of variable U_k. The allowed behavior of activity A is given as a relation over the allowed input and output values: $A(\overline{I}, \overline{O}) \subseteq D_{U_1} \times \cdots \times D_{U_s} \times D_{U_{s+1}} \times \cdots \times D_{U_t}$.*

We require that A is total, that is, $A(\widehat{v}, \overline{O})$ includes at least one tuple for each $\widehat{v} \in D_{U_1} \times \cdots \times D_{U_s}$. We describe the behavior relation of A extensionally by a set of literals. Value domains correspond to types and can appear in multiple behavior descriptions. For example, the domain of the data output of SAMPLE is the domain of the processing input of SEC1. We require processes to be well typed such that an activity is defined on all values that could be produced by its predecessors. Without loss of generality we assume that any two domains are either equal or mutually disjoint.

Definition 3 (Process Behavior). *A process behavior B_P for a process P is a vector of activity behavior relations $\langle A_1(\overline{I}_1, \overline{O}_1), \ldots, A_n(\overline{I}_n, \overline{O}_n) \rangle$. $\overline{I}_i, \overline{O}_i$ denote vectors of activity variables.*

To accurately model the flow of control in a process execution, we assume that each domain D_{U_k} contains a distinguished symbol *nil* that represents "no value" and that is different from any value produced by any execution of an activity. The control flow between activities is expressed as a shared variable connecting each predecessor activity to its successor(s). Control activities AND-split, AND-join, and XOR-join are defined as usual where control input and output variables have the binary domain $\{t, nil\}$. For processing activities (those which process inputs and pass the control flow), guards, and XOR-splits, we amend the relation $A(\overline{I}, \overline{O})$ to include all tuples $\langle \widehat{v}, nil, \ldots, nil \rangle$ where an input value in $\widehat{v}$ is *nil* and all other input variables are bound to values of their domain. For ϕ-activities the output is *nil* iff both inputs are *nil*. We refer to these sets of tuples as the *nil-description*. This model derived from SSA form ensures that an activity produces non-*nil* outputs only if it is activated with non-*nil* inputs along the control flow path and produces *nil* otherwise. As a result, the control and data flow in any process execution are captured correctly. Furthermore, the model ensures that the END activity receives a non-*nil* control input iff the process runs to completion and does not raise an exception.

Let us now investigate the case where the behavior of an activity A is partially unknown. This situation may arise if we must predict the execution of a process on partial input or in the presence of fault assumptions. For example, the outputs of X1 cannot be predicted precisely without knowing the values supplied by SEC1 and SEC2. However, even if the behavior of SEC1 is not known, it is still possible to conclude that any execution of SEC1 will result in an assignment for R_1 and the activation of X1. Let the hypothetical value of the assignment to R_1 be r. Then it is known that X1 will activate either the upper or the lower branch. Consequently, the behavior relation of X1 will contain either $x1(t, r, t, nil)$ or $x1(t, r, nil, t)$ where the behavior of an XOR-split activity is expressed by the relation $x1(C, W, Y, N)$ defined over control variables C, Y, N and decision input W. Since XOR-splits exhibit deterministic behavior (for given inputs) the behavior relation could not contain both tuples. To capture this form of incomplete knowledge, a model must be able to express a set of possible behavior relations where each relation reflects a different possible behavior if complete information was available.

We generalize our model of an activity from a single relation to a set of relations in order to model the behaviors that may arise if the behavior relation is not known completely. The possible behaviors of an activity A are expressed by a set of relations $\mathcal{A}(\overline{I}, \overline{O}) = \{A^1(\overline{I}, \overline{O}), \dots, A^z(\overline{I}, \overline{O})\}$, where each $A^k(\overline{I}, \overline{O})$ represents a behavior relation as defined previously.

E.g., the two possible behaviors of an XOR-split activity $x1(C, W, Y, N)$ with its decision input fixed to $W = x$ (where x may be nil) are

$$\{x1(nil, x, nil, nil), x1(t, nil, nil, nil), x1(t, x, t, nil)\} \text{ and}$$
$$\{x1(nil, x, nil, nil), x1(t, nil, nil, nil), x1(t, x, nil, t)\} \,.$$

More generally, if the value of variable W is not known, $\mathcal{A}_{X1}(\overline{I}_{X1}, \overline{O}_{X1})$ comprises all sets

$$\{\{x1(t, nil, nil, nil) \cup \bigcup_{x \in D_W} \{x1(nil, x, nil, nil), x1(t, x, Y, N)\}\} \mid$$
$$\langle Y, N \rangle = \langle t, nil \rangle \text{ or } \langle Y, N \rangle = \langle nil, t \rangle\}$$

The behavior of the entire process P is determined as a combination of specific behaviors, one each from $\mathcal{A}_i(\overline{I}_i, \overline{O}_i)$ for all activities A_i in P. By constructing the set of possible selections we define the set of all possible process behaviors.

Definition 4 (Possible Process Behaviors). *The set of all possible behaviors of P is given as*

$$\mathcal{B}_P = \left\{ \left\langle A_1^{k_1}, \dots, A_n^{k_n} \right\rangle \mid A_i^{k_i} \in \mathcal{A}_i(\overline{I}_i, \overline{O}_i) \right\} \,.$$

An element $B_P \in \mathcal{B}_P$ is a possible process behavior.

Assume an execution of P results in the following observed execution behavior of activities Obs:

$$\{start(t, spec_1), sample(t, spec_1, t, s_1), sec1(t, s_1, t, r1_1),$$
$$x1(t, r1_1, t, nil), sec2(t, s_1, t, r2_1), x1(t, r2_1, nil, t), \dots,$$
$$guard(t, s_1, nil), rem(t, s_1, t, s_2), guard(t, s_2, nil),$$
$$sample(t, spec_1, t, s_1), rem(t, s_1, t, s_3), guard(t, s_3, t)\}.$$

The same I/Os are observed for the executions of SAMPLE, while REM produces different outputs for the same input.

In absence of further information, the observed execution behaviors in Obs together with the nil-description comprise the behavior relations. Behavior relations of ϕ-activities and END are also included. Assume that REM may behave nondeterministically for some inputs, and that for the input value $r2_1$ the behavior of the

XOR is unknown; that is, *no* behavior matching $x1(t, r2_1, \_, \_)$ has been observed. Then there are two possible process behaviors B_P^U and B_P^L for P: in B_P^U, the second occurrence of X1 in P activates the upper branch on input $r2_1$, while in B_P^L the lower branch is taken.

A given process behavior $B_P \in \mathcal{B}_P$ determines the set of possible executions of P. We abstract from the concrete execution(s) implied by a given B_P and project the process behavior on its output values:

Definition 5 (Reachable assignment). *Let B_P be a behavior of a process $P = \langle A, V, I, O \rangle$. An assignment of value w to output variable $\widetilde{Q} \in O$ is reachable under B_P iff some execution admitted by $P(\widetilde{I}, \widetilde{X}, \widetilde{O})$ satisfies $\widetilde{Q} = w$. We write*
$$B_P \models \exists \widetilde{I}\, \widetilde{X}\, \widetilde{O} : P(\widetilde{I}, \widetilde{X}, \widetilde{O}) \wedge \widetilde{Q} = w.$$

For the scenario described above it holds that in both possible process behaviors $(B_P^U$ and $B_P^L)$ $E = nil$ is a reachable assignment: $B_P^L \models P(SPEC, R_1, R_2, S_1, \ldots, S_4, C_1, C_2, \ldots, E) \wedge E = nil$ (the variables of P are existentially quantified). That is because the guard signals an exception both for s_1 and s_2. Assignments $S_4 = s_2$ and $S_4 = s_3$ are both reachable in B_P^U.

If B_P^U determines the execution, $E = nil$, because the guard signals an exception if $S_4 = s_2$ is reached. If B_P^U is changed to $B_P'^U$ by removing $rem(t, s_1, t, s_2)$ from the behavior relation of REM, $E = nil$ is no longer reachable in $B_P'^U$ but is still reachable in B_P^L. The process behavior $B_P'^U$ specifies a process where –regardless of the concrete execution– no exception will be raised, whereas B_P^L admits an execution that fails. Consequently, if we assume that $SEC2_{t4}$ produces a different value than the observed value $r2_1$ and on this value the upper path of the second occurrence of X1 is taken, and REM produces a different value than s_1 or s_2 then we are guaranteed a process behavior which rules out exceptions.

4   Diagnosis Model

In "black box" application domains such as Web Services the complete behavior relation $A_i(\overline{I}_i, \overline{O}_i)$ is unknown. However, we can exploit the available knowledge which on one hand specifies the I/O tuples that *must* be contained in a behavior relation and on the other hand describes which I/O tuples are *forbidden*. For each activity A_i a behavior relation $A_i(\overline{I}_i, \overline{O}_i)$ is defined to include the *nil*-description, all observations gathered from executions of activities, and possibly other known concrete I/O behaviors. This set of predefined behaviors is denoted by Pre. Some domains of the variables of A_i may be known, e.g., control variables, while others are only partially known (e.g. the output of $SAMPLE$). If we observe a value v of a variable O whose domain is only partially known, and v is not contained in this domain, we extend the domain with a new symbol representing v.

Additional requirements constraints Re_i determine whether the behavior of an activity A_i must be deterministic. Re_i is a constraint expression over the variables in $A_i(\overline{I}_i, \overline{O}_i)$ specifying which value combinations for activity variables $\overline{I}_i, \overline{O}_i$ are allowed in the behavior relation. For our purposes it is sufficient if Re_i refers to known domain values of $\overline{I}_i, \overline{O}_i$. These constraints are local to an activity and do not depend on the behavior of any other activity. The set of requirements for all activities is denoted by Re. The requirement that activity behaviors must be totally defined is part of Re_i.

Definition 6 (Diagnosis Problem). *A diagnosis problem* $DP = \langle P, Obs, Pre, Re \rangle$ *consists of a process P, a set of I/O behaviors Obs observed from executions, a set of predefined behaviors Pre, and a set of requirements Re. Let* $P = \langle A, V, \emptyset, \{E\} \rangle$ *with activities* $A = \{A_1, \ldots, A_n\}$. *Let* $Obs = \{ob_1(\widehat{v}_1, \widehat{w}_1), \ldots, ob_q(\widehat{v}_q, \widehat{w}_q)\}$ *be the set of observed I/O behaviors of activity executions, where* $ob_j(\widehat{v}_j, \widehat{w}_j) \in Obs$ *is the observed execution of an activity occurrence* A_{i_j}. *The set of all observed execution behaviors of an activity* A_i *is denoted by* ob_i. $ob_i \subseteq A_i(\overline{I}_i, \overline{O}_i), A_i(\overline{I}_i, \overline{O}_i) \in Pre$ *for* $i \in \{1, \ldots, n\}$. *Process variable E indicates success or failure of any execution of P.*

Note that without loss of generality, the definition limits P to a single output and does not mention process inputs: the inputs that were observed in executions are modeled as outputs of the START activity. Furthermore, the decisions that establish if a process execution is successful (typically referred to as an "oracle") are explicitly encoded in the guard activities of the process. Note that we do *not* require that the criteria are completely known and formalized. Rather, the behavior of guard activities is also determined by observations in Obs. Our model implies that if a guard activity determines that its input values violate a process constraint, a vector containing nil values will be assigned to its output variables. By the definition of the SSA form and the behavioral relations, nil will be propagated to the END activity by the subsequent activities. Hence, it is sufficient to verify that the END activity does not receive a nil value to verify that the process execution complies with all guards.

For example, the behavior Pre_{X1} of $x1(C, W, Y, N)$ is given by the set $\{x1(t, nil, nil, nil), x1(nil, X, nil, nil) \mid X \in D_W\} \cup Obs$ where Obs contains the observations $\{x1(t, r1_1, t, nil), x1(t, r2_1, nil, t)\}$. The requirements Re_{X1} for the XOR behavior are given by the following sentence:

$$x1(C, W, Y, N) \Rightarrow$$
$$[(C = nil \vee W = nil) \Leftrightarrow Y = nil \wedge N = nil] \vee$$
$$[(C \neq nil \wedge W \neq nil) \Leftrightarrow Y \neq N]$$

In addition Re_{X1} includes the property that $X1$ must be deterministic and totally defined.

If a failure occurred (indicated by a guard raising an exception) either during process execution or repair planner guided re-execution, some activity executions must have produced incorrect values. In other words, specific activity behaviors in the process are faulty, and the behavior definition must be restricted so that the incorrect I/O behaviors cannot occur. Conversely, behaviors do not need to be removed if their execution cannot result in a failure.

Let B_P be a process behavior. For a set of tuples Δ, $B_P \setminus \Delta$ is the process behavior where from each behavior relation in B_P the tuples of Δ are removed.

Definition 7 (Diagnosis). *Let* $DP = \langle P, Obs, Pre, Re \rangle$ *be a diagnosis problem with* $P = \langle A, V, \emptyset, \{E\} \rangle$. *A subset* $\Delta \subseteq Obs$ *of activity executions is a diagnosis for* DP *iff there exists a process behavior* B_P *such that*

1. *Each $A_i'(\overline{I}_i, \overline{O}_i) \in B_P$ is a superset of $A_i(\overline{I}_i, \overline{O}_i) \setminus \Delta$ for $A_i(\overline{I}_i, \overline{O}_i) \in Pre$*
2. *Each $A_i'(\overline{I}_i, \overline{O}_i) \in B_P$ is consistent with $Re_i \in Re$*
3. $B_P \not\models \exists \widetilde{X} \, E : P(\emptyset, \widetilde{X}, E) \wedge E = nil.$

Δ *is* minimal *if no $\Delta' \subset \Delta$ is a diagnosis for DP.*

The first condition expresses the key concern that the executions should be consistent with existing non-faulty activity behaviors, but omit the faulty behavior tuples. The second condition formalizes the expectation that activity executions must also satisfy general known requirements like totally defined. The third is the error-freeness condition for the diagnosed and repaired execution.

Hence, a diagnosis Δ rules out certain observed behaviors of activities, such that *no process execution* conforming to the remaining assumed-correct behavior relations in B_P can lead to a failure. We say Δ is accepted as a diagnosis iff there exists a correct process behavior B_P that extends $Pre \setminus \Delta$. A minimal diagnosis preserves as much as possible the observed behavior. If the same behavior of an activity is observed multiple times in an execution (e.g. $sample(t, spec_1, t, s_1)$) then either all of these executions must be correct or all must be faulty. This assumption introduces dependencies between activity executions and may affect the diagnosis probability. Devising suitable probability models is beyond the scope of this paper.

As examples, consider the following diagnosis scenarios assuming that the process was executed until the first execution of the guard returns a failure. All the behavior relations of the activities contain just the observed I/O behaviors and the nil-description. Re contains the usual restrictions on the allowed behavior of processing activities and control activities. If $\Delta = \emptyset$ then $E = nil$ is reachable, so $\Delta = \emptyset$ is not a diagnosis. If $\Delta = \{sample(t, spec_1, t, s_1)\}$ then we can construct behavior relations for all activities such that $Pre \setminus \Delta$ is extended and the process behavior is correct. For example, the execution of SAMPLE generates a new value for which we can assume that the guard does not signal a failure. However, if $\Delta = \{sec1(t, s_1, t, r1_1)\}$ then it is not possible to generate a correct process behavior by extending $Pre \setminus \Delta$. Whatever value SEC1 generates, either the upper branch or the lower branch of the first occurrence of X1 in P is taken. In both cases, s_1 will be assigned to S_4 and therefore the guard will output nil (as in the original execution). Thus, $\Delta = \{sec1(t, s_1, t, r1_1)\}$ is not a diagnosis, as it does not prevent the exception.

In the following presentation we will assume that P is acyclic. This does not limit the representation of observed execution traces (traces are usually represented as partially ordered set of activities). But loops must be taken into account when projecting unseen behavior forward through the process, using common techniques to determine a sufficient number of unfoldings that cover all possible looping behaviors [7].

5   Symbolic Representation

To verify if Δ is a diagnosis, behavior relations $A_i'(\overline{I}_i, \overline{O}_i)$ of activities $A_i \in A$ must be found that include the tuples of $A_i(\overline{I}_i, \overline{O}_i) \setminus \Delta$, are consistent with Re_i, and no guard fails, i.e. $E = nil$ cannot be reached. If no such set of behavior relations exist then Δ is not a diagnosis. Consequently, all possible behavior relations of A_i have to be explored. If all domains of I/O variables of A_i are known we can enumerate all behaviors which are superset of $A_i(\overline{I}_i, \overline{O}_i) \setminus \Delta$ and consistent with Re_i. However, if domains are only partially known then we have to deal with unknown values.

We adopt the principle of *symbolic execution* [6] from program analysis to deal with unknown behaviors. In symbolic execution, unknown values of input and output variables of program statements are represented as symbols. Every occurrence of an activity A_i in the process P may produce a new, yet unseen value for a variable whose domain is partially unknown.

For an activity A_i and an output variable O of this activity, we inject unique symbols $s_1, \ldots, s_p$ into the domain D_O, where p is the number of occurrences of A_i in P. The domain D_O may be used multiple times by the same activity but also by other activities as a domain for output variables.

For example, assume that activities SEC1 and SEC2 use the same domain D for their data output. From observations we know that $\{r1_1, r2_1\} \subset D$. Both SEC1 and SEC2 can produce symbolic values $y1$ and $y2$ that represent yet unseen values in D. Since the symbolic values are not constrained further, both activities may output an arbitrarily chosen value —the same value or different values— in D. Hence the symbolic behavior relation must consider the cases where both activity executions result in the same symbolic value and where the values differ.

In the following we construct every possible behavior of activities given a diagnosis problem and a $\Delta \subseteq Obs$.

Let A be an activity with input variables $\overline{I} = \langle U_1, \ldots, U_s \rangle$ output variables $\overline{O} = \langle U_{s+1}, \ldots, U_t \rangle$, and let D_{U_k} denote the domain of variable U_k. The set of all input vectors of an activity is $w_{\overline{I}} = \{\langle w_1, \ldots, w_s \rangle \,|\, w_1 \in D_{U_1}, \ldots, w_s \in D_{U_s}\}$. Likewise the set of all output vectors of an activity is $w_{\overline{O}} = \{\langle w_{s+1}, \ldots, w_t \rangle \,|\, w_{s+1} \in D_{U_{s+1}}, \ldots, w_t \in D_{U_t}\}$.

Based on the I/O vectors we can construct all possible behavior relations of activities. However, in such a relation, for each input vector, at most p output vectors need to be defined, since the activity can only occur p times in P; on each occurrence a different output vector can be returned. If an activity is deterministic then just one output vector is created for each possible input vector. Consequently, the set of possible behaviors for an activity A_i is defined by behavior relations where for each input vector p output behaviors are chosen. The same output vector may be selected multiple times.

$$\mathcal{A}'_i(\overline{I}_i, \overline{O}_i) = \{\textstyle\bigcup_{w_{\overline{I}} \in w_{\overline{I}}}\{\langle w_{\overline{I}}, w_1 \rangle, \ldots, \langle w_{\overline{I}}, w_p \rangle\} \,|\, w_1 \in w_{\overline{O}}, \ldots, w_p \in w_{\overline{O}}\}$$

All the possible behavior descriptions in $\mathcal{A}'_i$ are extended by the set of tuples considered to be correct, i.e. $A_i(\overline{I}_i, \overline{O}_i) \setminus \Delta$ for $A_i(\overline{I}_i, \overline{O}_i) \in Pre$, and by the *nil*-description. In addition, we eliminate all behavior descriptions in $\mathcal{A}'_i$ that are inconsistent with requirements Re_i. We generate the possible behavior for all activities which have variables with a partially unknown domain, such as processing activities, guards, XOR-splits, and ϕ-activities. The result is a set of possible process behaviors $\mathcal{B}_P$ for a diagnosis problem and a $\Delta \subseteq Obs$.

For example, the domain D_W of $x1(C, W, Y, N)$ is extended to contain all of $\{r1_1, r2_1, y1, y2\}$ (and *nil* as the only other value). Every possible behavior of X1 includes the tuples in Pre_{X1} (shown earlier) and must be consistent with Re_{X1}. That is, the behavior on inputs $\{r1_1, r2_1, nil\}$ is fixed, but there are four different behaviors which differ just on the outputs provided for inputs $\{y1, y2\}$:

$$\{x1(t, y1, t, nil), x1(t, y2, t, nil)\}, \{x1(t, y1, nil, t), x1(t, y2, t, nil)\},$$
$$\{x1(t, y1, t, nil), x1(t, y2, nil, t)\}, \{x1(t, y1, nil, t), x1(t, y2, nil, t)\}.$$

Based on the possible process behaviors $\mathcal{B}_P$ for a diagnosis problem DP and a diagnosis Δ we can state the following property which is exploited for the generation of diagnoses:

Property 1. Let $DP = \langle P, Obs, Pre, Re \rangle$ be a diagnosis problem with $P = \langle A, V, \emptyset, \{E\} \rangle$ and $\mathcal{B}_P$ the set of possible process behaviors generated for a subset $\Delta \subseteq Obs$ as described above.

Δ is a diagnosis for diagnosis problem DP iff there is a process behavior $B_p \in \mathcal{B}_P$ s.t. $B_p \not\models \exists \widetilde{X} \, E : P(\emptyset, \widetilde{X}, E) \wedge E = nil$.

Proof sketch: ($\Leftarrow$) : This is trivially fulfilled by the construction of $\mathcal{B}_P$. All activity behaviors in $\mathcal{B}_P$ are supersets of $A_i(\overline{I}_i, \overline{O}_i) \setminus \Delta$, are consistent with Re_i, and B_p does not trigger an exception.

($\Rightarrow$) : If there exists a diagnosis Δ for DP then there exists a process behavior B_P s.t. $B_P \not\models \exists \widetilde{X} \, E : P(\emptyset, \widetilde{X}, E) \wedge E = nil$. An instantiation of the variables in $B_P \models \exists \widetilde{X} \, E : P(\emptyset, \widetilde{X}, E)$ corresponds to a process execution and defines behavior tuples for activities A_i. Values not covered by observations are replaced by a symbol. By construction, at least one symbolic value is available for each occurrence of A_i. The introduction of symbolic values cannot trigger an exception, and all constraints in Re_i remain satisfied, since both cannot contain symbolic values. Thus, if a constraint is fulfilled for an arbitrary unknown value it is also fulfilled for a symbolic value. A_i remains to be totally defined after the substitution. The tuples of all process executions where the unknown values are replaced by symbolic values define behavior relations which are included in some behavior relation generated by our construction of $\mathcal{B}_P$. It follows that if there is a process behavior B_P for which $Pre \setminus \Delta$ can be correctly extended, then there exists a process behavior B'_P in the set of generated possible process behaviors $\mathcal{B}_P$ which is also a correct extension of $Pre \setminus \Delta$. We have constructed a decision method which determines if a set $\Delta \subseteq Obs$ is a diagnosis. □

Given our example process, observations and the diagnosis candidate $\Delta = \emptyset$, all $A_i(\overline{I}_i, \overline{O}_i)$ in the process behaviors of the generated set $\mathcal{B}_P$ contain their observed execution behavior. Therefore, in each process behavior of $\mathcal{B}_P$, $E = nil$ is reachable. Consequently, there is no B'_P which is a correct extension of $Pre \setminus \Delta$. Hence, $\Delta = \emptyset$ is not a diagnosis. However, if the observed execution behavior $sample(t, spec_1, t, s_1)$ is removed, then only symbolic (unseen) output values remain to be assigned to S_1. Therefore, we can construct behaviors for REM, $GUARD$, and all other activities such that the guard is not triggered for any execution. Therefore, $\{sample(t, spec_1, t, s_1)\}$ is indeed a valid diagnosis.

6   Diagnosis Computation and Evaluation

Because all domains of the variables are finite, logic programming systems and model checkers can be used to concisely express all possible process behaviors and check whether $E = nil$ is reachable. The search for minimal, irreducible, or leading diagnoses can be implemented by standard methods, such as HS-tree generation, combined with appropriate minimization procedures, such as QuickXplain.

We conducted an empirical evaluation to determine the diagnostic accuracy that can be expected from our model, compare it with previous approaches, and assess the computational resources required. We sourced process examples from the literature, such as [4], and generated additional (artificial) processes to obtain a comprehensive benchmark suite of 200 processes. Each process comprised 5–79 activities chosen from 3–9 different types of activity, and each process included up to 22 xor decision nodes. Activities were assembled into complex processes based on a randomized graph grammar to ensure process control and data flow are well-defined. For each activity type, a set of observed behaviors was generated randomly to yield the observed process behaviors and exceptions. Two execution paths were generated for each process. The number of activities occurring in an execution path varied from 5–65 activities. The resulting benchmark suite of 400 process executions covers a wide range of different process structures, and, to the best of our knowledge, is more comprehensive than any other available benchmark.

We implemented the diagnosis framework in Eclipse Prolog. Each process was compiled into a finite domain constraint satisfaction problem which captured the structural and behavioral links between the activities. Concrete and symbolic values were encoded as integers to leverage efficient constraint solvers. We used additional variables to model correctness assumptions and the selection of possible behaviors. The constraint system was then used to isolate the maximal subsets of the observed process behaviors that did not result in an exception.

Table 1. Comparison of dependency- and symbolic diagnosis model

Size	N	Xor	Trace	Dep.	Symb.	Imp.	Time (s)
0–9	48	0.67	8.04	3.98	3.50	**0.10**	0.12
10–19	100	3.10	16.84	6.40	4.63	**0.16**	1.07
20–29	124	5.21	27.16	8.97	4.89	**0.45**	5.43
30–39	60	7.67	33.43	9.67	5.37	**0.59**	16.85
40–49	28	10.21	41.64	12.36	6.31	**0.50**	74.52
50–59	12	12.17	35.17	10.42	6.29	**0.32**	124.22
60–69	16	14.62	30.75	9.12	4.50	**0.40**	130.63
70–79	6	17.00	35.67	9.33	2.00		255.80
0–79	400	5.85	24.95	8.19	4.82	**0.29**	14.56

Our results are summarized in Table 1, aggregated by process size. The columns show the average number of activities in a process (*Size*), the number of process executions considered in our study (*N*), the average number of decision nodes in a process (*Xor*), the average number activities in each execution trace (*Trace*), the number of minimal diagnoses obtained from dependency-based models (*Dep*) and from our model (*Symb*), the mean relative improvement (*Imp*= $1 - Symb/Dep$), and the average diagnosis time in seconds (*Time*) to compute all diagnoses using the symbolic model. Accuracy is measured as the fraction of activity behaviors that need *not* be examined

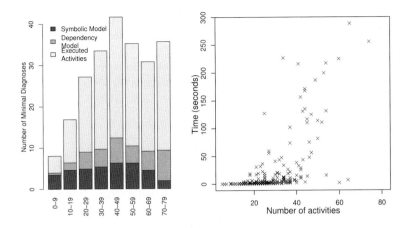

Fig. 2. Process size vs. result size and diagnosis time

given a set of diagnoses. Note that *Imp* may be larger than $1 - Symb/Dep$ since some instances exceeded the five minute time limit for the symbolic model. The blank cell denotes "no improvement" and is caused by too few symbolic results. Hence, *Imp* is a conservative estimate and may improve further with faster algorithms.

The results show that the symbolic model yields significantly more accurate results than simpler dependency-based models. The symbolic model on average eliminated three diagnoses, but could shorten the result by as much as 20 diagnoses. Overall, the number of diagnoses dropped by roughly 30% compared to dependency-based models. Our model on average implicated only 21% of the executed activities. Figure 2 shows a bar plot of the additional spurious diagnoses that are incurred when moving from a more precise diagnosis model (lower bars in the diagram) to a more abstract model (mid- and upper bars). The greatest reduction of the diagnosis ratio was observed for process executions that contained a large number of activities. Among all diagnoses, 90% were single-fault explanations, 9.5% double-faults, and 0.5% triple-faults.

The measured execution times indicate that the symbolic model also performed well in those scenarios that are most relevant for practical application. Figure 2 shows a scatter plot of the diagnosis times. In 75% of all cases, the result was obtained after just 5.3 seconds. On average, all minimal diagnoses were obtained after 14.56 seconds of CPU time.[1] Our results confirm that the model is sufficient to address the majority of practical process diagnosis scenarios, where the number of activities is virtually always less than 50. (Larger scenarios are usually decomposed hierarchically, where the number of activities on each level is small. Our model is particularly suited for hierarchical diagnosis, since no detailed specification of the abstract activities' behavior is required.) We believe that further optimization of our naïve implementation will improve these results.

Another area for future work lies in the more detailed incorporation of particular service properties. A significant paradigm adopted by most papers on Web services is

---

[1] The data were obtained from Eclipse 6.1 on Intel P4@1.86GHz with 6Gb RAM running Linux 2.6.

the CRP (compensatable, retriable, and pivot) model originally developed for Multi-database systems [10]. Though we have not addressed re-execution in detail this paper, the CRP model is easily compatible with our re-execution concept; we have worked on the default assumption that services are retriable, while pivot and compensatable services would be represented as additional constraints on the set of possible behaviors.

7 Related Work

Current approaches for dealing with runtime faults in composite service execution either assume the existence of an independent formal specification in the Event Calculus (e.g., [5]) or an explicit definition of detailed fault handling logic, relying on predefinition of detailed fault models and explicit specification of exception handling strategies to be followed in a particular situation [8].

Dependency tracking techniques are well-known techniques for model-based diagnosis of programs [14] and Web Services [1].

Expressive constraint models have been developed to increase the accuracy of model-based debugging of imperative programs [9,11]. While our processes are much simpler "programs", we cannot rely on the precise behavioral specification of the programs required by the earlier approaches. Instead, we exploit specific behavior instances observed at run time and embrace a symbolic representation to address the problem of incomplete information.

The repair planning problem in this paper, as it has been examined, e.g,. in [4,12]. The former assumes the existence of a diagnosis method to initiate the planning process, but does not specify it; our work therefore complements [4] and provides a basis for application of its methods. The latter requires explicit definition of planning operators representing application semantics to enable use of AI planners.

8 Conclusion

In many practical diagnosis/repair scenarios where service process executions have to be repaired, only partial knowledge about the behavior of activities is available. In order to recover from failures, repair-enabled process execution engines apply sequences of executions and re-executions, possibly resulting in exceptions signaling failures. For the construction of correct repair plans without extensive separate specification requirements, the appropriate diagnosis methods are a necessary precondition.

In this paper we pointed out the limitations of classic dependency tracing methods for process diagnosis and motivated the necessity to reason with multiple possible activity behaviors including the propagation of symbolic values. We have proposed a diagnosis approach which (1) can deal with partial knowledge about activity behaviors and (2) does not assume that activities are executed in an order as defined in the process. Both properties are necessary in diagnosis/repair scenarios where only limited behavior knowledge is available.

We presented a diagnosis method for process executions that relies only on observations gathered from concrete executions to infer possible faults in the execution of individual process steps. Our method can deal with partial information and non-deterministic activity behavior but requires only a structural model of the process and tolerates partially known behavior descriptions. We empirically confirmed the increased precision of our method and its feasibility for practical applications using a library of service processes. Thus our work lays the foundation for the overall goal of constructing complete and correct repair methods for processes where only partial behavior knowledge is available. We also address aspects of the repair process by seamlessly incorporating the repeated execution of activities.

This paper is an important first step towards a comprehensive diagnosis and repair framework for Web services. We intend to further explore the properties of our framework with respect to classical consistency-based and abductive diagnosis frameworks, and to further integrate the diagnosis method with recent work addressing the repair aspect of the problem [4].

Acknowledgements. The work is partially funded by the Australian Research Council (ARC) under Discovery Project DP0881854 and the Austrian National Science Fund (FWF) Project 813806 - C2DSAS.

References

1. Ardissono, L., et al.: Enhancing web services with diagnostic capabilities. In: European Conference on Web Services (2005)
2. Casati, F., Ceri, S., Paraboschi, S., Pozzi, G.: Specification and implementation of exceptions in workflow management systems. ACM Trans. Database Syst. 24(3), 405–451 (1999)
3. Cytron, R., et al.: Efficiently computing static single assignment form and the control dependence graph. ACM TOPLAS 13(4), 451–490 (1991)
4. Friedrich, G., Fugini, M., Mussi, E., Pernici, B., Tagni, G.: Exception handling for repair in service-based processes. In: IEEE TSE (2010)
5. Gaaloul, W., Bhiri, S., Rouached, M.: Event-based design and runtime verification of composite service transactional behavior. IEEE TSC 3(1), 32–45 (2010)
6. King, J.C.: Symbolic execution and program testing. CACM 19(7), 385–394 (1976)
7. Kroening, D., Strichman, O.: Efficient computation of recurrence diameters. In: Zuck, L.D., Attie, P.C., Cortesi, A., Mukhopadhyay, S. (eds.) VMCAI 2003. LNCS, vol. 2575, pp. 298–309. Springer, Heidelberg (2002)
8. Liu, A., Li, Q., Huang, L., Xiao, M.: Facts: A framework for fault-tolerant composition of transactional web services. IEEE TSC 3(1), 46–59 (2010)
9. Mayer, W., Stumptner, M.: Evaluating models for model-based debugging. In: Proc. ASE, pp. 128–137. IEEE, Los Alamitos (2008)
10. Mehrotra, S., Rastogi, R., Korth, H.F., Silberschatz, A.: A transaction model for multi-database systems. In: ICDCS, pp. 56–63 (1992)
11. Nica, M., Weber, J., Wotawa, F.: How to debug sequential code by means of constraint representation. In: Proc. DX Workshop (2008)
12. Rao, D., Jiang, Z., Jiang, Y.: Fault tolerant web services composition as planning. In: Proc. Int'l Conf.Intelligent Systems and Knoweldge Eng, ISKE 2007 (2007)
13. Reiter, R.: A theory of diagnosis from first principles. Artif. Intell. 23(1), 57–95 (1987)
14. Wotawa, F.: On the relationship between model-based debugging and program slicing. Artif. Intell. 135(1-2), 125–143 (2002)

Automatic Fragment Identification in Workflows Based on Sharing Analysis*

Dragan Ivanović,[1] Manuel Carro,[1] and Manuel Hermenegildo[1,2]

[1] School of Computer Science, T. University of Madrid (UPM)
idragan@clip.dia.fi.upm.es, {mcarro,herme}@fi.upm.es
[2] IMDEA Software Institute, Spain

Abstract. In Service-Oriented Computing (SOC), fragmentation and merging of workflows are motivated by a number of concerns, among which we can cite design issues, performance, and privacy. Fragmentation emphasizes the application of design and runtime methods for clustering workflow activities into fragments and for checking the correctness of such fragment identification w.r.t. to some predefined policy. We present a fragment identification approach based on sharing analysis and we show how it can be applied to abstract workflow representations that may include descriptions of data operations, logical link dependencies based on logical formulas, and complex control flow constructs, such as loops and branches. Activities are assigned to fragments (to infer how these fragments are made up or to check their well-formedness) by interpreting the sharing information obtained from the analysis according to a set of predefined policy constraints.

1   Introduction

Service-Oriented Computing (SOC) enables interoperability of components with low coupling which expose themselves using standardized interface definitions. In that context, service compositions are mechanisms for expressing in an executable form business processes (i.e., workflows) that include other services, and are exposed as services themselves. Compositions can be described using one of the several available notations and languages [Obj09, Jea07, Wor08, ZBDtH06, vdAP06, vdAtH05] which allow process modelers and designers to view a composition from the standpoint of business logic and processing requirements.

These service compositions are coarse-grained components that normally implement higher-level business logic, and allow streamlining and control over mission-critical business processes inside an organization and across organization boundaries. However, the centralized manner in which these processes are designed and engineered does not necessarily build in some properties which may be required in their run-time environment. In many cases defining subsets of activities (i.e., fragments inside the workflow)

* The research leading to these results has received funding from the European Community's Seventh Framework Programme under the Network of Excellence S-Cube - Grant Agreement n° 215483. Manuel Carro and Manuel Hermenegildo were also partially supported by Spanish MEC project 2008-05624/TIN *DOVES* and CM project P2009/TIC/1465 (*PROMETIDOS*). Manuel Hermegildo was also partially supported by FET IST-231620 *HATS*.

P.P. Maglio et al. (Eds.): ICSOC 2010, LNCS 6470, pp. 350–364, 2010.

according to some policy can be beneficial in order to increase reusability (by locating meaningful sets of activities), make it possible to farm, delegate, or subcontract part of the activities (if, e.g., resources and privacy of necessary data make it possible or even advisable), optimize network traffic (by finding out bottlenecks and adequately allocating activities to hosts), ensure privacy (by making sure that computing agents are not granted access to data whose privacy level is higher than their security clearance level), and others. To this end, various fragmentation approaches have been proposed [WRRM08, BMM06, TF07]. In the same line, mechanisms have been defined for refactoring existing monolithic processes into process fragments according to a given fragment definition while respecting the behavior and correctness aspects of the original process [Kha07, KL06].

This paper addresses the automatic identification of fragments given an input workflow, expressed in a rich notation. The kind of fragment identification policies we tackle is based on data accessibility / sharing, rather than, for example, mere structural properties. The latter simply try to deduce fragments or properties by matching parts of workflows with predefined patterns, as [AP08] does for deadlocks. In contrast, the design-time analysis we propose takes into account implicitly and automatically different workflow structures.

At the technical level, our proposal is based on the notion of *sharing* between activities. This is done by considering how these activities handle resources (such as data) that represent the state of an executing composition (i.e., process variables), external participants (such as partner services and external participants), resource identifiers, and mutual dependencies. In order to do so, we need to ensure that the workflow is deadlock free in order to infer a partial order between activities. This is used to construct a Horn clause program [Llo87] which captures the relevant information and which is then subject to sharing and groundness analysis [MH92, JL92, MS93, MH91] to detect the sharing patterns among its variables. The way in which this program is engineered makes it possible to infer, after analysis, which activities must be in the same fragment and which activities need / should not be in the same fragment. Even more interestingly, it can automatically uncover a *lattice* relating fragments of increasing size and complexity to each other and to simpler fragments, while respecting the fragment policy initially set.

2 Structuring Fragments with Lattices

We assume that any fragment definition is ultimately driven by a set of policies which determine whether two activities should / could belong to the same fragment. Fragment identification determines how to group activities so that the fragment policies are respected, while fragment checking ensures that predefined fragments abide by the policies. For example, data with some security level cannot be fed to activities with a lower security clearance level. This can be used to classify activities at different clearance levels according to the data they receive, and also to check that a previous classification is in accordance to the security level of the data received. This may have changed due, for example, to updates in an upstream part of the workflow.

Some approaches to process partitioning [FYG09, YG07] assume that the activities inside an abstractly described process can be *a priori* assigned to different organizational domains depending on the external service that is invoked from the workflow. These are concerned with ensuring that each fragment, corresponding to a projection of the workflow onto organizational domains, is correctly wired with other fragments to preserve both the correct behavior of the original workflow, and to satisfy externally specified constraints that describe legal conversations and data flows between services in the different domains. Rules for correctly separating fragments have also been devised for some concrete executable workflow languages, such as BPEL [Kha07]. In our approach we want to derive the fragmentation constraints from the workflow and the characterization of its inputs, without relying on other external policy sources. Also, we take a more flexible view of workflow activities, including different "local" data processing and structured constructs such as loops and nested sub-workflows, which, in principle, are not *a priori* organization domain specific.

Many fragmentation approaches assume *flat*, non-structured fragments: activities are just split into non-overlapping sets. However, for the sake of generality (which will be useful later), we assume that fragments can have a richer structure: a lattice, which means that in principle it is possible[1] to join activities belonging to two different fragments in a *super-fragment* which still respects the basic policies. For example, two activities with separate security clearance levels (because one deals with business profit data and the other one with medical problems in a company) can be put together in a new fragment whose clearance level has to be, at least, equal or higher than any of these two. It turns out that it may be possible that in order to have a consistent workflow, an "artificial" security level needs to be created if some activity is discovered to need both types of data. Of course, a lattice can also represent simpler fragmentation schemes, such as "flat" schemes (no order is induced by the properties of the fragments) or "linear" schemes (the properties induce a complete order).

Therefore we will assume that the fragmentation policies can be described using a complete lattice $\langle L, \sqsubseteq, \top, \bot, \sqcup, \sqcap \rangle$, where $\sqsubseteq$ is a partial order relation over the non-empty set L of elements which *tag* the fragments, $\top$ and $\bot$ are the top and bottom elements in the lattice, and $\sqcup$ and $\sqcap$ are the *least upper bound* (LUB) and the *greatest lower bound* (GLB) operations, respectively. In the examples we will deal with in this paper we will only use the LUB operation.

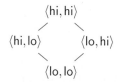

Fig. 1. Data confidentiality: two levels × two domains

As an example in the domain of data confidentiality, the simplest non-trivial case can be modeled using two levels $L_1 = \{lo, hi\}$ such that $lo \sqsubseteq hi$, and activities belong to these two classes depending on the level of data they operate on. In a more complex setting, we can have more degrees of confidentiality $L_2 = \{lo, med, hi\}$, which are still completely ordered ($lo \sqsubseteq med \sqsubseteq hi$) or, more interestingly, data belonging to different domains / departments in a company which each have different security levels, e.g., $L_3 = \{lo, hi\}^n$, where $n > 1$ is the number of domains. In this case $\sqsubseteq$ is to be defined to represent the company policy: maybe some department "dominates" the security in the company and therefore fragments marked with $\langle hi, \_ \rangle$ (where $\_$ stands for "any value") can access any data, or maybe there is no such a dominance and an activity

---

[1] But not *necessarily* permissible: it depends on the particular definition of the lattice.

marked with clearance $\langle \text{hi}, \text{lo} \rangle$ cannot read data marked with security level $\langle \text{lo}, \text{hi} \rangle$, and only activities with clearance level $\langle \text{hi}, \text{hi} \rangle$ can access all data in the organization. The corresponding lattice appears in Fig. 1.

The lattice formalism provides us with the necessary tools for identification of fragments. When a fragment is marked by some element $c \in L$, we can decide whether some activity a can be included in the fragment depending on whether its policy level $\hat{a}$ respects $\hat{a} \sqsubseteq c$ or not. Note that the direction of the partial order in the generic lattice is arbitrary and may need to be adjusted to match the needs of a real situation.

As anticipated earlier, in our approach policies which apply to data are reflected on the results of operations on data and on the activities that perform those operations. Thus, we assign policy levels to activities based on the policy levels of their input data flow. We on purpose abstract from the notion of program variables / storage locations and focus instead on pieces of the information flow, which are more important in distributed workflow enactment scenarios.

3   Derivation of Control and Data Dependencies

As a first step for the automatic fragmentation analysis proper, we need to find out a feasible order of activities which is coherent with their dependencies and which allows the workflow to finish successfully. How to do this obviously depends on the palette of allowed relationships between activities, with respect to which we opted for a notable freedom (Section 3.1). To find such an order we first establish a partial order between workflow activities which respects their dependencies; in doing this we also detect whether there are dependency loops that may result in deadlocks. While there is ample work in deadlock detection [BIZ04, AP08], we think that the technique we propose is clean, can be used for arbitrarily complex dependencies between activities, and uses well-proven, existing technology, which simplifies its implementation.

3.1   Workflow Representation

We first state which components we highlight in a workflow.

Definition 1 (Workflow). *A workflow W is a tuple $\langle A, C, D \rangle$, where A is a finite set of activities $\{a_1, a_2, \ldots, a_n\}$, $n \geq 0$, C is a set of control dependencies given as pre- and post-conditions for individual activities (see later), and D is a finite set of data dependencies expressed as pairs $\langle a_i, A^{(d)} \rangle \in D$ where $a_i \in A$ is an activity that produces (writes) data item d, and $A^{(d)} \subseteq A$ ($a_i \notin A^{(d)}$) is a set of activities that consume (read) data item d.*

This abstract workflow definition corresponds in general with the most frequently used models for distributed workflow enactment. However, the flexibility of the encoding we will use for the fragmentation analysis allows for two significant extensions compared to other workflow models.

- In our approach, the activities inside a workflow can be simple or structured. The latter include branching (*if-then-else*) and looping (*while* and *repeat-until*) constructs, arbitrarily nested. The body of a branch or a loop is a sub-workflow, and

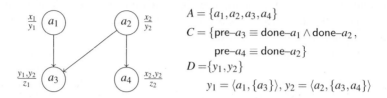

Fig. 2. An example workflow. Arrows indicate control dependencies.

activities in the main workflow cannot directly depend on activities inside that sub-workflow. Of course, any activity in such a sub-workflow is subject to the same treatment as activities in the parent workflow.

- Second, we allow an expressive repertoire of control dependencies between activities besides structured sequencing: AND split-join, OR split-join and XOR split-join. We express dependencies similarly to the link dependencies in BPEL but with fewer restrictions, thereby supporting OR- and XOR-join.

Definition 2 (Activity preconditions). *A precondition of an activity $a_i \in A$ is a propositional formula which can use the full set of logical connectives ($\wedge$, $\vee$, $\neg$, $\rightarrow$, and $\leftrightarrow$), the values 1 (for true) and 0 (for false), and the propositional symbols* done–a_j *and* succ–a_j, $a_j \in A$, *where* done–a_j *holds if a_j has completed and* succ–a_j *stands for a successful outcome of a_j when* done–a_j *holds (i.e.,* succ–a_j *is only meaningful when* done–a_j *is true).*

Definition 3 (Dependencies). *A set of control dependencies C that associates each $a_i \in A$ with its precondition, which we will term* pre–a_i. *We write C as a set of identities of the form* pre–$a_i \equiv \langle$formula$\rangle$. *Trivial cases of the form* pre–$a_i \equiv 1$ *are omitted.*

Commonly, the preconditions use "done" symbols, whereas "succ" symbols can be added to reflect the business logic in the structure of the workflow, and to distinguish mutually exclusive execution paths. We do not specify here how the "succ" indicators are exactly computed. Note that each activity in the workflow is executed at most once; repetitions are represented with the structured looping constructs (yet, within each iteration, an activity in the loop body sub-workflow can also be executed at most once).

Figure 2 shows an example. The activities are drawn as nodes, and control dependencies indicated by arrows. Data dependencies are textually shown in a "fraction" or "production rule" format next to the activities: items above the bar are used (read) by the activity, and the items below are produced. Note that only items y_1 and y_2 are data dependencies; others either come from the input message (x_1, x_2), or are the result of the workflow (z_1, z_2). Item y_1 is produced by a_1 and used by a_3, and y_2 is produced by a_2 and used by a_3 and a_4.

Many workflow patterns can be expressed in terms of such logical link dependencies. For instance, a sequence "a_j after a_i" boils down to pre–$a_j \equiv$ done–a_i. An AND-join after a_i and a_j into a_k becomes pre–$a_k \equiv$ done–$a_i \wedge$ done–a_j. An (X)OR-join of a_i and a_j into a_k is encoded as pre–$a_k \equiv$ done–$a_i \vee$ done–a_j. And an XOR split of a_i into a_j and a_k (based on the business outcome of a_i) becomes pre–$a_j \equiv$ done–$a_i \wedge$ succ–a_i, pre–$a_k \equiv$ done–$a_i \wedge \neg$succ–a_i. In terms of execution scheduling, we take the assumption that a workflow activity a_i may start executing as soon as its precondition is met.

3.2   Validity of Control Dependencies

The relative freedom given for specifying logic formulae for control dependencies comes at the cost of possible anomalies that may lead to deadlocks and other undesirable effects. These need to be detected beforehand, i.e., at design / compile time using some sort of static analysis. Here, we are primarily concerned with *deadlock-freeness*, i.e., elimination of the cases when activities can never start because they wait on events that cannot happen.

Whether a deadlock can happen or not depends on both topology and the logic of control dependencies. Figure 3 shows a simple example where the dependency arrows are drawn from a_i and a_j whenever pre–a_j depends on a_i finishing. That topological information is not sufficient for inferring deadlock freeness, unless there are no loops in the graph. If the connective marked with $\bullet$ in pre–a_3 is $\vee$, there is no deadlock: indeed, there is a possible execution sequence, $a_1 - a_2 - a_3 - a_4$. If, however, $\bullet$ denotes $\wedge$, there is a deadlock between a_3 and a_4.

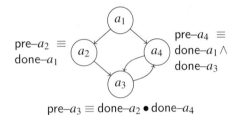

Fig. 3. An example of deadlock dependency on logic formula: $\bullet$ can be either $\wedge$ or $\vee$

Therefore, in general, checking for deadlock-freeness needs looking at the formulas. We present one such approach that relies on simple proofs of propositional formulas. We start by forming a logical theory Γ from the workflow by including all preconditions from C and adding axioms of the form done–$a_i \rightarrow$ pre–a_i for each $a_i \in A$. These additional axioms simply state that an activity a_i cannot finish if its preconditions were not met. On that basis, we introduce the following definition to help us detect deadlocks and infer a task order which respects the data and control dependencies:

Definition 4. *The dependency matrix Δ is a square Boolean matrix such that its element δ_{ij}, corresponding to $a_i, a_j \in A$, is defined as:*

$$\delta_{ij} = \begin{cases} 1, & \text{if } \Gamma \vdash \text{pre–}a_i \rightarrow \text{done–}a_j \\ 0, & \text{otherwise} \end{cases}$$

For every data dependency $\langle a_j, A^{(d)} \rangle \in D$, and for each $a_i \in A^{(d)}$, we wish to ensure that a_i cannot start unless a_j has completed, since otherwise the data item d would not be ready. Expressed with a logic formula, that condition is pre–$a_i \rightarrow$ done–a_j, as in the definition of Δ, above. Therefore, we require $\delta_{ij} = 1$.

The computation of Δ involves proving propositional formulas, which is best achieved using some form of SAT solvers, which are nowadays very mature and widely available either as libraries or standalone programs. It follows from the definition that $\delta_{ij} = 1$ if and only if the end of a_j is a necessary condition for the start of a_i. It can be easily shown that Δ is a transitive closure of C, and that is important for the ordering of activities in a logic program representation. However, the most important property can be summarized as follows.

Proposition 1 (Freedom from deadlocks). *The given workflow is deadlock-free if and only if $\forall a_i \in A$, $\delta_{ii} = 0$.*

Proposition 2 (Partial ordering). *In a deadlock-free workflow, the dependency matrix Δ induces a strict partial ordering $\prec$ such that for any two distinct $a_i, a_j \in A$, $a_j \prec a_i$ iff $\delta_{ij} = 1$.*

4   Translation and Analysis

To apply sharing analysis, we first transform the workflow into an appropriate logic program. The purpose of such program is not to operationally mimic the scheduling of workflow activities, but to express and convey relevant data and control dependency information to the sharing analysis stage.

4.1   Workflows as Horn Clauses

Based on the strict partial ordering $\prec$ induced by the dependency matrix Δ, in the deadlock-free case it is always possible to *totally* order the activities so that $\prec$ is respected. The choice of a particular order does not impact our analysis, because we assume that the control dependencies, from which the partial ordering derives, include the data dependencies. From this point on we will assume that activities are renumbered to follow the chosen total order. The workflow can then be translated into a Horn clause of the form:

$$w(V) \leftarrow T(a_1), T(a_2), \ldots, T(a_N)$$

where V is the set of all logic variables used in the clause, and $T(a_i)$ stands for the translation of the activity a_i.

As mentioned before, the logic program aims at representing data flow and dependencies in a sharing analysis-amenable way, which we will detail later. Logic variables are used to represent input data, data dependencies, output data, and the data sets read by individual activities. For each activity $a_i \in A$, we designate a set R_i of logic variables that represent data items read by a_i, and a set W_i of logic variables that stand for data items produced by a_i. We also designate a special variable $\hat{a}_i$ that represents the total inflow of data into a_i. The task of the translation is to connect R_i and $W_i \cup \{\hat{a}_i\}$ correctly.

A primer on logic programs. Data items in logic programs are called *terms*. A term t can be either a *variable*, an *atom* (i.e., a simple non-variable data item, such as the name of a object or a number), or a compound term of the form $f(t_1, t_2, \ldots, t_n)$, $(n \geq 0)$, where f is the *functor*, and $t_1, t_2, \ldots, t_n$ are the argument terms. $f(a, b)$ is not a function call, — it can be seen instead as a record named f with two fields containing items a and b. Terms that are not variables and do not contain variables are said to be *ground*. Procedure calls in a logic program are called *goals* and have the syntactic form

$p(t_1, t_2, \ldots, t_n)$ $(n \geq 0)$, where p is a *predicate name* of *arity* n (usually denoted as p/n), and the terms $t_1, t_2, \ldots, t_n$ are its arguments. In goals, the infix predicate $=/2$ is used to denote unification of terms (described later), as in $t_1 = t_2$.

In the execution of a logic program, variables serve as placeholders for terms that satisfy the logical conditions encoded in the program. Each successful execution step may map a previously free variable to a term. The set of such mappings at a program point is called a *substitution*. Thus, a substitution θ is a finite set of mappings of the form $x \mapsto t$ where x is a variable and t is a term. Each variable can appear only on one side of the mappings in a substitution. At any point during execution, the actual value of the variables in the program text is obtained by applying the current substitution to these (syntactical) variables. These applications may produce terms that are possibly more concrete (have fewer variables) than the ones which appear in the program text. If $\theta = \{x \mapsto 1, y \mapsto g(z)\}$, and $t = f(x, y)$, then the application $t\theta$ gives $f(1, g(z))$.

Substitutions at a subsequent program points are composed together to produce an aggregated substitution for the next program point (or the final substitution on exit). E.g., for the previous θ and $\theta' = \{z \mapsto a + 1\}$ (with a being an atom, not a variable), we have $\theta\theta' = \{x \mapsto 1, y \mapsto g(a + 1)\}$.

Substitutions are generated by *unifications*. Unifying t_1 and t_2 gives a substitution θ which ensures that $t_1\theta$ and $t_2\theta$ are identical terms by introducing the least amount of new information. Unifying x and $f(y)$ gives $\theta = \{x \mapsto f(y)\}$; unifying $f(x, a + 1)$ and $f(1, z + y)$ gives $\theta = \{x \mapsto 1, z \mapsto a, y \mapsto 1\}$; and the attempt to unify $f(x)$ and $g(y)$ fails, because the functors are different. When a goal calls a predicate, the actual and the formal arguments are unified, which may generate further mappings to be added to the accumulated ones.

Take, for instance, the Horn clause translation of the example workflow on Fig. 4. Variables in the listing are written in uppercase, and comments that start with "%" indicate workflow activity. The comma-separated goals in the body (after ":-") are executed one after another. If the initial substitution is $\theta_0 = \{x_1 \mapsto u_1, x_2 \mapsto u_2\}$, then the first unification produces $\theta_1 = \{\hat{a}_1 \mapsto f_1(x_1)\}$, so the aggregate substitution before the next goal is $\theta_0\theta_1 = \{x_1 \mapsto u_1, x_2 \mapsto u_2, \hat{a}_1 \mapsto f_1(u_1)\}$. The second unification in the body adds $\theta_2 = \{y_1 \mapsto f_2(x_1)\}$, and the result is $\theta_0\theta_1\theta_2 = \{x_1 \mapsto u_1, x_2 \mapsto u_2, \hat{a}_1 \mapsto f_1(u_1), y_1 \mapsto f_{1y_1}(u_1)\}$.

The process continues until the final substitution is reached: $\theta_0\theta_1 \cdots \theta_8 = \{x_1 \mapsto u_1, x_2 \mapsto u_2, \hat{a}_1 \mapsto f_1(u_1), y_1 \mapsto f_2(u_1), \hat{a}_2 \mapsto f_3(u_2), y_2 \mapsto f_4(u_2), \hat{a}_3 \mapsto f_5(f_2(u_1), f_4(u_2)), z_1 \mapsto f_6(f_2(u_1), f_4(u_2)), \hat{a}_4 \mapsto f_7(u_2, f_4(u_2)), z_2 \mapsto f_8(u_2, f_4(u_2))\}$.

Note that the program point substitutions are expressed based on u_1 and u_2, the terms to which x_1 and x_2 were initially bound to. In this case it is interesting that some variables (for example, y_1 and z_1) are bound to terms that contain a common variable (u_1, in this case), and so we say that y_1 and z_1 *share*.

Definition 5 (Sharing). *Given a runtime substitution θ, two syntactical variables x and y are said to share if the terms $x\theta$ and $y\theta$ contain some common variable z.*

In the preceding example $\hat{a}_1$ shares with x_1 via u_1; y_2 shares with x_2 via u_2; $\hat{a}_3$ shares both with x_1 via u_1, and with x_2 via u_2; etc. The basis for all sharing are u_1 and u_2, yet they do not appear in the program, but in the initial substitution. The key to the use of sharing analysis for the definition of fragments is, precisely, the introduction of such "hidden" variables, which act as "links" between workflow variables that represent data flows and activities.

Assignments, expression evaluations, and service invocations are translated into unifications that enforce sharing between the input and the output data items of the activity. Complex activities are translated into separate predicates, and an example of such translation (for a *repeat-until* loop construct) is given in the example in Section 5.

For each output data item $x \in W_i$ of the translated activity a_i, we introduce a unification between x and a compound term that involves the variables that are used in producing it, and which form a subset of R_i. If we do not know exactly which variables from R_i are necessary to produce x, we can safely use them all, at the cost of over-approximating sharing. The choice of functor name in the compound term is not significant. The same applies to the activity-level variable $\hat{a}_i$, which is unified

```
w(X1,X2,A1,Y1,A2,Y2,A3,Z1,A4,Z2):-
  A1=f1(X1),  % a1
  Y1=f1Y1(X1),
  A2=f2(X2),  % a2
  Y2=f2Y2(X2),
  A3=f3(Y1,Y2),  % a3
  Z1=f3Z1(Y1,Y2),
  A4=f4(X2,Y2),  % a4
  Z2=f4Z2(X2,Y2).
```

Fig. 4. Logic program encoding of the workflow from Fig. 2

with a compound term containing all variables from R_i, to model the dependency of a_i on all information that it uses as input.

4.2   Sharing Analysis

The sharing analysis we use here is an instance of abstract interpretation [CC77], a static analysis technique that interprets a program by mapping concrete, possibly infinite sets of variable values onto (usually finite) abstract domains, together with data operations, in a way that is correct with respect to the original semantics of the programming language. In the abstract domain, computations usually become finite and easier to analyze, at the cost of lack of precision, because abstract values typically cover (sometimes infinite) subsets of the concrete values. However, the abstract approximations of the concrete behavior are *safe*, in the sense that properties proven in the abstract domain necessarily hold in the concrete case. Whether abstract interpretation is precise enough for proving a given property depends on the problem and on the choice of the abstract domain. Yet, abstract interpretation provides a convenient and finite method for calculating approximations of otherwise, and in general, infinite fixpoint program semantics, as is typically the case in the presence of loops and/or recursion.

We use abstract interpretation-based sharing, freeness, and groundness analysis for logic programs. Instead of analyzing the infinite universe of possible substitutions during execution of a logic program, sharing analysis is concerned just with the question of which variables may possibly share in a given substitution. This analysis is helped by freeness and groundness analysis, because the former tells which variables are not substituted with a compound term, and the latter helps exclude ground variables from sharing. Some logic program analysis tools, like CiaoPP [HBC+10], have been developed which give users the possibility of running different analysis algorithms on input programs. We build on one of the sharing analyses available in CiaoPP.

function RECOVERSUBSTVARS(V, Θ)
    $n \leftarrow |\Theta|; U \leftarrow \{u_1, u_2, ..., u_n\}$ ▷ $n = |\Theta|$ fresh variables in U
    $S : V \rightarrow \wp(U); S \leftarrow \text{const}(\emptyset)$ ▷ the initial value for the result
    for $x \in V, i \in \{1..n\}$ **do**   ▷ for each variable and subst. setting
        if $x \in \Theta[i]$ **then**   ▷ if the variable appears in the setting
            $S \leftarrow S[x \mapsto S(x) \cup \{u_i\}]$ ▷ add u_i to its resulting set
        end if
    end for
    return U, S
end function

Fig. 5. The minimal substitution variable set recovery algorithm

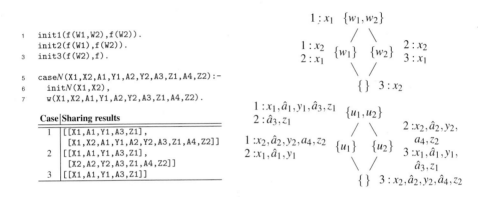

```
1   init1(f(W1,W2),f(W2)).
    init2(f(W1),f(W2)).
3   init3(f(W2),f).

5   caseN(X1,X2,A1,Y1,A2,Y2,A3,Z1,A4,Z2):-
6     initN(X1,X2),
7     w(X1,X2,A1,Y1,A2,Y2,A3,Z1,A4,Z2).
```

Case	Sharing results
1	[[X1,A1,Y1,A3,Z1],
	[X1,X2,A1,Y1,A2,Y2,A3,Z1,A4,Z2]]
2	[[X1,A1,Y1,A3,Z1],
	[X2,A2,Y2,A3,Z1,A4,Z2]]
3	[[X1,A1,Y1,A3,Z1]]

Fig. 6. The initial settings and the sharing results

In the sharing and freeness domain, an abstract substitution Θ is a subset of all possible sharing sets. Each sharing set is a subset of the variables in the program. The meaning of this set is that those variables may be bound at run-time to terms which share some common variable. E.g., if $\theta = \{x \mapsto f(u), y \mapsto g(u, v), z \mapsto w\}$, then the corresponding abstract substitution (projected over x, y, and z) is $\Theta = \{\{x, y\}, \{y\}, \{z\}\}$. Note that if u is further substituted (with some term t), x and y will be jointly affected; if v is further substituted, only y will be affected, and if w is further substituted only z will be affected.

Although an abstract substitution represents an infinite family of concrete substitutions (e.g., $\theta' = \{x \mapsto v, y \mapsto h(w, v), z \mapsto k(u)\}$ in the previous example), it is always possible to construct a minimal concrete substitution exhibiting that sharing, by taking as many auxiliary variables as there are sharing sets, and constructing terms over them. Furthermore, if one is only interested in the sets of shared auxiliary variables, not the exact shape of the substituted terms, the simple algorithm from Figure 5 suffices. Note that only a ground variable $x \in V$ can have $S(x) = \emptyset$.

4.3 Deriving Fragment Identification Information from Sharing

To derive fragment identification information from the sharing analysis results, the logic program workflow representation has to be analyzed in conjunction with some initial conditions that specify the policy levels of the input data. In our example from Figures 2 and 4, this applies to the input data items x_1 and x_2. We will assume that the policy lattice is isomorphic to or a sublattice of some lattice L induced by the powerset of a non-empty set $W = \{w_1, ..., w_n\}$ with the set inclusion relation.

The initial conditions are then represented by means of sharing between the input data variables and the corresponding subsets of W. Several initial conditions (labeled with 1, 2, and 3) are shown in Figure 6 (left). Each caseN (where N is in this case 1, 2, or 3) predicate starts with all variables independent (i.e., no sharing), and calls initN to set up the initial sharing pattern for x_1 and x_2 in terms of the hidden variables w_1 and w_2. How these different patterns place variables x_1 and x_2 in the policy lattice is shown in the figure at the right, top, by displaying the case number just before each variable. Below this lattice are the sharing results (as Prolog lists) obtained from the shfr analysis.[2] Right on the same figure are the projections of the initial sharing settings for x_1 and x_2 on the original policy lattice $L = \wp(W)$, $W = \{w_1, w_2\}$, and projections of the sharing results on the lattice $L' = \wp(U)$, $U = \{u_1, u_2\}$ derived using the algorithm in Figure 5.

Let us, for instance, interpret case 2. If we use variable names to mean their policy levels (with primes in L'), we see that initially $x_1 = \{w_1\}$ and $x_2 = \{w_2\}$ are disjoint, i.e., incomparable w.r.t. $\sqsubseteq$. Activity a_1 uses x_1 as the input, and produces y_1 from x_1; hence, $\hat{a}'_1 = y'_1 = x'_1 = \{u_1\}$. Analogously, $\hat{a}'_2 = y'_2 = x'_2 = \{u_2\}$. For a_3, both y_1 and y_2 are used to produce z_1. Hence, $\hat{a}'_3 = z'_1 = y'_1 \sqcup y'_2 = \{u_1, u_2\}$. Finally, a_4 uses x_2 and y_2 to produce z_2, and thus $\hat{a}'_4 = z'_2 = x'_2 \sqcup y'_2 = \{u_2\}$. Therefore, a_2 and a_4 are at the same clearance level, and a_3 is at a different (but non-comparable) level.

The most important feature of the derived lattice L' is that if for $x, y \in L$ we have $x \sqsubseteq y$, then for their respective images x', y' derived in L', we also have $x' \sqsubseteq y'$. This feature follows from the structure of the translation for simple activities (linear unifications), the fact that variables in W are hidden inside the initialization predicate (and thus remain mutually independent and free), and the semantics of unification in the shfr domain. Therefore, the two typical fragmentation inference tasks are:

- The policy level $\sqcup B$ of a subset of activities $B \subseteq A$ in L' is $\sqcup \{\hat{a}'_i \mid a_i \in B\}$.
- To check constraint compliance for $B \subseteq A$ in L, one needs to represent c as an input data item in the workflow, and then check $\sqcup B \sqsubseteq c'$ in L'.

Note that we have not defined at any moment the exact shape of the finally inferred lattice: we merely stated the relationship between two input flow streams (for three different possibilities, in this case) and the analysis algorithm built, for each of these cases, the abstract substitution which places every relevant program variable in its point.

The following section will present in more detail an example involving privacy and two types of data.

5   An Example of Application to Data Privacy

Figure 7 shows a simplified workflow for drug prescription in a health care organization. The input data are the identity of the patient (x), authorization to access the patient's medical history (d) and the authorization to access the patient's medication record (e).

---

[2] These results were obtained in 3.712ms (total) on a Intel Core Duo 2GHz machine with 2GB of RAM running CiaoPP 1.12 and Mac OS X 10.6.3.

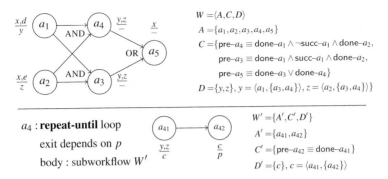

$W = \langle A, C, D \rangle$

$A = \{a_1, a_2, a_3, a_4, a_5\}$

$C = \{\text{pre-}a_4 \equiv \text{done-}a_1 \wedge \neg \text{succ-}a_1 \wedge \text{done-}a_2,$
$\quad \text{pre-}a_3 \equiv \text{done-}a_1 \wedge \text{succ-}a_1 \wedge \text{done-}a_2,$
$\quad \text{pre-}a_5 \equiv \text{done-}a_3 \vee \text{done-}a_4\}$

$D = \{y, z\}, y = \langle a_1, \{a_3, a_4\} \rangle, z = \langle a_2, \{a_3, a_4\} \rangle \}$

a_4 : **repeat-until** loop
exit depends on p
body : subworkflow W'

$W' = \{A', C', D'\}$

$A' = \{a_{41}, a_{42}\}$

$C' = \{\text{pre-}a_{42} \equiv \text{done-}a_{41}\}$

$D' = \{c\}, c = \langle a_{41}, \{a_{42}\} \rangle$

Fig. 7. A simplified drug prescription workflow

Based on the patient id and the corresponding authorization, activity a_1 retrieves the patient's medical history (y), and signals success (succ-a_1) iff the patient's health has been stable. Simultaneously, activity a_2 uses the patient's id and the corresponding authorization to retrieve the patient's medication record (z). Depending on the outcome of a_1, either a_3 or a_4 is executed. Activity a_3 continues the last medical prescription, based on the medical history and the medication record. Activity a_4, on the other hand, tries to select a new medication. Activity a_{41} runs some additional tests based on the medical history and the medication record to produce criteria c for the new medicine. Medication record z is used just for cross-checking, and does not affect the result c. Activity a_{42} searches the medication databases for a medicine matching c, which is prescribed if found; the search may fail if the criterion c is too vague. The search result p is used as the exit condition from the loop. Finally, activity a_5 records that the patient has been processed.

The fragmentation policies used in this example are based on the assumption that we want to distribute execution of this centralized workflow so that the fragments can be executed inside domains that need not have access to all patient's information. For instance, the health care organization may delegate some of the activities to an outside (or partner) service that keeps and integrates medical histories and runs medical checks, but should not (unless expressly authorized) be able to look into the patient's medication record, to minimize influence that the types and costs of earlier prescribed may have on the choice of medical checks. Other activities can be delegated to partners that handle only medication records. Finally, the organization owning the workflow wants to reserve to itself the right to access both the medical history and the medication record at the same time.

To formalize the policies, we introduce a set of two data privacy tags $W = \{w_1, w_2\}$, and the lattice of policies $L = \wp(W)$. The presence of tag w_1 indicates authorization to access medical history related data and the presence of tag w_2 indicates authorization to access medication record related data. Using variable names to indicate policy levels, we start with $d = \{w_1\}$, $e = \{w_2\}$, and $x = \{ \}$; the latter implies that consulting the identity of a patient does not require specific clearances.

It can be easily demonstrated that this workflow does not have deadlocks, and that one compatible ordering of activities is $\langle a_1, a_2, a_3, a_4, a_5 \rangle$. The translation of the

```
1   analysis(X,D,E,T,A1,Y,A2,Z,A3,A4,A41,C,A42,P,A5):-       a_4(Y,Z,A4,A41,C,A42,P):-
        init(X,D,E,T),                                 16         w2(Y,Z,A41,C2,A42,P2),
3       w(X,D,E,T,A1,Y,A2,Z,A3,A4,A41,C,A42,P,A5).                A4=f(P2),
                                                       18         a_4x(Y,Z,C2,P2,C,P,A4,A41,A42).
5   init(f,f(W1),f(W2),f(W1,W2)).
                                                       20   a_4x(_,_,C,P,C,P,_,_,_).
7   w(X,D,E,T,A1,Y,A2,Z,A3,A4,A41,C,A42,P,A5):-             a_4x(X,Z,_,_,C,P,A4,A41,A42):-
        A1=f1(X,D), % a_1                              22         a_4(X,Z,A4,A41,C,A42,P).
9       Y=f1_Y(X,D),
        A2=f2(X,E), % a_2                              24   w2(Y,Z,A41,C,A42,P):-
11      Z=f2_Z(X,E),                                              A41=f41(Y,Z), % a_41
        A3=f3(Y,Z), % a_3                              26         C=f41_C(Y),
13      a_4(Y,Z,A4,A41,C,A42,P), % a_4                           A42=f42(C), % a_42
        A5=f5(X). % a_5                                28         P=f42_P(C).
```

Fig. 8. Logic program encoding for the medication prescription workflow

workflow into a logic program is shown in Figure 8. Note the initial sharing setting in the predicate `init` before calling the workflow translation in predicate `w`. It corresponds to the lattice L from Figure 9. We have introduced the element $\top$ (variable `T` in the listing) that corresponds to the top element of the original lattice.

Also, note how the *repeat-until* has been translated into two predicates, a_4 and a_4x. Predicate a_4 invokes the sub-workflow w2, to produce data items c and p from the single iteration (logic variables C2 and P2). It then enforces sharing between $\hat{a}_4$ and the latest p on which the exit condition depends, and invokes a_4x. The latter predicate treats two cases: the first clause models exit from the loop, by passing the values of c and p from the last iteration as the final ones. The second clause of a_4x models repetition of the loop. The sub-workflow comprising the body of the loop is translated to w2 using the same rules as the main workflow.

The abstract substitution that is the result of the sharing analysis, as returned by the CiaoPP analyzer, is shown on Figure 11.[3] By interpreting these results using the algorithm for recovery of the minimal sets of variable substitutions from Figure 5, we obtain the resulting lattice L', shown on Figure 10. Variables X and A5 are ground and

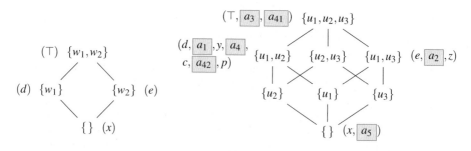

Fig. 9. The base sharing setting for the code from Fig. 11

Fig. 10. Interpretation of the sharing results from Fig. 11

[3] These results were obtained in 2.130ms on 2GHz Intel Core Duo machine with 2GB of RAM, running Mac OS X 10.6.3 and CiaoPP 1.12.

```
[[D,E,T,A1,Y,A2,Z,A3,A4,A41,C,A42,P],     (Corresponding to u₁)
 [D,T,A1,Y,A3,A4,A41,C,A42,P],            (Corresponding to u₂)
 [E,T,A2,Z,A3,A41]]                        (Corresponding to u₃)
```

Fig. 11. Sharing analysis result for the code from Fig. 8

do not appear in the result. Note that the relative ordering of the input data items (x, d, e, and $\top$) has been preserved in L'. Also, the assignment of policy levels to activities shows that the activities a_3 and a_{41} are critical because they need to have both the d and e clearance levels—i.e., the level $d \sqcup e$. Activities a_1, a_4 and a_{42} can be safely delegated to a partner that is authorized to look at the medical history of a patient, but not at the medication record. Activity a_2, by contrast, can be delegated to a partner that is authorized to look at the medication record, but not the medical history of a patient; and finally, a_5 can be entrusted to any partner, since it does not handle any private information.

Going in the other direction, we can look at the resulting lattice L' to deduce the policy level that corresponds to any subset of workflow activities. For $B_1 = \{a_1, a_2\}$, $\sqcup B_1 = \top$; for $B_2 = \{a_2, a_5\}$, $\sqcup B_2 = e$, etc.

6   Conclusions

We have shown how sharing analysis, a powerful program analysis technique, can be effectively used to identify fragments in service workflows. These are in our case represented using a rich notation featuring control and data dependencies between workflow activities, as well as nested structured constructs (such as branches and loops) that include sub-workflows. The policies that are the basis for the fragmentation are represented as points in a complete lattice, and the fragments to which input data / activities belong are stated with initial sharing patterns. The key to this use of sharing analysis is how workflows are represented: in our case we have used Horn clauses designed to adequately enforce sharing between inputs and outputs of the workflow activities. The results of the sharing analysis lead to the construction of a lattice that preserves the ordering of items from the original policy lattice and which contains inferred information which can be used for both deciding the compliance of individual activities with given fragmentation constraints, and to infer characteristics of potential fragments.

As future work, we want to attain a closer correspondence between the abstract workflow descriptions and well-known workflow patterns, as well as provide better support for languages used for workflow specification. Another line of future work concerns aspects of data sharing in stateful service conversations (such as accesses to databases, updates of persistent objects, etc.), as well as on composability of the results of sharing analysis across services involved in cross-domain business processes.

References

[AP08]   Awad, A., Puhlmann, F.: Structural Detection of Deadlocks in Business Process Models. In: Abramowicz, W., Fensel, D. (eds.) International Conference on Business Information Systems. LNBIP, vol. 7, pp. 239–250. Springer, Heidelberg (2008)

[BlZ04] Bi, H.H., leon Zhao, J.: Applying Propositional Logic to Workflow Verification. Information Technology and Management 5, 293–318 (2004)

[BMM06]   Baresi, L., Maurino, A., Modafferi, S.: Towards Distributed BPEL Orchestrations. ECEASST 3 (2006)

[CC77]   Cousot, P., Cousot, R.: Abstract Interpretation: a Unified Lattice Model for Static Analysis of Programs by Construction or Approximation of Fixpoints. In: ACM Symposium on Principles of Programming Languages (POPL 1977), pp. 238–252. ACM Press, New York (1977)

[FYG09]   Fdhila, W., Yildiz, U., Godart, C.: A Flexible Approach for Automatic Process Decentralization Using Dependency Tables. In: ICWS, pp. 847–855 (2009)

[HBC+10]   Hermenegildo, M.V., Bueno, F., Carro, M., López, P., Mera, E., Morales, J.F., Puebla, G.: An Overview of Ciao and its Design Philosophy. Technical Report CLIP2/2010.0, Technical University of Madrid (UPM), School of Computer Science, Under consideration for publication in Theory and Practice of Logic Programming (TPLP) (March 2010)

[Jea07]   Jordan, D et al.: Web Services Business Process Execution Language Version 2.0. Technical report, IBM, Microsoft, et. al (2007)

[JL92]   Jacobs, D., Langen, A.: Static Analysis of Logic Programs for Independent And-Parallelism. Journal of Logic Programming 13(2,3), 291–314 (1992)

[Kha07]   Khalaf, R.: Note on Syntactic Details of Split BPEL-D Business Processes. Technical Report 2007/2, Institut für Architektur von Anwendungssystemen, Universität Stuttgart, Universitätsstrasse 38, 70569 Stuttgart,Germany (July 2007)

[KL06]   Khalaf, R., Leymann, F.: E Role-based Decomposition of Business Processes using BPEL. In: IEEE International Conference on Web Services, ICWS 2006 (2006)

[Llo87]   Lloyd, J.W.: Foundations of Logic Programming, 2nd edn. Springer, Heidelberg (1987)

[MH91]   Muthukumar, K., Hermenegildo, M.: Combined Determination of Sharing and Freeness of Program Variables Through Abstract Interpretation. In: International Conference on Logic Programming (ICLP 1991), pp. 49–63. MIT Press, Cambridge (June 1991)

[MH92]   Muthukumar, K., Hermenegildo, M.: Compile-time Derivation of Variable Dependency Using Abstract Interpretation. Journal of Logic Programming 13(2/3), 315–347 (1992)

[MS93]   Marriott, K., Søndergaard, H.: Precise and efficient groundness analysis for logic programs. Technical report 93/7, Univ. of Melbourne (1993)

[Obj09]   Object Management Group. Business Process Modeling Notation (BPMN), Version 1.2 (January 2009)

[TF07]   Tan, W., Fan, Y.: Dynamic Workflow Model Fragmentation for Distributed Execution. Comput. Ind. 58(5), 381–391 (2007)

[vdAP06]   van der Aalst, W., Pesic, M.: DecSerFlow: Towards a Truly Declarative Service Flow Language. In: The Role of Business Processes in Service Oriented Architectures number 06291 in Dagstuhl Seminar Proceedings (2006)

[vdAtH05] van der Aalst, W.M.P., ter Hofstede, A.H.M.: YAWL: Yet Another Workflow Language. Information Systems 30(4), 245–275 (2005)

[Wor08]   The Workflow Management Coalition. XML Process Definition Language (XPDL) Version 2.1 (2008)

[WRRM08]   Weber, B., Reichert, M., Rinderle-Ma, S.: Change Patterns and Change Support Features - Enhancing Flexibility in Process-Aware Information Systems. Data Knowl. Eng. 66(3), 438–466 (2008)

[YG07]   Yildiz, U., Godart, C.: Information Flow Control with Decentralized Service Compositions. In: ICWS, pp. 9–17 (2007)

[ZBDtH06] Zaha, J.M., Barros, A.P., Dumas, M., ter Hofstede, A.H.M.: Let's Dance: A Language for Service Behavior Modeling. In: Meersman, R., Tari, Z. (eds.) OTM 2006. LNCS, vol. 4275, pp. 145–162. Springer, Heidelberg (2006)

Preventing SLA Violations in Service Compositions Using Aspect-Based Fragment Substitution

Philipp Leitner[1], Branimir Wetzstein[2], Dimka Karastoyanova[2], Waldemar Hummer[1], Schahram Dustdar[1], and Frank Leymann[2]

[1] Distributed Systems Group, Vienna University of Technology
Argentinierstrasse 8, 1040 Wien, Austria
lastname@infosys.tuwien.ac.at
[2] Institute of Architecture of Application Systems, University of Stuttgart, Germany
Universitätsstraße 38, 70569 Stuttgart, Germany
lastname@iaas.uni-stuttgart.de

Abstract. In this paper we show how the application of the aspect-oriented programming paradigm to runtime adaptation of service compositions can be used to prevent SLA violations. Adaptations are triggered by predicted violations, and are implemented as substitutions of fragments in the service composition. Fragments are full-fledged standalone compositions, and are linked into the original composition via special activities, which we refer to as virtual activities. Before substitution we evaluate fragments with respect to their expected impact on the performance of the composition, and choose those fragments which are best suited to prevent a predicted violation. We show how our approach can be implemented using Windows Workflow Foundation technology, and discuss our work based on an illustrative case study.

1 Introduction

As more and more companies shift towards a service-based model [1] of doing business, e.g., by providing coarse-grained value-added services as compositions of existing (external) Web services, management of service level agreements (SLAs) [2] is becoming increasingly important. SLAs are contractual agreements between a service provider and its customers, which govern the quality that the customers can expect. Violating SLAs is often associated with monetary penalties for the provider, i.e., the service provider generally has a strong interest in preventing SLA violations.

To this end, research in the area of SLA monitoring and compliance management [2, 3, 4] has so far mostly focused on detecting and explaining SLA violations after they have happened. While this is very useful to optimize service compositions in the long run, it does not prevent the problem in the first place. Therefore, we see the need for mechanisms to prevent violations at runtime, before they have happened. Basically, such mechanisms need both, a way

P.P. Maglio et al. (Eds.): ICSOC 2010, LNCS 6470, pp. 365–380, 2010.

to predict violations ahead of time, and a means to actually adapt the problematic composition instance in such a way that the violation is prevented. The former has already been covered in earlier work [5, 6].

The main contribution of this paper is a proposed solution for the latter problem. We apply the aspect-oriented programming (AOP) approach [7] to adaptation of running composition instances. Adaptations are triggered by predicted violations. Unlike in earlier work [8], aspects can contain composition fragments of arbitrary complexity, which can be applied before, after or instead of any subset of the original composition. We evaluate potential fragments based on their expected impact on SLA conformance, in order to identify the fragments which are best suited to prevent a predicted violation. Note that in this work we focus on performance-related service level objectives (SLOs). Our work is not directly applicable for most qualitative SLOs, such as security.

The rest of this paper is structured as follows. In Section 2 we present an example case, which we use as an illustrative example in the remainder of the paper. In Section 3 we present our approach to aspect-based adaptation in detail. In Section 4 we explain how our approach can be implemented using Windows Workflow Foundation [9] (Windows WF) technology. Section 5 contains an evaluation of our approach. In Section 6 we discuss related scientific work. Finally, Section 7 concludes the paper with a summary and an outlook on future work.

2   Case Study and Motivation

To illustrate the core ideas of the paper we use an order processing scenario. The scenario consists of a reseller who offers products to its customers. As shown in Figure 1 (left part of the figure), the reseller composes services from other providers (supplier, shipper, banking) to implement its process. After receiving the customer order, the list of needed parts is determined and parts which are not in stock are ordered from a supplier. After all the parts are gathered, the product is assembled and shipped to the customer. The reseller guarantees its customers a certain order processing time via an SLA. The goal of the reseller is to prevent cases of SLA violations, as this would lead to reduced customer satisfaction as well as penalty payments. The reseller can use SLA monitoring and prediction techniques as discussed in our previous work [5] to predict at process runtime whether the SLA with the customer is likely be violated, i.e., in our case, whether the order processing time will exceed the agreed value. If SLA prediction shows that the SLA with the customer will be violated, the reseller wants to adapt the service composition instance by using alternative, better performing services. Assume that in our scenario there are two alternative suppliers who offer faster delivery times, but do not provide all needed product types on their own. The full product range offered to the customer can only be realized by using both alternative suppliers in conjunction. Figure 1 shows a composition fragment consisting of a switch between those two suppliers, whereby supplier 2 is used if supplier 1 is unable to provide a certain part. Even though not the default case, this composition fragment can be used at runtime instead of the original supplier invocation if a given instance is likely to exceed the maximum processing time as promised to the customer in the SLA.

There are two approaches for supporting the execution of alternative composition fragments: (1) the straight-forward approach is to model all alternative fragments already at design time as part of the composition, e.g., using if-else branches; (2) the approach of this paper is to model alternative fragments separately from the original composition model, and dynamically substitute them based on prediction results at composition runtime. We will now explain this approach and its advantages in detail.

3   Aspect-Based Adaptation

In this paper we use the notion of aspect-based fragment substitution to model how service composition instances can be adapted at runtime in order to prevent predicted SLA violations. Our approach is general, in the sense that it is not specific to any concrete composition model. Instead, it can be applied to many existing block-structured composition models (for instance WS-BPEL or Windows Workflow Foundation [9]). In our work we reuse well-known AOP terminology to describe adaptations of service compositions. The most important of these terms are *aspects* (cross-cutting concerns, which are turned off and on at design or run-time, e.g., logging), *advices* (business logic which implements aspects, e.g., the code to implement logging), *joinpoints* (points in the application code where advices can potentially be inserted), and *weaving* (the process of dynamically inserting advices in jointpoints). Note that in literature AOP is often discussed as both a design time and a run time technology, i.e., weaving can

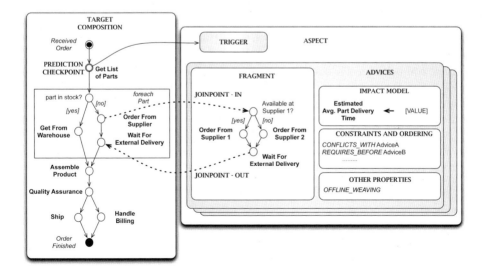

Fig. 1. Illustrative Example and Approach Overview

happen both statically or dynamically. In this paper we only consider weaving at runtime (at running instances), since our primary concern is the adaptation of composition instances, without modification of the underlying definition.

The main concepts of our work are summarized in Figure 1. *Aspects* are defined as an *adaptation trigger*, which is based on a predicted SLA violation, and any number of *advices*. Every advice in turn contains exactly one *composition fragment*, one *impact model* containing any number of impact clauses, a list of *constraints* on other advices of the same aspect, and any optional *other properties*. The fragment is linked to the service composition to adapt (denoted as *target composition* in the following) using two types of *joinpoints* – in-joinpoints mark the beginning of the composition segment to replace, while out-joinpoints mark the end of the segment. We will now discuss these components in more detail.

3.1   Adaptation Triggers

As discussed extensively in Section 1 and Section 2, our approach is motivated by the need to prevent SLA violations. Therefore, runtime adaptation is generally triggered by predictions of such violations. In the remainder of this paper we will assume that some means of prediction are available. This may be powerful prediction tooling as presented in [5] or [6], or simply some estimations provided by a human domain expert. The actual approach to prediction is out of scope of this paper, however, for the sake of completeness we give a very brief overview of our own earlier work.

We generate predictions using regression from runtime data. This data is collected using an event-based approach (i.e., components in the service-based system emit status events, which are collected and correlated). The actual regression is implemented as a black-box function, using methods from the field of machine learning, more precisely artificial neural networks [10] (ANNs). We sketch this in Figure 2. This prediction is carried out in predefined places in the service composition, the so-called checkpoints. Checkpoints should be selected in such a way that enough data is already available to generate useful predictions. Note that there is a strong relationship between the checkpoint selection and which actions can be associated with an advice – in earlier checkpoints a lot of adaptation actions are still available, while later checkpoints allow for more accurate predictions because of more data being available. The problem of selecting checkpoints is discussed in more detail elsewhere [5].

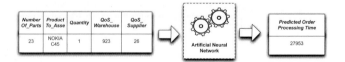

Fig. 2. Generating Predictions From Runtime Data

3.2   Composition Fragments

Composition fragments can be considered the core of our adaptation approach. In essence, fragments are full-fledged, even if usually small, service compositions. That is, fragments may contain variables, branches, Web service invocations, parallel execution, loops, scopes, fault handling, compensation, or any other construct which is legal in the composition model used. However, they do not have to follow the same syntactic and semantic rules as the target composition. For example, if WS-BPEL is used as composition model, designers of fragments may access e.g., variables defined in the target composition, even if the respective data is undefined in the fragment itself (syntactic rule). Also, they could specify a receive activity without a corresponding reply activity (semantic rule). The reason for this is that during weaving the fragment will be inserted into the composition model of the target composition, essentially becoming part of the composition itself. A fragment definition is valid if it results in an executable composition after weaving, which cannot be checked in isolation.

In addition to all activities provided by the composition metamodel, fragments may contain three additional activity types (FRAGMENT_START, in the following referred to as start, FRAGMENT_END, end, and TRANSPARENT_BLOCK, transparent) with a semantic specific to our approach. We refer to these activities as *virtual activities*, because they are never actually executed. Instead, virtual activities are dropped or replaced during weaving. Virtual activities are solely responsible for defining the joinpoints between the fragment and the target composition, marking the segment of the target composition to substitute.

Every fragment starts with exactly one start activity and ends with exactly one end activity. In-joinpoints, defined via the start activity, represent the start of substitution, and out-joinpoints, defined via the end activity, represent the end of substitution. All joinpoints can reference any activity in the service composition, either before or after the execution of the activity (i.e., both "immediately before executing Get List of Parts" and "immediately after executing Get List of Parts" are valid joinpoints). However, the in- and out-joinpoint of a fragment need to reference activities in the same sequence in the target composition, i.e., the joinpoints defined in Figure 1 are correct, but, for example, it would not be possible to move the in-joint point to the activity "Get List of Parts". The reason for this limitation is that semantic problems arise if in- and out-joinpoints are situated in different sequences. In the example, the branching activity "part in stock?" would be removed, but not the actual branches, rendering it impossible to decide which branch to execute.

It is not only possible to replace a segment of the target composition, even though this is the general case we discuss. Trivially, one may also just insert the fragment at a specific joinpoint (the in- and out-joinpoints are identical, and the fragment is non-empty), or remove a segment (substitution with an empty fragment). We refer to the sum of all joinpoints of a fragment as the *linking* of the fragment to the target composition. Figure 3 summarizes this linking. The start activity specifies that the fragment should be inserted before the activity "Schedule Assembling", while the end specifies that the end of the substitution

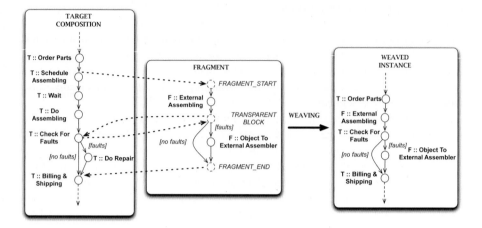

Fig. 3. Fragment Activities and Linking

segment is before the activity "Billing & Shipping". On the right-hand side, Figure 3 shows the dynamically constructed instance after the fragment has been weaved into the target composition. Activities depicted with the prefix T originate from the target composition, while activities with the prefix F are specified in the fragment.

Transparents are more complicated than start or end . They are a place-holder representing a part of the target composition in the fragment. This part is defined in the same way as the substitution segment, i.e., transparents have both out- and in-joinpoints. Additionally, the same restrictions apply (in and out-joinpoints need to reference activities in the same sequence). At runtime, transparents are replaced by a copy of the part that they represent. The purpose of transparent activities is threefold. Firstly, they allow for the definition of fragments which substitute segments, while still retaining some of this segment's functionality. One example of this usage is depicted in Figure 3, where the "Check for Faults" activity from the target composition is retained in the fragment. Note that it is not mandatory that a transparent references only a single activity. Secondly, transparent activities allow to essentially duplicate activities in the target composition. This is because transparents are in fact free to reference any part of the target composition, not only parts which are in the substitution segment (and hence removed during weaving). Additionally, many transparents may copy the same activities, multiplying them even further. Thirdly, transparent activities allow for the definition of generic fragments.

3.3   Generic Fragments

Generic fragments are (unlike the fragments discussed so far) not developed specifically for a given target composition. Instead, they can be applied to a number of compositions. Therefore, generic fragments do not contain any concrete case-specific business logics. They are used to implement adaptation scenarios which can be useful across several concrete target compositions and domains. Figure 4 exemplifies three generic fragments. The main property of generic fragments is that they consist only of virtual activities and control flow constructs, i.e., they do not contain any concrete activities such as Web service invocations. These generic fragments are instantiated by defining the linking (i.e., all in- and out-joinpoints) to concrete target compositions. As soon as this linking is defined, the fragment stops being generic, and is as case-specific as any other fragment.

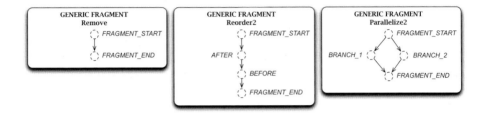

Fig. 4. Examples of Generic Fragments

The first and most simple generic fragment in Figure 4 (`Remove`) has been mentioned before – it is an empty fragment consisting only of a `start` and `end` activity. Using this generic fragment any segment of the target composition can be deleted. The second example is a generic fragment named `Reorder2`. It consists of `start`, `end`, and two `transparents` ("after" and "before"). Using this fragment two segments in the target composition can be rearranged, e.g., exchanging their order. Trivially, one can also implement similar generic fragments `ReorderX`, rearranging X segments instead of just two. Finally, `Parallelize2` consists again of `start`, `end`, and two `transparents` ("branch_1" and "branch_2"), however, this time "branch_1" and "branch_2" are executed in parallel. Using this generic fragment one can parallelize two segments from the target composition (which presumably have been executed in serial before). Of course, it is again possible to define `ParallelizeX` fragments to parallelize more than two segments at the same time.

3.4 Dynamic Weaving

At run-time, one or more previously selected fragments are weaved into the running instance of the target composition. The selection procedure will be discussed in Section 3.5. As we have sketched in Figure 5, the general weaving algorithm is a simple 2-step procedure. Firstly, the fragment is pre-processed, i.e., for each `transparent` in the fragment the linking to the target composition is resolved, and the `transparent` is replaced by a deep copy of the segment that it represents. Secondly, the linking of the fragment itself is resolved, and the

```
1   # input: instance, fragment, mode # output: weaved instance
2
3   if (mode == "OFFLINE") suspend(instance)
4
5   # step 1 - fragment preprocessing
6   foreach transparent in fragment
7       linking = resolve_linking(transparent,instance)
8       copy = copy_segment(linking,instance)
9       replace_fragments(fragment,transparent,copy)
10
11  # step 2 - fragment substitution
12  seqment := resolve_linking(fragment,instance)
13  remove_start_activity(fragment)
14  remove_end_activity(fragment)
15  replace_fragments(instance,segment,fragment)
16
17  if (mode == "OFFLINE") resume(instance)
18
19  return instance
```

Fig. 5. Weaving Algorithm

start and end virtual activities are removed from the fragment (they are not needed anymore). Finally, the segment of the target composition (indicated by the linking) is removed, and the fragment is inserted instead.

Weaving can be done either online or offline. For offline weaving the composition instance is halted while the adaptation is applied (see Line 4-5 in Listing 5), and resumed when the adaptation is finished (Lines 19-20). If online adaptation is used the instance continues running during weaving. This has the advantage that weaving does not introduce additional execution time overhead. However, if after weaving the running instance has already passed the entry point of the fragment (the linking of the fragment's start activity) the weaving fails and is rolled back. This is because our system needs to guarantee that a fragment is either executed as a whole, or not at all (which cannot be guaranteed after the instance has begun executing the substitution segment in the target composition). Our system falls back to offline adaptation as soon as at least one advice which needs to be applied requires it (i.e., if many advices are applied and only one of them requires offline weaving, we still need to suspend the composition instance before adaptation).

Generally, if more than one advice needs to be applied, we use recursive one-by-one weaving, that is, we start by weaving the first fragment into the instance (ignoring any other fragments). The result of this first weaving process is then the input to the weaving of the second fragment. This is continued until all fragments are weaved. The order in which fragments are applied is unimportant as long as all fragments are independent (i.e., as long as none of the segments indicated by any linking of either fragments or transparents overlaps). If this is not the case the user can specify a defined ordering of advices as part of the advice definition. The ordering can be defined using five different order predicates (REQUIRES_BEFORE, REQUIRES_AFTER, IF_PRESENT_BEFORE,

IF_PRESENT_AFTER, and CONFLICTS_WITH). REQUIRES_[BEFORE|AFTER] specifies that a given advice has to be applied before or after this advice (otherwise the advice cannot be applied at all). IF_PRESENT_[BEFORE|AFTER] specifies that if the other advice is present, it has to be applied before or after this one (but the other advice can also simply not be applied). Using REQUIRES_BEFORE one can specify complex fragments, whose linking does not actually point to the target composition itself, but to another fragment. This is possible since we can rely that the referenced fragment has already been weaved into the target composition before before the weaving of the dependent fragment starts. Another type of ordering predicate is CONFLICTS_WITH. This predicate specifies that two fragments are mutually exclusive, i.e., they cannot be applied together. At runtime, we construct a forest of directed graphs from these predicates, whose nodes are advices and whose edges are "is executed after" relationships. If the graphs in this forest are acyclic there is at least one allowed order of advices, which can be consructed using topological ordering. If the graphs contains at least one cycle the definition of advices is invalid, since the definition contains at least one cyclic dependency.

3.5   Impact Model and Advice Selection

As described briefly in Section 3.1, we build upon a predictor which estimates SLO values by assessing a set of lower level metrics. Examples include ordered product types, duration of branches of the composition, expected delivery times of suppliers and shipper, or QoS of services used. In order to being able to evaluate whether a given advice will actually help preventing the predicted SLA violation, we need to specify for each advice its impact on those lower-level base metrics (*impact model*). The impact model is used to identify which concrete advice (from all advices designed within an aspect) should be applied, i.e., which advices are best suited to prevent a predicted violation (*advice selection*).

The impact model contains a non-empty set of *impact clauses*. An impact clause relates to one base metric and specifies the expected value of that metric after adaptation (i.e., after this fragment has been applied). This value can be determined in several ways: (1) based on measured history data if the corresponding advice has already been used in past composition instances, e.g., using data mining techniques; (2) based on SLAs with external providers; or (3) by using QoS aggregation techniques as discussed in earlier research [11]. In QoS aggregation, based on the composition fragment structure, the properties of atomic activities are recursively aggregated (e.g., the duration of a sequence of activities is the sum of durations of those activities, the duration of the parallel execution of activities is given by the duration of the longest acitivity etc. [11]). The impact model should specify impact clauses for all metrics which the advice affects.

The impact model is specified as part of advice definition. Advice selection at runtime is performed as follows. If in a checkpoint a violation is predicted, we obtain the set of advices defined for this checkpoint. For each allowed combination of advices we evaluate if the usage of these advices would prevent the

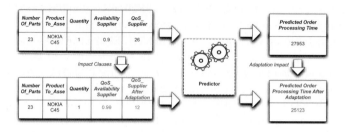

Fig. 6. Evaluation of Impact Models

SLA violation, i.e., all impact clauses are applied to the data which has originally been used to generate the prediction. The updated data (which essentially
represents the state after adaptation) is then again fed to the predictor, to re-
generate the prediction after adaptation. The difference between the original
prediction and the new prediction is the estimated impact of applying these advices. This is sketched in Figure 6. If more than one advice should be applied at
the same time, the impact clauses are applied in the same order to the data as
the weaving order of the fragments would be. If the predicted value complies to
the SLA, that advice or advice combination is put into a candidate set. In the
next step, we then select the best alternative from the candidate set by looking
at additionally specified criteria (in addition to the concrete predicted value). In
this step, complex evaluations can take place, taking into account and weighting
different dimensions (e.g., cost, customer satisfaction, reliability) according to a
user-defined utility function, which is currently left for future work. At the moment, we simply choose the candidate which brings the SLO value closest to the
target value, i.e., we apply "just as much" adaptation as necessary to prevent
the predicted violation.

4   Prototype Implementation

In our prototype we consider the aspect-based adaptation of service compositions implemented using the Windows Workflow Foundation [9] (WF) composition model. More concretely, our system can be applied to WF Sequential
Workflows[1]. WF Sequential Workflows are similar to e.g., Web service compositions implemented using WS-BPEL. However, unlike most WS-BPEL engines,
WF is deeply integrated with Microsoft .NET (starting with version 3.0), along
with strong tool support for developing compositions. Additionally, and most
importantly for this paper, Microsoft .NET supports the dynamic adaptation of
WF instances via an explicit API, the WorkflowChanges API[2]. This API allows
us to suspend, modify, and resume any running composition instance. Additionally, activities in the composition can easily be replicated. Implementation of

---

[1] http://msmvps.com/blogs/theproblemsolver/archive/2006/10/11/
Sequential-versus-State-workflows.aspx
[2] http://msdn.microsoft.com/en-us/library/ms734569(VS.85).aspx

the weaving algorithm as discussed in Section 3 is, therefore, straight-forward. Another important advantage of building the prototype based on WF is that we can reuse the tooling integrated in Visual Studio to support the development of fragments.

We have implemented the approach discussed in this paper within the larger VRESCo SOA runtime environment project. VRESCo is discussed in detail elsewhere [12], and will not be covered here. To trigger adaptations as briefly discussed in Section 3.1, we utilize our earlier work on prediction of violations, as discussed in [5]. The prototype has been designed to fit into PREVENT , an autonomous system for prevention of SLA violations [13]. The interested reader may download a recent snapshot of our VRESCo prototype, which includes an implementation of the case study used in this paper[3].

5   Evaluation

We will now evaluate our approach in two different ways. Firstly, we will qualitatively analyse the expressiveness of our approach by comparison with previously published adaptation patterns [14]. Secondly, we will have a look at performance implications. This is done by monitoring the weaving time in our prototype system, as well as comparing the execution time of dynamically weaved and statically defined composition instances.

5.1   Coverage of Adaptation Patterns

In order to discuss the expressiveness of our approach we have used the adaptation patterns defined in [14]. In this work, 14 patterns of structural changes in processes are identified. Using our approach 9 of these patterns are fully supported.

We have summarized the coverage of adaptation patterns in Table 1. The patterns **AP1**, **AP2** and **AP4** are the core feature of our approach, and can be implemented trivially. For **AP2** and **AP5** we specifically described a generic fragment in Section 3. Similarly, all of **AP3**, **AP5**, **AP8**, **AP9**, **AP10 AP14** can be implemented rather elegantly using transparents. The patterns concerning subprocesses (**AP6** and **AP7**) cannot be implemented since our approach does not support linking to more than one composition at the same time. **AP11** and **AP12** are in simple cases implementable using transparents, but our approach does not provide any explicit support for it, making the implementation rather cumbersome. Similarly, **AP13** can be implemented by replacing the branching node as a whole, but we do not consider this solution as in line with the idea of this pattern.

5.2   Performance Analysis

In a second step we have evaluated the runtime implications of our prototype. For this, we monitored the average execution time of dynamically weaved composition instances with an increasing number of activities, and compare them to

---

[3] http://sourceforge.net/projects/vresco/

Table 1. Coverage of Adaptation Patterns

ID	Pattern Name	Covered
AP1	Insert Fragment	✓
AP2	Delete Fragment	✓
AP3	Move Fragment	✓
AP4	Replace Fragment	✓
AP5	Swap Fragment	✓
AP6	Extract Sub Process	✗
AP7	Inline Sub Process	✗
AP8	Embed Fragment in Loop	✓
AP9	Parallelize Activities	✓
AP10	Embed Fragment in Conditional	✓
AP11	Add Control Dependency	✗
AP12	Remove Control Dependency	✗
AP13	Update Condition	✗
AP14	Copy Fragment	✓

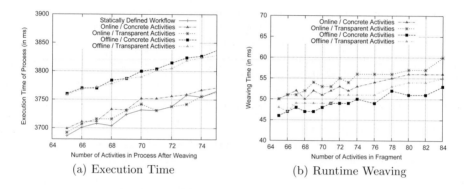

(a) Execution Time   (b) Runtime Weaving

Fig. 7. Performance Analysis Outcomes

the same instance defined statically. We also compare online and offline weaving, and distinguish between fragments defined using `transparent` activities and fragments defined without. For simplicity, all compositions and fragments are sequences of "wait" activities. Using different types of activities would not have an impact on the evaluation outcome, since our adaptation approach handles all non-virtual activities the same way, i.e., weaving an "invoke" activity has a similar overhead than weaving a "wait" activity. To mimimize external influences all results are the average of 50 independent test runs. We have also repeated the evaluation multiple times to make sure that the outcome is reproduceable. The outcomes of these experiments are summarized in Figure 7(a).

As can be seen, online weaved compositions exhibit very little overhead as compared to statically defined compositions. Of course, offline weaving introduces some overhead, which stems from the time necessary to select the fragments, to implement the actual weaving, and to suspend and unsuspend the composition. In our experiments, the largest part of these factors is the actual weaving time. Therefore, we have further analyzed this factor in Figure 7(b). We depict the weaving time depending on the number of activities to weave. Generally, concrete activities are faster to weave than `transparent` activities (since the logics of weaving `transparents` is more complicated), and offline weaving is faster than online weaving (since, in the online case, some additional sanity checks are done by the Windows Workflow runtime). In general, this increased weaving time for online weaving does not matter too much, since the online weaving time does not directly impact the execution time of the process. Overall, the overhead introduced by weaving is relatively constant in [45 : 80] ms, even for large fragments (more than 80 activities).

Summarizing, we can see that dynamic weaving does not introduce a big overhead, especially if online weaving is possible. If offline weaving has to be used, an additional weaving overhead, which is generally in [45 : 80] ms, is introduced. We argue that for most application areas this overhead is still far from being dramatic. Even though the concrete numbers are specific for our prototype implementation, they still show that implementing our ideas efficiently is well possible.

6   Related Work

In this paper we apply the AOP paradigm to adaptation of service compositions. On the level of atomic services earlier work in this direction has been presented by Kongdenfha et al [15]. In this work, they use the AOP paradigm to adapt the implementation of atomic Web services. A comparable approach has also been presented by Song et al. [16], who use the AOP approach to weave cross-cutting concerns, such as security, into all atomic Web services in a composition. A similar track has also been followed by Narendra et al., who used AOP-based adaptation of services in a composition to propagate changes in non-funtional properties through the composition [17]. Of course, all of these approaches assume that the developer has access to the implementation of these atomic services.

The general scope of our work is similar to work presented by Gmach et al. [18]. However, the focus of our contribution is purely on adaptation of service compositions, while Gmach et al. adapt on service infrastructure level (i.e., by moving services to different hosts, or by re-scheduling requests in the service bus). Finally, adaptation with the explicit goal of preventing SLA violations has been discussed by various authors, e.g., our own earlier work on PREVENT [13] or recent work by Metzger et al. [19]. The concrete execution of adaptation of compositions has in the past been covered by research in various directions. Earlier approaches often did not consider the adaptation of the composition structure at all, instead focusing solely on service rebinding. In a simplistic manner such adaptations can in fact be carried out using WS-BPEL alone, by using the *Dynamic Partner Link* feature. However, practical problems such as finding the right service to bind to (often based on QoS), or the need to resolve interface differences, demand for more sophisticated service rebinding approaches. Examples of such work include the WS-Binder [20] or the PAWS [21] frameworks.

More advanced service rebinding was also one of the contributions of Moser et al. in [22]. Finally, some work on service rebinding (dealing also with stateful services) has been presented by Mosincat and Binder in [23].

An early approach towards structural adaptation of compositions has been discussed in [24]. However, in this work no free-form adaptation is possible. Instead, predefined parameterizations are applied if certain conditions hold. Arguably, the AOP paradigm can provide a more powerful abstraction for adaptation in compositions. This idea has first been introduced by Charfi et al. [25,26]. However, unlike our work, Charfi et al. focus on the traditional AOP idea of weaving crosscutting concerns into the composition, while we apply the AOP paradigm with a different goal (adaptation for SLA compliance) in mind. Using aspects for runtime adaptation in WS-BPEL has been covered by the BPEL'n'-Aspects framework [8]. Our main contribution over this work is that in our case aspects can be composition fragments, while BPEL'n'Aspects supports only single Web service invocations as aspects. Work with similar goals, but specific to the telecommunications domain, has been presented Niemöller et al. [27]. An approach which deals with process fragment composition is presented by Eberle et al. [28]. Their idea is to exploit the redundancy in separately modeled composition fragments and use those redundant overlapping fragment parts to merge the fragments. In our approach we model how fragments should be merged explicitly by using virtual activities.

7   Conclusions and Future Work

In this paper we have presented an approach to runtime adaptation of service compositions for preventing SLA violations. The adaptation is based on composition fragments which are dynamically substitued at runtime using AOP techniques. Composition fragments are modeled separately and are explicitly linked into the original composition using virtual activities. In addition to their process logic, fragments specify also their expected impact on the composition performance. This is necessary in order to be able to choose the best fitting fragments for preventing a predicted SLA violation at composition runtime. We have implemented the approach using Windows Workflow Foundation technology and experiments show that the performance impact of dynamic weaving is acceptable.

While the current status of the approach is promising, there are still some open issues left for future work. Firstly, we do not take into account that adaptation which prevents the violation of one SLA metric could easily lead to the violation of another. In particular, we currently do not take the costs of adaptations into account (e.g., increased costs by using more expensive services in the weaved fragment) which in some cases could be higher than the gain of not violating the SLA. Therefore, we will extend the impact model and its evaluation in our future work. Secondly, we currently assume that the number of possible combinations of advices to apply is small, so that finding the best combination via full enumeration is possible. In future work we plan to embrace heuristic optimization for cases where full enumeration is not feasible.

Acknowledgments

The research leading to these results has received funding from the European Community's 7th Framework Programme under the Network of Excellence S-Cube (Grant Agreement no. 215483).

References

1. Papazoglou, M.P., Traverso, P., Dustdar, S., Leymann, F.: Service-Oriented Computing: State of the Art and Research Challenges. IEEE Computer 40(11) (2007)
2. Dan, A., Davis, D., Kearney, R., Keller, A., King, R., Kuebler, D., Ludwig, H., Polan, M., Spreitzer, M., Youssef, A.: Web Services on Demand: WSLA-Driven Automated Management. IBM Systems Journal 43(1), 136–158 (2004)
3. Bodenstaff, L., Wombacher, A., Reichert, M., Jaeger, M.C.: Analyzing Impact Factors on Composite Services. In: Proceedings of the 2009 IEEE International Conference on Services Computing (SCC 2009) (2009)
4. Wetzstein, B., Leitner, P., Rosenberg, F., Brandic, I., Leymann, F., Dustdar, S.: Monitoring and Analyzing Influential Factors of Business Process Performance. In: Proceedings of the 13th IEEE EDOC Conference (EDOC 2009) (2009)
5. Leitner, P., Wetzstein, B., Rosenberg, F., Michlmayr, A., Dustdar, S., Leymann, F.: Runtime Prediction of Service Level Agreement Violations for Composite Services. In: Proceedings of the 3rd Workshop on Non-Functional Properties and SLA Management in Service-Oriented Computing, NFPSLAM-SOC 2009 (2009)
6. Zeng, L., Lingenfelder, C., Lei, H., Chang, H.: Event-Driven Quality of Service Prediction. In: Bouguettaya, A., Krueger, I., Margaria, T. (eds.) ICSOC 2008. LNCS, vol. 5364, pp. 147–161. Springer, Heidelberg (2008)
7. Miller, F.P., Vandome, A.F., McBrewster, J.: Aspect-oriented Programming. Alphascript Publishing (2010)
8. Karastoyanova, D., Leymann, F.: BPEL'n'Aspects: Adapting Service Orchestration Logic. In: Proceedings of 7th IEEE International Conference on Web Services, ICWS 2009 (2009)
9. Shukla, D., Schmidt, B.: Essential Windows Workflow Foundation. Microsoft.Net Development Series (2006)
10. Haykin, S.: Neural Networks and Learning Machines: A Comprehensive Foundation, 3rd edn. Prentice-Hall, Englewood Cliffs (2008)
11. Jaeger, M.C., Rojec-Goldmann, G., Muhl, G.: QoS Aggregation in Web Service Compositions. In: Proceedings of the 2005 IEEE International Conference on eTechnology, eCommerce and eService, EEE 2005 (2005)
12. Michlmayr, A., Rosenberg, F., Leitner, P., Dustdar, S.: End-to-End Support for QoS-Aware Service Selection, Binding and Mediation in VRESCo. IEEE Transactions on Services Computing, TSC (2010)
13. Leitner, P., Michlmayr, A., Rosenberg, F., Dustdar, S.: Monitoring, Prediction and Prevention of SLA Violations in Composite Services. In: Proceedings of the 2010 IEEE International Conference on Web Services, ICWS 2010 (2010)
14. Weber, B., Reichert, M., Rinderle-Ma, S.: Change Patterns and Change Support Features - Enhancing Flexibility in Process-Aware Information Systems. Data and Knowledge Engineering 66(3), 438–466 (2008)
15. Kongdenfha, W., Saint-Paul, R., Benatallah, B., Casati, F.: An Aspect-Oriented Framework for Service Adaptation. In: Dan, A., Lamersdorf, W. (eds.) ICSOC 2006. LNCS, vol. 4294, pp. 15–26. Springer, Heidelberg (2006)

16. Song, H., Yin, Y., Zheng, S.: Dynamic Aspects Weaving in Service Composition. In: Proceedings of the International Conference on Intelligent Systems Design and Applications (2006)

17. Narendra, N.C., Ponnalagu, K., Krishnamurthy, J., Ramkumar, R.: Run-time adaptation of non-functional properties of composite web services using aspect-oriented programming. In: Krämer, B.J., Lin, K.-J., Narasimhan, P. (eds.) ICSOC 2007. LNCS, vol. 4749, pp. 546–557. Springer, Heidelberg (2007)

18. Gmach, D., Krompass, S., Scholz, A., Wimmer, M., Kemper, A.: Adaptive Quality of Service Management for Enterprise Services. ACM Transactions on the Web 2(1), 1–46 (2008)

19. Metzger, A., Sammodi, O., Pohl, K., Rzepka, M.: Towards Pro-Active Adaptation With Confidence: Augmenting Service Monitoring With Online Testing. In: Proceedings of the 2010 ICSE Workshop on Software Engineering for Adaptive and Self-Managing Systems, SEAMS 2010 (2010)

20. Penta, M.D., Esposito, R., Villani, M.L., Codato, R., Colombo, M., Nitto, E.D.: WS Binder: a Framework to Enable Dynamic Binding of Composite Web Services. In: Proceedings of the International Workshop on Service-Oriented Software Engineering, SOSE 2006 (2006)

21. Ardagna, D., Comuzzi, M., Mussi, E., Pernici, B., Plebani, P.: PAWS: A Framework for Executing Adaptive Web-Service Processes. IEEE Software 24(6), 39–46 (2007)

22. Moser, O., Rosenberg, F., Dustdar, S.: Non-Intrusive Monitoring and Service Adaptation for WS-BPEL. In: Proceedings of the 17th International Conference on World Wide Web, WWW 2008 (2008)

23. Mosincat, A., Binder, W.: Transparent Runtime Adaptability for BPEL Processes. In: Bouguettaya, A., Krueger, I., Margaria, T. (eds.) ICSOC 2008. LNCS, vol. 5364, pp. 241–255. Springer, Heidelberg (2008)

24. Karastoyanova, D., Leymann, F., Nitzsche, J., Wetzstein, B., Wutke, D.: Parameterized BPEL Processes: Concepts and Implementation. In: Dustdar, S., Fiadeiro, J.L., Sheth, A.P. (eds.) BPM 2006. LNCS, vol. 4102, pp. 471–476. Springer, Heidelberg (2006)

25. Charfi, A., Mezini, M.: AO4BPEL: An Aspect-oriented Extension to BPEL. World Wide Web 10(3), 309–344 (2007)

26. Charfi, A., Dinkelaker, T., Mezini, M.: A Plug-in Architecture for Self-Adaptive Web Service Compositions. In: Proceedings of the 2009 IEEE International Conference on Web Services, ICWS 2009 (2009)

27. Niemöller, J., Levenshteyn, R., Freiter, E., Vandikas, K., Quinet, R., Fikouras, I.: Aspect Orientation for Composite Services in the Telecommunication Domain. In: Baresi, L., Chi, C.-H., Suzuki, J. (eds.) ICSOC-ServiceWave 2009. LNCS, vol. 5900, pp. 19–33. Springer, Heidelberg (2009)

28. Eberle, H., Unger, T., Leymann, F.: Process Fragments. In: Meersman, R., Dillon, T., Herrero, P. (eds.) OTM 2009. LNCS, vol. 5870, pp. 398–405. Springer, Heidelberg (2009)

Adaptive Management of Composite Services under Percentile-Based Service Level Agreements

Valeria Cardellini, Emiliano Casalicchio, Vincenzo Grassi,
and Francesco Lo Presti

Università di Roma "Tor Vergata", Viale del Politecnico 1, 00133 Roma, Italy
{cardellini,casalicchio}@ing.uniroma2.it,
{vgrassi,lopresti}@info.uniroma2.it

Abstract. We present a brokering service for the adaptive management of composite services. The goal of this broker is to dynamically adapt at runtime the composite service configuration, to fulfill the Service Level Agreements (SLAs) negotiated with different classes of requestors, despite variations of the operating environment. Differently from most of the current approaches, where the performance guarantees are characterized only in terms of bounds on average QoS metrics, we consider SLAs that also specify upper bounds on the percentile of the service response time, which are expected to better capture user perceived QoS. The adaptive composite service management is based on a service selection scheme that minimizes the service broker cost while guaranteeing the negotiated QoS to the different service classes. The optimal service selection is determined by means of a linear programming problem that can be efficiently solved. As a result, the proposed approach is scalable and lends itself to an efficient implementation.

1 Introduction

The Service Oriented Architecture (SOA) paradigm encourages the construction of new applications through the composition of loosely coupled network-accessible services offered by independent providers. One of the underlying ideas is that different providers may offer different implementations of the same functionality, differentiated by their quality of service (QoS) and cost attributes, thus allowing a prospective user to choose the services that best suit his/her needs. To state the respective expectations and obligations concerning the delivered QoS and cost, users and providers of services engage in a negotiation process that culminates in the definition of a *Service Level Agreement* (SLA) contract.

Given a SOA system consisting of a composition of services, the fulfillment of the QoS requirements stated in its SLA is a challenging task that requires the system to take complex decisions within short time periods, because of the intrinsically dynamic and unpredictable nature of the SOA operational environment. A promising way to manage effectively this task is to make the system able to

P.P. Maglio et al. (Eds.): ICSOC 2010, LNCS 6470, pp. 381–395, 2010.

self-configure at runtime in response to changes in its operational environment. In this way, the system can timely react to environment changes (concerning for example the available resources or the type and amount of user requests), to keep the ability of fulfilling at runtime the QoS requirements stated in a SLA, thus avoiding SLA violations that could cause loss of income and reputation.

Several methodologies have been already proposed to drive the self-configuration of QoS-aware SOA systems. Most of them (*e.g.*, [1,2,4,15,16]) address this issue as a *service selection* problem: given the set of functionalities (*abstract services*) needed to compose a new added value service, the goal is to identify at runtime a set of *concrete services* (one for each abstract service) that implement them, selecting it from a pool of candidates. Each selected concrete service is then dynamically bound to the corresponding abstract service. Other methodologies [5,9,10] extend this idea by also considering the possibility of binding each abstract service to a set of functionally equivalent concrete services rather than a single service, coordinated according to some redundancy pattern (*e.g.*, 1-out-of-N or sequential retry), to achieve higher QoS at the expense of higher cost: in this case both the redundancy pattern and the set of equivalent concrete services must be selected at runtime.

The proposed methodologies also differ in the type of scenario they deal with: most of them (*e.g.*, [1,2,10,15,16]) deal with *single* requests for the composite service independently of each another. The goal in this case is to determine the concrete implementation of each abstract service for that request that is best suited to satisfy the requestor SLA given the current conditions of the operating environment. Others [4,5] jointly consider the aggregate *flow* of requests. In this case, the goal is to determine how to switch different flows of requests, possibly generated by several classes of users, to the different candidate implementations as to satisfy the different SLAs.

Most of the proposed approaches for self-configurable QoS-aware SOA systems consider SLAs where the performance guarantees are specified only in terms of bounds on the expected values of the QoS metrics of interests. A potential limitation of these approaches lies in the fact that the user perceived QoS is often better expressed in terms of bounds on the percentile of the QoS metrics, as also reflected in commercial practices. For example, the Amazon SOA-based e-commerce platform [7] includes SLAs concerning the 99.9 percentile of the response time under a given peak load of service requests per second. To the best of our knowledge, only the approaches proposed in [8,14] offer guarantees on the percentile of the response time. The results in [14], though, are limited to sequential patterns and only apply to the single request scenario, while [8] proposes a heuristic for request scheduling in a single database server which is based on the execution time prediction.

In this paper, we overcome this limitation of current methodologies for self-configurable QoS-aware SOA systems. We consider the *flow* scenario and propose a service selection scheme to drive the self-configuration of composite SOA applications, which considers SLAs that include performance guarantees on the percentiles of the QoS attributes. We present our solution from the perspective of an application implemented as a composite service and managed by an intermediary broker. We show that the application can efficiently provide the SLAs by selecting, among the pool of available services, those services that allow it to fulfill the SLAs negotiated with the users, given the constraints defined by the SLAs settled with the providers. The selection is driven by the goal of maximizing some broker utility goal. The search for a new solution is triggered by the occurrence of events that could make no longer valid a previously calculated solution, *e.g.*, the arrival or departure of a user or a change in the set of providers. We formulate the service selection problem as an optimization problem with non-linear constraints. For the solution, we linearize the constrains. The resulting linear programming problem can thus be efficiently solved via standard techniques. Hence the proposed approach is suitable for on-line operations.

The rest of the paper is organized as follows. In Sect. 2 we provide an overview of the system architecture offering the composite service with percentile-based SLAs and outline the SLA definition. In Sect. 3 we discuss how to compute the QoS attributes of the composite service. In Sect. 4 we present the formulation of the optimization problem that is solved to determined the percentile-based service selection. Then, in Sect. 5 we present the simulation experiments to assess the effectiveness of the proposed approach. Finally, we draw some conclusions and give hints for future work in Sect. 6.

2   System Architecture

We present our approach from the perspective of an application architected as a composite service and provided by an intermediary *service broker*. The service broker offers to prospective users a composite service with a range of different service classes. It acts as a full intermediary between users and concrete services, performing a role of service provider towards the users and being in turn a requestor to the concrete services offering the operations used to implement the composite service. Its main task is to drive the adaptation of the composite service it manages to fulfill the SLAs negotiated with its users, given the SLAs it has negotiated with the concrete services. Moreover, it also aims at optimizing a given utility goal.

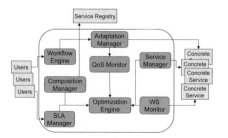

Fig. 1. Service broker high-level architecture

Figure 1 shows the core components of the broker high-level architecture and their interaction. A detailed description of the architecture can be found in [5]; in the next, we summarize the respective tasks of the components. The *Composition Manager* describes the composite service in some suitable workflow orchestration language (e.g., BPEL [13]) and identifies the concrete services implementing the required functionalities of the abstract composition (including their SLAs).

The *Workflow Engine* is the software platform executing the business process and represents the user front-end for the composite service provisioning. For each invocation of the component services it interacts with the *Adaptation Manager*. The latter binds dynamically the request to the real endpoint that represents the concrete service, which is identified through the solution of the optimization problem presented in Sect. 4. Together, the Workflow Engine and the Adaptation Manager manage the user requests flow, once the user has been admitted to the system with an established SLA. The *Optimization Engine* is the component that solves the broker optimization problem. The parameters values for this problem are derived from the parameters of the SLAs negotiated with the composite service users and concrete services, and from a monitoring activity carried out by the QoS Monitor and the WS Monitor.

The *QoS Monitor* collects information about the performance and availability levels (specified in the SLAs) perceived by the users and offered by the concrete services. This component is also in charge to observe and compute the distribution of the response time of the composite service for each service class and to estimate its z_α value (defined in Sect. 3). The *WS Monitor* checks periodically the responsiveness of the pool of concrete services and notifies if some of them becomes unavailable. Besides maintaining up to date the parameters of the optimization problem, the QoS Monitor and WS Monitor check and notify whether some relevant change occurs in the composite service environment. This may lead to the solution of a new instance of the optimization problem which accounts for the occurred changes. Events to be tracked include the arrival/departure of a user, an observed variation in the SLA parameters of the concrete services, and the addition/removal of concrete services.

The *Service Manager* and the *SLA Manager* are mainly responsible for the SLA negotiation processes in which the broker is involved as intermediary. The former negotiates the SLAs with the concrete services. The tasks of the latter are the user SLA negotiation and registration, that is, it is in charge to add, modify, and delete SLAs and users profiles. The SLA negotiation process towards the user side includes also the admission control of new users; to this end, it involves the use of the Optimization Engine in order to evaluate the broker capability to accept the incoming user. Most of the broker components access to a storage layer (not shown in Fig. 1) to know the model parameters of the composite service operations and environment.

2.1   Composite Service

We assume that the composite service structure is defined using BPEL [13]. In this paper, we actually refer to a significant subset of the whole BPEL definition, focusing on its structured style of modeling (rather than on its graph-based one, thus omitting to consider the use of control links). Specifically, in the definition of the workflow describing the composite service, besides the primitive `invoke` activity, which specifies the synchronous or asynchronous invocation of a Web service, we consider most of the structured activities: `sequence`, `switch`, `while`, and `pick`, whose meaning is summarized in Table 1. The percentile-based service selection proposed in this paper is not currently able to manage the `flow` structured activity, which is used for the concurrent execution of activities.

Table 1. Structured activities in BPEL

Activity	Meaning
`sequence`	Sequential execution of activities
`switch`	Conditional execution of activities
`while`	Repeated execution of activities in a loop
`pick`	Conditional execution of activities based on external event/alarm

Figure 2 shows an example of a BPEL workflow described as a UML2 activity diagram. With the exception of the `pick` construct, this example encompasses all the structured activities listed in Table 1.

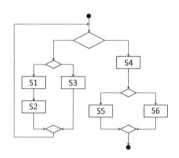

Fig. 2. An example of BPEL workflow

The business process for the composite service defines a set of abstract services $\{S_1, \ldots, S_n\}$. Each abstract service can be instanciated with a specific concrete service $k_{ij} \in \mathcal{K}_i$, where $\mathcal{K}_i$ is the set of functionally equivalent concrete services that have been identified by the Composition Manager as candidates to implement S_i.

2.2   SLA Negotiation

The Service Manager and SLA Manager components are involved in the SLA negotiation with two counterparts: on one side the requestors of the composite service, on the other side the providers of the concrete services. Let us first discuss the SLA settled with the latter. The QoS of each concrete service can be characterized according to various attributes of interest, such as response time, cost, reputation, availability, and throughput [6,16]. The values of these QoS attributes are advertised by the service providers as part of their SLA. Without loss of generality, in this paper we consider the following QoS attributes for each concrete service k_{ij}:

- the response time t_{ij}, which is the interval of time elapsed from the invocation to the completion of the concrete service k_{ij};
- the cost c_{ij}, which represents the price charged for each invocation of the concrete service k_{ij};
- the log of the availability, a_{ij}, i.e., the logarithm of the probability that the concrete service k_{ij} is available when invoked.

In the latter case, as in [16] we consider the *logarithm* of the availability, rather than the availability itself, in order to obtain linear expressions when composing the availability of different services.

For a given concrete service k_{ij}, the SLA established by the broker with the service provider defines the service cost (measured in money per invocation), availability, and expected response time (measured in time unit), provided the volume of requests generated by the broker does not exceed the negotiated average load. Therefore, the SLA for the concrete service k_{ij} is represented by the template $\langle t_{ij}, c_{ij}, a_{ij}, L_{ij} \rangle$, being L_{ij} the agreement on average load.

We denote by K the set of QoS classes offered by the broker. In the SLAs created with the requestors, the broker characterizes the QoS of the composite service in terms of bounds on the expected response time, quantile of the response time, expected cost, and excepted availability for each QoS class $k \in K$ (i.e., $T_{max}^k, T_{\alpha,max}^k, C_{max}^k, A_{min}^k$), where $T_{\alpha,max}^k$ is a bound on the α-quantile T_α^k of the response time. Observe that while the concrete service provides only guarantees on the expected response time t_{ij}, the composite service offered by the broker provides guarantees on the tail of the response time distribution.

Each requestor has to negotiate for each QoS class the volume of requests it will generate in that class (denoted by $\Delta\gamma^k$). The SLA established by the broker with the requestor for the QoS class $k \in K$ has therefore the template $\langle T_{max}^k, T_{\alpha,max}^k, C_{max}^k, A_{min}^k, \Delta\gamma^k \rangle$.

2.3   Admission Control

Upon the arrival of a new user, the SLA Manager determines whether it can be accepted for the required class of service, without violating the SLAs of already accepted requestors. Let γ be the aggregate arrival rate of already accepted requestors (i.e., $\gamma = (\gamma^1, ..., \gamma^{|K|})$) and denote by $\Delta\gamma$ the arrival rate requested by the new user for all the service classes (i.e., $\Delta\gamma = (\Delta\gamma^1, ..., \Delta\gamma^{|K|})$). The SLA Manager determines whether the new requestor can be accepted by invoking the Optimization Engine and asking for a new resolution of the optimization problem with $\gamma + \Delta\gamma$ as aggregate arrival rate. We have two possible cases. If a feasible solution to the optimization problem exists, it means that the additional requests can be satisfied - at the requested QoS - without violating the QoS of already accepted users. The new requestor can be thus accepted and the SLA finalized for the requested rate and QoS class. If, instead, a feasible solution does not exists, the broker can: 1) turn down the new requestor; 2) renegotiate the SLA with the requestor; 3) renegotiate the parameters of the SLAs with the service providers.

2.4   Service Selection Model

The Adaptation Manager determines, for each QoS class, the concrete service k_{ij} that must be used to fulfill a request for the abstract service S_i. We model this selection by associating with each abstract service S_i a service selection policy vector $\boldsymbol{x}_i = (\boldsymbol{x}_i^1, ..., \boldsymbol{x}_i^{|K|})$, where $\boldsymbol{x}_i^k = [x_{ij}^k]$ and $k_{ij} \in \mathcal{K}_i$. Each entry x_{ij}^k of $\boldsymbol{x}_i^k$ represents the probability that the class-k request will be bound to the concrete service k_{ij}. The x_{ij}^k values are determined by the Optimization Engine every time a new solution of the optimization problem is triggered by some environmental change and are then stored in the storage layer, from where they are accessed by the Adaptation Manager.

With this model, we assume that the Adaptation Manager can probabilistically bind to different concrete services the requests (belonging to a same QoS class k) for an abstract service S_i. As an example, consider the case $\mathcal{K}_i = \{k_{i1}, k_{i2}, k_{i3}\}$ and assume that the selection policy $\boldsymbol{x}_i^k$ for a given class k specifies the following values: $x_{i1}^k = x_{i2}^k = 0.3$, $x_{i3}^k = 0.4$. This strategy implies that 30% of the class-k requests for S_i are bound to k_{i1}, 30% are bound to k_{i2} while the remaining 40% are bound to k_{i3}. From this example we can see that, to get some overall QoS objective for a flow of requests of a given class, the Adaptation Manager may bind different requests to different concrete services.

3   Composite Service QoS Model

In this section, we present the QoS model for the composite service and show how to compute its QoS attributes.

Upon a composite service invocation, the broker executes a sequence of tasks as dictated by the service workflow. Each time a task S_i is invoked, the broker determines at runtime the concrete service k_{ij} to be bound to S_i and invokes it. We denote by N_i^k the number of times the task S_i is invoked by a class-k user service request.

For each class $k \in K$ offered by the broker, the overall QoS attributes, namely,

- the expected response time T^k, which is the time needed to fulfill a class-k request for the composite service;
- the α-quantile T_α^k of the response time;
- the expected execution cost C^k, which is the price to be paid to fulfill a class-k request;
- the expected availability A^k, which is the logarithm of the probability that the composite service is available for a class-k request

depend on: 1) the actual concrete service k_{ij} selected to perform each abstract service S_i, $i = 1, \ldots, n$, and 2) how the services are orchestrated.

Expected Value. To compute these quantities, let $Z_i^k(\boldsymbol{x})$ denote the QoS attribute of the abstract service S_i, $Z \in \{T, C, A\}$. We have

$$Z_i^k(\boldsymbol{x}) = \sum_{k_{ij} \in \mathcal{K}_i} x_{ij}^k z_{ij}^k$$

where z_{ij}^k, $z \in \{t, c, a\}$ is the corresponding QoS attribute offered by the concrete service $k_{ij} \in \mathcal{K}_i$ which can implement S_i.

From these quantities, we can derive closed form expressions for the QoS attributes of the composite service. Since all metrics, namely, the cost, the (logarithm of the) availability, and the response time QoS metrics are additive [6], for their expected value we readily obtain

$$Z^k(\boldsymbol{x}) = \sum_{i=1}^n V_i^k Z_i^k(\boldsymbol{x}) = \sum_{i=1}^n V_i^k \sum_{k_{ij} \in \mathcal{K}_i} x_{ij}^k z_{ij}^k$$

where $V_i^k = \mathrm{E}[N_i^k]$ is the expected number of times S_i is invoked for a class-k request.

Response Time α-quantile. It is not possible to find a general expression for a percentile of the response time. We assume to know - or to be able to estimate - the z_α^k-value of the distribution, *i.e.*, the α-quantile of the normalized response time, which is defined as $z_\alpha^k = \frac{T_\alpha^k - \mathrm{E}[T^k]}{\sqrt{\mathrm{Var}[T^k]}}$. Hence,

$$T_\alpha^k = \mathrm{E}[T^k] + z_\alpha^k \sqrt{\mathrm{Var}[T^k]} \tag{1}$$

i.e., we rewrite the percentile of the distribution as function of the expected value $\mathrm{E}[T^k]$, the variance $\mathrm{Var}[T^k]$, and the associated z_α^k-value. The response time variance takes the following form (the derivation of which, for its length, is omitted and can be found in [3]):

$$\mathrm{Var}[T^k] = \sum_{i=1}^n V_i^k \mathrm{Var}[T_i^k] + \sum_{i=1}^n \sum_{i'=1}^n \mathrm{Cov}[N_i^k N_{i'}^k] T_i^k(\boldsymbol{x}) T_{i'}^k(\boldsymbol{x}) \tag{2}$$

where

$$\mathrm{Var}[T_i^k] = \sum_{k_{ij} \in \mathcal{K}_i} x_{ij}(t_{ij}^2 + \sigma_{ij}^2) - \left(\sum_{k_{ij} \in \mathcal{K}_i} x_{ij} t_{ij} \right)^2 \tag{3}$$

is the variance of the response time of task S_i (being σ_{ij}^2 the response time variance of service k_{ij} which we also assume to estimate). Observe that the variance (2) comprises two terms: the first accounts for the variability of the response time of each task weighted by the expected number of times each task is invoked; the second term accounts for the variability of the number of tasks invocations (which are correlated), weighted by the tasks expected response time.

4   Optimization Problem

The Optimization Engine goal is to determine the service selection strategy x_{ij}^k, $i = 1, \ldots, n$, $k \in K$, $k_{ij} \in \mathcal{K}_i$ which maximizes a suitable utility function. For the sake of simplicity, here we consider the simple case that the broker wants to minimize the overall expected cost to offer the composite service, defined as $C(\boldsymbol{x}) = \frac{1}{\sum_{k \in K} \gamma^k} \sum_{k \in K} \gamma^k C^k(\boldsymbol{x})$. In general we could optimize multiple QoS attributes (which can be either mutually independent or possibly conflicting). Therefore, the optimal service selection would take the form of a multi-objective optimization which can be solved by reducing to a single objective problem using a scalarization method, $e.g.$, the Simple Additive Weighting technique.

The Optimization Engine task consists in finding the variables x_{ij}^k, $i = 1, \ldots, n$, $k \in K$, $k_{ij} \in \mathcal{K}_i$, which solve the following optimization problem:

$\quad$ **OPT : min** $C(\boldsymbol{x})$

$\quad$ **subject to:** $T^k(\boldsymbol{x}) \leq T_{\max}^k \quad k \in K$ $\hfill (4)$

$$C^k(\boldsymbol{x}) \leq C_{\max}^k \quad k \in K \tag{5}$$

$$A^k(\boldsymbol{x}) \geq A_{\min}^k \quad k \in K \tag{6}$$

$$\mathrm{P}[T^k > T_{\alpha,\max}^k] \leq 1 - \alpha \quad k \in K \tag{7}$$

$$\sum_{k \in K} x_{ij}^k V_i^k \gamma^k \leq L_{ij} \quad i = 1, \ldots, n, \, k_{ij} \in \mathcal{K}_i \tag{8}$$

$$x_{ij}^k \geq 0 \quad k_{ij} \in \mathcal{K}_i, \, \sum_{k_{ij} \in \mathcal{K}_i} x_{ij}^k = 1 \quad i = 1, \ldots, n, \, k \in K \tag{9}$$

Equations (4)-(6) are the QoS constraints for each service class on average response time, average cost and availability, where $T_{\max}^k$, $C_{\max}^k$, and $A_{\min}^k$ are respectively the maximum response time, the maximum cost and the minimum (logarithm of the) availability that characterize the QoS class k. Equation (7) is the QoS constraint on the percentile of the response time. Equations (8) are the broker-providers SLA constraints and ensure the broker does not exceed the SLA with the service providers. Finally, equations (9) are the functional constraints. The constraints $\mathrm{P}[T^k > T_{\alpha,\max}^k] \leq 1 - \alpha$ can be rewritten as $T_\alpha^k \leq T_{\alpha,max}^k$. Hence,

$$T_\alpha^k \leq T_{\alpha,\max}^k \iff \mathrm{E}[T^k] + z_\alpha \sqrt{\mathrm{Var}[T^k]} \leq T_{\alpha,\max}^k$$

Thus, the constraints on the response time percentile can be rewritten as:

$$z_\alpha \left(\sum_{i=1}^n \sum_{i'=1}^n \mathrm{Cov}[N_i N_{i'}] \sum_{k_{ij} \in \mathcal{K}_i} x_{ij} t_{ij} \sum_{k_{ij} \in \mathcal{K}_{i'}} x_{i'j} t_{i'j} + \ldots \right.$$

$$\left. \sum_{i=1}^n V_i^k \left(\sum_{k_{ij} \in \mathcal{K}_i} x_{ij}(t_{ij}^2 + \sigma_{ij}^2) - \left(\sum_{k_{ij} \in \mathcal{K}_i} x_{ij} t_{ij} \right)^2 \right) \right)^{\frac{1}{2}} \leq$$

$$T_{\alpha,\max}^k - \sum_{i=1}^n V_i^k \sum_{k_{ij} \in \mathcal{K}_i} x_{ij}^k t_{ij} \quad k \in K \tag{10}$$

Constraints Linearization. Because of the constraints (10), there is no known technique to solve problem $\mathbf{OPT}^1$. We tackle the problem by deriving a linear program (LP) which is obtained by linearizing (10) in two steps. First of all we eliminate the square root, which is not differentiable in zero by taking the square of both side of (2). Then, we linearize the constraints by approximating both sides with the first term of the Taylor expansion around a suitable point $\boldsymbol{x}_0$, which yields (for space limitation, the computation of the first term of the Taylor expansion is omitted; the details can be found in [3]):

$$\sum_{i=1}^{n} \sum_{k_{ij} \in \mathcal{K}_i} x_{ij}^k \left[z_\alpha^2 \left(2 \sum_{i'=1}^{n} \mathrm{Cov}[N_i N_{i'}] T_{i'}^k(\boldsymbol{x}_0) t_{ij} + \right. \right.$$
$$\left. V_i^k \left(t_{ij}^2 + \sigma_{ij}^2 - 2t_{ij} T_i^k(\boldsymbol{x}_0) \right) \right) + 2t_{ij} \left(T_{\alpha \max}^k - T^k(\boldsymbol{x}_0) \right) \right] \leq$$
$$z_\alpha^2 \left(\sum_{i=1}^{n} \sum_{i'}^{n} \mathrm{Cov}[N_i N_{i'}] T_{i'}^k(\boldsymbol{x}_0) T_i^k(\boldsymbol{x}_0) - \sum_{i=1}^{n} V_i^k T_i^{k2}(\boldsymbol{x}_0) \right) +$$
$$\left(T_{\alpha,\max}^k - T^k(\boldsymbol{x}_0) \right)^2 + 2 \left(T_{\alpha,\max}^k - T^k(\boldsymbol{x}_0) \right) T^k(\boldsymbol{x}_0) \qquad (11)$$

By replacing (7) with (11) in **OPT** we obtain the following LP **LINOPT** which we use to determine the optimal service selection policy:

LINOPT :   min $C(\boldsymbol{x})$

subject to:

$$\sum_{i=1}^{n} V_i^k \sum_{k_{ij} \in \mathcal{K}_i} x_{ij}^k t_{ij} \leq T_{\max}^k \quad k \in K \qquad (12)$$

$$\sum_{i=1}^{n} V_i^k \sum_{k_{ij} \in \mathcal{K}_i} x_{ij}^k c_{ij} \leq C_{\max}^k \quad k \in K \qquad (13)$$

$$\sum_{i=1}^{n} V_i^k \sum_{k_{ij} \in \mathcal{K}_i} x_{ij}^k a_{ij} \geq A_{\min}^k \quad k \in K \qquad (14)$$

percentile constraints (11) $k \in K$ \qquad (15)

$$\sum_{k \in K} x_{ij}^k V_i^k \gamma^k \leq L_{ij} \quad i = 1, \ldots, n, \, k_{ij} \in \mathcal{K}_i \qquad (16)$$

$$x_{ij}^k \geq 0 \quad k_{ij} \in \mathcal{K}_i, \sum_{k_{ij} \in \mathcal{K}_i} x_{ij}^k = 1 \quad i = 1, \ldots, n, \, k \in K \qquad (17)$$

LINOPT is a LP problem and can be efficiently solved via standard techniques. The solution thus lends itself to both on-line and off-line operations.

The choice of the linearization point $\boldsymbol{x}_0$ is crucial to obtain good solutions, *i.e.*, solutions close to those that would have been obtained by solving **OPT**. We found that a good choice for $\boldsymbol{x}_0$ is provided by a most recent solution $\boldsymbol{x}$ itself.

---

[1] Had the constraints be convex, we could have used semidefinite programming to solve the problem. Since convexity does not hold in general, we have resorted to linearization instead.

In case such a solution is not available, *e.g.*, when the broker is initialized, we simply do not consider the constraints (15) the first time **LINOPT** is executed.

5   Simulation Model and Experiments

In this section, we first describe the simulation model we have defined to study the effectiveness of the percentile-based adaptation policy and then present the results of simulation experiments.

5.1   Simulation Model

The broker simulation model comprises the same components of the architecture shown in Fig. 1. We consider an open system model, where new users belonging to a given service class $k \in K$ offered by the broker arrive at mean *user inter-arrival rate* Λ_k. Each class-k user is characterized by its SLA parameters defined in Sect. 2.2 and by the *contract duration* d_k. If admitted (according to the admission control mechanism explained in Sect. 2.3), the user will start generating requests to the composite service until its contract expires.

Differently from traditional Web workload, SOA workload characterization has been not deeply investigated up to now (some preliminary results are in [12]). Therefore, in our workload model we assume exponential distributions with parameters Λ_k and $1/d_k$ for the user inter-arrival time and contract duration, respectively, and a Gaussian distribution with parameters m_k and σ_k for the inter-arrival rate of requests to the composite service generated by each user. We also assume that the response times of the concrete services follow Erlang distributions with different shape parameters.

The discrete-event simulator has been implemented in C language using the CSIM package [11]. Multiple independent random number streams have been used for each stochastic model component. The experiments involved a minimum of 10,000 completed requests to the composite service; for all reported mean and percentile values the 95% confidence interval has been obtained using the run length control provided by CSIM.

5.2   Experimental Results

We illustrate the dynamic behavior of our adaptive service selection through the simple abstract workflow of Fig. 2. For the sake of simplicity we assume that two candidate concrete services (with their respective SLAs) have been identified for each abstract service, except for S_2 for which four concrete services have been identified. The respective SLAs differ in terms of cost, availability, and response time (all time values are measured in sec.). Table 2 summarizes for each concrete service k_{ij} the SLA parameters $\langle t_{ij}, c_{ij}, a_{ij} \rangle$ and the shape parameter Erl_{ij} of the Erlang distribution for the response time (for each k_{ij}, the mean value of the Erlang distribution corresponds to t_{ij}). The SLA and the Erlang shape parameters have been chosen so that for abstract service S_i, concrete service k_{i1}

Table 2. Concrete service SLA parameters and shape parameter of Erlang distribution

Service	c_{ij}	a_{ij}	t_{ij}	Erl_{ij}
k_{11}	6	0.995	2	4
k_{12}	3	0.99	4	2
k_{21}	4.5	0.99	1	4
k_{22}	4	0.99	2	4
k_{23}	2	0.95	4	2
k_{24}	1	0.95	5	2
k_{31}	2	0.995	1	4
k_{32}	1.8	0.95	2	2

Service	c_{ij}	a_{ij}	t_{ij}	Erl_{ij}
k_{41}	1	0.995	0.5	4
k_{42}	0.8	0.99	1	2
k_{51}	2	0.99	2	4
k_{52}	1.4	0.95	4	2
k_{61}	0.5	0.99	1.8	4
k_{62}	0.4	0.9	4	2

represents the best implementation, which at a higher cost guarantees higher availability and lower response time (in terms of mean as well as variance) with respect to concrete service k_{ij} for $j \geq 2$, which costs less but has lower availability and higher response time. For all concrete services, $L_{ij} = 10$.

On the user side, we assume a scenario where the broker offers the composite service with four QoS classes. The SLAs negotiated by the users are characterized by a wide range of QoS requirements as listed in Table 3, with users in class 1 having the most stringent requirements $A^1_{min} = 0.95$ and $T^1_{max} = 7$, and users in class 4 the least stringent requirements $A^4_{min} = 0.8$ and $T^4_{max} = 18$. With regard to the bound on the α-quantile $T^k_{\alpha,max}$ of the response time, we assume that for all classes $T^k_{\alpha,max} = \beta T^k_{max}$ and $\alpha = 0.95$ (i.e., we consider 95-percentile of the response time). The SLA costs parameters for the four classes have been set accordingly, where class 1 has the highest cost per request and class 4 is the cheapest. The expected number of service invocations for the different classes is: $V^k_1 = V^k_2 = V^k_3 = 1.5$, $V^k_4 = 1$, $k \in K$; $V^k_5 = 0.7$, $V^k_6 = 0.3$, $k \in \{1,3,4\}$; $V^2_5 = V^2_6 = 0.5$, that is, all classes have the same usage profile except users in class 2, who invoke S_5 and S_6 with different intensity. The values of the parameters that characterize the workload model are $d_k = 100$ and $(m_k, \sigma_k) = (3,1)$ for each k (Λ_k, d_k, and m_k values have to be set so that $\gamma^k = \Lambda_k m_k d_k$ for Little's formula).

We compare the performance obtained by the service selection with tight bounds on the percentile of the response time with that of the service selection where only guarantees on the mean values are offered to the users of the composite service. The problem formulation of the latter case is in [4] and we denote it with $\beta = \infty$ (i.e., the tail of the response time distribution is unbounded). We initially set $\beta = 2.2$, which represents a tight bound on the 95-percentile of the response time; we then analyze the sensitivity of the response time to β.

Table 3. User-side SLA parameters for each service class

Class k	C^k	A^k_{min}	T^k_{max}	$T^k_{0.95,max}$	γ^k
1	25	0.95	7	βT^1_{max}	10
2	18	0.9	11	βT^2_{max}	4
3	15	0.9	15	βT^3_{max}	2
4	12	0.8	18	βT^4_{max}	1

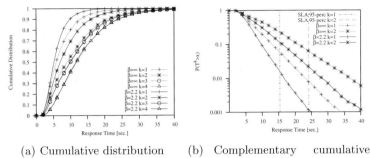

(a) Cumulative distribution   (b) Complementary   cumulative
                              distribution (lin-log scale)

Fig. 3. Response time

Figure 3(a) shows the cumulative distribution of the response time of the composite service for all the service classes when the percentile-based and mean-based optimizations are used, corresponding to $\beta = 2.2$ and $\beta = \infty$ curves, respectively. We can see that the percentile-based optimization achieves a better response time than the mean-based optimization for classes 1 and 2, which have the more stringent SLA requirements. Through Fig. 3(b) we further investigate the tendency of the response time for classes 1 and 2 by plotting its complementary cumulative distribution on a linear-logarithmic scale. The vertical lines represent the 95-percentile of the response time agreed in the SLA with the users of the composite services. We can see that the percentile-based service selection largely satisfies the 95-percentile SLA, that is only 1.6% and 2.1% of class 1 and class 2 requests respectively experience a response time greater than the 95-percentile value. The conservative behavior of the percentile-based approach is due to the constraints linearization explained in Sect. 4.

To compare in more detail the percentile-based and mean-based approaches, Fig. 4 shows how the mean and 95-percentile response times of the composite service vary over time for classes 1 and 2. The horizontal line is the agreed response time (both mean and 95-percentile values), as reported in Table 3. We observe that the mean-based approach leads to some violations of the agreed response time, while the percentile-based approach allows the broker to offer always a response time much better than that agreed.

We conducted a last set of experiments to analyze the sensitivity of the percentile-based service selection to the β parameter, which correlates in the SLA the 95-percentile to the mean of the composite service's response time (smaller values of β correspond to a tighter bound on the distribution tail). Figure 5 shows the trend of the 95-percentile response time to β for all classes (the corresponding SLA value is only shown for the most demanding classes 1 and 2). The percentile-based approach succeeds in respecting the agreed 95-percentile for all service classes and β values. The disadvantage of a tighter bound on the percentile (e.g., $\beta = 2.1$) is that a larger fraction of incoming contract requests are rejected.

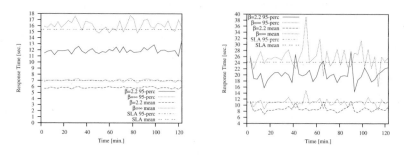

Fig. 4. 95-percentile and mean response time over time for classes 1 (left) and 2 (right)

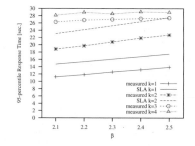

Fig. 5. Sensitivity of 95-percentile response time to β

6   Conclusions

In this paper, we have addressed the problem of selecting concrete services in a composite service offered by a brokering service which supports differentiated QoS service classes. Most of the existing approaches only consider SLAs based on bounds of the expected values of the relevant QoS metrics. A limitation of these solutions lies in the fact that the user perceived quality is often better expressed in terms of bounds on the percentile rather than the expected value of the QoS metrics. To overcome this limitation, in this paper we have considered SLAs which also specify bounds on the percentile of the response time. We have formulated the service selection problem as an optimization problem with non-linear constraints. For the solution, we have linearized the constrains. The resulting linear programming problem can be efficiently solved via standard techniques. Therefore, our approach can be used to efficiently manage the service selection in a real operating broker-based architecture, where the broker efficiency and scalability in replying to the users requests are important factors.

The model proposed in this paper provides statistical guarantees on the percentile of the response time. The results, though, only apply to the service selection scenario and only consider a subset, albeit significant, of the workflows' structured activities. Our future work includes the extension of these results to the use of redundant coordination patterns, the support of the `flow` BPEL activity, and the management of long term SLAs whose users cannot get their request rejected.

Acknowledgment

Work partially supported by the Italian PRIN project D-ASAP.

References

1. Ardagna, D., Pernici, B.: Adaptive service composition in flexible processes. IEEE Trans. Softw. Eng. 33(6), 369–384 (2007)
2. Canfora, G., Di Penta, M., Esposito, R., Villani, M.: A framework for qos-aware binding and re-binding of composite web services. J. Syst. Softw. 81(10) (2008)
3. Cardellini, V., Casalicchio, E., Grassi, V., Lo Presti, F.: Adaptive service selection in service oriented systems under percentile-based service level agreements. Tech. Rep. RR-10.85, DISP, Univ. of Roma Tor Vergata (2010), http://www.ce.uniroma2.it/publications/RR-10.85.pdf
4. Cardellini, V., Casalicchio, E., Grassi, V., Lo Presti, F., Mirandola, R.: Flow-based service selection for web service composition supporting multiple qos classes. In: Proc. IEEE ICWS 2007, pp. 743–750 (2007)
5. Cardellini, V., Casalicchio, E., Grassi, V., Lo Presti, F., Mirandola, R.: Qos-driven runtime adaptation of service oriented architectures. In: ACM ESEC/SIGSOFT FSE, pp. 131–140 (2009)
6. Cardoso, J., Sheth, A.P., Miller, J.A., Arnold, J., Kochut, K.J.: Modeling Quality of Service for Workflows and Web Service Processes. Web Semantics J. 1(3) (2004)
7. DeCandia, G., et al.: Dynamo: Amazon's highly available key-value store. SIGOPS Oper. Syst. Rev. 41(6), 205–220 (2007)
8. Gmach, D., Krompass, S., Scholz, A., Wimmer, M., Kemper, A.: Adaptive quality of service management for enterprise services. ACM Trans. Web 2(1), 1–46 (2008)
9. Grosspietsch, K.: Optimizing the reliability of component-based n-version approches. In: Proc. IEEE IPDPS 2002 Workshops (2002)
10. Guo, H., Huai, J., Li, H., Deng, T., Li, Y., Du, Z.: Angel: Optimal configuration for high available service composition. In: Proc. IEEE ICWS 2007, pp. 280–287 (2007)
11. Mesquite Software: http://www.mesquite.com/
12. Nagpurkar, P., Horn, W., Gopalakrishnan, U., Dubey, N., Jann, J., Pattnaik, P.: Workload characterization of selected jee-based web 2.0 applications. In: Proc. IEEE Int'l Symposium on Workload Characterization, pp. 109–118 (Septmeber 2008)
13. OASIS: Web Services Business Process Execution Language Version 2.0 (January 2007), http://docs.oasis-open.org/wsbpel/2.0/OS/wsbpel-v2.0-OS.html
14. Xiong, K., Perros, H.: Sla-based service composition in enterprise computing. In: IEEE Int'l Workshop on Quality of Service, pp. 35–44 (2008)
15. Yu, T., Zhang, Y., Lin, K.J.: Efficient algorithms for web services selection with end-to-end qos constraints. ACM Trans. Web 1(1), 1–26 (2007)
16. Zeng, L., Benatallah, B., Dumas, M., Kalagnamam, J., Chang, H.: QoS-aware middleware for web services composition. IEEE Trans. Softw. Eng. 30(5) (2004)

BPMN Modelling of Services with Dynamically Reconfigurable Transactions*

Laura Bocchi[1], Roberto Guanciale[2], Daniele Strollo[3], and Emilio Tuosto[1]

[1] Department of Computer Science, University of Leicester, UK
[2] Department of Computer Science, University of Pisa, Italy
[3] Istituto di Scienza e Tecnologie dell'Informazione "Alessandro Faedo", CNR, Pisa, Italy

Abstract. We promote the use of *transactional attributes* for modelling business processes in service-oriented scenarios. Transactional attributes have been introduced in Enterprise JavaBeans (EJB) to decorate the methods published in Java containers. Attributes describe "modalities" that discipline the reconfiguration of transactional scopes (i.e., of caller and callee) upon method invocation.

We define and study modelling and programming mechanisms to control dynamically reconfigurable transactional scopes in Service-Oriented Computing (SOC). On the one hand, we give evidence of the suitability of transactional attributes for modelling and programming SOC transactions. As a proof of concept, we show how BPMN can be enriched with a few annotations for transactional attributes. On the other hand, we show how the results of a theoretical framework enable us to make more effective the development of transactional service-oriented applications.

1 Introduction

In this paper we promote the use of *transactional attributes* for modelling transactional business processes in service-oriented systems. An original element of our research programme is the definition and study of modelling mechanisms for dynamically reconfigurable transactional scopes in SOC.

The long-lasting and cross-domain nature of activities in service-oriented systems contributed in characterising a novel powerful paradigm but imposed to re-think a number of classic concepts. Among these concepts, the notion of transaction had to be adapted in order to fit the requirements of the *Service-Oriented Computing* (SOC) paradigm. SOC transactions, which are often referred to as long-running transaction, ensure a weaker set of properties (e.g., no atomicity nor isolation) with respect to the classic ACID transactions used in database systems; on the other hand they do not require to lock resources.

The investigation of formal semantics for SOC transactions has been a topic of focus in the last few years (see § 5 for a non-exhaustive overview). Central to this investigation is the notion of *compensation*, a weaker and "ad hoc" version of the classic roll-back of database systems. Most of the research on long-running transactions has been focusing on providing suitable (formal) semantics of compensations while not much attention has been reserved to the inter-dependencies of failure propagation and dynamic

---

* This work has been supported by the project Leverhulme Trust Award "Tracing Networks".

P.P. Maglio et al. (Eds.): ICSOC 2010, LNCS 6470, pp. 396–410, 2010.

reconfiguration. This is a very critical issue in SOC, where dynamic reconfiguration is one of the key characteristics. In fact, the configuration of a service-oriented system can change at each service invocation to include new instances of invoked services in the ongoing computation. Notably, the reconfiguration affects the relationships between existing and newly created transactional scopes.

These issues have been first considered in [2,3,1] where it has been proposed a process calculus featuring *transactional attributes* (or attributes for short), inspired to the transactional mechanisms of EJB [15,13]. The theoretical framework in [2,3,1] aims to analyse different semantics of transactional scope reconfiguration, the observable behaviour of service-oriented system, failure propagation, and transactional scope reconfiguration.

We contend that transactional attributes represent a useful conceptual device also in the modelling phases and during the development of transactional SOC applications. In fact, we propose a methodology based on the features of transactional attributes and the theoretical framework of [2,3,1] to enable software architects and engineers to design and develop distributed applications with transactional properties in SOC. In this paper, we highlight the benefits of using transactional attributes for modelling and programming transactional service-oriented processes. As a proof of concept, we show how the Business Process Modelling Notation (BPMN) [12] can be enriched with transactional attributes and, through the use of a simple case study, we illustrate the suitability of an attribute-aware process modelling.

At design time, the software architect typically abstracts from the distribution of the activities, the communication mechanisms, and the technologies that will implement each activity. Also, a BPMN specification can describe a distributed workflow and its transactional properties both from *local* and *global* points of view; as a matter of fact, developers can create service-oriented applications from BPMN models by exploiting different strategies. One strategy consists of modelling a service-oriented process by means of an (e.g. BPEL4WS [10]) *orchestrator* by assembling tasks each representing a call to either a local or outsourced functionality (i.e., service). The orchestrator is a central entity that drives the interaction among services and manages their execution order. The other strategy has a more collaborative flavour and requires processes of BPMN designs to act as an ensemble that separately describe the role played by each participant. In this case, there is no single "controlling" process managing the interactions and the activity of each process consists of both invocations to other services and to an interactive conversation with them.

We illustrate how the development from abstract BPMN designs can be improved by the usage of transactional attributes. Intuitively, attribute-aware designs give information on the transactional support required from the different tasks; noteworthy, such information can be exploited when developing applications distributively. In fact, transactional attributes provide a useful set of preconditions which helps in preventing what is commonly known as defensive programming for those functionalities to be developed internally to an organisation[1]. The use of transactional attributes let programmers to rely on a set of preconditions and assumptions on the transactional context in which the task will be executed thus (s)he is relieved form the burden of considering all possible cases.

---

[1] In defensive programming the code is filled with unnecessary controls to validate data.

For functionalities provided by external parties, attribute-aware designs provide a useful set of non-functional requirements that allow to select the best match among the available services.

Also, we illustrate how an extension of BPMN allows software architects to specify the information for controlling the run-time reconfiguration of transactional scopes. More precisely, we consider the extension of BPMN with constructs for service invocation/instantiation associated to transactional attributes and constructs for representing distributed transactions.

Finally, we show how the results of a recently published theoretical framework [2,3,1] enable us to make more effective some common development activities of service-oriented applications. Actually, in [1] it has been proved that, under certain conditions, some of the proposed transactional attributes may be considered equivalent; this can be used to deduce that some scenarios may be ignored during the development.

Structure of the paper. In § 2 we summarise the key ingredients of our paper, namely BPMN, EJB attributes, and our case study. The description of our methodology and the use of attributes in BPMN designs is given in § 3. The extension of BPMN to incorporate service invocation and distributed transactional scope handling is reported in 4. Concluding remarks and considerations on future work are given in § 5.

2   Background

This section provides the background information used in the rest of the paper. In § 2.1 we give a brief introduction of the BPMN notation. In § 2.2 we give an intuition of the semantics of scope reconfiguration featured by EJB. Finally, in § 2.3 we introduce the case study used to illustrate our approach.

2.1   The Business Process Modeling Notation

The Business Process Modeling Notation [12] (BPMN) allows us to describe business processes through a graphical notation. We summarise here the main concepts of BPMN necessary in this paper; for a more complete presentation we refer the reader to [12].

The main building blocks of a BPMN design are *flow objects*, which represent activities and events involved in a business process. As illustrated in Figure 1, BPMN processes involve two special events: the *starting point* of the business process, graphically represented by an empty single-edge circle, and its *termination point* drawn as an empty double-edge circle; rounded-corner boxes represent tasks to be executed.

A BPMN task can be equipped with a *compensation* responsible for the (partial) recovery of the task upon failure of the process that includes the task. BPMN compensations are represented by tasks connected to the exception events by dotted dashed

Fig. 1. BPMN process with one task

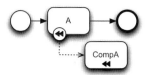

Fig. 2. A BPMN task with compensation

lines. For example, the process in Figure 2 describes that the compensation CompA can rectify the effects produced by task A.

Arrows connecting *flow objects* represent their dependencies, usually referred to as *forward-flow*. Standard arrows describe the temporal order of execution of the business process as opposed to the *backward-flow*, that describe the order of execution of compensations. In literature, the order in which compensation must be executed is usually "the inverse order" of the forward-flow. If the execution of a task fails, the forward-flow is stopped and the backward-flow started by executing first the compensation of the most recent successfully executed task back to the initial one. The BPMN process in Figure 3 describes the usage of arrows to compose tasks and defining the forward-flow. The process models a sequence of two tasks: task B can be executed only after the successfully termination of A.

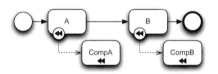

Fig. 3. Sequential composition of BPMN tasks

Figure 4 models a concurrent process. After the termination of task A, both tasks B and C can be executed independently, the crossed box on the left is used to regulate their parallel activation. The crossed box on the right represents a synchronization barrier, waiting for the termination of all elements connected by an incoming arrow before to propagate the forward-flow execution.

BPMN permits to design nested transactions, as depicted in Figure 5. A double edged box represents a transactional scope. Intuitively, this scoping mechanism allows transactional scopes to hide any fault of a contained task to external processes.

Finally, BPMN exploits "pools" to represent interactive participants in a business-to-business design. A pool can contain a process, which must be fully contained within the pool itself. Namely, forward-flow dependencies cannot cross the boundaries of a pool (participant). Interaction between participants is modelled via the *message flow* as illustrated in Figure 6 where the dashed arrow connecting the send and receive tasks represents a message flow. Similarly, transactional boxes cannot cross pools.

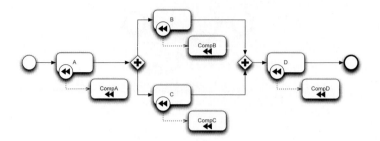

Fig. 4. BPMN concurrent tasks

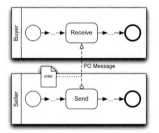

Fig. 5. BPMN sub-transaction

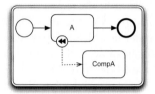

Fig. 6. BPMN pools

2.2   EJB Transactional Attributes

In EJB, objects can be assembled in specialised run-time environments called *contain-ers*. A container can be thought of as a configuration tool that allows to set up, at de-ployment time, a few characteristics of distributed applications. A *Java bean* can be thought of as on object amenable to be executed in a container (see e.g., [15,13]). An EJB container supports typical functionalities to manage e.g. the life-cycle of a bean and to make components accessible to other components by binding it to a naming service[2].

EJB containers feature a number of transactional features, namely *Container Man-aged Transactions* (CMT), whereby a container associates each method of a bean with

---

[2] http://docs.sun.com/app/docs/doc/819-3658/ablmw?a=view

a *transactional attribute* specifying the modality of reconfiguring transactional scopes. Namely, a transactional attribute determines:

- the transactional modality of the method calls. The modality expresses a requirement the invoking party must satisfy (e.g., *"calling the method* `fooBar` *from outside a transactional scope throws an exception"*),
- how the scope of transactions dynamically reconfigures (e.g., *"*`fooBar` *is always executed in a newly created transactional scope"*).

We denote the set of EJB transactional attributes as

$$\mathcal{A} \overset{def}{=} \{\texttt{requires}, \texttt{requires new}, \texttt{not supported}, \texttt{mandatory}, \texttt{never}, \texttt{supports}\}.$$

The intuitive semantics of EJB attributes $\mathcal{A}$ is illustrated in table below, where each row represents the behaviour of one transactional attribute and shows how the transactional scope of the caller and callee behave upon invocation. The first two columns show, respectively, invocations from outside and from within a scope. Scopes are represented by a box, callers by •, callee by ○, and failed activities by ⊗.

invoker **outside** a scope	invoker **inside** a scope	callee supports
(1) • ⟹ • [○]	[•] ⟹ [• ○]	requires
(2) • ⟹ • [○]	[•] ⟹ [•] [○]	requires new
(3) • ⟹ • ○	[•] ⟹ [•] ○	not supported
(4) • ⟹ ⊗	[•] ⟹ [• ○]	mandatory
(5) • ⟹ • ○	[•] ⟹ ⊗	never
(6) • ⟹ • ○	[•] ⟹ [• ○]	supports

More precisely, (1) a callee supporting `requires` is always executed in a transactional scope which happens to be the same as the caller's if the latter is already running in a transactional scope; (2) a callee supporting `requires new` is always executed in a new transactional scope; (3) a callee supporting `not supported` is always executed outside a transactional scope; (4) the invocation of a method supporting `mandatory` fails if the caller is not in a transactional scope (first column of the fourth row in the table), otherwise the method is executed in the transactional scope of the caller; (5) the invocation of a method supporting `never` is successful only if the caller is outside a transactional scope, and it fails if the caller is running in a transactional scope (in this case an exception is triggered in the caller); (6) a method supporting `supports` is executed inside (resp. outside) the caller's scope if the caller is executing in (resp. outside) a scope.

2.3 The Car Repair Case Study

We consider a case study where a car manufacturer offers a service that supports the driver in case of engine failure. Once the user's car breaks down, the service attempts to locate a garage, a tow truck, and a rental car service so that the car is towed to the

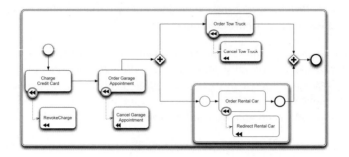

Fig. 7. The BPMN process for the Car Repair Scenario

garage and repaired, and the car owner may continue her/his travel with a substitutive vehicle.

Figure 7 illustrates a BPMN process modelling the car repair service. The whole process is included in a transactional scope. First, before any service lookup is made, the credit card of the driver is charged with a security deposit. Second, the process searches for a garage; the outcome of the search for the garage poses additional constraints to the candidate tow trucks. Third, a tow truck is called and, if the search for a tow truck fails then the garage appointment must be revoked (the dependencies among the bookings made by the services make it necessary to equip the orchestration with compensations). Finally, a car rental (which must in a reasonable proximity to the garage) is arranged. If renting a car succeeds and finding either a tow truck or a garage appointment fails, then car rental must be redirected to the actual location of the broken down car. We model *OrderRentalCar* inside a nested transactional scope because its failure should not affect the tow truck and garage appointments.

The BPMN design in Figure 7 uses a single BPMN pool. In fact, all activities and compensations are executed within a BPMN transactional scope, which can involve activities of only one participant. Namely, the design describes an orchestration that, whenever executed by a *leader* participant, regulates the execution of partner services. In the following section we extend the BPMN model in order to simplify modeling more collaborative approaches.

3   Modelling Transactional Processes with BPMN and Attributes

We propose a methodology for designing distributed transactions in BPMN consisting of the following phases:

phase 1 definition of the design of the system
phase 2 specification of (compensations and) transactional attributes
phase 3 refinement of transactional aspects of the design.

Before clarifying our methodology, it is worth emphasizing that, in phase 1, designs are supposed to provide a *local view* of the system where activities are supposed to reside within a same pool and the coordination strategy relies on an orchestrator (which is specified by the design). For example, the design in Figure 7 yields such a local view for the car repair scenario. The methodology could also be applied by using a diagram like the one in Figure 7 as an high level model for a global distributed process with no central orchestrator, abstracting form the mechanisms used by the participants to coordinate. This would require further extensions of BPMN; for instance using, instead of forward-flow connectors, a new kind of connector that subsumes both message and sequence flows. Such model could be then transformed into a global, more detailed, design where tasks are partitioned into pools and their coordination explicitly represented. In the next section we discuss global designs where we introduce service invocations and distributed scope handling.

A key element of transactional attributes is the separation of concerns they provide; EJB programmers, in fact, may develop their code independently of the transactional behaviour because attributes do not directly affect the behaviour of an object. Likewise, our methodology capitalises on this separation of concerns and makes attributes largely independent of other aspects of designs. In other words, transactional attributes can be specified once the software architect has designed the system. In a certain sense, we extend the design strategy that BPMN enables on compensations to attributes; indeed the BPMN architect could in principle give an initial model of a system without considering transactional aspects and introduce compensations at a later stage. Similarly, phase 2 of our methodology allows us to decorate designs with attributes as well as refine them (if necessary) subsequently.

For the moment, we just decorate BPMN designs with attributes assuming their intuitive semantics (cf. 2.2); in § 4 we extend BPMN so to illustrate the semantics of each attribute in a more precise way.

An attribute-aware design is simply a design where forward-flow arrows are labelled with a finite number of attributes. The idea is that if two activities T and T' are connected by a forward-flow arrow decorated with a set of attributes $A = \{a_1, \ldots, a_n\}$, the control is passed from T to T' if the latter "supports" at least one of the attributes in A. In other words, T and T' explicitly "agree" on their combined transactional behaviour; T requires T' to behave according to the set of transactional behaviours specified by A and, dually, T' guarantees that it is supporting some of such behaviours. Put in other terms, T' is aware of the transactional requirements of T which is in turn aware that the possible transactional behaviours of T' are included in A.

We illustrate our methodology and the use of how to add transactional attributes to BPMN designs considering the car repair scenario described in § 2.3. First, we extend the design of Figure 7 to incorporate the invocation of a new logging service; such extension allows us to explain the utility of the attributes not supported and never. The idea is that, upon completion of the transaction, logging information is sent to a logging service which outsources the calculation of some statistics to an external service.

The extended design is given in Figure 8 together with the annotations with transactional attributes. The BPMN design stays the same as in § 2.3 except for the newly added tasks and the attributes decorating the connectors. For simplicity, we assign a single attribute to each arrow except for the connector to the invocation of the tow truck which has three attributes.

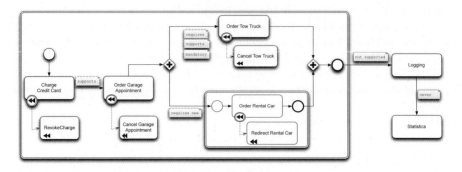

Fig. 8. Extended Car Rental with Attributes Annotations

- The attribute on the connector between the credit card check and garage activities is `supports`; it stipulates that the latter activity should be capable of engaging in the same transaction (if any) of the former one. In our scenario, since the credit card check is executed in a transactional scope, the garage endpoint will be part of the transaction of the check task.
- Once the garage is fixed, the process invokes a car rental that is able to start a new transaction; the attribute `requires new` specifies that the rental endpoint will be activated in new transaction whose failure will not cause the failure of the main transaction. Notice that in the global view, this correspond to confine the rental service in a subtransaction however, in the local view, the car rental will be a remote transactional scope (this issue will be considered in § 4).
- in parallel to the car rental activity, a two truck is searched; such service is required to support either of the attributes `mandatory`, `supports`, or `requires`; in fact, the expected behaviour is that a failure of the tow truck order has to trigger the failure of the whole transaction and such attributes will let the tow truck endpoint to be added in the scope of the transaction. Hence, a service supporting any of the remaining attributes should be ruled out.
- The logging service is specified to support the `not supported` attribute that will execute the logging endpoint outside any transaction as its failure is not crucial and should not affect the other transactional activities.
- The attribute `never` assigned to the connector to the statistics service specifies that such service should never be invoked from within a transaction.

It is worth to remark that, if an orchestrator were due to realise the workflow, it should also handle and coordinate possible failures of services and react according to the attributes assigned to each invocation; in other words, the orchestrator will also act as (or liaise with the) transaction manager.

Once the attributes have been assigned to a design, phase 3 of our methodology allows some refinement both at the design level and at later stages of the development. These refinements hinge on the theoretical framework of [1] where it has been proved that, in certain contexts, some attributes exhibit the same observational behaviour. Again we illustrate this on our running scenario.

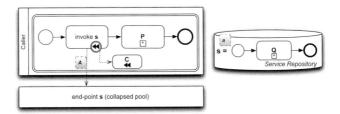

Fig. 9. Invocation of end-point **s**

Since an external observer cannot distinguish services supporting `mandatory`, `supports`, or `requires` when they are invoked from transactional scopes, the design of Figure 8 can be refined into one where only one of the attributes is assigned to the invocation of the tow truck service. Notice that this may provide a great simplification in the realisation of the design. For instance, the team developing the tow truck service may avoid to consider testing cases corresponding to the different attributes and chose the attribute that guarantees the smoother development.

Also, in a more complex scenario an activity may be invoked from many different other activities with different transactional requirements. The equivalences proved in [1] may again help in the refinement phase as the developers may factor out the invocations with equivalent attributes so limiting the development efforts.

4   Modelling Attribute-Based Services Invocation and Instantiation

An important feature in the service-oriented scenario is to allow invokers to specify their own requirements on the invoked services. In fact, a service invocation does not target a specific service but is resolved at run-time by selecting one of the available implementations matching a given description. Typically, both the service requester and the service provider express a set of requirements that need to be matched when defining the Service Level Agreement (SLA) for an invocation.

We consider a generalisation of the EJB mechanism for managing scope reconfiguration allowing both service requester and service provider to specify the transactional modality of each service instantiation. Namely, a service-oriented system is described as follows:

1. a process can contain a number of service invocations. Each service invocation specifies an abstract reference s[3]. Furthermore, service invocations specify a set of acceptable attributes, say $A \subseteq \mathcal{A}$. The execution of the invocation triggers, at run-time, the discovery/selection/binding of a service matching with s and A. Figure 9 (left-hand side) represents the process "*caller*" consisting of a transactional scope. The scope includes task `invoke` s, associated to compensation C, followed by sub-process P

---

[3] The service reference s can be thought as a service description that specifies the desired functional properties. Hereafter we refer to s simply as a *service*.

2. each provider can publish a number of services. The provider associates each service s to an implementation (e.g., a process) and a transactional attribute (e.g., a ∈ 𝒜). In Figure 9 the provider, represented by the repository on the right-hand side, implements s as a process consisting of a sub-process Q, and associates it to attribute a

3. upon service invocation, the matching/binding between caller and callee on s happens only if a ∈ A. In this case, the invocation of s triggers a (possibly remote) new instance s.

In other words, we threat attributes as non-functional properties that can be included as part of the SLA.

We present below a few examples of service invocation with attributes using a smooth extension of BPMN and following the semantics of EJB attributes. The BPMN extension will be described in more detail in the second part of this section. Intuitively, the system in Figure 9 may evolve to a number of different configurations depending on which attribute a the provider associates to s. We recall that the reconfiguration semantics, according to EJB, is decided by the provider through the definition of the attribute a. We allow also the service requester to specify the desired semantics by defining the set A.

The possible configurations follow from the semantics of transactional attributes illustrated in Section 2.2, when the invocation occurs inside a transactional scope.

- If a = not supported then the new instance of s is executed "as it is" outside any additional transactional scope. In this case the provider, by associating s with a specifies that no transactional support is provided and that the requester accepts such condition by including not supported in A. Figure 10a shows the reached configuration where the activity Q is executed outside any transactional scope.
- If a = requires new then the new instance of s is executed in a different, newly created scope. In this case, both provider and requester agree on the fact that the service will be executed in a newly created scope. Figure 10b shows the reached configuration where the activities P and Q are executed in different transactional scopes.
- If a = requires or a = mandatory or a = supported then the caller and the callee are executed in the same scope of the caller. Namely, caller and callee participate to the same distributed transaction. In Figure 10c both activities P and Q are executed in the same scope.
- If a = never then the invocation raises an exception which causes the execution of the compensation C.

Notice that teach alternative is desirable under certain circumstances, and has an impact on failure propagation. The configurations deriving from the invocation of s from outside a transactional scope can be defined similarly.

As mentioned before we used a smooth extension to BPMN to represent attribute aware service instantiation and distributed transactions.

Attribute-aware service instantiation. We represent the instantiation of a service as a task *invoke s* that sends a message to a collapsed pool. The collapsed pool represents the

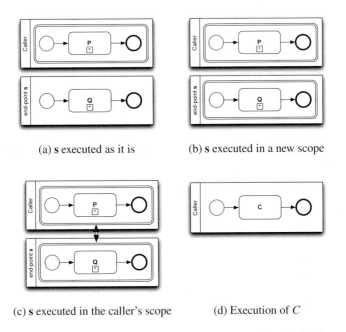

(a) **s** executed as it is   (b) **s** executed in a new scope

(c) **s** executed in the caller's scope   (d) Execution of *C*

Fig. 10. Scope reconfigurations following from the invocation of *s* in Figure 9

abstract reference of the service to be invoked. In general, the invoking process can have an interactive conversation with the invoked services, modelled as a message exchange with the collapsed pool (the messages are not shown in the examples for simplicity). We extend BPMN message flow by annotating the messages that spawn new processes to allow the caller to specify transactional requirements. Several implementations of a service can be available, each of them implemented by a different sub-process and satisfying different transactional properties. Upon an activation request, the callee activates only one of the processes satisfying caller requirement inside the right transactional scope.

Distributed transactions. Even if BPMN directly supports design of transactional processes, this features is limited to activities owned by a unique participant (e.g. confined into a pool). Architects must care about exceptions and explicitly model interactions performed by participants to implement distributed transactions. Moreover, BPMN provides a limited support to model service requirements and dependencies. In SOC, participants dynamically activates partners services (e.g. processes) that must respect the global transactional requirements.

To handle these issues we propose to extend BPMN to support the expressiveness of [2,3]. In order to represent distributed transaction, we introduce the double arrow connection. This artifact allows to represent that two (or more) participant transactions are confined by the same scope. Namely, a fault of one participant activity can automatically start the backward-flow of the linked transactions. Equipping BPMN with the distributed transaction artifact allows designer to statically define non functional properties of systems abstracting from the implementation details of the mechanisms for synchronising the outcomes. In fact, this artifact abstracts from the interactions required among participant to implement the correct behavior, that is demanded to the SOC frameworks (e.g. WS-TX [11] and BTP [9]).

5   Concluding Remarks and Related Work

We proposed an approach for the modelling of transactional service-oriented business processes that centres on the notion of transactional attribute. Our approach

1. features EJB-like mechanisms for the management of transactional scopes upon invocation; notably this allows a straightforward implementation of models as Java programs. Anyway, the approach we propose is not necessarily restricted to Java deployments. Our approach is based on the awareness of the semantics and conceptual relationship between transactional scopes and failure propagation. Such semantics can be implemented using different technologies.
2. is based on a generalisation of EJB transactions, that have been adapted to the SOC paradigm and can be used for the development of models in different technologies
3. builds on the theoretical results in [2,3] that allow to enhance and optimise software development and testing
4. can be adapted to a number of notations; as a proof of concept we have integrated our approach in BPMN.

Service development can benefit from transactional attributes for a number of reasons. In the implementation phase, transactional attributes provide the developer with a stronger set of preconditions on the (transactional) context in which a piece of software will be executed thus preventing defensive programming.

A service provider may want to publish different versions of the same service guaranteeing different transactional properties. This would allow the provider to maximise the number of matches for his/her portfolio of services. In [1] we proved equivalence of different transactional attributes under specific context. Starting from a registry that describes service versions, each associated with one transactional attribute, our theoretical results allow us to drive the implementation of the minimum set versions required to respect the BPMN design. Also, relying on the testing theory in [1] we can ease the testing of services-oriented artifacts since under certain conditions different transactional configuration have the same observed behaviour.

Finally we proposed an extension to the BPMN notation that focuses on service invocation and defines how the system should reconfigure at run-time. Notice that the structure of the transactional scopes describes the configuration of the whole execution of the transaction but does not details on how such configuration is achieved. Anyway, the information included in the models annotated with attributes can be used to define a semantics for dynamically reconfiguring BPMN processes. An interesting approach, that we leave as a future work, would be to use graph rewriting [14] to formalise such configurations.

Albeit our approach takes inspiration from EJB transactional attributes, our proposal abstract from the underling technology. Architects can specify transactional properties directly on the DSL that describe the business process.

Related Work. A number of formal models for long running transactions have been proposed in the last years. Saga [7] is one of the earlier proposal to manage LRTs by exploiting the notion of compensations. A recent work [8] provides a comparison of the expressiveness of different approaches to specify compensations. A formal model for failure propagation in dynamically reconfiguring systems has been proposed in [2] as a CCS-like process calculus called ATc (after *Attribute-based Transactional calculus*). The primitives of ATc are inspired to EJB [15] and allow to *determine* and *control* the dynamic reconfiguration of distributed transactions so to have consistent and predictable failure propagation. In [3] it has been proposed an observational theory (based on the theory of testing in [4]) yielding a formal framework for analysing the interplay between communication failures and the observable behaviour of a service-oriented system. In fact, the main result in [3] shows that the choice of different transactional attributes causes different system's behaviours and system's reactions to a failure. A comparison of the linguistic features of ATc wrt other calculi featuring distributed transactions has been given in [2].

BPMN allows to statically define the transactional activities. More expressive models have been investigated. For example the *dynamic recovery* approach allows compensations to be dynamically updated and replaced. It would be interesting to evaluate the effectiveness of BPMN artifacts to express dynamic recovery. A number of work tackled the lack of a formal semantics for BPMN (e.g., [6,17]). Our aim was rather to propose a methodology for the design of transactional processes that relies on a theoretical framework. The methodology centres on the fact that service invocations cause a reconfiguration of transactional scopes in a service-oriented scenario. Up to our knowledge, such aspects have not been included by existing formal models of BPMN. A promising approach to provide a formal account of BPMN in reconfiguring system would be to use graph rewriting techniques [14]. Some other work address the execution of BPMN models (e.g., [5] encodes them in executable YAWL [16] processes). We address an orthogonal issue by proposing a general approach for attribute-aware software development, that can be applied to many development techniques.

References

1. Bocchi, L., Tuosto, E.: A Java Inspired Semantics for Transactions in SOC, extended report (2009), http://www.cs.le.ac.uk/people/lb148/javatransactions.html
2. Bocchi, L., Tuosto, E.: A java inspired semantics for transactions in SOC. In: Wirsing, M., Hofmann, M., Rauschmayer, A. (eds.) TGC 2010, LNCS, vol. 6084, pp. 120–134. Springer, Heidelberg (2010)
3. Bocchi, L., Tuosto, E.: Testing attribute-based transactions in SOC. In: Hatcliff, J., Zucca, E. (eds.) Formal Techniques for Distributed Systems. LNCS, vol. 6117, Springer, Heidelberg (2010)
4. De Nicola, R., Hennessy, M.C.B.: Testing equivalences for processes. Theoretical Comput. Sci. 34(1–2), 83–133 (1984)

5. Decker, G., Dijkman, R., Dumas, M., García-Bañuelos, L.: Transforming BPMN Diagrams into YAWL Nets. In: Dumas, M., Reichert, M., Shan, M.-C. (eds.) BPM 2008. LNCS, vol. 5240, pp. 386–389. Springer, Heidelberg (2008)
6. Dijkman, R.M., Dumas, M., Ouyang, C.: Semantics and analysis of business process models in BPMN. Information & Software Technology 50(12), 1281–1294 (2008)
7. Garcia-Molina, H., Salem, K.: Sagas. In: Dayal, U., Traiger, I.L. (eds.) SIGMOD Conference, pp. 249–259. ACM Press, New York (1987)
8. Lanese, I., Vaz, C., Ferreira, C.: On the expressive power of primitives for compensation handling. In: Gordon, A.D. (ed.) ESOP. LNCS, vol. 6012, pp. 366–386. Springer, Heidelberg (2010)
9. OASIS. Business Transaction Protocol, BTP (2002),
   `http://www.oasisopen.org/committees/business-transactions/`
   `documents/primer/`
10. OASIS. Web Services Business Process Execution Language, WS-BPEL (2007),
    `http://docs.oasis-open.org/wsbpel/2.0/OS/wsbpel-v2.0-OS.html`
11. OASIS. Web Services Transaction, WS-TX (2009),
    `http://www.oasis-open.org/committees/ws-tx/`
12. OMG Group. Business Process Modeling Notation, BPMN (2002), `http://www.bpmn.org`
13. Panda, D., Rahman, R., Lane, D.: EJB 3 in action. Manning (2007)
14. Rozenberg, G. (ed.): Handbook of graph grammars and computing by graph transformation: vol. I. World Scientific Publishing Co., Inc., River Edge (1997)
15. Sun Microsystems. Enterprise JavaBeans (EJB) technology (2009),
    `http://java.sun.com/products/ejb/`
16. van der Aalst, W., Hofstede, A.H.M.T.: YAWL: Yet Another Workflow Language. Information Systems 30, 245–275 (2003)
17. Wong, P.Y., Gibbons, J.: A Process Semantics for BPMN. In: Liu, S., Maibaum, T., Araki, K. (eds.) ICFEM 2008. LNCS, vol. 5256, pp. 355–374. Springer, Heidelberg (2008)

Programmable Fault Injection Testbeds
for Complex SOA

Lukasz Juszczyk and Schahram Dustdar

Distributed Systems Group, Vienna University of Technology, Austria
{juszczyk,dustdar}@infosys.tuwien.ac.at

Abstract. The modularity of Service-oriented Architectures (SOA) allows to establish complex distributed systems comprising e.g., services, clients, brokers, and workflow engines. A growing complexity, however, automatically increases the number of potential fault sources which have effects on the whole SOA. Fault handling mechanisms must be applied in order to achieve a certain level of robustness. In this paper we do not deal with fault-tolerance itself but regard the problem from a different perspective: how can fault-tolerance be evaluated? We argue that this can be best done by testing the system at runtime and observing its reaction on occuring faults. Though, engineers are facing the problem of how to perform such tests in a realistic manner in order to get meaningful results. As our contribution to this issue we present an approach for generating fault injection testbeds for SOA. Our framework allows to model testbeds and program their behavior, to generate running instances out of it, and to inject diverse types of faults. The strength of our approach lies in the customizability of the testbeds and the ability to program the fault-injecting mechanisms in a convenient manner.

1 Introduction

The principles of SOA propagate building distributed systems based on modular and loosely-coupled components. The spectrum of these components ranges from stand-alone and composite Web services, clients, brokers and registries, workflow engines, monitors, governance systems, message dispatchers, service buses, etc. Considering the dependencies within a complex SOA, it becomes evident that each component is a potential fault source and has an impact on the whole system. Moreover, faults can happen at different levels, e.g., at the network layer, at the interaction level, or as errors in the exchanged messages. As a consequence, sophisticated fault handling mechanisms are required in order to mitigate the effects of faults, to prevent failures, and to guarantee a certain level of robustness. This problem has already been addressed in several works [1,2,3,4] and is out of the scope of this paper. Instead, we are facing it from a different perspective: how can engineers evaluate fault handling mechanisms of a SOA? How can they verify that their systems will behave as expected once deployed in their destination environment? These issues cannot be solved by simply performing simulations but require thorough tests at runtime. But how can engineers perform such tests *prior* to final deployment, without having access

P.P. Maglio et al. (Eds.): ICSOC 2010, LNCS 6470, pp. 411–425, 2010.

to a real(istic) environment which would serve as a testbed? In this paper we address this question and present our contribution.

In our previous work [5] we have introduced the *Genesis2* framework which supports engineers in setting up testbeds for SOA. *Genesis2* allows to model testbeds consisting of various types of components, to program their behavior, and to generate real instances of these on a distributed back-end. In the current paper we extend this approach in order to generate multi-level fault injection testbeds. We empower engineers to generate emulated SOA environments and to program fault injection behavior on diverse levels: *at the network layer, at the service execution level, and at the message layer.*

Our paper is structured as follows: in the next Section we present the motivation for our research. In Section 2 we present *Genesis2* and explain in Section 3 how we generate fault-injection testbeds. Section 4 covers the implementation the practical application of our approach. In Section 5 we review related work and outline our contribution. Finally, Section 6 concludes this paper.

1.1   Motivation

Today's SOAs comprise large numbers and varieties of components. This is not only limited to services, clients, and brokers (as conveyed in the famous Web service triangle [6]), but includes also more sophisticated components, such as governance systems and monitoring registries [7], which are performing complex tasks on the service-based environment. In general, we can divide SOA components into three groups: a) stand-alone components which are independent, b) complex services/components which have dependencies and, therefore, are affected by others, and c) clients which are simply consuming the offered services. Each of the components is prone to errors, but the complex ones are affected in a twofold manner as they have also to deal with remote faults of the components they depend on. As outlined correctly in [8] and [9], faults do happen on multiple levels, to be precise, on each layer of the communication stack. This includes low-level faults on the network layer (e.g., packet loss/delay), faults on the transport layer (e.g., middleware failures), on the interaction layer (quality of service), as well as directly at the exchanged messages which can get corrupted. Depending on the structure and configuration of the SOA, each of these faults can cause a chain of effects (also referred to as error propagation), ranging from simple execution delays to total denial of service. These challenges can only be met if engineers perform intense tests during the development phase, execute scenarios in erroneous SOA environments, and check their system's behavior on faults. However, the main problem remains how to set up such scenarios, in particular, the question how engineers can be provided with proper testbeds which emulate SOA infrastructures in a realistic way. We argue that engineers must be given a possibility to configure testbeds according to their requirements. Depending on the developed system, this includes the ability to customize the topology and composition of the testbed, to specify the behavior of all involved components, and to program individual fault injection models for each of these. In Section 5 we will show that research on fault injection for SOA has been already done by several groups, yet that these works mostly aim testing only individual Web services, for instance, by perturbing their communication channels. The problem of testing complex components which are operating on a whole SOA environment still remained unsolved. This has been our motivation for doing research on a solution which allows to generate large-scale fault-injection testbeds, provides high customizability, and offers an intuitive usage for engineers.

2 Genesis2 Testbed Generator Framework

The *Genesis2* framework (*Generating Service-oriented testbed InfrastructureS*, in short G2) [5] assists engineers in creating testbed infrastructures for SOA. It comprises a centralized front-end, from where testbeds are modeled and controlled, and a distributed back-end at which the models are transformed into real testbed instances. In a nutshell, the front-end provides a virtual view on the testbed, allowing engineers to manipulate it via scripts, and propagates changes to the back-end in order to adapt the running testbed. To ensure extensibility, the G2 framework follows a modular approach and provides the functional grounding for composable plugins that implement testbed generator features. The framework itself offers a) generic features for modeling and manipulating testbeds, b) extension points for plugins, c) inter-plugin communication among remote instances, and d) a runtime environment shared across the testbed. All in all, it provides the basic management and communication infrastructure which abstracts over the distributed nature of a testbed. The plugins, however, enhance the model schema by integrating custom model types and interpret these to generate deployable testbed instances at the back-end.

For a better understanding of the internal procedures inside G2, let us take a closer look at its architecture. Figure 1 depicts the layered components, comprising the framework, installed plugins, and, on top of it, the generated testbed:

- At the very bottom, the basic runtime consists of Java, Groovy, and 3rd-party libraries, such as Apache CXF [10].
- At the framework layer, G2 provides itself via an API and a shared runtime environment is established at which plugins and generated testbed elements can discover each other and interact. Moreover, an active repository distributes detected plugins among all hosts.
- Based on that grounding, installed plugins register themselves at the shared runtime and integrate their functionality into the framework.
- The top layer depicts the results of the engineer's activities. At the front-end he/she is operating the created testbed model. The model comprises virtual objects which act as a view on the real testbed and as proxies for manipulation commands. While at the back-end the actual testbed is generated according to the specified model.

In G2, the engineer creates models according to the provided schema at the front-end, specifying *what* shall be generated *where*, with *which customizations*, and the framework takes care of synchronizing the model with the corresponding

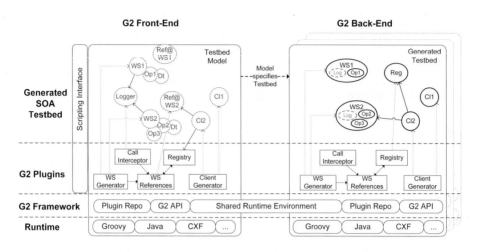

Fig. 1. Genesis2 architecture: infrastructure, plugins, and generated elements

back-end hosts on which the testbed elements are generated and deployed. The front-end, moreover, maintains a permanent view on the testbed, allowing to manipulate it on-the-fly by updating its model. Figure 2 illustrates the model schema used in this paper. By default, G2 provides model types for specifying Web services (which includes also Web service operations and used data types), clients, registries, and other basic SOA components. In this paper, we are extending this schema with models for specifying faulty behavior (marked gray), which are explained in more detail in the next section.

Listing 1 contains a sample specification for demonstrating how testbeds are modeled based on the applied model schema. Basically, G2 is controlled via Groovy scripts [11] that are executed on top of the *shared runtime environment* (SRE, see Figure 1). Each applied plugin extends the SRE by registering itself, its provided model types, additional macros and other artifacts via aliases. The

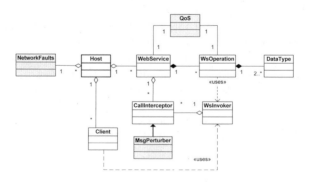

Fig. 2. Testbed model schema for fault injection

engineer references these in his/her scripts in order to make use of the provided features and to integrate them into his/her testbeds. Moreover, he/she is free to customize the testbed's behavior via Groovy code blocks.

The sample script starts with referencing remote back-end hosts and importing a data type definition from an XSD file. This is done via instantiating the corresponding types from the model schema via their aliases (host and datatype). In Lines 5 to 10 a simple Web service is created, which comprises only a single operation (named SayHi) and which uses the imported data type in its request message. By using the Builder feature [12] of Groovy, which simplifies the creation of nested datatypes, we are automatically binding the webservice to its wsperation and the used datatype's. In Line 12 the service is being deployed at two back-end hosts. In this step G2 serializes the service's model and propagates it to the remote back-ends where real Web service instances, which implement the modeled behavior, are being generated and deployed. Next, a simple client is started (Lines 14 to 21), which uses the registry plugin to discover a desired Web service and, eventually, invokes it. The main purpose of clients is to bootstrap activity into the testbed which would otherwise be purely passive and wait for invocations. Finally, in Lines 24 to 27 a callinterceptor is created and attached on-the-fly to the running Web service instances. Call interceptors step in to Web service invocations and allow, for instance, to extract the SOAP message (as done in the sample for logging) and to manipulate it. We have used this feature for implementing message perturbation in our fault injection testbeds.

All in all, G2 supports engineers in customizing testbeds, programming their behavior, and implementing extensions via plugins. Though, due to space constraints

```
1   def beHost1 = host.create("192.168.1.11:8080") //import BE host refs
2   def beHost2 = host.create("192.168.1.12:8080")
3   def vCard = datatype.create("/path/types.xsd","vCard") //import XSD type

5   def service = webservice.build { //model Web service via Groovy builder
6       //create model of TestService with one operation
7       TestService(binding: "doc,lit", tags: ["test"]) {
8           SayHi(card: vCard, result: String) { return "Hi ${card.name}" }
9       }
10  }[0]

12  service.deployAt(beHost1,beHost2) //deployment at two back-end hosts

14  def cl = client.create() //model simple client which calls TestService
15  cl.code = {
16      def refList=registry.get{ s-> s.name=="TestService"} //query
17      def ref=refList[0] //take first from result list
18      println ref.SayHi(vCard.newInstance()) //WS invocation
19  }

21  cl.deployAt(beHost2) //deployment at back-end

23  // attach call interceptor
24  def pi=callinterceptor.create()
25  pi.code={ ctx-> logger.logToDB(ctx.soapMsg) } //calling logger plugin

27  service.interceptors+=pi // on-the-fly attachement of interceptor
```

Listing 1. 'Sample script specifying a service, a client, and a call interceptor'

it is impossible to provide a closer introduction to G2 and, therefore, we direct interested readers to [5] which explains more details of our base framework.

3   Programmable Multi-level Fault Injection Testbeds

Taking into consideration the complexity of a typical SOA, which comprises diverse components being deployed on heterogeneous platforms and interacting with each others, it becomes evident that each host, each component, each communication channel, and each exchanged message is a potential source of faults, erroneous behavior, and service failures [13]. Basically, faults can occur at every level/layer of the communication stack and, therefore, if testbeds are supposed to emulate realistic scenarios they must be also able to emulate a wide range of fault types. Based on the G2 framework we have developed an approach for generating SOA testbeds and injecting programmable faults. Due to G2's generic nature and its extensibility it is possible to emulate a wide variety of faults by writing plugins which augment the testbed's components and impair their execution. However, in the current state of our work we have concentrated on the following:

1. **Faults at the message layer**, in terms of message data corruption.
2. **Faults at the service execution**, affecting Quality of Service (QoS).
3. **Faults at the network layer**, hampering the packet flow between hosts.

Each type of fault is affecting a different part of the overall SOA and, therefore, we have split their emulation into three independent plugins. Each plugin extends the model schema and offers possibilities to customize and program the fault injection behavior. Figure 2 depicts the provided model types and their position within the schema. Since network faults affect the whole communication between hosts, their model does directly extend the `Host` type. Service execution faults can be caused by the whole service (e.g., low availability) or only by individual operations (e.g., erroneous implementation), therefore their model is bound to both. Finally, for message faults we have extended the `CallInterceptor` which provides access to the request and response messages for perturbation purposes. In the following sections we are explaining the individual fault injection mechanisms in more detail.

3.1   Message Faults

SOAP Web services are using WSDL documents [14] to describe their interfaces. Consequently, the service can define the expected syntax of the request messages and the client is aware of the response message's syntax. However, malicious components can produce corrupted messages which either contain meaningless content (message errors on a semantical level), which violate the message's XML schema definition [15] (high-level syntax errors), or which even do not represent a correct XML document at all (low-level syntax errors). Depending on the degree of corruption, fault handling mechanisms can be applied to allow the integration of faulty components into a SOA. To test such mechanisms we have developed a plugin which allows to intercept exchanged SOAP messages and to perturb them on each of the mentioned levels. Engineers can program the perturbation via the `MsgPerturber` model and the plugin attaches the faulty behavior to Web services and clients, by using Apache CXF's interceptors [16]. We have built the perturbation mechanism upon the visitor pattern [17]. Perturbation code, wrapped in visitor objects, is propagated recursively along the XML tree and/or the unmarshalled objects and has full read/write access for performing manipulations.

For pure semantic perturbation the engineer can overwrite the message's values, but cannot violate the XML structure. The plugin unmarshalls the SOAP body arguments, as well as the headers, into Java objects and applies the visitor code on them. The first sample block in Listing 2 shows an interceptor that is programmed to assign random values to all integer fields named `sum`. Moreover, it deletes all postcodes for matching addresses.

For high-level syntax manipulation, the engineer can alternate both, the content and the structure of the XML document. In this case the visitor is applied on the DOM tree of the message. In the second sample block, the visitor is looking for nodes which have children named `country` and appends a new child which violates the message's XSD definition. However, the result is still a well-formated XML document. For low-level corruption, the message must be altered directly at the byte level, as demonstrated in the last snippet which corrupts XML closing tags. Finally, in Line 23, the interceptors get deployed at a Web service and start injecting faults into its request and response messages.

```
1   def valuePert = msgperturber.create("args") //pert. data values
2   valuePert.code = { it ->
3       if (it.name=="sum" && it.type==int) { //get by name and type
4           it.value*=new Random().nextInt()
5       } else if (it.name=="Address" && it.value.country=="AT") { //by value
6           it.value.postcode=null
7       }
8   }

10  def xmlPert = msgperturber.create("dom") //pert. XML structure
11  xmlPert.code = { node ->
12      if (node.children.any { c-> c.name=="country" }) {
13          Node newChild = node.appendNode("NotInXSD")
14          newChild.attributes.someAtt="123"
15      }
16  }

18  def bytePert = msgperturber.create("bytes") //pert. msg bytes
19  bytePert.code = { str ->
20      str.replaceFirst("</","<") //remove closing tag from XML doc
21  }

23  service.interceptors+=[bytePert, xmlPert, valuePert] //attach to service
```

Listing 2. 'Programming message perturbation'

3.2   Service Execution Faults

Service execution faults usually result in degraded Quality of Service (QoS) [18]. Examples are slower processing times which delay the SOA's execution, scalability problems regarding the number of incoming requests, availability failures which render parts of the SOA inaccessible, etc. Especially in the context of Web services, QoS covers a wide spectrum of properties, including also security, discoverability, and also costs. However, in our work we only deal with those concerning service execution, as defined in [19], comprising response time, scalability, throughput, and accuracy of Web service operations and the availability of the whole service. For emulating these, we developed the `QoSEmulator` plugin, which has access to the generated Web service instances in on the back-end and intercepts their invocations in order to simulate QoS. To model a service's QoS, engineers can either assign fixed values to the individual properties (e.g., processing time = 10 seconds) or define more sophisticated fault models via Groovy code closures [20], resulting in programmable QoS. The main advantage of closures consists in the ability to incorporate diverse factors into the fault models. For example, engineers can set the availability rate depending on the number of incoming requests or to define the processing time according to a statistical distribution function, supported via the *Java Distribution Functions* library [21].

Listing 3 contains a sample specification of two QoS models, one for defining the availability of a Web service and one for controlling the execution of its operations. The availability is defined according to the daytime in order to simulate a less overloaded service during the night (Lines 1 to 7). For the service operation, the response time is derived from a beta distribution (alias `dist`) while throughput and error rate (accuracy) are assigned with constant values. At the end, the models are bound to the service and its operations.

```
1    def svcQos = qos.create()
2    svcQos.availability = {
3        if (new Date().getHours()<8) { //from 0 to 7 AM
4            return 99/100 //set high availability of 99%
5        }
6        return 90/100 //otherwise, set lower availability rate
7    }

9    def opQos = qos.create()
10   opQos.responseTime = { dist.beta.random(5000,1,null) } //beta distrib.
11   opQos.throughput = 10/60 //restrict to 10 invocations per minute
12   opQos.errorRate = 15/100 //15% of invocations will fail with exceptions

14   service.qos=svcQos //attach QoS model to service definition

16   service.operations.grep { o-> o.returnType!=null }.each {
17       o.qos=opQos //and to all 2-way operations
18   }
```

Listing 3. 'Programming QoS emulation'

3.3   Low-Level Network Faults

Network faults, such as loss and corruption of IP packets, play a minor role in SOA fault handling, mainly because they are already handled well by the TCP/IP protocol which underlays most of the service-oriented communication. But they can cause delays and timeouts, and this way slow down the whole data flow. Apart from that, there exist Web service protocols which are built upon

UDP, such as *SOAP over UDP* [22] and *Web Service Dynamic Discovery* [23], which are, therefore, more vulnerable to network faults. Creating testbeds which emulate low-level faults requires a much deeper intrusion into the operating system, compared to the other plugins. It is necessary to intercept the packet flow, to perform dropping, duplication, reordering, slowing down, etc. This can hardly be done on top of the *Java Virtual Machine* which hosts the G2 framework. To by-pass this issue, we have developed our `NetworkFaultEmulator` plugin based on the Linux tool *Traffic Control* (tc) [24] (with *netem* module [25]) which allows to steer packet manipulation at the kernel level. Unfortunately, this deprives G2 of its platform independence but, on the other hand, allows to reuse tc's rich set of features. We have presented a first version of this approach in [26]. Similar to the previously presented plugins, engineers create fault models but, in this case, attach them directly to the back-end hosts. There the fault models are locally translated into tc commands for manipulating the host's packet flow.

Listings 4 and 5 comprise a sample for illustrating the mapping from the model to the resulting tc commands. The model is created by assigning self-explanatory parameters and is finally being attached to the hosts. At the back-end, the plugin first sets up a virtual network interface which hosts all generated instances, such as Web services, registries, etc. This step is necessary for limiting the effect of the fault emulation only on the testbed instances, instead of slowing down the whole physical system. Eventually, the modelled faults are translated into tc commands applied on the virtual IP.

```
1   def nf = networkfaults.create()
2   nf.loss = 2/100 //2% packet loss
3   nf.duplicate = 1/100 //1% packet duplication
4   nf.delay.value = 100 //100ms
5   nf.delay.variation = 20 //20ms of variation
6   nf.delay.distribution = "normal" //normal distribution

8   nf.deployAt(beHost1,beHost2) //attach to BE hosts
```

Listing 4. 'Programming network faults'

```
1   ifconfig lo:0 add 192.168.100.1 #set up virtual IP addr. for BE instances

3   tc qdisc change dev lo:0 root netem loss 2.0%
4   tc qdisc change dev lo:0 root netem duplicate 1.0%
5   tc qdisc change dev lo:0 root netem delay 100ms 20ms distribution normal
```

Listing 5. 'Network fault model translated to Traffic Control commands'

4   Implementation and Practical Application

4.1   Implementation and Extensibility of Genesis2 Prototype

The G2 framework has been developed in Java SE 6 [27] and Groovy [11]. The critical parts, which handle the framework's internal logic and the communication between front-end and back-end, are written in Java. Groovy, however, has been exploited for having a flexible scripting language for modelling the testbeds and for programming customizations via Groovy closures [20].

G2 provides a generic framework which outsources the generation of testbed instances to the corresponding plugins, supporting the procedure via its API. Based on that grounding, plugins define their extensions to the model schema and interpret their provided extensions for generating deployable testbed components. For instance, the `WebServiceGenerator` plugin analyzes `webservice` models and translates them into deployable Apache CXF-based [10] Web service instances. All plugins provide access to their generated components but offer also interfaces for customization, so that other plugins can intervene and/or extend their functionality. The fault injection plugins presented in this paper make intense use of this feature. Though, of course they do not cover all possible error sources in a SOA but only represent the current state of our work. For testing complex SOAs it would be also necessary to emulate, for example, middleware faults, fault in the execution of WS-* protocols, or misbehavior of human provided services [28] integrated into workflows. Depending on the next steps in our research, and which fault injection mechanisms will be required for evaluating our prototypes, we will develop further plugins in the future.

4.2   Practical Application in Testing of SOA Prototypes

The question how G2 should be used to generate fault injection testbeds depends strongly on the type of the tested SOA, its composition, purpose, as well as its internal fault handling mechanisms. In the end, engineers have to generate testbeds which emulate the SOA's final deployment environment as realistically as possible. While Groovy scripts are G2's primary interface for modeling testbeds, we are currently investigating techniques for importing external specifications of SOAs and their components into G2 models (e.g., from BPEL process definitions [29] and WSDL documents [14]). Independent on how the testbed got specified, whether from scratch or via imports, the engineer is always operating on a set of models describing SOA components which have their pendant generated instances located in the back-end. For providing a better conception of how a testbed is actually structured Figure 3 illustrates its layered topology. At the two bottom layers G2 connects the front-end to the distributed back-end and the plugins establish their own communication structures. Most important are the two top layers which comprise the results of the engineer's activities. Based on the provided model schema, he/she creates models of SOA components which are then being generated and deployed at the back-end hosts. At the very top layer the testbed instances are running and behave/interact according to the engineer's specification, which includes also fault injection behavior. The aggregation of these instances constitutes the actual testbed infrastructure on which the developed SOA can be evaluated.

Of course, the evaluation of a software system also comprises the monitoring of the test cases as well as the analysis of collected data. These data are, for instance, log files, performance statistics, captured messages, and other resources, depending on the tested SOA and the fault-handling mechanisms to be verified.

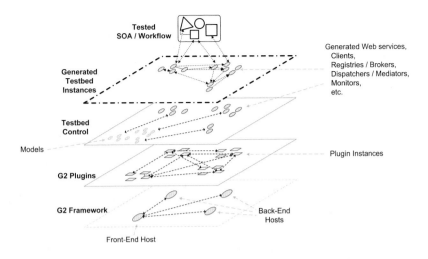

Fig. 3. Interactions within layers of a G2 testbed

These data must be also gathered from both, the tested SOA, to analyze internal procedures and reactions on faults, as well as from the testbed itself, to know which faults have been injected at which time. By correlating both, it is possible to narrow down errors in the SOA and to detect causes of misbehavior. G2 provides means for gathering relevant information about the execution inside the testbed, such as an eventing mechanism that allows to track and log all changes within the testbed configuration or call interceptors for logging of interactions. However, regarding the gathering of log data from the tested SOA system, we do not provide any tool support yet. Also, for the analysis of test results and the narrowing down of errors/bugs inside the SOA we have not come up yet with any novel contribution but regarded this problem as out of scope of the current paper which just describes how we generate the testbeds. But we intend to address these problems in future research.

4.3   Managing Large-Scale Testbeds

In [5] we have shown how G2 facilitates convenient generation of large-scale testbeds as well as manipulation of these in an efficient multicast-like manner. We are exploiting the multicast feature for adapting larger testbed on-the-fly, e.g., for injecting faults. Listing 6 demonstrates its usage for updating hosts and Web services. The command expects the type of the instances which shall be altered (in the sample: `webservice` and `host`) and two closure code blocks. The first closure specifies the filter which determines the designated instances, while the second one contains the manipulation commands. In the presented sample, fault models are attached to all Web services matching their namespace and annotation tags. Moreover, all hosts within a defined subnet are being enhanced with network fault emulation. As a result, multicast updates help to manage large-scale testbeds in a clear and compact manner.

```
1   webservice { ws-> //filter
2       "faulty" in ws.tags && ws.namespace =~ /www.infosys.tuwien.ac.at/
3   } { ws-> //command
4       ws.qos = qosModel
5       ws.interceptors += [xmlPertModel]
6   }

8   host { h-> //filter
9       h.location =~ /192.168.1./
10  } { h-> //command
11      netFaultModel.attachTo(h)
12  }
```

Listing 6. 'Injecting faults to hosts and Web services'

Regarding the performance of the framework and our fault injection mechanisms, we have omitted putting a detailed study into this paper, mainly due to space constraints and because we believe that it would not emphasize the message of our paper, which is the presentation of the concepts. Due to the fact that G2 is a programmable framework, the actual performance and system load also depend heavily on how it is applied and what kind of a testbed is being generated, with which components and functionality. Therefore, we believe that presenting a performance evaluation would be only of limited use for the readers.

4.4   Open-Source Prototype

As we did before with G2's predecessor, the first Genesis framework [30], we will also publish the current prototype as open-source via its homepage [31].

5   Related Research

Fault injection has been a well-established testing technique since decades. Numerous tools have been developed and applied for evaluating quality of software/systems. Due to the vast number of available tools, as well as due to their diversity, we do not present a survey on them but refer readers to [32] and [33], which provide a good introduction and overview of available solutions. In general, research on fault injection has produced a lot of results, covering sophisticated techniques for generating meaningful faults as well as for the analysis of their effects on the tested software.

In the domain of Web services and SOA, several works deal with fault injection. Xu et al. have presented an approach for perturbing the XML/SOAP-based messages exchanged by Web services in order to evaluate how well the tested systems can handle message corruption [34]. Moreover, Nik Looker has investigated fault injection techniques in his dissertation [35] and has developed the WS-FIT framework [9,36]. WS-FIT intercepts SOAP messages at the middleware level and supports a rich set of features for manipulating these. This includes discarding of messages, reordering of them in the interaction flows, perturbing the XML content, and other features. In general, works like those of Xu and Looker assume the presence of already existing Web services and inject faults for testing their runtime behavior and/or fault-handling mechanisms. However, we do not regard these works as direct competitors, since we have not developed any novel techniques for fault injection in the strict sense. Instead we empower engineers to generate SOA testbeds from scratch and to extend these with programmable faulty behavior. And this we regard as our most distinct contribution. Due to the novelty of our work, we have not identified many related works, but have only found SOABench, PUPPET, and ML-FIT to be relevant for testbed generation.

SOABench [37] provides sophisticated support for benchmarking of BPEL engines [29] via modeling experiments and generating service-based testbeds. It provides runtime control on test executions as well as mechanisms for test result evaluation. Regarding its features, SOABench is focused on performance evaluation and generates Web service stubs that emulate QoS properties, such as response time and throughput. Similar to SOABench, the authors of PUPPET [38,39] examine the generation of QoS-enriched testbeds for service compositions. PUPPET does not investigate the performance but verifies the fulfillment of Service Level Agreements (SLA) of composite services. This is done by analyzing WSDL [14] and WS-Agreement documents [40] and emulating the QoS of generated Web services in order to check the SLAs. Both tools, SOABench and Puppet, support the generation of Web service-based testbeds, but both are focused on evaluating workflows/compositions and do not support fault injection beyond emulating QoS.

Only the Multi-Level Fault-Injection Testbed (ML-FIT) [8] has a similar focus to our work. It also aims at emulating SOA faults at different levels, builds upon existing fault injection mechanisms, and the authors intend to use collected field data for creating realistic fault models. However, ML-FIT is still under development and, therefore, not much has been published about it yet. It is unclear how testbeds will be generated, which types of SOA components will be supported, and how faults will be modelled and injected. Without knowing these details it is difficult for us to compare our approach to ML-FIT.

6 Conclusion

In this paper we have presented our approach for generating programmable fault injection testbeds for SOA. Based on the Genesis2 framework, which allows engineers to model testbeds and to generate real instances of these, we have developed techniques for specifying faults and injecting them into running testbeds. Due to the extensibility of Genesis2, our approach supports the emulation of diverse types of faults. In the current state of our work, we have developed mechanisms for emulating network faults, service execution faults, and for corrupting exchanged messages. In a nutshell, our main contribution consists of the ability to generate SOA testbeds via scripts and the programmability of the injected faults. As a result, engineers can customize the fault behavior to their requirements, in order to have realistic testbeds for evaluating SOA systems.

For future plans, we will be working on further fault injection mechanisms to extend the spectrum of supported fault types and we will publish the prototype implementation as open-source.

Acknowledgments

The research leading to these results has received funding from the European Community Seventh Framework Programme FP7/2007-2013 under grant agreement 215483 (S-Cube).

The authors would also like to thank Philipp Leitner for contributing parts of the QoSEmulator plugin.

References

1. Goeschka, K.M., Froihofer, L., Dustdar, S.: What SOA can do for software dependability. In: DSN 2008: Supplementary Volume of the 38th Annual IEEE/IFIP International Conference on Dependable Systems and Networks, pp. D4–D9. IEEE Computer Society, Los Alamitos (2008)
2. Psaier, H., Skopik, F., Schall, D., Dustdar, S.: Behavior Monitoring in Self-healing Service-oriented Systems. In: COMPSAC. IEEE Computer Society Press, Los Alamitos (2010) (forthcoming)
3. Dialani, V., Miles, S., Moreau, L., Roure, D.D., Luck, M.: Transparent fault tolerance for web services based architectures. In: Monien, B., Feldmann, R.L. (eds.) Euro-Par 2002. LNCS, vol. 2400, pp. 889–898. Springer, Heidelberg (2002)
4. Modafferi, S., Mussi, E., Pernici, B.: Sh-bpel: a self-healing plug-in for ws-bpel engines. In: MW4SOC. ACM International Conference Proceeding Series, vol. 184, pp. 48–53. ACM, New York (2006)
5. Juszczyk, L., Dustdar, S.: Script-based generation of dynamic testbeds for soa. In: ICWS. IEEE Computer Society, Los Alamitos (2010) (forthcoming)
6. Gottschalk, K.D., Graham, S., Kreger, H., Snell, J.: Introduction to web services architecture. IBM Systems Journal 41(2), 170–177 (2002)
7. Michlmayr, A., Rosenberg, F., Leitner, P., Dustdar, S.: End-to-end support for qos-aware service selection, binding and mediation in vresco. IEEE T. Services Computing (2010) (forthcoming)
8. Reinecke, P., Wolter, K.: Towards a multi-level fault-injection test-bed for service-oriented architectures: Requirements for parameterisation. In: SRDS Workshop on Sharing Field Data and Experiment Measurements on Resilience of Distributed Computing Systems, Naples, Italy, AMBER (2008)
9. Looker, N., Munro, M., Xu, J.: Simulating errors in web services. International Journal of Simulation Systems 5(5), 29–37 (2004)
10. Apache CXF, http://cxf.apache.org/
11. Groovy Programming Language, http://groovy.codehaus.org/
12. Groovy Builders Guide, http://groovy.codehaus.org/Builders
13. Avizienis, A., Laprie, J.C., Randell, B., Landwehr, C.E.: Basic concepts and taxonomy of dependable and secure computing. IEEE Trans. Dependable Sec. Comput. 1(1), 11–33 (2004)
14. Web Services Description Language, http://www.w3.org/TR/wsdl

15. XML Schema Definition, http://www.w3.org/TR/xmlschema-0/
16. Apache CXF Interceptors, http://cxf.apache.org/docs/interceptors.html.
17. Palsberg, J., Jay, C.B.: The essence of the visitor pattern. In: COMPSAC, pp. 9–15. IEEE Computer Society, Los Alamitos (1998)
18. Menascé, D.A.: Qos issues in web services. IEEE Internet Computing 6(6), 72–75 (2002)
19. Rosenberg, F., Platzer, C., Dustdar, S.: Bootstrapping performance and dependability attributes of web services. In: ICWS, pp. 205–212. IEEE Computer Society, Los Alamitos (2006)
20. Groovy Closure Guide, http://groovy.codehaus.org/Closures
21. Java Distribution Functions library, http://statdistlib.sourceforge.net
22. SOAP Over UDP, http://docs.oasis-open.org/ws-dd/soapoverudp/1.1/os/wsdd-soapoverudp-1.1-spec-os.html
23. Web Services Dynamic Discovery, http://docs.oasis-open.org/ws-dd/discovery/1.1/os/wsdd-discovery-1.1-spec-os.pdf
24. Linux Advanced Routing & Traffic Control, http://lartc.org
25. Netem - Network Emulator, http://www.linuxfoundation.org/en/Net:Netem
26. Juszczyk, L., Dustdar, S.: Testbeds for emulating dependability issues of mobile web services. In: EMSOS. IEEE Computer Society, Los Alamitos (2010) (forthcoming)
27. Java 6 Standard Edition, http://java.sun.com/javase/6/
28. Schall, D., Truong, H.L., Dustdar, S.: The human-provided services framework. In: CEC/EEE, pp. 149–156. IEEE Computer Society, Los Alamitos (2008)
29. Business Process Execution Language for Web Services, http://www.oasis-open.org/committees/wsbpel/
30. Juszczyk, L., Truong, H.L., Dustdar, S.: Genesis - a framework for automatic generation and steering of testbeds of complex web services. In: ICECCS, pp. 131–140. IEEE Computer Society, Los Alamitos (2008)
31. Genesis Web site, http://www.infosys.tuwien.ac.at/prototype/Genesis/
32. Hsueh, M.C., Tsai, T.K., Iyer, R.K.: Fault injection techniques and tools. IEEE Computer 30(4), 75–82 (1997)
33. Wikipedia on Fault Injection, http://en.wikipedia.org/wiki/Fault_injection (accessed on June 13, 2010)
34. Xu, W., Offutt, J., Luo, J.: Testing web services by xml perturbation. In: ISSRE, pp. 257–266. IEEE Computer Society, Los Alamitos (2005)
35. Looker, N.: Dependability Assessment of Web Services. PhD dissertation, Durham University (2006)
36. Looker, N., Munro, M., Xu, J.: Ws-fit: A tool for dependability analysis of web services. In: COMPSAC Workshops, pp. 120–123. IEEE Computer Society, Los Alamitos (2004)
37. Bianculli, D., Binder, W., Drago, M.L.: Automated performance assessment for service-oriented middleware: a case study on bpel engines. In: WWW, pp. 141–150. ACM, New York (2010)
38. Bertolino, A., Angelis, G.D., Polini, A.: A qos test-bed generator for web services. In: Baresi, L., Fraternali, P., Houben, G.-J. (eds.) ICWE 2007. LNCS, vol. 4607, pp. 17–31. Springer, Heidelberg (2007)
39. Bertolino, A., Angelis, G.D., Frantzen, L., Polini, A.: Model-based generation of testbeds for web services. In: Suzuki, K., Higashino, T., Ulrich, A., Hasegawa, T. (eds.) TestCom/FATES 2008. LNCS, vol. 5047, pp. 266–282. Springer, Heidelberg (2008)
40. WS-Agreement, http://www.ogf.org/documents/GFD.107.pdf

Abstracting and Applying Business Modeling Patterns from RosettaNet[*]

Pankaj R. Telang[1,2] and Munindar P. Singh[2]

[1] Cisco Systems Inc., Research Triangle Park, NC 27709, USA
prtelang@ncsu.edu
[2] North Carolina State University, Raleigh, NC 27695-8206, USA
singh@ncsu.edu

Abstract. RosettaNet is a leading industry effort that creates standards for business interactions among the participants in a supply chain. The RosettaNet standard defines over 100 Partner Interface Processes (PIPs) through which the participants can exchange business documents necessary to enact a supply chain. However, each PIP specifies the business interactions at a syntactic level, but fails to capture the business meaning of the interactions to which they apply.

In contrast, this paper takes as its point of departure a commitment-based approach for business modeling that gives central position to interactions captured in terms of their meaning. This paper defines commitment-based business patterns abstracted from RosettaNet PIPs. Doing so yields models that are clearer, more flexible to changing requirements, and potentially enacted through multiple operationalizations. This paper validates the patterns by applying them to model the Order-to-Cash business process from the RosettaNet eBusiness Process Scenario Library.

1 Introduction

The intense competition in the global economy compels organizations to provide high-quality products and services at an attractive price. It forces organizations to innovate in how they define and deliver their services by identifying context-aware processes and activities, and operationalizing them flexibly, including by outsourcing them to other organizations that specialize in executing those processes. Important examples of such processes include human resources, workplace management, payroll, call centers, and IT infrastructure administration. By outsourcing such processes, an organization may reduce operational expenses, and at the same time gain access to any specialized resources it needs. Such outsourcing results in a network of organizations who engage in a complex set of service interactions.

RosettaNet [16], a leading industry effort, creates standards for business interactions. The RosettaNet consortium consists of over 500 organizations of various sizes, and from various industry sectors including electronics manufacturing from which domain RosettaNet began. These organizations use elements of the RosettaNet standard, named Partner Interface Processes (PIPs), to transact business that is worth billions of dollars.

---

[*] We thank the anonymous reviewers for helpful comments.

P.P. Maglio et al. (Eds.): ICSOC 2010, LNCS 6470, pp. 426–440, 2010.

A PIP specifies two-party interactions for some specific business purpose. For example, a buyer requests a quote from a seller using PIP 3A1, and a seller requests financing from a financing processor, on behalf of the buyer, using PIP 3C2. A PIP specification includes a natural language document that informally describes the purpose of the PIP, any underlying assumptions, the intended outcome of executing the PIP, and the message structures as XML DTD or XML Schema.

RosettaNet PIPs specify the business interactions well at a syntactic level, but they fail to capture the business meanings of those interactions. For example, in PIP 3A1, a buyer sends a request for quote to a seller, and the seller responds with either a quote or a referral. RosettaNet leaves important business details unspecified. If the seller responds with a quote, does the seller commit to the buyer to selling the goods at the quoted price? As an analogy, consider the price for a book you read on an online bookseller's (e.g., Amazon's) page versus the price you read for a stock on an online stock broker's (e.g., Ameritrade's) page. You can normally buy the book but not the stock for the quoted price, meaning that Amazon commits but Ameritrade doesn't. Likewise, does the buyer's acknowledging the quote commit it to buying the goods at the quoted price?

Thus, 3A1 and other RosettaNet PIPs leave such important questions regarding the business meanings of the interactions to human interpretation. Each group of analysts and developers working in the partner organizations would negotiate such considerations between themselves, but doing so has the effect of introducing idiosyncratic constraints through which the partners become inadvertently tightly coupled. This reduces their prospects for service innovation.

In previous work [22,24], we present a (1) high-level *business metamodel* to capture models that describe, purely in terms of business meaning, how cross-organizational service engagements are carried out and (2) a method based on temporal logic model checking [7] to establish that a particular operationalization satisfies a specified business model. This paper uses the business metamodel to abstract business *patterns* from the RosettaNet PIPs, and outlines a methodology for applying such patterns to develop business models of specific service encounters based on legacy models, such as based on activity models. The patterns developed here respect our previous metamodel and consequently can be used as a basis for model checking, as in our recent work [24].

Note that the patterns we propose are not operational patterns such as the well-known enterprise integration patterns [10] or workflow patterns [18]. Such operational patterns are useful for developing implementations of processes but would not address the challenge of encoding the business meaning that we pursue in this paper. In particular, developing operational patterns for the RosettaNet PIPs might offer implementation best practices but would not answer the questions of the type we ask above: who is committed to whom, for what, and when? Instead our patterns are high-level patterns that specify the essence of a business interaction, and may potentially map to multiple operational patterns depending upon other criteria.

There are two key motivations in abstracting commitment-based patterns from RosettaNet PIPs. First, since the patterns are at a business level, business analysts can easily understand and compose them to develop a desired business model. Second, a model composed from these patterns serves as a formal specification that can be used to verify an operational model defined in any technical standard, such as sequence diagrams [24]. Organizations frequently migrate their business process implementations to newer technologies to benefit from the improvements those technologies offer. In such cases of technology migration, the high-level formal specification provides a basis for establishing the correctness of the new implementation.

Contributions. The main contribution of this paper is business patterns abstracted from a key subset of the RosettaNet PIPs. Additionally, it outlines a simple methodology for applying the patterns to a real-life business scenario. The paper evaluates its contributions via a case study using the Order to Cash process, which has been addressed by conventional approaches—in particular, by the RosettaNet consortium using conventional means—yielding a ready basis for comparison.

Organization. Section 2 provides the necessary background on the RosettaNet PIP standard and introduces our business metamodel. Section 3 presents business patterns for a subset of the RosettaNet PIPs. Section 4 applies the patterns to model the Order-to-Cash scenario. Section 5 concludes the paper with a discussion of the related work and some future directions.

2   Background

We now review some key background on RosettaNet and on our approach.

2.1   RosettaNet

The RosettaNet standard specifies over 100 PIPs for various business processes in the eCommerce supply chain. The standard classifies the PIPs using clusters and segments. A cluster represents a major business process of the supply chain and comprises segments that represent subprocesses of the cluster's business process. Each segment contains many PIP specifications. For example, Cluster 3 represents the Order Management process. Segment A of Cluster 3 represents the subprocess Quote and Order Entry. Segment A contains PIPs such as for Request Quote (3A1), Request Shopping Cart Transfer (3A3), and Request Purchase Order (3A4). RosettaNet PIPs are commonly identified through their code names such as those in parentheses above.

The RosettaNet standard employs three views to specify a PIP: the Business Operational View (BOV), the Functional Service View (FSV), and the Implementation Framework View (IFV). The BOV informally describes the element of the business process that the PIP implements. It specifies a process flow diagram that shows the participant roles, business activities, and the flow of business messages among them. For each activity, the BOV specifies performance controls, such as the need to acknowledge receipt, the nonrepudiability of the receipt, and the timeout for the acknowledgment. For a PIP, the FSV derives from the BOV, and specifies the RosettaNet services. It specifies the message exchange sequence in a business transaction dialog, and for each message, it specifies message exchange controls. These controls include the time period within which an acknowledgment is required, the time within which a response to an action is required, and whether authorization is required for an action. The IFV specifies the formats of the messages exchanged in the PIP as XML DTDs or XML Schemas. For each message, it specifies the communication requirements such as whether it needs a digital signature or secure transport.

2.2   Business Metamodel

The following discussion is extracted from our previous work [22]. A business model specifies how business is conducted. We concern ourselves with business models that involve two or more participants. The business *participants*, abstracted as *roles*, participate in a *business relationship*. The participants create, manipulate, and satisfy *commitments* in a relationship. They execute *tasks* for each other that enable them to achieve their respective *goals*.

Three distinct phases characterize business execution. First, in the *agreement* phase, participants enter into an agreement, and *create* commitments toward each other. Second, in the *assembly* phase, the participants *delegate* or *assign* commitments to others. A participant may delegate a commitment that requires the execution of a task which is not a core competency of that participant, or due to some other economic motivation. Third, in the *enactment* phase, participants execute tasks to *satisfy* their commitments.

We now describe the concepts in our metamodel.

Agent: a computational representation of a business participant. An agent has goals [23], and executes business tasks. An agent enacts one or more roles in each business relationship in which it participates.

Role: an abstraction over agents that helps specify a business relationship. Each role specifies the commitments expected of the agents who play that role along with the tasks they must execute to function in that role.

Goal: a state of the world that an agent desires to be brought about [6]. An agent achieves a goal by executing appropriate tasks.

Task: a business activity viewed from the perspective of an agent.

Commitment: a normative relationship between a debtor and a creditor: a commitment C(DEBTOR, CREDITOR, antecedent, consequent) denotes that the DEBTOR commits to the CREDITOR for bringing about the consequent if the antecedent holds [19].

Business relationship: a set of interrelated commitments among two or more roles that describe how a business interaction is carried out among the participating roles.

Since our approach is centered on commitments, we discuss them at greater length. A commitment can be in one of the following states: *inactive*, *active*, *detached*, *pending*, *satisfied*, or *violated*. Before a commitment is created, it is inactive. A commitment may remain inactive forever if it is never created. Alternatively, if the debtor creates the commitment, it becomes active.

If the antecedent of an active commitment is brought about, then the commitment is detached. It is possible for a commitment to be created as detached—if its antecedent is true at the outset. When the consequent of a commitment, whether detached or not, is brought about, it is satisfied. After a commitment is satisfied, whether its antecedent is brought about or not has no effect.

For an active commitment, an active timeout occurs if neither its antecedent nor its consequent is brought about within the specified time period. In that case, the commitment expires. Similar to an active timeout, for a detached commitment, a detached timeout may occur if its consequent is not brought about, causing the commitment to be violated.

An active commitment functions like an obligation, but key differences include that a commitment is directed from a debtor to a creditor, arises in a (here, business) context, and may be manipulated. Manipulations of commitments are particularly important to business modeling. We discussed above how a commitment may be created (making an offer), discharged (satisfied), or canceled (withdrawing an offer). In addition, a commitment may be released (rejecting an offer), delegated to a new debtor (outsourcing), assigned (a reseller directing a shipment to the actual customer site). When a commitment is delegated or assigned, in some business patterns, we can place it in the pending state to enable it being revived if necessary [21].

3   Business Patterns from PIPs

A business pattern abstracts from operational details and, using the concepts of our business metamodel, captures the business-level interactions that underlie a PIP. We identify the business meanings that derive naturally from a PIP's description, and express them in terms of how they manipulate commitments. We now present the patterns for a selected subset of the PIPs that help us model the Order to Cash process from Section 4.

3.1   Request Quote (PIP 3A1)

Figure 1 shows the usage diagram extracted from the PIP 3A1 specification. The figure shows that a buyer desiring to purchase certain goods sends a request for a quote to a seller. If the seller is able to satisfy the requirements of the quote, the seller sends a quote response. Alternatively, if the seller is unable to satisfy the requirements of the quote request, the seller looks up and sends a referral to the buyer. In this case, the buyer at its own discretion may engage in business with the referred seller.

Figure 2 shows the business pattern we derive from PIP 3A1. Similar to the original RosettaNet specification for this PIP, the pattern specifies the two roles, the buyer and the seller. The business intent of PIP 3A1 is for the buyer to secure a price commitment from the seller for certain goods. The pattern captures this as a commitment C(SELLER, BUYER, pay, goods). Note that the PIP specifies *how* the roles interact in terms of the quote request, and the quote response. On the contrary, our pattern abstracts away from these operational details, and specifies *what* the interaction achieves in terms of the commitment that ensues from it.

At an operational level, the participants exchange messages to execute a PIP. The execution updates the state of the relevant commitments. Here, commitment C1 remains inactive if the buyer sends a request for quote, and either the seller fails to respond within certain timeout, or the seller responds with a referral. In case where the buyer requests a quote, and the seller responds with a quote, commitment C1 becomes active.

Note that PIP 3A1 requires the buyer to send a request for quote prior to the seller sending a quote. However, this is not always necessary. A seller may send an unsolicited quote as an advertisement to the buyer. Since our business pattern abstracts from operational details, it applies for the unsolicited quote scenario as well, thus offering operational flexibility beyond the traditional interpretation of the RosettaNet guidelines.

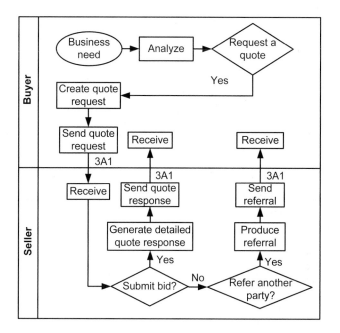

Fig. 1. Usage guideline for PIP 3A1 (verbatim from the RosettaNet specification [16])

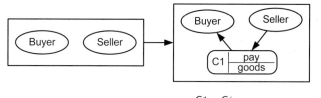

C1   C(SELLER, BUYER, pay, goods)

Fig. 2. Business pattern for PIP 3A1. Notice that the BUYER performs the task pay, and SELLER performs the task goods.

3.2   Request Purchase Order (PIP 3A4)

In PIP 3A4, a buyer sends a purchase order to a seller. The seller either accepts or rejects the order. This PIP presumes that the buyer and seller previously enacted another PIP to create a price commitment from the seller to the buyer. Figure 3 shows the business pattern for PIP 3A4. Similar to the original RosettaNet specification for this PIP, the pattern contains two roles: the buyer and the seller. The pattern presumes that a commitment C1 = C(SELLER, BUYER, pay, goods) exists from the seller to the buyer to sell the goods for certain price. In this pattern, the buyer commits to the seller to pay if the seller ships the goods. The pattern models this as the commitment C2 = C(BUYER, SELLER, goods, pay).

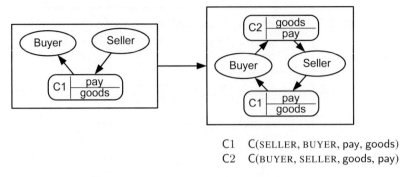

C1   C(SELLER, BUYER, pay, goods)
C2   C(BUYER, SELLER, goods, pay)

Fig. 3. Business pattern for PIP 3A4. Notice that the BUYER performs the task pay, and SELLER performs the task goods.

Table 1 shows the states of the commitments for some of the possible executions of PIP 3A4. Commitment C2 is not created and remains inactive if the buyer sends an order, and the timeout occurs. Further, in case where the buyer sends an order, and the seller rejects the order, the seller cancels its commitment C1 and thus C1 becomes inactive. When the buyer sends an order, and the seller accepts the order, commitment C2 is created, thereby making it active.

Table 1. Commitment state progression in alternative PIP 3A4 executions

Execution	Commitment State	
	C1	C2
sendOrder, timeout	Active	Inactive
sendOrder, rejectOrder	Inactive	Inactive
sendOrder, acceptOrder	Active	Active

3.3   Request Purchase Order Change (PIP 3A8)

A buyer may use PIP 3A8 to request a change to an order. This PIP presumes that the buyer and the seller have already negotiated, the buyer sent an order to the seller, and the seller accepted the order. The business pattern from Figure 3 models the precondition for this pattern. This pattern updates the antecedent and the consequent of commitments C1 and C2, and does not introduce any new commitments. Since the pattern is similar to the pattern from Figure 3, and to save space, we omit the details.

3.4   Request Shipping Order (PIP 3B12)

In this PIP, a shipper sends a shipping order to a shipping provider. The shipping provider either accepts or rejects the order. The shipper is the participant that sells goods to a customer, and employs the shipping provider for shipping the goods to the customer. Figure 4 shows the business pattern we abstract from this PIP. This PIP presumes that the shipper is committed to the customer to shipping the goods, as modeled by C1. The shipper outsources this commitment to a shipping provider. C4 is the outsourced commitment that models the shipping provider's commitment to the customer to ship the goods. It is unconditional (detached) since its antecedent is true ($\top$). To set up the outsourcing, the shipper and the shipping provider create commitments C2 and C3. In C2, the shipper commits to the shipping provider to paying if the shipping provider creates the outsourced commitment C4. Notice that commitment C3 is the converse of C2. We term such commitments *reciprocal* commitments; they arise often in practice.

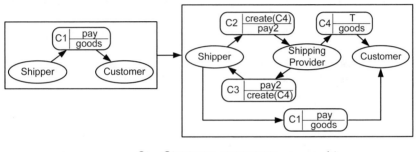

C1   C(SHIPPER, CUSTOMER, pay, goods)
C2   C(SHIPPER, SHIPPING PROVIDER, create(C4), pay2)
C3   C(SHIPPING PROVIDER, SHIPPER, pay2, create(C4))
C4   C(SHIPPING PROVIDER, CUSTOMER, $\top$, goods)

Fig. 4. Business pattern for PIP 3B12. Notice that the CUSTOMER performs task pay, SHIPPER performs pay2 and goods, and SHIPPING PROVIDER performs goods

Table 2 shows the progression of commitments corresponding to the possible executions of the PIP. In the case where the shipper sends a shipping order to the shipping provider, and either the timeout occurs or the shipping provider rejects the order, commitments C2, C3, and C4 remain inactive. When the shipping provider accepts a shipping order sent by a shipper, then the commitment C4 becomes active, commitment C3 becomes satisfied, and commitment C2 detaches. The original commitment C1 from the shipper to the customer becomes pending, since the outsourced commitment C4 is now

Table 2. Commitment state progression in alternative PIP 3B12 executions

Execution	Commitment State			
	C1	C2	C3	C4
sendShippingOrder, timeout	Active	Inactive	Inactive	Inactive
sendShippingOrder, rejectShippingOrder	Active	Inactive	Inactive	Inactive
sendShippingOrder, acceptShippingOrder	Pending	Detached	Satisfied	Active

active. Later, if the shipping provider fails to satisfy commitment C4, the original commitment C1 is reactivated. In that case, the shipper may engage with another shipping provider to bring about the shipping of the goods.

3.5   Notify of Advance Shipment (PIP 3B2) and Notify of Remittance Advice (PIP 3C6)

Using PIP 3B2, a shipper notifies a receiver about a shipment. This PIP presumes that the shipper and the receiver have negotiated, and agreed to exchanging goods for payment. At a business level, commitment C1 = C(SHIPPER, RECEIVER, pay, goods), and the commitment C2 = C(RECEIVER, SHIPPER, goods, pay) may be active prior to the shipper sending PIP 3B2. By executing this PIP, shipper satisfies commitment C1, and detaches commitment C2.

A buyer sends a remittance advice to a seller using PIP 3C6. Similar to PIP 3B2, this PIP presumes that the buyer and the seller earlier agreed to exchanging goods for payment. At a business level, commitment C1 = C(SELLER, BUYER, pay, goods), and commitment C2 = C(BUYER, SELLER, goods, pay) may be active prior to the buyer sending PIP 3C6. By executing this PIP, the buyer satisfies commitment C2, and detaches commitment C1.

3.6   Distribute Inventory Report (PIP 4C1), Notify of Shipment Receipt (PIP 4B2), and Notify of Invoice (PIP 3C3)

Using PIP 4C1, an inventory owner reports the inventory status to an inventory information user. We view this PIP as merely supporting information exchange between the participants. At a business level, such a PIP does not create or manipulate any commitments by either party to perform a tangible task for the other. In principle, we can create commitments for such notifications as well if necessary, such as Xing et al. [25] have done, but for simplicity we do not do so in this paper. Similarly, we view PIPs 4B2 and 3C3 as information exchange, and they do not create or manipulate any commitments.

4   Evaluation: Order to Cash Process

This section applies the above business patterns to model the Extended Order to Cash process, which is specified as an important scenario in the RosettaNet eBusiness Process Scenario Library [17].

Figure 5 shows the Order-to-Cash business process scenario. The participants of this process are a supplier, a customer, and a shipper. The customer orders products from the supplier. Later, the customer may request a change to the order. The supplier engages a shipper for shipping the goods to the customer. Additionally, the shipper periodically sends an inventory report to the supplier. Prior to shipping the goods, the shipper notifies the customer. The customer notifies the supplier upon receiving the goods. Subsequently, the supplier sends an invoice to the customer. The customer validates the invoice, and thereafter sends a remittance advice to the supplier. Figure 5 shows the RosettaNet PIPs that the participants employ for the above interactions.

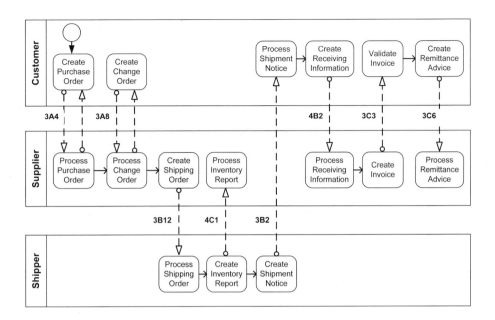

Fig. 5. The Order to Cash business process (verbatim from RosettaNet documentation [17])

We propose a simple bottom-up methodology to develop a business model for this scenario. In this methodology, we begin with a process flow diagram, such as that based on RosettaNet PIPs. The flow specifies the participating roles as swim lanes, and the interactions between the participants in terms of the PIPs that they execute. The methodology progressively composes the business patterns abstracted from the PIPs. The roles in the patterns are substituted by the corresponding roles in the modeled scenario. Further, the commitment labels in the composed patterns are updated to prevent spurious identification of distinct commitments. This methodology considers only those PIPs that pertain to the agreement and the assembly phase, that is, the PIPs that introduce new commitments.

Figure 6 applies the above methodology to the Order-to-Cash process, as described in Figure 5. Step 1 introduces the primary participant roles: the customer and the supplier. Notice that PIP 3A4 presumes that the buyer has previously secured a price commitment from the seller using a PIP such as PIP 3A1. However, the traditionally specified flow in Figure 5 fails to show such an interaction. Step 2 applies the business pattern of PIP 3A1, which introduces commitment C2 into the model. We substitute the buyer role with the customer role, and the seller role with the supplier role. Step 3 applies the business pattern of PIP 3A4, which introduces commitment C1. Step 4 applies the business pattern of PIP 3B12, and introduces commitments C3, C4, and C5 into the model. This step substitutes the pattern roles shipper, shipping provider, and customer with the scenario roles supplier, shipper, and customer, respectively. Since the remaining PIPs in the process flow do not pertain to the agreement or the assembly phases, the methodology stops here.

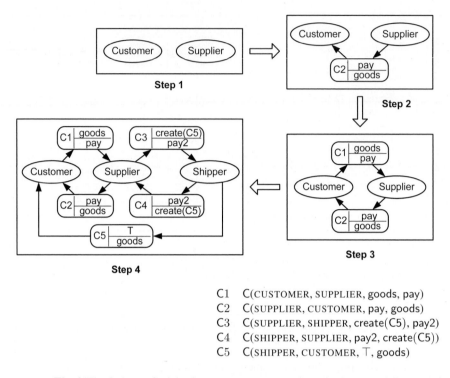

C1   C(CUSTOMER, SUPPLIER, goods, pay)
C2   C(SUPPLIER, CUSTOMER, pay, goods)
C3   C(SUPPLIER, SHIPPER, create(C5), pay2)
C4   C(SHIPPER, SUPPLIER, pay2, create(C5))
C5   C(SHIPPER, CUSTOMER, ⊤, goods)

Fig. 6. The Order-to-Cash business process expressed as a business model

The model in Figure 5 specifies the messages, in the form of PIPs, that the participants exchange and the temporal ordering of those messages. In this model, a participant complies with the model only if it exchanges messages in the prespecified temporal order. Such an operational restriction limits the flexibility that the participants have in executing the business. For example, the operational model mandates that the customer pays (3C6) only after receiving the shipment (3B2) and the invoice (3C3). At a business level, such a restriction may not be appropriate: e.g., for tax purposes, a customer may wish to pay prior to receiving the shipment.

Instead of imperatively specifying how the participants conduct business in terms of their messages and orderings, the business model in Figure 6 declaratively specifies how the business executes in terms of commitments. A participant complies with the business model if it satisfies all the detached commitments of which it is a debtor. Consider commitment C1(CUSTOMER, SUPPLIER, goods, pay). As per the operational semantics of a commitment, a customer can pay either before or after receiving the goods, thus benefiting from flexibility. A customer violates this commitment only if the supplier ships the goods, and the customer never pays.

Unlike RosettaNet's PIP-based flow model, our business model is based on the notion of commitments with a declarative semantics. A business model can formally detect if a given business execution is complete. An execution is complete if it leaves no commitments in detached state. Consider Table 3, which shows the commitment

Table 3. Commitment state progression (top to bottom) in the Order-to-Cash business process

PIP	C1	C2	C3	C4	C5
3A4 (sendOrder, acceptOrder)	Active	Active	Inactive	Inactive	Inactive
3A8 (sendChgOrder, acceptChgOrder)	Active	Active	Inactive	Inactive	Inactive
3B12 (sendShipOrder, acceptShipOrder)	Active	Detached	Satisfied	Detached	
4C1 (sendInventory)	Active	Active	Detached	Satisfied	Detached
3B2 (notifyShip)	Satisfied	Detached	Detached	Satisfied	Satisfied
4B2 (notifyGoodsReceipt)	Satisfied	Detached	Detached	Satisfied	Satisfied
3C3 (sendInvoice)	Satisfied	Detached	Detached	Satisfied	Satisfied
3C6 (sendRemitAdvice)	Satisfied	Satisfied	**Detached**	Satisfied	Satisfied

progression corresponding to the process flow of Figure 5. In the end, the process flow execution leaves commitment C3 in a detached state. That is, the shipper commits to shipping the goods, but is never paid by the supplier. This means that the flow shown in Figure 5 is incomplete. It lacks a PIP that enables the supplier to pay the shipper.

At runtime, a participant may violate a commitment. In such a case, a pattern that creates a penalty commitment [13] may apply. For example, if the supplier ships the goods but the customer fails to pay $10 within 15 days to the supplier, that is, the customer violates commitment C1, then the model can activate a new penalty commitment for the customer to pay $15 within 30 days to the supplier.

5 Discussion

This paper presents business patterns abstracted from a small subset of the RosettaNet PIPs. It outlines a simple methodology to apply these patterns to a real-life business scenario. The paper highlights the flexibility that our commitment-based model offers. For example, the business pattern for the Request Quote PIP 3A1 applies to the unsolicited quote scenario as well. The paper shows how our model detects incomplete executions. Our model allows several alternative executions so long as the execution leaves no commitments in the detached state.

RosettaNet PIPs can be divided into two broad categories: PIPs that create or manipulate commitments, and PIPs that merely enable the participants to exchange information. Section 3 describes how we abstract patterns from the PIPs that create or manipulate commitments. We can naturally expand our set of patterns to include PIPs used for information exchange, e.g., as described by Xing et al. [25], which would be suitable for capturing the PIPs focused on notifications. With this expansion, our approach will model all of the RosettaNet PIPs.

5.1 Related Work

Traditional business process modeling approaches, and several related industry standards, are based on low-level concepts of data, and control flows. For example, BPMN

[13] is a leading standard that expresses business processes in terms of sequence flow, and message flow. Such specifications do not capture the business meaning of the interactions, which is better described in terms of how the participants create and manipulate their commitments. Since traditional models ignore business intent of interactions, they over-constrain business behavior by mandating the exchange of a predetermined sequence of messages.

Existing works that aim at creating a catalog of reusable patterns for business interactions, such as the patterns that Zdun et al. [26] propose, concentrate on low-level abstractions. Although they are valuable for characterizing best practices of operationalizations, they do not specify the business relationships between the participants. It would be interesting to combine the patterns from this paper founded on the business relationships with Zdun et al.'s and other such approaches.

Singh et al. [21] propose a set of commitment patterns for business service interactions. They describe a pattern using a statechart that shows relevant elements of the life cycles of the commitments involved. In contrast, this paper describes patterns using a graphical language based on our business metamodel, which functions at a higher level of abstraction than statecharts, and indicates the design-time business relationships among the parties. Our graphical language emphasizes the roles and tasks in addition to showing the commitments. Singh et al. additionally outline a graphical notation based on business relationships: our approach can be thought of as applying in the same spirit, though offering additional refinement in terms of business relationships.

Nitto et al. [12] agree with us that systems in open environments need to be highly dynamic and self-adaptive. Toward that end, they identify the need for natural, high-level design abstractions for modeling such systems. Our research aims at developing such abstractions while satisfying the need for formalization. This paper extracts business patterns from RosettaNet PIPs in terms of the high-level abstractions from our business metamodel.

Kotinurmi et al. [11] and Haller et al. [8] incorporate semantics at the lower-level of data in RosettaNet PIPs. They develop an ontology using the Web Service Modeling Language (WSML) for the PIP payloads and choreographies. In contrast, our work identifies the business-level meaning of the PIPs in terms of the commitments.

Hofreiter et al. [9] present UN/CEFACT's methodology UMM for modeling global choreographies, that is, the business interactions realized by B2B scenarios. Similar to our approach, UMM intends to specify a choreography at a business level, independently of the underlying implementation technology. UMM's business domain view and business requirements view can benefit from our business metamodel by naturally modeling the collaborations in terms of commitments.

Redding et al. [15] propose an artifact-centric approach for flexible business process modeling called FlexConnect. This approach models a process as communicating state machines of the relevant business objects. In contrast, our approach models a business scenario more naturally in terms of business relationships founded upon commitments.

Work on agent-oriented approaches for services is also relevant here. We mentioned the notion of goals above. Although goals are not central to this paper, they are important in understanding why agents, i.e., independent parties, participate in a business interaction. At the design level, the work on Tropos [5] is relevant. At the implementation level, approaches such as Jadex [14] and others for agent programming [4] are crucial. It would be important to relate our approach to such works. With respect to design, we have taken some preliminary steps [23]. With respect to enactments, Avali and Huhns [2] show how to relate commitments to agents who reason based on representations such as beliefs, desires, and intentions.

Research on obligations, norms, and other deontic concepts is relevant here. Section 2.2 compares commitments with obligations. Other normative concepts, such as permissions and prohibitions, can be useful in describing high-level relationships among autonomous parties [19]. Although they are not as central to business transactions as commitments, it would be worth expanding our approach to accommodate them.

Research on temporal logic for representation and reasoning [7] is also relevant. Most temporal approaches for describing processes, however, apply at a lower level of abstraction [20,1]. Our recent effort [24] shows how to express a business model in a temporal language for model checking sequence diagrams. Baldoni et al. [3] draw deeper connections between commitments and time, which it would be interesting to synthesize with this paper.

5.2   Future Directions

This work opens up several interesting directions. Of these, we are pursuing the development of formal techniques that involve formalizing our business patterns so as to verify the compliance of a low-level operational model with respect to a specified business model. We expect also to develop a catalog of well-defined reusable patterns for business modeling, including those for notifications.

The methodology outlined above is a good start on an approach for developing business models based on traditional models. However, a more extensive and complete methodology to specify business models in high-level terms would also be crucial to the greater success of this effort. We hope to pursue such a methodology in future work.

References

1. van der Aalst, W.M.P., Pesic, M.: DecSerFlow: Towards a truly declarative service flow language. In: Bravetti, M., Núñez, M., Zavattaro, G. (eds.) WS-FM 2006. LNCS, vol. 4184, pp. 1–23. Springer, Heidelberg (2006)
2. Avali, V.R., Huhns, M.N.: Commitment-based multiagent decision making. In: Klusch, M., Pěchouček, M., Polleres, A. (eds.) CIA 2008. LNCS (LNAI), vol. 5180, pp. 249–263. Springer, Heidelberg (2008)
3. Baldoni, M., Baroglio, C., Marengo, E.: Commitment-based protocols with behavioral rules and correctness properties of MAS. In: Proc. Intl. Wkshp. Declarative Agent Languages and Technologies (DALT), pp. 66–83 (2010)
4. Bordini, R.H., Dastani, M., Dix, J., Fallah-Seghrouchni, A.E. (eds.): Multi-Agent Programming: Languages, Platforms and Applications. Springer, Heidelberg (2005)
5. Bresciani, P., Perini, A., Giorgini, P., Giunchiglia, F., Mylopoulos, J.: Tropos: An agent-oriented software development methodology. Autonomous Agents and Multi-Agent Systems 8(3), 203–236 (2004)
6. BRG: The business motivation model (2007)
7. Clarke, E.M., Grumberg, O., Peled, D.A.: Model Checking. MIT Press, Cambridge (1999)

8. Haller, A., Kotinurmi, P., Vitvar, T., Oren, E.: Handling heterogeneity in RosettaNet messages. In: Proc. 22nd ACM Symposium on Applied Computing, pp. 1368–1374 (2007)
9. Hofreiter, B., Huemer, C., Liegl, P., Schuster, R., Zapletal, M.: UN/CEFACT's Modeling Methodology (UMM): A UML Profile for B2B e-Commerce. In: Proc. 2nd Intl. Wkshp. Best Practices of UML (ER), pp. 19–31 (2006)
10. Hohpe, G., Woolf, B.: Enterprise Integration Patterns. Addison-Wesley, Boston (2004)
11. Kotinurmi, P., Vitvar, T.: Adding semantics to RosettaNet specifications. In: Proc. 15th Intl. Conf. World Wide Web, pp. 1059–1060 (2006)
12. Nitto, E.D., Ghezzi, C., Metzger, A., Papazoglou, M.P., Pohl, K.: A journey to highly dynamic, self-adaptive service-based applications. Automated Software Engineering 15(3-4), 313–341 (2008)
13. OMG: Business process management initiative (August 2009), http://bpmn.org/
14. Pokahr, A., Braubach, L., Lamersdorf, W.: Jadex: A BDI reasoning engine. In: [4], pp. 149–174 (2005)
15. Redding, G., Dumas, M., ter Hofstede, A.H.M., Iordachescu, A.: Modelling Flexible Processes with Business Objects. In: Proc. IEEE Conf. Comm. & Ent. Comp, pp. 41–48 (2009)
16. RosettaNet: Overview: Clusters, Segments, and PIPs (2008), http://www.rosettanet.org
17. RosettaNet: Extended order to cash (2010), http://www.rosettanet.org/
18. Russell, N., ter Hofstede, A.H.M., van der Aalst, W.M.P., Mulyar, N.: Workflow control-flow patterns: A revised view. Tech. rep., BPMcenter.org (2006)
19. Singh, M.P.: An ontology for commitments in multiagent systems: Toward a unification of normative concepts. Artificial Intelligence and Law 7(1), 97–113 (1999)
20. Singh, M.P.: Distributed enactment of multiagent workflows: Temporal logic for service composition. In: Proc. 2nd Intl. Joint Conf. Autonomous Agents and MultiAgent Systems (AAMAS), pp. 907–914 (July 2003)
21. Singh, M.P., Chopra, A.K., Desai, N.: Commitment-based service-oriented architecture. IEEE Computer 42(11), 72–79 (2009)
22. Telang, P.R., Singh, M.P.: Business modeling via commitments. In: Kowalczyk, R., Vo, Q.B., Maamar, Z., Huhns, M. (eds.) SOCASE 2009. LNCS, vol. 5907, pp. 111–125. Springer, Heidelberg (2009)
23. Telang, P.R., Singh, M.P.: Enhancing Tropos with commitments. In: Borgida, A.T., Chaudhri, V.K., Giorgini, P., Yu, E.S. (eds.) Conceptual Modeling: Foundations and Applications. LNCS, vol. 5600, pp. 417–435. Springer, Heidelberg (2009)
24. Telang, P.R., Singh, M.P.: Specifying and verifying cross-organizational business models: An agent-oriented approach. TR 12, North Carolina State University (May 2010)
25. Xing, J., Wan, F., Rustogi, S.K., Singh, M.P.: A commitment-based approach for business process interoperation. IEICE Trans. Info. & Syst. E84-D (10), 1324–1332 (2001)
26. Zdun, U., Hentrich, C., Dustdar, S.: Modeling process-driven and service-oriented architectures using patterns and pattern primitives. ACM Trans. Web 1(3), 14 (2007)

Heuristic Approaches for QoS-Based Service Selection

Diana Comes, Harun Baraki, Roland Reichle, Michael Zapf, and Kurt Geihs

Distributed Systems Group, University of Kassel,
Wilhelmshöher Allee 73, 34121 Kassel, Germany
{comes,baraki,reichle,zapf,geihs}@vs.uni-kassel.de

Abstract. In a Service Oriented Architecture (SOA) business processes are commonly implemented as orchestrations of web services, using the Web Services Business Process Execution Language (WS-BPEL). Business processes not only have to provide the required functionality, they also need to comply with certain Quality-of-Service (QoS) constraints which are part of a service-level agreement between the service provider and the client. Different service providers may offer services with the same functionality but different QoS properties, and clients can select from a large number of service offerings. However, choosing an optimal collection of services for the composition is known to be an NP-hard problem.

We present two different approaches for the selection of services within orchestrations required to satisfy certain QoS requirements. We developed two algorithms, OPTIM_HWeight and OPTIM_PRO, which perform a heuristic search on the candidate services. The OPTIM_HWeight algorithm is based on weight factors and the OPTIM_PRO algorithm is based on priority factors. We evaluate and compare the two algorithms with each other and also with a genetic algorithm.

1   Introduction

Web Services constitute the most spreaded technology that overcomes interoperability issues between applications from different partners using the Internet as the underlined infrastructure. In order to be trusted by their clients, services have to guarantee the fulfillment of the required functionality and also of the expected non-functional properties, known as Quality of Service (QoS). Service clients and providers come to an agreement where providers assure that the service complies with the promised service levels. Web Services from different partners can be composed to a service orchestration and realize a complex business process. The de facto standard for executing business processes is the *Web Services Business Process Execution Language* (WS-BPEL) [7] which specifies how service orchestrations are built. It describes how the interaction between web services takes place in order to realize a business process. The business workflow is described via activities triggered in the order defined within the BPEL description file. The language offers standard activities for specifying control structures (like

P.P. Maglio et al. (Eds.): ICSOC 2010, LNCS 6470, pp. 441–455, 2010.

while, repeatUntil, foreach activities), conditional structures (like *if, switch*) and basic activities like *invoke* for calling a web service or the *assign* activity for assigning values to variables. A process may start with the arrival of a message (like with a *receive* or a *pick* activity). It may send an answer back to the requestor with a *reply* activity. Activities may be grouped inside a *sequence* (sequential invocation) or a *flow* (parallel invocation) structure.

While WS-BPEL specifies the workflow and functionality of a business process, Quality of Service is not part of the BPEL specification and so needs to be treated separately. In this paper we address QoS properties like response time, availability, reliability, and cost. The malfunction of one single service might cause the failure of the entire process. Since enterprises offer services having the same functionality but at different QoS levels, the QoS properties become the key differentiator between multiple services. Therefore, other service offerings need to be searched in the service registry and bound to the service process dynamically at runtime, which is where the selection algorithm comes into play. The goal of the selection algorithm is to find an optimal choice of services that realize the service orchestration. The orchestration needs to satisfy certain QoS constraints and to optimize an objective function which depends on the QoS properties of the involved services. However, as soon as we have to optimize for several independent QoS properties, finding the optimal combination from all possible service candidates that might realize the service orchestration leads to an NP-hard problem [11,9].

In this paper, we propose two heuristic algorithms for the selection of services in service orchestrations. The *OPTIM_HWeight* algorithm is based on weight factors and the *OPTIM_PRO* algorithm considers priority factors for performing the service search. The OPTIM_HWeight is an extension of the OPTIM_S algorithm utilizing a specific heuristic function $f_{HWeight}$. The OPTIM_S algorithm can perform a heuristic search, a local, and a global (brute-force) search by only modifying its parameters. We evaluate and compare the algorithms OPTIM_HWeight and OPTIM_PRO with each other and also with the genetic algorithm proposed by [2] which we call GA_CAN. Our experiments revealed that our OPTIM_PRO and OPTIM_HWeight algorithms perform better than the genetic algorithm GA_CAN and reach optimization values at least as good as GA_CAN. Our OPTIM_PRO algorithm is the fastest of the presented algorithms.

The paper is structured as follows: In Section 2 we describe the selection algorithms OPTIM_S, OPTIM_HWeight, OPTIM_PRO and GA_CAN. Section 3 describes the experiments we run in order to compare the algorithms with each other and measure their performance and results. In Section 4 we compare our heuristic approaches to the related works.

2   Service Selection Algorithms

A service orchestration is a composition of multiple services that are required in order to execute the orchestration. An *abstract service* represents the functionality of the desired service and we assume that there are several *concrete services (candidates)* that provide this functionality but have different QoS properties. The QoS of the entire process is computed from the QoS of the services that build up the service composition. Finding the optimal solution means selecting those services that satisfy the QoS requirements, including the QoS constraints, and optimizing an objective function for the entire orchestration. Assuming that we have n abstract services and each abstract service may have m concrete service realizations, we get a total of m^n possible combinations. As we have to assume that all QoS dimensions are independent, the whole optimization problem turns out to be NP-hard [11,9].

We define the set S_a that contains the set of abstract services, the set S_c containing the concrete services and the set QD of QoS dimensions. The set V represents the set of service variants, meaning the possible combinations of service candidates. The vector $Q = (a, l, r, c) \in \mathbb{R}^4$ contains the QoS values of the QoS dimensions *availability* (a), *reliability* (l), *response time* (r), and *cost* (c) computed for the service variants $v \subseteq V$. As an example we consider the following QoS requirements for the orchestration:

$$f_{obj}(Q) = \frac{k_1 \cdot a + k_2 \cdot l}{k_3 \cdot r + k_4 \cdot c} \tag{1}$$

$$\text{maximize } f_{obj}(Q) \; \forall v \subseteq \mathbb{V} \text{ realizing the service orchestration} \tag{2}$$

$$a > b_1, \; l > b_2, \; r < b_3, \; c < b_4, \text{where } b_i \in \mathbb{R} \tag{3}$$

The factors k_i, $i = 1 \dots 4$ represent the weights for the $q \in QD$ variables depending on the user's preferences and b_i represent the bounds for the q variables. Within our approaches we address also non-linear objective functions, aggregation functions and constraints.

We developed the heuristic algorithms OPTIM_HWeight and OPTIM_PRO for the service selection problem. First, we will describe the tasks which are common for all our algorithms: (a) QoS aggregation and constraint checking, (b) creating the BPEL tree, and then we will present the specifics of the algorithms.

(a) QoS aggregation and constraint checking

The QoS of the service compositions depends on the QoS values of the services that build up the composition. The QoS value for a complex node (with children) is computed by the aggregation functions shown in table 1 (taken from [2]). The table is not complete but it provides examples for the structured activities *sequence, switch, flow* and *loop*. The aggregation formulas for the *switch* activity take into account the execution probabilities of the different branches to calculate the expected value for the quality dimensions. Still, the QoS constraints need to be fulfilled for every execution path, so for the *switch* activity we added an extra column (the last one) in the table where we consider the worst case of the QoS values over all of the branches of the *switch*. When we check the QoS constraints we use the aggregation formulas of the table (columns 2-4) and for the switch we take the formulas from the last column (*switch worst*). The QoS values of the candidate services are normalized to map the values onto the $[0, 1]$ interval. This is done with the formula adopted from [3]:

Table 1. Aggregation Functions

QoS Dimension	sequence	flow	loop	switch	switch worst
response time(r)	$\sum_{i=1}^{n} r_i$	$\max_{i\in 1..n}\{r_i\}$	$k \cdot r$	$\sum_{i=1}^{n} p_i \cdot r_i$	$\max_{i\in 1..n}\{r_i\}$
cost (c)	$\sum_{i=1}^{n} c_i$	$\sum_{i=1}^{n} c_i$	$k \cdot c$	$\sum_{i=1}^{n} p_i \cdot c_i$	$\max_{i\in 1..n}\{c_i\}$
availability (a)	$\prod_{i=1}^{n} a_i$	$\prod_{i=1}^{n} a_i$	a^k	$\sum_{i=1}^{n} p_i \cdot a_i$	$\min_{i\in 1..n}\{a_i\}$
reliability (l)	$\prod_{i=1}^{n} l_i$	$\prod_{i=1}^{n} l_i$	l^k	$\sum_{i=1}^{n} p_i \cdot l_i$	$\min_{i\in 1..n}\{l_i\}$

$$q' = \begin{cases} \frac{q-q^{min}}{q^{max}-q^{min}} & \text{if} \quad q^{max} - q^{min} \neq 0; \\ 1 & \text{if} \quad q^{max} - q^{min} = 0. \end{cases} \tag{4}$$

(b) Creating the tree

Both algorithms start with *creating a tree* out of the BPEL description file. The example in Figure 1 only serves to illustrate how our algorithms find a selection for a composition with four abstract services S_A, S_B, S_C, and S_D which can be realized by different concrete services. It does not show a realistic BPEL tree as this would be too complex here. The nodes of the BPEL tree contain the activities from the BPEL description file which are relevant for the execution of the BPEL process. It does not contain nodes for `partnerLinks`, for instance. We define S, the set of *simple element types* that contains the BPEL activities (e.g. `invoke`, `assign`) which we represent as leaves in the tree. The set C of *complex element types* contain the BPEL activities (e.g. `sequence`, `while`, `switch`) which we represent as inner nodes. Each node of the tree has the same structure and contains:

- the type *node.elem* $\in S \cup C$ of the node, the references *node.parent* to the parent node and *node.children* to the child nodes,
- the set of variants *node.V* containing combinations of the service candidates (e.g. $V = \{[v_1 = (S_2, S_4)], [v_2 = (S_2, S_5)]\}$),
- the set of QoS dimensions *node.QD* (e.g. *node.QD* $= \{a, l, c, r\}$),
- the set of QoS values *node.vQ* of variant v, where $v \in node.V$,
- the set *node.VQ* for all the variants $v \in node.V$ (e.g. $VQ = \{[v_1(c = 7, r = 3)], [v_2(c = 9, r = 4)]\}$), the objective values *node.VF_{obj}* computed for all the variants $v \in node.V$ having the QoS values *node.VQ*, (The objective value of variant v is vF_{obj} and is equivalent to $f_{obj}(vQ)$, analogously we define the heuristic value $f_{Heu}(vQ)$).

After being created, the BPEL tree has to be initialized with probabilities p and iterations k obtained from the runtime monitoring of the BPEL process during multiple executions. The probability p_i appears for conditional activities like *switch* and corresponds to the probability for executing the branch i of the activity during an execution. The nodes representing a loop (e.g. *repeatUntil*,

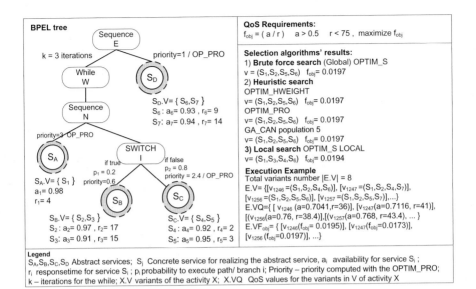

BPEL tree

k = 3 iterations — priority=1 / OP_PRO

QoS Requirements:
$f_{obj} = (a / r)$ $a > 0.5$ $r < 75$, maximize f_{obj}

Selection algorithms' results:
1) **Brute force search** (Global) OPTIM_S
v = (S_1,S_2,S_5,S_6) f_{obj}= 0.0197
2) **Heuristic search**
OPTIM_HWEIGHT
v= (S_1,S_2,S_5,S_6) f_{obj}= 0.0197
OPTIM_PRO
v= (S_1,S_2,S_5,S_6) f_{obj}= 0.0197
GA_CAN population 5
v= (S_1,S_2,S_5,S_6) f_{obj}= 0.0197
3) **Local search** OPTIM_S LOCAL
v= (S_1,S_3,S_4,S_6) f_{obj}= 0.0194

Execution Example
Total variants number |E.V| = 8
E.V= {[v_{1246} =(S_1,S_2,S_4,S_6)], [v_{1247} =(S_1,S_2,S_4,S_7)],
[v_{1256} =(S_1,S_2,S_5,S_6)], [v_{1257} =(S_1,S_2,S_5,S_7)],...}
E.VQ={[v_{1246} (a=0.7041,r=36)], [v_{1247}(a=0.7116, r=41)],
[(v_{1256}(a=0.76, r=38.4)],[(v_{1257}(a=0.768, r=43.4), ... }
E.VF$_{obj}$= { [v_{1246}(f_{obj}= 0.0195)], [v_{1247}(f_{obj}=0.0173)],
[v_{1256} (f_{obj}=0.0197)], ...}

S_D.V= { S_6,S_7 }
S_6 : a_6= 0.93 , r_6= 9
S_7: a_7= 0.94 , r_7= 14

S_A.V= { S_1 } priority=0.6
a_1= 0.98
r_1= 4

if true
p_1 = 0.2

if false
p_2 = 0.8
priority = 2.4 / OP_PRO

S_B.V= { S_2,S_3 }
S_2 : a_2= 0.97 , r_2= 17
S_3: a_3= 0.91 , r_3= 15

S_C.V= { S_4,S_5 }
S_4 : a_4= 0.92 , r_4= 2
S_5: a_5= 0.95 , r_5= 3

Legend
S_A,S_B,S_C,S_D Abstract services; S_i Concrete service for realizing the abstract service, a_i availability for service S_i ;
r_i responsetime for service S_i ; p_i probability to execute path/ branch i; Priority – priority computed with the OPTIM_PRO;
k – iterations for the while; X.V variants of the activity X; X.VQ QoS values for the variants in V of activity X

Fig. 1. Service selection example

while) receive an iteration number k that represents the average number of iterations monitored for that loop.

2.1 OPTIM_S Algorithm

Since our *OPTIM_HWeight algorithm* is an extension of our *OPTIM_S algorithm* we will first describe the OPTIM_S algorithm. We developed the *OPTIM_S algorithm* with the intention to allow for easy adaptation to the runtime environment, depending on the number of services that are available at runtime. The OPTIM_S algorithm permits different types of search (local, global, and heuristic search) for the service selection by only changing its parameters. Thus the algorithm allows for adjusting between shorter computation time of the algorithm and better solution quality. The choice of the service selection algorithm should depend on the number of services searched and available at runtime. For example, when the selection targets only few abstract services (like in a sub-orchestration) a brute-force search is sufficient. In contrast, when the search is performed for the entire process which contains many services, a suitable optimization algorithm is needed. The choice of the selection algorithm may differ between set-up time and runtime. At runtime, a quick and effective solution is usually preferred to an optimal but slow strategy. All these requirements have been considered in the development of our selection algorithms. As inputs, the algorithm receives the BPEL tree, the QoS constraints, the objective function f_{obj} to be minimized or maximized, the maximum number of selected variants (nr_v) for a node, and optionally a heuristic function f_{Heu} used within the

---

Algorithm 1: OPTIM_S(tree, qosConstraints, f_{obj}, nr_v, *optional* f_{Heu})

Input: tree- the BPEL tree ; *qosConstraints* – the QoS constraints, f_{obj} -objective function, f_{Heu} heuristic function, *nr_v* the maximal number of variants selected for a node
Output: the selected services

```
 1: Begin
 2:     initializeTree( tree) // initialize the tree nodes with probabilities (p) and iterations (k)
 3:     init(C,Sa) // initialize the set C with complex nodes and Sa with the abstract services
 4:     repeat  // traverse the tree from bottom to top
 5:         node ← treeTraverseBottomToTop(tree)
 6:         if node.elem in Sa // Sa- is an abstract service, a call to a service
 7:             node.V ← node.getConcreteServices()
 8:         else
 9:             if node.elem in C // node is a complex element with children
10:                 children ← node.children
11:                 childrenV ← { }
12:                 foreach child in children
13:                     child.VQ ← aggregateQoS(child.V)
14:                     // sort the variants with f_Heu and cut those that are too many
15:                     child.V ← sortAndCut(child.V, child.VQ, f_Heu, nr_v)
16:                     childrenV ← childrenV U child.V
17:                 endforeach
18:                 node.V ← combine(childrenV)
19:                 //compute QoS for each variant and eliminate those that don't meet QoS
20:                 foreach v in node.V
21:                     node.vQCons ←aggregateQoSCons(v) //aggregate with formulas for constraints check
22:                     if not (checkQoSConstraints(node.v, node.vQCons, qosConstraints))
23:                         node.V ←node.V \ v
24:                     endif
25:                 endforeach
26:             endif
27:         endif
28:     until node.parent = null
29:     node.VQ ← aggregateQoS(node.V)
30:     node.VFobj ← computeFobj(node.V, node.VQ, f_obj)
31:     node.V ← sort( node.V, node.VFobj) // sort the variants by the value of fobj
32:     return node.V[1]
33: End
```

Fig. 2. OPTIM_S Algorithm

selection process. The output of the algorithm will be the service selection fulfilling the QoS constraints and with the best found value for the objective function.

The basic idea of the algorithm is that for each of the nodes in the tree ($node.V$) starting with the leafs, we select only a subset of the variants of the children of this node so that the size $|node.V|$ of the variants set is at most nr_v. For each variant the QoS is computed by using the aggregation functions in Table 1. With this QoS value (vQ) the heuristic value is computed by applying the heuristic function ($f_{Heu}(vQ)$). The variants are sorted according to this heuristic value and those variants with better values are selected and propagated to the parent node. An example for a heuristic function is the objective function itself.

The different search types *heuristic*, *local*, and *global search* can be switched by modifying the parameters of the OPTIM_S algorithm nr_v and f_{Heu}. The *global search* is a simple brute force search without any heuristic function. The algorithm is invoked by calling it with $nr\_v = \infty$ (in Java we take Integer.MAX_VALUE). After sorting the variants on the root node with f_{obj}, the variant $node.V[1]$ will be the global optimum. This kind of search is suited when the search is performed on a small number of services. The *heuristic search* is triggered by calling the algorithm with $\infty > nr\_v \geq 2$ and a given heuristic function. The discovered solution is not necessarily the optimal solution, but a good heuristic could provide a near-optimal or even an optimal solution. The *local search* is triggered by calling the algorithm with $nr\_v = 1$ so that only one variant is selected at each node. While this is the fastest way, the solution quality is expected to be worse than from the heuristic search.

We describe the algorithm on the basis of the pseudocode (see Fig. 2). The service selection starts with traversing the tree from the bottom to its root node (line 5). We distinguish between nodes that represent a service call and complex nodes. If the node represents a call to a service, the variants of the node *node.V* are initialized with the concrete services (lines 6-7). The number nr_v represents the maximum number of variants that are selected for each node. This allows us to restrict the size of the search space considerably. For each of the non-leaf nodes in the tree, the variants are selected from the variants of the child nodes (lines 9-16) so that the number of combinations of the child variants is at most nr_v. The heuristic function helps us to select those candidates which are likely to perform better in the process (line 15). At selection time the child variants are already sorted by their heuristic values computed with f_{Heu}. Furthermore, the selected child variants are combined with their siblings (see the *combine* method in line 18) on their parent node. The QoS of the variants is computed (line 21) using the formulas in Table 1. The variants are checked against the QoS constraints and those which do not fulfill the constraints are eliminated (lines 22-23). In the final step, the variants of the root node are sorted with regard to the objective function and the variant on top of the sorted list (*node.V[1]*) represents the service selection that has won the evaluation.

2.2   OPTIM_HWeight Algorithm

The OPTIM_HWeight algorithm makes use of the OPTIM_S algorithm, providing a specific heuristic function $f_{HWeight}$ which is used to rank and sort the candidate services/variants. OPTIM_HWeight is a probabilistic iterative algorithm with the heuristic function $f_{HWeight}$ at its heart. By virtue of this function, the candidate variants are sorted at each node according to their *influence* on the overall process, ascending from the leaves to the root, and only the best rated variants are kept. The heuristic function $f_{HWeight}$ is defined for an arbitrary node N as follows:

$$f_{HWeight}(\boldsymbol{W_N}, q_N^c, q_N^s) = \boldsymbol{W_N} \cdot (\boldsymbol{q_N^c} - \boldsymbol{q_N^s}) = \nabla f_{obj} \cdot (\boldsymbol{q_N^c} - \boldsymbol{q_N^s})$$
$$= \left(\frac{\partial f_{obj}}{\partial q_1^N}, \frac{\partial f_{obj}}{\partial q_2^N}, \ldots, \frac{\partial f_{obj}}{\partial q_n^N} \right)^T \cdot (\boldsymbol{q_N^c} - \boldsymbol{q_N^s}) \quad (5)$$

with $\cdot$ being the scalar product, $\boldsymbol{q_N^s}$ the QoS vector of the current variant selection, $\boldsymbol{q_N^c}$ the QoS vector of the candidate variant, and the q_i^N being the QoS value of the node (aggregated value for complex nodes) of the ith QoS dimension. We denote the difference vector $\boldsymbol{q_{dif}} = \boldsymbol{q_N^c} - \boldsymbol{q_N^s}$. We take the gradient ∇f_{obj} computed at node N as the weight vector $\boldsymbol{W_N}$ considering the QoS values of the

```
Algorithm 2: OPTIM_HWeight(tree, qosConstraints, f_obj, nr_v, n_iter, n_steps)
 1: Procedure computeWeight(tree, variant) //computes the weights vector w for the heuristic f_HWeight
 2: begin
 3:   tree.InitToLastLeaf();
 4:   repeat  //Aggregate QoS for variant variant from the bottom to the top of the tree
 5:     node = treeTraverseBottomToTop(tree)
 6:     node.v = node.getSubVariant(variant) //get the sub-variant v of the node that coresponds to variant
 7:     node.vQ = aggregateQoS(node.v) //aggregate QoS values for v
 8:   until (node.parent == null)
 9:   repeat //propagate the QoS values from the top to the bottom of the tree and compute the weights
10:     node = treeTraverseTopToBottom(tree)
11:     foreach q in QD
12:       if(node == tree.Root)
13:         node.Weight(q) = partialDerivative(f_obj, q, node.vq);
14:       else
15:         node.Weight(q) = node.parent.Weight(q) * partialDerivative(Agg(node.parent, q), node.siblings.vq, node.vq));
16:       endif
17:     endforeach;
18:   until (node == tree.LastLeaf)
19:   return tree.Weight;
20: end;
    Procedure OPTIM_HWeight ( tree, qosConstraints, f_obj, nr_v, n_iter, n_steps)
21: begin //initialize multiple random variants, optimize with OPTIM_S, and select the best one
22:   init(v_best)
23:   for i = 1 to n_iter do
24:     v_0 = randomVariants(tree,Sc) //select a random variant from the set of concrete services
25:     tree.Weight = computeWeight(tree, v_0)
26:     v_prev = v_0;
27:     for j=1 to n_steps do//iterative improvement of weights, iterative steps of the gradient ascent
28:       f_HWeight = createFHWeight(tree.Weight, v_prev) //create the heuristic function f_HWeight
29:       v_s = OPTIM_S(tree, qosConstraints, f_obj, nr_v, f_HWeight)
30:       tree.Weight = computeWeight(tree,v_s)
31:       v_prev =v_s
32:     endfor
33:     if v_sFobj > v_bestFobj //from the found Variants select the one that optimizes fobj
34:       v_best = v_s
35:     endif
36:   endfor
37:   return v_best
38: end
```

Fig. 3. OPTIM_HWeight Algorithm

current selection. The result of the $f_{HWeight}$ function is used to deliver a score for the candidate service selection versus the current service selection; a higher value is ranked higher. The idea of this approach is essentially a *gradient ascent*. Given the current point represented by q_N^s, i.e. the QoS vector of the current selection, we calculate the gradient at that location. We try to find another variant which has "moved" from the point q_N^s in the direction of the gradient. As we have only discrete locations in our search space (the service selection variants) we can only choose another point with a minimal error. For this purpose, we compute the heuristic $f_{HWeight}$ as the scalar product between $\boldsymbol{W_N}$ and $\boldsymbol{q_{dif}}$. For the iteration we use the newly found point in the search space and retry (for n_steps).

In order to compute the derivatives for the gradient we have to consider that the objective function is a chain of aggregations, so we need to use the chain rule for partial differentiation. This can be explained by the fact that the QoS of a node in the tree is an aggregation of the QoS of its child nodes, and the QoS of each child node is again an aggregation of its child nodes, etc. For instance in Fig. 1, the tree has a root node E which has a child node W, and node W has a child node N which has a child S_A (abstract service) being a leaf. For the first quality dimension q_1 we may have the weight factor w_{S_A} computed at node S_A:

$$
w_{S_A} = \frac{\partial f_{obj}}{\partial q_1^{S_A}} = \frac{\partial f_{obj}(ag_E^{q_1}(ag_W^{q_1}(ag_N^{q_1}(q_1^{S_A}))))}{\partial q_1^{S_A}} = \frac{\partial f_{obj}}{\partial ag_E^{q_1}} \frac{\partial ag_E^{q_1}(ag_W^{q_1}(ag_N^{q_1}(q_1^{S_A})))}{\partial q_1^{S_A}}
$$
$$
= \ldots = \frac{\partial f_{obj}}{\partial ag_E^{q_1}} \frac{\partial ag_E^{q_1}}{\partial ag_W^{q_1}} \frac{\partial ag_W^{q_1}}{\partial ag_N^{q_1}} \frac{\partial ag_N^{q_1}(q_1^{S_A})}{\partial q_1^{S_A}} \tag{6}
$$

where $ag_X^{q_1}$ denotes the aggregation function for node X with regard to the QoS dimension q_1. The partial derivatives can be efficiently computed when traversing the tree top-down because we only need to reuse the last computed value at parent node and multiply the inner derivative for the current node.

In the following we explain the pseudocode of the algorithm (see Fig. 3). The weight factors of $f_{HWeight}$ differ dependent on the nodes in the tree where the heuristic is evaluated. At each node in the tree we need the partial derivatives for each QoS dimension. The weight vector $\boldsymbol{W_N}$ is computed (procedure $computeWeight$, lines 1-20) by aggregating the QoS values of a random variant v from the bottom of the tree to the top. Through backpropagation of the influence of the QoS dimensions from top to the bottom of the tree we compute the weight factors $\boldsymbol{W_N}$ for $f_{HWeight}$. This is done by calculating the partial derivatives, which requires the aggregated QoS values of the current selection as input.

$OPTIM\_HWeight$ performs two iterative processes, the external loop (lines 23-36, with n_iter iterations) and the internal loop (lines 27-32, with n_steps iterations). The internal loop can be interpreted in two different ways: (1) it implicitly performs a gradient ascent with regard to the objective function (2) it iteratively improves the weight factors $\boldsymbol{W_N}$ of the heuristic function. Starting from an initial random variant v_0, the $\boldsymbol{W_N}$ vector is computed (procedure $computeWeight$) through bottom-up aggregation of the QoS of v_0 in the tree and backpropagation of the influence of the QoS dimensions from top to the leafs of the tree. Knowing the weight factors $\boldsymbol{W_N}$ and the QoS of v_0 the heuristic function $f_{HWeight}$ can be created (line 28). The function $f_{HWeight}$ is used inside the $OPTIM\_S$ algorithm (in the $sortAndCut$ procedure, see $OPTIM\_S$ line 15) and calculates the scalar product between $\boldsymbol{W_N}$ and the difference vector $\boldsymbol{q_{dif}} = \boldsymbol{q_N^c} - \boldsymbol{q_N^{v\_0}}$, i.e. the difference of the QoS vector of the candidate variant at the actual node and the QoS vector of the current selection v_0. Now the $OPTIM\_S$ algorithm is called to find the (desired optimal) variant (v_s line 29) that optimizes the objective function. This selected variant (v_s) is considered in the next iteration step as starting variant to make a further improvement to the weights $\boldsymbol{W_N}$ and perform a further step of the gradient ascent. The computation of $\boldsymbol{W_N}$ and of the selection variant v_s starts again and the iterations continue until the n_steps iteration steps have been performed. In the external loop (line 23 - the for loop) all the steps described above are repeated n_iter times with different random variants as starting points for the inner loop. From the found variants during multiple iterations (i) the one with the best value for optimizing the objective function (lines 33-34) is finally selected.

Algorithm 3: OPTIM_PRO (tree, qosConstraints, f_{obj}, n_iter)

```
 1: Begin
 2: initializeTree( tree, p, k )  // initialize the tree nodes with probabilities (p) and iterations(k)
 3: init( root.v, C, Sa, vList)
 4: foreach node.elem in Sa // node is an abstract service
 5:     node.priority  ← computePriority(tree)  //compute priority = k * p
 6:     SaSet ← SaSet U node
 7: endforeach
 8: SaSet ← sortByPriority(SaSet , 'descendent')
 9: i ← 0
10: NEXT while (i < n_iter)
11:     i ← i + 1;
12:     foreach sa in SaSet
13:         c ← 0;  roottmp ← root
14:         foreach sc in sa.V  // sc is a concrete service that realizes the abstract service sa
15:             c ← c + 1
16:             roottmp.v(sa) ← sc //sc replaces the old candidate service of sa, in the root copy variant
17:             if (checkQoSConstraintsAggregate2 (roottmp.vQ, qosConstraints))
18:                 roottmp.vQ  ← aggregateQoS1 (roottmp.v)
19:                 roottmp.vFobj ← computeFobj (roottmp.vQ)
20:                 if (roottmp.vFobj > root.vFobj)  OR  ((i==1) AND(c==1))
21:                     //optimizing obj function OR first iteration, first candidate service
22:                     root ← roottmp
23:                 endif
24:             endif //else select the variant with the minimal distance to fulfill constraints
25:         endforeach
26:         if (root.v in vList )
27:             root.v ← chooseForAllRandomServices() //root.v receives random service candidates
28:             continue NEXT
29:         else
30:             vList ← vList U root.v   //save the root variant in the root variants list, vlist
31:         endif
32:     endforeach
33: endwhile
34: sortByFobj(vList) //sort the variants list by their objective values
35: return vList[1] //return the best variant
36: End
```

Fig. 4. OPTIM_PRO Algorithm

2.3   OPTIM_PRO Algorithm

The OPTIM_PRO heuristic algorithm calculates *priority factors* and uses the objective function to sort the variants. It is described in pseudocode in Figure 4. During monitoring of the execution, the nodes in the tree receive an iteration number k and a probability p as explained previously. Each of the nodes that represent an abstract service (Sa, lines 4-7) receive a priority as a product of k and p and the node is added to the set of abstract services $SaSet$. The *priority factor* states that those nodes which are executed more often should receive a higher priority. The algorithm proceeds with sorting the nodes from the $SaSet$ (line 8) in descendent order of the computed priorities such as the nodes with higher priorities are processed first. OPTIM_PRO is an iterative algorithm which improves the found variant (the objective value) of the root node with each iteration (lines 10-33) step. After selecting a variant for the root node in the first iteration, this variant is going to be improved during the next iterations. A copy of the root is created (*roottmp*, line 13) in order to check if the currently selected service candidate (*sc*) is an improvement to the objective function. In the root copy variant, the currently selected service candidate replaces the old service candidate. With this new service candidate value, the

QoS value of the root copy variant is aggregated ($roottmp.vQ$), checked against the constraints, and the objective function is computed ($roottmp.vFobj$). If the objective function yields a better value the root receives the value of its copy ($roottmp$), otherwise it remains the same. The variants that no longer can be improved are saved into the list $vlist$. When this is the case, the root variant receives random candidate services and the iterative process continues in the same way as described above. After reaching the maximal iteration number (n_iter), the iterative process stops. The list $vlist$ that contains the found variants is sorted due to their objective values. The first element in the list is returned as being the best variant that was found for optimizing the objective function.

2.4 GA_CAN Algorithm

In order to compare our heuristic algorithms we implemented a genetic algorithm as proposed by Canfora et al. [2]. Genetic algorithms are inspired by biology and use meta-heuristics in optimization problems. The reason why we chose this algorithm is because it can also be applied to non-linear functions and constraints, which is also our target. For more details we recommend [2]. The genome represents the service variants that realize the service orchestration and is encoded as an array. The length of the genome is equal to the number of abstract services. Each element within the array contains a reference to the list of the concrete candidate services that may realize the abstract service. The initial population is built with random individuals. The fitness of the individuals represents their utility as a solution and is computed using the fitness function defined in equation 7. It corresponds to the sum of the objective function calculated on the genome and the weighted distance $D(g)$ (multiplied with the penalty factor k_5) resulting from constraints satisfaction checking. This means that those individuals that do not fulfill the constraints are penalized with distance $D(g)$. Assuming that there are h missed constraints, the distance $D(g)$ is defined as the sum of all the deviations from each of the missed constraints.

$$f_{fit}(g) = f_{obj}(g) + k_5 \cdot D(g) \quad \text{with} \quad D(g) = \sum_{i=1}^{h} dev_i \qquad (7)$$

We build multiple generations over the population in an iterative way by applying the mutation and crossover operators. Through the mutation operator, the candidate services are varied randomly and an arbitrary concrete service is selected to realize the abstract service. The crossover operator combines service variants of different individuals. The algorithm stops when during multiple generations there is no improvement to the fitness function value.

3 Evaluation

Several experiments have been performed in order to compare our algorithms OPTIM_HWeight and OPTIM_PRO with the GA_CAN algorithm proposed

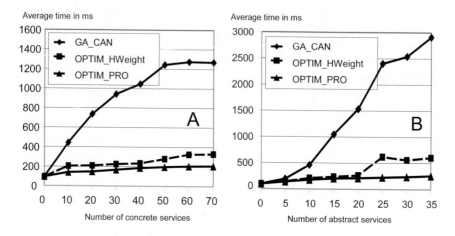

Fig. 5. Computation time OPTIM_HWeight, OPTIM_PRO and GA_CAN

in [2]. We have evaluated the three algorithms with regard to the required computation time and the optimization of the objective function. All tests have been performed on a Lenovo R60, 1.83 GHz, 2 GB RAM with Windows XP SP3 and JSDK 1.6.

As baseline for our experiments, we have randomly generated 10 different BPEL trees for each test case, with different structures and dimensions. The tree structures have been created in such a way that they contain the relevant BPEL activities, like *while, if, invoke, sequence* and *flow* with adjustable probabilities.

For the GA_CAN algorithm we set the mutation probability to 0.01 and the crossover probability to 0.7. The OPTIM_HWeight algorithm was triggered with $nr\_v = 12$ and $n\_iter = 12$. Since all the algorithms are probabilistic, we executed the algorithms 10 times (for each of the 10 BPEL trees, having 100 test runs in total) and took the average value. The results of our measurements are presented in Figures 5 and 6.

In our experiments A and B (Fig. 5, Fig. 6 Table A and B) we compared the computation time of OPTIM_HWeight and OPTIM_PRO with the computation time of the GA_CAN algorithm (with a population of 100) for reaching approximately the same value (difference less than 0.01 %) for the objective function.

In experiment A (Fig. 5, Fig. 6 Table A) we used a fixed number of abstract services (15) and measured how an increasing number of concrete services (from 10 to 70 per abstract service) influences the computation time. The results show that OPTIM_PRO is the fastest algorithm, requiring on average about 19% of the time of GA_CAN for reaching approximately the same optimization of f_{obj}. We observed that in average, our OPTIM_HWeight algorithm requires only about 28% of the time of the GA_CAN.

Experiment B is similar to experiment A, but this time we increased the abstract services from 0 to 35 while keeping the number of concrete services

Table A

Nr. Con. Serv	GA_CAN (G) Avg. timeG P100,[ms]	HWeight (H) Avg. timeH [ms]	Avg. timeH/ timeG	O_PRO (P) Avg. timeP [ms]	Avg. timeP/ timeG
10	443,10	205,10	46,29%	140,80	31,78%
20	736,10	210,10	28,54%	148,50	20,17%
30	942,20	225,80	23,97%	167,80	17,81%
40	1046,50	234,80	22,44%	186,90	17,86%
50	1244,00	280,10	22,52%	198,10	15,92%
60	1274,10	327,30	25,69%	206,50	16,21%
70	1269,00	331,30	26,11%	208,20	16,41%

Table C

Nr. Abs. Serv	Fobj_H/ Fobj_G	Fobj_P/ Fobj_G
5	100,00%	100,00%
10	101,22%	101,22%
15	100,01%	100,01%
20	103,29%	103,36%
25	110,78%	110,94%
30	107,31%	107,31%
35	107,10%	107,31%

Table B

Nr. Abs. Serv	GA_CAN Avg. timeG [ms]	HWeight (H) Avg. timeH [ms]	Avg. timeH/ timeG	O_PRO (P) Avg. timeP [ms]	Avg. timeP/ timeG
5	192,10	142,60	74,23%	136,80	71,21%
10	459,30	206,30	44,92%	176,10	38,34%
15	1046,50	234,80	22,44%	203,60	19,46%
20	1532,80	261,20	17,04%	210,40	13,73%
25	2404,70	621,80	25,86%	226,00	9,40%
30	2539,25	561,42	22,11%	238,30	9,38%
35	2909,92	606,25	20,83%	257,20	8,84%

Fig. 6. Algorithms evaluation: GA_CAN (G), OPTIM_PRO (P), OPT_HWeight (H)

constantly at 40. Experiment B (Fig. 5, Fig. 6 Table B) shows again that OPTIM_PRO is the fastest algorithm and needed in average about 24% of the GA_CAN time while the OPTIM_HWeight needed about 32% of the GA_CAN time.

In experiment C (Fig. 6 Table C) we evaluated how well the objective function was optimized by the different algorithms. We computed the value of f_{obj} reached by OPTIM_HWeight, OPTIM_PRO and GA_CAN, where the computation time limit for all of them was set to 4 seconds. The population size of GA_CAN during the evaluation was varied between 100 and 600 and the best result was chosen. The evaluation shows that our OPTIM_HWeight and OPTIM_PRO provides an optimization value at least as good as GA_CAN. With an increasing number of abstract services (the number of concrete services/possible realizations per abstract service is constantly 100) our algorithms provide even better optimization results than GA_CAN (e.g. above 25 abstract services, f_{obj} is about 7% better). Thus, according to our evaluation, the more possible combinations exist, the better are the optimization results of OPTIM_HWeight and OPTIM_PRO in comparison to GA_CAN.

4   Related Work

Zeng et al. describe in [3] a "QoS-Aware Middleware for Web Service Composition". For the service selection the authors describe two approaches for local and global optimization. In their global planning approach, the authors propose an Integer Programming (IP) solution, assuming that the objective function, the constraints, and the aggregation functions are linear. The multiplicative aggregation functions for availability and success rate are linearized by applying the logarithm. Our goal was to also consider non-linear objective functions and aggregation functions within both our heuristic algorithms. Due to the bad runtime performance of IP, their approach quickly becomes unfeasible when confronted with an increasing number of tasks and concrete services. An improvement of IP in respect to runtime performance is achieved in [6] by using relaxed integer programming and a backtracking algorithm. They have the same restrictions like [3] and address only sequential web service compositions and linear objective functions. In our approach we consider sequential and also parallel execution of activities and non-linear objective functions. In particular, OPTIM_HWeight utilizes gradient ascent and we perform the optimization on a tree.

Canfora et al. [2] propose a genetic approach for the selection problem. Since the authors consider also non-linear objective functions, we implemented their approach (within the GA_CAN algorithm) to compare it with our heuristic algorithms. The runtime behaviour was discussed in the previous section. We used the same aggregation functions as Canfora did. The authors select the genome with a fitness function containing a penalty factor. This penalty factor does not guarantee that the individuals will fulfill the QoS constraints for all possible execution paths. By checking the QoS constraints considering the worst case of QoS values throughout multiple branches, our algorithms ensure that the QoS constraints are met for all of the execution paths. In addition, our OPTIM_HWeight and OPTIM_PRO need less time than GA_CAN to find the same result or even a better one. An amendment of the genetic approach is introduced in [10] where the improvement is achieved by the usage of hybridization. The neighborhood of each individual of the genetic algorithm is explored iteratively to replace the actual individual with the best or the almost best neighbor. Still, this reduces the diversification of the population or the number of generations if the computation time shall not be increased. Thus, the authors come to the conclusion that for bigger problem instances the basic genetic algorithms perform better.

In [5] different heuristics are evaluated, including approaches which consider global constraints and obtain almost best possible QoS like the pattern-wise selection or the discarding subsets approach. Nevertheless the runtime performance can make them unsuitable for a growing number of tasks. Other heuristics like greedy selection or the bottom-up approximation proposed in [5] result in a loss of QoS up to 5% but lead to an acceptable runtime performance. In this context, especially our OPTIM_HWeight and OPTIM_PRO algorithms can provide an improvement in relation to shorter runtimes than *pattern-wise selection* and *discarding subsets*, and delivers a better QoS than greedy selection and bottom-up approximation. Besides, the user can configure the runtime-to-QoS ratio by setting few parameters like number of steps of OPTIM_HWeight or nr_v for OPTIM_S.

5   Conclusion

We presented two heuristic algorithms as solutions to the service selection problem in Web service orchestrations: the OPTIM_HWeight algorithm based on weighting factors inspired by gradient ascent approaches and the OPTIM_PRO algorithm utilizing priority factors. Both algorithms are iterative improving the found solution by every iteration step, and provide an easy way to trade computation time against the quality of the solution by merely changing their parameters. As our target was to optimize non-linear objective functions, we compared OPTIM_HWeight and OPTIM_PRO with the genetic algorithm GA_CAN proposed by Canfora [2]. Our experiments revealed that our OPTIM_PRO and OPTIM_HWeight are faster than GA_CAN (in average they needed about 22%, respectively 30% of the time of GA_CAN) and even achieve better values for the objective function (in our experiments up to 7% better) than GA_CAN in cases with a high number of combinations. The OPTIM_PRO algorithm turned out to be the fastest algorithm. In our future work we will also consider a combination of both algorithms, like having the solution of OPTIM_PRO as starting point for OPTIM_HWeight.

References

1. Bleul, S., Comes, D., Geihs, K.: Automatic Service Brokering in Service oriented Architectures, Homepage, `http://www.vs.uni-kassel.de/research/addo/`
2. Canfora, G., Penta, M., Esposito, R., Villani, M.L.: An approach for QoS-aware service composition based on genetic algorithms. In: Proceedings of the 2005 conference on Genetic and evolutionary computation, ACM, Washington (2005)
3. Zeng, L., Benatallah, B., Ngu, A.H., Dumas, M., Kalagnanam, J., Chang, H.: QoS-Aware Middleware for Web Services Composition. In: IEEE Transactions on Software Engineering, pp. 311–327. IEEE Press, Los Alamitos (2004)
4. Comes, D., Bleul, S., Weise, T., Geihs, K.: A Flexible Approach for Business Processes Monitoring. In: Senivongse, T., Oliveira, R. (eds.) DAIS 2009. LNCS, vol. 5523, pp. 116–128. Springer, Heidelberg (2009)
5. Jaeger, M., Múhl, G., Golze, S.: QoS-aware Composition of Web Services: An Evaluation of Selection Algorithms. In: International Symposium on Distributed Objects and Applications (DOA 2005), Springer, Heidelberg (2005)
6. Berbner, R., Spahn, M., Repp, N., Heckmann, O., Steinmetz, R.: Heuristics for QoS-aware Web Service Composition. In: IEEE International Conference on Web Services (ICWS 2006), IEEE Computer Society, Los Alamitos (2006)
7. Web Services Business Process Execution Language Version 2.0, OASIS standard (2007), `http://docs.oasis-open.org/wsbpel/2.0/OS/wsbpel-v2.0-OS.html`
8. Oracle BPEL Process Manager (2008), `http://www.oracle.com/technology/products/ias/bpel/index.html`
9. Baligand, F., Rivierre, N., Ledoux, T.: A Declarative Approach for QoS-Aware Web Service Compositions. In: Krämer, B.J., Lin, K.-J., Narasimhan, P. (eds.) ICSOC 2007. LNCS, vol. 4749, Springer, Heidelberg (2007)
10. Parejo, J., Fernandez, A., Cortes, P., QoS-Aware Services, A.: composition using Tabu Search and Hybrid Genetic Algorithms. Actas de los Talleres de las Jornadas de Ingeniería del Software y Bases de Datos 2(1) (2008)
11. Garey, M., Johnson, D.: Computers and Intractability; A Guide to the Theory of NP-Completeness. W.H. Freeman, New York (1979)

From Quality to Utility: Adaptive Service Selection Framework

Chung-Wei Hang and Munindar P. Singh

Department of Computer Science
North Carolina State University
Raleigh, NC 27695-8206, USA
{chang,singh}@ncsu.edu

Abstract. We consider an approach to service selection wherein service consumers choose services with desired nonfunctional properties to maximize their utility. A consumer's utility from using a service clearly depends upon the qualities offered by the service. Many existing service selection approaches support agents estimating trustworthiness of services based on their quality of service. However, existing approaches do not emphasize the relationship between a consumer's interests and the utility the consumer draws from a service. Further, they do not properly support consumers being able to compose services with desired quality (and utility) profiles.

We propose an adaptive service selection framework that offers three major benefits. First, our approach enables consumers to select services based on their individual utility functions, which reflect their preferences, and learn the providers' quality distributions. Second, our approach guides consumers to construct service compositions that satisfy their quality requirements. Third, an extension of our approach with contracts approximates Pareto optimality without the use of a market mechanism.

1 Introduction

We consider the problem of service selection. In service-oriented environments [16], consumers consume services for direct interaction or composition. How to select the "right" services to consume is one of the main challenges in service-oriented computing. The "right" services are determined based on two kinds of properties: functional and nonfunctional. *Service description matching* provides design-time automation for consumers to discover services with desired functionalities. By contrast, our emphasis is on *service selection*, which offers run-time automation for consumers to select services with the desired nonfunctional properties—quality of service (QoS), to meet consumers' preferences.

Three main challenges arise in service selection. First, <u>how do consumers collect information</u> about the QoS offered by a particular service? In open settings, quality information can be collected based on either consumers' direct experience or third-party referrals. However, learning from direct experience with

P.P. Maglio et al. (Eds.): ICSOC 2010, LNCS 6470, pp. 456–470, 2010.

a dynamic service (which delivers differing quality from time to time) is not trivial. Also, how consumers accommodate false referrals provided by malicious referrers is challenging. Second, how do consumers define their preferences for QoS? Potentially, each consumer may have a different requirements. For example, one may prefer high throughput, another low throughput, and yet another intermediate throughput. Another difficulty is accommodating the consumers' goals and context. For example, a latency of five seconds may be acceptable for a galaxy simulation but unacceptable for a web search. Third, how do consumers make selection decisions based on quality information and consumers' preferences? Selecting the apparently best services may not always lead to long-term success, because consumers have limited or incomplete knowledge, and services may change their behavior.

Trust models provide a promising solution to the first and third challenges. Trust models enable consumers to estimate the trustworthiness of dynamic services in terms of QoS based on both direct and indirect evidence. We particularly consider trust models, e.g., [10,19,21], that provide certainty measurement as an indicator of how confident the estimated trustworthiness is.

Many trust-based service selection approaches have been proposed [6,9,11,12,13,20]. However, many of them fail to deal with the second challenge practically. Maximilien and Singh [13] describe consumers' preferences of QoS in terms of utility theory. They only consider that consumer preferences follow a monotonic increasing function of QoS (i.e., the higher the quality the better). In practical cases, the utility function of QoS may not always be increasing (say, for price), or even monotonic. For example, a consumer may prefer medium over high or low capacity. Low capacity may lead to long response time because many consumers are waiting. In contrast, high capacity may lead to long latency because the service may not have sufficient buffer space to handle many requests at the same time.

Many service selection approaches, e.g., [9,12,13], guide consumers to select services for direct interaction but not for composition. Selecting for composition is nontrivial because the composition changes the context and thus can affect a consumer's preferences. For example, a consumer may prefer low latency for interaction but may prefer two subservices composed in parallel to have approximately equal latency so as to reduce the need for buffering. But in a sequential composition, the consumer may still prefer low latency for each service. Consequently, a service selection method should guide consumers to adjust their preferences based on the composition and quality being considered.

This paper proposes a service selection framework that enables consumers to select services based on the utility they expect to gain from the services. Our approach addresses all three of the above challenges. First, our approach incorporates any probabilistic trust model to collect quality information about the services. Second, our approach enables consumers to specify utility functions describing their preferences. Third, our approach provides a learning policy to explore and exploit desired services in order to maximize each consumer's utility based on its preferences and estimated quality of the services involved. We show experimentally that our approach helps achieve near Pareto optimality across the consumers. Besides, our approach can guide a consumer to adjust its preferences for desired compositions based on its quality requirements and composition types.

Section 2 surveys the relevant literature. Section 3 defines our problem and scope. Section 4 formalizes our approach. Section 5 evaluates our approach via simulations. Section 6 discusses our results and highlights future directions.

2   Related Work

Maximilien and Singh [13] study trust-based service selection involving multiple qualities. Their approach considers consumers' utility of each quality, and enables consumers to define preferences between qualities. However, Maximilien and Singh only consider two shapes of utility functions: *linear* and *sigmoid*. Our approach can take any utility function as input.

ServiceTrust [9] calculates reputations of services from all consumers. It introduces *transactional trust* to detect QoS abuse, where malicious services gain reputation from small transactions and cheat at large ones. However, ServiceTrust models transactions as binary events (success or failure), and combines reports from all consumers without taking their preferences into account.

Malik et al. [12] propose a reputation assessment approach based on Hidden Markov Models (HMMs). They maps qualities to each consumer's personal evaluations that incorporate its preferences by weighing preferred qualities higher. Next, they calculate an aggregated reputation based both on personal evaluations and ratings by others. Based on the aggregated reputation, Malik et al. apply HMM to predict future behavior. Instead of using weights, our approach reflects consumers preferences via utility functions. Our approach can also incorporate other consumers' quality ratings by choosing probabilistic trust models that support referrals to model our quality distribution. For example, our approach can adopt Wang and Singh's trust model [19], which provides trust propagation [8] and trust updates to deal with referrals from other consumers [7].

Li et al. [11] estimate the trustworthiness of composite services using Bayesian inference. They formalize a variety of service invocations and convert compositions into a service invocation graph. Then consumers can construct a desired composite service by finding the optimal service execution flow. Li et al. express trust as a normal distribution. and apply Bayesian inference to maintain trust. Our approach models a service's QoS as a probability distribution, which is also learned and updated via Bayesian inference. However, our approach deals with composition differently. Consumers select subservices for composition based on utility. More specifically, a consumer adjusts its utility function based on the already selected subservices to achieve better orchestration.

ServiceRank [20] ranks services from two aspects: quality of service and social information. ServiceRank considers two qualities: response time and availability. Social information includes (1) how many consumers a service has and (2) how frequently a service is invoked. Similar to ServiceTrust [9], ServiceRank models transactions as binary events. Our approach does not limit to any particular qualities and selects services with the highest expected utility of multiple qualities. In our approach, an analog of social information is characterized via the certainty of the quality distributions. Certainty measurements can be found in many probabilistic trust models [10,19,21]. Certainty reflects how much evidence a quality distribution has. If a service is seldom invoked or has few customers, then the certainty of its quality distribution will be low.

Hang and Singh [6] present a trust model for service selection. Their model focuses on how to estimate the trustworthiness of subservices based on the observed quality of composite services. Hang and Singh introduce *composition operators* that define how a quality is composed from subservices to compositions. They show their model can accurately estimate trustworthiness of subservices under various composition operators. Hang and Singh fail to specify how consumers interpret a quality as trust. Our approach builds trust based on the reputations of services (i.e., their quality distributions) and consumers' preferences (i.e., utility functions). Following Hang and Singh's formalization, our approach can be used to select services for composition by adjusting utility functions. Depending on the composition operator and existing subservices in the composition, the utility function is adjusted differently.

Gerding et al. [5] design mechanisms for service procurement. They consider the case where services may fail. Their mechanism guides consumers to procure services to form a workflow for completing a task with constraints, for example, within a certain time. The consumers aim to (1) maximize the probability of success given the constraints and (2) balance success probability with costs. Their work focuses on designing a mechanism to incentivise service providers to reveal their quality information, whereas, in our approach, consumers collect such information by themselves. Consumers apply probabilistic trust models to collect quality information of providers from direct interaction, referrals, and compositions. We show that our approach guides service procurement and leads to Pareto optimality, i.e., resources are allocated efficiently.

3   Problem Description and Scope

Environment. A service-oriented environment includes a set of providers $\mathcal{P} = \{ P_1, \ldots, P_m \}$ and a set of consumers $\mathcal{C} = \{ C_1, \ldots, C_n \}$. The providers provide services of the same underlying functionality, but each provider potentially offers different levels of the l qualities in $\mathcal{Q} = \{Q_1, \ldots, Q_l\}$. A service composition is defined as $\chi = \langle \mathcal{S}, \mathcal{T} \rangle$, where $\mathcal{S} \subseteq \mathcal{P}$ are services, and the composition type $\mathcal{T}$ is one of *sequence*, *flow*, and *case*, as in typical orchestrations [2].

Assumption. We assume the value of quality Q_k offered by provider P_j is governed by a probability distribution that is independent of the consumer and the service composition in consideration.

Objective. Each consumer defines a utility function for each quality to describe its preferences and selects services to maximize its utility.

Scenario 1: Select Services for Direct Interaction. A consumer C_i would like to interact with a service from $\mathcal{P}$ to maximize its utility regarding $\mathcal{Q}$.

Scenario 2: Select Services for Composition. We are given a partial composition $\chi' = \langle \mathcal{S}', \mathcal{T} \rangle$ with existing subservices $\mathcal{S}' \subseteq \mathcal{P}$, and a consumer C_i's utility function regarding $\mathcal{Q}$. Now, C_i would like to create a "supercomposition" of χ' as $\chi = \langle \mathcal{S}' \cup \mathcal{S}'', \mathcal{T} \rangle$ that builds on χ' by adding services $\mathcal{S}''$ to the composition.

4   Approach

We propose an adaptive service selection framework that enables consumers to select providers to maximize their utility based both on their preferences of qualities and what they learn about the providers' quality distributions.

Figure 1 illustrates the service selection process. For a consumer C_i, its *utility functions* with respect to each quality $Q_k \in \mathcal{Q}$ are given. Next C_i applies the following steps.

1. Collect quality information and learn the *quality distributions* of each provider $P_j \in \mathcal{P}$ with respect to each quality $Q_k \in \mathcal{Q}$.
2. Calculate *expected utility* of each provider $P_j \in \mathcal{P}$ with respect to all qualities $Q_k \in \mathcal{Q}$.
3. Select a provider $P_j \in \mathcal{P}$ to interact with.

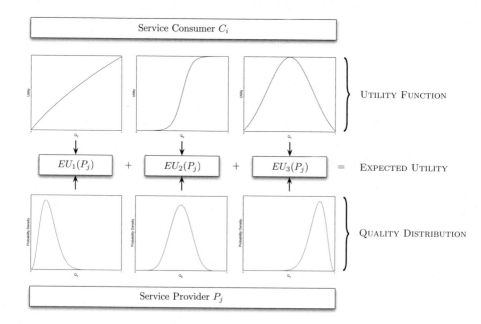

Fig. 1. Illustration of our approach. Consumer C_i describes its preferences of qualities via utility functions, collects information about and learns the distributions of all qualities of each provider, and calculates the expected utility of each provider.

4. Repeat Step 1.

In the remainder of this section, we (1) define utility functions and quality distributions; (2) introduce calculating expected utility involving multiple qualities; (3) relate the service selection strategy to the learning policy used in reinforcement learning; and (4) explain how our service selection can be used for selecting subservices in service compositions.

4.1 Describe Service Consumers: Utility Functions

We describe a consumer's preference of a particular quality by a utility function.

Definition 1. Utility function $U(x)$. *Let C_j be a consumer and random variable x be the volume of some quality of service Q_k. C_j's utility function $U(x)$ is defined as a function that maps Q_k's value x to C_j's utility.*

Table 1 shows some examples of utility functions.

Table 1. Example utility functions: Describing consumer preferences

Function	Plot	Description
Logistic [13] $$\frac{1}{1 + e^{-(x-u)/s}}$$		Rapid increase close to desired value, as for availability
Logarithm $$\log x$$		Diminishing returns, as for throughput
Gaussian $$\frac{1}{\sqrt{2\pi\sigma^2}} e^{-\frac{(x-\mu)^2}{2\sigma^2}}$$		Tradeoff between being idle or buffering heavily, as for throughput of subservice

4.2 Describe Service Providers: Quality Distributions

We capture the quality of service provided by a service provider P_j by introducing a quality distribution.

Definition 2. Quality distribution $Q_k(x)$. *Let P_j be a service and random variable x_j be the quality of service Q_k provided by P_j along some suitable dimension. Then P_j's quality function $Q_k(x_j)$ with respect to quality Q_k is defined as the probability density function of the probability distribution that governs x_j.*

The quality distributions can be learned by probabilistic trust models based on evidence regarding quality, which can be obtained through 1. direct experience [19], 2. referrals [8], or 3. composition [6,14].

4.3   Calculate Expected Utility of Providers

The consumers' decision making is based on the utility they expect to obtain from a provider.

Definition 3. Expected utility with respect to a quality. *Let P_j's quality distribution be $Q_k(x_j)$, and C_i be a consumer with utility function $U_k(x)$. The expected utility of quality Q_k that C_i can obtain from P_j is defined as*

$$EU_k^i(P_j) = \int_{x_j} U_k(x_j)Q_k(x_j)dx_j. \tag{1}$$

The expected utility of provider P_j based on all its qualities is as follows.

Definition 4. Expected utility with respect to all qualities. *Suppose $Q_1(x)$, ..., $Q_l(x)$ are quality distributions of provider P_j and $U_1(x)$, ..., $U_l(x)$ are utility functions of consumer C_i. Then C_i's expected utility of P_j is defined as*

$$EU^i(P_j) = \sum_{k=1,...,l} EU_k^i(P_j) = \sum_{k=1,...,l} \int_{x_j} U_k(x_j)Q_k(x_j)dx_j \tag{2}$$

4.4   Select Services: Exploration vs. Exploitation

Based on the expected utility of a provider with respect to all qualities, a consumer C_i can decide on which providers to interact with to maximize its utility as follows:

$$P_j = \arg\max_{P_j \in \mathcal{P}} EU^i(P_j) \tag{3}$$

However, given the assumption that the consumer can only learn the quality distributions from direct experience, selecting the provider that yields the most utility may not lead to long-term success. This is because the consumer lacks evidence (direct experience) to learn accurate quality distributions of the providers.

Here, we address this challenge by modeling the service selection problem as the multiarmed bandit problem [15,1]. An agent (gambler) seeks to maximize its reward by taking a series of actions (pulling levers from a multiarmed slot machine). At each instant, the reward is based on a probability distribution associated with each action. Notice that a myopic decision (choosing an action with the highest known reward) may not yield the most long-term reward. A *policy* is a function that predicts the (long-term) rewards from each action. Research in reinforcement learning [18] studies how to learn an optimal policy, by which the agent can select its actions. Doing so involves addressing the tradeoff between *exploration* (trying new alternatives that might lead to higher payoffs) and *exploitation* (making decision based on current knowledge).

We model the service-oriented environment as a multiarmed bandit, where the providers are the options and each consumer selects providers to maximize its long-term reward. Here, the reward is defined as the utility derived by the consumer and consumers learn a policy that maps actions (selecting a $P_j \in \mathcal{P}$) to their expected utility. To balance the above tradeoff between exploration and exploitation, we adopt *Boltzmann Exploration* [3], a widely used learning policy in reinforcement learning, written in our setting as:

$$Pr(P_j|EU^i) = \frac{e^{T*EU^i(P_j)}}{\sum_{P_i \in \mathcal{P}} e^{T*EU^i(P_i)}}, \qquad (4)$$

where $P_j \in \mathcal{P}$ is a service, $EU^i(P_j)$ is C_i's expected utility of P_j, and T is a *temperature parameter*. The consumer C_i chooses service P_j with probability $Pr(P_j|EU^i)$. The idea of Boltzmann Exploration is for consumers to choose services based on their expected utility. The services with low expected utility (i.e., exploration) are chosen less frequently than those with high expected utility (i.e., exploitation). The actual percentage of exploration and exploitation can be adjusted by T. There are two ways of choosing T. For stationary environments, T increases over time to reduce the probability of exploration after the policy is learned. In contrast, for nonstationary environments, consumers may use a fixed T to ensure continual exploration. Satinder Singh et al. [17] show a convergent result for choosing T. Applying their result to our case, we can define T as $\ln t/C_t$, where t is the timestep, $C_t = \max_{P_j \in \mathcal{P}} |EU^i(P_{max}) - EU^i(P_j)|$ and $P_{max} = \arg\max_{P_j \in \mathcal{P}} EU^i(P_j)$.

4.5 Selecting Services for Composition

Now we describe how our approach guides consumers to select services for composition. Section 3 mentions a scenario where a consumer C_i would like to add services $\mathcal{S}''$ from $\mathcal{P}$ to a current composition $\chi' = \langle \mathcal{S}', \mathcal{T} \rangle$ to maximize the utility of the resulting composition $\chi = \langle \mathcal{S}' \cup \mathcal{S}'', \mathcal{T} \rangle$ where $\mathcal{S}' \subseteq P$ is the set of constituent services of χ' and $\mathcal{T}$ is the composition type.

Following our previous work [6], we introduce the *composition operators* SWITCH, SUM, MAX, MIN, and PRODUCT. These operators determine the quality values of a composite service based on the quality values of the constituent services. They depend upon the composition type (*sequence, flow*, or *case*), and on the nature of the quality being considered. Table 2 shows examples of composition operators given the types of compositions and qualities.

Table 2. Mapping composition types and representative qualities to operators [6]

Quality	Sequence	Flow	Case
Latency	SUM	MAX	SWITCH
Throughput	MIN	SUM	SWITCH
Failure	PRODUCT	PRODUCT	SWITCH

Table 3. Utility function examples for composition operators based on two linear utility function: *prefer higher* and *prefer lower*. $E[x_i]$ is the expected quality from provide P_i.

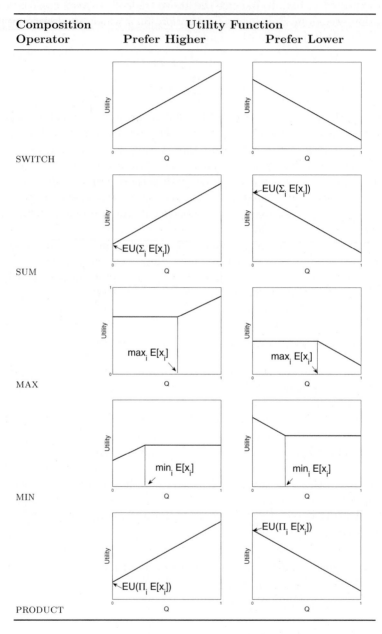

Based on the expected quality of the existing subservices $\mathcal{S}'$ in a composition χ, consumer C_i can adjust the utility function $U_k(x)$ of the composition with respect to Q_k. This adjustment depends on (1) the composition operator f, (2) composition χ's preferences of the quality Q_k, and (3) the expected quality $x_{\mathcal{S}'}$ of existing subservices $\mathcal{S}'$. For example, let f be MAX, the maximum of expected quality Q_k of $\mathcal{S}'$ be $E[x_{P_{max}}]$, and χ's original utility function be $U_k(x)$, Then the adjusted utility function U_k' should be

$$U_k'(x) = \begin{cases} U_k(E[x_{P_{max}}]) & \text{if } x < E[x_{P_{max}}] \\ U_k(x) & \text{otherwise.} \end{cases} \tag{5}$$

The idea behind this adjustment is that if the quality x provided by the new subservices is lower than $E[x_{P_{max}}]$, then the composite quality x_χ is dominated by P_{max} because $x_\chi = \max(x, E[x_{P_{max}}]) = E[x_{P_{max}}]$. Thus, the composite utility will be $U_k(E[x_{P_{max}}])$. Conversely, if $x > E[x_{P_{max}}]$, then the composite quality x_χ is dominated by x. The composite utility will be $U_k(x)$.

Table 3 shows utility function examples for various composition operators. It shows how monotonically increasing and decreasing utility functions are adjusted based on existing constituent services and the composition types. Note that our approach is not limited to these composition operators or utility functions.

5   Experiments

We conduct three experiments to evaluate the effectiveness of our approach. The first experiment examines how accurately the expected utility can predict the actual gained utility. The second experiment verifies the selection strategy described in Section 4.4 by checking if the consumers can quickly learn the quality distributions of all providers (exploration), and select the provider with the highest expected utility afterwards (exploitation). The third experiment adopts a resource allocation perspective and examines how closely our approach can lead to *Pareto optimal* allocations [4].

5.1   Two Consumers, Three Providers, One Quality, No Selection

We consider three providers: *Low, Medium*, and *High*, whose quality Q is governed by beta distributions with low, fair, and high means, respectively. We create two consumers, respectively with utility functions *Logistic* (prefers high over low Q) and *Gaussian* (prefers mid range Q over high or low values). At each timestep, each consumer interacts with all providers once, and learns their quality distributions. Figure 2 plots the expected and gained utility of the *Logistic* (left) and *Gaussian* (right) consumers from provider *Medium* at each timestep. *Medium* provides average Q_1 values, yielding utility around 0.50 for *Logistic*, whose gained utility has a high variance, because *Logistic* is highly sensitive to Q_1. *Medium* brings a fair amount of utility to *Gaussian*, who is less picky. The expected utility calculated by both consumers accurately predicts the actual gained utility. The experiment has total 100 timesteps. *Low* and *High* providers yield similar results. The result verifies that the expected utility is an effective basis to maximize consumers' utility.

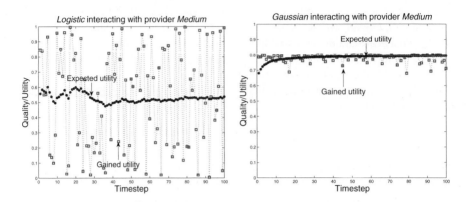

Fig. 2. The expected and gained utility of *Logistic* (left) and *Gaussian* (right) against *Medium*. Both consumers receive the same QoS from *Medium* but gain different utility based on their utility functions. *Logistic* is sensitive to quality, and thus has high variance in its gained utility. This experiment shows the expected utility correctly predicts the actual gained utility. The other providers yield similar results.

5.2   Two Consumers, Three Providers, One Quality, Selection

This experiment helps us evaluate the effectiveness of the strategy described in Section 4.4. Its setting follows Section 5.1, except that the consumers choose only one provider instead of all to interact with. Each consumer seeks to maximize its long-term utility. Figure 3 shows *Logistic*'s (left) and *Gaussian*'s (right) expected utilities of all providers and the actual utility gained from the sole provider each chooses to interact with at each timestep. *Logistic* explores all providers at the beginning,

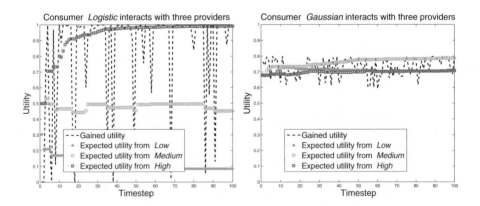

Fig. 3. The expected and gained utility of *Logistic* (left) and *Gaussian* (right) consumers against three providers. In each timestep, consumers select one of the providers to interact with. This shows each consumer learns the expected utility of all providers (exploration), and subsequently interacts with the desired provider to maximize its utility (exploitation).

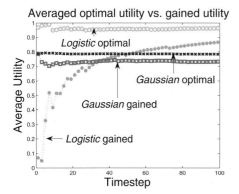

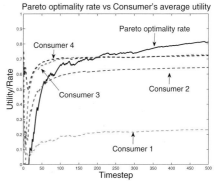

Fig. 4. Comparison of optimal and gained utilities of *Logistic* and *Gaussian*. Consumers choose nonoptimal services for exploration. This shows that when expected utilities of providers are close, the consumers are more willing to explore.

Fig. 5. The rates of Pareto optimality and consumers' average utility with four consumers and three providers, each of capacity two. This shows that even though consumers find desired services and maximize utility independently, together they achieve a Pareto optimal allocation 80% of the time.

gaining low utility at the beginning. After it determines *High* is its desired provider, *Logistic* selects *High* much more than the other providers. *Gaussian* has a similar strategy as *Logistic* at the beginning. However, since *Gaussian* is not as picky as *Logistic*, *Gaussian* chooses all providers almost equally often, but because *Medium* offers a slightly better expected utility, *Gaussian* selects *Medium* slightly more often than the other two. Both consumers gain utility close to optimal.

Figure 4 plots the comparison of optimal and actual gained utility of two consumers. Our approach learns the quality distribution through greater exploration at the beginning followed by greater exploitation subsequently. Because the gained utility is smaller than the optimal when the consumers choose to explore (or when the quality distribution is not learned accurately), the utility increases over time.

This result shows our service selection approach not only efficiently learns the quality distributions of the providers, but also exploits the desired provider to maximize each consumer's utility.

5.3 Contracts as a Means to Approximate Pareto Optimality

A resource allocation is *Pareto optimal* if and only if it is impossible to alter the allocation that would offer increased utility to one agent without offering reduced utility to another. In other words, no two agents can trade (their allocations) where they would both gain. Pareto optimality is a widely used indicator of economic efficiency. The intuition behind it is that we should allocate each resource to the party who values the resource the most. To ensure Pareto optimality typically requires some market mechanism such as an auction that takes bids from all consumers and allocates resources in a way to guarantee efficiency. For example, allocating each resource to the highest bidder means that the bidder who values the resource the most gets to use it.

We show how a natural extension of our approach with contracts leads to approximating Pareto optimality despite independent decision making by the consumers and without any central mechanism such as an auction clearinghouse. In an important departure from the previous experiments, here a consumer may sign a long-term contract with a provider. A contract is a way for a consumer to exploit (i.e., select the provider with most expected utility). We consider an exploitation strategy where the contract length is proportional to (ten times as) the expected utility. When a consumer chooses to explore, it interacts with the selected provider for one timestep. The intuitive motivation is that the consumers who value a provider the most will sign the longest contracts with it and thus gain the greatest utility from it for the longest time.

We create four consumers with different preferences of two qualities: throughput and price. Intuitively, the consumers vary from rich (prefers the highest throughput at any price) to poor (prefers to save money and accepts a little throughput). The consumers have *logistic* utility functions (monotonically increasing) for throughput with parameters $(\mu, s) = (0.8, 0.05), (0.6, 0.05), (0.4, 0.05), (0.2, 0.05)$, respectively. For price, each consumer has a negative exponentially decreasing utility function, with σ of 5, 4, 3, and 2, respectively:

$$U_{price}(x) = -\frac{x^{\sigma}}{100^{\sigma}} \tag{6}$$

Three providers provide throughput governed by beta distributions with means 0.75, 0.5, and 0.25, and asking \$75, \$50, and \$25 for their service, respectively.

The experiment runs for 500 timesteps. At each timestep, the consumers select one provider to interact with. A provider can serve two consumers at a time. We check if the resource allocation at each timestep is Pareto optimal.

For each timestep, Figure 5 shows the consumers' average utility and the cumulative percentage of instantaneous allocations that are Pareto optimal. We see that the rate of Pareto optimality increases as the average individual utility increases. This indicates that when the consumers maximize their utility, Pareto optimality is likely to be achieved. Pareto optimality is not achieved in every instance of exploitation because a consumer may not be able to sign a contract with its best provider who might be under another contract or because of the effects of randomness in quality. In general, though, this experiment shows that our approach can approximate Pareto optimality by selecting services in an economically efficient way.

6   Conclusions and Directions

This paper proposes an adaptive service selection approach, which enables service consumers to 1. collect quality information of service providers efficiently, 2. describe their preferences of quality by defining utility functions, and 3. select "right" service providers to maximize their long-term utility. Besides, our approach can guide consumers to select services for composition by defining utility functions for service compositions. Importantly, our approach yields a natural way to approximate Pareto optimality of service selection.

Important directions for future study include the generalization of our models of quality and utility. In particular, we hypothesize that if we allow the providers to change their quality profiles dynamically, that will yield protection against greedy consumers signing arbitrarily long contracts with the best current service and thus blocking other consumers.

Acknowledgment

This work is supported by the U.S. Army Research Office (ARO) under grant W911NF-08-1-0105 managed by NCSU Secure Open Systems Initiative (SOSI).

References

1. Berry, D.A., Fristedt, B.: Bandit Problems: Sequential Allocation of Experiments. Monographs on statistics and applied probability. Chapman and Hall, London (1985)
2. BPEL: Web services business process execution language, version 2.0 (July 2007), http://docs.oasis-open.org/wsbpel/2.0/
3. Bridle, J.S.: Training stochastic model recognition algorithms as networks can lead to maximum mutual information estimation of parameters. Advances in neural information processing systems 2, 211–217 (1990)
4. Feldman, A.M.: Welfare Economics and Social Choice Theory. Kluwer Nijhoff Publishing, Dordrecht (1980)
5. Gerding, E., Stein, S., Larson, K., Rogers, A., Jennings, N.R.: Scalable mechanism design for the procurement of services with uncertain durations. In: Proceedings of the 9th International Conference on Autonomous Agents and Multiagent Systems (AAMAS), pp. 649–656. IFAAMAS, Columbia (2010)
6. Hang, C.W., Singh, M.P.: Trustworthy service selection and composition. In: ACM Transactions on Autonomous and Adaptive Systems, TAAS (to appear 2010)
7. Hang, C.W., Wang, Y., Singh, M.P.: An adaptive probabilistic trust model and its evaluation. In: Proceedings of the 7th International Conference on Autonomous Agents and Multiagent Systems, pp. 1485–1488. IFAAMAS, Columbia (2008) (short paper)
8. Hang, C.W., Wang, Y., Singh, M.P.: Operators for propagating trust and their evaluation in social networks. In: Proceedings of the 8th International Conference on Autonomous Agents and Multiagent Systems (AAMAS), IFAAMAS, Columbia, SC, pp. 1025–1032 (2009)
9. He, Q., Yan, J., Jin, H., Yang, Y.: ServiceTrust: Supporting reputation-oriented service selection. In: Proceedings of the 7th International Conference on Service Oriented Computing, pp. 269–284 (2009)
10. Jøsang, A.: A subjective metric of authentication. In: Quisquater, J.-J., Deswarte, Y., Meadows, C., Gollmann, D. (eds.) ESORICS 1998. LNCS, vol. 1485, pp. 329–344. Springer, Heidelberg (1998)
11. Li, L., Wang, Y., Lim, E.P.: Trust-oriented composite service selection and discovery. In: Proceedings of the 7th International Conference on Service Oriented Computing, pp. 50–67 (2009)

12. Malik, Z., Akbar, I., Bouguettaya, A.: Web services reputation assessment using a hidden markov model. In: Proceedings of the 7th International Conference on Service Oriented Computing, pp. 576–591 (2009)
13. Maximilien, E.M., Singh, M.P.: Agent-based trust model involving multiple qualities. In: Proceedings of the 4th International Conference on Autonomous Agents and Multiagent Systems, pp. 519–526. IFAAMAS, Columbia (2005)
14. Nepal, S., Malik, Z., Bouguettaya, A.: Reputation propagation in composite services. In: Proceedings of the 7th IEEE International Conference on Web Services (ICWS), pp. 295–302. IEEE Computer Society, Los Alamitos (July 2009)
15. Robbins, H.: Some aspects of the sequential design of experiments. Bulletin of the American Mathematical Society 55, 527–535 (1952)
16. Singh, M.P., Huhns, M.N.: Service-Oriented Computing: Semantics, Processes, Agents. John Wiley & Sons, Chichester (2005)
17. Singh, S.P., Jaakkola, T., Littman, M.L., Szepesvári, C.: Convergence results for single-step on-policy reinforcement-learning algorithms. Machine Learning 38(3), 287–308 (2000)
18. Sutton, R.S., Barto, A.G.: Reinforcement Learning: An Introduction. MIT Press, Cambridge (1998)
19. Wang, Y., Singh, M.P.: Formal trust model for multiagent systems. In: Proceedings of the 20th International Joint Conference on Artificial Intelligence (IJCAI), Detroit, MI, USA, pp. 1551–1556 (2007)
20. Wu, Q., Iyengar, A., Subramanian, R., Rouvellou, I., Silva-Lepe, I., Mikalsen, T.A.: Combining quality of service and social information for ranking services. In: Proceedings of the 7th International Conference on Service Oriented Computing, pp. 561–575 (2009)
21. Zacharia, G., Maes, P.: Trust management through reputation mechanisms. Applied Artificial Intelligence 14(9), 881–907 (2000)

Trust Assessment for Web Services under Uncertainty

Zaki Malik[1] and Brahim Medjahed[2]

[1] Department of Computer Science, Wayne State University, MI. 48202
zaki@wayne.edu
[2] Department of Computer Science, University of Michigan-Dearborn, MI. 48120
brahim@umd.umich.edu

Abstract. We introduce a model for assessing the trust of providers in a service-oriented environment. Our model is cooperative in nature, such that Web services share their experiences of the service providers with their peers through ratings. The different ratings are aggregated using the "statistical cloud model" defined for uncertain situations. The model can uniformly describe the concepts of randomness, fuzziness, and their relationship in quantitative terms. By incorporating the credibility values of service raters in the model, we can assess a service provider's trust. Experiment results show that our proposed model performs in a fairly accurate manner.

1 Introduction

With the introduction of *Web services*, applications can now be automatically invoked by other Web clients. A Web service is a self-describing software application that can be advertised, located, and used across the Web using a set of standards (such as WSDL, UDDI, and SOAP) [29]. Businesses are increasingly using Web services to automate interactions both with their customers (B2C) and amongst each other (B2B). It is expected that future Web enterprises would exhibit a loose coupling of smaller applications offered by autonomous providers [26][29]. A primary goal of the Web services technology is therefore enabling the use of Web services as independent components in Web enterprises, that are automatically (i.e., without human intervention) formed as a result of consumer demand and which may dissolve post demand-completion [26].

Automatic Web services interactions entail that Web services have to determine to which extent they may *trust* other services to provide the required functionality, before they interact with them [20]. By definition, Web services are autonomous (i.e., provided by independent service providers), highly volatile (i.e., low reliability), and *a priori* unknown (i.e., new or no prior history) [29]. As a plethora of Web services are expected to compete in offering similar functionalities, a key requirement is then to provide mechanisms for the quality access and retrieval of services [25] [29]. Web services may make promises about the

P.P. Maglio et al. (Eds.): ICSOC 2010, LNCS 6470, pp. 471–485, 2010.
© Springer-Verlag Berlin Heidelberg 2010

provided service and its associated quality but may fail partially or fully to deliver on these promises bringing down the quality of the whole enterprise. Thus, the challenge lies in providing a framework for enabling the selection and composition of Web services based on trust parameters. The rationale behind the need for trust is the necessity to interact with unknown entities that have varied quality delivery levels [2]. There is a growing consensus that the Web service 'revolution' would not eventuate until trust related issues are resolved [4].

Trust has been defined as "an assured reliance on the character, ability, or strength of someone or something." Establishing trust is therefore a precondition for any transaction [2][22]. In a service-oriented environment, trust correlates to the ability of a service to perform the required functionality in an acceptable manner. The inherent open and large-scale nature of Web services means that traditional security approaches as confidentiality, authentication, authorization, etc. are insufficient for completely instilling trust. For instance, a provider's authentication or authorization credentials cannot guarantee that it will exercise these privileges in an expected manner [19]. When interacting with unknown providers, service consumers are thus usually interested in gaging provider reliability in delivering the required functionality (on top of traditional security mechanisms). Research results show that such a trust assessment process is facilitated by incorporating the "wisdom of crowds" through reputation ratings and recommendations [8] [20]. For example, several studies attribute eBay's commercial success to its reputation mechanism, known as eBay's Feedback Forum which has been effective in deterring dishonest behavior, and stimulating eBay's growth [30] [10]. Similar studies have investigated and generally confirmed that reputation systems benefit both sellers and buyers in e-auctions[15]. Reputation is defined as the confidence in the ability of a specific provider to fulfill a certain task [20]. It is a subjective assessment of a characteristic or an attribute ascribed to one entity by another based on observations or past experiences. Normally experiences from more than one source are assimilated to derive the reputation. This increases the subjectivity of trust and creates uncertainty.

In recent years, theoretical and experimental research has explored the subjective nature of trust. These works are primarily rooted in probability theory, evidence/belief models, or fuzzy logic. Probability based models usually do not consider the element of fuzziness in building trust [3] [34]. Since the reasoning is done in a purely statistical manner, they tend over-formalize trust's subjectiveness. For example, Bayesian systems take binary ratings as input and assess trust through updating of the beta probability density function [38] [33]. This process is fairly complex to comprehend and implement, and loses the component of fuzziness inherent in trust assessment. Models based on evidence and belief theory exhibit similar characteristics with added complexity [13] [34]. On the other hand, fuzzy logic based systems use precise set memberships for defining fuzziness of subjective trust. However, these solutions fail to consider the randomness and uncertainty of membership in those fuzzy sets [9] [27]. We propose a solution that incorporates uncertainty and fuzziness of trust to provide a more unified and holistic assessment. Our model employs the statistical cloud model which defines a way for modeling the transition between a linguistic term of a qualitative concept and its quantitative representation under uncertain and fuzzy conditions.

The paper is organized as follows. In Section 2, we provide an overview of a statistical model for predicting values in uncertain situations. In Section 3, we extend this model to evaluate trust of service providers. Section 4 provides experiment results, and verifies the applicability of our proposed model. Section 5 provides a brief overview of some related work, while Section 6 concludes the paper.

2   Statistical Cloud Model

The basis of the statistical cloud model (or simply, the cloud model) is that fuzziness and randomness are complementary and essentially inseparable concepts when considered in linguistic terms. It states that the concept of fuzzy membership functions is not sufficient for representing the uncertainty and imprecision in real world settings, and probability theory needs to be incorporated to overcome this inadequacy. In essence, a cloud model can uniformly describe the concepts of randomness, fuzziness, and their relationship in quantitative terms. Experiment results have shown that the cloud model exhibits higher levels of simplicity and robustness in comparison with traditional fuzzy logic and probability based methods [17] [18]. In the following, we provide a brief overview of the cloud model.

Let U be the quantitative universe of discourse, and C denote a qualitative concept associated with U. If $x \in U$ is a random realization of C, and $\mu(x) \in [0, 1]$ is a random variable with stable tendency denoting the degree of certainty for x belonging to C, that is:

$$\mu : U[0, 1] \qquad \forall x \in U \qquad x \to \mu(x)$$

The distribution of x in U is called the cloud (denoted $C(X)$) and each x is called a cloud drop. Note that in probabilistic terms, $x \in U$ is not a simple random number but it has a certainty degree, which itself is also random and not a fixed number. The cloud is composed of a number of drops, which are not necessarily ordered. The underlying character of the qualitative concept is expressed through all cloud drops. Hence the overall feature of the concept is more precisely represented by a large number of drops. The certainty degree of each cloud drop defines the extent to which the drop can represent the concept accurately. Formally, a cloud's quantitative representation is defined over a set of N ordered pairs (x_i, y_i), where x_i is a cloud drop, and y_i is its certainty degree, with $1 \leq i \leq N$.

A one-dimension normal cloud model's qualitative representation can be represented by a triple of quantitative characteristics: Expected value (Ex), Entropy (En) and Hyper-Entropy (He). Ex is the expectation of the cloud drops' distribution, i.e., it corresponds to the center of gravity of the cloud (containing elements fully compatible with the qualitative concept). En represents the uncertainty measurement of a qualitative concept. It is determined by both the randomness and fuzziness of the concept. En indicates how many elements could be accepted to the qualitative linguistic concept. He is a measure of the dispersion on the cloud drops. It can also be considered as En's uncertainty. Vector $v = (Ex, En, He)$ is called the eigenvector of a cloud [17].

The transformation of a qualitative concept expressed by Ex, En, and He to a quantitative representation expressed by the set of numerical cloud drops is performed by the forward cloud generator [18]. Given these three digital characteristics (Ex, En, He), and the number of cloud drops to be generated (N), the forward cloud generator can create these N cloud drops in the data space with a certainty degree for each drop that each drop can represent the qualitative concept. The procedure is:

1. Generate a normally distributed random number F with mean En and standard deviation He.
2. Generate a normally distributed random number x with mean Ex and standard deviation F.
3. Calculate $y = e^{-\frac{(x-Ex)^2}{2(F)^2}}$.
4. (x, y) represents a cloud drop in the universe of discourse.
5. Repeat Steps 1-4 until N cloud drops are generated.

Figure 1(a) shows the graph of a one-dimensional cloud whose digital characteristics are (0.7, 0.1, 0.01). A similar cloud with same Ex and En, but a different He (0.7, 0.1, 0.5) is shown in Figure 1(b). As defined in the above algorithm, the quantitative value of cloud drops is determined by the standard normal form distribution function. Hence, the certainty degree function adopts a bell-shaped curve. This is similar to the one adopted in fuzzy set theory. As mentioned earlier, the normal cloud model is therefore an inclusive model based on probability theory and fuzzy set theory, and is able to depict randomness in the former and fuzziness in the latter.

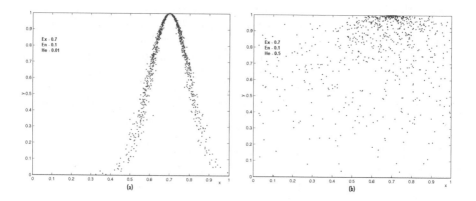

Fig. 1. Normal Cloud with Same Ex and En, but Different He Values

3   Statistical Cloud-Based Trust Model

We propose a trust model that is distributed in nature. In contrast to third-party-based traditional approaches for trust management, no single entity is responsible for collecting, updating, and disseminating ratings provided by different consumers. Each service consumer records its own perceptions of the reputation of only the services it actually invokes. This perception is called personal evaluation. For each service s_j that it has invoked, a service consumer t_x maintains a p-element vector $PerEval_j^x$ representing t_x's perception of s_j's behavior. Different strategies may be adopted in updating $PerEval_j^x$. A simple one may be a *per-invocation* update. Upon an invocation of service s_j, the delivered quality $QRef_d$ is compared to service s_j's promised quality $QRef_p$ and, if necessary, a trust updating algorithm is run to compute the new personal evaluation of service s_j. In essence, personal evaluation reflects the *Quality* performance of the provider in consumer's views. The personal evaluation $PerEval_j^x$, represents only consumer t_x's perception of the provider s_j's reputation. Other service consumers may differ or concur with t_x's observation of s_j. A service consumer that inquires about the reputation of a given service provider from its peers may get various differing personal evaluation "feedbacks." To get a correct assessment of the service provider's behavior, all the personal evaluations for s_j need to be aggregated. Assume L denotes the set of service consumers which have interacted with s_j in the past and are willing to share their personal evaluations of s_j. We assume that L is not empty, i.e., some service willing to share information can be found. Thus, $L \subseteq T$ with $L \neq \emptyset$ and each service x in L has $PerEval_j^x$ values for s_j. Then, consumer x's trust over s_j's ability to deliver is defined as:

$$Trust(s_j) = \bigwedge_{x \in L} (PerEval_j^x) \tag{1}$$

where $\bigwedge$ represents the aggregation function. Equation 1 provides a first approximation of how the trust may be assessed. However, it involves various factors that need to be precisely defined and measured.

The foremost drawback of feedback-only based systems is that all ratings are assumed to be honest and unbiased. However, in the real world we clearly distinguish between the testimonies of our sources and weigh the "trusted" ones more than others [36]. A Web service that provides satisfactory service (in accordance with its promised quality $(QRef_p)$), may get incorrect or false ratings from different evaluators due to several malicious motives. In order to cater for such "bad-mouthing" or collusion possibilities, a trust framework should weigh the ratings of highly credible raters more than consumers with low credibilities [7] [39] [20]. In our model, the final trust value is calculated according to the credibility scores of the raters (used as the weight).

After each interaction with the provider, apart from rating the provider s_j, the service consumer also updates the credibility of the raters that provided a rating for s_j. The service consumer computes the Euclidean distance (d) between the consumer's own experience (OE) and the provided rating (V_i). If d is less than a pre-defined threshold (δ), the credibility is increased in a linear manner. Otherwise, the rater's credibility is decreased exponentially by a factor of d, i.e., greater the d, more the rater credibility will decrease. This is in accordance with the sociological trust building process where it is difficult to gain inter-personal trust, but easy to lose it [6]. Since all transactions may not be equally weighed in terms of their importance, a service consumer may decide to decrease a dishonest rater's credibility according to the transaction's "impact". The transaction impact factor (τ) lies in the range [0, 1] and is assigned a low value for high impact transactions, and vice versa by the service consumer. The general formula for rater credibility is thus:

$$Cr^t = \begin{cases} Cr^{t-1} + c(\delta - d) & \text{if } d \leq \delta; \\ Cr^{t-1} \times e^{-(d+\tau)} & \text{otherwise.} \end{cases}$$

where c is the linear increment factor, weighted by the difference between δ and d. This implies that a lower value of δ will cause a lower increment in the value of c and hence the rater's credibility. Cr^t is the new credibility, and Cr^{t-1} is the rater's previous credibility value. The credibility of a service rater lies in the interval [0, 1] with 0 identifying a completely dishonest rater and 1 an honest one. In cases where no Cr^{t-1} exists, i.e., the rater and consumer have not previously interacted, the rater's initial credibility is set at the middle (0.5) to indicate impartiality. However, previous research has shown that assigning predefined high or average values may encourage "reputation white-washing" [21]. Therefore, we dampen the bootstrap value by weighing in the consumer's pessimistic/optimistic preferences towards services interactions, i.e.,

$$Cr_{bootstrap} = 0.5 \times \lambda$$

where λ denotes the consumer's pessimistic/optimistic preference in the range [0, 1]. A high λ value indicates an optimistic consumer, one that is willing to trust the testimony of a new rater. Alternatively, $\lambda \leq 0.5$ indicates a pessimistic consumer. The choice of λ is at the discretion of the service consumer. However, to provide a better estimate of the consumer's propensity to accept, we set λ as the *ratio* of the total number of times the ratings submissions (by all raters) are deemed useful (k) by the service consumer, over the total number of rating submissions received by the service consumer (n). This is similar to the manner in which peer recommendations are evaluated for usefulness in "recommender systems" [16][35]. The λ factor is:

$$\lambda = \frac{\sum_{i=1}^{k} U_i}{\sum_{x=1}^{n} V_x} \qquad (2)$$

where U_i is the submission where the rater was termed honest (i.e., $d \leq \delta$) and V_x denotes the total number of rating submissions.

Reputation information of a service provider decays with time [20], [23]. Hence all the past reputation data may be of little or no importance. For instance, a Web service performing inconsistently in the past may ameliorate its behavior. Alternatively, a service's performance may degrade over time. It may be the case that considering all historical data may provide incorrect reputation scores. In order to counter such discrepancies, we incorporate temporal sensitivity in our proposed model. The rating submissions are time-stamped to assign more weight to recent observations and less to older ones. This is termed as "reputation fading" where older perceptions gradually *fade* and fresh ones take their place. We adjust the value of the ratings as:

$$PerEval_j^{x:t} = PerEval_j^{x:t-1} * f_d \qquad (3)$$

where $PerEvall_j^x$ is as defined above and f_d is the reputation fader. In our model, the recent most rating has the fader value 1 while older observations are decremented for each time interval passed. When $f_d = 0$, the consumer's rating is not considered as it is outdated. The "time interval" is an assigned factor, which could be anywhere from a single reputation inquiry, ten inquiries or even more than that. All inquiries that are grouped in one time interval are assigned the same fader value. In this way, the service consumer can define its own temporal sensitivity degree. For example, a service can omit the fader value's effect altogether by assigning it a null value. We propose to use a fader value that can then be calculated as: $f_d = \frac{1}{\sqrt{P_u}}$, where P_u is the time interval difference between the present time and the time in which the rating was collected from the rater. This allows the convergence of reputation to a very small value as time passes. Note that the consumer can assign a group of ratings collected at different times to have the same time-stamp, and hence lie in the same time interval. As mentioned earlier, other calculated values for the fader are also acceptable.

Characteristics Extraction

The backward cloud generator allows transformation of the cloud model from its quantitative representation to a qualitative one. We incorporate rater credibility values and majority rating to produce the three digital characteristics of the cloud (Ex, En, He). Given a set of N ratings $PerEval_j^x (x = 1, 2, ..., N)$, we can extract the three characteristics as:

1. Update $PerEval_j^x$ values using f_d, for all ratings (including previous time instances).
2. For each rater x, update Cr_x (using equations defined previously).
3. Calculate

$$Ex = \frac{\sum_{x=1}^{N}(Cr_x PerEval_j^x)}{\sum_{x=1}^{N} Cr_x}$$

4. Calculate

$$En = \sqrt{\frac{\pi}{2}} \times \frac{\sum_{x=1}^{N} Cr_x |PerEval_j^x - Ex|}{\sum_{x=1}^{N} Cr_x}$$

5. Calculate

$$He = \sqrt{\frac{\sum_{x=1}^{N} Cr_x (PerEval_j^x - Ex)^2}{\frac{(N'-1)\sum_{x=1}^{N} Cr_x}{N'}} - (En)^2}$$

where N' is the number of non-zero credibilities.

Trust Decision

The next step is using the three discovered characteristics to make a subjective assessment of the provider's trust. Since He is a measure of En's uncertainty, we only use Ex and He to quantify the provider's trust and the associated uncertainty. This allows us to consider the latest majority view of the provider's reputation and the decentralization of ratings from it. A higher value of Ex therefore indicates high reputation, while a small He indicates the stability of the ratings around this decision. Intuitively this makes sense, but for a large N, making these comparisons is non-trivial. For instance, Ex and He can occur together in one of four forms: one is high/low the other is low/high, both are high, or both are low. Therefore, to quantify the relationship between the two characteristics, i.e., the provider (s_j)'s trust assessment, we use:

$$Trust(s_j) = \begin{cases} 1 - \frac{He}{Ex+He} & \text{if } Ex \neq 0 \text{ \& } He \neq 0; \\ Ex & \text{if He} = 0; \\ 0 & \text{if Ex} = 0; \end{cases}$$

where both $Ex \neq 0$ and $He \neq 0$.

4   Experiments

We have performed a number of experiments to show the applicability of the proposed statistical cloud-based trust model. We used Matlab for simulating the services interactions and ratings. The environment consists of five service providers and twenty service consumers (who act as raters) that interact over a period of twenty iterations. At each iteration, the raters report their past experiences (from the previous iteration) of the service providers. For simplicity, each rater interacts with all the service providers in each time instance. Therefore, the fader value (f_d) is set to 1.

The five service providers exhibit different dynamic behaviors. The first provider behaves consistently with high trust values, i.e., it behaves rationally and does not engage in any malicious activity. The next provider performs with consistently low trust values. It represents providers that are always looking to take advantage of the consumer. The third provider performs with high values for the first 10 iterations but then suffers a performance degradation. This strategic provider aims to build a reputation by initially performing honestly, and then starts "milking" [39] the attained reputation. The fourth provider acts in an opposite manner to the third provider where it performs with low values in the beginning. After the 10th iteration, it ameliorates its behavior and starts performing with high trust values. This provider represents the class of providers that learn from their mistakes. The provider performs in a random manner, oscillating between high (performing as promised) and low trust values (acting maliciously).

The service raters are distinguished into two classes: honest and dishonest raters. An honest rater provides the trust value it experiences, but a dishonest rater generates a rating that differs at least by 0.3 points from the actual rating. Say the provider's trust value was 0.9, then a dishonest rater would generate a value between [0.1 and 0.59]. These two classes of raters can be related to each other in one of three ways in the environment: the number of honest raters can exceed those of dishonest raters, honest and dishonest raters can be equal in number, or dishonest raters can out-number honest raters. We set the inequalities in rater behaviors (first and third scenario) to be significant (an 80-20 ratio imbalance is used). The different classes of raters and five provider behaviors mentioned above (and any combination thereof) cover any behavior that a service may exhibit. This ensures that the experiment samples are representative of the real world environment which contains a variety of provider and rater behaviors.

In the first experiment, honest raters (ones with high credibility values) outnumber dishonest raters, i.e., 80% of the raters are honest. Figure 2(a) shows the effect of this inequality in calculating the trust value for a provider that exhibits low values in a consistent manner. The dashed-line represents the trust value of the provider estimated using our proposed model, whereas the straight line represents the actual behavior experienced by the trust evaluator. It can be seen that due to the high number of honest ratings, the estimated trust value is almost equal to the actual provider behavior. The small variation in estimated and actual trust is due to the inconsistency brought in by the differences in opinions of credible raters and malicious attempts of non-credible raters. Figure 2(b) shows the case for the same provider (exhibiting same actual behavior) for the case where a large majority of raters are dishonest. In this case, the system "catches up" with dishonest testimonies after a few initial iterations. However, once this learning process is complete, the presence of dishonest raters is minimized and actual vs. estimated trust values become very close. Other classes of providers exhibit similar results, thus we omit those graphs (and associated discussions here).

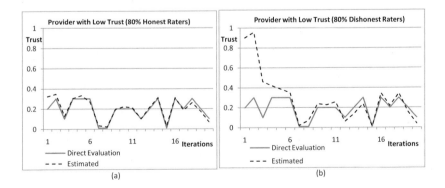

Fig. 2. Service Provider with Consistently Low Trust Values

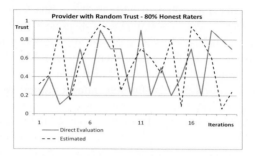

Fig. 3. Service Provider with Random Trust Values: 80% Raters are Honest

Figure 3 shows the trust evaluation process for a provider that exhibits random behavior in terms of trust values. Although the number of honest raters exceeds that of dishonest ones, the system still exhibits inconsistent results. This is due to the manner in which rater credibilities are evaluated and weighed. An honest rater that reports its experienced trust may have its credibility reduced in the next iteration due to the inconsistent behavior of the provider. Consequently, widening the gap between estimated and experienced trust.

We evaluate the error percentage of the proposed model by comparing the output (service provider chosen) against the "actual best service provider alternative" available. Note that since these are controlled experiments, we can identify the best providers for each iteration. A graph depicting these behaviors for all service interactions becomes convoluted. Thus, for brevity Figure 4(b) only shows a snapshot of actual service provider behaviors for interaction numbers 9 through 13. We can see that Service Provider 1 shows consistently high trust values, while Provider 3's performance (and hence trust) drops at 11th. iteration onwards. In contrast, Provider 4's trust values shift to higher values at the same point. Similarly, Provider 2 performs with consistently low values, while Provider 5 exhibits random behavior switching between high and low trust values. Figure 4(a) shows the trust values estimated using the proposed model for the same time period. The model chooses the service provider with the highest trust value at each iteration for interaction. For instance, at iteration 10, Service Provider 3 is estimated to be the "best" service available, while at iteration number 11 Provider 1 is chosen and Provider 5 is chosen at iteration 12 (and so on).

Table 1 shows all iterations, best provider alternatives for each iteration, and the service provider chosen by our model. The final column labeled "Error" places an X if the chosen service is incorrect. There are six instances in which our model chose an incorrect service as per the given data. Apart from iterations 3 and 4, the other four errors were reported because the model chose Provider 5. Note that this class of providers behaves randomly at each iteration. Thus, it is difficult for the system to predict or report correct trust values. However, such provider behavior is expected to be rare [20]. The errors of iterations 3 and 4 can be termed as "minor" since both Provider 1 and 3 have high trust values

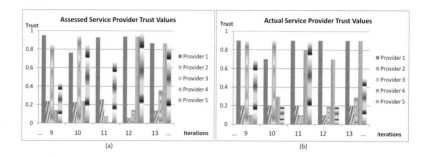

Fig. 4. Actual Service Provider Trust Values Compared for Iterations 9 through 13

Table 1. Error Evaluation of the Proposed Model

Iteration	Best Service Provider Available	Chosen Service Provider	Error
1	P1 or P3	P5	X
2	P1 or P3	P1	-
3	P3	P1	X
4	P1	P3	X
5	P1, P3 or P5	P3	-
6	P1 or P3	P3	-
7	P1, P3 or P5	P1	-
8	P1 or P3	P5	X
9	P1 or P3	P1	-
10	P3	P3	-
11	P1 or P5	P1	-
12	P1	P5	X
13	P1 or P4	P1	-
14	P4	P4	-
15	P4	P4	-
16	P1	P1	-
17	P4	P5	X
18	P1	P1	-
19	P4	P4	-
20	P1	P1	-

(note that Provider 3 switches behavior at the 11th. iteration). If we consider *all* reported errors, we can say the proposed model has 70% accuracy, while if we consider P1 and P3 comparable (which they are), then system accuracy jumps to 80%. Note that, these error evaluation results are for the case where 80% of the raters are dishonest. When 80% of the raters are honest, error percentage is reduced to less than 5%. In light of these results, we can conclude that our proposed model estimates a service provider's trust in a fairly accurate manner even under uncertainty.

5   Related Work

Trust assessment involves several components, including modeling, data collection, data storage, communication, assessment, and safeguards. Over the years, several research initiatives have worked on most of these problems. Similar to our model, most initiatives equate trust with reputation, i.e., the higher the reputation of a provider, the more trustworthy it is, and vice versa. Varied disciplines including economics, computer science, marketing, politics, sociology, and psychology have studied reputation-based trust in several contexts [8]. In the recent past, these research activities have gained momentum. In computer science, reputation has been studied both in theoretical areas and practical applications. Theoretical areas where reputation has been studied include game theory [12], Bayesian networks [37], overlay networks,[32] and social networks [6] to name a few. Theoretical literature that addressed reputation focused on proving properties of systems based on reputation. For example, results from game theory demonstrate that there are inherent limitations to the effectiveness of reputation systems when participants are allowed to start over with new names [31]. In [11], the authors study the dynamics of reputation, i.e., growth, decay, oscillation, and equilibria. Practical literature on reputation is mainly concerned with the applications of reputations. Major applications where reputation has been effectively used include e-business, peer-to-peer (P2P) networks, grid computing systems [1], multi-agent systems [33], Web search engines, and ad-hoc network routing [5]. In the following, we give a brief overview of a few reputation management frameworks for P2P systems and Web services since these are closely related to our research.

PeerTrust [39] is a P2P reputation management framework used to quantify and compare the trustworthiness of peers. In PeerTrust, the authors have proposed to decouple feedback trust from service trust, which is similar to the approach undertaken in this paper. Similarly, it is argued that peers use a similarity measure to weigh opinions of those peers highly who have provided similar ratings for a common set of past partners. However, this may not be feasible for large P2P systems, where finding a statistically significant set of such past partners is likely to be difficult. Consequently, peers will often have to make selection choices for peers which have no common information in the system.

In [14], the *EigenTrust* system is presented, which computes and publishes a global reputation rating for each node in a network using an algorithm similar to Google's *PageRank* [28]. Each peer is associated with a global trust value that reflects the experiences of all the peers in the network with that peer. EigenTrust centers around the notion of transitive trust, where feedback trust and service trust are coupled together. Peers that are deemed honest in resource sharing are also considered credible sources of ratings information. This is in contrast with our approach and we feel this approach may not be accurate. Moreover, the proposed algorithm is complex and requires strong coordination between the peers. A major limitation of EigenTrust is that it assumes existence of pre-trusted peers in the network.

PowerTrust [40] is a "distributed version" of EigenTrust. It states that the relationship between users and feedbacks on eBay follow a Power-law distribution.

It exploits the observation that most feedback comes from few "power" nodes to construct a robust and scalable trust modeling scheme. In PowerTrust, nodes rate each interaction and compute local trust values. These values are then aggregated to evaluate global trust through random walks in the system. Once power nodes are identified, these are used in a subsequent look-ahead random walk that is based on Markov chain to update the global trust values. Power nodes are used to assess the reputation of providers in a "system-wide absolute" manner. This is in contrast with our approach where each consumer maintains control over the aggregation of ratings to define a provider's reputation. Moreover, PowerTrust requires a structured overlay (for DHT), and the algorithms are dependent on this architecture. In contrast, service-oriented environments or the Web in general do not exhibit such structure.

Despite the abundance in reputation-related literature, little research has focused on the reputation of Web services. In [24], a distributed model for Web service reputation is presented. The model enables a service's clients to use their past interactions with that service to improve future decisions. It also enables services' clients to share their experience from past interactions with Web services. Agents are associated with each Web service, that act as proxies to collect information on and build a reputation of a Web service. The authors present an approach that provides a conceptual model for reputation that captures the semantics of attributes. The semantics includes characteristics, which describe how a given attribute contributes to the overall rating of a service provider and how its contribution decays over time. A similar reputation-based model using a node's first hand interaction experience is presented in [32]. The goal of the model is to increase/maintain QoS values in *selfish* overlay networks. The authors show that in presence of a reputation management system, an overlay network discourages *selfish* nodes. This increases the QoS guarantees in the network. The proposed model considers a node's first hand interaction experience and peer testimonials for deriving node reputations. In this regard, the reputation building process in [32] is similar to our approach. However, the proposed reputation model may not be completely robust and may not provide accurate results. First, the individual experience takes time to evolve over repeated interactions. Second, no distinction is made between the node's service credibility in satisfying consumer requests and its rating credibility. It may be the case that a node performs satisfactorily but does not provide authentic testimonials. We provide an extensive mechanism to overcome these and similar inadequacies.

6 Conclusion

We have presented a trust assessment model for Web services. We focused on an environment where Web services can act as both consumers (i.e., requesters) and providers of services, without the need of a *trusted third party*. This similarity with P2P systems, wireless networks, etc. means that the model is extensible and can be deployed in other contexts. We have also conducted extensive simulations to verify the proposed model. Results exhibit strong evidence that our approach provides a fairly accurate assessment of provider trust. In the future, we intend to implement the model in a real Web services environment. We also aim to extend the model to include service *compositions*.

References

1. Azzedin, F., Maheswaran, M.: Evolving and Managing Trust in Grid Cmputing Systems. In: Proc. of the IEEE Canadian Conference on Electrical and Computer Engineering, pp. 1424–1429 (May 2002)
2. Bertino, E., Ferrari, E., Squicciarini, A.C.: Trust-X: A Peer-to-Peer Framework for Trust Establishment. IEEE TKDE 16(7), 827–842 (2004)
3. Bharadwaj, K., Al-Shamri, M.: Fuzzy computational models for trust and reputation systems. Electron. Commer. Rec. Appl. 8(1), 37–47 (2009)
4. Birman, K.: The untrustworthy web services revolution. IEEE Computer 39(2), 113–115 (2006)
5. Buchegger, S., Le Boudec, J.-Y.: Performance Analysis of the CONFIDANT Protocol. In: Proc. of the 3rd ACM Intl. Symposium on Mobile Ad Hoc Networking and Computing, June 9-11, pp. 226–236 (2002)
6. Buskens, V.: Social Networks and the Effect of Reputation on Cooperation. In: Proc. of the 6th Intl. Conf. on Social Dilemmas (1998)
7. Delgado, J., Ishii, N.: Memory-Based Weighted-Majority Prediction for Recommender Systems. In: ACM Workshop on Recommender Systems (1999)
8. Dellarocas, C.: The Digitalization of Word-of-Mouth: Promise and Challeges of Online Feedback Mechanisms. In: Management Science (October 2003)
9. He, R., Niu, J., Yuan, M., Hu, J.: A novel cloud-based trust model for pervasive computing. In: International Conference on Computer and Information Technology, pp. 693–700 (2004)
10. Houser, D., Wooders, J.: Reputation in Auctions: Theory, and Evidence from eBay. Journal of Economics and Management Strategy (2005)
11. Huberman, B.A., Wu, F.: The Dynamics of Reputations. TR, Hewlett-Packard Laboratories and Stanford University (January 2003)
12. IBM. Aglet software development kit (2000), `http://www.trl.ibm.com/aglets`
13. Jøsang, A.: A logic for uncertain probabilities. Int. J. Uncertain. Fuzziness Knowl.-Based Syst. 9(3), 279–311 (2001)
14. Kamvar, S.D., Schlosser, M.T., Garcia-Molina, H.: The eigentrust algorithm for reputation management in p2p networks. In: Proceedings of the Twelfth International World Wide Web Conference (WWW) (2003)
15. Kesler, C.: Experimental Games for the Design of Reputation Management Systems. IBM Systems Journal 42(3) (2003)
16. Lam, S., Riedl, J.: Shilling Recommender Systems for Fun and Profit. In: Proc. of the 13th International World Wide Web Conference (WWW), New York, NY, USA, pp. 393–402 (2004)
17. Li, D., Han, J., Shi, X., Chan, M.: Knowledge representation and discovery based on linguistic atoms. Knowledge-Based Systems 10(7), 431–440 (1998), KDD: Techniques and Applications
18. Li, D., Liu, C., Gan, W.: A new cognitive model: Cloud model. Int. J. Intell. Syst. 24(3), 357–375 (2009)
19. Malik, Z., Bouguettaya, A.: Rater Credibility Assessment in Web Services Interactions. World Wide Web Journal 12(1), 3–25 (2009)
20. Malik, Z., Bouguettaya, A.: Reputation-based Trust Management for Service-Oriented Environments. VLDB Journal 18(4), 885–911 (2009)

21. Malik, Z., Bouguettaya, A.: Reputation Bootstrapping for Trust Establishment among Web Services. IEEE Internet Computing 13(1) (January-February 2009)
22. Malik, Z., Bouguettaya, A.: Trust Management for Service-Oriented Environments, 1st edn. Springer, Heidelberg (2009) ISBN:978-1-4419-0309-9
23. Marti, S., Garcia-Molina, H.: Limited Reputation Sharing in P2P Systems. In: Proc. of the 5th ACM Conference on Electronic Commerce, New York, NY, USA, pp. 91–101 (May 2004)
24. Maximillien, E.M., Singh, M.P.: Conceptual Model of Web Service Reputation. SIGMOD Record 31(4), 36–41 (2002)
25. Medjahed, B., Bouguettaya, A.: Customized delivery of e-government web services. IEEE Intelligent Systems 20(6) (November/December 2005)
26. Medjahed, B., Bouguettaya, A., Elmagarmid, A.: Composing Web Services on the Semantic Web. The VLDB Journal 12(4) (November 2003)
27. Niu, J., Chen, Z., Zhang, G.: Towards a subjective trust model with uncertainty for open network. In: Workshops, International Conference on Grid and Cooperative Computing, pp. 102–119 (2006)
28. Page, L., Brin, S., Motwani, R., Winograd, T.: The PageRank Citation Ranking: Bringing Order to the Web. Technical report, Stanford Digital Library Technologies Project (1998)
29. Papazoglou, M.P., Georgakopoulos, D.: Serive-Oriented Computing. Communcications of the ACM 46(10), 25–65 (2003)
30. Resnick, P., Zeckhauser, R.: Trust Among Strangers in Internet Transactions: Empirical Analysis of eBays Reputation System. Advances in Applied Microeconomics, vol. 11. Elsevier Science, Amsterdam (2002)
31. Resnick, P., Zeckhauser, R., Friedman, E., Kuwabara, K.: Reputation Systems. Communication of the ACM 43(12) (December 2000)
32. Rocha, B.G., Almeida, V., Guedes, D.: Increasing qos in selfish overlay networks. IEEE Internet Computing 10(3), 24–31 (2006)
33. Sabater, J., Sierra, C.: Bayesian Network-Based Trust Model. In: Proc. of the first Intl. Joint Conf. on Autonomous Agents and Multiagent Systems, Bologna, Italy, pp. 475–482 (2003)
34. Shibin, Z., Xiang, S., Zhi, Q.: Subjective trust evaluation model based on fuzzy reasoning. International Symposium Electronic Commerce and Security. 1, 328–332 (2009)
35. Sundaresan, N.: Online trust and reputation systems. In: EC 2007: Proceedings of the 8th ACM Conference on Electronic Commerce, pp. 366–367. ACM Press, New York (2007)
36. Tennenholtz, M.: Reputation systems: An axiomatic approach. In: AUAI 2004: Proceedings of the 20th Conference on Uncertainty in Artificial Intelligence, pp. 544–551. AUAI Press, Arlington (2004)
37. Wang, Y., Vassileva, J.: Trust and reputation model in peer-to-peer networks. In: Proc. of the Third International Conference on Peer-to-Peer Computing, pp. 150–158 (September 2003)
38. Whitby, A., Josang, A., Indulska, J.: Filtering Out Unfair Ratings in Bayesian Reputation Systems. The Icfain Journal of Management Research 4(2), 48–64 (2005)
39. Xiong, L., Liu, L.: PeerTrust: Supporting Reputation-based Trust for Peer-to-Peer Electronic Communities. IEEE Trans. on Knowledge and Data Engineering (TKDE) 16(7), 843–857 (2004)
40. Zhou, R., Hwang, K.: Powertrust: A robust and scalable reputation system for trusted peer-to-peer computing. IEEE Transactions on Parallel and Distributed Systems 18(4), 460–473 (2007)

Incorporating Expectations as a Basis for Business Service Selection

Adel M. ElMessiry, Xibin Gao, and Munindar P. Singh

North Carolina State University, Raleigh NC 27695, USA
{ammessir,xgao2,singh}@ncsu.edu

Abstract. The collaborative creation of value is the central tenet of services science. In particular, then, the quality of a service encounter would depend on the mutual expectations of the participants. Specifically, the quality of experience that a consumer derives from a service encounter would depend on how the consumer's expectations are refined and how well they are met by the provider during the encounter. We postulate that incorporating expectations ought therefore be a crucial element of business service selection.

Unfortunately, today's technical approaches to service selection disregard the above. They emphasize reputation measured via numeric ratings that consumers provide about service providers. Such ratings are easy to process computationally, but beg the question as to what the raters' frames of reference, i.e., expectations. When the frames of reference are not modeled, the resulting reputation scores are often not sufficiently predictive of a consumer's satisfaction.

We investigate the notion of expectations from a computational perspective. We claim that (1) expectations, despite being subjective, are a well-formed, reliably computable notion and (2) we can compute expectations and use them as a basis for improving the effectiveness of service selection. Our approach is as follows. First, we mine textual assessments of service encounters given by consumers to build a model of each consumer's expectations along with a model of each provider's ability to satisfy such expectations. Second, we apply expectations to predict a consumer's satisfaction for engaging a particular provider. We validate our claims based on real data obtained from eBay.

1   Introduction

This paper investigates the problem of business service selection based on an expanded notion of reputation and trust. It is widely recognized now that the collaborative creation of value is the central tenet of services science [13]. Specifically, the importance of understanding human behavior as a basis for service science is well-recognized, but is not necessarily reflected in the technical approaches developed by computer scientists. In particular, then, the quality of a service encounter would depend on the mutual expectations of the participants. Specifically, the quality of experience that a consumer derives from a service encounter would depend on how the consumer's expectations are refined and met by the provider during the encounter. Indeed, this is well-known in marketing theory as the service quality GAPS model as a basis of customer satisfaction [16]. This model, however, is traditionally applied from the perspective of the

P.P. Maglio et al. (Eds.): ICSOC 2010, LNCS 6470, pp. 486–500, 2010.

service provider in terms of its marketing and operations. In contrast, we postulate that incorporating expectations is a crucial element of business service selection as well.

Unfortunately, today's technical approaches to service selection rely upon combining numeric ratings without regard to what the raters' frames of reference, i.e., expectations, might have been. When the frames of reference are not modeled, the resulting reputation scores are often not sufficiently predictive of a consumer's satisfaction. Accordingly, the main claim of this paper is that reputation scores produced merely by an aggregation of context-free numeric ratings are not significantly effective in producing trust. Specifically, this paper proposes to explicitly consider the *expectations* of the parties involved in order to arrive at a finessed notion of reputation that an agent may use as a basis for trusting others.

Both to show the practicality of the above claim and to evaluate it rigorously, this paper considers the important setting of e-commerce interactions, such as the marketplaces of eBay and Amazon. E-commerce settings provide an immediate and widespread application for research into service selection. Further, they provide a source for independent, real-life data with which to objectively evaluate research claims. Such real-life evaluations are generally not prominent in the services literature.

To further motivate the problem, consider a buyer who is faced with a decision to select a seller from a group of sellers. Other things being equal, a buyer would rationally decide based on the experiences of previous buyers with the various sellers. For this reason, e-commerce sites include reputation systems whereby buyers can state a numeric rating of a seller with whom they interact (and sellers can rate buyers, but we do not consider those here). A subsequent buyer can use those ratings to select a suitable seller. This buyer too would rate the seller he chose, thus helping maintain the information in the reputation system. Current reputation systems aggregate numeric ratings and present a simple measure of a potential seller's quality.

In general, the better the reputation a seller accrues the more trustworthy it becomes. The fundamental deficiency of this approach lies in its presumption that we can simply combine ratings by different users. Doing so assumes that the different users have the same frame of reference. Such naïve aggregation may be acceptable in some cases, e.g., where a seller has obtained a large number of ratings from homogeneous buyers, but is not valid for many practical settings involving smaller sets of ratings, especially when the ratings differ in a way that can matter to a prospective buyer. Although reputation aggregated solely from numeric ratings can be useful, it often misses the point of what a buyer seeks. This is because the various ratings are given by different buyers based on their respective frames of reference. It would be surprising if simply aggregating such ratings would yield the most valuable information for a prospective buyer.

This paper is based on the idea that a key aspect of the frame of reference of a buyer is captured in the buyer's expectations. When a buyer's expectations are met, his experience is pleasant, and one would assume his rating of the seller is positive. More importantly, to predict the buyer's quality of a buyer's experience and his ultimate rating, we need to look beyond simply the ratings given by other buyers, and also incorporate the expectations that underlie those ratings. When we relate the expectations of a buyer with the expectations of previous raters, we would produce a more accurate recommendation and a more justifiable basis for the buyer to select a seller.

A natural challenge is how to estimate the expectations of a buyer. Fortunately, e-commerce settings provide a clue as to their users' expectations through text comments (termed *feedbacks*) that a user may produce in addition to a numeric rating. A user's feedback often describes the user's experience from a specific transaction and gives reasons for the associated rating. Although feedbacks are free form, we find that their vocabulary is generally quite restricted. Therefore, we can mine text feedback reasonably effectively to understand its author's expectations for the given interaction.

Contributions. We begin from the prima facie reasonable assumption that users with shared expectations would share a similar degree of satisfaction from their respective encounters with the same business services. Our main contribution is to refine and validate this assumption. We show that applying expectations in a common e-commerce setting yields better predictions of ratings than otherwise possible. Further, we show that the expectations of buyers can be reliably and effectively mined from the text feedbacks they produce. Additionally, through the use of abstract expectations, this approach can help match buyers and sellers even if there is no direct relationship between them. This is crucial in overcoming the sparsity of data, e.g., with respect to new buyers and sellers.

Organization. Section 2 introduces expectations, a representation for them, and our approach. Section 3 describes our evaluation methodology and presents our results. Section 4 discusses some relevant literature and some future research challenges.

2   Understanding Expectations

There is fairly strong support in the literature on consumer behavior for the notion of expectations. Kim et al. [11] observe that the fulfillment of a consumer's expectation is a key factor in the consumer's satisfaction, and may indirectly influence the consumer's intention to repurchase from the same seller. The approach of this paper reflects the intuitions of *Expectation-Confirmation Theory* due to Bhattacherjee [4], which is a leading model of consumer satisfaction. To understand the relation among expectations, satisfaction, and ratings, we consider a three-phase model.

Formulate expectations. The customer identifies his requirements and expectations.
Transact. The customer selects a seller and carries out the interaction.
Evaluate. The customer compares his expectations with his experience. The customer'
   expectations being met or *confirmed* correspond to greater satisfaction, and thus a
   higher rating of the seller. The customer' expectations not being met correspond to
   (partial or total) dissatisfaction, and thus a lower rating of the seller.

2.1   Expectation and Reputation Profiles

To realize the above approach computationally, we need to express expectations, automatically infer expectations, and compare them. A simple representation proves quite effective. We can think of each expectation as a name-value pair: the value describes the strength of the corresponding expectation as a real number in the interval $[0, 1]$.

It is convenient to write the expectation profile of a consumer as a row vector whose columns are interpreted as the expectation attributes and whose cells are the corresponding values. For example, in a two dimensional setting, we may interpret $\langle 0.9, 0.1 \rangle$ as the profile of a consumer who expects a high *Level of Service* and is relatively unconcerned with *Shipping Time*. The order in which the expectations are written is irrelevant, but we require that the order is (arbitrarily) fixed so we can perform sound calculations on the vectors. We use vector such as the above as the main representation in our approach:

Buyer's expectation profile based on the buyer's previous interactions. This represents the buyer's typical expectations as the buyer enters into an encounter.

Seller's reputation profile based on the previous interactions of buyers with this seller. This represents the typical preexisting expectations of a buyer who enters into an encounter with this seller.

We observe that feedbacks associated with negative ratings from a buyer yield a more meaningful estimation of the buyer's expectations. When buyers give negative ratings, they often elaborate on why. By contrast, with positive ratings, they often merely state that the experience is good. Some studies [19] also show that eBay auctions are mildly influenced by positive ratings, however, negative ratings emerged as highly influential and detrimental. Thus, in this paper, we focus exclusively on negative feedbacks to induce expectation and reputation vectors.

For each buyer, we create an expectation profile based on the buyer's comments. For each seller, we create a reputation profile based on the comments posted by the buyers who have interacted with that seller and given it negative feedbacks. Thus, the seller's reputation profile is negative: it captures expectations that the seller does not meet well. From a match between a prospective buyer and a target seller we can estimate how unsuccessful the buyer's experience with that seller will be. That is, *the stronger the match the greater the chances of the buyer's expectations not being met.*

2.2   Analyzing Feedback to Infer Expectations

We consider the following expectation attributes specialized for e-commerce services: *Item (is as described), Communications (are effective), Shipping time (is small), Shipping (and handling) charges (are appropriate), (Level of) service (is high).* For brevity, below, we omit the parenthesized parts of the names of each attribute. Notice that *Item, Communications,* and *Service* are subjective qualities.

As we remarked above, often in practical settings, the set of text feedbacks given by a user is the only source of knowledge we have of the user's expectations. We adopt the techniques of sentiment and affect analysis of text to infer a user's expectations. Sentiment analysis assesses the directionality of a text fragment and asserts if it is positively or negatively oriented [15]. Affect analysis [1] seeks to identify the emotions or affect classes indicated in a text fragment.

We analyze expectations in analogy with affect, and abstract the expectation vector construction process as a multiclass, multilabel text classification problem. An expectation vector has five dimensions corresponding to the above attributes. The value of each attribute represents its strength. For example, $\langle 0.1, 0.9, 0.0, 0.0, 0.0 \rangle$ means that the user has a strong concern with communication, and does not care about shipping time, shipping charges, or service. The expectation vector for a buyer is constructed by aggregating the class labels for all the feedbacks the buyer left.

For each textual feedback, the vector is assigned by a text classifier. The class labels are the above attributes plus *Others* because some feedbacks fall outside the five attributes. For example, some feedbacks are in Spanish, and some only contain symbols. Multiple class labels can be assigned to each feedback because multiple concerns can be expressed in each feedback. For example, "Dirty console. Did not respond. Non Working Console" alludes to *Item* ("Dirty console" and "Non Working Console") and to *Communication* ("Did not respond").

We apply text processing techniques to analyze the feedbacks and induce an expectation vector from these feedbacks.

Clean up the text using the Google Spell Checker service [8] to replace wrongly spelled words and thus reduce the noise in the input. The checker mostly suggests correct words, mapping "recieved" to "received" and "emials" to "emails." However, this step is not perfect. For example, it maps "wii" to "WI."

Remove stop words (such as "a," "the," and "all" [12]) because they carry little meaning. This process simplifies further text processing without sacrificing quality.

Reduce dimensionality of the data by stemming using Porter's algorithm [17]. Stemming maps several forms of a word to their common stem. For example, "receive," "received," and "receiving" are reduced to "receiv." Although "receiv" is not a dictionary word, it suffices for the purpose of classifying feedbacks as similar words are reduced to the same form.

Represent text computationally via two alternatives for representing text: unigram (bag of words) and bigram (bag of pairs of adjacent words).

Assign class labels to the textual feedback using a text classification module [20]. We evaluated two popular classification algorithms: Naïve Bayes and Support Vector Machine (SVM). We found that SVM outperforms Naïve Bayes. Therefore, we applied SVM over a combination of the unigram and bigram models.

Compute expectation profiles of the buyers using the results of the classification. For example, suppose a buyer has left three feedbacks that are assigned the class labels (1) *Item, Communication*; (2) *Others*; and (3) *Communication*. We disregard the *Others* label because it is outside our five main concerns. Then we aggregate the class labels from the other two feedbacks to obtain the initial vector $\langle 1.0, 2.0, 0.0, 0.0, 0.0 \rangle$. We divide this vector by the number of aggregated feedbacks to normalize it. The final expectation vector is $\langle 0.5, 1.0, 0.0, 0.0, 0.0 \rangle$.

2.3   Buyer-Buyer Profile Match

Our approach reflects the intuition that if two buyers have closely related expectation profiles, then each buyer is more predictive of the other's ratings of a seller. Consider a prospective buyer interested in purchasing a product offered by more then one seller. We collect the feedback and ratings given by previous buyers to the same seller. We analyze the feedback to extract the buyers' expectations.

We calculate the prospective buyer's predicted rating as the weighted sum of the previous buyers ratings for the same seller. The weight used for each previous buyer is calculated based on the Pearson correlation between the prospective buyer's expectation profile and the previous buyer's expectation profile, as used in conventional recommender systems [5]. The rating of each buyer is then weighted by how close his expectation profile matches the prospective buyer's expectation profile.

2.4 Buyer-Seller Profile Match

In addition to the above, we use the seller's reputation profile to predict the prospective buyer's rating. Since the seller's reputation profile indicates the expectations of an average buyer of this seller, comparing them with the prospective buyer's expectations helps us determine if the prospective buyer and the seller match.

To predict a prospective buyer's experience with a particular seller, collect the feedback and ratings given by previous buyers to this seller. Analyze the feedbacks to extract the buyers' expectations (for reasons motivated earlier, consider only buyers giving the seller negative ratings). Finally, use those profiles to generate the seller's reputation profile, which represents the average expectations of the buyers for that seller. Compare the seller's reputation profile to the prospective buyer's expectation profile, to predict what the prospective buyer's rating would be.

We develop a seller's reputation profile that reflects the feedbacks *received* by the seller from previous buyers. This is the seller's negative reputation profile from the standpoint of the expectations of the previous buyers. It represents the expectations most strongly arising in the buyers' negative feedbacks for this seller.

The seller's reputation profile represents the average buyer's expectation profile as the average buyer interacts with this seller. Intuitively, if the prospective buyer's expectation profile is close to the seller's reputation profile, the prospective buyer will have similar reaction. We apply this to the negative feedbacks, from which we can construct the (negative) reputation profile of the seller and the prospective buyer.

We determine the similarity between the profiles in terms of the cosine of the angle between them [18]. Below $\otimes$ refers to the inner product of two equal-length vectors, namely, the sum of their element-wise products. Then $\cos(V_1, V_2) = \frac{V_1 \otimes V_2}{\|V_1\| \times \|V_1\|}$. In order to convert similarity into a categorical value, we check if the cosine is larger than 0.87 (which corresponds to an angle of 30 degrees or less) to determine that the profiles are in agreement. Since we are focusing on the negative profiles, if those profiles are in agreement, we conjecture the buyer is likely to give the seller a negative rating. But if the buyer's main complaints from past purchases indicate different expectation attributes than what the seller's previous buyers have complained about, the buyer and seller's expectation profiles would not agree. Consequently, the buyer would be more likely to give a positive rating.

3   Evaluation

We conduct our evaluation using eBay, because it is one of the most popular online reputation systems for e-commerce, and because we can retrieve the ratings and feedbacks left by buyers after their actual transactions on eBay. On eBay, each party involved in a transaction can leave a feedback and a rating on the other. A rating can be of one of three values: $\{-1, 0, 1\}$. The numeric ratings help ground our approach.

3.1 Dataset

We explain below some important decisions necessary for the development of our dataset from the large amount of information available through eBay. Some of these decisions are pragmatic—to make the effort tractable. And, some decisions are necessary for the theme of our experiments.

Selecting a Category. We select data pertaining to a particular sales category so that we can find enough overlap among the buyers and sellers to conduct our experiments. We choose a category based on the following criteria.

- *Common*. The category needs to be for common items. This is so we can find sufficiently many buyers and find buyers with broad characteristics, so our results are not biased by any tight community we might happen to select. For example, if we chose a niche category, then there might be well-developed communities of interest with established patterns of expectations.
- *Affordable*. The category must be affordable to allow for repeat purchases. For example, not many buyers will be using the "Automotive" category repeatedly.

Thus, we focus our research on the categories *Music CDs* and *Cell Phones*.

Selecting the Sellers. Not all sellers would have meaningful data. We conjecture this is due to the positive feedback being often quite vague and not containing sufficient useful information. Thus we have followed the following criteria in selecting the sellers:

- *Not perfect*. The seller's score should be less than 100%, and preferably in the 95% to 99% range, so there is sufficient negative feedback to analyze. We remark in passing that the average feedback on eBay is high, about 95% positive: thus we identify sellers who are about average, not those who are unusually positive.
- *Adequate feedback*. In general, it is difficult to draw strong conclusions with only sporadic data. We select sellers who have received at least 40 negative feedbacks.

Selecting the Buyers. We seek buyers for whom meaningful data is available. We need buyer data for two experiments, and we select the buyers appropriately to suit the needs of each experiment. In each experiment, the previous buyers are extracted from eBay data. These buyers would give negative ratings in order for the feedback to be meaningful. The prospective buyer is treated differently in each experiment.

- *For Enhancing Ratings*. The prospective buyers' expectation profiles are determined in such a manner as to show their impact on the seller's rating.
- *Predicting the Buyer's Rating*. The prospective buyer can be positive or negative. We withhold the buyer's rating and use it as the ground truth to evaluate the predictions of our algorithm. The main criterion in selecting these buyers is that they would have given an adequate amount of negative feedback to sellers *other* than the one under consideration. The reason for this choice is that we need buyers with an adequate track record to be able to infer their expectation profiles.

Collecting the Data. For each of the selected sellers, we collect the feedback and rating left by each buyer. We consider all ratings and feedbacks received by a seller in a particular category. For each buyer, we collect the feedback and rating associated with each previous transaction. (Typically, such transactions are with different sellers.) This leaves us with a dataset that has sellers and buyers with sufficient history about their interactions with each other and with additional parties. The following are the instructions given to the human study participants.

- Consider the transactions with negative and neutral comments for each seller.
- For each transaction, determine which expectations of the buyer were not met—these would be the ones that the buyer complained about.

From the above data, we calculate the ratio of the expectations not met with the number of negative or neutral feedbacks.

Summary of the Data. Table 1 show a quick summary of our collected data.

Table 1. Statistics regarding feedbacks analyzed

Item	Count
Sellers	1,794
Buyers	147
Number of feedbacks	2,242
Unique buyer-seller interactions	2,048
Feedbacks left by buyers for a joint seller	1,195

The first important test is whether the buyers leaving feedback for a joint seller have matching profiles. If the expectation profile is not predictive, then buyers complaining about the same seller would not share the same profile. We compare each pair of buyers for the same seller across the entire data set, to find a relatively high percentage, 54%, of profile matching between buyers complaining about a joint seller in 649 cases.

3.2 Result: Robustness of Expectations as a Well-Formed Concept

We now show that even though expectations are subjective, they are a robust concept in that humans can extract buyers' expectations from feedbacks, and do so in a reliable manner. We show this by computing the *interrater agreement* among humans regarding the expectations that can be inferred from text feedbacks.

The Kappa measure of interrater agreement captures whether agreement among raters exceeds chance levels [9]. Given $P(a)$ as the relative observed agreement among raters, and $P(e)$ as the (hypothetical) probability of chance agreement, the Kappa measure is defined as $\frac{P(a)-P(e)}{1-P(e)}$, and ranges from 0 (complete disagreement) to 1 (complete agreement). For a setting involving multiple classifications and raters, the appropriate variants of Kappa have intricate definitions and we omit them for brevity.

Three raters independently assessed buyers' expectations from various text feedbacks. We selected 361 feedbacks that have three out of the six categories selected by the raters. We obtained a high level of interrater agreement with overall Kappa of 85.5% and fixed and free marginal Kappa of 80.0% and 82.6%, respectively.

3.3 Result: Effectiveness of Negative Feedback in Indicating Expectations

We selected five sellers with high ratings (over 95%), compiled their recent 16 positive and 16 negative feedbacks, thereby forming a sample of size 160 feedbacks. We submitted these 160 feedbacks to a human rater to rate each feedback's usefulness. The rater would assign the value of 1.0 if the feedback is useful in capturing the buyer's expectation associated with the feedback; otherwise, the rater would assign the value of 0.0. For each seller, the average is computed for both the positive and the negative feedbacks. From the summary Table 2, we infer that a negative feedback is more than twice as indicative of the expectations associated with the transaction than is a positive feedback.

Table 2. Relative effectiveness of positive and negative feedback in indicating expectations

Seller	Average Rating	Positive Feedback Usefulness	Negative Feedback Usefulness
Seller 1	99.7%	40.00%	73.33%
Seller 2	99.8%	33.33%	80.00%
Seller 3	99.5%	26.67%	60.00%
Seller 4	99.6%	26.67%	66.67%
Seller 5	98.6%	26.67%	60.00%
Average	**99.6%**	**30.67%**	**68.00%**

3.4 Result: Effectiveness of Automatically Computing Expectations

As remarked above, we apply supervised machine learning using Naïve Bayes (NB) and SVM techniques. Traditional text classification is often evaluated in terms of precision, recall, and F-measure. Because our problem involves multiple labels, we report these metrics as *macro-averaged* (calculating the average of a metric for each class) and *micro-averaged* (using a global contingency table for each class) [21].

Using 500 annotated feedbacks, we apply ten-fold cross validation. That is, we train our classifier on 90% of the data and test it on the remaining 10%, using a different 10% for testing each of ten times. Table 3 shows the results from different experimental settings. In particular, SVM classification on a combination of unigram and bigram yields the best performance. So we use that setting for the subsequent evaluation.

Notice that general text classification can yield better metrics than we obtained, but our approach proves quite effective in demonstrating the power of expectations. We conjecture that our classification results can be improved by using a larger training set, a better spelling checker, and considering those domains of business services where the feedbacks given are more complete.

3.5 Result: Buyer-Buyer Profile Match

In order to apply the buyer's expectations, we need to construct the expectation profile associated with the ratings.

Specifically, we select two sellers who sell under the *Cell Phones and PDAs, Bluetooth Wireless Accessories, Headsets-Wireless* category. Both sellers have a high Positive

Table 3. Feedback classifier performance in different experimental settings. All settings use stop words removal and stemming. They vary in using unigram (U), bigram: B, Naïve Bayes (NB), and Support Vector Machine (SVM). Each value is the mean of a ten-fold cross validation.

Setting	Micro P	Micro R	Micro F	Macro P	Macro R	Macro F	Error
B+U+SVM	0.67	0.76	0.71	0.66	0.76	0.67	0.14
B+SVM	0.72	0.53	0.61	0.70	0.45	0.50	0.16
U+SVM	0.67	0.73	0.70	0.68	0.73	0.66	0.15
B+U+NB	0.59	0.79	0.68	0.61	0.66	0.58	0.18
B+NB	0.40	0.82	0.54	0.39	0.65	0.42	0.32
U+NB	0.57	0.79	0.66	0.54	0.64	0.54	0.19

Table 4. Expectation profiles for prospective buyers

	Buyer 57	Buyer 119
Item	0.11	0.48
Communication	0.67	0.28
Shipping time	0.56	0.32
Shipping charges	0.11	0.04
Service	0.00	0.00

Feedback Percentage of 97.5%. In other words, the traditional eBay reputation cannot be used to distinguish between them. We claim that our approach can help a prospective buyer distinguish between such sellers.

From the negative feedback left for each seller by the previous buyers, we first determine the expectation profile of each of the previous buyers. Let us consider two prospective buyers with expectation profiles as shown in Table 4.

Table 5. Sellers' reputation profiles computed by mining feedbacks

	Item	Communication	Shipping time	Shipping charges	Service
Seller 1606	0.42	0.17	0.34	0.08	0.0
Seller 1321	0.25	0.75	0.50	0.25	0.0

To evaluate this approach, we select two sellers, collect the feedback left for them by previous buyers. Using the approach of Section 2.2, we compute the expectation profile for each feedback. We then average the profiles for all feedback received by each seller to compute the seller's reputation profile. Table 5 shows these results, normalized based on the total number of values. It is evident that whereas both sellers have relatively close results with respect to *Item* and *Communication*, they vary widely with respect to *Shipping time*, *Shipping charges*, and *Service*.

Next we calculate the predicted ratings for each buyer for each seller. Our approach yields the predicted ratings for the two sellers for each of the prospective buyers. It shows a clear distinction between the two sellers: Seller 1321 has a lower performance for *communication*, which is an important expectation attribute for Buyer 57. Thus its predicted rating is reduced, leading us to identify Seller 1606 as a better match than Seller 1321 for Buyer 57. Similarly, Buyer 119 would prefer Seller 1606.

3.6 Result: Buyer-Seller Profile Match

To validate the effectiveness of using expectation profiles, we select the top fifteen sellers with the most feedback (more than five negative feedbacks each). Their minimum rating is 97.2% with a mean of 98.4% and a standard deviation of 0.5 percentage points. We isolate the distinct buyers for those sellers to eliminate repeated seller-buyer interactions. We then apply the method of Section 2.2 to generate the buyers' expectation profiles and the reputation profile of each seller. Finally, we subject the resulting profiles to our buyer-seller matching. Our results show that in 73 cases out of the 116 available feedbacks, the buyer-seller profile matched, indicating a negative buyer experience. This is a hit ratio of 63% for our approach. Clearly, these 73 buyers would not have considered purchasing from the seller if our expectations-based approach were used. They interacted only because the traditional metric is not as effective in predicting outcomes in such cases.

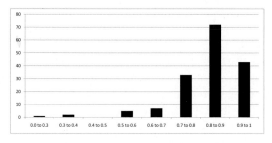

Fig. 1. Distribution of strength of matches between buyers and sellers for the top 15 sellers

Figure 1 shows that using the reputation profile of the seller and comparing it to the prospective buyer's expectation profile yields a significant advantage over using the traditional approach. Typically, the benefit of our approach is greatest when the profile match suggests a negative rating. This is because on eBay the average rating is overwhelmingly positive. For this reason, a true negative rating is highly indicative of an unsatisfied user, and an ability to predict accurately in cases of negative ratings is of extremely high value. We think of this as a major result from our study.

We next take a closer look at how a buyer may fare using the traditional approach compared to our approach. We selected a buyer (Buyer 60) who had already interacted with five sellers, apparently because the sellers had high overall ratings. Table 6 shows the profile we construct for each of these sellers in the usual way based on the feedback left by buyers other than Buyer 60.

All of the above sellers match Buyer 60's profile strongly (the cosines of the vectors are 0.87, 0.92, 0.97, 0.92, and 0.92, respectively), indicating that the buyer's expectations were not met. This result emphasizes our findings above that matching a buyer's expectations profile with a seller's (negative) expectations profile is an effective predictor of the buyer's expectations being unmet.

Table 6. Sellers' reputation profiles computed by mining feedbacks

Seller ID	Item	Communication	Shipping time	Shipping charges	Service	Other
235	0.5	0	0.5	0	0	0
805	1	1	1	0	0	0
838	0.50	0.17	0.58	0.08	0.25	0
1035	1	0	1	0	0	0
1620	1	0	1	0	0	0

4 Conclusions and Discussion

To summarize, our approach produces three important results. First, we show that incorporating expectations leads to improved predictions in ratings. These improvements arise precisely where they are the most valuable, which is when the prospective buyer would otherwise be likely to produce a negative rating. The key observation is that even if two sellers obtain similar numeric ratings, when they are viewed from a buyer's perspective, they may exhibit unique deficiencies and strengths with respect to that buyer's expectations. Capturing such variations is crucial for service selection.

Second, we show that even minimal text fragments can carry useful clues about a human's expectations that go beyond mere numeric ratings; it is possible to mine such text effectively to help bring cognitive models of trust to a new level.

Third, because the approach works at a level of abstraction, it can avoid the problem of sparsity of data, which plagues traditional approaches (and which might be the reason why content-free numeric ratings have become as popular as they have). We can predict the ratings of a buyer based on the feedbacks of other buyers even if prospective buyer has never shared a seller with them. This is important because finding adequate overlaps in the transactions of different pairs of parties can be incredibly difficult, especially as we approach the era of The Long Tail in e-commerce [2].

4.1 Threats to Validity

In general, it appears that the key elements of our approach are generalizable: most service settings involve rich notions of expectations and text feedbacks from users may often be our best path to access knowledge of such expectations. However, proving the above claim presupposes access to sufficiently large amounts of data from other settings. Such data is not readily available in vetted form with sufficient controls. It would be valuable if the research community were to develop curated datasets by collecting information from social websites regarding service interactions.

Our empirical study carries some inherent biases. First, we focus on negative ratings because our limited evaluation in Section 3.3 shows they are more useful than positive ratings. Second, the amount of data we consider is apparently fairly small in the scheme of things. We hope to scale up our approach in future studies. However, two important aspects of our study are human-intensive. One is to obtain human annotations of the ratings to judge the stability (interrater agreement) of the concept of expectations as reflected in text and the other is to use human annotations as a basis for supervised learning. Third, we have considered buyers who generally gave multiple feedbacks and sellers who received multiple feedbacks. We expect that a data mining approach such as ours is inherently limited to such cases: without adequate data, it would not get far.

4.2   Relevant Literature

Many efforts on the theme of trust and reputation in e-commerce address challenges such as malicious ratings or a seller employing others to provide false high ratings, or to provide false low ratings of another seller in order to distort the other seller's reputation [10]. Other efforts concentrate on the propagation of trust through several second-hand sources. Few have explored what other factors can influence the rating of a user and thus, influence the final computation of trust. To our belief, not much research has considered on the study of expectations and their relationship to reputation and trust.

Singh and Maximilien [14] introduce a trust model that is centered on a shared conceptualization for QoS (ontology) and a QoS preference model that considers consumer's tradeoffs among qualities as well as relationships between qualities. Their work could be combined with the present approach by modeling the users' expectations with regard to the various qualities.

At a practical level, an interesting direction for future work is to expand the techniques for sentiment and affect analysis that we have employed. We have considered the five most common domain-independent expectations attributes, four of which are now supported by eBay. However, the space of expectations is extremely broad. We would like to expand this work to accommodate more sophisticated expectations especially those that arise in specific domains. For example, the expectations of coin collector may be quite different from those of a business-woman purchasing a printer. When we broaden the scope of expectations, the problem naturally calls for sophisticated text processing and machine learning techniques.

The notion of expectations is central to trust. Bernard Barber [3] defines trust essentially in terms of expectations—regarding general social structures as well as the technical competence and intentions to meet obligations and responsibilities. The present paper has focused on the lower end of this scale of complexity and subtlety so as to demonstrate the effectiveness of several apparently simple techniques. However, the scope of the work could be naturally expanded, and we hope that the success of the approach and its results lead to greater interest in the study of expectations.

It is also interesting to consider trust, as Castelfranchi and colleagues [7] have argued, as a form of relationship capital that can be accumulated. The present approach could feed into such work. Meeting expectations strengthens the relational capital whereas violating expectations depletes it. We observe that a lot of the cognitively well-motivated research into trust and reputation such as [6] has not had practical applications in broader computational settings. This is because of the difficulty in inferring the cognitive states of users in open settings. The methodology developed here, of inferring expectations as a form of simplified sentiment and affect analysis of text fragments, could possibly develop into a more general approach that could handle the challenges of the cognitive approaches—in settings where some clues to the user's cognitive state are available in text or other media.

4.3 Future Work

We began from a motivation based on the importance of expectations from the services science standpoint, especially as applied to business services. The e-commerce interactions that we study are business as opposed to technical services, and the user experience they offer depends more on subjective expectations than on hard quality of service data such as latency. Therefore, although they are simple, they are a useful surrogate for business services at large. However, we imagine that more complex engagements would offer additional challenges, including the involvement of more than two parties and the evolution of expectations during negotiation. The latter would go beyond the exchange of messages as in the eBay setting.

Formulating a more general model of consumer expectations for service-centric systems along with a method for computationally inferring expectations in such settings are two significant challenges. We imagine that the computational method would again rely upon techniques such as text mining, but perhaps more sophisticated than the present approach. We hope to address some of these conceptual and technical challenges in future work.

Acknowledgments

We thank the anonymous reviewers for their helpful comments.

References

1. Abbasi, A., Chen, H., Thoms, S., Fu, T.: Affect analysis of web forums and blogs using correlation ensembles. IEEE Transactions on Knowledge and Data Engineering 20(9), 1168–1180 (2008)
2. Anderson, C.: The Long Tail: Why the Future of Business is Selling Less of More. Hyperion, New York (2008)
3. Barber, B.: Logic and Limits of Trust. Rutgers University Press, New Brunswick (1986)
4. Bhattacherjee, A.: Understanding information systems continuance: An expectation-confirmation model. MIS Quarterly 25(3), 351–370 (2001)
5. Breese, J.S., Heckerman, D., Kadie, C.: Empirical analysis of predictive algorithms for collaborative filtering. In: Proceedings of the 14th Annual Conference on Uncertainty in Artificial Intelligence, pp. 43–52. American Association for Artificial Intelligence, Menlo Park (1998)
6. Castelfranchi, C., Falcone, R.: Principles of trust for MAS: cognitive anatomy, social importance, and quantification. In: Proceedings of the 3rd International Conference on Multiagent Systems, pp. 72–79. IEEE Computer Society Press, Los Alamitos (1998)
7. Castelfranchi, C., Falcone, R., Marzo, F.: Being trusted in a social network: Trust as relational capital. In: Stølen, K., Winsborough, W.H., Martinelli, F., Massacci, F. (eds.) iTrust 2006. LNCS, vol. 3986, pp. 19–32. Springer, Heidelberg (2006)
8. Checker, G.S.:
   http://code.google.com/apis/soapsearch/reference.htm#1_3
9. Eugenio, B.D., Glass, M.: The kappa statistic: a second look. Computational Linguistics 30(1), 95–101 (2004)

10. Kerr, R., Cohen, R.: Smart cheaters do prosper: defeating trust and reputation systems. In: Proceedings of the 8th International Conference on Autonomous Agents and Multiagent Systems (AAMAS), pp. 993–1000. IFAAMAS, Budapest (2009)
11. Kim, D.J., Ferrin, D.L., Rao, H.R.: A study of the effect of consumer trust on consumer expectations and satisfaction: the Korean experience. In: Proceedings of the 5th international conference on Electronic commerce (ICEC), pp. 310–315. ACM Press, New York (2003)
12. Project stop words list, S.:
    `http://jmlr.csail.mit.edu/papers/volume5/lewis04a/`
    `all-smart-stop-list/english.stop`
13. Maglio, P.P., Spohrer, J.: Fundamentals of service science. Journal of the Academy of Marketing Science 36(1), 18–20 (2008)
14. Maximilien, E.M., Singh, M.P.: Agent-based trust model involving multiple qualities. In: Proceedings of the 4th International Joint Conference on Autonomous Agents and MultiAgent Systems (AAMAS), pp. 519–526. ACM Press, New York (July 2005)
15. Pang, B., Lee, L.: A sentimental education: Sentiment analysis using subjectivity summarization based on minimum cuts. In: Proceedings of the 42nd Meeting of the Association for Computational Linguistics (ACL), pp. 271–278. Association for Computational Linguistics, Barcelona (2004)
16. Parasuraman, A., Zeithaml, V.A., Berry, L.L.: A conceptual model of service quality and its implications for future research. Journal of Marketing 49(4), 41–50 (Fall 1985)
17. Porter, M.F.: An algorithm for suffix stripping. Information Systems 40(3), 211–218 (2006)
18. Salton, G., McGill, M.J.: An Introduction to Modern Information Retrieval. McGraw-Hill, New York (1983)
19. Standifird, S.: Reputation and e-commerce: ebay auctions and the asymmetrical impact of positive and negative ratings. Journal of Management 27(3), 279–295 (2001)
20. Williams, K.:
    `http://search.cpan.org/~kwilliams/ai-categorizer-0.09/`
21. Yang, Y., Liu, X.: A re-examination of text categorization methods. In: Proceedings of the 22nd Annual International ACM SIGIR Conference on Research and Development in Information Retrieval, pp. 42–49. ACM, New York (1999)

Enhancing Collaboration with IBM's Rational Jazz^{tm}

Laura Anderson[1], Bala Jegadeesan[2], Kenneth Johns[2],
Mario Lichtsinn[2], Priti Mullan [2], James Rhodes[2],
Akhilesh Sharma[2], Ray Strong[2], and Ruoyi Zhou[2]

[1] Doctoral Student, Gateway PhD program, San Jose State University,
Queensland University of Technology, Brisbane, Australia
[2] Almaden Services Research, IBM Research - Almaden
650 Harry Road, San Jose, California, 95120
111.anderson@student.qut.edu.au,balaj@us.ibm.com,kjusf@us.ibm.com,
lichtsin@us.ibm.com,pritim@us.ibm.com,jjrhodes@us.ibm.com,
akhi@us.ibm.com,strong@almaden.ibm.com,ruoyi@us.ibm.com

Abstract. This paper describes our experience with IBM's Rational Jazz^{tm} platform for collaboration and for coordinating software development in the context of a medium sized service research and development project. We discuss the observed advantages of Jazz in systematizing the development process, especially when we are operating with extreme agility and the team is widely distributed around the world. We cover both narrative observations and quantitative measurements of Jazz usage. We demonstrate an objective measure of the value of such a software development management system. And we study the extent to which Jazz interfaces can replace ad hoc communication. While Jazz provides sufficient structure to replace all other communication within a geographically distributed research and development team, we conclude that redundant team communication in the forms of email and telephone meetings is necessary to maintain team motivation.

Keywords: Agile Software Development, Collaboration, Service System.

1 Introduction

The service system concept provides a valuable abstraction for evaluating and understanding the activities of a service provider, client, and the intrinsic value co-creation [3], [8]. Software development is perhaps one of the best examples of a service system today from several vantage points: the software under development is most certainly destined to be a part of a larger service system, the overall project team is a service provider to a customer within the enterprise, and the extended team formed to create the software is itself a stand-alone operational service system.

This practitioner paper examines the operation of a globally distributed virtual team responsible for the research and development of a complex financial

P.P. Maglio et al. (Eds.): ICSOC 2010, LNCS 6470, pp. 501–514, 2010.

system which includes applications, a data repository and advanced data analytics capabilities. Activities start from initial concept, requirements gathering, all the way through the lifecycle to deployment and maintenance. Work is performed collaboratively and dynamically by an organizationally matrixed team, with members coming together from a wide variety of disciplines and professions. The team is globally distributed, with some parts of the team co-located, and others dispersed in individual locations. Primary team members and stakeholders include the business process owners, the business transformation members, architectural, development, and quality assurance professionals, and the target customers. In addition, an agile software development methodology is utilized to provide rapid prototyping and development as well as flexibility and responsiveness to changing business requirements [11].

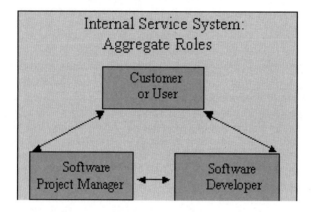

Fig. 1. Communication and Collaboration among roles within the SDM Software Development Service System

The project is named Solution Definition Manager (SDM), which includes multiple subprojects producing IBM^{tm} software for multiple customers within IBM. Each project encompasses multiple roles and crosses various organizational and geographic boundaries. In this study we aggregate these multiple roles and projects into three roles with short names: Customer, Manager, and Developer. The software being produced is used by solution architects and others within IBM to prepare bids for IBM's external service clients. Modifications and new features in the software are requested by these solution architects, by executives responsible for sales and service delivery, and by executives responsible for funding the research and development that produces the desired software. Our focus in this paper is on the software development process, so we consolidate all these users and executives into one role: Customer. We group all those who participate in the research and development process by writing or testing code into one role: Developer. And we collect a relatively small group of participants in the development process who do not write or test code into one role: Manager.

(Note that there is no particular correlation between IBM Management and any of these roles.)

Managers are trained in software development project management. There are very roughly ten times as many Developers as Managers. There are potentially at least a thousand times as many Customers as Developers; but we are only focused on the set of Customers who participate in the software development service system to co-create value. The size of this set is roughly the same as the size of the set of Developers.

The combination of Customers, Developers, and Managers constitutes a highly geographically dispersed virtual team. Managers and Developers who reside on different continents work closely together to produce software in spite of global scale time differences and intervening organizational boundaries.

Our goal is to produce reliable, innovative software both punctually and with agility [11]. Of course agility, reliability, and punctuality compete and cannot be simultaneously maximized. In this paper we will describe our experience as we, somewhat dynamically, explore tradeoffs toward the ultimate goal of optimizing the value we are co-creating.

Work is organized into work streams that are included in research and development projects. The output of several projects is combined into a release. The frequency of releases varies from quarterly to annually depending on agreements reached among all the roles (part of the exploration of tradeoffs mentioned above). In addition, more frequent internal "prototyping and iteration" releases can also be managed through this agile process to rapidly gather feedback on user interfaces and functionality.

We will report qualitative experience over several years and many releases of multiple software systems; but we will focus on one year of work involving multiple releases of a single system for a report consisting of the interpretation of quantitative data. During this year, the code base for this system was moved from a previous management platform to Jazz, a program product from IBM Rational. We will report on our experience with Jazz as a platform for collaboration and co-creation of value within our service system.

Jazz is an integrated software development environment that includes a central database, client applications and a web portal. It allows a virtual team to track custom defined items related to software development. In our case, we track defects (reported software problems), tasks (within work streams), requested enhancements, requirements, and cross-line-of-business conflicts. Our selections allow Jazz to function as a workload manager, a software source code file manager, a software release content manager/scheduler, and a source code integration manager, a communication platform, and a project information repository. The workload manager provides a view of work items and their associated status (e.g., open closed) as well as the software developer that is assigned to the work item. It also provides a cross-team view of workloads and assignments to enable workload balancing. A software source code file manager enables programmers to utilize a shared code base and add to it or modify code elements. It provides a central code repository and a foundation for producing software builds. The software release content manager/scheduler provides the capability to group individual work items together into an iteration plan, or release. The communication platform and project information repository allow all team members to access information about project work items without having to go through e-mail trails, phone calls or other means of ad hoc communication.

2   Relevant Software Development Research

Two important enablers of close collaboration across the dimensions of physical space, disparate time zones, and differing knowledge bases and disciplines are 1. the establishment and active maintenance of "situation awareness"; the ability of team members to perceive the activities and work items of their colleagues [10], and 2. the creation of a common base or context around which to bring together diverse disciplines, expertise, and viewpoints to a focused project objective. [7].

The computer supported cooperative work (CSCW) literature has addressed these challenges from multiple angles: the exploration of collaboration support systems, from general "communication" systems to ones tightly integrated with workflow and contextual tasks [1], formal and semi-formal frameworks [2], [5].

Integrated development environments, such as Jazz, have also been studied and evaluated for their effectiveness in core technical activities such as coding, as well as corollary tasks such as project management.[2], [9], [12], [13]. Our practical experience utilizing Jazz as a project activity and information hub, builds on these previous studies and extends research to include other stakeholders in the software development process, such as customers, business process owners, and project managers.

Agile software development methodologies [4], [6] are characterized by iterative, interactive, and highly collaborative practices. They provide a high degree of customer value throughout the project, through this co-creation process, particularly when compared with traditional waterfall methodologies. However, agile methodologies can pose some practical challenges when the virtual team is dispersed geographically, since the affordances of co-location, such as serendipitous informal meetings, are not present. The fast-paced and rapidly changing priorities of an agile project put particular pressure on the capability to rapidly synchronize the work activities of dispersed technical team members across multiple time zones. Similarly, the close collaboration required between the technical team and the customers can also be negatively impacted by these same factors. Jazz addresses these issues through an integrated software development environment coupled with an information hub for related project information and activities.

3   Narrative Observations

Qualitative data was gathered through a questionnaire completed by people serving in the project manager role for different workstreams in the project, a small subset of the full development team for this multi-year agile development project. They were asked to objectively provide information about their experiences using Jazz in their daily work during the past year by responding to the following questions.

1. How effective is Jazz at tracking defects, tasks, enhancements, requirements, and cross-line-of-business conflicts?
2. How effective is Jazz in collaborating with a geographically dispersed team?
3. Does Jazz increase, reduce, or eliminate the time spent communicating synchronously (in meetings, on the phone, and instant messaging)? Can you estimate weekly meeting frequency before and after adopting Jazz?
4. Does Jazz increase, reduce, or eliminate the total time spent communicating asynchronously (including email, Jazz, any other non-instant messaging)?
5. Does Jazz improve workload balance? How?
6. Does Jazz make more agility possible? How?
7. Does Jazz improve communication between developers and customers or users? Do you use pie charts or trend graphs generated from Jazz data to communicate with customers? Do you use similar visualizations to communicate with developers?
8. Does Jazz improve programmer productivity? How?
9. Does Jazz reduce the numbers of defects? How?
10. Does Jazz make source code integration (merge) easier and more defect free? How?
11. How long did it take for you to learn how to use Jazz (in your PM role)? Did you have to learn Jazz for all roles (PM, developer, customer, ...)?
12. What, if any, is your experience with the Jazz web portal? Why do developers use a Jazz client and customers, a web portal?

This section provides the consolidated results of the responses to these questions and is structured as an interview with one composite answer representing the entire service system rather than answers from each role.

1. How effective is Jazz at tracking the items of interest to SDM stakeholders (defects, tasks, enhancements, requirements, and cross-line-of-business conflicts)?

Answer: During the previous three years of SDM development and research, we have used different tools for tracking these items including spreadsheets, MS Project^{tm}, Lotus Notes Teamroom^{tm}, and CVS^{tm}. None of them are as effective as Jazz. Jazz integrates the development and project management processes into one tool, reducing cross-process overhead. We use Jazz to log enhancements (requests and new ideas) and requirements. Then we generate and track the associated development work items (tasks and defects). We rarely use the conflicts selection, which was designed to track conflicting business requirements.

We have to define our own development process, including agility tradeoffs. Jazz provides the framework. We are still exploring potential improvements to our process. Requirement conflict tracking and resolution is an example area where more work is needed before the item will be useful.

Sometimes a Customer creates a defect item or adds comments indicating a problem on a development work item in order to suggest a change to an original requirement. This provides a challenge because we need to detect this particular category and treat it differently than we would a defect indicating a failure to meet an original requirement. This is simply an overhead price the service system pays for agility.

Overall, Jazz serves as a customizable, flexible, and easy to use information hub, activity center, and status console, simultaneously providing high and low level views of a project.

2. How effective is Jazz in collaborating with a geographically dispersed team?

Answer: Jazz provides shared access to a common view of the state of the service system. It facilitates context specific communication and work flow management (assigning and reassigning work items). The particular value of Jazz is that it provides relevant access to all the different roles in the service system, promoting co-creation of value between each pair of roles, across geographies, time zones, and organizational boundaries. People from different organizations with varied roles tend to have their own tools for collaboration and project tracking. Jazz breaks the silos and horizontally integrates different teams to focus on the project.

3. Does Jazz change the time spent communicating synchronously (in meetings, on the phone, and instant messaging)?

Answer: Jazz provides email notification for lists of people subscribed to specific work items. We use Jazz to keep people informed and to record updates to plans. However, Developers in particular are likely subscribed to large numbers of items at any given time; so Managers use telephone or instant message as a redundant communication medium for high priority information that might otherwise be lost in a flood of emails. By serving as the definitive plan repository, Jazz does reduce time that is otherwise wasted in meetings when information about plans has not been synchronized. But Jazz does not replace the need for meetings and other synchronous communication. On balance it may reduce synchronous communication time slightly. It does provide a common authority and framework for improving the overall project effectiveness. Project management processes need to be aligned and integrated with the use of Jazz.

4. Does Jazz change the total time spent communicating asynchronously (including email, Jazz, any other non-instant messaging)?

Answer: When items are updated with appropriate and timely information, it does help reduce the time spent communicating asynchronously. It definitely reduces coordination time among Managers who need to act on status information including the number of requirements completed, the defect backlog, and Developer work load. There is a significant reduction in total time spent in asynchronous communication by Managers. In addition, providing a "level playing field" for easily obtaining information between team members from different organizations addresses the problem of varying knowledge levels about a particular situation or activity, as can be the case with email distribution.

5. Does Jazz improve workload balance? How?

Answer: Jazz provides work load information across teams so that Managers have some general visibility. This is especially helpful when one work stream needs help from the team working on another. This is an area where we expect significant improvement when we upgrade to Jazz 2.0 and can explore new processes corresponding to new Jazz function.

One feature we're particularly interested in evaluating is plan risk assessment. It takes a minimum/maximum time estimate for a work item and provides a probability estimate for on time completion. If the probability is low, we can reassign the item based on general work load information.

6. Does Jazz make more agility possible? How?

Answer: Yes. Jazz provides a platform for direct and documented communication within the entire service system. We build agile processes on top of this platform. Without it, the communication channel for requirements and conflicts becomes a bottleneck, inhibiting agility.

7. Does Jazz improve service system communication? Does anyone use pie charts or trend graphs generated from Jazz data?

Answer: Jazz definitely improves communication by providing a shared view of service system state as described above. We do not currently use the Jazz visualization tools for service system communication. This is part of the tradeoff in favor of agility.

8. Does Jazz improve programmer productivity? How?

Answer: Yes, here are two specific features jazz offers that have proven invaluable:

1) The ability to associate a change-set to a work item and be able to later reference why certain changes were made. It's common to come across code and wonder "why is this here?" In Jazz, one can simply annotate the class file and jazz will color code the file indicating the last change-set associated with every line of code in the file. This makes it easy to pinpoint the person to contact if further explanation is necessary. We've used this feature countless times and it's saved us from introducing regression bugs.

2) The suspend change-set feature allows a developer to remove changes from the workspace, but keeps them available to resume at a later time. This eliminates the need to maintain multiple development workspaces. If we're working on a new feature and we're notified of a very high priority defect that needs to be resolved ASAP, This feature allows us to suspend the changes for the new feature and work on resolving the defect, without the new feature code getting in the way. When the defect is resolved, we simply resume the change-set and continue working. Prior to Jazz, this would require setting up a new workspace, which consumes valuable time.

9. Does Jazz reduce the numbers of defects? How?

Answer: Jazz can help to reduce the number of defects if the developers use the functions designed to do so. In Jazz we set up a status called "ready for review" indicating the item should be reviewed by a technical lead Developer before the Developer can check in the code. We're also looking into the using build/test capabilities offered by Jazz. Once enabled, any developer will be able to kick off a build and have automated test scripts performed before ever delivering code for the rest of the team to consume.

10. Does Jazz make source code integration (merge) easier and more defect free? How?

Answer: Without a question, Yes. The code merge process itself is very challenging. Especially for a project such as ours that's very fast paced. The concept of change-sets and the process of flowing them to various other work streams saves a lot of time. The flow change-set process in Jazz identifies new change-sets that have been added since the last merge. These change-sets can be accepted into the stream and any conflicts are identified by Jazz. Jazz has a built-in feature that attempts to auto merge conflicts. When it's unable to merge automatically, a manual merge is required.

11. How long did it take to learn how to use Jazz? Did you have to learn Jazz for all roles?

Answer: It generally takes about a week to become proficient at one role. One does not need to learn the other roles. At a basic level, the Jazz concepts were simple to pick up. We had a working test environment set up for evaluation within a day.

12. What, if any, is your experience with the Jazz web portal? Why do developers use a Jazz client and customers, a web portal?

Answer: The web portal allows any jazz registered users to access project artifacts without having to install the client. Typically, Developers prefer the client because it's integrated with their IDE. Some non-Developers also prefer the client because of speed and an integrated screen capturing feature.

4   Jazz Usage Measurements

Our working hypothesis is that increasing usage is an indication of perceived value, particularly in the dimension of time savings through consolidated information and global team presence awareness. Jazz puts every item created by any Jazz user in its central database, so it provides us with a relatively easy way to measure usage. However, it does not provide us with the number of times an item is accessed or modified – it only maintains the most recent state of the item. We rely on our experience to suggest that item creation activity provides a reasonable proxy for all Jazz activity.

In this section we report on a little over one year of development work, beginning with the introduction of Jazz as the new integrated development

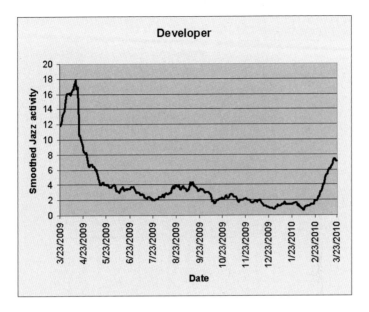

Fig. 2. Smoothed trace of Developer-created Jazz items per work day in monthly increments (March, 2009 to March, 2010)

environment. Three releases of one system involving multiple projects and project managers are covered. The dates of these releases are late August, early December, and early May (planned).

Figures 2, 3, and 4 are the plots of Jazz item creation activity by role.

During this time period, the three projects progressed through milestones that generally included: a sequence of iteration releases to the Quality Assurance team who performed functional verification tests; requirements and scope agreements with the customer; a sequence of defect fixes and code build cycles; release to a user acceptance test environment; and deployment to a pilot or production environment.

The work schedules of members of this service system covered almost all of the available hours of every day for the duration of our data; but there were many days when no items were created, especially during the winter holiday period in December, 2009. In order to represent items created per day in a visually intelligible way, we have smoothed the raw data and applied a uniform scaling factor of 10:7 to account for vacation, weekends, etc. The smoothing is accomplished by taking a simple moving average of seven days (each data point in figures 2, 3, and 4 is thus the average of the raw data points in the week leading to the corresponding date, multiplied by the factor of 10/7).

Our experience suggests that the initial flurry of Developer and Manager activity corresponds to the period in which Jazz was introduced to the already ongoing effort. It also suggests that the delay before the beginning of Customer

Fig. 3. Smoothed trace of Manager-created Jazz items per work day in monthly increments (March, 2009 to March, 2010)

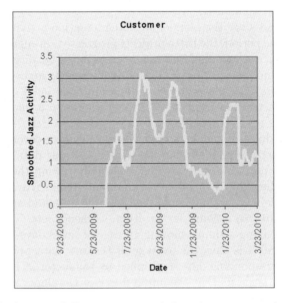

Fig. 4. Smoothed trace of Customer created Jazz items per work day in 2 month increments (March, 2009 to March, 2010)

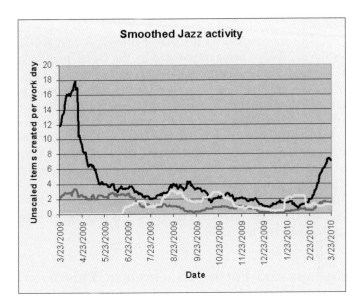

Fig. 5. Smoothed trace of Jazz items created per work day by role - a combination of Figures 2, 3, and 4

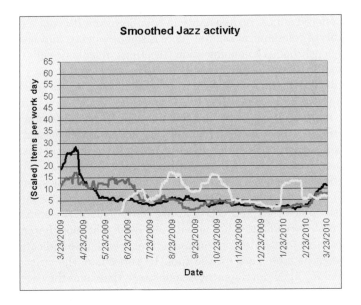

Fig. 6. Smoothed trace of Jazz items created per work day by role, scaled to compare trends (as if equal numbers of items were produced - a scaling of Figure 5

creation activity also corresponds to the introduction of Jazz to the customer via the web portal.

Figure 5 contains the stacked results from figures 2, 3, and 4. It is harder to read because the number of items introduced by the Developers far outnumbers the numbers of items introduced by the other roles so that scaling hides most of the information about the relative trends for the roles. In order to provide a visual representation of the relative trends (to compare roles independent of the absolute numbers of items they create), we provide a scaled version of Figure 5 in Figure 6. In the case of Figure 6 data for each role is independently scaled by factors that correspond to each role creating the same total number of items. Thus Figure 6 shows the relative trends of Jazz item creation activity but not the relative numbers of items produced.

If we ignore the first three months of reported activity as corresponding to initialization, then the trend for each of the roles is increasing, with the Customer providing the most increasing trend.

5   Conclusions and Future Research in This Area

We report from our experience that Jazz provides excellent value in terms of its use as a manager of code files and integration as well as its use for communication and collaboration. Our positive report on use of Jazz should be viewed as a comparison with the use of a much less elaborate simple check-out and check-in system that offered almost no assistance in collaboration. It is not a replacement for other forms of communication; but there is some evidence that it does at least reduce total synchronous communication (meetings, telephone calls, and instant messages) and improve the effectiveness of those interactions.

We described how the two distinct methods of Jazz access (client and web portal) each provided specific value to specific roles. Each has its strengths: the client being more appropriately connected to the Developer's other tools; the portal requiring no client installation and easy access for the casual user.

Our study provides confirmation to our working hypothesis that usage is correlated with perceived value. We were surprised to see the dramatically increasing usage trend for Customers relative to the trends for other roles; but take it as confirmation that Customers appreciate the value represented by Jazz: the more they use it the more they appreciate it. We have dealt with sophisticated systems before that were adopted but never really used. The most important aspect of this paper is the initial report on usage that we believe indicates the value different classes of user place on the tool. In particular, the customers in our service system for agile development demonstrate the value they see in the tool by their increasing rate of usage. We suggest this criterion as a way to assess such tools that goes beyond a comparison of features.

We did not find that the tool replaced all other types of communication or that it dramatically reduced the frequency of communication outside the tool. Since we introduced the tool in the middle of our project, we could compare at least individual subjective reports, which we synthesized into the virtual Q and A. We had and still have no way to collect and measure out-of-band communication, and our ability to measure the in-band communication begins with the tool introduction. Our simple criterion of trend in tool usage is generally available and seems to be a useful and inexpensive way to assess tool value. Future research activities in this area include collection of more detailed quantitiative usage data from Jazz by role and geography, survey data from customers and developers, and in-depth examination of the role of email, phone converations and conferences, and web conferences in conjunction with Jazz usage.

Acknowledgement. Special thanks to our colleagues and partners for their many contributions to the project: Henri Naccache, Julian Jones, George De-Candio, Roger Andrews, Rajesh Singi, Michael VanAmburgh, Roslyn Highsmith, Kevin Janasak, and Isaac Councill.

References

1. Bernstein, A.: How can cooperative work tools support dynamic group process? bridging the specificity frontier. In: Proceedings of the 2000 ACM conference on Computer supported cooperative work, pp. 279–288. ACM, Philadelphia (2000), doi:10.1145/358916.358999
2. Cheng, L., Souza, C.R.D., Hupfer, S., Patterson, J., Ross, S.: Building Collaboration into IDEs. Queue 1(9), 40–50 (2004)
3. Councill, I.G., Hacigumus, H., Johns, K., Kreulen, J.T., Lehman, T.J., Rhodes, J., Strong, R., et al.: An analysis of a service system supporting IBM's global service delivery. In: 2009 IEEE/INFORMS International Conference on Service Operations, Logistics and Informatics, Presented at the 2009 IEEE/INFORMS International Conference on Service Operations, Logistics and Informatics (SOLI), Chicago, StateIL,USA, pp. 317–322 (2009), doi:10.1109/SOLI.2009.5203952
4. Dyba, T., Dingsøyer, T.: Empirical studies of agile software development: A systematic review. Information and Software Technology 50(9-10), 833–859 (2008)
5. Hayes, J.H., Dekhtyar, A., Janzen, D.S.: Towards traceable test-driven development. In: Proceedings of the 2009 ICSE Workshop on Traceability in Emerging Forms of Software Engineering, pp. 26–30. IEEE Computer Society, Los Alamitos (2009)
6. Highsmith, D., Cockburn, A.: Agile Software Development: The Business of Innovation. In: Computer, pp. 120–122 (September 2001)
7. Larsson, A.: Making sense of collaboration: the challenge of thinking together in global design teams. In: Proceedings of the 2003 international ACM SIGGROUP conference on Supporting group work, pp. 153–160. ACM, Sanibel Island (2003), doi:10.1145/958160.958184
8. Maglio, P.P., Srinivasan, S., Kreulen, J.T., Spohrer, J.: Service systems, service scientists, SSME, and innovation. Commun. ACM 49(7), 81–85 (2006), doi:10.1145/1139922.1139955
9. Meneely, A., Williams, L.: On preparing students for distributed software development with a synchronous, collaborative development platform. In: Proceedings of the 40th ACM technical symposium on Computer science education, pp. 529–533. ACM, USA (2009), doi:10.1145/1508865.1509047

10. Neale, D.C., Carroll, J.M., Rosson, M.B.: Evaluating computer-supported cooperative work: models and frameworks. In: Proceedings of the 2004 ACM conference on Computer supported cooperative work, pp. 112–121. ACM, USA (2004), doi:10.1145/1031607.1031626
11. Nerur, S., Balijepally, V.: Theoretical reflections on agile development methodologies. Commun. ACM 50(3), 79–83 (2007)
12. Sengupta, B., Chandra, S., Sinha, V.: A research agenda for distributed software development. In: Proceedings of the 28th international conference on Software engineering. ACM, China (2006), doi:10.1145/1134285.1134402
13. Yaeli, A., Klinger, T.: Enacting responsibility assignment in software development environments. In: Proceedings of the 1st international workshop on Software development governance, pp. 7–10. ACM, Leipzig (2008), doi:10.1145/1370720.1370724

Discovering Business Process Similarities: An Empirical Study with SAP Best Practice Business Processes

Rama Akkiraju and Anca Ivan

IBM Almaden Research Center,
650 Harry Rd, San Jose, CA 95120

Abstract. Large organizations tend to have hundreds of business processes. Discovering and understanding the similarities among these business processes are useful to organizations for a number of reasons: (a) business processes can be managed and maintained more efficiently, (b) business processes can be reused in new or changed implementations, and (c) investment guidance on which aspects of business processes to improve can be obtained. In this empirical paper, we present the results of our study on over five thousand business processes obtained from SAP's standardized business process repository divided up into two groups: Industry-specific and Cross-industry. The results are encouraging. We found that 39% of cross-industry processes and 43% of SAP-industry processes have commonalities. Additionally, we found that 20% of all processes studied have at least 50% similarity with other processes. We use the notion of semantic similarity on process and process activity labels to determine similarity. These results indicate that there is enough similarity among business processes in organizations to take advantage of. While this is anecdotally stated, to our knowledge, this is the first attempt to empirically validate this hypothesis using real-world business processes of this size. We present the implications and future research directions on this topic and call for further empirical studies in this area.

Keywords: business processes, process maps, discovery.

1 Introduction

For the purposes of this paper, a business process means those 'structured activities or tasks' in an organization which, when executed in a specific way, 'produce a specific product or service for a specific customer' [14]. Examples of business processes include: accounts payable, accounts receivable, demand planning, order processing, employee payroll management, new-hire on boarding, sales promotion management, drug discovery management, clinical trial management etc. As can be noted in the example business process names above, some of them are applicable to most companies (cross-industry), while some are specific to some industries (industry-specific). For example, most companies have some kind of

P.P. Maglio et al. (Eds.): ICSOC 2010, LNCS 6470, pp. 515–526, 2010.
© Springer-Verlag Berlin Heidelberg 2010

employee payroll management, new hire on boarding, accounts payable and accounts receivable kind of processes. They are the cross-industry processes. Processes such as drug discovery and clinical trial management are processes that are specific to pharmaceutical industry. Demand planning business process is typically used in manufacturing oriented industries and sales promotion management is most typical in retail industry context. These are typically referred to as industry specific business processes.

A business process is said to be documented or modeled if the structure of the collection of process activities involved is represented and can be visualized as a model (eg: flowchart like diagram). A simplest form of such a representation could be a sequence of activities. More complex representations include forks, joins, parallel paths, decision nodes etc. A business process is said to be formally documented if its flowchart-like model adheres to formal rules of any one chosen business process representation language (eg: Business Process Modeling Notation BPMN [12], Unified Modeling Language [13], Petrinets).

Large organizations tend to have hundreds and sometimes even thousands of business processes. Organizations that are mature and disciplined in the way they run their business processes may maintain models of their business processes in repositories for reference and maintenance purposes. These repositories could be valuable assets for organizational learning. Analyzing these business process models and discovering and understanding the similarities among them can be useful to organizations in a number of ways. First, if similar aspects/tasks/activities of business processes are known business processes can be managed more efficiently. For example, if a software patch is to be applied to an application that supports a specific process activity, then knowing what all business processes use the same process activity is very helpful. This information helps in planning the business process unavailability and therefore eventually scheduling the business process unavailability optimally. Second, during new business process implementations or changes to existing business processes, those aspects of process activities that might be common with or similar to any of the existing process activities can be readily reused or leveraged for efficient implementations. Third, during mergers and acquisitions, knowing the similarities among the business processes of the two organizations involved can help with identifying opportunities for process standardization and consolidation. Finally, knowing similar process activities can also guide investment decisions if the identified similar process steps are associated with metrics that need further improvements. In summary, the need for understanding business process similarities within an organization is well-established.

Discovering business process similarities can be viewed from IT services provider perspective as well. Information Technology (IT) services companies are under constant pressure to deliver solutions quickly and cost effectively to their clients. One way to achieve this is by reusing assets developed for past clients after appropriate cleansing in the context of a new client project. Most IT services providers have some internal mechanisms in place to maintain assets from projects in some repositories. Business processes stored in these repositories could contain a wealth of knowledge and assets related to business process models, best practices, time taken to implement solutions etc. Leveraging the assets around these existing business process models can reduce project delivery times and improve project efficiencies. For example, some aspects of campaign management process in pharmaceutical industry might be similar to a trade promotions management process in retail industry. Therefore, the assets related to the campaign management processes such as best-practices, process definition documents, implementation guides, test scripts, and possibly even some code implemented for a specific client in pharmaceutical industry might be useful when implementing a trade promotions management process for another client in retail industry.

Thus far in this introduction, we have presented several arguments for why discovering and understanding similarities among business processes can be useful for organizations. However, an important question that we feel is not answered well in literature so far is: is there much similarity among business processes in organizations, in real-world or is it merely a topic of academic interest? We have not found any empirical studies presenting evidence one way or another. That is what motivated our work.

In this empirical study, we explore business process similarity with the aim of discovering similarities among a given set of business processes in an industry setting. We have analyzed over one thousand publicly available best practice business processes from SAP's business process repository to discover similarities among them within and across industries. The results are encouraging. We found that 20% of all processes studied have at least 0.5 similarity with other processes. We use the notion of semantic similarity on process and process activity labels to determine similarity. While this is a simple start, the results indicate that there is enough similarity among business processes in real-world organizations to take advantage of. While this is anecdotally observed thus far, to our knowledge, this is the first attempt to empirically prove this hypothesis using real business processes of this size. We present the implications and future research directions on this topic. The results can be applied and used by large organizations with many business processes and also for IT services companies that provide business process implementation services for their clients.

The rest of the paper is organized as follows. We discuss various aspects of business process similarities in Section 2 and discuss some of the techniques used in literature. We present the details of our experimental setup in Section 3. Section 4 presents our analysis of process similarities in SAP best practice processes. Finally, in Section 5 we discuss limitations of our study and call for additional empirical studies to substantiate the need for more research on this topic.

2 Background and Related Work on Process Similarity

What information about business processes can be used to discover similarities? Business processes operate in specific contexts in organizations. Business processes have *names(labels), structure, semantics, and data flow*. They use *resources* and manipulate resources(*system, people, and data*) and leave *traces* behind when executed. The efficiency and effectiveness of business processes can be measured by *metrics*. Business processes serve specific *business objectives* that can be measured by *key performance indicators*. Business process designers and analysts document information about processes and process steps in plain text in *design documents*. Sometimes there might be rich text (attachments, diagrams with annotations etc) about processes in process design documents. Business processes can be *classified* along many dimensions: *industry, scenario groups, scenarios, functional areas, organizations (that are responsible for managing and maintaining them), user groups and roles (that use the processes).* Business processes have *dependencies* on other processes and are *related* to other business process. When business processes are not functioning normally or as desired, certain aspects of business will be at *risk*. Business processes need to be maintained and updated and when *outages (planned or unplanned)* occur, there will be *business impact*. All of this information about processes can be used for determining process similarity.

Obtaining all of the information about business processes at once is hard. The organizational structure of companies makes it difficult to go to one single source to obtain comprehensive information about business processes. In the past, there weren't enough mature tools that supported formal business process modeling, analysis, and simulation. Even if they existed, they were considered academic and didn't receive much adoption in the industry. So, not many companies formally documented their business processes. Recent emergence of industry standards such as Business Process Modeling Notation [12] and Business Process Execution Language [15] combined with the maturity and accessibility of vendor tools make the goal of discovering business process similarities more achievable than it was in the past.

Our related work analysis on business process similarity matching is not comprehensive since we are concerned with presenting the results of our empirical study. We note that much of the past work done in business process similarity matching is done based on matching of process labels, process structure (control flow) and process execution semantics. Dumas et al. [4] present a nice summary of various techniques that have been applied to conduct process similarity matching in their paper. They note the usage of string-edit distance based approaches for label matching, graph matching techniques [1,2,3] for process control flow matching and process mining techniques for matching execution semantics (traces, logs) [5,6]. Simulation and causal footprint analysis [7] have also been used for matching. Much of this work focuses on matching pairs of business processes. However, in our work, we are concerned with matching a query with a repository of business processes.

Clustering and machine learning communities have looked at repositories of business processes. For example, Lee H.S [8] generates hierarchical clusters from a set of business processes using the notions of cohesion and coupling. The author uses clustering as a means to find out related and dependent processes. This work does not directly focus on finding a set of matching processes (from a repository of processes) with the purpose of reuse in mind. J. Melcher and Sees [9] applied clustering to SAP reference models using process metrics values for finding (structurally) similar processes among business process collections. The process metric values of various processes are compared to obtain a heatmap. This visual technique is used for clustering. This is one empirical work that we are aware of on SAP reference models. We perform semantic matching using process and process step labels whereas this work used process metrics information. In another work Jung and Bae et al [10] apply hierarchical machine learning to discover process similarities among a group of processes. In their work they first transform business process models to vector models based on their structures such as activities and transitions, and the vectors are compared by Cosine similarity measure. Finally, the models are clustered by the agglomerative hierarchical clustering algorithm. B. Srivastava [11] uses process features to derive summaries on groups of processes. These latter two works aim to address the same problem of leveraging existing processes for future process implementations.

Although, it not the main focus of this empirical paper, it is interesting to note that there is no body of work leveraging multiple attributes of business processes (listed in Figure 2) at the same time - perhaps because of the difficulty of obtaining that data. But it is increasingly becoming possible to obtain that information. We believe that a combination of text analytics, clustering and structure matching that takes into account data, resource flows into account will yield more accurate and precise matches. This is the subject of our next study. For now, we turn our attention to our study.

3   Empirical Study Setup and Discussion

We believe that there is enough similarity among business processes within a company and within and across industries that discovering and understanding these similarities is beneficial for individual organizations as well as IT services providers. We want to test this hypothesis with our experiments.

To test our hypothesis we need access to a large number of business processes that might exist either within a company or across various companies in various industries. Because of the ease of accessing the data, we have chosen the latter. Enterprise Resource Planning vendors such as SAP and Oracle offer models of best practice business processes for various industries and cross industries. We have chosen SAP's best practice processes that are publicly available via SAP's Solution Composer tool. These business processes are classified across various industries (eg: Pharmaceuticals, Retail, Financial Services etc) and cross industries (eg: Finance, Accounting, Human Resource Management etc). These best practice business proccess have the following attributes: name of the business process, any known process variants, names of the process steps (or activities), and description. The industry classification, the process hierachies, names, descriptions and names of process steps can all be visualized in SAP's Solution composer tool. For programmatic parsing, this data is also available as XML files with several references and links (perhaps to avoid duplication). We did not have access to the formal process model representations of these best practice processes via the SAP Solution Composer tool. We are aware that EPC (Event Process Chain) models of these best practice processes exist but they are not public. We also did not have access to the data flow through these processes. Therefore, our study has several limitations which are cited below. Since writing this paper, we have had access to many business processes of a large company with formal business process models and data flows. Currently, we are working on several extensions to this study by considering the structure, data and resource flow in discovering similarities among business processes. However, we believe that even with the known limitations of our current study, the results are of great significance since very limited, if any, empirical studies exist in this important space. First we list the limitations of our study and then describe the nature of the data before presenting our analysis.

Limitations of our study

- In this study, our business process similarity matching approach does not consider the structure of the processes into account. This is due to the lack of availability of this data at the time of this study.

- In this study, we do not consider the data and resource flow through business processes. Again, this is due to the lack of availability of this data at the time of this study.

- We assume that name similarity of either processes or process steps implies some underlying similarities. Currently, we do not account for the scenarios where the names of processes or process steps might be the same but the underlying behavior is very different.

Process complexity. The data analysis was peformed on 21 solution best practice maps from the SAP Solution Composer tool [16]. Solution Composer keeps these maps as XML files. Unfortunately, the XML files have no consistent schema. Our first challenge was extracting the processes and their structure for every map. Once the data was extracted and saved a consistent computer readable form, we ran several experiments to determine the nature of the data. Our conclusions are presented next.

On average, the solution maps have 160 processes. The cross-industry maps have 1916 processes, the SAP industry maps have 3383 processes (total of 5299 processes). Table 1 shows the number of processes defined for a sample set of cross-industry and industry maps.

Each process has an average 6 or 7 process steps; Figure 1 shows the distribution of processes as a function of number of steps contained in the process. A very small number of processes have more than 20 steps: for example, the *Campaign Planning and Execution in CRM* process from the *SAP Service and Asset Management* cross-industry map has 27 steps, and 13 processes from industry maps including *Management of Internal Controls* from *Mining* industry map which has 56 steps, and *Local Close* from *Banking* industry map which has 37 steps).

Table 1. Number of processes for a sample set of industry and cross-industry maps

Cross Industry Map	No.	Industry Map	No.
mySAP Product Lifecycle Management	47	Aerospace	192
Channel Management	377	Banking	244
SAP Business One integration for SAP NetWeaver	19	Defense	149
SAP Radio Frequency Identification (RFID)	62	Defense Logistics	220
SAP Business One 2005	239	Mining	236
Field Applications	344	Public Sector	177
E-Commerce	256	Higher Education	171
SAP Business One 2004	239	Hospitality	272
SAP CRM Powered by SAP NetWeaver	208	Insurance	113
SAP NetWeaver	82	Research	106
SAP Global Trade Services	43	Utilities Retail	239

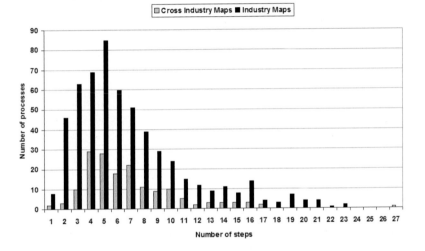

Fig. 1. Process complexity as a function of number of steps

Process duplication. Given the large number of processes defined by both industry and cross-industry maps, the next question is whether these processes are unique to their respective domains. Figure 2 highlights the process duplication across maps. In this experiment, two processes are considered to be duplicates if their names are identical. The Y axis represents the number of processes that belong to 1, 2, 3 or more industries. In the case of cross-industry maps, 648 processes are unique to a single map, 295 processes can be found in 2 maps, 140 can be found in 3 maps, and 65 processes can be found in more than 3 maps. For example, the *Self-Service Support through FAQ and Solution Search* process belongs to the following cross-industry maps: *SAP Service and Asset Management, E-Commerce,* and *Channel Management.* In the case of cross industry

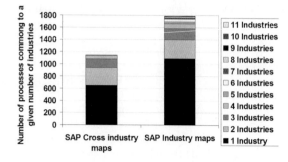

Fig. 2. Process duplication across industry and cross-industry maps

maps, 39% of process are duplicated across maps; in the case of SAP-industry maps, 43% are duplicated across maps.

4 Data Analysis

In order to evaluate the process similarity, we are using 3 approaches: (1) identify process duplication (as described above), (2) identify common steps amongst processes, and (3) compute the semantic similarity score for the process names.

The semantic similarity score is given by the following equation:

$$S = 2 * n_{CS}/(n_P + n_Q)$$

where n_P and n_Q are the numbers of steps contained in the structures of processes P and Q, and n_{CS} is the number of common steps.

Step-based similarity. Figure 3 shows how often business processes share process steps. The X axis represents the number of process steps shared by two processes. The Y axis represents the number of processes that share the given number of process steps. In the SAP industry maps data set, the *Complaints*

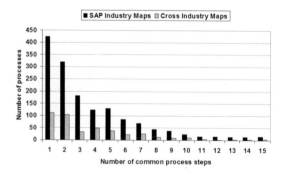

Fig. 3. Process commonality across industries as a function of number of steps

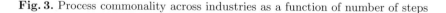

Processing with CRM Mobile Service for Handheld process from the *Logistics Service Providers* map and the *Service Order Processing with CRM Mobile Service for Handheld* process from *Utilities* map have 3 steps in common (similarity score of 0.5): (1) Synchronize data, (2) System replicates data, and (3) Assign business partner and contact person.

Process similarity scores. Figure 4 shows the process similarity trends for both data sets; we computed the similarity scores between all pairs of processes defined in each domain (cross-industry, and industry-specific). The similarity scores are high for a small number of processes, and then they drop. Only about 20% of processes have similarity scores higher than 0.5: for example, in the cross-industry maps, the similarity score between *Quotation Processing with CRM Mobile Sales* and *Activity Processing with CRM Mobile Sales* is 0.8. This means that 80% of the processes either have no variant or the variant is so different in name that semantic matching is not discovering the variant.

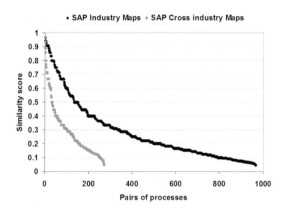

Fig. 4. Similarity scores

Process variants. In order to find process variants, we used the semantic similarity algorithm previously described for our experiments. Both graphs show only a subset of the processes that have variants. For presentation purposes, we only show a subset of the process variants that have representative variants (many of the processes have very low similarity scores). In the case of cross-industry maps, most processes are not connected (similarity scores are very low). This makes sense because an enterprise runs only one instance of a process. There are only a few processes that have variants and were found by the semantic similarity engine; for example, "Complaints Processing with CRM Mobile Service" and "Complaints Processing with CRM Mobile Service for Handheld". In the case of industry maps, the similarity scores are higher because there are more processes related across multiple industries.

The results indicate the following. (1) There is enough similarity among these processes studied. 39% of cross-industry processes and 43% of SAP-industry

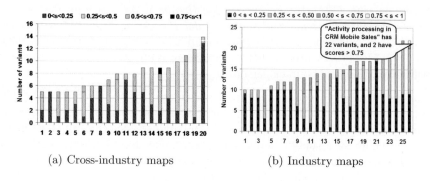

(a) Cross-industry maps   (b) Industry maps

Fig. 5. Process variants

processes are re-used across maps. Additionally, we found that 20% of all processes studied have at least 50% similarity with other processes. (2) The amount of similarity among processes in cross-industry segment is a little bit smaller than (39%) that discovered among processes in industry segment (43%). While it would be too early to draw any conclusions based on these experiments which only consider the process and process step labels as similarity metrics, the results reveal opportunities for some further areas of study. This result when substantiated further might mean that there are fewer opportunities to leverage similarities among business processes within an organization than among best practice processes developed for many industries by IT services provider. IT services providers might benefit more from conducting business process similarity matching than individual organizations. This result makes one assumption that individual organizations all have non-duplicating common best practices. We know that that is seldom the case. Often companies end up with duplicate processes and systems due to mergers and acquisitions. So, this result does not apply to that case since the data assumes that there are standardized processes within an organization. In any case, this calls for further empirical studies with business process data within individual organizations as well as with data of best practices from IT services providers to really understand the nature of similarities in business processes within companies, within industries and across industries.

5   Discussions and Conclusions

The data used for analysis in this work is from the best practice process repository of a business process implementation software vendor, SAP. Individual companies implement business processes that pertain to their industry. They don't implement all processes for all industries. Therefore, the results from analyzing industry-specific processes apply more to IT services providers' that implement business process software for companies than to individual companies. The cross-industry business processes apply more generally to companies in any industry. So, these results apply to both individual companies and IT services providers.

Our study, presently, uses semantic similarity of process and process activity labels to determine similarities among processes. One might argue that semantic matching of labels alone is a weak indication of similarity if the structure is not considered. While we acknowledge that in general, we argue that for the specific data set we considered that is not an issue. This is because SAP business process repository uses vocabulary that is standardized across all of SAP's software. For example, the word 'sales order' in a process activity would mean the same when it is found in any other process activity in any business process within SAP domain. Therefore, label matching works well in this domain. We acknowledge the limitations of this study both in the amount of information about business processes that was used and in the simplicity of technical approaches used to discover similarities among business processes. The main reason for limiting the study to these aspects is the lack of publicly available data on some of the other aspects of business processes (such as control flow, data flow, resource flow etc) for the data we considered. The results presented in this paper can be treated as a call for further empirical studies to discover similarities among business processes in an industry setting. As of the time of writing of this paper, we were fortunate to get access to a large repository of internal business processes of a large company (one of the 30 Dow Jones companies who guide the Dow Jones Industrial Average Index) with detailed control flow, data flow, resource flow and detailed design documentation. We are currently studying that data and are exploring the application of machine learning, clustering and a combination of graph matching, text analysis techniques and semantic matching algorithms to determine process similarities.

References

1. Dijkman, R., Dumas, M., Garcia-Banuelos, L.: Graph matching algorithms for business process model similarity search. In: Dayal, U., Eder, J., Koehler, J., Reijers, H.A. (eds.) Business Process Management. LNCS, vol. 5701, pp. 48–63. Springer, Heidelberg (2009)
2. Melnik, S., Garcia-Molina, H., Rahm, E.: Similarity flooding: A versatile graph matching algorithm (extended technical report). Technical Report 2001-25, Stanford InfoLab (2001)
3. Li, C., Reichert, M.U., Wombacher, A.: On measuring process model similarity based on high-level change operations. Technical Report TR-CTIT-07-89, CTIT, Enschede, The Netherlands (2007)
4. Dumas, M., Garcia-Banuelos, L., Dijkman, R.: Similarity Search of Business Process Models, http://sites.computer.org/debull/A09sept/marlon.pdf
5. van der Aalst, W., Weijters, A., Maruster, L.: Workflow Mining: Discovering Process Models from Event Logs. IEEE Transactions on Knowledge and Data Engineering 16(9), 1128–1142 (2004)
6. Agrawal, R., Gunopulos, D., Leymann, F.: Mining Process Models from Workflow Logs. In: Schek, H.-J., Saltor, F., Ramos, I., Alonso, G. (eds.) EDBT 1998. LNCS, vol. 1377, pp. 469–483. Springer, Heidelberg (1998)
7. van Dongen, B.F., Dijkman, R.M., Mendling, J.: Measuring similarity between business process models. In: Bellahsène, Z., Léonard, M. (eds.) CAiSE 2008. LNCS, vol. 5074, pp. 450–464. Springer, Heidelberg (2008)

 8. Lee, H.S.: Automatic clustering of business processes. Business systems planning European Journal of Operational Research 114(2), 354–362 (1999)
 9. Melcher, J., Seese, D.: Visualization and Clustering of Business Process Collections Based on Process Metric Values. In: 10th International Symposium on Symbolic and Numeric Algorithms for Scientific Computing, pp. 572–575 (2008)
10. Jung, J.Y., Bae, J., Liu, L.: Hierarchical Clustering of Business Process Models. International Journal of Innovative Computing, Information and Control 5(12) (2009)
11. Srivastava, B.: Summarizing Business Processes; Manuscript (2009)
12. Business Process Model and Notation, http://www.omg.org/spec/BPMN/
13. Unified Modeling Language,
    http://www.omg.org/technology/documents/formal/uml.htm
14. Wikipedia, http://www.wikipedia.org/
15. Web Services Business Process Execution Language,
    http://docs.oasis-open.org/wsbpel/2.0/wsbpel-specification-draft.html
16. SAP Business Maps, Solution Composer,
    http://www.sap.com/solutions/businessmaps/composer/index.epx

A Scalable and Highly Available Brokering Service for SLA-Based Composite Services

Alessandro Bellucci, Valeria Cardellini, Valerio Di Valerio, and Stefano Iannucci

Università di Roma "Tor Vergata", Viale del Politecnico 1, 00133 Roma, Italy
{cardellini,iannucci}@ing.uniroma2.it

Abstract. The introduction of self-adaptation and self-management techniques in a service-oriented system can allow to meet in a changing environment the levels of service formally defined with the system users in a Service Level Agreement (SLA). However, a self-adaptive SOA system has to be carefully designed in order not to compromise the system scalability and availability. In this paper we present the design and performance evaluation of a brokering service that supports at runtime the self-adaptation of composite services offered to several concurrent users with different service levels. To evaluate the performance of the brokering service, we have carried out an extensive set of experiments on different implementations of the system architecture using workload generators that are based on open and closed system models. The experimental results demonstrate the effectiveness of the brokering service design in achieving scalability and high availability.

1 Introduction

The complexity of service-oriented systems poses an increasing emphasis on the need of introducing runtime adaptation features, so that a SOA-based system can meet its quality of service (QoS) requirements even when operating in highly changing environments. In addition, the SOA paradigm allows to build new applications by composing network-accessible services offered by loosely coupled independent providers. A service functionality, e.g., booking an hotel, may be implemented by several competing services (referred to as *concrete services*) with different QoS and cost attributes, thus allowing a prospective user to select the services that best suit his/her requirements. Hence, being able to effectively deliver and guarantee the QoS levels required by differentiated classes of users may bring competitive advantage to a composite service provider over the others.

In this paper, we present the design and performance evaluation of MOSES (MOdel-based SElf-adaptation of SOA systems), a runtime adaptation framework for a SOA system architected as a brokering service and operating in a sustained traffic scenario. MOSES offers to prospective users various composite services, each of which presents a range of service classes that differ for the QoS performance parameters and cost. Its goal is to drive the adaptation of the composite services it manages to fulfill the SLAs negotiated with its users, given

P.P. Maglio et al. (Eds.): ICSOC 2010, LNCS 6470, pp. 527–541, 2010.
© Springer-Verlag Berlin Heidelberg 2010

the SLAs it has negotiated with the concrete services used to implement the composite services, and to optimize a utility goal (e.g., the broker revenue).

The major goals of the MOSES brokering service are: (1) its ability to manage in an adaptive manner the concrete services so that it guarantees the QoS parameters agreed in the SLAs with the composite service users; (2) its scalability and availability, being the brokering service subject to a sustained traffic of requests; therefore, its architecture should not affect the performance of the managed composite services. To achieve these goals, we have designed the MOSES architecture as an instantiation for the SOA environment of a self-adaptive software system, where the software components are organized in a feedback loop aiming to adjust the SOA system to internal and external changes that occur during its operation. Moreover, the MOSES prototype exploits the rich capabilities offered by OpenESB (an implementation of the JBI standard) and MySQL, which both provide interesting features to enhance the scalability and availability of complex systems. We have evaluated the performance and scalability of the MOSES prototype through an extensive set of experiments using workload generators that are based on open and closed system models. The results show that under every load condition the MOSES prototype based on OpenESB and MySQL achieves a significant performance improvement in terms of scalability and reliability with respect to a previously developed version of MOSES [4]. In addition, the clustered version of the prototype further enhances the performance introducing only a negligible overhead due to the load balancing.

The MOSES architecture is inspired by existing implementation of frameworks for QoS brokering of Web services (e.g., [1,2,10]). Menascé et al. have proposed a SOA-based broker for negotiating QoS goals [10] but their broker does not offer a composite service and its components are not organized as a self-adaptive system. PAWS [1] is a framework for flexible and adaptive execution of business processes but some of its modules work at design time, while MOSES adaptation operates only at runtime. Proxy-based approaches, similar to that used by MOSES for the runtime binding to concrete services, have been previously proposed, either for re-binding purposes [2] or for handling runtime failures in composite services as in the TRAP/BPEL framework [5]. The SASSY framework for self-adaptive SOA systems has been recently proposed in [11]: it self-architects at run-time a SOA system to optimize a system utility function. Nonetheless, to the best of our knowledge none of the previous works in the SOA field has evaluated the proposed prototype in terms of performance and scalability, but this kind of evaluation is needed for any prototype to be adopted and developed in an industrial environment.

The methodology at the basis of MOSES has been presented in [3]; its distinguishing features are the *per-flow* approach to adaptation and the combination of *service selection* and *coordination pattern selection*. The per-flow approach means that MOSES jointly considers the aggregate flow of requests, generated by multiple classes of users; to the contrary, most of the proposed adaptation methodologies (e.g., [1,2,14]) deal with single requests to the composite service, which are managed independently one from another. The second feature regards the adaptation mechanisms used by MOSES, that combine service selection with coordination pattern selection. The first mechanism aims at identifying for each abstract functionality in the composite service one corresponding concrete service, selecting it from a set of candidates (e.g., [1,2,14]), The coordination pattern selection allows to increase the offered QoS by binding at runtime each functionality to a properly chosen subset of concrete services, coordinating them according to some redundancy pattern.

The paper is organized as follows. In Sect. 2 we present an overview of the MOSES architecture. The MOSES design and implementation are discussed in Sect. 3. We present the testing environment and analyze the experimental results assessing the effectiveness of MOSES design in Sect. 4. Finally, we draw some conclusions and give hints for future work in Sect. 5.

2   Overview of the MOSES Architecture

The MOSES architecture represents an instantiation for the SOA environment of a self-adaptive software system [8], focused on the fulfillment of QoS requirements. The architecture of an autonomic system comprises a set of managed resources and managers, that operate as part of the IBM's MAPE-K (Monitor, Analyze, Plan, Execute and Knowledge) reference model [9]. This autonomic loop collects information from the system, makes decisions and then organizes the adaptation actions needed to achieve goals and objectives, and controls the execution. Figure 1 shows the MOSES architecture, whose core components are organized in parts according to the MAPE-K cycle. In the following we provide a functional overview of the tasks carried out by the MOSES components, while in Sect. 3 we discuss in details their design and implementation.

The Execute part comprises the *Composition Manager*, *BPEL Engine*, and *Adaptation Manager*. The first component receives from the brokering service

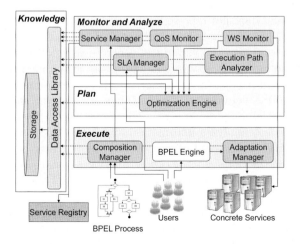

Fig. 1. MOSES high-level architecture

administrator a new BPEL process to be deployed inside MOSES and builds its corresponding behavioral model. To this end, it interacts with the Service Manager to identify the concrete services that implement the functionalities required by the service composition. Once created, the behavioral model, which also includes information about the discovered concrete services, is stored in the Knowledge part to make it accessible to the other system components.

While the Composition Manager is invoked rarely, the BPEL Engine and Adaptation Manager are the core modules for the execution and runtime adaptation of the composite service. The first is the software platform that actually executes the business process and represents the user front-end for the composite service provisioning. It interacts with the Adaptation Manager to invoke the proper component services: for each abstract functionality required during the process execution (i.e., invoke BPEL activity), the Adaptation Manager dynamically binds the request to the real endpoint that represents the service. The latter is identified by the solution of a linear programming (LP) optimization problem [3] and can be either a single service instance or a subset of service instances coordinated through some pattern. The MOSES methodology currently supports as coordination patterns the 1-out-of-n parallel redundancy and the alternate service [3]. With the former, the Adaptation Manager invokes the concurrent execution of the concrete services in the subset identified by the solution of the LP problem, waiting for the first successful completion. With the latter, the Adaptation Manager sequentially invokes the concrete services in the subset, until either one of them successfully completes, or the list is exhausted.

The *Optimization Engine* realizes the planning aspect of the autonomic loop. It solves the LP optimization problem, which is based on the behavioral model initially built by the Composition Manager and instantiated with the parameters of the SLAs negotiated with the composite service users and the concrete services. The model is kept up to date by the monitoring activity carried out by the components in the Monitor-and-Analyze part. Since the optimization problem is formulated as an LP problem, it is suitable to be solved at runtime because of its efficiency [3] and does not represent a bottleneck for MOSES scalability. The problem solution provides indications about the adaptation actions that must be performed to optimize the use of the concrete services with respect to the utility goal of the brokering service and within the SLA constraints.

The Monitor-and-Analyze part comprises all the components that capture changes in the MOSES environment and, if they are relevant, modify at runtime the behavioral model and trigger a new adaptation plan. Specifically, the *QoS Monitor* collects and analyzes information about the QoS levels perceived by the composite service users and offered by the concrete services providers. The *WS Monitor* checks periodically the concrete services availability. The *Execution Path Analyzer* monitors variations in the usage profile of the composite service functionalities by examining the business process executed by the BPEL Engine; it determines the expected number of times that each functionality is invoked by each service class. The *Service Manager* and the *SLA Manager* are responsible for the SLA negotiation processes in which the brokering service is involved.

Specifically, the first negotiates the SLAs with the concrete services, while the latter is in charge to add, modify, and delete users SLAs and profiles. The SLA negotiation process towards the user side includes the admission control of new users; to this end, it involves the use of the Optimization Engine to evaluate MOSES capability to accept the incoming user, given the associated SLA and without violating already existing SLAs. Since the Service and SLA Managers can determine the need to modify the behavioral model and solve a new instance of the LP problem, we have included them within the Monitor-and-Analyze part.

In the current MOSES prototype, each component in the Monitor-and-Analyze part, independently from the others, senses the composite service environment, checks whether some relevant change has occured on the basis of event-condition-action rules and, if certain conditions are met, triggers the solution of a new LP problem instance. Tracked changes include the arrival/departure of a user with the associated SLA (SLA Manager), observed variations in the SLA parameters of the concrete services (QoS Monitor), addition/removal of concrete services corresponding to functionalities of the abstract composition (WS Monitor and Service Manager), variations in the usage profile of the functionalities in the abstract composition (Execution Path Analyzer).

Finally, the Knowledge part is accessed through the *Data Access Library*, which allows to access the parameters of the composite service operations and environment, among which the solution of the optimization problem and the monitored model parameters.

3   MOSES Design

We have designed the MOSES architecture on the basis of the Java Business Integration (JBI) specification. JBI is a messaging-based pluggable architecture, whose components describe their capabilities through WSDL. Its major goal is to provide an architecture and an enabling framework that facilitates the dynamic composition and deployment of loosely coupled participating applications and service-oriented integration components. The key components of the JBI environment are: (1) the Service Engines (SEs) that enable pluggable business logic; (2) the Binding Components (BCs) that enable pluggable external connectivity; (3) the Normalized Message Router (NMR), which directs normalized messages from source to destination components according to specified policies.

After thoroughly comparing the available and stable open source implementations for JBI, we chose *OpenESB*[1], developed by an open source community under the direction of Sun Microsystems, because it is an implementation and extension of the JBI standard. It implements JBI because it provides binding components, service engines, and the NMR; it extends JBI because it enables a set of distributed JBI instances to communicate as a single logical entity that can be managed through a centralized administrative interface. GlassFish application server is the default runtime environment, although OpenESB can be integrated in several JEE application servers.

---

[1] ESB stands for Enterprise Service Bus.

3.1   MOSES within the JBI Environment

Each MOSES component is executed by one Service Engine, that can be either Sun BPEL Service Engine for executing the business processes logic and internal orchestration needs, or J2EE Engine for executing the business logic of all the MOSES components except the BPEL Engine. Developing the components with J2EE Engine improves the flexibility, because they can be accessed either as standard Web services or as EJB modules through the NMR.

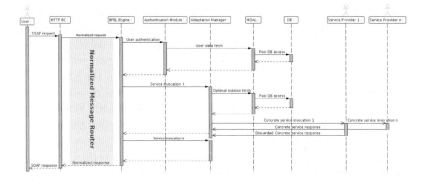

Fig. 2. Typical execution flow in the ESB-based MOSES prototype

The typical execution flow of a request to the composite service is illustrated by the sequence diagram in Fig. 2. As first step, the registered user issues a SOAP request to the MOSES front-end, that is the HTTP BC; the request format follows what expected by the BPEL process to whom the request is addressed. The HTTP BC normalizes the HTTP request and sends it to the BPEL Engine through the NMR. Upon receipt of the message, the BPEL Engine denormalizes the message and starts to serve the request. The first task performed within the process is the invocation of the authentication module (not shown in the high-level architecture of MOSES) to verify that the user issuing the request is properly registred. If not, an exception is forwarded to the user. Otherwise, for each invoke activity within the BPEL process, the Adaptation Manager reads the solution of the LP problem from the storage layer and for that abstract functionality invokes the subset of concrete services using the coordination pattern as determined by the solution (Fig. 2 shows the use of the 1-out-of-n parallel redundancy pattern for one service invocation). Finally, when the response is ready for the user (these steps are not shown in Fig. 2), the BPEL Engine puts the response message on the NMR, the HTTP BC de-normalizes it, obtaining a plain SOAP response message that is finally forwarded to the user.

Alternative execution flows can be split in monitoring and administration flows. The former denotes each flow that is related to the resources monitoring and can trigger the execution of the Optimization Engine to determine a new optimal solution. The WS Monitor, QoS Monitor, and Execution Path Analyzer are periodically invoked by the Scheduler BC, and each of them can trigger the

Optimization Engine when a new adaptation plan is needed. The Service Manager can be invoked either by the Scheduler BC or by the Composition Manager when new concrete services are needed. The SLA Manager is invoked by users when they register or establish new SLAs with MOSES; the Composition Manager is invoked by the MOSES administrator to manage new BPEL processes.

We observe that MOSES requires that only the BPEL Engine, the Adaptation Manager and the storage layer must be up and running to complete the request-response cycle. When only these components work, the broker can orchestrate the composite service (although in a sub-optimal way, being not able to solve a new instance of the optimization problem), but it still succeeds in providing a response to the users.

3.2   MOSES Components

We analyze in detail only the Adaptation Manager and storage layer design, because these are the components that mostly influence the MOSES performance and scalability. We have designed and implemented all the other components, except the Service Manager; their detailed description can be found in [4]. We note that all inter-module communications exploit the NMR presence: message exchanges are faster than those based on SOAP communication, because they are "in-process", thus avoiding to pass through the network protocol stack. However, thanks to OpenESB we can expose every MOSES component as a Web service.

The tasks of the Adaptation Manager are to modify the request payload in order to make it compatible with the subset of invoked concrete services and to invoke these services according to the coordination pattern determined by the solution of the optimization problem.

Being the Adaptation Manager the MOSES component that receives the highest request rate, its design is crucial for scalability and availability. We have investigated three alternative solutions for its implementation. The first realizes the component directly in BPEL, but we discarded it because the Sun BPEL Service Engine does not currently support the forEach BPEL structured activity with the attribute parallel set to 'yes'. We needed this activity to realize in BPEL the 1-out-of-n coordination pattern. With the second alternative we investigated how to realize the Adaptation Manager as a Java EE Web service. We found a feasible solution (based on the *Provider* interface offered by the JAX-WS API) but we discarded it because it causes a non negligible and useless performance overhead for the service invocation itself. The solution we finally implemented realizes the Adaptation Manager as a Java class which is directly invoked inside the BPEL process. The advantage is the higher communication efficiency and the consequent reduction of the response time perceived by the users of the composite service, as shown in Sect. 4.

The storage layer represents a critical component of a multi-tier distributed system, because the right tradeoff between responsiveness and other performance indexes (like availability and scalability) has to be found.

We have investigated various alternatives to implement the MOSES storage layer and decided to rely on the well-known relational database MySQL, which

offers reliability and supports clustering and replication. However, to free the
MOSES future developers from knowing the storage layer internals, we have
developed a data access library, named MOSES Data Access Library (MDAL),
that completely hides the data backend. This library currently implements a
specific logic for MySQL, but its interfaces can be enhanced with other logics.

3.3   MOSES Clustered Architecture

In designing the clustered architecture of MOSES we made a tradeoff between
flexibility and performance. By flexibility we mean the ability to distribute the
MOSES components at the finest level of granularity (i.e., each component on a
different machine); however, we have found that having a high degree of flexibility
impacts negatively on the overall MOSES performance [4]. Therefore, we have
carefully distributed the MOSES components in order to minimize the network
overheads for inter-module communications and storage access. Following this
guideline, we have collocated the BPEL Engine and the Adaptation Manager
on the same machine; in such a way, for each invoked external service whose
binding is executed at runtime by the Adaptation Manager, the BPEL Engine
does not need to communicate through the network. In addition, being these two
components executed by the same JVM, the Adaptation Manager is called as a
Java class rather than as a Web service, with consequent performance speedup.

Figure 3 illustrates the MOSES clustered architecture composed by three
clusters, where each one owns two replicas of the components placed in that
cluster. The BPEL Engine and the Adaptation Manager constitute the *core*
cluster, while the other two clusters provide additional features that are not
mandatory for the basic execution. The *front-end* cluster provides the broker
with the ability to receive new BPEL processes and negotiate SLAs with users.
The *back-end* cluster comprises the components to monitor and analyze the
environment and to determine a new adaptation plan. In front of those clusters
that are accessed by the composite service users, there is an HTTP load balancer
that distributes the requests among the replicas.

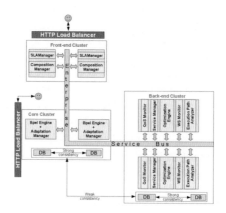

Fig. 3. MOSES clustered architecture

As regards the distribution of the storage layer, the core cluster hosts its own high available DB server with strong consistency to execute the DB queries as fastest as possible. The back-end cluster's DB is instead synchronized with the core cluster's DB using an external weak consistency policy and an internal strong consistency policy. Finally, the front-end cluster does not own a DB at all: we assume that the request rate directed to it is much lower than that directed to the core cluster; therefore, we prefer to pay a penalty for the DB accesses generated by the front-end cluster rather than having on it a new MySQL instance with its own replication strategy and related overhead.

4   Experimental Results

In this section we present the results of the experiments we have conducted on the MOSES prototype based on OpenESB. We compare its performance to that of a previous version of the MOSES prototype, whose components have been developed in Java as Web services. We refer to the latter as **MOSES WS**, while the current version is referred to as **MOSES ESB**. We also analyze the performance of the clustered MOSES ESB. Prior to present the experimental environment and the tools supporting the performance testing, we briefly review the main features of MOSES WS, whose detailed discussion can be found in [4].

4.1   MOSES WS

MOSES WS was entirely designed and implemented using the Web services stack as core technology. It included each component of the high-level MOSES architecture in Sect. 2; we also realized its replicated version.

Some choices we made during the MOSES WS design have turned out not to be appropriate, especially from the performance point of view. First of all, the adoption of *Apache ZooKeeper* [15] for the storage layer. ZooKeeper is a distributed coordination system for distributed applications, that provides synchronization primitives as well as a shared tree data structure. We relied on it to have an uniform data view from every application instance and to build mechanisms such as distributed counters and distributed locks. However, the penalty for this choice is a significant performance overhead, caused by a large amount of disk I/O operations. Secondly, we used *ActiveBPEL* from Active Endpoints as BPEL engine. Although we chose it for its better performance with respect to Apache ODE and for its usage in many research works on SOA systems, it turned not to be sufficiently stable; moreover, it was also suddenly retired. Finally, the adoption of SOAP as the core application protocol for the components inter-communications gave us a great flexibility, because we could place the components everywhere, even in a geographically distributed fashion. However, the cost paid for such flexibility is the overhead for managing the SOAP messages.

4.2   Experimental Setup

The testing environment is composed by 3 Intel Xeon quad-core servers (2 Ghz/core) with 8 GB RAM each (referred to as nodes 1, 2, and 3); 2

dual-processor Athlon MP servers with 1 GB RAM each (nodes 4 and 5); a Gb Ethernet connection for the quad-core machines, 100Mbps for the others.

We have analyzed the performance of MOSES ESB in the non-clustered and clustered versions: for each of these configurations we have executed the experiments using two different workload generators that are based on closed and open system models. Using the closed system model, we have identified the maximum system throughput. The open system model has been useful to find the effective response time in a real world SOA environment, where the generation of new requests does not depend on the completion of previous ones, and to establish how MOSES response time changes according to a controlled variation in the request rate. Closed and open system models can lead to different system behaviors, as discussed in [13]: therefore, using both we can analyze MOSES performance in a more complete way. The closed-model experiments have been performed with *The Grinder* [6], while *httperf* was used for the open-model load testing [7]. The first is an open source powerful load testing framework, that allows to test every application accessible through a Java API. For our testing purposes, we have used the Grinder plugin HTTPlugin, therefore encapsulating the SOAP request message to the composite service inside the HTTP request message. The latter is an open-source tool largely used for measuring the performance of Web servers: therefore, it can be also used to measure the performance of Web services when they can be accessed through HTTP.

Differently from traditional Web workload, SOA workload characterization has been not deeply investigated up to now (some results have been published in [12]). Therefore, to evaluate the performance of our SOA system, we have defined a BPEL process that mimics a "trip planner" SOA application, with 6 `invoke` activities (corresponding to 6 functionalities of the abstract composition). The tasks are orchestrated using most of the BPEL structured activities, including `flow`, which is used for the concurrent execution of the activities. Two concrete services can be selected for each functionality in the abstract composition and the binding is carried out at runtime by the Adaptation Manager; the used service(s) and the coordination pattern depend on the solution of the LP optimization problem managed by the Optimization Engine. For the experiments, we disabled the monitoring activities executed by the QoS and WS Monitors. The invoked Web services are simple stubs with no internal logic, being the analysis of MOSES scalability the goal of our performance study.

In the next sections we present the performance results, first considering the non-clustered version of MOSES ESB and MOSES WS under closed and open system models. Then, we analyze the performance of the MOSES ESB clustered architecture. We anticipate that the experimental results show that MOSES ESB outperforms MOSES WS for every load condition. The choice of MySQL and the optimization of some components (e.g., the Adaptation Manager) allows to remove most performance problems of MOSES WS; furthermore, from the stability point of view GlassFish proved to have a high availability: even after many stress tests no response error was received.

4.3 Closed-Model Experiments

In a closed system model, there is a fixed number of users who use the system forever. Each user repeats two steps: (a) submits a job; (b) receives the response and "thinks" for some amount of time. In a closed system, a new request is only triggered by the completion of a previous one. We set a think time equal to 0, because our aim is to perform a stress testing of the system to determine its effective throughput. Each closed-model test was performed on a three-machine environment, where node 1 hosted a full MOSES instance without data backend, node 2 the data backend together with the concrete services, and node 3 The Grinder. The latter generates an increasing number of client processes named "worker processes", each of which behaves like a user above described.

Figure 4(a) shows the MOSES WS throughput in terms of Transactions Per Second (TPS), which represents the mean number of transactions per second for a given number of worker processes. MOSES WS does not achieve a high TPS: the maximum value is around 21 TPS, which is definitely too low to cope with a relatively sustained incoming request rate. Furthermore, the maximum TPS value is reached with a relatively high number of worker processes. The motivation is that we get high response times (on average equal to the number of worker processes divided by the TPS value) and a non-optimal CPU utilization. By analyzing the components of the response time, we found that a large fraction of the response time is spent in waiting for the data storage layer, which is based on Apache ZooKeeper. Figure 4(a) illustrates the performance reason that lead us to design and develop the second version of our prototype, i.e., MOSES ESB.

Figure 4(b) shows the MOSES ESB performance in terms of TPS within the same testing environment. MOSES ESB achieves a significant performance improvement with respect to MOSES WS: the maximum TPS value is around 140 and this maximum is achieved with only 9 worker processes.

As regards the availability of the two prototypes, MOSES ESB is again the winner: MOSES WS reported an error percentage equal to 1.87 (2593 errors on a total of 139030 requests), while MOSES ESB never returned an error message for the entire experiment duration.

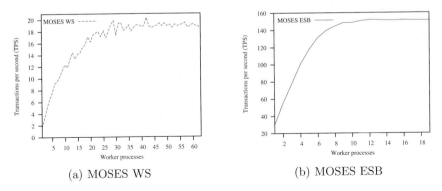

(a) MOSES WS   (b) MOSES ESB

Fig. 4. Throughput in the closed system model

4.4   Open-Model Experiments

In an open system model there is a stream of arriving users with an average arrival rate. Each user submits one job to the system under test, waits for the response, and then leaves. The main difference between open and closed systems is that the arrival of a new request is only determined by a new user arrival and does not depend on the completion of a previously issued request. We believe that the real world SOA environment in which MOSES can operate is closer to an open system model, because users with already established SLAs can generate new requests independently of the completion of previously issued requests.

The overall experiment is composed by a maximum of 140 runs, each one lasting 180 seconds, during which httperf generates HTTP requests at a constant rate. We note that there is a 1-to-1 mapping between an HTTP request and a request to the composite service provided by MOSES. The main performance metric we collected for each run is the mean response time, i.e., the time spent on average for the entire request-response cycle. The deployment environment for the open-model experiment is the same of the closed one.

Figure 5(a) shows the response time achieved by MOSES WS in the open model testing environment. When the system is stable (corresponding to a rate ranging from 1 to 19 requests per second), the response time varies between 600 ms and 3 sec. When the request rate reaches 20, the system becomes unstable and we observe an uncontrolled grow of the queues length. We have found that the high response times of MOSES WS is due to I/O waits. In preliminary experiments, we have also compared the response time of the composite service managed by MOSES with that of the same service offered by a standalone BPEL engine [4]. When the system is stable, we found that the response time of MOSES WS is on average 266% higher than that achieved by the ActiveBPEL engine. This overhead is very similar to that reported in [5] for the TRAP/BPEL framework, which has a simpler architecture and provides less adaptation functionalities than MOSES WS. Although the SOA system manager expects to pay some performance penalty for the system self-adaptiveness, our effort in designing MOSES ESB has been to reduce such overhead.

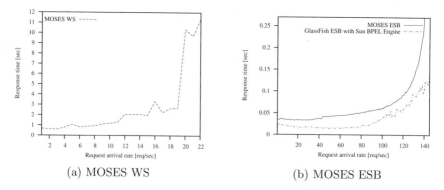

(a) MOSES WS   (b) MOSES ESB

Fig. 5. Response time in the open system model

Figure 5(b) shows the results for MOSES ESB. First, we observe that in this case the overall experiment is composed by almost 140 runs against 22 runs for MOSES WS. The system is stable up to 130 requests per second, which represents the saturation point. The I/O waits are now reduced to less than 1% of the overall CPU execution time and this positively impacts on the smoothness of the curve with respect to that of MOSES WS. Figure 5(b) also shows the response time obtained by the standard GlassFish ESB with Sun BPEL Engine when no self-adaptive capability is provided. When the composite service is managed by MOSES ESB, the response time is on average 108% higher than that served by GlassFish ESB (the percentage increase ranges from a minimum of 30% to a maximum of 209%). Therefore, the careful design of MOSES ESB allows us to substantially reduce the overhead introduced by the self-adaptiveness.

Figure 6 compares the performance achieved by MOSES ESB and MOSES WS, using a logarithmic axes scale (base 2 and 10 for x and y axes, respectively). The performance improvement achieved by MOSES ESB is clearly evident. As regards the availability of the two prototypes, MOSES ESB again returned no error message, while MOSES WS reported 21 errors in 3600 seconds.

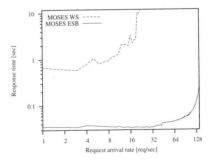

Fig. 6. Comparison of the response time in the open system model

4.5   Performance of MOSES ESB Clustered

The experiments for the clustered version of MOSES ESB have also been based on the open and closed system models. These sets of experiments were executed with the same hardware already used for the non-clustered version, but we slightly changed the component deployment schema. We used 5 machines, where nodes 1 and 2 hosted a GlassFish instance, node 3 the data backend and the concrete services, node 4 the load balancer, and node 5 either The Grinder or httperf. GlassFish allows the system administrator to choose between two load balancers: Sun Java Web Server or Apache Web Server with a load balancing plugin. The first is a closed-source Web server; therefore, we have chosen the latter being open-source. Nevertheless, we were constrained to use a closed-source plugin in order to have an active load-balancing subsystem, which allows to react at the load-balancer level to any failure of the connected GlassFish instances, for example by re-issuing the request to an active instance.

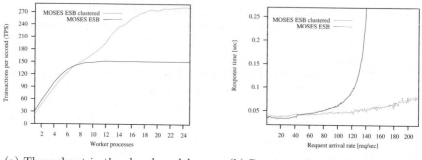

(a) Throughput in the closed model   (b) Response time in the open model

Fig. 7. Performance comparison of MOSES ESB and MOSES ESB Clustered

Figure 7(a) shows the throughput improvement achieved by adding a Glass-Fish instance to the MOSES cluster. The load balancer introduces a negligible overhead and the overall performance is incremented by almost a factor of 2. Figure 7(b) compares the clustered version of MOSES ESB with its non-clustered counterpart using the open system model. Similarly to what obtained in the closed-model experiment, we can see that for a low request load, the clustered version is a bit slower than the non-clustered one because of the load balancer component. However, this gap is rapidly filled starting from the request rate equal to 50. After this point, the clustered version is clearly the winner, achieving a response time that halves that of the non-clustered prototype.

5   Conclusions

In this paper we have presented an OpenESB-based prototype for a scalable and highly available brokering service that provides runtime QoS-driven adaptation of composite services. We have analyzed its performance and scalability, comparing them to those of a previous version of the prototype. The experimental results demonstrate that the key choices made during the MOSES ESB development have allowed to obtain significant performance improvements with respect to MOSES WS, which presents some similarities with other prototypes developed for service selection in SOA applications. With respect to MOSES WS, the response time achieved by MOSES ESB is two orders of magnitude lower, while the throughput is one order of magnitude higher. Furthermore, MOSES ESB clustered obtains a nearly linear performance improvement according to the number of installed GlassFish instances.

We are planning new experiments using MySQL cluster, that allows to increase the system availability and to improve further the performance through its in-memory DB feature. We will also extend MOSES to support stateful as well as asynchronous long-running services and to proactively monitor SLA violations.

Acknowledgment. Work partially supported by the Italian PRIN project D-ASAP.

References

1. Ardagna, D., Comuzzi, M., Mussi, E., Pernici, B., Plebani, P.: PAWS: A framework for executing adaptive Web-service processes. IEEE Softw. 24(6), 39–46 (2007)
2. Canfora, G., Di Penta, M., Esposito, R., Villani, M.: A framework for QoS-aware binding and re-binding of composite web services. J. Syst. Softw. 81(10) (2008)
3. Cardellini, V., Casalicchio, E., Grassi, V., Lo Presti, F., Mirandola, R.: QoS-driven runtime adaptation of service oriented architectures. In: ACM ESEC/SIGSOFT FSE, pp. 131–140 (2009)
4. Cardellini, V., Iannucci, S.: Designing a broker for QoS-driven runtime adaptation of SOA applications. In: IEEE ICWS 2010 (July 2010)
5. Ezenwoye, O., Sadjadi, S.: A proxy-based approach to enhancing the autonomic behavior in composite services. J. of Networks 3(5), 42–53 (2008)
6. The Grinder, http://sourceforge.net/projects/grinder/
7. httperf, http://www.hpl.hp.com/research/linux/httperf/
8. Huebscher, M.C., McCann, J.A.: A survey of autonomic computing - degrees, models, and applications. ACM Comput. Surv. 40(3), 1–28 (2008)
9. Kephart, J.O., Chess, D.M.: The vision of autonomic computing. IEEE Computer 36(1), 41–50 (2003)
10. Menascé, D.A., Ruan, H., Gomaa, H.: QoS management in service oriented architectures. Perform 7-8(64), 646–663 (2007)
11. Menascé, D.A., Ewing, J.M., Gomaa, H., Malek, S., Sousa, J.P.: A framework for utility-based service oriented design in sassy. In: WOSP/SIPEW 2010 (2010)
12. Nagpurkar, P., Horn, W., Gopalakrishnan, U., Dubey, N., Jann, J., Pattnaik, P.: Workload characterization of selected JEE-based Web 2.0 applications. In: Proc. IEEE Int'l Symposium on Workload Characterization, pp. 109–118 (September 2008)
13. Schroeder, B., Wierman, A., Harchol-Balter, M.: Open versus closed system models: a cautionary tale. In: USENIX NSDI 2006 (2006)
14. Yu, T., Zhang, Y., Lin, K.J.: Efficient algorithms for Web services selection with end-to-end QoS constraints. ACM Trans. Web 1(1), 1–26 (2007)
15. Apache ZooKeeper, http://hadoop.apache.org/zookeeper/

Business Artifacts Discovery and Modeling

Zakaria Maamar[1], Youakim Badr[2], and Nanjangud C. Narendra[3]

[1] Zayed University, Dubai, U.A.E.
[2] INSA-Lyon, Lyon, France
[3] IBM Research India, Bangalore, India

Abstract. Changes in business conditions have forced enterprises to continuously re-engineer their business processes. Traditional business process modeling approaches, being activity-centric, have proven to be inadequate for handling this re-engineering. Recent research has focused on developing data-centric business process modeling approaches based on (business) artifacts. However, formal approaches for deriving artifacts out of business requirements currently do not exist. This paper describes a method for artifact discovery and modeling. The method is illustrated with an example in the purchase order domain.

Keywords: Artifact, Data, Discovery, Process, Operation.

1 Introduction

Continuous changes in market opportunities and conditions have led enterprises to re-engineer their business processes. Typically, these business processes are modeled in an activity-centric manner. While this way of modeling is popular, it has several limitations, e.g., aligning business requirements to business processes is not simple and modifying these processes mid-stream is cumbersome. A data-centric approach through *(business) artifacts* [3] can address these limitations.

As in our earlier work [2], we adopt the definition of artifact from [3] as a *"concrete, identifiable, self-describing chunk of information that can be used by a business person to actually run a business"*. That is to say that an artifact is a self-describing collection of closely related data that represent a business record, which describes details of goods and services provided or used by the business. One would consider order and menu as artifacts when modeling a restaurant. An artifact is subject to changes that are reflected on a state transition system called $\mathcal{A}$rtifact $\mathcal{L}$ife-$\mathcal{C}$ycle ($\mathcal{ALC}$). Transitions between successive states in an $\mathcal{ALC}$ are the result of executing specific tasks in a business process.

There is an abundant literature on artifacts [1,3,4]. However, there is still a lack of rigorous approaches that assist those in charge of discovering and modeling artifacts We propose a method that examines the discovery of artifacts from three perspectives. The data perspective capitalizes on the data in a system and the dependencies between these data. The operation perspective capitalizes on the operations in a system and the dependencies between these operations. Out of the data and operation perspectives, two separate lists of candidate business

P.P. Maglio et al. (Eds.): ICSOC 2010, LNCS 6470, pp. 542–550, 2010.

artifacts start to emerge. Finally, the connection perspective establishes links between these two lists so that a list of final artifacts upon which the future system will be built is identified.

Our running example is a simplified purchase order scenario. A customer places an order of products via *Customer-App*. Based on this order, *Customer-App* obtains details on the customer's purchase history from *CRM-App*. Then *Customer-App* forwards these details to *Billing-App*, which calculates the bill based on this history (e.g., discount eligibility), and then sends the bill to *CRM-App*. The latter prepares the detailed purchase order and sends it to *Inventory-App* for order fulfillment. For the in-stock products, *Inventory-App* sends a shipment request to *Shipper-App*, which will deliver the products to the customer. For the out-of-stock products, *Inventory-App* sends a supply message to the requisite *Supplier-App*, which provides *Shipper-App* with the products for subsequent shipments to the customer.

The rest of this paper is organized as follows. Section 2 introduces the method along with a short description of the proof-of-concept prototype. Concluding remarks and future work elements are included in Section 3.

2   Our Method

Fig. 1 shows our proposed method for business artifacts discovery and modeling. The cloudy shape represents the business case-study. The ovals correspond to the beginning and end states of this method. The dashed bold-line rectangles correspond to the three perspectives mentioned in Section 1. The regular plain-line rectangles correspond to the steps to carry out in each perspective. The arrowed plain-lines connect the steps of the same perspective. Finally, the arrowed dashed-lines connect the steps of separate perspectives.

In the method, the data and operation perspectives rely on the description of the case study along with a complete understanding of other elements such as types of users and nature of business. The data perspective identifies the core

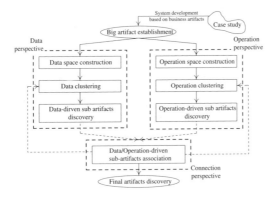

Fig. 1. Method for business artifacts discovery and modeling

data that are manipulated during users' needs satisfaction, and the dependencies between these data. This perspective leads into the *data space* of the case study. In parallel, the operation perspective identifies the core operations that are executed to satisfy users' needs, and the dependencies between these operations. This perspective leads into the *operation space* of the case study. Putting the data and operations together constitutes the basis for establishing different elements namely $\mathcal{B}$ig $\mathcal{A}$rtifact ($\mathcal{BA}$), $\mathcal{S}$ub $\mathcal{A}$rtifact ($\mathcal{SA}$), $\mathcal{F}$inal $\mathcal{A}$rtifact ($\mathcal{FA}$), $\mathcal{D}$ata $\mathcal{S}$pace ($\mathcal{DS}$), and $\mathcal{O}$peration $\mathcal{S}$pace ($\mathcal{OS}$).

The connection perspective connects the data-driven $\mathcal{SA}$s and the operation-driven $\mathcal{SA}$s together. By doing this, the $\mathcal{SA}$s are refined by (1) finalizing the structure of the $\mathcal{SA}$s in terms of data and operations, (2) identifying the possible interactions between the $\mathcal{SA}$s, or (3) either identifying new $\mathcal{SA}$s or combining some $\mathcal{SA}$s into other $\mathcal{SA}$s. Through this refinement, the $\mathcal{FA}$s are now available.

In the method, there is one $\mathcal{BA}$ that represents the business case-study to examine. A $\mathcal{BA}$ is like a melting pot that includes all the data and operations of the case study without any distinction to their types, natures, etc. $\mathcal{BA}$ = $\langle \mathcal{DATA}, \mathcal{OPERATION} \rangle$ where $\mathcal{DATA}$ is a finite set of data $d_{i,i=1..n}$ and $\mathcal{OPERATION}$ is a finite set of operations $op_{j,j=1..m}$.   □

2.1   Data Perspective

Establishing the data perspective requires three steps to be detailed hereafter.

Data space construction space step. The construction of a data space requires (1) extracting all the data $d_{i,i=0,\cdots,n}$ of the case study from $\mathcal{DATA}$ of the $\mathcal{BA}$, (2) pruning these data from synonyms, homonyms, and antinomes, and 3 describing each $d_i \in \mathcal{DATA}$ using $\langle id, l, t, i, u, e \rangle$ structure where: (*id*: is a unique *id*entifier of the data), (*l*: is the *l*abel of the data), (*t*: is the *t*ype of the data whether atomic (e.g., real) or composite (e.g., address); in case of composite, identify recursively all the constituent data until the type of these constituent data is atomic; atomic is assigned by default to any data whose type is unknown), (*i*: is the *i*nput value of the data whether this value is assigned or calculated), (*u*: is the expected *u*se of the data, i.e., update, consultation, or both), and (*e*: is the *r*estrictions put on the receiver of the data, e.g., read only, no transfer, etc.). Product, order, bill, and order_list_of_products are examples of data extracted from the running example.

Data clustering within the data space step. To identify data-driven $\mathcal{SA}$s, the different data in the data space are grouped into clusters. A cluster is a potential candidate to be a data-driven $\mathcal{SA}$ although the mapping is not always one-to-one. For data clustering we use *dependencies* between data. We define the following dependency types: $\mathcal{U}$pdate $\mathcal{D}$ependency ($\mathcal{UD}$), $\mathcal{S}$ubstitution $\mathcal{D}$ependency ($\mathcal{SD}$), and $\mathcal{R}$emoval $\mathcal{D}$ependency ($\mathcal{RD}$). We refine each type of dependency into *strong* and *weak*. The *weak* type is motivated by the restrictions that can be put on data.

An $\mathcal{UD}$ from d_i to d_j exists if the successful update of d_i (i.e., value modification) triggers the update of d_j. $\mathcal{UD}$ is weak if the successful update of d_j is guaranteed regardless of the artifact that will host it once d_j is separated from the artifact of d_i. $\mathcal{UD}$ is strong if the successful update of d_j is not guaranteed. By moving d_j to an artifact different from the artifact of d_i, there is a risk of not updating d_j (due to some restrictions). Both d_i and d_j have to remain in the same artifact.

A $\mathcal{SD}$ from d_i to d_j exists if the unavailability of d_i (due to some restrictions) makes d_j available for use. $\mathcal{SD}$ is weak if d_j is made available for consultation, only. d_j could be moved to a new artifact as long as there is no-strong $\mathcal{UD}$ from d_i to d_j. $\mathcal{SD}$ is strong if d_j is made available for both consultation and modification. Both d_i and d_j have to remain in the same artifact.

A $\mathcal{RD}$ from d_i to d_j exists if the deletion of d_i is declared complete subject to the successful deletion of d_j. $\mathcal{RD}$ is weak if the successful deletion of d_j is guaranteed regardless of which artifact hosts d_j and as long there is no-strong $\mathcal{UD}$ from d_i to d_j. $\mathcal{RD}$ is strong if the successful deletion of d_j is not guaranteed. By moving d_j to an artifact different from the artifact of d_i, there is a risk of not deleting d_j (due to some restrictions). Both d_i and d_j have to remain in the same artifact.

Before we continue describing the data clustering, some assumptions are made: (#1) If there is a dependency of type $\mathcal{X}$ from d_i to d_j, then a dependency of the same type from d_j to d_i will not be allowed, i.e., not commutative; (#2) If there exists a strong dependency of type $\mathcal{X}$ from d_i to d_j and another strong dependency of the same type from d_j to d_k, then a similar strong dependency from d_i to d_k will not be allowed or will be broken. The no-transitivity eases the ungrouping of data into separate clusters. Contrarily, if there exists a *weak* dependency of type $\mathcal{X}$ from d_i to d_j and another weak dependency of the same type from d_j to d_k, then a similar weak dependency from d_i to d_k will be formed. The transitivity eases the grouping of data into clusters; And, (#3) An artifact can limit the access to its data whether for consultation or update needs. This access concerns the operations that require artifacts in their processing.

We have developed two algorithms. The first algorithm identifies the necessary dependencies between the data of the data space. First, the algorithm determines whether the type of d_i is atomic or composite. If it is composite, then the data $\{d_{j,j \neq i}\}$ that make up d_i are determined. For each d_j, a $\mathcal{RD}$ from d_i to each d_j is then established. This is because the removal of d_i causes the removal of all its constituent data $\{d_j\}$. It is noted that if d_j had to be removed, this would make d_i incomplete calling for a $\mathcal{RD}$ from this d_j to d_i. However, this contradicts Assumption #1. If the type of d_i is atomic, then the algorithm determines whether the value of d_i is assigned or calculated automatically. If it is the latter, then the data $\{d_{j,j \neq i}\}$ that contribute to the calculation of the value of d_i are determined, and an $\mathcal{UD}$ from each d_j to d_i is established. In addition to the $\mathcal{UD}$, a $\mathcal{SD}$ is established from d_i to each d_j. Table 1 depicts some data dependencies from the running example. Strong (+) and weak (-) types of each dependency is done by the system engineer.

The second algorithm checks the consistency between the different dependencies. The purpose is to modify the respective types of these dependencies suitably from *strong* to *weak* and *vice-versa* so as to ensure that dependencies

Table 1. Some data dependencies before consistency checking

$d_i \rightarrow d_j$	pp	ota	**oda**	**omdd**	bn	ba	$\cdots$
order_date_approval (oda)	—	—	n/a	n/a	—	—	...
order_maximum_date_delivery (omdd)	—	—	**SD(-)**	n/a	—	—	...

Table 2. Some data dependencies after consistency checking

$d_i \rightarrow d_j$	$\cdots$	$\cdots$	oda	omdd	$\cdots$
omdd	—	—	SD(+)	n/a	...

are consistent and deadlock free. For example, in Table 2, the weak substitution dependency from omdd to oda is changed into strong (for the sake of clarity, Table 2 does not show all the dependencies.

Data-driven $\mathcal{SA}$s discovery step. Using Table 2, a *data dependency graph* is built. In this graph, each node is an atomic data, and each edge is a dependency with emphasis on update. Strong dependencies are depicted by plain lines, whereas weak dependencies are depicted by dashed lines. We, also, assume the existence of "default" strong dependencies between atomic data that belong to the same composite data, and this is done purely for consistency. These "default" dependencies are regarded as similar to strong update dependencies while determining the connected components of the graph; the connected components can be determined in linear time based on the number of nodes of the graph [5], and this is explained below. Fig. 2 shows an example of such a graph.

Fig. 2 shows that if the weak edges in the dependency graph are omitted, the resultant graph is a disconnected one, partitioned into one or more connected Clusters (C_i). Each cluster is a candidate to become a data-driven $\mathcal{SA}$. Connecting the different data-driven $\mathcal{SA}$s can happen through the dashed edges that symbolize weak dependencies. Later we show that the weak edges can be modeled via message passing between the different data-driven $\mathcal{SA}$s [2]. The interesting insight about Fig. 2 is that product and order composite data are merged into one cluster, i.e., one potentially separate data-driven $\mathcal{SA}$.

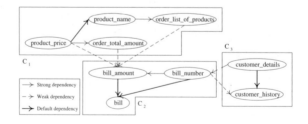

Fig. 2. Partial data dependency graph for the running example

Proposition 1. If weak edges are removed from a data dependency graph, then the graph is transformed into a disconnected one, with at least two connected clusters, (proof omitted).

Proposition 1 shows that each data dependency graph that contains at least one dashed edge can be partitioned into at least two connected clusters by removing the dashed edges. This proposition provides the justification for decomposing a data dependency graph into conceptually separate clusters, with each cluster depicting the data of a data-driven $\mathcal{SA}$, i.e., a "container" of the data that makes up the data-driven $\mathcal{SA}$. It should be noted that each data-driven $\mathcal{SA}$ is strongly coupled internally and weakly coupled externally, in line with well-known software engineering principles of high cohesion and low coupling. In this figure, $C_{1,2,3}$ can refer to *OrderContent*, *Bill*, and *Customer*, respectively.

2.2   Operation Perspective

Establishing the operation perspective of a case study requires three steps to be detailed hereafter.

Operation space construction step. The construction of an operation space requires (1) extracting all the operations $o_{i,i=0,\cdots,m}$ from $\mathcal{OPERATION}$ of the $\mathcal{BA}$, (2) pruning these operations' names from synonyms and homonyms, and (3) describing each operation using $\langle I, O, P, E \rangle$ structure, where: (I: is a set of input data reported in $\mathcal{DATA}$ of the $\mathcal{BA}$), (O: is a set of output data reported in $\mathcal{DATA}$ of the $\mathcal{BA}$), (P: is a set of preconditions, which are boolean formulae that must hold true if operation o_i is to start execution; these formulae are in CNF,and (E: is a set of effects, which are boolean formulae that hold true after operation o_i finishes execution; these formulae are in CNF as well).

We say that o_j is dependent on o_i if one of the outputs of o_i is an input for o_j, and if $e_i \in E$ is an effect of o_i and $p_j \in P$ is a precondition of o_j, then $e_i \Rightarrow p_j$; i.e., the effect e_i subsumes the pre-condition p_j.

We therefore define an *operation dependency graph* as a graph whose nodes correspond to operations, and whose edges correspond to dependencies between operations. Some operations from the running example are (o_1: place_order_submission), (o_2: customer_history_verification), and (o_3: bill_preparation).

Operation clustering within the operation space step. With an operation dependency graph in place, we have developed an algorithm to cluster operations. It groups the operations that use the same set of input data into clusters and then, relates these clusters to potential operation-driven $\mathcal{SA}$.

To illustrate the operation clustering algorithm, Fig. 3 depicts the operation dependency graph for some operations identified earlier. Initially, all the nodes belong to cluster C_1. Each operation o_i has a unique index starting with 1. The algorithm treats o_1 and checks its successor, i.e., o_2. Since both operations share common input data (namely order_list_of_products), o_2 is assigned to C_1. The algorithm continues with the successors of o_2, i.e., o_3, and so on until all the operations are processed. The various clusters created by the algorithm are depicted as C'_1, C'_2, and C'_3 in Fig. 3. The algorithm takes $O(n)$ time, where n is the number of nodes in the operation dependency graph. In this figure, plain lines represent intra-dependencies between operations in the same clusters, while the dashed lines represent inter-dependencies between operations in separate clusters.

Operation-driven sub-artifacts discovery step. Each cluster derived using the operation clustering algorithm is a potential operation-driven $\mathcal{SA}$. The reason is to link the operations that manipulate a common set of data into a common container.

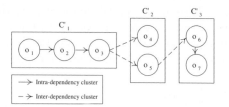

Fig. 3. Partial operation dependency graph for the running example

2.3   Connection Perspective

In this perspective the data-driven $\mathcal{SA}$s and operation-driven $\mathcal{SA}$s obtained previously are combined to form the future data-driven $\mathcal{FA}$s of the future system. Data in the $\mathcal{DATA}$ set are common to both $\mathcal{SA}$s. The idea of the connection perspective is that the data-driven $\mathcal{SA}$s provide the necessary data, and the operation-driven $\mathcal{SA}$s provide the necessary operations that act on these data.

Fig. 4 shows the connection perspective that leads into obtaining $\mathcal{FA}$s. In Fig. 4 (a) each data-driven $\mathcal{SA}$ (e.g., d-$\mathcal{SA}_1$) along with its related operation-driven $\mathcal{SA}$ (e.g., o-$\mathcal{SA}_1$) form a specific $\mathcal{FA}$ for instance $\mathcal{FA}_1$. As a result if n data-driven $\mathcal{SA}$s exist in the data perspective, the same number of $\mathcal{FA}$s will exist too. To obtain the states and life cycle of a $\mathcal{FA}$ we capitalize on the input and

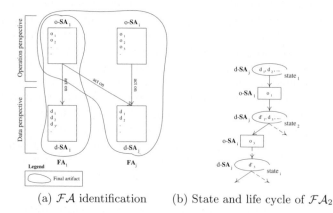

(a) $\mathcal{FA}$ identification   (b) State and life cycle of $\mathcal{FA}_2$

Fig. 4. Connecting the data and operation perspectives

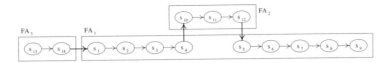

Fig. 5. Final artifacts

output data (e.g., $d\text{-}\mathcal{SA}_1.\{d_1, d_2, d_3\}$) that the operations (e.g., $o\text{-}\mathcal{SA}_1.\{o_1, o_2\}$) consume and produce, respectively. A state represents the data that are taken as input and modified later by an operation as output. As per Fig. 4 the intra-dependency between operations constitute the life cycle of a $\mathcal{FA}$, whereas the inter-dependency between operations constitute message passing between the respective life cycles of the different $\mathcal{FA}$s [2].

The set of final artifacts' lifecycles - modeled via their states - is depicted in Fig. 5. Operation o_1 is represented via $\mathcal{FA}_3$, and refers to the customer placing the purchase order. Further processing of the purchase order, described as per operations o_2 and o_3, are represented by states s_1 through s_4 in $\mathcal{FA}_1$. Operations o_4 and o_5, which deal with billing, are represented with sub-artifact $\mathcal{FA}_2$, after which control returns to $\mathcal{FA}_1$ for fulfilling the purchase order via states s_5 through s_9. These latter states pertain to operations o_6 and o_7.

2.4   Proof of Concept Implementation

We are now validating our business artifacts discovery and modeling method through a proof-of-concept prototype. It is implemented in Java on top of Eclipse 3.5.2. *Data Perspective*, *Operation Perspective*, and *Connection Perspective*

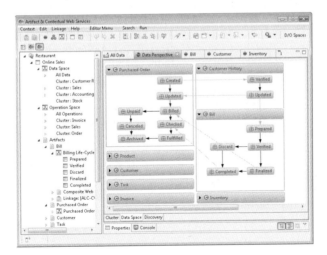

Fig. 6. Data clustering snapshot

modules constitute the prototype. Each module is accessible via interfaces based on SWT/JFace components, and a graphical editor built on GEF/EMF Frameworks. Currently we can model the data and operation perspectives, run the algorithms, and derive the final artifacts (Fig. 6).

3   Conclusion

Activity-centric modeling approaches, which mainly deal with business processes, fail to quickly respond to business changes. However, data-centric modeling approaches stand out as a serious alternative to model businesses by only focusing on data instead of activities. Data are often well-defined and stable regardless of the activities that manipulate them. Based on user requirements, our discovery and modeling method identifies business artifacts. The method applies a bottom-up analysis to assess and then gather fine-grained data into clusters before defining business artifacts. Concurrently, operations are identified and gathered into clusters with respect to their common input and output data. The final step consolidates data and operations. In term of future work, three areas are identified: compliance analysis of derived business artifacts with user requirements, impact of changes in user requirements on these artifacts, and exception handling analysis.

Acknowledgements. The authors thank Anil Nigam for his feedback.

References

1. Liu, R., Bhattacharya, K., Wu, F.Y.: Modeling Business Contexture and Behavior Using Business Artifacts. In: Krogstie, J., Opdahl, A.L., Sindre, G. (eds.) CAiSE 2007 and WES 2007. LNCS, vol. 4495, pp. 324–339. Springer, Heidelberg (2007)
2. Narendra, N.C., Badr, Y., Thiran, P., Maamar, Z.: Towards a Unified Approach for Business Process Modeling Using Context-Based Artifacts and Web Services. In: Proceedings of SCC 2009, Bangalore, India (2009)
3. Nigam, A., Caswell, N.S.: Business Artifacts: An Approach to Operational Specification. IBM Systems Journal 42(3) (2003)
4. Santhosh, K., Rong, L., Wu, W., Frederick, Y.: On the Duality of Information- Centric and Activity-Centric Models of Business Processes. In: Bellahsène, Z., Léonard, M. (eds.) CAiSE 2008. LNCS, vol. 5074, pp. 32–47. Springer, Heidelberg (2008)
5. West, D.B.: Introduction to Graph Theory, 2nd edn. Prentice-Hall, Englewood Cliffs (2000)

Carbon-Aware Business Process Design in Abnoba

Konstantin Hoesch-Klohe and Aditya Ghose

Decision Systems Lab (DSL),
School of Computer Science and Software Engineering,
University of Wollongong

Abstract. A key element of any approach to meeting the climate change challenge is the ability to improve *operational efficiency* in a pervasive fashion. The notion of a *business process* is a particularly useful unit of analysis in this context. This article describes a subset of the *Abnoba framework* for green business process management and shows how an algebraic framework can be leveraged to enable an environmental assessment on multiple heterogeneous dimensions (of qualitative or quantitative nature). Furthermore, a machinery for process improvement is outlined.

1 Introduction

The *Abnoba framework* enables business process management with explicit support for the environmental sustainability aspects of processes (represented in the Business Process Modeling Notation (BPMN) standard [1]). In particular we are concerned with business process design and re-design/improvement. This article extends our earlier work in the space [2,3] by describing a machinery for assessing the sustainability performance of a process design (which may be potentially incomplete) by aggregating task-level measures. These measures could include the carbon-footprint of a process (as assessed at design time), but also others, such as amount of water consumed, or the extent of waste generated. Our machinery uses an abstract algebraic framework (the c-semiring framework [4]) that enables assessment on multiple heterogeneous dimensions, which could be either qualitative or quantitative. The resulting framework extends the results of [5] and represents an improvement over other approaches to Quality of Service (QoS) modeling for processes [6,7]. We further outline how sustainability-driven process improvement can be achieved by leveraging a library of process fragments. This machinery requires us to leverage the ProcessSEER framework for semantic effect annotation of process designs [8,9,10].

2 A Framework for Dealing with Green QoS Measures

A key driver for process analysis, re-design and optimization is to satisfy or improve certain QoS measures. However, in practice QoS measures are often not commonly agreed upon and assessed on heterogeneous and multidimensional scales, which reduces their applicability (e.g. different machineries for each QoS measure have to

P.P. Maglio et al. (Eds.): ICSOC 2010, LNCS 6470, pp. 551–556, 2010.

be defined)[5]. We address these issues by deploying the algebraic c-semiring structure, which permits a multi-dimensional assessment of both qualitative and quantitative QoS factors. The framework generalizes many useful scales (real-valued, fuzzy-valued, probabilistic, qualitative and so on) and permits the integration of multiple heterogeneous scales into a single composite scale with the same abstract properties. Thus, while we might assess the carbon footprint of a process (or process step) on a real-valued scale, we might assess the impact of a process on flora/fauna on a qualitative scale of $\{high, medium, low\}$. In this article we do not describe how to determine the values for the QoS measures, but note that they can be derived in a context specific manner, by correlating (rich) resource models with process designs (as described in our earlier work [3]).

A c-semiring, which adds additional properties to the classic mathematical definition of a semiring, is defined as follows:

Definition 1. *(C-Semiring[4])*
A semiring is a 5-tuple $\langle A, \oplus, \otimes, 0, 1 \rangle$ such that A is a set of preference values, where $0, 1 \in A$. 0 denotes the "worst" element and 1 denotes the "best" element in A. $\oplus$ is a cumulative, associative and idempotent comparison operator with 0 as identity element $(a \oplus 0 = a)$ and 1 as absorbing element $(a \oplus 1 = 1)$, closed over A. $\otimes$ is an associative and commutative combination operator with 0 as its absorbing element $(a \otimes 0 = 0)$ and 1 as identity element $(a \otimes 1 = a)$, closed over the set A. $\otimes$ distributes over $\oplus$.

The "$\oplus$" comparing operator is used to define a partial order $\geq_S$ over the set of preference values A, enabling us to compare different elements of the semiring. On principle $a \geq_S b$ if and only if $a \oplus b = a$, denoting that the $\oplus$ operator choses a over b. The $\otimes$ operator is used to combine elements of the set A. We have $a \otimes b \geq_S a$ (1 is the maximum element of A), denoting that combining more elements of A leads to a "worse" result with respect to $\geq_S$.

We require each activity to be annotated with its specific (local) QoS measures, represented by a vector $\langle m_1, m_2, ..., m_k \rangle$ where each m_i is an element of A, of the c-semiring associated with the i-th QoS measure. We accumulate QoS values across a process design, using the "$\otimes$" combination operator, to receive the cumulative QoS values for each distinct QoS measure of the process design (see subsection 2.3 for more details).

2.1   Green QoS Measures

Our particular interest is in green QoS measures. In the following we list a (incomplete) list of green scales and illustrate their instantiation in the c-semiring structure. Other, QoS measures instantiated in the c-semiring structure can be found in [5].

1. *Water consumption:* $\langle R^+, min, +, \infty_+, 0 \rangle$
2. *$CO2$-e[1] emission:* $\langle R^+, min, +, \infty_+, 0 \rangle$

---

[1] Carbon dioxide equivalent (CO2-e) is an expression of other greenhouse gases in their carbon dioxide equivalent by their global warming potential (CO2 itself has a global warming potential of 1).

3. *Waste generation*: $\langle R^+, min, +, \infty_+, 0 \rangle$
4. *Damage to fauna and flora*: $\langle \{low, ..., high\}, min, max, high, low \rangle$
5. *Air Quality* : $\langle \{normal, ..., dangerous\}, min, max, dangerous, normal \rangle$
6. *Environmental performance*: $\langle \{AAA, ..., D\}, min, max, D, AAA \rangle$

While "Water consumption", "CO2-e emission" and "Waste generation" are generally quantifiable, other measures like "damage to fauna and flora" are assessed in a qualitative scale, since their "real impact" can only be assessed in long term studies. Therefore, these values are often determined by an educated guesses of some expert. On the other hand "Air Quality" and "Environmental Performance" are qualitative measures, representing a combination of measures. In the next subsection we show how different heterogeneous c-semiring scales can be combined.

2.2   Combining C-Semirings

Each QoS scale is of individual interest. However, there is often the need to combine different measures to asses the overall environmental performance of a process design, considering all, or some subset of the green QoS scales. This results in a multidimensional QoS assessment. The resulting composite scale can be shown to have the same abstract properties (it is a c-semiring as well). More details and the corresponding proofs can be found in [4].

Definition 2. *(Composition of C-Semirings)[4]*
   Given n semirings $S_i = \langle A_i, \oplus_i, \otimes_i, 0_i, 1_i \rangle$, for $i = 1, ..., n$, let us define the structure $Comp(S_1, ..., S_n) = \langle \langle A_1, ..., A_n \rangle, \oplus, \otimes, \langle 0_1, ..., 0_n \rangle, \langle 1_1, ..., 1_n \rangle \rangle$. Given $\langle a_1, ..., a_n \rangle$ and $\langle b_1, ..., b_n \rangle$ such that $a_i, b_i \in A_i$ for $i = 1, ..., n$, $\langle a_1, ..., a_n \rangle \oplus \langle b_1, ..., b_n \rangle = \langle a_1 \oplus_1 b_1, ..., a_n \oplus_n b_n \rangle$, and $\langle a_1, ..., a_n \rangle \otimes \langle b_1, ..., b_n \rangle = \langle a_1 \otimes_1 b_1, ..., a_n \otimes_n b_n \rangle$.

Accordingly, the order $\geq_S$ over $\langle A_1, ..., A_n \rangle$ is $\langle a_1, ..., a_n \rangle \geq_S \langle b_1, ..., b_n \rangle$ if and only if $\langle a_1 +_1 b_1, ..., a_n +_n b_n \rangle = \langle b_1, ..., b_n \rangle$. Since we have only defined the least upper bound ($\langle 0_1, ..., 0_n \rangle$) and greatest lower bound ($\langle 1_1, ..., 1_n \rangle$) not all elements of the composed c-semiring structure can be compared or combined. For example, consider the following composition of c-semiring instantiations for CO2-e and damage to fauna and flora. $\langle \langle R^+, \{l, m, h\} \rangle, \oplus, \otimes, \langle \infty_+, h \rangle, \langle 0, l \rangle \rangle$. Let us first compare the elements $\langle 5, m \rangle \oplus \langle 4, l \rangle = \langle 4, l \rangle$, hence $\langle 4, l \rangle \geq_S \langle 5, m \rangle$ ($a + b = a$). However, $\langle 5, l \rangle \oplus \langle 4, h \rangle = \langle 4, l \rangle$ ($a + b = c$) is not comparable, since there is no order for these two tuples. We can solve this by defining a new order $\geq'_S$ over each tuple in $\langle A_1, ..., A_n \rangle$ such that there does not exist a situation where $a \geq_S b$ and $a \neq b$ and $b \geq'_S a$ (the orders contradict each other).
   On the other hand, we can map each tuple of the combined c-semiring into a set A of another c-semiring and define the order over this new structure. For example, scales for "fine particles in the air", "ground-level ozone", and "carbon monoxide" (besides others) can be composed and the resulting composition be mapped into the "Air Quality" c-semiring. Such a mapping is particularly appealing when a combination of different scales have to be communicated to stakeholders like the government, business partners or costumers. Similar, the measure "Environmental

performance" $\langle \{AAA, ..., D\}, min, max, D, AAA \rangle$, listed in subsection 2.1, subsumes other environmental scales for ease of communication, where AAA denotes the "best" environmental performance and D the "worst" (similar scales are used to rate credits in the financial sector).

2.3   QoS Measure Accumulation

In this subsection we show how the QoS values (annotated at each activity) for distinct QoS measures can be accumulated across a process design to receive cumulative QoS values for each path through the process design.

The task of accumulating QoS measures across business process designs is not trivial since there might be various paths that can be traversed during process execution. We refer to each path through the process model, starting from a "start event" to a (user) selected activity, as a *scenario label*. A scenario label consists of a sequence ($\langle \rangle$) or a set ($\{\}$) or a combination of both. Sets can be processed in any order and are used to represent parallel splits, while the sequence dictates an order to account for the sequence in which the activities of a design are modeled.

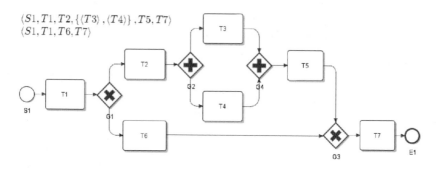

Fig. 1. BPMN Process Design

Figure 1 shows a BPMN process design with an exclusive split after activity $T1$ denoting that during process execution either the "upper path" $(T2, T3, T4, T5)$ or the "lower path" $(T6)$ can be taken, before both scenarios continue with activity $T7$ and terminate at $E1$. The corresponding scenario labels for selecting activity $T7$ are shown at the upper left corner of the Figure 1.

We accumulate as follows. Let S be a set of c-semiring, each denoting a distinct QoS measure for a given process design. We accumulate annotated QoS values, where each value corresponds to an element of the set A of each $s \in S$, between a pair of contiguous activities Ti and Tj (Ti pointing to Tj) as follows. The (cumulative) QoS values of a measure $s \in S$ at Tj consists of $a_i^{cu}(s) \otimes_s a_j^{lo}(s)$, where $a_i^{cu}(s)$ is a cumulative QoS value associated with Ti and $a_j^{lo}(s)$ is a local QoS value of Tj. The operator '$\otimes_s$' is the corresponding combination operator for c-semiring $s \in S$. We deal with *XOR merges* (see Figure 1 label $G3$) in the following manner. If Ti and Tj are the only two activities immediately preceding an XOR-merge, and

Tm is the activity immediately following it, we proceed by $a_i^{cu}(s) \otimes a_m^{lo}(s) = a_m^{cu}(s)$ and $a_j^{cu}(s) \otimes_s a_m^{lo}(s) = a_m^{cu}(s)'$. To deal with *AND merges* (see Figure 1 label *G4*) we have to add an additional *parallel combination operator* "$\circledast$" to the semiring structure. This operator allows us to specify how the QoS measures are propagated along a parallel branch and combined together at the merge gateway. For example, such an operator is needed when dealing with cycle time, where the "worst" time value of each branch in a parallel environment is picked. Let Ti and Tj be the only two activities immediately preceding an AND-merge, and Tm is the activity immediately following it, we proceed by $\left(a_i^{cu}(s) \circledast_s a_j^{cu}(s)\right) \otimes_s a_m^{lo}(s) = a_m^{cu}(s)$. In the case of cycle time, the $\circledast$ operator (choose max value) is idempotent, therefore $\otimes$ distributes over $\circledast$.

3   Green Process Improvement

In this section we outline (space constraints do not permit a more detailed elaboration) a machinery for identifying process re-designs with a more desired sustainability profile and the same functional outcome as the original design, using a library of process fragments. A process fragment is a (sub)process graph with a single entry and exit point (using process fragments any composition of well formed fragments results in a well formed process design).

First we require the activities of a process design to be annotated with semantic effects (denoting the post-conditions of the individual activity). These semantic *effect annotations* are represented in conjunctive normal form (CNF) and are accumulated along the execution paths of a process design (as described in [8,9] and implemented in the ProcessSEER[10] tool), to obtain the *cumulative effects* at the end-event of the process design. The final cumulative effects (representing *intended effects*) determine functional requirements for the re-designed processes. Consequently, any process re-design has to meet these the functional requirements.

Second, we define a library of (semantic annotated) process fragments. These fragments can denote single activities, processes, or potentially services derived from a service broker. Essentially, we enable the replacement of fragments of a process design with other fragments drawn from the library in an (exhaustive search) procedure that ensures that the original functionality of the process is still realized, but the sustainability profile of the resulting process design is improved.

Third, in the context of process improvement, there is often a requirement of *minimally change* existing process designs, i.e., maximizing process improvement while minimizing disruption to the status quo. This is particularly important if we are interested in protecting investment put in existing process infrastructure and minimizing the ancillary costs associated with any change to process designs. The requirement for minimal change could be dealt with by *design proximity* as a tie breaker when multiple alternative process re-designs achieve the same quantum of process improvement. Instances of proximity relations and measures can be found in [8] and [11].

4   Conclusion

In this article we described a subset of the *Abnoba framework* for green business process management. In this context we first showed how the abstract algebraic c-semiring structure can be leveraged to deal with heterogeneous and multidimensional green measures. We further sketched a machinery for green business process improvement. A first evaluation with a handcrafted library, confirms the soundness of the approach, but its applicability in an industry setting remains future work.

References

1. Object Management Group: Business process modeling notation (bpmn) 1.2. , (2009), http://www.omg.org/spec/BPMN/1.2/PDF last checked 21.02
2. Ghose, A., Hoesch-Klohe, K., Hinsche, L., Le, L.S.: Green business process management: A research agenda. Australian Journal of Information Systems 16 (2009)
3. Hoesch-Klohe, K., Ghose, A.: Towards Green Business Process Management. In: Proc. of the 7th International Conference on Services Computing (Industry and Application Track) (2010)
4. Bistarelli, S., Montanari, U., Rossi, F.: Semiring-based constraint satisfaction and optimization. Journal of the ACM (JACM) 44(2), 236 (1997)
5. Ghose, A., Koliadis, G.: Pctk: A toolkit for managing business process compliance. In: Proc. of the Second International Workshop on Juris-informatics (2008)
6. Pavlovski, C., Zou, J.: Non-functional requirements in business process modeling. In: Proc. of the fifth on Asia-Pacific conference on conceptual modelling (2008)
7. Gorton, S., Reiff-Marganiec, S.: Towards a task-oriented, policy-driven business requirements specification for web services. In: Dustdar, S., Fiadeiro, J.L., Sheth, A.P. (eds.) BPM 2006. LNCS, vol. 4102, p. 465. Springer, Heidelberg (2006)
8. Ghose, A., Koliadis, G.: Auditing business process compliance. In: Krämer, B.J., Lin, K.-J., Narasimhan, P. (eds.) ICSOC 2007. LNCS, vol. 4749, pp. 169–180. Springer, Heidelberg (2007)
9. Ghose, A., Koliadis, G.: Pctk: A toolkit for managing business process compliance. In: Proc. of the 2008 International Workshop on Juris Informatics (2008)
10. Hinge, K., Ghose, A., Koliadis, G.: Process seer: A tool for semantic effect annotation of business process models. In: Proc. of the 13th IEEE International EDOC Conference, EDOC 2009 (2009)
11. Morrison, E.D., Menzies, A., Koliadis, G., Ghose, A.K.: Business process integration: Method and analysis. In: Proc. Sixth Asia-Pacific Conference on Conceptual Modelling, APCCM 2009 (2009)

On Predicting Impacts of Customizations to Standard Business Processes

Pietro Mazzoleni, Aubrey Rembert, Rama Akkiraju, and Rong (Emily) Liu

IBM T.J. Watson research Center

Abstract. Adopting standard business processes and then customizing them to suit specific business requirements is a common business practice. However, often, organizations don't fully know the impact of their customizations until after processes are implemented. In this paper, we present an algorithm for predicting the impact of customizations made to standard business processes by leveraging a repository of similar customizations made to the same standard processes. For a customized process whose impact needs to be predicted, similar impact trees are located in a repository using the notion of *impact nodes*. The algorithm returns a ranked list of impacts predicted for the customizations.

Keywords: Process Re-engineering, Process Comparison, Best practices, Tree Comparison.

1 Introduction

In this paper, we consider the problem of predicting the impact of a given set of customizations to a standard business process. We look at the problem from an IT services providers perspective. IT services providers typically implement the desired customizations to standard processes offered by ERP vendors for many companies. In our solution, we assume that IT service providers maintain a repository of anonymized customizations, each with its associated impact. We predict the impact of changes done on a standard process by comparing a query customization with all customizations (with associated impacts) available in the repository. The set of retrieved customizations are ranked based on closeness to the query customization.

2 Process Difference and Impact Representations

In this section, we describe delta trees and impact trees, which are both derivations of process structure trees. A Process Structure Tree (PST) is a hierarchical representation of business process. PSTs are used to represent both standard and customized processes because there are established algorithms for detecting differences between trees [1]. The output of our PST difference detection algorithm is a delta tree. Impact trees are delta trees that have been annotated with impact information.

P.P. Maglio et al. (Eds.): ICSOC 2010, LNCS 6470, pp. 557–562, 2010.

2.1   Delta Tree

A delta tree is a PST difference representation that is annotated with customization operations. To create delta trees, we only consider the customization operations *insert* and *delete*. We do not consider the *move* and *relabel* operations because their effects can be replicated with combinations of delete and insert operations. *Customization tags* are labels on leaf nodes of a delta tree that represent customization operations (i.e. whether a node has been inserted or deleted), and *customization summary tags* are labels on interior nodes which summarize the changes that were made to its descendents. The algorithm for constructing a delta tree has three phases.

The first phase is a modification of the algorithm by Küster et. al. [7], which determines the differences between two PSTs and represents those differences with a Joint PST (JPST). The modification decomposes the move portion of the algorithm into a series of insertions and deletions. The second phase involves reducing the JPST by finding the *delta root*. The delta root is the least common uncustomized ancestor of all the nodes in the JPST that have a customization tag. Let ℓ be the least common ancestor of the two customization tagged nodes that are the farthest distance apart in JPST, J. Thus, ℓ is also the ancestor of all the customization tagged nodes in that Joint PST. There are, however, situations when ℓ could itself be a customization tagged node, and thus not the delta root. When this happens, the delta root is the parent of ℓ in the Joint PST. Once the delta root, ℓ, is found the subtree J/ℓ becomes the delta tree. The reduction procedure continues by finding all of the untagged nodes that are not ancestors of customization tagged nodes and removing them from the delta tree. The procedure recursively removes all of the untagged leaves from the delta tree. The last phase in constructing a delta tree is adding *customization summary tags* (CSTs) to each interior node. The CST of an interior node, x, denoted by $CST(x)$, can take on one of three different values: "+", "-", and "M". Let x be an interior node in a delta tree and v be a descendant of x.

Definition 1 (Insertion Summary Tag). *If there exist at least one descendent of x with a customization tag of $"+"$, and no descendant of x with a customization tag of $"-"$, then $CST(x) =" +"$.*

Definition 2 (Deletion Summary Tag). *If there exist at least one descendent of x with a customization tag of $"-"$, and no descendant of x with a customization tag of $"+"$, then $CST(x) =" -"$.*

Definition 3 (Mixed Summary Tag). *If there is at least one descendant of x with a customization tag of "+", and at least one descendant of x with a customization tag of "-", then $CST(x) = "M"$.*

2.2   Impact Trees

An *impact tree* is a delta tree that has user-specified nodes called *impact nodes*. An impact node characterizes the effect the set of change operations defined by the customization tagged descendents have on a business. There is at least one impact node in an impact tree.

If a query delta tree matches an impact tree in the repository, then the impact associated with the impact nodes is the impact predicted for the query.

Definition 4. *Delta (Sub)Tree Compatibility. Let r be a node in impact tree $\hat{R}$, and X be the set of customization tagged descendents of r. Additionally, let q be a node in delta tree $\hat{Q}$ and Y be the set of customization tagged descendents of q. Subtree $\hat{R}/r$ is* incompatible *with subtree $\hat{Q}/q$, if $X \not\subseteq Y$. Otherwise, $\hat{R}/r$ is* compatible *with $\hat{Q}/q$.*

It should be noted that compatibility is directional. Therefore, if $\hat{R}/r$ is compatible with $\hat{Q}/q$, it does not imply that $\hat{Q}/q$ is compatible with $\hat{R}/r$. Based on the customization summary tags on delta trees, we can determine whether or not a subtree of an impact tree is compatible with a subtree of a delta tree. Given two trees R and Q, let r be in R and q and a be in Q. If a is an ancestor of q in Q and $id(a) = id(r)$, then a is an *r-matched ancestor* of q.

Property 1. Let $\hat{Q}$ and $\hat{R}$ be a query delta tree and an impact tree in the repository, respectively, created from the same standard process. Additionally, let q and r be interior nodes in $\hat{Q}$ and $\hat{R}$, respectively. Subtree $\hat{R}/r$ is compatible with $\hat{Q}/q$, if q does not have an r-matched ancestor and $CST(r) = CST(q)$ or q does not have an r-matched anscestor and $CST(q) = M$.

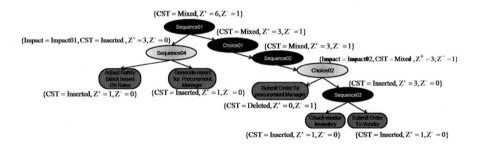

Fig. 1. Impact Tree Representation - Customized Process

3   Impact Prediction Algorithm

Our notion of tree matching is, as such, not new and is grounded in the methods noted in literature. But, the innovative rubber-banding of sub-trees/nodes as impact nodes for the customized processes in the repository is what differentiates our approach. This enables us to apply conditions to prune the search space by recognizing unfruitful paths. This allows us to speed up the performance. Our match starts with the basic query delta tree on the left hand side and the impact trees from a repository on the right hand side.

Algorithm 1. ImpactTreeTraversal($\hat{Q}$, $\hat{R}$)

$r \leftarrow$ Root node of $\hat{R}$;
$q \leftarrow$ Root node of $\hat{Q}$;
$matched \leftarrow$ FALSE ;
if $id(r) == id(q)$ **then**
   | $matched \leftarrow$ TRUE ;

if r *is an impact node* **then**
   | ImpactTreeSearch($\hat{Q}$, $\hat{R}$);

for *each child node* $r_j \in children(\hat{R})$ *do* **do**
   | **if** $matched == FALSE$ **then**
   | | ImpactTreeTraversal($\hat{Q}$, $\hat{R}/r_j$);

The algorithm to predict impacts for a delta tree $\hat{Q}$ consists of three steps to be repeated for all impact trees in the repository.

Step 1 described in Algorithm 1 performs a pre-order traversal of all impact nodes r in $\hat{R}$, where $\hat{R}$ is an impact tree in the repository. For each impact node, *ImpactTreeSearch*() (to be described in Step 2) traverses $\hat{Q}$ searching for a subtree matching the selected impact node in $\hat{R}/r$. If such matching subtree is found, the corresponding subtree, $\hat{Q}/q$, is annotated with the impacts associated with r. The algorithm terminates when there are no more impact nodes to be searched in $\hat{R}$.

In *Step 2*, ImpactTreeSearch(), which is illustrated in Algorithm 2, does a pre-order traversal of $\hat{Q}$ searching for a node q_i in $\hat{Q}$ such that $\hat{Q}/q_i$ and $\hat{R}/r_j$ are a *compatible* . Step 2 primarily checks the compatibility of the sub-trees and hands over the actual tree comparison to Step 3. The recursive comparison of $\hat{Q}/q_i$ and $\hat{R}/r_j$ will stop under two conditions: (1) all the nodes in $\hat{Q}$ have been searched and no compatible subtree was found, or (2) $\hat{R}/r_j$ is *incompatible* with $\hat{Q}/q_i$.

In *Step 3*, DeltaTreeSimilarityMatch() is invoked to compare compatible trees. The algorithm traverses the query and impact tree sub-trees to find similarity. When matching leaf nodes, only the nodes with the same id are matched. Let m be the number of leaf nodes in $\hat{Q}/q_i$ and let n be the number of leaf nodes in $\hat{R}/r_j$. Let k denote the number of *matched leaf nodes* between $\hat{Q}/q_i$ and $\hat{R}/r_j$. Then, the similarity match score M between these two sub-trees is:

$$M(\hat{R}/r_j, \hat{Q}/q_i) = \min(k/m, k/n)$$

Once all the matching is complete, repository customizations are ranked based on the overall similarity score attributed to the parent query node. The impact lists associated with each of the ranked repository customizations are the predicted impacts of the desired customizations in the query process.

Algorithm 2. ImpactTreeSearch($\hat{Q}$, $\hat{R}$)

$q \leftarrow$ Root of $\hat{Q}$;
$r \leftarrow$ Root of $\hat{R}$;
if $CST(q) == CST(r)$ **then**
    if $id(q) == id(r)$ **then**
        DeltaTreeSimilarityMatch(q, r);
        return();
    else
        for *each node $q_i \in children(\hat{Q}/q)$* **do**
            ImpactTreeSearch($\hat{Q}/q_i$, $\hat{R}$);
            return();

if $CST(q) ==$ "M'' **then**
    for *each node $q_i \in children(\hat{Q}/q)$* **do**
        ImpactTreeSearch($\hat{Q}/q_i$, $\hat{R}$);
else
    return();

---

4 Related Work

A large number of publications have addressed the problem of process matching, impact analysis, and tree comparison. However, they differ in domain, goal, medium, or approach.

We are not the first to leverage the PST representation for detecting the differences between process models. As example, the paper by Küsteret. al. [7] detects the differences between PSTs and represents those differences in a JPST, which is similar to our notion of delta trees. However, their work is concerned with obtaining a change log when one is not available. The paper by Eshuis and Grefen [3], which proposes a heuristic approach for matching BPEL processes represented in Program Structure Tree [5,6], is similar but, once again, the goal of their work (to find executable services exposing a certain behavior) is different than ours. The work of Dijkman et. al. [2] compares four approaches to the process similarity problem using a graph-based representation of process models. Their work is similar to ours in that they explore the process similarity problem. However, our approach differs in that we use a tree-based representation. The authors of Provop [4] present an approach for managing process variants by constraining the variations to select change operators such as insert, delete, move and modify. Te main motivation for our work is to improve the overall discoverability of variations on processes and also to predict the impact of these variations.

5 Conclusion

In this paper we have presented an algorithm to predict the impact of customizations made to standard business processes. We assumed that (a) all customizations are to the same standard business processes and (b) a repository of such customizations exists. For a given customized process whose impact needs to be predicted, we searched the repository of existing customizations to find similar customizations for that prediction. The algorithm presented takes advantage of two characteristics of our problem domain (a) the set of operations to customize a standard process is constrained, and (b) not all changes result in impact worthy of consideration. Together, these characteristics limit the scope and speeds up the runtime of the algorithm.

For future research, we would like to explore if given a desired business impact to be achieved, could we predict the customizations that need to be made to a standard process by analyzing customizations with similar impacts in the repository. This could help IT service providers in assessing what needs to be done to a standard process to meet customer requirements.

References

1. Bille, P.: A survey on tree edit distance and related problems. Theoretical Computer Science 337(1-3), 217–239 (2005)
2. Dijkman, R., Dumas, M., García-Banuelos, L.: Graph matching algorithms for business process model similarity search. In: Dayal, U., Eder, J., Koehler, J., Reijers, H.A. (eds.) Business Process Management. LNCS, vol. 5701, pp. 48–63. Springer, Heidelberg (2009)
3. Eshuis, R., Grefen, P.: Structural matching of BPEL processes. In: Fifth European Conference on Web Services, ECOWS 2007, pp. 171–180 (2007)
4. Hallerbach, A., Bauer, T., Reichert, M.: Managing process variants in the process lifecycle. In: ICEIS 2008 (2008)
5. Johnson, R., Pearson, D., Pingali, K.: The program structure tree: Computing control regions in linear time. In: Proceedings of the ACM SIGPLAN 1994 Conference on Programming Language Design and Implementation, pp. 171–185. ACM, New York (1994)
6. Johnson, R.C.: Efficient program analysis using dependence flow graphs (1995)
7. Küster, J.M., Gerth, C., Förster, A., Engels, G.: Detecting and resolving process model differences in the absence of a change log. In: Dumas, M., Reichert, M., Shan, M.-C. (eds.) BPM 2008. LNCS, vol. 5240, pp. 244–260. Springer, Heidelberg (2008)

Extended WS-Agreement Protocol to Support Multi-round Negotiations and Renegotiations[*]

Christoph Langguth and Heiko Schuldt

Databases and Information Systems Group,
University of Basel, Switzerland

Abstract. WS-Agreement is a well-established and widely adopted protocol that helps service providers and consumers to agree on constraints under which a service is made available. However, the original protocol is limited to a simple interaction pattern for establishing agreements: the requester suggests the Quality of Service (QoS) details, the responder either accepts or declines. This is no longer sufficient when several rounds of negotiations are needed before both parties agree on the QoS level to be provided, or when an already established agreement needs to be changed based on mutual consent (renegotiation). This paper presents an extension to WS-Agreement which jointly addresses these limitations.

1 Introduction

As Service-oriented Architectures (SOA), and in particular Web Services (WS), are constantly gaining in popularity and adoption, the research focus is broadening more and more towards non-functional service properties. A prime example is Quality of Service (QoS): in a production system, customers may demand for guarantees about a service's QoS, for instance because a best-effort-only provision of the service could lead to untolerable latencies when the system gets heavily loaded. If guarantees can be given, they are generally expressed in a Service Level Agreement (SLA), which can be considered a binding contract between provider and consumer.

WS-Agreement [2] is a well-established specification that allows to express and manage such SLAs. It defines a standardized protocol for managing agreements, while being flexible concerning their actual (domain-specific) content. However, it has a few shortcomings that we point out in the following use case.

Consider the example of a workflow engine W that orchestrates a process consisting of several service invocations – say, service S_1 followed by S_2. If each individual service provider participating in the workflow could assure proper QoS guarantees (e.g., on the availability of local resources to guarantee a certain execution time; or to guarantee an upper bound on the cost incurring during execution), the predictability of the individual service calls – and therefore also of the process as a whole – would be greatly improved. Thus, W could support the negotiation of QoS agreements for the overall process with its own client C.

---

[*] This work has been partly supported by the Hasler Foundation in the *COSA* project.

P.P. Maglio et al. (Eds.): ICSOC 2010, LNCS 6470, pp. 563–570, 2010.
© Springer-Verlag Berlin Heidelberg 2010

However, as the workflow engine needs to act as a kind of mediator and has to rely on QoS guarantees of the actual service providers, it has to individually negotiate agreements with the service providers as well. The QoS guarantees of the overall process need to be derived from "internal" negotiations with the service providers. In the case of long-running workflows encompassing resource-intensive services, each QoS agreement with a service provider might include several parameters (run-time, local resources, execution cost) that need to be jointly negotiated in a single agreement.

We have used the term *negotiation* in its literal sense, as this is a desirable feature: C could send an agreement offer to W, which, in trying to find a configuration that can satisfy the SLA terms, in turn needs to negotiate with providers offering S_1 and S_2. Clearly, if an agreement responder is able to send "counter-offers" to proposals, instead of just rejecting them (and forcing a subsequent attempt with a different proposal), the negotiation process is significantly facilitated. One shortcoming of WS-Agreement is that the specification does not allow for such multi-round negotiations, but only considers "one-shot" agreement creation, i.e., the responder has to immediately accept or reject an offer.

Furthermore, existing and valid agreements cannot be modified once established, except by terminating the existing SLA and creating a new one. Yet, the likeliness of "things going wrong" increases with the complexity of a workflow. Suppose that the provider of S_1 realizes it cannot assure the QoS it committed to. Being able to renegotiate with W (which may in turn trigger other renegotiations with providers of subsequent workflow activities) might limit the negative effects, whereas being forced to terminate the SLA inevitably leads to all agreements – and thus the workflow execution as well – having to be terminated.

This scenario stems directly from our ongoing research on DWARFS[4], which uses Advance Reservations for delivering QoS guarantees at workflow level, particularly for complex, long-running and resource-intensive scientific workflows. We consider the limitations of the WS-Agreement specification crucial. Thus, we devised and implemented an extension which: a) allows for multi-round agreement negotiations, as opposed to the existing single-shot "offer-accept-or-reject" creation; b) supports renegotiations, i.e., changing SLA terms while an agreement is in effect; c) is symmetric concerning the options that the involved parties have to operate on an agreement (e.g., allows also the agreement responder to terminate it); d) strives for maximum possible downward-compatibility.

The remainder of this paper is structured as follows: Section 2 analyzes the original WS-Agreement specification and its limitations. Section 3 provides detailed information about our extensions to the specification. Section 4 presents related work. Finally, Section 5 concludes.

2   The Original WS-Agreement Specification

Figure 1 shows a high-level overview of the lifecycle of an agreement (for the moment, consider only the "non-bold" part of the figure). The lifecycle states can be related to the port types defined in the specification as follows. An agreement passes through the **negotiating** state by two possible sequences of actions:

- The agreement initiator invokes the `createAgreement` operation of the `AgreementFactory` port type. This operation either returns an EPR to an `Agreement` resource, which corresponds to the **accept** transition, or it throws a fault, which corresponds to the **reject** transition.
- The agreement initiator invokes the `createPendingAgreement` operation of the `PendingAgreementFactory` port type, passing it an EPR to an `AgreementAcceptance` resource. The `PendingAgreementFactory` decides on whether it accepts the offer, and calls back the respective operation (`accept` or `reject`) on the `AgreementAcceptance`. This callback invocation directly corresponds to the transition of the same name.

If the agreement ends up in state **void**, the semantics are the same as if the agreement never existed, i.e., a contract has never taken place. Once an agreement is in state **effective**, the specification allows for two further transitions: The agreement comes to its "normal" end of lifetime, i.e., it *successfully* passes its expiration time. The transition is implicit in the specification, and is taking place when "[...] an agreement is no longer valid, and the parties are no-longer obligated by the terms of the agreement" [2]. This transition is made explicit in the figure, leading to the **completed** state. The second possible transition can only be triggered by the agreement initiator by calling the `terminate` operation on the `Agreement` resource. This leads to the **terminated** state, signifying that the agreement was terminated *unsuccessfully*.

There are several implications of this protocol design. First, the negotiation is in fact a simple request/response operation, in which the agreement initiator sends an offer that the responder either accepts or rejects. Second, only the initiator may terminate an agreement. There is no possibility for the agreement responder to terminate an agreement. Third, an agreement may not be modified after its creation – neither by the initiator nor by the responder. Fourth, when an agreement is created using the callback mechanism (`PendingAgreementFactory`/`AgreementAcceptance`), no provision is taken for the possible case of the responder not answering.

The first three issues share one common aspect: they can only be fully addressed if the asymmetry of the protocol is broken. By asymmetry we mean that

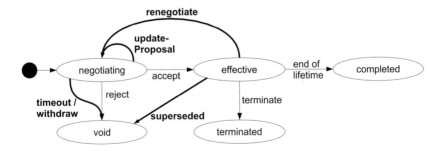

Fig. 1. Lifecycle of an Agreement (extensions in **bold**)

Table 1. Modified Port Types in the extended WS-Agreement Protocol

Port Type	Operations	Resource Properties
PendingAgreementFactory	createPendingAgreement	Template
Agreement	*accept*	Name
	reject	Id
	terminate	Context
	updateProposal	Terms
	extendDecisionDeadline	*AgreementState*
	withdraw	*ServiceTermStateList*
	renegotiate	*GuaranteeTermStateList*
		AgreementServiceReferenceList
AgreementAcceptance	accept	*Name*
	reject	*Id*
	terminate	*Context*
	updateProposal	*Terms*
	extendDecisionDeadline	*AgreementState*
	withdraw	
	renegotiate	

Operations/Resource Properties: unchanged, *reused*, **new**

according to the specification, only the responder keeps track of the agreement, while only the initiator may operate on it (e.g., call the `terminate` operation).

3   Extended WS-Agreement Protocol

Overcoming these limitations is possible by promoting the agreement initiator role to actually (also) *represent* the SLA. This is already partially done in the original specification by the definition of the `AgreementAcceptance` port type, albeit it is defined to only provide callback methods. As an example, consider the second issue: if an `AgreementAcceptance` also provides a `terminate` operation, then it becomes possible for the responder to terminate an agreement.

3.1   Modifications of Port Types

In that spirit, we have modified the WS-Agreement port types as shown in Table 1. The `Agreement` and `AgreementAcceptance` port types now present a much more symmetric interface: both provide exactly the same operations, and the `AgreementAcceptance` "mirrors" to a large extent the resource properties (RP) of the `Agreement` port type. While we describe the operations in more detail in Section 3.2, in the following we make a few important observations.

First, the `AgreementFactory` port type is not used. Even in the specification, this port type merely presents a simpler alternative to the use of the `Pending-AgreementFactory` in conjunction with the `AgreementAcceptance`. Since we heavily rely on the latter, the `AgreementFactory` is simply superfluous. While the `AgreementState` port type is not mentioned explicitly in Table 1, it is actually being used: according to [2], this port type "is not meant to be used as is but instead, its resource properties may be composed into a domain-specific Agreement port type". In our proposal, the `Agreement` and `AgreementAccep-tance` both represent the agreement, therefore we integrate the additional RPs into these port types. As we do not want our system to permanently "synchronize" system state from one port type to another, the `ServiceTermStateList` and the `GuaranteeTermStateList` RPs are only available at the service provider side (`Agreement`), while the `AgreementState` RP is part of both `Agreement` and `AgreementAcceptance`.

The full state diagram that the modified port types allow is shown in Figure 1. We have not introduced new states, but several new transitions. Most notably, the agreement can stay in state **negotiating** for arbitrarily long, by repeatedly following the **updateProposal** transition. Thus, the agreement responder no longer needs to immediately accept or reject an agreement, but may instead send a counter-offer to the initiator, who then has to accept or reject it, or in turn come up with another proposal. This "ping-pong" style is the reason why the operations and RPs of `Agreement` and `AgreementAcceptance` are to a large extent symmetric: both agreement partners now have equal roles in the negotiation. The concept of having this alternation of responsibility to decide about the "fate" of an agreement means that while the agreement is in the **negotiating** state, there is always one involved party waiting for a decision from its partner. To cope with the possible case of that partner not answering anymore, we have introduced a *decision deadline*: this is the time by which a decision must have been taken, or the agreement is cancelled by the waiting party (transition **timeout** into state **void**).

3.2   Operations in Detail

The following list gives an overview of the newly introduced operations. In the interest of space, operations which were merely "copied" from the `Agreement` to the `AgreementAcceptance` or vice-versa, are not discussed, as their semantics remains the same. Figure 2 shows sequence diagrams of how these operations may play together during the initial negotiation and renegotiation of agreements.[1]

- `updateProposal`: This operation allows for a multi-round negotiation process. If one of the agreement partners receives an agreement proposal that it neither accepts nor rejects, it responds by sending a proposal which would be accepted instead, by invoking the `updateProposal` operation at the partner's endpoint. The method has one parameter, which is the proposal, and it does not return any value. An invocation of the `updateProposal` operation should always be responded to by invoking either the `accept` or `reject` operation, or by sending yet another proposal.
- `extendDecisionDeadline`: As described earlier, there is a deadline to prevent timeouts and to give agreement partners the possibility to limit the time for decision making. It is initially defined by the service provider, but either of the negotiation parties can request an extension by invoking the `extendDecisionDeadline` operation on its partner's endpoint. The operation does not

---

[1] To avoid clutter, illustration of the decision making process is limited to the initiator's side. The analogous parts on the responder's side have been omitted.

expect any parameters. If the invoked party is willing to accept the extension, it returns the new deadline or else throws a fault.

- `withdraw`: If one of the parties has sent a proposal to the other partner and has not yet received an answer, it still has the possibility to abort the negotiation process by calling the `withdraw` operation at the partner's endpoint.
- `renegotiate`: Either partner can request renegotiation of an existing agreement. This is described in more detail in Section 3.3.

3.3 Renegotiation

As we have mentioned, the possibility to renegotiate an existing agreement is of fundamental importance. As shown in Figure 2, invocation of the `renegotiate` operation creates two new resources (`Agreement` and `AgreementAcceptance`).[2] The partners then carry out the renegotiation in exactly the same style as a normal multi-round negotiation, using these new endpoints. Once that negotiation process comes to an end, the following actions depend on its outcome. In case of a successful negotiation, the newly created agreement enters the **effective** state, superseding the existing one, which gets discarded (transition **superseded**). If the negotiation process is not successful, the existing agreement stays in place unchanged (and the newly created one is **void**).

3.4 Compatibility with the Original Specification

With the exception of the (dispensable) `AgreementFactory` port type, our extension is completely downward-compatible with the existing WS-Agreement specification. In other words, if none of our extensions are being used, i.e., the responder immediately accepts or rejects the first proposal, and no renegotiation takes place, the interaction patterns correspond exactly to the original specification. The only additional data that needs to be communicated is the decision deadline; it was added to the `wsag:Context` (which allows for `xs:any`). Thus, we ensure interoperability with endpoints not using our extension – but it should be noted that this will not hold anymore if one party *requires* our extension.

4   Related Work

The shortcomings of WS-Agreement that our extension deals with have been addressed at various levels. A formal analysis of the structure of an agreement and its internal state is presented in [3]. The authors analyze in detail *when* an agreement may need to be renegotiated, and propose an extension to the agreement representation that allows for (in-place) modification of existing agreement terms; however, *how* a renegotiation can be performed is not addressed. Multi-round negotiation is discussed in [7,8] using an approach similar to ours, but

---

[2] The figure only shows the case of the initiator triggering a renegotiation. The symmetric case is, of course, also possible.

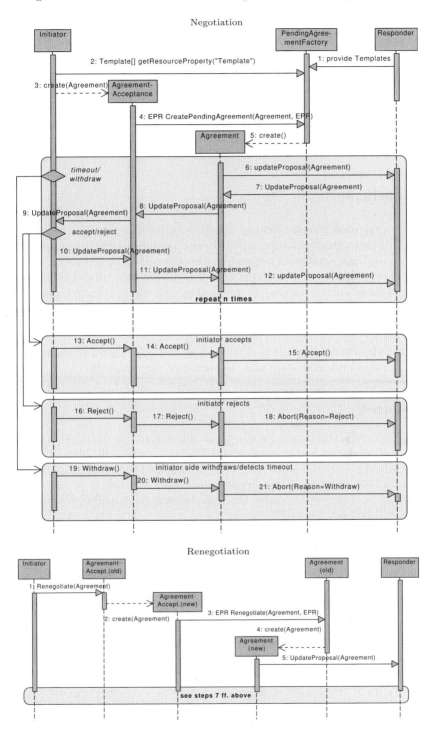

Fig. 2. Sequence Diagrams: Agreement Negotiation and Renegotiation

performing the negotiation using agreement templates rather than actual agreement offers. A protocol that focuses on renegotiation only is described in [6]. It proposes multiple operations that allow for renegotiation, whereas our approach mostly reuses the multi-round negotiation capabilities for renegotiation; also, the inherent asymmetry is not addressed, thus enabling only the agreement initiator to request a renegotiation. Finally, [5] proposes new port types that allow for a (symmetric) renegotiation, whereas we extend the existing port types. In addition, our proposal does not require any changes to the structure of an agreement representation, but deliberately strives to be "agnostic" of the SLA content.

5   Conclusions

We have described an extension of the WS-Agreement protocol which allows for multi-round agreement negotiation. It also enables renegotiation of existing SLAs, giving both agreement partners the opportunity to trigger such renegotiations. Our proposal requires no modifications to the structure of an agreement and, to a large extent, reuses the operations and resource properties defined in the specification, assigning them in a symmetric fashion to the original port types. This approach allows us to stay compatible with the original specification.

Acknowledgement. The authors would like to thank David Ammann for his support in the implementation and evaluation of this proposal.

References

1. Ammann, D.: Design and Implementation of a Negotiation Protocol for Scientific Workflows based on WS-Agreement. Master's thesis, University of Basel (2009)
2. Andrieux, A.: et al. Web Services Agreement Specification. Specification, Open Grid Forum (2007), http://www.ogf.org/documents/GFD.107.pdf
3. Frankova, G., Malfatti, D., Aiello, M.: Semantics and Extensions of WS-Agreement. Journal of Software 1(1) (2006)
4. Langguth, C., Ranaldi, P., Schuldt, H.: Towards Quality of Service in Scientific Workflows by using Advance Resource Reservations. In: IEEE 2009 Third International Workshop on Scientific Workflows, (SWF 2009) (2009)
5. Modica, G.D., Tomarchio, O., Vita, L.: Dynamic SLAs management in service oriented environments. Journal of Systems and Software 82(5), 759–771 (2009)
6. Parkin, M., Hasselmeyer, P., Koller, B., Wieder, P.: An SLA Re-Negotiation Protocol. In: 2nd Non Functional Properties and Service Level Agreements in Service Oriented Computing Workshop, NFPSLA-SOC 2008 (November 2008)
7. Pichot, A., Wäldrich, O., Ziegler, W., Wieder, P.: Towards Dynamic Service Level Agreement Negotiation: An Approach Based on WS-Agreement. In: WEBIST (Selected Papers), pp. 107–119 (2008)
8. Ziegler, W., Wieder, P., Battr, D.: Extending WS-Agreement for dynamic negotiation of Service Level Agreements. Technical Report TR-0172, Institute on Resource Management and Scheduling, CoreGRID - Network of Excellence (August 2008)

Event-Driven Virtual Machine for Business Integration Middleware

Joachim H. Frank[1], Liangzhao Zeng[2], and Henry Chang[2]

[1] IBM Software Group
jhfrank@us.ibm.com
[2] IBM T.J. Watson Research Center
{lzeng,hychang}@us.ibm.com

Abstract. Business integration middleware uses a variety of programming models to enable business process automation, business activity monitoring, business object state management, service mediation, etc. Different kinds of engines have been developed in support of these programming models. At their core however, all of these engines implement the same kind of behavior: formatted messages (or events) are received, processed in the context of managed objects, and new messages are emitted. These messages can represent service invocations and responses, tracking events, notifications, or point-to-point messages between applications. The managed objects can represent process instances, state machines, monitors, or service mediations. Developing separate engines for each programming model results in redundant implementation efforts, and may even cause an "integration problem" for the integration middleware itself. To address these issues, we propose to use an event-driven virtual machine that implements the fundamental behavior of all business integration middleware as the sole execution platform, and provide compilers for higher level programming models. Conceptually, this is similar to passing from CISC to RISC architecture in CPU design: efficiently implement a small instruction set, and support higher level languages via compilers.

1 Introduction

The key observation leading to this work was that event-driven systems [1] [2] [3] implement all of the key mechanisms used by integration middleware components: event/message[1] identification, correlation, updates of stateful objects, and emission. In a business integration environment, which can include components for business process automation, business activity monitoring, service mediation, and so on, events are typically transmitted over a network, for example in the SOAP [4] format. While event-driven systems are gaining considerable momentum in both academia and industry, no unified architecture has been proposed for a generic event processor in the business integration middleware domain. Instead, different engines are developed for different high-level programming models, all of which implement the same fundamental set of operations. For example, in a business process management (BPM) system events

---

[1] Throughout this paper we use the term "event" synonymously with "one-way message".

P.P. Maglio et al. (Eds.): ICSOC 2010, LNCS 6470, pp. 571–578, 2010.

indicating that a process should be started or an activity has completed are received, correlated, and used to update process instances. As another example, in a business activity monitoring (BAM) system, tracking events are received, correlated, and update metrics in an observer object (monitoring context). While the need for different high-level programming models in the business integration domain seems obvious, developing separate engines for each of those models results in: (i) redundant development efforts; (ii) high installation and maintenance cost for a variety of engines; and (iii) possibly additional work to "integrate the integration platform".

After analyzing various business integration programming models, six fundamental capabilities emerged that they all had in common: identifying and receiving events; correlating events; creating, updating, and deleting stateful objects; and emitting events. These basic capabilities were captured in a concise machine language with six instructions. A virtual machine for this language was developed and tested with a variety of event processing applications. The main contributions of this paper are thus:

- **A machine language for event-driven applications.** We propose a machine language for event processing called ICE (for *I*ntermediate *C*od*E*). It has six instructions that cover the fundamental spectrum of capabilities required by business integration middleware. The small instruction set facilitates building virtual machines for this language on different hardware platforms and operating systems.
- **A componentized ICE virtual machine.** We present a virtual machine for the ICE language, written in Java. It can be embedded in event-processing applications, or be at the core of a business integration hub or event processing service. Its component architecture allows to easily replace functional parts (for example, the expression evaluator or the persistence manager) which helps portability.
- **A collection of ICE compilers.** We discuss how to write ICE compilers for higher level programming models, so that business integration software written in a variety of high-level languages (processes, mediations, monitor models, etc.) can run on the same virtual machine.

2   ICE Language

2.1   Overview

An ICE virtual machine ("ICE machine") provides an execution environment for processing events in the context of target objects. A target object may represent a state machine, a process execution, a stateful mediation, a monitoring context, and so on. Events are processed in an ICE machine using five basic steps: (1) Event filtering, to determine the kind of the incoming event. (2) Event correlation processing, to find target objects, and instantiate new ones if necessary. (3) Update operations, to change the state of the target objects. (4) Event emission, to send out requests, replies, alerts, etc. (5) Terminating target objects. The ICE instruction set reflects these five operations, with a sixth instruction added for conditional branching.

2.2   Instruction Set

Following a "reduced instruction set" paradigm (similar to the RISC philosophy in CPU design) we defined a small but fundamental set of event processing instructions. It appears that the following six instructions are necessary and sufficient to support any event-driven application:

1. **onEvent.** An *onEvent* statement represents an event subscription. It has a Boolean filter condition which defines the subscription criteria: events that pass the filter, and only those, will be processed by the onEvent statement. The statement can nest an instruction sequence, and when an incoming event passes the filter, that sequence is executed. The nested statements can be any of the following:

2. **forAll.** A *forAll* statement selects target objects based on a target object type and a correlation predicate. The correlation predicate is evaluated for all target objects of the given type. It typically compares a key value in the incoming event with a field containing this key in all candidate target objects. Zero, one, or several matches can result, and the forAll specifies what to do in each case. Here are some examples: create a new target object if none was found; process the event for all matching target objects; ignore the event if no target is found; raise an error if more than one target is found; etc. A forAll can nest a statement sequence, which is executed once in the context of each target object. If forAll statements are nested, a tree of target objects results with each nested forAll contributing a new set of child nodes.

3. **assign.** An *assign* statement has a left hand side expression whose evaluation must yield a slot in the target object's data structure ("target slot") and a right hand side expression that can depend on target object data and the current event. The target slot is updated with the result of the right-hand side, and created if it did not exist.

4. **branch.** A *branch* statement allows for conditional branching within an ICE program. It has a Boolean branch condition. If it evaluates to true the branch is taken, otherwise execution continues with the following statement. A branch may specify a positive (forward) or negative (backward) branching distance.

5. **emit.** An *emit* statement specifies that an outbound event will be sent, whose payload will be taken from a specified target slot.

6. **terminate.** A *terminate* statement specifies that the current target object (identified by the nearest enclosing forAll) is to be removed from the set of objects under control of the ICE machine after the current event has been processed completely.

The instruction set of the ICE machine is "minimal" for a virtual machine that processes events in the context of target objects: Obviously, an instruction is needed to receive and classify events (onEvent) and to send them out (emit); a correlation step is required for target identification (forAll); there must be instructions for target object creation (forAll, implicit), update (assign), and deletion (terminate). Target object creation is covered by forAll with the "no correlation matches" option set to "create new target". Finally, a statement is needed to permit conditional logic (branching) and for a machine language, GOTO semantics seemed adequate.

3   ICE Machine

3.1   Component Architecture

Two considerations guided our design: (i) *Pluggability of Components.* A modular structure as in Fig. 1 allows to vary implementation options and facilitates portability. For example, different Expression Managers can support a variety of expression languages and evaluators. Different ICE Cube Managers (persistence managers) can provide interfaces to a variety of databases. (ii) *Usability in Different Environments.* It should be possible to use an ICE machine as a universal event processor in a variety of environments: embedded in applications; as a stand-alone middleware component; or as an event processing service in a cloud environment.

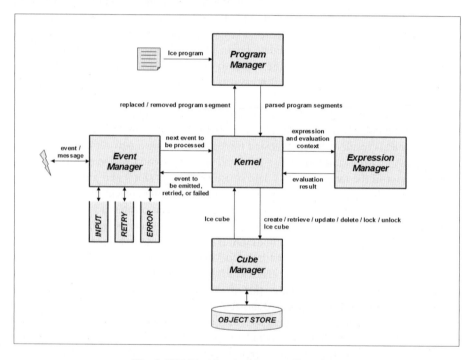

Fig. 1. ICE Machine Architecture Overview

3.2   Components

As shown in Fig 1. an ICE machine has five components: *program manager, event manager, cube manager, expression manager* and *kernel*. They interact as follows:

1. The **Program Manager** receives ICE program segments. A program segment is the smallest unit of logic that can be deployed to or removed from an ICE machine. The program manager parses the program segments and constructs an in-memory model of the code, which the kernel will use to control execution.

2. The **Event Manager** receives incoming events and puts them in the input bucket, from where they are consumed by the kernel. Events can be returned to the event manager if correlation processing ends with a "retry" condition (typically, when an expected target object does not yet exist) or when unrecoverable errors occur; they are then put in the retry or error bucket, respectively. Events in the retry bucket are moved back to the input bucket after some wait time. An event that has exceeded the maximum number of retries goes to the error bucket. The event manager also publishes outbound events produced by emit statements. Their further processing and routing, for example via an ESB or pub-sub infrastructure, depends on the environment in which the ICE machine operates.

3. The **Cube Manager** handles the creation, persistence, locking, updating, and termination of target objects. The target objects in an ICE machine are dubbed "ICE cubes" which explains the name of this component.

4. The **Expression Manager** is called by the kernel to evaluate filters, correlation predicates, branch conditions, and right hand sides of assigns. It is passed an expression and its evaluation context, which consists of the current event, any target objects, and any local variables. It returns the evaluation result.

5. The **Kernel** is the actual virtual machine. It fetches an event from the input bucket, initiates a new ICE program execution, and runs it by interpreting the ICE program. It calls the event manager, the cube manager, and the expression manager to use their services as needed.

3.3 Compilers

A detailed description of ICE compiler algorithmss for the programming models commonly used in business integration would exceed the realm of this paper, but here is an outline:

The simplest use case is stateless *message transformation (mediation)* which is translated into an ICE program with a onEvent statement for each type of message to be transformed. It contains a sequence of assigns updating a local variable, and an emit to send out the content of that variable at the end. No target objects are used.

A *monitor model* [2] [3] is compiled by mapping each event subscription to an onEvent (for filtering) followed by a forAll (for correlation). The target object now represents a "monitoring context" whose fields (representing metrics) are updated by assign statements based on the content of the incoming event. Outbound events are sent via emit statements; their triggers are translated into branch statements, which skip the emit if the trigger condition is false.

A *business state machine* is compiled by generating an onEvent/forAll pair for each kind of event that the state machine can process. The target objects are state machine instances. State machine start events will find no target instance, and their forAll will create a new instance in an initial state. Other events, once their target object has been identified by a forAll, will drive assigns that put those target instances in a new state, followed by emits for any events to be sent as part of the state transition.

A *business process* [5] can be considered a state machine whose states are given by token placements on the process graph. Process start events create a new instance corresponding to an initial token placement. Events representing activity completions, or (BPMN) process events, cause transitions to new states by tokens being added and/or moved to subsequent nodes of the graph. As tokens enter nodes, outbound events may be sent representing service invocations or process event emissions.

An illustration is shown in Fig. 2, where a business integration solution comprising a business process, a monitor model, and a service mediation runs on a single ICE machine after all of the higher level logic has been compiled into ICE programs.

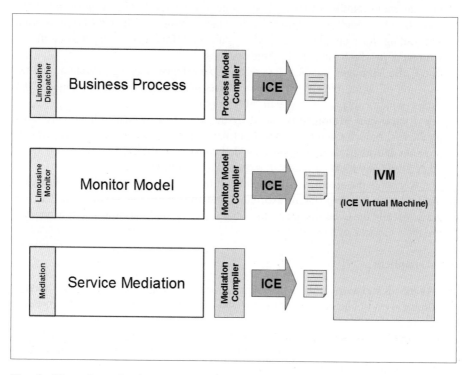

Fig. 2. Illustration of using common intermediate code (ICE) for different high-level programming models

4   Implementation Aspects

Our ICE machine prototype was developed in Java. Any well-formed XML can be processed as an event. We currently have two event managers, one using JMS and one using in-memory queues. The program manager and the kernel are pure Java. The expression manager uses an XPath 2.0 [6] evaluator, and is the most performance-critical component at this time. There are two versions of the cube manager, one that holds target objects in memory and one based on Apache Cassandra [8]. Assemblies of these components into a full ICE machine are currently available as a stand-alone Java program, as a Java EE application on IBM WebSphere Application Server [7], and as an event processing stage in Apache Cassandra.

An implementation of the cube manager using an XML database is in preparation, and we expect that pushing expressions to the database will result in significant performance benefits: correlation predicates for example become queries that return the keys of matching target objects, which can benefit from indexes on those keys.

The ICE machine has an external control interface, which allows to deploy and remove ICE program segments, submit events, inspect the three event buckets, browse the object store, and control the virtual machine. In the WebSphere based implementation the control interface is exposed as a REST API. This version of the ICE machine is also used in an interactive debugger for monitor models [3].

5 Related Work

We review some related event-processing systems, including active databases, complex event processing applications and event stream processors.

Modern database systems support triggers as a means of reacting to certain conditions (or "events"). Triggers are part of the SQL3 standard [9] and use Event Condition Action (ECA) rules to specify their logic. However, the events in database ECA rules are limited to database state transitions. It should be noted that an ICE machine can also be considered an ECA rule engine, because ECA rules can be complied into ICE programs—thus adding to the set of high-level programming models that an ICE machine can handle and affirming its role as a "universal" event processor. An ICE machine imposes no limitations on the format of the events processed (our current implementation accepts any well-formed XML).

Unlike active database systems, which provide a data-centric approach to event processing, complex event processing systems [13] are usually considered middleware. They can enrich and extend the event processing semantics in active databases, and provide a collection of event operators that allow to define complex event patterns. These operators include and, or, sequence, not, periodic, etc. Note however that event patterns can also be compiled into ICE programs. For example, the complex event Event_A and Event_B would be realized as two onEvent statements, with subsequent logic to register the arrival of each event in a stateful target object, and emit the "combined" event after both have arrived.

Event stream processors [10] [11] [12] consider a collection of events in a time window as relations, using SQL like languages to process the event streams. Unlike traditional database systems, which assume that data is persisted first and processed later, event stream processors process events in memory, following a paradigm of "read and read only once". Event-driven systems on the other hand, including the ICE machine, focus on individual events rather than collections, and perhaps the most distinguishing feature of the ICE machine is its correlation logic, putting events in the context of target objects that persist the processing result.

6 Conclusion

We have introduced an event-driven virtual machine as a universal runtime for business-integration middleware. It features a minimal instruction set and a componentized engine. We briefly discussed compiler algorithms for a number of programming models used in the business integration domain. Going forward, we plan to improve the performance and scalability of the ICE machine, provide improved tool support, an open testbed, and study its usability as an event-processing service in a cloud environment.

References

[1] Zeng, L., Lei, H., Chang, H.: Model-analysis for Business Event Processing. IBM Systems journal (2007)
[2] Zeng, L., Lei, H., Dikun, M.J., Chang, H., Bhaskaran, K.: Model-Driven Business Performance Management. In: ICEBE 2005, pp. 295–304 (2005)
[3] IBM WebSphere Business Monitor,
   http://publib.boulder.ibm.com/infocenter/dmndhelp/v7r0mx/
   topic/com.ibm.btools.help.monitor.doc/home/home.html
[4] SOAP specification, http://www.w3.org/TR/soap/
[5] BPMN 2.0 specification, http://schema.omg.org/spec/BPMN/2.0/Beta2/
[6] XPath 2.0, http://www.w3.org/TR/xpath20/
[7] IBM WebSphere Application Server,
   http://www-01.ibm.com/software/webservers/appserv/was/
[8] Apache Cassandra, http://cassandra.apache.org/
[9] Kulkarni, K., Mattos, N.M., Cochrane, R.: Active database features in SQL3. In: Paton, N.W., Gries, D., Schneider, F. (eds.) Active rules in database systems. Monographs in computer science, pp. 197–219. Springer, Heidelberg (1999)
[10] Babu, S., Widom, J.: Continuous queries over data streams. In: SIGMOD Rec. 30,3,2
[11] Fjording the Stream: An Architecture for Queries over Streaming Sensor Data. In: ICDE 2002 (2002)
[12] Chandrasekaran, S., Franklin, M.J.: Streaming Queries over Streaming Data. In: VLDB 2002 (2002)
[13] Luckham, D.C.: The Power of Events: an Introduction to Complex Event Proc-essing, in Distributed Enterprise Systems. Addison-Wesley Longman, Inc, Amsterdam

Consistent Integration of Selection and Replacement Methods under Different Expectations in Service Composition and Partner Management Life-Cycle

Fuyuki Ishikawa

GRACE Center, National Institute of Informatics,
2-1-2 Hitotsubashi, Chiyoda-ku, Tokyo 101-8430, Japan
f-ishikawa@nii.ac.jp

Abstract. Active efforts on Service-Oriented Computing have involved a variety of proposals on service selection and replacement methods to achieve quality assurance with adaptability in service composition. However, each method has specific expectations on when it is activated and how it affects service composition. Blind use of such methods can thus lead to inconsistency. This paper proposes a framework to integrate selection and replacement methods. The framework supports to clarify and analyze expectations in service composition and partner management life-cycle as well as to construct a consistent implementation accordingly. The proposed framework facilitates to test, introduce and replace service selection and replacement methods according to the environment and its change, for a variety of application domains.

Keywords: WS-BPEL, Service Composition, Service Selection, Service Replacement, Service Management.

1   Introduction

Service-Oriented Computing (SOC) aims at facilitating agile and flexible system composition by combining services published on the web [8]. Here "services" mean software components that are published on networks with machine-accessible self-description and interface. A variety of services have been explored, not only classical web-based applications such as travel reservation and stock information access but emerging services (cloud services, ambient services, etc.).

Process-based approaches are often considered where control and data flows are specified among a set of tasks to compose a new service. In those approaches, process languages such as WS-BPEL, or just BPEL, (Web Services Business Process Execution Language) are used to define the control and data flows [7]. At this point, only interfaces of the involved services are often defined so that decisions on concrete bindings with service providers be made at deployment time or runtime. On the basis of such approaches, a variety of methods have been proposed to select services according QoS (Quality of Service) aspects as

P.P. Maglio et al. (Eds.): ICSOC 2010, LNCS 6470, pp. 579–586, 2010.

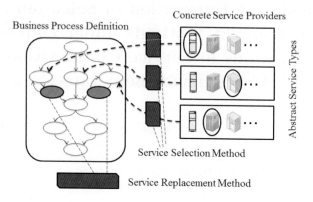

Fig. 1. Underlying Architecture for BPEL-based Services

well as to replace them according to runtime situations. Figure 1 illustrates this architecture, which has become somewhat common in research activities for SOC.

Each of such selection and replace methods has specific expectations for environments where it is applied. For example, many selection methods have expectations on available QoS data and their formats, such as conditional statements in SLA (Service Level Agreement) and accumulation of third-party or user scores. Selection methods may also differ in scalability against the number of candidate services. Environmental characteristics, such as QoS data availability and the number of service providers, are continuously changing over time while depending on the application targets (e.g., services provided in Japan). It is therefore desirable to make use of service selection and replace methods by selecting and replacing themselves as well. This is also useful in terms of testing where developers can test a variety of methods, whose effectiveness is difficult to assess and compare with each other without testing against actual data sets.

The above discussion might seem to just imply that selection and replacement methods should be also modeled and implemented as services (or components). However, actually each method has specific expectations on its expected use, when it is activated and how it affects the composition. It is thus necessary to integrate selection and replacement behaviors to a service composition process in a consistent way. For example, typical replacement methods transparently replace a service upon some events during execution of the composition process. However, blind use of such methods can lead to inconsistency, when the replaced service has states or protocols (e.g., requires a cancellation message), or when a selection method was used together that chose a set of multiple providers to make their QoS balanced to satisfy some constraints.

In response to the problem, this paper proposes a framework to integrate selection and replacement methods into a service composition process. The framework is based on analysis of different expectations in service composition and partner management life-cycle. The framework supports to clarify and analyze such expectations, and then to construct a consistent implementation accordingly. It facilitates to test, introduce and replace service selection and replacement methods according to the environment and its change. This paper reports the approach of the framework (Section 2) and case studies (Section 3) as well as discussion on advantages and limitations (Section 4).

2 Framework for Integration of Selection and Replacement Methods

In the proposed framework, expectations are first analyzed and clarified in service composition as well as selection and replacement methods (Section 2.1). Patterns are then determined to weave selection and replacement behaviors into process execution and management, and actually implemented with a policy description provided by the framework (Section 2.2).

2.1 Classification of Expectations in Service Composition and Partner Management Life-Cycle

Expectations in Use of Each Component Service. A component service used by a composition process sometimes has states, which the composition process needs to manage carefully. Below two types of states are discussed, states within one session, a unit of interaction a process instance has with the service, and states among multiple sessions.

Session States. Some services can be used through one-shot invocation of their operations (e.g., get the current stock price). Others require specific sequences of message exchanges to complete some functionality (e.g., login, then add an item to cart, check out, and finally logout). These different expectations are referred to as **Session States: No (One-Shot Invocation)** and **Session States: Yes(Conversational Interaction)**. In the latter case, service replacement during process execution can lead to inconsistencies. As the simplest example, suppose a choreography where an operation opA is first invoked then another operation opB is invoked. It is nonsense to invoke opA of $serviceA$, then switch the service and invoke opB of $serviceB$. In this case, opA of $serviceB$ should be invoked before opB, thus requiring some rollback or replay mechanism. In addition, explicit compensation or cancellation activities may be necessary for $serviceA$. In this way, service replacement at an intermediate state of the choreography requires careful state management in the case of Conversational Interaction.

Persistent States. Some services provide functionality that is closed within one instance of interaction, which means instances of interaction with the services do not affect each other. Others provide functionality to operate on service-side states (e.g., photo upload service), whose effects are persistent and shared by succeeding instances of interaction with the services. These different expectations are referred to as **Persistent States: No (No Persistent Service States)** and **Persistent States: Yes (Persistent Service States)**. In the latter case, service replacement may require state migration. For example, migration may be required by downloading data from a service to be replaced, uploading it to the alternative service, and deleting the data on the original service. It is notable that service contracts can be also considered as this kind of states, as initiation of contracts have persistent effects such as permission to use the service and billing while service replacement requires termination of a contract and initiation of a contract with another service.

Expectations in Service Selection and Replacement. As a variety of selection and replacement methods have been proposed, each of them has specific expectations on when it is activated and how it affects during process execution and management. In other words, these method vary in terms of when to modify which partner references, which developers need to consider when incorporating these methods into process execution and management.

Inter-Service Dependency. In some cases, a service for each service type is selected or replaced one by one, independently of the other service types. This kind of methods matches with the situations where QoS constraints or optimization is considered for each of the service types. In other cases, selection or replacement of multiple services is considered to deal with inter-service dependencies in QoS aspects. For example, suppose constraints are imposed on the composite QoS of the whole process (e.g., upper bound of the total cost and upper bound of the total processing time) [5]. In such a case, QoS of each service cannot be examined solely and it is necessary to consider sets of services for all the involved service types. Other examples of inter-service dependencies include discounts when using services provided by the same company and better communication performance when using services that within the same area (e.g., data center). These different expectations are referred to as **Inter-Service Dependency: No (One-by-One Service Selection)** and **Inter-Service Dependency: Yes (Service Set Selection)**. When consideration of inter-service dependency is essentially required by the composer's intention or characteristics of available services, selection methods should be used that can deal with the aspect. Here the expected benefits of such a method can be lost if a replacement method would replace one service with another without consideration of the aspect. Selection methods and replacement methods should not be blindly used in combination actually, while they have been often discussed and proposed independently.

Target of Selected References. As multiple instances run for one definition of a service composition process, it is necessary to clarify the target scope in which a certain partner reference chosen by a selection method (or re-selection within a replacement method) is used. In some cases, service selection is conducted for each process instance, when the selection method considers properties specific to the instance such as its request parameters. In other cases, the results of service selection are shared among multiple process instances. These different expectations are referred to as **Selection per Instance: No (Instance-Independent**

Selection) and Selection per Instance: Yes (Instance-Specific Selection). In the latter case, it is necessary to activate the selection method in every process instance. In the case of Instance-Independent Selection, selection methods may be repeatedly activated upon some events or periodically. This type of re-selection does not affect the running process instances and the new references are used for process instances initiated after the replacement.

Replacement during Process Execution. Many methods have been proposed for service replacement during execution of a process instance. Typically replacement upon failure in service invocation is considered, to retry the invocation with an alternative (e.g., [2]). Other methods consider replacement of services to be used successively. For example, such replacement may aim at covering a loss in QoS (e.g., more processing time than estimated) of the precedent services (e.g., [1]). These different expectations are referred to as **Replacement Type: Retry (Replacement for Retry)** and **Replacement Type: Re-selection (Replacement for Re-Selection)**. Actually none, either, or both of these types of replacement methods can be used for each of the involved service types. It is necessary to replace services in a consistent way in complying with the state management (if required). Especially, in the case of Retry, it is necessary to properly rollback the states in the case of Conversational Interaction.

2.2   Implementation according to the Classification

Depending on the expectations classified according to the criteria presented in Section 2.1, it is sometimes possible that the chosen methods essentially lead to inconsistency. For example, suppose a replacement methods that expect **One-Shot Invocation** is used for a service type that involves **Conversational Interaction**. In this case, message sequences can become invalid against the choreography with replacement at an intermediate state, for both of the original service and the alternative service.

For the other cases, the framework provides interfaces of components and notations for policy description to weave selection and replacement behaviors that modify partner references (and have additional state transitions in the composition process) according to the expectations. For example, it is necessary to implement components that define service selection methods. Use of the components is declared in the policy description. One component may be used for selection of services for multiple service types, when **Service Set Selection** is considered. Otherwise (**One-by-One Selection**), one component is allocated with one service type. Triggering events are also declared in the policy description for each of these selection components. Those events can be user-defined, specific to the environment or the application, such as time passage, user command, and a specific notification by a monitoring service. In the case of **Instance-Specific Selection**, triggering events defined in the framework can also be used. One of the defined events denotes instantiation of a process so that selection per process instance is activated as soon as a new process instance is initiated. Another one denotes activation of a specific activity so that election per process instance is activated as soon as the branch is chosen and it turns out that interaction with the service type is required.

Due to the page limitation, only a few examples have been shown to illustrate the approach. but the essential intention has been discussed in Section 2.1.

The framework provides a mechanism for generation of a BPEL process where additional behaviors are woven as described above, given an original BPEL process and the policy description. It is thus possible to use any BPEL engine if references of the involved components are configured adequately. On the other hand, as many selection and replacement methods require logs or statistics of QoS and other aspects, it is sometimes necessary to accumulate such data and make it available for the components that implement selection or replacement methods. Use of a certain BPEL engine can be inadequate regarding this point, depending on its capabilities for logging, insertion of additional behaviors, or programmable management through API. The presented framework also accompanies its own implementation of a custom BPEL engine, which can interpret the policy description directly and insert additional behaviors.

3   Case Studies

Five cases from different application domains have been investigated in order to illustrate and discuss different usages of the proposed framework, or different combinations of the expectations discussed in Section 2.1. Due to the page limitation, below illustrates only the essential aspects of each case study.

Stock Information: the composition process receives a list of company names as input. It returns their stock information (e.g., current prices) and latest news on the companies, by using a stock service and a news service. This case is discussed as the simplest situation where the best service is just chosen for each service type and replacement upon failure is taken.

Travel Planning: the composition process receives a request including the destination and period for a travel. It returns several sets of recommended flights and hotels with their price information, by using a flight search service and a hotel search service. This time, the composer intends to use a selection method that evaluates the number of hotels covered by each hotel search service within the target area, which means the selection depends on the destination given in the request (**Selection per Instance: Yes**).

Logistics: given a request for shipping, the composition process conducts the actual delivery by using a domestic delivery service for the source side, an international (air/sea) delivery service and a domestic delivery service for the destination side. The composite service and the involved delivery services have adhesive terms and conditions that specify the price and the maximum time required for the delivery, with some penalty statements. The composer thus intends to carefully select a set of services to be used to satisfy the constraint of the maximum delivery time (**Inter-Service Dependency: Yes**). In addition, the composer also considers adaptation during process execution to replace the succeeding service(s) to be used, when delay occurs in the precedent service(s) or some trouble is found in the succeeding service to be used [1] (**Replacement Type: Re-selection**).

Storage for Mobile Phone: the composition process receives a movie or music file as its input and put it on a storage service after some transformation by a conversion service so that the users can access the file later by using their mobile devices. In this case, re-selection of the storage service after a long term may happen with migration of the accumulated data (**Persistent States: Yes**).

Smart Space: the composition process receives a file as its input and plays it using a display service and an audio service that are located nearby the user. So the composer selects the services according to their locations and replaces them upon user movement as well as upon device failures. In this case, both of the two service types have expected control sequences, e.g., initially to switch on, then to start playing the content, and finally to stop it (**Session States: Yes**), and their selection is meaningful only if both of the service types are provided in the space where the user is (**Selection per Instance: Yes, Inter-Service Dependency: Yes**). Although omitted in Section 2.2, this case leads to the most complex implementation pattern. The two services need to be replaced at the same time, e.g., in response to user movement, while both require management of the session states. So it is necessary to define a process that includes the behavior to rollback by canceling and replacing both of the two services in response to the partner switch fault, which is defined and thrown by the framework when replacement is activated.

4   Discussion and Concluding Remarks

Although there have been a variety of proposals on selection and replacement methods, each proposal is often incremental to cover additional aspects that had not been discussed before. Such state-of-the-art methods often require finer-grained QoS data to meet finer-grained requirements (e.g., conditional statements in SLAs [3]). Those methods also differ in their purposes, e.g., optimization, constraint satisfaction or both of them. This fact implies selection and replacement of the selection and replacement methods themselves are also desirable, in terms of customization and adaptation as well as testing. On the other hand, such methods have stronger support by dealing with selection of multiple services as well as automated replacement transparent to the process. This fact means that those methods may involve possibilities to have side effects that invalidates effects of other methods or original behaviors of the composition process. The primary contribution of the paper is a comprehensive framework to deal with different expectations in selection and replacement methods.

The implementation approach of the proposed framework is essentially not so novel, which uses configuration to define how to incorporate additional behaviors for adaptation. Specifically, it is now common to use such an approach to handle faults by defining behavior patterns such as retry and replace (e.g.,

[4]). However, the patterns have not been explored for the various expectations, specifically Inter-Service Dependency introduced in the state-of-the-art selection methods. This paper has discussed even so complex a case where multiple services are replaced upon a failure of one service, leading to a partial rollback caused by different triggers. On the other hand, many frameworks have been proposed and used for separation of concerns, based on aspect-oriented programming (e.g., [6]). However, they have only discussed value-added functionality such as logging, which does not affect the essential service composition logic, e.g., by rewriting partner references. This paper has focused on and discussed insertion of additional behaviors that essentially affect partner references.

In summary, this paper proposed a framework to integrate selection and replacement methods. The framework supports to clarify and analyze expectations in service composition and partner management life-cycle as well as to construct a consistent implementation accordingly. The proposed framework facilitates to test, introduce and replace service selection and replacement methods according to the environment and its change, for a variety of application domains. This is the first step to integrate a variety of selection and replacement methods, and future work involves construction of actual libraries of existing methods.

References

1. He, Q., Yan, J., Jin, H., Yang, Y.: Adaptation of web service composition based on workflow patterns. In: Bouguettaya, A., Krueger, I., Margaria, T. (eds.) ICSOC 2008. LNCS, vol. 5364, pp. 22–37. Springer, Heidelberg (2008)
2. Kalayci, S., Ezenwoye, O., Viswanathan, B., Dasgupta, G., Sadjadi, S.M., Fong, L.: Design and implementation of a fault tolerant job flow manager using job flow patterns and recovery policies. In: Bouguettaya, A., Krueger, I., Margaria, T. (eds.) ICSOC 2008. LNCS, vol. 5364, pp. 54–69. Springer, Heidelberg (2008)
3. Klein, A., Ishikawa, F., Bauer, B.: A probabilistic approach to service selection with conditional contracts and usage patterns. In: Baresi, L., Chi, C.-H., Suzuki, J. (eds.) ICSOC-ServiceWave 2009. LNCS, vol. 5900, pp. 253–268. Springer, Heidelberg (2009)
4. Mosincat, A., Binder, W.: Transparent runtime adaptability for bpel processes. In: Bouguettaya, A., Krueger, I., Margaria, T. (eds.) ICSOC 2008. LNCS, vol. 5364, pp. 241–255. Springer, Heidelberg (2008)
5. Mukherjee, D., Jalote, P., Nanda, M.G.: Determining QoS of ws-bpel compositions. In: Bouguettaya, A., Krueger, I., Margaria, T. (eds.) ICSOC 2008. LNCS, vol. 5364, pp. 378–393. Springer, Heidelberg (2008)
6. Niemoller, J., Levenshteyn, R., Freiter, E., Vandikas, K., Quinet, R., Fikouras, I.: Aspect orientation for composite services in the telecommunication domain. In: Baresi, L., Chi, C.-H., Suzuki, J. (eds.) ICSOC-ServiceWave 2009. LNCS, vol. 5900, pp. 19–33. Springer, Heidelberg (2009)
7. OASIS: Web Services Business Process Execution Language Version 2.0. (April 2007), http://docs.oasis-open.org/wsbpel/2.0/OS/wsbpel-v2.0-OS.html
8. Papazoglou, M.P., Traverso, P., Dustdar, S., Leymann, F.: Service-oriented computing: State of the art and research challenges. Computer 40(11), 38–45 (2007)

Optimizing the Configuration of Web Service Monitors

Garth Heward[1], Jun Han[1], Ingo Müller[1],
Jean-Guy Schneider[1], and Steve Versteeg[2]

[1] Swinburne University of Technology, Hawthorn, Victoria, Australia
[2] CA Labs, Melbourne, Victoria, Australia
{gheward,jhan,imueller,jschneider}@swin.edu.au,
Steve.Versteeg@ca.com

Abstract. Service monitoring is required for meeting regulatory requirements and verifying compliance to Service Level Agreements (SLAs). As
such, monitoring is an essential part of web service-based systems. However, service monitoring comes with a cost, including an impact on the
quality of monitored services and systems. To deliver the best value to a
service provider, it is important to balance meeting monitoring requirements and reducing monitoring impacts. We introduce a novel approach
to configuring the web service monitors deployed in a system so that they
provide an adequate level of monitoring but with minimized quality impacts, delivering the best value proposition in terms of monitoring benefits
and costs. We use a prototype system to demonstrate that by optimizing
a web service monitoring system, we can reduce the impact of a set of deployed web service monitors by up to two thirds.

Keywords: Web Services, Monitoring, Monitoring Optimization.

1 Introduction

Web service providers give quality guarantees for their services, so that consumers know the expected Quality of Service (QoS) of services prior to using
them. To demonstrate that they have met these guarantees, providers monitor
their services. Whilst achieving this goal, service monitoring creates a problem
because the monitoring itself reduces the quality of the web services. This impact has been demonstrated to be as much as 40% (for response time) for a
single monitor[1]. As such, there is a conflict between the goal of performing
monitoring, and the goal of maintaining acceptable quality levels.

To meet these conflicting goals, a web service provider should carefully select
what monitoring is performed in the system in order to meet their monitoring
obligations without violating any quality guarantees or requirements. Achieving a balance between meeting monitoring requirements and achieving required
quality levels by manual configuration is difficult, time-consuming, and unveri-
fied for optimality. We propose an automated approach, which allows a service
provider to discover an optimal monitoring configuration with less human effort.

P.P. Maglio et al. (Eds.): ICSOC 2010, LNCS 6470, pp. 587–595, 2010.

Methods exist for optimizing the performance of web service systems through selective execution or load balancing, e.g. [2,3]. Whilst highlighting the need to optimize the performance of web service systems, none of these techniques relate to the management of deployed service monitors. Only Baresi and Guinea [4] discuss the configuration of web service monitors in order to achieve a trade-off between performance and monitoring. However, they only go as far as manually assigning a resolution of monitoring to each individual service in the system.

We introduce a novel approach that takes as inputs the monitoring requirements (benefits) and the monitoring impacts on system performance (costs), and determines an optimal monitoring configuration that delivers the best value by trading-off these benefits and costs. It considers the quality aspects and monitoring levels for each monitor and service. The optimal monitoring configuration consists of which monitors should be enabled, for what measures of quality, and at what sampling rates, in order to meet monitoring requirements whilst not reducing delivered qualities of service to unacceptable levels.

We demonstrate the benefits (the performance and utility increases) of applying our approach to the deployed monitors of a web service system. We have shown that in the best case, the web services under an optimal monitoring configuration had a response time impact just one third of the impact that a standard monitoring configuration had on the same services.

In Section 2, we introduce our approach to automated monitoring optimization. In Section 3, we discuss the experiments conducted to demonstrate the possible performance benefits of our approach.

2   Monitoring Optimization

As discussed above, to optimize the configuration of deployed web service monitors, their impact on system performance must be minimised, whilst meeting monitoring requirements. As such, the optimization problem is to find a monitoring configuration that gives the maximum value (utility) in terms of performance impact (costs) and monitoring coverage (benefits). Figure 1 shows a framework illustrating our approach to monitoring optimization, annotated with the ordering of activities of the optimization process. In step **1**, the set of deployed monitors is identified based on IT records, and then the Enumerator generates all the possible monitoring configurations for this set of monitors. In step **2**, the performance impacts of each monitor are identified from IT Records or benchmarking, and the Impact Analyser derives the total performance impact of each possible monitoring configuration. In step **3**, the monitoring requirements and associated penalties for not meeting them are identified from analysing SLAs, policies and laws, and the Requirements Analyser transforms requirements into a set of utility functions that define the benefit gained from monitoring a quality whilst a specific level of performance is being achieved. In step **4**, the Optimizer uses the set of utility functions from the Requirements Analyser to score all monitoring configurations with impacts from the Impact Analyser, and the monitoring configuration that yields the highest utility is selected and applied to the monitoring system. Each framework component is described below in more detail.

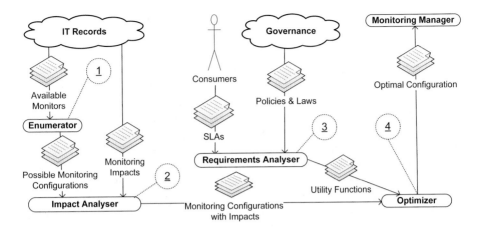

Fig. 1. Monitoring Optimization Framework

Enumerator. The Enumerator takes as input the set of available monitors, and outputs the set of all possible monitoring configurations.

A monitor can monitor one or more quality types of one or more services, simultaneously or separately. We refer to the set of all quality types of a system as Q, and the set of all services as S. A *monitoring capability, mcap* $= (m, s, q) \mapsto SR$ represents the ability of a monitor $m \in M$ to monitor a quality $q \in Q$ of a service $s \in S$ at a sampling rate $sr \in SR$. A *monitoring setting, ms* $= ((m, s, q) \mapsto sr, sr \in mcap(m, s, q)$ represents a monitoring capability set at a particular sampling rate sr. MS represents the set of all possible monitoring settings. A set of monitoring settings obtained by assigning every monitoring capability to a sampling rate is called a monitoring configuration, $mc \in MC$ and $mc = \{(m, s, q) \mapsto sr \in mcap(m, s, q) | \forall (m, s, q) \in MCAP\}$, where $MCAP$ is the set of all the deployed monitoring capabilities in the system.

For example, if we have monitor m_1 capable of monitoring quality q_1 of service s_1 at sampling rates of 0, 0.5, or 1.0, and monitor m_2, capable of monitoring quality q_1 and q_2 of service s_1 at sampling rates of 0 or 1.0, the three monitoring capabilities are $\{(m_1, s_1, q_1) \mapsto (0, 0.5, 1.0), (m_2, s_1, q_1) \mapsto (0, 1.0), (m_2, s_1, q_2) \mapsto (0, 1.0)\}$. One of the monitoring configurations is $mc = \{(m_1, s_1, q_1) \mapsto 0.5, (m_2, s_1, q_1) \mapsto 0, (m_2, s_1, q_2) \mapsto 1.0\}\}$. The Enumerator generates all possible monitoring configurations MC by stepping through all the allowable combinations of monitors, services, qualities and sampling rates. For the above example, the output from the Enumerator is presented in Table 1, where a row corresponds to a monitoring capability, a column corresponds to a monitoring configuration, and a cell is the specific sampling rate of the corresponding monitoring capability in the relevant monitoring configuration. The monitoring configuration mentioned above is column mc_8 in Table 1.

Table 1. Monitoring Enumeration

	mc_1	mc_2	mc_3	mc_4	mc_5	mc_6	mc_7	mc_8	mc_9	mc_{10}	mc_{11}	mc_{12}
$m_1s_1q_1$	0	0.5	1.0	0	0.5	1.0	0	0.5	1.0	0	0.5	1.0
$m_2s_1q_1$	0	0	0	1.0	1.0	1.0	0	0	0	1.0	1.0	1.0
$m_2s_1q_2$	0	0	0	0	0	0	1.0	1.0	1.0	1.0	1.0	1.0

Impact Analyser. The Impact Analyser takes as input all possible monitoring configurations MC, all monitor setting impacts MI and monitor overheads MO, and outputs the set of monitoring configurations with impacts MCI.

il denotes the *impact level* on a quality q of a service s, $(s, q) \mapsto il$. Impact level $il \in IL$ is an impact as a percentage on the original quality. For example, the impact of $((s_1, q_1) \mapsto 0.5)$ means the level of q_1 of s_1 is halved.

Monitoring has both overhead and monitor setting impacts. The overhead mo of a monitor m on a service s occurs whenever the monitor is in use, regardless of the activities of the monitor. Let SQ be all the service-quality pairs of concern in the system, the overheads a monitor has on every relevant quality q of every service s are $mo = \{(s, q) \mapsto il : IL | \forall (s, q) \in SQ\}$. For example, an interceptor m_1 that redirects messages of services s_1 and s_2 for analysis may reduce response time of all messages passing through it by 10%, whether or not those messages are actually analysed. Let $MIS = SQ \rightarrow IL$, the set of all monitor overheads is the collection of all the monitors' overheads, $MO = \{m \mapsto \mathcal{P}(MIS) | \forall m \in M\}$.

The monitoring setting impacts msi represent the impacts that a monitoring setting ms has on each quality q of each service s in the system. That is, $msi = \{(s, q) \mapsto il : IL | \forall (s, q) \in SQ\}$. For example, IT records may show that when monitor m_1 is configured to measure q_1 of s_1 at sampling rate 0.5, it reduces q_1 of services s_1 and s_2 by 10%. The impacts of this monitor setting are $\{(s_1, q_1) \mapsto 0.1, (s_2, q_1) \mapsto 0.1\}$. The set of impacts of all possible monitor settings in MS is: $MI = \{ms \mapsto msi : \mathcal{P}(MIS) | \forall ms \in MS\}$.

The impact of a monitoring configuration mc on quality q of service s is made up the following components: (1) the sum of the impacts of all monitoring settings on q of s: $I_{s,q}(mc) = \sum_{ms \in mc} MI(ms)(s, q)$; and (2) the sum of all the monitors' overheads on q of service s: $O_{s,q}(mc) = \sum_{m \in M} MO(m)(s, q) \times inUse(m)$, where $inUse(m) = \{^{1 \text{iff} \exists mc_i \in mc, mc_i.m=m, mc_i.sr>0}_{0 \text{iff} \nexists mc_i \in mc, mc_i.m=m, mc_i.sr>0}\}$. Therefore, mc's impacts on q of s are: $IM(mc)(s, q) = I_{s,q}(mc) + O_{s,q}(mc)$, and mc's impacts on all (s, q) pairs are: $IM(mc) = \{(s, q) \mapsto IM(mc)(s, q) | \forall (s, q) \in SQ\}$. Finally, the set of all monitoring configurations with impacts (on service-quality pairs) is: $MCI = \{mc \mapsto IM(mc) | \forall mc \in MC\}$.

Requirements Analyser. The Requirements Analyser takes requirements from SLAs and other sources such as corporate governance as input, and outputs a set of utility functions representing the values of achieving those requirements.

We assume that requirements can be translated into statements that describe a fine for not meeting or not monitoring a QoS. For example, an SLA may require a service s_1 to have response time of 15 seconds and sampling rate of 50% to demonstrate a QoS has been met, with a penalty of \$100 for exceeding this.

We say that the benefit is \$100 for monitoring service s_1 for response time whilst that response time is less than 15 seconds with a sampling rate of at least 0.5.

A requirement that the quality q of service s must be at least ql and monitored with a sampling rate at least sr can be represented as $r = (s, q, ql, sr)$, and the requirement r with a *fine* for non-compliance can be represented as $rp = ((s, q, ql, sr) \mapsto fine)$. The quality level ql is a fraction of the required quality level over the *ideal quality level* that is provided by the service. For example, if the best possible response time of a service is 10 seconds, and the required response time is 20 seconds, then the quality level ql is 0.5. The *fine* is the penalty that must be paid if the sampling rate sr and the quality level ql are not met. The set of all requirements with fines is $RP = \{(s, q, ql, sr) \mapsto fine : \mathbb{R}|\forall(s, q, ql, sr) \in R\}$, where R is the set of all requirements.

Consider the requirements that the quality q of service s should be monitored all the time and achieve a quality level of 0.75, with a fine of \$60 if the quality level goes below 0.75, and a fine of \$90 if the quality level goes below 0.5. This set of requirements with fines can be represented as $rps = \{(s_1, q_1, .50, 1) \mapsto \$90, (s_1, q_1, .75, 1) \mapsto \$60, (s_1, q_1, 1, 1) \mapsto \$0\}$.

We transform each monitoring requirement describing fines for non-compliance into *utility functions* describing benefit (utility) for compliance. Since our utilities are cumulative, for $rp = ((s, q, ql, sr) \mapsto fine)$, we have the corresponding utility $util(s, q, ql, sr) = (curmax - RP(s, q, ql, sr)) - \sum_{lr \in LR(s,q,sq,sr)}(curmax - util(lr))$, where $curmax$ is the benefit of achieving the quality level ql and sampling rate sr, and LR is the set of requirements with a quality level $lr.ql < ql$ or sampling rate $lr.sr < sr$, $LR(s, q, ql, sr) = \{(s, q, ql_1, sr_1)|\forall(s, q, ql_1, sr_1) \in R((ql_1 < q_1) \wedge (sr_1 \le sr)) \vee ((ql_1 \le q_1) \wedge (sr_1 < sr))\}$. Therefore, the utility function covering all the monitoring requirements is $U = \{(s, q, ql, sr) \mapsto util(s, q, ql, sr)|(s, q, ql, sr) \in R\}$.

For the above set of example requirements rps, we have the following corresponding utilities: $us = \{(s_1, q_1, .50, 1) \mapsto \$0, (s_1, q_1, .75, 1) \mapsto \$30, (s_1, q_1, 1, 1) \mapsto \$60\}$. The last element $((s_1, q_1, 1, 1) \mapsto \$60)$ of the utility set us is read as "achieving quality level greater than .75 of quality q_1 for service s_1 with a sampling rate of 1 is worth an additional \$60 (relative to the next lower quality level of 0.75), since fines of that amount will not have to be paid". The absolute utility for the $ql = 1$ level is \$90, including the utility at the lower quality level (\$30). Designers may also add utilities that are not directly derived from requirements.

Optimizer. The Optimizer takes as input the set of utilities U, the set of monitoring configurations with impacts MCI, and the *ideal service quality levels* for all qualities of all services $IQL = \{(s, q) \mapsto iql : QL|\forall s \in S, \forall q \in Q\}$, where iql is the pre-determined best achievable quality level for quality q of service s. The Optimizer outputs a monitoring configuration that gives the best utility in terms of meeting requirements and reducing monitoring impacts.

For a monitoring configuration mc with impacts, the Optimizer first obtains the Final Quality Levels FQL of all (s, q) pairs by subtracting all relevant impacts from their ideal quality levels IQL, i.e., $FQL(mc) = \{(s, q) \mapsto fql : QL|iql = IQL(s, q) - MCI(mc)(s, q)\}$.

The utility of the (s, q) pair under monitoring configuration mc, $u(mc)(s, q)$, is the sum of those utilities of (s, q), (1) whose required quality level ql has been met by the pair's final quality level $FQL(mc)(s, q)$ and (2) whose sampling rate sr is met by at least one monitor setting in mc.

Let $R_{(s,q)}$ be the set of all requirements concerning (s, q), i.e., $R_{(s,q)} = \{(s_1, q_1, ql, sr) | (s_1, q_1, ql, sr) \in R \land s_1 = s \land q_1 = q\}$. Then, $u(mc)(s, q) = \sum_{(s,q,ql,sr) \in R_{(s,q)}} (util(m, s, ql, sr) \times a \times b$, where

$$a = \{{}^{1 iff\ FQL(s,q) \geq ql}_{0 iff\ FQL(s,q) < ql}\}, b = \{{}^{1 iff\ \exists m \in M, ms(m,s,q) \geq sr}_{0 iff\ \nexists m \in M, ms(m,s,q) \geq sr}\}.$$

The total utility for the monitoring configuration mc will be the sum of the utilities for all (s, q) pairs under the configuration, $u(mc)$. Let $SQ_{mc} = \{(s, q) | \forall (m, s, q, l) \in mc\}$. Then, $u(mc) = \sum_{(s,q) \in SQ_{mc}} u(mc)(s, q)$. The set of all monitoring configurations with utility is, $MCU = \{mc \mapsto u(mc) | mc \in MC\}$. A monitoring configuration that gives the highest total utility will be an optimal monitoring configuration, $optimal_{mc} \in \{mc_1 | \forall mc_2 \in MC, MCU(mc_1) \geq MCU(mc_2)\}$, which may be applied to the monitors in the system either manually or automatically (if available via methods such as SNMP or WS-Management).

Optimization Complexity. The number of monitoring configurations is the product of the number of monitoring levels (ML_{mcap}) for all monitoring capabilities in the system ($mcap \in MCAP$). The size of this search space is bounded by $\mathcal{O}(avg(|ML_{mcap}|)^{|MCAP|})$. Since we step through the search space once for each of Impact Analysis and Optimization, this is also the time complexity for our optimization technique. The problem is a combinatorial optimization problem with both overhead (fixed) and instance (variable) costs, a case of an integer fixed charge network flow (FCNFP) problem, demonstrated to be NP-hard [5]. We have provided a brute force technique to demonstrate the possible performance and utility benefits of applying optimization. This also provides a baseline of a 'perfect' optimization against which to compare future heuristic algorithms.

3   Performance Evaluation

A prototype[1] of a travel agency with two web services, five monitors, four quality types, six SLA requirements, four Corporate Governance requirements, and 2.5×10^5 possible monitoring configurations has been implemented to verify our optimization technique and measure possible performance benefits of monitoring optimization. There always exists one or more optimal monitoring configurations (yielding the highest utility) in terms of monitoring coverage and performance. The purpose of these experiments is to discover these optimal monitoring configurations, and compare the utility and performance of each optimal configuration to the utility and performance of each corresponding maximum (un-optimized) monitoring configuration, in which all monitors run at a 100% sampling rate.

---

[1] Full details at http://www.ict.swin.edu.au/personal/gheward/

The performance measurements are based on a series of simulated service executions, which use response time measured through real service invocations to determine what the performance will be for a given monitoring configuration.

3.1   Results

We report average response times and utilities to demonstrate that system performance has increased whilst monitoring requirements have been met. Utility increased in each experiment, as only the minimum valuable monitoring level was met, allowing for a performance increase which minimised the chance of breaching requirements for response time. Figure 2 shows response time versus load level with unmonitored, maximum, and optimal monitoring configurations. The load levels on the horizontal axis represent the average number of active client requests, and the vertical axis is the average response time over both services.

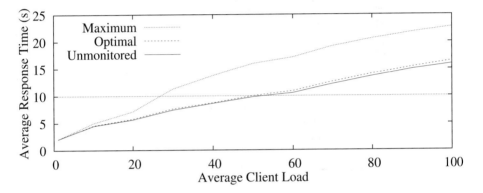

Fig. 2. Performance Evaluation

Optimization reduced the average response time by approximately 30% from maximum monitoring, and reduced the average response time impact by 80%.

The horizontal line on Figure 2 shows the 10-second boundary, for which penalties apply in the test system. The optimized monitoring configuration stays under this 10-second boundary for approximately twice as long as the maximum monitoring configuration, i.e. the system with optimized monitoring dealt with twice as much load before a penalty would have been paid.

The utility provided by the unmonitored solution was 0, since no requirements could be verified. The Maximum and Optimal monitoring configurations both included complete monitoring coverage. For each of these two configurations, the utility at or below 10 seconds response time was 4.245, and the utility above 10 seconds response time was 3.75. We repeated all experiments with randomly generated utility functions and monitoring impacts ranging from mild (less than .01% per monitoring instance on average) to severe (up to 20% per monitoring instance), under various load levels. The response times for the optimized solutions were on average 40% lower than maximum monitoring, and the optimized response time impacts were on average 70% lower than maximum monitoring. Utility values were on average 30% higher for the optimized solutions.

4   Related Work

Ranganathan and Dan present a Web Services management system to monitor and reallocate local system resources for services based on comparing their current QoS to their SLAs[6]. Whilst performing system-level administration, this method does not re-configure the web service monitoring system.

Baresi and Guinea present a method for dynamic monitoring of WS-BPEL processes, which uses high level monitoring rules [4]. These Monitoring Rules are used to control the monitoring of each WS-BPEL process. The rules are created with an equivalent of debug levels (one to five), which allows for optimization in terms of performance versus monitoring trade-offs at run-time. The monitoring level must be set for each service as a unit. Rather than assigning a monitoring resolution (debug level) to each individual service in the system, we assign a monitoring resolution to each quality of each service, directly reflecting requirements from SLAs. Furthermore, we enhance the optimization by selecting those monitors which will most efficiently monitor each service.

Overall, there have been numerous efforts for optimizing the QoS of web services and web service compositions, which consider the selection of services in order to optimize QoS. We have discovered no work that optimizes a web services monitoring system by trading off between monitoring costs and benefits, directly translated from SLAs and other requirements for monitoring.

5   Conclusions and Future Work

We have presented a framework and techniques for optimizing the configuration of web service monitors, in order to maximise utility for a web services provider.

A prototype instantiation of our proposed framework was used for a series of experiments, which demonstrated that both utility and performance can be improved by optimally configuring a web services monitoring system. Results indicate that the performance impact of web service monitoring can be significantly reduced, whilst meeting monitoring requirements.

We plan to extend the framework and implementation so that run-time properties of the system being monitored are fed back into the monitoring optimization framework, for re-optimization at run-time. We will also develop a heuristic approach to optimization in order to ensure scalability of the technique.

Acknowledgements. This work is supported by the Australian Research Council in collaboration with CA Labs.

References

1. Heward, G., Müller, I., Han, J., Schneider, J.G., Versteeg, S.: Assessing the performance impact of service monitoring. In: Australian Software Engineering Conference (ASWEC 2010), pp. 192–201 (2010)

2. Ludwig, H., Dan, A., Kearney, R.: Cremona: An architecture and library for creation and monitoring of ws-agreements. In: International Conference on Service Oriented Computing (ICSOC 2004), vol. 74, pp. 65–74 (2004)
3. Cardellini, V., Casalicchio, E., Grassi, V., Lo Presti, F.: Flow-based service selection for web service composition supporting multiple qos classes. In: International Conference on Web Services (ICWS 2007), pp. 743–750 (2007)
4. Baresi, L., Guinea, S.: Towards dynamic monitoring of ws-bpel processes. In: Benatallah, B., Casati, F., Traverso, P. (eds.) ICSOC 2005. LNCS, vol. 3826, pp. 269–282. Springer, Heidelberg (2005)
5. Stevens, T., Vermeir, J., Leenheer, M.D., Develder, C., Turck, F.D., Dhoedt, B., Demeester, P.: Distributed service provisioning using stateful anycast communications. In: Annual IEEE Conference on Local Computer Networks (LCN 2007), pp. 165–174 (2007)
6. Ranganathan, K., Dan, A.: Proactive management of service instance pools for meeting service level agreements. In: Benatallah, B., Casati, F., Traverso, P. (eds.) ICSOC 2005. LNCS, vol. 3826, pp. 296–309. Springer, Heidelberg (2005)

A Soft Constraint-Based Approach
to Qos-Aware Service Selection[*]

Mohamed Anis Zemni[1], Salima Benbernou[1], and Manuel Carro[2]

[1] LIPADE, Université Paris Descartes, France
[2] Facultad de Informática, Universidad Politécnica de Madrid, Spain
mohamedaniszemni@gmail.com, salima.benbenrou@paridescartes.fr,
mcarro@fi.upm.es

Abstract. Service-based systems should be able to dynamically seek replacements for faulty or underperforming services, thus performing self-healing. It may however be the case that available services do not match all requirements, leading the system to grind to a halt. In similar situations it would be better to choose alternative candidates which, while not fulfilling all the constraints, allow the system to proceed. *Soft constraints*, instead of the traditional *crisp* constraints, can help naturally model and solve replacement problems of this sort. In this work we apply soft constraints to model SLAs and to decide how to rebuild compositions which may not satisfy all the requirements, in order not to completely stop running systems.

Keywords: Service Level Agreement, Soft Constraints.

1 Introduction

A (web) service can be defined as a remotely accessible software implementation of a resource, identified by a URL. A set of protocols and standards, such as WSDL, facilitate invocation and information exchange in heterogeneous environments. Software services expose not only functional characteristics, but also non-functional attributes describing their Quality of Service (QoS) such as availability, reputation, etc. Due to the increasing agreement on the implementation and management of the functional aspects of services, interest is shifting towards non-functional attributes describing the QoS. Establishing QoS contracts, described in the Service Level Agreement (SLA), that can be monitored at runtime, is therefore of paramount importance. Various techniques [1] to select services fulfilling functional and non-functional requirements have been explored, some of them based on expressing these requirements as a constraint solving problem [2,3] (CSP). Traditional CSPs can either be fully solved (when all requirements are satisfied) or not solved at all (some requirements cannot be satisfied). In real-life cases, however, over-constraining is common (e.g., because available services offer a quality below that required by the composition), and problems are likely

[*] The research leading to these results has received funds from the European Community's Seventh Framework Programme FP7/2007-20013 under grant agreement 215483 (S-CUBE). Manuel Carro was also partially supported by Spanish MEC project 2008-05624/TIN *DOVES* and CM project P2009/TIC/1465 (*PROMETIDOS*).

P.P. Maglio et al. (Eds.): ICSOC 2010, LNCS 6470, pp. 596–602, 2010.

A C-semiring is a tuple $\langle A, +, \times, \mathbf{0}, \mathbf{1} \rangle$ s.t.

- A is a set and $\mathbf{0} \in A$, $\mathbf{1} \in A$.
- $\sum$ (the *additive* operation)[a] is defined on subsets of A as follows:
  - $+$ is commutative ($a + b = b + a$), associative ($a + (b + c) = (a + b) + c$), with unit element $\mathbf{0}$ ($a + \mathbf{0} = a$) and absorbing element $\mathbf{1}$ ($a + \mathbf{1} = \mathbf{1}$).
  - $\sum \emptyset = \mathbf{0}$ and for all $a \in A$, $\sum \{a\} = a$.
  - Given any set of indices S, $\sum_{i \in S}(\bigcup A_i) = \sum(\{\sum_{i \in S} A_i\})$ (flattening).
- $\times$ (the *multiplicative* operation) is associative, commutative, $a \times \mathbf{1} = a$ and $a \times \mathbf{0} = \mathbf{0}$.
- $\times$ distributes over $+$, i.e., $a \times (b + c) = (a \times b) + (a \times c)$.

---

[a] Written as infix $+$ when applied to a two-element set.

Fig. 1. Definition of a C-Semiring for Soft Constraints

not to have a classical, crisp solution. Solving techniques for *soft* CSPs (SCSP) [4,5,6] can generate solutions for overconstrained problems by allowing some constraints to remain unsatisfied.

Our framework takes into consideration the penalties agreed upon on the SLA by building a new (Soft) Service Level Agreement (SSLA) based on preferences where strict customer requirements are replaced by soft requirements allowing a suitable composition. This agreement has to include penalty terms to be applied while the contract terms are violated.

2   Soft Constraints in a Nutshell

A CSP defines a set of variables whose ranges we assume a finite domain (FD)[1] and a set of constraints which restrict the values these variables can take. A solution for a CSP is an assignment of a value to *every* variable s.t. all the constraints are simultaneously satisfied. Soft constraints [5,6] generalize classical CSPs by adding a preference level to every tuple in the domain of the constraint variables. This level can be used to obtain a suitable solution which may not fulfill all constraints, which optimizes some metrics, and which in our case will be naturally applied to the requirements of the users.

The basic operations on soft constraints (building a constraint conjunctions and projecting on variables) need to handle preferences in a homogeneous way. This requires the underlying mathematical structure of classical CSPs to change from a cylindrical algebra to a semiring algebra, enriched with additional properties and termed a *C-semiring* (Figure 1). In it, A provides the levels of preference of the solutions and it can be proved that it is a lattice with partial order $a \preceq b$ iff $a + b = b$, minimum $\mathbf{0}$, and maximum $\mathbf{1}$. When solutions are combined or compared, preferences are accordingly managed using the operations $\times$ and $+$. Note that the theory makes no assumptions as to what the preferences mean, or how they are actually handled: $\times$ and $+$ are placeholders for

---

[1] CSPs can be defined on infinite domains, but assume a FD here because it can accommodate many real-life problems, as witnessed by the relevance of FD in industrial applications, and because soft constraint theory requires finiteness.

Definition 1 (Constraint). *Given a c-semiring* $\langle A, +, \times, 0, 1 \rangle$, *a set of variables* V, *and a set of domains* D, *one for every variable in* V, *a constraint is the pair* $\langle def, con \rangle$ *where* $con \subseteq V$ *and* $def : D^{|con|} \rightarrow A$.

Definition 2 (Soft Constraint Satisfaction Problem SCSP). *A SCSP is a pair* $\langle C, con \rangle$ *where* $con \subseteq V$ *and* C *is a set of constraints.* C *may contain variables which are not in* con, *i.e., they are not interesting for the final result. In this case the constraints in* C *have to be projected onto the variables in* con.

Definition 3 (Constraint combination). *Two constraints* $c_1 \langle def_1, con_1 \rangle$ *and* $c_2 = \langle def_2, con_2 \rangle$ *can be combined in* $c_1 \otimes c_2 = \langle def, con \rangle$ *by taking all the variables in the original constraints* $(con = con_1 \bigcup con_2)$ *and assigning to every tuple in the new constraint a preference value which comes from combining the values in the original constraints:* $def(t) = def_1(t \downarrow_{con_1}^{con}) \times def_2(t \downarrow_{con_2}^{con})$, *with* $t \downarrow_Y^X$ *denoting the projection of tuple* t, *which is defined on the set of variables* X, *over the set of variables* $Y \subseteq X$.

Definition 4 (Projection). *Given a soft constraint* $c = \langle def, con \rangle$ *and a set of variables* $I \subseteq V$, *the projection of* c *over* I, *denoted by* $c \Downarrow_I$ *is the constraint* $\langle def', con' \rangle$ *where* $con' = con \bigcap I$ *and* $def'(t') = \sum_{\{t|t\downarrow_{con \bigcap I}^{con}=t'\}} def(t)$.

Definition 5 (Solution). *A solution of a SCSP problem* $\langle C, con \rangle$ *is the constraint* $(\otimes C) \Downarrow_{con}$, *i.e., the combination (conjunction) of all the constraints in* C *projected over all the variables* con *of interest.*

Fig. 2. Definitions for Soft Constraints

concrete definitions which can give rise to different constraint systems, such as fuzzy constraints, traditional constraints, etc.

Figure 2 summarizes some basic definitions regarding soft constraints. A constraint takes a tuple of variables and assigns it a tuple of concrete values in the domain of the variables, plus a preference value (belonging to the set A). Constraints can be combined into other constraints (with $\otimes$, similar to conjunction) and projected ($\Downarrow_Y^X$) onto a tuple of variables. The preference value of every tuple in a constraint conjunction is worked out by applying $\times$ to the preference values of the tuples in the individual constraints. Projections eliminate "columns" from tuples and retain only the non-removed tuple components. Repeated rows may then appear, but only one is retained, and its preference is calculated applying $+$ to the preferences of the repeated tuples. Since a solution is a projection on some selected set of variables, the preferences of solutions are naturally calculated using the projection operation. Usually the tuple with the highest preference value is selected as the "optimal" solution.

3   Soft Service Level Agreement and SCSPs

A Service Level Agreement (SLA) [7] is a contract between provider(s) and client(s) specifying the guarantees of a service, the expected quality level, and the penalties to be applied in case of unfulfillment of duties, and it is therefore an important quality management artifact. The SLA can be used to identify the responsible of a malfunction

---

Definition 6 (Preference). *The set* $Pr = \{\langle \delta_i, v_i, a_i \rangle | \delta_i \in \Delta, v_i \in \Upsilon, a_i \in A\}$ *where* δ_i *is the sub-domain that the* i*-th preference belongs to,* v_i *is the variable defining the preferences, and* a_i *is semiring value, representing the preferences in an SSLA.*

Definition 7 (Penalty). *The set* $Pn = \{pn_i \mid \exists pr_i \; s.t. \; v_i \notin \delta_i\}$ *represents the penalties.*

Definition 8 (SSLA document). *A SSLA document is a tuple* $\zeta = \langle \Upsilon, \Delta, A, Pr, Pn, T \rangle$ *where* Υ *is a set of variables* v_i, Δ *is a set of variable domains* δ_i *(one for each variable),* Pr *is a set of preferences* Pr_i, Pn *is a set of penalties* Pn_i *to apply when the preferences are not satisfied and* T *is a set of pairs* $\langle pr_i, pn_i \rangle$ *which associates preferences with the penalties to apply in case of violation.*

Fig. 3. Definitions related to a soft SLA

and to decide which action (if any) has to be taken. An SLA should, therefore, be realistic, achievable, and maintainable.

An SLA has a rich structure from which we underline the properties of the services, including those measurable aimed at expressing guarantees. This part provides a set Υ of variables v_i (whose meaning is explained in the service description) and their domains $\delta_i \in \Delta$, which can be established by the metric attribute. A Soft SLA (SSLA) is similar to a SLA but with the addition of a set of user preferences and of penalties associated to contract breaking (respectively, Pr and Pn). The preferences are used to make a composition in the presence of unsatisfied requirements and the penalties are used to refine found solutions and to protect each party from the violation of the contract terms. These notions are depicted in Figure 3. The i-th penalty $pn_i \in Pn$ is applied when the i-th preference $pr_i \in Pr$ is not satisfied.

3.1 Extending SCSP Using Penalties

We will adapt the SCSP framework to handle explicitly penalties for service selection and to build a Soft Service Level Agreement including preferences and penalties. In this framework, service selection has three phases:

1. Model the characteristics for the selection using soft constraints.
2. Assuming a pre-selection is made using functional requirements, rank candidate services using non-functional requirements and the constraint preferences.
3. We assign penalties to unmet user preferences, and these penalties are used to rank solutions having the same constraint preferences.

Figure 4 shows the definitions for this extended SCSP framework. We extend the application of semiring operations to penalties. Variables are assumed to take values over subdomains which discretize a continuous domain, and which for brevity we represent using identifiers in $D_{\{\}}$. The constraint preference function *def* is also adapted in order to apply it both to preferences and to penalties. The projection operation is kept as in the SCSP framework.

Definition 9 (CP-semiring). *A CP-semiring is a tuple $S = \langle A, Pn, +, \times, 0, 1 \rangle$, extending a C-semiring. A and Pn are two sets with lattice structure stating preference values for solutions and penalties. Operations $\times$ and $+$ are applied when constraints are combined or projected.*

Definition 10 (Constraint System). *A constraint system is a tuple $CS = \langle S, D_{\{\}}, V \rangle$, where S is c-semiring, $D_{\{\}}$ represents the set of identifiers of subdomains, and V is the ordered set of variables.*

Definition 11 (Constraint). *Given a constraint system $CS = \langle S_p, D_{\{\}}, V \rangle$ and a problem $P = \langle C, con \rangle$, a constraint is the tuple $c = \langle def_c, type \rangle$, where type represents the type of constraint and def_c is the definition function of the constraint, which returns the tuple*

$$def : D_{\{\}}^{|con|} \to \langle p_r, p_n \rangle,$$

Definition 12 (Soft Constraint Satisfaction Problem SCSP). *Given a constraint system $CS = \langle S, D_{\{\}}, V \rangle$, an SCSP over CS is a pair $P = \langle C, con \rangle$, where con, called set of variables of interest for C, is a subset of V and C is a finite set of constraints, which may contain some constraints defined on variables not in con.*

Fig. 4. CP-Semiring

3.2 An Example

A delivery service has an order-tracking web service. Companies wishing to hire this service want to have in the contract non-functional criteria such as availability, reputation, response time and cost.

Phase 1. Let $CS = \langle S_p, D_{\{\}}, V \rangle$ be a constraint system and $P = \langle C, con \rangle$ be the problem to be solved, where $V = con = \{\underline{A}vailability, \underline{R}eputation, response \underline{T}ime, co\underline{S}t\}$, $D_{\{\}} = \{\{a_1, a_2\}, \{r_1, r_2\}, \{t_1, t_2, t_3\}, \{s_1, s_2\}\}$, $S_p = \langle [0, 1], Pn, \max, \min, 0, 1 \rangle$, $C = \{c_1, c_2, c_3, c_4\}$. For simplicity, variables and their domains have been written in the same order.

A set of penalties, ranked from the most to then less important one, has been set: $pn_i \preceq pn_j$ if $i \leq j$. The above shown values of the variable domains comes from a discretization such as $availability \in \{[0, 0.5[, [0.5, 1]\}, reputation \in \{[0, 0.6[, [0.6, 1]\}$, $response\ time \in \{[20, \infty[, [5, 20[, [0, 5[\}, cost \in \{[1000, 1500[, [1500, 3000]\}$.

Table 1. Constraint definitions

$\langle A, R \rangle$	def_{c1}	$\langle T \rangle$	def_{c2}	$\langle A, R, S \rangle$	def_{c3}	$\langle R, T \rangle$	def_{c4}
$\langle a_1, r_1 \rangle$	$\langle 0, - \rangle$	$\langle t_1 \rangle$	$\langle 0.25, pn_6 \rangle$	$\langle a_1, r_1, s_1 \rangle$	$\langle 0.25, pn_8 \rangle$	$\langle r_1, t_1 \rangle$	$\langle 0.5, pn_6 \rangle$
$\langle a_1, r_2 \rangle$	$\langle 0.25, pn_1 \rangle$	$\langle t_2 \rangle$	$\langle 0.5, pn_5 \rangle$	$\langle a_1, r_1, s_2 \rangle$	$\langle 0.25, pn_1 \rangle$	$\langle r_1, t_2 \rangle$	$\langle 0.5, pn_5 \rangle$
$\langle a_2, r_1 \rangle$	$\langle 0.5, pn_3 \rangle$	$\langle t_3 \rangle$	$\langle 1, pn_7 \rangle$	$\langle a_1, r_2, s_1 \rangle$	$\langle 0.5, pn_1 \rangle$	$\langle r_1, t_3 \rangle$	$\langle 0, - \rangle$
$\langle a_2, r_2 \rangle$	$\langle 0.75, pn_3 \rangle$			$\langle a_1, r_2, s_2 \rangle$	$\langle 0.25, pn_3 \rangle$	$\langle r_2, t_1 \rangle$	$\langle 0.75, pn_2 \rangle$
				$\langle a_2, r_1, s_1 \rangle$	$\langle 0.75, pn_9 \rangle$	$\langle r_2, t_2 \rangle$	$\langle 0.75, pn_4 \rangle$
				$\langle a_2, r_1, s_2 \rangle$	$\langle 0.5, pn_8 \rangle$	$\langle r_2, t_3 \rangle$	$\langle 1, pn_2 \rangle$
				$\langle a_2, r_2, s_1 \rangle$	$\langle 0.75, pn_2 \rangle$		
				$\langle a_2, r_2, s_2 \rangle$	$\langle 0.25, pn_1 \rangle$		

Table 2. Ordered constraint combinations with preferences and penalties

$\langle A,R,T,S\rangle$	$\langle pr,pn\rangle$	$\langle A,R,T,S\rangle$	$\langle pr,pn\rangle$	$\langle A,R,T,S\rangle$	$\langle pr,pn\rangle$	$\langle A,R,T,S\rangle$	$\langle pr,pn\rangle$
$\langle 2,2,3,1\rangle$	$\langle 0.75, pn_2\rangle$	$\langle 2,2,1,2\rangle$	$\langle 0.25, pn_1\rangle$	$\langle 1,2,1,1\rangle$	$\langle 0.25, pn_1\rangle$	$\langle 1,1,3,2\rangle$	$\langle 0.0, -\rangle$
$\langle 2,2,2,1\rangle$	$\langle 0.50, pn_2\rangle$	$\langle 1,2,3,2\rangle$	$\langle 0.25, pn_1\rangle$	$\langle 2,2,1,1\rangle$	$\langle 0.25, pn_2\rangle$	$\langle 1,1,3,1\rangle$	$\langle 0.0, -\rangle$
$\langle 2,1,2,2\rangle$	$\langle 0.50, pn_3\rangle$	$\langle 1,2,3,1\rangle$	$\langle 0.25, pn_1\rangle$	$\langle 2,1,1,2\rangle$	$\langle 0.25, pn_3\rangle$	$\langle 1,1,2,2\rangle$	$\langle 0.0, -\rangle$
$\langle 2,1,2,1\rangle$	$\langle 0.50, pn_3\rangle$	$\langle 1,2,2,2\rangle$	$\langle 0.25, pn_1\rangle$	$\langle 2,1,1,1\rangle$	$\langle 0.25, pn_3\rangle$	$\langle 1,1,2,1\rangle$	$\langle 0.0, -\rangle$
$\langle 2,2,2,2\rangle$	$\langle 0.25, pn_1\rangle$	$\langle 1,2,2,1\rangle$	$\langle 0.25, pn_1\rangle$	$\langle 2,1,3,2\rangle$	$\langle 0.0, -\rangle$	$\langle 1,1,1,2\rangle$	$\langle 0.0, -\rangle$
$\langle 2,2,3,2\rangle$	$\langle 0.25, pn_1\rangle$	$\langle 1,2,1,2\rangle$	$\langle 0.25, pn_1\rangle$	$\langle 2,1,3,1\rangle$	$\langle 0.0, -\rangle$	$\langle 1,1,1,1\rangle$	$\langle 0.0, -\rangle$

Let us consider the following constraints: $c_1 = \langle def_{c1}, \{\text{availability, reputation}\}\rangle$, $c_2 = \langle def_{c2}, \{\text{response time}\}\rangle$, $c_3 = \langle def_{c3}, \{\text{availability, reputation, cost}\}\rangle$, $c_4 = \langle def_{c4}, \{\text{reputation, response time}\}\rangle$, where the preference values and corresponding penalties are in Table 1. For example, for the tuple $\langle a_2, r_1\rangle$, attributes "availability" and "reputation" are respectively assigned subdomains $[0.5, 1]$ and $[0, 0.6[$. The function $def_{c1}(\langle a_2, r_1\rangle) = \langle 0.5, pn_3\rangle$ shows that these attribute values have a preference 0.5 and company is ready to sign away this preference for a penalty pn_3.

Phase 2. Given the model, we define constraint combination to keep the minimum value of preferences (resp. for the penalties). For example $def_{c1}(\langle a_2, r_1\rangle) \otimes def_{c2}$ $(\langle t_3\rangle) = \min(\langle 0.5, pn_3\rangle, \langle 0.25, pn_6\rangle) = \langle 0.25, pn_3\rangle$ and so on with all the tuples to obtain $c_{1,2}$. Next, we would combine $c_{1,2}$ and c_3 to get $c_{1,2,3} = c_{1,2} \otimes c_3$ and so on, until all constraints have been combined. Table 2 shows the results of combining all the constraints.

Phase 3. The set of solutions is ranked by preferences and then by penalties (already in Table 2). The solution with highest rank is chosen first. If it turns out not to be feasible, the associated penalty is applied and the next solution is chosen, and so on.

3.3 Mapping SSLA onto SCSP Solvers

Given the our design of an SSLA, mapping it into a SCSP is very easy: variables v_i in the SSLA are mapped onto the corresponding v_i in the SCSP; SSLA domains δ_i are discretized and every discrete identifier is a domain for a SCSP variable; and preferences and penalties (both lattices) are handled together by the def function, so they can be mapped to the A set in a C-semiring with an adequate definition of the def function.

4 Conclusion

We have presented a soft constraint-based framework to seamlessly express QoS properties reflecting both customer preferences and penalties applied to unfitting situations. The application of soft constraints makes it possible to work around overconstrained problems and offer a feasible solution. Our approach makes easier this activity thanks to ranked choices. Introducing the concept of penalty in the Classical SCSP can also be useful during the finding and matching process. We plan to extend this framework to also deal with behavioral penalties.

References

1. Müller, C., Ruiz-Cortés, A., Resinas, M.: An Initial Approach to Explaining SLA Inconsistencies. In: Bouguettaya, A., Krueger, I., Margaria, T. (eds.) ICSOC 2008. LNCS, vol. 5364, pp. 394–406. Springer, Heidelberg (2008)
2. Montanari, U.: Networks of Constraints: Fundamental Properties and Application to Picture Processing. Information Sciences 7, 95–132 (1974)
3. Dechter, R.: Constraint Processing. Morgan Kaufmann, San Francisco (2003)
4. Bistarelli, S.: Semirings for Soft Constraint Solving and Programming. Springer, Heidelberg (2004)
5. Bistarelli, S., Montanari, U., Rossi, F.: Semiring-based constraint satisfaction and optimization. J. ACM 44(2), 201–236 (1997)
6. Bistarelli, S., Montanari, U., Rossi, F.: Constraint Solving over Semirings. In: Proc. IJCAI 1995 (1995)
7. Bianco, P., Lewis, G.A., Merson, P.: Service Level Agreements in Service-Oriented Architecture Environment. Technical Report CMU/SEI-2008-TN-021, Carnegie Mellon (September 2008)

Timed Conversational Protocol Based Approach for Web Services Analysis

Nawal Guermouche and Claude Godart

LORIA-INRIA-UMR 7503
F-54506 Vandoeuvre-les-Nancy, France
{Nawal.Guermouche,Claude.Godart}@loria.fr

Abstract. Choreography is one of the most important features of Web services. It allows to capture collaborative processes involving multiple services. In this paper, we are interested in analyzing the interoperability of Web services that support asynchronous communications which are constrained by data and timed constraints, using a model checking based approach. In particular, we deal with the compatibility problem. To do so, we have developed a set of abstractions and transformations on which we propose a set of primitives characterizing a set of compatibility classes of Web services. This paper is about the specification and implementation of this approach using the UPPAAL model checker.

Keywords: Asynchronous Web service, Timed properties, Compatibility analysis.

1 Introduction

Web services are the main pillar of the Service Oriented Computing (SOC) paradigm. Based on standard interfaces, they facilitate application-to-application interactions thanks to the notion of *choreography* of message exchanges between services. Such a feature offers the possibility to capture collaborative processes involving multiple services where the interactions between these services are seen from a global perspective. In this context, one of the important elements is the *compatibility analysis*. By compatibility we mean the capability of a set of services of actually fulfilling successful interactions by exchanging messages.

It is commonly agreed that in general the interaction of Web services and in particular the compatibility of Web services depends not only on the supported sequences of messages but also on crucial quantitative properties such as timed properties [8,10]. We mean by timed properties the required delays to exchange messages (e.g., in an e-government application, a prefecture must send its final decision to grant an handicapped pension to a requester after 7 days and within 14 days).

Some works have dealt with the problem of compatibility of two services. In [4,3,2], authors consider the sequence of messages that can be exchanged between two synchronous Web services to analyze compatibility of two services.

P.P. Maglio et al. (Eds.): ICSOC 2010, LNCS 6470, pp. 603–611, 2010.
© Springer-Verlag Berlin Heidelberg 2010

Considering only the message exchange sequences is not sufficient. To succeed a conversation, other metrics can have an impact such as timed properties which are not considered in [4]. Another important remark is that in [4], authors consider synchronous Web services. Such assumption is very restrictive since two services can succeed a conversation despite that they do not support the same branching structure.

The compatibility framework presented in [10] considers a more expressive timed constraints model. Although powerful, in some cases, the compatibility framework cannot detect some timed conflicts due to non-cancellation constraints. In fact, the authors deal only with synchronous communicating services and discover timed conflicts based on synchronizing the corresponding timed properties over messages. However, in case of asynchronous Web services, this framework cannot be applied to discover timed conflicts.

In [5], the authors handle the timed conformance problem. The timed conformance problem consists in checking if a given timed orchestration satisfies a global timed choreography. In this framework, the authors deal with timed cost (i.e., the delay) of operations. Our aim is to detect deadlocks that can arise when a set of Web services are interacting altogether. While authors of [5] are not interested in analyzing the compatibility of a choreography but only in checking if a given orchestration conforms to a choreography. So, one of the assumption on which the work presented in [5] relies, is that the choreography does not hold timed conflicts.

Regarding our previous work, [6] presents a framework for analyzing the compatibility of Web services. [6], presents an algorithm to analyze the compatibility of Web services based on the clock ordering process. This work is limited to discover only some kind of timed conflicts that do not consider other eventual timed conflicts that can arise when Web services interact together.

In this paper, we propose an analyzing choreography compatibility framework which is based on our previous work [6,7]. This approach is based on the model checker UPPAAL[1]. In this framework we take into account data flow involved when exchanging messages. Furthermore, we consider constraints over data and timed properties that specify delays concerning message exchanges. By studying the possible impacts of timed properties on a choreography, we remarked that when Web services are interacting together, implicit timed dependencies can be derived from the different timed properties of the different services [6,7]. Such dependencies can give rise to implicit timed conflicts. In order to catch the possible timed deadlocks, we propose a set of model checking based primitives.

More precisely, in order to be able to analyze the compatibility of a set of timed and asynchronous Web services, we propose a set of primitives which consists in: (1) extending the model of conversational protocols proposed in [7,6] to consider together messages, data flow, data constraints, and timed constraints, (2) extending the transformation process we proposed in [7] to allow applying model checking to asynchronous Web services composition analysis, particularly, considering timed properties and data constraints when analyzing asynchronous services, (3) finally, we propose new fine grained asynchronous compatibility classes.

---

[1] http://www.uppaal.com/

The remainder of the paper is organized as follows. The next section presents how we model the timed behaviour of Web services. In order to be able to handle asynchronous services with the UPPAAL model checker, we present a set of abstractions and transformations. Before concluding, we present our formal choreography compatibility investigations.

2   Modeling Timed Behaviour of Web Services

The model we consider is based on timed automata. Intuitively, the states represent the different phases a service may go through during its interaction. Transitions enable sending or receiving a message. An output message is denoted by $!m$, whilst an input one is denoted by $?m$. A message involving a list of data types is denoted by $m(d1, \ldots, dn)$, or $m(\overline{d})$ for short. These automata are equipped with a set of clocks [1]. Transitions are labelled by timed constraints, called guards, and resets of clocks. The former represent simple conditions over clocks, and the latter are used to reset values of certain clocks to zero. The guards specify that a transition can be fired if the corresponding guards are satisfied.

A timed constraint is a conjunction of atomic formula that compares the value of a clock $x \in X$, to a positive real constant $a \in \mathbb{R}_{\geq 0}$.

The set of Web services are equipped with a bounded queue to store the incoming messages.

Figure 2 shows the timed conversational protocols of an e-government application we consider. The goal is to manage handicapped pension requests. Such a request involves three Web services: (1) a prefecture service (PS) (2) a health authority service (HAS), and (3) a town hall service (TH). A citizen can apply for a pension. The prefecture solicits the medical entity to examine the requester. On the other side, the prefecture asks the town hall to deliver the domiciliation attestation. After studying the received file, the prefecture sends the notification of the final decision to the citizen after 48 hours and within 96 hours from receiving the pension request. To specify such constraint, we associate a reset of the clock t_1 ($t_1 = 0$) to the transition that enables to receive the request of the pension and we associate the constraint $48 \leq t_1 \leq 96$ to the transition that enables to send the final decision.

As the approach we propose is based on the model checker UPPAAL, next, we present the required process we propose to adapt this general model to the UPPAAL one to be able to perform the compatibility cheking.

3   From Conversational Protocols to UPPAAL Timed Automata

UPPAAL is a model checker for the verification and simulation of real time systems. An UPPAAL model is a set of timed automata, clocks, channels for systems (automata) synchronization, variables and additional elements [9,7].

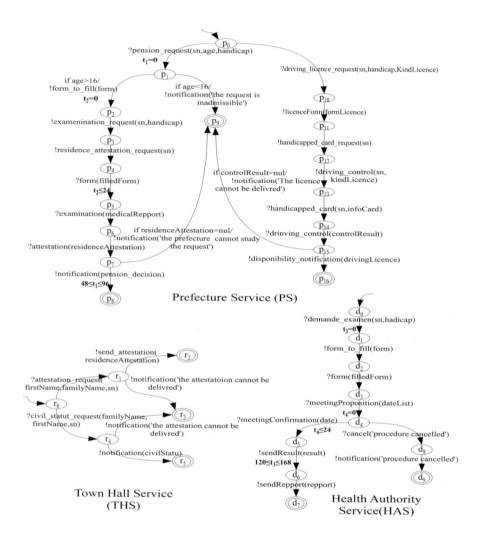

Fig. 1. Web services of the e-government scenario

In order to perform a model checking using UPPAAL, we use a set of transformation steps, which are: (1) Messages abstraction, (2) data constraints abstraction, (3) final states specification. The steps of messages abstraction and final states specification are presented in [7].

3.1 Abstraction of Data Constraints

As said previously, our model considers constraints over data. To analyze these constraints with UPPAAL, the values of the data must be known. However, as the compatibility analysis we propose is done at design time, the values of the data cannot be known in advance. Consequently, the constraints over data cannot be correctly considered. To consider constraints over data, we propose to abstract the variables of messages resulting from the process of message abstraction described in [7] with information about data constraints. The idea is to compute the set of transitions that hold the same variable. If the set of solutions of the data constraints associated to these transitions is disjoined, then we abstract differently the variables. Whilst, if the set of solution is not disjoined, then we remove only the data constraints without changing the variables. To explain this issue, let us present the following example.

Example 1. Via this example, we are going to show how we apply the data constraints abstraction process. As we can see, the two services, illustrated in Figure 2, have the following two common transitions (i.e., transitions that hold the same variable):

- $(s_0, m_0 + +, d_0 < 100, s_1)$ and $(p_1, m_0 + +, d_0 > 120, p_2)$
- $(s_2, m_{21} - -, m_{21} > 0, d_1 < 50, s_3)$ and $(p_0, m_{21} + +, d_1 < 80, p_1)$

Let us start with the first pair of transitions $(s_0, m_0 + +, d_0 < 100, s_1)$ and $(p_1, m_0 + +, d_0 > 120, p_2)$. We can remark that the set of solutions of the constraints $d_0 < 100$ and $d_0 > 120$ is disjoint, i.e., $Sol(d_0 < 100) \cap Sol(d_0 > 120) = \emptyset$. Hence, by applying the data constraints abstraction process, we substitute $m_0 + +$ of the transition $(p_1, m_0 + +, d_0 > 120, p_2)$ by another variable m_0'. So the transition becomes $(p_1, m_0' + +, p_2)$

Now, we check the second pair of transitions $(s_2, m_{21} - -, m_{21} > 0, d_1 < 50, s_3)$ and $(p_0, m_{21} + +, d_1 < 80, p_1)$. We can see that the set of solutions of data constraints $d_1 < 50$ and $d_1 < 80$ is not disjoint. The two constraints have a common set of solutions, i.e., $Sol(d1 < 50) \cap Sol(d1 < 80) \neq \emptyset$. Consequently, when abstracting data constraints, we do not substitute the variable m_{21}.

The result of the transformation steps we described above is a set of abstract UPPAAL timed automata. These automata preserve the semantic we consider in timed conversational protocol of asynchronous services.

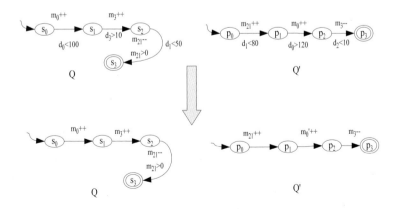

Fig. 2. Abstraction of data constraints

Next, we present the formal primitives we propose to characterize the compatibility class of a set of timed asynchronous Web services.

4   Formal Asynchronous Compatibility Checking

Based on the previous transformations, we present in this section a compatibility checking using UPPAAL. We define the following fine grained timed asynchronous compatibility classes: (1) *full and perfect compatibility*, (2) *full but non-perfect compatibility*, (3) *perfect partial compatibility*, (4) *partial but non-perfect compatibility*, and (5) *full incompatibility*.

4.1   Perfect Full Compatibility

In general, a set of Web services constitute a full compatible choreography if they can interact without an eventual blocking. As we deal with asynchronous services, the output messages are sent without synchronization with the corresponding input. Thus, it is not sufficient to check only if there is no deadlock when services interact together, but, it is important too to check if all the sent messages are consumed. So, a set of services constitute a full and perfect compatible choreography if: (1) they collaborate together without any eventual blocking and (2) at the same time, all the generated messages are consumed.

Formally, checking if a set of Web services interact without an eventual blocking is equivalent to checking if the services reach their final states in all interactions. At the same time, when the services reach their final states, the fact that all the sent messages must be consumed is formally equivalent to checking that, when the services reach their final states, all the variable values are equal to zero.

Let $P_1, \ldots, P_n$ be n (asynchronous) services and $R_1, \ldots, R_n$ be the corresponding set of variables. The set of fully and perfect compatible Web services is specified by the following CTL formulas:

$$AF\ P_1.final\ \wedge\ \ldots\ \wedge\ P_n.final \wedge AG\ (P_1.final\ \wedge\ \ldots\ \wedge\ P_n.final \Rightarrow AF$$
$$r_1 == 0\ and\ \ldots \wedge r_m == 0)\ where\ r_i \in \{R_1, \ldots R_i, \ldots, R_n\} \tag{1}$$

4.2   Non-perfect Full Compatibility

When a set of Web services can collaborate together without an eventual blocking but at the same time, during their interaction, there are messages that cannot be consumed, i.e., extra messages, we say that the services are fully but non-perfectly compatible.

Formally, a set of Web services are said to be fully and non-perfectly compatible if via all the paths, the services reach their final state and at the same time, and in this state, there exists at least one variable whose value is bigger than zero. This latter can be specified by the following CTL formulas:

$$AF(P_1.final \wedge \ldots \wedge P_n.final) \wedge EF(P_1.final \wedge \ldots \wedge P_n.final \Rightarrow r_1 > 0 \vee \ldots \vee r_n > 0)$$
$$\text{where } r_i \in \{R_1, \ldots R_i, \ldots, R_n\}$$
$$(2)$$

4.3 Partial But Non-perfect Compatibility

As services are heterogeneous they can fulfil incorrect conversations. A conversation during which a service remains blocked is called incorrect. A set of Web services are not fully compatible when the set of possible conversations of the services hold at least one incorrect conversation.

Formally, a set of Web services are not fully compatible if there exists at least a path of their automata that cannot reach the final state. This later can be specified as the following formula:

$$EG \neg P_1.final \vee \ldots \vee EG \neg P_n.final$$
$$(3)$$

When a set of Web services can achieve correctly a set of conversations and at the same time they fail other conversations, we say that the services are partially compatible. In this section, we define particularly the partial but non-perfect compatibility class. This class is assigned to a set of Web services that are partially compatible and at the same time, there is at least one correct conversation during which there is at least one extra message. This is formally specified by the following CTL formulas:

$$EF \ P_1.final \wedge \ldots \wedge P_n.final \wedge$$
$$(EF \ P_1.final \wedge \ldots \wedge P_n.final \Rightarrow r_1 > 0 \wedge \ldots \wedge r_m > 0) \text{ where } r_i \in$$
$$\{R_1, \ldots R_i, \ldots, R_n\}$$
$$(4)$$

Formally, a set of Web services is said to be partially but non-perfectly compatible if the formulas (3) and (4) are satisfied.

4.4 Partial and Perfect Compatibility

The partial and perfect compatibility class characterizes the fact that services are not fully compatible but at the same time, they can fulfil correctly conversations during which all the produced messages are consumed.

Formally, a set of Web services can achieve correctly at least one conversation so that all produced messages are consumed is equivalent to checking that there exists at least one path so that all the services reach their final state and at the same time, when the final state is reached, the value of all variables is equal to zero. This is specified by the following CTL formula:

$$EF \ P_1.final \wedge \ldots \wedge P_n.final \wedge$$
$$(EF \ P_1.final \wedge \ldots \wedge P_n.final \Rightarrow r_1 == 0 \wedge \ldots \wedge r_m == 0) \text{ where } r_i \in$$
$$\{R_1, \ldots R_i, \ldots, R_n\}$$
$$(5)$$

A set of Web services whose conversational protocols do not verify the formula 4 and at the same time, verify the formulas 3 and 5 is said to be partially and perfectly compatible.

4.5 Full Incompatibility

Full incompatibility characterizes the fact that the set of services cannot, absolutely, collaborate together. Formally, a set of services are fully incompatible, if for all the paths, all the services cannot reach the state 'final'. This property is specified as the following CTL formulas:

$$AG \neg P_1.final \wedge \ldots \wedge AG \neg P_n.final$$

$$(6)$$

5   Conclusion

In this paper, we presented a formal framework for analyzing the timed compatibility of a choreography. Unlike the existing approaches, this framework caters for timed properties and data constraints of asynchronous Web services. In order to handle timed and data constraints deadlocks, we proposed an approach based on the model checker UPPAAL. The model checker UPPAAL does not take into account constraints over data semantics. In order to handle asynchronous services augmented with data flow and data constraints, we proposed to extend our previous work [7] by the data constraints abstraction process. By using the result of the abstractions, we presented a set of CTL formulas that characterize the different choreography compatibility classes we have defined.

In our ongoing work, we are interested in analyzing the compatibility of a choreography in which the instances of the involved services is not known in advance. Our aim is to provide primitives for defining dynamically the required instances for a successful choreography. Moreover, we plan to extend the proposed approach to support more complex timed properties when analyzing the compatibility of a set of Web services.

References

1. Alur, R., Dill, D.L.: A theory of timed automata. Theoretical Computer Science 126(2), 183–235 (1994)
2. Benatallah, B., Casati, F., Toumani, F.: Analysis and management of web service protocols. In: Atzeni, P., Chu, W., Lu, H., Zhou, S., Ling, T.-W. (eds.) ER 2004. LNCS, vol. 3288, pp. 524–541. Springer, Heidelberg (2004)
3. Benatallah, B., Casati, F., Toumani, F.: Web service conversation modeling: A cornerstone for e-business automation. IEEE Internet Computing 8(1), 46–54 (2004)
4. Bordeaux, L., Salaün, G., Berardi, D., Mecella, M.: When are two web services compatible? In: Shan, M.-C., Dayal, U., Hsu, M. (eds.) TES 2004. LNCS, vol. 3324, pp. 15–28. Springer, Heidelberg (2005)

5. Eder, J., Tahamtan, A.: Temporal conformance of federated choreographies. In: Bhowmick, S.S., Küng, J., Wagner, R. (eds.) DEXA 2008. LNCS, vol. 5181, Springer, Heidelberg (2008)
6. Guermouche, N., Godart, C.: Asynchronous timed web service-aware choreography analysis. In: van Eck, P., Gordijn, J., Wieringa, R. (eds.) CAiSE 2009. LNCS, vol. 5565, pp. 364–378. Springer, Heidelberg (2009)
7. Guermouche, N., Godart, C.: Timed model checking based approach for web services analysis. In: IEEE International Conference on Web Services (ICWS 2009), Los Angeles, CA, USA, July 6-10, pp. 213–221 (2009)
8. Kazhamiakin, R., Pandya, P.K., Pistore, M.: Representation, verification, and computation of timed properties in web service compositions. In: Proceedings of the IEEE International Conference on Web Services (ICWS), pp. 497–504 (2006)
9. Larsen, K.G., Pettersson, P., Yi, W.: Uppaal in a nutshell. International Journal on Software Tools for Technology Transfer (1997)
10. Ponge, J., Benatallah, B., Casati, F., Toumani, F.: Fine-grained compatibility and replaceability analysis of timed web service protocols. In: Parent, C., Schewe, K.-D., Storey, V.C., Thalheim, B. (eds.) ER 2007. LNCS, vol. 4801, pp. 599–614. Springer, Heidelberg (2007)

Service Discovery Using Communication Fingerprints*

Olivia Oanea[1], Jan Sürmeli[2], and Karsten Wolf[1]

[1] Universität Rostock
18051 Rostock, Germany
{olivia.oanea,karsten.wolf}@uni-rostock.de
[2] Humboldt-Universität zu Berlin
Unter den Linden 6
10099 Berlin, Germany
suermeli@informatik.hu-berlin.de

Abstract. A request to a service registry must be answered with a service that fits in several regards, including semantic compatibility, non-functional compatibility, and interface compatibility. In the case of stateful services, there is the additional need to check behavioral (i.e. protocol) compatibility. This paper is concerned with the latter aspect. For speeding up compatibility checks which need to be performed on many candidate services, we propose an abstraction of the behavior of each published service that we call communication fingerprint. The technique is based on linear programming and is thus extremely efficient. We validate our approach on a large set of services that we cut out of real world business processes.

1   Introduction

In a service oriented architecture, we expect a service *broker* to manage a service *registry*. The broker can be approached by a service *provider* or a service *requester*. Service providers want their service to be published such that it can later on be bound to a service requester. The service broker may extract useful information about the provided service. A service requester approaches the broker for extracting one of the registered services. Besides all kind of functional and non-functional properties that should match the request, it is important that the requesting service R and the service P selected by the broker have compatible behavior, i.e. their interaction should not run into problems such as deadlocks and livelocks. In this article, we propose an approach for supporting a service broker in this regard.

An apparent method for asserting deadlock and livelock freedom would be to model check [2] the composition $R \oplus P$ before shipping the URI of P to R. This is a rather expensive procedure which has a strong negative impact on the response time of the broker. For this purpose, we proposed an alternative check [3] which preprocesses fragments of the state space to be checked at publish time. However, even this check must in worst case be applied to all compositions $R \oplus P_i$ where $\{P_1, \ldots, P_n\}$ is the set of registered services. Consequently, we need a complementing technique which narrows the set of registered services to be checked with R to a subset as small as possible.

---

* An extended version of this paper is available as technical report [1].

P.P. Maglio et al. (Eds.): ICSOC 2010, LNCS 6470, pp. 612–618, 2010.

To this end, we propose *communication fingerprints*. A communication fingerprint of service P collects constraints on the number of occurrences of messages in any correct run of a composed system that involves P. The fingerprint of a registered service is computed upon publishing a service. When a requester approaches the registry, its fingerprint is computed as well and matched with the fingerprints of the registered services. We show that fingerprint matching is a necessary condition for correct interaction, so the expensive model checking procedures need only be executed for matching services.

For computing communication fingerprints, we rely on Petri net models of services which can be automatically obtained [4] from specifications in the industrial language WS_BPEL [5]. We apply a technique called the *state equation* to the Petri net models. The state equation provides a linear algebraic relation between two markings (states) m and m' as well as a sequence of transitions that transforms m into m'. Using the state equation, we derive constraints on the number of message occurrences. For matching fingerprints, we rely on a relation between the state equations of components and the state equation of the composed system that has been observed in [6,7,8].

The paper is organized as follows. We introduce Petri net models for services and formally define compatibility of services. We continue with the formal definition of fingerprints, their computation, and their application in deciding compatibility. We present a case study that underpins the performance gain of our approach. Finally, we discuss further use cases for communication fingerprints.

2   Compatibility of Services

We model services as *open nets*, which are Petri net models with classical syntax and semantics, enriched with a simple notion to support message exchange and composition. Figure 1 shows two example open nets D and S and their composite D $\oplus$ S: Initially, transition s_1 is enabled. Firing s_1, a message is sent by S over channel **document**, enabling transition d_1. Firing d_1, D consumes the message from the **document** channel and results in a state that allows D to make a decision: It fires either d_2, d_3 or d_4, resulting in a message either on the channel **feedback**, **reject** or **accept**. If d_2 fires, D is in a state waiting for a new message over channel **document**; otherwise it is in a final state $[\omega_D]$. Before this decision, S is in a state waiting for a message over channel **feedback**.

The composite S $\oplus$ D can not reach a common final state from any other reachable state. We thus call D and S *incompatible*: In this paper, we inspect the compatibility criterion *weak termination* of a closed composite. Weak termination is similar to *soundness* which is applied as a correctness criterion in the field of business processes. A closed composite is *weakly terminating*, if from each reachable state, some final state is *reachable*. We call two partner services N and Q *compatible* if either (1) their composite is closed and weakly terminating or (2) there exists a partner P of $N \oplus Q$, such that $(N \oplus Q) \oplus P$ is closed and weakly terminating. For finite state services, (1) can be decided by model checking; case (2) is exploited in [9].

Since all known techniques to decide compatibility base on state space computation, they result in a high complexity and runtime. In our scenario, many such decisions need to be done subsequently. We thus suggest a necessary condition for compatibility to preselect potential partners. The condition is based on the observation that, in a terminating

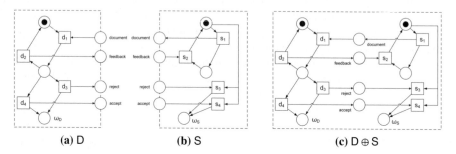

Fig. 1. Two example services D and S, and their composition D⊕S. The final markings are defined as follows: $\Omega_S = \{[\omega_S]\}$, $\Omega_D = \{[\omega_D]\}$, and $\Omega_{D⊕S} = \{[\omega_D, \omega_S]\}$.

run, the number of *send* events for some message type must match the number of *receive* events for that type. Consequently, it is necessary for compatibility that the range of send event occurrences permitted by the internal control flow of one service must intersect with the range of receive event occurrences permitted by the internal control flow of the other service. The same is true for more complicated expressions involving send and receive events, e.g. the difference between the number of send events. Such more complicated expressions are quite useful for services with loops where the absolute number of occurrences of some event may be unbounded. The mentioned ranges for occurrence numbers can be computed for each service independently.

3   Communication Fingerprints

The objective of a fingerprint [1] is to represent the terminating behavior of an open net finitely on an abstraction level which is applicable for preselecting a set of compatible partner services. Since compatibility bases on proper interaction, we focus on *message dependencies* and abstract from private activites. More precisely, we take into account boolean combinations of integer linear constraints, counting messages that are sent over specific channels and the relations thereof.

Formally, a *linear constraint* $c = f * b$ consists of a formal sum f containing channel name variables, a comparison operator $* \in \{\leq, \geq, =, <, >\}$, and an integer b. To decide whether a transition sequence σ *satisfies* a linear constraint c, we abstract σ to its channel usage $\alpha(\sigma)$: A function mapping each channel a to the number of messages exchanged over a while executing σ. Obviously, $\alpha(\sigma)$ is a variable assignment for f. Based thereon, σ *satisfies* c, written $\sigma \models c$, if and only if substitution of the variables in f according to $\alpha(\sigma)$ leads to a true sentence. An example linear constraint for open net D in Fig. 1 is accept $+ 2 \cdot$ reject ≤ 2 which is satisfied by any transition sequence with $\alpha(\sigma)(\text{accept}) = 0$ and $\alpha(\sigma)(\text{reject}) = 1$. We call c *satisfiable* if there exists some σ satisfying c. We combine such linear constraints with the boolean operators $\vee, \wedge, \neg$ to *formulas* with the obvious semantics. Example formulas are $\varphi_1 = $ accept $\leq 1 \wedge$ accept $+$ reject ≤ 1 and $\varphi_2 = $ accept $\leq 1 \wedge -$accept ≤ -2. Any transition sequence σ with $\alpha(\sigma)(\text{accept}) = 0$ and $\alpha(\sigma)(\text{reject}) = 1$ satisfies φ_1, but φ_2 is not satisfiable.

A formula φ can be used to describe the channel usage of an open net N: Each terminating firing sequence $\sigma \in \mathcal{L}(N)$ needs to satisfy φ. We call such a formula *fingerprint* of N. Example fingerprints for D and S in Fig. 1 are $\varphi_D =$ document $-$ (feedback + accept + reject) $= 0 \wedge$ accept + reject $= 1$ and $\varphi_S =$ document $-$ feedback $= 0$.

Services may have infinitely many fingerprints. We can classify a fingerprint based on the formal sums that appear on left hand sides in its constraints: A fingerprint containing only formal sums from a set F is called F-fingerprint. Fingerprint φ_D is a {document $-$ (feedback + accept + reject), accept + reject}-fingerprint. The idea is to *compute* a F-fingerprint for a given set of formal sums F. Our algorithm yields a fingerprint of the form $\bigvee_{m \in \Omega} \bigwedge_{f \in F}((f \geq l_m^f) \wedge (f \leq u_m^f))$: Each conjunctive clause represents the firing sequences resulting in a specific final marking m by specifying two inequalities per formal sum f. We sketch our algorithm for computing l_m^f and u_m^f for some given f and m: The set of firing sequences resulting in a specific final marking m is over-approximated by a system of linear equations, called the *state equation* for m [10]. The state equation is derived from the structure of N, its solutions are vectors over transition variables, which we transform to channel variables. This yields a valid base to minimize and maximize a formal sum of channel variables, resulting in valid l_m^S and u_m^S. If the solver returns *unbounded*, we skip this result. If the solver returns *infeasible*, we skip this final marking. This may result in an empty fingerprint: N might not be compatible to any partner. The complexity for computing such a F-fingerprint of N is that of solving $2 \cdot |\Omega| \cdot |F|$ integer linear programs. In [1], we discuss different generic parameter sets, i.e. sets of formal sums that can be canonically derived from an interface or an open net structure. As a rule of thumb, the complexity of the formal sums has an impact on the precision of the fingerprint: φ_D is more precise than $\varphi_D' =$ document $-$ (feedback + accept + reject) $= 0$.

Matching fingerprints φ_N and φ_Q is a method to semi-decide compatibility of N and Q by deciding satisfiability of $\varphi_N \wedge \varphi_Q$. We assume that φ_N and φ_Q have the above introduced structure. We transform $\varphi_N \wedge \varphi_Q$ into an equivalent formula in disjunctive normal form by applying the distributivity rule. We then check satisfiability for each conjunction which is equivalent to solving a system of linear inequalities. As soon as one satisfiable conjunction is found, we terminate the matching process with *inconclusive*, otherwise with *incompatible*. Different variants of matching, for example matching a φ_N directly with Q, are discussed in [1]. For example, taking the fingerprints φ_D and φ_S, we find that $\varphi_D \wedge \varphi_S$ is unsatisfiable and thus N and Q are incompatible. Turning to φ_D', we notice that $\varphi_D' \wedge \varphi_S$ is satisfiable, which proves that matching is not a sufficient condition.

4   Case study

For validating our approach, we had to build up a large number of services. As a sufficiently large set of actual services was not available to us, we generated "close to real" services as follows. We started with a large set of *real* industrial business processes available to us. They have been modeled using the IBM WEBSPHERE BUSINESS MODELER, then anonymized so they could be made available to us and finally translated into anonymized Petri net models. The used set of business processes has been analyzed

Table 1. Testbed statistics and analysis results

Library	# Processes	# Composites	# Weakly terminating	# Matching inconclusive
A	127	2412	252	672
B1	43	2066	20	597
B2	49	592	25	209
B3	105	3460	210	1165

Table 2. State-based approach vs. fingerprint approach

Library	State-based	Fingerprint			
	Total	Computation	Matching	Model checking	Total
A	>48h	2m49s	30s	28h	≈28h
B1	18m3s	2m57s	29s	6m9s	6m38s
B2	30m43s	53s	12s	16s	28s
B3	>36h	11m6s	1m29s	2h	≈2h

in [11]. We decomposed the processes into asynchronously communicating services following the idea of [6,12] using DIANE. Due to different decomposition options, we obtain a rather big set of services. Two services that each have been obtained from a weakly terminating business process model are not necessarily compatible. In addition, several original models have not been weakly terminating in the first place. The original process set is organized into libraries, each containing models from similar business fields, we thus experimented with one sample set for each library. As the final preparation, we paired interface matching services inside the same sample set. In a first run, we model checked each composite with LoLA. In a second run, we computed the fingerprints of the components with LINDA and matched them with YASMINA. Table 1 lists statistics of the used testbed and analysis results: For each library, we list the number of processes and service pairs, i.e. composites. The fourth column shows how many of those composites were actually weakly terminating, while the fifth displays for how many composites the fingerprint matching of the components returned inconclusive.

In Table 2, we compare the run times of a pure state based approach with the run times of the proposed fingerprint based approach. To this end, we checked all pairs of partner services that stem from the same library. The reported times are the overall times for executing all these checks within a library: The second column lists total amount of time for model checking the composites. The third column states the run time of the fingerprint computation. The fourth column displays the time needed for fingerprint matching. For all inconclusive results, we used model checking, resulting in run times as given in the fifth column. Finally, the sixth column displays the total amount for the fingerprint based compatibility check, which does not include the run time for fingerprint computation.

We see that for about two thirds of the individual problems, the fingerprint check tells that these services are incompatible. These are the problem instances for which it is not necessary to perform a subsequent model checking. For the remaining services, model checking must be applied in any case. Hence, the speed-up can be seen in comparing the overall time of model checking *all instances* with the overall time of all fingerprint matchings plus the overall time for those model checking runs where the fingerprint check was inconclusive. The runtime of the fingerprint matching alone does not contribute significantly to the overall run time and the fingerprint approach requires only about one third of the state-based approach. The used tools DIANE, LoLA, LINDA, and YASMINA are open source tools available at `http://service-technology.org/tools`.

5   Conclusion

In this paper we have considered service communication fingerprints as an approach for pre-selecting appropriate interaction partners with respect to weak termination. We used the state equation of the underlying Petri net to derive constraints over the set of synchronous and asynchronous message event occurrences. Communication fingerprints are considerably small in comparison to the state space of a service. We considered a simple and efficient procedure for obtaining a suitable (not necessarily optimal) communication fingerprint. Matching fingerprints amounts to solving linear programming problems. Our experiments show that the fingerprint approach can significantly speed up service discovery. Our approach is complementary to testing observed behavior against model behavior using frequency profiles [13] and keeping repositories of behavioral profiles [14,15]. Both approaches apply to monolithic workflow and are restricted to transition occurrences. Our approach is different from compositional analysis of invariants of functional nets [6]: We analyze communication patterns which are inherently related to communication.

For future work, we shall consider the application of fingerprints in the synthesis of livelock-free partners. Further, we shall experiment how service communication fingerprint registries created to store subclasses of potentially compatible partners contributes to speeding up operations on behavioral registry [16].

Acknowledgments. Olivia Oanea and Karsten Wolf are supported by the German Research Foundation (DFG) under grant WO 1466/11-1.

References

1. Oanea, O., Sürmeli, J., Wolf, K.: Service discovery using communication fingerprints. Informatik-Berichte 236, Humboldt-Universität zu Berlin (2010)
2. Clarke, E.M., Peled, D., Grumberg, O.: Model Checking. MIT Press, Cambridge (1999)
3. Wolf, K., Stahl, C., Ott, J., Danitz, R.: Verifying livelock freedom in an SOA scenario. In: ACSD 2009, pp. 168–177. IEEE, Los Alamitos (2009)
4. Lohmann, N.: A feature-complete Petri net semantics for WS-BPEL 2.0. In: Dumas, M., Heckel, R. (eds.) WS-FM 2007. LNCS, vol. 4937, pp. 77–91. Springer, Heidelberg (2008)
5. Alves, A., et al.: Web Services Business Process Execution Language Version 2.0. Technical Report CS-02-08, OASIS (2007)

6. Zaitsev, D.A.: Compositional analysis of Petri nets. Cybernetics and Systems Analysis 42(1), 126–136 (2006)
7. Sürmeli, J.: Profiling services with static analysis. In: AWPN 2009 Proceedings, of CEUR Workshop Proceedings, vol. 501, pp. 35–40 CEUR-WS.org (2009)
8. Oanea, O., Wolf, K.: An efficient necessary condition for compatibility. In: ZEUS, of CEUR Workshop Proceedings, vol. 438, pp. 81–87 CEUR-WS.org (2009)
9. Wolf, K.: Does my service have partners? In: Jensen, K., van der Aalst, W.M.P. (eds.) Transactions on Petri Nets. LNCS, vol. 5460, pp. 152–171. Springer, Heidelberg (2009)
10. Lautenbach, K.: Liveness in Petri Nets. St. Augustin: Gesellschaft für Mathematik und Datenverarbeitung Bonn, Interner Bericht ISF-75-02.1 (1975)
11. Fahland, D., Favre, C., Jobstmann, B., Koehler, J., Lohmann, N., Völzer, H., Wolf, K.: Instantaneous soundness checking of industrial business process models. In: Dayal, U., Eder, J., Koehler, J., Reijers, H.A. (eds.) BPM 2009. LNCS, vol. 5701, Springer, Heidelberg (2009)
12. Mennicke, S., Oanea, O., Wolf, K.: Decomposition into open nets. In: AWPN 2009, Proceedings of CEUR Workshop, pp. 29–34 CEUR-WS.org (2009)
13. van der Aalst, W.M.P.: Matching observed behavior and modeled behavior: an approach based on Petri nets and integer programming. Decis. Support Syst. 42(3), 1843–1859 (2006)
14. Weidlich, M., Weske, M., Mendling, J.: Change propagation in process models using behavioural profiles. In: SCC 20209, pp. 33–40. IEEE, Los Alamitos (2009)
15. Weidlich, M., Polyvyanyy, A., Mendling, J., Weske, M.: Efficient computation of causal behavioural profiles using structural decomposition. In: Lilius, J., Penczek, W. (eds.) PETRI NETS 2010. LNCS, vol. 6128, Springer, Heidelberg (2010)
16. Kaschner, K., Wolf, K.: Set algebra for service behavior: Applications and constructions. In: Dayal, U., Eder, J., Koehler, J., Reijers, H.A. (eds.) BPM 2009. LNCS, vol. 5701, pp. 193–210. Springer, Heidelberg (2009)

Quantifying Service Compatibility: A Step beyond the Boolean Approaches

Meriem Ouederni[1], Gwen Salaün[2], and Ernesto Pimentel[1]

[1] University of Málaga, Spain
{meriem,ernesto}@lcc.uma.es
[2] Grenoble, INP–INRIA–LIG, France
Gwen.Salaun@inria.fr

Abstract. Checking the compatibility of service interfaces allows one to avoid erroneous executions when composing services together. In this paper, we propose a flooding-based approach for measuring the compatibility degree of service interfaces specified using interaction protocols. This proposal is fully automated by a prototype tool we have implmented.

1 Introduction

Checking the compatibility of service interfaces guarantees the safe reuse and the successful interoperation of services in the context of Service Oriented Computing (SOC). In this paper, we focus on the interaction protocol level of service interfaces. Checking the compatibility of interaction protocols is a tedious and hard task even though this is of utmost importance to avoid run-time errors, *e.g.*, deadlock situations or unmatched messages. Most of the existing approaches (see for instance [5,17,2,8,6,3]) return a "True" or "False" result to detect whether services are compatible or not. Unfortunately, a Boolean answer is not very helpful for many reasons. First, in real world case studies, there will seldom be a perfect match, and when service protocols are not compatible, it is useful to differentiate between services that are slightly incompatible and those that are totally incompatible. Furthermore, a Boolean result does not give a detailed measure of which parts of service protocols are compatible or not.

To overcome the aforementioned limits, a very few works (see for instance [16]) recently aim at measuring the compatibility degree of service interfaces. However, most of them are based upon description models of service interfaces which do not consider value-passing and internal behaviours (τ transitions). Moreover, they often measure the interface compatibility using a simple (*i.e.*, not iterative) traversal of protocols, and consider a unique compatibility notion making their application quite restricted.

In this paper, we propose a generic framework where the compatibility degree of service interfaces can be automatically measured according to different compatibility notions. We illustrate our approach using a bidirectional compatibility notion, namely *unspecified receptions*. Additional notions can easily be added to our framework. We consider a formal model for describing service interfaces with interaction protocols (messages and their application order, but

P.P. Maglio et al. (Eds.): ICSOC 2010, LNCS 6470, pp. 619–626, 2010.

also value-passing and internal actions). In our approach, the compatibility degree is computed in two steps. A first step computes a set of static compatibility degrees where the execution order of messages is not taken into account. Then, a flooding algorithm computes the compatibility degree of interaction protocols using the static compatibility results. The computation process also returns the mismatch list indicating the interoperability issues. The proposed framework is fully automated by a prototype tool (called Comparator) we have implemented.

The remainder of this paper is structured as follows. Section 2 describes our model of services. Section 3 introduces the compatibility notion we use in this paper for illustration purposes. In Section 4, we present our solution for measuring the service compatibility. Section 5 introduces our prototype tool. Finally, concluding remarks are presented in Section 6. All the formal definitions and more details are given in a companion technical report available at Meriem Ouederni's Webpage.

2   Service Model

We assume service interfaces are described using their interaction protocols represented by *Symbolic Transition Systems* (STSs) which are Labelled Transition Systems extended with value-passing (parameters coming with messages). In particular, a STS is a tuple (A, S, I, F, T) where: A is an alphabet which corresponds to the set of labels associated to transitions, S is a set of states, $I \in S$ is the initial state, $F \subseteq S$ is a nonempty set of final states, and $T \subseteq S \backslash F \times A \times S$ is the transition relation. In our model, a *label* is either an (internal) τ action or a tuple (m, d, pl) where m is the message name, d stands for the communication direction (either an emission ! or a reception ?), and pl is either a list of typed data terms if the label corresponds to an emission (output action), or a list of typed variables if the label is a reception (input action).[1]

It is worth noticing that communication between services relies on a synchronous and binary communication model. The operational semantics of this model is given in [6]. STSs can also be easily derived from higher-level description languages such as Abstract BPEL, see for instance [7,14,4] where such abstractions were used for verification, composition or adaptation of Web services.

3   Unspecified Receptions Compatibility

Compatibility checking verifies the successful interaction between services *wrt.* a criterion set on their observable actions. This criterion is referred to as a compatibility notion. We distinguish two classes of notions depending on the direction of the compatibility checking, that are, bidirectional and unidirectional analysis. Our approach supports both classes; here we particularly illustrate it with a bidirectional compatibility notion, namely *unspecified receptions* (*UR* for short). This notion is inspired from [17] and requires that two services are compatible (i) if they are deadlock-free, and (ii) if one service can send a message at a reachable state, then its partner must eventually receive that emission such that both

---

[1] The message names and parameter types respect the service signature.

services evolve into states where the *UR* notion is preserved. In real-life cases, one service must receive all the requests from its partner, but can also accept more receptions, because the service could interoperate with other partners.

4   Measuring Protocol Compatibility

This section presents our techniques for measuring the compatibility of two service protocols. In what follows, we describe a transition using a tuple (s, l, s') such that s and s' denote the source and target states, respectively, and l stands for its label. We suppose that for all transitions (s, τ, s'), $s \neq s'$. Given two services described using STSs $STS_{i \in \{1,2\}} = (A_i, S_i, I_i, F_i, T_i)$, we define a global state as a pair of states $(s_1, s_2) \in S_1 \times S_2$. All the compatibility measures we present in the sequel belong to $[0..1]$ where 1 means a perfect compatibility. The approach overviewed in Figure 1 consists first in computing a set of static compatibility measures (Section 4.1). In a second step, these static measures are used for computing the behavioural compatibility degree for all global state in $S_1 \times S_2$ (Section 4.2). Last, the result is analysed and a global compatibility degree is returned (Section 4.3).

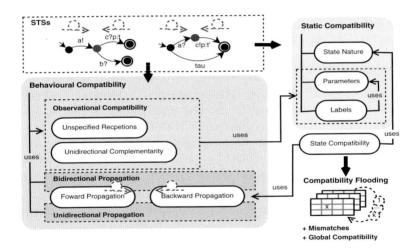

Fig. 1. Compatibility Measuring Process

4.1   Static Compatibility

We use three auxiliary static compatibility measures, namely state nature, labels, and exchanged parameters.

State Nature. The comparison of state nature assigns 1 to each pair of states which have the same nature, *i.e.*, both states are initial, final or none of them. Otherwise, the measure is equal to 0.

Parameters. The compatibility degree of two parameter lists pl_1 and pl_2 depends on three auxiliary measures, namely: (i) the compatibility of parameter number comparing the list sizes; (ii) the compatibility of parameter order measuring the number of types which does not appear in the same order, and (iii) the compatibility of parameter type using the set of unshared types in both lists. These measures must be set to 1 if these lists are empty.

Labels. Protocol synchronisation requires that compatible labels must have opposite directions. Therefore, given a pair $(l_1, l_2) \in A_1 \times A_2$, the label compatibility – $lab\text{-}comp(l_1, l_2)$ – is measured as 0 if these labels have same directions. Otherwise, the computation of this measure uses the semantic distance between message names and the parameter compatibility degree presented above. Here, message names are compared using the Wordnet similarity package [13].

4.2   Behavioural Compatibility

We consider a flooding algorithm which performs an iterative measuring of behavioural compatibility for every global state in $S_1 \times S_2$. This algorithm incrementally propagates the compatibility between neighbouring states using backward and forward processing. The compatibility propagation is based on the intuition that two states are compatible if their backward and forward neighbouring states are compatible, where the backward and forward neighbours of global state (s'_1, s'_2) in transition relations $T_1 = \{(s_1, l_1, s'_1), (s'_1, l'_1, s''_1)\}$ and $T_2 = \{(s_2, l_2, s'_2), (s'_2, l'_2, s''_2)\}$ are the states (s_1, s_2) and (s''_1, s''_2), respectively. The flooding algorithm returns a matrix denoted $COMP^k_{CN,D}$ where each entry $COMP^k_{CN,D}[s_1, s_2]$ stands for the compatibility measure of global state (s_1, s_2) at the kth iteration. The parameter CN refers to the considered compatibility notion which must be checked according to D, that is, a bidirectional ($\leftrightarrow$) protocol analysis in this paper. $COMP^0_{CN,D}$ represents the initial compatibility matrix where all states are supposed to be perfectly compatible, i.e., $\forall (s_1, s_2) \in S_1 \times S_2$, $COMP^0_{CN,D}[s_1, s_2] = 1$. Then, in order to compute $COMP^k_{CN,D}[s_1, s_2]$, we consider the observational compatibility function, $obs\text{-}comp^k_{CN,D}$, and the state compatibility function, $state\text{-}comp^k_{CN,D}$, which combines the forward and backward propagations. In this paper, we only present the forward compatibility for lack of space, the backward compatibility can be handled in a similar way based upon incoming rather than outgoing transitions.

Unspecified Receptions. For all global state (s_1, s_2): (i) $obs\text{-}comp^k_{UR,\leftrightarrow}$ returns 1 if and only if every outgoing emission at state s_1 (and s_2) perfectly matches an outgoing reception at state s_2 (and s_1) and all synchronisations on those emissions lead to compatible states; (ii) $obs\text{-}comp^k_{UR,\leftrightarrow}$ returns 0 if there is a deadlock; (iii) otherwise, $obs\text{-}comp^k_{UR,\leftrightarrow}$ measures the best compatibility of every outgoing emission at s_1 with the outgoing receptions at s_2, leading to the neighbouring states which have the highest compatibility degree, and vice-versa.

Example 1. Let us consider the global state (s_0, c_0) in Figure 2. Here, there is a unique emission seek! at c_0 which perfectly matches with search? at s_0, $lab\text{-}comp(seek!, search?) = 1$ using Wordnet similarity package. The synchronisation on these compatible labels leads to (s_1, c_1) where $COMP^0_{UR,\leftrightarrow}[s_1, c_1] = 1$.

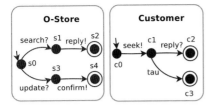

	c_0	c_1	c_2	c_3
s_0	**0.95**	0.17	0.01	0.01
s_1	0.01	0.82	0.01	0.32
s_2	0.01	0.26	0.95	0.51
s_3	0.01	0.47	0.01	0.16
s_4	0.01	0.26	0.75	**0.51**

Fig. 2. Online Store

Fig. 3. Matrix $COMP_{UR,\leftrightarrow}^{7}$

Thus, at the first iteration, $obs\text{-}comp_{UR,\leftrightarrow}^{1}((s_0,c_0)) = lab\text{-}comp(seek!,search?) * COMP_{UR,\leftrightarrow}^{0}[s_1,c_1] = 1$.

Forward Propagation. The compatibility is computed from both services point of view. The function $fw\text{-}propag_{CN,\leftrightarrow}^{k}((s_1,s_2))$ propagates to (s_1,s_2) the compatibility degrees obtained for the forward neighbours of state s_1 with those of state s_2, and vice-versa. For each τ transition, $fw\text{-}propag_{CN,\leftrightarrow}^{k}$ must be checked on the target state. Observable transitions going out from (s_1,s_2) are compared using $obs\text{-}comp_{CN,\leftrightarrow}^{k}((s_1,s_2))$.

Example 2. Let us consider the global state (s_1,c_1) in Figure 2. We show below the computation of $fw\text{-}propag_{UR,\leftrightarrow}^{1}((s_1,c_1))$ which results in the average of the auxiliary values computed from each protocol point of view:

$$fw\text{-}propag_{UR,\leftrightarrow}^{1}((s_1,c_1)) = \frac{1}{2}*$$

$$[\frac{fw\text{-}propag_{UR,\leftrightarrow}^{1}((s_1,c_3))+obs\text{-}comp_{UR,\leftrightarrow}^{1}((s_1,c_1))}{2} + obs\text{-}comp_{UR,\leftrightarrow}^{1}((s_1,c_1))]$$

where:

- $fw\text{-}propag_{UR,\leftrightarrow}^{1}((s_1,c_3)) = obs\text{-}comp_{UR,\leftrightarrow}^{1}((s_1,c_3)) = 0$ due to the deadlock that can occur at the state (s_1,c_3).
- $obs\text{-}comp_{UR,\leftrightarrow}^{1}((s_1,c_1)) = lab\text{-}comp(reply?,reply!) * COMP_{UR,\leftrightarrow}^{0}[s_2,c_2] = 1$.

As a consequence, $fw\text{-}propag_{UR,\leftrightarrow}^{1}((s_0,c_0)) = \frac{3}{4}$.

State Compatibility. The function $state\text{-}comp_{CN,D}^{k}((s_1,s_2))$ computes the weighted average of three measures: the forward and backward compatibilities, and the value returned by the function comparing state natures.

Compatibility Flooding. As a final measuring step, $COMP_{CN,D}^{k}[s_1,s_2]$ is computed as the average of its previous value $COMP_{CN,D}^{k-1}[s_1,s_2]$ and the current state compatibility degree. Our iterative process terminates when the Euclidean difference $\varepsilon_k = \|COMP_{CN,D}^{k} - COMP_{CN,D}^{k-1}\|$ converges.

Example 3. Figure 3 shows the matrix computed for the example depicted in Figure 2. This matrix was obtained after 7 iterations. Let us comment the compatibility of states c_0 and s_0. The measure is quite high because both states are initial and the emission seek! at c_0 perfectly matches the reception search? at s_0. However, the compatibility degree is less than 1 due to the backward propagation of the deadlock from the global state (s_1,c_3) to (s_1,c_1), and then from (s_1,c_1) to (s_0,c_0).

Mismatch Detection. Our compatibility measure comes with a list of mismatches which identifies the incompatibility sources, *e.g.,* unmatched message names or unshared parameter types. For instance, the states s_0 and c_1 in Figure 2 present several mismatches, *e.g.,* the first state is initial while the second is not, and their outgoing transition labels have the same directions.

Extensibility. Our approach is generic and can be easily extended to integrate other compatibility notions. Adding a compatibility notion CN only requires to define a new function $obs\text{-}comp^k_{CN,D}$.

4.3   Analysis of Compatibility Measures

Compatible Protocols. Our flooding algorithm ensures that every time a mismatch is detected in a reachable global state, its effect will be propagated to the initial states. Hence, the forward and backward compatibility propagation between neighbouring states implies that protocols are compatible if and only if their initial states are also compatible. Such information is useful for automatically discovering available services that can be composed without using any adaptor service for compensating mismatches [10].

Global Protocol Compatibility. As regard incompatible protocols, this global measure is helpful to differentiate between services that are slightly incompatible and those which are totally incompatible, and for service ranking and selection. Seeking for services with high global compatibility degree enables to simplify further processing to compensate existing mismatches, *e.g.,* using service adaptation. In our approach we compute the global compatibility degree as the weighted average of all behavioural compatibility degrees that are higher than a threshold t. The weight is the rate of states having a compatibility degree higher than t, among all states compared in one service, with the states in the partner service.

5   Prototype Tool

Our approach for measuring the compatibility degree of service protocols has been fully implemented in a prototype tool called Comparator which has been

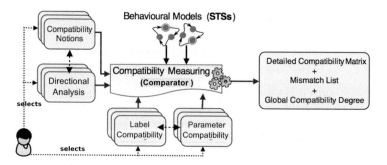

Fig. 4. Comparator Architecture

validated on more than 110 examples. The framework architecture is given in Figure 4. The Comparator tool, implemented in Python, accepts as input two XML files corresponding to the service interfaces and an initial configuration, *i.e.*, the compatibility notion, the checking direction, and a threshold t. The tool returns the compatibility matrix, the mismatch list, and the global compatibility degree which indicates how compatible both services are. The implementation of our proposal is highly modular which makes easy its extension with new compatibility notions, or other strategies for comparing message names and parameters.

6   Concluding Remarks

Existing quantitative analysis of service behaviours have been devoted to two related issues in SOC. A first research line measures the compatibility, that is, how much interacting services fulfill each other's requirements. The second research line checks the substitutability, that is, the correspondences between similar service behaviours. The techniques used for measuring the simulation-based correspondences in [15], and the global compatibility degree based on checking the deadlock-freedom in [16] of two protocols, rely on a simple (not iterative), forward, and parallel traversal. In [9,1], the authors compute the minimal edit distance between two similar versions of one service interface. Other works [11,12] rely on a similarity flooding algorithm for computing the matrix of correspondences between models such as labelled graphs and statecharts.

Our work advances the state-of-the-art as follows. Our behavioural model takes value passing and internal behaviours into account. Our framework is generic, supports different compatibility notions, and can be extended with other ones. Considering both the forward and backward compatibility propagations makes our flooding algorithm more precise, and also enables to detect the boolean compatibility. Our proposal is fully supported by the Comparator tool which has been validated on many examples. The global compatibility degree is helpful for service selection and ranking. The returned matrix and the mismatch list have some straightforward applications in the software adaptation area [10,17]. Our tool was already integrated into an environment for the interactive specification of adaptation contracts [4]. Our main perspective is to apply our compatibility measuring approach for the automatic generation of adaptor protocols.

Acknowledgements. This work has been partially supported by the project TIN2008-05932 funded by the Spanish Ministry of Innovation and Science and FEDER, and by the project P06-TIC220, funded by the Andalusian government.

References

1. Aït-Bachir, A.: Measuring Similarity of Service Interfaces. In: Bouguettaya, A., Krueger, I., Margaria, T. (eds.) ICSOC 2008. LNCS, vol. 5364. Springer, Heidelberg (2008)

2. Bordeaux, L., Salaün, G., Berardi, D., Mecella, M.: When are Two Web Services Compatible?. In: Shan, M.-C., Dayal, U., Hsu, M. (eds.) TES 2004. LNCS, vol. 3324, pp. 15–28. Springer, Heidelberg (2005)

3. Bravetti, M., Zavattaro, G.: Contract-Based Discovery and Composition of Web Services. In: Bernardo, M., Padovani, L., Zavattaro, G. (eds.) SFM 2009. LNCS, vol. 5569, pp. 261–295. Springer, Heidelberg (2009)

4. Cámara, J., Salaün, G., Canal, C., Ouederni, M.: Interactive Specification and Verification of Behavioural Adaptation Contracts. In: Proc. of QSIC 2009, pp. 65–75. IEEE Computer Society, Los Alamitos (2009)

5. de Alfaro, L., Henzinger, T.: Interface Automata. In: Proc. of ESEC/FSE 2001, pp. 109–120. ACM Press, New York (2001)

6. Durán, F., Ouederni, M., Salaün, G.: Checking Protocol Compatibility using Maude. In: Proc. of FOCLASA 2009. ENTCS, vol. 255, pp. 65–81 (2009)

7. Fu, X., Bultan, T., Su, J.: Analysis of Interacting BPEL Web Services. In: Proc. of WWW 2004, pp. 621–630. ACM Press, New York (2004)

8. Hameurlain, N.: Flexible Behavioural Compatibility and Substitutability for Component Protocols: A Formal Specification. In: Proc. of SEFM 2007, pp. 391–400. IEEE Computer Society, Los Alamitos (2007)

9. Lohmann, N.: Correcting Deadlocking Service Choreographies Using a Simulation-Based Graph Edit Distance. In: Dumas, M., Reichert, M., Shan, M.-C. (eds.) BPM 2008. LNCS, vol. 5240, pp. 132–147. Springer, Heidelberg (2008)

10. Mateescu, R., Poizat, P., Salaün, G.: Adaptation of Service Protocols Using Process Algebra and On-the-Fly Reduction Techniques. In: Bouguettaya, A., Krueger, I., Margaria, T. (eds.) ICSOC 2008. LNCS, vol. 5364, pp. 84–99. Springer, Heidelberg (2008)

11. Melnik, S., Garcia-Molina, H., Rahm, E.: Similarity Flooding: A Versatile Graph Matching Algorithm and Its Application to Schema Matching. In: Proc. of ICDE 2002, pp. 117–128. IEEE Computer Society, Los Alamitos (2002)

12. Nejati, S., Sabetzadeh, M., Chechik, M., Easterbrook, S.M., Zave, P.: Matching and Merging of Statecharts Specifications. In: Proc. of ICSE 2007, pp. 54–64. ACM Press, New York (2007)

13. Pedersen, T., Patwardhan, S., Michelizzi, J.: WordNet:Similarity - Measuring the Relatedness of Concepts. In: Proc. of AAAI 2004, pp. 1024–1025. AAAI, Menlo Park (2004)

14. Salaün, G., Bordeaux, L., Schaerf, M.: Describing and Reasoning on Web Services using Process Algebra. IJBPIM 1(2), 116–128 (2006)

15. Sokolsky, O., Kannan, S., Lee, I.: Simulation-Based Graph Similarity. In: Hermanns, H., Palsberg, J. (eds.) TACAS 2006. LNCS, vol. 3920, pp. 426–440. Springer, Heidelberg (2006)

16. Wu, Z., Deng, S., Li, Y., Wu, J.: Computing Compatibility in Dynamic Service Composition. Knowledge and Information Systems 19(1), 107–129 (2009)

17. Yellin, D.M., Strom, R.E.: Protocol Specifications and Component Adaptors. ACM Trans. Program. Lang. Syst. 19(2), 292–333 (1997)

Consistency Benchmarking: Evaluating the Consistency Behavior of Middleware Services in the Cloud

Markus Klems[1], Michael Menzel[2], and Robin Fischer[1]

[1] Karlsruhe Institute of Technology (KIT),
76131 Karlsruhe, Germany
markus.klems@kit.edu, robin.fischer@kit.edu
http://www.kit.edu

[2] FZI Forschungszentrum Informatik,
Haid-und-Neu-Straße 10-14,
76131 Karlsruhe, Germany
menzel@fzi.de
http://www.fzi.de

Abstract. Cloud service providers such as Amazon Web Services offer a set of next-generation storage and messaging middleware services that can be utilized on-demand over the Internet. Outsourcing software into the cloud, however, confronts application developers with the challenge of understanding the behavior of distributed systems, which are out of their control. This work proposes an approach to benchmark the consistency behavior of services by example of Amazon Simple Queue Service (SQS), a hosted, Web-scale, distributed message queue that is exposed as a Web service. The data of our consistency benchmarking tests are evaluated with the metric *harvest* as described by Fox and Brewer (1999). Our tests with SQS indicate that the client-service interaction intensity has an influence on harvest.

Keywords: cloud computing, distributed systems, service-oriented computing.

1 Background and Motivation

Leveraging the seemingly infinite resources of cloud computing needs software to scale out and, hence, run in multiple, replicated instances. Coordination and collaboration between multiple replicas is required to allow distributed software acting as a whole. Middleware promises a solution by delivering distribution transparency for heterogeneous distributed systems [1]. Middleware is typically applied to integrate client-server architectures that have been deployed in Local Area Networks (LANs) or in Wide Area Networks (WANs). Unfortunately, additional software layers increase the size and complexity of technology and infrastructure that is required to support these new programming abstractions.

Cloud-based middleware services follow a different paradigm by using the Web as a platform. The success of RESTful services (in particular for mashups)

P.P. Maglio et al. (Eds.): ICSOC 2010, LNCS 6470, pp. 627–634, 2010.

demonstrates that applications on the Web strive for less features in favor of simplicity and scalability. Although traditional middleware services might be ported into the cloud, substantial modifications would be required to fulfill availability and scalability characteristics commonly associated with the cloud. On the other side, cloud service providers already offer scalable services of basic middleware capabilities, such as Amazon Simple Queue Service (SQS), a Web-scale distributed message queue. We discuss new challenges that arise from using cloud-based middleware services, particularly the less predictable consistency behavior. Then we present a prototypical benchmarking tool that we designed and used in order to conduct experiments on SQS.

2   Approach

Cloud-based middleware service promise improvements over traditional middleware, such as reduced complexity, better re-use, scalability, world wide access and high availability. On the other side, new challenges arise when using cloud-based middleware services.

2.1   Consistency-Availability Trade-off Challenges

Cloud-based middleware services are built of large-scale systems which are possibly distributed over multiple datacenters in different availability zones, connected by the Internet. Distribution of storage infrastructure provokes a fundamental trade-off challenge known as the *strong CAP principle* [2] [3]: only two out of the three properties of a distributed system, strong consistency (C), high availability (A), and partition-tolerance (P), can be achieved at the same time. The *weak CAP principle* generalizes the strong CAP principle by characterizing the trade-off as a continuum instead of binary choices. In particular, relaxing consistency requirements to a certain degree and trading them for higher availability has become a successful modus operandi for large-scale systems [4] [5]. Understanding and addressing the weak CAP principle in application design and development – as there seems to be no general-purpose solution – becomes increasingly important.

The Amazon Web Service developer guides raise explicit awareness for challenges that software developers must face if they want their software to work correctly [6]. SQS stores multiple replicas of the same message on multiple storage servers with the goal to provide fault-tolerance and high availability. Due to the distributed nature of SQS, message delivery order cannot be guaranteed. Moreover, on rare occasions, it may happen that messages are delivered more than once. Therefore, it is important to design SQS-based applications with idempotent "receive message" operations. Behind the scenes, SQS uses weighted random server sampling. Not all available server replicas are queried, but only a randomly chosen subset. Repeated receive requests will eventually retrieve all messages.

2.2   Consistency Behavior

We define the *consistency behavior* of a cloud-based middleware service along the lines of *temporary inconsistencies* and *conflicts*. Temporary inconsistencies can emerge as a consequence of optimistic and probabilistic replication techniques. Temporary inconsistencies are non-deterministic and disappear eventually over time. Conflicts are server-side inconsistencies between replicas that require reconciliation. Our work focuses on temporary inconsistencies.

Fox and Brewer introduced the two metrics *harvest* and *yield* to differentiate the behaviour of applications which are capable of graceful availability degradation [2]. Yield measures the amount of successfully completed requests, whereas harvest measures the fraction of data reflected in the responses in relation to the data that could have been delivered in a failure-free world. Besides graceful degradation, we believe that harvest and yield are well-suited metrics to measure the client-side consistency behavior of those middleware services which relax consistency requirements on purpose. The metrics can easily be recorded by observing communication interactions between client and service.

2.3   Consistency Benchmarking of SQS

With our approach to consistency benchmarking, we attempt to better understand the significance of eventual consistency from an application programmer perspective. Although the qualitative nature of software development challenges has been described in the SQS developer guide, their gravity is unknown. Based on a qualitative description of the consistency behavior of SQS, we propose to measure the following indicators:

Y: How many requests return a valid response?
H: How many messages are received with a receive request?
O: To which degree are messages out-of-order?
D: How often are duplicate messages received?

Furthermore, we want to evaluate whether these indicators depend on the following application properties:

P1: The location of application clients,
P2: the maximum number of messages fetched with a single receive request,
P3: the timespan between subsequent Web service requests,
P4: the availability zone of the SQS service endpoint, and
P5: the average amount of messages stored in SQS.

3   Experiment and Evaluation

We implemented a benchmarking tool prototype to conduct experiments on Amazon SQS. First, we describe the basic benchmarking test setup. Then we discuss the metrics for the indicators under evaluation. The test case is described with pseudocode, and our results are presented and discussed.

3.1   Benchmarking Test Setup

The test case is executed by a local client who triggers remote Web services deployed on Amazon EC2 instances in four different availability zones: Ireland (EU), Singapore (ASIA), Virginia (US-EAST), and North California (US-WEST). In the example depicted in figure 1, the local client triggers synchronous requests of the benchmarking Web services, which, in turn, call the SQS Web service with endpoint US-EAST. The local client triggers two servers in EU and ASIA to send messages with ids "7214c..." and "6f7ab..." to the SQS queue. Two servers in US-EAST and US-WEST are triggered to request receiving messages from the queue. All response messages are collected by the local client and aggregated for statistic evaluation.

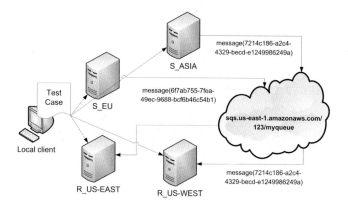

Fig. 1. Example of a benchmark test run

3.2   Test Case Algorithm

The basic test case is described with pseudocode shown in Algorithm 1. Required input parameters are the Web services "Sender S" and "Receiver R", particularly the respective availability zones where they are deployed (property P1). The service endpoint E determines to which of the four availability zones currently provided by SQS a service request should be routed (property P4). Other required input parameters are the maximum number of messages received with a single "receive" request max_R (property P2), the number of messages nos_S sent by S within a single test run (property P5), the number of test runs T performed in a single test case, and the waiting period w between subsequent requests (property P3). Output parameters of the algorithm are a "yield" vector $\mathbf{Y}$ of dimension T (number of test runs), and similarly "harvest" $\mathbf{H}$, "order error" $\mathbf{O}$, and "number of duplicate messages" $\mathbf{D}$.

Each test case begins with the creation of a new queue Q_E (line 3). The for-loop from line 5 to 31 encloses a single test run. With the first inner for-loop, nos_S messages are sent to Q_E and the message id that is created for each sent message is added to Set_{sent}. Then the for-loop starting in line 12 tries to retrieve all messages stored in Q_E. In line 15, a check for duplicate messages is performed. The following conditional statement in line 17 checks whether a previously sent message has been received. If none of these two conditional statements are true, a stale message from a previous test run has been received. In the basic version of the algorithm, stale messages are simply discarded. However, one could evaluate how many requests it takes on average to retrieve a specific message from Q_E. For each test run, the metrics yield Y_t, harvest H_t, order error O_t, and duplicate messages D_t are recorded. After all test runs have been performed, the queue Q_E is deleted (line 32).

Algorithm 1. SQS Consistency Benchmarking Algorithm

Require: $S, R, E, max_R, nos, T, w$
Ensure: $\mathbf{Y} \in [\mathbf{0,1}], \mathbf{H} \in [\mathbf{0,1}], \mathbf{O} \geq \mathbf{0}, \mathbf{D} \geq \mathbf{0}$
1: $\mathbf{Y} \Leftarrow \mathbf{1}, \mathbf{H} \Leftarrow \mathbf{1}, \mathbf{O} \Leftarrow \mathbf{0}, \mathbf{D} \Leftarrow \mathbf{0}$
2: $Set_{sent} \Leftarrow \emptyset, Set_{deleted} \Leftarrow \emptyset, \textbf{sequence} \Leftarrow \emptyset$
3: Create queue Q_E
4: Wait w seconds.
5: **for** $t = 1$ to T **do**
6:    **for** $s = 1$ to nos **do**
7:       Sender S requests to send a new message to Q_E with sequence number s in message body.
8:       Add message id to Set_{sent}.
9:       Wait w seconds.
10:    **end for**
11:    $h \Leftarrow 0$
12:    **for** $r = 1$ to nos/max_R **do**
13:       Client R requests to receive at most max_R messages from queue Q_E as $Set_{received}$.
14:       **for all** messages $\in Set_{received}$ **do**
15:          **if** message id $\in Set_{deleted}$ **then**
16:             $D_t \Leftarrow D_t + 1$
17:          **else if** message id $\in Set_{sent}$ **then**
18:             $h \Leftarrow h + 1$
19:             Append s to $sequence$.
20:             Remove message id from Set_{sent}.
21:             Add message id to $Set_{deleted}$.
22:          **else**
23:             Evaluate stale messages from previous test run.
24:          **end if**
25:          Wait w seconds.
26:       **end for**
27:    **end for**
28:    $Y_t \Leftarrow$ the fraction of HTTP requests that return with code 200.
29:    $H_t \Leftarrow h/nos$
30:    $O_t \Leftarrow$ complexity of sorting algorithm applied on $sequence$.
31: **end for**
32: Delete queue Q_E.
33: **return** $\mathbf{Y}, \mathbf{H}, \mathbf{O}, \mathbf{D}$

3.3   Data and Discussion

We perform tests based on a ceteris paribus assumption where four of the five properties presented in section 2.3 remain fixed. Thereby, the influence of a single independent variable (properties P1-P5) on the dependent variables (indicators Y,H,O,D) can be measured. The results of our tests never recorded duplicate messages or invalid responses; in other words, the results showed 0 duplicates and 100% yield.

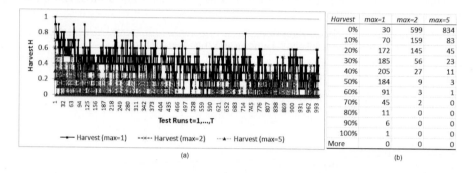

Harvest	max=1	max=2	max=5
0%	30	599	834
10%	70	159	83
20%	172	145	45
30%	185	56	23
40%	205	27	11
50%	184	9	3
60%	91	3	1
70%	45	2	0
80%	11	0	0
90%	6	0	0
100%	1	0	0
More	0	0	0

(a)   (b)

Fig. 2. Charts showing harvest depending on maximum number of messages to be retrieved with a single request for $max_R = 1$, $max_R = 2$, and $max_R = 5$ (a). Histogram of harvest depending on max_R (b).

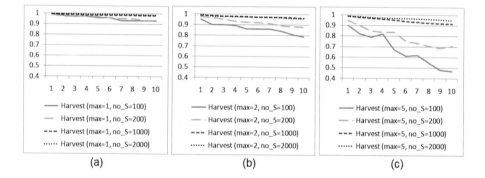

(a)   (b)   (c)

Fig. 3. Chart (a) showing how harvest improves for $max_R = 1$ when the number of sent messages no_S, and thereby average queue size increases. Chart (b) shows the same effect for $max_R = 2$, and chart (c) for $max_R = 5$.

Influence of Property P2 (max_R) on Harvest (H). For each of three test cases, the maximum number of messages to be retrieved with a single request, max_R, is set to 1,2, and 5, respectively, while sender and receiver client location (P1), waiting time (P3), service endpoint (P4), and average number of queued messages (P5) remain fixed for all test cases.

The local client performs $T = 1000$ test runs with $no_S = 10$ messages sent in each test run. Test results show that "receive" requests with $max_R = 1$ achieve better harvest than those with $max_R = 2$, and $max_R = 2$ achieves better harvest than $max_R = 5$ (figure 2). The results suggest that lower max_R leads to larger harvest. Subsequent tests with other values of the fixed properties were in accordance with this observation.

We interpret these results in the context of our benchmarking algorithm (Algorithm 1). In the for-loop starting in line 12 that encloses a statement issuing "receive" requests, iterating from $r = 1$ to no_S/max_R, a larger value of max_R means that less "receive" requests are issued. Based on the weighted random server sampling algorithm employed by SQS, with each request a new server sample is chosen. Therefore, the coverage of servers increases with the number of requests, since more potentially different server samples are addressed.

Interestingly, the harvest of all three test cases decreases in the beginning. We interpret this effect as a result of how stale messages are dealt with: the basic algorithm simply discards stale messages and does not count them as harvest. After a few test runs that do not return 100% harvest, stale messages accumulate in the queue Q.

Other Results. We measured the influence of average queue size (P5), in terms of number of messages sent to and stored in the queue no_S, on harvest H, while the other properties remain fixed. Tests with $T = 10$ indicate that harvest improves considerably when more messages are sent to the message queue (figure 3). We believe that this is the case because more messages sent to and stored in the queue clearly imply a higher probability to retrieve any harvest messages. The margin by which harvest can be improved apparently converges toward a number near zero.

Tests did not indicate evidence of harvest (H) depending on client location (P1) and service endpoint (P4), respectively.

4   Related Work

Garfinkel described early hands-on experience with Amazon Simple Storage Service (S3), Elastic Compute Cloud (EC2), and Simple Queue Service (SQS) in a technical report [7]. The author performed thorough performance benchmarking of S3 and EC2 and found that EC2 and S3 delivered on their promises to provide scalability and high availability. In some tests, S3 did not provide good through-put, though. Garfinkel also tested SQS, however not as extensively as the other two Web services.

Binning et al. are the first to suggest that cloud services require a benchmarking approach and tools that are considerably different from traditional benchmarking [8]. The authors point out that cloud services are different from traditional software systems with respect to cost model, performance, scalability, consistency guarantees, fault-tolerance, and other properties. For our benchmarking tests we focused on the metric harvest, introduced by Fox and Brewer

[2] to measure client-side consistency behavior. Yu and Vahdat suggest the concept of a *consistency unit* (conit) as a means to quantitatively express and measure a continuous consistency range and *continuous consistency programming* as a software development approach to create consistency-aware applications [9]. This approach is viable for on-premise systems, but not for hosted services like Amazon SQS.

5   Conclusion and Future Work

Software developers are confronted with a general problem when using cloud-based middleware services: eventual consistency. We proposed an approach to consistency benchmarking along with a prototypical implementation and used the prototype to conduct experiments on Amazaon SQS. The results show that frequent service requests result in better harvest, probably due to the fact that SQS uses server sampling. Client location and service endpoint location, on the other hand, did not appear to have an influence on harvest. With our tests, we never detected duplicate messages or unavailability of service. Future work will extend our basic approach to measure a richer set of properties of more complex software stacks.

References

1. Bernstein, P.A.: Middleware: A model for distributed system services. ACM Commun 39(2) (1996)
2. Fox, A., Brewer, E.A.: Harvest, yield, and scalable tolerant systems. In: Proceedings of the 7th Workshop on Hot Topics in Operating Systems (1999)
3. Gilbert, S., Lynch, N.: Brewer's conjecture and the feasibility of consistent available partition-tolerant web services. ACM SIGACT News 3(2), 51–59 (2002)
4. Vogels, W.: Eventually consistent. ACM Comm. 52(1), 40–44 (2009)
5. Pritchett, D.: BASE: An ACID alternative. Queue 6(3), 48–55 (2008)
6. Amazon Web Services LLC: Amazon Simple Queue Service developer guide - API version 2009-02-01 (2010)
7. Garfinkel, S.: An evaluation of Amazon's grid computing services: EC2, S3 and SQS. Tech. Rep. TR-08-07, Harvard University (2007)
8. Binnig, C., Kossmann, D., Kraska, T., Loesing, S.: How is the Weather tomorrow? Towards a Benchmark for the Cloud. In: DBTest Workshop (ACM SIGMOD), Providence, USA (2009)
9. Yu, H., Vahdat, A.: Design and evaluation of a conit-based continuous consistency model for replicated services. ACM Transactions on Computer Systems 20(3), 239–282 (2002)

Service Composition with Pareto-Optimality of Time-Dependent QoS Attributes

Benjamin Klöpper*, Fuyuki Ishikawa, and Shinichi Honiden

National Institute of Informatics, 2-1-2 Hitotsubashi, Chiyoda-ku, Tokyo, Japan

Abstract. Quality of Services (QoS) plays an essential role in realizing user tasks by service composition. Most QoS-aware service composition approaches have ignored the fact that QoS values can depend on the time of execution. Common QoS attributes such as response time may depend for instance on daytime, due to access tendency or conditional Service of Level Agreements. Application-specific QoS attributes often have tight relationships with the current state of resources, such as availability of hotel rooms. In response to these problems, this paper proposes an integrated multi-objective approach to QoS-aware service composition and selection.

Keywords: Service Composition, Multi-objective Optimization.

1 Introduction

Both, functional and non-functional properties - the latter expressed by Quality of Service (QoS) Attributes - have to be taking into account when identifying a suitable composition of a user task. Current approaches consider these QoS attributes to be static, so they do not change over time. Hence, these approaches cannot properly reflect certain business models or the interaction with scarce resources. For instance, service providers maybe use flexible price models in order to level the utilization of their computational resources. Furthermore, the availability and hence the price of goods and non-computational services are also time-dependent, e.g. flight tickets or hotel rooms get less overtime. Hence, composition approaches should be able to consider the time-dependency of QoS attributes. Furthermore, this time dependency makes the decision problem more complex and hardly comprehensible for human users. A composition process is desirable that presents a set of relevant solutions to the user.

2 The Timed Service Composition Problem

To realize a user task by a composed service, two problems must be solved. First, a workflow must be identified that implements the user task. Often, alternative workflows can be found. Second, specific service instances must be selected to implement the workflow. If these problems are solved subsequently, only local optima can be found. Hence, we introduce an integrated solution approach.

---

* Benjamin Klöpper is a visiting researcher and scholarship holder of the (DAAD).

P.P. Maglio et al. (Eds.): ICSOC 2010, LNCS 6470, pp. 635–640, 2010.

2.1   Workflow Model

The service model used throughout the paper follows basically a model introduced by Kalasapur et al. [3]. A user service s is described by a workflow schema, a directed acyclic graph (DAG) $w = (ST, D, Source, Sink)$ where the vertex set ST represents the services required to implement the user service and the edge set D describes input-output relation or dependencies between two services. If there is a $d = (st_a, st_b) \in D$ and $st_a, st_b \in ST$, the service st_a has to be accomplished before st_b can start. To include alternative workflow schemes for the implementation of user services, we extend the model from [3]. Two different types of *services* are considered:

1. Atomic services (S_A): services offered by a service provider
2. Complex services (S_C): services with alternative workflow schemes

A complex service $cs \in S_C$ is a set of alternative workflow schemes W_{cs}. The composition of a complex service cs consists of the implementation of all services s_t in one of the workflows $w_{cs} \in W_{cs}$. An implementation of an atomic service is defined by the selection of a service instance offered by a service provider and a corresponding start time. A specific implementation of a service s is referred to as i_s.

2.2   Solution of the Timed-Composition Problem

A timed composition plan CP of a user service or complex service cs is the set of all service instances $s_o, ..., s_k$ from a workflow schema $w_{cs} \in W_{cs}$ with start time $start_i$ and finishing time $finish_i$ of each service instance s_i in the list. A feasible composition plan contains no service instances s_i and s_j such that there is a directed edge from s_j to s_i in the workflow schema w_{cs} and s_i starts before s_j ends. A number of QoS attributes qa [1..n-1] and the response time of the user service i_{cs} establish a n-dimensional vector PV, describing the performance of the composition plan. Given the n-dimensional vector, the pareto-optimality of composition plans can be defined. A composition plan with performance vector PV is pareto-optimal or non-dominated if there is no other composition plan with performance vector PV' such that:

$$PV_i' \leq PV_i \; \forall i, 1 \leq i \leq n+1 \text{ and } PV_i' < PV_i \; \exists i, 1 \leq i \leq n+1 \qquad (1)$$

If FS is the set of feasible solutions, a pareto-optimal composition process returns a set PO with all performance vectors that satisfy two conditions:

$$\forall pv_{po} \in PO : \nexists s \in FS : pv_s \prec pv_{po} \qquad (2)$$
$$\forall pv_{po} \in PO : \exists s \in FS : pv_s = pv_{po} \qquad (3)$$

2.3   Monotone Quality of Service Attributes

If QoS attributes depend in execution time and response time is a relevant QoS attribute, a potential trade-off occurs: It is possible to achieve a gain in some QoS attributes by delaying the execution of a service. To catch this trade-off properly in the composition problem, we will assume that the QoS attributes of service instances are monotonically decreasing. Any service instance without this property will be split into several logical service instances with an earliest and latest start time. These logical services are encapsulated in a complex service, where each alternative workflow consists of exactly one atomic service with the corresponding earliest and latest start time.

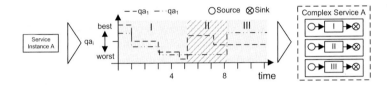

Fig. 1. Service Instance split into Logical Instances I, II, III with Monotony Property

3   Partial Composition Plan Search Tree

This section maps the timed composition problem defined above to a search problem. Each node in the search tree represents a partial composition plan of the complex service to be composed, selecting a number of specific services for composition. Starting from an empty composition (no services are selected) the partial composition plans subsequently are extended until a complete composition is found.

A partial composition plan is a tuple $(S_{pc}, A_{pc}, N_{pc}, ST_{pc}, FT_{pc})$, where S_{pc} is the set of services selected for the composition plan (complex services and atomic service), A_{pc} is the set of services available for expansion, and N_{pc} contains all services that are not yet available. A service is available for expansion, if all its predecessors from the corresponding service graph are already included in S_{pc}. ST_{pc} and FT_{pc} are two functions mapping the service S_{pc} to their start and finishing times. The start time of any service is determined by the latest finishing time of any of its predecessors in the workflow schema and the earliest start time of the service. The root of the search tree is the partial composition plan which contains the services from the user specified service and S_{pc} is empty, A_{pc} contains only the source of the user service workflow and N_{pc} contains all remaining services.

Partial composition plans are extended towards a complete composition plan by two repeated steps. In the first step, a service s from A_{pc} is selected for expansion. In the second step, all offspring pc' regarding parent pc and selected service s are generated. Regarding the generation of offspring, two cases have to be distinguished. In the *first case* a service instance as from the set A_{pc} is added to the partial composition plan. The result is one offspring for each service instance. In each of these new partial composition plans, as is added to the set of selected services S_{pc}. The earliest start time depends on the latest finishing time of any predecessor service, the finish time as well as the QoS attributes q_a depend on the performance offered by the service provider at start time. In this way, the QoS attributes of a service instance depends of the selected start time of its predecessor. After adding as to the set C_{pc}, all services from N_{pc} that are now available are moved to A_{pc}.

In the *second case*, a complex service cs from the set A_{pc} is added to the composition plan. The result is one offspring for each decomposition d of the complex service. In each new partial composition plan, the source node of the decomposition d is added to the set of selected services S_{pc}. The remaining services from the decomposition are added to A_{pc} if the source is their only predecessor or to N_{pc} otherwise. The complex service cs will be finally moved to A_{pc}, when the sink node of d is moved to A_{pc}. Hence, all successors of cs can become available, when the decomposition d is entirely included in the partial composition plan. Given these two expansion operations, a search tree is defined. The leaves of the tree are complete composition plans of the user specified service. A composition plan is complete, when the two sets A_{pc} and N_{pc} are empty. We refer to the set of leaves reachable from partial composition pc as CP_{pc}.

Given an admissible heuristic function that systematically underestimates the distance towards a complete schedule; heuristic search algorithms can be used to identify optimal compositions. The extension to the multi-objective case is done by not optimizing a scalar value (e.g. weighted sum over all QoS attributes), but identifying all non-dominated compositions regarding the n-dimensional objective vector. In [4] we introduced a suitable heuristic function. Hence, multi-objective heuristic search algorithms (for instance, cf. [6,5]) can be used to identify the set of non-dominated compositions.

3.1   Use Case with Multi-objective Search Based Composition

Figure 2 shows an example user task with two alternative workflows. As well, the complex task E_1 encompasses two alternative workflows, the first one consisting of a single task and the second one consisting of two subsequent tasks.

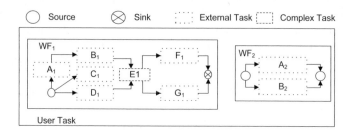

Fig. 2. User Task

For the evaluation regarding the use case, the time-dependent QoS attributes and the execution time were randomly chosen. The QoS attributes for each service instance were generated for a time horizon with 100 time points. The attributes were generated as monotone increasing on time intervals between 3 and 7 time steps. Hence, each service instance is split into 15 up to 34 logical service instances.

Figure 3 shows results from experiments[1] with different of service instances. Each experiment consisted in 50 randomly generated problem instances. Figure 3(a) shows that the run-times do not solely depend on the size of the problem, but also on the relation between the objective functions. The maximum run-times for bigger instances are significantly too long for interactive systems. Figure 3(b) on the other hand shows that a feasible solution can be found rather fast (below one second). This is a strong hint, that anytime algorithms could be developed for interactive systems.

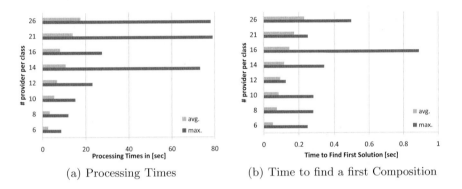

(a) Processing Times   (b) Time to find a first Composition

Fig. 3. Experimental Results from the Example Problem

4   Related Work

The introduced service model and solution procedure are in between *staged composition and execution* and *template-based composition* [1]. The composition is not as static as in template based approaches, but the structure of complex services resembles predefined workflow scheme. The hierarchical structure and the subsequent refinement of complex tasks resembles Hierarchical Task Network Planning (HTN) that is quite popular in the service community [2]. HTN based approaches do not consider time-dependent attributes and cannot find the set of non-dominated compositions regarding a set of QoS attributes. Multi-objective approaches for service composition were until now limited to template-based approaches [7,8].

---

[1] Performed on a PC with an Intel Core 2 Quad CPU (2.99Ghz), 8GB RAM, Windows 7 64 Bit, JVM 1.6 using a single thread implementation.

5   Conclusion

In this paper we introduced the *timed service composition problem* that considers time-dependent QoS attributes. Furthermore, we mapped the problem to a search problem and showed first results of the implementation of a composition algorithms based on multi-objective heuristic search. In our opinion, the *timed service composition problem* is an important step towards the proper consideration of complex business models of service providers as well as scarce physical resources and services, such as hotel rooms or flight tickets. The employment of the multi-objective composition algorithm is more straightforward then classical single objective approaches because a priori definition of an objective function is not necessary. To use the approach in practical application, approximation algorithms have to be developed and implemented.

References

1. Argarwal, V., Chafle, G., Mittal, S., Srivastava, B.: Understanding Approaches for Web Service Composition and Execution. In: Proceedings of the 1st Bangalore Annual Compute Conference, ACN (2008)
2. Chen, K., Xu, J., Reiff-Marganiec, S.: Markov-HTN Planning Approach to Enhance Flexibility of Automatic Web Service Composition. In: IEEE International Conference on Web Services, pp. 9–16 (2009)
3. Kalasupur, S., Kumar, M., Behrooz, A.: Dynamic Service Composition in Pervasive Computing. IEEE Transactions on Parallel and Distributed System 18, 907–917 (2007)
4. Klöpper, B.: First Steps Towards Distributed Multiobjective Scheduling for Self-Optimizing Manufacturing Systems. In: 10th IFAC Workshop on Intelligent Manufacturing Systems (2010)
5. Mandow, L., Pérez de la Cruz, J. L.: A new approach to multiobjective A* Search. In: Proceedings of the Nineteenth International Joint Conference on Artificial Intelligence (IJCAI 2005). pp. 218–223. Edinburgh, Scotland (2005)
6. Stewart, B.S., White, C.C.: Multiobjective A*. Journal of the Association for Computing Machinery 38(4), 775–814 (1991)
7. Wang, J., Hou, Y.: Optimal Web Service Selection based on Multi-Objective Genetic Algorithm. In: International Symposium on Computational Intelligence and Design (2008)
8. Zeng, L., Benatallah, B., Ngu., A., Dumas, M., Kalagnanam, Chang, H.: QoS-Aware Middleware for Web Services Composition. IEEE Transactions on Software Engineering 30, 311–327 (2004)

QoS-Based Optimization of Service Compositions for Complex Workflows

Dieter Schuller, André Miede, Julian Eckert, Ulrich Lampe,
Apostolos Papageorgiou, and Ralf Steinmetz

Multimedia Communications Lab (KOM),
Technische Universität Darmstadt, Germany
firstname.lastname@KOM.tu-darmstadt.de

Abstract. In Service-oriented Architectures, business processes can be realized by composing loosely coupled services. If services in the Internet of Services with comparable functionalities but varying quality levels are available at different costs on service marketplaces, service requesters can decide, which services from which service providers to select. The work at hand addresses computing an optimal solution to this service-selection-problem considering complex workflow patterns. For this, a linear optimization problem is formulated, which can be solved by applying integer linear programming techniques.

Keywords: Optimization, Service Selection, Quality of Service, Complex Workflows.

1 Introduction

In highly competitive markets with similar products and services, enterprises are facing a tough cost pressure. Their offered products and services need to be constructed and provided efficiently. Therefore, efficient process execution is mandatory. With respect to the globalization and the deregulation of markets, enterprises are forced to react quickly to changing environments, driven by market forces, and adapt their business processes. This requires the business processes to be flexible. But as IT architectures within an enterprise are often heterogeneous, the required flexibility is hard to achieve. Even within a single enterprise, a certain amount of legacy systems and a couple of applications exist running on different operating systems and middleware platforms, implemented with different programming languages. An approach for integrating these legacy systems and applications is necessary in order to realize the required flexible and efficient business processes.

In Service-oriented Architectures (SOA), business processes can be realized by composing loosely coupled services, which autonomously provide a more or less complex functionality depending on their granularity (cf. [1]). To support and enable agile business processes, the SOA paradigm is often recommended [2]. In the Internet of Services, typically multiple service providers offer equal or rather similar services regarding the services' functionalities at different Quality

P.P. Maglio et al. (Eds.): ICSOC 2010, LNCS 6470, pp. 641–648, 2010.
© Springer-Verlag Berlin Heidelberg 2010

of Service (QoS) levels and at different costs on service marketplaces. This gives
enterprises the opportunity to select those services which meet their business
and QoS requirements best. The problem of selecting appropriate services which
meet specified QoS and cost conditions and restrictions for business processes
– the service-selection-problem – is well known in the literature and has been
discussed recently by several authors [3,4,5]. An optimal selection of services and
their invocation results in an efficient business process execution. Therefore, the
work at hand addresses the computation of an optimal solution to the service-
selection-problem for complex workflows by formulating a linear optimization
problem, which can be solved optimally by applying integer linear programming
(ILP) [6]. It extends our approach in [7] by taking recursive interlacings of these
patterns into account.

The rest of this work is structured as follows. In Section 2, we distinguish our
approach from related work in this field. The considered workflow patterns and
the applied system model is depicted in Section 3. An approach for recursively interlacing the required QoS aggregation functions is discussed in Section 4. In Section 5, the computation of an optimal execution plan taking recursive workflow
pattern interlacings into account is addressed. Finally, in Section 6, conclusions
are drawn and future work is discussed.

2   Related Work

A lot of work has been done regarding the service-selection-problem. Several authors propose and implement heuristic solutions to this problem [3,8,9]. Further,
also tree-based algorithms are proposed in [4]. Here, the complex workflow is
transformed into a tree-like execution structure (BPTree) based on the alignment of the considered workflow patterns. An optimal solution to the service-
selection-problem is proposed in [10,11]. The respective authors solve this problem for complex workflows by unfolding arbitrary cycles and computing optimal
execution plans for each possible path in the complex workflow, thereby formulating and solving a linear optimization problem using ILP solely for sequential
workflows.

This is overcome in the work at hand, as (in our approach) the knowledge of
all possible execution paths is not necessary in advance. Our aim is to describe
and implement an approach that enables the computation of an optimal solution
to the service-selection-problem for complex workflows without considering each
execution path separately and for recursive interlacings of these patterns, which
– to the best of our knowledge – has not been addressed in the literature so far.
Thus, we create a sort of benchmark, enabling other (heuristic) approaches to
evaluate their achieved solution quality without having to calculate the optimal
solution with brute force algorithms (checking out the whole solution space)
but by (simply) applying ILP. In case, scalability issues are foregrounded, the
heuristic solution method proposed in [12] can be applied to our approach.

3   System Model

In order to formulate the mentioned linear optimization problem – consisting of an objective function and a set of process conditions – in Section 5, we present the applied system model in this section. Thereby, an abstract business process (written, e.g., in Business Process Modeling Notation – BPMN) consisting of n abstract process steps respectively tasks (we will use these terms synonymously) is assumed. In the work at hand, the process steps may be arraged according to the workflow patterns *sequence*, *parallel split* (AND-split), *synchronization* (AND-join), *exclusive choice* (XOR-split), *simple merge* (XOR-join), which are described in [13]. Additionally, the *simple loop* pattern (cf. [14]) is considered. Besides concatenating these patterns, they can be interlaced recursively to create complex workflows respectively complex business processes. An example for such a complex workflow is given in Figure 1. The process steps in this figure are abbreviated with *PS*.

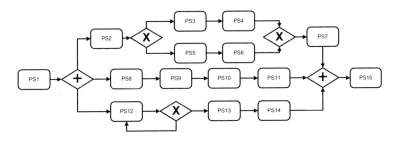

Fig. 1. Example Workflow

The set of all tasks is labeled with I, $i \in I = \{1, ..., n\}$. Each task is accomplished by exactly one service $j \in J_i = \{1, ..., m_i\}$. The decision-variables $x_{ij} \in \{0, 1\}$ state, whether service j is selected for task i or not. As QoS parameters, we take execution time e (the time it takes to execute the service), costs c (costs for the invocation of a service), reliability r (the probability that the service successfully executes), and throughput d (number of parallel service invocations) into account. These parameters – in fact, even a subset of these parameters – are sufficient to cover the aggregation types summation, multiplication and min/max-operator, so that the integration of further QoS parameters into the optimization problem is straightforward. The respective restrictions (bounds) are labeled with $b_{[index]}$. We further consider a pay-per-use pricing model.

When it comes to branchings, we define the set L of paths l as $l \in L = \{1, ..., l^\#\}$. Thus, l represents the respective path number within a branching. To make this clear, we refer to Figure 1. After a successful execution of PS_1, the following AND-split branches into three paths l (so $L = \{1, 2, 3\}$), beginning with PS_2, PS_8, PS_{12}. The set $IW_L \subseteq I$ represents the set of tasks within a branching and $IW_l \subseteq IW_L$ the set of tasks within path $l \in L$. The remaining tasks (not located within a branching) are covered in the set $IS = I \backslash (IW_l | l \in L)$.

The parameter p_l indicates the probability that path l is executed. We thereby assume $\sum_{l \in L} p_l = 1$.

4 Recursive Workflow Pattern Interlacing

In order to formulate the optimization problem, it is necessary to aggregate the considered QoS parameters and to restrict them to their respective process conditions. Referring to our work in [7], we propose the aggregation functions in Table 1 to address the workflow patterns mentioned in Section 3.

Table 1. Aggregation Functions

QoS	Sequence	AND-split/-join	XOR-split/-join
e	$\sum\limits_{i \in IS} \sum\limits_{j \in J_i} e_{ij} x_{ij}$	$\max\limits_{l \in L} \left(\sum\limits_{i \in IW_l} \sum\limits_{j \in J_i} e_{ij} x_{ij} \right)$	$\sum\limits_{l \in L} p_l \sum\limits_{i \in IW_l} \sum\limits_{j \in J_i} e_{ij} x_{ij}$
c	$\sum\limits_{i \in IS} \sum\limits_{j \in J_i} c_{ij} x_{ij}$	$\sum\limits_{l \in L} \sum\limits_{i \in IW_l} \sum\limits_{j \in J_i} c_{ij} x_{ij}$	$\sum\limits_{l \in L} p_l \sum\limits_{i \in IW_l} \sum\limits_{j \in J_i} c_{ij} x_{ij}$
r	$\prod\limits_{i \in IS} \sum\limits_{j \in J_i} r_{ij} x_{ij}$	$\prod\limits_{l \in L} \prod\limits_{i \in IW_l} \sum\limits_{j \in J_i} r_{ij} x_{ij}$	$\sum\limits_{l \in L} p_l \prod\limits_{i \in IW_l} \sum\limits_{j \in J_i} r_{ij} x_{ij}$
d	$\min\limits_{i \in IS} \left(\sum\limits_{j \in J_i} d_{ij} x_{ij} \right)$	$\min\limits_{l \in L} \left(\min\limits_{i \in IW_l} \left(\sum\limits_{j \in J_i} d_{ij} x_{ij} \right) \right)$	$\sum\limits_{l \in L} p_l \min\limits_{i \in IW_l} \left(\sum\limits_{j \in J_i} d_{ij} x_{ij} \right)$

But applying these aggregation functions for the optimization implies a sequential arrangement of the process steps within a split and join (cf. [7]). Therefore, we describe in this section an approach to account for recursive interlacings of workflow patterns to overcome this shortcoming. An example for such an interlacing is given in Figure 1. Here, after the AND-split, the process steps in the path starting with PS_2 are not arranged sequentially. Subsequent to PS_2, another split and join follows. To cope with this situation, we abstract from the interlacing by creating a "new" service which represents a composition of the services able to realize the respective tasks within the interlacing. Referring to Figure 1, we build a service by loosely coupling the alternative services for PS_3, PS_4, PS_5, PS_6 according to the structural arrangement of these process steps in the workflow, i.e., XOR-split with XOR-join. This way, we exchange PS_3, PS_4, PS_5, PS_6 for PS_{3456} to obtain a sequential arrangement of the "remaining" process steps PS_2, PS_{3456}, PS_7. To compute the QoS values of the newly composed service, we introduce variables e'_l, c'_l, r'_l, d'_l (with respect to the considered QoS parameters) and apply the appropriate aggregation functions from Table 1 – depending on the kind of split and join. Regarding Figure 1, we specify e'_l, r'_l, d'_l in (1) to (3) – c'_l is specified analogously to e'_l – by applying the respective aggregation functions for XOR-split with XOR-join. Integrating these variables into the optimization problem and performing the described abstraction enables the application of the aggregation functions Table 1 for the optimization.

$$e'_l := \begin{cases} \sum\limits_{l \in L} p_l \sum\limits_{i \in IW_l} \sum\limits_{j \in J_i} e_{ij} x_{ij} & \text{, if interlacing at path } l \\ 0 & \text{, else} \end{cases} \qquad (1)$$

$$r'_l := \begin{cases} \sum_{l \in L} p_l \prod_{i \in IW_l} \sum_{j \in J_i} r_{ij} x_{ij} & \text{, if interlacing at path } l \\ 1 & \text{, else} \end{cases} \tag{2}$$

$$d'_l := \begin{cases} \sum_{l \in L} p_l \cdot \min_{i \in IW_l} (\sum_{j \in J_i} d_{ij} x_{ij}) & \text{, if interlacing at path } l \\ \infty & \text{, else} \end{cases} \tag{3}$$

5 Optimization Problem

In this section, we formulate a non-linear optimization problem in Model 1 by specifying the target function in (4) – aiming at minimizing overall costs of the selected services – and restrictions for the aggregated QoS values addressing workflows arbitrarily compiled by combining sequences, AND-splits/-joins, XOR-splits/-joins and Loops. Due to column width, we define $y_{ij} = d_{ij} x_{ij}$ and introduce c_s, c_a, c_x representing the costs for the respective patterns. Further, we use L_a, L_x to separate AND-splits from XOR-splits. In order to consider Loops, we would exchange the QoS parameters e, c, r for the adapted parameters e^*, c^*, r^* defined in Table 2 (c^* is defined analogously to e^*; d is not affected by a Loop) (cf. [7]).

In conditions (5) to (8), the restrictions for the regarded QoS parameters are depicted. By integrating e'_l, c'_l, r'_l, d'_l in (5) to (8), we take additional interlacings within the AND-split/-join part into account. The values of e'_l, c'_l, r'_l, d'_l are determined in (9) to (12) by applying the respective aggregation functions for an XOR-split with XOR-join. This way, also other (and more complex) interlacings can be considered. Condition (13) ensures that exactly one service is selected to realize a process step and condition (14) represents the integrality condition.

As the min/max-operator as well as the multiplication are non-linear aggregation types regarding the decision-variables x_{ij}, we require to adapt these non-linear functions and terms in order to obtain a linear optimization problem, which can be solved optimally by applying ILP techniques. To linearize the term with the max-operator in (5), we exchange this term for e_a^{max} and add condition (15) to Model 1. Analogously, additional variables d^{min} are specified and appropriate conditions for each min-operator in (8) are added to Model 1. Regarding condition (7), we apply the approximation in (16) to (7) – which is very accurate for parameter values z_{ij} very close to 1 (such as reliability) – and exchange (7) for (17), which is linear regarding x_{ij}.

$$e'_l + \sum_{i \in IW_l} \sum_{j \in J_i} e_{ij} x_{ij} \leq e_a^{max} \qquad \forall l \in L \tag{15}$$

$$\prod_{i \in I} \sum_{j \in J_i} z_{ij} x_{ij} \approx 1 - \sum_{i \in I} (1 - \sum_{j \in J_i} z_{ij} x_{ij}) \tag{16}$$

$$1 - \sum_{l \in L_x} (p_l \sum_{i \in (IS \vee IW_{L_a} \vee IW_l)} (1 - \sum_{j \in J_i} r_{ij} x_{ij})) \geq b_r \tag{17}$$

Model 1. Optimization Problem

Objective Function

$$\text{minimize } F(x) = c_s + c_a + c_x \tag{4}$$

so that

$$\sum_{i \in IS} \sum_{j \in J_i} e_{ij} x_{ij} + \max_{l \in L_a}(e'_l + \sum_{i \in IW_l} \sum_{j \in J_i} e_{ij} x_{ij}) + \sum_{l \in L_x} p_l \sum_{i \in IW_l} \sum_{j \in J_i} e_{ij} x_{ij} \le b_e \tag{5}$$

$$\sum_{i \in IS} \sum_{j \in J_i} c_{ij} x_{ij} + \sum_{l \in L_a}(c'_l + \sum_{i \in IW_l} \sum_{j \in J_i} c_{ij} x_{ij}) + \sum_{l \in L_x} p_l \sum_{i \in IW_l} \sum_{j \in J_i} c_{ij} x_{ij} \le b_c \tag{6}$$

$$\left(\prod_{i \in IS} \sum_{j \in J_i} r_{ij} x_{ij} \right) \cdot \left(\prod_{l \in L_a}(r'_l \cdot \prod_{i \in IW_l} \sum_{j \in J_i} r_{ij} x_{ij}) \right) \cdot \left(\sum_{l \in L_x} p_l \prod_{i \in IW_l} \sum_{j \in J_i} r_{ij} x_{ij} \right) \ge b_r \tag{7}$$

$$\min \left(\min_{i \in IS}(\sum_{j \in J_i} y_{ij}), \min_{l \in L_a}(d'_l, \min_{i \in IW_l}(\sum_{j \in J_i} y_{ij})), \sum_{l \in L_x} p_l \cdot \min_{i \in IW_l}(\sum_{j \in J_i} y_{ij}) \right) \ge b_d \tag{8}$$

$$\sum_{l \in L} p_l \sum_{i \in IW_l} \sum_{j \in J_i} e_{ij} x_{ij} = e'_l \qquad \forall l \in L_a | \text{ interlacing at path } l \tag{9}$$

$$\sum_{l \in L} p_l \sum_{i \in IW_l} \sum_{j \in J_i} c_{ij} x_{ij} = c'_l \qquad \forall l \in L_a | \text{ interlacing at path } l \tag{10}$$

$$\sum_{l \in L} p_l \prod_{i \in IW_l} \sum_{j \in J_i} r_{ij} x_{ij} = r'_l \qquad \forall l \in L_a | \text{ interlacing at path } l \tag{11}$$

$$\sum_{l \in L} p_l \cdot \min_{i \in IW_l}(\sum_{j \in J_i} d_{ij} x_{ij}) = d'_l \qquad \forall l \in L_a | \text{ interlacing at path } l \tag{12}$$

$$\sum_{j \in J_i} x_{ij} = 1 \qquad \forall i \in I \tag{13}$$

$$x_{ij} \in \{0, 1\} \qquad \forall i \in I, \forall j \in J_i \tag{14}$$

By performing these adaptation and substitution steps, we transform Model 1 into a linear optimization problem. To compute an optimal solution to this problem – if a solution exists – ILP can be applied. In order to address scalability issues we propose to relax the integrality conditions for the decision-variables x_{ij} and calculate an optimal solution using mixed integer linear programming (MILP) (cf. [6]). A valid (probably non-optimal) solution – containing integer values for x_{ij} – is obtained afterwards by selecting those services, which satisfy the constraints, based on the decision-variables' values. A possible heuristic

Table 2. Aggregation Functions

	Ex. time	Reliability
Loop	$e^*_{ij} := \begin{cases} \frac{1}{1-\rho_i} e_{ij} & \text{, if } i \in I_{loop} \\ e_{ij} & \text{, else} \end{cases}$	$r^*_{ij} := \begin{cases} \frac{(1-\rho_i)r_{ij}}{1-\rho_i r_{ij}} & \text{, if } i \in I_{loop} \\ r_{ij} & \text{, else} \end{cases}$

approach could be H1_RELAX_IP [12], which is not performing significantly worse compared to the optimal solution (cf. [15]).

6   Conclusion and Outlook

In highly competitive markets, flexible and efficient business process execution is mandatory. By applying service-based processes and selecting services which meet the enterprises' business and QoS requirements best, the mentioned flexibility and efficiency can be increased. This leads to the service-selection-problem which has attracted a lot of research efforts recently. But complex workflows have thereby only insufficiently been addressed in the literature (cf. Section 2). The work at hand enables the computation of the optimal solution to the service-selection-problem without requiring to consider all possible execution paths. It extends previous solutions in this field by allowing arbitrary combinations (including recursive interlacings) of the workflow patterns sequence, AND-split with AND-join, XOR-split with XOR-join, and Loops. We presented an approach to compute an optimal solution to the service-selection-problem by formulating a linear optimization problem for complex workflows, which can be solved optimally using ILP techniques. Applying the optimal service selection increases the mentioned efficiency regarding business process execution.

In our future work, we will focus on integrating security features as qualitative service properties into the optimization. The aim is to arrive at a more or less *secure* communication between service requester, provider and broker, and to ascertain and assess the achieved Quality of Protection (QoP). This achieved QoP will then be considered as additional QoS parameter in the optimization.

Acknowledgements. This work is supported in part by E-Finance Lab e. V., Frankfurt am Main, Germany (http://www.efinancelab.com).

References

1. Krafzig, D., Banke, K., Slama, D.: Enterprise SOA: Service-Oriented Architecture Best Practices. Prentice Hall PTR, Upper Saddle River (2004)
2. Papazoglou, M.P.: Service-Oriented Computing: Concepts, Characteristics and Directions. In: Proceedings of WISE, pp. 3–12 (2003)
3. Anselmi, J., Ardagna, D., Cremonesi, P.: A QoS-based Selection Approach of Autonomic Grid Services. In: Proceedings of ICSOC, pp. 1–8 (2007)
4. Menascé, D.A., Casalicchio, E., Dubey, V.: A Heuristic Approach to optimal Service Selection in Service-oriented Architectures. In: Proceedings of WOSP, pp. 13–24 (2008)
5. Huang, A.F.M., Lan, C.W., Yang, S.J.H.: An optimal QoS-based Web Service Selection Scheme. Information Sciences 179(19), 3309–3322 (2009)
6. Domschke, W., Drexl, A.: Einführung in Operations Research. Springer, Heidelberg (2007)
7. Schuller, D., Eckert, J., Miede, A., Schulte, S., Steinmetz, R.: QoS-Aware Service Composition for Complex Workflows. In: Proceedings of ICIW (2010)

8. Jaeger, M.C., Rojec-Goldmann, G.: SENECA-Simulation of Algorithms for Selection of Web Services for Composition. In: Proceedings of TES, pp. 84–97 (2005)
9. Mabrouk, N.B., Georgantas, N., Issarny, V.: A semantic end-to-end QoS Model for dynamic Service oriented Environments. In: Proceedings of PESOS, pp. 34–41 (2009)
10. Ardagna, D., Pernici, B.: Adaptive Service Composition in Flexible Processes. Transactions on Software Engineering 33(6), 369–384 (2007)
11. Zeng, L., Benatallah, B., Ngu, A.H., Dumas, M., Kalagnanam, J., Chang, H.: QoS-Aware Middleware for Web Services Composition. Transactions on Software Engineering 30(5), 311–327 (2004)
12. Berbner, R., Spahn, M., Repp, N., Heckmann, O., Steinmetz, R.: Heuristics for QoS-aware Web Service Composition. In: Proceedings of ICWS, pp. 72–82 (2006)
13. Van Der Aalst, W.M.P., Ter Hofstede, A.H.M., Kiepuszewski, B., Barros, A.P.: Workflow Patterns. Distributed Parallel Databases 14(1), 5–51 (2003)
14. Cardoso, J., Sheth, A.P., Miller, J.A., Arnold, J., Kochut, K.: QoS for Workflows and Web Service Processes. Journal of Web Semantics 1(3), 281–308 (2004)
15. Berbner, R., Spahn, M., Repp, N., Heckmann, O., Steinmetz, R.: Dynamic Replanning of Web Service Workflows. In: Proceedings of DEST, pp. 211–216 (2007)

Privacy-Aware Device Identifier through a Trusted Web Service

Marcelo da Cruz Pinto, Ricardo Morin,
Maria Emilia Torino, and Danny Varner

Intel Corporation
{juan.m.da.cruz.pinto,ricardo.a.morin,maria.e.torino,
danny.varner}@intel.com

Abstract. Device identifiers can be used to enhance authentication mechanisms for conducting online business. However, personal computers (PC) today are not equipped with standardized, privacy-aware hardware-based device identifiers for general use. This paper describes the implementation of privacy-aware device identifiers using the capabilities of the Trusted Platform Module (TPM) and extending the trust boundary of the device using a Web Service. It also describes a case study based on a device reputation service.

Keywords: device identifiers, identity, privacy, protected execution, reputation systems, TPM, Web Services.

1 Introduction

Internet usage is permeating many aspects of our life. E-Commerce, online communities, media services and many other sectors are growing at a rapid pace. At the same time, issues such as fraud, identity theft and spoofing are real problems [7]. For example, in 2009 the online revenue loss due to fraud has been estimated at USD 3.3 billion [5].

To help address these issues, multifactor authentication can be used to enhance the ability of identifying parties engaged in online business, but it usually requires the issuance of tokens or other devices as a supplemental mechanism for identity proof [9]. One way of enhancing authentication is to use platform-specific device identifiers in lieu of tokens, but these are not standardized in commodity personal computers (PC). This leads to the usage of proprietary software-based methods that attempt to generate device identifiers through multiple sources such as IP address, MAC address, and browser cookies, all of which can be easily spoofed. It is therefore desirable to have the ability to establish and use device identifiers that are hard to tamper with by strongly rooting them in the device's hardware.

One of the key challenges with unique device identifiers is how to preserve the user's privacy, i.e., ensuring complete control over the usage of artifacts that may expose their identity. Users should be able to opt-in and opt-out of requests to release device identifiers for authentication or tracking applications. In addition,

P.P. Maglio et al. (Eds.): ICSOC 2010, LNCS 6470, pp. 649–656, 2010.

device identifiers should be protected from being used to link interactions across multiple sites or domains without the explicit consent of the user.

Today, an increasing number of PCs are being furnished with a Trusted Platform Module (TPM) [6]. The TPM provides hardware assisted key generation, secure storage of keys and hashes, and basic cryptographic functions. However, the TPM does not provide a general purpose protected execution environment for deploying algorithms needed to deliver privacy aware device identifiers. While it is possible to establish multiple, unlinkable device identifiers using the TPM through multiple attestation keys [4], the system is vulnerable to malware software extracting various identifiers or keys and sending them to a remote server for linking, thus compromising the users privacy.

In this paper, we describe the implementation of a strong device identifier (Device ID) that could be used by service providers to make decisions on the trustworthiness of transactions emanating from a device, while protecting the privacy of the user. We explore extending the trust boundary of a TPM-equipped device out to a trusted Web Service hosted in the cloud thus leveraging an execution environment that is protected from local attacks.

Our approach is privacy-aware because it a) requires user opt-in, b) protects device unique keys generated by the TPM, c) ensures that Device IDs are application, site and/or domain specific under the control of the user, and d) users can opt-out by removing Device IDs if desired.

To illustrate the proposed solution we describe a use case based on a hypothetical device reputation system that uses a tamper-proof persistent Device ID as the basis for its identity system.

2   Requirements

Access control: The user shall be in control of the Device ID feature (e.g. opt-int/opt-out and access control for third parties).

Unlinkability: The Device ID shall be site and/or domain specific in that no two (or more) third parties should be able to link users from their respective domains by solely using the Device ID feature. This prevents unscrupulous third parties from damaging the privacy of the user.

Malware protection: Unprotected Device IDs could lead to identity theft and damaging the user's reputation. The solution needs to mitigate these attacks.

Context: The Device ID itself is of no use without some context information such as longevity (i.e., the time elapsed since the creation of identity). This can help a third party better infer trust based on historical records.

Trust & Integrity: In order for a third party to make a trustworthy decision based on the Device ID, the solution needs to provide a proof of origin and tamper evidence in the form of a digital signature.

Confidentiality: The Device ID information shall be protected against eavesdropping and replay attacks while transferred from the device to a third party.

Integration and ease of deployment: The proposed solution shall be easy to integrate to existing Web applications via standards such as XML and HTTP.

3   Architecture

The proposed architecture is depicted in Figure 1. The *Device* that requires
the identity feature contains a Web browser that acts as a nexus between the
Security Hardware (SH), the *Device Identity Provider* (DIP) and the *Service
Provider* (SP).

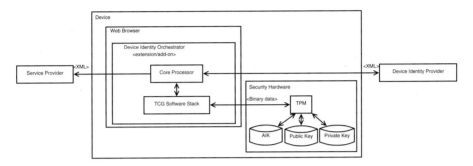

Fig. 1. Proposed architecture

The SH is a component that provides support for digital signature, protection
of the involved private keys, and a proof of the hardware support behind it. A
good example of SH is the TPM [2].

The DIP is a Web Service that takes the digital signature value generated
by the Device (using the SH) and binds this information to some calculation
performed in the protected environment of the Web Service. In our solution, the
DIP calculates a "pseudonym" identity for the device to meet the *Unlinkability*
and *Context* requirements listed in section 2.

The SP is a Web entity that is interested in using the Device ID produced by
the DIP for weighing some decision. This entity could be an e-Commerce Web
site, social network, banking Web site, etc. that requires strong authentication or
an intermediate entity which manages device reputation for the aforementioned
(in section 6 we present this as a case study).

The Web browser orchestrates these components while also providing an
overall smooth user experience. This configuration effectively extends the trust
boundary of the device to the cloud, more specifically to the DIP. The DIP
acts as an extension of the device by performing some calculation that would
otherwise require a protected execution environment in the device.

4   Security Protocol

As mentioned in section 3, we separate the DIP from the actual platform by
using a Web Service. Therefore, we need a secure communication protocol which
ensures the correct binding between these components. We achieve this binding
by using TPM's support for attestation, and creating a pseudonym identity for
the device in the context of the requesting SP. In this section we describe this
protocol using a simplified version of the notation from [8].

Declarations

- Let D be the device
- Let SP be the Service Provider
- Let DIP be the Device Identity Provider
- Let T_A be the timestamp for the identity request
- Let N_A be the nonce for the identity request
- Let T_E be the timestamp in which the device was first seen by the DIP ("Enrollment" timestamp)
- Let T_R be the timestamp of the last identity reset
- Let T_S be the current time on the DIP server
- Let RC be the reset count (times the user has requested an identity reset)
- Let $DevSeed$ be a unique number which represents the universal device identity of D for a given DIP. This unique number is randomly generated the first time D accesses the services of the DIP
- Let $pub(X)$ be the public key and $priv(X)$ the private (secret) key of entity X

Pre-conditions

- At least one TPM AIK has been provisioned on D, and a signature key has been generated which is rooted on said AIK. $(pub(D), priv(D))$ refers to the aforementioned signature key pair.
- SP has generated a private/public key pair, and has shared the public portion (or certificate) with the DIP service. $(pub(SP), priv(SP))$ refers to the aforementioned key pair.
- DIP has generated a private/public key pair, and has shared the public portion (or certificate) with the SP. $(pub(DIP), priv(DIP))$ refers to the aforementioned key pair.
- Given the two previous pre-conditions, SP trusts DIP and vice-versa

Protocol

1. $SP \rightarrow D : \{N_A, T_A\}_{priv(SP)}, pub(SP)$
2. $D \rightarrow DIP : \{N_A, T_A\}_{priv(SP)}, \{N_A, T_A\}_{priv(D)}, \{pub(D)\}_{pub(DIP)}$
3. $DIP \rightarrow D :$
   $\{\{N_A, T_E, T_R, RC, hash(DevSeed|pub(SP)), T_S\}_{pub(SP)}\}_{priv(DIP)}$

In the above flow, the Device ID of device D requested by service provider SP in the context of Device Identity Provider DIP is denoted as $hash(DevSeed|pub(SP))$: This enforces the *Unlinkability* requirement from section 2, since two SPs who share information about device identities will not be able to correlate any transactions solely based on this identity. The $DevSeed$ value will be generated by the DIP in step 2, only for devices that are new to the DIP. Once generated, this value will be stored in the DIP's database using D's public key as the index, and recalled every time the same device requests the identity service. This protocol also ensures the requirements of *Trust & Integrity* and *Confidentiality* by using digital signatures and encryption, and the *Context* requirement is met by attaching the timestamps and reset count information corresponding to the device.

5   Implementation

Our implementation uses the TPM as the SH component. We are particularly interested in the Attestation Identity Key (AIK)/Direct Anonymous Attestation (DAA) feature of the TPM specification, which provides support for remote attestation. We use this capability as the proof that the SH component is protecting the signature keys used by the DIP to derive trust in the device.

We assume that the TPM chip inside a device will be provisioned with at least one attestation key. For our implementation, we use the AIK scheme and a Privacy CA (Certification Authority) to attest the TPM hardware, but our architecture does not impose this model. Since the AIK cannot be used to sign artifacts generated outside the TPM hardware, the TPM is instructed to create a generic signing key and sign it with the AIK. The key pair $(AIK, SigningKey)$ is our effective trust anchor for the device.

The proposed implementation uses a Web browser add-on for orchestrating the information flow between the SP and the DIP, including the communication with the TPM for the digital signature primitive.

The DIP exposes a Web Service interface, which provides a TPM AIK signature consumption service and creates unlinkable identifiers for each SP.

TCG Software Stack. A TCG Software Stack (TSS) [1] implementation was used as the interface to the TPM for creating and protecting the Device IDs and represents the SH as described in section 3. The TSS can create a complete PKI (Public Key Infrastructure) tree using an AIK (Attestation Identity Key) as the trust anchor, but for the purpose of this paper and to fulfill the requirement of *Malware Protection* by having the Device ID protected, we only require a single RSA key, issued by an AIK. This TPM public key, which will be pseudonymized by the DIP, forms the basis of the Device ID. It is important to note that this key is never exposed to an SP.

Web browser extension. The Web browser extension is responsible for orchestrating the device identity generation process through the *Device Identity Orchestrator*(DIO) and for providing device identity management abilities through a graphical interface. This allows for standard Web protocols to be used fulfilling the requirement of *Integration* as described in section 2.

This extension also includes improvements in user experience, facilitating the opt-in and opt-out from the service as desired, meeting the *Access control* requirement also described in section 2.

The DIO is made up of two main components that manage the entire device identity generation process: A core communication protocol stack, which ensures that the messages from the SP and DIP are exchanged correctly (see message list in section 4), and the TSS wrapper which allows the interaction with the SH to access the device credentials.

Device Identity Provider (DIP). It provides the implementation of the message exchange protocol described in section 4 as a RESTful Web Service, mapping all the messages to XML structures. All of the cryptography described in section 4 is implemented with XML Security standards (see [3]).

The DIP verifies the identity of the SP and of the Device. SPs participating in the device identification service must enroll with the DIP through a prior exchange of certificates in order to be considered trusted. The certificate embedded in the XML Digital Signature is then extracted and looked up in the list of trusted SPs to ensure communication was initiated by a valid SP.

The DIP authenticates the identity of the device itself using embedded TPM based credentials rooted into the Privacy CA. The TPM public key is used as a primary key for accessing the DIP database and storing data associated to the device (timestamps and reset count as described in section 4).

A possible extension of this work would be to maintain a list of all identity requests by Service Providers to give the user full transparency in how their Device ID is being accessed.

6   Case Study: A Device Reputation Example

As online fraud costs to online vendors is significant [5] there is a vested community interest in the prevention of processing fraudulent transactions through secure data sharing without impeding on user privacy. To put our proposed system in context, we developed a case study providing an end-to-end scenario demonstrating the strength and value of the solution coupled with a device reputation service. The result is a reputation service that is unique in two ways. The first is user privacy, as the solution is designed to be opt-in only through collecting and rewarding positive behavior. The second is device trust, since the online SP can guarantee the device identity is legitimate.

The case study consists of four actors as seen in Fig. 2: a reputation service, an online vendor subscribed to the reputation service, a client device operated by a user wishing to execute a transaction with the online vendor, and the DIP.

The device reputation service collects data on the Device ID longevity and transaction history of the device to determine the device's reputation in online commerce. The user is in effect relinquishing control of the longevity of their Device ID tied to online transactions to provide evidence the device is not involved in fraudulent activities. The benefit for the user in relinquishing this control can simply be gained confidence in initiating transactions within a trusted web of

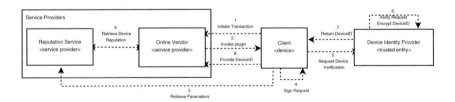

Fig. 2. Case study

SPs. This trusted web of the DIP, SPs subscribed to the DIP, and the user will be defined as a 'trusted computing community.'

The user wishing to participate in the trusted computing community installs a browser plug-in provided by the DIP, the user consents to the opt-in policy and initiates the process of obtaining device identity trust. The wizard walks the user through provisioning of the TPM and provides the user the ability to set an access control list on their Device ID. The plug-in will also expose a menu option for the user to fully reset their device identity, with the associated consequence of resetting any reputation they have built up. The user is now ready to initiate a transaction with an online vendor participating in the trusted computing community. It is worth noting the reputation service and the online vendor can be a single entity or separate SPs. By separating the reputation service from the online vendor, it provides the benefit that a single online vendor can access the reputation history of the device in question for all the device's transactions within the trusted computing community.

The user initiates an online transaction with the online vendor and the device trust process is activated. A nonce from the reputation service is generated, the TPM performs the signature and attestation process, the payload is signed by the reputation service certificate and sent to the DIP. The DIP performs the device verification and then hashes and encrypts the Device ID with the reputation service certificate in order to send it back to the client to be embedded in the response to the online vendor. At this point the online vendor has the verified Device ID in possession however is unable to access any details as it is encrypted by the reputation service key. The online vendor forwards this data to the reputation service to receive a user consented feedback report on the trusted Device ID. The reputation report is generated by the number of successful transactions the device has completed and the longevity of the Device ID. After the transaction is complete the online vendor provides feedback on the results of the transaction to the reputation service, affecting the device's overall reputation.

This case study demonstrates how: a) an online vendor can achieve a trusted network based reputation report on a device without obtaining any additional personally identifiable information; b) the user is able to maintain full control over their privacy through an opt-in only approach and the ability to reset the identity/reputation of the device; and c) the reputation service maintains data integrity by only tracking data on verified devices.

7   Conclusions

We introduced a privacy-aware Device ID system that can be implemented using off-the-shelf TPM capabilities present in many commodity PCs, enhanced with a Web Service that extends the trust boundary of the device. The Web Service is used to protect the user's privacy in addition to providing additional security to prevent tampering attacks. We described an end-to-end implementation of a fully functional proof-of-concept in the context of a device reputation application that can be deployed with today's available technologies. Our contribution is innovative in two ways. First, through a security protocol, we extend the trust boundary of a device to a Web Service that can be hosted in the cloud. Second, using cryptographic techniques we generate unlinkable identities that are fully controllable by the user.

Future work opportunities would involve the replacement of the trusted external Web Service by utilizing a local secure execution environment. This capability is not available in commodity PC today. However, the system we describe would provide a valuable application of such capability. By describing this solution and its applications, we hope to encourage PC manufacturers to consider the inclusion of secure execution environments in their product offerings in the future.

References

1. Trusted computing group software stack (2010),
   http://www.trustedcomputinggroup.org/developers/software_stack
2. Trusted platform module (2010),
   http://www.trustedcomputinggroup.org/developers/trusted_platform_module
3. Xml digital signature (2010),
   http://www.xml.com/pub/a/2001/08/08/xmldsig.html
4. Balfe, S., Lakhani, A.D., Paterson, K.G.: Trusted computing: Providing security for peer-to-peer networks. In: IEEE International Conference on Peer-to-Peer Computing, pp. 117–124 (2005)
5. CyberSource: 2010 fraud report (2010),
   http://www.cybersource.com/cgi-bin/resource_center/resources.cgi
6. McFadden, T.: Tpm matrix (2006),
   http://www.tonymcfadden.net/tpmvendors_arc.html
7. Ahamad, M., et al: Emerging cyber threats report for 2009 (2008),
   http://www.gtisc.gatech.edu/pdf/CyberThreatsReport2009.pdf
8. Needham, R.M., Schroeder, M.D.: Using encryption for authentication in large networks of computers. Commun. ACM 21(12), 993–999 (1978)
9. O'Gorman, L.: Comparing passwords, tokens, and biometrics for user authentication. Proceedings of the IEEE 91(12), 2021–2040 (2003)

Towards Mitigating Human Errors in IT Change Management Process

Venkateswara R. Madduri[1], Manish Gupta[1], Pradipta De[1], and Vishal Anand[2]

[1] IBM Research India, Delhi
[2] IBM Integrated Technology Delivery, Bangalore, India

Abstract. IT service delivery is heavily dependent on skilled labor. This opens the scope for errors due to human mistakes. We propose a framework for minimizing errors due to human mistakes in Change Management process, focusing on change preparation and change execution. We developed a tool that brings better structure to the change plan, as well as, helps the change plan creator in developing a plan faster through use of knowledge-base and automatic guidance. At the change execution phase, we designed and implemented an architecture that intercepts and validates operator actions, thereby significantly reducing operator mistakes. The system can be tuned to vary the involvement of the operator. We have tested the system in a large IT delivery environment and report potential benefits.

1 Introduction

IT service delivery has seen unprecedented growth. To tackle the surge, IT service management has become a human labor intensive industry. The strong dependence on human workforce leads to several outages which can be traced back to human mistakes [5,3,2,4]. Outage in service delivery stems from several factors, starting from hardware failures to simple misconfiguration of an application, leading to service downtime.

This paper proposes a framework for minimizing outages, that are triggered by human errors, in service delivery environment. We look closely at the *change management process*, as defined by ITIL [1]. A typical change management lifecycle involves: (i) a change request is raised and logged into a change request system, (ii) an expert team reviews the problem and draws up a change plan, (iii) designated change assignee executes the steps as documented in the change plan, (iv) changes are validated and the change ticket is closed. *Starting from change plan preparation to change execution, the process is heavily dependent on skills of the human workforce.*

We propose a solution targeted at two levels: change preparation and change execution. At change preparation, errors could be due to inadequately specified instructions, reuse of older change plans, and omission of instructions for rarely used stages, like pre-validation and backout. We introduce a column-based structure for change plan creation. An MS-Excel plugin based wizard, referred

P.P. Maglio et al. (Eds.): ICSOC 2010, LNCS 6470, pp. 657–662, 2010.

to as TexExpeditor, helps in building a structured change plan. Standardized structure, along with several functionalities to guide the change plan creation.

The proposed method to prevent errors during change execution is based on the idea of intercepting operator actions. The system, referred henceforth as Facade, checks the correct time window for the change execution, as well as, validates the server address on which the change must be acted. The interceptor is also capable of automating command execution by matching command outputs. Facade can also run in supervised mode where it waits for the user to indicate successful command execution.

In this paper, our key contributions are two-fold: we propose a standardization for change plan creation, and provide a tool to create standard change plans; and based on this standard template, we have designed and implemented a change execution engine, called Facade, which can be tuned to run at different levels of automation. In the rest of the paper, we present a broad overview of the tools (Section 2), followed by details of the implementation. We also present a set of results from our limited engagement with accounts (Section 4).

2   System Overview

We have developed a system that addresses the challenges of Change Management at two levels: change preparation and change execution. In this section, we describe the overall design of two complementary tools: TexExpeditor used for change plan creation, and Facade used for mitigating errors during execution of the plan.

2.1   Change Plan Creation

In most service delivery environments, Subject-Matter-Expert (SME) creates the change plan. A change plan is usually a set of instructions in unstructured text. Use of unstructured text leaves scope for misinterpretation during execution. Keeping the current state in mind, the key goal of the change plan creation phase is two-pronged: (i) to reduce ambiguity in the definition of execution instructions in a change plan, and (ii) reduce the effort, as well as, chance of mistakes in the creation of change plan.

We introduce a structure in the change plan to reduce ambiguity. The proposed change plan is a set of tasks, with each step in the task described as a record with fixed number of fields. The fields are <command, node to execute on, type of command, comments>. To aid the process of plan creation, we have implemented a MS-Excel based wizard to guide in plan creation (details in Section 3.1). Figure 1 shows the workflow of change plan creation and that of new change plan template generation. During the plan creation, a user can provide the keywords describing the change, which will pull out relevant plans for reference.

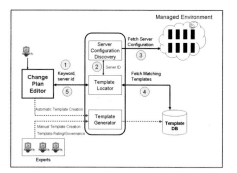

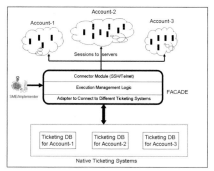

Fig. 1. Steps in Change Plan Creation using TexExpeditor tool

Fig. 2. Overall Architecture of Facade

2.2   Change Plan Execution

At present, a change plan is written in an unstructured manner leading to misinterpretation of the instructions, and errors in execution. Other sources of error in this manual mode of change execution are, (i) the user mistakenly logs into the incorrect server and performs changes, (ii) being in a different time zone from the target servers, the implementer may start execution at wrong change window,

Facade execution engine is a gateway before any change action reaches the target server, as shown in Figure 2. The ticketing system holds the change requests and change plans for target servers. Facade architecture has three important modules which makes it flexible to incorporate new ticketing systems and new connection types. The adapters to the ticketing system perform the task of fetching relevant tickets for display to the user. The connector module opens sessions to the target hosts specified in the change plan. Since the connections are opened automatically by reading in the hostname from the change plan directly, this eliminates possibility of wrong server login. Before executing any change command on the target host, the change time window is checked with the server time to ensure that a change is restricted within its change window. In order to make the transformation from the current state-of-the-art to a fully automated change plan execution, we have implemented an extensible framework. The flexibility provided in the semi-automatic mode is that the user analyzes the output of a command and decides on the progress of the change, while in the automatic mode the command is pushed to the endhost, output analyzed and the next command is executed.

3   Design Choices and Implementation

The design choices and implementation of the change preparation tool (TexExpeditor) and change execution engine (Facade) are guided by several business and practical constraints. In this section, we will present the requirements that shaped our design choices, followed by the implementation of the tool.

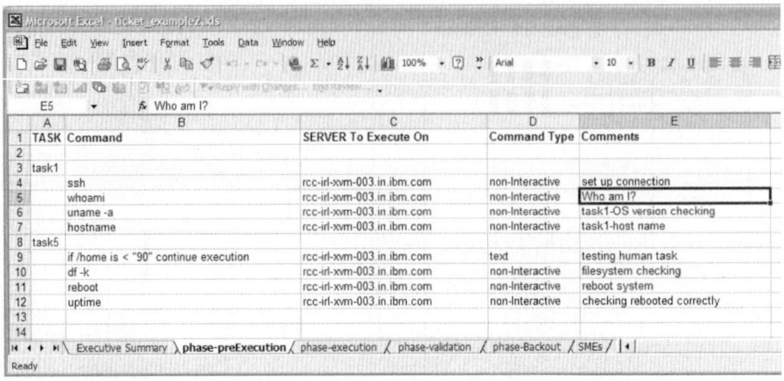

Microsoft Excel - ticket_example2.xls

E5 Who am I?

	A	B	C	D	E
1	TASK	Command	SERVER To Execute On	Command Type	Comments
2					
3	task1				
4		ssh	rcc-irl-xvm-003.in.ibm.com	non-Interactive	set up connection
5		whoami	rcc-irl-xvm-003.in.ibm.com	non-Interactive	Who am I?
6		uname -a	rcc-irl-xvm-003.in.ibm.com	non-Interactive	task1-OS version checking
7		hostname	rcc-irl-xvm-003.in.ibm.com	non-Interactive	task1-host name
8	task5				
9		if /home is < "90" continue execution	rcc-irl-xvm-003.in.ibm.com	text	testing human task
10		df -k	rcc-irl-xvm-003.in.ibm.com	non-Interactive	filesystem checking
11		reboot	rcc-irl-xvm-003.in.ibm.com	non-Interactive	reboot system
12		uptime	rcc-irl-xvm-003.in.ibm.com	non-Interactive	checking rebooted correctly
13					
14					

Executive Summary | phase-preExecution | phase-execution | phase-validation | phase-Backout | SMEs

Ready

Fig. 3. A typical change plan along with the wizard for creating a plan

3.1 TexExpeditor: Design and Implementation

Several factors lead to making mistakes during change plan creation. *Cut-Paste error* is the classic case of reusing old plans to create new ones, and forgetting to change a parameter in the new plan. *Omission error* happens when an important field, like patch version, is omitted during plan creation. Another common practice is to *omit backout plan* for simple changes, assuming there will be no complication during change.

TexExpeditor tool forces a structure while building the change plan, as well guides the user with recommendations. It is built on top of MS-Excel, and opens a wizard to guide the plan creation. Six mandatory worksheets are defined: *Executive Summary, Pre-execution Phase, Execution Phase, Validation Phase, Backout Plan, SME list.* Any violation of the structure alerts the user. For example, while filling out a sheet, if incorrect type is entered in a column, e.g. host address does not match IP format, then an error is raised. The wizard is shown in Figure 3. We also create a change plan store which can be searched based on keyword. Search for a relevant plan is based on keywords. The task store is a 3-way dictionary with keywords describing *Actions, Software and Platform.* Sample keywords for Action are Install, Upgrade, Update, Modify, Patch, etc; for Software is DB2, Oracle, Websphere, etc,; and for platform are Linux, Windows, AIX, etc.

3.2 Facade: Change Plan Execution Engine

Several observations guide the Facade design. Complex changes often require human intervention, and therefore, Facade must be tuned to switch from automatic to supervised mode. Multiple changes could be implemented simultaneously. Once a change has started, Facade must ensure that no other person by mistake accesses the same ticket; this requires maintaining session state of the ticket. An alerting mechanism is necessary to intimate relevant stakeholders on exception scenarios.

Facade is a web application with a web-based Graphical User Interface (GUI), as shown in Figure 4. The web UI allows several features, viz. Role-based access control, Multiple ticket execution, Failed execution handling. Different users, like Subject-Matter-Expert(SME) and an implementer, get different views of

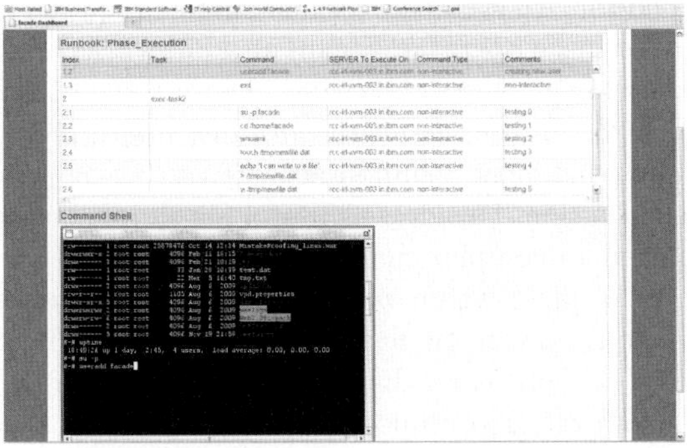

Fig. 4. Facade Graphical User Interface for executing a change plan

the ticket. Separate tabs are opened for each ticket, so that a user implementing multiple changes can navigate across tickets. When exception occurs during a change, Facade allows user to abort a ticket, and triggers the backout plan. It also alerts the list of SMEs mentioned along with the ticket, and updates are sent to the Ticketing system.

Three key building blocks in Facade framework are interface to the native ticketing systems, the session management and interceptor modules, and end-host connection manager. Tickets are accessed from ticketing system using web-service interfaces. For example, BMC Remedy ARS [6] exposes web service APIs, that is used to implement access to the ticketing database.

Once a change begins, Facade maintains a session for the ticket to guide the user with the progress. Facade maintains the current command being executed on the endhost, and proceeds to the next command when previous command is successfully completed. In supervised mode, user indicates successful completion; in automatic mode, it is detected by Facade. There are two types of commands in a change plan, non-interactive, and interactive/text based. For the text based commands, Facade opens a putty session to the designated endhost and allows the user to execute the change directly on the target host. However, the chance of an error in terms of execution on a wrong node is precluded by opening the putty session to defined host.

The connection management to the target host is the other important functionality in Facade. Since all target hosts are now accessed through Facade, this allows the ability to control access to endhosts. If due to incorrect scheduling of change, multiple tickets try to access the same endhost, Facade can easily intercept and prevent. For connecting to the endhost, Facade uses the same authentication method, like ssh or telnet, and asks the user for the credentials.

4   Results and Observations

This section presents preliminary results collected from a test engagement. The results are indicative of the benefits of the tools. In order to understand the benefit of TexExpeditor, we studied over 300 change requests over a period of 6 months raised for database operations team at a large telecom account. Approximately 60% of the changes were repeating, where some of the major keyword classes were *dba, patch, update, database, upgrade, migration*, with changing tablespace in DB being the most common activity.

During change execution, Facade was useful for simple changes, but more supervision was required for complex changes. Facade was able to prevent execution of about 50% of the changes which were attempted. We prevented execution of tickets whose change time window has not been reached, and those which were pending approval. The web based display of the execution result is difficult to read for the user. However, in our upcoming version, we are integrating a VT100 terminal emulator to maintain the standard look-and-feel for the user.

5   Conclusion

In the current human labor intensive IT delivery model, scope for errors due to human mistakes cannot be precluded. We designed a framework that minimizes the chance of human mistakes in Change Management process. We target two key stages to restrict the errors: change preparation and change execution. TexExpeditor tool introduces a structure in change plan creation, and guides the user during change plan creation, thereby reducing the chances of making common mistakes. Facade execution engine acts like a validation system before a user can start executing change on the target host. It intercepts operator actions, and allows execution only after validating the correct execution parameters, like correct time window, correct target host. Facade can be tuned to run in a semi-supervised mode, as well as, execute changes automatically on the endhost. We envision that commonly occurring changes will benefit significantly from the automated execution framework of Facade, while complex changes will involve human intervention.

References

1. It infrastructure library. itil service support, version 2.3. In: Office of Government Commerce (2000)
2. Benson, T., Sahu, S., Akella, A., Shaikh, A.: A first look at problems in the cloud. In: Proceedings of the 2nd Workshop on Hot Topics in Cloud (2010)
3. Gray, J.: Why do computers stop and what can be done about it. In: Proc of SRDS (1986)
4. Oliveira, F., Tjang, A., Bianchini, R., Martin, R.P., Nguyen, T.D.: Barricade: Defending systems against operator mistakes. In: Proc. of Eurosys (2010)
5. Oppenheimer, D., Ganapathi, A., Patterson, D.: Why do internet services fail, and what can be done about it. In: Proc. of Usenix Symposium on Internet Technologies and Systems (2003)
6. BMC Remedy IT Service Management Suite,
   http://www.bmc.com/products/offering/
   bmc-remedy-it-service-management-suite.html.

A Service-Based Architecture for Multi-domain Search on the Web

Alessandro Bozzon, Marco Brambilla,
Francesco Corcoglioniti, and Salvatore Vadacca

Dipartimento di Elettronica e Informazione - Politecnico di Milano
via Ponzio, 34/5 - 20133 Milano, Italy
{bozzon,mbrambil,corcoglioniti,vadacca}@elet.polimi.it

Abstract. Current search engines lack in support for multi-domain queries, i.e., queries that can be answered by combining information from
two or more knowledge domains. Questions such as "Find a theater close
to Times Square, NYC, showing a recent thriller movie, close to a pizza
restaurant" have no answer unless the user individually queries different
vertical search engines for each domain and then manually combines results. Therefore, the need arises for a special class of search applications
that combine different search services. In this paper we propose an architecture aiming at answering multi-domain queries through composition
of search services and we provide facilities for the execution of multi-
domain queries and the visualization of their results, at the purpose of
simplifying the access to the information. We describe our service-based
architecture and the implemented optimization and distribution options,
and we evaluate the feasibility and performance of our approach.

1 Introduction

Throughout the last decade, search has become the most adopted way to access
information over the Internet. User queries are becoming more and more engaging for search engines: the single query itself becomes more complex (both in
terms of amount and extension of queried information), the user interaction assumes the form of a process instead of a single query and search sessions tend to
become longer and focus not only on documents but also on structured objects.
The information to be retrieved is often hidden in the so called "deep Web".
While vertical domain-specific search engines provide access to this information,
a whole class of queries spanning multiple domains, possibly covered by distinct
vertical engines, is unsupported and requires the manual intervention of the user.

We define *search computing applications* [6] the new class of applications
aimed at responding to multi-domain queries, i.e., queries over multiple semantic
fields of interest, by helping users (or by substituting to them) in decomposing
queries and manually assembling complete results from partial answers, provided
by domain-specific search services.

The motivation for a novel approach to search service composition is due
to: the peculiar characteristics of search services (i.e., ranking and chunking of

P.P. Maglio et al. (Eds.): ICSOC 2010, LNCS 6470, pp. 663–669, 2010.
© Springer-Verlag Berlin Heidelberg 2010

results), the data-intensive essence of the orchestration, the ad-hoc optimization strategies of query plans, the algorithms for the computation of composite results (based on different join strategies), and the novel user interaction paradigms that let users access queries and interact with results. These aspects also challenge the performance and scalability issues of traditional SOA solutions.

2 Architecture

In this section we present an overview of the reference architecture (see Figure 1) of a search computing system, and we provide some details of the main modules. Components are partitioned in three deployment environments (*client, server* and *services*) organized as on-line (see Section 3.1) and off-line (see Section 3.2) components.

The search infrastructure is built on top of search services, which may consist of wrapped websites, relational databases, Web services, ReST APIs, SPARQL endpoints, or any other data resources.

Data produced by search services are extracted and combined according to a query execution plan. The query processor accepts users' queries as input, defines the execution plan and orchestrates the invocation of services. The orchestration is performed according to user and service statistics collected and analyzed by means of an off-line profiler. When needed, service materialization increases the overall performance of the system, thanks to local replication.

Finally, a set of tools allows administrators to manage the system and to configure search applications. Caching techniques and the use of multiple query processor instances, together with a load balancer, increase availability and performance of the overall system.

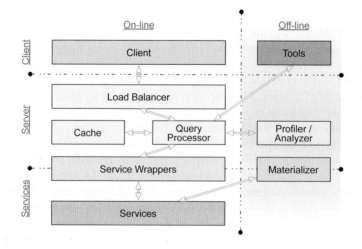

Fig. 1. Overview of the Search Computing architecture

2.1   Client Tier

The client tier comprises the Search Computing user interface. It is based on the *Liquid Query* [2] approach, a "search as a process" information seeking paradigm based on two distinct interaction steps: the initial query submission and the result browsing and query refinement.

At *initial query submission* time, the user specifies the actual parameters of his search, either by filling up a search form or by expressing her needs via natural language queries. The result set computed by the server is shown by the client according to the user's data visualization choices.

Result browsing and query refinement options are offered as a set of interaction primitives that support manipulation, exploration and expansion of the search results, thus allowing for continuous evolution of the query and of the result set itself. The user can also apply data-driven operations to results such as: attribute projection, filtering, sorting, grouping, clustering, and so on. Finally, users can switch between alternative data visualization options such as maps and graphs.

The client is designed as a Rich Internet Application (RIA) architecture running in a Web browser, providing local data storage and manipulation, off-line functioning, and asynchronous, bidirectional client-server communications. Application designers can configure the default data visualization and interaction paradigm, leaving to end users the possibility to dynamically select and download additional visualization components providing alternative views of result sets.

2.2   Server Tier

The Server side mainly comprises the Query Processor, plus a set of caching and balancing facilities. The Query Processor is the component devoted to the management and orchestration of users' queries. The component is accessed by external users and tools through a ReST API and comprises the following modules.

Query Analyzer and Optimizer. It translates user-specified queries into an internal format, which is then optimized by the Query Optimizer [4] according to expected invocation costs and intermediate and final result sizes, as calculated by the offline Profiler/Analyzer. Eventually, the optimization process produces a query plan; query optimization can take place on-line (providing optimized plans in response to user queries) and off-line (refining recurring plans for reuse by other users).

Execution Engine. It executes Panta Rhei query plans [3]. The role of the engine is to produce an execution environment where results from service calls flow within the engine to generate new result combinations at the maximum speed, at the same time also supporting adaptation to changes in the search process and to other runtime factors. The system provides users with both synchronous (pull) and asynchronous (push of results to the user) search mechanisms and fine-grained control to allow for interaction with the search process, in order to dynamically orchestrate it (e.g., to react to the results being produced).

Query Registry. The aim of the Query Registry is to store optimized query execution plans for future reuse.

Mart Registry. We define the abstraction of a search service by means of the notion of Service Mart [5]. The purpose of the Mart Registry is to store *Service Marts*, with expected attributes and their data types; *Connection Patterns*, introducing pair-wise couplings of service marts that define possible join paths; and pointers to the concrete *Service Interfaces* that implement the marts, together with the profiling information collected by the analyzer component.

Service Invoker. When invocations to search services are requested, the invoker looks up the Mart registry and, based on the information at hand, performs the physical invocation of services, possibly through service wrappers.

2.3 Services Tier

While Services consist of the actual search service implementations made available by third party providers, Service Wrappers are components that expose a homogeneous interface to search services, providing retrieved data in a common format processable by the higher layers of the architecture.

In the picture, the component is half-way between the server and the service side to represent two different usage scenarios: the wrappers can be deployed either at the service provider premises or at server side within the Search Computing environment.

3   Distribution Issues

The proposed architecture could be easily compared to a distributed Web retrieval system [1]. We classify the operations executed within the system in the two typical classes of *on-line processing* of queries and *off-line indexing and analysis* of user and service data and metadata. Both on-line and off-line aspects require hardware and software able to cope with high data volumes and to handle high query throughput. Indeed, the number of existing sites and services and the rapidly growing amount of user generated content pose several challenges to the system in terms of result quality and scalability.

3.1   On-Line Query Processing

The system allows users to submit multi-domain queries by means of the Liquid Query UI or by exploiting the available ReST API.

The architecture takes advantage of caching mechanisms. Cache servers hold results of frequent and popular queries, thus reducing the load of the query processor and the latency of the query. Partial results obtained after service calls are also stored in cache. This allows shortening the query latency whenever the execution plan partially overlaps with a previously executed one. Since service invocations are the bottleneck of the architecture, a careful planning and organization of the cache boosts the performance of the overall system, reduces the bandwidth requirements and also increases the availability and fault tolerance of the infrastructure. A load balancer assigns queries to processors according to the availability of the nodes and their internal load. In the future we also plan to take into account geographical position of clients, nodes, and services, so as to route queries to the appropriate query processor according to the geographical proximity of the client to the processor node and the distance of the processor node from the service provider. The architecture exploits a set of registries to store execution plan descriptions and metadata of the services. The system currently supports several distributed stores; their adoption allows several instances of the query processor to share the data, taking advantage of the partitioning and replication features of the underlying back-end.

3.2   Off-Line Data Indexing and Analysis

User and service profiling is a time-consuming and computation-intensive task, which must be performed off-line and requires ad-hoc hardware and software. Profiling improves the user experience and the efficiency, as we describe below.

User profiling. The user is part and parcel of the search process. He submits queries, expands results, chooses the combinations which best fit to her needs and expresses her preferences. Tracking users' behaviors allows providing high-quality answers: the query execution plan comprises user's favorite services, ranking of result combinations is defined on a per-user basis [8] and result diversification [7] is promoted to address the interests of the user.

Service profiling. Services are subject to a variable load in the space of a day, according to the provenance of users accessing it. If services are correctly profiled, the system can apply more precise load balancing, by querying services with lower load. Moreover, data coming from different services may not be updated with the same frequency. If the update frequency is profiled, ad-hoc time-to-live values can be fixed for the cached data in order to avoid stale data and maximizing the use of the cache at the same time.

Data prefetch. The system implements some proactive behavior by anticipating possible user needs. Recurring usage patterns can be identified and some tasks can be anticipated. The system can decide either to show prefetched data anticipating the user input or to react to the user input with prefetched data.

Service materialization. Service materialization is a bulk operation that is useful whenever there is the need for invoking a service with heavy load. The a-priori download of its data is the best way to provide the answer in a reasonable amount of time. When materialization is performed, the Search Computing infrastructure exposes its own surrogate of the service, guaranteeing better performance due to the locality and replication of data.

4   Experimental Evaluation

In this section we evaluate functionalities and performance of our system. We consider the scenario in which the user is looking for a cinema displaying a thriller movie near Times Square in New York City and a pizza restaurant nearby.

A prototype, together with a few other examples in different scenarios, is available at the following URL: http://demo.search-computing.com/. In the prototype, movie information is retrieved through the IMDb archive API, showtimes and theaters through Google Movie Search, and restaurants through the Yahoo Local source. The user interface allows customers to submit their search criteria and to get a set of results, that can be further explored by asking for more combinations, expanding to other concepts, and so on.

Service invocation is the most time-consuming task, requiring respectively 0.2, 0.4 and 0.7 seconds for the Theater, Restaurant and Movie services. The first query result is computed after 4.368 seconds. The system suggests as a first result combination the movie "Iron Man 2" at the "Regal E-Walk 13" theater (which is 0.4 miles far from Times Square) and then a pizza at "Times Square Deli" (300 feet far from the cinema). Globally, the system retrieves 308 results in 18.752 seconds, with 15 invocations of Movie, 7 of Theater and 111 of Restaurant.

Figure 2(a) shows the average number of service invocations required to obtain the top-k query results, with k ranging from 1 to 100, averaging out over multiple random query inputs. The number of invocations of the Restaurant service is almost linear in k, since each one produces an average of 10 query results (its chunk size). Fewer invocations of the Movie and Theater services are required since the number of combinations generated after the parallel join of the two is enough to invoke the Restaurant service to produce the desired amount of results. In some cases, an increase of k may also correspond to a lower number of invocations of some services, due to the impact of other services and compositions on the combination number. In the example, this happens for the Movie and Theater services, due to variations in the number of combinations extracted after the parallel join.

Figure 2(b) shows the impact of caching on the average query execution time, for cache hit probabilities ranging from 0 to 1. Experimental results were obtained by testing our prototype with 20 concurrent clients, running the query of

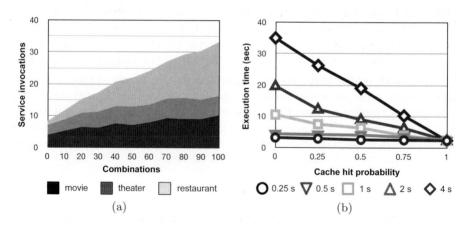

Fig. 2. (a) Required service invocations vs. desired number k of results; (b) Response time vs. probability of cache hit for different average service response times

our scenario to extract the top 10 results from synthetic services whose response time can be configured and ranges from 0.25 sec to 4 sec. Average query execution times dramatically decrease with the growth of cache hit probabilities. Ideally, a cache hit probability of 1 lends to the same execution time regardless of service performance, which depends only on the overhead introduced by our system and, therefore, represents a measure of its efficiency.

5   Conclusion

In this paper we presented a distributed architecture for multi-domain web search applications, according to the Search Computing vision [6]. From a functional standpoint, our approach allows for exploratory search of composite concepts in a service-based environment with no navigational constraints. Our implementation and experimental results demonstrate the feasibility of the approach and show how standard optimization techniques such as distribution, load balancing and caching can be proficiently applied to the multi-domain search problem and are actually needed in a realistic setting to grant performances acceptable for the end user.

Acknowledgments. This research is part of the Search Computing (SeCo) project [www.search-computing.org], funded by the European Research Council. We wish to thank all the members of the SeCo team for their contributions.

References

1. Baeza-Yates, R.A., Castillo, C., Junqueira, F., Plachouras, V., Silvestri, F.: Challenges on Distributed Web Retrieval. In: 23rd International Conference on Data Engineering, ICDE 2007, Istanbul, April 15-20, pp. 6–20 (2007)
2. Bozzon, A., Brambilla, M., Ceri, S., Fraternali, P.: Liquid Query: Multi-domain Exploratory Search on the Web. In: WWW 2010: Proceedings of the 19th international conference on World wide web, pp. 161–170. ACM, New York (2010)
3. Braga, D., Ceri, S., Corcoglioniti, F., Grossniklaus, M.: Panta Rhei: Flexible Execution Engine for Search Computing Queries. In: Ceri, S., Brambilla, M. (eds.) Search Computing Challenges and Directions. LNCS, vol. 5950, pp. 225–243. Springer, Heidelberg (2010)
4. Braga, D., Ceri, S., Daniel, F., Martinenghi, D.: Optimization of Multi-domain Queries on the Web. PVLDB 1(1), 562–573 (2008)
5. Campi, A., Ceri, S., Maesani, A., Ronchi, S.: Designing Service Marts for Engineering Search Computing Applications. In: Benatallah, B., Casati, F., Kappel, G., Rossi, G. (eds.) ICWE 2010. LNCS, vol. 6189, pp. 50–65. Springer, Heidelberg (2010)
6. Ceri, S., Brambilla, M. (eds.): Search Computing. LNCS, vol. 5950. Springer, Heidelberg (2010)
7. Gollapudi, S., Sharma, A.: An Axiomatic Approach for Result Diversification. In: Proceedings of the 18th International Conference on World Wide Web, WWW 2009, Madrid, Spain, April 20-24, pp. 381–390 (2009)
8. You, G., Hwang, S.: Personalized Ranking: a Contextual Ranking Approach. In: Proceedings of the 2007 ACM Symposium on Applied Computing (SAC), Seoul, Korea, March 11-15, pp. 506–510 (2007)

Natural Language Service Composition with Request Disambiguation

Florin-Claudiu Pop[1], Marcel Cremene[1], Mircea Vaida[1], and Michel Riveill[2]

[1] Technical University of Cluj-Napoca, Romania
{florin.pop,cremene,mircea.vaida}@com.utcluj.ro
[2] University of Nice, Sophia-Antipolis, France
riveill@unice.fr

Abstract. The aim of our research is to create a service composition system that is able to detect and deal with the imperfections of a natural language user request while keeping it as unrestricted as possible. Our solution consists in three steps: first, service prototypes are generated based on grammatical relations; second, semantic matching is used to discover actual services; third, the composed service is generated in the form of an executable plan. Experimental results have shown that inaccurately requested services can be matched in more than 95% of user queries. When missing service inputs are detected, the user is asked to provide more details.

1 Introduction

The major issue for a natural language composition system is to understand the user request, knowing that natural language implies a diversity of expressions, may be inaccurate and incomplete. Some user queries may contain indications about how to achieve a goal (i.e. *book flight from Paris to London*) but other expressions (i.e. *get me to London*) will just indicate a goal without giving an indication about how to achieve it. The user request needs to be interpreted in a specific context; some of the user needs are implicit, etc.

To overcome these problems, current natural language service composition approaches impose restrictions like: a narrow dictionary (a subset of natural language), the use of keywords as boundaries for different sentence blocks, a specific grammatical structure (e.g a verb and a noun).

Service composition based on restricted natural language is not convenient for the end user. In order to keep the format of the request unrestricted, we need a more reliable way to deal with the ambiguous nature of the language. When using the term *ambiguity* in the context of this paper, we refer to inaccurate (inexact) or incomplete user requests.

This paper proposes a service composition system that is able to detect and deal with the imperfections of a natural language user request while keeping it unrestricted, in the context of current Web services technologies. The next section presents the proposed solution, while section 3 shows the evaluation of our implementation. In Section 4, we discuss related approaches. Finally, the conclusions and perspectives are summarized in Section 5.

P.P. Maglio et al. (Eds.): ICSOC 2010, LNCS 6470, pp. 670–677, 2010.

2   Proposed Solution

Our service composition system, called *NLSCd - Natural Language Service Composer with request disambiguation* is the second release of NLSC [1]. Its architecture is depicted in Fig. 1.

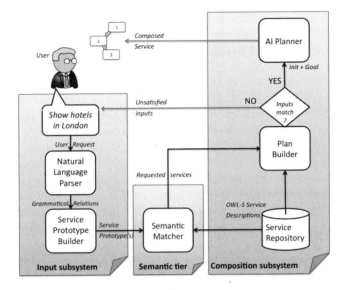

Fig. 1. NLSCd architecture

The **input subsystem** receives a natural language query from the user. A *natural language parser* extracts grammatical relations (GR) between the parts of speech in the request. Based on GRs, the *Service Prototype Builder* transforms the user input into a machine readable, formal request - a list of *service prototypes*.

A **semantic tier** is used as a bridge between natural language and the services ontology. In order to identify actual Web services based on their natural language prototypes, we use the *Semantic Matcher*. Services in the *Service Repository* are annotated using OWL-S [3].

Composition subsystem. The list of actual services identified by the matcher represents the input for the *Plan Builder*. First, the *Plan Builder* finds other services, on which required services depend on. Second, it matches the input values of the prototypes with the inputs of actual services. Values for the inputs that can't be satisfied is requested from the user. Finally, an initial state and a goal is defined, which the *AI Planner* uses to generate the composed service.

2.1   From a Natural Language Request to a Service Prototype

NLSCd's input subsystem accepts imperative natural language requests. According to Portner [4], an imperative construct can be modeled as function which assigns a set of imperative denotations (a To-Do List with properties P) to the addressee (A): *Requiring TDL(A) U {P}*.

In service composition, the addressee is implicit (the computer), and each property *P* describes a service (process) to be invoked. Current natural language interfaces rely on parts of speech (mainly verbs and nouns) to extract such properties. But in cases of more complex user requests, parts of speech by themselves are not sufficient to correctly identify services. For example, in a request with two or more verbs and several nouns, it would be impossible to find which noun is related to each verb without taking into account the syntax of the sentence.

In a sentence, the action is expressed by a predicate, which must contain a verb. Other parts of speech (direct/indirect/prepositional objects, complements, adverbials, etc.) may complete the predicate of the sentence. To identify the parts of speech and the grammatical relations between them, we use a natural language parser called RASP - Robust Accurate Statistical Parser [2].

First, the parser finds the predicate of the sentence, which becomes the root node in a grammatical relations (GR) tree. Then, parts of speech (PoS) that are related to the predicate are added as leaves to this tree. The process continues for parts of PoS related to the ones added in the previous step, and so on.

For example, the predicate of the sentence *Print directions from Paris to London* contains the verb *print* and its direct object (**dobj**) is the noun *directions*. Prepositions *to* and *from* complete the predicate *print*, while themselves are completed by the nouns *Paris* and *London*, therefore these nouns are indirectly related to the predicate.

The GR tree is used by the *Service Prototype Builder* component to generate *service prototypes*. A service prototype corresponds to a property *P* in the request function and consists in a *process name* and its *input values*.

To create prototypes, the *Service Prototype Builder* component finds *dobj* (direct object) relations that include the predicate of the sentence. Then, the predicate and its direct object represent the process name. Other PoS that are related to either the predicate or its direct object (except other predicates) represent inputs for the process. For the previous example, the process is *print directions* and its inputs are *Paris* and *London*.

2.2   Semantic Matching

Information about services is published at a service registry. In Service Oriented Computing, the act of locating a machine-processable description of a resource that can be reached through a service that may have been previously unknown and that meets certain functional criteria is called *service discovery*. In essence, the discovery activity is comprised of matching the requirements of a service requester with the properties of a service provider.

Services are annotated using OWL-S [3], which is a standard ontology for describing the semantics of Web services. In order to find concrete services based on the user request, the concepts in the OWL-S service profiles are matched against their natural language service prototypes. Semantic matching evaluates the semantic similarity between a prototype and a concrete service. The metric we use, called the *conceptual distance*, was presented in paper [1].

The *conceptual distance* is a measure of the relatedness between two concepts. It is based on the WordNet [6] lexical database for the English language. The distance is zero for two synonyms and increases for remotely related terms. The use of related terms compensates for the **inexact** (inaccurate) user requests. Based on the conceptual distance, the distance between a prototype and a concrete service is evaluated as follows:

$$\frac{1}{2}min\{D(Ppn, Sn), D(Ppn, Pn))\} + \frac{1}{4}D(Ppi, Pi) + \frac{1}{4}(1 - \frac{min(Npp, Np)}{max(Npp, Np)}) \quad (1)$$

where Ppn is the prototype process name, Sn is the OWL-S service name, Pn is the OWL-S process name, Ppi are the prototype input names, Pi are the OWL-S input names, Npp is the number of prototype inputs, Np is the number of the actual service inputs.

For example, let's consider that the service prototype is *reserve flight (John Doe)*, where *reserve flight* is the prototype process name and *John Doe* and is the prototype process input. Also, the service repository contains 3 services:

1. Book Flight Service: Book Flight Atomic Process (Customer, Account Data, Flight), where the OWL-S service name is *Book Flight Service*, the OWL-S process name is *Book Flight Atomic Process* and the process input names are: *Customer, Account Data, Flight*

2. Book Flight Service 2: Book Flight Atomic Process (Flight, Account Data)

3. Book Medical Flight Service: Book Medical Flight Atomic Process (Attendant, Patient, Flight)

The distances for the prototype and named services are: D1 = 0.516, D2 = 0.75 and D3 = 0.75. The first service is the match for the given prototype. Even though the request is inexact, the matcher identifies the correct service as the verb *to book* is a related term to the verb *to reserve*. Also, *John Doe* is a *Person*, which is a related term to *Customer* and *Attendant*, therefore they match better than with other inputs.

2.3   Service Composition and Dealing with Request Incompleteness

Having identified the services requested by the user, a composed service can be created. Since generating workflows would be practically impossible without control constructs, we chose to use AI planning to keep the format of the user request unrestricted. But, in order for a planner to function, it requires complete knowledge of the world - a description of the initial state and goal, the set of services.

To specify the initial state and the user goal, first we determine the list of all services required for the composition. Semantic matching only retrieves services that are indicated by the user. But these services may require data provided by other services. For example, the *flight booking* service may require a valid account, therefore the *create account service* (which was not mentioned in the user request) needs to be invoked first.

To solve this, we use XPlan's [7] OWL reasoner. In AI planning, the reasoner is used to store the world state, answer the planner's queries regarding the evaluation of preconditions, and update the state when the planner simulates the effects of services. [8] When the complete list of required services is available, their inputs are matched against the inputs from the service prototypes. An input can have one of two sources: a value from the user, or the result of invoking another service. The value from the user can be part of the user request or acquired based on the user context / profile. For simplification, we assume that the user request is the only source of values for user provided inputs.

First, the inputs that result from invoking other services are resolved. What remains after this step is the list of inputs that need to be satisfied by the user. These are compared to the types and values of the service prototype inputs. If all the inputs are satisfied, the initial state and the user goal are created and provided to the planner for composition. Unsatisfied inputs, if any, are caused by **incomplete requests**. In a case when such a request is detected, the user is prompted for the value of unsatisfied inputs. This way, he is engaged in a dialog with the system, which keeps the service composition process intuitive and unrestricted.

3   Evaluation and Results

We approached two aspects of ambiguity - incompleteness and inexactness - for which we used two separate methods. Therefore, a separate evaluation is required for each of these methods. Instead of creating a new ontology from scratch, we extended the Health-SCALLOPS (H-S) ontology, that was proposed for evaluating XPlan. We chose this ontology, because it already provides support for various transportation services.

For the evaluation of semantic matching, we used 23 most common user queries, some that request a transportation service, others completely out of the context of the H-S ontology. Prototypes based on five of these queries and their similarity with services in the repository are summarized in Table 1.

The smallest semantic distance corresponds to a match. Matches for 95% of tested prototypes were correctly identified. One particular case is that of the prototype *create account (John)*, when the semantic matcher finds two candidate services. Situations like this are solved by picking the service that has the minimum $D(Ppn, Sn)$ from equation (1).

For the evaluation of service composition we used the same set of user queries. Following, we present a scenario for the where the user request is *Book medical flight from Paris to London*. Based on this request, the service prototype is *book medical flight (Paris, London)*. The matching service in this case is *Book Medical Flight Service*.

The OWL reasoner selects 3 extra services for composition: *Find Nearest Airport Service*, *Propose Medical Flight Service* and *Create Medical Flight Account Service*. Following inputs need to be satisfied: *1.* Provided Flight (isBookedFor : Person, hasDepartureLocation : Location, hasDestinationLocation : Location) and *2.* Person (hasAddress : Address).

Table 1. Similarity matching results

Service URI / Service Prototype	book flight alternative (John)	book flight (Paris, London)	create account (John)	find airport (Paris)	transport person (John)
../BookFlight.owl	0.458333333	**0.516666667**	0.683333333	0.783333333	0.495833333
../BookFlight2.owl	0.458333333	0.75	0.833333333	0.789583333	0.633333333
../BookFlightAlternative.owl	**0.404761905**	0.75	0.833333333	0.789583333	0.633333333
../BookMedicalFlight.owl	0.526785714	0.708333333	0.8125	0.7875	0.625
../BookMedicalFlight2.owl	0.609375	0.732142857	0.8125	0.8125	0.651785714
../CreateFlightAccount.owl	0.583333333	0.791666667	**0.666666667**	0.808333333	0.6875
../CreateFlightAccount2.owl	6.61E-01	0.80952381	0.69047619	0.833333333	0.672619048
../CreateMedicalFlightAccount.owl	0.583333333	0.791666667	**0.666666667**	0.808333333	0.697916667
../CreateMedicalFlightAccount2.owl	0.680555556	0.80952381	0.69047619	0.833333333	0.681547619
../CreateMedicalTransportAccount.owl	0.722222222	0.863095238	0.69047619	0.833333333	0.645833333
../CreateVehicleTransportAccount.owl	0.722222222	0.863095238	0.69047619	0.833333333	0.645833333
../CreateVehicleTransportAccount2.owl	0.722222222	0.916666667	0.833333333	0.833333333	0.731770833
../FindNearestAirport.owl	0.895833333	0.7	0.95	**0.75**	0.6
../ProposeFlight.owl	0.5625	0.591666667	0.758333333	0.802083333	0.558333333
../ProposeFlight2.owl	0.601190476	0.8125	0.833333333	0.808333333	0.645833333
../ProposeMedicalFlight.owl	0.601190476	0.8125	0.833333333	0.808333333	0.6875
../ProposeMedicalFlight2.owl	0.708333333	0.827380952	0.833333333	0.833333333	0.672619048
../RegisterPersonWithMedicalTransport.owl	0.736111111	0.880952381	0.833333333	0.833333333	0.606547619
../RegisterPersonWithTransport.owl	0.625	0.666666667	0.708333333	0.786458333	0.420833333
../RequestMedicalTransport.owl	0.654761905	0.875	0.833333333	0.795833333	0.614583333
../RequestTransport.owl	0.583333333	0.666666667	0.708333333	0.786458333	**0.470833333**

The *isBookedFor* field of the *Provided Flight* input is satisfied by the *Person* input. The remaining fields are compared to the service prototype input values: *hasDepartureLocation, hasDestinationLocation, hasAddress*. But the service prototype has only two inputs: *Paris, London*. Since input matching also uses the conceptual distance, and *location* and *address* are synonyms and *Paris* and *London* can be the value of both an address and a location, the system assigns *Paris* to the *hasDepartureLocation* field and *London* to the *hasDestinationLocation* of the *Provided Flight* input, then it asks the user to provide the value of the *hasAddress* field for the *Person* input. The composition plan the AI planner generates is shown in figure 2.

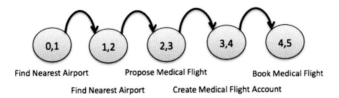

Fig. 2. The composition plan

4   Related Work

Several natural language service composition systems have been proposed in literature. The most relevant solutions related to our work are discussed below.

A solution based on restricted natural language and sentence templates. The system described in [5] assumes that the user request is expressed using a controlled vocabulary and is according to patterns like: *if ... then ... else, when ... do* and others. Based on verbs and patterns, the user request is transformed into a flow model. The major limitation of this solution derives from the restrictions imposed on how the user request is formulated. Another limitation is that, according to this approach, it is not clear how to create a new service if the user request specifies only a goal, without indications about how to achieve it.

Constructing workflows from natural language requests. Lim & Lee [9] propose a method for extracting a workflow from a natural language request. First, the user sentence is split into blocks based on control constructs (*if, then, else, etc.*) and verbs. Workflow templates are extracted by applying basic workflow patterns to control constructs. Second, for each sentence block, the service type and a list of candidate services are determined. Third, a service is selected from the candidate service list by calculating a similarity with the sentence block. Finally, an abstract workflow is generated by combining the workflow templates and the selected services. Control constructs and the lack of a semantic similarity measure (services need to be specified using words exactly as in their ontology) are the main disadvantages of this solution.

A solution based on AI Planning. The solution called SPICE ACE (Automatic Composition Engine) [10] is proposed as a development and a deployment platform for value-added services. The user request is transformed into a formal service request, specific to the ACE platform, a process which is not detailed in the paper. A causal link matrix models all possible interactions between all the known Web services as semantic connections. A semantic connection or a causal link consists of a triple: the output, the input and the semantic meaning of the link. An ontology is used to infer concept matching. The backward chaining technique is used for service composition: a plan of Web services is generated for finding an optimal plan among various compositions. The main drawbacks of this approach derive from the proposal's initial assumptions: a) the set of Web services is closed; situations like non-determinism, implicit goal, fuzzy service description are not considered.

5   Conclusion and Perspectives

In this paper, we propose an efficient method to compose a service, based on natural language requests. We focus on dealing with inexact and incomplete requests, while keeping them unrestricted. Inexactly named services are discovered using a semantic matcher that is able to measure the similarity between a natural language term and a concept from an ontology. Taking into account preconditions and effects, a reasoner discovers services related to those pointed by the user. When invoking these services, if missing inputs are detected, as in an incomplete request, the user is prompted to provide the required values.

The original aspect of our work is that by dealing with inexact and incomplete user requests, we manage to keep the query unrestricted in the context of current

Web service standards. Also, the user is actively involved into the composition process, through a dialog with the machine.

A few assumptions have been made: the user request is a form of imperative, a service prototype only matches a service from the repository and a contextual source of inputs is out of scope. The first two assumptions are justified, as most English requests are a form of imperative, and additional input sources can be implemented with ease.

The condition that a service prototype only matches a service from the repository is the major limitation of our system. Our semantic matching algorithm is intended to compensate for inexactness, which requires a compromise between a relaxed similarity metric and a small number of matches. The number of matches is linked to the number of candidate services. Instead of using a single candidate, the system could provide the user with a list of potential candidates to select from. But this is a challenge we intend to approach in the future.

Acknowledgments. This work was supported by CNCSIS-UEFISCSU, project code 1062/2007 and 1083/2007 and Brancusi PHC 301 project.

References

1. Cremene, M., Tigli, J.Y., Lavirotte, S., Pop, F.C., Riveill, M., Rey, G.: Service composition based on natural language requests. In: IEEE International Conference on Services Computing, pp. 486–489 (2009)
2. Martin, D., Burstein, M., Hobbs, J., Lassila, O., McDermott, D., McIlraith, S., et al.: OWL-S: Semantic Markup for Web Services (2004)
3. Portner, P.: The semantics of imperatives within a theory of clause types. In: Young, R.B. (ed.) Proceedings of SALT XIV, pp. 235–252. CLC Publications, Ithaca (2004)
4. Briscoe, T., Carroll, J., Watson, R.: The second release of the rasp system. In: Proceedings of the COLING/ACL on Interactive presentation sessions, Morristown, NJ, USA. Association for Computational Linguistics, pp. 77–80 (2006)
5. Christiane Fellbaum, E.: WordNet An Electronic Lexical Database. The MIT Press, Cambridge (1998), http://wordnet.princeton.edu/
6. Klusch, M., Gerber, A.: Evaluation of service composition planning with owls-xplan. In: WI-IATW 2006: Proceedings of the 2006 IEEE/WIC/ACM international conference on Web Intelligence and Intelligent Agent Technology, Washington, DC, USA, pp. 117–120. IEEE Computer Society, Los Alamitos (2006)
7. Sirin, E., Sirin, E., Parsia, B.: Planning for semantic web services. In: Semantic Web Services Workshop at 3rd International Semantic Web Conference (2004)
8. Bosca, A., Corno, F., Valetto, G., Maglione, R.: On-the-fly construction of web services compositions from natural language requests. JSW 1(1), 40–50 (2006)
9. Lim, J., Lee, K.H.: Constructing composite web services from natural language requests. Web Semant 8(1), 1–13 (2010)
10. Lécué, F., da Silva, E.G., Pires, L.F.: A framework for dynamic web services composition. In: WEWST (2007)

Families of SOA Migration

Maryam Razavian* and Patricia Lago

Department of Computer Science, VU University Amsterdam, The Netherlands
{m.razavian,p.lago}@few.vu.nl

Abstract. Migration of legacy systems to SOA constitutes a key challenge of service-oriented system engineering. Despite the many works around such migration, there is still little conceptual characterization on what SOA migration entails. To solve this problem, we conducted a systematic literature review that extracts main categories of SOA migration, called SOA migration families, from the approaches proposed in the research community. Based on the results of the systematic review, we describe eight distinct families along with their characteristics and goals.

1 Introduction

One of the key promises of service oriented paradigm is facilitating reuse of enterprise assets in legacy systems. Migration of legacy systems to service-based systems enables achieving advantages offered by SOA while still reusing the embedded capabilities in the legacy systems. Various studies present an approach for such migration. These studies mainly differ in the way they provide solutions for two challenging problems of what can be migrated (i.e. the legacy elements) and how the migration is performed (i.e. the migration process). Such differences can hinder achieving a general understanding of 'what SOA migration entails' and therefore making it difficult to determine how to migrate.

To obtain such understanding, we conducted a systematic literature review that extracts main migration categories existing in the field. Due to its methodological rigor, we chose systematic review as our research method in aggregating existing SOA migration approaches. Furthermore, the strength of systematic reviews in minimizing the bias in the review process enhances the extraction of sound and meaningful migration categories. By devising a coding procedure, we analyzed the studies and extracted eight distinct categories. Using a holistic conceptual framework that reflects distinct conceptual elements involved in the migration process, SOA migration families are typified in a unified manner. As such, these families act as a frame of reference for SOA migration which brings order and enhances understanding in how such migration can be carried out. Accordingly, this frame of reference increases awareness of the ways in which a legacy system can be migrated to SOA.

* This research has been partially sponsored by the Dutch Jacquard program on Software Engineering Research via contract 638.001.206 SAPIENSA: Service-enAbling PreexIsting ENterprISe Assets; and the European Community's FP7/2007-2013 under grant agreement 215483 (S-Cube).

P.P. Maglio et al. (Eds.): ICSOC 2010, LNCS 6470, pp. 678–679, 2010.

2   SOA Migration Families

By applying the pre-defined protocol of the systematic review, we identified 39 primary studies. Using qualitative analysis techniques, each of the primary studies was mapped to a framework represented in Fig. 1 called SOA-MF. By considering similar SOA-MF coverage patterns, out of 39 different mappings eight distinct families of SOA migration approaches were extracted. Fig. 1.III illustrates the schematic form of distinguished mappings that are dedicated to each family. As an example, F4.b is a schematic form of the mapping shown in Fig 1.II. At first glance, a SOA migration family represents a set of approaches with graphically similar mappings on SOA-MF. Despite their simplicity, the mappings reflect the following information about the migration process: to what extent the reverse engineering, transformation and forward engineering occur, what activities are carried out, what artifacts are used or produced, and what abstraction levels are covered. By positioning a migration approach on these families, insight in the following aspects can be achieved: what is migrated, how the migration is carried out, what is the main objective of migration, and finally, what are the available solutions. More details are outlined at `http://www.few.vu.nl/~mrazavi/SOAMigrationAppendix.pdf`.

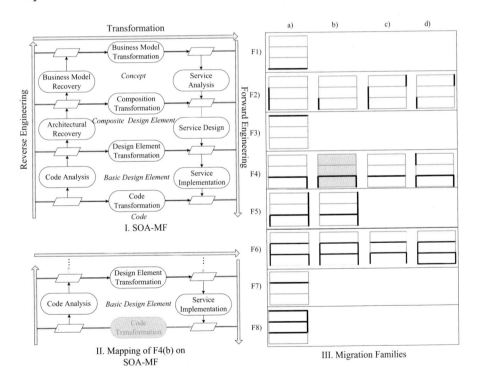

Fig. 1. SOA Migration Families

An Ontology Based Approach for Cloud Services Catalog Management

Yu Deng, Michael R. Head, Andrzej Kochut, Jonathan Munson,
Anca Sailer, and Hidayatullah Shaikh

IBM T.J. Watson Research Center,
P.O. Box 704, Yorktown Heights, NY 10598 USA
{dengy,mrhead,akochut,jpmunson,ancas,hshaikh}@us.ibm.com

Abstract. As more and more service providers choose to deliver services
on common Cloud infrastructures, it becomes important to formally represent knowledge in a services catalog to enable automatic answering of
user requests and sharing of building blocks across service offerings. In
this paper, we propose an ontology-driven methodology for formal modeling of the service offerings and associated processes.

Keywords: Ontology, Process composition, Catalog management, Cloud
services, Service composibility.

1   Introduction

Cloud computing, as a new computing model delivering on demand services regardless of time and location, hides complexities of large scale systems from its consumers. The services delivered on Cloud are normally presented to customers in a
service catalog. As more and more service providers leverage Cloud environments
to deliver their services, it becomes important to formally represent the knowledge
in these service catalogs. Such knowledge may include the definition of service offerings, relationships between offerings, processes to implement operations on the
offerings as well as related constraints and rules. We propose an ontology based
approach to formally model the service offerings and associated processes.

2   Ontology Model for Services Catalog

Ontology has received a lot of attention in the last few years. For example, the
Web Service Modeling Language (WSML)[1] provides a syntax and semantics
for modeling Web Service. In the process support aspect, Task ontologies [3] and
enterprise ontologies [2] enable process description as part of the problem and
respectively enterprise structure description. Recently, Youseff et al. [5] proposed
a unified ontology for Cloud computing, which is a layered classification of Cloud
services. In the business-process modeling and workflow automation arena, the
authors in [4] developed an workflow ontology. When integrated with a workflow
execution engine, they can map the top level of their ontology to a process-
modeling language as required by a workflow execution engine.

P.P. Maglio et al. (Eds.): ICSOC 2010, LNCS 6470, pp. 680–681, 2010.

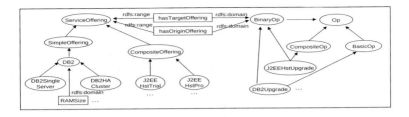

Fig. 1. An Simplified Catalog Ontology

We propose modeling the composibility of Cloud service offerings with common requirements for user actions in the services catalog. The composibility refers to the ability to compose a service offering from one or more other offerings. By examining common actions (e.g., onboarding, subscription, upgrade) taken by a user in a catalog across Cloud service offerings, we cover the following concepts in our ontology model: (1) Simple offering that is defined through properties (e.g., service functional requirements) and basic operations; (2) Basic operation that is a catalog action or internal atomic process; (3) Composite offering that leverages operations provided by simple or composite offerings; (4) Composite operation that is defined on top of simple or composite operations and corresponds to a user action when related to catalog offerings.

Figure 1 shows a simplified catalog ontology, where the links without any labels represent *rdfs:subClassOf* property. In the figure, *DB2SingleServer* and *DB2HACluster* are simple offerings and *DB2Upgrade* is a basic operation between these two offerings. In addition, *J2EEHstTrial* is a composite offering based on *DB2SingleServer* while *J2EEHstPro* is a composite offering based on *DB2HACluster*. The upgrade operation *J2EEHstUpgrade* between *J2EEHstTrial* and *J2EEHstPro* can be defined as a composite operation leveraging *DB2Upgrade*. Using our ontology model, we have developed algorithms to decompose user catalog actions into sequences of basic operations. Thus, the execution of complex actions can be automated using the sequenced operations on a Cloud platform.

References

1. WSML Language Reference, http://www.wsmo.org/TR/d16/d16.1/v1.0/
2. Grüninger, M., Atefi, K., Fox, M.S.: Ontologies to support process integration in enterprise engineering. Comput. Math. Organ. Theory 6(4), 381–394 (2000)
3. Mizoguchi, R., Vanwelkenhuysen, J., Ikeda, M.: Task ontology for reuse of problem solving knowledge. In: Proceedings of 2nd International Conference on Very Large-Scale Knowledge Bases (1995)
4. Sebastian, A., Noy, N.F., Tudorache, T., Musen, M.A.: A generic ontology for collaborative ontology-development workflows. In: Gangemi, A., Euzenat, J. (eds.) EKAW 2008. LNCS (LNAI), vol. 5268, pp. 318–328. Springer, Heidelberg (2008)
5. Youseff, L., Butrico, M., Silva, D.D.: Towards a unified ontology of cloud computing. In: Proceedings of GCE 2008, held in conjunction with SC 2008 (2008)

A Scalable Cloud-Based Queueing Service with Improved Consistency Levels

Han Chen, Fan Ye, Minkyong Kim, and Hui Lei

IBM T.J. Watson Research Center, 19 Skyline Drive, Hawthorne, NY 10532
{chenhan,fanye,minkyong,hlei}@us.ibm.com

Queuing, an asynchronous messaging paradigm, is used to connect loosely coupled components to form large-scale, highly-distributed, and fault-tolerant applications. As cloud computing continues to gain traction, a number of vendors currently operate cloud-based shared queuing services. These services provide high availability and network partition tolerance with reduced consistency—at-least once delivery (no-loss) with no effort in message order. This paper presents the design and implementation of BlueDove Queuing Service (BDQS), a scalable cloud-based queuing service with improved queuing consistency. BDQS provides at-least once and best-effort in-order message delivery model, while preserving high availability and partition tolerance. It also offers clients a flexible trade-off between message duplication and message order. Performance evaluation shows that BDQS achieves linear throughput scalability and offers significantly reduced out-of-order messages compared to no-order queuing services.

BDQS consists of three main components. Cassandra, an open source distributed key-value store, provides highly available and partition tolerant *persistence*. The *queue operations* component implements a queue API using Cassandra API. The queue operations component stores all states in Cassandra; therefore, multiple instances can be deployed to maximize overall system throughput. To enable a wide variety of clients to access the service, an *HTTP REST* component provides a RESTful interface of the native queue API via HTTP binding. In a cloud-based deployment, VM images consisting of one instance of each component described above are deployed on an Infrastructure-as-a-service cloud, as shown in Figure 1. A dispatching mechanism routes client requests to a REST interface instance. To provide adequate service level, a separate monitoring mechanism controls the dynamic scaling of the cluster.

Messages in BDQS are distributed among all available nodes. To provide best-effort in-order delivery, an index of message sequence is maintained for each queue. In order to maximize system throughput and assure availability, no distributed locks are used among the multiple queue operations instances. The result is that, when multiple clients invoke `ReceiveMessage` operation on the same queue object using different entry points into the system, the same message may be returned to these clients. BDQS uses a collision avoidance algorithm to balance the probability of duplication and the message delivery order. Instead of always retrieving the first message in the index, the system retrieves a random one among the first K messages. The larger the value of K, the less likely that concurrent receivers will obtain the same message, but the more out-of-order

P.P. Maglio et al. (Eds.): ICSOC 2010, LNCS 6470, pp. 682–683, 2010.

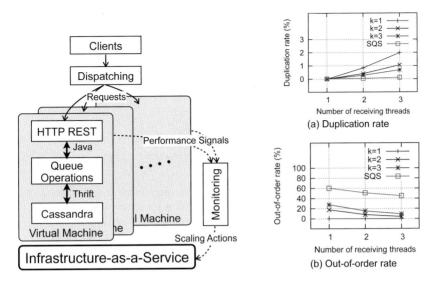

Fig. 1. Deployment architecture of BDQS on an IaaS cloud

Fig. 2. Consistency level hint (K) controls the tradeoff between order and duplication

the returned message sequence will be. Thus K acts as a consistency level hint, which the system exposes as a configurable parameter for each queue.

A prototype of BDQS has been implemented and deployed on an IaaS platform. Simulation drivers are used to generate a synthetic workload to benchmark the system's performance. Evaluation results show that the system's throughput scales linearly versus the cluster size. (Details are not reported here.) To quantify the improvement in consistency, we vary the number of receiver threads per queue, T_{recv}, from 1 to 3 to generate different levels of concurrency in ReceiveMessage operations. Three consistency level hints are used, $K = 1, 2, 3$. To compare the consistency level against a no-order system, the same workload is tested on Amazon SQS. Figure 2(a) shows that with no concurrency $(T_{recv} = 1)$, both BDQS and the no-order system produce negligible amount of duplication. When concurrency increases, duplication rate increases for BDQS. The rate of increase depends on the consistency level hint—the more order is favored, the more duplicates are produced. In a no-order system, random sampling is used to retrieve message. Therefore the duplication rate remains low when concurrency increases. On the other hand, Figure 2(b) shows that BDQS produces significantly fewer out-of-order messages. With consistency level hint $K = 1$, almost all messages are delivered in order, whereas the no-order system delivers about 50% of messages out of order. Out-of-order measures increase as K increases, but they are much smaller than those of the no-order system. This result shows that BDQS offers client a flexible way to specify the desired tradeoff between the two aspects of consistency—order and duplication. In fact, the no-effort approach can be viewed as a special case of BDQS, where $K = \infty$.

Exploring Simulation-Based Configuration Decisions

Michael Smit and Eleni Stroulia*

Department of Computing Science
University of Alberta
Edmonton, AB, Canada
{msmit,stroulia}@cs.ualberta.ca

Abstract. As service compositions grow larger and more complex, so does the challenge of configuring the underlying hardware infrastructure on which the component services are deployed. With more configuration options (virtualized systems, cloud-based systems, *etc.*), the challenge grows more difficult. Configuring service-oriented systems involves balancing a competing set of priorities and choosing trade-offs to achieve high-priority goals. We describe a simulation-based methodology for supporting administrators in making these decisions by providing them with relevant information obtained using inexpensive simulation-generated data. From our existing services-aware simulation framework, we generated millions of performance metrics for a given system in varying configurations. We describe how we structured our simulation experiments to answer specific questions such as optimal service distribution across multiple servers; we relate a general methodology for assisting administrators in balancing trade-offs; and we present results establishing benchmarks for the cost and performance improvements we can expect from run-time configuration adaptation for this application.

Deciding on the size, scale, and configuration of computing infrastructure is complex even for technical experts. Decisions must be made about trade-offs between many different attributes and configuration parameters. Configuration assistance supports decision-making about systems; our focus is on the domain of service-oriented software infrastructure, particularly trade-offs involving quality versus cost, where "quality" means attributes that fall within the domain of quality of service (QoS), and "cost" means financial cost.

We offer three novel contributions in the area of configuration assistance, each on a path toward autonomic assistance based on models built by reasoning with simulation-generated data. These methodologies are applicable to other applications and data sets. We describe a proof-of-concept based on data generated by a simulated service-oriented system (running on our existing simulation framework [1,2]), run in a variety of configurations and usage scenarios.

The first contribution is question answering, where the simulation is run in specific scenarios designed to explore the system behavior under alternative conditions. For example, we considered the challenge of distributing the operations

---

* The authors acknowledge the generous support of iCORE, NSERC, and IBM.

P.P. Maglio et al. (Eds.): ICSOC 2010, LNCS 6470, pp. 684–685, 2010.

of a web service among a number of servers to identify the configuration that produced the best performance versus cost trade-off. For all possible distributions on 1, 2, or 3 servers, we simulated a two hour block of realistic traffic. The single-server configuration took 277 minutes to process all of the requests. The fastest two-server configurations took 140 minutes (50% less time); twice the cost, twice the performance. The fastest three-server configurations completed shortly after the traffic generator stopped generating requests (120 minutes), 57% less time than the single server. This represents 3 times the cost but only 2.3 times the performance: a more expensive improvement. An expert manually created a three-server configuration using the same information available to the simulation. His suggestion took 137 minutes: worse than the best three-server configurations but better than two servers.

Second, we present our method for undirected exploration of potentially conflicting configuration goals and trade-offs, where we assist in establishing service-level agreements (SLAs), appropriate thresholds, accurate costing models, or appropriate configurations to meet a specific SLA or cost model. The foundation is our visual comparison tool for viewing the trade-off between two potentially conflicting metrics. For example, to identify an SLA with appropriate thresholds, a user is shown a series of such comparisons for relevant metrics, and for each selects the configurations with the balance they desire. Each configuration is given a fitness score based not only on how frequently that configuration is selected, but also by both how close to the "ideal" trade-offs identified by the user and how important each trade-off is to the user (estimated automatically). This identified plausible ideal configurations; a full user study of satisfaction with the results is pending.

Finally, we explored the effect of run-time configuration adaptation on the simulated application, determining the benefit of and targets for a future autonomic system. The tool developed for this exploration could also be used to train administrators to adapt configurations to changing situations, or to help administrators understand how the system behaves in various configurations. Using our simulation, we sent an identical set of requests to 5 configurations: fixed 3, 4, 5, and 6 server configurations, and a configuration where the number of servers was manually adapted based on the performance of the application. Compared to a fixed 3-server configuration, a manually varied configuration with 1 to 6 servers was 3% more expensive but performed 75% better. 5 and 6 server configurations performed 78% and 88% better, but cost 22% and 38% more (respectively).

References

1. Smit, M., Nisbet, A., Stroulia, E., Edgar, A., Iszlai, G., Litoiu, M.: Capacity planning for service-oriented architectures. In: CASCON 2008: Proceedings of the 2008 conference of the Center for Advanced Studies on collaborative research, pp. 144–156. ACM, New York (2008)
2. Smit, M., Nisbet, A., Stroulia, E., Iszlai, G., Edgar, A.: Toward a simulation-generated knowledge base of service performance. In: Proceedings of the 4th International Workshop on Middleware for Service Oriented Computing (November 2009)

Efficient, Failure-Resilient Semantic Web Service Planning

Florian Wagner[1]
(Advisors: Fuyuki Ishikawa[2] and Shinichi Honiden[1,2])

[1] The University of Tokyo, Japan
[2] National Institute of Informatics, Tokyo, Japan
{florian,f-ishikawa,honiden}@nii.ac.jp

Abstract. Over the past years service-oriented architectures have been widely adopted by stakeholders from research and industry. Since the number of services increases rapidly, effective methods are required to automatically discover and compose services according to user requirements. For this purpose, machine-understandable semantic annotations have to be applied in order to enable logical reasoning on the functional aspects of services. However, current approaches are not capable of composing workflows in reasonable time, except for planning tools that require domain-dependent heuristics or constrain the expressiveness of the description language. In addition to that, these tools neglect alternative plans, concealing the danger of creating a workflow having insufficient reliability. Therefore, we propose an approach to efficiently pre-cluster similar services according to their parameters. This way the search space is limited and vulnerable intermediate steps in the workflow can be effectively avoided.

1 Introduction

The service-oriented paradigm envisions the discovery and composition of reusable services by using widely accepted standards such as XML and HTTP. This way loosely coupled components can be dynamically integrated into an infrastructure of e.g. a company, independent of the given hardware and software.

In order to further enhance the automatic selection and composition of services, machine-processable descriptions based on service ontologies such as WSMO and OWL-S and the annotation language SAWSDL have been proposed. Web services that provide semantic descriptions are called *semantic web services*.

Semantic annotations are mandatory for AI planning, that can be incorporated in order to create service workflows automatically. Instead of offering a restricted set of predefined composite services, the user can request customized composite services by providing a set of input and output parameters plus preconditions and the intended effects. Service planning is an active research field that poses one central challenge in service computing research [4].

In this paper we tackle the problems of insufficient performance and lacking reliability of current service planning algorithms. Many registries contain services that have the same intended purpose. Therefore, we will show how the

P.P. Maglio et al. (Eds.): ICSOC 2010, LNCS 6470, pp. 686–689, 2010.

performance and reliability issues can be addressed by identifying and clustering these services beforehand.

2   Problem Statement

In this section we present the two main phases in service planning, the composition of abstract workflows and the subsequent service grouping for each task.

In the composition phase, a planning tool attempts to compute a composite service from a set of given services. For this purpose, the user provides a set of input and output parameters including the guaranteed preconditions and the intended effects to the planer. Since the search space is exponential, the runtime performance and memory usage are central issues in current planning tools and therefore AI algorithms cannot be applied blindfolded. In order to prune the search space, heuristics can be employed but these are in most cases tailored for a particular domain and therefore are only of limited reusability.

After computing an appropriate workflow, for each task all applicable services are selected and grouped in so-called service classes. If in the execution phase one service crashes, then any other service from the same class can be used to compensate the erroneous services (failure resilience). Moreover, QoS-(Quality-of-Service) aware service selection algorithms [7] can be applied to choose a specific service for each class in order to optimize the utility function of the user. However, current planning tools do not take the reliability of the service classes into account but instead attempt to find the shortest possible plan in order to simplify the planning task. If a service class contains only very few services, then these class might comprise the whole workflow, in other words pose a so-called *single point of failure*.

If a service fault occurs, re-planning can be instantiated [2], invoking additional services in order to obtain the desired output parameters and effects. This might include services that try to revert some recent world state changes caused by previous services, entailing additional costs for the user.

3   Proposed Approach

Our approach towards service planning is divided into two steps. First, functional similar services are pre-clustered and arranged in a hierarchical structure beforehand. Second, in the composition stage a planning tool is incorporated, taking only the representatives of each cluster into consideration. This way the search space is limited efficiently and heuristics that take the reliability into consideration can be integrated easily.

3.1   Pre-clustering of Services

Registries often contain services that have the same intended purpose, e.g. booking of a hotel room or requesting stock market information. By clustering these services automatically, we can avoid redundant computations in the planning phase and moreover evaluate the reliability of every type of service. In order to identify such clusters we propose to use the partial order relation that is given by *Exact* and *Plug-in* matches and was first introduced as a clustering method in pervasive service computing [3]. Given a specific service s, all services that have an *Exact* or *Plug-in* match with this service can be used as a replacement.

In the end, services are grouped in a hierarchical structure, turning the registry into a set of trees. Roots are called *representatives* since their functionality can be considered as a "least common denominator" of its corresponding subtree.

3.2   Planning Algorithm Outline

In the planning stage only the computed representatives are taken into account. In case no feasible plan could be computed, large service classes are split up by removing the root and adding the subtrees into the registry (cf. Figure 1).

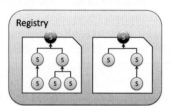

(a) Original service classes

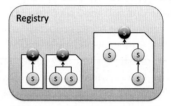

(b) After splitting the biggest class

Fig. 1. A split operation on the service classes

Afterwards, the planning algorithm iteratively attempts to compute a plan with the modified classes until a plan was found. In the end, the workflow containing the corresponding classes is returned.

3.3   Expected Outcome

We expect to shrink the search space to a size that can be solved by planning tools in reasonable time. In contrast to related search algorithms, that employ a domain-specific heuristic, our approach is domain-independent.

Single points of failure can be avoided effectively since each service in the service class can be used as a replacement service in case of a failure.

Selection algorithms, mentioned in Section 2, benefit from our approach as well. Since we attempt to extend the number of services per task, these algorithms have more services to choose from. Using our approach, these algorithms can be reused and therefore bridge the gap between automatic composition and service selection research.

4   Related Work

AI planning has a long history in computer science and various approaches have been introduced to the service domain [5].

The approach described in [6] uses the HTN planner SHOP2, requiring a plan library that contains decomposition rules for dedicated domains, thus this approach cannot be applied to arbitrary domains.

In [1] the HTN planner Xplan is employed, combining forward and HTN planning. It uses a graph plan algorithm if no decomposition rules can be applied. Thereby, it will always find a plan, but the search space is also exponential.

Apart from that, several researchers focus on the problem of crashing services. For instance, in [2] a re-planning scope is defined and iteratively extended until all faulty services have been successfully compensated. Our approach attempts to avoid re-planning, since it entails additional costs for the user.

Our approach is based on [3] that originally introduced the hierarchical structure implied by *Exact* and *Plug-in* matches for the service matchmaking domain.

5 Conclusion and Future Work

In this paper we have presented our approach towards semantic web service planning. Thereby, we addressed performance and reliability issues by pre-clustering functional similar services and determining representatives for the planning stage.

As a next step we intend to further develop the current pre-clustering and planning algorithm. Subsequently, we will examine how to integrate both into given planning tools and evaluate our approach.

References

1. Klusch, M., Gerber, A.: Semantic web service composition planning with OWLS-XPlan. In: Proceedings of the 1st Int. AAAI Fall Symposium on Agents and the Semantic Web, pp. 55–62 (2005)
2. Lin, K.J., Zhang, J., Zhai, Y.: An efficient approach for service process reconfiguration in SOA with End-to-End QoS constraints. In: Hofreiter, B., Werthner, H. (eds.) CEC, pp. 146–153. IEEE Computer Society, Los Alamitos (2009)
3. Mokhtar, S.B., Preuveneers, D., Georgantas, N., Issarny, V., Berbers, Y.: EASY: Efficient semantic service discovery in pervasive computing environments with QoS and context support. Journal of Systems and Software 81(5), 785–808 (2008)
4. Papazoglou, M.P., Traverso, P., Dustdar, S., Leymann, F.: Service-oriented computing: State of the art and research challenges. IEEE Computer 40(11) (2007)
5. Peer, J.: Web service composition as AI planning - a survey. Tech. rep., University of St. Gallen, Switzerland (2005)
6. Wu, D., Parsia, B., Sirin, E., Hendler, J.A., Nau, D.S.: Automating DAML-S web services composition using SHOP2. In: Fensel, D., Sycara, K., Mylopoulos, J. (eds.) ISWC 2003. LNCS, vol. 2870, pp. 195–210. Springer, Heidelberg (2003)
7. Zeng, L., Benatallah, B., Dumas, M., Kalagnanam, J., Sheng, Q.Z.: Quality driven web services composition. In: WWW 2003: Proceedings of the 12th International Conference on World Wide Web, pp. 411–421. ACM, New York (2003)

Integrated Service Process Adaptation

Zhe Shan
(Advisor: Dr. Akhil Kumar)

Department of Supply Chain and Information Systems,
Smeal College of Business, Penn State University, USA
zheshan@psu.edu

Abstract. With more automation in inter-organizational supply chains and proliferation of Web services technology, the need for organizations to link their business services and processes is becoming increasingly important. Using adapters to
reconcile incompatibilities between multiple interacting business processes is an
efficient and low-cost way to enable automatic and friction-free supply chain
collaboration in an IT-enabled environment. My dissertation proposes a new
framework and novel techniques for integrated service process adaptation. For the
control flow adaptation, we propose an algorithm based on Message Interaction
Graph to create an optimal adapter. For message adaptation, we identify a set of
extendible message adaptation patterns to solve typical message mismatches. In
addition new message adapter can be generated on the fly so as to integrate
control flow considerations into message adaptation. Finally we design another
algorithm to integrate individual message adaptation patterns with control flow
adapters to create a full adapter for multiple processes. We implement all these algorithms in a Java-based prototype system and show the advantages of our methods by performance experiment and case study.

Keywords: business process composition, service process adaptation, message
interaction graph, optimal adapter, message adaptation patterns.

1 Introduction

Organizations rely on effective supply chains to successfully compete in the global
market. Successful supply chain management integrates individual functions within
organization or across difference parties. Supply chain business process integration
involves collaborative work between supply chain partners. The concept of business
collaboration seeks to organize entire business processes throughout a value chain of
multiple parties. In recent years, the concentration of supply chain collaboration has
shifted from the inputs and outputs of the processes to the process semantics of individual players. Furthermore, market forces demand changes with supply chain partners. This variability has significant effect on the design and configuration of the
processes. Therefore, how to analyze the correctness and robustness of business collaboration has become a key factor of supply chain success.

During the past decades, information technology has enabled many organizations
to successfully operate solid collaborative supply networks. Recently, E-services and
cloud computing technologies prevail to increase creativity, information sharing, and

P.P. Maglio et al. (Eds.): ICSOC 2010, LNCS 6470, pp. 690–694, 2010.

collaboration among supply chain network. The grand vision of those revolutionary technologies is leading to considerable inner- or cross-organization interactions in a real-time and ad-hoc way. Therefore, how to achieve automated, "on-the-fly" composition of two or more processes to create new collaboration, and new technologies for designing and offering business processes is the key challenge in this new business environment. The traditional approaches based on process re-design or re-engineering cannot fulfill those new requirements due to their long lifecycle and high cost. By comparison, creating adapters to enable conflict-free collaborations is a much more efficient and cost-saving solution.

The purpose of service process adaptation is to mediate the communication between multiple processes to overcome the mismatches in the message and control flow aspects. Our goal in this work is to develop a framework and new techniques for creating highly flexible, dynamic, general purpose adapters that can be written on-the-fly to allow interaction between multiple services. This framework (Figure 1) can integrate two major dimensions of adaptation, i.e. control flow adaptation and message adaptation.

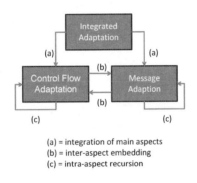

(a) = integration of main aspects
(b) = inter-aspect embedding
(c) = intra-aspect recursion

Fig. 1. Framework for service process adaptation

2   Control Flow Adaptation Based on Message Interaction Graph

In this work, we assume that each process is well structured, i.e. each split for a pattern has a corresponding join, and also that the patterns are properly nested inside one another. We focus on the analysis of Sequence and Parallel (SP) structure, because Choice and Loop structures are eventually composed of branches of these structures. It has been shown in previous work that for two processes to be compatible their choice and loop structures must be matched [1]. Moreover, it is assumed that the messages in interacting processes (and along branches of choice and loop structures) are well matched, i.e. each send activity in process i has a corresponding receive activity in process j, and vice versa. Additionally, we assume for ease of exposition that each send or receive activity is unique and is not repeated in the process.

The incompatibilities in SP processes are mainly due to crossovers in message flows. We explain all these incompatibilities in a new tool named *Message Interaction Graph* (MIG), and generalize the incompatibility analysis for multiple messages and multiple processes.

A *Message Interaction Graph* (MIG) consists of nodes and directed edges, where a node denotes a unique message in a multiple-process interaction, labeled with message ID or name. There are one or two arcs between each two nodes. Each arc denotes a control-flow link between two messages, labeled with activity information (S for Send and R for Receive.). Figure 2 shows one incompatibility example and its corresponding MIG.

Based on MIG, we have the following results for incompatibility detection and adapter creation. The proofs of these results are available in [2].

Result 1: In a MIG, if all the links in a cycle are of type RS or RR, then the process interaction represented by the MIG is deadlocked and it cannot be broken with an adapter.

Result 2: Multiple interacting processes are compatible without an adapter if and only if their MIG does not contain any cycle.

Result 3: In a MIG cycle, message m can be adapted to break the cycle if its outgoing arc is labeled with S* (SR or SS), and its incoming arc is labeled with *R (SR or RR).

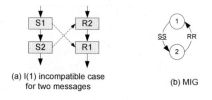

(a) I(1) incompatible case for two messages

(b) MIG

Fig. 2. Incompatible case and MIG

From result 2 and 3, we know that to check whether multiple processes are compatible in an interaction, we transform them into a MIG and check for cycles in it. If there is no cycle in the MIG, then these processes are compatible without an adapter. If there exists at least one cycle in which no Send is adaptable (Type I(0) incompatibility), these interacting processes are deadlocked. If all cycles in the MIG contains at least one adaptable Send (from result 3), then we can always create an adapter to make these processes compatible in interaction. Two variants of the optimal adapter creation algorithm are discussed in [2].

3 Message Adaptation

After the discussion on the control flow adaptation, we focus on the message adaptation in this section. Due to independent design efforts or non-standardized industry practices, generally the message interfaces between multiple services are not well matched. Message adapters are needed to reconcile this incompatibility. We propose a set of patterns for message adaptation. a) Message data generation: It generates default information for it based on specific scenario semantics. b) Message data casting: It calculates or transforms the data based on available information. c) Message Fragmentation and Aggregation: *Message fragmentation* means that a large message is divided into sub-elements in a 1-to-n relationship, while *message aggregation* means the opposite. Some typical patterns are shown in Figure 3.

These patterns can be further concatenated, nested, or extended by users. In general, the interaction between two subgroups of activities is quite complex if one subgroup contains a mix of sequence and parallel structures. Basic adaptation patterns cannot cover all such situations. A new algorithm is introduced in [3] to create an message adapter on the fly. Furthermore, an adapter integration algorithm is presented in [3] to integrate individual message adaptation patterns with control flow adapters to create a full adapter.

4   Related Work and Conclusion

In the control flow adaptation part, [4] and [5] are closely related work to ours. But they create non-minimal adapters. There is very limited research involving integration of both control flow and message aspects in service process adaptation. [6], [7], and [8] are valuable work in this area. We compare our approach with them in [3].

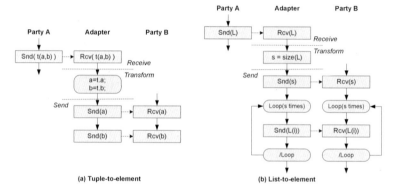

Fig. 3. Selected message adaptation patterns

In this work, we propose a new framework and novel techniques for service process adaptation, which integrates both message and control flow adaptation. It is based on the recognition that message adaptation can affect control flow and vice versa. Hence, a tight integration is required between these two aspects. For control flow adaptation, our algorithms are based on using a pattern compatibility matrix and matching rules to reduce the search space. Furthermore, we described algorithms based on MIG to generate an optimal adapter. For message adaptation, we identify common message mismatch patterns and also show how adapters can be created on the fly for matching parts of two services where basic adapter patterns do not exist. Last, we show how message adapters can themselves be combined to create an aggregate adapter for the complete service process integration. We implemented all these algorithms in a Java-based prototype system and show the advantages of our methods by performance experiment and case study in [2, 3].

References

1. Kumar, A., Shan, Z.: Algorithms Based on Pattern Analysis for Verification and Adapter Creation for Business Process Composition. In: CoopIS 2008, pp. 120–138 (2008)
2. Shan, Z., Kumar, A., Liu, R.: Creating a Minimal Adapter for Multiple Business Process Composition. Under review (2010)
3. Shan, Z., Kumar, A., Grefen, P.: Towards Integrated Service Adaptation – A New Approach Combining Message and Control Flow Adaptation. In: ICWS 2010, pp. 385–392 (2010)
4. Brogi, A., Popescu, R.: Automated Generation of BPEL Adapters. In: Dan, A., Lamersdorf, W. (eds.) ICSOC 2006. LNCS, vol. 4294, pp. 27–39. Springer, Heidelberg (2006)
5. Seguel, R., Eshuis, R., Grefen, P.: Constructing minimal protocol adaptors for service composition. In: WEWST 2009, pp. 29–38 (2009)
6. Motahari Nezhad, H.R., Benatallah, B., Martens, A., Curbera, F., Casati, F.: Semi-automated adaptation of service interactions. In: WWW 2007, pp. 993–1002 (2007)
7. Kongdenfha, W., Motahari-Nezhad, H.R., Benatallah, B., Casati, F., Saint-Paul, R.: Mismatch Patterns and Adaptation Aspects: A Foundation for Rapid Development of Web Service Adapters. IEEE Transactions on Services Computing 2, 94–107 (2009)
8. Li, X., Fan, Y., Madnick, S., Sheng, Q.Z.: A Pattern-based Approach to Procotol Mediation for Web Services Composition. Working Paper, 4716-08, MIT Sloan School of Management (2008)

Contract Based, Non-invasive, Black-Box Testing of Web Services

Michael Averstegge

(Advisor: Bernd J. Kraemer)

FernUniversitt Hagen, Germany
Department of Electrical Engineering
Michael.Averstegge@web.de

Abstract. The Web service standard represents a prominent conversion of the SOA paradigm increasingly used in practice. The (not so knew) technical aspects in combination with the practices introducded by the WEB, lead new challanges in testing Web services often stated in literature. Introduced in this paper is a not invasive functional testing approach for Web services based on the Design by Contract (DbC) paradigm. By using formal semantic specification in a consequent manner we can present a generic testing approach which enables us to introduce quality metric measurements not before viable in traditional testing in a practicable way. We present results of our first basic study at the Schweizer Bundesbahn (SBB) Informatik in Bern.

Keywords: Web service, design by contract, generic testdriver, generic oracle, semantic specification, conformity, black-box test, monitoring, contract checker, test data generation, non-invasive.

1   Introduction

Web services are the main realization of service oriented architecture (SOA) and are widely considered to be the strategic model for loose coupled, distributed computing ([9], [7], [4], [13]).

Its often stated that unforseen dynamically use of Web services leads to new challanges in the field of testing ([5], [1]). The WSDL specification ([12]) is a syntactical contract of a Web service and ist therefor on the first level of contracts ([3]). New conceptual enhancements of the traditional test techniques and methods is postulated ([8], [6]).

Immens growing dependencies and fast changing interfaces make it impossible to test bug fixes as well as newly added interfaces in manifold usage environments. Our answer to the challanges is a new fully generic, non-invasive functional test-technique method of contract based Web service functions. Test oracle and test driver are generally derived from the contract and the WSDL specification. By this newly introduced technique we can use the structural coverage proof of the formal semantic specification as a quality metric ([2]).

One basic side effect is the economic efficiency: writing testdrivers manually is obsolete.

P.P. Maglio et al. (Eds.): ICSOC 2010, LNCS 6470, pp. 695–698, 2010.

2   Contract-Based Testing

We connote a contract to a WSDL and its correspondig Web service. The contract is given in XML-syntax specified by an XSD definition. The expression of contract conditions are given in OCL. This language is used to be adoptable to model based approaches.

The technical architecture for the interaction of any client, VWS, monitor agents and WSUT is depicted in figure 1.

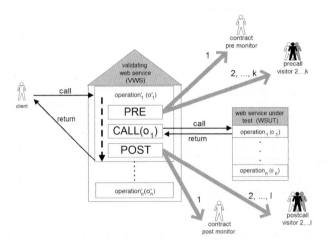

Fig. 1. VWS-Proxy and Monitor

The framework includes following functional kernels:

1. Proxy and monitor-agents generation,
2. Type-system analysis and persisting,
3. Runtime monitoring of the Web service under test (WSUT),
4. Testdriver generation,
5. Oracle generation,
6. Testdata import,
7. Test executing. i.e.:
   (a) running generic testdriver,
   (b) agent monitors and persists runtime values,
   (c) generic oracle,
       i. verifies pre-/post-conditions and invariants,
       ii. determines coverage metrics qualities of expression and atomic expression and
       iii. determines functional correctness of the particular WSUT function.

The observer pattern allows to plug in in further agents, especially ones that break the proxy conformity by, e.g., refusing calls with actual parameter values which don't achieve the preconditions and can be used to implement Meyer's *Modular Protection* ([10], pp. 345). We tested this first and necessary condition in a study at real business WSUT applications (ticketing system) at the Schweizer Bundesbahn (SBB).

2.1   An Example: Bookflight

We give a simple example to demonstrate the functionality and the benefit of using business rules in form of contracts right from the start.

Let's take the often used example of booking a flight.

precondition	`flight_nof > children_nof` and
	`children_nof >= 0` and
	`location_from <> location_to`
postcondition	`result.akzeptedOrder.flight_nof > 0`

Fig. 2. Simple contract (3)

From the VWS-System GUI we start the test run by clicking a button to start to formentioned mechanism.

The result is depicted in figure 3. We focus on branche coverage (Branch), simple condition coverage (SCC), modified decision condition coverage (MCDC) and multiple condition coverage (MCC).

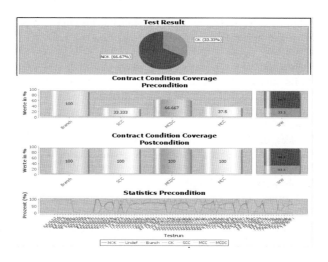

Fig. 3. Oracle Report (3)

In a study we implemented a testdata generator which uses the contract, transforms it to an equation with n unknowns (n = number of distinct atomar conditions) and calling the solver GlassTT ([11]). This works for about 80% of conditions used in the WSDL interfaces. This technique is also very effective in evaluating boundary values.

In further studies we will collect data in professional projects to measure and prove the aformentioned benefits in terms of numerary.

3 Summary

We presented the non-invasive validating system VWS framework, with which Web services can be supervised and tested based on contract in a contract-based way.

The non-invasive approach is realized by inserting an intermediate, transparent layer between caller and supplier that serves for validating the WSUT.

We introduce with the VWS testing framework a new technical and methodic way of testing Web services, based on behavioral contractual level. Conceptually this is not limited to a specific component technology, but for Web service testing it generates the most dramatic earnings. This method enables us to adopt structural quality metrics in thorough generic functional testing. The aforementioned metrics could not be measured practicable without formal semantic specification before.

References

1. Andrikopoulos, V., Benbernou, S., Papazoglou, M.P.: Evolving services from a contractual perspective. In: van Eck, P., Gordijn, J., Wieringa, R. (eds.) CAiSE 2009. LNCS, vol. 5565, pp. 290–304. Springer, Heidelberg (2009)
2. Averstegge, M.: Generisches testen von webservices. OBJEKTspektrum 4(4) (2010)
3. Beugnard, A., Jézéquel, J.-M., Plouzeau, N., Watkins, D.: Making components contract aware. Computer 32(7), 38–45 (1999)
4. Dustdar, S., Haslinger, S.: Testing of service-oriented architectures - a practical approach. In: Weske, M., Liggesmeyer, P. (eds.) NODe 2004. LNCS, vol. 3263, pp. 97–109. Springer, Heidelberg (2004)
5. Farooq, A., Dumke Reiner, R., Georgieva, K.: Challenges in evaluating soa test processes. In: Dumke, R.R., Braungarten, R., Büren, G., Abran, A., Cuadrado-Gallego, J.J. (eds.) IWSM 2008. LNCS, vol. 5338, pp. 107–113. Springer, Heidelberg (2008)
6. Heckel, R., Lohmann, M.: Towards contract-based testing of web services (2004)
7. Huang, H., Tsai, W.-T., Paul, R., Chen, Y.: Automated model checking and testing for composite web services. In: ISORC , pp. 300–307 (2005)
8. Martin, E., Basu, T.X.S.: Automated testing and response analysis of web services. In: Proc. the IEEE International Conference on Web Services (ICWS 2007), Application Services and Industry Track, July 2007, pp. 647–654 (2007)
9. Martínez, A., Martínez, M.P., Jiménez-Peris, R., Pérez-Sorrosal, F.: Zenflow: A visualweb service composition tool for bpel4ws. In: Proceedings of the 2005 IEEE Symposium on Visual Languages and Human-Centric Computing, VL/HCC 2005 (2005)
10. Meyer, B.: Object-Oriented Software Construction, 2nd edn. Prentice-Hall, Englewood Cliffs (1997)
11. Kuchen, H., Müller, R., Lembeck, C.: GlassTT – a Symbolic Java Virtual Machine Using Constraint Solving Techniques for Glass-Box Test Case Generation. Technical Report 102, Universität Münster, Institut für Informatik (2003)
12. W3C. Web Services Description Language (WSDL) 1.1 (2001), http://www.w3.org/TR/wsdl (last visited (2010.06.03))
13. Yang, J.: Web service componentization. Commun. ACM 46(10), 35–40 (2003)

Managing Process Model Collections with AProMoRe

M.C. Fauvet[1,*], M. La Rosa[2], M. Sadegh[2], A. Alshareef[2], R.M. Dijkman[3],
Luciano García-Bañuelos[4], H.A. Reijers[3], W.M.P. van der Aalst[3],
Marlon Dumas[4], and Jan Mendling[5]

[1] University of Grenoble, France
[2] Queensland University of Technology, Australia
[3] Eindhoven University of Technology, The Netherlands
[4] University of Tartu, Estonia
[5] Humboldt-Universität zu Berlin, Germany

Abstract. As organizations reach higher levels of Business Process Management
maturity, they tend to collect numerous business process models. Such models
may be linked with each other or mutually overlap, supersede one another and
evolve over time. Moreover, they may be represented at different abstraction levels depending on the target audience and modeling purpose, and may be available
in multiple languages (e.g. due to company mergers). Thus, it is common that organizations struggle with keeping track of their process models. This demonstration introduces AProMoRe (Advanced Process Model Repository) which aims to
facilitate the management of (large) process model collections.

1 Introduction

AProMoRe is a process model repository which goes beyond the typical amenities of
traditional repositories, such as model import/export and version control. First, it supports a variety of process modeling languages, including EPCs, BPMN, YAWL, BPEL.
Second, it offers an open and extensible platform to build advanced features that specifically deal with large process model collections, such as similarity search, process merging and efficient model querying. These features can be classified according to four
main service areas: i) *evaluation*, concerned with establishing the adherence of process
models to various quality notions such as syntactic quality and usability issues; ii) *comparison*, offering capabilities to compute the degree of similarity between models and
to merge similar models; iii) *management*, supporting the creation, modification and
completion of process models, based on the reuse of existing content; and iv) *presentation*, providing visual support for improving the understanding of process models, e.g.
via abstraction or coloring techniques. The possibility to operate over process models
irrespective of their language and abstraction level, is made possible via the use of an
internal *canonical process format* [1]. This format provides a common, unambiguous
representation of business processes so that all process models can be treated alike.
The idea is to represent only the structural characteristics of a process model that are
common to the majority of modeling languages. Language-specific concepts are omitted because they cannot be meaningfully interpreted when dealing with process models

---

* This work was done while she was visiting Queensland University of Technology, Australia.

P.P. Maglio et al. (Eds.): ICSOC 2010, LNCS 6470, pp. 699–701, 2010.

originating from different notations, i.e. when cross-language operations need to be performed such as comparing process models that are in BPMN with models that are in EPCs. Moreover, this canonical format is agnostic of graphical information (e.g. layout, shapes, line thickness). Instead, this information is stored separately in the form of *annotations* linked to files in canonical format. These annotations are used when a canonical model needs to be presented to the user or converted back to a process modeling language.

2   System Overview

AProMoRe is implemented via a three-layered Service Oriented Architecture (SOA) and deployed over the internet (see Fig. 1). The Enterprise layer hosts the *Manager*—a public enterprise service which exposes all the repository features via Web service operations for integration with third-party applications, e.g. a BPM System. Moreover, these operations can be accessed via a Web *Portal*, which in turn delegates model editing functionality to Oryx (http://bpt.hpi.uni-potsdam.de/Oryx/WebHome).

The Intermediary layer hosts the *Canonizer* which is an adapter responsible for (de-)canonizing process models as they are imported/exported into/from the repository. The *Toolbox* is a façade over the advanced operations that can be performed on the stored process model collections. Access to these models is achieved via the *Data access* service in the Basic layer, which encapsulates data-centric operations for reading/writing data upon requests made by the other services. Finally, the *Access Control* service controls security aspects such as user authentication and authorization. In future work, we plan

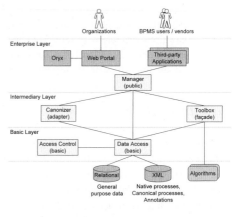

Fig. 1. AProMoRe's SOA.

to also store process logs and to integrate AProMoRe with the process mining tool ProM (http://www.processmining.org). AProMoRe's portal is accessible at http://brahms0.imag.fr:8080/Apromore-portal (login: icsoc, no password). The source code, manuals and a demonstration screencast can be found at http://code.google.com/p/apromore (under Downloads).

3   Demo Script

This demonstration focuses on the similarity search and merging functionality. After a quick overview of AProMoRe's basic features—e.g. import/export and editing of process models in various formats—we will show how AProMoRe is able to retrieve models from a repository that are similar to a given model. Next, we will show how the repository can be queried according to various parameters. Finally, we will retrieve two similar models and show how they can be merged into a single model—a feature that has been used in a real process model consolidation project.

Reference

1. La Rosa, M., Reijers, H.A., van der Aalst, W.M.P., Dijkman, R.M., Mendling, J., Dumas, M., Garcia-Banuelos, L.: Apromore: An advanced process model repository. QUT ePrints Technical Report (2009), http://eprints.qut.edu.au/27448

Managing Long-Tail Processes Using FormSys*

Ingo Weber, Hye-Young Paik, Boualem Benatallah, Corren Vorwerk,
Zifei Gong, Liangliang Zheng, and Sung Wook Kim

School of Computer Science and Engineering
University of New South Wales, Sydney, Australia
{ingo.weber,hpaik,boualem}@cse.unsw.edu.au

Efforts and tools aiming to automate business processes promise the highest potential gains on business processes with a well-defined structure and high degree of repetition [1]. Despite successes in this area, the reality is that today many processes are in fact *not* automated. This is because, among other reasons, Business Process Management Suites (BPMSs) are not well suited for ad-hoc and human-centric processes [2]; and automating processes demands high cost and skills. This affects primarily the "long tail of processes" [3], i.e. processes that are less structured, or that do not affect many people uniformly, or that are not considered critical to an organization: those are rarely automated. One of the consequences of this state is that still today organisations rely on templates and paper-based forms to manage the long tail processes.

In this paper, we present a novel tool for enabling end-users to model and deploy processes they encounter in their daily work. We thus focus on a subset of long-tail processes, which we refer to as *personal processes*, i.e., business processes as experienced and described by a single person. Hence we can avoid many complicated modelling constructs, and devise simple process representations which can be as easily understood as a cooking recipe or an audio playlist. By focusing our efforts on a smaller set of usage scenarios, we aim to enable end-users to design their own executable processes, to support their everyday tasks. In earlier work, we built a system named *FormSys* [4] for creating form-filling Web services. Herein we present a completely new development as an extension of the earlier tool, therefore named *FormSys Process Designer*, for modeling and executing processes over such form-filling (and related) services. This can be useful to automate processes that involve filling the same information into multiple forms. E.g., when a new employee is hired at UNSW, the following units need to be informed: HR, IT support, procurement, the faculty, facilities, etc. Filling all different forms manually is a time-consuming task.

In order to enable end-users to design executable process models, we devised a simple control flow language for sequential process steps and conditional execution (or skipping) of process steps. The processes can be represented graphically or textually, as shown in Fig. 1. For the textual representation, we tried to stay close to natural language descriptions of how a process is executed; for the graphical representation we followed the analogy to composing a playlist in an audio player, such as using "cover flow". Data field equivalence between forms used in different process steps can be specified in a *mapping* part. Once the editing

---

* This work has been supported by a grant from the SmartServices CRC.

P.P. Maglio et al. (Eds.): ICSOC 2010, LNCS 6470, pp. 702–703, 2010.

is completed, the process can be translated to BPEL. By doing so, an input Web form is automatically created, from which the data is distributed to the various steps in the process. Together with other artifacts, the BPEL process and the input form comprise an Intalio deployable package. By currently restricting focusing this work on processes around form-filling services, we achieve the desired simplicity but limit the scope of application to long-tail form-based processes. More details can be found in a technical report [5] and a screencast video, available at http://www.cse.unsw.edu.au/~FormSys/FormSys/.

To our knowledge, no related end-user process modeling tool features the creation of executable processes. CoScripter (http://coscripter.researchlabs.ibm.com) in contrast is a tool for recording and automating processes performed in a Web browser. While closely related to our textual representation, it does not support Web service invocation or conditional execution.

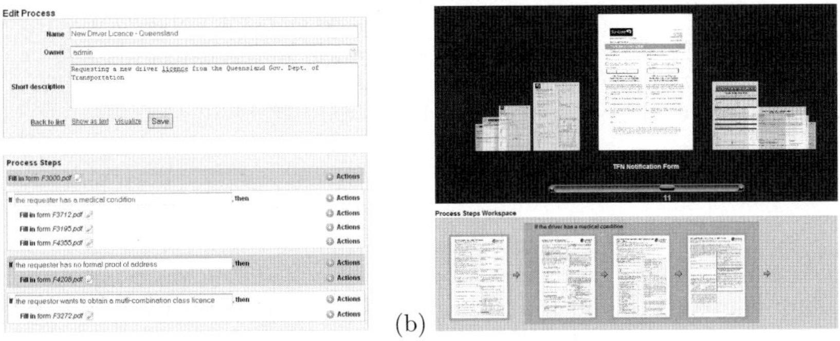

Fig. 1. Screenshots of the tool: textual (a) and graphical (b) process editing

The demonstration includes viewing, editing, translating, and executing processes using our system. While the control flow part seems intuitive to the users, the mapping task requires further support, e.g., by semi-automatically creating the mappings, re-using mappings created by other users. From this work we want to expand the concepts, so as to support more generic scenarios involving arbitrary kinds of services and interactions between multiple people.

References

1. Leymann, F., Roller, D.: Production Workflow - Concepts and Techniques. Prentice Hall, Englewood Cliffs (2000)
2. Schurter, T.: BPM state of the nation 2009. bpm.com (2009), http://www.bpm.com/bpm-state-of-the-nation-2009.html (accessed 25/11/2009)
3. Oracle White Paper: State of the business process management market (August 2008), http://www.oracle.com/technologies/bpm/docs/state-of-bpm-market-whitepaper.pdf (accessed 20/11/2009)
4. Weber, I., Paik, H., Benatallah, B., Gong, Z., Zheng, L., Vorwerk, C.: FormSys: Form-processing web services. In: WWW, Demo Track (2010)
5. Weber, I., Paik, H.Y., Benatallah, B., et al.: Personal process management: Design and execution for end-users. Technical report, UNSW-CSE-TR-1018 (2010)

Managing Web Services: An Application in Bioinformatics

Athman Bouguettaya, Shiping Chen, Lily Li, Dongxi Liu, Qing Liu,
Surya Nepal, Wanita Sherchan, Jemma Wu, and Xuan Zhou

CSIRO ICT Centre, Australia
{firstname.lastname}@csiro.au

Abstract. We propose to treat Web services as first-class objects that
can be manipulated as if they were data in DBMS. We provide an integrated way for service users to query, compose and evaluate Web services. The resulting system is called Web Service Management System
(WSMS). We deployed WSMS as the backbone of a bioinformatics experiment framework named Genome Tracker. In this demonstration, we
show how WSMS helps biologists conduct experiments easily and effectively using a service-oriented architecture.

1 Introduction of WSMS

Fully delivering on the potential of Service Oriented Architecture (SOA) requires
building fundamental technologies for efficiently modeling, querying, composing,
monitoring, trusting, and optimizing access to services. We have deployed these
technologies into an integrated framework called Web Service Management Systems (WSMS). In this framework, Web services are treated as first-class objects
that can be manipulated as if they were pieces of data. WSMS provides a single
entry point for customers to find, compose and use services.

WSMS is composed of a number of key components that work collaboratively
to manage the life-cycles of Web services. They include service organizer, service
query processor, service composition generator, service optimizer and service
trust manager. To use WSMS, a user declares the requirements using a service
query language. Taking the user's request, the WSMS guides the user to create
and consume a customized composite service. For instance, the service query
processor interprets the service query by mapping it to a set of relevant services.
Based on interpretation, the composition generator creates a composition plan,
which is then instantiated into a composite service by the service optimizer.
During the optimization, the trust manager is consulted to obtain services' reputation. Finally, the composite service is executed by the service executor to
satisfies the user's requirements. The workflow of WSMS is shown in Figure 1.
The detailed technologies of WSMS have been reported in [2,3,1].

2 The Application Scenario

We have deployed WSMS as the back-end of the Genome Tracker system, which
aims to help biologists conduct bioinformatics experiments easily and effectively
using a service oriented architecture.

P.P. Maglio et al. (Eds.): ICSOC 2010, LNCS 6470, pp. 704–705, 2010.

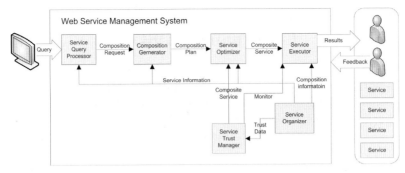

Fig. 1. WSMS Architecture

A bioinformatics study conducted in Genome Tracker usually involves a series of statistical analysis and functional analysis. There are a number of databases and software packages on the Web providing facilities for these analysis. However, it is difficult for a biologist to utilize these tools. First, they are not aware of what tools can help in their study. Second, they are not informed about the quality of the tools. Last but not the least, hey have to manually assemble the tools into an analysis process, which requires a considerable amount of expertise.

To support biologists in bioinformatics study, we developed the Genome Tracker system on top of WSMS. All the datasets and analytic services in Genome Tracker are encapsulated as services and managed by WSMS. A biologist accesses these services by simply issuing queries to WSMS. WSMS help the user to easily find, compose, optimize and invoke services.

3   The Demonstration

In our demonstration[1], we will showcase how Genome Tracker supports a biologist to conduct bioinformatic experiments. Our purpose is to demonstrate the strength of WSMS. We use the analysis of colorectal cancer as the user scenario. We show how a biologist uses our system to quickly compose workflows that aim to analyze the genetic causes of colorectal cancer.

The demonstration will show the following benefits of WSMS: first, prior knowledge about the available tools or datasets is not mandatory for biologists; second, a biologist does not need to be aware the quality of service, and WSMS is intelligent enough to select the best services for her; finally, WSMS is able to guide the user to construct a workflow through intuitive interactions.

References

1. Malik, Z., Bouguettaya, A.: Evaluating rater credibility for reputation assessment of web services. In: WISE, pp. 38–49 (2007)
2. Medjahed, B., Bouguettaya, A.: A multilevel composability model for semantic web services. IEEE TKDE 17(7), 954–968 (2005)
3. Yu, Q., Bouguettaya, A.: Framework for web service query algebra and optimization. TWEB 2(1) (2008)

---

[1] A video can be found at: http://www.youtube.com/watch?v=U84ZGr-otkE

An Integrated Solution for Runtime Compliance Governance in SOA

Aliaksandr Birukou[1], Agnieszka Betkowska Cavalcante[2], Fabio Casati[1],
Soudip Roy Chowdhury[1], Vincenzo D'Andrea[1], Frank Leymann[3],
Ernst Oberortner[4], Jacek Serafinski[2], Patricia Silveira[1],
Steve Strauch[3], and Marek Tluczek[2,*]

[1] DISI, University of Trento, TN 38123, Italy
[2] Telcordia Poland, Poznan
[3] IAAS, University of Stuttgart, 70569, Germany
[4] Distributed Systems Group, Vienna University of Technology, 1040, Austria

Abstract. Compliance governance in organizations has been recently
gaining importance because of new regulations and the diversity of compliance sources. In this demo we will show an integrated solution for runtime compliance governance in Service-Oriented Architectures (SOAs).
The proposed solution supports the whole cycle of compliance management and has been tested in a real world case study.

Keywords: compliance governance, DSL, monitoring, SOA, CEP.

1 Introduction and Contributions

Compliance governance refers to the overall management approach for controlling the state of compliance in the entire organization and, in general, consists
of: (1) selecting the sources to be compliant with and designing corresponding
compliance requirements; (2) (re-)designing business processes compliant with
the selected requirements; (3) monitoring compliance of processes during their
execution; (4) informing interested parties (managers, auditors) on the current
state of compliance; (5) taking specific actions or changing the processes in
cases of (predicted or happened) non-compliance. Compliance governance has
been gaining importance in organizations because of new regulations appeared
recently (e.g., Sarbanes-Oxley Act, Basel III, Solvency II), non-compliance bringing money loss and reputation damage, and the diversity of compliance sources:
business owners consider legislature and regulatory bodies, standards and codes
of practice, business partner contracts. Existing approaches rarely deal with different types of compliance sources and cover only few steps of the compliance
governance.

In this demo we will show how service-oriented technology can be used as the
basis for an integrated solution for runtime compliance governance in a company.

* This work was supported by funds from the European Commission (contract no.
215175 for the FP7-ICT-2007-1 project COMPAS).

P.P. Maglio et al. (Eds.): ICSOC 2010, LNCS 6470, pp. 706–707, 2010.

The framework includes tools for: modeling compliance requirements for different compliance sources in domain-specific languages; linking the requirements to the business processes; monitoring process execution using Complex Event Processing (CEP); displaying the current state of compliance in dashboards, and analyzing cases of non-compliance to find what caused them. The framework is targeted at people dealing with compliance in an organization, ranging from people specifying compliance requirements (process analysts, compliance officers, technical specialists) to those controling the compliance (managers, auditors) and it helps them to deal with various compliance aspects in a uniform and automated manner. The framework has been applied in a real case study in the context of the EU FP7 project COMPAS[1] (Compliance-driven Models, Languages, and Architectures for Services). The case study focuses on the compliance of telecom service provider to licenses of its business partners. The framework provides the following unique contributions:

- handling requirements from different source in a uniform manner within an integrated solution;
- covering whole compliance governance lifecycle;
- the model-driven approach reduces user inputs by transforming information defined in requirements to further steps - up to monitoring;
- supporting traceability and access to information during runtime execution, monitoring and mining, thus enabling drill-down in non-compliant cases.

2   Demonstration Storyboard

The live demonstration introduces the contributions of the compliance governance framework by means of a joint use of slides (for the conceptual aspects) and hands-on framework demos (for the practical aspects):

1. Advanced Telecom Services scenario: a company provides customers with on-demand aggregated audio/video streaming by combining services from different providers
2. Design aspects: identifying compliance sources and requirements, modelling business process, expressing compliance requirements in QoS and Licensing Domain-Specific Languages (DSLs), generating events and CEP rules for monitoring.
3. Runtime aspects: deployment of the process in the process engine, executing the process, showing the use of the online dashboard for monitoring and the offline dashboard for the historical analysis of the processes.
4. Runtime Compliance Governance architecture: explanation of the architecture and showing that framework in general is more than what is shown in the demo.

The video illustrating this demo is available at
http://disi.unitn.it/~birukou/2010runtime-compas-demo.zip

---

[1] http://www.compas-ict.eu

Event-Driven Privacy Aware Infrastructure for Social and Health Systems Interoperability: CSS Platform

Giampaolo Armellin[1], Dario Betti[1], Fabio Casati[2], Annamaria Chiasera[1,2], Gloria Martinez[2], Jovan Stevovic[1,2], and Tefo James Toai[1]

[1] GPI SpA, Via Ragazzi del '99, 13, Trento, Italy,
`{garmellin,dbetti,achiasera,jstevovic,ttoai}@gpi.it`
[2] Information Engineering and Computer Science Department,
University of Trento, Italy,
`casati@disi.unitn.eu, glomarin@gmail.com`

Abstract. Assistive processes in healthcare and socio-assistive domains typically span multiple institutions which usually communicate manually with the exchange of documents. Despite the needs of cooperation it is difficult to provide an integrated solution to improve data exchange and allow comprehensive monitoring of the processes due to the complexity of the domains and the privacy issues derived by the use of sensitive data. In this demo we show how we approached the problem in designing and deploying a platform for the interoperability and monitoring of multi-organization healthcare processes in Italy. Our solution provides an event-based platform that assures privacy enforcement with a fine-grained control on the data that is distributed and minimizes the effort required to join the platform providing components that automates the data exchange.

Keywords: EDA, interoperability, cooperation, privacy, business intelligence.

1   Introduction and Contributions

In this demo we describe a solution to manage and partially automate the integration between social and healthcare institutions to deliver social and health services. The work is the result of a large, multi-million dollar effort, the CSS (Cartella Socio-Sanitaria) project, undertaken by the autonomous province of Trento, Italy[1]. The context in which CSS is born is characterized by many heterogeneous and very complex systems with different level of evolution and owned by different institutions with new partners joining the scenario over time. The data used in this domain is particularly sensitive and related to the health status of citizens. This imposes strict legal constraints on the way data is collected, stored, distributed and processed in a context with multiple data controllers collecting the data of citizens and their consent.

[1] This work was supported by the CSS project, funded by the Autonomous Province of Trento (Italo della Noce, Cinzia Boniatti) and coordinated by Fondazione Bruno Kessler (Giuliano Muzio). Besides the authors of this paper, the CSS project includes as participants: Municipality of Trento (Claudio Covelli) and Rovereto (Mauro Viesi), Local Healthcare Agency of Trento-APSS (Leonardo Sartori), CNR-ISTC (Nicola Guarino), Informatica Trentina (Luca Mion), Dedagroup (Michele Brugnara), Engineering (Stefano Scamuzzo).

P.P. Maglio et al. (Eds.): ICSOC 2010, LNCS 6470, pp. 708–710, 2010.

We approached the analysis problem in a lighter way than for classical integration approaches. We analyzed processes of assistance isolating interesting events in a Business Intelligence (BI) and interoperability perspective. We used those events as unit of information and developed a platform based on SOA and EDA that enables the routing of data among involved institutions and also to the BI that becomes an Event Based BI. Privacy is assured via a fine-grained, purpose-based, two-phase access control mechanism: each source produces notification of events that are only partially specified (with no sensitive data) and CSS notifies them to interested consumers; each consumer must explicitly request the details to the source (along with a purpose statement) via the CSS platform; the source returns only the allowed details always via the CSS platform. This protocol allows sources to specify different visibility rules based on explicitly stated purposes in compliance with privacy regulations [1] and to CSS to trace the requests for auditing. The main contributions of CSS are:

- an event-based interoperability infrastructure that allows the different institutions to interoperate easily with minimum effort;
- a fine-grained privacy control over the exchanged information among involved partners;
- an event based Business Intelligence analysis over processes of assistance that span different organizations available to the Governance.

2   Demonstration Storyboard

In the demo we will explain the main concepts of the architecture (with some slides) and simulate some concrete usage scenarios of the event-base CSS platform. In particular, the demo will be as follow:

1. *Intro*: explains the real context, its challenges, CSS goals and contributions
2. *Approach*: presents our analysis approach and its points of innovation
3. *Architecture*: explains the CSS components and their interactions, simplicity of installation, privacy management visibility rule wizard to define privacy policies on events
4. *Event creation demo*: we simulate a patient using the tele-care and tele-assistance service requesting a rest home service. A social assistant approves the request and edits the social profile of the patient generating an event that is automatically notified by the platform to the destination rest home and tele-care/tele-assistance system for interoperability and BI module for reporting.
5. *Privacy-aware event routing*: explains the routing of notifications and the privacy-aware retrieval of the details
6. *Event consumption demo*: we show how the detailed acceptance event is accessed differently depending on roles and purposes. A doctor of the rest home can see all the details of the patient while the reception does not receive the social profile. We show the operator at the tele-care and tele-assistance service searching the events to know where the patient is and his destination rest home. Finally we show the BI module for the Governance receiving only aggregated data to create the report in a near real time fashion.
7. Conclusions and future works: a summary of the lessons learned and future extensions.

Reference

1. Armellin, G., Betti, D., Casati, F., Chiasera, A., Martinez, G., Stevovic, J.: Privacy preserving event driven integration for interoperating social and health systems. In: Jonker, W., Petković, M. (eds.) SDM 2010. LNCS, vol. 6358, pp. 54–69. Springer, Heidelberg (2010)

Mashups with Mashlight*

Luciano Baresi and Sam Guinea

Politecnico di Milano
Deep-SE Group - Dipartimento di Elettronica e Informazione
Piazza L. da Vinci, 32 - 20133 Milano, Italy
{baresi,guinea}@elet.polimi.it

Abstract. Mashlight is a framework for creating process mashups out of Web 2.0 widgets. In our demo we show how Mashlight can be used to simplify patient management in a hospital. We illustrate the design-time tools for creating mashups, a desktop execution environment, and mobile environments for iPhones and Android smartphones.

1 Mashlight

The web is becoming a user-centric platform. Social networks, video-sharing sites, blogs, and wikis have converted millions of users from spectators to contributors. People use the Web to collaborate, share information, and solve their everyday needs. This ecosystem has placed the grounds for mashups, i.e., applications that combine data and functionality from different sources to meet user goals. Mashlight [1] presents a flexible solution that supports data, logic, and presentation mashups both on the desktop and on mobile devices. It encourages creativity by taking inspiration from widgets, i.e., interactive and single-service auto-contained web applications such as those provided by Apple's Dashboard and Google's Gadgets.

In Mashlight widgets can exchange data and be sequenced in a process-like fashion. Widgets exchange data through input and output parameters, while their sequencing determines the order in which they are presented to the user. For greater flexibility, Mashlight introduces the notion of *super-widget*, an abstraction for aggregating widgets that need to be shown to the user at the same time. Inside a super-widget there is no process flow, and the user is free to interact with the internal widgets in any order; however, there are data flows that allow widgets to collaborate by exchanging information. Externally, a super-widget exchanges data and is sequenced just like any other regular widget.

The "Mashlight Suite" (see Figure 1) provides two design-time tools[1]. The "Widget Builder" is an Eclipse plugin for creating composable widgets. The

---

* This research has been funded by the European Commission, Programme IDEAS-ERC, Project 227077-SMScom (http://www.erc-smscom.org) and the Network of Excellence S-Cube (http://www.s-cube-network.eu/)

[1] The Mashlight Suite can be experienced online at
http://home.dei.polimi.it/guinea/mashlight/index.html, while a video can be seen at
http://home.dei.polimi.it/guinea/mashlight/demo.mov

P.P. Maglio et al. (Eds.): ICSOC 2010, LNCS 6470, pp. 711–712, 2010.

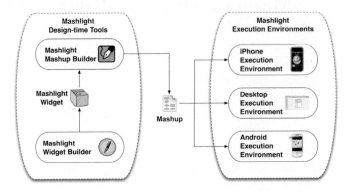

Fig. 1. The Mashlight Suite

"Mashup Builder" provides designers with a drag-and-drop canvas in which they can define process and data flows. Mashlight also provides three execution environments. The first is intended for Webkit browsers and is implemented in JavaScript. The other two environments are intended for iOS and Android mobile devices. For each we have developed special-purpose widgets that take advantage of their capabilities (e.g., GPS geolocation, contact lists, etc.).

2   Demo Proposal

In our demo we improve patient service in a fictional public hospital. Through Mashlight doctors setup personalized management processes for their patients that nurses carry out. Doctors interact with the "Patient Management Process Creator" (PMPC), a mashup created by Mashlight experts that acts as a domain-specific mashup creation environment. Through the PMPC doctors state their patient's needs; the result is a dynamically generated process for that patient, one that nurses can run on the mobile devices provided by the hospital. The demo will start with a brief overview of the Mashlight Suite, and proceed to present the scenario and its requirements. The demo will then illustrate how the Mashup Builder was used to create the PMPC mashup, and conclude with a presentation of the runtime environments. The PMPC will be executed in a browser, and we will run a personalized management process within an iOS device.

Reference

1. Albinola, M., Baresi, L., Carcano, M., Guinea, S.: Mashlight: a Lightweight Mashup Framework for Everyone. In: 2nd Workshop on Mashups, Enterprise Mashups and Lightweight Composition on the Web - 18th International World Wide Web Conference (2009)

A Service Mashup Tool for
Open Document Collaboration

Nelly Schuster, Raffael Stein, Christian Zirpins, and Stefan Tai

eOrganization Group, Karlsruhe Institute of Technology (KIT),
Englerstraße 11, Karlsruhe, Germany
{firstname.lastname}@kit.edu

Abstract. Mashup technologies enable end-users to compose situational applications from Web-based services. A particular problem is to find high-level service composition models that a) are intuitive and expressive enough to be easily used by end-users and b) allow for efficient runtime support and integration on the Web. We propose a novel approach that leverages a metaphor of document collaboration: end-users declare the coordination and aggregation of peer contributions into a joint document. Peers provide contributions as Web-based services that allow a) integrating any Web-accessible resource and b) orchestrating the collaboration process. Thus, collaborative document mashups enable lightweight, situational collaboration that is not addressed by most BPM or CSCW systems. In this demo we present our document service infrastructure and collaboration RIA, which allows collaborators to declare and participate in document collaborations in an interactive, intuitive and dynamic way.

Keywords: service mashups, open document collaboration.

1   Introduction

Service mashups offer end-user-oriented compositions of APIs, content and data sources from the Web. However, early approaches that built on simplified programming languages (scripting) or software composition techniques (pipes, workflows) saw limited commercial success. To tap their full potential, service mashups need to become more intuitive, beneficial and easy-to-use for end-users. This requires higher-level models closer to end-user applications. In this work we present a novel mashup approach called MoSaiC that is based on a document metaphor and tailored to support open collaboration of end-users. Document mashups do not only provide an intuitive means to utilize service composition techniques but also enable so far missing support for human-centric situational ad-hoc processes. The demo illustrates the utilization of the MoSaiC Web application, execution platform and integration infrastructure.

2   Concept, Implementation and Benefits of MoSaiC

MoSaiC supports *coordinators* to decompose collaborative tasks into *contributions* to be provided by *collaborators* or *robots* as Web-based services. MoSaiC *mashups* define the aggregation and orchestration of contributions into a joint document [1]. To this end, contribution services are mapped to formatted *elements* of the document

P.P. Maglio et al. (Eds.): ICSOC 2010, LNCS 6470, pp. 713–714, 2010.
© Springer-Verlag Berlin Heidelberg 2010

structure. The coordination of different collaborators (e.g. causal or temporal relations of their contributions) is declared by ECA-based *rules* associating incoming and outgoing service messages.

Mashups are one-way document instances that are evolved by collaborating individuals in terms of structure, behavior and contents. This flexible model fits a variety of application scenarios including financial reporting, process documentation, product specification, research publication, education material/exercises and many more.

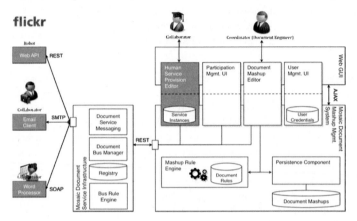

Fig. 1. Document Mashup System Architecture Overview (see screencast[1] for UI pictures)

Figure 1 shows the MoSaiC architecture consisting of a) the *mashup management system* providing a rule-driven mashup engine and a Web GUI to initiate, maintain and participate in open document collaborations, b) the *document service infrastructure* enabling *interaction* (asynchronous messaging, dynamic routing) as well as *management* (service registry) and *integration* (adapters) of various Web-resources.

The MoSaiC approach offers an application-specific mashup model that is more pragmatic and intuitive than simplified software composition models. It leverages the potential of service mashups for unique support of open document collaborations. Beyond the specific MoSaiC application, we anticipate that the document metaphor is a promising basis to be leveraged by a future class of mashup approaches.

3 Demonstration Overview

The demo will showcase the utilization of MoSaiC for the use case of supporting collaborative research resulting in a paper. It illustrates the use of many concepts and features of the tool and infrastructure like ad hoc integration of human-provided and Web-based services or usage of coordination rules. We provide a screencast online[1].

Reference

1. Schuster, N., Zirpins, C., Tai, S., et al.: A Service-Oriented Approach to Document-Centric Situational Collaboration Processes. In: Proc. WETICE 2009, pp. 221–226. IEEE, Los Alamitos (2009)

---

[1] www.zirpins.de/downloads/MosaicScreenCast.m4v (subject to frequent updates)

Panta Rhei: Optimized and Ranked Data Processing over Heterogeneous Sources

Daniele Braga, Francesco Corcoglioniti,
Michael Grossniklaus, and Salvatore Vadacca

Dipartimento di Elettronica e Informazione - Politecnico di Milano
Via Ponzio, 34/5 - 20133 Milano, Italy
{braga,corcoglioniti,grossniklaus,vadacca}@elet.polimi.it

Abstract. In the era of digital information, the value of data resides not only in its volume and quality, but also in the additional information that can be inferred from the combination (aggregation, comparison and join) of such data. There is a concrete need for data processing solutions that combine distributed and heterogeneous data sources, such as Web services, relational databases, and even search engines, that can all be modeled as services. In this demonstration, we show how our *Panta Rhei* model addresses the challenge of processing data over heterogeneous sources to provide feasible and ranked combinations of these services.

Keywords: Panta Rhei, data processing, search computing.

1 Introduction and Contributions

Users have the need to express complex queries over multiple sources and heterogeneous domains. We define *search computing systems* [1] as a new class of systems aimed at responding to multi-domain queries, i.e., queries over multiple semantic fields of interest.

Data sources currently available on the Web share some common features: results are brought to the user as small chunks of information, data is retrieved in a given order and more or less sophisticated interfaces allow querying the data. We model these sources as Web "services" to be composed in order to solve a multi-domain query. Currently existing solutions to the problem, such as BPEL, lack in real-time adaptivity to failure and on-line statistics, optimization and performance of the process, and definition of a "global" ranking.

These requirements led us to the definition of *Panta Rhei*, an execution model supporting multi-domain queries, whose contribution is three-fold.

- a *physical query algebra*, representing query plans as a workflow (comprising both data and control) where the basic node is the service implementation and composition of nodes is performed according to a set of simple and recursive production rules (parallel and pipe join of nodes and concatenation of modifiers, such as selection, projection and sorting).
- an *optimization layer*, choosing a feasible plan topology and defining the optimal parameters based on off-line service statistics.

P.P. Maglio et al. (Eds.): ICSOC 2010, LNCS 6470, pp. 715–716, 2010.

- a *runtime environment*, executing plans expressed by means of the physical algebra and adapting the execution according to possible failure events and on-line service statistics.

A query workbench has been deployed to highlight internal details of the model and to ease debugging and testing of optimization heuristics.

2   Demonstration Storyboard

Our demonstration highlights the four steps of the query process. The conceptual aspects our model will be presented with the joint use of slides, whereas the practical aspects will be showcased by means of a query execution workbench. To be more precise, the demonstration is organized as follows:

1. *Introduction.* Introduction of the *Panta Rhei* model, its conceptual background and novelty of our approach.
2. *Query design.* Specification of the query in a Datalog-like conjunctive form and definition of the optimization parameters to be applied. We will show how different optimization parameters and statistics lead to different topologies.
3. *Logical query plan.* Specification of a workflow with quantitative estimates of the size of partial results determined by the planner which exploits the available degrees of freedom to fix the topology, the number and sequence of service invocations, the join strategies, etc.
4. *Physical query plan.* Definition of both data and control flow in the execution of a query. The execution engine instantiates physical operators (units) of the compiled plan and the query is orchestrated accordingly.
5. *Query execution.* Execution of the physical plan and specification of the input attributes. Plan execution can be constrained in terms of number of commands, resulting combinations or execution time.
6. *Conclusion and future work.* Summary and possible future directions.

A preview of the demo can be found at *http://www.search-computing.it/demo/qp*.

Acknowledgments. This research is part of the Search Computing (SeCo) project [*www.search-computing.it*], funded by the European Research Council (ERC). We thank all the members of the SeCo team for their contributions.

Reference

1. Ceri, S., Brambilla, M. (eds.): Search Computing. LNCS, vol. 5950. Springer, Heidelberg (2010)

RnR: A System for Extracting Rationale from Online Reviews and Ratings

Dwi A.P. Rahayu[1], Shonali Krishnaswamy[1], Cyril Labbe[2], and Oshadi Alhakoon[1]

[1] Centre of Distributed System and Software Engineering, Monash University, Australia
[2] University of Genoble, France
dwi.ap.rahayu@gmail.com, {Shonali.Krishanswamy,
Oshadi.Alhakoon}@monash.edu.au, Cyril.Labbe@imag.fr

Abstract. In this paper we present a web based system as well as web service based application to summarise and extract the rationale that underpins online ratings and reviews. The web-based version of RnR system is available for testing from http://rnrsystem.com/RnRSystem. RnR system web service is available from http://rnrsystem.com/axis2/services/RnRData?wsdl.

Keywords: Review mining, Online Reviews/Ratings.

1 Introduction

The phenomenal growth of online social networking and Web 2.0 has led to an unprecedented increase in opinions/reviews on a wide range of topics, products and services being available and accessible both through websites or review service APIs [1]. In fact, these reviews and opinions are now a *de facto* basis and contributing factors for a range of daily activities such as buying products (e.g., electronic goods), choosing restaurants, booking hotels and planning holidays. Thus, there is an increasing reliance on online opinions for selection of product and services. This in turn is leading to an increasing focus in the area of opinion/review mining. The main of aim of review/opinion analysis is to firstly identify the product/service and its key features and then to distill whether a review expresses positive/negative sentiments towards the object that is being reviewed.

In this paper, we present our RnR system that in addition to feature identification and sentiment analysis, focuses on explicating the rationale and reasoning that underpins an opinion expressed with respect to a product/service or its specific features. This can be easily justified as follows. Consider the example of a hotel which has very clean rooms, with a good view – but which is rather small in size. It is quite possible that for certain users, this hotel could be rated very positively because of the cleanliness or the view. However, it is also possible that some users have negative opinions based on the size of the room. Thus, it is important to understand what drives users to rate things differently since this makes selections based on such reviews more personalized and appropriate.

It is interesting to note that while many online reviews/opinions typically have a rating to specify the extent of positive or negative affinity for the product/service. We take the position those ratings (when available) along with textual descriptions provide a holistic representation of the opinion. Together, they combine an objective/directly measurable opinion along with a subjective/qualitative view which underpins the

P.P. Maglio et al. (Eds.): ICSOC 2010, LNCS 6470, pp. 717–718, 2010.

rationale for the opinion [2]. We also take the view that in opinion analysis, "positive" opinions that indicate certain negative aspects or "negative" opinions that bring to the positive features are significant and worthy of highlighting. Finally, we take the position that in analyzing reviews/opinions, it is important to factor in the changing views over time. This temporal dimension captures the essential improvement or decline in the general perception of a product or service. In this paper, we present our RnR system for extracting rationale from online reviews/ratings. The system captures and summarizes the key rationale for positive and negative opinions expressed in a corpus of reviews. It highlights the negative features among positive reviews and vice versa. It also displays the changing perceptions of reviewers over time with respect to the entity that is being reviewed. We have developed as part of the RnR approach, innovative algorithms that leverage a new support metric in conjunction with a domain ontology to improve the computational overheads associated with sentiment identification. We have implemented the RnR system for a hotel review mining application. The RnR system uses reviews in the TripAdvisor.com as its corpus.

2   Architecture and Operation of the RnR System

RnR is implemented as web based system as well as web service application. Users can access the system using the web based application or embed RnR system in their websites using it as a web service. The user enters the product/service name, for which a performance summary based on online customer reviews is determined, either using RnR webpage or RnR service request. RnR main system connects to and accesses a corpus of previous reviews for the queried product/service. RnR system has a local cache for recently retrieved reviews. If the cached data is valid (in terms of being recent, as determined by a user threshold), and valid for the query, then the cached data is used rather than performing an online crawling and retrieval. Otherwise, the query is sent to an external site where online reviews are maintained (e.g. TripAdvisor.com, Expedia.com.au) via their service API. The retrieved set of reviews is then locally processed to extract the requisite rationale. The current implementation accesses TripAdvisor.com. An important feature of RnR is to identify "good" opinions in the negative group and "bad" opinions in the positive group. The RnR system highlights in grey negative adjectives within positive group and positive adjectives within negative group. The results are presented in four quadrants showing *an overall summary, a detailed summary of positive features (highlighting negative aspects within positive reviews), a detailed summary of negative features (highlighting positive aspects within negative reviews), and a chart showing temporal evolution of ratings.* Each point on the chart represents one rating given for a date of stay. The straight line within the scattered chart is the linear regression line showing the trend of performance.

References

[1] Hu, M., Liu, B.: Mining opinion features in customer reviews. In: Proceedings of National Conference of Artificial Intelligent, pp. 755–760. AAAI Press, San Jose (2004)
[2] Sherchan, W., Loke, S.W., Krishnaswamy, S.: Explanation aware service selection: Rationale and reputation. Service Oriented Computing and Applications 2(4), 203–218 (2008)

Liquid Course Artifacts Software Platform

Marcos Baez[1], Boualem Benatallah[2], Fabio Casati[1], Van M. Chhieng[2], Alejandro Mussi[1], and Qamal Kosim Satyaputra[2]

[1] Dipartimento di Ingegneria e Scienza dell'Informazione, University of Trento, Italy
[2] School of Computer Science and Engineering, UNSW, Sydney, Australia
{baez,casati,mussi}@disi.unitn.it, {boualem,vmc,qamalk}@cse.unsw.edu.au

Abstract. Liquid Course Artifacts Software Platform aims to improve social productivity and enhance interactive experience for teaching and collaborating by using suppliment materials such as slides, exercises, audios, videos and books.

1 Introduction

Teaching a course involves preparing notes, tutorials, exercises, exams, slides and others teaching materials. It is very common that besides preparing the core teaching artifacts such as notes and tutorials, it is useful to provide access to complementary materials that add to the student experience and improve learning such as additional non conventional supplement materials (exercises, slides, books, tags, audios, videos).

Services like Wikipedia, Q&A services (Yahoo Answers), Google Wave, Search Engines and various vertical social networks are making it possible for people to access and contribute content, as well as collaborating over the web. While there are advancements in Web 2.0 [1], cloud computing, and service oriented architectures which have techniques, services, tools, content accessibility and sharing in general to foster collaboration, there no effective support to foster sharing and collaboration on course materials [2] and artifacts. These include co-editing slides and notes, sharing tutorials and references, reusing complementary materials, comments and feedbacks from external students and colleagues.

This paper presents a Web 2.0 social productivity platform, called Crowd Learning and Teaching (CrowdL&T), which supports effective collaboration among teachers and students. The vision of CrowdL&T is to promote a comprehensive, end-to-end framework and Web 2.0 social productivity platform [3] that unlock teaching and learning knowledge. This can be done by empowering teachers and students with robust techniques, efficient services, easy to use tools that allow them to share course artifacts and to collaborate on building a free knowledge base about teaching and learning based on lecture notes, slides, tutorials, video presentations, quizzes, and experiences. The CrowdL&T platform aims to develop services for evaluating contribution of knowledge from collaborators.

P.P. Maglio et al. (Eds.): ICSOC 2010, LNCS 6470, pp. 719–721, 2010.

2   Architecture

The following diagram depicts the overall architecture of our system. It consists of services, open APIs and portals that allow live interaction between users such as teachers and students. An open service is called CoreDB. It contains several modules. The first module is used as the basis for artifacts browsing and editing. The second module is used to enable traceability where changes to artifacts are traced. The third module is used for security where access control level (ACL) policy are created to manage access to entities representing artifacts and relationships. The forth module provides fulltext search capability over artifact database.

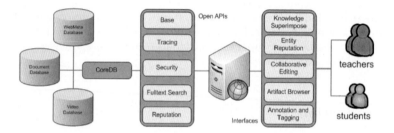

Fig. 1. Overall Architecture

Collaborative editing is a service provided by our system. It is a browser based tool that allows both private and live-collaborate editing of artifacts such as lecture notes and slides. Its functionalities include content importation from and exportation to well-known document formats (PDF and PowerPoint). Another feature that makes our system unique is tagging [4] artifacts with other various form of artifacts includes text books, research papers, video and audio lectures.

Another service provided by the system is knowledge improvement. This service is achieved by using the combination of the annotation tool and the creation of semantic relation technique that improve the second order knowledge. Another service is the artifact reputation. This service allows the system makes use of information from the sharing artifacts such as annotations, artifacts and artifact relations that compute the reputation of individual artifacts such as persons, files and folders. This improves search accuracy and provides incentives to users to collaborate.

3   Demo Routine

First, we show how teachers create, upload and organise courses. From a course workspace, teachers create course artifacts, namely lecture notes and slides using the notes collaborative editor featuring real-time. Users tag slides using terms automatically extracted from PDF, text books and online video lectures. Second, we show the organisation of course artifacts and the continuous superimposition of additional information through links to other artifacts forming dynamic folders. In doing this, the course knowledge base is incrementally enriched and provide valuable learning experiences to students and colleagues. Third, we demonstrate how feedback and ranking are used to improve artifacts quality and reputation. Demo Link: http://www.youtube.com/watch?v=yqBhQRFfinE

References

1. Ullrich, C., Borau, K., Luo, H., Tan, X., Shen, L., Shen, R.: Why web 2.0 is good for learning and for research: principles and prototypes. In: Proc. WWW 2008, pp. 705–714 (2008)
2. Bercovitz, B., Kaliszan, F., Koutrika, G., Liou, H., Mohammadi Zadeh, Z., Garcia-Molina, H.: CourseRank: a social system for course planning. In: Proc.SIGMOD 2009, pp. 1107–1110 (2009)
3. Huberman, B.A., Romero, D.M., Wu, F.: Crowdsourcing, attention and productivity. J. Inf. Sci. 35(6), 758–765 (2009)
4. Golder, S.A., Huberman, B.A.: Usage patterns of collaborative tagging systems. J. Inf. Sci. 32(2), 198–208 (2006)

A Programmble Fault Injection Testbed Generator for SOA

Lukasz Juszczyk and Schahram Dustdar

Distributed Systems Group, Vienna University of Technology, Austria
{juszczyk,dustdar}@infosys.tuwien.ac.at

Abstract. In this demo paper we present the prototype of our fault injection testbed generator. Our tool empowers engineers to generate emulated SOA environments and to program fault injection behavior on diverse levels: at the network layer, at the execution level, and at the message layer. Engineers can specify the structure of testbeds via scripts, attach fault models, and generate running testbed instances from that. As a result, our tool facilitates the setup of customizable testbeds for evaluating fault-handling mechanisms of SOA-based systems.

1 Motivation

Today service-oriented architectures (SOAs) do not only comprise Web services, clients, and brokers, but also diverse complex components that operate on distributed service-based environments, e.g., workflow engines executing business processes or governance systems managing whole large-scale systems. Usually, these components carry out critical tasks and, therefore, must be dependable. However, if one considers that SOA-based infrastructures often have complex dependency structures and each service is a potential fault source, it becomes obvious that single faults can trigger chains of harmful effects. Consequently, complex SOA components must provide fault handling mechanisms in order to guarantee a certain level of dependability.

In our current research, we regard this challenge from the perspective of how such mechanisms can be evaluated in order to verify their correct execution. We argue that this can only be achieved by testing the developed component at runtime, in an environment which comprises faulty elements, and by observing the component's reaction on occurring faults. Yet, the main obstacle remains how to get access to such an environment which exhibits faulty behavior and, therefore, can be used as a testbed infrastructure. As a contribution to solving this issue we have developed the *Genesis2* testbed generator framework and extended it with fault emulation techniques. Our tool provides SOA engineers the facility to generate customizable testbeds for evaluating their complex components.

2 Fault Injection Testbed Generator Framework

The presented prototype uses the *Genesis2* testbed generator framework [1] (in short, G2) as a base grounding for emulating testbeds for SOA. Engineers model

P.P. Maglio et al. (Eds.): ICSOC 2010, LNCS 6470, pp. 722–723, 2010.

the composition of required testbeds via a *Groovy*-based [2] scripting language, define the communication topology among the testbed's components, and program the functional behavior of these. G2 interprets these models, generates real SOA components, and deploys them on a distributed back-end environment, creating this way testbed infrastructures on-demand. For the sake of extensibility G2 comprises a modular architecture and applies composable plugins that extend the framework's functionality and augment the generated testbeds, for instance by providing the generation of additional SOA artifacts.

Based on G2 framework we have developed techniques for injecting multi-level faults into running testbeds in order to emulate typical failures in service-oriented computing. In the current state we support the following fault types:

- faults at the *message layer*, in terms of message data corruption,
- faults in *service execution*, for simulating quality of service (QoS) issues, and
- faults at the *network layer*, hampering the IP packet flow between hosts.

A distinct feature of our tool is the ability to program fault models via the scripting language. It provides fine grained control on the fault injection mechanisms and allows engineers to customize the functionality of their testbeds to their requirements of the tested complex SOA component.

For a mode detailed description of how we perform fault injection we refer readers to [3] and for learning how G2 generates testbeds we recommend to read [1].

3   Prototype Demonstration

In the demo we will present the prototype implementation of our testbed generator. Via sample scripts we will demonstrate how testbeds are modeled, how faulty components are specified, and, eventually, how faults are injected into running testbeds. Particular focus will be put on the programmability of the fault models, which is the most novel contribution of our approach. We will show the effects of injected faults on a deployed complex SOA component (e.g., a BPEL workflow engine) by visualizing the intercepted communication and pointing out occurring misbehavior.

The provision of our prototype as open source software (downloadable at [4]) will be an additional asset of our demonstration.

References

1. Juszczyk, L., Dustdar, S.: Script-based generation of dynamic testbeds for soa. In: ICWS, pp. 195–202. IEEE Computer Society, Los Alamitos (2010)
2. Groovy Programming Language, http://groovy.codehaus.org/
3. Juszczyk, L., Dustdar, S.: Programmable Fault Injection Testbeds for Complex SOA. In: ICSOC. LNCS, Springer, Heidelberg (2010)
4. Genesis Web site, http://www.infosys.tuwien.ac.at/prototype/Genesis/

BPEL'n'Aspects&Compensation: Adapted Service Orchestration Logic and Its Compensation Using Aspects

Mirko Sonntag and Dimka Karastoyanova

Institute of Architecture of Application Systems, University of Stuttgart
Universitaetsstrasse 38
70569 Stuttgart, Germany
{sonntag,karastoyanova}@iaas.uni-stuttgart.de

Abstract. One of the main weaknesses of workflow management systems is their inflexibility regarding process changes. To address this drawback in our work on the BPEL'n'Aspects approach we developed a standards-based mechanism to adapt the control flow of BPEL processes [1]. It uses AOP techniques to non-intrusively weave Web service invocations in terms of aspects into BPEL processes. Aspects can be inserted before, instead or after BPEL elements and that way adaptation of running processes is enabled. In this work we want to present a novel extension of the BPEL'n'Aspects prototype that deals with the compensation of weaved-in aspects in a straight-forward manner. The extension enormously improves the applicability of the approach in real-world scenarios: processes in production need the means to compensate behavior that was inserted into the process in the course of adaptation steps. The ability to compensate weaved-in aspects distinguishes our approach from other existing concepts that introduce AOP techniques to business processes.

Keywords: Service orchestration, BPEL, compensation, aspect-orientation, adaptability.

1 System Overview

The BPEL'n'Aspects system consists of four components (see Fig. 1) described in the following: A *BPEL engine* with an extension event system to publish a set of events (e.g. navigation events). Process instance data such as variable instances can be accessed through an engine adapter. A *broker* conducts the actual weaving of aspects into processes. After deployment of an aspect it subscribes to the engine's event system and waits for an event that signals the correct position of the aspect (as given in the aspect definition). Execution of an advice of an aspect (i.e. invocation of a service) is done by the *service bus*. It consists of several wrappers that act as gateways to invoke services. This design decouples the broker from the service invocations. The results of these invocations are routed to the broker that propagates them back to the engine. The user can create, edit, delete, deploy and undeploy aspects with the help of the *aspect management tool*.

In order to account for compensation of weaved-in aspects, we extended the existing prototype as follows: (1) the aspect management tool now allows to attach compensation

P.P. Maglio et al. (Eds.): ICSOC 2010, LNCS 6470, pp. 724–725, 2010.

aspects to aspects to be executed during compensation of the associated scope; (2) engine events that signal states of compensation handlers (ready, executing, finished) can be generated; (3) the engine adapter now provides functionality to dynamically register events that block process instance execution. This is needed to weave in compensation aspects; (4) the new auditor component stores the audit trail of processes (especially execution timestamps of activities and weaved-in aspects, and variable snapshots); (5) the weaver is capable of registering compensation aspects.

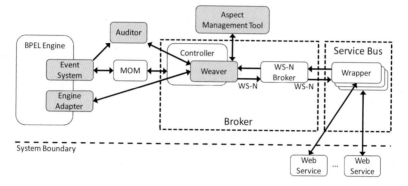

Fig. 1. Overview of the BPEL'n'Aspects system. Gray components were developed or adapted during this work.

2   Functions to Be Demonstrated

We demonstrate the extended BPEL'n'Aspects prototype with an example scenario of an online book store: (1) we show how users create aspects with the aspect management tool; (2) how a compensation aspect is attached to an aspect; (3) how aspects are deployed to the book store process model; (4) we prepare three different kinds of aspects that cover the most important use cases of our approach. For these three cases we show the deployment, normal execution with the changed process logic, and faulty execution with the compensation of the changed process logic.

Acknowledgments. The authors would like to thank the German Research Foundation (DFG) for financial support of the project within the Cluster of Excellence in Simulation Technology (EXC 310/1) at the University of Stuttgart.

Reference

1. Karastoyanova, D., Leymann, F.: BPEL'n'Aspects: Adapting Service Orchestration Logic. In: Proceedings of the 7th International Conference on Web Services, ICWS 2009 (2009)

A Tool for Integrating Pervasive Services and Simulating Their Composition

Ehsan Ullah Warriach, Eirini Kaldeli, Jaap Bresser,
Alexander Lazovik, and Marco Aiello*

Distributed Systems Group, Johann Bernoulli Institute
University of Groningen, Nijenborgh 9, 9747 AG, The Netherlands
{e.u.warriach,e.kaldeli,j.bresser,a.lazovik,m.aiello}@rug.nl

Abstract. As computation and services are pervading our working and living environments, it is important for researchers and developers to have tools to simulate and visualize possible executions of the services and their compositions. The major challenge for such tools is to integrate highly heterogeneous components and to provide a link with the physical environment. We extend our previous work on the RuG ViSi tool [4], in a number of ways: first, we provide a customizable and interactive middleware based on open standards (UPnP and OSGi) [3]; second, we allow any composition engine to guide the simulation and visualization (not only predefined compositions using BPEL) [3]; third, the interaction with simulated or physical devices is modular and bidirectional, i.e., a device can change the state of the simulation. In the demo, we use an AI planner to guide the simulation, a number of simulated UPnP devices, a real device running Java, and a two room apartment. The related video is available at http://www.youtube.com/watch?v=2w_UIwRqtBY.

Domotics is concerned with the automation of the home in order to improve the safety and comfort of its inhabitants, by having numerous loosely-coupled and heterogeneous devices working together. The EU Smart Homes for All (SM4All) project provides a Service Oriented Computing approach to have the smart home respond to user needs by performing a set of actions and being aware of the home context. The objective is to realise a domotic infrastructure that is highly interactive and adaptive to the needs of different users and environments. The main components of the SM4ALL framework are the building blocks of the implementation presented here and include the pervasive platform, the composition module, and the visualisation and simulation tool. Figure 1 illustrates how these components interact with each other. The pervasive platform is where the devices of the house live. The devices are described following the UPnP (www.upnp.org) protocol, and are wrapped as service components at the OSGi (www.osgi.org) platform. Non-UPnP devices are also supported by deploying a UPnP proxy. In Figure 1 the pervasive platform includes a set of simulated

---

* The research is supported by the EU project Smart Homes for All (http://www.sm4all-project.eu), contract FP7-224332.

P.P. Maglio et al. (Eds.): ICSOC 2010, LNCS 6470, pp. 726–727, 2010.

devices (door, window and TV) that use the UPnP protocol, as well as a physical Sentilla mote (www.sentilla.com) with a ZigBee interface. Several clients can subscribe to the server built on top of the OSGi framework, and interact with the service components by exchanging SOAP messages, as well as receive notifications about new devices and contextual changes.

The composition module we use in the current demo to drive the simulation and visualization is registered as a client, and is responsible for registering the state of the home, as well as for coordinating the available services. The most important part of the composition component is the planner, which is domain-independent and builds upon constraint satisfaction techniques [2]. A rule engine is responsible for identifying whether certain conditions hold, and accordingly triggering some appropriate pre-defined goals, e.g.

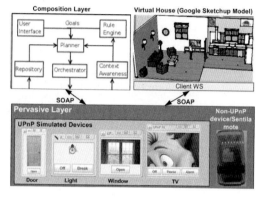

Fig. 1. Architectural Overview

to deal with an event of fire. The user can also issue his own goals through the Brain-Computer Interface (BCI) [1] and web interfaces, e.g. a request to watch TV. The computed plan is then passed to an orchestrator that executes it by invoking the corresponding operations at the pervasive layer, which are in turn visualised at the simulated home environment.

The simulation and visualisation platform –the *RuG ViSi tool*– is an extension of our initial work presented last year at the ICSOC Demo session [4]. It is based on Google SketchUp for the 3D rendering. The most notable improvements are: first, we provide a customizable and interactive middleware based on open standards (UPnP and OGSi); second, we allow any composition engine to guide the simulation and visualization third, the interaction with simulated or physical devices is modular and bidirectional. In addition, we now fully comply with the modular SM4ALL architecture.

References

1. Babiloni, F., Cincotti, F., Marciani, M., Astolfi, L., Aloise, F., Fallani, F., Mattia, D.: On the use of bci outside scientific laboratories: Toward an app. in domotic environments. Int. Review of Neurobiology (2009)
2. Kaldeli, E., Lazovik, A., Aiello, M.: Extended goals for composing services. In: Int. Conf. on Automated Planning and Scheduling (ICAPS 2009), AAAI Press, Menlo Park (2009)
3. Kaldeli, E., Warriach, E.U., Bresser, J., Lazovik, A., Aiello, M.: Interoperation, composition and simulation of services at home. In: ICSOC (2010)
4. Lazovik, E., den Dulk, P., de Groote, M., Lazovik, A., Aiello, M.: Services inside the smart home: A simulation and visualization tool. In: ICSOC, pp. 651–652 (2009)

BPEL4Pegasus: Combining Business and Scientific Workflows

Mirko Sonntag[1], Dimka Karastoyanova[1], and Ewa Deelman[2]

[1] Institute of Architecture of Application Systems, University of Stuttgart
Universitaetsstrasse 38
70569 Stuttgart, Germany
{sonntag,karastoyanova}@iaas.uni-stuttgart.de
[2] Information Science Institutes, University of Southern California
Admiralty Way 4676
90292 Marina Del Rey, California, USA
deelman@isi.edu

Abstract. Business and scientific workflow management systems (WfMS) offer different features to their users because they are developed for different application areas with different requirements. Research is currently being done to extend business WfMSs by functionality that meets requirements of scientists and scientific applications. The idea is to bring the strengths of business WfMSs to e-Science. This means great effort in re-implementing features already offered by scientific WfMSs. In our work, we investigated another approach, namely combining business and scientific workflows and thus harnessing the advantages of both. We demonstrate a prototype that implements this idea with BPEL as business workflow language and Pegasus as scientific WfMS. Our motivation is the fact that the manual work to correctly install and configure Pegasus can be supervised by a BPEL workflow to minimize sources of failures and automate the overall process of scientific experimenting.

Keywords: Scientific workflows, business workflows, human tasks, Pegasus, BPEL.

1 System Overview

The main idea of the work is allowing a business workflow to orchestrate and supervise one or more scientific workflows that in combination represent a whole scientific experiment with all its stages. Fig. 1 shows how this concept is implemented in the prototype to demonstrate. Note that the dotted lines represent possible machine borders. Pegasus relies on Condor DAGMan and Condor to execute scientific workflows on Grids. A BPEL engine (we used the open source engine Apache ODE 2.0, http://ode.apache.org/) runs a business process that supervises the Pegasus workflow's planning and execution phase. In order to invoke Pegasus by BPEL we created a Web service (WS) that wraps and offers Pegasus' functionality. Apache ODE currently does not implement a direct support for human activities and hence there is no human task (HT) client. That is the reason why we developed a Web application as

P.P. Maglio et al. (Eds.): ICSOC 2010, LNCS 6470, pp. 728–729, 2010.

GUI for the users. It is a HT client and monitoring tool in one, and HTs are called by BPEL in terms of WS calls. Since scientific workflows executed by Pegasus can be long-running, we follow an asynchronous communication model between the GUI, BPEL engine and Pegasus.

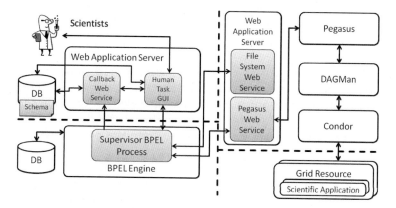

Fig. 1. Overview of the system. Gray ingredients were developed as part of this work.

Contributions of the prototype can be summarized as follows: (1) the correlation between BPEL workflow instances and Pegasus workflows; (2) providing Pegasus' original interface that is a mix of shell commands and file operations as WS; (3) a GUI for preparing and executing Pegasus workflows; and (4) GUI support for users to setup Pegasus' site, transformation and replica catalogs. These contributions enormously simplify the work of scientists since it is more straightforward to use and lowers the learning curve, automates manual tasks and supports decision making.

2 Functions to Be Demonstrated

The demonstration has two parts: (1) All aspects of the GUI are shown: The *work list* containing all work items assigned to a user, the *monitor* that shows the current state of workflow instances, and the *view* to select a Pegasus server, and to choose and start a *Pegasus workflow*. (2) Pegasus workflow execution: It is shown how a user can follow the progress of scientific experiments with the help of the monitor, how work items are assigned to users, and how they can handle these work items. Moreover, we present how a user is assisted during the configuration of Pegasus catalogs and how he can react to failures in the Pegasus planning phase and can ensure convergence of result files. A video of the demonstration can be found here: http://www.iaas.uni-stuttgart.de/institut/mitarbeiter/sonntag/indexE.php.

Acknowledgments. The authors M.S. and D.K. would like to thank the German Research Foundation (DFG) for financial support of the project within the Cluster of Excellence in Simulation Technology (EXC 310/1) at the University of Stuttgart.

Multidisciplinary Views of Business Contracts

Munindar P. Singh[1] and Nirmit Desai[2]

[1] North Carolina State University, Raleigh, NC 27695-8206, USA
[2] IBM Research, Bangalore 560071, India

Several major trends in the services industry drive toward an increasing importance of contracts. These include the formalization of business processes across the client and the provider organizations; resource administration in cloud computing environments; service-level agreements as they arise in infrastructure and networking services; and services viewed from the perspective of real-life engagements.

Previous work on e-commerce architectures and on technical services (such as web and grid services) has focused on low-level aspects of computation. In contrast, the emerging trend toward contracts recognizes the importance of high-level, flexible specifications of interactions. It is clear that contracts make sense only when the contracting parties are autonomous. Further, contracts help shield the organizational heterogeneity of the contracting parties from one another. In this manner, contracts provide a natural match for a variety of real-world problems that service scientists are beginning to recognize.

By developing and studying contracts from perspectives of multiagent systems, legal and jurisprudence literature, and economics, we would not only find compelling new applications for the concepts and techniques of multiagent systems but also discover new and multidisciplinary methods driven by contracts for architecting service systems.

This tutorial introduces the key ideas and techniques of contracts as they arise in major real-world service engagements; the benefits of formalizing contracts to realize them computationally; and the opportunities and challenges contracts offer for researchers and practitioners. We are seeing increasing interest in contracts from the services research community. Recently, several high-profile research projects have been centered on contracts. While most members of the ICSOC community may be familiar with WS-Agreement, Service-Level, Agreements, and Quality of Service, the attendees may benefit from alternative, multidisciplinary, perspectives into contracts such as the theory and practice of multiagent systems, the legal and jurisprudence literatures, and ideas from social sciences and economics. This tutorial eill enable studies of contracts by explaining why contracts are needed, how they can be represented, and which concepts and techniques support contracts naturally. This tutorial will provide the key background, which attendees can use as a launching pad for their investigations.

P.P. Maglio et al. (Eds.): ICSOC 2010, LNCS 6470, p. 730, 2010.
© Springer-Verlag Berlin Heidelberg 2010

Quantitative Service Analysis

Naveen Kulkarni, Deepti Parachuri, and Shashank Trivedi

Software Engineering and Technology Labs, Infosys Technologies Ltd, India
{Naveen_Kulkarni,Deepti_Parachuri,Shshank_Trivedi}@infosys.com

Abstract. Service Orientation has become popular due to dynamic market conditions and changing customer needs. A successful service oriented architecture implementation requires the need for right identification of services from business process models. Service identification is considered to be the main activity in the modeling of service oriented solution, as errors made during service identification flows down through detailed design and implementation of activities.

Though service orientation has been an important milestone in many enterprise transformation initiatives, there hasn't been much work on identification of services. Services have been identified and are used in day to day transactions, but they are limited to exchange of information between partners (two different organizations) or infrastructure related. Functionalities that are widely used across all applications such as security, auditing has been considered for servicification. In some other cases, business processes have been considered as simple orchestrated set of web services with each activity mapping to a single web service.

Adopting any service identification approach for Service Orientation without verification would rather be impractical for the simple reason being that no common notion of service can be established among stakeholders. It is essential to assert if all services identified provide necessary value and exhibit acceptable technical health (flexibility, reuse etc). To be more effective, there is a need for a methodology that can quantitatively measure the candidature of services with respect to business process models. With such automation, a platform can be provided to bootstrap service analysis where stakeholders can continually model and refine services based on predefined criteria.

This tutorial is intended for researchers and industry practitioners who are interested in Service Oriented Architecture and Service Analysis. The tutorial gives a deeper insight on service analysis and service identification methodologies. Though our methodology follows the prescribed top down approach while recognizing the importance of starting with business models for service identification, it stands different as it is based on mathematical model rather than heuristics or questionnaire based. Our method adopts quantitative way of groping set of business activities and measuring the service candidacy of those groups based on well defined principles. It also demonstrates an automated tool for service analysis.
abstract environment.

P.P. Maglio et al. (Eds.): ICSOC 2010, LNCS 6470, p. 731, 2010.

Scalable Services:
Understanding Architecture Trade-off

Markus Klems and Stefan Tai

Karlsruhe Institute of Technology, Germany
{markus.klems,stefan.tai}@kit.edu
http://www.kit.edu

Abstract. Creating Internet-scale services is a critical challenge for many organizations today. Data storage is a key component and factor to scalability, and data partitioning and replication along with loose coupling and simple service interfaces have become successful architecture guidelines to preventing scalability issues.

Partitioning realizes incremental scalability by splitting up large data sets and distributing smaller data shards across multiple servers. Replication and loose coupling help tolerate server failures and improve service availability. Replica synchronization, however, can produce substantial volumes of server-to-server traffic and delay service response time.

Distribution of storage infrastructure, consequently, provokes fundamental trade-off challenges, known as the strong CAP principle: only two out of the three properties of a distributed system, strong consistency (C), high availability (A), and partition-tolerance (P), can be achieved at the same time. For example, a transactional database on a single node provides CA without P, a distributed database system with pessimistic locking provides CP without A, and the Domain Name System provides AP without C. The weak CAP principle generalizes the strong CAP principle by characterizing the trade-off as a continuum instead of binary choices. In particular, relaxing consistency requirements and trading consistency for higher availability has become a successful modus operandi for Internet-scale systems.

Key-value data stores provide storage capabilities for a wide range of applications and services, from Amazon's shopping carts to Zynga's social gaming engine. We explore common mechanisms employed by Internet-scale key-value data stores, such as Dynamo, Cassandra, and Membase, and discuss how key-value data stores are used in support of representative Internet applications and services.

To evaluate and compare eventually consistent data stores, metrics and benchmarking tools are needed. We review metrics proposed by the distributed systems community and argue for a novel consistency benchmarking model as a systematic approach to measure relaxed consistency.

Keywords: Service-Oriented Computing, Cloud Computing, Data Store Architecture.

P.P. Maglio et al. (Eds.): ICSOC 2010, LNCS 6470, p. 732, 2010.
© Springer-Verlag Berlin Heidelberg 2010

Crowd-Driven Processes:
State of the Art and Research Challenges

Maja Vukovic[1] and Claudio Bartolini[2]

[1] IBM Research, 19 Skyline Dr, Hawthorne, NY 10532, USA
maja@us.ibm.com
[2] HP Labs, 1501 Page Mill Road, Palo Alto, CA 94304, USA
claudio.bartolini@hp.com

Abstract. Over the past few years the crowdsourcing paradigm has evolved from its humble beginnings as isolated purpose-built initiatives, such as Wikipedia and Elance and Mechanical Turk to a growth industry employing over 2 million knowledge workers, contributing over half a billion dollars to the digital economy. Web 2.0 provides the technological foundations upon which the crowdsourcing paradigm evolves and operates, enabling networked experts to work collaboratively to complete a specific task.

Crowdsourcing has a potential to significantly transform the business processes, by incorporating the knowledge and skills of globally distributed experts to drive business objectives, at shorter cycles and lower cost. Many interesting and successful examples exist, such as Gold-Corp, TopCoder, Threadless, etc. However, to fully adopt this mechanism enterprises, and benefit from appealing value propositions, in terms of reducing the time-to-value, a set of challenges remain, in order for enterprises to retain the brand, achieve high quality contributions, and deploy crowdsourcing at the minimum cost.

Enterprise crowdsourcing poses interesting challenges for both academic and industrial research along the social, legal, and technological dimensions. In this tutorial we present a landscape of existing crowdsourcing applications, targeted to the enterprise domain. We describe the challenges that researchers and practitioners face when thinking about various aspects of enterprise crowdsourcing. First, to establish technological foundations, what are the interaction models and protocols between the Enterprise and the crowd (including different types of crowd, such as internal, external and hybrid models). Secondly, how is crowdsourcing going to face the challenges in quality assurance, enabling Enterprises to optimally leverage the scalable workforce. Thirdly, what are the novel (Web) applications enabled by Enterprise crowdsourcing, and how can existing business processes be transformed for crowd consumption.

P.P. Maglio et al. (Eds.): ICSOC 2010, LNCS 6470, p. 733, 2010.

Author Index

Printing: Mercedes-Druck, Berlin
Binding: Stein+Lehmann, Berlin